CASSELL'S
CLASSIFIED QUOTATIONS

Cassell's Classified Quotations

From Authors of all Nations and Periods, grouped under Subject - Headings, with full Index of Cross - References and Annotated List of Authors

By

W. GURNEY BENHAM

Compiler of " Cassell's Book of Quotations "

CASSELL AND COMPANY, LIMITED
London, Toronto, Melbourne and Sydney

**BOOK
PRODUCTION
WAR ECONOMY
STANDARD**

THE PAPER AND BINDING OF
THIS BOOK CONFORM TO THE
AUTHORIZED ECONOMY STANDARDS

Fifth	„	.	*May*	1941
Sixth	„	.	*January*	1944
Seventh	„	.	*September*	1946

MADE AND PRINTED IN GREAT BRITAIN
AT GREYCAINES (TAYLOR GARNETT
EVANS AND CO. LTD.), WATFORD, HERTS.
746

PREFACE

DICTIONARIES of Quotations are usually bought for one of two purposes—either to assist in finding the exact *locale* and wording of some well- or half-remembered line, or to help a writer or speaker to do with effect what Montaigne spoke of when he said "I quote others only the better to express myself."

This book of CLASSIFIED QUOTATIONS is intended primarily for the use of those who write, speak, or teach ; and the compiler confidently anticipates that, owing to its arrangement and to the very large number of subjects of which it treats, it will be of value alike to the clergyman, the lecturer, the journalist, and the author ; that it will not only recall to writers and to speakers the most striking phrases of their predecessors on almost any subject, but will also guide them to ideas which otherwise might not suggest themselves ; that it will save the after-dinner speaker time, trouble, and anxiety in the preparation of his speech; and that it will prove itself a continuous source of interest and of useful information to the general reader.

Whilst including the favourite household words, which can never wear out with use, the present volume contains many thousands of quotable passages and sayings not hitherto included in any similar collection. These have been chosen with care, and often as the result of extensive research. Extracts from the Greek, Latin, French, German, Spanish, Italian, and other languages are given in English form ; and a large amount of time and trouble has been spent in locating the quotations with such exactitude as will enable the student to refer to their setting in the work from which they come.

"The art of quotation," said Isaac D'Israeli, "requires more delicacy in the practice than those conceive who see nothing more in a quotation than an extract." All definitions are dangerous, and to define a "quotation" is a thing as elusive and difficult as to explain precisely what constitutes an article of *virtu*. In the end the humble, unpopular test of "utility" is the best, let the connoisseurs rail as they will, provided always that we realize that not the least useful things in this world are those that can give pleasure, enlightenment, and inspiration.

This same utility is also the reason for attempting the difficult— sometimes impossible—task of "classifying" a collection of literary gems and curiosities. Not a few quotations object to be classified ; others demand classification under many different headings. But on the whole the advantages of a system of classification outweigh the disadvantages. Busy men and women require to be helped in their quest for the word in season, or for the inspiration which may be obtained from the varied ideas of the world's thinkers, of different periods, nationalities, religions, politics, and temperaments.

Nearly two thousand separate subject-headings have been introduced in this book, some of them necessarily overlapping one another. Readers who do not at once find the lucky words under the particular heading which they have selected, should turn to the Index of Cross-References (p. 565), which will guide them to other passages appropriate for their purpose. But in using this or any similar work of reference D'Israeli's saying, quoted above, should be borne in mind, for it must be remembered that the art of quotation depends very largely on the taste, discernment, and ingenuity of those who practise it.

W. GURNEY BENHAM.

Whitefriars Club,
London.

CONTENTS

CONTENTS

CASSELL'S
CLASSIFIED QUOTATIONS

A

ABASEMENT

At whose sight all the stars hide their
diminished heads.
MILTON.—*Paradise Lost, Bk.* 4, 34.

Ye little stars! hide your diminished
rays! POPE.—*Moral Essays, Ep.* 3, 282.

ABILITY

The winds and waves are always on
the side of the ablest navigators.
GIBBON.—*Decline and Fall, ch.* 68.

ABSENCE

Absence makes the heart grow fonder.
T. H. BAYLY.—*Isle of Beauty.*

To that loved land, where'er he goes,
His tenderest thoughts are cast;
And dearer still, through absence, grows
The memory of the past.
J. D. BURNS.—*Song.*

But aye the tear comes in my ee,
To think on him that's far awa'.
BURNS.—*Oh, how can I be Blithe?*

Absence is to love what wind is to
fire; it puts out the little and kindles
the great. BUSSY.

Absence! Is not the heart torn by it.
From more than light, or life, or
breath?
'Tis Lethe's gloom, but not its quiet,
The pain without the peace of death.
CAMPBELL.—*Absence.*

That out of sight is out of mind
Is true of most we leave behind.
A. H. CLOUGH.—*Songs of Absence.*

Absence from whom we love is worse than
death,
And frustrate hope severer than despair.
COWLEY.—*Despair at his Separation.*

Love reckons hours for months, and days
for years;
And every little absence is an age.
DRYDEN.—*Amphitryon.*

The farther off, the more desired;
thus lovers tie their knot.
HENRY HOWARD, EARL OF SURREY.
—*The Faithful Lover.*

Though lost to sight, to memory dear.
GEO. LINLEY.—*Song (c.* 1835), *but
found as an " axiom " in " Gentleman's
Magazine," Jan.,* 1827. *" The absent
claim a sigh, the dead a tear," has been
added as a second line.*

Absence not long enough to root out quite
All love, increases love at second sight.
THOS. MAY.—*Henry II.*

Alas, what winds can happy prove
That bear me far from her I love?
PRIOR.—*Song.*

A bright adieu
For a brief absence proves that love is
true;
Ne'er can the way be irksome or forlorn
That winds into itself for sweet return.
WORDSWORTH.—*Memorials of a Tour
in Scotland.*

Absent in body, but present in spirit.
1 *Corinthians* v, 3.

Herte soon forgets what the eye sees
not. *Cursor Mundi (c.* 1250).

ABSTINENCE

And made almost a sin of abstinence.
DRYDEN.—*A Good Parson, l.* 11.

And must I wholly banish hence
These red and golden juices,
And pay my vows to Abstinence,
That pallidest of Muses?
SIR W. WATSON.—*To a Maiden who
bade me shun Wine.*

ABSTRUSENESS

This young man expresses himself in
terms too deep for me.
SIR W. S. GILBERT.—*Patience.*

Who, too deep for his hearers, still went
on refining,
And thought of convincing while they
thought of dining.
GOLDSMITH.—*Retaliation.*

B

I

When he to whom one speaks does not understand, and when he who speaks does not understand himself, that is metaphysics.   VOLTAIRE.

Abstrusest matter, reasonings of the mind
Turned inward.
  WORDSWORTH.—*Excursion, Bk. 1.*

ABSURDITY

They are of all most subject to it [absurdity] that profess philosophy. For it is most true that Cicero saith of them somewhere, that there can be nothing so absurd but may be found in the books of philosophers.
  HOBBES.—*Leviathan, Bk. 1, ch. 5.*

ABUNDANCE

Not more than others I deserve,
Yet God has given me more.
  I. WATTS.—*Praise for Mercies.*

ABUSE

Letting the rank tongue blossom into speech. BROWNING.—*Caliban.*

Never slang a cabman—he can beat you.   H. J. BYRON.—*Mirth.*

Poets, like disputants, when reasons fail,
Have one sure refuge left—and that's to rail.   DRYDEN.—*All for Love, Ep.*

There must be something good in you, I know,
Or why does everyone abuse you so?
  SIR OWEN SEAMAN.—*Praise of Fog.*

The ears can endure an injury better than the eyes.   PUBLILIUS SYRUS.

If it is abuse, why, one is sure to hear of it from one damned good-natured friend or another.
  SHERIDAN.—*The Critic, Act 1, 1.*

But from sharp words and wits men pluck no fruit;
And gathering thorns they shake the tree at root;
For words divide and rend,
But silence is most noble till the end.
  SWINBURNE.—*Atalanta.*

Detraction and spitefulness are eagerly received.   TACITUS.—*Hist. Bk. 1.*

He should have a hail pow
  [a sound head],
That calls his neighbour nikkienow.
  Scottish prov. (Ray).

Keep your kiln-dried taunts for your mouldy-haired maidens.   *Scottish prov.*

Sticks and stanes may break my banes,
But names will never hurt me.
  Scottish saying.

ABUSES

There are four good mothers, of whom are often born four unhappy daughters. Truth begets Hatred; Happiness, Pride; Security, Danger; and Familiarity, Contempt.
  STEELE.—*Guardian*, No. 6 (Mar. 17, 1713).

The older the abuse the more sacred it is.   VOLTAIRE.—*Les Guèbres.*

ACCOMPLISHMENT

To stretch the octave 'twixt the dream and deed,
Ah, that's the thrill!
  R. LE GALLIENNE.—*The Decadent to his Soul.*

ACCOMPLISHMENTS

All his perfections were so rare,
The wit of man could not declare
Which single virtue, or which grace
Above the rest had any place.
  BUTLER.—*Miscell. Thoughts.*

A man of letters, manners, morals, parts.
  COWPER.—*Tirocinium*, 673.

He combined the manners of a marquis with the morals of a Methodist.
  SIR W. S. GILBERT.—*Ruddigore.*

A combination, and a form, indeed,
Where every god did seem to set his seal,
To give the world assurance of a man.
  SHAKESPEARE.—*Hamlet*, Act 3, 4.

ACCOUNTANCY

What is an inaccurate accountant good for? "Silly man, that dost not know thy own silly trade!" was once well said; but the trade here is not silly.
  BURKE.—*Impeachment of Hastings* (May 7, 1789).

ACCUSATION

Heedless of grammar they all cried "That's him!"
  R. H. BARHAM.—*Jackdaw of Rheims.*

Demon—with the highest respect for you—behold your work!
  DICKENS.—*Our Mutual Friend, Bk. 4, ch. 5*

The charge is prepared, the lawyers are met;
The judges all ranged—a terrible show!
  GAY.—*Beggar's Opera*, Act 2, 2.

I will make a Star-Chamber matter of it.
  SHAKESPEARE.—*Merry Wives*, Act 1, 1.

Believe not each accusing tongue,
As most weak persons do;
But still believe that story wrong,
Which ought not to be true.
  SHERIDAN (*Attributed*).

ACHIEVEMENT

I did some excellent things indifferently,
Some bad things excellently. Both were
   praised ;
The latter loudest.
   E. B. BROWNING.—*Aurora Leigh, Bk.* 3.

I die, but first I have possessed,
And come what may, I *have been* blessed.
   BYRON.—*The Giaour, l.* 1113.

The hand that rounded Peter's dome,
And groined the aisles of Christian Rome,
Wrought in a sad sincerity ;
Himself from God he could not free ;
He builded better than he knew ;—
The conscious stone to beauty grew.
   EMERSON.—*The Problem.*

I've touched the height of human
   happiness,
And here I fix *nil ultra.*
   FLETCHER and MASSINGER.—*Prophetess,*
      Act 4.

Each morning sees some task begun,
   Each evening sees it close ;
Something attempted, something done,
   Has earned a night's repose.
   LONGFELLOW.—*Village Blacksmith.*

I write *nil ultra* to my proudest hopes.
   MASSINGER.—*New Way to Pay Old Debts,*
      Act 4.

She whom I love is hard to catch and
   conquer,
Hard, but O the glory of the winning were
   she won !
   GEO. MEREDITH.—*Love in the Valley, st.* 2.

Nothing is here for tears, nothing to wail
Or knock the breast ; no weakness, no
   contempt,
Dispraise or blame, nothing but well and
   fair
And what may quiet us in a death so noble.
   MILTON.—*Samson Agonistes, l.* 1721.

Discoveries old of Wisdom's ways,
And works still pregnant with the in-
   ventor's praise.
   PINDAR.—*Olympian Odes,* 13, 17
      (*Moore tr.*).

The more the marble wastes,
   The more the statue grows.
   MRS. H. ROSCOE (*tr. of Michael Angelo*).

Yet through good heart, and our Lady's
   grace,
At length he gained the landing-place.
   SCOTT.—*Lay of the Last Minstrel, c.* 1, *st.* 29.

If you have writ your annals true, 'tis there,
That like an eagle in a dove-cote, I
Fluttered your Volscians in Corioli :
Alone I did it.
   SHAKESPEARE.—*Coriolanus,* Act 5, 5.

And now the matchless deed's achieved,
Determined, dared, and done.
   CHRISTOPHER SMART.—*To David, st.* 86.

The vulgar is content if he has fulfilled
his duty. To the hero more is necessary.
He must exceed that ; he must exceed
our hope.   VOLTAIRE.—*Tancrède.*

He set his face against the blast,
   His feet against the flinty shard,
Till the hard service grew at last
   Its own exceeding great reward.
   WHITTIER.—*Sumner, st.* 10.

Much done, and much designed, and
more desired.
   WORDSWORTH.—*Evening Walk.*

And all may do what has by man been
   done.   YOUNG.—*Night Thoughts,* 6.

ACQUAINTANCESHIP

We met—'twas in a crowd.
   T. H. BAYLY.—*Song.*

To meet, to know, to love—and then to
   part,
Is the sad tale of many a human heart.
   COLERIDGE.—*Couplet.*

Acquaintance I would have, but when't
   depends
Not on the number but the choice of
   friends.   A. COWLEY.—*Of Myself.*

Wery glad to see you, indeed, and hope
our acquaintance may be a long 'un, as the
gen'l'm'n said to the fi' pun' note.
   DICKENS.—*Pickwick, ch.* 25.

Ships that pass in the night, and speak
   each other in passing ;
Only a signal shown, and a distant voice
   in the darkness.
So on the ocean of life we pass and speak
   one another,
Only a look and a voice, then darkness
   again and silence.
   LONGFELLOW.—*Elizabeth, c.* 4.

ACQUIESCENCE

The habit of agreeing seems to be
dangerous and slippery.
   CICERO.—*Acad.,* 2, 21.

ACQUISITIVENESS

Ye come o' the McTabs, but no o' the
McGies.   *Scottish prov.*

ACTION

Let every action be directed to some
definite object, and perfect in its way.
   MARCUS AURELIUS.—*Meditations, Bk.* 4, 2.

He that works and *does* some Poem,
not he that merely *says* one, is worthy of
the name of Poet.
   CARLYLE.—*Cromwell, Intro.*

The whole praise of virtue lies in action.
CICERO.—*De Officiis, Book 1, 6.*

Not one of those men who in words are valiant,
But when it comes to action, skulk away.
COLERIDGE.—*Piccolomini, Act 5, 4.*

And all agog
To dash through thick and thin.
COWPER.—*John Gilpin, st. 10.*

Oh give my youth, my faith, my sword,
Choice of the heart's desire ;
A short life in the saddle, Lord,
Not long life by the fire !
LOUISE I. GUINEY (b. 1861).—*Knight Errant*

Thinking the deed, and not the creed,
Would help us in our utmost need.
LONGFELLOW.—*Tales of a Wayside Inn, Part 1, Prelude.*

So much one man can do,
That does both act and know.
MARVELL.—*Horatian Ode.*

For bragging time was over and fighting time was come.
SIR H. NEWBOLT.—*Hawke.*

To all the sensual world proclaim,
One crowded hour of glorious life
Is worth an age without a name.
Used by SCOTT as heading to ch. 34 of *Old Mortality*, first published in *The Bee* (Edinburgh, 1791) as one of a set of verses by MAJOR T. O. MORDAUNT (1730-1809).

To harps preferring swords,
And everlasting deeds to burning words !
WORDSWORTH.—*Eccles. Sonnets, Pt 1, 10.*

ACTIONS

In idle wishes fools supinely stay ;
Be there a will, and wisdom finds a way.
CRABBE.—*Birth of Flattery.*

Our deeds still travel with us from afar,
And what we have been makes us what we are.
GEO. ELIOT.—*Middlemarch, Heading to Chapter 70.*

He who does a good deed is instantly ennobled. He who does a mean deed is by the action itself contracted.
EMERSON.—*Address, July 15, 1838.*

Man is his own star, and the soul that can
Render an honest and a perfect man,
Commands all light, all influence, all fate ;
Nothing to him falls early or too late.

Our acts our angels are, or good or ill,
Our fatal shadows that walk by us still.
JOHN FLETCHER.—*On an Honest Man's Fortune.*

If thou do ill, the joy fades, not the pains ;
If well, the pain doth fade, the joy remains.
HERBERT.—*Church Porch (ad fin.).*

Virtue's achievement, Folly's crime,
Whate'er of guilt or good the past has known,
Not e'en the Sire of all things, mighty Time,
Hath power to change, or make the deed undone.
PINDAR.—*Olympian Odes, 2, 29 (Moore tr.).*

But the gods hear men's hands before their lips. SWINBURNE.—*Atalanta Althœa.*

ACTIVITY

There are indeed some spirits so ardent that change of employment to them is rest, and their only fatigue a cessation from activity. C. C. COLTON.—*Lacon.*

A generous ardour boils within my breast,
Eager of action, enemy to rest.
VIRGIL.—*Æneid, Bk. 9 (Dryden tr.).*

A ganging foot is aye getting—an it were but a thorn. *Scottish prov.*

ACTORS

The Poet, to the end of time,
Breathes in his works and lives in rhyme ;
But when the Actor sinks to rest,
And the turf lies upon his breast,
A poor traditionary fame
Is all that's left to grace his name.
W. COMBE.—*Dr. Syntax, c. 24.*

On the stage he was natural, simple, affecting ;
'Twas only that, when he was off, he was acting. GOLDSMITH.—*Retaliation.*

What are the hopes of man ? I am disappointed by that stroke of death which has eclipsed the gaiety of nations, and impoverished the public stock of harmless pleasure.
JOHNSON.—*Alluding to Garrick's Death.*

The drama's laws the drama's patrons give,
For we that live to please must please to live. JOHNSON.—*Prologue, 1747.*

Let them be well used, for they are the abstracts and brief chronicles of the time ; after your death you were better have a bad epitaph than their ill report while you live. SHAKESPEARE.—*Hamlet, Act 2, 2.*

I have thought some of nature's journeymen had made men, and not made them well, they imitated humanity so abominably. SHAKESPEARE.—*Hamlet, Act 3, 2.*

Tear a passion to tatters, to very rags, to split the ears of the groundlings; who for the most part are capable of nothing but inexplicable dumb shows and noise. SHAKESPEARE.—*Ib., Act 3, 2.*

The best in this kind are but shadows. SHAKESPEARE.—*Midsummer Night's Dream, Act 5, 1.*

French comedians, expert troubadours in the high science, the greatest of all the arts, the great art of pleasure. VOLTAIRE.—*Princesse de Navarre.*

ACTS OF PARLIAMENT

There is something picturesque in an Act of Parliament. SIR A. HELPS.—*Friends in Council, Slavery, ch. 1.*

ADAM AND EVE

Adam, the goodliest man of men since born His sons; the fairest of her daughters Eve. MILTON.—*Paradise Lost, Bk. 4, 323.*

ADAPTABILITY

Read in the temper that he wrote, And may his gentle spirit guide thee! ROGERS.—*Voyage of Columbus.*

Every time
Serves for the matter that is then born in it. SHAKESPEARE—*Antony and Cleopatra, Act 2, 2.*

Be soople, Davie, in things immaterial. R. L. STEVENSON.—*Kidnapped.*

I am made all things to all men. 1 *Corinthians ix.* 22 (I am become all things to all men. *R. V*).

ADMIRATION

A fool always finds a greater fool to admire him. BOILEAU.—*Art Poétique.*

It seems to me that men do not love what they are compelled to admire. DUCLOS.—*On the Manners of the Age.*

There is a species of benevolence which ought to have an appropriate name,..... a love of excellence,—a benevolence excited by all superiority in good, as envy is the hatred excited by that superiority, ...an admiration which no disparity of situation, no spirit of party, none of the hateful and disuniting feelings can extinguish. SYDNEY SMITH.—*Lectures on Moral Philosophy, No. 22.*

We indeed hear it not seldom said that ignorance is the mother of admiration. No falser word was ever spoken, and hardly a more mischievous one. ARCHBP. TRENCH.—*Study of Words.*

Small is the worth
Of beauty from the light retired;
Bid her come forth,
Suffer herself to be desired
And not blush so to be admired. WALLER.—*Go, Lovely Rose.*

ADMISSION

The very head and front of my offending Hath this extent, no more. SHAKESPEARE.—*Othello, Act 1, 3.*

Fain would I dwell on form, fain, fain deny
What I have spoke: but farewell, compliment. SHAKESPEARE.—*Romeo and Juliet, Act 2, 2.*

I own the soft impeachment [Mrs. Malaprop]. SHERIDAN.—*Rivals, Act 5, 3.*

ADMONITION

Admonish your friends in private; praise them in public. PUBLILIUS SYRUS.

ADORNMENT

But who is this? What thing of sea or land?
Female of sex it seems,
That so bedecked, ornate, and gay,
Comes this way sailing. MILTON.—*Samson Agonistes, l.* 710.

ADSUM

As the last bell struck, a peculiar sweet smile shone over his face, and he lifted up his head a little, and quickly said, "Adsum!" and fell back. It was the word we used at school, when names were called; and lo, he, whose heart was as that of a little child, had answered to his name, and stood in the presence of The Master. THACKERAY.—*Newcomes, Bk. 2, c. 42.*

ADVANTAGE

It's them as takes advantage that gets advantage i' this world. GEO. ELIOT.—*Adam Bede, ch. 32.*

Advantage is a better soldier than rashness. SHAKESPEARE.—*Henry V, Act 3, 6.*

Coigne of vantage. SHAKESPEARE.—*Macbeth, Act 1, 6.*

ADVENTURE

Mortals, who sought and found, by dangerous roads,
A path to perpetuity of fame. BYRON.—*Childe Harold, c. 3, st.* 105.

The fruit of my tree of knowledge is plucked, and it is this, " Adventures are to the Adventurous." Written in the Album of Minerva, by Ixion in Heaven.
DISRAELI.—*Ixion, Pt.* 2, 2.

Wherein I spoke of most disastrous chances,
Of moving accidents by flood and field,
Of hair-breadth 'scapes i' the imminent deadly breach,
Of being taken by the insolent foe
And sold to slavery.
SHAKESPEARE.—*Othello,* Act 1, 3.

She gave me for my pains a world of sighs ;
She swore,—In faith, 'twas strange, 'twas passing strange ;
'Twas pitiful, 'twas wondrous pitiful ;
She wished she had not heard it.
SHAKESPEARE.—*Ib.,* Act. 1, 3.

ADVERSITY

Ah, life of man ! When most it prospereth,
It is but limned in outline ; and when brought
To low estate, then doth the sponge, full soaked,
Wipe out the picture with its frequent touch ;
And this I count more piteous e'en than that.
ÆSCHYLUS.—*Agamemnon,* 1327
(*Plumptre tr.*).

Prosperity is the blessing of the Old Testament. Adversity is the blessing of the New, which carrieth the greater benediction. BACON.—*Essays,* 5, *Adversity.*

Virtue is like precious odours, most fragrant when they are incensed and crushed ; for prosperity does best discover vice, but adversity doth best discover virtue. BACON.—*Ib.*

No greater grief than to remember days Of joy, when misery is at hand.
H. F. CARY.—*Tr. Dante, c.* 5, *l.* 118.

O sodeyn wo ! that ever art successour To worldly blisse !
CHAUCER.—*Man of Law's Tale, l.* 4841.

For of fortunes sharp adversitee
The worst kinde of infortune is this,
A man to have been in prosperitee
And it remembren, whan it passed is.
CHAUCER.—*Troilus and Cressid, Bk.* 3,
v. 1625.

Let Fortune empty her whole quiver on me,
I have a soul that, like an ample shield,
Can take in all, and verge enough for more.
DRYDEN.—*Don Sebastian,* Act 1, 1.

For friendship, of itself a holy tie,
Is made more sacred by adversity.
DRYDEN.—*Hind and Panther, Pt.* 3, 47.

Bad times have a scientific value. These are occasions a good learner would not miss.
EMERSON.—*Conduct of Life,*
Considerations by the way.

The greatest object in the universe, says a certain philosopher, is a good man struggling with adversity ; yet there is a still greater, which is the good man that comes to relieve it.
GOLDSMITH.—*Vicar of Wakefield, c.* 30.

In his adversity I ever prayed that God would give him strength ; for greatness he could not want. BEN JONSON.—*Of Bacon.*

In the adversity of our best friends we ever find something not displeasing to us.
LA ROCHEFOUCAULD.—*Maxim* 99.

Sweet are the uses of adversity ;
Which like the toad, ugly and venomous,
Wears yet a precious jewel in his head.
SHAKESPEARE.—*As You Like It,* Act 2, 1.

A man I am crossed with adversity.
SHAKESPEARE.—*Two Gentlemen of Verona,*
Act 4, 1.

I have been near, I have been far, my back's been at the wall,
Yet aye and ever shone the star to guide me through it all ;
The love of God, the help of man, they both shall make me bold,
Against the gates of darkness as beside the Gates of Gold. R. L. STEVENSON.

In the day of prosperity be joyful, but in the day of adversity consider.
Ecclesiastes vii, 14.

The wind in one's face makes one wise.
Prov. (*Geo. Herbert*).

ADVERTISEMENT

If you wish in this world to advance,
Your merits you're bound to enhance ;
You must stir it and stump it,
And blow your own trumpet,
Or, trust me, you haven't a chance.
SIR W. S. GILBERT.—*Ruddigore.*

Great is advertisement ! 'tis almost fate ;
But, little mushroom men, of puff-ball fame,
Ah, do you dream to be mistaken great
And to be really great are just the same ?
R. LE GALLIENNE.—*Tennyson.*

Great is advertisement with little men.
SIR OWEN SEAMAN.—*Ode to Spring.*

Yes, sir, puffing is of various sorts; the principal are the puff direct, the puff preliminary, the puff collateral, the puff collusive, and the puff oblique, or puff by implication.

SHERIDAN.—*Critic*, Act 1, 2.

ADVICE

A woman seldom asks advice before she has bought her wedding clothes.

ADDISON.—*Spectator*, 518.

Woman's advice is either too dear or too cheap.

ALBERTANO OF BRESCIA.—*Liber Consolationis.*

The worst men give oft the best advice.

P. J. BAILEY.—*Festus.*

In ploughman phrase, "God send you speed,"
Still daily to grow wiser ;
And may ye better reck the rede
Than ever did th' adviser.

BURNS.—*Epistle to a Young Friend.*

Ah, gentle dames ! it gars me greet
To think how mony counsels sweet,
How mony lengthened, sage advices
The husband frae the wife despises !

BURNS.—*Tam o' Shanter.*

Good but rarely came from good advice.

BYRON.—*Don Juan*, 14, 66.

Advice is seldom welcome ; and those who want it the most, always like it the least.

LORD CHESTERFIELD.—*Letter to his Son*, Jan. 29, 1748.

We ask advice, but we mean approbation.   C. C. COLTON.—*Lacon.*

They first condemn that first advised the ill.   DRYDEN.—*Absalom*, Pt. 2, 183.

It is easier to give advice than to bear sufferings manfully.

EURIPIDES.—*Alcestis.*

We ask advice, but we are not particular about its being good. Quite the reverse. Good advice is often annoying ; bad advice never is.

E. GONDINET.—*Gavaut, Minard, et Cie.*

Extremely foolish criticism is likely to be uttered by those who are looking at the labouring vessel from the land.

SIR A. HELPS.—*Friends in Council*, Bk. 2, ch. 2.

One gives nothing so liberally as advice.

LA ROCHEFOUCAULD.—*Maxim* 110.

I know your worship's wise, and needs no counsel ;
Yet, if in my desire to do you service,

I humbly offer my advice (but still Under correction), I hope I shall not Incur your high displeasure.

MASSINGER.—*New Way to Pay Old Debts*, Act 2.

Giving advice is many times only the privilege of saying a foolish thing oneself, under pretence of hindering another from doing one.

POPE.—*Thoughts on Various Subjects.*

A man is badly in need of advice when he has many advisers.

PUBLILIUS SYRUS.

An angry man regards even advice as a crime.   PUBLILIUS SYRUS.

Ann will do just exactly what she likes. And what's more, she'll force us to advise her to do it ; and she'll put the blame on us if it turns out badly.

G. B. SHAW.—*Man and Superman.*

Advice gratis seldom great is.

C. H. SPURGEON.—*" Salt-Cellars."*

He had only one vanity ; he thought he could give advice better than any other person.

MARK TWAIN.—*Man that Corrupted Hadleyburg.*

It is always a silly thing to give advice, but to give good advice is absolutely fatal.

OSCAR WILDE.—*Soul of Man under Socialism.*

Women's counsels are often fatal.
Icelandic prov. (Quoted by *Chauc..* *Nun Priest's Tale*, 436).

Advice most needed is least heeded.
Prov.

Who works in the public square will have many advisers.   *Spanish prov.*

ADVOCACY

A certain lawyer, on being asked why he defended so many bad causes, replied that he did so because he had lost so many good ones. C. C. COLTON.—*Lacon.*

Doubt not, my lad, I'll play the orator, As if the golden fee, for which I plead, Were for myself.

SHAKESPEARE.—*Richard III.*, Act 3, 5.

AFFABILITY

He is a Gentleman, because his nature Is kinde and affable to everie Creature.

BARNFIELD.—*Shepherd's Content* (1594).

The fient a pride, nae pride had he, Nor sauce, nor state, that I could see.

BURNS.—*On meeting with Lord Daer.*

Bear in mind then that by pleasing men it becomes possible to accomplish something ; but austerity might as well dwell in a desert.
PLATO.—*Epistle* 4 (To *Dion of Syracuse*).

AFFECTATION

I would give the universe for a disposition less hard to please. Yet after all, what is pleasure ? When one has seen one thing, one has seen everything. O, 'tis heavy work ! [Mr. Meadows, " Man of the Ton."]
MME. D'ARBLAY (MISS BURNEY).— *Cecilia, Bk.* 2, *c.* 6.

Papa, potatoes, poultry, prunes and prism are all very good words for the lips ; especially prunes and prism.
DICKENS.—*Little Dorrit, Pt.* 2, *ch.* 5.

They are the affectation of affectation.
FIELDING.—*Joseph Andrews, Bk.* 3, *c.* 3.

A most intense young man,
A soul-ful eyed young man,
An ultra-poetical, super-æsthetical
Out-of-the-way young man.
SIR W. S. GILBERT.—*Patience.*

Die of a rose in aromatic pain.
POPE.—*Essay on Man, Ep.* 1, 200.

Why, is it not a lamentable thing, grandsire, that we should be thus afflicted with these strange flies, these fashion-mongers, these *pardon-mes* ?
SHAKESPEARE.—*Romeo and Juliet,* Act 2, 4.

AFFECTION

The world has little to bestow
Where two fond hearts in equal love are joined. MRS. BARBAULD.—*Delia.*

None are so desolate but something dear,
Dearer than self, possesses or possessed
A thought, and claims the homage of a tear.
BYRON.—*Childe Harold, c.* 1, *st.* 24.

It behoves
Those who are wise to love their children first,
Their aged parents next, and native land,
Whose growing fortunes they are bound to improve,
And not dismember it.
EURIPIDES.—*Suppliants,* 508 (*Woodhull tr.*).

Dear lost companions of my tuneful art,
Dear, as the light that visits these sad eyes,
Dear, as the ruddy drops that warm my heart. GRAY.—*Bard c.* 1.

Scorn no man's love, though of a mean degree ;
Love is a present for a mighty king.
HERBERT.—*Church Porch.*

Was there a nearer one
Still, and a dearer one,
Yet, than all other ?
HOOD.—*Bridge of Sighs.*

Talk not of wasted affection, affection never was wasted ;
If it enrich not the heart of another, its waters, returning
Back to their springs, like the rain, shall fill them full of refreshment.
LONGFELLOW.—*Evangeline, Pt.* 2.

Something the heart must have to cherish. LONGFELLOW.—*Wilhelm Meister.*

Come, live in my heart and pay no rent !
S. LOVER.—*Song " Vourneen."*

If you have any care for me, take care of yourself. OVID.—*Heroides,* 13.

I do receive your offered love, like love,
And will not wrong it.
SHAKESPEARE.—*Hamlet,* Act 5, 2.

Love comforteth, like sunshine after rain.
SHAKESPEARE.—*Venus and Adonis, st.* 134.

The affection of young ladies is of as rapid growth as Jack's beanstalk, and reaches up to the sky in a night.
THACKERAY.—*Vanity Fair, ch.* 4.

AFFECTIONS

Of all the tyrants that the world affords
Our own affections are the fiercest lords.
WM. ALEXANDER (EARL OF STIRLING).—*Julius Cæsar.*

A woman's whole existence is a history of the affections.
WASHINGTON IRVING.—*The Broken Heart.*

Glorious is the blending
Of right affections, climbing or descending
Along a scale of light and life, with cares
Alternate, carrying holy thoughts and prayers. WORDSWORTH.—*Humanity, l.* 28.

AFFECTION, PARTIALITY OF

The apples she had gathered smelt most sweet,
The cake she kneaded was the savoury meat:
But fruits their odour lost, and meats their taste,
If gentle Abra had not decked the feast ;
Dishonoured did the sparkling goblet stand,
Unless received from gentle Abra's hand.
PRIOR.—*Solomon, Bk.* 2, 495.

AFFECTION, UNREQUITED

If you could see my legs when I take
my boots off, you'd form some idea of
what unrequited affection is.
DICKENS.—*Dombey, c.* 48.

AFFINITIES

There is a story told [said Diotima to
Socrates] that they who are in love are in
search of their other half.
PLATO.—*The Banquet*, 31.

The fountains mingle with the river,
  And the rivers with the ocean.
The winds of heaven mix for ever,
  With a sweet emotion ;
Nothing in the world is single ;
  All things, by a law divine,
In one another's being mingle—
  Why not I with thine ?
    SHELLEY.—*Love's Philosophy.*

Two shall be born the whole wide world
    apart,
And speak in different tongues, and have
    no thought
Each of the other's being, and no heed.
. . . . . .
And all unconsciously, shape every act
And bend each wandering step to this
    one end,
That one day, out of darkness, they shall
    meet
And read life's meaning in each other's
  eyes. SUSAN MARR SPALDING.—*Fate.*

AFFLICTION

For the tear is an intellectual thing,
And a sigh is the sword of an Angel King ;
And the bitter groan of a martyr's woe
Is an arrow from God Almighty's bow.
    WM. BLAKE.—*The Grey Monk.*

For the poet saith that we oughte
paciently to take the tribulacions that
come to us, when we think and consider
that we have deserved to have them.
  CHAUCER.—*Tale of Melibeus, sec.* 46.
  (*The name of "the poet" is not known.*)

Pain after pain, and woe succeeding woe—
Is my heart destined for another blow ?
  COLERIDGE.—*On his Sister's Death.*

But misery still delights to trace
  Its semblance in another's case.
    COWPER.—*The Castaway.*

If aught can teach us aught, Affliction's
    looks,
(Making us pry into ourselves so near),
Teach us to know ourselves, beyond all
    books,
Or all the learned schools that ever
    were.
    SIR JOHN DAVIES.—*Nosce Teipsum,*
            sec. 1, *st.* 38.

O suffering, sad humanity !
O ye afflicted ones who lie
Steeped to the lips in misery,
Longing, and yet afraid to die,
Patient, though sorely tried !
  LONGFELLOW.—*Goblet of Life.*

Alas ! by some degree of woe
  We every bliss must gain ;
The heart can ne'er a transport know,
  That never feels a pain.
  GEO. LORD LYTTELTON.—*Song.*

We bear it calmly, though a ponderous
    woe,
And still adore the hand that gives the
  blow. J. POMFRET.—*To his Friend*, 45.

Heaven is not always angry when He
    strikes,
But most chastises those whom most He
  likes. J. POMFRET.—*Ib.*, 89.

Our griefs how swift ! our remedies how
slow !   PRIOR.—*Solomon*, Bk. 2, 352.

'Tis a cruelty
  To load a falling man.
  SHAKESPEARE.—*Henry VIII.*, Act 5, 2.

For our light affliction, which is but for
a moment, worketh for us a far more
exceeding and eternal weight of glory.
    2 *Corinthians* iv, 17.

AFFRONTS

Young men soon give and soon forget
    affronts ;
Old age is slow in both.
    ADDISON.—*Cato*, Act 2.

A moral, sensible, and well-bred man
Will not affront me, and no other can.
    COWPER.—*Conversation.*

To one well-born the affront is worse and
    more,
When he's abused and baffled by a boor.
  DRYDEN.—*Satire on the Dutch, l.* 27.

If slighted, slight the slight and love the
  slighter.
Given by C. H. SPURGEON *as " conduct
    worthy of a noble mind."*

AFRICA

Africa ever brings evil.   ARISTOTLE.

Always something new out of Africa.
    PLINY.—*Nat. Hist.* 8, 6.

AFTERNOON

In the posteriors of this day ; which
the rude multitude call the afternoon.
  SHAKESPEARE.—*Love's Labour's Lost,*
           Act 5, 1.

B*

AFTER-THOUGHTS

Second thoughts are admissible in painting and poetry only as dressers of the first conception. No great idea was ever formed in fragments.
HENRY FUSELI.—*Aphorisms of Art.*

His sayings are generally like women's letters ; all the pith is in the postscript. [*In reference to Chas. Lamb.*]
HAZLITT.—*Boswell Redivivus.*

AFTER-WISDOM

Of all the horrid, hideous sounds of woe,
Sadder than owl-songs on the midnight blast,
Is that portentous phrase, " I told you so."
BYRON.—*Don Juan, c.* 14, *st.* 50.

AGE

Age will not be defied.
BACON.—*Of Regiment of Health.*

Alonzo of Arragon was wont to say in commendation of age, " That age appeared to be best in four things : old wood best to burn ; old wine to drink ; old friends to trust ; and old authors to read."
BACON.—*Apophthegms* 134.

I've seen sae mony changefu' years,
On earth I am a stranger grown ;
I wander in the ways of men,
Alike unknowing and unknown.
BURNS.—*Lament for Earl of Glencairn.*

Years steal
Fire from the mind, as vigour from the limb ;
And life's enchanted cup but sparkles near the brim.
BYRON.—*Childe Harold, c* 3, *st.* 8.

And wrinkles, the d—d democrats, won't flatter.
BYRON.—*Don Juan, c.* 10, *st.* 24.

'Tis well to give honour and glory to Age,
With its lessons of wisdom and truth ;
Yet who would not back to the fanciful page,
And the fairy tale read but in youth ?
ELIZA COOK.—*Stanzas.*

Age is like love, it cannot be hid.
DEKKER.—*Old Fortunatus.*

For never any man was yet so old
But hoped his life one winter more might hold.
SIR J. DENHAM, *Old Age,* Pt. 1, *l.* 135.

Our nature here is not unlike our wine ;
Some sorts, when old, continue brisk and fine.
SIR J. DENHAM.—*Ib.,* Pt. 3, *l.* 245.

She may very well pass for forty-three
In the dusk with a light behind her.
SIR W. S. GILBERT.—*Trial by Jury.*

Women and music should never be dated.
GOLDSMITH.—*She Stoops to Conquer,*
Act 3.

I'm wearin' awa'
To the land o' the leal.
BARONESS NAIRN.—*Land o' the Leal.*

My age is as a lusty winter,
Frosty, but kindly.
SHAKESPEARE.—*As You Like It,*
Act 2, 3.

The lean and slippered pantaloon,
With spectacles on nose and pouch on side ;
His youthful hose, well saved, a world too wide
For his shrunk shank.
SHAKESPEARE.—*Ib.,* Act 2, 7.

Men are as old as they feel, women are as old as they seem.   *Italian prov.*

AGES, THE SEVEN

And one man in his time plays many parts,
His acts being seven ages. At first the infant,
Mewling and puking in the nurse's arms.
And then the whining schoolboy with his satchel,
And shining morning face, creeping like snail
Unwillingly to school. And then the lover,
Sighing like furnace, with a woful ballad
Made to his mistress' eyebrow. Then a soldier,
Full of strange oaths, and bearded like the pard,
Jealous in honour, sudden and quick in quarrel,
Seeking the bubble reputation
Even in the cannon's mouth. And then the justice,
In fair round belly, with good capon lined,
With eyes severe, and beard of formal cut,
Full of wise saws and modern instances ;
And so he plays his part. The sixth age shifts.
Into the lean and slippered pantaloon,
With spectacles on nose, and pouch on side ;
His youthful hose, well saved, a world too wide
For his shrunk shank ; and his big manly voice,
Turning again toward childish treble, pipes
And whistles in his sound. Last scene of all,
That ends this strange eventful history,—
Is second childishness, and mere oblivion,—
Sans teeth, sans eyes, sans taste, sans everything.
SHAKESPEARE.—*As You Like It,* Act 2, 7.

AGREEABLENESS

"My idea of an agreeable person," said Hugo Bohun, "is a person who agrees with me." Disraeli.—*Lothair, c.* 41.

Whate'er you think, good words, I think, were best.
Shakespeare.—*K. John*, Act 4, 2.

I laugh not at another's loss,
I grudge not at another's gain.
Byrd's Collection (c. 1585).

AGREEMENT

By agreement small things grow; by discord great things go to pieces.
Sallust.—*Jugurtha.*

Where they *do* agree on the stage, their unanimity is wonderful.
Sheridan.—*Critic*, Act 2, 2.

Ah! don't say that you agree with me. When people agree with me I always feel that I must be wrong.
Oscar Wilde.—*Intentions.*

It's my earnest desire to see a' the haill warld shakin' hauns.
J. Wilson—*Noctes (Ettrick Shepherd).*

Transcendent over time, unbound by place,
Concord and Charity in circles move.
Wordsworth.—*Eccles. Sonnets, Pt.* 3, 14.

Gentlemen, I say ditto to Mr. Burke.—
Speech by Mr. Cruger on returning thanks for election as Burke's colleague.

Can two walk together, except they be agreed?
Amos iii, 3.

Agree with thine adversary quickly, whiles thou art in the way with him.
St. Matthew v, 25.

AGRICULTURE

In agriculture if you do one thing late, you are late in all things.
Cato.

Of all things from which gain is obtained, nothing is better than agriculture, nothing more productive, more delightful, more worthy of a man or of a freeman.
Cicero.—*De Officiis.*

Cows are my passion.
Dickens.—*Dombey, c.* 21.

Men do not like hard work, but every man has an exceptional respect for tillage, and a feeling that this is the original calling of his race.
Emerson.—*Farming.*

Agriculture is the foundation of manufactures, since the productions of nature are the materials of art.
Gibbon.—*Decline and Fall.*

All taxes must, at last, fall upon agriculture.
Gibbon.—*Ib.*

A time there was, ere England's griefs began,
When every rood of ground maintained its man.
Goldsmith.—*Deserted Village.*

O happy life! if that their good
The husbandmen but understood.
Herrick *(From Virgil).*

Earth is so kindly there (Australia) that tickle her with a hoe and she laughs with a harvest.
D. Jerrold.—*Letter.*

In every way agriculture is the first calling of mankind; it is the most honest, the most useful, and consequently the noblest which he can exercise.
Rousseau.—*Emile.*

There is no ancient gentlemen but gardeners, ditchers, and gravemakers; they hold up Adam's profession.
Shakespeare.—*Hamlet*, Act 5, 1.

He gave it for his opinion, "that whoever could make two ears of corn, or two blades of grass, to grow upon a spot of land where only one grew before, would deserve better of mankind, and do more essential service to his country, than the whole race of politicians put together.
Swift.—*Brobdingnag.*

The sire of gods and men, with hard decrees,
Forbids our plenty to be bought with ease,
And wills that mortal men, inured to toil,
Should exercise with pains the grudging soil.
Virgil.—*Georgics, Bk.* 1 *(Dryden tr.).*

O husbandmen, happy beyond measure if they only knew their own good fortune!
Virgil.—*Ib.*, 2.

No laws, divine or human, can restrain
From necessary works the labouring swain;
E'en holy-days and feasts permission yield
To float the meadows or to fence the field.
Virgil.—*Ib., Bk.* 1 *(Dryden tr.).*

O happy, if he knew his happy state,
The swain, who, free from business and debate,
Receives his easy food from Nature's hand,
And just returns of cultivated land!
Virgil.—*Ib., Bk.* 2 *(Dryden tr.).*

Their soil was barren and their hearts were hard.
Virgil.—*Æneid, Bk.* 7 *(Dryden tr.).*

The art which feeds the world is a thankless calling. VOLTAIRE.—*Le Temps Present.*

I believe that a sensible peasant knows more about agriculture than authors who from the seclusion of their libraries issue instructions as to how the earth is to be ploughed. VOLTAIRE.—*Letter.*

Give fools their gold, and knaves their
    power ;
Let fortune's bubbles rise and fall ;
Who sows a field or trains a flower
Or plants a tree is more than all.
        WHITTIER.—*Lines (Amesbury).*

He who sows the ground with care and diligence acquires a greater stock of religious merit than he could gain by the repetition of ten thousand prayers.
        ZOROASTER (*as quoted by Gibbon*).

Whose talk is of bullocks.
        Ecclesiasticus xxxviii, 25.

Hope sustains the husbandman.
        Latin prov.

The first men in the world were a gardener, a ploughman, and a grazier.
        Old Saying.

Corn and horn go together [Referring to prices of corn and cattle]. *Prov. (Ray).*

Where there is muck there is luck.
Quoted by Dr. Sheridan as a Scottish saying.
        Letter, 1735.

He that by the plough would thrive,
Himself must either hold or drive.
        Old Saying (Ray).

To break a pasture will make a man,
To make a pasture will break a man.
        Suffolk Saying.

Nae hurry wi' your corns,
Nae hurry wi' your harrows ;
Snaw lies ahint the dike,
Mair may come and fill the furrows.
        Scottish prov.

As ane flits, anither sits, and that keeps mailins [farms] dear. *Scottish prov.*

AILMENTS

Most of those evils we poor mortals know
From doctors and imagination flow.
        C. CHURCHILL.—*Night, v.* 69.

We are so fond of each other, because our ailments are the same.
        SWIFT.—*To Stella,* Feb. 1, 1711.

AIM

The aim, if reached or not, makes great
    the life ;
Try to be Shakespeare, leave the rest to
    fate ! BROWNING.—*Bishop Blougram.*

Who aimeth at the sky,
Shoots higher much than he that means a
    tree. HERBERT.—*Church Porch.*

Who shoots at the midday sun, though he be sure he shall never hit the mark, yet as sure he is he shall shoot higher than he who aims at a bush.
        SIR P. SIDNEY, *Arcadia, Bk.* 2.

A noble aim,
Faithfully kept, is as a noble deed.
        WORDSWORTH.—*Poems to National
            Independence, Pt.* 2, *No.* 19.

All in a row,
Bend the bow,
Shoot at the pigeon and kill the crow.
        Old Nursery Rhyme.

ALARMS

What man dare, I dare :
Approach thou like the rugged Russian
    bear,
The armed rhinoceros, or the Hyrcan tiger ;
Take any shape but that, and my firm
    nerve
Shall never tremble.
        SHAKESPEARE.—*Macbeth,* Act 3, 4.

Or in the night, imagining some fear,
How easy is a bush supposed a bear !
        SHAKESPEARE.—*Midsummer Night's
            Dream,* Act 5, 1.

ALCOHOL

O madness, to think use of strongest wines
And strongest drinks our chief support of
    health ;
When God, with these forbidden, made
    choice to rear
His mighty champion, strong beyond
    compare,
Whose drink was only from the liquid
    brook. MILTON.—*Samson Agonistes.*

ALE

Your best barley wine, the good liquor that our honest forefathers did use to drink of.
        IZAAK WALTON.—*Complete Angler, c.* 5.

Bring us in no beef for there is many bones,
But bring us in good ale, for that goth
    down at once.
        Song (14*th or* 15*th Century*).

ALIBI

Oh, Sammy, Sammy, vy worn't there a alleybi ? DICKENS.—*Pickwick, c.* 34.

ALLEGORICAL ART

I had rather see the portrait of a dog that I know than all the allegorical paintings they can show me in the world.
        JOHNSON.—*Remark as recorded by Sir
            John Hawkins.*

ALLIANCE

A sudden thought strikes me ; let us
swear an eternal friendship.
J. H. FRERE.—*Rovers*, Act 1, 1.

United thoughts and counsels, equal hope,
And hazard in the glorious enterprise.
MILTON.—*Paradise Lost, Bk. 1, l.* 88.

ALLITERATION

Who often, but without success, have
prayed,
For apt alliteration's artful aid.
C. CHURCHILL.—*Prophecy of Famine, v.* 86.

Begot by butchers and by beggars bred,
How high his Honour holds his haughty
head.   *Anon.*—*Anthologia Oxoniensis*
(1846). *On Cardinal Wolsey.*

ALLUREMENT

The look of love alarms,
Because 'tis filled with fire ;
But the look of soft deceit
Shall win the lover's hire ;
Soft deceit and idleness,
These are beauty's sweetest dress.
WM. BLAKE.—*Couplets and Fragments.*

How cheerfully he seems to grin,
How neatly spreads his claws,
And welcomes little fishes in
With gently smiling jaws !
C. L. DODGSON.—*Alice in Wonderland, c.* 2.

ALMANAC

The cheap convenience of an almanac,
which enters into the comforts of every
fireside in the country, could not be enjoyed but for the labours and studies of
the profoundest philosophers.
EDW. EVERETT.—*Lecture on the Working
Man's Party (c.* 1835).

ALOOFNESS

His was the lofty port, the distant mien,
That seems to shun the sight—and awes
if seen.   BYRON.—*Corsair, c.* 1, 16.

I strove with none, for none was worth my
strife ;
Nature I loved ; and next to Nature, Art.
I warmed both hands before the fire of
life ;
It sinks, and I am ready to depart.
W. S. LANDOR.—*Last Fruit.*

And stood aloof from other minds
In impotence of fancied power.
TENNYSON.—*A Character.*

ALTERNATIVES

It's very hard to lose your cash,
But harder to be shot.
O. W. HOLMES.—*Music Grinders.*

A door must be either open or shut.
French prov.

ALTRUISM

The eternal, *not ourselves,* which makes
for righteousness.
M. ARNOLD.—*Literature and Dogma, c.* 8.

Each man should bear his own discom-
forts rather than abridge the comforts of
another man.
CICERO *(adapted). See De Amic.,* 16, 57.

He never errs who sacrifices self.
(1st) LORD LYTTON.—*New Timon, Part* 4, 3

This is the highest learning,
The hardest and the best :
From self to keep still turning,
And honour all the rest.
G. MACDONALD.—*After Thomas à Kempis.*

Through self-forgetfulness divine.
GEO. MEREDITH.—*Lark Ascending.*

AMATEURS

Every artist was first an amateur.
EMERSON.—*Progress of Culture.*

AMBASSADORS

An ambassador is an honest man sent
to lie abroad for the commonwealth.
SIR H. WOTTON.—*In an Album.*

AMBIGUITY

Obscurity illustrated by a further
obscurity.   BURKE.—*Impeachment of
Hastings* (May 5, 1789).

Thus Oracles of old were still received,
The more ambiguous, still the more
believed.
GEO. FARQUHAR.—*Letter from Gray's Inn.*

Out of the same mouth proceedeth
blessing and cursing. My brethren, these
things ought not so to be.
St. James iii, 10.

Thou shalt go thou shalt return never
in battle shalt thou perish.
*Utterance of the Oracle capable of
favourable or unfavourable construction,
according to punctuation.*

There's mair knavery amang kirkmen
than honesty amang courtiers.
Scottish saying.

AMBITION

To bliss unknown my lofty soul aspires,
My lot unequal to my vast desires.
DR. J. ARBUTHNOT.—*Gnothi Seauton, l.* 53.

He would have been greater to posterity
if he had been willing to be smaller.
AUBROTUS MIRÆUS (*said of Erasmus*).

The strongest poison ever known
Came from Cæsar's laurel crown.
WM. BLAKE.—*Proverb.*

The same sun which gilds all nature,
and exhilarates the whole creation, does
not shine upon disappointed ambition.
BURKE.—*Present State of Nation.*

This Siren song of ambition.
BURKE.—*Speech* (1780).

Ambition can creep as well as soar.
BURKE.—*Letters on a Regicide Peace.*

Whose game was empires and whose
stakes were thrones ?
Whose table earth—whose dice were
human bones ?
BYRON.—*Age of Bronze*, 3.

Affection chained her to that heart ;
Ambition tore the links apart.
BYRON.—*Bride of Abydos, c.* 1, 6.

Ambition is the only power that combats
love. C. CIBBER.—*Cæsar in Egypt*, Act 1.

For what are riches, empire, power,
But larger means to gratify the will ?
CONGREVE.—*Mourning Bride*, Act 2, 3.

What shall I do to be for ever known,
And make the age to come my own ?
COWLEY.—*The Moth.*

Glory and empire are to female blood
More tempting dangerous rivals than a god.
J. CROWNE.—*Destruction of Jerusalem,
Pt.* 1, Act 3, 2.

Be not with honour's gilded baits beguiled,
Nor think ambition wise because 'tis brave.
SIR W. D'AVENANT.—*Gondibert,
Bk.* 1, 5, 75.

Remember Milo's end,
Wedged in the timber which he strove to
rend.
WENTWORTH DILLON (4TH EARL OF
ROSCOMMON).—*On Translated Verse.*

Desire of greatness is a godlike sin.
DRYDEN.—*Absalom and Achitophel,
Pt.* 1, *l.* 372.

Either I am
The foremost horse in the team, or I am
none.
FLETCHER (and SHAKESPEARE ?).—*Two
Noble Kinsmen*, Act 1.

Not to swim
I' the lead o' th' current were almost to
sink.
FLETCHER (and SHAKESPEARE ?).—*Ib.*

Ambition is but Avarice on stilts and
masked.
W. S. LANDOR.—*Imaginary
Conversations.*

The greatest ambition has not the least
appearance of being ambition, when it
is found in a position where it is absolutely
impossible to realise its aspirations.
LA ROCHEFOUCAULD, *Maxim* 91. —
(*Declared by George Eliot to be one of
his most acute sayings.*)

But what will not ambition and revenge
Descend to ?
MILTON.—*Paradise Lost, Bk.* 9, *l.* 168.

His trust was with th' Eternal to be
deemed
Equal in strength ; and rather than be
less,
Cared not to be at all.
MILTON.—*Ib., Bk.* 2, 44.

Vain hopes, vain aims, inordinate
desires.   MILTON.—*Ib., Bk.* 4, 808.

Those who write against glory desire
to have the glory of having written well ;
and those who read wish for the glory of
having read ; and I myself, in writing
this, have perhaps that yearning, and so
also perhaps have those who read me.
PASCAL.—*Pensées.*

You thought to grasp the world ; but
you shall keep
Its curses only crowned upon your brow.
EDEN PHILLPOTTS.—*Unto this Last.*

If Wealth and Worth and Happiness and
Fame
Be thine, among the Gods seek not to
inscribe thy name.
PINDAR.—*Olympic Odes*, 5, 55 (*Moore tr.*).

Pride still is aiming at the blest abodes,
Men would be angels, angels would be gods.
POPE.—*Essay on Man, Ep.* 1, 125.

Who pants for glory finds but short repose,
A breath revives him or a breath o'erthrows.
POPE.—*Ep. of Horace, Ep.* 1, 300.

The glorious fault of angels and of
gods.   POPE.—*Elegy, l.* 14.

I hold ambition of so airy and light a
quality that it is but a shadow's shadow.
SHAKESPEARE.—*Hamlet*, Act 2, 2.

The very substance of the ambitious
is merely the shadow of a dream.
SHAKESPEARE.—*Ib.*, Act 2, 2.

Fare thee well, great heart !
Ill-weaved ambition, how much art thou
shrunk !
When that this body did contain a spirit,
A kingdom for it was too small a bound :
But now two paces of the vilest earth
Is room enough.
SHAKESPEARE.—*Henry IV., Pt.* 1, Act 5.

I have touched the highest point of all
  my greatness,
And from that full meridian of my glory
I haste now to my setting: I shall fall
Like a bright exhalation in the evening,
And no man see me more.
    SHAKESPEARE.—*Henry VIII.*, Act 3, 2.

I have ventured,
Like little wanton boys that swim on
  bladders,
This many summers in a sea of glory ;
But far beyond my depth.
    SHAKESPEARE.—*Ib.*

Cromwell, I charge thee, fling away ambition :
By that sin fell the angels.
    SHAKESPEARE.—*Ib.*

Lowliness is young ambition's ladder,
Whereto the climber-upward turns his
  face ;
But when he once attains the upmost
  round,
He then unto the ladder turns his back,
Looks in the clouds, scorning the base
  degrees
By which he did ascend.
    SHAKESPEARE.—*Julius Cæsar*, Act 2,1.

I have no spur
To prick the sides of my intent, but only
Vaulting ambition, which o'erleaps itself,
And falls on the other.
    SHAKESPEARE.—*Macbeth*, Act 1, 7.

Yet peace begins just where ambition ends.
    YOUNG.—*Night Thoughts*, 5.

Ambition ! powerful source of good and ill !
    YOUNG.—*Ib.*, 6.

The trap to the highborn is ambition.
    Ancient British or Welsh prov. (Ray).

No priestling, small as he may be,
But wishes some day Pope to be.
    Prov. (cited by Heine, in his
        " Confessions ").

He that hews over high,
The chips will fall into his eye.
    Prov. (Scottish ?).

AMENABILITY

I am of a constitution so general, that
it consorts and sympathiseth with all
things.   I have no antipathy or, rather,
Idiosyncrasy.
    SIR THOS. BROWNE.—*Religio Medici*,
        Pt. 2, sec. 1.

He needs not fear to be chidden,
That sits where he is bidden.
    Tr. of French prov. (Cotgrave).

AMERICA

Yet still from either beach
The voice of blood shall reach,
More audible than speech,
  " We are one ! "
W. ALLSTON.—*America to Great Britain.*

Westward the course of empire takes
its way.
    BISHOP BERKELEY.—*Prospect of
    Planting Arts and Learning in America.*

I called the New World into existence
to redress the balance of the Old.
    GEO. CANNING.—*King's Message*, 1826.

Columbia, Columbia, to glory arise,
The queen of the world and the child of
  the skies.
    DR. T. DWIGHT.—*Columbia.*

In America the geography is sublime,
but the men are not ; the inventions are
excellent, but the inventors one is sometimes ashamed of.
    EMERSON.—*Conduct of Life,
    Considerations by the Way.*

One of our statesmen said, " The curse
of this country is eloquent men."
    EMERSON.—*Eloquence.*

Thou, O my country, hast thy foolish
  ways,
Too apt to purr at every stranger's
  praise.
    O. W. HOLMES.—*After-dinner Poem*

Boston State-house is the hub of the
Solar System.
    O. W. HOLMES.—*Autocrat of Breakfast
        Table.*

Hail, Columbia ! happy land !
Hail, ye heroes ! heavenborn land !
Who fought and bled in Freedom's cause.
    DR. J. HOPKINSON.—*Hail, Columbia.*

Oh ! but for such, Columbia's days were
  done ;
Rank without ripeness, quickened without
  sun,
Crude at the surface, rotten at the core,
Her fruits would fall before her spring
  was o'er.
    T. MOORE.—*To the Hon. W. R. Spencer.*

The indignant land,
Where Washington hath left
His awful memory,
A light for after times.
    SOUTHEY.—*Ode*, 1814.

God sifted a whole Nation that He might
send choice grain over into this wilderness.
    WM. STOUGHTON.—*Sermon : New
        England's True Interests.*

The youth of America is their oldest tradition. It has been going on now for three hundred years.
OSCAR WILDE.—*Woman of no Importance,*
Act I.

AMERICANS

Our American people cannot be taxed with slowness in performance, or in praising their performance.
EMERSON.—*Success.*

And ne'er shall the sons of Columbia be slaves
While the earth bears a plant, or the sea rolls its waves.
ROBT. TREAT PAINE.—*Adams and Liberty.*

He [Jonathan] was rather an odd-looking chap, in truth, and had many queer ways; but everybody that had seen John Bull saw a great likeness between them, and swore he was John's own boy, and a true chip of the old block.
J. K. PAULDING.—*History of John Bull and Brother Jonathan* (1816).

Be proud of those strong sons of thine
Who wrenched their rights from thee !
TENNYSON.—*England and America in* 1782.

AMIABILITY

God has given us tongues that we may say something pleasant to our fellow-men.
HEINE.—*Confessions.*

That you may be loved, be lovable.
OVID.—*Ars Amat.*

And if thou wouldst be happy, learn to please.
PRIOR.—*Solomon,* 2, 266.

AMOROUSNESS

The landlady and Tam grew gracious,
Wi' favours secret, sweet, and precious.
BURNS.—*Tam o' Shanter.*

Still amorous, and fond, and billing,
Like Philip and Mary on a shilling.
BUTLER.—*Hudibras, Pt.* 3, *c.* 1.

Of temper amorous as the first of May.
TENNYSON.—*Princess, c.* 1, 2.

AMUSEMENT

Amusement is the happiness of those that cannot think.
POPE.—*Thoughts on Various Subjects.*

Who lives without folly is not so wise as he thinks.   *French prov.*

ANACHRONISMS

He [Apollo after hearing the accusation against Virgil of making Æneas and Dido cotemporary] decreed for the future no

poet should presume to make a lady die for love two hundred years before her birth.   DRYDEN.—*Dedic. of Æneid.*

ANALYSIS

Analysis kills love, as well as other things.
DR. J. BROWN.—*Horæ Subsecivæ,*
Oh, I'm Wat.

ANARCHY

I am of his mind that said, " Better it is to live where nothing is lawful than where all things are lawful."
BACON.—*Church Controversies.*

O what a parish, what a terrible parish,
O what a parish is Little Dunkel !
They hae hangit the minister, drowned the precentor,
Dung down the steeple and drucken the bell.   ANON.

ANECDOTAGE

When a man fell into his anecdotage it was a sign for him to retire from the world.
DISRAELI.—*Lothair, c.* 29.

But oh ! the biggest muff afloat
Is he who takes to anecdote.
H. S. LEIGH.—*Men I Dislike.*

The world is in its anecdotage.
ROGERS (*Attributed*).

ANGELS

'Tis only when they spring to Heaven that angels
Reveal themselves to you.
BROWNING.—*Paracelsus, Pt.* 5.

This world had angels all too few,
And heaven is overflowing.
COLERIDGE.—*To a Young Lady.*

ANGER

On my heart's prow a blast blows mightily,
Keen wrath and loathing fierce.
ÆSCHYLUS.—*Choephoræ,* 387 (*Plumptre tr.*).

The angry man always thinks that he can do more than he can.
ALBERTANO OF BRESCIA.—*Liber Consolationis.*

When most angry and vexed remember that life lasts but a moment and that we shall be soon all in our graves.
MARCUS AURELIUS.—*Bk.* 11, 18.

Anger makes dull men witty, but it keeps them poor.
BACON.—*Certain Apophthegms (Attributed to Queen Elizabeth).*

Few men can afford to be angry.
A. BIRRELL.—*Edmund Burke.*

I was angry with my friend:
I told my wrath, my wrath did end.
I was angry with my foe:
I told it not, my wrath did grow.
WM. BLAKE.—*A Poison Tree.*

To be in a passion you good may do,
But no good if a passion is in you.
WM. BLAKE.—*Proverbs.*

The thing I pity most
In men is—action prompted by surprise
Of anger.   BROWNING.—*A Forgiveness.*

Where sits our sulky, sullen dame,
Gathering her brows like gathering storm,
Nursing her wrath to keep it warm.
BURNS.—*Tam o' Shanter.*

Is nat this [anger] a cursed vice? Yis,
certes. Allas! it binimeth [taketh away]
from man his wit and his resoun and al
his debonaire [gentle] lyf espirituel, that
should kepe his soule.
CHAUCER.—*Parson's Tale, sec.* 34.

He who quells an angry thought is
greater than a King.
ELIZA COOK.—*Anger.*

Of all bad things by which mankind
are cursed,
Their own bad tempers surely are the
worst. R. CUMBERLAND.—*Menander.*

Call for the grandest of all human
sentiments, what is that? It is that a
man should forget his anger before he
lies down to sleep.
DE QUINCEY.—*Opium Eater.*

Beware the fury of a patient man.
DRYDEN.—*Absalom and Achitophel.*

Like women's anger, impotent and
loud.   DRYDEN.—*To Sir G. Kneller.*

Jupiter is always in the wrong, you
know, when he has recourse to his thunder.
MISS EDGEWORTH.—*Griselda, c.* 15.

Well,—no offence:
Thar ain't no sense
In gittin riled.
BRET HARTE.—*Jim.*

Anger is short madness.
HORACE.—*Ep., Bk.* 1.

As bodies through a mist, so actions
through anger, seem greater than they are.
PLUTARCH.—*Morals, Bk.* 1.

To be angry is to revenge the fault of
others upon ourselves.
POPE.—*Thoughts on Various Subjects.*

He who conquers his wrath overcomes
his greatest enemy.   PUBLILIUS SYRUS.

The law sees the angry man; the angry
man does not see the law.
PUBLILIUS SYRUS.

When an angry man comes to himself,
then he is angry with himself.
PUBLILIUS SYRUS.

Delay is the best remedy for anger.
SENECA.—*De Ira.*

Carries anger as the flint bears fire;
Who, much enforcèd, shows a hasty
spark,
And straight is cold again.
SHAKESPEARE—*Julius Cæsar*, Act 4, 3.

Think when you are enraged with
anyone, what would probably become
your sentiments should he die during the
dispute.
SHENSTONE.—*Men and Manners.*

'Tis the noblest mood
That takes least hold on anger.
SWINBURNE.—*Bothwell*, Act 2, 4.

Can heavenly minds such high resentment
show,
Or exercise their spite in human woe?
VIRGIL.—*Æneid, Bk.* 1 (*Dryden*).

Is there such rage in heavenly minds?
VIRGIL.—*Ib.*

But, children, you should never let
Your angry passions rise;
Your little hands were never made
To tear each other's eyes.
I. WATTS.—*Against Quarrelling.*

I canna be angry for lauchin.
J. WILSON.—*Noctes,* 35 (*Ettrick
Shepherd*).

Be not as a lion in thy house, nor
frantick among thy servants.
Ecclesiasticus iv, 30.

Envy and wrath shorten the life.
Ib. xxx, 24.

ANGLERS AND ANGLING

And angling too, that solitary vice,
Whatever Izaak Walton sings or says:
The quaint old cruel coxcomb, in his
gullet
Should have a hook, and a small trout to
pull it.
BYRON.—*Don Juan, c.* 13, *st.* 106.

He minded not his friends' advice
But followed his own wishes;
But one most cruel trick of his
Was that of catching fishes.
JANE TAYLOR.—*Little Fisherman.*

Angling is somewhat like poetry, men
are to be born so.
> I. WALTON.—*Complete Angler, ch.* 1.

I am, sir, a brother of the angle.
> I. WALTON.—*Ib.*

We may say of angling as Dr. Boteler
said of strawberries, " Doubtless God
could have made a better berry, but
doubtless God never did "; and so, if
I might be judge, " God never did make
a more calm, quiet, innocent recreation
than angling." I. WALTON.—*Ib., c.* 5.

This dish of meat is too good for any
but anglers, or very honest men.
> I. WALTON.—*Complete Angler, The
> Angler's Wish, ch.* 8.

ANGUISH, MENTAL

While the vexed mind, her own tormentor
plies
A scorpion scourge, unmarked by human
eyes.
> JUVENAL.—13, 195 (*Gifford tr.*).

Canst thou not minister to a mind
diseased ;
Pluck from the memory a rooted sorrow,
Raze out the written troubles of the brain ;
And, with some sweet oblivious antidote,
Cleanse the stuffed bosom of that perilous
stuff,
Which weighs upon the heart?
> SHAKESPEARE.—*Macbeth,* Act 5, 3.

Not poppy, nor mandragora,
Nor all the drowsy syrups of the world,
Shall ever medicine thee to that sweet
sleep,
Which thou ow'dst yesterday.
> SHAKESPEARE.—*Othello,* Act 3, 3.

ANIMALS

Animals are such agreeable friends—
they ask no questions, they pass no
criticisms.
> GEO. ELIOT.—*Scenes of Clerical
> Life. Mr. Gilfil's Love Story.*

ANIMALS, FUTURE EXISTENCE OF

Though I am far from denying that to
this day the counsels of Divine Goodness
regarding dumb creatures are, for us,
involved in deep obscurity, yet we see
nevertheless that Scripture foretells for
them a " glorious liberty "; and we are
assured that the compassion of Heaven,
to which we owe so much, will not be
wanting to them.
> KEBLE.—*Lectures on Poetry, No.* 19
> (*E. K. Francis tr.*).

There is another world
For all that live and move . . . a better
one !

Where the proud bipeds, who would fain
confine
Infinite goodness to the little bounds
Of their own charity, may envy thee.
> SOUTHEY.—*On the Death of a Spaniel.*

ANNIHILATION

Oh threats of Hell and hopes of Paradise !
One thing at least is certain—*This* life
flies ;
One thing is certain, and the rest is Lies ;
The flower that once has blown for ever
dies. FITZGERALD.—*Omar.*

ANNOTATION

Notes are often necessary, but they are
necessary evils.
> JOHNSON.—*Pref. to Shakespeare.*

Note this before my notes.
There is not a note of mine that's worth
the noting.
> SHAKESPEARE.—*Much Ado,* Act 2, 3.

ANONYMITY

While he [Junius] walks like Jack the
Giant-Killer in a coat of darkness, he
may do much mischief with little strength.
> JOHNSON.—*Falkland's Islands.*

ANSWER

Ambiguous, and with double sense deluding,
Which they who asked have seldom
understood.
> MILTON.—*Paradise Regained, Bk.* 1, 435.

Had I as many mouths as Hydra, such
an answer would stop them all.
> SHAKESPEARE.—*Othello,* Act 2, 3.

ANTICIPATION

Like one that on a lonesome road
Doth walk in fear and dread,
And having once turned round, walks
on,
And turns no more his head ;
Because he knows a frightful fiend
Doth close behind him tread.
> COLERIDGE.—*Ancient Mariner, Pt.* 6.

Why should we
Anticipate our sorrows ? 'Tis like those
That die for fear of death.
> SIR J. DENHAM.—*The Sophy.*

Nothing is so good as it seems beforehand.
> GEO. ELIOT.—*Silas Marner, c.* 18.

Truth is for other worlds, and hope for
this ;
The cheating future lends the present's
bliss. O. W. HOLMES.—*Old Player.*

ANTI-CLIMAX

The mountains laboured with prodigious throes,
And lo! a mouse ridiculous arose.
P. FRANCIS.—*Horace, Art of Poetry.*

ANTIQUITIES

Antiquities are history defaced, or some remnants of history which have casually escaped the shipwreck of time.
BACON.—*Advancement of Learning, Bk.* 2.

Who studies ancient laws and rites,
Tongues, arts and arms, and history,
Must drudge, like Selden, days and nights,
And in the endless labour die.
BENTLEY.—*Who Strives to Mount Parnassus' Hill.*

Veneration of antiquity is congenial to the human mind.
BURKE.—*Tracts on Popery Laws, c.* 3, *Pt.* 2.

Age shakes Athena's tower, but spares grey Marathon.
BYRON.—*Childe Harold, c.* 2, *st.* 88.

To look back to antiquity is one thing; to go back to it is another.
C. C. COLTON.—*Lacon.*

Nothing can be preserved that is not good. EMERSON.—*Books.*

I love everything that's old: old friends, old times, old manners, old books, old wine.
GOLDSMITH.—*She Stoops to Conquer,* Act 1.

The ridiculous part of John's [John Bull's] character is his love of an absurdity, an injustice—it may be an acute inconvenience—from its very antiquity.
D. JERROLD.—*Heads of the People.*

Woodman, spare that tree!
Touch not a single bough!
In youth it sheltered me,
And I'll protect it now.
G. P. MORRIS.—*Woodman, Spare that Tree.*

Whatever authority antiquity may possess, truth always has the advantage, however newly discovered, because she is always more ancient than all the opinions man has held on the matter.
PASCAL.—*Pensées.*

By many a temple half as old as Time.
ROGERS.—*Italy, A Farewell* (1839).

Your modern antiques and your antiquated moderns.
SCOTT.—*Tales of Crusaders.*

Old thanks, old thoughts, old aspirations,
Outlive men's lives and lives of nations.
SWINBURNE.—*Age and Song.*

Is not old wine wholesomest, old pippins toothsomest, old wood burn brightest, old linen wash whitest?
WEBSTER.—*West-Ward Hoe.*

While poring antiquarians search the ground,
Upturned with curious pains, the Bard, a Seer,
Takes fire. The men that have been reappear.
WORDSWORTH.—*Miscellaneous Sonnets, Pt.* 3, 20.

As statues moulder into worth.
Ascribed to Paul Whitehead.

Everything ancient is to be respected.
Greek prov.

ANXIETY

And slowly dropping on the heart in sleep
Comes woe-recording care,
And makes the unwilling yield to wiser thoughts.
ÆSCHYLUS.—*Agamemnon (Plumptre tr.).*

Suspense, the only insupportable misfortune of life.
LORD BOLINGBROKE.—*Letter,* 1725.

One morn a Peri at the gate
Of Eden stood disconsolate.
MOORE.—*Lalla Rookh.*

I would it were bed-time, Hal, and all well. SHAKESPEARE.—*Henry IV.,* Act 5, 1.

APATHY

But not to understand a treasure's worth
Till time has stolen away the slighted good,
Is cause of half the poverty we feel,
And makes the world the wilderness it is.
COWPER.—*Winter Walk at Noon,* 50.

A people sunk in apathy and fear.
WORDSWORTH.—*Poems to National Independence, Pt.* 2, *No.* 25 (1805).

APOLOGY

No 'polligy ain't gwine ter make hair come back where the biling water hit.
J. C. HARRIS.—*Uncle Remus.*

APPARITIONS

Ghost, kelpie, wraith,
And all the trumpery of vulgar faith.
CAMPBELL.—*Pilgrim of Glencoe.*

Whence and what art thou, execrable shape?
MILTON.—*Paradise Lost, Bk.* 2, *l.* 81.

Be thy intents wicked or charitable,
Thou com'st in such a questionable shape
That I will speak to thee.
SHAKESPEARE.—*Hamlet,* Act 1, 4.

APPEAL

Awake, arise, or be for ever fallen !
MILTON.—*Paradise Lost, Bk.* 1, 330.

Strike, but hear.
THEMISTOCLES (*according to Plutarch*).

I would appeal to Philip, but to Philip
sober.   VAL. MAXIMUS.—*Bk.* 6.

I appeal unto Cæsar. *Acts* xxv, 11.

APPEARANCE

A thing may look specious in theory
and yet be ruinous in practice. A thing
may look evil in theory and yet be in
practice excellent.
BURKE.—*Impeachment of Hastings,*
Feb., 1788.

The world that never sets esteem
On what things are, but what they seem.
BUTLER.—*Elephant in the Moon.*

The world is an old woman, and mistakes any gilt farthing for a gold coin.
CARLYLE.—*Sartor, Bk.* 2, *ch.* 4.

And be ye wys, as ye ben fair to see,
Wel in the ring then is the ruby set.
CHAUCER.—*Troilus, Bk.* 2.

Keep up appearances ; there lies the test ;
The world will give thee credit for the rest.
Outward be fair, however foul within ;
Sin, if thou wilt, but then in secret sin.
C. CHURCHILL.—*Night,* 311.

Things are seldom what they seem ;
Skim milk masquerades as cream.
SIR W. S. GILBERT.—*Pinafore.*

Men are valued not for what they are,
but for what they seem to be.
(1st) LORD LYTTON.—*Money,* Act 1.

Be not afraid of every stranger ;
Start not aside at every danger ;
Things that seem are not the same ;
Blow a blast at every flame.
G. PEELE.—*Old Wives' Tale.*

Whether the fellow do this out of kindness or knavery, I cannot tell ; but it is
pretty to observe.
PEPYS.—*Diary,* Oct. 7, 1665.

We'll have a swashing and a martial
outside.
SHAKESPEARE.—*As You Like It,* Act 1, 3.

Seems, madam ? Nay, it is, I know
not seems.
SHAKESPEARE.—*Hamlet,* Act 1, 2.

The devil hath power
To assume a pleasing shape.
SHAKESPEARE.—*Ib.,* Act 2, 2.

Assume a virtue, if you have it not.
SHAKESPEARE.—*Ib.,* Act 3, 4.

The world is still deceived with orna-
ment.
SHAKESPEARE.—*Merchant of Venice,*
Act 3, 2.

Was ever book, containing such vile
matter,
So fairly bound ? O that deceit should
dwell
In such a gorgeous palace !
SHAKESPEARE.—*Romeo and Juliet,* Act 3, 2.

Ye are like unto whited sepulchres,
which indeed appear beautiful outward,
but are within full of dead men's bones,
and of all uncleanness.
St. Matthew xxiii, 27.

Judge not according to the appearance.
St. John vii, 24.

APPETITE

Cursed with an appetite keen I am,
And I'll subdue it—
And I'll subdue it—
And I'll subdue it—with cold roast lamb.
SIR W. S. GILBERT.—*Princess Ida.*

He is a very valiant trencher-man.
SHAKESPEARE.—*Much Ado,* Act 1, 1.

APPLAUSE

Envy itself is dumb, in wonder lost,
And factions strive which shall applaud
him most.
ADDISON.—*The Campaign.*

Applause is the spur of noble minds,
the end and aim of weak ones.
C. C. COLTON.—*Lacon.*

And even the ranks of Tuscany
Could scarce forbear to cheer.
MACAULAY.—*Horatius.*

Fate cannot rob you of deserved applause,
Whether you win or lose in such a cause.
MASSINGER.—*Bashful Lover,* Act 1, 2.

I love the people,
But do not like to stage me to their eyes.
Though it do well, I do not relish well
Their loud applause and *aves* vehement ;
Nor do I think the man of safe discretion,
That does affect it.
SHAKESPEARE.—*Measure for Measure,*
Act 1, 1.

I would applaud thee to the very echo,
That should applaud again.
SHAKESPEARE.—*Macbeth,* Act 5, 3.

He only is a great man who can neglect
the applause of the multitude, and enjoy
himself independent of its favour.
STEELE.—*Spectator, vol.* 3, 172.

APPREHENSION

Some of your griefs you have cured,
And the sharpest you still have sur-
vived,
But what torments of pain you endured
From evils that never arrived !
EMERSON.—*From the French.*

We will not woo foul weather all too soon,
Or nurse November in the lap of June.
HOOD.—*Plea of the Midsummer Fairies.*

What you fear happens sooner than
what you hope. PUBLILIUS SYRUS.

Present fears
Are less than horrible misgivings.
SHAKESPEARE.—*Macbeth*, Act 1, 3.

All things are less dreadful than they
seem. WORDSWORTH.—*Eccles. Sonnets,*
Pt. 1, 7.

I would it were not as I think,
I would I thought it were not.
SIR T. WYATT.—*He lamenteth.*

APPROBATION

Reproof on her lips but a smile in her eye.
S. LOVER.—*Rory O'More.*

Approbation from Sir Hubert Stanley
is praise indeed.
T. MORTON.—*Cure for Heartache.*

APRIL

Oh, to be in England now that April's
there !
BROWNING.—*Home Thoughts*
from Abroad.

'Tis a month before the month of May,
And the spring comes slowly up this way.
COLERIDGE.—*Christabel, Pt. 1.*

When well apparelled April on the heel
Of limping winter treads.
SHAKESPEARE.—*Romeo and Juliet*, Act 1, 2.

The uncertain glory of an April day.
SHAKESPEARE.—*Two Gentlemen of Verona,*
Act 1, 1.

April, April,
Laugh thy girlish laughter ;
Then, the moment after,
Weep thy girlish tears !
SIR W. WATSON.—*April.*

When the cuckoo comes to the bare thorn,
Sell your cow and buy your corn ;
But when she comes to the full bit,
Sell your corn and buy your sheep.
North England saying (Halliwell).

When April blows his horn,
It's good both for hay and corn.
Old Saying (Ray).

ARBITRATORS

Men who are engaged in settling difficult
questions should be devoid of hatred, of
friendship, of anger, and of soft hearted-
ness. SALLUST.—*Catilina*, 51, 1 (*From*
Cæsar's Oration).

ARCHBISHOPS

I have no illusion left but the Archbishop
of Canterbury.
SYDNEY SMITH.—*Saying.*

ARCHITECTURE

How reverend is the face of this tall pile,
Whose ancient pillars rear their marble
heads
To bear aloft its arched and ponderous
roof,
By its own weight made steadfast and
immoveable,
Looking tranquillity !
CONGREVE.—*Mourning Bride*, Act 2, 1.

The Gothic cathedrals were built when
the builder and the priest and the people
were overpowered by their faith. Love
and fear laid every stone.
EMERSON.—*Art.*

A thing of ugliness is potent for evil.
It deforms the taste of the thoughtless ;
it frets the man who knows how bad it is ;
it is a disgrace to the people who raised
it—an example and an occasion for more
monstrosities.
SIR A. HELPS.—*Friends in Council, Bk. 1,*
ch. 10.

A style of Architecture [Gothic Deco-
rated] which, to me at least, is, in comparison with all others, the most beautiful
of all, and by far the most in harmony
with the mysteries of religion.
KEBLE.—*Lectures on Poetry*, No. 3
(*E. K. Francis tr.*).

With antique pillars massy proof,
And storied windows richly dight,
Casting a dim religious light.
MILTON.—*Il Penseroso*, 159.

Good architecture is essentially religious
—the production of a faithful and virtuous,
not of an infidel and corrupted people.
But . . . good architecture is not ecclesiastical. . . . It has always been the
work of the commonalty, not of the
clergy. RUSKIN.—*Lecture No. 2, Crown*
of Wild Olive.

Among the first habits that a young
architect should learn, is that of thinking
in shadow.
RUSKIN.—*Seven Lamps, c. 3, 13.*

No architecture is so haughty as that
which is simple.
RUSKIN.—*Stones of Venice, c. 6, 73.*

Architecture is frozen music.
SCHELLING.—*Philosophie der Kunst.*

Built ere the art was known
By pointed aisles, and shafted stalk,
The arcades of an alleyed walk
To emulate in stone.
SCOTT.—*Marmion, 2, 10.*

In Saxon strength that abbey frowned,
With massive arches broad and round.
SCOTT.—*Ib.*

Built
To music; therefore never built at all,
And therefore built for ever.
TENNYSON.—*Gareth and Lynette.*

They dreamt not of a perishable home
Who thus could build.
WORDSWORTH.—*Eccles. Sonnets, Pt. 3, 45*
(Of Westminster Abbey).

ARCHIVES

Of all countries England is, without
contradiction, the one which has the most
ancient archives, and the most consecutive.
VOLTAIRE.—*Pyrrhonism of History.*

ARGUMENT

For still the longer we contend,
We are but further off the end.
BUTLER.—*Hudibras, Pt. 3, c. 1.*

Though syllogisms hang not on my tongue,
I am not surely always in the wrong;
'Tis hard if all is false that I advance;
A fool must now and then be right by
chance.
COWPER.—*Conversation, l. 93.*

Rather a tough customer in argeyment,
Joe, if anybody was to try and tackle him.
DICKENS.—*Barnaby Rudge, ch. 1.*

It is in the nature of foolish reason to
seem good to the foolish reasoner.
GEO. ELIOT.—*Theophrastus Such,
Looking Inward.*

It's only d—d fools who argue. Never
contradict, never explain, never apologize.
These are the secrets of a happy life.
LORD FISHER.—*Letter to Times, Sept. 5,
1919.*

He argued high, he argued low,
He also argued round about him.
SIR W. S. GILBERT.—*Sir Macklin.*

In arguing too the parson owned his skill,
For ev'n when vanquished, he could argue
still. GOLDSMITH.—*Deserted Village.*

I find you want me to furnish you with
argument and intellects too. No, sir,
there I protest you are too hard for me.
GOLDSMITH.—*Vicar of Wakefield.*

Be calm in arguing; for fierceness makes
Error a fault and truth discourtesie.
HERBERT.—*Church Porch.*

His [Berkeley's] arguments admit of
no answer and produce no conviction.
HUME.—*Of Bishop Berkeley.*

In argument with men a woman ever
Goes by the worse, whatever be her cause.
MILTON.—*Samson Agonistes, 903.*

You have not converted a man because
you have silenced him.
LORD MORLEY.—*On Compromise.*

In overmuch disputation the truth is
lost. PUBLILIUS SYRUS.

You shall never take her without her
answer, unless you take her without her
tongue.
SHAKESPEARE.—*As You Like It, Act 4, 1.*

The Retort courteous . . . the Quip
modest . . . the Reproof valiant . . . the
Countercheck quarrelsome . . . the Lie circumstantial . . . the Lie direct.
SHAKESPEARE.—*Ib., Act 5, 4.*

Heat is in proportion to the want of
true knowledge.
STERNE.—*Tristram Shandy, Vol. 4.*

The sombre Englishman, even in his
love affairs, always wants to reason.
The Frenchman is more reasonable than
that. VOLTAIRE.—*Les Originaux.*

I hate a' argling and hargarbargling
o' argument ower ane's toddy.
J. WILSON.—*Noctes, 13.*

Bluster, splutter, question, cavil! But
be sure your argument be intricate enough
to confound the court.
WYCHERLEY.—*Plain Dealer.*

ARITHMETIC

What is the meaning of these damned
little dots?
LORD RANDOLPH CHURCHILL.—
*Remark attributed to him on being
presented with some official returns
worked out in decimal points.*

" Well done, my boy ! " the joyful father
cries;
" Addition and subtraction make us wise."
P. FRANCIS.—*Horace, Art of Poetry.*

That arithmetic is the basest of all the
mental activities is proved by the fact that
it is the only one that can be accomplished
by a machine.
SCHOPENHAUER.—*Psychological Observations.*

Lucy, dear child, mind your arithmetic.
. . . In that first sum you had carried two
(as a cab is licensed to do), and you ought,
dear Lucy, to have carried but one. Is
this a trifle ? What would life be without
arithmetic, but a scene of horrors ?
SYDNEY SMITH.—*Letter, July 22,* 1835.

ARMOUR

They carved at the meal
With gloves of steel ;
And they drank the red wine through
the helmet barred.
ScoTT.—*Lay of the Last Minstrel.*

ARRIVAL

We're here because we're here,
Because we're here, because we're here ;
Oh, here we are, oh, here we are,
Oh, here we are again.
Popular Soldier Song (c. 1916).

ART

Art still has truth, take refuge there.
M. ARNOLD.—*Memorial Verses.*

The lyf so short, the craft so long to lerne,
Th' assay so hard, so sharp the conquering.
CHAUCER.—*Assembly of Foules, v.* 1.

Careless she is with artful care,
Affecting to seem unaffected.
CONGREVE.—*Amoret.*

The conscious utterance of thought, by
speech or action, to any end, is Art.
EMERSON.—*Art.*

The statue is then beautiful when it
begins to be incomprehensible.
EMERSON.—*Love.*

When they talked of their Raphaels,
Correggios, and stuff,
He shifted his trumpet and only took
snuff.   GOLDSMITH.—*Retaliation.*

Rules and models destroy genius and
art.   HAZLITT.—*Essay on Taste.*

Deeds are the offspring of words, but
Goethe's pretty words are childless. That
is the curse of all which has originated
in mere art.
HEINE.—*The Romantic School.*

Art is the application of knowledge to
a practical end. If the knowledge be
merely accumulated exper ence, the art
is empirical.
SIR J. HERSCHEL.—*Influence of Science.*

Life is short and the art is long.
HIPPOCRATES.—*Aphorisms (In reference to the art of healing).*

But the Devil whoops, as he whooped of
old :
" It's clever, but is it Art ? "
KIPLING.—*Conundrum of the Workshop.*

And what is art ; whereto we press,
Through pain and prose and rhyme,
When Nature in her nakedness
Defeats us every time ?
KIPLING.—*Edge of the Evening.*

'Tis the fault of all art to seem antiquated
and faded in the eyes of the succeeding
generation.   A. LANG.—*Letters to Dead
Authors—Jane Austen.*

Nietzsche says : " Art is with us that we
shall not perish of too much truth " ;
but there is no fear of any such surfeit.
Truth is a rare bird still—so rare that
few recognise it even if the artist show
it to them.
EDEN PHILLPOTTS.—*A Shadow Passes.*

They [the sportsmen] doubted and mis-
trusted artists, dividing them roughly
into two classes. Some they held harmless lunatics ; some, who employed art in
propaganda, they regarded as dangerous
lunatics. But they agreed that all must
be lunatic.   EDEN PHILLPOTTS.—*Ib.*

The learned understand the theory of
art, the unlearned its pleasure.
QUINTILIAN.

Art should set itself a goal which is
unceasingly retiring.   A. DE RIVAROL.

Art, properly so called, is no recreation.
It cannot be learned at spare moments,
nor pursued when we have nothing better
to do. RUSKIN.—*Modern Painters, Vol.* 2,
sec. 1, *ch.* 1, 2.

Every art is an imitation of nature.
SENECA.—*Ep.* 65.

He does it with a better grace, but I
do it more natural.
SHAKESPEARE.—*Twelfth Night,* Act 2, 3.

Roebuck believes in the fine arts with
all the earnestness of a man who does
not understand them.
G. B. SHAW.—*Man and Superman.*

There is no Art delivered to mankind
that hath not the works of Nature for
his principal object.
SIR PHILIP SIDNEY.—*Apologie for
Poetrie.*

And, that which all faire workes doth most
aggrace,
The art, which all that wrought, appearèd
in no place.
SPENSER.—*Faerie Queene,
bk.* 2, *c.* 12, *st.* 58.

The assertion that art may be good
art and at the same time incomprehensible
to a great number of people, is extremely
unjust ; and its consequences are ruinous
to art itself.   TOLSTOY.

To keep in sight Perfection, and adore
The vision, is the artist's best delight.
        SIR W. WATSON.—*Epigram*

There never was an artistic period. There
never was an art-loving nation.
        J. McN. WHISTLER.—*Ten o'Clock.*

The secret of life is in art.
        OSCAR WILDE.—*English Renaissance.*

A true artist takes no notice whatever
of the public.
        OSCAR WILDE.—*Soul of Man under
                Socialism.*

Art should never try to be popular.
        OSCAR WILDE.—*Ib.*

Where art is too conspicuous, truth
seems to be wanting.   *Latin prov.*

ARTFULNESS

The dodgerest of all the dodgers.
        DICKENS.—*Mutual Friend, Bk. 2, c. 13.*

ARTIFICES

"Chops and Tomata Sauce. Yours,
Pickwick." Chops! Gracious heavens!
and Tomata Sauce! Gentlemen, is the
happiness of a sensitive and confiding
female to be trifled away by such shallow
artifices as these?
        DICKENS.—*Pickwick, ch. 34.*

ARTISTRY

That's the wise thrush; he sings each
        song twice over
Lest you should think he never could re-
        capture
The first fine careless rapture.
        BROWNING.—*Home Thoughts from
                Abroad.*

ARTISTS

The poison of the honey-bee
Is the artist's jealousy.
        WM. BLAKE.—*Proverbs.*

The number of pure artists is small.
Few souls are so finely tempered as to
preserve the delicacy of meditative
feeling, untainted by the allurements of
accidental suggestion.
        DR. J. BROWN.—*Horæ Subsecivæ
                (A. H. Hallam).*

The artist who is to produce a work
which is to be admired . . . by all men,
. . . must disindividualize himself, and
be a man of no party, and no manner,
and no age, but one through whom the
soul of all men circulates, as the common
air through his lungs.
        EMERSON.—*Art.*

Every artist has got to be a man,
woman, and child rolled into one.
        EDEN PHILLPOTTS.

The true artist will let his wife starve,
his children go barefoot, his mother drudge
for his living at seventy, sooner than work
at anything but his art.
        G. B. SHAW.—*Man and Superman.*

A great painter is not satisfied with
being sought after and admired because
his hands can do more than ordinary
hands, . . . but he wants to be fed
as if his stomach needed more food than
ordinary stomachs. . . . A day's work is
a day's work, neither more nor less, and
the man who does it needs a day's susten-
ance, a night's repose, and due leisure,
whether he be painter or ploughman.
        G. B. SHAW.—*Unsocial Socialist,
                ch. 5 (Sidney Trefusis).*

The rascal of a painter, poet, novelist,
or other voluptuary in labour, is not
content with his advantage in popular
esteem over the ploughman; he also
wants an advantage in money.
        G. B. SHAW.—*Ib.*

I have seen no men in life loving their
profession so much as painters, except,
perhaps, actors, who, when not engaged
themselves, always go to the play.
        THACKERAY.—*Philip, Bk. 1, 17.*

The Grecian artist gleaned from many
        faces,
And in a perfect whole the parts com-
        bined.   H. T. TUCKERMAN.—*Mary.*

Artists, like the Greek gods, are only
revealed to one another.
        OSCAR WILDE.—*Lecture on the English
                Renaissance.*

High is our calling, Friend! Creative Art
Demands the service of a mind and heart,
And oh, when Nature sinks, as oft she
        may,
Still to be strenuous for the great reward
And in the soul admit of no decay,—
Great is the glory, for the strife is hard!
        WORDSWORTH.—*From Sonnets, Pt. 2,
                No. 3 (To B. R. Haydon).*

ARTS, THE

All liberal and humane studies are linked
together by a certain bond of union.
        CICERO.—*De Oratore 3, 6.*

All the arts have a sort of common
bond, and are connected by a sort of
relationship.   CICERO.—*Pro Archia.*

Honour nourishes the arts, and all are
kindled to study by love of glory.
        CICERO.—*Tusc. Quæst.*

Our arts are happy hits. We are like
the musician on the lake, whose melody
is sweeter than he knows.
        EMERSON.—*Art.*

The Arts are sisters; Languages are close kindred; Sciences are fellow-workmen. SIR A. HELPS.—*Friends in Council, Bk. 2, ch. 1.*

All the arts are brothers. Each of them lights up another, and thence results a universal light.
VOLTAIRE.—*Note on Ode upon the death of the Princess de Bareith.*

This island [Britain], which has produced the greatest philosophers in the world, is not so fertile as regards the fine arts. Unless the English apply themselves to follow the precepts of Pope and Addison, they will not approach other nations in matters of taste and literature.
VOLTAIRE.—*Pref. Letter to Mérope.*

Those who love the arts are all fellow-citizens.
VOLTAIRE.—*Zaire, Dedication to Mr. Falkener.*

ASCETICISM

In hope to merit Heaven by making earth a Hell.
BYRON.—*Childe Harold, c. 1, st. 20.*

We need not bid, for cloistered cell, Our neighbour and our work farewell.
KEBLE.—*Morning.*

If all the world
Should, in a pet of temperance, feed on pulse,
Drink the clear stream, and nothing wear but frieze,
Th' All-giver would be unthanked, would be unpraised.
MILTON.—*Comus, l. 720.*

Great things are granted unto those
That love not—far off things brought close,
Things of great seeming brought to nought,
And miracles for them are wrought.
WM. MORRIS.—*Earthly Paradise, Story of Acontius and Cydippe, 997.*

ASIA MINOR

There is no trust to be placed in the populations of Asia Minor.
Founded on passages in Cicero's "Oratio pro Flacco," in which deceit is ascribed to the Greek race.

ASPIRATION

We ought to live with the gods. This a man does whose soul is always content with the appointments of Providence.
M. AURELIUS.—*Meditations, Bk. 5, 27.*

By aspiring to a similitude of God in goodness or love, neither man nor angel ever transgressed or shall transgress.
BACON.—*Advancement of Learning, Bk. 2.*

Great things are done when men and mountains meet;
These are not done by jostling in the street.
WM. BLAKE.—*Couplets and Fragments.*

O youth whose hope is high,
Who dost to Truth aspire,
Whether thou live or die,
O look not back nor tire.
ROBERT BRIDGES.—*Song.*

Carpet-dusting, though a pretty trade,
Is not the imperative labour, after all.
E. B. BROWNING.—*Aurora Leigh, Bk. 1.*

Ah, but a man's reach should exceed his grasp,
Or what's a heaven for?
BROWNING.—*Andrea del Sarto.*

For thence,—a paradox
Which comforts while it mocks,—
Shall life succeed in that it seems to fail:
What I aspired to be
And was not, comforts me.
BROWNING.—*Rabbi Ben Ezra, 7.*

'Tis not what man Does which exalts him, but what man Would do.
BROWNING.—*Saul, st. 18.*

The love of higher things and better days;
The unbounded hope, and heavenly ignorance
Of what is called the world, and the world's ways. BYRON.—*Don Juan, 16, 108.*

Hitch your waggon to a star.
EMERSON.—*Society and Solitude.*

The restless throbbings and burnings
That hope unsatisfied brings;
The weary longings and yearnings
For the mystical better things.
A. L. GORDON.—*Wormwood and Nightshade.*

Our heart is in heaven, our home is not here. BISHOP HEBER.—*Hymn.*

She [Io] teaches us [in " Prometheus "] that in some way or other a sort of Nemesis hangs over men who are overbold in aspiration : whether, like Prometheus, they devise methods and expedients for alleviation of common ills; or, as Io, indulge in building castles in the air, which is the way with most of us in the ignorance of our early years.
KEBLE.—*Lectures on Poetry, No. 23 (E. K. Francis tr.).*

The shades of night were falling fast,
As through an Alpine village passed
A youth, who bore, 'mid snow and ice,
A banner, with the strange device,
Excelsior !
LONGFELLOW.—*Excelsior.*

Long is the way
And hard, that out of hell leads up to
light.
MILTON.—*Paradise Lost, Bk.* 2, 432.

Higher, higher will we climb
Up the mount of glory,
That our names may live through time
In our country's story.
MOORE.—*Aspirations of Youth.*

Paternal Jove ! the wish that fires his
breast
His lip reveals not : but all things in thee
End and begin : by dangers none
repressed,
His toil-trained heart but asks what all
the brave would be.
PINDAR.—*Nemesis,* 10, 55 (*Moore tr.*).

If the company will be persuaded by me,
remembering the soul to be immortal, able
to bear all evil and all good, we shall
always persevere in the road which leads
upwards, that so we may be friends both
to ourselves and to the gods, even whilst
we remain on this earth, and afterwards
when we receive the rewards of justice,
like victors assembled together.
PLATO.—*Republic, Bk.* 10, 16.

Agatha . . . often endured the mortification of the successful clown, who believes,
whilst the public roars with laughter at
him, that he was born a tragedian.
G. B. SHAW.—*Unsocial Socialist, ch.* 4.

The desire of the moth for the star,
Of the night for the morrow,
The devotion to something afar
From the sphere of our sorrow.
SHELLEY.—*To* ———.

For to the highest she did still aspyre.
SPENSER.—*Faerie Queene, c.* 3, 11.

I held it truth with him who sings
To one clear harp in divers tones,
That men may rise on stepping-stones
Of their dead selves to higher things.
TENNYSON.—*In Memoriam, c.* 1.

The thirst to know and understand,
A large and liberal discontent :
These are the goods in life's rich hand,
The things that are more excellent.
SIR W. WATSON.—*Things that are
more Excellent.*

We live by admiration, hope, and love,
And even as these are well and wisely
fixed
In dignity of being, we ascend.
WORDSWORTH.—*Excursion, Bk.* 4.

We know the arduous strife, the eternal
laws,
To which the triumph of all good is given,
High sacrifice, and labour without pause,

Even to the death : else wherefore should
the eye
Of man converse with immortality ?
WORDSWORTH.—*Poems to National
Independence, Pt.* 2, 14.

Too low they build who build beneath
the stars.   YOUNG.—*Night Thoughts,* 8,

ASSASSINATION

But now some demon, or evil spirit
surely, with iniquity and impiety, and,
more important still, with the audacity of
ignorance, in which all evils are rooted,
and whence they all spring up and afterwards produce most bitter fruit, has again
subverted and destroyed everything.
PLATO.—*Epistle* 7 (*Of the Assassination
of Dion*).

If I could find example
Of thousands that had struck anointed
kings,
And flourished after, I'd not do 't ; but
since
Nor brass, nor stone, nor parchment bears
not one,
Let villainy forswear 't.
SHAKESPEARE.—*Winter's Tale,* Act 1, 2.

ASSEVERATION

How haughtily he cocks his nose,
To tell what every schoolboy knows ;
And with his finger and his thumb
Explaining, strikes opposers dumb.
SWIFT.—*Country Life.*

By G——, gentlemen, I tell you nothing
but the truth ; and the d—l broil them
eternally that will not believe me.
SWIFT.—*Tale of a Tub.*

ASSIDUITY

Ease from this noble miser of his time
No moments steals ; pain narrows not
his cares.
WORDSWORTH.—*Eccles. Sonnets,
Pt.* 1, 26 (*Alfred*).

ASSOCIATION

I love it—I love it, and who shall dare
To chide me for loving that old Arm-chair ?
ELIZA COOK.—*The Old Arm-chair.*

Men who are rascals severally are highly
worthy people in the mass.
MONTESQUIEU.

Things worthless singly are useful
collectively.   OVID.—*Rem. Am.,* 420.

Oh ! while along the stream of time thy
name
Expanded flies, and gathers all its fame,
Say, shall my little bark attendant sail,
Pursue the triumph and partake the gale ?
POPE.—*Essay on Man, Ep.* 4, 383.

One bunch of grapes ripens another.
SUIDAS (*Greek*).

ASTRONOMY

For ever singing, as they shine,
" The Hand that made us is divine."
ADDISON.—*Spectator, Ode*, 466.

These earthly godfathers of heaven's
lights,
That give a name to every fixèd star,
Have no more profit of their shining
nights
Than those that walk and wot not what
they are.
SHAKESPEARE.—*Love's Labour's Lost*,
Act 1, 1.

Give me the ways of wandering stars to
know,
The depths of heaven above, and earth
below ;
Teach me the various labours of the moon,
And whence proceed the eclipses of the sun.
VIRGIL.—*Georgics, Bk.* 2 (*Dryden tr.*).

ATHEISM

God never wrought miracle to convince
atheism, because his ordinary works
convince it. BACON.—*Essays, Of Atheism.*

Atheism is rather in the lip than in the
heart of man.   BACON.—*Ib.*

An atheist's laugh's a poor exchange
For Deity offended.
BURNS.—*Epistle to a Young Friend.*

Forth from his dark and lonely hiding-
place
(Portentous sight !) the owlet Atheism,
Sailing on obscene wings athwart the
noon,
Drops his blue fringèd lids, and holds
them close,
And hooting at the glorious sun in Heaven,
Cries out, " Where is it ? "
COLERIDGE.—*Fears in Solitude.*

Virtue in distress and vice in triumph,
Make atheists of mankind.
DRYDEN.—*Cleomenes*, Act 4.

ATHENS

Athens, the eye of Greece, mother of arts
And eloquence.
MILTON.—*Paradise Regained, Bk.* 4, 240.

ATHLETICISM

His limbs were cast in manly mould,
For hardy sports or contest bold.
SCOTT.—*Lady of the Lake*, 1, 21.

ATOMS

An accidental and fortuitous concourse
of atoms.   LORD PALMERSTON (1857).

ATTACK

No skill in swordsmanship, however just,
Can be secure against a madman's thrust.
COWPER.—*Charity.*

Once more into the breach, dear friends,
once more,
Or close the wall up with our English
dead.   SHAKESPEARE.—*Henry V.*

ATTAINMENT

What at a distance charmed our eyes,
Upon attainment droops and dies.
J. CUNNINGHAM.—*Hymen.*

ATTENTION

That ancient and patient request,
Verbera, sed audi [Strike, but hear].
BACON.—*Advancement of Learning, Bk.* 2.

These things to hear
Would Desdemona seriously incline.
SHAKESPEARE.—*Othello*, Act 1, 3.

All speech, written or spoken, is a dead
language, until it finds a willing and
prepared hearer.
R. L. STEVENSON.—*Lay Morals.*

And listens like a three years' child.
WORDSWORTH.—*Lines added to the
Ancient Mariner.*

ATTRACTIVENESS

Saith he, " Yet are you too unkind,
If in your heart you cannot find
To love us now and then."
DRAYTON.—*Pastorals, Eclogue*, 4.

Here's metal more attractive.
SHAKESPEARE.—*Hamlet*, Act 3, 2.

A sweet attractive kind of grace :
A full assurance given by looks—
Continual comfort of a face,
The lineaments of Gospel books.
SIR P. SIDNEY.—*Friend's Passion.*

AUDACITY

You have deeply ventured ;
But all must do so who would greatly win.
BYRON.—*Marino Faliero*, 1, 2.

What we need for victory is audacity,
audacity, and for ever audacity.
DANTON.—*September*, 1792.

" To dare " is the secret of success in
literature, as it is in revolutions—and in
love.   HEINE.—*Religion and Philosophy.*

Be stirring as the time ; be fire with fire ;
Threaten the threatener, and outface the
brow
Of bragging horror.
SHAKESPEARE.—*King John*, Act 5.

O, what men dare do ! What men may
do !
What men daily do, not knowing what
they do !
SHAKESPEARE.—*Much Ado*, Act 4, 1.

AUGURIES

Hear ye not the hum
Of mighty workings ?
KEATS.—*To Haydon.*

According to fates and destinies, and
such odd sayings, the sisters three, and
other branches of learning.
SHAKESPEARE.—*Merchant of Venice*,
Act 2, 2.

Against ill chances men are ever merry ;
But heaviness foreruns the good event.
SHAKESPEARE.—*Henry IV., Pt.* 2, Act 4.

AUSTRALIA

Britannia, when thy heart's a-cold,
When o'er thy grave has grown the
moss,
Still " Rule Australia " shall be trolled
In Islands of the Southern Cross.
A. LANG.—*Ballade of the Southern Cross.*

AUTHORITY

Authority is a disease and cure,
Which men can neither want nor well
endure.
S. BUTLER.—*Miscellaneous Thoughts.*

I would rather err with Plato than perceive the truth with these others.
CICERO.—*Tusc. Quæst.*

Time has made this question without
question.
SIR E. COKE.—*Institutes, No.* 3, 302.

I am monarch of all I survey,
My right there is none to dispute.
COWPER.—*Alex. Selkirk.*

Young folks are smart, but all ain't good
thet's new ;
I guess the gran'thers they knowed sun-
thin', tu.   J. R. LOWELL.—*Biglow
Papers,* 2nd *Ser.,* 2.

And Art made tongue-tied by authority.
SHAKESPEARE.—*Sonnet* 66.

AUTHORS

Indeed I should doubt if my drama
throughout
Exhibit an instance of woman in love.
ARISTOPHANES.—*Frogs,* 1335 (*Frere tr.*).

Time, which is the author of authors.
BACON.—*Advancement of Learning, Bk.* 1.

No man was ever written out of reputation but by himself.
R. BENTLEY.—*Monk's Life of Bentley, p.* 90.

The author of " Amelia," . . . whose
works it has long been the fashion to
abuse in public and to read in secret.
BORROW.—*Bible in Spain.*

Then read my fancies ; they will stick
like burrs.
BUNYAN.—*Pilgrim's Progress, Pt.* 1.

One hates an author that's *all author,*
fellows
In foolscap uniform turned up with ink.
BYRON.—*Beppo, st.* 75.

The Ariosto of the North (Sir Walter
Scott).   BYRON.—*Childe Harold, c.* 4,
st. 40.

What is writ is writ,—
Would it were worthier ! but I am not
now
What I have been.
BYRON.—*Ib., st.* 185.

Sighing that Nature formed but one such
man,
And broke the die—in moulding Sheridan.
BYRON.—*Death of Sheridan.*

That unspeakable shoeblack-seraph
Army of Authors.   CARLYLE.—*Boswell.*

Little do such men know—the toil, the
pains,
The daily, nightly racking of the brains,
To range the thoughts, the matter to
digest,
To cull fit phrases, and reject the rest.
C. CHURCHILL.—*Gotham, Bk.* 2, 11.

There are three difficulties in authorship
—to write anything worth the publishing
—to find honest men to publish it—and
to get sensible men to read it.
C. C. COLTON.—*Lacon. Preface.*

Literature has her quacks no less than
medicine, and they are divided into two
classes,—those who have erudition without
genius, and those who have volubility
without depth.   C. C. COLTON.—*Lacon.*

Let authors write for glory and reward ;
Truth is well paid when she is sung and
heard.
BISHOP CORBET.—*On Lord W. Howard.*

Whose prose was eloquence, by wisdom
taught,
The graceful vehicle of virtuous thought ;
Whose verse may claim, grave masculine
and strong,
Superior praise to the mere poet's song.
COWPER.—*On Dr. S. Johnson.*

None but an author knows an author's
cares,
Or Fancy's fondness for the child she
bears.
COWPER.—*Progress of Error, l.* 515.

Till authors hear at length one general
cry,
Tickle and entertain us, or we die!
COWPER.—*Retirement, l.* 707.

Who often reads will sometimes wish
to write. CRABBE.—*Edward Shore.*

But years had done this wrong,
To make me write too much, and live too
long.
DANIEL.—*Philotas, Dedication, l.* 106.

The character of a good writer, wherever
he is to be found, is this, namely, that he
writes so as to please and serve at the same
time. DEFOE.—*Universal Spectator,* 1728.

To him no author was unknown,
Yet what he wrote was all his own.
SIR J. DENHAM.—*On A. Cowley's Death.*

I think the author who speaks about his
own books is almost as bad as a mother
who talks about her own children.
DISRAELI.—*Speech, Nov.* 19, 1870.

When a poet is thoroughly provoked,
he will do himself justice, however dear
it cost him ; *animamque in vulnere ponit*
[and he puts his whole soul into the
wound]. DRYDEN.—*Dedication of Æneas.*

The pleasing punishment of publication.
GEO. ELIOT.—*Theophrastus Such,
Looking Inward.*

Talent alone cannot make a writer.
There must be a man behind the book.
EMERSON.—*On Goethe.*

Authors and readers are separated by
a great gulf of which happily neither is
conscious. GOETHE.—*Autob., Bk.* 13.

Thou source of all my bliss and all my
woe,
That found'st me poor at first, and
keep'st me so.
GOLDSMITH.—*Deserted Village.*

The pen of a man of genius is always
greater than himself ; it extends far
beyond his temporary purpose.
HEINE.—*Don Quixote.*

A writer of course cannot get beyond
his own ideal, but at least he should see
that he works up to it ; and if it is a poor
one, he had better write histories of the
utmost concentration of dulness, than
amuse us with unjust and untrue imaginings. SIR A. HELPS.—*Friends in Council,
Bk.* 1, *ch.* 6.

With the greatest possible solicitude
avoid authorship. Too early or immoder-
ately employed it makes the head waste
and the heart empty.
HERDER.—*Tr. by S. T. Coleridge.*

If it be well considered, the praise of
ancient authors proceeds not from the
reverence of the dead, but from the competition and mutual envy of the living.
HOBBES.—*Leviathan Conclusion.*

All writers love the groves and flee from
cities. HORACE.—*Ep.* 2, 2.

Corneille is to Shakespeare as a clipped
hedge is to a forest.
JOHNSON.—*Remark recorded by
Mrs. Piozzi.*

The chief glory of every people arises
from its authors.
JOHNSON.—*Dictionary (Pref.).*

For we that live to please must please
to live. JOHNSON.—*Prologue.*

A man will turn over half a library to
make one book. JOHNSON.—*Remark.*

No man but a blockhead ever wrote
except for money. JOHNSON.—*Remark.*

There marks what ill the scholar's life assail,
Toil, envy, want, the patron, and the gaol.
JOHNSON.—*Vanity of Human Wishes.*

Many are possessed by the incurable
itch of writing. JUVENAL.—*Sat.* 7.

In a word too much applause is given
to wit and smartness, too little to reality
and truth. KEBLE.—*Lectures on Poetry,
No.* 1 (*E. K. Francis tr.*).

An author, like a host, shows his ability
most surely if his readers are dismissed
with an appetite whetted but not satisfied.
KEBLE.—*Ib., No.* 5.

There are two literary maladies—
writer's cramp and swelled head. The
worst of writer's cramp is that it is never
cured ; the worst of swelled head is that
it never kills.
COULSON KERNAHAN.—*Lecture.*

It is not a question of my being an
author—but it seems to me that a man of
the world may have thoughts and record
them in a little notebook.
LABICHE.—*Perrichon in " Le Voyage
de M. Perrichon."*

Slave-merchants, scalpers, cannibals agree:
In Letter-land no brotherhood must be.
If there were living upon earth but twain,
One would be Abel and the other Cain,
W. S. LANDOR.—*Miscell.,* 278.

For as from sweetest flowers the labouring
bee
Extracts the precious juice, Great Soul,
from thee
We all our Golden Sentences derive—
Golden, and fit eternally to live.
LUCRETIUS.—*De Rerum Natura,* 3, 11
(*Creech. tr.*)

Write something great.
MARTIAL.—*Epig., Bk.* 1, 108.

Things unattempted yet in prose or rhyme. MILTON.—*Paradise Lost, Bk.* 1, 16.

He who would not be frustrate of his hope to write well hereafter in laudable things ought himself to be a true Poem.
MILTON.—*Apology against a pamphlet called Smectymnuus* (1642).

He [Rudyard Kipling] possesses the inkpot which turns the vilest tin idiom into gold. GEO. MOORE.—*Avowals* (1919).

Whate'er my fate is, 'tis my fate to write. J. OLDHAM.—*To a Friend*

Good sense must be the certain standard still
To all that will pretend to writing well.
J. OLDHAM.—*Ode on St. Cecilia's Day.*

Let others write for glory or reward;
Truth is well paid when she is sung and heard.
SIR T. OVERBURY.—*On Lord Effingham.*

To great poets there is no need of a gentle reader; they hold him captive, however unwilling and unmanageable.
OVID.—*Ep. ex Pont.*, 3, 4, 9.

Be sure, whatever you propose to write, Let the chief motive be your own delight.
C. PITT.—*Tr. of Vida's Art of Poetry, Bk.* 1.

" 'S death, I'll print it,
And shame the fools."
POPE.—*Prol. to Satires, l.* 61.

Who shames a scribbler? break one cob-web through,
He spins the slight, self-pleasing thread anew;
Destroy his fib or sophistry, in vain,
The creature's at his dirty work again.
POPE.—*Ib., l.* 89.

The mob of gentlemen who wrote with ease. POPE.—*Satires, Bk.* 2, *Ep.* 1, 108.

Authors in France seldom speak ill of each other but when they have a personal pique; authors in England seldom speak well of each other but when they have a personal friendship.
POPE.—*Thoughts on Various Subjects.*

In an age
Of savage warfare and blind bigotry,
He cultured all that could refine, exalt,
Leading to better things.
ROGERS.—*Italy, Arquà (Of Petrarch).*

It is too difficult to think nobly when one only thinks to get a living.
ROUSSEAU.—*Confessions*, 2, 9.

There are two kinds of authors—those who write for the subject's sake, and those who write for the sake of writing.
SCHOPENHAUER.—*On Authorship.*

I have perhaps been the most voluminous author of the day; and it *is* a comfort to me to think I have tried to unsettle no man's faith, to corrupt no man's principle, and that I have written nothing which on my death-bed I should wish blotted.
SCOTT.—*Remark to Lockhart, May* 10, 1832 (*He died Sept.* 21, 1832).

I envy the old hermit of Prague, who never saw paper or ink.
SCOTT.—*Diary, Feb.*, 1826.

Devise, wit! write, pen! for I am for whole volumes in folio.
SHAKESPEARE.—*Love's Labour's Lost,* Act 1, 2.

The poetry of despair will not outlive despair itself. Your nineteenth century novelists are only the tail of Shakespeare. Don't tie yourself to it; it is fast wriggling into oblivion.
G. B. SHAW.—*Unsocial Socialist, Appendix.*

Learn to write well, or not to write at all. J. SHEFFIELD.—*On Satire.*

You write with ease to show your breeding, But easy writing's curst hard reading.
SHERIDAN.—*Clio's Protest.*

I that . . . am admitted into the company of the Paper-blurrers do find the very true cause of our wanting estimation is want of desert.
SIR P. SIDNEY.—*Apologie for Poetrie.*

I know of no reason why he [Dugald Stewart] is not ranked among the first writers of the English language, except that he is still alive; and my most earnest and hearty wish is that that cause of his depreciation may operate for many years.
SYDNEY SMITH.—*Lectures on Moral Philosophy, No.* 3.

Ask my pen; it governs me—I govern not it.
STERNE.—*Tristram Shandy, Vol.* 6, ch. 6.

Blot out, correct, insert, refine,
Enlarge, diminish, interline;
Be mindful, when invention fails,
To scratch your head and bite your nails.
SWIFT.—*On Poetry.*

He [Lord Macaulay] reads twenty books to write a sentence; he travels a hundred miles to make a line of description.
THACKERAY.—*Nil nisi Bonum (Cornhill, Feb.*, 1860).

Tutored by thee, hence poetry exalts
Her voice to ages, and informs the page
With music, image, sentiment, and thought,
Never to die.
THOMSON.—*Summer (Used for his epitaph
                    in Westminster Abbey).*

If writing was drink I should be a
drunkard ; I simply could not refrain
from it. It has filled my life with happiness. KATHARINE TYNAN.—*Years of the
                    Shadow* (1919).

Bitten by the dog Metromania (mania
for versification), I was taken with the
disease and became an author also.
VOLTAIRE.—*Le Pauvre Diable.*

Their faults [those of the Greek dramatists] are due to the age in which they
lived ; their beauties belong to themselves
alone.
VOLTAIRE.—*Prefatory Letter to Œdipus.*

This great man (Corneille) is always
superior to others, but he is not always
equal to himself.   VOLTAIRE.—*Ib.*

An author may be good in spite of some
faults, but not in spite of many faults.
VOLTAIRE.—*Letters on the English.*

Nature's refuse and the dregs of men,
Compose the black militia of the pen.
YOUNG.—*Epistle to Pope.*

He was the interpreter of nature,
dipping his pen into his mind.
Old Greek Saying.

It was well known that the Dean
[Swift] could write finely upon a broomstick.
*Remark attributed to Stella (Mrs.
Johnson) in reference to Dean Swift's
poems to Vanessa (Miss Vanhomrigh).*

AUTOCRACY

Law and arbitrary power are in eternal
enmity.   BURKE.—*Speech,* 1788.

AUTOMOBILES

It didn't want no stable, it didn't ask no
        groom,
It didn't need no nothin' but a bit o'
        standin' room.
Just fill it up with paraffin an' it would
        go all day ;
Which the same should be agin the law,
        if I could 'ave my way.
SIR A. C. DOYLE.—*The Groom's Story.*

AUTUMN

Now autumn's fire burns slowly along the
        woods,
And day by day the dead leaves fall and
        melt.
W. ALLINGHAM.—*Autumnal Sonnet.*

The melancholy days are come,
    The saddest of the year,
Of wailing winds, and naked woods,
    And meadows brown and sere.
W. CULLEN BRYANT.—*Death of the
                    Flowers.*

Of seasons of the year the autumn is
most melancholy.
    BURTON.—*Anatomy of Melancholy,
                    Pt. 1, sec. 1.*

Touched with the dewy sadness of the
    time,
To think how the sweet months had spent
    their prime.
HOOD.—*Plea of the Midsummer Fairies.*

Boughs are daily rifled
    By the gusty thieves,
And the Book of Nature
    Getteth short of leaves.
            HOOD.—*Seasons.*

Autumnal frosts enchant the pool,
And make the cart ruts beautiful.
R. L. STEVENSON.—*House Beautiful.*

What pensive beauty autumn shows,
    Before she hears the sound
Of winter rushing in, to close
    The emblematic round !
WORDSWORTH.—*Thoughts on the Seasons.*

AVARICE

In all the world there is no vice
Less prone to excess than avarice.
S. BUTLER.—*Miscellaneous Thoughts.*

So for a good old-gentlemanly vice,
I think I must take up with avarice.
BYRON.—*Don Juan, c.* 1, *st.* 216.

He lives poor, to die rich, and is the mere
jailor of his house, and the turnkey of his
wealth. C. C. COLTON.—*Lacon, No.* 24.

It is evident insanity to live in penury
in order that you may die rich.
            JUVENAL.—*Sat.* 14.

A very few pounds a year would ease
a man of the scandal [reproach] of avarice.
POPE.—*Thoughts on Various Subjects.*

The miser is as much in want of what
he has, as what he has not.
            PUBLILIUS SYRUS.

Many things are wanting to poverty,
all things to avarice. PUBLILIUS SYRUS.

The name of the servant of Mammon is
Miser, that is, miserable.
C. H. SPURGEON.—*Salt-cellars.*

It is sad to grow old ; one has less time
left for growing rich.
VOLTAIRE.—*Gripon in " La Femme qui a
Raison."*

AVERSION

I do not love thee, Dr. Fell,
The reason why, I cannot tell;
But this I know, and know full well,
I do not love thee, Dr. Fell.
TOM BROWN.—*After Martial.*

My aversion, my aversion, my aversion
of all aversions !
WYCHERLEY.—*Plain Dealer*, Act 2, I.

What things we see when we don't have
a gun !
*American Colloquialism, published in this
form in "Troy Times," Dec. 26, 1883.*

AVIATION

He shall have chariots easier than air,
That I will have invented.
BEAUMONT AND FLETCHER.—*A King and
no King* (1610 ?), Act 5.

God never meant that man should scale
the heavens
By strides of human wisdom.
COWPER.—*Garden*, 221.

Possibly this was only a figure of speech,
like that of Bishop Wilkins [1614-1672],
who prophesied that the time would come
when gentlemen, when they were to go a
journey, would call for their wings as
regularly as they call for their boots.
MISS EDGEWORTH.—*Essay on Irish
Bulls*, ch. 2.

Volatile spirits, light mercurial humours,
Oh give us soon your sky adventures truly
With full particulars, correcting duly
All flying rumours.
HOOD.—*To Messrs. Green, Holland, and
Monck Mason on their late Balloon
Expedition (Comic Annual*, 1837).

Above the smoke and stir of this dim spot,
Which men call Earth.
MILTON.—*Comus*, 5.

O, for a horse with wings !
SHAKESPEARE.—*Cymbeline*, Act 3, 2.

Guarded with ships, and all the sea our
own,
From heaven this mischief on our heads
is thrown.
WALLER.—*To Lord Falkland.*

AWKWARDNESS

God may forgive sins, he said, but
awkwardness has no forgiveness in
heaven or earth.
EMERSON.—*Society and Solitude.*

He stood a spell on one foot fust,
Then stood a spell on t'other,
An' on which one he felt the wust
He couldn't ha' told ye nuther.
J. R. LOWELL.—*Biglow Papers*, series 2.
The Courtin'.

There is always war between Ungraceful-
ness and Love.   PLATO.—*Banquet*, 21.

It is very pleasantly said of the awkwardness of Englishwomen that they seem
to have two left arms.
A. DE RIVAROL.—*Traits et Bons Mots.*

B

BABIES

Every baby born into the world is a
finer one than the last.
DICKENS.—*Nicholas Nickleby*, ch. 26.

" Where did you come from, baby dear ? "
" Out of the everywhere into the here."
GEO. MACDONALD.—*Baby.*

BACHELORS

One was never married, and that's his
hell ; another is, and that's his plague.
BURTON.—*Anat. of Melan.*, Pt. I.

At three score winters' end I died,
A cheerless being, lone and sad ;
The nuptial knot I never tied,
And wish my father never had.
COWPER.—*Tr. of Greek Epitaph
on an old Bachelor.*

Lord of yourself, uncumbered with a
wife.   DRYDEN.—*To John Dryden.*

The only comfort of my life
Is that I never yet had wife.
HERRICK.—*Hesperides*, No. 1053.

A bachelor is a man who shirks responsibilities and duties.
G. B. SHAW.—*Unsocial Socialist*, ch. 18.

BACK NUMBERS

And then like almanacs, whose dates are
gone,
They are thrown by and no more looked
upon.   DEKKER.—*Honest Whore,
Pt.* 2, Act 4, I.

BANISHMENT

Eating the bitter bread of banishment.
SHAKESPEARE.—*Richard II.*, Act 3, I.

BANQUETS

" Music hath charms to soothe a savage
beast,"
And therefore proper at a sheriff's feast.
JAMES BRAMSTON.

Truth that peeps
Over the glass's edge when dinner's done,
And body gets its sop, and holds its noise,
And leaves the soul free a little.
BROWNING.—*Bishop Blougram.*

Keen appetite
And quick digestion wait on you and
  yours. DRYDEN.—*Cleomenes*, Act 4, 1.

London's the dining-room of civilisation.
  MIDDLETON.—*City Pageant* (1617).

You'll have no scandal while you dine,
But honest talk and wholesome wine.
  TENNYSON.—*To the Rev. F. D. Maurice.*

BARGAINS

Here's the rule for bargains : "Do
other men, for they would do you."
  DICKENS.—*Martin Chuzzlewit.*

The propensity to truck, barter and
exchange one thing for another . . . is
common to all men, and to be found in
no other race of animals.
ADAM SMITH.—*Wealth of Nations*, Bk. 1, 2.

It is naught, it is naught, saith the
buyer : but when he is gone his way, then
he boasteth.   *Proverbs* xx, 14.

There are more foolish buyers than
foolish sellers.   *Prov.*

BARONETS

  All baronets are bad.
  SIR W. S. GILBERT.—*Ruddigore.*

BARRISTERS

My learned profession I'll never disgrace
By taking a fee with a grin on my face,
When I haven't been there to attend to the
  case. SIR W. S. GILBERT.—*Iolanthe.*

And many a burglar I've restored
  To his friends and his relations.
  SIR W. S. GILBERT.—*Trial by Jury.*

He (a barrister) hires out his anger and
his words. SENECA.—*Hercules Furens,* 173.

    O perilous mouths,
That bear in them one and the selfsame
  tongue,
Either of condemnation or approof,
Bidding the law make courtesy to their
  will !
SHAKESPEARE.—*Measure for Measure,*
                          Act 2, 4.

BATHOS

So in this way of writing without thinking
Thou hast a strange alacrity in sinking.
  T. SACKVILLE (LORD DORSET).—*Satire.*

I have a kind of alacrity in sinking.
  SHAKESPEARE.—*Merry Wives,* Act 3, 5.

From Flecknoe down to Howard's time,
How few have reached the low sublime !
  SWIFT.—*On Poetry.*

BATTLES

There's some say that we wan, some say
  that they wan,

Some say that nane wan at a', man,
But one thing I'm sure, that at Sheriff-
  Muir,
  A battle there was which I saw, man.
And we ran and they ran, and they ran
  and we ran,
And we ran, and they ran awa', man.
  MURDOCH MCLENNAN.—*Sheriff-Muir*
  (*referring to an indecisive battle in the
  valley of Sheriff-Muir, Nov.,* 1715).

When the hurly-burly's done,
When the battle's lost and won.
  SHAKESPEARE.—*Macbeth,* Act 1, 1.

A captain forth to battle went,
With soldiers neat and trim.
  ANN and JANE TAYLOR.—*Hymns for
                    Infant Minds, No.* 91.

The glory and grief of battle won or lost
Solders a race together—yea, though they
  fail,
The names of those who fought and fell
  are like
A banked-up fire that flashes out again
From century to century.
  TENNYSON.—*The Cup.*

God of battles, was ever a battle like
this in the world before ?
  TENNYSON.—*The Revenge.*

Nothing except a battle lost can be half
so melancholy as a battle won.
  DUKE OF WELLINGTON.—*Despatch,* 1815.

He saith among the trumpets, Ha, ha ;
and he smelleth the battle afar off.
                        Job xxxix, 25.

BEACH

On Margate beach, where the sick one
  roams,
And the sentimental reads ;
Where the maiden flirts, and the widow
  comes,
Like the ocean—to cast her weeds.
  HOOD.—*Mermaid of Margate.*

Come unto these yellow sands,
  And then take hands :
Curtsied when you have, and kissed,
  The wild waves whist. ["whist" =
                            silenced.]
  SHAKESPEARE.—*Tempest,* Act 1, 2.

BEATING

A woman, a dog, and a walnut tree,
The more you beat them the better they'll
  be.
      *Old Saying found in Danish and
                    other languages.*

BEAUTY

The best part of beauty is that which
a picture cannot express.
  BACON.—*Collection of Sentences.*

Sure there is music even in Beauty,
and the silent note which Cupid strikes,
far sweeter than the sound of an instrument. For there is a music wherever
there is harmony, order, or proportion.
SIR T. BROWNE.—*Religio Medici, Pt. 2, 9.*

A worthless woman ! mere cold clay,
As all false things are, but so fair
She takes the breath of men away,
Who gaze upon her unaware.
E. B. BROWNING.—*Bianca.*

If you get simple beauty, and nought else,
You get about the best thing God invents.
BROWNING.—*Fra Lippo Lippi.*

Too bright, too beautiful to last.
W. CULLEN BRYANT.—*The Rivulet.*

All that is beautiful shall abide,
All that is base shall die.
R. BUCHANAN.—*Balder, Pt. 7, 5.*

A pretty woman is a welcome guest.
BYRON.—*Beppo, 23.*

The light of love, the purity of grace,
The mind, the Music breathing from her
face. BYRON.—*Bride of Abydos, c. 1, 6.*

Who hath not proved how feebly words
essay
To fix one spark of Beauty's heavenly ray ?
BYRON.—*Ib.*

His changing cheek, his sinking heart
confess
The might—the majesty of Loveliness.
BYRON.—*Ib.*

Whose large blue eyes, fair locks, and
snowy hands
Might shake the saintship of an anchorite.
BYRON.—*Childe Harold, c. 1, st. 11.*

The fatal gift of beauty.
BYRON.—*Ib., c. 4, st. 42.*

The women pardoned all except her
face. BYRON.—*Don Juan, c. 5, st. 113.*

He could not slay a thing so fair.
BYRON.—*Parisina, st. 7.*

Without the smile from partial beauty
won,
Oh, what were man ?—a world without a
sun.
CAMPBELL.—*Pleasures of Hope, Pt. 2.*

There is a garden in her face,
Where roses and white lilies grow.
T. CAMPION.—*Cherry Ripe.*

The beautiful is vanished and returns
not. COLERIDGE.—*Death of
Wallenstein, 5, 1.*

No beauty's like the beauty of the mind.
JOSHUA COOKE.—*A Good Wife.*

Beauty, like sorrow, dwelleth everywhere.
T. DEKKER.—*Old Fortunatus, Act 3, 1.*

Trust not too much to that enchanting
face ;
Beauty's a charm, but soon the charm will
pass. DRYDEN.—*Virgil, Pastoral 2.*

Beauty, truth, and goodness are not
obsolete ; they spring eternal in the
breast of man. EMERSON.—*Art.*

One more text from the mythologists ...
" Beauty rides upon a lion ! " Beauty rests
on necessities. The line of beauty is the
result of perfect economy.
EMERSON.—*Conduct of Life.*

Rhodora ! if the sages ask thee why
This charm is wasted on the marsh and
sky,
Tell them, dear, that if eyes were made
for seeing,
Then Beauty is its own excuse for being.
EMERSON.—*The Rhodora.*

Beauties they are, but beauties out of
place. P. FRANCIS.—*Horace, Art of Poetry.*

Nature, that wisely nothing made in vain,
Did make you lovely to be loved again.
R. HEATH.—*To Clarastella.*

Beauty and beauteous words should go
together. GEO. HERBERT.—*Forerunners.*

O lovelier daughter of a lovely mother !
HORACE.—*Odes, Bk. 1.*

Beauty enough to make a world to dote.
JAMES I (of Scotland).—*King's Quair.*

Rare is the agreement between beauty
and modesty. JUVENAL.—*Sat., 10.*

A thing of beauty is a joy for ever ;
Its loveliness increases ; it will never
Pass into nothingness ; but still will keep
A bower quiet for us, and a sleep
Full of sweet dreams, and health, and quiet
breathing. KEATS.—*Endymion, Bk. 1.*

" Beauty is truth, truth beauty,"—that
is all
Ye know on earth, and all ye need to know.
KEATS.—*Grecian Urn.*

Oh ! could you view the melody
Of every grace,
And music of her face,
You'd drop a tear,
Seeing more harmony
In her bright eye,
Than now you hear.
R. LOVELACE.—*Orpheus to Beasts.*

Beauty and sadness always go together.
G. MACDONALD.—*Within and Without,
Pt. 4, sec. 3.*

All the eminent and canonised beauties,
By truth recorded, or by poets feigned.
MASSINGER.—*Bashful Lover*, Act 4, 1.

At the best, my lord, she is a handsome
picture,
And, that said, all is spoken.
MASSINGER.—*Gt. Duke*, Act 3, 1.

Beauty is the elimination of super-
fluities.   MICHAEL ANGELO.

Where perhaps some beauty lies,
The Cynosure of neighbouring eyes.
MILTON.—*L'Allegro*, *l*. 79.

Beauty stands
In the admiration only of weak minds
Led captive.
MILTON.—*Paradise Regained*, *Bk*. 2, 220.

As rich and purposeless as is the rose,
Thy simple doom is to be beautiful.
STEPHEN PHILLIPS.—*Marpessa*, *l*. 51.

The beautiful consists in utility and
fitness for the production of some good
purpose.   PLATO.—*Hippias Major*, 37.

If to her share some female errors fall,
Look on her face, and you'll forget them
all. POPE.—*Rape of the Lock*, *c*. 2, 17.

And beauty draws us with a single
hair.   POPE.—*Ib.*, *c*. 2, 28.

Take away from our hearts the love
of the beautiful and you take away the
charm of life.   ROUSSEAU.—*Émile*.

I have always believed that good is
only the beautiful put into action, that
one is intimately linked with the other,
and that they both have one common
source in well-ordered nature.
ROUSSEAU.—*Julie*.

Is she not more than painting can express,
Or youthful poets fancy when they love ?
N. ROWE.—*Fair Penitent*, Act 3, 1.

It is evident that the sensation of
beauty is not sensual on the one hand,
nor is it intellectual on the other ; but is
dependent on a pure, right, and open
state of the heart.
RUSKIN.—*Modern Painters*, vol. 2,
sec. 1, ch. 2, 8.

Neither is there any better test of
beauty than its surviving or annihilating
the love of change, a test which the
best judges of art have need frequently
to use. RUSKIN.—*Ib.*, vol. 2, sec. 2, ch. 2, 7.

It [Repose] is the most unfailing test of
beauty, whether of matter or of motion.
Nothing can be ignoble that possesses it ;
nothing right that has it not.
RUSKIN.—*Ib.*, vol. 2, sec. 2, ch. 3, 5.

Many very sublime pictures derive their
sublimity from the want of it [symmetry],
but they lose proportionally in the diviner
quality of beauty.
RUSKIN.—*Ib.*, vol. 2, sec. 2, ch. 4, 4.

Beautiful things are useful to men because they are beautiful, and for the sake
of their beauty only ; and not to sell,
or pawn—or in any other way turn into
money.   RUSKIN.—*Pref. to Revised edition
of " Modern Painters," vol. 2 (1882).
Described by him as "the beginning
of all my political economy."*

And ne'er did Grecian chisel trace
A Nymph, a Naiad, or a Grace,/
Of finer form or lovelier face !
SCOTT.—*Lady of the Lake*, *c*. 1, *st*. 18.

If ladies be but young and fair,
They have the gift to know it.
SHAKESPEARE.—*As You Like It*, Act 2, 7.

Well, I am not fair, and therefore I
pray the gods make me honest.
SHAKESPEARE.—*Ib.*, Act 3, 2.

Beauty itself doth of itself persuade
The eyes of men without an orator.
SHAKESPEARE.—*Lucrece*, *st*. 5.

Beauty is but a vain and doubtful good.
SHAKESPEARE.—*Passionate Pilgrim*, *st*. 11.

There's nothing ill can dwell in such a
temple ;
If the ill spirit have so fair a house,
Good things will strive to dwell with 't.
SHAKESPEARE.—*Tempest*, Act 1, 2.

For he being dead, with him is beauty
slain,
And, beauty dead, black chaos comes
again.
SHAKESPEARE.—*Venus and Adonis*, 170.

And narcissi, the fairest among them all,
Who gaze on their eyes in the stream's
recess,
Till they die of their own dear loveliness.
SHELLEY.—*Sensitive Plant*, Pt. 1, *st*. 5.

The saying that beauty is but skin
deep is but a skin deep saying.
HERBERT SPENCER.—*Personal Beauty*.

The hearts of men, which fondly here
admyre
Fair seeming shewes, . . . may lift them-
selves up hyer,
And learn to love, with zealous humble
dewty,
Th' Eternall Fountaine of that heavenly
Beauty.
SPENSER.—*Hymn of Heavenly Beauty*.

A rosebud set with little wilful thorns,
And sweet as English air could make her,
she. TENNYSON.—*Princess*, Prol., 153

Beauty, madam, pleases only the eyes;
sweetness charms the mind.
VOLTAIRE.—*Nanine.*

How small a part of time they share
That are so wondrous sweet and fair!
E. WALLER.—*Go, Lovely Rose.*

O be less beautiful, or be less brief!
SIR WM. WATSON.—*Autumn.*

Beauty is the only thing that time
cannot harm. Philosophies fall away
like sand, creeds follow one another, but
what is beautiful is a joy for all seasons,
a possession for all eternity.
OSCAR WILDE.—*Lecture on the English
Renaissance.*

If she be not so to me,
What care I how fair she be?
G. WITHER.—*Shepherd's Resolution.*

She seemed a thing that could not feel
The touch of earthly years.
WORDSWORTH.—*Poems of the Imagination,
No. 11.*

And beauty born of murmuring sound
Shall pass into her face.
WORDSWORTH.—*Three Years.*

Beautiful as sweet!
And young as beautiful! and soft as
young!
And gay as soft! and innocent as gay!
YOUNG.—*Night Thoughts,* 3.

Beauty without virtue is a flower
without perfume.   *French prov.*

Every woman would rather be beautiful
than good.   *German prov.*

Everything beautiful is lovable.
Latin prov.

The fairer the hostess the fouler the
reckoning.   *Prov. (Ray).*

A handsome hostess makes a dear
reckoning. *Saying quoted by Bishop
Corbet (c. 1632) and derived from the French.*

BED

Bed is a bundle of paradoxes: we go
to it with reluctance, yet we quit it with
regret; and we make up our minds every
night to leave it early, but we make up
our bodies every morning to keep it late.
C. C. COLTON.—*Lacon.*

Oh, bed! oh, bed! delicious bed!
That heaven upon earth to the weary
head!   HOOD.—*Miss Kilmansegg.*

Whoever thinks of going to bed before
twelve o'clock is a scoundrel.
JOHNSON.—*Remark as recorded by
Sir John Hawkins.*

In bed we laugh, in bed we cry,
And born in bed, in bed we die;
The near approach a bed may show
Of human bliss to human woe.
JOHNSON.—*tr. of Benserade.*

'Tis very warm weather when one's
in bed.   SWIFT.—*Letter,* 1710.

BEER

Yes, my soul sentimentally craves
British beer. CAMPBELL.—*From Algiers.*

For a quart of ale is a dish for a king.
SHAKESPEARE.—*Winter's Tale,* Act 4, 2.

They who drink beer will think beer.
*Attr. to Warburton. (Parodied: "They
who drink water will think water.")*

BEES

Nature's confectioner, the bee.
J. CLEVELAND.

Swarm o' bees i' May
'S woth a load o' hay;
Swarm o' bees i' June
'S woth a silver spune;
Swarm o' bees i' July
'S not woth a fly.
*Derbyshire Saying, as recorded in "Notes
and Queries," May 27,* 1911.

BEGGARS

He was the beste beggere in his hous.
CHAUCER.—*Cant. Tales, Prol.*

Of avaryce and of swich cursednesse
Is al my preching, for to make them free
To give their pence, and namely unto me.
CHAUCER.—*Pardoner's Tale, V.* 12335.

A beggar's life is for a king.
F. DAVISON.—*Song.*

Patience, the beggar's virtue.
MASSINGER.—*New Way to Pay Old Debts.*

Pity the sorrows of a poor old man,
Whose trembling limbs have brought him
to your door.
T. MOSS.—*Beggar's Petition.*

You taught me first to beg, and now,
methinks,
You teach me how a beggar should be
answered. SHAKESPEARE.—*Merchant
of Venice,* Act 4, 1.

It is one beggar's woe,
To see another by the door go.
Prov. (Ray).

BEGINNINGS

"The contrast of beginning and end,"
said the general [Kinsale], "is almost
always melancholy."
MME. D'ARBLAY.—*Camilla, Bk.* 3, *c.* 12.

My way is to begin with the beginning.
BYRON.—*Don Juan, Canto* 1, *st.* 7.

Nothing so difficult as a beginning
In poesy, unless perhaps the end.
BYRON.—*Ib., c.* 4, *st.* 1.

The beginnings of all things are small.
CICERO.—*De Finibus.*

Every evil thing is easily stifled at its
birth; allowed to become old it generally
becomes too powerful.
CICERO.—*Philippics, Bk.* 5, 11.

The bud may have a bitter taste,
But sweet will be the flower.
COWPER.—*Hymn.*

Run a moist pen slick through everything and start afresh.
DICKENS.—*M. Chuzzlewit, c.* 17.

Every beginning is cheerful. GOETHE.

Withstand the beginnings; when the
evils have become rooted the remedies
are too late. OVID.—*Rem. Am.*

Things are always at their best in their
beginning. PASCAL.—*Lettres provinciales.*

Whilst we deliberate about beginning,
it becomes too late to begin. QUINTILIAN.

That is the true beginning of our end.
SHAKESPEARE.—*Midsummer Night's
Dream,* Act 5, 1.

Every man must submit to be slow
before he is quick; and insignificant
before he is important.
SYDNEY SMITH.—*Lectures on Moral
Philosophy, No.* 19.

Each goodly thing is hardest to begin.
SPENSER.—*Faerie Queene, c.* 5, *st.* 6.

Few men, drinking at a rivulet, stop
to consider its source.
M. F. TUPPER.—*Of Gifts.*

Others shall sing the song,
Others shall right the wrong,
Finish what I begin,
And all I fail of win.
J. G. WHITTIER.—*Triumph.*

The beginning is half of the whole.
Greek saying (ascribed to Pythagoras).

The difficult thing is to get your foot
in the stirrup.   *Old saying.*

The deil's aye gude to beginners.
Scottish prov.

Begin on porridge that you may end
with chicken.   *Scottish saying.*

The first dish pleaseth all.
Prov. (Geo. Herbert).

BELIEF

To its own impulse every creature stirs:
Live by thy light, and Earth will live by
hers.   M. ARNOLD.—*Religious
Isolation.*

We are born believing. A man bears
beliefs, as a tree bears apples.
EMERSON.—*Conduct of Life, Worship.*

Ah me! we believe in evil,
Where once we believed in good;
The world, the flesh, and the devil
Are easily understood.
A. L. GORDON.—*Wormwood and
Nightshade.*

All I can say is you are not " experte
credo," or expert at believing.
HOOD.—*The Rope Dancer,* 1834.

A thing that nobody believes cannot be
proved too often.
G. B. SHAW.—*Devil's Disciple.*

He in his heart
Felt that misgiving which precedes belief
In what was disbelieved.
SOUTHEY.—*Joan of Arc, Bk.* 1.

No soul can believe but by the permission of God . . . but signs are of no avail,
neither preachers, unto people who will
not believe.   *Koran,* ch. 10.

BELLS

The vesper bell from far
That seems to mourn for the expiring day.
H. F. CARY.—*Dante's Purgatory, c.* 8, 6.

The sound of the church-going bell.
COWPER.—*Alex. Selkirk.*

How soft the music of those village bells,
Falling at intervals upon the ear,
In cadence sweet!
COWPER.—*Winter Morning Walk.*

Sundays observe; think when the bells
do chime,
'Tis angels' music.
HERBERT.—*Church Porch.*

Bells are Music's laughter.
HOOD.—*Miss Kilmansegg.*

Dear bells! how sweet the sound of
village bells,
When on the undulating air they swim!
Now loud as welcome! faint now, as
farewells. HOOD.—*Ode to R. Wilson.*

They went and told the sexton,
And the sexton tolled the bell.
HOOD.—*Sally Brown.*

Those evening bells! those evening bells!
How many a tale their music tells
Of youth and home and that sweet time
When last I heard their soothing chime.
MOORE.—*Evening Bells.*

Silence that dreadful bell !
> SHAKESPEARE.—*Othello*, Act 2, 3.

Ring out wild bells to the wild sky.
> TENNYSON.—*In Memoriam, c.* 106.

Differing in size,
In note and weight,
Yet, small or great,
We harmonise.
Inscription on bell, Colchester Town Hall.

BENEFITS

A benefit loses its grace in being too much published. CORNEILLE.—*Théodore.*

On adamant our wrongs we all engrave,
But write our benefits upon the wave.
> DR. W. KING.—*Art of Love.*

To do well to a bad man is as great a danger as to do ill to a good one.
> PLAUTUS.—*Pœnulus*, Act 3, 3.

Much of what is great, and to all men beneficial, has been wrought by those who neither intended nor knew the good they did.   RUSKIN.—*Modern Painters,*
> *vol.* 2, *sec.* 3, *ch.* 4, 8.

He has received a favour who has granted one to a worthy person.
> PUBLILIUS SYRUS.

Benefits are pleasing up to that point when they seem to be capable of requital ; when they far exceed that possibility hatred is returned instead of gratitude.
> TACITUS.—*Annals, Bk.* 4, 18.

BENEVOLENCE

A heart to pity and a hand to bless.
> C. CHURCHILL.—*Prophecy of Famine,*
> *l.* 178.

Careless their merits or their faults to scan,
His pity gave ere charity began.
> GOLDSMITH.—*Deserted Village.*

He chid their wanderings but relieved their pain.   GOLDSMITH.—*Ib.*

Large was his bounty and his soul sincere.   GRAY.—*Elegy.*

Officious, innocent, sincere,
Of every friendless name the friend.
> JOHNSON.—*On R. Levett.*

To relieve the oppressed is the most glorious act a man is capable of. It is in some measure doing the business of God and Providence.
> POPE.—*Thoughts on Various Subjects.*

When that the poor have cried, Cæsar hath wept :
Ambition should be made of sterner stuff.
> SHAKESPEARE.—*Julius Cæsar*, Act 3, 2.

Miracles are good, but to comfort one's brother, to extricate a friend from the depths of misery, to pardon one's enemies their virtues—that is the greater miracle which no longer takes place.
> VOLTAIRE.—*Discours 7.*

BEQUESTS

He that defers his charity until he is dead, is, if a man weighs it rightly, rather liberal of another man's than of his own.
> BACON.—*Collection of Sentences.*

This seems to me to be ambition, not charity. (Of charitable bequests.)
> ERASMUS.—*Convivium Religiosum.*

Die and endow a college, or a cat.
> POPE.—*Ep.,* 3.

The man who has not made his will at forty is worse than a fool—almost a knave.   J. WILSON.—*Noctes.*

BEREAVEMENT

Dreams dawn and fly, friends smile and die
Like spring flowers ;
Our vaunted life is one long funeral.
> M. ARNOLD.—*A Question.*

Something is broken which we cannot mend.
God has done more than take away a friend
In taking you ; for all that we have left
Is bruised and irremediably bereft. . .
Here is no waste,
No burning might-have-been,
No bitter after-taste,
None to censure, none to screen,
Nothing awry, nor anything misspent ;
Only content, content beyond content,
Which hath not any room for betterment.
> M. BARING.—*On the death of Lord*
> *Lucas, R.F.C.*

Fled, like the sun eclipsed at noon appears,
And left us darkling in a world of tears.
> BURNS.—*3rd Epistle to R. Graham.*

Hark ! to the hurried question of Despair,
" Where is my child ? "—an echo answers " Where ? "
> BYRON.—*Bride of Abydos, c.* 2, *st.* 27.

Could not the grave forget thee, and lay low
Some less majestic, less beloved head?
> BYRON.—*Childe Harold, c.* 4, *st.* 168.

Thee to deplore were grief misspent indeed ;
It were to weep that goodness has its meed,
That there is bliss prepared in yonder sky,
And glory for the virtuous when they die.
> COWPER.—*In Memory of J. Thornton.*

Oh, that those lips had language. Life
  has passed
With me but roughly since I heard thee
  last.
    Cowper.—*On his mother's picture.*

The Leaves of Life keep falling one by
  one.   Fitzgerald.—*Rubaiyat, st.* 8.
              (*Not in* 1st *Ed.*)

Our light is flown,
Our beautiful, that seemed too much our
  own
Ever to die !
    Mrs. Hemans.—*The Two Voices.*

'Tis sweet, as year by year we lose
Friends out of sight, in faith to muse
How grows in Paradise our store.
              Keble.—*Burial.*

Then fell upon the house a sudden gloom,
  A shadow on those features fair and thin,
And softly, from that hushed and dark-
  ened room,
  Two angels issued where but one went in.
    Longfellow.—*Death of Maria Lovell.*

Oh, not in cruelty, not in wrath,
  The Reaper came that day ;
'Twas an angel visited the green earth,
  And took the flowers away.
    Longfellow.—*The Reaper.*

The air is full of farewells to the dying,
And mournings for the dead.
    Longfellow.—*Resignation.*

There is no flock, however watched and
  tended,
But one dead lamb is there !
There is no fireside, howsoe'er defended,
  But has one vacant chair.
              Longfellow.—*Ib.*

In this dim world of clouding cares,
We rarely know, till 'wildered eyes
See white wings lessening up the skies,
The angels with us unawares.
    G. Massey.—*Babe Christabel.*

Although my life is left so dim,
The morning crowns the mountain rim ;
Joy is not gone from summer skies,
Nor innocence from children's eyes,
And all these things are part of him.
    Alice Meynell.—*Parted.*

Angels, as 'tis but seldom they appear,
So neither do they make long stay ;
They do but visit, and away.
    John Norris.—*To the Memory of my
                    dear Niece.*

Weep not for friends departed,
  But shed the bitter tear
For those who, broken-hearted,
  Are doomed to linger here.
    Thos. Oliphant.—*Imitated from the
        German of Franz Schubert.*

Those whom he loved so long, and sees
  no more ;
Loved and still loves—not dead, but
  gone before. Rogers.—*Human Life.*

Weep not, O friend, we should not weep ;
  Our friend of friends lies full of rest ;
  No sorrow rankles in her breast,
Fallen fast asleep.
She sleeps below,
  She wakes and laughs above ;
To-day, as she walked, let us walk in
  love ;
To-morrow, follow so.
    Christina Rossetti.—*My Friend.*

Grief fills the room up of my vacant child,
Lies in his bed, walks up and down with
  me,
Puts on his pretty looks, repeats his words,
Remembers me of all his gracious parts,
Stuffs out his vacant garments with his
  form.
    Shakespeare.—*King John,* Act 3, 4.

What, all my pretty chickens and their
  dam,
At one fell swoop ?
    Shakespeare.—*Macbeth,* Act 4, 3.

But I must also feel it as a man :
I cannot but remember such things were,
That were most precious to me.
              Shakespeare.—*Ib.*

Oh ! when a Mother meets on high
  The Babe she lost in infancy,
Hath she not then, for pains and fears,
  The day of woe, the watchful night,
For all her sorrow, all her tears,
  An overpayment of delight.
    Southey.—*Curse of Kehama,* Pt. 10, 11.

  Birds sing on a bare bough ;
  O believer, canst not thou ?
    C. H. Spurgeon.—"*Salt-Cellars.*"

The thorns he spares when the rose is
  taken ;
  The rocks are left when he wastes the
  plain ;
The wind that wanders, the weeds wind-
  shaken,
  These remain.
    Swinburne.—*Forsaken Garden.*

Farewell : how should not such as thou
  fare well,
  Though we fare ill that love thee, and
  that live,
And know, whate'er the days wherein we
  dwell
  May give us, thee again they will not
  give.
    Swinburne.—*In Memory of
                J. W. Inchbold.*

As often as a man loses his own relatives
so often he dies.   Publilius Syrus.

I am in some little disorder by reason of the death of a little child of mine, a boy that lately made us very glad: but now he rejoices in his little robe, while we think, and sigh, and long to be as safe as he is.   JEREMY TAYLOR.—*Letter to John Evelyn.*

As those we love decay, we die in part,
String after string is severed from the heart.
    THOMSON.—*Death of Mr. Aikman.*

How fast has brother followed brother
From sunshine to the sunless land!
    WORDSWORTH.—*On the death of James Hogg.*

But she is in her grave, and oh,
The difference to me!
    WORDSWORTH.—*She dwelt among the untrodden ways.*

BETRAYAL

Just for a handful of silver he left us,
Just for a riband to stick in his coat.
    BROWNING.—*The Lost Leader.*

We never are but by ourselves betrayed.
    CONGREVE.—*Old Bachelor*, Act 3, 1.

When lovely woman stoops to folly,
  And finds, too late, that men betray,
What charm can soothe her melancholy,
  What art can wash her guilt away?
    GOLDSMITH.—*On Woman.*

When a man talks of love, with caution hear him;
But if he swears, he'll certainly deceive thee.   T. OTWAY.—*Orphan.*

Call you that backing of your friends?
A plague upon such backing! Give me them that will face me.
    SHAKESPEARE.—*Henry IV.*, Act 2, 4.

He who betrays his friend shall never be
Under one roof, or in one ship, with me.
    SWIFT.—*Horace, Odes*, 3, 2.

Authority forgets a dying king.
    TENNYSON.—*Passing of Arthur, l.* 289.

BIBLE

If most of Genesis be hopeless fiction,
  Yet hath that fiction more poetic worth,
(This one may say, defying contradiction),
Than any scientific " truth " on earth.
    G. BARLOW.—*Poetry and Science*, 31.

Holy Bible, book divine,
Precious treasure, thou art mine.
    JOHN BARTON, SEN. (*b.* 1773).

The sire turns o'er, wi' patriarchal grace,
The big ha' Bible, ance his father's pride.
    BURNS.—*Cotter's Saturday Night.*

Perverts the Prophets and purloins the Psalms.   BYRON.—*English Bards.*

His studie was but litel on the Bible.
    CHAUCER.—*Cant. Tales, Prol.*

The sacred book no longer suffers wrong,
Bound in the fetters of an unknown tongue,
But speaks with plainness art could never mend,
That simplest minds can soonest comprehend.   COWPER.—*Hope,* 450.

And of all arts sagacious dupes invent,
To cheat themselves and gain the world's assent,
The worst is—Scripture warped from its intent.   COWPER.—*Progress of Error.*

Just knows, and knows no more, her Bible true,
A truth the brilliant Frenchman never knew.   COWPER.—*Truth,* 328.

What none can prove a forgery may be true;
What none but bad men wish exploded, must.
    COWPER.—*Winter Morning Walk,* 617.

You rule the Scripture, not the Scripture you.
DRYDEN.—*Hind and the Panther, Pt.* 2, 187.

He that has lost his God can find Him again in this book, and towards the man who has never known Him it wafts the breath of the divine word.
    HEINE.—*Religion and Philosophy, Pref.* (1852).

Bibles laid open, millions of surprises.
    HERBERT.—*Church Porch.*

The book of books, the storehouse and magazine of life and comfort, the Holy Scriptures.
    HERBERT.—*Priest to the Temple, c.* 4.

It is not the bare words but the scope of the writer that giveth the true light by which any writing is to be interpreted; and they that insist upon single texts, without considering the main design, can derive nothing from them clearly; but rather by casting atoms of Scripture, as dust before men's eyes, make everything more obscure than it is.
    HOBBES.—*Leviathan, ch.* 43.

On Bible stilts I don't affect to stalk,
Nor lard with Scripture my familiar talk.
    HOOD.—*Ode to R. Wilson.*

If I am not mistaken, nearly half the sacred volume was written in metre.
    KEBLE.—*Lectures on Poetry, No.* 40 (*E. K. Francis tr.*).

There is a book, who runs may read,
Which heavenly truth imparts,
And all the lore its scholars need,
Pure eyes and Christian hearts.
KEBLE.—*Septuagesima.*

A man of confined education, but of
good parts, by constant reading of the
Bible will naturally form a more winning
and commanding rhetoric than those that
are learned. HENRY MORE (1614-1687).

The Scripture, in time of disputes, is
like an open town in time of war, which
serves indifferently the occasions of both
parties. Each makes use of it for the
present turn and then resigns it to the
next comer to do the same.
POPE.—*Thoughts on Various Subjects.*

This bears the seed of immortality,
For every soul that reads it feels the
search
Of answering thought, and thousands
there may be
Saying at once, "How straight that
looks at me!"
EDNA D. PROCTOR.—*The Living Book.*

Within that awful volume lies
The mystery of mysteries.
. . . . .
And better had they ne'er been born,
Who read to doubt or read to scorn.
SCOTT.—*Monastery, ch.* 12.

Scrutamini Scripturas. These two words
have undone the world.
SELDEN.—*Bible.*

The devil can cite scripture for his purpose.
SHAKESPEARE.—*Merchant of Venice,*
Act 1, 3.

And he who guides the plough, or wields
the crook,
With understanding spirit now may look
Upon her records, listen to her song,
And sift her laws.
WORDSWORTH.—*Eccles. Sonnets, Pt.* 2, 29.

Mighty in the Scriptures.
Acts xviii, 24.

BIGOTRY

Bigotry murders Religion, to frighten
fools with her ghost.
C. C. COLTON.—*Lacon.*

When too much zeal doth fire devotion,
Love is not love, but superstition.
BISHOP CORBET.—*To Lord Mordant.*

Fanatic fools, that in those twilight
times,
With wild religion cloaked the worst of
crimes.
J. LANGHORNE.—*Country Justice.*

But oh, what mighty magic can assuage
A woman's envy and a bigot's rage?
LORD LANSDOWNE.—*Progress of Beauty,*
l. 161.

The worst of madmen is a saint run mad.
POPE.—*Satires, Ep.* 6, 27.

Singly he faced the bigot brood,
The meanly wise, the feebly good;
He pelted them with pearl, with mud;
He fought them well,—
But ah, the stupid million stood,
And he,—he fell!
SIR W. WATSON.—*Tomb of Burns.*

BILLIARDS

A man who wants to play billiards must
have no other ambition. Billiards is all.
E. V. LUCAS.—*Character and Comedy.*

Half the time often lost in learning to
play the beautiful but pernicious game of
billiards would be sufficient to give a
youth mastery of that art [of drawing].
JOHN WILSON.—*Noctes,* 12.

To play billiards well is the sign of a
mis-spent youth.
Saying quoted by Herbert Spencer.

BIOGRAPHERS

Would that every Johnson in the
world had his veridical Boswell, or leash
of Boswells! CARLYLE.—*Voltaire.*

A well-written life is almost as rare as
a well-spent one. CARLYLE.—*Richter.*

The talents of a biographer are often
fatal to his reader.
MISS EDGEWORTH.—*Castle Rackrent, Pref.*

There is properly no history, only biography. EMERSON.—*History.*

After my death I wish no other herald,
No other speaker of my living actions,
To keep mine honour from corruption,
Than such an honest chronicler as
Griffith.
SHAKESPEARE.—*Henry VIII.*, Act 4, 2.

Reader, pass on, nor idly waste your time,
In bad biography or bitter rhyme,
For what I am this cumbrous clay insures,
And what I was is no affair of yours.
Epitaph, said to be in Peterborough
Churchyard.

BIRDS

I value my garden more for being full
of blackbirds than of cherries, and very
frankly give them fruit for their songs.
ADDISON.—*Spectator,* 477.

Proof they give, too, primal powers,
Of a prescience more than ours,
Teach us, while they come and go,
When to sail and when to sow.
M. ARNOLD.—*Poor Matthias.*

He who shall hurt the little wren
Shall never be beloved by men.
WM. BLAKE.—*Proverbs.*

And many a silly thing
  That hops and cheeps,
And perks his tiny tail,
  And sideways peeps,
And flitters little wing,
  Seems in his consequential way
    To tell of Spring.
R. LE GALLIENNE.—*Ode to Spring.*

" None but the lark so shrill and clear !
Now at Heaven's gate she claps her wings,
The morn not waking till she sings."
JOHN LYLY.—*Alexander and Campaspe*, Act 1.

A bird knows nothing of gladness,
Is only a song-machine.
G. MACDONALD.—*Book of Dreams, Pt.* 2, 2.

Quaintest, richest carol of all the singing
  throats. [The blackbird.]
GEO. MEREDITH.—*Love in the Valley*, st. 17.

Gone to the world where birds are blest !
Where never cat glides o'er the green.
ROGERS.—*Epitaph on a Robin.*

At earliest dawn his thrilling pipe was
  heard ;
And when the light of evening died away,
That blithe and indefatigable bird
Still his redundant song of joy and love
  preferred. [The thrush.]
SOUTHEY.—*Tale of Paraguay, Dedication.*

The sober-suited songstress. [The nightingale.]   THOMSON.—*Summer*, 746.

The bird whom man loves best,
The pious bird with the scarlet breast,
  Our little English robin.
WORDSWORTH.—*The Redbreast.*

If the cock moult before the hen,
We shall have weather thick and thin ;
But if the hen moult before the cock,
We shall have weather hard as a block.
North England saying.

Robins and wrens
Are God Almighty's friends ;
Martins and swallows
Are God Almighty's scholars.
*From A. S. Cooke's " Off the Beaten
  Track in Sussex " (1912).*

The robin redbreast and the wren
Are God Almighty's cock and hen.
Old English saying.

Seagull, seagull, sit on the sand ;
It's never good weather when you're on
  the land.   *Old Scottish rhyme.*

On the first of March, the crows begin to
  search ;
By the first of April, they are sitting still ;
By the first of May, they're a' flown away ;
Croupin' greedy back again in October's
  wind and rain.
Old Scottish rhyme (Cheviot's Collection).

One magpie's joy ;
Two's grief ;
Three's a marriage ;
Four's death.
Old Scottish saying (Cheviot's Collection).

BIRTH

For the child's gone that never came.
W. COMBE.—*Syntax in Search of
  Consolation.*

The pleasing punishment that women
  bear.
SHAKESPEARE.—*Comedy of Errors*, Act 1, 1.

What ailed thee then to be born ?
SWINBURNE.—*Atalanta.*

Our birth is but a sleep and a forgetting ;
The Soul that rises with us, our life's Star,
  Hath had elsewhere its setting,
    And cometh from afar ;
Not in entire forgetfulness,
And not in utter nakedness,
But trailing clouds of glory do we come
From God, who is our home.
WORDSWORTH.—*Intimations of Immortality, c.* 5.

BIRTH, NOBLE

Do, as your great progenitors have done,
And, by their virtues, prove yourself their
  son. DRYDEN.—*Wife of Bath, l.* 398.

In some, greatness of birth is apt to
produce meanness of mind.
GREGORY.—*Dial.*

What can ennoble sots, or slaves, or
  cowards ?
Alas ! not all the blood of all the Howards.
POPE.—*Essay on Man, Ep.* 4, 215.

Nothing like blood, sir, in hosses,
dawgs, and men. [James Crawley.]
THACKERAY.—*Vanity Fair, c.* 35.

The first king was a fortunate soldier.
He who serves his country well has no
need of ancestors.
VOLTAIRE.—*Mérope.*

BIRTHDAYS

Born of a Monday, fair in face ;
Born of a Tuesday, full of God's grace ;
Born of a Wednesday, merry and glad ;

Born of a Thursday, sour and sad ;
Born of a Friday, godly given ;
Born of a Saturday, work for your living ;
Born of a Sunday, ne'er shall we want,
So there ends the week and there's an
end on 't.
BRAND's *Popular Antiquities.*

Monday's child is fair in face,
Tuesday's child is full of grace,
Wednesday's child is full of woe,
Thursday's child has far to go,
Friday's child is loving and giving,
Saturday's child works for its living ;
And a child that's born on Christmas day,
Is fair and wise, and good and gay.
Old Rhyme (Halliwell).

BIRTHPLACE

And for their birthplace moan, as moans
the ocean-shell.
MRS. HEMANS.—*Forest Sanctuary, st.* 4.

Seven cities warred for Homer being dead,
Who living had no roof to shroud his head.
THOS. HEYWOOD.—*Hierarchie.*

Every man has a lurking wish to appear
considerable in his native place.
JOHNSON.—*Letter,* 1770.

There may be fairer spots of earth,
But all their glories are not worth
The virtue of the native sod.
J. R. LOWELL.—*An Invitation.*

The first requisite to happiness is that
a man be born in a famous city.
"*Euripides or some other,*" *according to
Plutarch.*

It matters less to a man where he is
born than how he can live.
Turkish prov.

BIRTH-RATE

Every minute dies a man
And one and one-sixteenth is born.
Parody (by BABBAGE, the mathematician)
of Tennyson's "Every moment dies a man."

BIRTHRIGHT

His birthright sold, some pottage so to
gain.   EARL OF STIRLING.—
Doomsday, 6th Hour, 39.

BISHOPS

In the days of gold,
The days of old,
Crozier of wood,
And bishop of gold !
Now we have changed
That law so good
To crozier of gold
And bishop of wood.
LONGFELLOW.—*Golden Legend,* 4 (*Friar
Paul's song*).

Come then, my brethren, and be glad,
And eke rejoice with me ;
Lawn sleeves and rochets shall go down,
And hey ! then up go we !
F. QUARLES.—*Shepherd's Oracles.*

Now hear an allusion :—A mitre, you
know,
Is divided above but united below.
If this you consider, our emblem is right ;
The bishops divide, but the clergy unite.
SWIFT.—*On the Irish Bishops,* 1731.

A bishop then must be blameless.
1 *Timothy* iii, 2.

Weel's him and wae's him, that has a
bishop in his kin.   *Scottish prov.*

BITTERNESS

Much I muse,
How bitter can spring up where sweet is
sown.
DANTE.—*Paradise, c.* 8 (*Cary's tr.*).

His acrid words
Turn the sweet milk of kindness into curds.
O. W. HOLMES.—*The Moral Bully.*

And taunts he casten forth most bitterly.
THOMSON.—*Castle of Indolence, c.* 2, *st.* 80.

But hushed be every thought that springs
From out the bitterness of things.
WORDSWORTH.—*Elegiac Stanzas,* 1824.

The iron entered into his soul.
Church Psalter, CV, 18.

BLACKBALLING

A custom was of old and still remains,
Which life or death by suffrages ordains :
White stones and black within an urn are
cast ;
The first absolve, but fate is in the last.
DRYDEN.—*Tr. Ovid Metam., Bk.* 15.

BLARNEY STONE

The stone this is,
Whoever kisses,
He never misses
To grow eloquent.
'Tis he may clamber
To my lady's chamber,
Or be a member
Of Parliament.
ANON.—*Quoted in Lockhart's Life of Scott,*
ch. 63.

BLASPHEMY

That they may be considered wise they
rail at heaven.
PHÆDRUS.—*Fables, Bk.* 4.

To blaspheme the gods is a hateful form
of cleverness.   PINDAR.—*Pythian Odes,*
c. 9, 40.

BLESSING

A double blessing is a double grace.
SHAKESPEARE.—*Hamlet*, Act 1, 3.

BLINDNESS

Blinder
Than a trebly-bandaged mole.
C. S. CALVERLEY.—*On hearing the Organ.*

Dear to the Muse was he,
Who yet appointed him both good and ill ;
Took from him sight, but gave him strains
divine.
HOMER.—*Odyssey, Bk.* 8, 62 (*Cowper tr.*).

A blind man is a poor man, and blind a
poor man is ;
For the former seeth no man, and the
latter no man sees.
LONGFELLOW.—*From Friedrich von Logan.*

Seasons return, but not to me returns
Day or the sweet approach of even or
morn,
Or sight of vernal bloom, or summer's rose,
Or flocks, or herds, or human face divine.
MILTON.—*Paradise Lost, Bk.* 3, 41.

From the cheerful ways of men
Cut off, and for the book of knowledge fair
Presented with an universal blank
Of Nature's works, to me expunged and
razed,
And wisdom at one entrance quite shut
out.   MILTON.—*Ib., Bk.* 3, 46.

To live a life half dead, a living death.
MILTON.—*Samson Agonistes*, 100.

He that is strucken blind, cannot forget
The precious treasure of his eyesight lost.
SHAKESPEARE.—*Romeo and Juliet*, Act 1, 1.

A picture gallery is a dull place for a
blind man.
G. B. SHAW.—*Man and Superman.*

Being too blind to have desire to see.
TENNYSON.—*Holy Grail, l.* 868.

BLOCKADE

The British blockade won the war ;
but the wonder is that the British blockhead did not lose it.
G. B. SHAW.—*O'Flaherty, V.C., Pref.*
(1919).

Our stern foe
Had made a league with Famine.
SOUTHEY.—*Joan of Arc, Bk.* 2.

BLOODTHIRSTINESS

I love a dire revenge :
Give me the man that will all others kill,
And last himself.
BEAUMONT and FLETCHER.—*Little French
Lawyer*, Act 4, 1.

His word was still—Fie, foh and fum,
I smell the blood of a British man.
SHAKESPEARE.—*Lear*, Act 3, 4.

Brutes never meet in bloody fray,
Nor cut each other's throats for pay.
SWIFT.—*Logicians Refuted.*

And he that was of mildest mood
Did slaye the other there.
Children in the Wood (Old Ballad).

BLOWS

Another's sword has laid him low,
Another's and another's,
And every hand that dealt the blow—
Ah me ! it was a brother's.
CAMPBELL.—*O'Connor's Child*, 10.

Gregory, remember thy swashing blow.
SHAKESPEARE.—*Romeo and Juliet*, Act 1, 1.

BLUNDERS

Your blunderer is as sturdy as a rock.
COWPER.—*Progress of Error*, 538.

It was worse than a crime ; it was a
blunder.   FOUCHÉ (1763-1820).

It is not allowable to make a mistake
twice in war.
PLUTARCH (*A maxim attributed to Lama-
chus, Athenian general*).

You have made this hash ; it is for you
to swallow it all.   TERENCE.—*Phormio.*

Against a foe I can myself defend,
But Heaven protect me from a blunder-
ing friend.
D. W. THOMPSON.—*Sales Attici.*

It is disgraceful to stumble twice against
the same stone.   *Greek prov.*

BLUNTNESS

He would not flatter Neptune for his
trident,
Or Jove for's power to thunder.
SHAKESPEARE.—*Coriolanus*, Act 3, 1.

This rudeness is a sauce to his good wit,
Which gives men stomach to digest his
words
With better appetite.
SHAKESPEARE.—*Julius Cæsar*, Act 1, 2.

He cannot flatter, he—
An honest mind and plain—he must speak
truth !
An they will take it, so ; if not, he's plain.
These kind of knaves I know.
SHAKESPEARE.—*Lear*, Act 2, 2.

BLUSHES

The question [with Mr. Podsnap] about
everything was, would it bring a blush
into the cheek of the young person ?
DICKENS.—*Our Mutual Friend.*

With a smile that glowed
Celestial rosy red, love's proper hue.
MILTON.—*Paradise Lost, Bk.* 8, 618.

The man that blushes is not quite a
brute.   YOUNG.—*Night Thoughts.*

BLUSTER

A noisy man is always in the right.
COWPER.—*Conversation.*

A foutra for the world and worldlings
base !
I speak of Africa and golden joys.
SHAKESPEARE.—*Henry IV.*, Act 5, 3.

From my heart-string
I love the lovely bully.
SHAKESPEARE.—*Henry V.*, Act 4, 1.

He speaks plain cannon—fire and smoke
and bounce.
SHAKESPEARE.—*King John*, Act 2, 2.

BOASTING

Man often indulges too much in vainglory about his contempt of vainglory.
ST. AUGUSTINE.

Quoth she, I told thee what would come
Of all thy vapouring, base scum.
BUTLER.—*Hudibras, Pt.* 1, *c.* 3.

For bragging-time was over, and fighting time was come.
SIR H. NEWBOLT.—*Hawke.*

Ah, this thou should'st have done,
And not have spoke on't !
SHAKESPEARE.—*Antony and Cleopatra*,
Act 2, 7.

Let not him that girdeth on his armour
boast himself as he that putteth it off.
I *Kings* xx, 11 (*Revised Version*).

Brag's a good dog, but he hath lost his
tail.   *Prov.*

Brag's a good dog, but Holdfast is a
better.   *Prov;*

BOATING

Drifting down on the dear old river,
O, the music that interweaves !
The ripples run and the sedges shiver ;
O, the song of the lazy leaves !
J. ASHBY-STERRY.—*Drifting Down.*

And all the way to guide their chime
With falling oars they kept the time.
A. MARVELL.—*Bermudas.*

BOGIES

I'm ole man Spewter-Splutter wid long
claws, en scales on my back ! I'm
snaggle-toofed en double-j'inted ! Gimme
room ! J. C. HARRIS.—*Nights with Uncle
Remus, ch.* 22.

Why does the nurse tell the child of
Rawhead and Bloody-bones ? To keep
it in awe.   SELDEN.—*Priests of Rome.*

BOLDNESS

In civil business, what first ?—Boldness.
What second and third ?—Boldness.
And yet boldness is a child of ignorance
and baseness. BACON.—*Of Boldness*, 12.

What action is to the orator, that
boldness is to the public man—first,
second, and third.
BACON.—*Instauratio, Pt.* 1, *Bk.* 6, 33.

Boldness be my friend !
SHAKESPEARE.—*Cymbeline*, Act 1, 7.

Virtue is bold and goodness never
fearful.
SHAKESPEARE.—*Measure for Measure*,
Act 3, 1.

But flies an eagle flight, bold, and forth on,
Leaving no track behind.
SHAKESPEARE.—*Timon, Act* 1, 1.

Be bolde, Be bolde, and everywhere, *Be
bolde.*
SPENSER.—*Faerie Queene, c.* 11, *st.* 54.

Be not too bolde.
SPENSER.—*Ib.*

BOMBAST

With ravished ears
The monarch hears,
Assumes the god,
Affects to nod,
And seems to shake the spheres.
DRYDEN.—*Alexander's Feast, st.* 2.

Bombast and words a foot-and-a-half long.
HORACE.—*De Arte Poetica.*

Be exceeding proud. Stand upon your
gentility, and scorn every man. Speak
nothing humbly.
BEN JONSON.—*Every Man in his Humour*,
Act 3.

And thou Dalhousie, the great God of
War,
Lieutenant-Colonel to the Earl of Mar.
POPE.—*Art of Sinking, ch.* 9.

I will do it in King Cambyses' vein.
SHAKESPEARE.—*Henry IV., Pt.* 1,
Act 2, 4.

This is Ercles' vein.
SHAKESPEARE.—*Midsummer Night's
Dream*, Act 1, 2.

BONDAGE

So free we seem, so fettered fast we are !
BROWNING.—*Andrea del Sarto.*

A fool I do him firmely hold
That loves his fetters, though they were
　of gold.
　　SPENSER.—*Faerie Queene, Bk. 3, c. 9.*

BOOK INSCRIPTIONS

This book is one thing,
And hemp is another ;
Steal not the one
For fear of the other ;
For if you steal this book,
It is very true
A harder thing hereafter
Will ensue to you.　*MS. (c.* 1693).

This book, a child of Adam's race,
Among my human friends I place,
Whereof this label on his face
　The token and the pledge is.
Then, gentle reader, of your grace,
Preserve my friend from usage base,
Have pity on his helpless case,
　And reverence his edges.　ANON.

Small is the wren ;
　Black is the rook ;
Blacker the sinner
　Who steals this book.
　　　Traditional Rhyme.

Steal not this book for fear of shame,
For in it is the owner's name,
And when you die the Lord will say,
Where is that book you stole away ?
　　Old Schoolbook Inscription.

BOOK LEARNING

And let a scholar all Earth's volumes carry,
He will be but a walking dictionary.
　　CHAPMAN.—*Tears of Peace.*

He that takes up conclusions on the
trust of authors, and doth not fetch them
from the first items in every reckoning,
which are the significations of names
settled by definitions, loses his labour
and does not know anything, but only
believeth.　HOBBES.—*Leviathan, ch.* 5.

Deep versed in books and shallow in
himself.
　MILTON.—*Paradise Regained, Bk.* 4, 327.

The bookful blockhead, ignorantly read,
With loads of learned lumber in his head.
　　POPE.—*Criticism, l.* 612.

His knowledge of books had in some
degree diminished his knowledge of the
world.　W. SHENSTONE.—*A Character.*

Nature's fair table-book, our tender souls,
We scrawl all o'er with old and empty
　rules,
Stale memorandums of the schools ;
For learning's mighty treasures look
　Into that deep grave, a book.
　　SWIFT.—*To Sir W. Temple.*

BOOKS

A man of one book (i.e. a learned man).
　　THOS. AQUINAS.

Libraries . . . are as the shrines where
all the relics of the ancient saints, full
of true virtue, and that without delusion
or imposture, are preserved and reposed.
BACON.—*Advancement of Learning, Bk.* 2.

Books will speak plain when counsellors
blanch.　　BACON.—*Of Counsel,* 20.

Some books are to be tasted, others to
be swallowed, and some few to be chewed
and digested.　BACON.—*Of Studies,* 50.

Histories make men wise ; poets, witty ;
the mathematics, subtile ; natural philosophy, deep ; moral, grave ; logic and
rhetoric, able to contend.　BACON.—*Ib.*

Books are the shrine where the saint
is, or is believed to be.
　　BACON.—*To Sir T. Bodley.*

A borrowed book is but a cheap pleasure,
an　unappreciated　and　unsatisfactory
tool.　To know the true value of books
. . . you must first feel the sweet delight
of buying them.　　J. M. BALDWIN.

Read bookes, hate Ignorance, the foe
　to Art,
The dam of Error, Envy of the hart.
　　R. BARNFIELD.—*Affectionate
　　　　　Shepheard* (1594).

A home without books is like a house
without windows; no man has the right
to bring up children without books to
surround them.　　H. W. BEECHER.

Books are men of higher stature.
　　E. B. BROWNING.—*Lady Geraldine's
　　　　　Courtship.*

Some said, John, print it ; others said,
　Not so ;
Some said, It might do good ; others
　said No.
　　BUNYAN.—*Pilgrim's Progress, Pt.* 2.

You only, O books, are liberal and independent.　You give to all who ask, and
enfranchise all who serve you assiduously.
　RICHARD DE BURY, BISHOP OF DURHAM
　　　(1281-1345).—*Philobiblon.*

Affects all books of past and modern ages,
But reads no further than their title pages.
　　S. BUTLER.—*Human Learning.*

'Tis pleasant sure to see one's name in
　print ;
A book's a book, although there's nothing
　in 't.　BYRON.—*English Bards, l.* 51.

A big book is a big evil.
　　CALLIMACHUS (*Greek*).

For him was lever have at his beddes heed.
Twenty bokes, clad in black or reed,
Of Aristotle and his philosophye,
Than robes riche, or fithele or gay sautrye.
CHAUCER.—*Cant. Tales, Prol.*

In books a prodigal, they say,
A living cyclopedia.
COTTON MATHER.—*On Anne Bradstreet.*

Come, my best friends, my books, and
lead me on ! COWLEY.—*The Motto.*

'Twere well with most if books that could
engage
Their childhood, pleased them at a riper
age. COWPER.—*Tirocinium,* 147.

Books cannot always please, however
good ;
Minds are not ever craving for their food.
CRABBE.—*The Borough, Letter* 24.

These are the tombs of such as cannot
die. CRABBE.—*Library.*

Books should to one of these four ends
conduce,
For wisdom, piety, delight, or use.
SIR J. DENHAM.—*Prudence, l.* 83.

Choose an author as you choose a friend.
W. DILLON (E. of Roscommon).—*On
Translated Verse,* 96.

An author may influence the fortunes
of the world to as great an extent as a
statesman or a warrior. A book may be
as great a thing as a battle.
DISRAELI.

The three practical rules, then, which I
have to offer, are : 1. Never read any book
that is not a year old. 2. Never read any
but famed books. 3. Never read any
but what you like. EMERSON.—*Books.*

There must be a man behind the book.
EMERSON.—*Goethe.*

'Tis the good reader that makes the
good book. EMERSON.—*Success.*

The princeps copy, bound in blue and
gold. J. FERRIAR.—*Bibliomania.*

That place that does contain
My books, the best companions, is to me
A glorious court, where hourly I converse
With the old sages and philosophers.
FLETCHER and MASSINGER.—*Elder
Brother, Act* 1, 2.

He breaks his fast
With Aristotle, dines with Tully, takes
His watering with the Muses, sups with
Livy. FLETCHER and MASSINGER.—*Ib.*

Learning hath gained most by those
books by which the printers have lost.
T. FULLER.—*Of Books.*

Books teach us very little of the world.
GOLDSMITH.—*Letter,* 1739.

A book may be amusing with numerous
errors, or it may be very dull without a
single absurdity.
GOLDSMITH.—*Vicar of Wakefield, Preface.*

The scholar only knows how dear these
silent yet eloquent companions of pure
thoughts and innocent hours become
in the season of adversity. When all
that is worldly turns to dross around us,
these only retain their steady value.
WASHINGTON IRVING.

Was there ever yet anything written
long that was wished longer by its readers ?
—except Don Quixote, Robinson Crusoe,
and the Pilgrim's Progress.
JOHNSON.—*Remark as recorded by
Mrs. Piozzi.*

Books without the knowledge of life
are useless, for what should books teach
but the art of living ?
JOHNSON.—*Remark as recorded by
Mrs. Piozzi.*

As in feeling a pulse it is not always
easy for a doctor to detect whether the
beating comes from himself or from his
patient, so the case is exactly the same
in the close union and mingling of the
minds of author and reader.
KEBLE.—*Lectures on Poetry, No.* 31
(*E. K. Francis tr.*).

Books which are no books . . . things
in books' clothing. LAMB.—*On Books.*

I love to lose myself in other men's
minds. LAMB.—*Ib.*

I mean your borrowers of books—those
mutilators of collections, spoilers of the
symmetry of shelves, and creators of
odd volumes. LAMB.—*Two Races.*

One gift the Fairies gave me . . .
The love of Books, the Golden Key
That opens the Enchanted Door.
ANDREW LANG.—*Ballads of the
Bookworm.*

What are my books ? My friends, my
loves,
My church, my tavern, and my only
wealth.
R. LE GALLIENNE.—*My Books.*

A reading-machine, always wound up and
going,
He mastered whatever was not worth the
knowing.
J. R. LOWELL.—*Fable for Critics.*

When the dim presence of the awful night
Clasps in its jewelled arms the slumber-
ing earth,
Alone I sit beside the lowly light,

That like a dream-fire flickers on my
    hearth,
With some joy-teeming volume in my
    hand—
A peopled planet, opulent and grand.
    JAMES MACFARLAN.—*The Book World*
                                (1859).

A good book is the precious life-blood
of a master-spirit, imbalmed and treasured
up on purpose to a Life beyond Life.
    MILTON.—*Areopagitica.*

As good almost kill a Man as kill a
good Book. Who kills a Man kills a
reasonable creature, God's image; but
he who destroys a good Book, kills reason
itself, kills the image of God, as it were,
in the die.   MILTON.—*Ib.*

Every abridgment of a book is a stupid
abridgment.   MONTAIGNE.—*Bk.* 3.

The best books are those which every
reader feels that he could have written ;
the natural, which alone is good, is entirely
familiar and common.
    PASCAL.—*Pensées.*

I have for my friends books, friends
extremely agreeable, of all ages, of every
land ; of easy access, for they are always
at my service ; I admit them to my company, and dismiss them from it, whenever
I please. They are never troublesome,
but immediately answer every question
I ask them.   PETRARCH.

A book is a friend that never betrays
us.   GUILBERT DE PIXÉRÉCOURT.

He [Pliny the Elder] read no books
without making extracts ; and he used to
say there was no book so bad but that
profit might be derived from some part
of it.   PLINY THE YOUNGER.—*Ep.*

Timotheus said that they who dine
with Plato never complain the next
morning.   PLUTARCH.—*Morals, Bk.* 1.

While I pondered, weak and weary,
Over many a quaint and curious volume
    of forgotten lore.
    E. A. POE.—*Raven, st.* 1.

For some in ancient books delight ;
Others prefer what moderns write ;
Now I should be extremely loth
Not to be thought expert in both.
    PRIOR.—*Alma, c.* 1, 519.

Holds secret converse with the Mighty
Dead.   ROGERS.—*Human Life.*

The Frenchman reads much, but he
only reads new books, or rather he runs
through them, less for the sake of reading
them than to say that he has read them.
    ROUSSEAU.—*Julie.*

How learned many a man would be if
he knew all that is in his own books !
    SCHOPENHAUER.—*On Authorship.*

It would be a good thing to buy books
if we could also buy the time to read them.
    SCHOPENHAUER.—*On Reading.*

Waverley drove through the sea of
books, like a vessel without a pilot or
a rudder.   SCOTT.—*Waverley, ch.* 36.

A crowd of books distracts the mind.
    SENECA.—*Ep.* 2.

Leisure without books is death, and the
burial of a man alive.   SENECA.—*Ep.* 82.

As painfully to pore upon a book,
    To seek the light of truth ; while truth
        the while
Doth falsely blind the eyesight of his look :
    Light, seeking light, doth light of light
        beguile.
    SHAKESPEARE.—*Love's Labour's Lost,*
                                Act 1, 1.

    My library
Was dukedom large enough.
    SHAKESPEARE.—*Tempest,* Act 1, 2.

I always know when Lady Slattern has
been before me. She has a most observing thumb.   SHERIDAN.—*Rivals,* Act 1, 2.

As I never return books, I make a rule
never to borrow them.
    SYDNEY SMITH.—*Letter, Sept.* 17, 1844.

No furniture so charming as books.
    SYDNEY SMITH.—*Sayings, Vol.* 1.

My days among the dead are passed ;
    Around me I behold,
Where'er these casual eyes are cast,
    The mighty minds of old ;
My never-failing friends are they,
With whom I converse day by day.
    SOUTHEY.—*Occas. Pieces,* 18.

If there should be another flood,
    For refuge hither fly ;
Though all the world should be submerged,
This book will still be dry.
    Saying quoted or invented by
                                C. H. SPURGEON.

Books, like proverbs, receive their chief
value from the stamp and esteem of
ages through which they have passed.
    SIR W. TEMPLE.—*Ancient and Modern
                                Learning.*

But every page having an ample marge,
And every marge enclosing in the midst
A square of text that looks a little blot.
    TENNYSON.—*Merlin and Vivien,* 667.

There studious let me sit,
And hold high converse with the Mighty
Dead.
THOMSON.—*Seasons, Winter*, 431.

Book love, my friends, is your pass to
the greatest, the purest, and the most
perfect pleasure that God hath prepared
for His creatures.   A. TROLLOPE.

This little book fed me in a very hungry
place.   MARK TWAIN.—*Tramp Abroad.*

Is a book bad? Nothing can plead for
it. Is it good? All the kings cannot
crush it. They suppress it at Rome,
and in London they admire it; the Pope
proscribes it, and all Europe wants to
read it.
VOLTAIRE.—*To the King of Denmark.*

The multitude of useless books is so
immense that the life of a man would not
suffice to make a catalogue of them.
VOLTAIRE.—*Letter to M. Marin, July* 5,
1769.

Books should be treated like men.
Choose the most reasonable, examine
them, and never give up your judgment
except to evidence.
VOLTAIRE.—*L'Homme aux Quarante Écus.*

Books govern the world, or at any rate
all nations which possess the faculty of
writing. VOLTAIRE.—*On the Old Testament.*

Titles of books are like those of men,
in the eyes of a philosopher. He judges
nothing by titles.
VOLTAIRE.—*On the Will of Cardinal
Alberoni.*

It is necessary to be on one's guard
against books, even more than judges
are against advocates.
VOLTAIRE.—*Printed Falsehoods.*

To lend a byuck is to lose it—an'
borrowin's but a hypocritical excuse for
stealin' and should be punished wi' death.
JOHN WILSON.—*Noctes* 30 (*The
Ettrick Shepherd*).

Go forth, my little book! pursue thy way!
Go forth, and please the gentle and the
good.
WORDSWORTH.—*Desultory Stanzas.*

More sweet than odours caught by him
who sails
Near spicy shores of Araby the blest,
A thousand times more exquisitely sweet,
The freight of holy feeling which we meet,
In thoughtful moments, wafted by the
gales
From fields where good men walk, or
bowers wherein they rest.
WORDSWORTH.—*Eccles. Sonnets, Pt.* 2, 39.

If in this book Fancy and Truth agree;
If simple Nature, trained by careful
Art,
Through it have won a passage to thy
heart,
Grant me thy love—I claim no other fee.
WORDSWORTH.—*Miscell. Sonnets,
Pt.* 3, 39.

Dreams, books, are each a world; and
books, we know,
Are a substantial world, both pure and
good.
WORDSWORTH.—*Personal Talk,* 3.

Of making many books there is no end;
and much study is a weariness of the flesh.
Ecclesiastes xii, 12.

Behold, my desire is . . . that mine
adversary had written a book.
Job xxxi, 35.

The dead are the best advisers.
Latin saying.

Woe be to him that reads but one book!
Prov. (*Geo. Herbert*) *from the Latin.*

Books and friends should be few and
good.   *Spanish prov.*

O! for a booke and a shadie nooke,
Eyther indore or out;
With the grene leaves whispering over-
heade,
Or the street cryes all about.
*Quoted by Lord Avebury as "An Old
Song," but probably modern and said
to be written by John Wilson, London
bookseller (d.* 1889), *as a "motto"
for his second-hand catalogue, c.* 1888.

BOREDOM

By thy long grey beard and glittering
eye,
Now wherefore stopp'st thou me?
COLERIDGE.—*Ancient Mariner.*

We almost always get bored with those
whom we bore.
LA ROCHEFOUCAULD.—*Maxim* 634.

People always get tired of one another.
I grow tired of myself whenever I am
left alone for ten minutes, and I am certain
that I am fonder of myself than anyone
can be of another person.
G. B. SHAW.—*Unsocial Socialist, ch.* 4.

In order not to displease too much, one
must submit to be frequently bored.
VOLTAIRE.—*Le Dépositaire.*

The secret of boring is the practice of
saying everything.
VOLTAIRE.—*Discourse on Man.*

Repose is a good thing, but boredom is its
brother.   VOLTAIRE.

BORROWERS AND LENDERS

The human species, according to the best theory I can form of it, is composed of two distinct races, *the men who borrow*, and *the men who lend*.   LAMB.—*Two Races*.

Neither a borrower nor a lender be,
For loan oft loses both itself and friend,
And borrowing dulls the edge of husbandry.
SHAKESPEARE.—*Hamlet*, Act 1, 3.

Let us all be happy and live within our means, even if we have to borrer the money to do it with.
ARTEMUS WARD (C. F. BROWNE).—*Natural History*.

The borrower is servant to the lender.
Proverbs xxii, 7.

BOUNDARIES

Mountains interposed,
Make enemies of nations, who had else,
Like kindred drops, been mingled into one.   COWPER.—*Time Piece, l.* 17.

BOYHOOD

Not when the sense is dim,
  But now from the heart of joy,
I would remember Him :
  Take the thanks of a boy.
    H. C. BEECHING.—*Prayers*.

The schoolboy spot
We ne'er forget, though there we are forgot.   BYRON.—*Don Juan*, 1, 130.

Few boys are born with talents that excel,
But all are capable of living well.
COWPER.—*Tirocinium*, 509.

I only know two sorts of boys : mealy boys and beef-faced boys.
DICKENS.—*Oliver Twist, c.* 14.

The microcosm of a public school.
DISRAELI.—*Vivian Grey, c.* 2.

Far happier is thy head that wears
That hat without a crown.
HOOD.—*Clapham Academy*.

O dearest, dearest boy ! my heart
For better lore would seldom yearn,
Could I but teach the hundredth part
Of what from thee I learn.
WORDSWORTH.—*Anecdote for Fathers*.

An angelic boyhood becomes a Satanic old age. *Latin Mediæval prov., described by Erasmus as " invented by Satan."*

Forty years on, growing older and older,
  Shorter in wind as in memory long,
Feeble of foot and rheumatic of shoulder,
  What will it help you that once you were young ?
Harrow School Song, " Forty Years On."

BRAGGADOCIO

'Tis easier far to flourish than to fight.
DRYDEN.—*Hind and the Panther*.

Gross feeders, lion-talkers, lamb-like fighters. DRYDEN.—*Spanish Friar*, Act 4, 2.

BRAINS

I abhor brains
As I do tools : they're things mechanical.
J. S. KNOWLES.—*Hunchback*, Act 3, 1.

I mix them with my brains, sir.
JOHN OPIE.—*Reply to question " With what do you mix your colours ? "*

BREAD

Man doth not live by bread only.
Deuteronomy viii, 3.

BREAKFAST

And then to breakfast, with what appetite you have.
SHAKESPEARE.—*Henry VIII.*, Act 3, 2.

I think breakfasts so pleasant because no one is conceited before one o'clock.
SYDNEY SMITH.—*Saying*.

When a man 'as breakfast every day, he don't know what it is.
R. L. STEVENSON (and L. OSBORNE).—*Ebb-Tide, ch.* 2.

BREEDING

Good breeding is the blossom of good sense.   YOUNG.—*Love of Fame*.

Meat feeds, claith cleeds (clothes), but breeding maks the man.   *Scottish prov.*

BREVITY

Would'st thou foil the censurer's sneer,
Thy copious theme in narrowest pale
Confine ; nor pall the impatient ear
That throbs for fresh delights, and loathes
  the lengthening tale.
PINDAR.—*Pythian Odes*, 9, 133 (*Moore tr.*).

The Lacedæmonian wisdom consisted of brief and memorable sayings [uttered by the seven Wise Men] . . . This was the manner of philosophy among the ancients—a certain laconic brevity of speech.   PLATO.—*Protagoras*, 82.

Brevity is the soul of wit.
SHAKESPEARE.—*Hamlet*, Act 2, 2.

Not that the story need be long, but it will take a long while to make it short.
H. D. THOREAU.—*Letter to a Friend*.

BRIBERY

Moved by the rhetoric of a silver fee.
GAY.—*Trivia, Bk.* 3, 318.

Turn from the glittering bribe thy scornful
    eye,
Nor sell for gold what gold could never
    buy.   JOHNSON.—*London.*

Omnes diligunt munera. They all love
bribes. Bribery is a princely kind of
thieving. . . . Nowadays they call them
gentle rewards. Let them leave their
colouring, and call them by their Christian
name—bribes.
      BISHOP LATIMER.—*Sermon.*

Let speculative men reason or rather
refine as they please, it will ever be true
among us, that as long as men engage in
the public service upon private ends . . .
it will be safer to trust our property and
constitution in the hands of such who have
paid for their election, than of those who
have obtained them by servile flatteries
of the people.
    SWIFT.—*Contests and Dissensions, ch.* 4.

It is an old maxim that every man has
his price.   *The Bee* (1733-4).

A hoarseness caused by swallowing
gold and silver.
    *Plutarch says that this was said of
    Demosthenes, when he pretended in-
    ability to plead owing to having lost his
                voice.*

Yet one of them, more hard of heart,
    Did vowe to do his charge,
Because the wretch, that hired him,
    Had paid him very large.
     The Children in the Wood.
     Black-letter ballad, st. 12.

BRIDES AND BRIDEGROOMS

That Adam, called " the happiest of
men."   BYRON.—*Don Juan*, 14, 55.

The bride hath paced into the hall,
Red as a rose is she.
    COLERIDGE.—*Ancient Mariner, Pt.* 1.

Holy and pure are the drops that fall
When the young bride goes from her
    father's hall ;
She goes unto love yet untried and new ;
She parts from love which hath still been
    true.
    MRS. HEMANS.—*Bride of the Greek Isle.*

Blest is the Bride on whom the sun
doth shine.
    HERRICK.—284, *Nuptial Song.*

Nothing is to me more distasteful than
that entire complacency and satisfaction
which beam in the faces of a new-married
couple—in that of the lady particularly.
    LAMB.—*A Bachelor's Complaint.*

And doubtful joys the father move,
    And tears are on the mother's face,
    As, parting with a long embrace,
She enters other realms of love.
    TENNYSON.—*In Memoriam, c.* 40.

BRIDESMAIDS

Bridesmaids may soon be made brides.
One wedding brings on another.
    C. H. SPURGEON.—" *Salt-Cellars.*"

A happy bridesmaid makes a happy
bride.   TENNYSON.—*The Bridesmaid.*

BRILLIANCY

How inferior for seeing with is your
brightest train of fireworks to the humblest
farthing candle.   CARLYLE.—*Diderot.*

BRITAIN

This most happy and glorious event,
that this Island of Britain, divided from
all the world, should be united in itself.
BACON.—*Advancement of Learning, Bk.* 2.

There are no countries in the world less
known by the British than these self-same
British Islands.   G. BORROW.—*Lavengro.*

Be Britain still to Britain true,
    Among oursels united ;
For never but by British hands
    Maun British wrangs be righted !
    BURNS.—*Dumfries Volunteers.*

Britannia needs no bulwarks,
    No towers along the steep,
Her march is on the mountain waves,
    Her home is on the deep.
    CAMPBELL.—*Ye Mariners.*

Oh it's a snug little island,
A right little, tight little island !
Search the globe round, none can be found
So happy as this little island.
    THOS. DIBDIN.—*Snug Little Island.*

What should they know of England
    Who only England know ?
        KIPLING.—*English Flag.*

Rejoice, O Albion ! severed from the world
By Nature's wise indulgence.
    JOHN PHILIPS.—*Cider, Bk.* 2.

Britain is
A world by itself ; and we will nothing
        pay
For wearing our own noses.
    SHAKESPEARE.—*Cymbeline*, Act 3, 1.

You shall find us in our salt-water
girdle.   SHAKESPEARE.—*Ib.*

Prithee, think
There's livers out of Britain.
    SHAKESPEARE.—*Ib.*, Act 3, 4.

Hath Britain all the sun that shines ?
  SHAKESPEARE.—*Cymbeline*, Act 3, 4.

Hail, happy Britain ! highly favoured
  isle,
And Heaven's peculiar care !
  W. SOMERVILLE.—*The Chase, Bk.* 1.

Thank Him who isled us here, and roughly
  set
His Britain in blown seas and storming
  showers.
  TENNYSON.—*On Wellington, st.* 7.

God bless the narrow sea which keeps
  her off,
And keeps our Britain, whole within
  herself,
A nation yet, the rulers and the ruled.
  TENNYSON.—*Princess, Conclusion.*

No little German state are we,
  But the one voice of Europe ; we *must*
  speak.
  TENNYSON.—*Third of February.*

Broad-based upon her people's will,
And compassed by the inviolate sea.
  TENNYSON.—*To the Queen.*

This was the charter of the land,
  And guardian angels sung the strain ;
  " Rule, Britannia ! rule the waves !
  Britons never will be slaves."
  THOMSON.—*Mask of Alfred*
  (authorship disputed).

Whether this portion of the world were
  rent
By the rude ocean from the continent,
Or thus created, it was sure designed
To be the sacred refuge of mankind.
  WALLER.—*To my Lord Protector,*
  st. 7.

Rome, though her eagle through the world
  had flown,
Could never make this island all her own.
  WALLER.—*Ib., st.* 17.

BRITISH FLAG

Whose flag has braved a thousand years,
The battle and the breeze !
  CAMPBELL.—*Ye Mariners.*

The meteor flag of England shall yet
  terrific burn. CAMPBELL.—*Ib.* 4.

With Freedom's lion-banner
Britannia rules the waves.
  CAMPBELL.—*To the Germans.*

Take 'old o' the Wings o' the Mornin',
  An' flop round the earth till you're
  dead ;
But you won't get away from the tune
  that they play
  To the bloomin' old rag overhead.
  KIPLING.—*Widow at Windsor.*

BRITONS

As long as faith and freedom last,
  And earth goes round the sun,
This stands—The British line held fast,
  And so the fight was won.
  H. BEGBIE.—*The Living Line (April* 2,
  1918).

The fickleness which is attributed to
us as we are islanders.
  MILTON.—*Ready and Easy Way* (1660).

Britons, strike home ! Revenge your
country's wrongs !
  GEO. POWELL.—*Bonduca* (1696 *version*).

BROADMINDEDNESS

Just as he [Homer] could speak of the
rich and royal without envy, so he could
deal with the poorest of the poor without
a touch of slight or contempt.
  KEBLE.—*Lectures on Poetry, No.* 14
  (E. K. Francis tr.).

BROTHERHOOD

For 'a that, and a' that,
  It's comin' yet for a' that,
That man to man, the warld o'er,
  Shall brothers be for a' that.
  BURNS.—*Is there, for Honest Poverty ?*

Father and mother
Ask reverence ; a brother, only love.
  T. CAMPION.—*Fortune and Glory.*

The political brotherhood which philosophy teaches us is more beneficial to us
than the merely spiritual brotherhood,
for which we are indebted to Christianity.
  HEINE.—*The Romantic School.*

No distance breaks the tie of blood ;
Brothers are brothers evermore.
  KEBLE.—*Christian Year,* 2nd
  Sunday after Trinity.

A brother is a friend given by nature.
  J. B. LEGOUVÉ.

We few, we happy few, we band of
  brothers.
  SHAKESPEARE.—*Henry V.,* Act 4, 3.

And when, with grief, you see your brother
  stray,
Or in a night of error lose his way,
Direct his wandering and restore the day.
To guide his steps afford your kindest aid,
And gently pity whom ye can't persuade ;
Leave to avenging Heaven his stubborn
  will,
For, O remember, he's your brother still,
  SWIFT.—*Swan Tripe Club.*

Let brotherly love continue.
  2 *Timothy* xiii, 1.

BRUTALITY

They are neither man nor woman—
They are neither brute nor human,
They are Ghouls !
E. A. POE.—*The Bells.*

The time and my intents are savage-wild ;
More fierce, and more inexorable far,
Than empty tigers, or the roaring sea.
SHAKESPEARE.—*Romeo and Juliet,*
Act 3, 5.

Like brute beasts that have no understanding.
Common Prayer, Marriage Service.

BUILDING

A noble craft, that of a mason ! A
good building will last longer than most
books—longer than one book in a million.
CARLYLE.—*Remark referring to
Auldgarth Bridge.*

Build houses of five hundred by a hundred feet, forgetting that of six by two.
FIELDING.—*Tom Jones, Bk. 2, c. 8.*

No hammers fell, no ponderous axes rung ;
Like some tall palm the mystic fabric
sprung.
Majestic silence.   HEBER.—*Palestine.*

Anon out of the earth a fabric huge
Rose like an exhalation.
MILTON.—*Paradise Lost, Bk. 1, 710.*

I seldom see a noble building, or any
other piece of magnificence and pomp,
but I think how little is all this to satisfy
the ambition or to fill the idea of an immortal soul.
POPE.—*Thoughts on Various Subjects.*

The man who builds, and wants where-
with to pay,
Provides a home from which to run away.
YOUNG.—*Love of Fame.*

Building is a sweet impoverishing.
Prov. (Geo. Herbert).

The grandsire buys, the father bigs
(builds), the son sells, and the grandson
thigs (begs).   *Scottish saying.*

BULLIES

He was a coward to the strong ;
He was a tyrant to the weak.
SHELLEY.—*Rosalind.*

BURDENS

Respect the burden.   NAPOLEON.

For every man shall bear his own burden.
Galatians vi, 5.

BURGLARS

A terrier tyke and a rusty key
Were Johnnie Armstrong's Jeddart fee.
*Scottish saying, founded on a statement
that Johnnie Armstrong, a convicted
moss trooper, was offered his life if he
would disclose the best safeguards
against marauders. He replied, " A
terrier and rusty locks."*

BURIAL

So peaceful rests, without a stone, a name,
What once had beauty, titles, wealth, and
fame.   POPE.—*Elegy,* 69.

We carved not a line and we raised not
a stone,
But we left him alone with his glory.
C. WOLFE.—*Burial of Sir John Moore.*

Denied the charity of dust, to spread
O'er dust.   YOUNG.—*Night Thoughts,* 3.

BUSINESS

The playthings of our elders are called
business.
ST. AUGUSTINE.—*Conf., Bk.* 1.

No-wher so bisy a man as he ther nas,
And yet he semed bisier than he was.
CHAUCER.—*Cant. Tales, Prol.*

Hackneyed in business, wearied at that
oar,
Which thousands, once fast chained to,
quit no more.
COWPER.—*Retirement.*

You Irish gentlemen [said the attorney]
are rather in too great a hurry in doing
business. Business, sir, is a thing that
must be done slowly to be done well.
MISS EDGEWORTH.—*Essay on Irish
Bulls, ch.* 3.

A business that makes nothing but
money is a poor kind of business.
HENRY FORD (*American millionaire*),
Jan. 1919.

Curse on that man that business first
designed,
And by 't enthralled a freeborn lover's
mind.   J. OLDHAM.—*Absence.*

Being asked whether he was at leisure,
Dionysius the elder said, " No, nor do
I ever expect to be."
PLUTARCH.—*Morals, Bk.* 1.

A man of wit is not incapable of business,
but above it. A sprightly, generous horse
is able to carry a pack saddle as well as
an ass, but he is too good to be put to
the drudgery.
POPE.—*Thoughts on Various Subjects.*

BUSY-BODIES

But so many books thou readest,
But so many schemes thou breedest,
But so many wishes feedest,
  That thy poor head almost turns.
        M. ARNOLD.—*Second Best.*

Zeus hates busy-bodies and those who
do too much.
    EURIPIDES.—*As quoted by Emerson,
        in essay on " Success."*

There is nothing in the world more un-
seemly than an aged busy-body.
        MARTIAL.—4, 79.

" O Hercules," said Phocion, when
busy-bodies tried to interfere with his
military dispositions and alter his plans,
" how many generals we have, and how few
soldiers ! " PLUTARCH.—*Life of Phocion.*

BUTTER

Butter is mad twice a year [in the extremes of temperature].   *Prov.*

Butter is gold in the morning, silver at
noon, lead at night.   *Prov. (Ray).*

  Butter to butter's nae kitchen.
  *Scottish prov., meaning " like to like
        is no relish."*

BUTTONS

My father was an eminent button-maker
at Birmingham . . . but I had a soul
above buttons.
    G. COLMAN.—*Sylvester Daggerwood.*

C

CABALS

O my soul, come not thou into their
secret ; unto their assembly, mine honour,
be not thou united.   *Genesis* xlix, 6.

CALAMITY

        Calamity
  Is man's true touchstone.
    BEAUMONT AND FLETCHER.—*Triumph
        of Honour, Sc.* 1.

Never did any public misery
Rise of itself ; God's plagues still grounded
  are
On common stains of our humanity.
    F. GREVILLE.—*Treatie of Warres.*

Romeo, come forth ; come forth, thou
  fearful man ;
Affliction is enamoured of thy parts,
And thou art wedded to calamity.
    SHAKESPEARE.—*Romeo and Juliet,
        Act 3, 3.*

CALCULATION

For he by geometric scale
Could take the size of pots of ale,
And wisely tell what hour o' the day
The clock does strike by algebra.
    BUTLER.—*Hudibras, Pt.* 1, *c.* 1.

CALLOUSNESS

So perish all whose breast ne'er learned to
  glow
For other's good or melt at other's woe.
    POPE.—*Elegy to the Memory of an
        Unfortunate Lady,* 45.

You blocks, you stones, you worse than
  senseless things !
O you hard hearts, you cruel men of Rome,
Knew you not Pompey ?
    SHAKESPEARE.—*Julius Caesar,* Act 1, 1.

He jests at scars that never felt a wound.
    SHAKESPEARE.—*Romeo and Juliet,* Act 2, 2.

    Hearts which lapse of years,
And that half-wisdom half-experience
  gives,
Make slow to feel.
    WORDSWORTH.—*The Old Cumberland
        Beggar.*

CALM

The torrent's smoothness, ere it dash
below. CAMPBELL.—*Gertrude of Wyoming,
        Pt.* 3, 5.

Calmness is great advantage ; he that lets
Another chafe, may warm him at his fire.
    HERBERT.—*Church Porch.*

Hence in a season of calm weather,
  Though inland far we be,
Our souls have sight of that immortal
  sea
Which brought us hither.
    WORDSWORTH.—*Intimations of
        Immortality.*

No motion but the moving tide, a breeze,
Or merely silent nature's breathing life.
    WORDSWORTH.—*Elegiac Stanzas,* 1805.

With heart as calm as lakes that sleep
In frosty moonlight glistening ;
Or mountain rivers, where they creep
Along a channel smooth and deep,
To their own far-off murmurs listening.
    WORDSWORTH.—*Memory.*

CALUMNY

It is a royal experience to be ill-spoken
of for good deeds.
    ANTISTHENES.—*As quoted by Marcus
        Aurelius,* 7, 36.

Calumniate, calumniate ! Something will
always stick.
    BEAUMARCHAIS.—*Barbier de Seville.*

Innocence is a defence
For nothing else but patience.
'Twill not bear out the blows of fate
Nor fence against the tricks of state;
Nor from the oppression of the laws
Protect the plain'st and justest cause;
Nor keep unspotted a good name
Against the obloquies of fame.
S. BUTLER.—*Miscellaneous Thoughts.*

As long as there are readers to be delighted with calumny, there will be found
reviewers to calumniate.
COLERIDGE.—*Biographia
Literaria, ch.* 3.

Calumny always makes the calumniator
worse, but the calumniated—never.
C. C. COLTON.—*Lacon.*

The man that dares to traduce, because
he can
With safety to himself, is not a man.
COWPER.—*Expostulation, l.* 432.

Assailed by scandal and the tongue of
strife,
His only answer was a blameless life.
COWPER.—*Hope, l.* 578.

He turneth praising into blame,
And worship into worldes shame.
GOWER.—*Confessio Amantis, Bk.* 2.

Slander, that worst of poisons, ever finds
An easy entrance to ignoble minds.
LORD J. HERVEY.—*Juvenal.*

With favour graced, the evil-doer stands,
Nor curbs with shame nor equity his hands;
With crooked slanders wounds the virtuous
man,
And stamps with perjury what hate began.
HESIOD.—*Works and Days (Elton tr.).*

Calumnies are answered best with
silence.
BEN JONSON.—*Volpone, Act* 2, 2.

For good deeds, evil report—that is the
King's portion.
MARCUS AURELIUS.—7, 36.

A mind conscious of rectitude laughs
at the lies of rumour.   OVID.—*Fast.*

Those who convey and those who listen
to calumnies, should, if I had my way,
all hang, the former by their tongues, the
latter by their ears. PLAUTUS.—*Pseudolus.*

At every word a reputation dies.
POPE.—*Rape of the Lock, c.* 3, 16.

It often happens that those are the best
people whose characters have been most
injured by slanders; as we usually find
it to be the sweetest fruit which the birds
have been picking at.
POPE.—*Thoughts on Various Subjects.*

The malice of one man quickly becomes
the ill word of all.   PUBLILIUS SYRUS.

The chariest maid is prodigal enough,
If she unmask her beauty to the moon;
Virtue itself 'scapes not calumnious
strokes.
SHAKESPEARE.—*Hamlet, Act* 1, 3.

Be thou as chaste as ice, as pure as
snow, thou shalt not escape calumny.
SHAKESPEARE.—*Ib.*, Act 3, 1.

Back-wounding calumny
The whitest virtue strikes.
SHAKESPEARE.—*Measure for Measure,
Act* 3, 2.

Through slander, meanest spawn of hell,—
And women's slander is the worst.
TENNYSON.—*Letters,* 5.

I am small and scandalous
And love to hear bad tales.
TENNYSON.—*Queen Mary, Act* 5, 2.

Evil-speaking is the immortal daughter
of Self-love and Idleness.
VOLTAIRE.—*To the Marquise de Chatelet.*

If there were no hearers, there would be
no back-biters.   *Prov. (Geo. Herbert).*

Half the world delights in slander and
the other half in believing it. *French prov.*

CAMBRIDGESHIRE

For England's the one land I know
Where men with Splendid Hearts may go;
And Cambridgeshire, of all England,
The shire for Men who Understand.
RUPERT BROOKE.—*Grantchester.*

CANDIDATES

Candidates are creatures not very susceptible of affronts, and would rather,
I suppose, climb in at a window than be
absolutely excluded.   COWPER.—
Letter, c. 1775.

Mr. Grenville [the parliamentary candidate] squeezed me by the hand again,
kissed the ladies, and withdrew. He
kissed likewise the maid in the kitchen,
and seemed upon the whole a most loving,
kissing, kind-hearted gentleman.   *Ib.*

Sertin citizens of Baldinsville axed me
to run fur the Legislater. Sez I, "My
frends, dostest think I'd stoop to that
there?" ARTEMUS WARD.—*Interview with
President Lincoln.*

CANDOUR

The artlessness of unadorned truth,
however sure in theory of extorting admiration, rarely in practice fails inflicting
pain or mortification.
MME. D'ARBLAY.—*Camilla, Bk.* 7, c. 8.

Give me the avowed, the erect, the manly
  foe ;
Bold I can meet—perhaps may turn—
  his blow ;
But of all plagues, good Heaven, thy wrath
  can send,
Save, save, oh ! save me from the Candid
  Friend.
      G. CANNING.—*New Mortality.*

I hate him that my vices telleth me.
    CHAUCER.—*Wife of Bath's Prologue.*

CANNON

The last argument of Kings.
*Inscription (Latin) on a French cannon,
    temp. Louis XIV.*

CANT

Till Cant cease nothing else can begin.
    CARLYLE.—*French Revolution, Bk.* 3,
                      ch. 7.

It is now almost my sole rule of life to
clear myself of cants and formulas, as of
poisonous Nessus shirts.
        CARLYLE.—*Letter,* 1835.

The English and the Americans cant
beyond all other nations.
  EMERSON.—*English Traits,* 13, *Religion.*

My dear friend, clear your mind of
cant. JOHNSON.—*Remark to Boswell,* 1783.

CAPITAL

Their money is their plough.
    CHAUCER.—*Shipman's Tale, v.* 13218.

CAPITAL PUNISHMENT

Hasn't a doubt—zample—far better
hang wrong fler than no fler. (*The
" debilitated cousin."*)
    DICKENS.—*Bleak House, ch.* 53.

All greatness, all power, all authority
depends on the executioner. . . . Take
away this incomprehensible agent from
the world, and in the same moment order
gives place to chaos, thrones crash, and
society disappears.
JOSEPH DE MAISTRE (1753–1821).—*Soirées
            de St. Pétersbourg.*

Hanging is the worst use a man can be
put to. SIR H. WOTTON.—*A Parallel.*

CAPTIVITY

A Robin Redbreast in a cage
Puts all heaven in a rage.
    WM. BLAKE.—*Proverbs.*

Although his cage of gold be never so gay
Yet had this bird, by **twenty thousandfold**
Lever in a forest, that is rude and cold,
Go eten wormes, and swich wrecchednesse.
    CHAUCER.—*Manciple's Tale, v.* 17112.

Who can divine what impulses from God
Reach the caged lark within a town abode,
From his poor inch or two of daisied sod ?
O yield him back his privilege ! No sea
Swells like the bosom of a man set free ;
A wilderness is rich with liberty.
      WORDSWORTH.—*Liberty.*

CARDS

With spots quadrangular of diamond form,
Ensanguined hearts, clubs typical of strife,
And spades the emblem of untimely graves.
    COWPER.—*Winter Evening,* 217.

A clear fire, a clean hearth, and the
rigour of the game. LAMB.—*Mrs. Battle
                     on Whist.*

They do not play at cards, but only
play at playing at them.   LAMB.—*Ib.*

See how the world its veterans rewards !
A youth of frolics, an old age of cards.
    POPE.—*Moral Essays, Ep.* 2, 243.

You do not play at whist, sir ?   Alas, what
a sad old age you are preparing for yourself !   TALLEYRAND.

Cards are the devil's prayer book.
  *German prov. (A Dutch saying describes
    cards as " the Bible of* 52 *leaves.")*

CARE

They say it was care killed the cat,
That starved her and caused her to die ;
But I'll be much wiser than that,
For the devil a care will care I.
    MISS EDGEWORTH.—*Rose, Thistle, and
      Shamrock, Act* 3, 2 *(Old Rhyme ?).*

Care that is entered once into the breast,
Will have the whole possession, ere it
  rest.
  BEN JONSON.—*Tale of a Tub, Act* 1, 7.

           Care
Sat on his faded cheek ; but under brows
Of dauntless courage.
    MILTON.—*Paradise Lost, Bk.* 1, 601.

Care killed the cat, but sobered the
kit.   *Prov. (Spurgeon's version in " Salt-
                      Cellars.")*

CARELESSNESS

We do not what we ought,
  What we ought not, we do,
And lean upon the thought
  That chance will bring us through.
    M. ARNOLD.—*Empedocles.*

I hae naething to lend,
  I'll borrow from naebody.
If naebody care for me,
  I'll care for naebody.
    BURNS.—*I hae a wife.*

Life is all a variorum,
  We regard not how it goes !
Let them cant about decorum
  Who have characters to lose.
          BURNS.—*Jolly Beggars*.

Alas, regardless of their doom,
  The little victims play !
No sense have they of ills to come
  Nor care beyond to-day.
          GRAY.—*Eton College*.

Time to me this truth has taught,
  ('Tis a treasure worth revealing)—
More offend by want of thought
  Than by any want of feeling.
          CHARLES SWAIN.

CASTLES IN THE AIR

For a' sae sage he looks, what can the
    laddie ken ?
He's thinking upon naething, like mony
    mighty men ;
A wee thing maks us think, a sma' thing
    maks us stare ;
There are mair folks than him biggin'
    castles in the air.
    JAS. BALLANTINE.—*Castles in the Air*.

Castles in the air cost a vast deal to
keep up.   (1st) LORD LYTTON.—*Lady
                    of Lyons*, Act 1, 3.

CASUALNESS

He was fresh, and full of faith that
" something would turn up."
    DISRAELI.—*Tancred*, Bk. 3, c. 6.

I suppose, to use our national motto,
" something will turn up " [Motto of
Vraibleusia].   DISRAELI.—*Popanilla*, c. 7.

CASUISTRY

But all was false and hollow, though his
    tongue
Dropped manna, and could make the
    worse appear
The better reason, to perplex and dash
Matured counsels.
    MILTON.—*Paradise Lost*, Bk. 2, 112.

Vain wisdom all, and false philosophy ;
Yet with a pleasing sorcery could charm
Pain for a while, or anguish, and excite
Fallacious hope, or arm th' obdured breast
With stubborn patience as with triple
    steel.   MILTON.—*Ib.*, Bk. 2, 565.

To prove by reason, in reason's despite,
That right is wrong, and wrong is right,
And white is black, and black is white.
    SOUTHEY.—*All for Love*, Pt. 9.

CATCHWORDS

Man is a creature who lives not upon
bread alone, but principally by catch-
words.   R. L. STEVENSON.—*Virginibus*.

CATS

A harmless necessary cat.
    SHAKESPEARE.—*Merchant of Venice*,
                      Act 4, 1.

CAUSE

This is not the cause of faction, or of
party, or of any individual, but the common interest of every man in Britain.
          JUNIUS.—*Letter* 1.

It is the cause, it is the cause, my soul—
Let me not name it to you, you chaste
    stars !—
It is the cause.
    SHAKESPEARE.—*Othello*, Act 5, 1.

CAUSE AND EFFECT

Happy the man, who, studying Nature's
    laws,
Through known effects can trace the
    secret cause.
    VIRGIL.—*Georgics*, Bk. 2 (*Dryden tr.*).

Let Pheelosophers ken causes—Poets
effecks.   JOHN WILSON.—*Noctes*, 16
                      (*Ettrick Shepherd*).

As if a wheel had been within a wheel.
          Ezekiel x, 10 (*R.V.*).

Behold, how great a matter a little
fire kindleth !   *St. James* iii, 5.

CAUTION

Sir Roger told them, with the air of a
man who would not give his judgment
rashly, that much might be said on both
sides.   ADDISON.—*Spectator* (112).

Early and provident fear is the mother
of safety.   BURKE.—*Speech*, 1792.

But cautious Queensberry left the war.
The unmannered dust might soil his star ;
Besides, he hated bleeding.
    BURNS.—*Second Epistle to Robert
                      Graham*.

There for bihoveth him a ful long spoon,
That shall ete with a feend.
          CHAUCER.—*Squire's Tale*.

He would not with a peremptory tone
Assert the nose upon his face his own.
    COWPER.—*Conversation*, l. 121.

One who by delay restored our affairs
to us ; for he did not esteem public rumour
above public safety.
    ENNIUS (*of Quintus Maximus, as cited
        by Cicero, De Senectute*, 4, 10).

He who by discretion
His conduct regulates, desists in time;
And caution I esteem the truest valour.
    EURIPIDES.—*Suppliants*, 516
                      (*Woodhull tr.*).

Brer Fox, he lay low.
J. C. HARRIS.—*Old Planter Legend.*

Hear all men speak ; but credit few or
none.   HERRICK.—*Hesperides*, No. 177.

Give thy thoughts no tongue,
Nor any unproportioned thought his act.
SHAKESPEARE.—*Hamlet*, Act 1, 3.

Wisely and slow ; they stumble that run
fast.   SHAKESPEARE.—*Romeo and Juliet*,
Act 2, 3.

Somewhat is sure designed by fraud or
force ;
Trust not their presents nor admit the
horse.
VIRGIL.—*Æneid, Bk.* 2 (*Dryden*).

Sleep over it or you may weep over it.
Old saying.

Little boats must keep the shore ;
Larger ships may venture more.
Prov. (*Ray*).

CAVILLERS

So those who play a game of state,
And only cavil in debate,
Although there's nothing lost or won,
The public business is undone.
BUTLER.—*Hudibras*, Pt. 3, c. 2.

Wilt thou show the whole wealth of
thy wit in an instant ? I pray thee, understand a plain man in his plain meaning.
SHAKESPEARE.—*Merchant of Venice*,
Act 3, 5.

A fault-mender is better than a fault-
finder.   *Prov.*

They who only seek for faults find
nothing else.   *Prov.*

Stones are thrown only at fruitful
trees.   *French prov.*

Any silly little soul
Easily can pick a hole.
Old saying.

CELIBACY

Marriage has many pains, but celibacy
has no pleasures.   JOHNSON.—*Rasselas.*

CELTS

It is not the question of race ; it is the
land itself that makes the Celt.
G. MOORE.—*Bending of the Bough*, Act 3.

CENSORIOUSNESS

I am not of those miserable males
Who sniff at vice, and daring not to snap,
Do therefore hope for heaven.
GEO. MEREDITH.—*Modern Love.*

Jupiter gives us two wallets. Hanging
behind each man's back is one full of his
own faults ; in front is a heavy one full
of other people's.
PHÆDRUS.—*Fab., Bk.* 4 (*see Shakespeare's
Troilus and Cressida*, Act 3, 3).

Attacking, when he took the whim,
Court, city, camp—all one to him.
SWIFT.—*On the Death of Dr. Swift.*

Our two eyes do not improve our lot.
One serves us to see the good things and
the other the evil things of life. Many
folk have the habit of closing the former.
Happy are the one-eyed who have lost
their evil eye. Mesrour was an example.
He was one-eyed from birth. He did
not possess the eye which sees the bad
side of things.
VOLTAIRE.—*The One-eyed Porter.*

CENSURE

He who discommendeth others obliquely
commendeth himself.
SIR T. BROWNE.—*Christian Morals.*

No man can justly censure or condemn
another, because indeed no man truly
knows another.
SIR T. BROWNE.—*Religio Medici, Pt.* 2, 4.

O mortal men ! be wary how ye judge !
H. F. CARY.—*Dante's "Paradise,"*
c. 20, 125.

Thou best humoured man with the
worst humoured muse.
GOLDSMITH.—*Retaliation.*

No further seek his merits to disclose,
Or draw his frailties from their dread
abode.   GRAY.—*Elegy.*

CEREMONY

Ceremony keeps up all things.
SELDEN.—*Table Talk.*

CHALLENGE

He swore by a' was swearing worth,
To speet him like a pliver,
Unless he wad, from that time forth,
Relinquish her for ever.
BURNS.—*Jolly Beggars.*

" Who dares this pair of boots displace
Must meet Bombastes face to face."
Thus do I challenge all the human race.
W. B. RHODES.—*Bombastes.*

I'll speak to it, though hell itself should
gape,
And bid me hold my peace.
SHAKESPEARE.—*Hamlet*, Act 1, 2.

" Dar'st thou, Cassius, now,
Leap in with me into this angry flood,

And swim to yonder point ? " Upon the
    word,
Accoutred as I was, I plunged in,
And bade him follow.
    SHAKESPEARE.—*Julius Cæsar*, Act 1, 2.

CHAMPAGNE

Produced, rightly deeming he would not
    object to it,
An orbicular bulb with a very long neck
    to it.
    R. H. BARHAM.—*Mr. Peters's Story.*

The foaming grape of Eastern France.
    TENNYSON.—*In Memoriam,*
                Conclusion, 20.

CHAMPIONS

Greatly unfortunate, he fights the cause
Of honour, virtue, liberty, and Rome.
    ADDISON.—*Cato,* Act 1.

For thou wert still the poor man's stay,
The poor man's heart, the poor man's
    hand ;
And all the oppressed who wanted strength
    Had thine at their command.
    WORDSWORTH.—*Memorials of Tour in*
    Scotland, No. 11 (*Rob Roy's Grave*).

CHANCE

Yet they, believe me, who await
No gifts from chance, have conquered fate.
    M. ARNOLD —*Resignation, l.* 247.

For " up an' down an' round," said 'e,
    " goes all appointed things,
An' losses on the roundabouts means
    profits on the swings ! "
    P. R. CHALMERS.—*Roundabouts and*
                  Swings.

Chance fights on the side of the prudent.
    EURIPIDES.—*Pirithous.*

The happés over mannés head
Ben hongé [are hanging] with a tender
    thread.
    GOWER.—*Confessio Amantis, Bk.* 6.

I shot an arrow into the air,
It fell to earth, I know not where.
    LONGFELLOW.—*The Arrow and the Song.*

Always have an eye to the mayne,
whatsoever thou art chaunced at the buy.
    LYLY.—*Euphues.*

The slings and arrows of outrageous
fortune. SHAKESPEARE.—*Hamlet,* Act 3, 1.

If Hercules and Lichas play at dice,
Which is the better man ? The greater
    throw
May turn by fortune from the weaker
    hand !
    SHAKESPEARE.—*Merchant of Venice,*
                    Act 2, 1.

A chance may win that by mischance
was lost.
    R. SOUTHWELL.—*Times go by Turns.*

It chaunst (eternall God that chaunce
did guide).
    SPENSER.—*Faerie Queene, Bk.* 1 2.

There is no such thing as chance. We
have invented this word to express the
known effect of every unknown cause.
VOLTAIRE.—*The Ignorant Philosopher,* 13.

The race is not to the swift, nor the battle
to the strong, neither yet bread to the
wise, nor yet riches to men of understanding, nor yet favour to men of skill ; but
time and chance happeneth to them all.
    Ecclesiastes ix, 11.

    Our cause God's is,
    But the odds is
    Ten times ten to one.
Royalist lines in MS. (c. 1649) *found
in Archdeacon Plume's Library, Maldon,
Essex.*

CHANGE

I loved thee once, I'll love no more ;
    Thine be the grief as is the blame :
Thou art not what thou wast before—
    What reason I should be the same ?
    SIR R. AYTON.—*I do Confess.*

It were good, therefore, that men in
their innovations would follow the example
of time itself, which indeed innovateth
greatly, but quietly and by degrees scarce
to be perceived.
    BACON.—*Essays, Innovation.*

In government change is suspected,
though to the better.
    BACON.—*Valerius Terminus.*

This world has been harsh and strange ;
Something is wrong : there needeth a
 change. BROWNING.—*Holy Cross Day.*

Rejoice that man is hurled
From change to change unceasingly,
His soul's wings never furled.
    BROWNING.—*James Lee's Wife,* 6, 14.

A change came o'er the spirit of my
dream. BYRON.—*The Dream, st.* 5.

Change is not made without inconvenience, even from worse to better.
    *Quoted by Johnson, as from Hooker, in
    Preface to " English Dictionary."*

It is best not to swap horses while
crossing a river.
    ABR. LINCOLN.—*Speech,* 1864 (*given as
    the remark of* " *an old Dutch farmer*").

Change the strongest son of Life.
    GEO. MEREDITH.—*Woods of Wester main*

To-morrow to fresh woods and pastures
new.   MILTON.—*Lycidas, l.* 193.

All things change ; nothing perishes.
                OVID.—*Metam.*

It will be found that they are the weakest-
minded and the hardest-hearted men that
most love variety and change.
        RUSKIN.—*Modern Painters, vol.* 2,
                sec. 2, *ch.* 2, 7.

Old times were changed, old manners
gone.
        SCOTT.—*Lay of the Last Minstrel,*
                Introduction.

Bless thee, Bottom ! bless thee ! thou
art translated.
        SHAKESPEARE.—*Midsummer Night's*
                Dream, Act 3. 1.

Nought may endure but Mutability.
        SHELLEY.—*Mutability.*

Political changes should never be made
save after overcoming great resistance.
        HERBERT SPENCER.—*Ethics, sec.* 468.

Right now is wrong, and wrong that was
        is right ;
As all things else in time are changed
        quight.
SPENSER.—*Faerie Queene, Bk.* 5, *Introd.*

The old order changeth, yielding place
        to new.
        TENNYSON.—*Coming of Arthur, l.* 284.

O earth, what changes hast thou seen !
        TENNYSON.—*In Memoriam,* 123.

The old order changeth, giving place
        to new,
And God fulfils Himself in many ways,
Lest one good custom should corrupt the
        world. TENNYSON.—*Morte d'Arthur.*

        Nothing was born,
        Nothing will die,
        All things will change.
        TENNYSON.—*Nothing will die.*

The sundry and manifold changes of
the world.   *Common Prayer.—Collect.*

Weathercocks turn more easily when
placed very high.   *French prov.*

CHANGE OF OPINION

" Yes ! " I answered you last night ;
" No ! " this morning, sir, I say :
Colours seen by candle-light
Will not look the same by day.
        E. B. BROWNING.—*The Lady's Yes.*

He was a man who had seen many changes,
And always changed, as true as any needle.
        BYRON.—*Don Juan,* 3, 80.

Who can believe what varies every day,
Nor ever was, nor will be at a stay ?
        DRYDEN.—*Hind and Panther, Pt.* 2, 36.

It is natural for a wise man to change
his opinion ; a fool keeps on changing like
the moon.   *Latin prov.*

CHAOS

Lo ! thy dread empire, Chaos ! is restored ;
Light dies before thy uncreating word ;
Thy hand, great Anarch ! lets the curtain
        fall ;
And universal darkness buries all.
        POPE.—*Dunciad,* 4, 649.

CHARACTER

There was never a bad man that had
ability for good service.
        BURKE.—*Impeachment of Hastings*
                (*Feb.* 17, 1788).

That there is falsehood in his looks,
        I must and will deny ;
They say their master is a knave,
        And sure they do not lie.
        BURNS.—*The Parson's Looks.*

Everyone is as God made him, and often
a great deal worse.
        CERVANTES.—*Don Quixote.*

Colonel Chartres . . . was once heard to
say that although he would not give one
farthing for virtue, he would give ten
thousand pounds for a character ; because he should get a hundred thousand
pounds by it.
        LORD CHESTERFIELD.—*Advice to his Son.*

Good and bad men are each less so
than they seem.
        COLERIDGE.—*Table Talk.*

Character is simply a habit long continued.   PLUTARCH.

Not swaying to this faction or to that,
Not making his high place the lawless
        perch
For winged ambitions, nor a vantage
        ground
For pleasure ; but through all this tract
        of years
Wearing the white flower of a blameless
        life. TENNYSON.—*Idylls, Dedication.*

The only way to make men speak good
of us is to do it.
        VOLTAIRE.—*History of Charles XII.,*
                Prel. Discourse.

Wha ever saw either a book or a man
worth praisin, that wasna as weel worth
abusin ?
        JOHN WILSON.—*Noctes,* 21 (*Ettrick*
                Shepherd).

CHARACTERISTICS

Fair and sluttish, black and proud ;
Long and lazy, little and loud ;
Fat and merry, lean and sad ;
Pale and pettish, red and bad.
Old saying.

CHARITY

In charity there is no excess.
BACON.—*Goodness.*

He that defers his charity until he is
dead, is, if a man weighs it rightly, rather
liberal of another man's than of his own.
BACON.—*Collection of Sentences.*

And from the prayer of Want, and plaint
of Woe,
O never, never turn away thine ear.
BEATTIE.—*The Minstrel, Bk.* 1, 29.

'Twas a thief said the last kind word to
Christ :
Christ took the kindness and forgave the
theft.
BROWNING.—*Ring and the Book,* 6, 869.

Want passed for merit at her open door.
DRYDEN.—*Eleonora.*

In Faith and Hope the world will disagree,
But all mankind's concern is Charity.
POPE.—*Essay on Man, Ep.* 3, 307.

Thou art gone :
And he that would assail thee in thy grave,
Oh, let him pause ! For who among us all,
Tried as thou wert, even from thine
earliest years,
When wandering, yet unspoilt, a highland
boy—
Tried as thou wert, and with thy soul of
flame ;
Pleasure, while yet the down was on thy
cheek,
Uplifting, pressing, and to lips like thine,
Her charmèd cup—ah, who among us
all
Could say he had not erred as much, and
more ? ROGERS.—*Italy (On Byron).*

Harsh towards herself, towards others
full of ruth.
CHRISTINA ROSSETTI.—*Portrait.*

Our charity begins at home,
And mostly ends where it begins.
HORACE SMITH.—*Moral Alchemy.*

You find plenty of people willing
enough to do the good Samaritan, without
the oil and the twopence.
SYDNEY SMITH.—*Saying.*

It is better to feed five drones than
starve one bee.
C. H. SPURGEON.—*"Salt-Cellars."*

To learn how to love better, hate yourself. VOLTAIRE.—*Fête de Bellébat.*

Charity creates a multitude of sins.
OSCAR WILDE.—*Soul of Man under
Socialism.*

He only judges right,who weighs,compares,
And, in the sternest sentence which his
voice
Pronounces, ne'er abandons charity.
WORDSWORTH.—*Eccles. Sonnets, Pt.* 2, 1.

Whate'er we look on, at our side
Be Charity, to bid us think,
And feel, if we would know.
WORDSWORTH.—*In one of the Catholic
Cantons.*

Knowledge puffeth up, but charity
edifieth. 1 *Corinthians* viii, 1.

Charity shall cover the multitude of
sins. 1 *St. Peter* iv, 8.

CHARM

Here lies David Garrick, describe him
who can,
An abridgment of all that was pleasant
in man. GOLDSMITH.—*Retaliation.*

Give me a look, give me a face,
That makes simplicity a grace.
BEN JONSON.—*Epicœne,* Act 1.

When she had passed it seemed like
the ceasing of exquisite music.
LONGFELLOW.—*Evangeline, Pt.* 1, *c.* 1.

The angel ended, and in Adam's ear
So charming left his voice, that he awhile
Thought him still speaking, still stood
fixed to hear.
MILTON.—*Paradise Lost, Bk.* 8, 1.

Grace was in all her steps, Heaven in her
eye ;
In every gesture, dignity and love.
MILTON.—*Ib., Bk.* 8, 488;

Those graceful acts,
Those thousand decencies, that daily flow
From all her words and actions.
MILTON.—*Ib., Bk.* 8, 600.

Thy sweet obligingness could supple hate,
And out of it, its contrary create.
J. OLDHAM.—*On C. Morwent, st.* 17.

Her pleasure in her power to charm.
C. PATMORE.—*Angel in the House, c.* 12.

You have sae saft a voice and slid a tongue,
You are the darling of baith auld and
young. ALLAN RAMSAY.—*Eclogue.*

Angels listen when she speaks ;
She's my delight, all mankind's wonder.
EARL OF ROCHESTER.—*Song.*

Blessed with that charm, the certainty
to please.   ROGERS.—*Human Life.*

Her voice, whate'er she said, enchanted ;
Like music to the heart it went.
And her dark eyes—how eloquent !
Ask what they would, 'twas granted.
     ROGERS.—*Jacqueline, Pt.* i.

See, what a grace was seated on his brow ;
Hyperion's curls ; the front of Jove himself :
An eye like Mars, to threaten and command.
     SHAKESPEARE.—*Hamlet,* Act 3, 4.

She told him stories to delight his ear ;
She showed him favours to allure his eye.
     SHAKESPEARE.—*Passionate Pilgrim, st.* i.

Bid me discourse, I will enchant thine ear,
Or, like a fairy, trip upon the green,
Or, like a nymph, with long dishevelled
   hair,
Dance on the sands, and yet no footing
   seen.
     SHAKESPEARE.—*Venus and Adonis, st.* 25.

Had I a heart for falsehood framed,
   I ne'er could injure you.
     SHERIDAN.—*Duenna,* Act 1, 5.

Pray present my benediction to your
charming wife, who I am sure would bring
any plant in the garden into full flower by
looking at it and smiling upon it.
     SYDNEY SMITH.—*Letter to Lord Mahon,*
                      July 4, 1843.

Her feet beneath her petticoat,
Like little mice, stole in and out,
   As if they feared the light.
But oh ! she dances such a way—
No sun upon an Easter day
   Is half so fine a sight !
SIR J. SUCKLING.—*Ballad on a Wedding,*
                           st. 8.

She was born to make hash of men's
buzzums.
     ARTEMUS WARD.—*Piccolomini.*

All charming people, I fancy, are spoiled.
It is the secret of their attraction.
     OSCAR WILDE.—*Soul of Man under*
                       Socialism.

Whose life was like the violet sweet,
Or climbing jasmine pure.
     WORDSWORTH.—*Elegiac Stanzas* (1824).

She was a phantom of delight
   When first she gleamed upon my sight.
     WORDSWORTH.—*She was a Phantom.*

CHASE, THE

Back limped, with slow and crippled pace,
The sulky leaders of the chase.
     SCOTT.—*Lady of the Lake,* 10.

CHASTITY

Abstain wholly, or wed.
     HERBERT.—*Church Porch.*

'Tis Chastity, my brother, Chastity :
She that has that, is clad in complete
   steel.   MILTON.—*Comus,* 420.

So dear to Heaven is saintly Chastity,
That when a soul is found sincerely so,
A thousand liveried angels lackey her.
     MILTON.—*Ib.,* 453.

Let this great maxim be my virtue's
   guide :
In part she is to blame that has been tried ;
He comes too near that comes to be denied.
     LADY M. W. MONTAGU.—*Lady's*
     Resolve (*quoted from Sir T. Overbury*).

In part to blame is she
Which hath without consent been only
   tried ;
He comes too near that comes to be denied.
     SIR T. OVERBURY.—*A Wife, st.* 36.

Chaste as the icicle,
That's curded by the frost from purest
   snow,
And hangs on Dian's temple.
     SHAKESPEARE.—*Coriolanus,* Act 5, 3.

CHAUCER

Dan Chaucer, well of English undefyled,
On fame's eternall bead-roll worthie to
   be fyled.
     SPENSER.—*Faerie Queene, Bk.* 4, 2, 32.

CHEATING

Doubtless the pleasure is as great
Of being cheated, as to cheat.
     BUTLER.—*Hudibras, Pt.* 2, *c.* 3.

He is not cheated who knows that he
is being cheated.   COKE.

Thus do I ever make my fool my purse.
     SHAKESPEARE.—*Othello,* Act 1, 3.

CHEERFULNESS

Know then whate'er of cheerful and serene
Supports the mind, supports the body too.
J. ARMSTRONG.—*Art of Preserving Health.*

One can be a soldier without dying, and
a lover without sighing.
     SIR E. ARNOLD.—*Adzuma,* Act 2, 5.

With a wink of his eye his friend made
   reply,
In his jocular manner, sly, caustic, and dry,
" Still the same boy, Bassanio—never say
   ' die ' ! "
     R. H. BARHAM.—*Merchant of Venice.*

A happy-tempered bringer of the best
Out of the worst.
     BROWNING.—*Soul's Tragedy,* Act 1.

Sweet bird ! thy bower is ever green,
  Thy sky is ever clear ;
Thou hast no sorrow in thy song,
  No winter in thy year.
      M. BRUCE.—*To the Cuckoo.*

And warl'ly cares and warl'ly men
  May a' gae tapsalteerie, O !
      BURNS.—*Green grow the Rashes.*

He had no wish but—to be glad,
  Nor want but—when he thirsted.
      BURNS.—*Jolly Beggars.*

He hated naught but—to be sad.
      BURNS.—*Ib.*

When the days are sad and lonely,
  And life hardly seems worth while,
Keep on pegging—think there's only
  Just one other stile.
      G. BUSHNELL.—*Emptyings of my Ash
          Tray* (1918).

I am of Ben's mind, madam ; resolve
to be merry though the ship were sinking.
  MRS. CENTLIVRE.—*The Artifice.*

That man, I trow, is doubly curst,
Who of the best doth make the worst ;
And he, I'm sure, is doubly blest,
Who of the worst can make the best.
      W. COMBE.—*Dr. Syntax, c. 26.*

In came Mrs. Fezziwig, one vast substantial smile. DICKENS.—*Christmas Carol.*

Some credit in being jolly (Mark Tapley).
  DICKENS.—*Martin Chuzzlewit, ch. 5.*

Be merry, man, and tak not sair in mind
  The wavering of this wretchit warld of
    sorrow ;
To God be humble, and to thy friend be
    kind,
And with thy neighbours gladly lend
    and borrow ;
His chance to-nicht, it may be thine to-
    morrow.
    W. DUNBAR.—*No Treasure without
          Gladness.*

Every journey has an end ;
When at the worst, affairs will mend ;
Dark the dawn when day is nigh ;
Hustle your horse and don't say die !
    SIR W. S. GILBERT.—*Iolanthe.*

Little by little the time goes by—
Short if you sing through it, long if you
  sigh.
    LEON HERBERT.—*Hymns for Heart
    and Voice (Sunday School Association).*

Let the world slide, let the world go !
A fig for care and a fig for woe !
If I can't pay, why I can owe,
And death makes equal the high and low.
  JOHN HEYWOOD.—*Be Merry, Friends.*

There was an old man who said, How
Shall I flee from this horrible Cow ?
  I will sit on this stile
  And continue to smile,
Which may soften the heart of that Cow.
    EDWARD LEAR.—*Book of Nonsense.*

Laugh, for the time is brief, a thread the
  length of a span.
Laugh, and be proud to belong to the old
  proud pageant of man.
  JOHN MASEFIELD.—*Laugh and be Merry.*

So buxom, blithe and debonair.
    MILTON.—*L'Allegro, l. 24.*

Some folks seem glad even to draw their
breath.
  W. MORRIS.—*Bellerophon at Argos, 472.*

Be merry ! Think upon the lives of men,
And with what troubles three score years
  and ten
Are crowded oft, yea, even unto him
Who sits at home, nor fears for life and
  limb.
    W. MORRIS.—*Jason, Bk. 10, 101.*

Weep not, nor pity thine own life too
  much. W. MORRIS.—*Ib., Bk. 13, 315.*

Jog on, jog on, the footpath way,
  And merrily hent the stile-a :
A merry heart goes all the day,
  Your sad tires in a mile-a.
  SHAKESPEARE.—*Winter's Tale, Act 4, 2.*

As long liveth the merry man, they say,
As doth the sorry man—and longer by a
  day.   N. UDALL.—*Ralph Roister
          Doister, Act 1, 1.*

Everything succeeds with people of
sweet and cheerful disposition.
    VOLTAIRE.—*Le Dépositaire.*

Woe to the philosophers who cannot
laugh away their learned wrinkles ! I
look on solemnity as a disease. It
appears to me that morality, study and
gaiety are three sisters who should never
be separated. They are your servants ;
I take them as my mistresses.
    VOLTAIRE.—*To Frederick the Great.*

Some day soon something nice is going to
  happen ;
Be a good little girl and take this hint :
Swallow with a smile your cod-liver ile
  And the first thing you know you will
    have a peppermint.
    JEAN WEBSTER.—*Dear Enemy.*

Laugh, and the world laughs with you,
  Weep, and you weep alone ;
For sad old earth must borrow its mirth,
  But has trouble enough of its own.
    ELLA W. WILCOX.—*Way of the World
    (The first two lines are also claimed by
          Col. J. A. Joyce).*

Care to our coffin adds a nail, no doubt,
And every grin, so merry, draws one out.
           J. WOLCOT.—*Ode* 15.

A man he seems of cheerful yesterdays
And confident to-morrows.
           WORDSWORTH.—*Excursion, Bk. 7.*

And cheerful songs, and suns that shine
On busy days, with thankful nights, be
mine !
           WORDSWORTH.—*To Enterprise.*

Go not half way to meet a coming sorrow,
   But thankful be for blessings of to-day,
And pray that thou mayst blessèd be
     to-morrow ;
So shalt thou go with joy upon thy way.
      ANON.—(*Enquired for without result in
          " Notes and Queries,"* 1901).

Whichever way the wind doth blow,
   Some heart is glad to have it so ;
Then blow it east or blow it west,
The wind that blows, that wind is best.
                 Old saying.

The saddest dog sometimes wags its tail.
                           Prov.

   Fortune will be fortune still,
   Let the weather blow as it will ;
For the laddie has his lease and the lassie
     has her ring,
And there's mony a merry heart beneath
     a mourning string.
                 Scottish saying.

CHEESE

     Cheese it is a peevish elf,
     It digests all things but itself.
         Prov. (from *Mediæval Latin*).

CHESS

     Life's too short for chess.
     H. J. BYRON.—*Our Boys,* Act 1.

He [Ned Connolly] hates chess. He
says it is a foolish expedient for making
idle people believe they are doing something very clever, when they are only
wasting their time.
     G. B. SHAW.—*Irrational Knot, ch.* 14.

CHILBLAINS

Another weepeth over chilblains fell,
Always upon the heel, yet never to be
   well.   HOOD.—*Irish Schoolmaster.*

CHILDHOOD

     A child may say Amen
To a bishop's prayer, and feel the way it
   goes.
E. B. BROWNING.—*Aurora Leigh, Bk.* 2.

Ah, could I be once more a careless
   child !
     COLERIDGE.—*To the River Otter.*

The growth of flesh is but a blister ;
   Childhood is health.
         HERBERT.—*Holy Baptism.*

I remember, I remember,
   The fir trees dark and high ;
I used to think their slender tops
   Were close against the sky ;
It was a childish ignorance,
   But now 'tis little joy
To know I'm further off from heaven
   Than when I was a boy.
            HOOD.—*I Remember.*

   The childhood shows the man
   As morning shows the day.
MILTON.—*Paradise Regained, Bk.* 4, 220.

A sudden wakin', a sudden weepin' ;
A li'l suckin', a li'l sleepin' ;
A cheel's full joys an' a cheel's short
   sorrows,
Wi' a power o' faith in gert to-morrows.
     EDEN PHILLPOTTS.—*Man's Days.*

   I remember, I remember,
     How my childhood fleeted by,
   The mirth of its December,
     And the warmth of its July.
     W. M. PRAED.—*I Remember.*

Respect childhood and do not be too
hasty in judging it, whether in good or
in evil.   ROUSSEAU.—*Emile.*

The round little flower of a face that
exults in the sunshine of shadowless days.
   SWINBURNE.—*After a Reading, st.* 3.

In books, or work, or healthful play,
   Let my first years be passed,
That I may give for every day
   Some good account at last.
   I. WATTS.—*Against Idleness.*

Heaven lies about us in our infancy !
Shades of the prison-house begin to close
   Upon the growing Boy.
       WORDSWORTH.—*Intimations of
                  Immortality, c.* 5.

The child is father of the man ;
And I could wish my days and years to be
Bound each to each by natural piety.
   WORDSWORTH.—*My heart leaps up.*

Sweet childish days, that were as long
As twenty days are now.
       WORDSWORTH.—*To a Butterfly.*

   A simple child
That lightly draws its breath,
And feels its life in every limb,
   What should it know of death ?
      WORDSWORTH.—*We are Seven.*

CHILDISHNESS

Genius has somewhat of the infantine,
But of the childish not a touch or taint.
     BROWNING.—*Prince Hohenstiel.*

CHILDREN

Children sweeten labours ; but they make misfortunes more bitter.
BACON.—7, *Of Parents and Children.*

He that hath a wife and children hath given hostages to fortune.
BACON.—8, *Of Marriage.*

Children mothered by the street,
Blossoms of humanity,
Poor soiled blossoms in the dust,
In your features may be traced
Childhood's beauty half effaced.
MATHILDE BLIND.—*Street-children's Dance.*

Do you hear the children weeping, O my brothers,
Ere the sorrow comes with years ?
E. B. BROWNING.—*Cry of the Children.*

But the young, young children, O my brothers,
They are weeping bitterly !
They are weeping in the playtime of the others,
In the country of the free.
E. B. BROWNING.—*Ib.*

The many-tattered,
Little, old-faced, peaking, sister-turned-mother.
BROWNING.—*Christmas Eve, c. 2.*

A mother who boasts two boys was ever accounted rich.
BROWNING.—*Ivàn Ivànovitch*, 154.

Go practise if you please
With men and women ; leave a child alone,
For Christ's particular love's sake.
BROWNING.—*Ring and the Book*, 3, 88.

No sound of tiny footfalls filled the house with happy cheer.
R. BUCHANAN.—*Scaith o' Bartle.*

Th' expectant wee things, toddlin' stacher through
To meet their dad, wi' flichterin' noise and glee.
BURNS.—*Cotter's Saturday Night.*

The lisping infant prattling on his knee,
Does a' his weary carking cares beguile,
And makes him quite forget his labour and his toil.   BURNS.—*Ib.*

To whom nor relative nor blood remains,
No !—not a kindred drop that runs in human veins.
CAMPBELL.—*Gertrude*, 17.

So for the mother's sake the child was dear,
And dearer was the mother for the child.
COLERIDGE.—*Sonnet.*

And when, with envy Time transported,
Shall think to rob us of our joys ;
You'll in your girls again be courted,
And I'll go wooing in my boys.
J. G. COOPER.—*To his Wife.*

Speak roughly to your little boy,
And beat him when he sneezes ;
He only does it to annoy,
Because he knows it teases.
C. L. DODGSON.—*Alice in Wonderland, ch. 6.*

How many troubles are with children born !
Yet he that wants them counts himself forlorn.
WM. DRUMMOND.—*Translation.*

I was the first
To call thee father ; me thou first didst call
Thy child ; I was the first that on thy knees
Fondly caressed thee.
EURIPIDES.—*Iphigenia in Aul.*, 1230 (*R. Potter tr.*).

Where yet was ever found a mother
Who'd give her booby for another ?
GAY.—*Fables, Pt.* 1, 3.

A little sorrowful deserted thing,
Begot of love, and yet no love begetting.
HOOD.—*Midsummer Fairies.*

Ye are better than all the ballads
That ever were sung or said ;
For ye are the living poems,
And all the rest are dead.
LONGFELLOW.—*Children.*

This child is not mine as the first one was,
I cannot sing it to rest.
J. R. LOWELL.—*Changeling.*

Of all people children are the most imaginative.   MACAULAY.—*Milton.*

A little child with laughing look
A lovely white, unwritten book.
J. MASEFIELD.—*Everlasting Mercy*, 427.

And he who gives a child a treat
Makes joy-bells ring in Heaven's street ;
And he who gives a child a home
Builds palaces in Kingdom come.
JOHN MASEFIELD.—*Ib.*

Children blessings seem, but torments are ;
When young our folly, and when old our fear.
OTWAY.—*Don Carlos.*

Children know,
Instinctive taught, the friend and foe.
SCOTT.—*Lady of the Lake, c.* 2, 14.

How sharper than a serpent's tooth it is
To have a thankless child !
SHAKESPEARE.—*Lear*, Act 1, 4.

Upon my head they placed a fruitless
crown,
And put a barren sceptre in my gripe,
Thence to be wrenched with an unlineal
hand,
No son of mine succeeding.
SHAKESPEARE.—*Macbeth*, Act 3, 1.

A little bench of heedless bishops here,
And there a chancellor in embryo,
Or bard sublime, if bard may e'er be so.
SHENSTONE.—*Schoolmistress.*

I am glad it is a girl; all little boys ought
to be put to death.
SYDNEY SMITH.—*Letter to Countess
Grey, Feb. 4, 1835 (on the birth of his
granddaughter).*

O may our house be still a garrison
Of smiling children, and for evermore
The tune of little feet be heard along the
floor.
R. L. STEVENSON.—*Before this little
gift was come.*

The child that is not clean and neat,
With lots of toys and things to eat,
He is a naughty child, I'm sure—
Or else his dear papa is poor.
R. L. STEVENSON.—*System.*

Man, a dunce uncouth,
Errs in age and youth,
Babies know the truth.
SWINBURNE.—*Cradle Songs*, 4.

The world has no such flower in any land,
And no such pearl in any gulf the sea,
As any babe on any mother's knee.
SWINBURNE.—*Pelagius*, 2.

The painless and stainless love of little
children. SWINBURNE.—*Social Verse.*

Where children are not, heaven is not.
SWINBURNE.—*Song of Welcome, l. 37.*

The bearing and the training of a child
Is woman's wisdom.
TENNYSON.—*Princess, c. 4, 455.*

Good chicks from a good hen
And good sons from good men.
D. W. THOMPSON.—*From Euripides.*

It were better for him that a millstone
were hanged about his neck, and he cast
into the sea, than that he should offend
one of these little ones.
St. Luke xvii, 2.

Oh, think what joy my heart shall know,
How bright the expiring lamp shall glow
When quivering o'er the tomb,
If, in the evening of my days,
I live to hear thy well-earned praise,
And see thy honours bloom.
ANON. (? Thomas Hood).

Better bairns greet than bearded men.
Scottish prov.

A beltless bairn cannot lie. *Ib.*

When bairns are young they gar their
parents' heads ache; when they are auld
they make their hearts ache. *Scottish prov.*

The best that can happen a poor man is
that ae bairn dee, and the rest follow.
Scottish prov.

Twa to fight and one to redd (settle
the dispute). *Scottish prov. (The ideal
number for a family.)*

Speak when ye're spoken to, do what ye're
bidden;
Come when ye're ca'd, an' ye'll no be
chidden. *Scottish rhyme.*

Waly, waly! bairns are bonny!
Ane's enough, and twa's ower mony.
Scottish rhyme.

As the auld cock crows the young cock
learns;
Aye tak' care what ye do afore the bairns.
Scottish saying.

He is happy who has children; he is
not unhappy who has none. *French prov.*

Circles, though small, are yet complete.
*On a monument to two children, North-
leigh, Oxfordshire (c. 1800).*

Children pick up words as pigeons peas,
And utter them again as God shall please.
Old Saying (Ray).

CHINA

Now ain't they utterly too-too,
Them flymy little bits of Blue?
W. E. HENLEY.—*Villanelle (Culture in
the Slums, 2).*

CHINAMAN

A disorderly Chinaman is rare, and a
lazy one does not exist.
MARK TWAIN.—*Innocents at Home,
ch. 9.*

CHIVALRY

I will not steal a victory.
ALEXANDER THE GREAT (*Plutarch*).

Honour has come back, as a king to earth,
And paid his subjects with a royal wage;
And Nobleness walks in our ways again;
And we have come into our heritage.
RUPERT BROOKE.—*The Dead* (1914).

The age of chivalry is gone. That of
sophisters, economists, and calculators,
has succeeded; and the glory of Europe
is extinguished for ever.
BURKE.—*Reflections on French Revolution.*

Cervantes smiled Spain's chivalry away.
BYRON.—*Don Juan, c.* 13, 11.

Misfortune ever claimed the pity of
the brave.   C. DIBDIN.—*Veterans.*

For he wants worth who dares not
praise a foe.
DRYDEN.—*Conquest of Granada, Pt.* 2,
Act 2.

To set the Cause above renown,
To love the game beyond the prize,
To honour, while you strike him down,
The foe that comes with fearless eyes,
SIR H. J. NEWBOLT.—*Island Race.
Clifton Chapel.*

Not hate, but glory, made these chiefs
contend,
And each brave foe was in his soul a friend.
POPE.—*Iliad, Bk.* 7, 364.

I love to hear of worthy foes.
SCOTT.—*Lady of the Lake,* 4, 8.

Yet, rest thee God ! for well I know
I ne'er shall find a nobler foe.
SCOTT.—*Lay of the Last Minstrel, c.* 5, 29.

And I will say, as still I've said,
Though by ambition far misled,
Thou art a noble knight.
SCOTT.—*Lord of the Isles, c.* 3, 5.

Thus, then, my noble foe I greet:
Health and high fortune till we meet,
And then—what pleases Heaven.
SCOTT.—*Ib., c.* 3, st. 6.

O goodly usage of those antique times,
In which the sword was servaunt unto
right.
SPENSER.—*Faerie Queene, Bk.* 3, 1, 13.

'Tis true old times are dead,
When every morning brought a noble
chance,
And every chance brought out a noble
knight.
TENNYSON.—*Passing of Arthur, l.* 397.

CHOICE

She's left the guid fellow and ta'en the
churl.   BURNS.—*Meg o' the Mill.*

The miller he hecht her a heart leal and
loving ;
The laird did address her wi' matter mair
moving,
A fine-pacing horse, wi' a clear-chainèd
bridle,
A whip by her side, and a bonny side-
saddle.   BURNS.—*Ib.*

Oh, how hard it is to find
The one just suited to our mind !
CAMPBELL.—*Song, " Oh, how Hard ! "*

How happy could I be with either,
Were t'other dear charmer away !
GAY.—*Beggar's Opera,* Act 2, 2.

Maidens, why should you worry in choosing
whom you should marry ?
Choose whom you may, you will find you
have got somebody else.
JOHN HAY.—*Distichs,* 10.

The difficulty in life is the choice.
GEO. MOORE.—*Bending of the Bough,*
Act 4.

The mountain sheep are sweeter,
But the valley sheep are fatter ;
We therefore deemed it meeter
To carry off the latter.
T. L. PEACOCK.—*Elphin, ch.* 2.

It is like washing bushels of sand for
a grain of gold.   SCOTT.—*Diary,* 1826.

Under which king, Bezonian ? speak,
or die !
SHAKESPEARE.—*Henry IV., Pt.* 2, Act 5, 3.

There's small choice in rotten apples.
SHAKESPEARE.—*Taming of the Shrew,*
Act 1, 1.

For not that, which men covet most, is
best ;
Nor that thing worst, which men doe most
refuse.
SPENSER.—*Faerie Queene, Bk.* 6, c. 9.

Choose your love and then love your
choice.   *Prov.*

There are more maids than Maukin
and more men than Michael. *Prov.* (*Ray*).

God made me choose, and I like my
choice.   *Ring posy (c.* 1650).

Speak weel o' the Hielands, but dwell in
the Laigh (low).   *Scottish saying.*

CHRIST

The Vision of Christ that thou dost see
Is my vision's greatest enemy.
Thine is the Friend of all Mankind,
Mine speaks in Parables to the blind.
WM. BLAKE.—*The Everlasting Gospel.*

Hold fast His hand,
Though the nails pierce thee too.
HARRIET ELEANOR HAMILTON-KING.—
The Disciples.

O Son of Man ! if Thou and not another
I here have known,
If I may see Thee then, our First-born
Brother,
Upon Thy throne,
How stern soe'er, how terrible in brightness
That dawn shall break,
I shall be satisfied with Thy dear likeness,
When I awake.
DR. T. HODGKIN.—*Christianity.*

I believe that all who are acquainted with the range of sacred art will admit not only that no representation of Christ ever has been even partially successful, but that the greatest painters fall therein below their accustomed level.
RUSKIN.—*Modern Painters, vol. 2, pt. 3, ch. 5, 7.*

Thou hast conquered, O pale Galilean.
SWINBURNE.—*To Proserpine.*

CHRISTIANITY

I dare without usurpation assume the honourable style of a Christian.
SIR T. BROWNE.—*Religio Medici, Pt. 1, 1.*

Dear Christian people, one and all,
When will you cease your sinning?
CARLYLE (*tr. of Goethe*).

Philosophy makes us wiser, but Christianity makes us better men.
FIELDING.—*Tom Jones, Bk. 8, c. 13.*

The New Testament was less a Christiad than a Pauliad to his intelligence.
T. HARDY.—*Tess of the D'Urbervilles, 4, 1.*

Christianity is an idea, and as such is immortal, like every idea.
HEINE.—*Religion and Philosophy.*

It is well known how much this story about Christ has profited us and ours.
Attributed to LEO X.

He that shall collect all the moral rules of the philosophers, and compare them with those contained in the New Testament, will find them to come short of the morality delivered by our Saviour and taught by His apostles.
LOCKE.—*Reasonableness of Christianity.*

It [the teaching of Christ] is all pure; all sincere; nothing too much, nothing wanting; but such a complete rule of life as the wisest men must acknowledge tends entirely to the good of mankind, and that all would be happy if all would practise it.   LOCKE.—*Ib.*

O father Abraham! what these Christians are!
Whose own hard dealings teach them to suspect
The thoughts of others!
SHAKESPEARE.—*Merchant of Venice, Act 1, 3.*

Christianity, in its abstract purity, became the exoteric expression of the esoteric doctrines of the poetry and wisdom of antiquity.
SHELLEY.—*Defence of Poetry (1821).*

As to the Christian creed, if true
Or false, I never questioned it;
I took it as the vulgar do.
SHELLEY.—*Rosalind and Helen.*

Christ bless thee, brother, for that Christian speech.
SOUTHEY.—*Roderick, sec. 5.*

See how these Christians love one another! TERTULLIAN.—*Apol. adv. Gent.*

Scratch the Christian and you find the pagan—spoiled.
I. ZANGWILL.—*Children of the Ghetto, Bk. 2, ch. 6.*

CHRISTMAS

I have often thought, said Sir Roger, it happens very well that Christmas should fall out in the middle of the winter.
ADDISON.—*Spectator, 269.*

Christians awake, salute the happy morn
Whereon the Saviour of the world was born.   J. BYROM.—*Hymn.*

Though some are dead and some are fled
To lands of summer over sea,
The holly berry keeps his red,
The merry children keep their glee.
A. LANG.—*Ballade of Yule.*

Glorious time of great Too-much!
Too much heat and too much noise,
Too much babblement of boys,
Too much eating, too much drinking,
Too much everything but thinking.
LEIGH HUNT.—*Christmas.*

Right thy most unthrifty glee,
And pious thy mince-piety.
LEIGH HUNT.—*Ib.*

New every year,
New born and newly dear,
He comes with tidings and a song,
The ages long, the ages long.
ALICE MEYNELL.—*Unto us a Son is given.*

Sudden as sweet
Come the expected feet.
All joy is young, and new all art,
And He, too, Whom we have by heart.
ALICE MEYNELL.—*Ib.*

Heap on more wood! the wind is chill;
But let it whistle as it will,
We'll keep our Christmas merry still.
SCOTT.—*Marmion, c. 6, Introduction.*

England was merry England, when
Old Christmas brought his sports again.
'Twas Christmas broached the mightiest ale,
'Twas Christmas told the merriest tale;
A Christmas gambol oft could cheer
The poor man's heart through half the year.   SCOTT.—*Ib.*

So hallowed and so gracious is the time.
SHAKESPEARE.—*Hamlet, Act* 1, 1.

Long-winded schismatics shall rule the roast,
And father Christmas mourn his revels lost.
SWIFT.—*Swan Tripe Club.*

As fits the holy Christmas birth,
Be this, good friends, our carol still;
Be peace on earth, be peace on earth,
To men of gentle will!
THACKERAY.—*End of the Play.*

At Christmas play and make good cheer,
For Christmas comes but once a year.
T. TUSSER.—*Good Husbandry.*

Life still hath one romance that naught can vary—
Not Time himself, who coffins Life's romances—
For still will Christmas gild the year's mischances,
If Christmas comes, as here, to make him merry.
T. WATTS-DUNTON.—*Christmas Tree.*

So now is come our joyfullest feast;
Let every man be jolly;
Each room with ivy leaves be dressed,
And every post with holly.
G. WITHER.—*Christmas.*

With an old fashion, when Christmas is come,
To call in his neighbors with bagpipe and drum,
And good cheer enough to furnish every old room,
And old liquor able to make a cat speak,
and a wise man dumb.
ANON.—*Old Song, " Of an Old Courtier and a New."*

With a new fashion, when Christmas is come on,
With a journey up to London we must be gone,
And leave nobody at home but our new porter John,
Who relieves the poor with a thump on the back with a stone.
ANON.—*Ibid.*

Yule's come and Yule's gane,
And we hae feasted weel;
Sae Jock maun to his flail again,
And Jenny to her wheel.
Fifeshire rhyme (Cheviot's Collection).

Men who fished in Yule week
Fortune never mair did seek.
Fishermen's saying (Scottish).

For Christmas comes but once a year,
And when it comes it brings good cheer,
And when it goes it laves us here,
And what shall we do for the rest of the year?
Irish version of Old Carol.

CHRONIC

" Don't repine, my friends," said Mr. Pecksniff, tenderly. " Do not weep for me. It is chronic."
DICKENS.—*Martin Chuzzlewit, c.* 9.

CHRONICLERS

In endless night they sleep, unwept, unknown,
No bard had they to make all time their own.
P. FRANCIS.—*Tr. of Horace, Odes, Bk.* 4, 9.

CHURCH AND CHURCHYARD

One place there is—beneath the burial sod—
Where all mankind are equalised by death;
Another place there is—the Fane of God,
Where all are equal who draw living breath. HOOD.—*Ode to Rae Wilson.*

CHURCH AND STATE

Necessity, thou tyrant conscience of the great,
Say why the Church is still led blindfold by the State;
Why should the first be ruined and laid waste,
To mend dilapidations in the last?
SWIFT.—*Ode to Sancroft.*

CHURCH OF ENGLAND

" The Church of England," I said, seeing that Mr. Inglesant paused, " is no doubt a compromise."
J. H. SHORTHOUSE.—*John Inglesant.*

Place before your eyes two precepts, and two only. One is " Preach the Gospel," and the other is " Put down enthusiasm." [Attributed to Archdeacon Manners Sutton] . . . The Church of England in a nutshell!
MRS. HUMPHRY WARD.—*Robert Elsmere, Bk.* 2, 16.

CHURCH MUSIC

Some to church repair,
Not for the doctrine, but the music there.
POPE.—*Essay on Criticism,* 342.

CHURCHES (Buildings)

An I have not forgotten what the inside of a church is made of, I am a peppercorn, a brewer's horse.
SHAKESPEARE.—*Henry IV., Pt.* 1, Act 3.

I never weary of great churches. It is my favourite kind of mountain scenery.
R. L. STEVENSON.—*Inland Voyage.*

Such to this British Isle her Christian fanes,
Each linked to each for kindred services;
Her spires, her steeple-towers with glittering vanes

Far-kenned, her chapels lurking among
    trees,
Where a few villagers, on bended knees,
Find solace which a busy world disdains.
WORDSWORTH.—*Eccles. Sonnets, Pt.* 3, 17.

CHURCHES, THE

Surely the church is a place where one
day's truce ought to be allowed to the
dissensions and animosities of mankind.
    BURKE.—*Reflections on the Revolutions.*

To be of no church is dangerous.
        JOHNSON.—*Life of Milton.*

So clomb this first grand thief into God's
    fold ;
So since into his church lewd hirelings
    climb.
    MILTON.—*Paradise Lost, Bk.* 4, 192.

Her force and fire all spent and gone,
Like the dead moon, she still shines on.
SIR WM. WATSON.—*The Church To-day.*

CIPHERS

Then sat summe, as siphre doth in awgrym
    (arithmetic),
That noteth (marks) a place and nothing
    availeth.
LANGLAND (?).—*Richard the Redeless,* 4, 53.

CIRCLES

And as when
A stone is flung into some sleeping tarn,
The circle widens till it lip the marge,
Spread the slow smile through all her
    company.
    TENNYSON.—*Pelleas and Ettarre,* 88.

CIRCUMLOCUTION

Whatever was required to be done, the
Circumlocution Office was beforehand
with all the public departments in the
art of perceiving—HOW NOT TO DO IT.
    DICKENS.—*Little Dorrit, Pt.* 1, *ch.* 10.

CIRCUMSPECTION

High-reaching Buckingham grows cir-
cumspect.
    SHAKESPEARE.—*Richard III.,* Act 4, 2.

CIRCUMSTANCES

Men are the sport of circumstances, when
The circumstances seem the sport of men.
    BYRON.—*Don Juan, c.* 5, 17.

Man is not the creature of circumstances.
Circumstances are the creatures of man.
    DISRAELI.—*Vivian Grey, Bk.* 6, *ch.* 7.

I endeavour to subdue circumstances
to myself, and not myself to circumstances.   HORACE.—*Ep., Bk.* 1, 1, 191.

Circumstances never made the man do
right who didn't do right in spite of them.
    C. KERNAHAN.—*Book of Strange Sins.*

CITIES

A rose-red city half as old as Time.
    DEAN BURGON.—*Petra.*

In great cities men are more callous
both to the happiness and the misery of
others, than in the country ; for they are
constantly in the habit of seeing both
extremes.   C. C. COLTON.—*Lacon.*

In cities vice is hidden with most ease,
Or seen with least reproach.
        COWPER.—*Task,* 689.

Cities give us collision. 'Tis said
London and New York take the nonsense
out of a man.
    EMERSON.—*Conduct of Life, Culture.*

The ecclesiastics have their cathedral
churches, which, in what town soever they
be erected, by virtue of holy water and
certain charms called exorcisms, have the
power to make those towns cities, that is
to say, seats of empire.
    HOBBES.—*Leviathan, ch.* 47.

Surely in toil or fray,
  Under an alien sky,
Comfort it is to say,
  Of no mean city am I.
RUDYARD KIPLING.—*Seven Seas.*

Paris, half Angel, half Grisette,
I would that I were with thee yet ;
But London waits me, like a wife,
London, the love of my whole life.
    R. LE GALLIENNE.—*Paris Day by Day.*

Towered cities please us then,
  And the busy hum of men.
    MILTON.—*L'Allegro, l.* 117.

As one who, long in populous city pent,
Where houses thick and sewers annoy the
    air.
    MILTON.—*Paradise Lost, Bk.* 9, 445.

A house is much more to my taste than a
    tree ;
And for groves ! O, a good grove of
    chimneys for me !
    CAPT. CHAS. MORRIS.—*The Contrast.*

O give me the sweet shady side of Pall
Mall !   CAPT. C. MORRIS.—*Ib.*

I [Socrates] am a lover of learning.
Now the fields and trees will not teach
me anything, but men in the city do.
    PLATO.—*Phædrus,* 10 (*Cary tr.*).

An age builds up cities ; an hour destroys them.   SENECA.—*Nat. Quæst.*

Augustus Cæsar found a city of brick ;
he left it a city of marble.
SUETONIUS.—*Cæs. Aug.*

I never learned to tune a harp or play
a lute ; but I know how to raise a small
city to glory and greatness.
THEMISTOCLES (*as ascribed by Plutarch*).

I am more convinced every day that
there is not only no knowledge of the
world out of a great city, but no decency,
no practicable society—I had almost said
not a virtue. HORACE WALPOLE.—*Letter.*

A city that is at unity in itself.
Church Psalter cxxii, 3.

Without these [the handicrafts] cannot a
city be inhabited. *Ecclesiasticus* xxxviii, 32.

A great city is a great solitude.
Ancient Greek prov.

CITIZENSHIP

Man is by nature a civic animal.
ARISTOTLE.

Here once the embattled farmers stood,
And fired the shot heard round the world.
EMERSON.—*Hymn at Completion of
Concord Monument.*

If we would persuade them that never
at all should one citizen hate another, and
that it is not holy, such teaching as this
is desirable for early childhood.
PLATO.—*Republic, Bk.* 2, 17.

We are all soldiers of the state. We are
all in the pay of society ; we become
deserters if we leave it.
VOLTAIRE.—*L'Homme aux Quarante Ecus.*

CIVILISATION

The three great elements of modern
civilisation, gunpowder, printing, and the
Protestant religion.
CARLYLE.—*State of German Literature.*

The resources of civilisation are not
yet exhausted.
GLADSTONE.—*Leeds, Oct.* 7, 1881.

It is so sweet to find one's self free from
the stale civilisation of Europe.
A. W. KINGLAKE.—*Eöthen.*

I am not aware that any community
has a right to force another to be civilised.
J. S. MILL.—*Liberty, ch.* 4.

Soap and education are not as sudden
as a massacre, but they are more deadly
in the long run. MARK TWAIN.—*Facts
concerning the Recent Resignation.*

The civilized savage is the worst of all
savages. C. J. WEBER.

CLAMOUR

Because half a dozen grasshoppers under
a fern make the field ring with their importunate chink, whilst thousands of
great cattle, reposed beneath the shadow
of the British oak, chew the cud and are
silent, pray do not imagine that those who
make the noise are the only inhabitants
of the field ; that, of course, they are many
in number ; or that, after all, they are
other than the little, shrivelled, meagre,
hopping, though loud and troublesome
insects of the hour.
BURKE.—*Reflections on the Revolution.*

CLASSES

Of all the lunacies earth can boast,
The one that must please the devils the
most
Is pride reduced to the whimsical terms
Of causing the slugs to despise the worms.
R. BROUGH.—*Tent-Maker's Story.*

Thus, it has been said, does society
divide itself into four classes—noblemen,
gentlemen, gigmen, and men.
CARLYLE.—*On Johnson.*

For ever must the rich man hate the
poor. W. MORRIS.—*Earthly Paradise,
Bellerophon at Argos, l.* 515.

Ring out the feud of rich and poor.
TENNYSON.—*In Memoriam, c.* 106.

The rich is born to spend much ; the
poor is made to amass much.
VOLTAIRE.—*Défense du Mondain.*

The worst enemy of his country and
of his kind is he who seeks to set one order
against the other by false aspersions on
their prevalent character.
JOHN WILSON.—*Noctes,* 29.

CLASSICAL LEARNING

Small skill in Latin, and still less in Greek,
Is more than adequate to all I seek.
COWPER.—*Tirocinium,* 385.

Classical quotation is the parole of
literary men all over the world.
JOHNSON.—*Remark,* 1781.

And though thou hadst small Latin
and less Greek.
BEN JONSON.—*On Shakespeare.*

To the glory that was Greece,
And the grandeur that was Rome.
E. A. POE.—*To Helen.*

CLEANLINESS

I'm sorry for you,
You very imperfect ablutioner !
SIR W. S. GILBERT.—*Mikado.*

Cleanliness is indeed next to godliness.
JOHN WESLEY.—*Sermon* 93 (*given as
a quotation*).

CLEARNESS

Meaning, however, is no great matter.
C. S. CALVERLEY.—*Lovers.*

Oh ! rather give me commentators plain,
Who with no deep researches vex the
brain ;
Who from the dark and doubtful love to
run,
And hold their glimmering tapers to the
sun.
CRABBE.—*Parish Register, Pt.* 1.

When Phœbus touched the Poet's trem-
bling ear
With one supreme commandment, " Be
thou clear."
AUSTIN DOBSON.—*Dialogue to the
Memory of Alex. Pope.*

And if the mind with clear conceptions
glow,
The willing words in just expressions flow.
P. FRANCIS.—*Horace, Art of Poetry.*

Unless one is a genius, it is best to aim
at being intelligible.
SIR A. HOPE HAWKINS.—*Dolly Dialogues.*

Socrates : Do we understand, or how ?
Protarchus : I endeavour to understand,
Socrates ; but do you endeavour likewise
to speak still more clearly.
PLATO.—*Philebus,* 117.

To be intelligible is to be found out.
OSCAR WILDE.—*Lady Windermere's Fan.*

CLERGY AND CLERICS

Wyd was his parisshe, and houses fer
a-sonder.
CHAUCER.—*Cant. Tales, Prol., v.* 493.

But Cristes lore and his apostles twelve
He taughte, but first he folwed it him-
selve. CHAUCER.—*Ib., Prol., v.* 529.

I conceive that priests are extremely
like other men, and neither the better
nor the worse for wearing a gown or a
surplice.
LORD CHESTERFIELD.—*Advice to his Son.*

There is not in the universe a more
ridiculous nor a more contemptible animal
than a proud clergyman.
FIELDING.—*Amelia, Bk.* 9, *ch.* 10.

A Protestant country clergyman is
perhaps the most beautiful subject for
a modern idyl. Like Melchisedek he appears as priest and king in one person.
GOETHE.—*Autob., Bk.* 10.

A man he was to all the country dear,
And passing rich with forty pounds a year.
Remote from towns he ran his godly race,
Nor e'er had changed nor wished to change
his place ;
Unskilful he to fawn or seek for power,
By doctrines fashioned to the varying
hour. GOLDSMITH.—*Deserted Village.*

And as a bird each fond endearment tries,
To tempt its new-fledged offspring to the
skies,
He tried each art, reproved each dull delay,
Allured to brighter worlds, and led the
way. GOLDSMITH.—*Ib.*

Still, for all you've so gentle a soul,
Gad ! you've your flock in the grandest
control,
Checkin' the crazy ones,
Coaxin' onaisy ones,
Liftin' the lazy ones on wid the shtick.
A. P. GRAVES.—*Father O'Flynn.*

And sometimes comes she with a tithe-
pig's tail,
Tickling a parson's nose as 'a lies asleep,
Then dreams he of another benefice.
SHAKESPEARE.—*Romeo and Juliet,* Act 1, 4.

What bishops like best in their clergy
is a dropping-down-deadness of manner.
SYDNEY SMITH.—*First Letter to
Archdeacon Singleton.*

From long residence upon your living
[you] are become a kind of holy vegetable.
SYDNEY SMITH.—*Peter Plymley's Letters,
No.* 1.

As the French say, there are three sexes
—men, women, and clergymen.
SYDNEY SMITH.—*Sayings.*

You have met, I hear, with an agreeable
clergyman. The existence of such a
being has been hitherto denied by the
naturalists ; measure him, and put down
on paper what he eats.
SYDNEY SMITH.—*Letter to R. Sharpe,* 1835.

I have seen nobody since I saw you,
but persons in orders. My only varieties
are vicars, rectors, curates, and every
now and then (by way of turbot) an
archdeacon. SYDNEY SMITH.—*Letter to
Miss Berry, Jan.* 28, 1843.

A genius in the reverend gown
Must ever keep its owner down ;
'Tis an unnatural conjunction,
And spoils the credit of the function.
SWIFT.—*To Dr. Delany,* 1729.

I never saw, heard, nor read that the
clergy were beloved in any nation where
Christianity was the religion of the country.
Nothing can render them popular but some
degree of persecution.
SWIFT.—*Thoughts on Religion.*

The snowy-banded dilettante,
Delicate-handed priest intone.
TENNYSON.—*Maud, Pt.* 1, 8.

To convert a cleric (docteur) is an impossible task.   VOLTAIRE.—*Discours* 6.

The English clergy have a pious ambition for being masters. What village vicar would not wish to be pope ?
VOLTAIRE.—*Letters on the English.*

CLERKS

A votary of the desk.
LAMB.—*Oxford in Vacation.*

CLEVERNESS

Ye're a vera clever chiel, man, but ye wad be nane the waur of a hanging.
LORD BRAXFIELD (ROBERT MACQUEEN).— *Remark to "an eloquent culprit at the bar."*

An' you've gut to git up airly
Ef you want to take in God.
J. R. LOWELL.—*Biglow Papers,* 1st Series, 1.

But John P.
Robinson, he
Ses they didn't know everythin' down in Judee.
J. R. LOWELL.—*Ib.,* 1st Series, 3.

If all the good people were clever,
And all clever people were good,
The world would be nicer than ever
We thought that it possibly could.
But somehow 'tis seldom or never
The two hit it off as they should ;
The good are so harsh to the clever,
The clever so rude to the good !
ELIZ. WORDSWORTH.—*St. Christopher and Other Poems.*

CLIFFS

Half-way down
Hangs one that gathers samphire, dreadful trade !
Methinks he seems no bigger than his head ;
The fishermen, that walk upon the beach,
Appear like mice. . . . The murmuring surge,
That on the unnumbered idle pebbles chafes,
Cannot be heard so high.
SHAKESPEARE.—*Lear,* Act 4, 6.

CLIMATE

The cold in clime are cold in blood ;
Their love can scarce deserve the name.
BYRON.—*The Giaour, l.* 1098.

The English winter—ending in July,
To recommence in August.
BYRON.—*Don Juan, c.* 13, 42.

Though thy clime
Be fickle, and thy year, most part deformed
With dripping rains, or withered by a frost,
I would not yet exchange thy sullen skies,
And fields without a flower, for warmer France,
With all her vines.
COWPER.—*Time Piece,* 209.

Wherever snow falls there is usually civil freedom.
EMERSON.—*Civilization.*

Heat, ma'am ! It was so dreadful here that I found there was nothing left for it but to take off my flesh and sit in my bones.   SYDNEY SMITH.—*Saying.*

A listless climate made, where, sooth to say,
No living wight could work, ne caréd even for play.
THOMSON.—*Castle of Indolence, c.* 1, *st.* 2.

England is windy ; when it is not windy it is pestilent.   *Mediæval saying.*

CLOTHING

His very serviceable suit of black
Was courtly once, and conscientious still.
BROWNING.—*How it strikes a Contemporary.*

She just wore
Enough for modesty—no more.
R. BUCHANAN.—*White Rose and Red.*

A silk suit which cost me much money, and I pray God to make me able to pay for it.   PEPYS.—*Diary,* 1660.

When you would select a wife,
Do not call on Sunday ;
If you'd know her as she is,
Better seek on Monday.
C. H. SPURGEON.—*" Salt-Cellars."*

Clothed in white samite, mystic, wonderful.   TENNYSON.—*Coming of Arthur.*

CLOUDS

The clouds in thousand liveries dight.
MILTON.—*L'Allegro, l.* 62.

I am the daughter of earth and water,
And the nurseling of the sky ;
I pass through the pores of the ocean and shores,
I change but I cannot die.
SHELLEY.—*The Cloud,* 6.

When clouds appear like rocks and towers,
The earth's refreshed with frequent showers.   *Old Saying.*

If woolly fleeces strew the heavenly way,
Be sure no rain disturbs the summer's day.
Old Saying.

D*

Hen scarts and filly tails
Make lofty ships wear low sails.
*Scottish prov. (of light clouds resem-
bling hen's claw-marks and tails of
young mares).*

CLUBS

Oh, to the club, the scene of savage joys,
The school of coarse good-fellowship and
noise. Cowper.—*Conversation, l. 421.*

Boswell (said he) is a very clubbable
man. Johnson.—*Remark, 1783.*

A very unclubbable man.
Johnson.—*Of Sir J. Hawkins.*

Indian clubs are good for the liver ;
London clubs are not.
Sir A. W. Pinero.—*The Magistrate*, Act 1
(*Mrs. Pocket*).

COALITIONS

England does not love coalitions.
Disraeli.—*Speech, 1852.*

COARSENESS

Whose laughs are hearty, though his jests
are coarse,
And loves you best of all things—but his
horse. Pope.—*To Mrs. Blount.*

COCKNEYS

I'm one of those whose infant ears have
heard the chimes of Bow.
Thos. Hood.—*The Desert-Born, 1837.*

Oh, mine in snows and summer-heats,
These good old Tory brick-built streets !
My eye is pleased with all it meets
In Bloomsbury.
Wilfred Whitten.—*Bloomsbury.*

COCKSURENESS

I wish I were as cock-sure of anything
as Tom Macaulay is of everything.
Lord Melbourne.—*Remark concerning Lord Macaulay.*

The cock is at his best on his own
dunghill. Seneca.—*De Morte Claudii.*

There is no doubt in this book.
Koran, ch. 2.

COERCION

Themistocles told the Adrians that he
brought two gods with him, Persuasion and
Force. They replied : " We also, have two
gods on our side, Poverty and Despair."
Herodotus.

The more the fire is covered up the more
it burns. Ovid.—*Metam., Bk. 4.*

The current that with gentle murmur
glides,

Thou know'st, being stopped, impatiently
doth rage. Shakespeare.—*Two
Gentlemen of Verona*, Act 2, 7.

COFFEE

Coffee, which makes the politician wise,
And see through all things with his half-
shut eyes.
Pope.—*Rape of the Lock, c. 3, 117.*

COGITATION

His cogitative faculties immersed
In cogibundity of cogitation.
H. Carey.—*Chrononhotonthologos, 1, 1.*

COINCIDENCE

The long arm of coincidence.
C. H. Chambers.—*Capt. Swift.*

COLD WEATHER

It is a nipping and an eager air.
Shakespeare.—*Hamlet*, Act 1, 4.

A' the months with an R in them
[Months for household fires in Scotland].
Scottish saying.

COLLEAGUES

It did so happen, that persons had a
single office divided between them, who
had never spoke to each other in their
lives, until they found themselves, they
knew not how, pigging together, heads
and points, in the same truckle-bed.
Burke.—*Speech on American
Taxation.*

COLLECTIONS

If a good story will not answer [to
disorganize an unfriendly audience], still
milder remedies sometimes serve to dis-
perse a mob. Try sending round the
contribution-box. Emerson.—*Resources.*

It cannot be,—it is—it is—
A hat is going round.
O. W. Holmes.—*Music Grinders.*

COLLECTORS

A snapper-up of unconsidered trifles.
Shakespeare.—*Winter's Tale*, Act 4, 2.

This snug little chamber is crammed in
all nooks
With worthless old knick-knacks and silly
old books,
And foolish old odds and foolish old ends,
Cracked bargains from brokers, cheap
keepsakes from friends.
Thackeray.—*Cane-bottomed Chair.*

COLLEGES

I do not recognize as a public institution
those laughable establishments called
colleges. Rousseau,—*Emile.*

If rudeness be the effect of knowledge,
My son shall never see a college.
　　SWIFT.—*Apology to Lady Carteret.*

COLONIES

We view the establishment of the English
colonies on principles of liberty as that
which is to render this kingdom venerable
to future ages.
　　BURKE.—*Address to Colonies* (1777).

Through a wise and salutary neglect [of
the British colonies] a generous nature
has been suffered to take her own way
to perfection.
　　BURKE.—*Speech on Conciliation.*

The English sway of their colonies has
no root of kindness. They govern by
their arts and ability; they are more
just than kind.
　　EMERSON.—*English Traits*, 9,
　　　　　Cockayne (1833).

The reluctant obedience of distant provinces generally costs more than it is
worth.　　MACAULAY.—*Mahon's
　　　　　War of the Succession.*

Remote compatriots, wheresoe'er ye
　dwell,
By your prompt voices, ringing clear and
　true,
We know that with our England all is
　well:
Young is she yet, her world-task but
　begun;
By you we know her safe, and know by
　you
Her veins are million but her heart is one.
　　SIR WM. WATSON.—*Ver Tenebrosum.*

Hands across the sea,
　Feet on English ground,
The old blood is bold blood, the wide
　world round.
　　BYRON WEBBER.—*Hands across the Sea.*

In deep and awful channel runs
This sympathy of Sire and Sons;
Untried our brothers have been loved
With heart by simple nature moved;
And now their faithfulness is proved.
　　WORDSWORTH.—*White Doe of Rylstone*,
　　　　　c. 2.

COLOURS

The purest and most thoughtful minds
are those which love colour the most.
　　RUSKIN.—*Stones of Venice*, 2,
　　　　　ch. 5, *sec.* 30.

　　Blue is true,
　　Yellow is jealous,
　　Green's forsaken,
　　Red's brazen,
　　White is love,
　　And black is death.
　　Colour Superstitions (E. *of England*).

COMBAT

Dim is the rumour of a common fight,
Where host meets host, and many names
　are sunk;
But of a single combat fame speaks clear.
　　M. ARNOLD.—*Sohrab and Rustum.*

Give us this day good hearts, good enemies,
Good blows o' both sides.
　　BEAUMONT AND FLETCHER.—*Bonduca*,
　　　　　Act 3, 1.

He hath sounded forth the trumpet that
　shall never call retreat,
He is sifting out the hearts of men before
　His judgment seat,
Oh, be swift, my soul, to answer Him!
　be jubilant, my feet!
　　Our God is marching on!
　　JULIA WARD HOWE.—*Battle Hymn
　　　　　of the Republic* (U.S.A.).

One of us two, Herminius,
　Shall never more go home;
I will lay on for Tusculum,
　And lay thou on for Rome!
　　MACAULAY.—*Lake Regillus*, st. 27.

So frowned the mighty combatants, that
　hell
Grew darker at their frown.
　　MILTON.—*Paradise Lost*, Bk. 2, 719.

Full many a bloody day
　In toilsome fight he spent;
And many a wakeful night
　In battle's management.
　　J. PHILIPS.—*Tr. of Plutarch.*

Now truce, farewell, and ruth, begone!
　　SCOTT.—*Lady of the Lake.*

What god can tell, what numbers can
　display
The various labours of that fatal day,
What chiefs and champions fell on either
　side,
In combat slain, or by what deaths they
　died?
　　VIRGIL.—*Æneid*, Bk. 2 (*Dryden tr.*).

Whosoever fighteth for the religion of
God, whether he be slain or be victorious,
we will surely give him a great reward.
　　Koran, ch. 4.

There's some say that we wan,
　Some say that they wan,
Some say that nane wan at a', man;
　But one thing I'm sure,
　That at the Shirra Muir
A battle there was, which I saw, man.
　And we ran and they ran,
　And they ran and we ran,
And we ran, and they ran awa', man.
　　*Old Scottish Song, referring to the battle
　　of Sheriff-Muir* (*November* 13, 1715).

COMBATIVENESS

I was ever a fighter, so—one fight more,
The best and the last !
        BROWNING.—*Prospice.*

He that wrestles with us strengthens
our nerves and sharpens our skill. Our
antagonist is our helper.
BURKE.—*Thoughts on French Revolution.*

A controversy that affords
Actions for arguments, not words.
        BUTLER.—*Hudibras, Pt.* 1, *c.* 1.

Away he scours and lays about him,
Resolved no fray should be without him.
        GAY.—*Fables,* 34.

I welcome the fight as if it were a
holiday. [*Falk.*]
        IBSEN.—*Love's Comedy,* Act 2 (1862).

So, ere's *to* you, Fuzzy-Wuzzy, at your
'ome in the Soudan ;
You're a pore benighted 'eathen but a
first-class fightin' man.
        RUDYARD KIPLING.—*Fuzzy-Wuzzy.*

COMBINATION

When bad men combine, the good must
associate.
        BURKE.—*Cause of Present Discontents.*

COMEDY

The literature of joy is infinitely more
difficult, more rare, and more triumphant
than the black and white literature of
pain.
G. K. CHESTERTON.—*The Defendant :
                Defence of Farce.*

COMFORT

It's grand, and you canna expect to
be baith grand and comfortable.
SIR J. M. BARRIE.—*Little Minister, c.* 10.

Them as ha' never had a cushion don't
miss it. GEO. ELIOT.—*Adam Bede, ch.* 49.

A house full of books, and a garden of
flowers.
        A. LANG.—*Ballade of True Wisdom.*

COMFORTERS

By his sovereign might
That works no ill, was she from evil freed ;
And by his breath divine
She findeth rest, and weeps in floods of
        tears
Her sorrowing shame away.
ÆSCHYLUS.—*Suppliants,* 571 (*Plump-
tre tr.*). (*Of the cure of Io by Jove.*)

Most of our misfortunes are more sup-
portable than the comments of our friends
upon them.   C. C. COLTON.—*Lacon.*

He receives comfort like cold porridge.
        SHAKESPEARE.—*Tempest,* Act 2, 1.

Miserable comforters are ye all.
        Job xvi, 2.

COMMANDS

All her commands were gracious, sweet
        requests.
How could it be then, but that her requests
Must need have sounded to me as com-
        mands ?
        COLERIDGE.—*Zapolya, Pt.* 2, Act 1.

Yet seemed that tone and gesture bland
Less used to sue than to command.
        SCOTT.—*Lady of the Lake, c.* 1, *st.* 21.

COMMENTATORS

Distinctions, that had been at first
        designed
To regulate the errors of the mind,
By being too nicely overstrained and
        vexed
Have made the comment harder than the
        text.
S. BUTLER.—*Upon the Abuse of Human
                        Learning.*

Commentaries are commonly more
subject to cavil than the text, and therefore need other commentaries ; and so
there will be no end of such interpretation.   HOBBES.—*Leviathan, ch.* 2, 6.

I heard a whisper from a ghost who
shall be nameless, " that these commentators always kept in the most distant
quarters from their principals in the lower
world, through a consciousness of shame
and guilt, because they had so horribly
misrepresented the meaning of these
authors to posterity." SWIFT.—*Laputa.*

As learned commentators view
In Homer more than Homer knew.
        SWIFT.—*On Poetry.*

How commentators each dark passage
        shun,
And hold their farthing candles to the
        Sun.
        YOUNG.—*Love of Fame, Sat.* 7.

COMMERCE

For Commerce, though the child of Agri-
        culture,
Fosters his parent, who else must sweat
        and toil
And gain but scanty fare.
        WM. BLAKE.—*Edward III.*

In little trades more cheats and lying
Are used in selling than in buying ;
But in the great, unjuster dealing
Is used in buying than in selling.
        S. BUTLER.—*Miscellaneous Thoughts.*

Business men boast of their skill and
  cunning,
But in philosophy they are like little
  children.
Bragging to each other of successful
  depredations,
They neglect to consider the ultimate fate
  of the body.
  Ch'en Tzu-agig (*Chinese poet, 7th
  century*) (*Arthur Waley's translation*).

Down the river did glide, with wind and
  tide,
  A pig with vast celerity ;
And the Devil looked wise as he saw how
  the while
It cut its own throat. " There," quoth
  he, with a smile,
" Goes England's commercial prosperity."
  Coleridge.—*Devil's Thoughts*, st. 8.

  Art thrives most
Where commerce has enriched the busy
  coast.   Cowper.—*Charity*, 114.

East and west, and north and south,
  Under the crescent or under the cross,
One song you hear in every mouth—
Profit and loss, profit and loss.
  J. Davidson.—*Scaramouch in Naxos, sec.*3.

A true-bred merchant is the best
gentleman in the nation.
  Defoe.—*Robinson Crusoe. The Further
  Adventures.*

No nation was ever ruined by trade.
  B. Franklin.

Commerce ! beneath whose poison-breath-
  ing shade
No solitary virtue dares to spring ;
But poverty and wealth, with equal hand,
Scatter their withering curses.
  Shelley.—*Queen Mab, c. 5.*

If a man knew what would be dear,
He would be merchant but for a year.
  Old Saying.

COMMITTEES

Committee is a noun of multitude,
signifying many ; but not signifying much.
  C. H. Spurgeon.—" *Salt-Cellars.*"

The committee sat and sat and sat,
till every sensible plan was crushed as
flat as a pancake. C. H. Spurgeon.—*Ib.*

Noah built the ark, for he was one man ;
but all the men in the world, formed into
a committee, could not finish a tower.
  C. H. Spurgeon.—*Ib.*

COMMONPLACE

It is right and meet that there should
be an abundant utterance of commonplaces. Part of an agreeable talker's

charm is that he lets them fall continually
with no more than their due emphasis.
  Geo. Eliot.—*Theophrastus Such.
  A Too Deferential Man.*

A common-place book contains many
Notions in Garrison, whence the owner
may draw out an army into the field on
competent warning. T. Fuller.—*Holy
  State and Profane State. (Of Tombs.)*

An everyday young man ;
  A commonplace type
With a stick and a pipe,
And a half-bred black-and-tan.
  Sir W. S. Gilbert.—*Patience.*

It is difficult to speak commonplaces
effectively. Horace.—*De Arte Poetica*, 218.

He has more than anyone the wit which
everyone possesses. Montesquieu.

He learns how stocks will fall or rise ;
Holds poverty the greatest vice ;
Thinks wit the bane of conversation ;
And says that learning spoils a nation.
  Prior.—*Chameleon.*

To suckle fools and chronicle small
beer. Shakespeare.—*Othello*, Act 2, 1.

It's deadly commonplace, but after all
the commonplaces are the great poetic
truths.
  R. L. Stevenson.—*Weir of Hermiston.*

It is always the unreadable that occurs.
  Oscar Wilde.—*Intentions.*

The common growth of Mother Earth
Suffices me—her tears, her mirth,
Her humblest mirth and tears.
  Wordsworth.—*Peter Bell, Prologue.*

COMMON SENSE

Be neither saint nor sophist-led, but
be a man. M. Arnold.—*Empedocles.*

He knew what's what, and that's as high
As metaphysic wit can fly.
  Butler.—*Hudibras, Pt. 1, c. 1.*

Nothing astonishes men so much as
common sense and plain dealing.
  Emerson.—*Art.*

The cure for false theology is mother-wit.
Forget your books and traditions and
obey your moral perceptions at this hour.
  Emerson.—*Conduct of Life, Worship.*

On fire that glows
  With heat intense
I turn the hose
  Of common sense,
And out it goes
  At small expense.
  Sir W. S. Gilbert.—*Iolanthe.*

Sword of Common Sense !
Our surest gift.
                  GEO. MEREDITH.—*Ode.*

Good sense, which only is the gift of
    Heaven,
And, though no science, fairly worth
    the seven.   POPE.—*Ep.* 4.

Fine sense and exalted sense are not
half so useful as common sense. There
are forty men of wit to one man of sense,
and he that will carry nothing about
him but gold will be every day at a loss
for want of readier change.
POPE.—*Thoughts on Various Subjects.*

Common sense is a bad judge when it
deals with great matters.   RENAN.

Common sense is a kind of sixth sense,
less because it is common to all men than
because it results from the well-ordered
use of the other senses.
                  ROUSSEAU.—*Emile.*

No Englishman has any common sense,
or ever had or ever will have.
G. B. SHAW.—*John Bull's Other Island.*

Steer your ship by the stars, but don't
forget the sands.
C. H. SPURGEON.—*John Ploughman.*

Foremost captain of his time,
Rich in saving common-sense,
And, as the greatest only are,
In his simplicity sublime.
TENNYSON.—*On the Duke of Wellington.*

Common sense is not so common.
                  VOLTAIRE.

Plain sense but rarely leads us far
astray.   YOUNG.—*Night Thoughts,* 6.

COMMON THINGS

A thing is not vulgar because it is merely
common.   HAZLITT.—*On Vulgarity.*

COMMUNICATIVENESS

In trying to achieve success
No envy racks our heart ;
And all the knowledge we possess
We mutually impart.
SIR W. S. GILBERT.—*Princess Ida.*

COMMUNISM

The right of all to all things, and consequently the war of all against all.
                  HOBBES.

COMPANIONSHIP AND COMPANY

Above all things endeavour to keep
company with people above you.
LORD CHESTERFIELD.—*Advice to his Son.*

Society we must have ; but let it be
society, and not exchanging news or
eating from the same dish.
EMERSON.—*Society and Solitude.*

When he is here,
    I sigh with pleasure—
When he is gone,
    I sigh with grief.
SIR W. S. GILBERT.—*Sorcerer.*

If you would be loved as a companion,
avoid unnecessary criticism upon those
with whom you live.
SIR A. HELPS.—*Friends in Council,*
                  Bk. 1, *ch.* 7.

Crowd not your table : let your number be
Not more than seven, and never less than
    three.
DR. W. KING.—*Art of Cookery.*

It costs far more trouble to be admitted
or continued in ill company than in good.
POPE.—*Thoughts on Various Subjects.*

Banish plump Jack, and banish all the
world.
SHAKESPEARE.—*Henry IV., Pt.* 1, Act 2, 4.

Company, villainous company, hath
been the spoil of me.
          SHAKESPEARE.—*Ib.,* Act 3, 3.

Therefore 'tis meet
That noble minds keep ever with their
    likes ;
For who so firm that cannot be seduced ?
SHAKESPEARE.—*Julius Cæsar,* Act 1, 2.

Best company consists of five persons.
                  STEELE.—*Tatler.*

I love good creditable acquaintance ;
I love to be the worst of the company.
          SWIFT.—*Letter,* 1711.

He showed me his bill of fare to tempt
me to dine with him   " Foh ! " said I,
" I value not your bill of fare ; give me
your bill of company."   SWIFT.—*Ib.*

One sickly sheep infects the flock,
And poisons all the rest.
I. WATTS.—*Against Evil Company.*

Evil company doth corrupt good
manners.   1 *Corinthians* xv, 33 (*R.V.*).

COMPARISONS

Her goodness doth disdain comparison,
And, but herself, admits no parallel.
MASSINGER.—*Duke of Milan,* Act 4, 3.

To compare
Great things with small.
MILTON.—*Paradise Lost Bk.* 2, 921.

Our discontent is from comparison.
        J. NORRIS.—*Consolation.*

Comparing what thou art
With what thou mightst have been.
        SCOTT.—*Waterloo,* 18.

Hyperion to a satyr.
        SHAKESPEARE, *Hamlet,* Act 1, 2.

Comparisons are odorous.
        SHAKESPEARE.—*Much Ado,* Act 3, 5.

Let us like merchants show our foulest
    wares,
And think, perchance, they'll sell; if not,
The lustre of the better shall exceed
By showing the worse first.
        SHAKESPEARE.—*Troilus,* Act 1, 3.

Rome only might to Rome comparèd be.
        SPENSER.—*Ruines of Rome.*

None but himself can be his parallel.
        L. THEOBALD.—*Double Falsehood.*

COMPASSION

Take her up tenderly,
Lift her with care;
Fashioned so slenderly,
Young and so fair!
        HOOD.—*Bridge of Sighs*

Teach me to feel another's woe,
To hide the fault I see;
That mercy I to others show,
That mercy show to me.
        POPE.—*Universal Prayer.*

First Murderer : Relent! 'tis cowardly,
and womanish. *Clarence :* Not to relent
is beastly, savage, devilish.
        SHAKESPEARE.—*Richard III.,* Act 1.

COMPATIBILITY

" My idea of an agreeable person,"
said Hugo Bohun, " is a person who agrees
with me." DISRAELI.—*Lothair, ch.* 41.

COMPENSATION

Thy fame, thy worth, thy filial love at last,
Shall soothe his aching heart for all the past.
    CAMPBELL.—*Pleasures of Hope, Pt.* 1.

One moment may with bliss repay
Unnumbered hours of pain.
        CAMPBELL.—*Ritter Bann.*

Men may scoff and men may pray,
  But they pay
Every pleasure with a pain.
    W. E. HENLEY.—*Ballade of Truisms.*

There is some soul of goodness in things
    evil
Would men observingly distil it out.
    SHAKESPEARE.—*Henry V.,* Act 4, 1.

Many a green isle needs must be
In the deep wide sea of misery,
Or the mariner, worn and wan,
Never thus could voyage on.
        SHELLEY.—*Euganean Hills.*

This was an hour
That sweetened life, repaid and recom-
    pensed
All losses ; and although it could not heal
All griefs, yet laid them for awhile to rest.
        SOUTHEY.—*Roderick, sec.* 18.

A little evil is often necessary for ob-
taining a great good.
        VOLTAIRE.—*Baron d'Otrante.*

COMPETENCE

Meanwhile, allowing things below your
    merit
Yet, doctor, you've a philosophic spirit ;
Your wants are few, and, like your income,
    small,
And you've enough to gratify them all.
    P. DELANY.—*To Lord Carteret,* 1729.

How much richer are you than millions
of people who are in want of nothing !
        FIELDING.—*Amelia, Bk.* 3, *c.* 11.

O grant me, heaven, a middle state,
Neither too humble nor too great ;
More than enough for nature's ends,
With something left to treat my friends.
        D. MALLET.—*Tr. of Horace.*

I've often wished that I had clear,
For life, six hundred pounds a year.
POPE.—*Imit. of Horace, Bk.* 2, *Sat.* 6, *l.* 1.

Him for a happy man I own
Whose fortune is not overgrown,
And happy he who wisely knows
To use the gifts that heaven bestows.
        SWIFT.—*Horace, Odes,* 4, 9.

An elegant sufficiency, content,
Retirement, rural quiet, friendship, books.
        THOMSON.—*Seasons.*

What limits shall we fix to the vague and
shifting notion of a competency ? The
truth is that everything is a competency
which a man is inclined to live on, and
therefore it varies as his desires are
more or less reasonable.
    J. TRUSLER.—*System of Etiquette* (1804).

A competence is vital to content ;
Much wealth is corpulence, if not disease.
        YOUNG.—*Night Thoughts,* 6.

A competence is all we can enjoy.
        YOUNG.—*Ib.,* 6.

COMPETITION

So nice a difference in your singing lies,
That both have won, or both deserved, the
    prize. DRYDEN.—*Virgil, Pastoral,* 3.

Nothing is ever done beautifully which is done in rivalship, nor nobly which is done in pride. RUSKIN.—*Ethics of the Dust.*

COMPLACENCY

Had that calm look which seemed to all assent,
And that complacent speech which nothing meant.
  CRABBE.—*Parish Register, Pt.* 1.

One truth is clear, whatever is is right.
  POPE.—*Essay on Man.*

To observations, which ourselves we make,
We grow more partial, for the observer's sake. POPE.—*Moral Essays, Ep.* 1.

Woe unto them that are wise in their own eyes!   *Isaiah* v, 21.

COMPLAINT

Do not suppose that you are hurt and your complaint will cease. Cease complaint and you are no longer hurt.
  MARCUS AURELIUS.—*Meditations, Bk.* 4, 7.

Can anybody remember when the times were not hard, and money not scarce?
  EMERSON.—*Works and Days.*

There is no fortune so good that you can find nothing in it to complain of.
  PUBLILIUS SYRUS.

The worst wheel always creaks most.
  French prov.

COMPLETENESS AND COMPLETION

But now my task is smoothly done,
I can fly, or I can run.
  MILTON.—*Comus, l.* 1012.

Joy, joy for ever!—my task is done—
The Gates are past and Heaven is won.
  MOORE.—*Lalla Rookh.*

The last act crowns the play.
  QUARLES.—*Emblems.*

The wheel has come full circle.
  SHAKESPEARE.—*Lear,* Act 5, 3.

COMPLEXION

There is a garden in her face
Where roses and white lilies grow.
  R. ALISON.—*Recreation in Music.*

Her face! oh, call it fair, not pale.
  COLERIDGE.—*Christabel, Pt.* 2.

Her brow was fair, but *very* pale, and looked
Like stainless marble; a touch methought would soil
Its whiteness.
  BARRY CORNWALL.—*Magdalen.*

What though the sun, with ardent frown,
Had slightly tinged her cheek with brown?
  SCOTT.—*Lady of the Lake.*

Mislike me not for my complexion,
The shadowed livery of the burnished sun.
  SHAKESPEARE.—*Merchant of Venice,* Act 2, 1.

With a red man rede thy rede;
With a brown man break thy bread;
At a pale man draw thy knife;
From a black man keep thy wife.
  Old Rhyme, Wright's "Passions of the Mind," 1604.

COMPLEXITY OF CHARACTER

With knowledge so vast, and with judgment so strong,
No man with the half of 'em e'er went far wrong;
With passions so potent, and fancies so bright,
No man with the half of 'em e'er went quite right.
  BURNS.—*Sketch : inscribed to C. J. Fox.*

In him, inexplicably mixed, appeared
Much to be loved, much hated, sought, and feared. BYRON.—*Lara, c.* 1, 17.

COMPLIANCE

A short and certain way to obtain the character of a reasonable and wise man is, whenever anyone tells you his opinion, to comply with it.
  POPE.—*Thoughts on Various Subjects.*

COMPLIMENT

You're exceedingly polite,
And I think it only right
To return the compliment.
  SIR W. S. GILBERT.—*H.M.S. Pinafore.*

To compliments inflated I've a withering reply,
And vanity I always do my best to mortify.
  SIR W. S. GILBERT.—*Princess Ida.*

This barren verbiage, current among men,
Light coin, the tinsel clink of compliment.
  TENNYSON.—*Princess, c.* 2, 40.

When quality meets, compliments pass.
  Prov.

COMPRESSION

Even copious Dryden wanted, or forgot,
The last and greatest art, the art to blot.
  POPE.—*Satires and Epistles Imitated, 2nd Bk. Ep. of Horace,* 267.

COMPROMISE

All government, indeed every human benefit and enjoyment, every virtue,

and every prudent act, is founded on compromise and barter.
BURKE.—*Speech on Conciliation.*

The half is better than the whole.
HESIOD.—*Works and Days.*

They enslave their children's children who make compromise with sin.
J. R. LOWELL.—*Present Crisis.*

That bastard verdict, " Not proven."
I hate that Caledonian *medium quid.* One who is not proved guilty is innocent in the eyes of the law.
SCOTT.—*Diary, Feb.* 20, 1827.

All great alterations in human affairs are produced by compromise.
SYDNEY SMITH.—*Catholic Question.*

Is not compromise of old a god among you ?
SWINBURNE.—*Word from the Psalmist.*

COMPULSION

Nothing is pleasant
Joined with a must.
R. BRIDGES.—*Nero, Pt.* 1, Act 5, 1.

He that complies against his will
Is of his own opinion still.
BUTLER.—*Hudibras, c.* 3.

All that makes existence valuable to anyone depends on the enforcement of restraints upon the actions of other people.
J. S. MILL.—*Liberty, Introduction.*

On what compulsion must I ? tell me that. SHAKESPEARE.—*Merchant of Venice,* Act 4, 1.

If you cannot make a man think as you do, make him do as you think.
American Saying.

One thing thinketh the bear, but all another thinketh his leader.
Saying (Chaucer, Troilus, Bk. 4).

COMRADES

For danger levels man and brute,
And all are fellows in their need.
BYRON.—*Mazeppa, st.* 3.

Though I don't like the crew, I won't sink the ship. I'll do my best to save the ship. I'll pump and heave and haul and do anything I can, though he that pulls with me were my enemy. The reason is plain. We are all in the ship and must sink or swim together.
DEFOE.—*The Review,* 1708.

But 'tis always the way on 't ; one scarce finds a brother,
Fond as pitch, honest, hearty, and true to the core,

But by battle or storm or some damned thing or other
He's popped off the hooks and we ne'er see him more.
C. DIBDIN.—*Grieving's a Folly.*

Matilda : A sudden thought strikes me. Let us swear an eternal friendship !
Cecilia : Let us agree to live together !
J. H. FRERE.—*The Rovers,* Act 1, 1.

Every man,
To aid his clan,
Should plot and plan
As well as he can.
SIR W. S. GILBERT.—*Mikado.*

As unto the bow the cord is,
So unto the man is woman ;
Though she bends him, she obeys him,
Though she draws him, yet she follows ;
Useless each without the other !
LONGFELLOW.—*Hiawatha, Pt.* 10.

Be no one's boon companion. You will have less pleasure and less pain.
MARTIAL.—*Bk.* 12.

For we were nursed upon the self-same hill. MILTON.—*Lycidas,* 23.

Draw near together ; none be last or first ;
We are no longer names, but one desire ;
With the same burning of the soul we thirst,
And the same wine to-night shall quench our fire.
SIR H. NEWBOLT.—*Sacramentum Supremum* (1905).

There is nothing wanting to make all rational and disinterested people in the world of one religion, but that they should walk together every day.
POPE.—*Thoughts on Various Subjects.*

A pleasant possession is useless without a comrade. SENECA, *Ep.* 6.

One writ with me in sour misfortune's book.
SHAKESPEARE.—*Romeo and Juliet,* 5, 3.

Where are the boys of the old Brigade,
Who fought with us side by side ?
F. E. WEATHERLEY.—*Old Brigade.*

Horses he loved and laughter and the sun,
A song, wide spaces and the open air.
The trust of all dumb living things he won,
And never knew the luck too good to share.
Now, though he will not ride with us again,
His merry spirit seems our comrade yet,
Freed from the power of weariness and pain,
Forbidding us to mourn or to forget.
ANON.—*Quoted* 1916.

Thy people shall be my people, and thy
God my God. Where thou diest, will I
die, and there will I be buried : the Lord
do so to me, and more also, if aught
but death part thee and me.
Ruth i, 16 *and* 17.

Saul and Jonathan were lovely and
pleasant in their lives, and in their death
they were not divided.   2 *Samuel* i, 23.

CONCEALMENT

I canna tell, I mauna tell,
   I darena for your anger ;
But secret love will break my heart,
   If I conceal it langer.
       BURNS.—*Craigie-burn Wood.*

It is in truth a most contagious game :
HIDING THE SKELETON, shall be its name.
GEO. MEREDITH.—*Modern Love*, st. 17.

Duke :   And what's her history ?
Viola :   A blank, my lord. She never
   told her love,
But let concealment, like a worm i' the
   bud,
Feed on her damask cheek.
SHAKESPEARE.—*Twelfth Night*, Act 2, 4.

However deep you might embower the
   nest,
Some boy would spy it.
       TENNYSON.—*Princess, Prol.*, 148.

To hide disease is fatal.   *Latin prov.*

CONCEIT

The arch-flatterer, which is a man's self.
       BACON.—*Essays, Of Ceremonies.*

It was prettily devised of Æsop : The
fly sat upon the axle-tree of the chariot-
wheel, and said, " What a dust do I raise ! "
       BACON.—*Of Vain-Glory.*

He was like a cock who thought the
sun had risen to hear him crow.
       GEO. ELIOT.—*Adam Bede, ch.* 33.

Conceit is the finest armour a man can
wear.   J. K. JEROME.—*Idle Thoughts.*

The surest way to be taken in is to
think yourself cleverer than others.
       LA ROCHEFOUCAULD.

There never was so wise a man before ;
He seemed the incarnate " Well, I told you
   so ! "
       LONGFELLOW.—*Poet's Tale*, st. 9.

Of all speculations the market holds forth,
   The best that I know for a lover of pelf,
Is to buy —— up, at the price he is worth,
   And then sell him at that which he sets
     on himself.
       MOORE.—*A Speculation.*

Almost everybody is capable of thinking
he has done more than another deserves,
while the other thinks he has received less
than he deserves.
       POPE.—*Thoughts on Various Subjects.*

Conceit in weakest bodies strongest works.
       SHAKESPEARE.—*Hamlet*, Act 3, 4.

As who should say, I am Sir Oracle,
And when I ope my lips let no dog bark !
       SHAKESPEARE.—*Merchant of Venice,*
            Act 1, 1.

CONCENTRATION

Who keeps one end in view makes all
   things serve.
       BROWNING.—*In a Balcony.*

Concentration is the secret of success
in politics, in war, in trade, in short in
all the management of human affairs.
       EMERSON.—*Power.*

Once science only will one genius fit,
So vast is art, so narrow human wit.
       POPE.—*Essay on Criticism*, 60.

Have the courage to be ignorant of a
great number of things, in order to avoid
the calamity of being ignorant of everything.
       SYDNEY SMITH.—*Lectures on Moral
           Philosophy, No.* 9.

CONCESSIONS

The concessions of the weak are the
concessions of fear.
       BURKE.—*Speech on Conciliation.*

CONCILIATION

With reconciling words and courteous
   mien
Turning into sweet milk the sophist's
   spleen.   KEATS.—*Lamia, Pt.* 2.

Still in thy right hand carry gentle peace,
To silence envious tongues.
       SHAKESPEARE.—*Henry VIII.*, Act 3, 2.

Give him all kindness : I had rather have
Such men my friends, than enemies.
       SHAKESPEARE.—*Julius Cæsar*, Act 5, 4.

To Cerberus they give a sop,
   His triple barking mouth to stop.
       SWIFT.—*On Poetry.*

CONCISENESS

In few but sweetest numbers, Muse,
   rehearse :
My few shall far exceed more numerous
   verse.
       LUCRETIUS.—*De Rerum Natura*, 4,
           181 (*Creech tr.*).

He had a wonderful talent for packing
thought close, and rendering it portable.
       MACAULAY.—*Bacon.*

He speaks reserv'dly, but he speaks with
force,
Nor can one word be changed but for a
worse.   POPE.—*Odyssey, Bk.* 8, 191.

Sum up thy speech, many things in
few words.
   Ecclesiasticus 32, 8 (*R.V.*).

CONCORD

Of divers voices is sweet music made :
So in our life the different degrees
Render sweet harmony among these wheels.
H. F. CARY.—*Dante's Paradise, c.* 6, 127.

CONDEMNATION

We ought not to be so rash and rigorous
in our censures as some are : charity will
judge and hope the best.   God be merciful
unto us all !
BURTON.—*Anatomy of Melancholy, Pt.* 1.

The world is full of pots calling the
kettles black.
   LA ROCHEFOUCAULD.—*Maxim* 586.

He hears
On all sides, from innumerable tongues,
A dismal universal hiss, the sound
Of public scorn
   MILTON.—*Paradise Lost, Bk.* 10, 506.

More matter with less art.
   SHAKESPEARE.—*Hamlet,* Act 2, 2.

CONDOLENCE

Funeral grief loathes words.
T. DEKKER.—*Honest Whore, Pt.* 1, Act 1, 1.

CONDUCT

When we are asked further, What is
conduct ? let us answer, Three-fourths of
life.
M. ARNOLD.—*Literature and Dogma, ch.* 1.

Conduct is three-fourths of our life and
its largest concern.   M. ARNOLD.—*Ib.*

Our ingress into the world
Was naked and bare ;
Our progress through the world
Is trouble and care ;
Our egress from the world
Will be nobody knows where :
But if we do well here
We shall do well there.
   LONGFELLOW.—*Tales of a Wayside Inn,*
   Pt. 2.

Love all, trust a few,
Do wrong to none.
   SHAKESPEARE.—*All's Well,* Act 1, 1.

The system in everything ought to be,
—do as you please—so long as you please
to do what is right.   SYDNEY SMITH.—
Lectures on Moral Philosophy, No. 19.

From another's evil qualities a wise man
corrects his own.   PUBLILIUS SYRUS.

Be sparing of four things, *lingua, loculis,
oculis, et poculis*—your tongue, your purse,
your eyes, and your cups.
   J. TRUSLER.—*System of Etiquette.*

Fear thy God, speak ill of none,
Stick to the truth and don't be done !
   Old Maxim.

CONFEDERATES

" Arcades ambo," *id est*—blackguards
both.
   BYRON.—*Don Juan, c.* 4, *st.* 93.

CONFESSION

All shame is cowardice. The bravest
spirit is the best qualified for a penitent.
He then that will be honest must dare to
confess that he has been a knave.
   DEFOE.—*Serious Reflections.*

A fault confessed
Is a new virtue added to a man.
J. S. KNOWLES.—*Love-Chase,* Act 1, 2.

He's half absolved who has confessed.
   PRIOR.—*Alma,* 2, 22.

It is a greater thing to know how to
acknowledge a fault than to know how
not to commit one.
CARDINAL DE RETZ.—*Memoirs, vol.* 2, 13.

And now am I, if a man should speak
truly, little better than one of the wicked.
SHAKESPEARE.—*Henry IV., Pt.* 1, Act 1, 2.

CONFIDENCE

I felt so young, so strong, so sure of God.
   E. B. BROWNING.—*Aurora Leigh, Bk.* 2.

Self-trust is the first secret of success.
   EMERSON.—*Success.*

Confidence placed in another often compels
confidence in return. LIVY.—22, 22.

And, confident we have the better cause,
Why should we fear the trial ?
   MASSINGER.—*Bashful Lover,* Act 1.

Like Cato, give his little senate laws,
And sit attentive to his own applause.
   POPE.—*Prol. to Satires,* 209.

My dreams presage some joyful news at
hand ;
My bosom's lord sits lightly in his throne.
   SHAKESPEARE.—*Romeo and Juliet,*
   Act 5, 1.

Ferd : Here's my hand,
Miranda : And mine, with my heart in't.
    SHAKESPEARE.—*Tempest*, Act 2, 1.

In a just cause it is right to be confident.
    SOPHOCLES.

Youth is confident, manhood wary, and
old age confident again.
    M. F. TUPPER.—*Proverbial
Philosophy. Of Experience.*

For they can conquer who believe they
can.
    VIRGIL.—*Æneid, Bk.* 5 (*Dryden tr.*).

If he has been capable of believing me
unworthy of his trust, then it is he who is
for ever unworthy of me.
    VOLTAIRE.—*Tancrède (Armenaïde).*

A man of hope and forward-looking
mind. WORDSWORTH.—*Excursion, Bk.* 7.

The past unsighed for, and the future
sure.   WORDSWORTH.—*Laodamia.*

CONFIDENCE, MISPLACED

Now, behold, thou trustest upon the
staff of this bruised reed, even upon
Egypt, on which if a man lean, it will go
into his hand and pierce it.
    2 *Kings* xviii, 21.

CONFISCATION

A fine method !
This is neither begging, borrowing, nor
  robbery ;
Yet it hath a fine twang of all of them.
    MASSINGER.—*Guardian*, Act 5, 4.

CONFLICT

The meeting of these champions proud
Seemed like the bursting thunder-cloud.
SCOTT.—*Lay of the Last Minstrel, c.* 3, *st.* 5.

CONFLICT OF PASSIONS

Who can be wise, amazed, temperate,
  and furious,
Loyal and neutral, in a moment ? No
  man.
    SHAKESPEARE.—*Macbeth*, Act 2, 3.

CONFORMABILITY AND CON-
FORMITY

They make it a principle of their
irreligion outwardly to conform to any
religion.
    BURKE.—*Speech on Bill for Relief
of Dissenters* (1773).

My son ! the road the human being travels,
That, on which BLESSING comes and goes,
  doth follow
The river's course, the valley's playful
  windings,

Curves round the cornfield and the hill
  of vines,
Honouring the holy bounds of property ;
And thus secure, though late, leads to its
  end.
    COLERIDGE.—*Piccolomini*, Act 1, 4.

It is often the shorter way and the more
useful to conform to other people, rather
than to make other people conform to us.
    LA BRUYÈRE.—*De la Société*, 48.

The world's wicked.
We are men, not saints, sweet lady ;
  you must practise
The manners of the time if you intend
To have favour from it.
  MASSINGER.—*Unnatural Combat*, Act 1, 1.

It is the rule of rules and the general
law of laws that everyone should observe
that of the place where he is.
    MONTAIGNE.—*Bk.* 1, 22.

CONFUSION

Feels himself spent and fumbles for his
brains.   COWPER.—*Table Talk*, 536.

Chaos umpire sits,
And by decision more embroils the fray
By which he reigns : next him high arbiter
Chance governs all.
    MILTON.—*Paradise Lost, Bk.* 2, 907.

Confusion worse confounded.
    MILTON.—*Ib., Bk.* 2, 996.

They whose affairs are in a dangerous
or confused state, proceed to make them
more confused, so that nothing can be
settled.   PLAUTUS.—*Mostellaria*, Act 5, 1.

CONGÉ D'ÉLIRE

A *congé d'élire* is just such a recom-
mendation as if I should throw you out
of a three-pair-of-stairs window and recommend you to fall to the ground.
    JOHNSON.—*Remark as recorded by
Sir John Hawkins.*

CONJECTURE

Say first, of God above, of man below,
What can we reason, but from what we
  know ?
    POPE.—*Essay on Man, Ep.* 1, 8.

CONNOISSEURS

If they could forget for a moment the
correggiosity of Correggio.
    CARLYLE.—*Frederick the Great, Bk.* 4, 3.

For a male person *bric-à-brac* hunting is
about as robust a business as making
doll-clothes.
    MARK TWAIN.—*Tramp Abroad, c.* 20.

CONQUEST

Then fly betimes, for only they
Conquer Love, that run away.
T. CAREW.—*Conquest by Flight.*

The vanquished have no friends.
SOUTHEY.—*Vision of Maid of Orleans.*

The gates of hell are open night and day;
Smooth the descent, and easy is the way;
But to return and view the cheerful skies—
In this the task and mighty labour lies.
To few great Jupiter imparts this grace,
And those of shining worth and heavenly
race.
VIRGIL.—*Æneid, Bk.* 6 (*Dryden tr.*).

Great let me call him, for he conquered
me. YOUNG.—*The Revenge,* Act 1, 1.

CONSCIENCE

Ah, what an embarrassment is a conscience, and how happy one might be if
one were without it!
E. AUGIER.—*Homme de Bien.*

Good conscience you owe to yourself;
good fame to your neighbour.
ST. AUGUSTINE.

The great beacon-light God sets in all,
The conscience of each bosom.
BROWNING.—*Strafford,* Act 4, 2.

Conscience wakened in a fever,
Just a day too late, as ever.
R. BUCHANAN.—*White and Red.*

Nor ear can hear, nor tongue can tell
The tortures of that inward hell.
BYRON.—*Giaour,* 753.

Whatever creed be taught or land be trod,
Man's conscience is the oracle of God.
BYRON.—*The Island, c.* 1, 6.

Hence, babbling dreams! you threaten
here in vain.
Conscience, avaunt! Richard's himself
again!
C. CIBBER.—*Richard III.* (*adaptation*),
Act 5, 3.

Conscience, good my lord,
Is but the pulse of reason.
COLERIDGE.—*Zapolya, Pt.* 1, 1.

In early days the Conscience has in most
A quickness which in later life is lost.
COWPER.—*Tirocinium,* 109.

Men vehemently in love with their own
new opinions, though never so absurd,
and obstinately bent to maintain them,
give those opinions also that reverenced
name of conscience . . . and so pretend
to know they are true, when they know
at most but that they think so.
HOBBES.—*Leviathan, c.* 7.

A man's conscience and his judgment
is the same thing, and as the judgment,
so also the conscience, may be erroneous.
HOBBES.—*Ib., c.* 29.

To all mortals conscience is a God.
MENANDER (*Greek*).

Now Conscience wakes Despair
That slumbered; wakes the bitter memory
Of what he was, what is, and what must
be.
MILTON.—*Paradise Lost, Bk.* 4, 23.

All fame is foreign, but of true desert;
Plays round the head, but comes not to
the heart:
One self-approving hour whole years out-
weighs
Of stupid starers, and of loud huzzas;
And more true joy Marcellus exiled feels,
Than Cæsar with a senate at his heels.
POPE.—*Essay on Man, Ep.* 4, 253.

What conscience dictates to be done,
Or warns me not to do,
This, teach me more than hell to shun,
That, more than heaven pursue.
POPE.—*Universal Prayer.*

On he moves,
Careless of blame, while his own heart
approves. ROGERS.—*Human Life.*

Conscience! Conscience! divine instinct, immortal and heavenly voice;
the sure guide of an ignorant and limited
but intelligent and free existence; infallible judge of good and evil, who render
man like to God! It is you who make the
excellence of his nature and the moral
goodness of his actions; without you I
feel nothing in me which raises me above
the brutes,—nothing but the sad privilege
of leading myself astray, from errors to
errors, by the help of an understanding
without rule, and a reason without
principle. ROUSSEAU.—*Emile.*

There is a degree of debasement which
takes the life out of the soul. The internal
voice can no longer make itself heard to
him whose only thought is to nourish
himself. ROUSSEAU.—*Ib.*

A man has less conscience when in love
than in any other condition.
SCHOPENHAUER.—*Metaphysics of Love.*

A sinful heart makes feeble hand.
SCOTT.—*Marmion, c.* 3, *st.* 31.

A conscience that ne'er did him any harm.
SCOTT.—*Waverley* (*referring
to an easy-going conscience*).

Thus conscience doth make cowards of
us all.
SHAKESPEARE.—*Hamlet,* Act 3, 1.

A peace above all earthly dignities,
A still and quiet conscience.
SHAKESPEARE.—*Henry VIII.*, Act 3, 2.

Some certain dregs of conscience are yet
within me.
SHAKESPEARE.—*Richard III.*, Act 1, 4.

Love is too young to know what conscience
is ;
Yet, who knows not conscience is born
of love.
SHAKESPEARE.—*Sonnet* 151.

And conscience, that undying serpent,
calls
Her venomous brood to their nocturnal
task.
SHELLEY.—*Queen Mab, c.* 3.

Nay truly, learned men have learnedly
thought that . . . the inward light each
mind hath in itself, is as good as a Philosopher's book.
SIR P. SIDNEY.—*Apologie for Poetrie.*

What better bed than conscience good,
to pass the night with sleep ?
What better work than daily care fro' sin
thyself to keep ?
What better thought than think on God,
and daily him to serve ?
What better gift than to the poor that
ready be to sterve ?
T. TUSSER.—*Posies for the Bed Chamber.*

Conscience, a terrifying little sprite,
That bat-like winks by day and wakes by
night.   J. WOLCOT.—*Lousiad, c.* 3.

CONSCIENTIOUSNESS

Not always right in all men's eyes,
But faithful to the light within.
O. W. HOLMES.—*Birthday Tribute.*

CONSENT

Now what could artless Jeanie do ;
She had nae will to say him na :
At length she blushed a sweet consent,
And love was aye between them twa.
BURNS.—*There was a lass.*

A little while she strove, and much repented,
And whispering " I will ne'er consent,"
consented.
BYRON.—*Don Juan, c.* 1, st. 117.

He hath, my lord, wrung from me my
slow leave
By laboursome petition ; and, at last,
Upon his will I sealed my hard consent.
SHAKESPEARE.—*Hamlet*, Act 1, 2.

I must marry the girl first and ask his
consent afterwards.
SHERIDAN.—*St. Patrick's Day.*

CONSERVATISM

It seems to me a barren thing this
Conservatism—an unhappy cross-breed,
the mule of politics that engenders nothing.
DISRAELI.—*Coningsby, Bk.* 3,
c. 5 (*Eustace Lyle*).

The staid, conservative,
Came-over-with-the-Conqueror type of
mind.
SIR WM. WATSON.—*Study in Contrasts,*
1, 42.

Toryism is an innate principle o' human
nature—Whiggism but an evil habit.
JOHN WILSON.—*Noctes Ambrosianæ.*

CONSIDERATION

Let us cease shrieking and begin con-
sidering !
CARLYLE.—*French Revolution, Pt.* 3,
Bk 1, *ch.* 6.

CONSISTENCY

But Consistency still wuz a part of his
plan,—
He's been true to *one* party—an' thet
is himself.
J. R. LOWELL.—*Biglow Papers, No.* 3.

CONSOLATION

There is a day of sunny rest
For every dark and troubled night :
And grief may hide an evening guest,
But joy shall come with early light.
W. C. BRYANT.—*Blessed are they
that Mourn.*

Words that will solace him while life
endures.   CAMPBELL.—*Theodric.*

Never a tear bedims the eye
That time and patience will not dry ;
Never a lip is curved with pain
That can't be kissed into smiles again.
BRET HARTE.—*Lost Galleon.*

Watching, not as a fellow sufferer,
but as it were from afar, with dispassionate
vision, he [Simonides] tried to lighten
men's cares by such pathetic melodies
as taught men by their very sweetness,
that the gift of tears is (as has been said)
[by Juvenal 15, 131] the best gift of God
to suffering man.
KEBLE.—*Lectures on Poetry, No.* 16
(*E. K. Francis tr.*).

The philosophic brain soothes not the
stricken heart.
SIR L. MORRIS.—*Rhyme, the Consoler.*

There is no consolation, except in
truth alone.   PASCAL.—*On Death.*

This is the comfort of friends, that
though they may be said to die, yet

their friendship and society are, in the best sense, ever present, because immortal.
PENN.—*Fruits of Solitude.*

Everyone can master a grief but he that has it.
SHAKESPEARE.—*Much Ado,* Act 3, 2.

Over the bridge of sighs we pass to the palace of peace.
C. H. SPURGEON.—" *Salt-Cellars.*"

In all distresses of our friends
We first consult our private ends ;
While Nature, kindly bent to ease us,
Points out some circumstance to please us.
SWIFT.—*On the Death of Dr. Swift.*

What shall be said ? for words are thorns to grief. SWINBURNE.—*Atalanta.*

They are worse treated than we are ; but that is the consolation of the damned.
VOLTAIRE.—*Letter to D'Alembert, July 8,* 1771.

For sunlight gleams upon this shadowed earth ;
Sunlight and shadow waver to and fro,
And sadness echoes in the voice of mirth,
And music murmurs through the wail of woe.
AUGUSTA WEBSTER.—*A Woman Sold,* 3, To and Fro.

There is a comfort in the strength of love :
'Twill make a thing endurable, which else
Would overset the brain or break the heart. WORDSWORTH.—*Michael.*

Not without hope we suffer and we mourn.
WORDSWORTH.—*On a picture of Peele Castle* (1805).

CONSPIRACIES

When two or three were gathered to declaim
Against the monarch of Jerusalem,
Shimei was always in the midst of them.
DRYDEN.—*Absalom,* 601.

O the curst fate of all conspiracies !
They move on many springs ; if one but fail
The restive machine stops.
DRYDEN.—*Don Sebastian,* Act 4.

CONSTANCY

Except that household virtue, most uncommon,
Of Constancy to a bad, ugly woman.
BYRON.—*Vision of Judgment,* st. 12.

Seasons may roll,
But the true soul
Burns the same where'er it goes.
MOORE.—*Irish Melodies.*

When change itself can give no more,
'Tis easy to be true.
SIR C. SEDLEY.—*Constancy.*

To love one maiden only, cleave to her,
And worship her by years of noble deeds,
Until they won her.
TENNYSON.—*Guinevere,* 471.

Woman is like a weathercock which, when it is new, glistens in the sun and turns at every wind, but becomes fixed at last when time has rusted it.
VOLTAIRE.—*Le Dépositaire.*

There is no other, and I am he,
That loves no other, and thou art she.
Ring Posy.

Kepe Fayth till deth. *Old Ring Posy.*

It is good to be merry and wise,
It is good to be honest and true,
It is best to be off with the old love,
Before you are on with the new.
Published in " Songs of England and Scotland," London, 1835.

CONSTITUENTS

The king, and his faithful subjects, the Lords and Commons of this realm—the triple cord, which no man can break.
BURKE.—*Letter to a Noble Lord* (1796).

The principles of a free constitution are irrecoverably lost when the legislative power is nominated by the executive.
GIBBON.—*Decline and Fall, ch.* 3.

Like the British Constitution, she owes her success in practice to her inconsistencies in principle.
T. HARDY.—*Hand of Ethelberta, ch.* 9.

Constitoounts air hendy to help a man in,
But afterwards don't weigh the heft of a pin.
J. R. LOWELL.—*Biglow Papers,* No. 5.

There is a higher law than the Constitution. W. H. SEWARD.—*Speech,* 1850.

CONSUMMATION

'Tis a consummation
Devoutly to be wished.
SHAKESPEARE.—*Hamlet,* Act 3, 1.

CONTEMPLATIVE FACULTIES

Perfect happiness is some sort of energy of Contemplation, for all the life of the gods is therein glad, and that of men glad in the degree in which some likeness to the gods in this energy belongs to them. For none other of living creatures (but men only) can be happy, since in no way they have any part in Contemplation.
ARISTOTLE.—*Ethics, Bk.* 10 (*As translated by Ruskin*).

CONTEMPORARIES

Every age
Appears to souls who live in it (ask Carlyle)
Most unheroic.
E. B. BROWNING.—*Aurora Leigh, Bk. 5.*

I do distrust the poet who discerns
No character or glory in his times.
E. B. BROWNING.—*Ib.*

Contemporaries appreciate the man rather than the merit; but posterity will regard the merit rather than the man.
C. C. COLTON.—*Lacon.*

Speaking generally no man appears great to his cotemporaries, for the same reason that no man is great to his servants —they know too much of him.
C. C. COLTON.—*Ib.*

The way of this world is to praise dead saints and persecute living ones.
DR. N. HOWE.—*Sermon.*

CONTEMPT

Who despises all displeases all.
ALBERTANO OF BRESCIA.—*Lib. Cons.*

The Sacristan, he says no word that indicates a doubt,
But he puts his thumb unto his nose, and spreads his fingers out.
R. H. BARHAM.—*Nell Cook.*

I will not descend to a world I despise.
BYRON.—*Hours of Idleness, To Rev. J. T. Becher.*

I pity his ignorance and despise him [*Fanny Squeers*].
DICKENS.—*Nickleby, ch. 15.*

Let Sporus tremble!—*A.* What that thing of silk?
Sporus, that mere white curd of ass's milk?
Satire or sense, alas! can Sporus feel?
Who breaks a butterfly upon a wheel?
POPE.—*Prol. to Satires.*

I had rather be a dog, and bay the moon,
Than such a Roman.
SHAKESPEARE.—*Julius Cæsar, Act 4, 3.*

Scorned! to be scorned by one that I scorn,
Is that a matter to make me fret?
TENNYSON.—*Maud, Pt. 1, 13, 1.*

Gorgonised me from head to foot
With a stony British stare.
TENNYSON.—*Ib., Pt. 1, 13, 2.*

No one can boast of having never been despised.
VAUVENARGUES.—*Maxim 888.*

Disdainfully she looked; then turning round,
She fixed her eyes unmoved upon the ground,
And what he says and swears regards no more
Than the deaf rocks, when the loud billows roar.
VIRGIL.—*Æneid, Bk. 6 (Dryden tr.).*

CONTENT

Blesses his stars and thinks it luxury.
ADDISON.—*Cato, Act 1.*

But if I'm content with a little,
Enough is as good as a feast.
I. BICKERSTAFFE.—*Love in a Village, Act 3, 1.*

The countless gold of a merry heart,
The rubies and pearls of a loving eye,
The idle man never can bring to the mart,
Nor the cunning hoard up in his treasury.
WM. BLAKE.—*Two Kinds of Riches.*

Enough if we may wait in calm content
The hour that bears us to the silent sod;
Blameless improve the time that heaven has lent,
And leave the issue to Thy will, O God!
W. L. BOWLES.—*Sundial in a Churchyard.*

Then let us cheerfu' acquiesce
Nor make our scanty pleasures less,
By pining at our state.
BURNS.—*Epistle to Davie.*

Hope not sunshine every hour,
Fear not clouds will always lower.
Happiness is but a name,
Make content and ease thy aim.
BURNS.—*Lines on Friars-Carse Hermitage.*

Life is with such all beer and skittles;
They are not difficult to please
About their victuals.
C. S. CALVERLEY.—*Contentment.*

The all-in-all of life—Content.
CAMPBELL.—*To a Lady.*

God hath made none (that all might be) contented.
CHAPMAN.—*Tears of Peace.*

'Tis want of courage not to be content.
C. CHURCHILL.—*The Farewell, 70.*

Let not what I cannot have
My peace of mind destroy.
COLLEY CIBBER.—*The Blind Boy.*

Men live best on little. Nature gives all men happiness if they only knew how to use it.   CLAUDIAN.—*In Rufinum.*

A happy soul, that all the way
To heaven hath a summer day.
R. CRASHAW.—*Praise of Lessius.*

Grief never mended no broken bones,
and, as good people's very scarce, what I
says is, make the most on 'em.
    DICKENS.—*Sketches by Boz. Gin-Shops.*

On earth's wide thoroughfares below
Two only men contented go ;
Who knows what's right and what's forbid,
And he from whom is knowledge hid.
    EMERSON.—*Trans. from " Omar Chiam "*
                (Essay on Persian Poetry).

Him whom a little will not content,
nothing will content.
    EPICURUS (*as quoted by Ælian*).

Happy the man, and he alone,
    Who, master of himself, can say
" To-day at least hath been my own,
    For I have clearly lived to-day."
    P. FRANCIS.—*Horace, Odes, Bk.* 3, 29.

Let us draw upon content for the
deficiencies of fortune.
    GOLDSMITH.—*Vicar of Wakefield, c.* 3.

Sweet are the thoughts that savour of
    content ;
The quiet mind is richer than a crown.
    R. GREENE.—*Farewell to Folly.*

A mind content both crown and king-
    dom is.   R. GREENE.—*Ib.*

Few things are necessary to make a
wise man happy, but nothing can render
a fool contented. That is why nearly
all men are miserable.
    LA ROCHEFOUCAULD.—*Maxim* 617.

But live content, which is the calmest life.
    MILTON.—*Paradise Lost, Bk.* 6, 461.

    Taught to live
The easiest way, nor with perplexing
    thoughts
To interrupt the sweet of life.
    MILTON.—*Ib., Bk.* 8, 182.

Then, when the world is born again
    And the sweet year before thee lies,
Shall thy heart think of coming pain,
    Or vex itself with memories ?
    W. MORRIS.—*Jason, Bk* 14, 213.

It's good for a man to be contented, but
no good for the place he lives in. Contented people never stir up things, or
throw light into dark corners, or let air
into stuffy places.   EDEN PHILLPOTTS.

For myself I think that the surest sign
of true contentment of mind is the retired
and domestic life.
    ROUSSEAU.—*Julie.*

Poor and content is rich, and rich enough.
    SHAKESPEARE.—*Othello, Act* 3, 3.

Let me arise and open the gate,
To breathe the wild warm air of the heath,
And to let in Love, and to let out Hate,
And anger at living, and scorn of Fate ;
To let in Life, and let out Death.
    MRS. M. M. SINGLETON (VIOLET
                FANE).—*Time.*

I hold that to need nothing is divine,
and the less a man needs the nearer does
he approach divinity.
    SOCRATES (*as quoted by Xenophon*).

The noblest mind the best contentment
    has.
    SPENSER.—*Faerie Queene, Bk.* 1, c. 1, 35.

But fittest is that all contented rest
With what they hold : each hath his for-
    tune in his brest.
    SPENSER.—*Ib., Bk.* 6, c. 9, st. 29.

What better fare than well content ?
    T. TUSSER.—*Posies for thine own
                Bedchamber.*

As long liveth the merry man, they say,
As doth the sorry man—and longer by
    a day.
    N. UDALL.—*Ralph Roister Doister,* Act 1, 1.

When all is done and said,
In the end thus you shall find,
He most of all doth bathe in bliss
That hath a quiet mind.
    THOS. LORD VAUX.—*A Contented Mind.*

I'll not willingly offend,
Nor be easily offended ;
What's amiss I'll strive to mend,
And endure what can't be mended.
    I. WATTS.—*Good Resolution.*

I know indeed that wealth is good,
But lowly roof and simple food,
    With love that hath no doubt,
    Are more than gold without.
    WHITTIER.—*Maids of Attitash, st.* 1.

Content is the true philosopher's stone.
                                    Prov.

CONTENTION

Rest springs from strife, and dissonant
    chords beget
Divinest harmonies.
    SIR L. MORRIS.—*Love's Suicide.*

Contention with an equal is doubtful ;
with a superior, madness ; with an inferior,
a degradation.   SENECA.—*De Ira,* 2, 34.

CONTENTIOUSNESS

Some there are debate that seek,
    Making trouble their content,
Happy if they wrong the meek,
    Vex them that to peace are bent ;
Such undo the common tie
Of mankind, society.
    T. CAMPION.—*Wise Men.*

In every heart
Are sown the sparks that kindle fiery war.
COWPER.—*Winter Morning Walk*, 205.

CONTEST

He that is valiant and dares fight,
Though drubbed, can lose no honour by't.
BUTLER.—*Hudibras, Pt.* 1, *c.* 3.

In a wrong fight fell a good knight :
So a good night to Sir Bevil !
Who gained his laurel in an ill quarrel,
And whose cause went to the devil.
L. HOUSMAN.—*On Lansdown Hill.*

As if men fought upon the earth,
And fiends in upper air.
SCOTT.—*Marmion, c.* 6, 25.

CONTINUANCE

For men may come and men may go,
But I go on for ever.
TENNYSON.—*Brook.*

CONTRADICTION

But when the Crier cried, " O Yes ! " the
people cried " O No ! "
R. H. BARHAM.—*Misadventures at
Margate.*

Asseveration blustering in your face
Makes contradiction such a hopeless case.
COWPER.—*Conversation, l.* 59.

It is the instinct of understanding to
contradict reason.
JACOBI (*as quoted by Carlyle*).

Be dumb,
Thou spirit of contradiction !
MASSINGER.—*Picture,* Act 1, 2.

The evangelists may contradict each
other, provided only that the gospel does
not contradict itself.
Quoted as a "wholesome word" by GOETHE.

CONTRAST

Did He who made the lamb make thee ?
WM. BLAKE.—*The Tiger.*

Look here, upon this picture, and on
this,
The counterfeit presentment of two
brothers.
SHAKESPEARE.—*Hamlet,* Act 3, 4.

Could you on this fair mountain leave to
feed,
And batten on this moor ?
SHAKESPEARE.—*Ib.*

O, the more angel she,
And you the blacker devil !
SHAKESPEARE.—*Othello,* Act 5, 2.

CONTRITION

Mercy, for praise ;—to be forgiven, for
fame ;
He asked and hoped, through Christ. Do
thou the same.
COLERIDGE.—*Epitaph on himself.*

Ah ! happy they whose hearts can break
And peace of pardon win !
How else may man make straight his plan
And cleanse his soul from Sin ?
How else but through a broken heart
May Lord Christ enter in ?
OSCAR WILDE.—*Ballad of Reading Gaol.*

CONTROVERSIALISTS

Our disputants put me in mind of the
scuttle fish, that when he is unable to
extricate himself, blackens the water about
him till he becomes invisible.
ADDISON.—*Spectator, vol.* 7, 476.

Too dull for laughter, for reply too mad.
POPE.—*Epigram.*

CONTROVERSY

Some thrilling view of the surplice
question.
BROWNING.—*Christmas Eve, c.* 14.

Old religious factions are volcanoes
burnt out.   BURKE.—*Speech* (1792).

He'd run in debt by disputation,
And pay by ratiocination.
BUTLER.—*Hudibras, Pt.* 1, *c.* 1.

To hear
Such wrangling is a joy for vulgar minds.
H. F. CARY.—*Dante's "Hell," c.* 30, 145.

Pelting each other for the public good.
COWPER.—*Charity*, 623.

Religion should extinguish strife,
And make a calm of human life ;
But friends that chance to differ
On points which God has left at large,
How fiercely will they meet and charge !
No combatants are stiffer.
COWPER.—*Friendship, st.* 23.

Great contest follows, and much learned
dust.   COWPER.—*Garden*, 161.

But most she fears the controversial pen,
The holy strife of disputatious men.
CRABBE.—*Library.*

The ecclesiastical writers, in the heat
of religious faction, are apt to despise the
profane virtues of sincerity and moderation. GIBBON.—*Decline and Fall, ch.* 26.

I never think I have hit hard, unless it
rebounds.   JOHNSON.—*Remark,* 1775.

So high at last the contest rose,
From words they almost came to blows.
    J. MERRICK.—*Chameleon.*

Truth often suffers more by the heat of
its defenders than from the arguments
of its opposers.
    PENN.—*Some Fruits of Solitude.*

Generally true disputants are like true
sportsmen—their whole delight is in the
pursuit; and a disputant no more cares
for the truth than the sportsman for
the hare.
    POPE.—*Thoughts on Various Subjects.*

There is consolation in the fact that in
controversies and in taking mineral waters,
it is the after effects that are the real
effects.   SCHOPENHAUER.—*Dialogue on
        Religion (Philalethes).*

He would not waken old debate,
For he was void of rancorous hate.
    SCOTT.—*Lay of the Last Minstrel,* 5, 28.

'Faith, there has been much to do on
both sides; and the nation holds it no
sin, to tarre them to controversy.
    SHAKESPEARE.—*Hamlet,* Act 2, 2.

And do as adversaries do in law,
Strive mightily, but eat and drink as
   friends.   SHAKESPEARE.—*Taming
    of the Shrew,* Act 1, 2.

In this quarrel whole rivulets of ink
have been exhausted, and the virulence
of both parties enormously augmented.
    SWIFT.—*Battle of the Books.*

Anathemas are hurled
From both sides; veteran thunders (the
   brute test
Of truth) are met by fulminations new.
WORDSWORTH.—*Eccles. Sonnets, Pt.* 2, 36.

The itch of disputing will prove the
scab of churches.
SIR H. WOTTON.—*Panegyric to Charles I.*

God save the king, and bless the land
   In plenty, joy, and peace,
And grant henceforth that foul debate
   'Twixt noblemen may cease!
    Old Ballad.—Chevy Chase.

CONVENTION

Society . . . being in its nature a
convention, it loves what is conventional,
or what belongs to coming together.
    EMERSON.—*Manners.*

We pray to be conventional. But the
wary Heaven takes care you shall not be,
if there is anything good in you. Dante
was very bad company and was never
invited to dinner.
    EMERSON.—*Society and Solitude.*

No man [in Paris] dares to be himself.
"We must do as others do," that is the
first maxim of the country's wisdom.
"So and so is done; so and so is not done"
—behold this is the supreme law.
    ROUSSEAU.—*Julie.*

Somehow the grace, the bloom of things
   has flown,
And of all men we are most wretched,
   who
Must live each other's lives and not our
   own. OSCAR WILDE.—*Humanitad.*

CONVERSATION

Were we as eloquent as angels, yet
we should please some men, some women,
and some children, much more by listening
than by talking.   C. C. COLTON.—*Lacon.*

Conversation in its better part,
May be esteemed a gift, and not an art.
    COWPER.—*Conversation,* 3.

Words learned by rote a parrot may
   rehearse,
But talking is not always to converse.
    COWPER.—*Ib.,* 7.

The insignificant click-clack of modish
conversation [*Mr. Gosport*].
    MME. D'ARBLAY.—*Cecilia, Bk.* 1, 3.

"There are amusing people who do
not interest," said the Monsignore, "and
interesting people who do not amuse."
    DISRAELI.—*Lothair, ch.* 41.

Conversation is an art in which a man
has all mankind for his competitors,
for it is that which all are practising every
day while they live.
    EMERSON.—*Conduct of Life,
    Considerations by the Way.*

With thee conversing I forget the way.
    GAY.—*Trivia, Bk.* 2, 480.

Like precious stones his sensible remarks
Derive their value from their scarcity.
    SIR W. S. GILBERT.—*Princess Ida.*

He [Coleridge] talked on for ever; and
you wished him to talk for ever.
    W. HAZLITT.—*Living Poets.*

Confidence does more to make conversation than wit.   LA ROCHEFOUCAULD.

With thee conversing, I forget all time.
    MILTON.—*Paradise Lost, Bk.* 4, 639.

Silence and modesty are very valuable
qualities in conversation.
    MONTAIGNE, *Bk.* 1, 25.

If you your lips would keep from slips,
Five things observe with care—
To whom you speak, of whom you speak,
And how and when and where.
Version of old rhyme as given by W. E.
NORRIS *in " Thirlby Hall."*

Formed by thy converse, happily to steer
From grave to gay, from lively to severe.
POPE.—*Essay on Man, Ep.* 4, 379.

Discourse, the sweeter banquet of the
mind. POPE.—*Odyssey, Bk.* 15, 433.

That character in conversation which
commonly passes for agreeable is made up
of civility and falsehood.
POPE.—*Thoughts on Various Subjects.*

His talk was like a stream which runs
With rapid change from rocks to roses ;
It slipped from politics to puns :
It passed from Mahomet to Moses.
W. M. PRAED.—*Vicar, st.* 5.

To hear him speak, and sweetly smile
You were in Paradise the while.
SIR P. SIDNEY.—*Friend's Passion.*

Macaulay is like a book in breeches.
He has occasional flashes of silence that
make his conversation perfectly delightful.
SYDNEY SMITH.—*Saying.*

Don't talk all the talk, nor eat all the
meat. C. H. SPURGEON.—*" Salt-Cellars."*

Would you both please and be instructed
too,
Watch well the rage of shining to subdue ;
Hear every man upon his favourite theme,
And ever be more knowing than you seem.
B. STILLINGFLEET.—*Conversation.*

I am not one who oft or much delight
To season my fireside with personal talk.
WORDSWORTH.—*Personal Talk.*

CONVERSION

A convert's but a fly, that turns about
After his head's cut off, to find it out.
S. BUTLER.—*Miscellaneous Thoughts.*

To become properly acquainted with
a truth we must first have disbelieved it,
and disputed against it.
NOVALIS (*tr. by Carlyle*).

CONVICTION

But dash my buttons, though you put it
strong,
It's my opinion you're more right than
wrong.
R. BUCHANAN.—*Last of the Hangmen.*

CONVIVIALITY

If all be true that I do think,
There are five reasons we should drink ;

Good wine, a friend, or being dry,
Or lest we should be by and by,
Or any other reason why.
H. ALDRICH (*from the Latin*).

Nose, nose, jolly red nose,
And who gave thee that jolly red nose ?
Nutmegs and ginger, cinammon and cloves,
And they gave me this jolly red nose.
BEAUMONT AND FLETCHER.—*Knight
of the Burning Pestle,* Act 1, 3 (*also
in* RAVENCROFT'S *Deuteromela,* 1609).

Their hearts and sentiments were free,
their appetites were hearty.
R. BUCHANAN.—*City of the Saints.*

I wasna' fou, but just had plenty.
BURNS.—*Death and Dr. Hornbook.*

We are na fou, we're nae that fou,
But just a drappie in our ee.
BURNS.—*Song.*

Tam lo'ed him like a vera brither—
They had been fou for weeks thegither.
BURNS.—*Tam o' Shanter.*

Kings may be blest, but Tam was glorious,
O'er a' the ills o' life victorious !
BURNS.—*Ib.*

Inspiring bold John Barleycorn !
What dangers thou canst mak us scorn !
Wi' tippenny, we fear nae evil ;
Wi' usquebae, we'll face the devil.
BURNS.—*Ib.*

A man may drink and no be drunk ;
A man may fight and no be slain ;
A man may kiss a bonny lass
And aye be welcome back again.
BURNS.—*There was a Lass.*

Should every creature drink but I ?
Why, man of morals, tell me why.
COWLEY.—*Drinking.*

To drink healths is to drink sickness.
T. DEKKER.—*Honest Whore.*

Did you ever hear of Captain Wattle ?
He was all for love and a little for the
bottle. C. DIBDIN.—*Capt. Wattle.*

" It wasn't the wine," murmured Mr.
Snodgrass, in a broken voice. " It was
the salmon."
DICKENS.—*Pickwick Papers, ch.* 8.

A very merry, dancing, drinking,
Laughing, quaffing and unthinking time.
DRYDEN.—*Secular Masque, l.* 40.

Let other hours be set apart for business !
To-day it is our pleasure to be drunk.
FIELDING.—*Tom Thumb,* Act 1, 2.

The warm champagny, old-particular,
brandy-punchy feeling.
O. W. HOLMES.—*Nux Postcœnatica.*

The rapturous, wild, and ineffable pleasure
Of drinking at somebody else's expense.
H. S. Leigh.—*To an Intoxicated Fly.*

When thirsty grief in wine we steep,
When healths and draughts go free,—
Fishes, that tipple in the deep,
Know no such liberty.
R. Lovelace.—*To Althea.*

Fill the bumper fair!
Every drop we sprinkle
O'er the brow of Care
Smooths away a wrinkle.
Moore.—*Irish Melodies.*

It being reported to Pyrrhus (B.C. 318 c.-
B.C. 272), that certain young men had
spoken disrespectfully of him, he asked
them, "Did you really say these things?"
"We did, sir," replied one, "and we
should have said a good deal more, if we
had had more wine." Whereupon he
laughed and dismissed them.
Plutarch.—*Life of Pyrrhus.*

As Doctor Martin Luther sang:
"Who loves not wine, woman, and song,
He is a fool his whole life long."
Thackeray.—*A Credo.* (*The saying
is wrongly attributed to Luther.*)

I love such mirth as does not make
friends ashamed to look upon one another
next morning.
I. Walton.—*Complete Angler, ch.* 5.

They drink with impunity, or anybody
who invites them.
Artemus Ward.—*Moses the Sassy.*

CONVULSION

Unhurt amidst the war of elements,
The wrecks of matter, and the crash of
worlds. Addison.—*Cato,* Act 5, 1.

COOKERY

Until the nature of man is completely
altered, cooking is the most important
thing for a woman.
Arnold Bennett.—*The Title* (1918),
Act 1.

Home-made dishes that drive one from
home. Hood.—*Miss Kilmansegg.*

The greatest animal in creation, the
animal who cooks.
Douglas Jerrold.—*Attributed.*

Of herbs, and other country messes
Which the neat-handed Phyllis dresses.
Milton.—*L'Allegro,* 85.

Ilka man as he like, I'm for the cook.
Scottish prov.

CO-OPERATION

Nature works on a method of all for each
and each for all. Emerson.—*Farming.*

But when was honey ever made
With one bee in the hive?
Hood.—*Last Man.*

The Ox said to his fellow-servant the
Camel, when he refused help in carrying
his burden, "It will not be long before
you carry my burden and me too."
Which came to pass when the ox died.
Plutarch.—*Morals, Bk.* 1.

Hold the fort! I am coming!
Signal to General Corse (Oct. 5, 1864)
by William F. Sherman.

CORDIALITY

The music that can deepest reach,
And cure all ill, is cordial speech.
Emerson.—*Conduct of Life,
Considerations by the Way.*

CORNWALL

I love thee, Cornwall, and will ever,
And hope to see thee once again!
For why?—thine equal knew I never
For honest minds and active men.
T. Freeman.—*Encomion Cornubiæ* (1614).

And have they fixed the where and when,
And shall Trelawny die?
Then twenty thousand Cornish men
Shall know the reason why.
Song. Trelawny (1688).

In Cornwall are the best gentlemen.
Cornish prov., as quoted by Borrow
(*Lavengro*).

CORPORAL PUNISHMENT

Too much Cain is apt to kill Abel.
C. H. Spurgeon.—"*Salt-Cellars.*"

Never known, during eight years at
school, to be subject to that punishment
which it is generally thought none but a
cherub can escape.
Thackeray.—*Vanity Fair, Bk.* 1, *ch.* 9.

CORPORATIONS

They [corporations] cannot commit
treason nor be outlawed nor ex-com-
municate, for they have no souls.
Coke.—*Case of Sutton's Hospital.*

Corporations have neither bodies to
be punished, nor souls to be damned.
Lord Thurlow (*according to
Poynder's* "*Literary Extracts*").

CORPSE

A demd damp, moist, unpleasant body.
Dickens.—*Nickleby, ch.* 34.

CORRESPONDENCE

Another success is the post-office, with
its educating energy augmented by cheap-

ness and guarded by a certain religious
sentiment in mankind ; so that the power
of a wafer or a drop of wax or gluten,
to guard a letter, as it flies over sea, over
land, as if a battalion of artillery brought
it, I look upon as a fine meter of civilization.   EMERSON.—*Civilization.*

CORRUPTION

When vice prevails, and impious men
    bear sway,
The post of honour is a private station.
             ADDISON.—*Cato, Act* 4, 4.

For this is the true strength of guilty
    kings,
When they corrupt the souls of those they
    rule.   M. ARNOLD.—*Merope.*

Among a people generally corrupt
liberty cannot long exist.
                  BURKE.—*Letter.*

Corrupt influence, which is in itself the
perennial spring of all prodigality, and of
all disorder ; which loads us, more than
millions of debt ; which takes away vigour
from our arms, wisdom from our councils,
and every shadow of authority and credit
from the most venerable parts of our
constitution.
      BURKE.—*Speech on Economical
          Reform (Feb.,* 1780).

Corrupted freemen are the worst of
slaves.   GARRICK.—*Gamesters, Prologue.*

Corruption, the most infallible symptom
of constitutional liberty.
      GIBBON.—*Decline and Fall, ch.* 21.

Robbery and depeculation of the public
treasure or revenues is a greater crime
than the robbing or defrauding of a private
man ; because to rob the public is to rob
many at once.
          HOBBES.—*Leviathan, ch.* 27.

Justice is such a fine thing that one
cannot buy it too dearly.
             LE SAGE.—*Crispin.*

In vain doth valour bleed,
While avarice and rapine share the land.
          MILTON.—*To Fairfax.*

Some flowerets of Eden ye still inherit
But the trail of the Serpent is over them
    all.
      MOORE.—*Lalla Rookh, Paradise
            and the Peri.*

You yourself
Are much condemned to have an itching
    palm.
SHAKESPEARE.—*Julius Cæsar, Act* 4, 3.

Though authority be a stubborn bear,
yet he is often led by the nose with gold.
SHAKESPEARE.—*Winter's Tale, Act* 4, 3.

And loathsome canker lives in sweetest
    bud.   SHAKESPEARE.—*Sonnet* 35.

All men have their price.
Attributed to SIR R. WALPOLE, *but current
                before his time.*

He that toucheth pitch shall be defiled.
           Ecclesiasticus xiii, 1.

There was never any thing by the wit
of man so well devised, or so sure established, which in continuance of time hath
not been corrupted.
         Common Prayer, Preface.

COSMOPOLITANISM

Socrates, when asked of what country
he called himself, said, " Of the world " ;
for he considered himself an inhabitant
and a citizen of the whole world.
      CICERO.—*Tusc. Quæst., Bk.* 5, 37.

He made all countries where he came his
    own.   DRYDEN.—*Astræa Redux,* 76.

Go where he will, the wise man is at
    home,
His hearth the earth, his hall the azure
    dome.
      EMERSON.—*Wood-Notes, Pt.* 1, 3.

The whole world is my native land.
             SENECA.—*Ep.* 28.

All places that the eye of heaven visits,
Are to a wise man ports and happy havens.
      SHAKESPEARE.—*Richard II., Act* 1, 3.

Whoever seeks for truth should be of
no country.
    VOLTAIRE.—*Reply to an Academician.*

COTTAGES

Well would it be if every landowner
carried in his mind a resolve in conson-
ance with an Act passed, I believe, in
Elizabeth's reign, which forbade cottages
to be erected unless a certain quantity
of land were laid to each cottage, and
denominated all cottages failing in this
respect, " silly cottages."
      SIR A. HELPS.—*Friends in Council,
              Bk.* 2, *ch.* 4.

COUNCILS

This council I establish pure from bribe,
Reverend, and keen to act ; for those
    that sleep
An ever watchful sentry of the land.
      ÆSCHYLUS.—*Eumenides,* 232
              (*Plumptre tr.*).

But yet beware of councils when too full ;
Number makes long disputes.
      SIR J. DENHAM.—*Of Prudence,* 59.

COUNSEL

Ask counsel of both times : of the ancient time what is best ; and of the latter time what is fittest. BACON.—*Of Great Place.*

They are too old to learn, and I too young
To give them counsel.
 MASSINGER.—*Fatal Dowry*, Act 1, 1.

In the multitude of counsellors there is safety.   *Proverbs* xi, 14 ; xxiv, 6.

"Twa heads are better than ane," as the wife said when she and her dog gaed to the market.   *Scottish prov.*

COUNTERPLOT

For 'tis the sport to have the engineer
Hoist with his own petard ; and it shall
   go hard
But I will delve one yard below their mines,
And blow them to the moon.
 SHAKESPEARE.—*Hamlet*, Act 3, 4.

COUNTRY, THE

'Tis sweet to him, who all the week
  Through city crowds must push his way,
To stroll alone through fields and woods,
  And hallow thus the Sabbath-day.
 COLERIDGE.—*Home-Sick.*

God made the country and man made
   the town. COWPER.—*The Sofa*
 (*bor-rowed from Varro*).

For him light labour spread her wholesome store,
Just gave what life required, and gave
   no more.
 GOLDSMITH.—*Deserted Village.*

All country people hate each other.
 HAZLITT.—*Wordsworth's " Excursion."*

There is nothing good to be had in the country, or, if there be, they will not let you have it.   HAZLITT.—*Ib.*

The gift of country life, near hills and
   woods,
Where happy waters sing in solitudes.
 JOHN MASEFIELD.—*Biography.*

It is good to be out on the road, and
   going one knows not where,
Going through meadow and village, one
   knows not whither or why.
 JOHN MASEFIELD.—*Tewkesbury Road.*

Meadows trim with daisies pied.
 MILTON.—*L'Allegro*, 75.

Abroad in the meadows to see the young
   lambs
Run sporting about by the side of their
   dams,
With fleeces so clean and so white.
 I. WATTS.—*Innocent Play*

COURAGE

That is well said, John, an honest man, that is not quite sober, has nothing to fear. ADDISON.—*The Drummer Boy.*

The man so bravely played the man,
He made the fiend to fly.
 J. BUNYAN.—*Pilgrim's Progress, Pt. 2.*

And let us mind, " Faint heart ne'er wan
   A lady fair ; "
Wha does the utmost that he can,
   Will whiles do mair.
 BURNS.—*Epistle to Dr. Blacklock.*

I see before me the Gladiator lie ;
He leans upon his hand—his manly brow
Consents to death, but conquers agony.
 BYRON.—*Childe Harold, c.* 4, *st.* 140.

Blessed are the valiant that have lived in the Lord.
 CARLYLE.—*Cromwell, vol.* 5, *Pt.* 10.

True valour lies half way between cowardice and rashness.
 CERVANTES.—*Don Quixote.*

None but the brave deserves the fair.
 DRYDEN.—*Alexander's Feast, st.* 1.

Whistling to keep myself from being afraid.
 DRYDEN.—*Amphitryon.*

Courage consists in equality to the problem before us.
 EMERSON.—*Courage.*

Counsel that I once heard given to a young person, " Always do what you are afraid to do." EMERSON.—*Heroism.*

Conquest pursues, where courage leads
   the way.
 SIR S. GARTH.—*Dispensary, c.* 4, 198.

Unto it boldly let us stand ;
God will give right the upper hand.
 H. GIFFORD.—*For Soldiers.*

Question not, but live and labour
   Till yon goal be won,
Helping every feeble neighbour,
   Seeking help from none ;
Life is mostly froth and bubble,
   Two things stand like stone—
Kindness in another's trouble,
   Courage in your own.
 A. L. GORDON.—*Wearie Wayfarer, Pt.* 8.

Though all we knew depart,
The old commandments stand ;
" In courage keep your heart,
In strength lift up your hand."
 RUDYARD KIPLING.—*For all we have
   and are (Sept.,* 1914).

Instead of rage
Deliberate valour breathed, firm and
    unmoved
With dread of death, to flight or foul
    retreat.
    MILTON.—*Paradise Lost, Bk. 1,* 553.

I do not call a wild beast or anything
else brave, which, through ignorance,
has no fear of things of dread ; " fearless "
is not the same thing as " brave."
    PLATO.—*Laches,* 28.

You will find many men who are most
unjust, most unholy, most intemperate,
and most ignorant, yet eminently courageous.   PLATO.—*Protagoras,* 96.

The first in danger as the first in fame.
    POPE.—*Iliad, Bk.* 6, 637.

I dare do all that may become a man ;
Who dares do more is none.
    SHAKESPEARE.—*Macbeth,* Act 1, 7.

Courage respects courage.
R. L. STEVENSON.—*Travels with a Donkey.*

A brave man, were he seven times king,
Is but a brave man's peer.
    SWINBURNE.—*Marino Faliero,* Act 2, 2.

Valour grows by daring, fear by holding
back.   PUBLILIUS SYRUS.

The courage that lifted their hearts shall
    leaven
All who in England's name go forth
From east and west, from south and north,
Under the great Godspeed of Heaven.
    SIR WM. WATSON.—*Charge of the 9th
        Lancers, Sept.* 5, 1914.

Only be thou strong and very courageous.   *Joshua* 1, 7.

Be strong, and quit yourselves like men.
    1 *Samuel* iv, 9.

COURTESY

If a man be gracious and courteous
to strangers, it shows he is a citizen of the
world.   BACON.—*Of Goodness.*

Of Courtesy it is much less
Than Courage of Heart or Holiness,
Yet in my Walks it seems to me
That the Grace of God is in Courtesy.
    HILAIRE BELLOC.—*Courtesy.*

Life is not so short but that there is
always room for courtesy.
    EMERSON.—*Social Aims.*

His ready speech flowed fair and free
In phrase of gentlest courtesy ;
Yet seemed that tone and gesture bland
Less used to sue than to command.
    SCOTT.—*Lady of the Lake, c.* 1, st. 21.

I am the very pink of courtesy.
    SHAKESPEARE.—*Romeo and Juliet,*
        Act 2, 4.

The greater man, the greater courtesy.
    TENNYSON.—*Last Tournament,* 630

For courtesy wins woman all as well
As valour.   TENNYSON.—*Ib.*

It's aye good to be ceevil,
As the auld wife said when she becked
    (curtseyed) to the deevil.
    Scottish prov.

Put your hand quickly to your hat and
slowly to your purse.   *Danish prov.*

Hech how [an expression of grief, a sigh]
    is heavysome,
An auld wife is dowiesome [dismal],
And courtesy is cumbersome
    To them that canna show it.
    Scottish saying.

COURTING

Thrice happy's the wooing that's not long
    a doing,
So much time is saved in the billing and
    cooing.
    R. H. BARHAM.—*Sir Rupert.*

Perhaps if you address the lady
    Most politely, most politely,
Flatter and impress the lady
    Most politely, most politely.
Humbly beg and humbly sue,
She may deign to look on you.
    SIR W. S. GILBERT.—*Princess Ida.*

Whaur hae ye been a' day,
    My boy Tammy ?
I've been by burn and flowery brae,
Meadow green and mountain grey,
Courting of this young thing
Just come frae her mammy.
    HECTOR MACNEILL.—*Song.*

I will now court her in the conqueror's
    style ;
" Come, see, and overcome."
    MASSINGER.—*Maid of Honour,* Act 2, 1.

Friendship is constant in all other things,
Save in the office and affairs of love ;
Therefore all hearts in love use their own
    tongues ;
Let every eye negotiate for itself
And trust no agent.
    SHAKESPEARE.—*Much Ado,* Act 2, 1.

Was ever woman in this humour wooed ?
Was ever woman in this humour won ?
    SHAKESPEARE.—*Richard III.,* Act 1, 2.

A whispering tale in a fair lady's ear,
Such as would please.
    SHAKESPEARE.—*Romeo and Juliet,* Act 1, 5.

That man that hath a tongue, I say, is
no man,
If with his tongue he cannot win a woman.
>SHAKESPEARE.—*Two Gentlemen of
Verona*, Act 3, 1.

Since first I saw your face, I resolved
To honour and renown you;
If now I be disdained, I wish
My heart had never known you.
>*Old Song* (c. 1600).

COVETOUSNESS

As thorough an Englishman as ever
coveted his neighbour's goods.
>C. KINGSLEY.—*Water Babies*.

Get place and wealth, if possible with
grace;
If not, by any means get wealth and place.
>POPE.—*Satires, Ep.* 1, 108.

When Naboth's vineyard looked so fine,
The King cried out, "Would this were
mine!"
And yet no reason could prevail
To bring the owner to a sale.
>SWIFT.—*Garden Plot*, 1709.

Old age brings this vice,—that we are
all more eager than we should be about
acquiring property. TERENCE.—*Adelphi*.

COWARDICE

There needs no other charm nor conjurer
To raise infernal spirits up, but fear.
>S. BUTLER.—*Miscellaneous Thoughts*.

That all men would be cowards, if they
dare,
Some men have had the courage to declare.
>CRABBE.—*Tales of the Hall*, 1, 1.

For anything I know, I am an arrant
coward.
>FLETCHER AND MASSINGER.—*Little
French Lawyer*, Act 2.

Whilst you are fighting (said Panurge)
I will pray God for your victory, after the
example of the chivalrous Captain Moses,
leader of the people of Israel.
>RABELAIS.—*Pantagruel, Bk.* 4, c. 37.

For all men would be cowards if they
durst. EARL OF ROCHESTER.—*Satire*.

Instinct is a great matter; I was a
coward on instinct.
>SHAKESPEARE.—*Henry IV.*, Act 2, 4.

Cowards die many times before their
deaths;
The valiant never taste of death but once.
>SHAKESPEARE.—*Julius Cæsar*, Act 2, 2.

When our actions do not,
Our fears do make us traitors.
>SHAKESPEARE.—*Macbeth*, Act 4, 2.

The devil damn thee black, thou cream-
faced loon!
Where gott'st thou that goose look?
>SHAKESPEARE.—*Ib.*, Act 5, 3.

An I thought he had been valiant, and
so cunning in fence, I'd have seen him
damned ere I'd have challenged him.
>SHAKESPEARE.—*Twelfth Night*, Act 3, 4.

I know them to be as true-bred cowards
as ever turned back.
>SHAKESPEARE, *Henry IV.*, Pt. 1,
Act 1, 2.

As an old soldier I admit the cowardice:
it's as universal as sea-sickness, and
matters just as little.
>G. B. SHAW.—*Man and Superman*.

My valour is certainly going! It is
sneaking off! I feel it oozing out, as it
were, at the palms of my hands.
>SHERIDAN.—*Rivals*, Act 5, 3.

There grows
No herb of help to heal a coward
heart.
>SWINBURNE.—*Bothwell*, Act 2, 13.

The wicked flee when no man pursueth:
but the righteous are bold as a lion.
>*Proverbs*, xxviii, 1.

Many would be cowards if they had
courage enough. *Prov.*

COYNESS

Yielded with coy submission, modest pride,
And sweet reluctant amorous delay.
>MILTON.—*Paradise Lost, Bk.* 4, 307.

Flee, and she follows; follow, and she'll
flee;
Than she there's none more coy; there's
none more fond than she.
>QUARLES.—*Emblems, Bk.* 1, 4.

Yet she was coy, and would not believe
That he did love her so;
No, nor at any time would she
Any countenance to him show.
>*Bailiff's Daughter of Islington* (*Ancient
Ballad*).

CRAFTINESS

He's tough, ma'am, tough is J. B. Tough
and de-vilish sly. DICKENS.—*Dombey, c.* 7.

That's the common fate of your Machi-
avellians; they draw their designs so
subtle that their very fineness breaks
them. DRYDEN.—*Sir Martin Mar-All*.

The devil knew not what he did when
he made man politic; he crossed himself
by 't. SHAKESPEARE.—*Timon*, Act 3, 3.

CRANKS

A crank is a little thing that makes revolutions. *Anonymous saying.*

CREATIVE FACULTY

Only God and the Poet deserve the name of Creator.   TASSO.

Of that which is more than Creature, no Creature ever conceived.
RUSKIN.—*Modern Painters, vol. 2, Pt. 2, sec. 3, ad fin.*

Genius invents, wit merely discovers.
WEBER.

CREDULITY

A credulous man is a deceiver.
BACON.—*Adv. of Learning, Pt.* 1.

Between craft and credulity, the voice of reason is stifled.
BURKE.—*Letter to Sheriffs of Bristol.*

As a rule men freely believe what they wish.   CÆSAR.—*De Bello Gallico.*

Confidence is a plant of slow growth in an aged bosom ; youth is the season of credulity. LORD CHATHAM.—*Speech,* 1766.

The most positive men are the most credulous, since they most believe themselves.
POPE.—*Thoughts on Various Subjects.*

We have believed in too many things, we men of little faith.   JULES ROMAINE.

Wearied from doubt to doubt to flee,
We welcome fond credulity,
Guide confident, though blind.
SCOTT.—*Marmion, c.* 3, *st.* 30.

There is nothing that cannot be imagined by people of no imagination.
EDITH SICHEL.

That only disadvantage of honest hearts, credulity.
SIR P. SIDNEY.—*Arcadia.*

Let any man speak long enough, he will get believers.
R. L. STEVENSON.—*Master of Ballantrae.*

Like simple, noble natures, credulous
Of what they long for, good in friend or foe.
TENNYSON.—*Geraint and Enid,* 877.

CREEDS

Unduped of fancy, henceforth man
Must labour !—must resign
His all too human creeds, and scan
Simply the way divine !
M. ARNOLD.—*Obermann Once More.*

Light half-believers of our casual creeds,
Who never deeply felt, nor clearly willed.
M. ARNOLD.—*Scholar Gipsy.*

Creeds are as thistle-down wind-tossed and blown,
But deeds abide throughout eternity.
G. BARLOW.—*Dawn to Sunset, Bk.* 2.

Uncursed by doubt our earliest creed we take ;
We love the precepts for the teacher's sake.
O. W. HOLMES.—*Rhymed Lesson.*

All creeds I view with toleration thorough,
And have a horror of regarding heaven
As anybody's rotten borough.
HOOD.—*Ode to Rae Wilson.*

Shall I ask the brave soldier who fights by my side
In the cause of mankind, if our creeds agree ?
MOORE.—*Come send round the wine.*

We have a Calvinistic creed, a Popish liturgy, and an Arminian clergy.
W. PITT.—*Speech,* 1790.

For modes of faith let graceless zealots fight,
He can't be wrong whose life is in the right.
POPE.—*Essay on Man.*

Ye are but purblind leaders, who preach that our utmost need
Can be met by a faith in a Semite book and the Athanasian Creed !
Who damn with a text in this world and the next, if we stray from the Church's path,
And believe that creeds shall be more than deeds, when God gathers His aftermath.
LT.-COLONEL DUDLEY SAMPSON.—*Songs of Love and Life.*

From the dust of creeds out-worn.
SHELLEY.—*Prometheus,* Act 1.

All creeds and opinions are nothing but the mere result of chance and temperament. J. H. SHORTHOUSE.—*John Inglesant.*

It was his [Tom Bowling's] opinion that no honest man would swerve from the principles in which he was bred, whether Turkish, Protestant, or Roman.
SMOLLETT.—*Roderick Random, ch.* 42.

Give each his creed, let each proclaim
His catalogue of curses ;
I trust in Thee and not in them,
In Thee and in Thy mercies.
W. M. THACKERAY.—*Jolly Jack.*

Truth has never been, can never be, contained in any one creed or system.
MRS. HUMPHRY WARD.—*Robert Elsmere, Bk.* 4, *ch.* 28.

When whelmed are altar, priest, and creed,
  When all the faiths have passed,
Perhaps, from darkening incense freed,
God may emerge at last.
          SIR W. WATSON.—*Revelation*

From the death of the old the new proceeds,
And the life of truth from the rot of creeds.
          J. G. WHITTIER.—*Preacher.*

CRICKET

Casting a ball at three straight sticks
  and defending the same with a fourth.
          R. KIPLING.—*Kitchener's School.*

CRIME

Nor florid prose, nor honied lies of rhyme,
Can blazon evil deeds, or consecrate a
crime.   BYRON.—*Childe Harold, c.* I, 3.

My ear is pained,
My soul is sick with every day's report
Of wrong and outrage with which earth
  is filled.   COWPER.—*Time Piece.*

His virtues lie so mingled with his crimes,
As would confound their choice to punish
  one
And not reward the other.
          DRYDEN.—*All for Love*, Act 3, 1.

More men are hanged in England in
one year than in France in seven, because
the English have better hearts; the
Scotchmen likewise never dare rob, but
only commit larcenies.
          SIR J. FORTESCUE (*Lord Chief Justice,*
          1442), *De laudibus Legum Angliæ.*

It is worse than a crime; it is a blunder.
          Attrib. to FOUCHÉ.

There are crimes which become inno
cent, and even glorious, by their fame,
their number, and their excess.
          LA ROCHEFOUCAULD.—*Maxim* 550.

It was the destiny of Medea to be criminal, but her heart was formed to love
virtue.   QUINAULT.

Foul deeds will rise,
Though all the earth o'erwhelm them, to
  men's eyes.
          SHAKESPEARE.—*Hamlet*, Act I, 2.

Flat burglary as ever was committed!
          SHAKESPEARE.—*Much Ado*, Act 4, 2.

Had I a hundred mouths, a hundred
  tongues,
And throats of brass inspired with iron
  lungs,
I could not half those horrid crimes repeat
Nor half the punishments those crimes
  have met.
          VIRGIL.—*Æneid, Bk.* 6 (*Dryden tr.*).

Divided by interests, united in crime.
          VOLTAIRE.—*Artémire (also in Mérope).*

CRIMINALITY

He hath no drowning mark upon him;
his complexion is perfect gallows.
          SHAKESPEARE.—*Tempest*, Act I, I.

CRISIS

This hour's the very crisis of your fate,
Your good or ill, your infamy or fame,
And the whole colour of your life depends
On this important now.
          DRYDEN.—*Spanish Friar.*

Ye see our danger on the utmost edge
Of hazard, which admits no long debate.
          MILTON.—*Paradise Regained, Bk.* I, 94.

This push
Will cheer me ever, or disseat me now.
          SHAKESPEARE.—*Macbeth*, Act 5, 3.

This is the night
That either makes me, or fordoes me quite.
          SHAKESPEARE.—*Othello*, Act 5, I.

The fack can't be no longer disgised that
a Krysis is onto us.
          ARTEMUS WARD.—*The Crisis.*

CRITICISM

You have no leisure to read books?
What then? You have leisure to check
your own insolence.
          MARCUS AURELIUS.—*Bk.* 8, 8.

Good critics who have stamped out poet's
                              hope;
    .   .   .   .   .   .
Now may the good God pardon all good
  men!
          E. B. BROWNING.—*Aurora Leigh, Bk.* 4.

When the prophet beats the ass,
The angel intercedes.
          E. B. BROWNING.—*Ib., Bk.* 8.

The mair they talk I'm kenned the better,
  E'en let them clash!
          BURNS.—*Welcome to his Illegitimate*
                              Child.

While brave and noble writers vainly
  strive
To such a height of glory to arrive;
But still with all they do unsatisfied,
Ne'er please themselves, though all the
  world beside.
          BUTLER.—*On Rhyme (tr. from Boileau).*

'Tis strange the mind, that very fiery
  particle,
Should let itself be snuffed out by an
  article.
          BYRON.—*Don Juan, c.* II, *st.* 60.

There is only one writer who can really injure any author, and that writer is himself. SIR HALL CAINE.—*My Story*.

How blind is Pride! What eagles we are still
In matters that belong to other men!
What beetles in our own!
CHAPMAN.—*All Fools*, Act 4, 1.

Criticism is easy and art is difficult.
DESTOUCHES.

You know who the critics are? The men who have failed in literature and art.
DISRAELI.—*Lothair*, ch. 35.

It is much easier to be critical than correct. DISRAELI.—*Speech*, 1860.

Errors, like straws, upon the surface flow;
He who would search for pearls must dive below. DRYDEN.—*Prologue*.

Blame is safer than praise.
EMERSON.—*Compensation*.

One is led astray alike by sympathy and coldness, by praise and by blame.
GOETHE.—*Autob.*, Bk. 13.

The absence of humility in critics is something wonderful.
SIR A. HELPS.—*Friends in Council,
Bk. 2, ch. 2.*

'Tis hard to say if greater want of skill
Appear in writing or in judging ill.
POPE.—*Essay on Criticism*, 1.

Ten censure wrong for one who writes amiss. POPE.—*Ib.*, 6.

Let such teach others who themselves excel,
And censure freely who have written well.
POPE.—*Ib.*, 15.

Those oft are stratagems which errors seem,
Nor is it Homer nods, but we that dream.
POPE.—*Ib.*, 179.

In every work regard the writer's end,
Since none can compass more than they intend;
And if the means be just, the conduct true,
Applause, in spite of trivial faults, is due. POPE.—*Ib.*, 253.

Eye nature's walks, shoot folly as it flies,
And catch the manners living as they rise;
Laugh where we must, be candid where we can;
But vindicate the ways of God to man.
POPE.—*Essay on Man*.

The eye of a critic is often, like a micro-scope, made so very fine and nice that it discovers the atoms, grains, and minutest particles, without ever comprehending the whole, comparing the parts, or seeing all at once the harmony.
POPE.—*Thoughts on Various Subjects*.

I must have liberty
Withal, as large a charter as the winds,
To blow on whom I please.
SHAKESPEARE.—*As You Like It*, Act 2, 7.

A friendly eye would never see such faults.
SHAKESPEARE.—*Julius Cæsar*, Act 4, 3.

Shall quips, and sentences, and these paper bullets, awe a man from the career of his humour?
SHAKESPEARE.—*Much Ado*, Act 2, 3.

Do not put me to 't,
For I am nothing if not critical.
SHAKESPEARE.—*Othello*, Act 2, 1.

Embrace your reproaches: they are often glories in disguise.
G. B. SHAW.—*Annajanska* (1918), *Pref.*

No one minds what Jeffrey says. It is not more than a week ago that I heard him speak disrespectfully of the equator.
SYDNEY SMITH.—*Saying*.

Thou speakest always ill of me;
I speak always well of thee:
But spite of all our noise and pother,
The world believes nor one nor t'other.
STEELE.—*Guardian*, No. 16 (*March
30, 1713) (Tr. of French epigram*).

Of all the cants which are canted in this canting world, though the cant of hypocrisy may be the worst, the cant of criticism is the most tormenting.
STERNE.—*Tristram Shandy*.

When things are as pretty as that, criticism is out of season.
R. L. STEVENSON.—*Some portraits by
Raeburn.*

Yet malice never was his aim;
He lashed the vice, but spared the name.
No individual could resent,
Where thousands equally were meant.
SWIFT.—*On the death of Dr. Swift*.

The aim of criticism is to distinguish what is essential in the work of a writer.
A. SYMONS.—*Intro. to Coleridge's
Biographia Literaria.*

What we ask of him [the critic] is that he should find out for us more than we can find out for ourselves.
A. SYMONS.—*Ib.*

I paints and paints,
Hears no complaints,
And sells before I'm dry,
Till savage Ruskin
Sticks his tusk in,
And nobody will buy.
TOM TAYLOR (?).—*Punch, c.* 1850
(*Said to be in allusion to Ruskin's family
crest—a boar's head*).

To tame criticism it is said that one must die. But this is fallacious. Its insatiable tooth gnaws our memory even in the tomb.
VOLTAIRE.—*Les Trois Empereurs.*

But our invectives must despair success, For, next to praise, she values nothing less.
YOUNG.—*Love of Fame.*

Faithful are the wounds of a friend.
Proverbs xxvii, 6.

CRITICS

Critics,—appalled I venture on the name, Those cut-throat bandits on the paths of fame.
BURNS.—*3rd Epistle to R. Graham.*

Teasing with blame, excruciating with praise. BYRON.—*Beppo, st. 74.*

A man must serve his time to every trade
Save censure—critics all are ready made.
BYRON.—*English Bards, 63.*

Believe a woman or an epitaph, Or any other thing that's false, before You trust in critics, who themselves are sore. BYRON.—*Ib., 78.*

Dull, superstitious readers they deceive, Who pin their easy faith on critic's sleeve, And knowing nothing, everything believe.
CHURCHILL.—*Apology.*

No private grudge they need, no personal spite :
The *viva sectio* is its own delight !
All enmity, all envy they disclaim, Disinterested thieves of our good name :
Cool, sober, murderers of their neighbour's fame.
COLERIDGE.—*Biog. Literaria, c. 21.*

Too nicely Jonson knew the critic's part ; Nature in him was almost lost in Art.
COLLINS.—*To Sir T. Hanmer.*

Impartially speaking, the French are much better as critics than the English, as they are worse poets.
DRYDEN.—*Dedication of Æneid.*

Every critic in the town
Runs the minor poet down ;
Every critic—don't you know it ?—
Is himself a minor poet.
R. F. MURRAY.—*Poems* (1893).

It is interesting to note how most art-lovers and critics are town-bred and town-minded.
EDEN PHILLPOTTS.—*A Shadow Passes.*

Get your enemies to read your works in order to mend them ; for your friend is so much your second self that he will judge too like you.
POPE.—*Thoughts on Various Subjects.*

Little wits triumph over the errors of great geniuses, just as owls rejoice in an eclipse of the sun.   A. DE RIVAROL.

Never is anything more unjust than an ignorant man, who thinks nothing done properly unless he himself has done it.
TERENCE.—*Adelphi*, 1, 2.

If four play whist
And I look on,
They make blunders
And I make none.
D. W. THOMPSON.—*Sales Attici.*

There is more profit in a dozen verses by Homer or Virgil than in all the criticisms which have been written on those two great men. VOLTAIRE.—*Letters on the English.*

The world takes a poet as it finds him, and seats him above or below the salt. The world is as obstinate as a million mules, and will not turn its head on one side or another for all the shouting of the critical population that ever was shouted.   JOHN WILSON.—*Noctes.*

From such sad readers Heaven the muse protect !
Proud to find fault and raptured with defect.
J. WOLCOT.—*Ep. to Sylvanus Urban.*

CROSS

He that had no cross deserves no crown.
QUARLES.—*Esther.*

And on his brest a bloodie crosse he bore, The dear remembrance of his dying Lord.
SPENSER.—*Faerie Queene, Bk. 1, 2.*

The cross if rightly borne shall be
No burden, but support to thee.
J. G. WHITTIER.—*The Cross (tr. of Thomas Kempis).*

CROWNS

Every noble crown is, and on earth will forever be, a crown of thorns.
CARLYLE.—*Past and Present, Bk. 3, c. 8.*

O polished perturbation ! golden care !
SHAKESPEARE.—*Henry IV., Pt. 2, Act 4, 4.*

How sweet a thing it is to wear a crown, Within whose circuit is Elysium, And all that poets feign of bliss and joy.
SHAKESPEARE.—*Henry VI., Pt. 3, Act 1, 2*

CRUELTY

Of all beasts the man-beast is the worst ;
To others and himself the cruellest foe.
R. BAXTER.—*Hypocrisy.*

A horse misused upon the road
Calls to heaven for human blood
WM. BLAKE.—*Proverbs.*

I said, " You must have been most miserable
To be so cruel."
E. B. BROWNING.—*Aurora Leigh, Bk.* 3.

Whose most tender mercy is neglect.
CRABBE.—*Village, Bk.* 1.

Cowards are cruel, but the brave
Love mercy, and delight to save.
GAY.—*Fables, Pt.* 1, *No.* 1.

Man kills to obtain his food, kills to
clothe himself, kills to adorn himself, kills
to defend himself, kills to attack, kills to
instruct himself, kills to amuse himself,
kills for the sake of killing.
JOSEPH DE MAISTRE (1753–1821).—*Soirées
de Saint Pétersbourg.*

Cruel as death and hungry as the grave.
THOMSON.—*Seasons, Winter,* 393.

CUCKOO

O blithe new comer ! I have heard,
I hear thee and rejoice.
O Cuckoo ! Shall I call thee bird,
Or but a wandering voice ?
WORDSWORTH.—*To the Cuckoo.*

The cuckoo's a bonny bird ; he sings as
he flies ;
He brings us good things, he tells us nae
lies ;
He drinks the cold water to keep his voice
clear,
And he'll come again in the spring o' the
year.   *Old Scottish rhyme.*

CULTURE

Culture is the passion for sweetness
and light, and (what is more) the passion
for making them prevail. M. ARNOLD.—
Literature and Dogma, Pref.

The more of kindly strength is in the soil,
So much doth evil seed and lack of culture
Mar it the more, and make it run to wild-
ness.   DANTE.—" *Purgatory* "
(*Cary's tr.*), *c.* 30, 119.

The great law of culture is : Let each
become all that he was created capable of
being.   CARLYLE.—*Richter.*

Child of Nature, learn to unlearn.
DISRAELI.—*Contarini Fleming, c.* 1.

If there be one whose wisdom crowned
The unerring paths of Truth has found,
'Tis his, with heart uplift to Heaven,
To improve the gift its grace has given.
PINDAR.—*Pythian Odes,* 3, 182 (*Moore tr.*).

The play, I remember, pleased not the
million. 'Twas caviare to the general.
SHAKESPEARE.—*Hamlet,* Act 2, 2.

The two noblest of things, which are
sweetness and light.
SWIFT.—*Battle of the Books.*

A Society that sets up to be polite, and
ignores Arts and Letters, I hold to be a
Snobbish Society.
THACKERAY.—*Book of Snobs.*

CUNNING

The brave, impetuous heart yields every-
where
To the subtle, contriving head.
M. ARNOLD.—*Empedocles.*

Nothing doth more hurt in a state than
that cunning men pass for wise.
BACON.—*Of Cunning.*

How like a hateful ape,
Detected, grinning, 'midst his pilfered
hoard,
A cunning man appears, whose secret
frauds
Are opened to the day !
JOANNA BAILLIE.—*Basil,* Act 5, 3.

The weak in courage is strong in cunning.
WM. BLAKE.—*Proverbs of Hell.*

And still the less they understand,
The more they admire his sleight of hand.
BUTLER.—*Hudibras, Pt.* 2.

Nick Machiavel had ne'er a trick
(Though he gave his name to our old
Nick).   BUTLER.—*Ib., Pt.* 3, *c.* 1.

A sly old fish, too cunning for the hook.
CRABBE.—*Parish Register.*

Bless yo' soul, honey, Brer Rabbit
mought er bin kinder fibble [feeble] in
de legs, but he wa'n't no ways cripple
und' de hat.   J. C. HARRIS.—*Nights
with Uncle Remus, ch.* 35.

Which I wish to remark,
And my language is plain,
That for ways that are dark,
And for tricks that are vain,
The Heathen Chinee is peculiar.
BRET HARTE.—*Plain Language.*

It is to have made great progress in
cunning when you have made people
think that you are only moderately
cunning. LA BRUYÈRE.—*De la Cour,* 85.

Cunning is only a poor kind of skill.
LA ROCHEFOUCAULD.—*Maxim* 608.

The foxes find themselves at the furrier's at last.   *French prov.*

Air day or late day, the fox's hide finds aye the flaying knife.
Scottish prov. (Scott's " Rob Roy ").

CURATES

A curate—there is something which excites compassion in the very name of a Curate !
SYDNEY SMITH.—*Persecuting Bishops.*

The curate ; he was fatter than his cure.
TENNYSON.—*Edwin Morris.*

CURIOSITY

Much curiousness is a perpetual wooing,
Nothing with labour, folly long a-doing.
HERBERT.—*Church Porch.*

Curiosity is only vanity. Most often we only wish to know in order to talk about it.   PASCAL.—*Pensées.*

Born in an age more curious than devout.
YOUNG.—*Night Thoughts, 9.*

Be not curious in unnecessary matters.
Ecclesiasticus iii, 23.

Lift me up and I'll tell you more.
Lay me down as I was before.
Scottish rhyme. The first line is inscribed on the upper part of a big stone ; the second on its underside.

CURSES

Those which have not sufficiently learned out of Solomon that " the causeless curse shall not come."
BACON.—*Adv. of Learning.*

Never was heard such a terrible curse ;
But what gave rise to no little surprise,
Nobody seemed one penny the worse !
R. H. BARHAM.—*Jackdaw of Rheims.*

The bad man's charity (cursing).
BEAUMONT AND FLETCHER.—*Spanish Curate.*

There's a great text in Galatians,
Once you trip on it, entails
Twenty-nine distinct damnations,
One sure, if another fails.
BROWNING.—*Soliloquy.*

Curse and be cursed ! It is the fruit of cursing.
JOHN FLETCHER.—*Valentinian.*

Curses, not loud but deep.
SHAKESPEARE.—*Macbeth,* Act 5, 3.

I called thee to curse mine enemies, and, behold, thou hast altogether blessed them these three times.
Numbers xxiv, 10.

Curses are like processions ; they return whence they started.   *Italian prov.*

CUSTOM

What custom hath endeared
We part with sadly, though we prize it not.
JOANNA BAILLIE.—*Basil,* Act 1.

Custom reconciles us to everything.
BURKE.—*Vindication of Natural Society.*

As custom arbitrates, whose shifting sway
Our life and manners must alike obey.
BYRON.—*Hints from Horace.*

Custom's idiot sway.
COWPER.—*Retirement, 49.*

Such dupes are men to custom, and so prone
To reverence what is ancient, and can plead
A course of long observance for its use.
COWPER.—*Winter Morning Walk.*

Custom, that is before all law; Nature, that is above all art.
S. DANIEL.—*Defence of Rhyme.*

Custom, that unwritten law,
By which the people keep even kings in awe.
SIR W. D'AVENANT.—*Circe,* Act 2.

Custom then is the great guide of human life.   HUME.—*Human Understanding.*

Custom . . . is not only, as the proverb says, a second nature, but is continually mistaken for the first.
J. S. MILL.—*Liberty, Introd.*

The despotism of custom is everywhere the standing hindrance to human advancement.   J. S. MILL.—*Ib., ch.* 3.

Custom is not a small thing.
PLATO (*cited by Montaigne, Essays, Bk. 1, 23*).

Custom, the world's great idol, we adore.
J. POMFRET.—*Reason, 99.*

Take the course opposite to custom and you will almost always do well.
ROUSSEAU.—*Emile.*

But, to my mind, though I am native here,
And to the manner born, it is a custom
More honoured in the breach than in th' observance.
SHAKESPEARE.—*Hamlet,* Act 1, 4.

That monster, custom, who all sense
    doth eat.   SHAKESPEARE.—*Hamlet*,
                        Act 3, 4.

All his successors, gone before him, have
done't ; and all his ancestors that come
after him, may.
    SHAKESPEARE.—*Merry Wives*, Act 1, 1.

How use doth breed a habit in a man !
    SHAKESPEARE.—*Two Gentlemen of
                    Verona*, Act 5, 4.

CYCLES

In all things there is a kind of law of
cycles.   TACITUS.—*Annals, Bk.* 2.

CYCLISTS

I [Lady Brandon] think the most
ridiculous sight in the world is a man
on a bicycle, working away with his feet as
hard as he possibly can, and believing that
his horse is carrying him, instead of,
as any one can see, he carrying his horse.
G. B. SHAW.—*Unsocial Socialist, c.* 11.

CYNICISM

I do distrust the poet who discerns
No character or glory in his times.
E. B. BROWNING.—*Aurora Leigh*, Bk. 5.

And I must say I ne'er could see the very
Great happiness of the " Nil admirari."
    BYRON.—*Don Juan*, 5, 100.

Life is too short to waste
In critic peep or cynic bark,
Quarrel or reprimand :
'Twill soon be dark.
    EMERSON.—*To J. W.*

I've an irritating chuckle, I've a celebrated
    sneer,
I've an entertaining snigger, I've a fas-
    cinating leer.
    SIR W. S. GILBERT.—*Princess Ida*.

I was born sneering, but I struggle hard
to overcome this defect.
    SIR W. S. GILBERT.—*Mikado*.

Cynicism is intellectual dandyism.
    GEO. MEREDITH.—*Egoist, c.* 7.

Nothing's new and nothing's true and
nothing matters.
Attributed to SYDNEY (LADY) MORGAN,
                        *novelist.**

The reason we controvert maxims
which discover the human heart is that
we are afraid of being discovered ourselves.
    LA ROCHEFOUCAULD.—*Maxim* 603.

---

* " Ah," said my languid gentleman at Oxford, " there's nothing new or true—and no
matter."—EMERSON, *Representative Men. Montaigne* (1849).

I love to cope him in these sullen fits,
For then he's full of matter.
SHAKESPEARE.—*As You Like It*, Act 2, 1.

Seldom he smiles, and smiles in such a sort
As if he mocked himself, and scorned his
        spirit,
That could be moved to smile at anything.
    SHAKESPEARE.—*Julius Cæsar*, Act 1, 2.

What is the use of straining after an
amiable view of things, Marian, when a
cynical view is most likely to be the true
one ?   G. B. SHAW.—*Irrational Knot, c.* 3.

I hate cynicism a great deal worse than
I do the devil ; unless, perhaps, the two
were the same thing.
        R. L. STEVENSON.—*W. Whitman*.

Cecil Graham : What is a cynic ?
Lord Darlington : A man who knows the
price of everything and the value of
nothing.
    OSCAR WILDE.—*Lady Windermere's Fan*.

D

DAISIES

Myriads of daisies have shone forth in
        flower,
Near the lark's nest, and in their natural
        hour
Have passed away; less happy than the one
That, by the unwilling ploughshare,
        died to prove
The tender charm of poetry and love.
    WORDSWORTH.—*Poems during a
            Summer Tour*, 1833, *No.* 37

Thou art indeed by many a claim
    The poet's darling.
    WORDSWORTH.—*To the Daisy*.

DALLIANCE

To sport with Amaryllis in the shade,
Or with the tangles of Neæra's hair.
        MILTON.—*Lycidas*, 68.

The primrose path of dalliance.
    SHAKESPEARE.—*Hamlet*, Act 1, 3

DANCING

On with the dance; let joy be unconfined ;
No sleep till morn, when Youth and
        Pleasure meet
To chase the glowing hours with flying
        feet.
    BYRON.—*Childe Harold, c.* 3, *st.* 22.

Muse of the many twinkling feet, whose
        charms
Are now extended up from legs to arms.
        BYRON.—*The Waltz*.

How inimitably graceful children are
before they learn to dance !
COLERIDGE.—*Table Talk.*

Dancing, the child of Music and of Love.
SIR JOHN DAVIES.—*Orchestra.*

The poetry of the foot.
DRYDEN.—*Rival Ladies.*

The greater the fool the better the
dancer.   THEODORE HOOK.—*Maxim.*

Come, and trip it as you go,
On the light fantastic toe.
MILTON.—*L'Allegro,* 31.

When you do dance, I wish you
A wave i' the sea, that you might ever do
Nothing but that.
SHAKESPEARE.—*Winter's Tale,* Act 4, 3.

DANGER

There may be danger in the deed,
But there is honour too.
W. E. AYTOUN.—*Island of the Scots.*

If the danger seems slight, then it is not
slight.
BACON.—*Instauratio,* Pt. 1, Bk. 6, 43.

Tiger, tiger, burning bright
In the forests of the night.
WM. BLAKE.—*The Tiger.*

Dangers by being despised grow great.
BURKE.—*Speech,* 1792.

Or whispering, with white lips—" The
foe !
They come ! They come ! "
BYRON.—*Childe Harold,* c. 3, st. 25.

For danger levels man and brute,
And all are fellows in their need.
BYRON.—*Mazeppa,* 3.

Danger, the spur of all great minds.
CHAPMAN.—*Bussy d'Ambois.*

The absent danger greater still appears ;
Less fears he who is near the thing he fears.
S. DANIEL.—*Cleopatra,* Act 4, 1.

This danger that all of us foresee so
clearly will not happen. Nothing does
that we foresee.
SIR A. HELPS.—*Friends in Council,
Slavery, c. 5.*

In worst extremes, and on the perilous
edge
Of battle.
MILTON.—*Paradise Lost,* Bk. 1, 276.

But boundless risk must pay for boundless
gain.
W. MORRIS.—*Earthly Paradise,
Wanderers,* 1581.

Should you find yourself strike upon the
rock of danger, cast obstinacy overboard
and call wisdom to the helm.
FRANCIS OSBORNE.—*Advice to a Son*
(1656).

Danger is never overcome without
danger.   PUBLILIUS SYRUS.

Thy mirth refrain,
Thy hand is on a lion's mane.
SCOTT.—*Lady of the Lake,* 2, 12.

Something is rotten in the state of
Denmark.
SHAKESPEARE.—*Hamlet,* Act 1, 4.

Sir, though I am not splenetive and rash,
Yet have I in me something dangerous.
SHAKESPEARE.—*Ib.,* Act 5, 1.

Out of this nettle, danger, we pluck
this flower, safety.
SHAKESPEARE.—*Henry IV.,* Pt. 1,
Act 2, 3.

By a divine instinct men's minds mistrust
Ensuing danger.
SHAKESPEARE.—*Richard III.,* Act 2, 3.

Danger deviseth shifts ; wit waits on
fear. SHAKESPEARE.—*Venus and Adonis.*

Cannon to right of them,
Cannon to left of them,
Cannon in front of them,
Volleyed and thundered.
TENNYSON.—*Charge of Light Brigade.*

Into the jaws of Death,
Into the mouth of Hell.
TENNYSON.—*Ib.*

Now when our land to ruin's brink is
verging,
In God's name, let us speak while there
is time !
Now, when the padlocks for our lips are
forging,
Silence is crime.
J. G. WHITTIER.—*Lines on the
adoption of Pinckney's Resolutions.*

He that has a head of wax must not
walk in the sun.   *Prov. (Geo. Herbert).*

DARING

And darest thou then
To beard the lion in his den,
The Douglas in his hall ?
SCOTT.—*Marmion,* c. 6, st. 14.

DARKNESS

Yet from those flames
No light ; but rather darkness visible.
MILTON.—*Paradise Lost,* Bk. 1, 62.

O dark, dark, dark, amid the blaze of
    noon,
* Irrecoverably dark, total eclipse,
    Without all hope of day !
        MILTON.—*Samson Agonistes,* 80.

And all around was darkness like a wall.
        W. MORRIS.—*Jason, Bk.* 7, 157.

Darkness there, and nothing more.
        E. A. POE.—*Raven, st.* 4.

    There's husbandry in heaven ;
    Their candles are all out.
        SHAKESPEARE.—*Macbeth,* Act 2, 1.

With hue like that when some great
    painter dips
His pencil in the gloom of earthquake
    and eclipse.
        SHELLEY.—*Islam, c.* 5, 23.

DATES

    "W'en you come to ax me 'bout de
year en day er de mont'," said the old man
[Uncle Remus] . . . " den I'm done,
kase the almanick w'at dey got in dem
times won't pass muster deze days."
        J. C. HARRIS.—*Nights with Uncle
                Remus, c.* 13.

DAUGHTERS

    Marry thy daughters in time lest they
marry themselves.
        WM. CECIL (LORD BURGHLEY).—
                Precepts to his Son.

It was a lording's daughter, the fairest
    one of three.
        Attrib. to SHAKESPEARE.—*Passionate
                Pilgrim, No.* 14.

I am all the daughters of my father's
    house,
And all the brothers too.
SHAKESPEARE.—*Twelfth Night,* Act 2, 4.

Mother, a maiden is a tender thing,
And best by her that bore her understood.
        TENNYSON.—*Marriage of Geraint,* 509.

DAYS

The great, th' important day, big with
    the fate
Of Cato and of Rome.
        ADDISON.—*Cato,* Act 1.

    The days are ever divine—as to the
first Aryans. . . . They come and go like
muffled and veiled figures, sent from a
distant friendly party, but they say
nothing, and if we do not use the gifts
they bring they carry them as silently
away.   EMERSON.—*Works and Days.*

Write it on your heart that every day
is the best day in the year. No man
has learned anything rightly until he
knows that every day is Doomsday.
        EMERSON.—*Works and Days.*

There's a feast undated yet :
    Both our true lives hold it fast—
The first day we ever met,
    What a great day came and passed !
Unknown then, but known at last.
        ALICE MEYNELL.—*An Unmarked
                        Festival.*

Every day is the pupil of the day before.
        PUBLILIUS SYRUS.

The spirit walks of every day deceased,
And smiles an angel, or a fury frowns.
        YOUNG.—*Night Thoughts,* 2.

What then is man ?   The smallest part of
    nothing.
Day buries day, month month, and year
    the year.
        YOUNG.—*Revenge,* Act 4, 1.

    Monday for wealth,
    Tuesday for health,
Wednesday the best day of all ;
    Thursday for crosses,
    Friday for losses,
Saturday, no luck at all.
    " *Days Lucky or Unlucky* " (*for
        Marriage*), *Brand's Antiquities.*

DEAD, THE

And through thee I believe
In the noble and great who are gone ;
Pure souls honoured and blest.
        M. ARNOLD.—*Rugby Chapel.*

They shall not grow old, as we that are
    left grow old ;
Age shall not weary them, nor the years
    condemn.
At the going down of the sun, and in the
    morning,
We will remember them.
        LAURENCE BINYON.—*For the Fallen,
                Sept.,* 1915.

But never be a tear-drop shed
    For them, the pure enfranchised dead.
MARY E. BROOKS.—*Weep not for the Dead.*

        All that tread
The globe, are but a handful to the tribes
That slumber in its bosom.
        W. C. BRYANT.—*Thanatopsis,* 48.

    The shroud is forgiveness' token,
        And death makes saints of all.
W. CARLETON.—*Festival of Memory,* 3, 15.

    Is he then dead ?
What, dead at last ? quite, quite, for
    ever dead !
        CONGREVE.—*Mourning Bride,* Act 5, 3.

---

* " Irrecoverably " in all printed editions.
" Irrevocably " may possibly have been the word
actually dictated by Milton.

I should ill requite thee to constrain
Thy unbound spirit into bonds again.
    COWPER.—*On Receipt of his Mother's
                           Picture, 86.*

Hail and farewell ; the laurels with the
    dust
Are levelled, but thou hast thy surer crown,
Peace, and immortal calm, the victory
    won.
Somewhere serene thy watchful power
    inspires ;
Thou art a living purpose, being dead,
A fruit of nobleness in lesser lives,
A guardian and a guide ; Hail and fare-
    well !
    J. G. FAIRFAX.—*On Sir Stanley
                    Maude, 1917.*

For some we loved, the loveliest and the
    best
That from his Vintage rolling Time hath
    prest,
Have drunk their Cup a Round or two
    before,
And one by one crept silently to rest.
    E. FITZGERALD.—*Rubáiyát, st.* 22.

Strange, is it not ? that of the myriads who
Before us passed the door of Darkness
    through,
Not one returns to tell us of the Road,
Which to discover we must travel too.
    E. FITZGERALD.—*Ib., st.* 64.

Their tears, their little triumphs o'er,
Their human passions now no more.
    GRAY.—*Ode for Music,* 48.

Yet saw he something in the lives
Of those who ceased to live
That rounded them with majesty,
Which living failed to give.
    T. HARDY.—*Casterbridge Captains.*

Go, stranger ! track the deep,
Free, free the white sail spread !
Wave may not foam nor wild wind sweep
Where rest not England's dead.
    MRS. HEMANS.—*England's Dead.*

Gone before
To that unknown and silent shore.
    LAMB.—*Hester.*

I think of the friends who are dead, who
    were dear long ago in the past,
Beautiful friends who are dead, though
    I know that death cannot last ;
Friends with the beautiful eyes that the
    dust has defiled,
Beautiful souls who were gentle when I
    was a child.
    JOHN MASEFIELD.—*Twilight.*

There is something—something—
Something which gives me
Loathing, terror,

To leave the dead
So alone, so wretched.
    JOHN MASEFIELD.—*From the Spanish
        of Don Gustavo A. Becquèr.*

They whose course on earth is o'er
Think they on their brethren more ?
    J. M. NEALE.—*All Souls.*

When the dust of the workshop is still,
The dust of the workman at rest,
May some generous heart find a will
To seek and to treasure his best.
    EDEN PHILLPOTTS.

That law of Solon's is justly to be com-
    mended, which forbids man to speak ill
of the dead.   PLUTARCH.—*Solon.*

There is no music more for him,
    His lights are out, his feast is done :
His bowl that sparkled at the brim
    Is drained, is broken, cannot hold.
    CHRISTINA ROSSETTI.—*Peal of Bells.*

Our respect for the dead, when they are
just dead, is something wonderful, and the
way we show it more wonderful still.
    RUSKIN.—*Political Economy of Art,
                      Lecture* 2.

Imperial Cæsar, dead, and turned to clay,
Might stop a hole to keep the wind away.
    SHAKESPEARE.—*Hamlet,* Act 5, 1.

He has outsoared the shadow of our night,
Envy and calumny and hate and pain,
And that unrest which men miscall
    delight,
Can touch him not, and torture not again ;
From the contagion of the world's slow
    stain
He is secure, and now can never mourn
A heart grown cold, a head grown grey
    in vain.
    SHELLEY.—*Adonais, st.* 40.

Not a kindlier life or sweeter
    Time, that lights and quenches men,
Now may quench or light again.
    SWINBURNE.—*Epicede.*

For if, beyond the shadow and the sleep
    A place there be for souls without a
        stain,
Where peace is perfect, and delight more
      deep
Than seas or skies that change and
      shine again,
There none of all unsullied souls that live
    May hold a surer station : none may
      lend
More light to hope's or memory's lamp,
      nor give
More joy than thine to those who
      called thee friend.
    SWINBURNE.—*In Memory of J. W.
                        Inchbold.*

Time takes them home that we loved,
    fair names and famous,
To the soft long sleep, to the broad
    sweet bosom of death ;
But the flower of their souls he shall not
    take away to shame us,
Nor the lips lack song for ever that now
    lack breath.
    SWINBURNE.—*In Memory of Barry*
                 Cornwall, st. 6.

But O for the touch of a vanished hand,
And the sound of a voice that is still !
    TENNYSON.—*Break, Break.*

We have lost him ; he is gone :
We know him now : all narrow jealousies
Are silent ; and we see him as he moved.
    TENNYSON.—*Idylls, Dedication.*

But trust that those we call the dead
Are breathers of an ampler day
For ever nobler ends.
    TENNYSON.—*In Memoriam, c.* 118.

Speak no more of his renown,
Lay your earthly fancies down,
And in the vast cathedral leave him,
God accept him, Christ receive him.
    TENNYSON.—*On Wellington.*

Ne'er to these chambers, where the mighty
    rest,
Since their foundation, came a nobler
    guest,
Nor e'er was to the bowers of bliss con-
    veyed
A fairer spirit, or more welcome shade.
    T. TICKELL.—*On Addison.*

They are all gone into the world of light,
And I alone sit lingering here ;
Their very memory is fair and bright,
And my sad thoughts doth cheer.
    H. VAUGHAN.—*Departed Friends.*

Lightly they'll talk of the spirit that's
    gone,
And o'er his cold ashes upbraid him—
But little he'll reck if they let him sleep on
In the grave where a Briton has laid
    him.
    WOLFE.—*Burial of Sir J. Moore.*

They whom death has hidden from our
    sight
Are worthiest of the mind's regard.
    WORDSWORTH.—*Excursion, Bk.* 5.

How fast has brother followed brother
From sunshine to the sunless land !
    WORDSWORTH.—*On the death of*
              James Hogg.

Dead men open the eyes of the living.
    Spanish prov.

DEAD, ATTACKS ON THE

Vile is the vengeance on the ashes cold ;
And envy base to barke at sleeping fame.
    SPENSER.—*Faerie Queene, Bk.* 2, *c.* 8.

DEAD, THE DISTINGUISHED

All these were honoured in their generations, and were the glory of their times.
    Ecclesiasticus xliv, 7.

DEAD, TRIBUTES TO THE

Be kind to my remains : and O defend,
Against your judgment, your departed
    friend ! DRYDEN.—*To Congreve,* 73.

Green be the turf above thee,
    Friend of my better days ;
None knew thee but to love thee,
    Nor named thee but to praise.
    F. HALLECK.—*On the death of J. R.*
                      Drake.

Yet once more, O ye laurels, and once
    more,
Ye myrtles brown, with ivy never sere,
I come to pluck your berries harsh and
    crude,
And with forced fingers rude,
Shatter your leaves before the mellowing
    year. MILTON.—*Lycidas,* 1.

DEADNESS

And ships were drifting with the dead
To shores where all was dumb !
    CAMPBELL.—*The Last Man.*

DEANS

A canon ! That's a place too mean :
No, doctor, you shall be a dean ;
Two dozen canons round your stall,
And you the tyrant of them all.
    SWIFT.—*Horace, Bk.* 1, *Ep.* 7.

DEATH

Stern law of every mortal lot !
Which man, proud man, finds hard to
    bear,
And builds himself I know not what
Of second life, I know not where.
    M. ARNOLD.—*Geist's Grave.*

And truly he who here
Hath run his bright career,
And served men nobly and acceptance
    found,
And borne to light and right his witness
    high,
What could he better wish than then
    to die,
And wait the issue, sleeping underground ?
    M. ARNOLD.—*Westminster Abbey.*

I have often thought upon death and
I find it the least of all evils.
    BACON.—*Essay on Death, Sec.* 1

Above all, believe it, the sweetest
canticle is " Nunc Dimittis," when a
man hath attained worthy ends and expectations. BACON.—*Ib.*

It is as natural to die as to be born.
BACON.—*Essay on Death, Sec.* 1.

Death . . . openeth the gate to good
fame and extinguisheth envy.
BACON.—*Ib.*

Men fear death as children fear to go in
the dark.   BACON.—*Ib.*

Endless parting
With all we can call ours, with all our
    sweetness,
With youth, strength, pleasure, people,
    time, nay reason !
For in the silent grave, no conversation,
No joyful tread of friends, no voice of
    lovers,
No careful father's counsels, nothing's
    heard,
For nothing is, but all oblivion.
BEAUMONT AND FLETCHER.—*Thierry
        and Theodoret, Act* 4, 1.

Why be heavy of heart, my brother ;
    Why be weary or weep ?
For death ends all things, one with another,
And death is a dreamless sleep.
E. F. M. BENEKE.—*Cross beneath
        the Ring.*

The Angel of Death has been abroad
throughout the land ; you may almost
hear the beating of his wings.
JOHN BRIGHT.—*Speech, Feb.,* 1855.

We shall start up, at last awake
From Life, that insane dream we take
For waking now, because it seems.
BROWNING.—*Easter Day Eve, c.* 17.

Strict and close are the ties that bind
In death the children of human kind,
Yea, stricter and closer than those of
life.
W. C. BRYANT.—*Two Graves,* 2.

The finest sight beneath the sky
Is to see how bravely a MAN can die.
R. BUCHANAN.—*O'Murtagh.*

He hath got beyond the gunshot of
his enemies.
BUNYAN.—*Pilgrim's Progress, Pt.* 1.

O Death ! the poor man's dearest friend,
The kindest and the best.
BURNS.—*Man was made to mourn.*

The silence of that dreamless sleep
I envy now too much to weep.
BYRON.—*And thou art Dead.*

Thus lived—thus died she ; never more on
    her
Shall sorrow light, or shame.
BYRON.—*Don Juan,* 4, 71.

He died as erring man should die,
Without display, without parade ;
Meekly had he bowed and prayed,
As not disdaining priestly aid,
Nor desperate of all hope on high.
BYRON.—*Parisina, st.* 17.

Oh, God ! it is a fearful thing
To see the human soul take wing
In any shape, in any mood.
BYRON.—*Prisoner of Chillon.*

O Death ! if there be quiet in thy arms,
    And I must cease—gently, O, gently
        come
To me ! and let my soul learn no alarms,
    But strike me, ere a shriek can echo,
        dumb,
Senseless, and breathless.
CAMPBELL.—*Lines in Sickness.*

Never weather-beaten sail more willing
    bent to shore ;
Never tired pilgrim's limbs affected
    slumber more.
CAMPION.—*Never Weather-beaten Sail.*

Time for him had merged itself into
eternity ; he was, as we say, no more.
CARLYLE.—*Characteristics.*

The crash of the whole solar and stellar
systems could only kill you once.
CARLYLE.—*Letter,* 1831.

There is a remedy for everything
excepting death.   CERVANTES (*Prov.*).

Then is it best, as for a worthy fame,
To dyen when a man is best of name.
CHAUCER.—*Knight's Tale, v.* 3057.

I depart from life as from an inn, and
not as from my home.
CICERO.—*De Senectute.*

We ought to assemble and lament at
the house where one has been born, having
regard to the varied woes of human life ;
but when one has by death finished his
weary labours, him should all his friends
follow to the grave with honour and rejoicing.
CICERO (*tr. of Euripides*). *Tusc. Quæst.,
        Bk.* 1, 48.

O what a wonder seems the fear of death,
Seeing how gladly we all sink to sleep !
COLERIDGE.—*Monody on the
        Death of Chatterton.*

The debt which cancels all others.
C. C. COLTON.—*Vol.* 2, *No.* 49.

Two hands upon the breast,
    And labour's done ;
Two pale feet crossed in rest,
    The race is won.
D. M. CRAIK.—*On the Russian prov.
"Two hands upon the breast and labour
                    is past."*

And, when life's sweet fable ends,
Soul and body part like friends :—
No quarrels, murmurs, no delay ;
A kiss, a sigh, and so away.
    R. CRASHAW.—*Praise of Lessius.*

So gentle was her death, so blest,
    Under the covering cross,
That even those who loved her best
    Could scarcely mourn their loss.
[SIR F. H. DOYLE.—*Lady Agnes, st.* 62.

Welcome, Death !
Thou best of thieves ! who, with an easy
    key,
Dost open life, and unperceived by us
Even steal us from ourselves !
    DRYDEN.—*All for Love,* Act 5, 1.

He was exhaled ; his great Creator drew
His spirit, as the sun the morning dew.
    DRYDEN.—*Elegy.*

So soon was she exhaled, and vanished
    hence ;
As a sweet odour of a vast expense,
She vanished, we can scarcely say she
    died.   DRYDEN.—*Eleonora.*

A little trust that when we die
We reap our sowing, and so—Good-bye.
    G. DU MAURIER.—*Trilby.*

Now the labourer's task is o'er ;
    Now the battle day is past ;
Now upon the farther shore
    Stands the voyager at last.
    E. ELLERTON.—*Hymn.*

That silent organ loudest chants
    The master's requiem.
    EMERSON.—*Dirge.*

To die is landing on some silent shore,
Where billows never break nor tempests
    roar ;
Ere well we feel the friendly stroke, 'tis
    o'er. S. GARTH.—*Dispensary,* 3, 225.

Death rides on every passing breeze,
    He lurks in every flower ;
Each season has its own disease,
    Its peril every hour.
    BISHOP HEBER.—*At a Funeral.*

Thou art gone to the grave, but we will
    not deplore thee,
    Though sorrows and darkness encom-
    pass the tomb.
    BISHOP HEBER.—*Ib.*

Leaves have their time to fall,
And flowers to wither at the north wind's
    breath,
And stars to set—but all,
Thou hast *all* seasons for thine own, O
Death ! MRS. HEMANS.—*Hour of Death.*

Our light is flown,
Our beautiful, that seemed too much our
    own,
Ever to die.
    MRS. HEMANS.—*Two Voices.*

We watched her breathing through the
    night,
    Her breathing soft and low,
As in her breast the wave of life
    Kept heaving to and fro.
    HOOD.—*Death-Bed.*

Our very hopes belied our fears,
    Our fears our hopes belied,
We thought her dying when she slept,
    And sleeping when she died.
    HOOD.—*Ib.*

Past all dishonour,
Death has left on her
Only the beautiful.
    HOOD.—*Bridge of Sighs.*

'Tis horrible to die
And come down with our little all of dust,
That Dun of all the duns to satisfy.
    HOOD.—*Bianca's Dream.*

No one can obtain from the pope a
dispensation for never dying.
    THOS. KEMPIS.

We hurry to the river we must cross,
    And swifter downward every footstep
    wends ;
Happy who reach it ere they count the
    loss
Of half their faculties and half their
    friends.
    W. S. LANDOR.—*Ode to Southey* (1833).

And, as she looked around, she saw how
    Death, the consoler,
Laying his hand upon many a heart, had
    healed it for ever.
    LONGFELLOW.—*Evangeline, Pt.* 2, *c.* 5.

There is a reaper, whose name is Death.
    LONGFELLOW.—*The Reaper.*

There is no death ! What seems so is
    transition.
This life of mortal breath
Is but a suburb of the life Elysian,
    Whose portal we call Death.
    LONGFELLOW.—*Resignation.*

The gods conceal from those who are
to live how happy a thing it is to die,
so that they may continue to live.
    LUCANUS.—*Pharsalia,* 4, 519.

And Life is all the sweeter that he lived,
And all he loved more sacred for his sake ;
And Death is all the brighter that he died,
And Heaven is all the happier that he's
    there.
    G. MASSEY.—*On Earl Brownlow.*

There are so many ways to let out life.
MASSINGER.—*Duke of Milan*, Act 1, 3.

Death hath a thousand doors to let out
   life;
I shall find one.
MASSINGER.—*Very Woman*, Act 5, 4.

Fortune and Hope farewell! I've found
   the port:
You've done with me; go now with others
   sport.
J. H. MERIVALE.—*Tr. of Greek.*

Comes the blind Fury with the abhorrèd
   shears,
And slits the thin-spun life.
MILTON.—*Lycidas, l.* 64.

Death, who sets all free,
Hath paid his ransom now, and full dis-
   charge.
MILTON.—*Samson Agonistes, l.* 1,572.

Hell trembled at the hideous name, and
   sighed
From all her caves, and back resounded
   Death.
MILTON.—*Paradise Lost, Bk.* **2,** 788.

Death
Grinned horrible a ghastly smile, to
   hear
His famine should be filled.
MILTON.—*Ib., Bk.* **2,** 845.

And over them triumphant Death his dart
Shook, but delayed to strike, though oft
   invoked
With vows, as their chief good and final
   hope. MILTON.—*Ib., Bk.* 11, 491.

A deathlike sleep,
A gentle wafting to immortal life.
MILTON.—*Ib., Bk.* 12, 434.

When faith and love, which parted from
   thee never,
Had ripened thy just soul to dwell
   with God,
Meekly thou didst resign this earthly
   load
Of death, called life; which us from death
   doth sever. MILTON.—*Sonnet.*

Boys, are ye calling a toast to-night?
   (Hear what the sea-wind saith)
Fill for a bumper strong and bright,
   And here's to Admiral Death!
He's sailed in a hundred builds o' boat,
He's fought in a thousand kinds o' coat,
He's the senior flag of all that float,
   And his name's Admiral Death!
SIR H. NEWBOLT.—*Admiral Death.*

Life's race well run,
Life's work well done,
Life's victory won,
   Now cometh rest.
E. H. PARKER.—*Pres. Garfield.*

No one knows but that death is the
greatest of all goods to man; but men
fear it, as if they well knew that it is the
greatest of evils.
PLATO.—*Apol. of Socrates*, 17 (*Cary tr.*).

"In reality then," he [Socrates] continued, "those who pursue philosophy
rightly, study to die; and to them of
all men death is least formidable."
PLATO.—*Phœdo*, 33 (*Cary tr.*).

Death sets us free even from the greatest
evils. PLUTARCH.—*Cons. to Apollonius.*

No man is certain whether death be not
the greatest good that can befal a man.
PLUTARCH.—*Ib.*

Tell me, my soul, can this be death?
POPE.—*Dying Christian.*

A heap of dust alone remains of thee;
'Tis all thou art and all the proud shall be.
POPE.—*Elegy.*

The hour concealed, and so remote the
   fear,
Death still draws nearer, never seeming
   near. POPE.—*Essay on Man*, 3, 76.

Death aims with fouler spite
At fairer marks.
QUARLES.—*Divine Poems*

O eloquent, just, and mighty Death!
Whom none could advise, thou hast persuaded; what none hath dared thou hast
done . . . Thou hast drawn together all
the far-stretched greatness, all the pride,
cruelty, and ambition of man; and covered
it all over with these two narrow words:
Hic jacet.
SIR W. RALEGH.—*Hist. of World.*

He is now at rest;
And praise and blame fall on his ear alike.
ROGERS.—*On Byron.*

Sleep that no pain shall wake,
Night that no morn can break,
Till joy shall overtake
   Her perfect peace.
CHRISTINA ROSSETTI.—*Dream Land.*

O fading honours of the dead!
O high ambition, lowly laid!
SCOTT.—*Lay of the Last Minstrel, c.* **2,** 10.

And come he slow or come he fast,
It is but Death who comes at last.
SCOTT.—*Marmion, c.* **2,** 30.

Death had he seen by sudden blow,
By wasting plague, by tortures slow,
By mine or breach, by steel or ball,
Knew all his shapes and scorned them all.
SCOTT.—*Rokeby, c.* 1, 8.

The pomp of death alarms us more than death itself.

> SENECA (*according to Francis Bacon. The actual passage in Seneca is, " It is folly to die of the fear of death," Ep.*69).

Thou hast finished joy and moan.

> SHAKESPEARE.—*Cymbeline*, Act 4, 2.

He had rather
Groan so in perpetuity, than be cured
By the sure physician, death.

> SHAKESPEARE.—*Ib.*, Act 5, 4.

Thou know'st 'tis common, all that live must die,
Passing through nature to eternity.

> SHAKESPEARE.—*Hamlet*, Act 1, 2.

To sleep! perchance to dream ;—ay, there's the rub ;
For in that sleep of death, what dreams may come
When we have shuffled off this mortal coil

> SHAKESPEARE.—*Ib.*, Act 3, 1.

This fell sergeant, Death,
Is strict in his arrest.

> SHAKESPEARE.—*Ib.*, Act 5, 2.

He's in Arthur's bosom, if ever man went to Arthur's bosom. 'A made a finer end, and went away, an it had been any christom child.

> SHAKESPEARE.—*Henry V.*, Act 2, 3.

He gave his honours to the world again,
His blessed part to Heaven, and slept in peace.

> SHAKESPEARE.—*Henry VIII.*, Act 4, 2.

O mighty Cæsar! dost thou lie so low?
Are all thy conquests, glories, triumphs, spoils,
Shrunk to this little measure?

> SHAKESPEARE.—*Julius Cæsar*, Act 3, 1.

He is gone indeed.
The wonder is he hath endured so long :
He but usurped his life.

> SHAKESPEARE.—*Lear*, Act 5, 3.

Nothing in his life
Became him like the leaving it ; he died
As one that had been studied in his death,
To throw away the dearest thing he owed
As 'twere a careless trifle.

> SHAKESPEARE.—*Macbeth*, Act 1, 4.

The fatal bellman, which gives the stern'st good-night.

> SHAKESPEARE.—*Ib.*, Act 2, 2.

After life's fitful fever he sleeps well.

> SHAKESPEARE.—*Ib.*, Act 3, 2.

Treason hath done his worst ; nor steel, nor poison,
Malice domestic, foreign levy, nothing
Can touch him further.

> SHAKESPEARE.—*Ib.*, Act 3, 2.

Blow wind! come wrack!
At least we'll die with harness on our back.

> SHAKESPEARE.—*Macbeth*, Act 5, 5.

If I must die,
I will encounter darkness as a bride,
And hug it in mine arms.

> SHAKESPEARE.—*Measure for Measure*, Act 3, 1.

The sense of death is most in apprehension;
And the poor beetle, that we tread upon,
In corporal sufferance finds a pang as great
As when a giant dies.

> SHAKESPEARE.—*Ib.*

Ay, but to die, and go we know not where ;
To lie in cold obstruction, and to rot ;
This sensible warm motion to become
A kneaded clod ; and the delighted spirit
To bathe in fiery floods, or to reside
In thrilling region of thick-ribbèd ice ;
To be imprisoned in the viewless winds,
And blown with restless violence round about
The pendent world!   SHAKESPEARE.—*Ib.*

Ay, past all surgery.

> SHAKESPEARE.—*Othello*, Act 2, 3.

Gave
His body to that pleasant country's earth,
And his pure soul unto his captain, Christ,
Under whose colours he had fought so long.

> SHAKESPEARE.—*Richard II.*, Act 4, 1.

This [Death] is what I am hastening toward at the express speed of sixty minutes an hour.

> G. B. SHAW.—*Unsocial Socialist*, ch. 5 (*Sidney Trefusis*).

Death is the veil which those who live call life :
They sleep, and it is lifted.

> SHELLEY.—*Prometheus*, Act 3, 3.

How wonderful is Death,
Death—and his brother Sleep !

> SHELLEY.—*Queen Mab*, c. 1.

He was within a few hours of giving his enemies the slip for ever.

> STERNE.—*Tristram Shandy*, vol. 1, ch. 12.

Death is the port where all may refuge find,
The end of labour, entry into rest.

> EARL OF STIRLING.—*Darius*.

His time was come ; he ran his race ;
We hope he's in a better place.

> SWIFT.—*On the death of Dr. Swift.*

Peace, rest, and sleep are all we know of
  death,
And all we dream of comfort.
    SWINBURNE.—*In Memory of J. W.
                  Inchbold.*

At the doors of life, by the gate of breath,
There are worse things waiting for men
  than death.
    SWINBURNE.—*Triumph of Time.*

The Shadow, cloaked from head to foot,
Who keeps the keys of all the creeds.
    TENNYSON.—*In Memoriam, c.* 23.

Half-dead to know that I shall die.
    TENNYSON.—*Ib., c.* 35.

And so through those dark gates across
  the wild
That no man knows.
    TENNYSON.—*Princess, c.* 7, 341.

Let us have a quiet hour,
Let us hob-and-nob with Death.
    TENNYSON—*Vision of Sin, Pt.* 4, 3.

May be our life is death, and death is
  life ;
One thing I know,—Life wakes to grief
  and pain,
And Death, the healer, lulls to sleep
  again.
    D. W. THOMPSON.—*Tr. of Euripides.*

A quiet passage to a welcome grave.
    I. WALTON.—*Complete Angler.*

Who die of having lived too much
  In their large hours.
    SIR W. WATSON.—*Tomb of Burns.*

Death hath ten thousand several doors
For men to take their exits.
    WEBSTER.—*Duchess of Malfi.*

And now he rests ; his greatness and his
  sweetness
No more shall seem at strife ;
And death has moulded into calm com-
  pleteness
The statue of his life.
    J. G. WHITTIER.—*Joseph Sturge.*

A Power is passing from the earth
To breathless Nature's dark abyss ;
But when the great and good depart,
What is it more than this—
That man, who is from God sent forth,
Doth yet again to God return ?
Such ebb and flow must ever be ;
Then wherefore should we mourn ?
    WORDSWORTH.—*Lines at Grasmere
(written when C. J. Fox was dying)* (1806).

Death is the crown of life.
    YOUNG.—*Night Thoughts,* 3.

Death, of all pain the period, not of
  joy.   YOUNG.—*Ib.*

Were death denied, e'en fools would
  wish to die.   YOUNG.—*Ib.,* 4.

Man makes a death which Nature never
  made ;
Then on the point of his own fancy falls ;
And feels a thousand deaths, in fearing
  one.   YOUNG.—*Ib.*

Death loves a shining mark, a signal
  blow.   YOUNG.—*Ib.,* 5.

Nothing is dead but that which wished
  to die ;
Nothing is dead but wretchedness and
  pain.   YOUNG.—*Ib.,* 6.

And, round us, Death's inexorable hand
Draws the dark curtain close ; undrawn
  no more.   YOUNG.—*Ib.,* 7.

Life is the desert, life the solitude ;
Death joins us to the great majority.
    YOUNG.—*The Revenge, Act* 4, 1.

Judge none blessed before his death.
    Ecclesiasticus xi, 28.

Let me die the death of the righteous,
and let my last end be like his !
    Numbers xxiii, 10.

Come, gentle death, the ebb of care,
The ebb of care, the flood of life.
    Tottel's Miscellany (1557).

DEATH, PREMATURE

Brief, brave, and glorious was his young
  career.
    BYRON.—*Childe Harold, c.* 3, *st.* 57.

Heaven gives its favourites—early death.
    BYRON.—*Ib., c.* 4, *st.* 102.

" Whom the gods love die young," was
  said of yore.
    BYRON.—*Don Juan,* 4, 12.

Grieve not that I die young. Is it not
  well
To pass away ere life hath lost its brightness ?
    LADY FLORA E. HASTINGS.—*Swan Song.*

How happier far than life, the end
Of souls that infant-like beneath their
  burden bend.
    KEBLE.—*Holy Innocents.*

He whom the gods love dies young.
    MENANDER.—*Dis Exapaton.*

He whom the gods love dies young,
whilst he is full of health, perception, and
judgment.
    PLAUTUS.—*Bacchides, Act* 4, 7.

A dirge for her, the doubly-dead,
  In that she died so young.
    E. A. POE.—*Lenore.*

His bright and brief career is o'er,
And mute his tuneful strains.
SCOTT.—*Lord of the Isles*, 4, 11.

Sweet rose, fair flower, untimely plucked,
soon faded ;
Plucked in the bud, and faded in the spring.
Attrib. to SHAKESPEARE.—*Passionate
Pilgrim, No.* 8.

As is the bud bit with an envious worm,
Ere he can spread his sweet leaves to the
air,
Or dedicate his beauty to the sun.
SHAKESPEARE.—*Romeo and Juliet*,
Act 1, 1.

Death lies on her, like an untimely frost
Upon the sweetest flower of all the field.
SHAKESPEARE.—*Ib.*, Act 4, 5.

She died in beauty—like a rose, blown
from its parent stem.
C. D. SILLERY.—*Song*.

The good die first . . .
And they whose hearts are dry as summer
dust
Burn to the socket.
WORDSWORTH.—*Excursion, Bk.* 1.

Early, bright, transient, chaste, as morning dew
She sparkled, was exhaled, and went
to Heaven.
YOUNG.—*Night Thoughts*, 5.

Therefore a heaven's gift she was,
Because the best are soonest hence bereft.
Tottel's Miscellany (1557). *On the death
of Lord Pembroke.*

DEATH, SUDDEN

Oh, sunderings short of body and breath !
Oh, " battle and murder and sudden
death ! "
Against which the Liturgy preaches ;
By the will of a just yet a merciful Power,
Less bitter perchance, in the mystic hour,
When the wings of the shadowy angel
lower,
Than man in his blindness teaches.
A. L. GORDON.—*Wearie Wayfarer*, 5.

Then with no fiery throbbing pain,
No cold gradations of decay,
Death broke at once the vital chain,
And freed his soul the nearest way.
JOHNSON.—*Death of R. Levett.*

Cut off even in the blossoms of my sin,
Unhouseled, disappointed, unaneled ;
No reckoning made, but sent to my account
With all my imperfections on my head.
SHAKESPEARE.—*Hamlet*, Act 1, 5.

DEATH, UNITED IN

Saul and Jonathan were lovely and
pleasant in their lives, and in their death
they were not divided. *2 Samuel* i, 23.

DEATH-BED

A death-bed's a detector of the heart.
Here tired dissimulation drops her mask.
YOUNG.—*Night Thoughts*, 2.

DEBATERS

Frank, haughty, rash—the Rupert of
debate.
(1st) LORD LYTTON.—*New Timon,
Pt.* 1 (*Lord Stanley was previously
described by B. Disraeli as " the
Rupert of debate* ").

DEBT

He (Vaugeron) argues that the floating
debt must be light because it floats.
D. DAIGNE.—*Les Repus.*

A person who can't pay gets another
person who can't pay to guarantee that he
can pay. Like a person with two wooden
legs getting another person with two
wooden legs to guarantee that he has got
two natural legs. It don't make either
of them able to do a walking match.
DICKENS.—*Little Dorrit, c.* 23.

Debt is the prolific mother of folly and
of crime.
DISRAELI.—*Henrietta Temple,
Bk.* 2, *c.* 1.

The second vice is lying ; the first is
running into debt.
B. FRANKLIN.—*Poor Richard.*

Debts and lies are generally mixed
together. RABELAIS.—*Pantagruel, Bk.* 3.

I pay debts of honour—not honourable
debts.
F. REYNOLDS.—*The Will*, Act 3, 2.

He that dies pays all debts.
SHAKESPEARE.—*Tempest*, Act 2, 2.

When once a people have tasted the
luxury of not paying their debts, it is
impossible to bring them back to the
black broth of honesty.
SYDNEY SMITH.—*Letter to Mrs. Grote,
Aug.* 31, 1843.

He [Sir Pitt Crawley] had an almost
invincible repugnance to paying anybody,
and could only be brought by force to
discharge his debts.
THACKERAY.—*Vanity Fair, Bk.* 1, *c.* 9.

DECADENCE

Shrine of the mighty ! can it be
That this is all remains of thee ?
BYRON.—*The Giaour, l.* 103.

His heart was formed for softness—warped
to wrong ;
Betrayed too early, and beguiled too long.
BYRON.—*Corsair* 3, 23.

I am ashes where once I was fire.
BYRON.—*To Lady Blessington.*

Fears of the brave and follies of the wise !
From Marlborough's eyes the streams of
   dotage flow,
And Swift expires a driveller and a show.
JOHNSON.—*Vanity of Human Wishes.*

But O how fallen ! how changed
From him, who, in the happy realms of
   light,
Clothed in transcendent brightness, didst
   outshine
Myriads, though bright !
MILTON.—*Paradise Lost, Bk.* 1, 84.

And bitter memory cursed with idle rage
The greed that coveted gold above renown,
The feeble hearts that feared their heritage,
The hands that cast the sea-king's sceptre
   down,
And left to alien brows their famed an-
   cestral crown.
SIR H. J. NEWBOLT.—*Væ victis.*

Thus all below, whether by Nature's
   curse,
Or Fate's decree, degenerate still to worse
VIRGIL.—*Georgics, Bk.* 1 (*Dryden tr.*)

Milton ! thou shouldst be living at this
   hour :
England hath need of thee ; she is a fen
Of stagnant waters.
WORDSWORTH.—*London.*

Shame followed shame, and woe supplanted
   woe—
Is this the only change that time can show?
WORDSWORTH.—*Ode.*

Perpetual emptiness ! unceasing change !
No single volume paramount, no code,
No master spirit, no determined road :
But equally a want of books and men.
WORDSWORTH.—*Poems to National
   Independence, Pt.* 1, 15.

I find nothing great :
Nothing is left which I can venerate ;
So that a doubt almost within me springs
Of Providence, such emptiness at length
Seems at the heart of all things.
WORDSWORTH.—*Ib., Pt.* 1, 22.

The great events with which old story
   rings
Seem vain and hollow.
WORDSWORTH.—*Ib.*

DECAY

I would not mind being dead, but I
would not die out.
EPICHARMUS (*quoted by Cicero*).

There will be a day when even sacred
Troy shall be no more. HOMER.—*Iliad.*

While man is growing, life is in decrease ;
And cradles rock us nearer to the tomb.
Our birth is nothing but our death begun.
YOUNG.—*Night Thoughts,* 5.

DECEIT

Fraud that in every conscience leaves a
   sting. DANTE.—*Hell, c.* 11 (*Cary tr.*).

Who dares think one thing, and another
   tell,
My heart detests him as the gates of hell.
HOMER.—*Iliad, Bk.* 9, 412 (*Pope tr.*).

'Tis in vain to find fault with those arts
of deceiving, wherein men find pleasure
to be deceived.
LOCKE.—*Human Understanding, Bk.* 3.

I open an old book, and there I find,
That " Women still may love whom they
   deceive."
Such love I prize not.
GEO. MEREDITH.—*Modern Love, st.* 14.

Oh, what a tangled web we weave
When first we practise to deceive !
SCOTT.—*Marmion, c.* 6, *st.* 17.

She has deceived her father, and may thee.
SHAKESPEARE.—*Othello,* Act 1, 3.

If a man deceive me once, shame on
him ; if twice, shame on me. *Prov.*

Since you wish to deceive me, deceive
me better than you are doing it.
*French Opera, " Phénix de la Poésie
   chantante."*

Speak unto us smooth things ; prophesy
deceits. *Isaiah* xxx, 10.

The heart is deceitful above all things,
and desperately wicked.
Jeremiah xvii, 9.

DECENCY

Not one immoral, one corrupted thought,
One line which, dying, he could wish to
   blot.
GEO. LORD LYTTELTON.—*Prologue.*

Immodest words admit of no defence,
For want of decency is want of sense.
EARL OF ROSCOMMON.—*On Translated
   Verse.*

DECEPTION

If such as came for wool, sir, went home
   shorn,
Where is the wrong I did them ?
BROWNING.—*Mr. Sludge.*

Between craft and credulity the voice
of reason is stifled.
BURKE.—*Letter to Sheriffs of Bristol.*

What a world of gammon and spinnage
it is, though, ain't it ?
> DICKENS.—*David Copperfield, ch.* 22.

Sure men were born to lie, and women
to believe them.
> GAY.—*Beggar's Opera*, Act 2, 2.

Lest men suspect our tale untrue,
Keep probability in view.
> GAY.—*Fables, Pt.* 1, 14.

DECISION

When desperate ills demand a speedy
cure,
Distrust is cowardice and prudence folly.
> JOHNSON.—*Irene.*

I tell thee, God is in that man's right hand,
Whose heart knows when to strike, and
when to stay.
> SWINBURNE.—*Bothwell.*

Let your yea be yea ; and your nay, nay.
> *St. James* v, 12.

DECORUM

Nor will virtue herself look beautiful,
unless she be bedecked with the outward
ornaments of decency and decorum.
> FIELDING.—*Tom Jones, Bk.* 3, *c.* 7.

DEEDS

We live in deeds, not years ; in thoughts,
not breaths ;
In feelings, not in figures on a dial.
> P. J. BAILEY.—*Festus.*

All dies, as we often say ; except the
spirit of man, of what man *does.*
> CARLYLE.—*French Revolution, Pt.* 2,
> *Bk.* 1, *ch.* 5.

The only things in life in which we can
be said to have any property, are *our
actions.* C. C. COLTON.—*Lacon, No.* 52.

Without doubt it is a delightful harmony when doing and saying go together.
> MONTAIGNE.—*Essays*, 2, 31.

Think nothing done while aught remains
to do.   ROGERS.—*Human Life.*

Deeds are fruits, words are but leaves.
> *Prov.* (*Ray*).

Deeds are males and words are females.
> *Prov.* (*Ray*).

DEFEAT

He smiled a kind of sickly smile, and curled
up on the floor,
And the subsequent proceedings interested
him no more.
> BRET HARTE.—*Stanislaus.*

I would rather suffer defeat than have
cause to be ashamed of victory.
> QUINTUS CURTIUS.

The conquering cause was pleasing to
the gods, but the conquered to Cato.
> LUCANUS.—*Pharsalia.*

They'll wondering ask how hands so vile
Could conquer hearts so brave.
> MOORE.—*Weep On.*

In the lost battle,
Borne down by the flying,
Where mingles war's rattle,
With groans of the dying.
> SCOTT.—*Marmion*, 3, 11.

Great is the facile conqueror ;
Yet happy he, who, wounded sore,
Breathless, unhorsed, all covered o'er
With blood and sweat,
Sinks foiled, but fighting evermore,—
Is greater yet.   SIR W. WATSON.—
> *Laleham Churchyard*, 14.

DEFENCE

Self-defence is nature's oldest law.
> DRYDEN.—*Absalom and Achitophel.*

Self-preservation is the first of laws.
> DRYDEN.—*The Spanish Friar,*
> Act 4, 2 (1681).

The first and fundamental law of Nature
. . . is " to seek peace, and follow it."
The second, the sum of the right of Nature :
which is, " by all means we can to defend
ourselves." HOBBES.—*Leviathan, ch.* 14.

Self-preservation, nature's first great law,
All the creation, except man, doth awe.
> MARVELL.—*Hodge's Vision.*

What boots it at one gate to make defence,
And at another to let in the foe ?
> MILTON.—*Samson Agonistes*, 5, 60.

This animal is very vicious. When you
attack it, it defends itself. *French (Anon).*

DEFERENCE

Deference to others obtains friends ;
truth brings hatred. TERENCE.—*Andria.*

DEFIANCE

With his back to the field, and his feet to
the foe. CAMPBELL.—*Lochiel's Warning.*

Juletta. Why, slaves, 'tis in our power
to hang ye.
Master. Very likely :
'Tis in our powers then to be hanged
and scorn ye.
> FLETCHER.—*Sea Voyage*, Act 4.

Though changed in outward lustre, that
   fixed mind
And high disdain from sense of injured
   merit.
      MILTON.—*Paradise Lost, Bk.* 1, 97.

He manned himself with dauntless air,
Returned the Chief his haughty stare.
      SCOTT.—*Lady of the Lake, c.* 5, *st.* 10.

Come one, come all! This rock shall fly
From its firm base as soon as I!
      SCOTT.—*Ib.*

Hang out our banners on the outward
   walls;
The cry is still, "They come."
      SHAKESPEARE.—*Macbeth,* Act 5, 5.

Lay on, Macduff!
And damned be he that first cries, "Hold,
   enough!"
      SHAKESPEARE.—*Ib.,* Act 5, 7.

Nor fate I fear, but all the gods defy.
Forbear thy threats; my business is to die;
But first receive this parting legacy.
      VIRGIL.—*Æneid, Bk.* 10 (*Dryden tr.*).

DEFINITIONS

I have no great opinion of a definition,
the celebrated remedy for the cure of this
disorder [uncertainty and confusion].
      BURKE.—*On the Sublime and
      Beautiful, Pt.* 1, *Introduction.*

I hate definitions.
   DISRAELI.—*Vivian Grey, Bk.* 2, *ch.* 6.

Every definition is dangerous.
      Latin prov.

DEGENERACY

A nation swollen with ignorance and pride,
Who lick yet loathe the hand that waves
   the sword.
   BYRON.—*Childe Harold, c.* 1, *st.* 16.

The age of our fathers, who were worse
than our grandfathers, produced us still
more vicious, and we are about to raise
a still more iniquitous progeny.
   HORACE.—*Odes, Bk.* 3, 6, 46.

Degenerate Douglas! Oh, the unworthy
   lord!
   WORDSWORTH.—*Composed at Castle.*

DEGRADATION

A man that could look no way but
downwards, with a muck-rake in his hand.
   BUNYAN.—*Pilgrim's Progress.*

Let Gryll be Gryll and have his hoggish
   minde.
   SPENSER.—*Faerie Queene, Bk.* 3, *c.* 1.

DEJECTION

One discovers a consolation in unhappi-
ness by a certain pleasure one finds in
appearing unhappy.
   LA ROCHEFOUCAULD.—*Maxim* 515.

Alas! how changed from him,
That life of pleasure and that soul of
   whim!   POPE.—*Ep.* 3.

But as it sometimes chanceth, from the
   might
Of joy in minds that can no further go,
As high as we have mounted in delight
In our dejection do we sink as low.
   WORDSWORTH.—*Resolution and
      Independence.*

DELAY

Justice deferred enhances the price
at which you must purchase safety and
peace.
   LORD BROUGHAM.—*Speech on Par-
      liamentary Reform, Oct.* 7, 1831.

All delays are dangerous in war.
   DRYDEN.—*Tyrannic Love,* Act 1, 1.

Delay of justice is injustice.
   W. S. LANDOR.—*Du Paty.*

Woman indeed was born of delay itself.
   PLAUTUS.—*Miles.*

With sweet, reluctant, amorous delay.
   POPE.—*Odyssey, Bk.* 1, 23.

Now fitted the halter, now traversed the
   cart,
And often took leave, but was loth to
   depart.
   PRIOR.—*Thief and Cordelier.*

When fair occasion calls, 'tis fatal to delay.
   N. ROWE.—*Pharsalia, Bk.* 1, 513.

Do you not come your tardy son to chide?
   SHAKESPEARE.—*Hamlet,* Act 3, 4.

And Mecca saddens at the long delay.
   THOMSON.—*Summer,* 979.

Delay is cowardice and doubt despair.
   W. WHITEHEAD.—*Atys and Adrastus.*

When my house burns, it is not good
playing at chess.   *Prov.* (*Geo. Herbert*)

DELIBERATENESS

The woman that deliberates is lost.
      ADDISON.—*Cato.*

Take time enough; all other graces
Will soon fill up their proper places.
   JOHN BYROM.—*Advice to Preach Slow.*

Take a little time—count five-and-
twenty, Tattycoram.
      DICKENS.—*Dorrit, c.* 14.

Wise emblem of our politic world,
Sage snail, within thine own self curled,
Instruct me softly to make haste,
Whilst these my feet go slowly fast.
> R. LOVELACE.—*The Snail.*

The road to resolution lies by doubt ;
The next way home's the farthest way
about.   QUARLES.—*Emblems.*

Truth thrives with examination and
delay ; things which are false thrive on
haste and uncertainty.
> TACITUS.—*Annals*, 2.

DELIVERANCE

When the tale of bricks is doubled,
then comes Moses.
> *Mediæval proverb* (*Latin*).

DELUSION

The people wish to be deceived ; let
them be deceived.
> *Attrib. to* CARDINAL CARAFA (*d.* 1591).

A delusion that distance creates, and
that contiguity destroys.
> C. C. COLTON.—*Lacon, Reflections*, 190.

A delusion, a mockery, and a snare.
> THOS. LORD DENMAN.—*O'Connell v.*
> *The Queen.*

I was never much displeased with those
harmless delusions that tend to make us
more happy.
> GOLDSMITH.—*Vicar of Wakefield, c.* 3.

We must have done with delusive hopes.
If we sow a crop of lies we shall reap a
harvest of tares.
> IBSEN.—*Love's Comedy*, Act 3 (1862).

Where is the philosopher who, for his
own glory, will not willingly deceive the
human race ?   ROUSSEAU.—*Emile.*

Lay not that flattering unction to your
soul.
> SHAKESPEARE.—*Hamlet*, Act 3, 4.

He that is robbed not wanting what is
stolen,
Let him not know't, and he's not robbed
at all.
> SHAKESPEARE.—*Othello*, Act 3, 3.

Hence, dear delusion, sweet enchantment,
hence !
> H. AND J. SMITH.—*Rejected Addresses.*

This is the sublime and refined point
of felicity, called the possession, of being
well deceived ; the serene peaceful state
of being a fool among knaves.
> SWIFT.—*Tale of a Tub.*

DEMAGOGUES

Flattery corrupts both the receiver and
giver ; and adulation is not of more service
to the people than to kings.
> BURKE.—*Reflections on the Revolution.*

To the people they're ollers ez slick ez
molasses,
An' butter their bread on both sides with
The Masses.
> J. R. LOWELL.—*Biglow Papers, No.* 5.

In every age the vilest specimens of
human nature are to be found among
demagogues.
> MACAULAY.—*Hist. of England.*

Faith, there have been many great men
that have flattered the people, who ne'er
loved them.
> SHAKESPEARE.—*Coriolanus*, Act 2, 2.

Spite of this modern fret for Liberty,
  Better the rule of One, whom all obey,
  Than to let clamorous demagogues
  betray
Our freedom with the kiss of anarchy.
> OSCAR WILDE.—*Libertatis Sacra Fames.*

DEMOCRACY

I think I hear a little bird, that sings
  The people by-and-by will be the
  stronger.
> BYRON.—*Don Juan, c.* 8, *st.* 50.

Popular governments have hitherto
uniformly glided into democracies, and
democracies as uniformly perish of their
own excess.
> J. A. FROUDE.—*Short Studies, Party*
> *Politics.*

Corruption, the most infallible sign of
constitutional liberty.
> GIBBON.—*Decline and Fall, ch.* 21.

Of course everything has its wrong side ;
and from this number of people let in
comes declamation and clap-trap and mob-
service, which is much the same thing as
courtiership was in other times.
> SIR A. HELPS.—*Friends in Council,*
> *Bk.* 1, *ch.* 6.

The common crowd is wiser because it
is just as wise as it need be.
> LACTANTIUS.—*Div. Institut.*

Government of the people, by the people,
for the people. A. LINCOLN.—*Speech*, 1863.

Democracy gives every man
The right to be his own oppressor.
> J. R. LOWELL.—*Biglow Papers, Series* 2, 7.

The many-headed monster, multitude.
> MASSINGER.—*Emperor of East*, Act 2, 1.

The only remedy against democrats is soldiers.
W. VON MERCKELS.—*Poem* (1848).

Let the People think they govern and they will be governed.
PENN.—*Some Fruits of Solitude.*

That worst of tyrants, an usurping crowd.
POPE.—*Iliad, Bk.* 2, 242.

The populace is a sovereign which only asks something to eat ; His Majesty is tranquil while digesting.
DE RIVAROL.—*Traits et Bons Mots.*

Supremacy of the people tends to liberty.
TACITUS.—*Annals, Bk.* 6.

Democracy means simply the bludgeoning of the people, by the people, for the people.
OSCAR WILDE.—*Soul of Man under Socialism.*

The voice of the people is the voice of a God.
Quoted by Alcuin, c. A.D. 800, as a saying.

DEMONS

Cob was the strongest, Mob was the wrongest ;
Chittabob's tail was the finest and longest.
R. H. BARHAM.—*Truants.*

DEMONSTRATION

Almost everyone knows this, but it has not occurred to everyone's mind.
ERASMUS.—*Epicureus.*

DENSENESS

Fortunately we have strong heads, we Highcastles. Nothing has ever penetrated to our brains.
G. B. SHAW.—*Augustus does his Bit* (1917).

DEPARTURE

Good-bye, proud world ! I'm going home ;
Thou art not my friend, and I'm not thine.
EMERSON.—*Good-bye, Proud World.*

For who, to dumb Forgetfulness a prey,
This pleasing anxious being e'er resigned,
Left the warm precincts of the cheerful day,
Nor cast one longing, lingering look behind ?   GRAY.—*Elegy.*

Why dost thou not then, like a thankful guest,
Rise cheerfully from Life's abundant feast,
And with a quiet mind go take thy rest ?
LUCRETIUS.—*De Rerum Natura,* 3, 953 (*Creech tr.*).

But, O the heavy change, now thou art gone,
Now thou art gone, and never must return !
MILTON.—*Lycidas,* 37.

Must I thus leave thee, Paradise ! thus leave
Thee, native soil, these happy walks and shades,
Fit haunt of Gods !
MILTON.—*Paradise Lost, Bk.* 11, 269.

They, hand in hand, with wandering steps and slow
Through Eden took their solitary way.
MILTON.—*Ib., Bk.* 12, 647.

In vain you tell your parting lover
You wish fair winds may waft him over :
Alas ! what winds can happy prove
That bear me far from what I love ?
PRIOR.—*Song.*

Stand not upon the order of your going,
But go at once.
SHAKESPEARE.—*Macbeth,* Act 3, 4.

The hopeless word of—never to return.
SHAKESPEARE.—*Richard II.,* Act 1, 3.

I hear a voice you cannot hear
Which says I must not stay ;
I see a hand you cannot see
Which beckons me away.
T. TICKELL.—*Lucy and Colin.*

A power is passing from the earth.
WORDSWORTH.—*Lines on the expected Dissolution of Mr. Fox.*

DEPORTMENT

No dancing bear was so genteel
Or half so *dégagé.* COWPER.—*Of Himself.*

DEPRAVITY

He left a Corsair's name to other times,
Linked with one virtue and a thousand crimes. BYRON.—*Corsair, c.* 3, *st.* 24.

Thy mind, reverting still to things of earth,
Strikes darkness from true light.
H. F. CARY.—*Dante's " Purgatory,"* c. 15, 62

A Being, erect upon two legs, and bearing all the outward semblance of a man, and not of a monster.
DICKENS.—*Pickwick, c.* 34.

No one ever became thoroughly bad all at once.   JUVENAL.—*Sat.* 8.

My imaginations are as foul
As Vulcan's stithy.
SHAKESPEARE.—*Hamlet,* Act 3, 2.

Zounds, sir, you are one of those that will not serve God if the devil bid you.
SHAKESPEARE.—*Othello,* Act 1, 1.

DEPRESSION

You never yet saw
Such an awfully marked elongation of
jaw.
    R. H. BARHAM.—*Merchant of Venice.*

I would that I were low laid in my grave ;
I am not worth this coil that's made for
me.
    SHAKESPEARE.—*King John*, Act 2, 1.

DEPTH

A gulf profound as that Serbonian bog.
    MILTON.—*Paradise Lost*, Bk. 2, 592.

DEPUTATIONS

A deputation is a noun of magnitude
which signifies many but not much.
    W. E. GLADSTONE.—(*Attrib.*
    See " Committees.")

DESCRIPTION

I won't describe ; description is my forte,
But every fool describes in these bright
days.
    BYRON.—*Don Juan*, c. 5, st. 52.

I feel, but want the power to paint.
    JUVENAL.—*Sat.* 7, 56 (*Gifford tr.*).

DESERT

The less they deserve, the more merit
in your bounty.
    SHAKESPEARE.—*Hamlet*, Act 2, 2.

Use every man after his desert, and who
should 'scape whipping ?
    SHAKESPEARE.—*Ib.*

For others say thou dost deserve, and I
Believe it better than reportingly.
    SHAKESPEARE.—*Much Ado*, Act 3, 1.

DESERTION

Deserted at his utmost need
By those his former bounty fed.
    DRYDEN.—*Alexander's Feast*, st. 4.

He felt towards those whom he had
deserted that peculiar malignity which has,
in all ages, been characteristic of apostates.
    MACAULAY.—*History of England*, ch. 1.

That, sir, which serves and seeks for gain,
    And follows but for form,
Will pack when it begins to rain,
    And leave thee in the storm.
    SHAKESPEARE.—*Lear*, Act 2, 4.

    The very rats
Instinctively had quit it.
    SHAKESPEARE.—*Tempest*, Act 1, 2.

DESIRE

Sighed and looked, and sighed again.
    DRYDEN.—*Alexander's Feast*, st. 5.

The sea hath bounds, but deep desire
    hath none.
    SHAKESPEARE.—*Venus and Adonis*, st. 65.

The delight that consumes the desire,
The desire that outruns the delight.
    SWINBURNE.—*Dolores.*

Most women have small waists the world
    throughout,
But their desires are thousand miles
    about.
    C. TOURNEUR.—*Revenger's Tragedy*, Act 5.

DESPAIR

However sad man's lot,
    Despair should enter not
      Into the heart of man.
God, by one single stroke,
    Can heal the heart He broke,
      So carrying out His plan.
    G. BARLOW.—*Pageant of Life*, Bk. 5.

Let me not know that all is lost,
Though lost it be—leave me not tied
To this despair, this corpse-like bride.
    BROWNING.—*Easter Day*, c. 31

Our last and best defence, despair.
    BUTLER.—*Hudibras*, Pt. 3, c. 2.

Despair, by which the gallantest feats,
Have been achieved in greatest straits.
    BUTLER.—*Ib.*

Hope withering fled—and Mercy sighed
farewell. BYRON.—*Corsair*, c. 1, st. 9.

All hope abandon ye who enter here.
    H. F. CARY.—*Tr. Dante.*

Certes above all sinnes is this
sinne [" Wanhope " or Despair] most
displesant to Crist and most adversarie.
    CHAUCER.—*Parson's Tale*, sec. 56

What do the damned endure, but to
    despair ?
    CONGREVE.—*Mourning Bride*, Act 3, 1.

Darkness our guide, Despair our leader
    was.
    SIR J. DENHAM.—*On Virgil's Æneis.*

Night was our friend, our leader was
    Despair.
    DRYDEN.—*Æneid*, Bk. 2, 487.

Despair in vain sits brooding over the
putrid eggs of hope.
    J. H. FRERE.—*Rovers*, Act 1.

Mad from life's history,
Glad to death's mystery
Swift to be hurled—
Anywhere, anywhere
Out of the world !
    HOOD.—*Bridge of Sighs.*

There is no vulture like despair.
LORD LANSDOWNE.—*Peleus.*

Vaunting aloud, but racked with deep despair.
MILTON.—*Paradise Lost, Bk.* 1, 126.

What re-inforcement we may gain from hope ;
If not, what resolution from despair.
MILTON.—*Ib., Bk.* 1, 190.

The strongest and the fiercest Spirit
That fought in Heaven, now fiercer by despair.   MILTON.—*Ib., Bk.* 2, 44.

Me miserable ! which way shall I fly
Infinite wrath, and infinite despair ?
Which way I fly is Hell ; myself am Hell ;
And in the lowest deep a lower deep,
Still threatening to devour me opens wide,
To which the Hell I suffer seems a Heaven.
MILTON.—*Ib., Bk.* 4, 73.

So farewell hope, and with hope farewell fear,
Farewell remorse ; all good to me is lost ;
Evil, be thou my good !
MILTON.—*Ib., Bk.* 4, 108.

The thunders roar, the lightnings glare ;
Vain is it now to strive or dare ;
A cry goes up of great despair,—
Miserere, Domine !
ADELAIDE A. PROCTER.—*The Storm.*

Hard toil can roughen form and face,
And want can quench the eye's bright grace ;
Nor does old age a wrinkle trace
More deeply than despair.
SCOTT.—*Marmion, c.* 1, *st.* 28.

O now, for ever
Farewell the tranquil mind, farewell content.
SHAKESPEARE.—*Othello,* Act 3, 3.

Then black despair,
The shadow of a starless night, was thrown
Over the world in which I moved alone.
SHELLEY.—*Revolt of Islam, Dedication.*

" And must I die ? " she said,
" And unrevenged ? 'Tis doubly to be dead !
Yet even this death with pleasure I receive :
On any terms 'tis better than to live.
VIRGIL.—*Æneid, Bk.* 4 (*Dryden tr.*).

Nor flight was left, nor hopes to force his way.
Emboldened by despair, he stood at bay.
VIRGIL.—*Ib., Bk.* 9 (*Dryden tr.*).

Despair has often gained battles.
VOLTAIRE.—*Henriade.*

DESPATCH

There is nothing more requisite in business than despatch.
ADDISON.—*The Drummer,* Act 5, 1.

There is no secrecy comparable to celerity.
BACON.—*Of Delays.*

Despatch is the soul of business and nothing contributes more to despatch than method.
LORD CHESTERFIELD.—*Advice to his Son.*

" Dash and through with it ! "—That's the better watchword.
COLERIDGE.—*Piccolomini,* Act 1, 2.

Tout de suite—and the touter the sweeter.
STEPHEN GRAHAM.—*A Private in the Guards* (1919) (*an example of soldiers' slang*).

If it were done, when 'tis done, then 'twere well
It were done quickly.
SHAKESPEARE.—*Macbeth,* Act 1, 7.

Cecil's despatch of business was extraordinary, his maxim being, " The shortest way to do many things is to do only one thing at a time."   S. SMILES.—*Self-Help.*

Blessed is the wooing
That is not long a-doing.
Prov. (*quoted in Burton's " Anatomy of Melancholy,"* 1621).

" Now " is the watchword of the wise.
Saying (*Spurgeon's " Salt-Cellars "*).

DESPERATION

Beware of desperate steps.   The darkest day,
Live till to-morrow, will have passed away.
COWPER.—*The Needless Alarm.*

Though rashness can hope for but one result,
We are heedless when fate draws nigh us,
And the maxim holds good, " Quem perdere vult
Deus, dementat prius."
A. L. GORDON.—*Wearie Wayfarer,* 2.

I am driven
Into a desperate strait, and cannot steer
A middle course.
MASSINGER.—*Great Duke of Florence,* Act 3, 1.

And he that stands upon a slippery place
Makes nice of no vile hold to stay him up.
SHAKESPEARE.—*King John,* Act 3, 4.

I am one, my liege,
Whom the vile blows and buffets of the world
Have so incensed, that I am reckless what I do to spite the world.
SHAKESPEARE.—*Macbeth,* Act 3, 1.

Slave! I have set my life upon a cast,
And I will stand the hazard of the die.
SHAKESPEARE.—*Richard III.*, Act 5, 4.

Tempt not a desperate man.
SHAKESPEARE.—*Romeo and Juliet*, Act 5, 3.

The determined foe
Fought for revenge, not hoping victory.
SOUTHEY.—*Joan of Arc, Bk.* 2.

DESPONDENCY

O chide not my heart for its sighing;
I cannot be always gay:
There's a blight in the rosebud lying,
A cloud in the sunniest day.
MRS. AYLMER.—*Song.*

It is the Slough of Despond still, and
so will be when they have done what
they can.
BUNYAN.—*Pilgrim's Progress, Pt.* I.

No night is so utterly cheerless
That we may not look for the dawn.
PHŒBE CAREY.—*Light in Darkness.*

" I feel it more than other people,"
said Mrs. Gummidge.
DICKENS.—*Copperfield, c.* 3.

The day is cold and dark and dreary;
It rains, and the wind is never weary.
LONGFELLOW.—*Rainy Day*

I have not that alacrity of spirit,
Nor cheer of mind, that I was wont to
have.
SHAKESPEARE.—*Richard III.*, Act 5, 3.

Great God! I'd rather be
A pagan suckled in a creed outworn,
So might I, standing on this pleasant lea,
Have glimpses that would make me less
forlorn!
WORDSWORTH.—*The World is too much
with us.*

DESPOTISM

Step by step and word by word : who is
ruled may read,
Suffer not the old Kings—for we know the
breed.   KIPLING.—*The Old Issue.*

DESTINY

Long tarries destiny,
But comes to those who pray.
ÆSCHYLUS.—*Choephoræ,* 462
(*Plumptre tr.*).

A man can have but one life, and one death,
One heaven, one hell.
BROWNING.—*In a Balcony.*

How little do we know that which we are!
How less what we may be! The
eternal surge
Of time and tide rolls on and bears afar
Our bubbles.
BYRON.—*Don Juan,* 15, 99.

" If thou," he answered, " follow but thy
star,
Thou canst not miss at last a glorious
haven."
H. F. CARY.—*Dante's " Hell,"* c. 15, 55.

Whoe'er she be,
That not impossible she,
That shall command my heart and me;
Where'er she lie,
Locked up from mortal eye,
In shady leaves of destiny.
R. CRASHAW.—*To his Supposed Mistress.*

O Sairey, Sairey, little do we know what
lays before us [Mrs. Harris].
DICKENS.—*M. Chuzzlewit, c.* 40.

The Moving Finger writes; and, having
writ,
Moves on : nor all your Piety nor Wit
Shall lure it back to cancel half a Line,
Nor all your Tears wash out a Word of it.
E. FITZGERALD.—*Rubáiyát, st.* 71.

Weave the warp, and weave the woof,
The winding sheet of Edward's race.
GRAY.—*The Bard, c.* I.

What different lots our stars accord!
This babe to be hailed and wooed as a
Lord!
And that to be shunned like a leper!
One, to the world's wine, honey, and corn,
Another, like Colchester native, born
To its vinegar only, and pepper.
HOOD.—*Miss Kilmansegg.*

Oh no! 'tis only Destiny or Fate
Fashions our wills to either love or hate.
R. LOVELACE.—*On a Lost Heart.*

Be not amazed at life; 'tis still
The mode of God with His elect,
Their hopes exactly to fulfil
In times and ways they least expect.
C. PATMORE.

Who sees with equal eye, as God of all,
A hero perish, or a sparrow fall,
Atoms or systems into ruin hurled,
And now a bubble burst, and now a world.
POPE.—*Essay on Man, Ep.* I, 87.

What shall be the maiden's fate?
Who shall be the maiden's mate?
SCOTT.—*Lay of the Last Minstrel,* I, 16.

If we could push ajar the gates of life,
And stand within, and all God's work-
ings see,
We could interpret all this doubt and
strife,
And for each mystery could find a key.
But not to-day. Then be content, poor
heart!
God's plans, like lilies pure and white,
unfold;

We must not tear the close-shut leaves
apart—
Time will reveal the calyxes of gold.
MAY RILEY SMITH.—*Sometime.*

Come wealth or want, or good or ill,
Let young and old accept their part,
And bow before the Awful Will,
And bear it with an honest heart.
THACKERAY.—*End of the Play.*

Thou cam'st not to thy place by accident;
It is the very place God meant for thee.
ARCHBISHOP TRENCH.—*Sonnet.*

The gods sell things at a fair price.
Prov. (from the Greek).

DESTITUTION

My lodging is on the cold ground,
And very hard is my fare.
SIR W. D'AVENANT.—*Rivals.*

Alas, for the rarity
Of Christian charity
Under the sun!
Oh, it was pitiful!
Near a whole city full,
Home had she none.
HOOD.—*Bridge of Sighs.*

And hopeless near a thousand homes I
stood,
And near a thousand tables pined and
wanted food.
WORDSWORTH.—*Guilt and Sorrow.*

DESTRUCTION

A thousand years scarce serve to form a
state;
An hour may lay it in the dust.
BYRON.—*Childe Harold, c. 2, st.* 84.

One minute gives invention to destroy
What to rebuild will a whole age employ.
CONGREVE.—*Double Dealer,* Act I.

As dreadful as the Manichean god,*
Adored through fear, strong only to
destroy.
COWPER.—*Winter Morning Walk,* 499.

Havoc, and spoil, and ruin are my gain.
MILTON.—*Paradise Lost, Bk.* 2, 1,009.

The children in Holland take pleasure in
making
What the children in England take pleasure
in breaking.   *Nursery proverb.*

DETACHMENT

I stood
Among them, but not of them.
BYRON.—*Childe Harold, c.* 3, *st.* 113.

---

* The god of Evil.

He heard it, but he heeded not—his eyes
Were with his heart, and that was far
away.
BYRON.—*Childe Harold, c.* 4, *st.* 140.

We
Are that which we would contemplate
from far.
WORDSWORTH.—*Excursion, Bk.* 5.

DETERMINATION

To-morrow let us do or die!
CAMPBELL.—*Gertrude, Pt.* 3, *st.* 37.

His way once chose, he forward thrust
outright,
Nor stepped aside for dangers or delight.
COWLEY.—*Davideis, Bk.* 4, 361.

If you'd pooh-pooh this monarch's plan,
Pooh-pooh it;
But when he says he'll hang a man,
He'll do it.
SIR W. S. GILBERT.—*Princess Ida.*

Think not
Our counsel's based upon so weak a base,
As to be overturned, or shaken with
Tempestuous winds of words.
MASSINGER.—*Maid of Honour,* Act I;

What though the field be lost?
All is not lost; th' unconquerable will,
And study of revenge, immortal hate,
And courage never to submit or yield;
And what is else not to be overcome?
MILTON.—*Paradise Lost, Bk.* 1, 105.

DETRACTION

Black detraction
Will find faults where they are not.
MASSINGER.—*Guardian,* Act I.

Let there be gall enough in thy ink;
though thou write with a goose pen, no
matter.
SHAKESPEARE.—*Twelfth Night,* Act 2, 3.

DEVASTATION

Mark where his carnage and his conquests
cease;
He makes a solitude, and calls it—peace!
BYRON.—*Bride of Abydos, c.* 1, *st.* 20.

The Assyrian came down like a wolf on
the fold,
And his cohorts were gleaming in purple
and gold.
BYRON.—*Destruction of Sennacherib.*

They make a desert and call it peace.
TACITUS.—*Agricola.*

DEVIL

And backward and forward he switched
his long tail,
As a gentleman switches his cane.
COLERIDGE.—*Devil's Thoughts, st.* 1.

His jacket was red and his breeches were
    blue,
And there was a hole where the tail came
    through.
    COLERIDGE.—*Devil's Thoughts, st.* 3.

The prince of darkness is a gentleman.
    SHAKESPEARE.—*Lear,* Act 3, 4.

Gie the deil his due, and ye'll gang to
him.   *Scottish prov.*

The deil's nae waur than he's ca'd.
                          Scottish prov.

DEVONSHIRE

For me, there's nought I would not leave
For the good Devon land.
    SIR H. J. NEWBOLT.—*Laudabunt alii.*

DEVOTION

'Tis sweeter for thee despairing
Than aught in the world besides.
              BURNS.—*Jessy.*

Madam, I do, as is my duty,
Honour the shadow of your shoe-tie.
    BUTLER.—*Hudibras, Pt.* 3, *c.* 1.

Devotion, mother of obedience.
    S. DANIEL.—*Civil War, Bk.* 6, *st.* 33.

She kissed his brow, he kissed her feet—
    He kissed the ground her feet did kiss.
J. DAVIDSON.—*New Ballad of Tannhäuser.*

I do honour the very flea of his dog.
BEN JONSON.—*Every Man in his Humour,*
                        Act 4.

No, the heart that has truly loved never
    forgets,
But as truly loves on to the close!
As the sunflower turns on her god, when
    he sets,
The same look which she turned when
    he rose.
    MOORE.—*Believe me, if all.*

Pleased to the last he crops the flowery
    food,
And licks the hand just raised to shed his
    blood.
    POPE.—*Essay on Man, Ep.* 1, 83.

And all my fortunes at thy foot I'll lay,
And follow thee, my lord, throughout the
    world.
    SHAKESPEARE.—*Romeo and Juliet,*
                      Act 2, 2.

I say no man has ever yet been half
    devout enough,
None has ever yet adored or worshipped
    half enough,
None has begun to think how divine he
    himself is, and how certain the future
is.   WALT WHITMAN.

DIALECT

Dialect-words—those terrible marks of
the beast to the truly genteel.
    THOS. HARDY.—*Mayor of Casterbridge.*

DIARIES

If you make too much of diaries you
blur every beautiful sight by thinking
what you should write about it.
    SIR A. HELPS.—*Friends in Council,*
                    Bk. 2, c. 3.

DIET

If you wish to grow thinner, diminish
    your dinner,
    And take to light claret instead of
      pale ale ;
Look down with an utter contempt upon
    butter,
    And never touch bread till it's wasted—
      or stale.   H. S. LEIGH.—*Wishing.*

Whatsoever was the father of the
disease, an ill-diet was the mother.
             Prov. (Geo. Herbert).

DIFFERENCE

Some say that Signor Bononchini,
Compared to Handel's a mere ninny ;
Others aver, to him that Handel
Is scarcely fit to hold a candle.
Strange that such high disputes should be
'Twixt Tweedledum and Tweedledee.
The Contest (*London Journal, June,* 1725).

DIFFICULTY

There's difficulty, there's danger, there's
the dear spirit of contradiction in it.
        I. BICKERSTAFFE.—*Hypocrite.*

Difficulty is a severe instructor.
    BURKE.—*Reflections on French*
                    Revolution.

Quoth he, In all my past adventures
I ne'er was set so on the tenters.
    BUTLER.—*Hudibras, Pt.* 2, *c.* 3.

So he with difficulty and labour hard
Moved on, with difficulty and labour he.
    MILTON.—*Paradise Lost, Bk.* 2, 1,021.

Sith never ought was excellent assayde,
Which was not hard t'atchieve and bring
    to end.   SPENSER.—*Amoretti,* 51.

For a stone of stumbling and for a rock
of offence.   *Isaiah* viii, 14.

DIFFIDENCE

Ever with the best desert goes diffidence.
    BROWNING.—*Blot in the 'Scutcheon.*

Now Giant Despair had a wife and her
name was Diffidence.
    BUNYAN.—*Pilgrim's Progress, Pt.* 1.

Whatever I try, sir,
I fail in—and why, sir ?
I'm modesty personified.
Sir W. S. Gilbert.—*Ruddigore.*

Archly the maiden smiled, and with eyes
over-running with laughter,
Said, in a tremulous voice, " Why don't
you speak for yourself, John ? "
Longfellow.—*Miles Standish,*
Pt. 3 (*ad fin.*).

He either fears his fate too much
Or his deserts are small,
That dares not put it to the touch,
To gain or lose it all.
Marquis of Montrose.—*My dear and
only Love.*

His trembling hand had lost the ease
Which marks security to please.
Scott.—*Lay of the Last Minstrel, Intro.*

The cat is fain the fish to eat,
But hath no will to wet her feet.
Old Saying.

More I could tell, but more I dare not say ;
The text is old, the orator too green.
Shakespeare.—*Venus and Adonis, st.* 135.

DIGESTION

I am in the great catalogue of the satisfied, under the section of the people who
can digest.   E. Goudinet.—*The Club.*

DIGNITY

A life both dull and dignified.
Scott.—*Marmion, c.* 6, *st.* 1.

Who, taking counsel of unbending truth,
By one example hath set forth to all
How they with dignity may stand ; or fall,
If fall they must.
Wordsworth.—*King of Sweden.*

DIGRESSIONS

Full thoughts cause long parentheses.
Letter from Buckingham to James I.
(*c.* 1622) (*apparently a proverbial
saying*).

I am of Beroaldus's opinion, " Such
digressions do mightily delight and refresh
a weary reader."
Burton.—*Anatomy of Melancholy,*
Pt. 1, sec. 2, mem. 3, 1.

I think there is a fatality in it : I seldom
go to the place I set out for.
Sterne.—*Sent. Journey, The address,
Versailles.*

Digressions, incontestably, are the sunshine,—they are the life, the soul of reading.
Sterne.—*Tristram Shandy, vol.* 1, *ch.* 22.

One of the principal features of my
Entertainment is that it contains so many
things that don't have anything to do
with it.   Artemus Ward.

DILETTANTI

Seeks painted trifles and fantastic toys,
And eagerly pursues imaginary joys.
M. Akenside.—*Virtuoso.*

We all draw a little and compose a little,
and none of us have any idea of time or
money. (*Mr. Skimpole.*)
Dickens.—*Bleak House, c.* 43.

Did nothing in particular,
And did it very well.
Sir W. S. Gilbert.—*Iolanthe.*

DILIGENCE

That which ordinary men are fit for,
I am qualified in ; and the best of me is
diligence.
Shakespeare.—*King Lear*, Act 1, 4.

Seest thou a man diligent in his business ? he shall stand before kings.
Proverbs, xxii, 29.

DINNER

That all-softening, overpowering knell,
The tocsin of the soul—the dinner-bell.
Byron.—*Don Juan, c.* 5, 49.

Let's warm our brains with half-a-dozen
healths,
And then hang cold discourse, for we'll
speak fireworks.
Fletcher and Massinger.—*Elder
Brother*, Act 1.

If an earthquake were to engulf England
to-morrow, the English would manage
to meet and dine somewhere among the
rubbish, just to celebrate the event.
D. Jerrold.

A man seldom thinks with more earnest-
ness of anything than he does of his dinner.
Johnson.—*Remark as recorded by
Mrs. Piozzi.*

Even the great Napoleon could not dine
twice.
Alphonse Karr.—*Chemin le plus court.*

Thou wouldst do well
To wait at my trencher, and tell me lies
at dinner-time ;
And as I like your discoursing, I'll have
you. Marlowe.—*Edward II.*, Act 1.

A dinner lubricates business.
Lord Stowell.—*Saying.*

Where I dines I sleeps.
R. S. Surtees.—*Handley Cross.*

We were to do more business after dinner ; but after dinner is after dinner—an old saying and a true, Much drinking, little thinking.   SWIFT.—*Letter*, 1712.

Across the walnuts and the wine.
    TENNYSON.—*Miller's Daughter*, st. 4.

Dinner was made for eatin', not for talkin'.   THACKERAY.—*Fashionable Fax.*

. Sir, respect your dinner ! Idolise it ; enjoy it properly. You will be by many hours in the week, many weeks in the year, and many years in your life, the happier if you do.
       THACKERAY.—*Memorials of Gormandising.*

After a good dinner one can forgive anybody, even one's own relations.
OSCAR WILDE.—*Woman of No Importance.*

It's a mighty deaf nigger that doesn't hear the dinner-horn.   *Negro prov.*

DIRECTION

Not there, not there, my child.
     HEMANS.—*The Better Land.*

Who point, like finger-posts, the way
They never go.   MOORE.—*Song.*

DIRECTNESS

Mark now, how a plain tale shall put you down.
SHAKESPEARE.—*Henry IV.*, Pt. 1, *Act* 2, 4.

In russet yeas and honest kersey noes.
    SHAKESPEARE.—*Love's Labour's Lost*, *Act* 5, 2.

DIRT

The sailors have an uncouth proverb that every man must eat a peck of dirt in his life.
SIR W. SCOTT.—*Letter, Oct.* 31, 1830.

DISAFFECTION

The right hon. gentleman . . . has retired into what may be called his political cave of Adullam, and he has called about him everyone that was in distress and everyone that was discontented.
     JOHN BRIGHT.—*Speech*, 1866.

To complain of the age we live in, to murmur at the present possessors of power, to lament the past, to conceive extravagant hopes of the future, are the common dispositions of the greatest part of mankind.   BURKE.—*Thoughts on Present Discontents.*

Man has been set against man, Washed against Unwashed.
     CARLYLE.—*French Revolution.*

In every deed of mischief he had a heart to resolve, a head to contrive, and a hand to execute.
     GIBBON.—*Decline and Fall*, ch. 48.

Thou art the Mars of malcontents.
    SHAKESPEARE.—*Merry Wives*, Act 1, 3.

Fortune can give no greater advantage than disaffection amongst the enemy.
       TACITUS.—*Germania*, 33.

The glance
That only seems half-loyal to command,
A manner somewhat fallen from reverence.
     TENNYSON.—*Last Tournament.*

She that gangs to the well wi' an ill will,
Either the pig [jug] breaks or the water will spill.   *Scottish prov.*

DISAGREEMENT

Thy heaven-doors are my hell-gates.
   WM. BLAKE.—*The Everlasting Gospel.*

In every age and clime, we see
Two of a trade can ne'er agree.
       GAY.—*Fables.*

Who shall decide, when doctors disagree,
And soundest casuists, like you and me ?
   POPE.—*Moral Essays, Ep.* 3.

DISAPPEARANCE

Though like a demon of the night
He passed, and vanished from my sight.
     BYRON.—*Giaour, l.* 202.

Slowly she faded. Day by day
Her step grew weaker in our hall,
And fainter, at each even-fall,
Her sad voice died away.
     J. G. WHITTIER.—*Mogg Megone.*

DISAPPOINTMENT

The worldly hope men set their hearts upon
Turns ashes—or it prospers ; and anon,
Like snow upon the desert's dusty face,
Lighting a little hour or two—is gone.
     E. FITZGERALD.—*Omar*, st. 16.

As for disappointing them, I should not so much mind ; but I can't abide to disappoint myself.
GOLDSMITH.—*She Stoops to Conquer*, Act 1.

Oh ! 'ever thus from Childhood's hour,
I've seen my fondest hopes decay ;
I never loved a tree or flower
But 'twas the first to fade away.
I never nursed a dear gazelle,
To glad me with its soft, black eye,
But when it came to know me well,
And love me, it was sure to die.
     MOORE.—*Lalla Rookh.*

Against experience willing to believe,
Desirous to rejoice, condemned to grieve.
     PRIOR.—*Solomon, Bk.* 3, 223.

The hour when you too learn that all is
vain,
And that Hope sows what Love shall never
reap.   D. G. ROSSETTI.—*Sonnet.*

And some sad thoughts lie heavy in the
breast
Such as by hope deceived are left
behind ;
But like a shadow these will pass away
From the pure sunshine of the peaceful
mind.
       SOUTHEY.—*Oliver Newman, 4.*

For of all sad words of tongue or pen,
The saddest are these : " It might have
been."
       WHITTIER.—*Maud Muller.*

I never had a piece of toast,
Particularly long and wide,
But fell upon the sanded floor,
And always on the buttered side.
       Anon. parody.

DISASTER

He went like one that hath been stunned,
And is of sense forlorn.
       COLERIDGE.—*Ancient Mariner.*

Me, howling blasts drive devious, tempest-
tossed,
Sails ripped, seams opening wide, and
compass lost.
       COWPER.—*His Mother's Picture.*

Earth felt the wound ; and Nature from
her seat
Sighing, through all her works gave signs
of woe.
       MILTON.—*Paradise Lost,* 9, 782.

The medicine for disaster is equanimity.
       PUBLILIUS SYRUS.

To be abused in disaster is worse than
the disaster.   PUBLILIUS SYRUS.

Night was our friend ; our leader was
despair.
       VIRGIL.—*Æneid, Bk.* 2 *(Dryden).*

DISCIPLINE

But discipline, that rock that bears the
world,
Breaking disorder back like unknit waves.
       J. DAVIDSON.—*Bruce,* Act 4, 2.

It's my old girl that advises. She has
the head. But I never own to it before
her. Discipline must be maintained. [*Mr.
Bagnet.*] DICKENS.—*Bleak House, c.* 27.

We must do the thing we *must*
Before the thing we *may* ;
We are unfit for any trust
Till we can and do obey.
G. MACDONALD.—*Willie's Question, Pt.* 4.

In time the savage bull doth bear the
yoke.
       SHAKESPEARE.—*Much Ado,* Act 1, 1;

Their's not to make reply
Their's not to reason why,
Their's but to do and die.
TENNYSON.—*Charge of the Light Brigade.*

DISCLAIMER

There was no such stuff in my thoughts.
       SHAKESPEARE.—*Hamlet,* Act 2, 2.

DISCONTENT

Complaint of present days
Is not the certain path to future praise.
       BYRON.—*Don Juan, c.* 1, *Dedic.,* 8.

O we are querulous creatures ! Little less
Than all things can suffice to make us
happy :
And little more than nothing is enough
To make us wretched.
       COLERIDGE.—*Zapolya,* Pt. 2, Act 1, 1;

Thus always teasing others, always teased,
His only pleasure is—to be displeased.
       COWPER.—*Conversation, l.* 345.

" I'm a lone lorn creetur " were Mrs.
Gummidge's words, " and everythink goes
contrairy with me;"
       DICKENS.—*David Copperfield, ch.* 3.

Some folks rail against other folks because other folks have what some folks
would be glad of.
       FIELDING.—*Joseph Andrews, Bk.* 4, *ch.* 6.

When thou hast thanked thy God for
every blessing sent,
What time will then remain for murmurs
or lament ?   W. FRENCH.

Oh, don't the days seem lank and long,
When all goes right, and nothing goes
wrong ?
And isn't your life extremely flat
With nothing whatever to grumble at ?
SIR W. S. GILBERT.—*Princess Ida.*

Men are suspicious ; prone to discontent :
Subjects still loathe the present Government.
       HERRICK.—*Present Government Grievous.*

Borrow trouble for yourself if that's
your nature, but don't lend it to your
neighbours.
       KIPLING.—*Rewards and Fairies.*

A man whom no one pleases is much
more unhappy than a man who pleases no
one. LA ROCHEFOUCAULD.—*Maxim* 640.

Like a melancholy malcontent.
       SHAKESPEARE.—*Venus and Adonis, st.* 53.

Regent of love rhymes, lord of folded
   arms,
Th' anointed sovereign of sighs and groans,
Liege of all loiterers and malcontents.
   SHAKESPEARE.—*Love's Labour's Lost*,
                Act 3, 1.

I feel at my heart that it is not right—
" Nothing is right and nothing is just ;
We sow in ashes and reap the dust."
   MRS. M. M. SINGLETON (VIOLET FANE).
               —*Time.*

When nothing is enjoyed, can there
be greater waste ?
   THOMSON.—*Castle of Indolence*,
               c. 1, st. 49.

The splendid discontent of God
  With Chaos, made the world.
   ELLA W. WILCOX.—*Discontent.*

Discontent is the first step in the progress of a man or a nation.
   OSCAR WILDE.—*Woman of No Importance.*

And he that knoweth what is what
  Saith he is wretched that weens him so.
   SIR T. WYATT.—*Despair Counselleth.*

Pills are to be swallowed, not chewed.
               French prov.

DISCORD

What dire effects from civil discord flow !
   ADDISON.—*Cato*, Act 5, 4.

Now cometh the sinne of them that
sowen and maken discord amonges folk,
which is a sinne that Crist hateth outrely
[utterly], and no wonder is. For he
deyde [died] to make concord.
   CHAUCER.—*Parson's Tale*, sec. 45.

Therfore a philosophre seyde, when men
axed him how that men should plese the
peple. And he answerde, " Do many
good workes and speak few Iangles [idle
talk]."   CHAUCER.—*Ib.*, sec. 47.

If that worm Discord gnaw the root
Of England's old and stately tree,
  Graces and gifts, like blighted fruit
From wasting boughs, will fall and lie
On the rank earth, foredoomed to die.
   SIR F. H. C. DOYLE.—*Robin Hood's
             Bay*, c. 1.

Our offspring, like the seed of dragons'
  teeth,
Shall issue armed, and fight themselves
  to death.
   DRYDEN.—*Don Sebastian*, Act 2, 1.

You think they are crusaders sent
  From some infernal clime,
To pluck the eyes of Sentiment,
  And dock the tail of Rhyme,
To crack the voice of Melody,
  And break the legs of Time.
   O. W. HOLMES.—*Music Grinders.*

And filled the air with barbarous dis-
  sonance.   MILTON.—*Comus*, 550.

O shame to men ! devil with devil damned
Firm concord holds ; men only disagree
Of creatures rational.
   MILTON.—*Paradise Lost*, Bk. 2, 496.

And Discord, with a thousand various
  mouths.   MILTON.—*Ib.*, Bk. 2, 967.

Like sweet bells jangled, out of tune and
  harsh.
   SHAKESPEARE.—*Hamlet*, Act 3, 1.

By this time the Demon of Discord,
with her sooty wings, had breathed her
influence upon our counsels.
   SMOLLETT.—*Roderick Random*, c. 33.

Dischord ofte in musick makes the
  sweeter lay.
   SPENSER.—*Faerie Queene*, Bk. 3, c. 2, st. 15.

This Fury, fit for her intent, she chose ;
One who delights in wars and human woes.
   VIRGIL.—*Æneid*, Bk. 7 (*Dryden tr.*).

Now shake, from out thy fruitful breast,
  the seeds
Of envy, discord, and of cruel deeds ;
Confound the peace established, and prepare
Their souls to hatred and their hands to
  war.   VIRGIL.—*Ib.*

Dissenting clamours in the town arise ;
Each will be heard and all at once advise.
One part for peace and one for war con-
  tends ;
Some would exclude their foes, and some
  admit their friends.
The helpless king is hurried in the throng,
And (whate'er tide prevails) is borne
  along.
   VIRGIL.—*Ib.*, Bk. 12 (*Dryden tr.*).

DISCOURAGEMENT

Ah ! who can tell how hard it is to climb
The steep where Fame's proud temple
  shines afar ;
Ah ! who can tell how many a soul sublime
Has felt the influence of malignant star,
And waged with Fortune an eternal war ;
Checked by the scoff of Pride, by Envy's
  frown,
And Poverty's unconquerable bar,
In life's low vale remote has pined alone,
Then dropped into the grave, unpitied
  and unknown ?
   BEATTIE.—*The Minstrel*, Bk. 1, 1.

DISCOURSE

Perhaps it may turn out a song,
  Perhaps turn out a sermon.
   BURNS.—*Epistle to a Young Friend.*

Nor wanted sweet discourse, the banquet
  of the mind.
   DRYDEN.—*Flower and the Leaf*, l. 432.

DISCOURTESY

Ill manners were best courtesy to him.
DANTE.—*Inferno* (tr. *H. F. Cary*),
c. 33, 148 (*To the Friar Alberigo*).

DISCOVERERS

They are ill discoverers that think there
is no land when they can see nothing but
sea.   BACON.—*Adv. of Learning, Bk.* 2.

I journeyed far, I journeyed fast; I
glad I found de place at last.
J. C. HARRIS.—*Uncle Remus,* 35.

Then felt I like some watcher of the skies,
    When a new planet swims into his ken;
Or like stout Cortez, when, with eagle
        eyes,
    He stared at the Pacific—and all his
        men
Looked at each other with a wild surmise—
    Silent, upon a peak in Darien.
KEATS.—*Chapman's Homer.*

Whether my discoveries will be read by
posterity, or by my contemporaries, is
a matter that concerns them more than
me.   I may well be contented to wait
one century for a reader, when God himself,
during so many thousand years, has
waited for an observer.
JOHN KEPLER (*d.* 1631).

I seem to have been only like a boy
playing on the sea-shore and diverting
myself in now and then finding a smoother
pebble, or a prettier shell, than ordinary,
whilst the great ocean of truth lay all
undiscovered before me.
SIR I. NEWTON.—*Memoirs.*

'Twas his to make, but not share, the
morrow. T. WATTS-DUNTON.—*Columbus.*

God hath made man upright; but they
have sought out many inventions.
Ecclesiastes vii, 29.

DISCRETION

Distrust yourself, and sleep before you
fight.
'Tis not too late to-morrow to be brave.
ARMSTRONG.—*Art of Preserving
Health, Bk.* 4.

            The man that cries
"Consider," is our foe.
BEAUMONT AND FLETCHER.—*Scornful
Lady, Act* 2.

You put too much wind to your sail;
discretion
And hardy valour are the twins of honour.
FLETCHER.—*Bonduca, Act* 1, 1.

Be wary, then; best safety lies in fear.
SHAKESPEARE.—*Hamlet, Act* 1, 3.

DISCRIMINATION

Though it make the unskilful laugh,
cannot but make the judicious grieve;
the censure of which one must, in your
allowance, o'erweigh a whole theatre of
others. SHAKESPEARE.—*Hamlet, Act* 3, 2.

DISCURSIVENESS

" The time has come," the Walrus said,
    " To talk of many things;
Of ships and shoes and sealing-wax,
    Of cabbages and kings."
"L. CARROLL" (REV. C. L. DODGSON).
    —*Alice through the Looking-glass.*

From whatever place I write you will
expect that part of my " Travels " will
consist of excursions in my own mind.
COLERIDGE.—*Satyrane's Letters,
No.* 2.

DISDAIN

When love does meet with injury and
pain,
Disdain's the only medicine for disdain.
BUTLER.—*Cat and Puss.*

I have learned thy arts, and now
Can disdain as much as thou.
T. CAREW.—*Disdain returned.*

What, my dear lady Disdain!
SHAKESPEARE.—*Much Ado, Act* 1, 1.

DISEASES

Dangers stand thick through all the ground,
    To push us to the tomb;
And fierce diseases wait around
    To hurry mortals home.
I. WATTS.—*Hymn, Thee we adore.*

If the head is sick all the limbs are
affected.   *Latin prov.*

DISGRACE

        Alas, to make me
A fixèd figure, for the time of scorn
To point his slow unmoving finger at!
SHAKESPEARE.—*Othello, Act* 4, 2.

I cannot tell, good sir, for which of
his virtues it was, but he was certainly
whipped out of the court.
SHAKESPEARE.—*Winter's Tale, Act* 4, 2.

DISGUST

        O vile,
Intolerable, not to be endured!
SHAKESPEARE.—*Taming of the Shrew,
Act* 5, 2.

DISHONESTY

But for your petty, picking, downright
thievery
We scorn it as we do board wages.
BYRON.—*Werner, Act* 2, 1.

What ain't missed ain't mourned.
SIR A. W. PINERO.—*The Magistrate*
(Wyke, the Butler).

It is a pretty thing to endure so much
misfortune to be a brigand; it would
not cost more to be an honest man, and
there are moments when I am tempted to
become one, even if only as a speculation.
E. SCRIBE.—*Cascaro in " Les Frères*
invincibles."

What, man! more water glideth by the
mill
Than wots the miller of; and easy it is
Of a cut loaf to steal a shive, we know.
SHAKESPEARE.—*Titus Andronicus,*
Act 2.

A little stealing is a dangerous part,
But stealing largely is a noble art;
'Tis mean to rob a hen-roost or a hen,
But stealing thousands makes us gentle-
men.
C. H. SPURGEON.—*" Salt-Cellars "*
(a quotation?).

Why should I deprive my neighbour
Of his goods against his will?
Hands were made for honest labour,
Not to plunder or to steal.
I. WATTS.—*The Thief.*

Stolen waters are sweet. *Proverbs* ix, 17.

DISHONOUR

An idiot race, to honour lost;
Who know them best despise them most.
BURNS.—*Lines on viewing Stirling*
Palace.

Unfaith in aught is want of faith in all.
TENNYSON.—*Merlin and Vivien.*

The shame is in the crime not in the
punishment.
VOLTAIRE.—*Artèmire,* Act 3.

I have known all misfortunes; valour
can surmount them, but what generous
heart can endure dishonour?
VOLTAIRE.—*Zulime.*

When faith is lost, when honour dies,
The man is dead.
WHITTIER.—*Ichabod!*

DISILLUSIONMENT

The glory dropped from their youth and
love,
And both perceived they had dreamed
a dream.
BROWNING.—*Statue and the Bust.*

The only difference is this,—
The gilt is off the chain;
And what was once a golden bliss
Is now an iron pain.
E. R. BULWER-LYTTON (EARL OF
LYTTON).—*Marah.*

My days are in the yellow leaf;
The flowers and fruits of love are gone;
The worm, the canker, and the grief
Are mine alone!
BYRON.—*On his* 36th *Birthday.*

Long toils, long perils, in their cause I bore,
But now the unfruitful glories charm no
more. . . .
Of all my dangers, all my glories, pains,
A life of labours, lo, what fruit remains?
HOMER.—*Iliad, Bk.* 17, 670 *(Pope tr.)*
(said by Achilles).

There is between that smile we would
aspire to,
That sweet aspect of princes, and their
ruin,
More pangs and fears than wars and women
have.
SHAKESPEARE.—*Henry VIII.,* Act 3, 2.

The world is not sweet in the end;
For the old faiths loosen and fall, the new
years ruin and rend.
SWINBURNE.—*To Proserpine.*

There was a time when meadow, grove
and stream,
The earth, and every common sight,
To me did seem
Apparelled in celestial light,
The glory and the freshness of a dream.
It is not now as it hath been of yore;—
Turn wheresoe'er I may,
By night or day,
The things which I have seen I now can
see no more.
WORDSWORTH.—*Intimations of*
Immortality, c. 1.

The sunshine is a glorious birth;
But yet I know, where'er I go,
That there hath passed away a glory from
the earth. WORDSWORTH.—*Ib.,* c. 2.

Whither is fled the visionary gleam?
Where is it now, the glory and the dream?
WORDSWORTH.—*Ib.,* c. 4.

At length the Man perceives it die away,
And fade into the light of common day.
WORDSWORTH.—*Ib.,* c. 5.

A power is gone which nothing can restore;
A deep distress hath humanised my soul.
Not for a moment could I now behold
A smiling sea, and be what I have been;
The feeling of my loss will ne'er be old;
This which I know I speak with mind
serene.
WORDSWORTH.—*On a picture of*
Peele Castle (1805).

DISINTERESTEDNESS

The only reward of virtue is virtue;
the only way to have a friend is to be
one.   EMERSON.—*Friendship.*

Not that I loved Cæsar less, but that
I loved Rome more.
SHAKESPEARE.—*Julius Cæsar*, Act 3, 2.

DISLIKE

I dote on his very absence.
SHAKESPEARE.—*Merchant of Venice*,
Act 1, 2.

I see, lady, the gentleman is not in your
good books.
SHAKESPEARE.—*Much Ado*, Act 1, 1.

DISMISSAL

Out of my sight, and trouble me no more !
MARLOWE.—*Edward II.*, Act 2.

I do desire we may be better strangers.
SHAKESPEARE.—*As You Like It*,
Act 3, 2.

And so without more circumstance at all,
I hold it fit that we shake hands and part.
SHAKESPEARE.—*Hamlet*, Act 1, 5.

Cassio, I love thee,
But never more be officer of mine.
SHAKESPEARE.—*Othello*, Act 2, 3.

DISORGANISATION

This party of two reminds me of the
Scotch terrier, which was so covered with
hair that you could not tell which was the
head, and which was the tail of it.
JOHN BRIGHT.—*Speech*, 1866.

DISPARAGEMENT

The words she spoke of Mrs. Harris,
lambs could not forgive nor worms forget.
[*Mrs. Gamp.*]
DICKENS.—*M. Chuzzlewit*, c. 49.

The idiot who praises, with enthusiastic
tone,
All centuries but this and every country
but his own.
SIR W. S. GILBERT.—*Mikado*.

For whoso will another blame,
He seketh ofte his ownè shame.
GOWER.—*Confessio Amantis*, Bk. 2.

I never told a lie yet ; and I hold it
In some degree blasphemous to dispraise
What's worthy admiration : yet, for once,
I will dispraise a little.
MASSINGER.—*Gt. Duke of Florence*, Act 3.

Of whom to be dispraised were no small
praise.
MILTON.—*Paradise Regained*, Bk. 3, 56.

Damn with faint praise, assent with civil
leer,
And, without sneering, teach the rest to
sneer.   POPE.—*Prol. to Satires*.

Just hint a fault and hesitate dislike.
POPE.—*Ib*.

Who but must laugh, if such a man there
be ?
Who would not weep if Atticus were he ?
POPE.—*Ib*.

With silent smiles of slow disparagement.
TENNYSON.—*Guinevere*, 14.

I don't see no p'ints about that frog
that's any better'n any other frog.
MARK TWAIN.—*Jumping Frog*.

There is a luxury in self-dispraise.
WORDSWORTH.—*Excursion, Bk.* 4.

DISPLAY

The boast of heraldry, the pomp of
power.   GRAY.—*Elegy*.

She that a clinquant outside doth adore,
Dotes on a gilded statue and no more.
R. LOVELACE.—*Song, " Strive not."*

And tape-tied curtains never meant to
draw.   POPE.—*Ep.* 3.

The wealthiest man amongst us is the best :
No grandeur now in Nature or in book
Delights us.   Rapine, avarice, expense,—
This is idolatry, and these we adore ;
Plain living and high thinking are no more.
WORDSWORTH.—*Poems to National
Indep.*, Pt. 1, 13.

DISPOSITION

There was a little girl, and she had a
little curl
Right in the middle of her forehead ;
When she was good, she was very very
good,
But when she was bad she was horrid.
LONGFELLOW (*According to his
biographer, Blanche Roosevelt*, 1882).

Lofty and sour to them that loved him not;
But, to those men that sought him, sweet
as summer.
SHAKESPEARE.—*Henry VIII.*, Act 4, 2.

It is the mynd that maketh good or ill,
That maketh wretch or happie, rich or
poore.
SPENSER.—*Faerie Queene, Bk.* 6,
c. 9, st. 30.

DISPROPORTION

As if an eagle flew aloft, and then—
Stooped from its highest pitch to pounce a
wren.   COWPER.—*Table Talk*, 551.

O monstrous ! but one half-pennyworth
of bread to this intolerable deal of sack !
SHAKESPEARE.—*Henry IV.*, Pt. 1, Act 2, 4.

DISPUTES

He could distinguish, and divide
A hair 'twixt south and south-west side ;
On either which he would dispute,
Confute, change hands, and still confute.
    BUTLER.—*Hudibras, Pt.* 1, *c.* 1.

He'd run in debt by disputation,
And pay by ratiocination.
    BUTLER.—*Ib.*

Quoth he, That man is sure to lose
That fouls his hands with dirty foes ;
For where no honour's to be gained
'Tis thrown away in being maintained.
    BUTLER.—*Ib., Pt.* 2, *c.* 2.

This is no time ,nor fitting place to mar
The mirthful meeting with a wordy war.
    BYRON.—*Lara, c.* 1, 23.

An Irishman fights before he reasons,
a Scotchman reasons before he fights,
an Englishman is not particular as to the
order of precedence, but will do either
to accommodate his customers.
    C. C. COLTON.—*Lacon.*

To hear
Such wrangling is a joy for vulgar minds.
    DANTE.—*Inferno, c.* 30 (*Cary's tr.*).

He who discusses is in the right, he
who disputes is in the wrong.
    DE RULHIÈRES.—*Disputes.*

And of their vain contest appeared no end.
    MILTON.—*Paradise Lost, Bk.* 9, *l.* 1189.

Like doctors thus, when much dispute has
    past,
We find our tenets just the same as last.
    POPE.—*Moral Essays,* 3, 15.

What Tully says of war may be applied
to disputing: it should always be so
managed as to remember that the only
end of it is peace.
    POPE.—*Thoughts on Various Subjects.*

Respect was mingled with surprise,
And the stern joy which warriors feel
In foemen worthy of their steel.
    SCOTT.—*Lady of the Lake, c.* 5, *st.* 10.

But in the way of bargain, mark you me,
I'll cavil on the ninth part of a hair.
    SHAKESPEARE.—*Henry IV., Pt.* 1, Act 3, 1.

And 'tis not hard, I think,
For men so old as we to keep the peace.
    SHAKESPEARE.—*Romeo and Juliet,* Act 1, 2.

The itch of disputation will break out
Into a scab of error.
    R. WATKYNS.—*Flamma sine Fumo.*

Very foolish children of God, have
brotherly love to each other, and do not
devour one another any more for vain
chimeras.
    VOLTAIRE.—*To the Author of The Three
    Impostors.*

Yes and No are the cause of all disputes.
    Prov.

DISQUIET

Alas ! my everlasting peace
Is broken into pieces.
    HOOD.—*Sea Spell.*

DISSENSION

What foreign arms could never quell
By civil rage and rancour fell.
    SMOLLETT.—*Tears of Scotland.*

'Tis thine to ruin realms, o'erturn a state,
Betwixt the dearest friends to raise debate,
And kindle kindred blood to mutual hate.
    VIRGIL.—*Æneid, Bk.* 7 (*Dryden tr.*).

Let now your immature dissension cease ;
Sit quiet, and compose your souls in peace.
    VIRGIL.—*Ib., Bk.* 10 (*Dryden tr.*).

DISSIMULATION

Clothe thy feigned zeal in rage, in fire, in
    fury.   ADDISON.—*Cato,* Act 1, 3.

The continual habit of dissimulation is
but a weak and sluggish cunning, and not
greatly politic.
    BACON.—*Adv. of Learning, Bk.* 2.

Dissimulation invites dissimulation.
    BACON.—*Instauratio, Pt.* 1, *Bk.* 6.

The carl spak oo [one] thing but he
thoghte another.
    CHAUCER.—*Wife of Bath's Tale.*

Hang art, madam, and trust to nature
for dissimulation !
    CONGREVE.—*Old Bachelor,* Act 3.

" Frank and explicit " —that is the
right line to take when you wish to conceal
your own mind and to confuse the minds
of others. [*The Gentleman in Downing
Street.*]   DISRAELI, *Sybil, Bk.* 6, *c.* 1.

"I weep for you," the Walrus said,
" I deeply sympathize ; "
With sobs and tears he sorted out
Those of the largest size,
Holding his pocket-handkerchief
Before his streaming eyes.
    C. L. DODGSON.—*Through the
    Looking-glass.*

. . . Love no man. Trust no man.
Speak ill of no man to his face ; nor well
of any man behind his back. . . . Spread
yourself on his bosom publicly, whose
heart you would eat in private.
    BEN JONSON.—*Every Man in His
    Humour,* Act 3, 4.

All seemed well pleased ; all seemed,
but were not all.
      MILTON.—*Paradise Lost, Bk.* 5, 617.

But good God ! What an age is this
and what a world is this, that a man
cannot live without playing the knave
and dissimulation !
            PEPYS.—*Diary*, 1661.

Euphelia serves to grace my measure,
But Chloe is my real flame.
            PRIOR.—*Ode.*

Look like the innocent flower,
But be the serpent under it.
      SHAKESPEARE.—*Macbeth*, Act 1, 5.

She that could think, and ne'er disclose
      her mind ;
See suitors following, and not look behind.
      SHAKESPEARE.—*Othello*, Act 2, 1.

This art (dissimulation) is the virtue
of the coward.   VOLTAIRE.—*Don Pèdre.*

The words of his mouth were smoother
than butter, but war was in his heart ;
his words were softer than oil, yet were
they drawn swords.   *Psalms* lv, 21.

Nothing is more like an honest man than
a rascal.   *French prov.*

Who does not know how to dissemble
does not know how to reign.
      *Maxim ascribed to Louis XI. Also to
      the Emperor Frederick (Sigismund).
      (Quoted by R. Burton as " He who does
      not know how to dissemble does not
      know how to live.")*

DISSIPATION

The excesses of our youth are drafts
upon our old age, payable with interest
about thirty years after date.
            C. C. COLTON.—*Lacon.*

The wildest colts make the best horses.
      PLUTARCH.—*Themistocles.*

DISTANCE

'Tis distance lends enchantment to the
      view,
And robes the mountain in its azure hue.
      CAMPBELL.—*Pleasures of Hope, Pt.* 1.

To the vulgar eye few things are wonderful that are not distant.
            CARLYLE.—*Burns.*

Distance sometimes endears friendship,
and absence sweeteneth it.
      J. HOWELL.—*Familiar Letters, Bk.* 1.

Far awa' fowls hae fair feathers.
Scottish prov. (Fergusson collection, c. 1580).

DISTINCTION

Robust, but not Herculean—to the sight.
No giant frame sets forth his common
      height ;
Yet, in the whole, who paused to look
      again
Saw more than marks the crowd of vulgar
      men.   BYRON.—*Corsair, c.* 1, 9.

That constellation set, the world in vain
Must hope to look upon their like again.
      COWPER.—*Table Talk*, 659.

You could not stand five minutes with
that man (Edmund Burke) beneath a
shed, while it rained, but you must be
convinced that you had been standing with
the greatest man you had ever yet seen.
      JOHNSON.—*Remark as recorded by Mrs.
                              Piozzi.*

He nothing common did, or mean,
Upon that memorable scene.
            MARVELL.—*Horatian Ode.*

First of the first he shone
'Mongst all the Hellenian host in Pythos
      groves ;
Isthmian and Nemean crowns his prowess
      won ;
Fortune still follows as he moves.
      PINDAR.—*Nem.*, 10, 46 (*Moore tr.*).

A bright particular star.
      SHAKESPEARE.—*All's Well*, Act 1, 1.

There be many Cæsars
Ere such another Julius.
      SHAKESPEARE.—*Cymbeline*, Act 3, 1.

He was a man, take him for all in all,
I shall not look upon his like again.
      SHAKESPEARE.—*Hamlet*, Act 1, 2.

The expectancy and rose of the fair state,
The glass of fashion, and the mould of
      form,
The observed of all observers.
      SHAKESPEARE.—*Ib.*, Act 3, 1.

A hooded eagle among blinking owls
[*Coleridge*]. SHELLEY.—*To Maria Gisborne.*

In fields of air he writes his name,
      And treads the chambers of the sky ;
He reads the stars, and grasps the flame
      That quivers round the throne on high.
            C. SPRAGUE.—*Art.*

For thou, if ever godlike foot there trod
These fields of ours, went surely like a
      god.   SWINBURNE.—*In the Bay.*

He is master and lord of his brothers
Who is worthier and wiser than they.
SWINBURNE.—*Word for the Country*, 18.

Scarce of earth, nor all divine.
            TENNYSON.—*Adeline.*

Men endowed with highest gifts,
The vision and the faculty divine,
Yet wanting the accomplishment of verse.
WORDSWORTH.—*Excursion, Bk.* 1.

Thy soul was like a Star, and dwelt apart.
WORDSWORTH.—*Poems to National
Indep., Pt.* 1, 14 (*Of Milton*) (*Also in
" London "*).

A noticeable man with large grey eyes.
WORDSWORTH.—*Written in Thomson's
" Castle of Indolence."*

He was a burning and a shining light.
St. John v, 35.

Of whom the world was not worthy.
Hebrews xi, 38.

DISTRESS

Beauty in distress is much the most
affecting beauty.
BURKE.—*Vindication of Natural Society.*

Affliction's sons are brothers in distress,
A brother to relieve, how exquisite the
bliss !   BURNS.—*A Winter Night.*

Nor be, what man should ever be,
The friend of Beauty in distress.
BYRON.—*To Florence.*

DISTRUST

Here must thou all distrust behind thee
leave.
DANTE.—*Inferno* (*tr. H. F. Cary*), *c.* 3, 14.

It is a rule in friendship, when Distrust
enters in at the foregate, Love goes out
at the postern.
J. HOWELL.—*Familiar Letters, Bk.* 1.

Distrust that man who tells you to
distrust. ELLA W. WILCOX.—*Distrust.*

Do weel and doubt nae man ; do ill
and doubt a' men.   *Scottish prov.*

DIVINE PRESENCE

It rests upon the verdict of all true-
hearted and good men that there is not a
nook or corner of the world, in which
something cannot be found which will
touch or comfort men's minds with a
sense of the divine presence.
J. KEBLE.—*Lectures on Poetry, No.* 38
(*E. K. Francis tr.*).

DIVINITY IN MAN

There is a God within us and intercourse with heaven.
OVID.—*Art of Love,* 3, 549.

DIVISION

This arithmetic is perfect in its kind,
and is beyond question—equal portions !
VOLTAIRE.—*Le Dépositaire.*

DOCTRINE

Accuse a man of being a Socinian and
it is all over with him, for the country
gentlemen all think it has something to
do with poaching.
SYDNEY SMITH.—*Saying.*

As thou these ashes, little brook, wilt bear
Into the Avon, Avon to the tide
Of Severn, Severn to the narrow seas,
Into main ocean they, this deed accurst
An emblem yields to friends and enemies,
How the bold teacher's doctrine, sanctified
By truth, shall spread throughout the
world dispersed.
WORDSWORTH.—*Eccles. Sonnets,
Pt.* 2, 17 (*From Fuller*).

Carried away with every blast of vain
doctrine.   *Common Prayer, Collect.*

DOGGEDNESS

It's dogged as does it.   It ain't thinking
about it.
ANTHONY TROLLOPE.—*Last Chronicles
of Barset, Vol.* 1, *p.* 201.

DOGMA

It is certain because it is impossible.
TERTULLIAN.—*De Carne Curisti.*

The interpretation of two or three
words have flooded the earth with blood.
Dogma is often devilish, as you know ;
Morality is divine !
VOLTAIRE.—*Remonstrances.*

Reason arrives late ; she finds the place
occupied by folly. She does not chase
away the ancient mistress of the house,
but lives with her on good terms. . . .
That is how the most absurd dogmas
contrive to exist among the most instructed
peoples.   VOLTAIRE.—*Chinese Letters.*

DOGMATISM

You are the men and wisdom shall die
with you,
And none of the old Seven Churches vie
with you.
BROWNING.—*Christmas Eve, c.* 2.

Dogmatism is Puppyism come to its
full growth.
D. JERROLD.—*Man Made of Money.*

Rome has spoken ; the case is ended.
Founded on St. Augustine, Sermon, 131.

DOGS

'Tis sweet to hear the honest watch-dog's
bark
Bay deep-mouthed welcome, as we draw
near home.
BYRON.—*Don Juan, c.* 1, *st.* 123.

But the poor dog, in life the firmest friend,
The first to welcome, foremost to defend !
    BYRON.—*Inscription on a*
        Newfoundland Dog.

And in that town a dog was found,
  As many dogs there be,
Both mongrel, puppy, whelp and hound,
  And curs of low degree.
    GOLDSMITH.—*Mad Dog.*

Two dogs of black St. Hubert's breed,
Unmatched for courage, breath, and
    speed.
    SCOTT.—*Lady of the Lake, c.* 1, *st.* 7.

    The little dogs and all,
Tray, Blanch, and Sweet-heart, see, they
  bark at me. . . .
Mastiff, greyhound, mongrel grim,
Hound or spaniel, brach or lym,
Or bobtail tyke, or trundle-tail.
    SHAKESPEARE.—*Lear, Act* 3, 6.

The more I see of men, the more I
admire dogs.
French saying, Attrib. to Mme. Roland.

DOLES

The man who first ruined the Roman
people was he who first gave them treats
and gratuities.
    Quoted by Plutarch (Life of Coriolanus)
    as " a shrewd remark, whoever said it."

DOMESTICITY

From quiet homes and first beginning,
  Out to the undiscovered ends,
There's nothing worth the wear of winning,
  But laughter and the love of friends.
    H. BELLOC.

In her very style of looking
  There was cognisance of cooking!
From her very dress were peeping
  Indications of housekeeping.
  R. BUCHANAN.—*White Rose and Red,*
    Pt. 3, 3.

In all the necessaries of life there is not
a greater plague than servants.
  C. CIBBER.—*She would and she would*
    not, Act 1.

Domestic happiness, thou only bliss
Of Paradise that has survived the Fall !
    COWPER.—*Garden,* 41.

    Parlour twilight ; such a gloom
Suits well the thoughtful or unthinking
  mind.
  COWPER.—*Winter Evening,* 278.

Domesticity is the tap-root which
enables the [British] nation to branch wide
and high. The motive and end of their

trade and empire is to guard the independence and privacy of their homes.
    EMERSON.—*English Traits,* 6,
        Manners.

Sweet is the smile of home ; the mutual
  look
When hearts are of each other sure.
    J. KEBLE.—*1st. Sun. in Lent.*

Where glowing embers through the room
Teach light to counterfeit a gloom.
    MILTON.—*Il Penseroso,* 79.

Some dish more sharply spiced than this
Milk-soup men call domestic bliss.
    COVENTRY PATMORE.—*Olympus.*

To love the peaceable and domestic life
it is necessary to have known it ; one
must have felt its sweetnesses in childhood.   ROUSSEAU.—*Emile.*

When the black-lettered list to the Gods
  was presented
  (The list of what Fate for each mortal
    intends),
At the long string of ills a kind goddess
  relented
And slipped in three blessings—wife,
  children, and friends.
  HON. W. R. SPENCER.—*Wife, Children,*
    Friends.

DOOM

Hell from beneath is moved for thee to
meet thee at thy coming.   *Isaiah xiv,* 9.

DOOMSDAY

That day of wrath, that dreadful day,
When heaven and earth shall pass away.
    SCOTT.—*Lay of the Last Minstrel, c.* 6,
        st. 31.

Till the sun grows cold,
And the stars are old,
And the leaves of the Judgment Book
  unfold.
    B. TAYLOR.—*Bedouin Song.*

DOTAGE

Thus in glory was he seen,
  While his years as yet were green ;
But now that his dotage is on him,
  God help him ! for no eye
Of all those who pass him by
Throws a look of compassion upon him.
  ARISTOPHANES.—*The Knights,* 529
    (*Mitchell's tr.*).

Second childishness and mere oblivion,
Sans teeth, sans eyes, sans taste, sans
  everything.
  SHAKESPEARE.—*As You Like It,* Act 2, 7.

DOUBT

To doubt is to decide.
  H. ADDINGTON (LORD SIDMOUTH).—
    (*c.* 1802).

If a man will begin with certainties,
he shall end in doubts; but if he will be
content to begin with doubts, he shall end
in certainties
      BACON.—*Adv. of Learning.*

Who never doubted, never half believed;
Where doubt, there truth is—'tis her
   shadow.   P. J. BAILEY.—*Festus.*

If the sun and moon should doubt,
They'd immediately go out.
      WM. BLAKE.—*Proverbs.*

God help all poor souls lost in the dark!
   BROWNING.—*Heretic's Tragedy*, st. 10.

Who knows most, doubts not.
     BROWNING.—*Two Poets*, 158.

A castle called Doubting Castle, the
owner whereof was Giant Despair.
   BUNYAN.—*Pilgrim's Progress*, Pt. 1.

I've stood upon Achilles' tomb
And heard Troy doubted; time will doubt
   of Rome.
     BYRON.—*Don Juan, c. 4, st.* 101.

Melt and dispel, ye spectre-doubts that
   roll
Cimmerian darkness on the parting soul!
   CAMPBELL.—*Pleasures of Hope*, 2.

By doubting we come at the truth.
      CICERO.

The more generous construction is to
be preferred in words which are general
or doubtful.   COKE.

My mind is in a state of philosophic
doubt.   COLERIDGE.—*Table Talk.*

Dubius is such a scrupulous good man.
   COWPER.—*Conversation, l.* 119.

Uncertain ways unsafest are,
And doubt a greater mischief than despair.
   SIR J. DENHAM.—*The Sophy.*

Unbelief is a belief, a very exacting
religion.   ALPHONSE KARR.

The man that feareth, Lord, to doubt,
In that fear doubteth Thee.
   GEO. MACDONALD.—*Disciple.*

To doubt is safer than to be secure.
MASSINGER.—*A Very Woman*, Act 1, 1.

Though thus, my friend, so long employed,
And so much midnight oil destroyed,
I must confess, my searches past,
I only learned to doubt at last.
     T. MOORE.—*Morality.*

We doubt our doubts,
We hug our faiths, and fancy we are free.
   SIR L. MORRIS.—*Gwen*, Act 6, 1.

I [Meno] heard of you, Socrates, before
I met you, that you are always doubting
yourself, and causing others to doubt.
     PLATO.—*Meno*, 13.

Doubt on matters important for us
to know is a state too violent for the
human mind. It cannot resist long;
in spite of itself it decides for itself in some
way or other and loves rather to deceive
itself than not to believe.
     ROUSSEAU.—*Emile.*

Our doubts are traitors
And make us lose the good we oft might
   win,
By fearing to attempt.
   SHAKESPEARE.—*Measure for Measure,*
         Act 1, 5.

To be once in doubt
Is once to be resolved.
   SHAKESPEARE.—*Othello*, Act 3, 3.

Modest doubt is called
The beacon of the wise.
   SHAKESPEARE.—*Troilus*, Act 2, 2.

Nor can belief touch, kindle, smite, reprieve
His heart who had not heart to disbelieve.
   SWINBURNE.—*In the Bay*, st. 31.

You tell me Doubt is devil-born.
   TENNYSON.—*In Memoriam*, 96.

There lives more faith in honest doubt,
Believe me, than in half the creeds.
     TENNYSON.—*Ib.*

The slow-consenting Academic doubt.
   J. THOMSON.—*Liberty*, Pt. 2, 240.

In philosophy you must doubt things
which you understand too easily, as much
as things which you do not understand at
all.   VOLTAIRE.—*Letters on the English*, 15.

I have lived in doubt; I die in anxiety;
I know not whither I go.
     Attrib. to a Pope of Rome.

DOWRY

Oh, gie me the lass that has acres o'
   charms,
Oh, gie me the lass wi' the well-stockit
   farms.
   BURNS.—*Hey for a Lass wi' a Tocher.*

DRAMA

Plays make mankind no better, and no
   worse.
     BYRON.—*English Bards.*

If you would have your play deserve
   success,
Give it five acts complete, nor more nor
   less.
   P. FRANCIS.—*Horace, Art of Poetry.*

There are three sorts of spectators who compose " the public " so-called : firstly women, secondly thinkers, thirdly what is described as the crowd. The crowd demands almost exclusively action ; the women desire above all other things passion ; the thinkers specially look for " character."

VICTOR HUGO.—*Pref. to Ruy Blas* (1838).

All spectators desire pleasure—the crowd the pleasure of the eyes ; the women the pleasure of the heart ; the thinkers the pleasure of the intellect.

VICTOR HUGO.—*Ib.*

Melodrama for the crowd ; tragedy for women ; comedy, which depicts humanity, for thinkers.   VICTOR HUGO.—*Ib.*

The stage but echoes back the public voice ; The drama's laws, the drama's patrons give.   JOHNSON.—*London.*

The actors are, it seems, the usual three, Husband, and wife, and lover.

GEO. MEREDITH.—*Modern Love, st.* 35.

Have you not perceived the tendency of your soul during a comedy, how a mixture of pain and pleasure is found therein.   PLATO.—*Philebus,* 106.

There still remains, to mortify a wit, The many-headed monster of the pit.

POPE.—*Satires.*

The play's the thing Wherein I'll catch the conscience of the king.

SHAKESPEARE.—*Hamlet,* Act 2, 2.

The purpose of playing . . . to hold, as 'twere, the mirror up to nature.

SHAKESPEARE.—*Ib.,* Act 3, 2.

The awful legitimacy of the highbrow theatre.

G. B. SHAW.—*Annajanska* (1918), *Pref.*

If the best actors are only Horatios, the authors will have to leave Hamlet out, and be content with Horatios for heroes.

G. B. SHAW.—*Great Catherine, Pref.*

In London we have no theatres for the welfare of the people : they are all for the sole purpose of producing the utmost obtainable rent for the proprietor.

G. B. SHAW.—*Heartbreak House, Pref., Commerce in the Theatre.*

Through all the drama—whether damned or not— Love gilds the scene, and women guide the plot.

SHERIDAN.—*Rivals, Epilogue,* 5.

Lo, where the stage, the poor, degraded stage, Holds its warped mirror to a gaping age.

C. SPRAGUE.—*Curiosity,* 127.

The drama which has no religious element as its foundation is not merely not an important and not a good thing, but the most trivial and despicable of things.

TOLSTOY.—*Shakespeare and the Drama.*

What the devil does the plot signify, except to bring in fine things ?

GEO. VILLIERS (DUKE OF BUCKING- HAM).—*Rehearsal.*

Raillery apart, I am persuaded that religion has more effect on people in the theatre, when set forth in splendid verse, than in the church, where it is never dis- played without kitchen-Latin.

VOLTAIRE.—*Letter to Comte D'Argental,* Jan. 4, 1756.

DREAMS

I dreamt that I dwelt in marble halls.

A. BUNN.—*Bohemian Girl.*

I had a dream which was not all a dream.   BYRON.—*Darkness.*

A straw for alle swevenes [dreams'] significaunce ! God helpe me so, I counte hem not a bene ; Ther woot no man aright what dremes mene.

CHAUCER.—*Troilus, Bk.* 5, 362.

Some dreams we have are nothing else but dreams, Unnatural and full of contradictions.

HOOD.—*Haunted House.*

After midnight visions are true.

HORACE.—*Sat., Bk.* 1, 10.

Drames always go by conthrairies, my dear.   S. LOVER.—*Rory O'More.*

Dreams that bring us little comfort, heavenly promises that lapse Into some remote It-may-be, into some forlorn Perhaps.

S. R. LYSAGHT.—*A Ritual, Confession of Unfaith, st.* 32.

But O, as to embrace me she inclined I waked, she fled, and day brought back my night.

MILTON.—*On his deceased wife.*

Those dreams are true which we chance to have in the morning.

OVID.—*Epist.* 19.

Dreams grow holy put in action ; work grows fair through starry dreaming ; But where each flows on unmingling, both are fruitless and in vain.

A. A. PROCTER.—*Philip and Mildred.*

This morn, as sleeping in my bed I lay,
I dreamt (and morning dreams come true,
    they say).
    W. B. RHODES.—*Bombastes Furioso.*

Oh I have passed a miserable night,
So full of fearful dreams, of ugly sights,
That, as I am a Christian faithful man,
I would not spend another such a night,
Though 'twere to buy a world of happy
    days ;
So full of dismal terror was the time !
    SHAKESPEARE.—*Richard III.*, Act 1, 4.

        I talk of dreams,
Which are the children of an idle brain,
Begot of nothing but vain fantasy.
SHAKESPEARE.—*Romeo and Juliet*, Act 1, 4.

        All this is but a dream,
Too flattering-sweet to be substantial.
    SHAKESPEARE.—*Ib.*, Act 2, 2.

Did I hear it half in a doze
    Long since, I know not where ?
Did I dream it an hour ago,
    When asleep in this armchair ?
    TENNYSON.—*Maud*, Pt. 1, 7.

All the wild trash of sleep, without the
    rest.   YOUNG.—*Night Thoughts*, 8.

DRESS

Love's special lesson is to please the eye.
    CHAPMAN.—*Hero and Leander (con-
    tinuation of Marlowe's poem)*, st. 5.

Th' adorning thee with so much art
    Is but a barbarous skill ;
'Tis like the poisoning of a dart
    Too apt before to kill.
    COWLEY.—*The Waiting-maid.*

We know, Mr. Weller, we, who are men
of the world, that a good uniform must
work its way with the women, sooner or
later.
    DICKENS.—*Pickwick Papers*, c. 37.

Those who make their dress a principal
part of themselves, will, in general, become
of no more value than their dress.
    HAZLITT.—*On the Clerical Character.*

A sweet disorder in the dress.
    HERRICK.—*Delight in Disorder.*

As if to show that love had made him
    smart
All over, and not merely round his heart.
    HOOD.—*Bianca's Dream.*

For gowns, and gloves, and caps, and
    tippets,
Are beauty's sauces, spice, and sippets.
    HOOD.—*Recipe.*

The world must be getting old, I think ;
it dresses so very soberly now.
J. K. JEROME.—*Idle Thoughts (On Dress).*

Still to be neat, still to be drest,
As you were going to a feast ;
Still to be powdered, still perfumed,
Lady, it is to be presumed,
Though art's hid causes are not found,
All is not sweet, all is not sound.
    BEN JONSON.—*Epicœne.*

To show the form it seemed to hide.
    SCOTT.—*Lord of the Isles*, c. 1, st. 5.

Costly thy habit as thy purse can buy,
But not expressed in fancy ; rich, not
    gaudy ;
For the apparel oft proclaims the man.
    SHAKESPEARE.—*Hamlet*, Act 1, 3.

As martyrs burn for Christ, so ladies
freeze for fashion.
    C. H. SPURGEON.—*"Salt-Cellars."*

'Tis a *credit* to any good girl to be neat,
    But quite a disgrace to be *fine.*
    ANN AND JANE TAYLOR.—*Folly of
                                    Finery.*

I love that beauty should go beautifully.
    TENNYSON.—*Geraint and Enid*, l. 682.

O fair undress, best dress ! it checks no
    vein,
But every flowing limb in pleasure drowns,
And heightens ease with grace.
    THOMSON.—*Castle of Indolence*, 1, 26.

Dress being a compliment we owe to
society, you should not show a remissness
therein, unless you would be thought a
sloven.   REV. J. TRUSLER.—*System of
                                Etiquette* (1804).

Let me be dressed fine as I will,
Flies, worms, and flowers exceed me
    still.   I. WATTS.—*Against Pride.*

Women were made to give our eyes
    delight ;
A female sloven is an odious sight.
    YOUNG.—*Love of Fame.*

It's the life o' an auld hat to be weel
cockit.   *Scottish prov.*

DRINKING

Thirst comes with drinking when the
wine is good.   E. AUGIER.—*La Cigue.*

There's naught, no doubt, so much the
    spirit calms,
As rum and true religion.
    BYRON.—*Don Juan*, c. 2, 34.

Man being reasonable, must get drunk ;
The best of life is but intoxication.
    BYRON.—*Ib.*, c. 2, 179.

For dronkenesse is verray sepulture
Of mannes wit and his discrecioun.
    CHAUCER.—*Pardoner's Tale.*

As for a Drunkard, who is *voluntarius dæmon*, he hath (as hath been said) no privilege thereby, but what hurt or ill so ever he doeth, his drunkenness doth aggravate it.   SIR E. COKE.—*Institutes*.

To drink is a Christian diversion, Unknown to the Turk or the Persian. CONGREVE.—*Way of the World*, Act 4, 2.

The thirsty earth soaks up the rain, And drinks and gapes for drink again ; The plants suck in the earth, and are With constant drinking fresh and fair. COWLEY.—*Drinking*.

Therefore I *do* require it, which I makes confession, to be brought reg'lar and drawed mild [*Mrs. Gamp*]. DICKENS.—*M. Chuzzlewit, c.* 25.

"Wery good power o' suction, Sammy," said Mr. Weller the elder. . . . "You'd ha' made an uncommon fine oyster, Sammy, if you'd been born in that station o' life."   DICKENS.—*Pickwick, c.* 23.

From wine what sudden friendship springs !   GAY.—*Fables*, 50.

Man wants but little drink below, But wants that little strong. O. W. HOLMES.—*Song of Other Days*.

Hundreds of men were turned into beasts, Like the guests at Circe's horrible feasts, By the magic of ale and cider. HOOD.—*Miss Kilmansegg*.

Long quaffing maketh a short lyfe. JOHN LYLY.—*Euphues*.

Oh some are fond of Spanish wine, and some are fond of French, And some 'll swallow tay and stuff fit only for a wench. J. MASEFIELD.—*Capt. Stratton's Fancy*.

Oh some that's good and godly ones they holds that it's a sin To troll the jolly bowl around, and let the dollars spin ; But I'm for toleration and for drinking at an inn, Says the old bold mate of Harry Morgan. JOHN MASEFIELD.—*Ib.*

Busy, curious, thirsty fly, Drink with me, and drink as I. W. OLDYS.—*Song*.

Potations pottle deep. SHAKESPEARE.—*Othello*, Act 2, 3.

O thou invisible spirit of wine, if thou hast no name to be known by, let us call thee devil.   SHAKESPEARE.—*Ib.*

O that men should put an enemy in their mouths, to steal away their brains ! SHAKESPEARE.—*Ib.*

Every inordinate cup is unblessed, and the ingredient is a devil. SHAKESPEARE.—*Ib.*

"A little drop" may end in a great fall. C. H. SPURGEON.—*John Ploughman*.

I cannot eat but little meat, My stomach is not good : But sure I think that I can drink With him that wears a hood. WM. STEVENSON (?).—*Gammer Gurton* (*c.* 1550).

The dew was falling fast, the stars began to blink ; I heard a voice ; it said, "Drink, pretty creature, drink." WORDSWORTH.—*Pet Lamb*.

We're gaily yet, we're gaily yet, And we're not very fow, but we're gaily yet ; Then set ye awhile, and tipple a bit, For we's not very fow, but we're gaily yet. "Colonel Bully," in "*The Provoked Wife*," Covent Garden version, *c.* 1800. (*The song is not in Vanbrugh's original version.*)

There are five reasons for drinking : the visit of a friend, present thirst, future thirst, the goodness of the wine, or any other reason. *Attrib. to Père Sirmond* (16th *cent.*).

Drink or begone. *Ancient Greek maxim of Topers*.

If you get the best of whiskey it will get the best of you.   *American saying*.

He that goes to bed thirsty rises healthy. *Prov.* (*Geo. Herbert*), *from the French*.

Whiskey is a bad thing—especially bad whiskey. *Highland saying* (*quoted by C. H. Spurgeon*).

Nae luck till the second tumbler, and nae peace after the fourth.   *Scottish prov.*

Fair fa' gude drink, For it gars folk speak as they think. *Scottish saying*

Wine wears no breeches. *Spanish prov. equiv. to the English,* "*What soberness conceals drunkenness reveals.*"

DROWNING

A solitary shriek, the bubbling cry Of some strong swimmer in his agony. BYRON.—*Don Juan, c.* 2, *st.* 53.

And Christians love in the turf to lie,
Not in watery graves to be ;
Nay, the very fishes will sooner die
On the land than in the sea.
HOOD.—*Mermaid of Margate.*

O Lord ! methought what pain it was to
drown.
SHAKESPEARE.—*Richard III.*, Act 1, 4.

It's best to let saut water tak its ain
gate ; luck never came o' crossin' it.
*Shetland prov., in excuse for not
attempting to rescue a drowning person.*

Luck never came of a half drowned man
or a half hanged one either.
*Scottish prov. (a superstitious excuse
for not rescuing a drowning man or a
hanging man).*

DRUDGERY

A captive fettered to the oar of gain.
W. FALCONER.—*Shipwreck.*

Curse on the man who business first designed,
And by 't enthralled a freeborn lover's
mind.
OLDHAM.—*Complaining of Absence.*

DRUGS

The insane root
That takes the reason prisoner.
SHAKESPEARE.—*Macbeth*, Act 1, 3.

DRYNESS

Dry as the remainder biscuit,
After a voyage.
SHAKESPEARE.—*As You Like It*, Act 2, 7.

DUALISM

God be thanked, the meanest of his
creatures
Boasts two soul-sides—one to face the
world with,
One to show a woman when he loves her.
BROWNING.—*One Word More.*

Like two single gentlemen rolled into
one.
G. COLMAN, JR.—*Lodgings for Single
Gentlemen.*

United, yet divided, twain at once ;
So sit two Kings of Brentford on one
throne.   COWPER.—*The Sofa.*

The chest, contrived a double debt to pay,
A bed by night, a chest of drawers by day.
GOLDSMITH.—*Deserted Village.*

Where the Rug's twofold use we might
display,
By night a blanket and a plaid by day.
E. B. GREENE.—*Juvenal Imitated.*

There's a double beauty whenever a
Swan
Swims on a lake with her double thereon.
HOOD.—*Miss Kilmansegg.*

In form and feature, face and limb,
I grew so like my brother,
That folks got taking me for him,
And each for one another.
H. S. LEIGH.—*Twins.*

Man is not truly one, but truly two.
R. L. STEVENSON.—*Jekyll and Hyde.*

As if within his frame
Two several souls alternately had lodged,
Two sets of manners could the youth put
on. WORDSWORTH.—*Excursion*, Bk. 6.

"Are they no a bonny pair ? " as the
deil said to his hoofs.   *Scottish prov.*

DUBLIN

It's as true as the deil's in Dublin city.
Scottish prov.

DUELS

So up into the harmless air
Their bullets they did send;
And may all other duels have
That upshot in the end.
HOOD.—*The Duel*, 1831.

The Christless code
That must have Life for a blow.
TENNYSON.—*Maud, Pt.* 2, 1, 1.

DUES

Crito, we owe a cock to Æsculapius.
Pay it, therefore, and do not neglect it.
SOCRATES.—*His last words, according
to Plato (Phædo, c.* 155) *(Cary tr.).*

DULLNESS

O Dullness ! portion of the truly blest !
Calm shattered haven of eternal rest !
BURNS.—*3rd Ep. to Mr. Graham.*

The petrifactions of a plodding brain.
BYRON.—*English Bards and Scotch
Reviewers*, 416.

I find that we are growing serious, and
then we are in great danger of being dull.
CONGREVE.—*Old Bachelor.*

And gentle dullness ever loves a joke.
POPE.—*Dunciad, Bk.* 2, 34.

Dullness is sacred in a sound divine.
POPE.—*Ib.*, Bk. 2, 352.

For thee we dim the eyes, and stuff the
head
With all such reading as was never read ;
For thee explain a thing till all men doubt
it,
And write about it, goddess, and about it.
POPE.—*Ib.*, Bk. 4, 248.

You beat your pate, and fancy wit will
    come ;
Knock as you please, there's nobody at
    home.   POPE.—*Epigram.*

A dull and muddy-mettled rascal.
    SHAKESPEARE.—*Hamlet*, Act 2, 2.

Cudgel thy brains no more about it ;
for your dull ass will not mend his pace with
beating.   SHAKESPEARE.—*Ib.*, Act 5, 1.

It is to be noted that when any part of
this paper appears dull, there is a design
in it.   STEELE.—*Tatler*, No. 38.

Accept a miracle instead of wit,—
See two dull lines with Stanhope's pencil
writ.
    YOUNG.—*Written with Lord Chesterfield's
                    diamond pencil.*

DUNCES

Such as take lodgings in a head
That's to be let unfurnishèd.
    BUTLER.—*Hudibras, Pt. 1, 1.*

DUPES

You fancy he is your dupe, but if he
is only pretending to be, which is the
greater dupe ?
    LA BRUYÈRE.—*De la Société.*

What web too weak to catch a modern
brain ?   COWPER.—*Expostulation*, 629.

Men seem to be born to make dupes, one
of another. VAUVENARGUES.—*Maxim* 522.

DUPLICITY

Beware alway of doubleness.
    LYDGATE.—*Balade.*

" It's gude to be merry and wise," as the
miller said when he moutered (took toll)
twice.   *Scottish prov.*

DUTCH

In matters of commerce the fault of the
    Dutch
Is offering too little and asking too much.
    GEO. CANNING.—*Despatch*, 1826.

DUTY

        Like as a Star
    That maketh not haste,
    That taketh not rest,
    Be each one fulfilling
    His God-given Hest.
        CARLYLE (*tr. of Goethe*).

Do the duty which lies nearest thee,
which thou knowest to be a duty ! The
second duty will already become clearer.
    CARLYLE.—*Sartor.*

So nigh is grandeur to our dust,
    So near is God to man,
When duty whispers low, " Thou must,"
    The youth replies, " I can."
        EMERSON.—*Voluntaries.*

For duty, duty must be done ;
The rule applies to everyone ;
And painful though that duty be,
To shirk the task were fiddle-de-dee.
    SIR W. S. GILBERT.—*Ruddigore.*

I slept, and dreamed that life was Beauty ;
I woke, and found that life was Duty.
    ELLEN HOOPER.—*The Dial.*

If on our daily course our mind
Be set to hallow all we find,
New treasures still, of countless price,
God will provide for sacrifice.
        KEBLE.—*Morning Hymn.*

The trivial round, the common task
Would furnish all we ought to ask ;
Room to deny ourselves, a road
To bring us daily nearer God.
                KEBLE.—*Ib.*

Then draw we nearer, day by day,
Each to his brethren, all to God ;
Let the world take us as she may,
We must not change our road.
    KEBLE.—*2nd Sun. after Trin.*

Do the work that's nearest,
    Though it's dull at whiles,
Helping, when we meet them,
    Lame dogs over stiles.
        C. KINGSLEY.—*Invitation.*

The only way to regenerate the world is
to do the duty which lies nearest us, and
not hunt after grand, far-fetched ones for
ourselves.
    C. KINGSLEY.—*Letters and Memories.*

Straight is the line of duty ;
Curved is the line of beauty ;
Follow the straight line, thou shalt see
The curved line ever follow thee.
    WM. MACCALL (*c.* 1830). *But attrib. by
    Douglas Jerrold to "N.W." with the
    first two lines transposed and the others
    given : "Walk by the last, and thou
    wilt see The other ever follow thee."*

But here I am not left to choose,
    My duty is my lot ;
And weighty things will glory lose,
    If small ones are forgot.
        G. MACDONALD.

You would not think any duty small
    If you yourself were great.
    G MACDONALD.—*Willie's Question.*

This world is full of beauty, as other
    worlds above,
And if we did our duty, it might be as
    full of love.
    G. MASSEY.—*This World.*

As ever in my great Taskmaster's
eye.   MILTON.—*On being arrived to
the age of twenty-three.*

To know
That which before us lies in daily life,
Is the prime wisdom ; what is more is
fume,
Or emptiness, or fond impertinence.
MILTON.—*Paradise Lost, Bk.* 8, 192.

Knowledge is a steep which few may
climb,
While Duty is a path which all may tread.
SIR L. MORRIS.—*Epic of Hades.*

In matters of duty first thoughts are
commonly best. They have more in
them of the voice of God.
CARDINAL NEWMAN.—*See " N. and Q.,"
May* 21, 1898.

This then, my friend, said I [Socrates],
somehow seems to be justice,—to attend
to one's own business, . . . when child
and woman, bond and free, artificer,
magistrate, and subject, everyone in
short, attends to his own business and does
not meddle.
PLATO.—*Republic, Bk.* 4, 11 (*Davis tr.*).

God never imposes a duty without giving
time to do it.
RUSKIN.—*Lectures on Architecture.*

For never anything can be amiss
When simpleness and duty tender it.
SHAKESPEARE.—*Midsummer Night's
Dream,* Act 5, 1.

In the modesty of fearful duty
I read as much as from the rattling
tongue
Of saucy and audacious eloquence.
SHAKESPEARE.—*Ib.*

I do perceive here a divided duty.
SHAKESPEARE.—*Othello,* Act 1, 3.

Thy path is plain and straight,—that light
is given ;
Onward in faith,—and leave the rest to
Heaven.   SOUTHEY.—*Retrospect.*

" England expects every man to do
his duty." England will not get all it
expects. Every man will do his duty—if
he likes. C. H. SPURGEON.—"*Salt-Cellars.*"

Duty, that strong spur of earnest souls.
BISHOP C. W. STUBBS.—*Conscience.
Una and her Paupers.*

There's life alone in duty done,
And rest alone in striving.
J. G. WHITTIER.—*Drovers.*

A light of duty shines on every day
For all ; and yet how few are warmed or
cheered !
WORDSWORTH.—*Excursion, Bk.* 5.

The primal duties shine aloft like stars.
WORDSWORTH.—*Ib., Bk.* 9.

Stern Daughter of the Voice of God !
O Duty ! WORDSWORTH.—*Ode to Duty.*

Be thankful, even though tired and faint,
For the rich bounties of constraint ;
Whence oft invigorating transports flow,
That choice lacked courage to bestow.
WORDSWORTH.—*Pass of Kirkstone.*

To do my duty in that state of life
unto which it shall please God to call me.
Church Catechism.

O mortal race,
Our lesson learn ;
Each has his turn
And time and place.
*Inscription on Tenor Bell, Colchester
Town Hall.*

England expects every officer and man
to do his duty.
*Actual words of Nelson's signal,
Oct.* 26, 1805.

DYING, THE

Truth sits upon the lips of dying men.
M. ARNOLD.—*Sohrab.*

But she was journeying to the land of
souls.   CAMPBELL.—*Gertrude.*

The slender debt to Nature's quickly paid,
Discharged, perchance, with greater ease
than made.
F. QUARLES.—*Emblems, Bk.* 2, 13.

Oh, but they say the tongues of dying men
Enforce attention, like deep harmony.
SHAKESPEARE.—*Richard II.,* Act 2, 1.

Sweet peace conduct his sweet soul to
the bosom
Of good old Abraham !
SHAKESPEARE.—*Ib.,* Act 4, 1.

And may there be no moaning of the bar,
When I put out to sea !
TENNYSON.—*Crossing the Bar.*

The passing of the sweetest soul
That ever looked with human eyes.
TENNYSON.—*In Memoriam, c.* 57.

E

EAGERNESS

My soul's in arms and eager for the fray.
COLLEY CIBBER.—*Richard III.
(adaptation),* Act 5, 3.

I see you stand like greyhounds in the slips,
Straining upon the start.
SHAKESPEARE.—*Henry V.,* Act 3, 1.

EARLS

Earls that dated from early years.
HOOD.—*Miss Kilmansegg.*

EARLY RISING

Plough deep, while sluggards sleep,
And you shall have corn to sell or keep.
B. FRANKLIN.—*Poor Richard.*

Cheerful at morn he wakes from short repose,
Breathes the keen air and carols as he goes.   GOLDSMITH.—*Traveller.*

Oh! timely happy, timely wise,
Hearts that with rising morn arise!
KEBLE.—*Morning.*

He that would thrive
Must rise by five;
He that hath thriven
May lie till seven.
*Prov. quoted in this form by Sir W.
Scott, 1807.*

They that rise wi' the sun hae their
work weel begun.   *Scottish prov.*

Wash thy face in morning dew,
Thus thou wilt thy health renew.
Old saying.

EARLY TO BED

Would you have a settled head,
You must early go to bed;
I tell you, and I tell 't again,
You must be in bed at ten.
N. CULPEPPER.—*As quoted by Swift in
Letter, Jan. 19, 1710.*

EARTH

Earth fills her lap with pleasures of her own; . . .
The homely Nurse doth all she can
To make her foster-child, her Inmate Man,
Forget the glories he hath known
And that imperial palace whence he came.
WORDSWORTH.—*Intimations of
Immortality.*

Back to earth, the dear green earth.
WORDSWORTH.—*Peter Bell, Prologue.*

Lean not on Earth; 'twill pierce thee to the heart;
A broken reed at best; but oft a spear;
On its sharp point peace bleeds and hope expires.
YOUNG.—*Night Thoughts*, 3.

EARTHQUAKES

The exquisitely polite expression of a correspondent of the English Royal Society, who talks of "the earthquake that had the honour to be noticed by the Royal Society."
MISS EDGEWORTH.—*Essay on Irish
Bulls, ch.* 2.

EASE

An easy-minded soul, and always was.
ARISTOPHANES.—*Frogs,* 82 *(Frere tr.).*
(Of Sophocles.)

Studious of laborious ease.
COWPER.—*The Garden.*

Like a coy maiden, Ease, when courted most,
Farthest retires.   COWPER.—*The Sofa.*

For not to live at ease is not to live.
DRYDEN.—*Persius.*

Studious of ease, and fond of humble things. A. PHILIPS.—*From Holland.*

'Tis as easy as lying.
SHAKESPEARE.—*Hamlet,* Act 3, 2.

To the latter end of a fray, and the beginning of a feast,
Fits a dull fighter, and a keen guest.
SHAKESPEARE.—*Henry IV., Pt.* 1, Act 4.

EAST, THE

Oh, East is East, and West is West, and never the twain shall meet,
Till earth and sky stand presently at God's great judgment seat.
KIPLING.—*Ballad of East and West.*

Ship me somewhere east of Suez, where the best is like the worst,
Where there aren't no Ten Commandments, an' a man can raise a thirst.
KIPLING.—*Mandalay.*

The departure of the wise men from the East seems to have been on a more extensive scale than is generally supposed, for no one of that description seems to have been left behind.
SYDNEY SMITH.—*Letter to Sir. W.
Horton, Jan.* 15, 1835.

EASTER

When Yule comes, dule comes—
Cauld feet and legs;
When Pasch comes, grace comes—
Butter, milk and eggs.
Scottish rhyme.

EATING

Tell me what you eat, and I will tell you what you are.   BRILLAT-SAVARIN.

You ought to eat to live, and not live to eat.   CICERO.—*Ad Herrenium.*

Man is what he eats.   L. FEUERBACH.

I maun confess that I like the Englishers, if they wadna be sae pernicketty about what they eat.
JOHN WILSON.—*Noctes (Ettrick Shepherd).*

The cattle are grazing,
Their heads never raising,
There are forty feeding like one.
      WORDSWORTH.—*In March.*

You may know a carpenter by his chips.   *Suffolk prov. (Of great eaters).*

ECCENTRICITY

Some deemed him wondrous wise, and
  some believed him mad.
      BEATTIE.—*The Minstrel, Bk.* 1, 16.

In truth he was a strange and wayward
  wight.   BEATTIE.—*Ib.*, 1, 22.

"Eccentricities of genius, Sam," said
Mr. Pickwick.
      DICKENS.—*Pickwick, c.* 30.

Free from all meaning, whether good or
  bad,
And, in one word, heroically mad.
      DRYDEN.—*Absalom*, 413.

Our attitude's queer and quaint;
You're wrong if you think it ain't.
      SIR W. S. GILBERT.—*Mikado.*

That so few now dare to be eccentric
marks the chief danger of the time.
      J. S. MILL.—*Liberty, c.* 3.

Having neither the accent of Christians,
nor the gait of Christian, pagan, nor man.
      SHAKESPEARE.—*Hamlet,* Act 3, 2.

ECCLESIASTICISM

And of all plagues with which mankind
  are curst,
Ecclesiastic tyranny's the worst.
      DEFOE.—*True-Born Englishman.*

I like a church; I like a cowl;
I like a prophet of the soul;
And on my heart monastic aisles
Fall like sweet strains, or pensive smiles:
Yet not for all his faith can see,
Would I that cowlèd churchman be.
      EMERSON.—*The Problem.*

Help us to save free conscience from the
  paw
Of hireling wolves, whose gospel is their
  maw.   MILTON.—*To Cromwell.*

But the churchmen fain would kill their
  church,
As the churches have killed their Christ.
      TENNYSON.—*Maud, Pt.* 2, 5, 2.

ECCLESIASTICS

The eagle never lost so much time as
when he submitted to learn of the crow.
      WM. BLAKE.—*Proverbs of Hell.*

Mothers, wives, and maids,
These be the tools wherewith priests
manage men.
      BROWNING.—*Ring and the Book,* 4, 503.

Cleric before and Lay behind;
A lawless linsey-woolsey brother;
Half of one order, half another.
      BUTLER.—*Hudibras, Pt.* 1, c. 3.

That pride to pampered priesthood dear.
      BYRON.—*Childe Harold, c.* 2, 44.

Ful swetely herde he confession,
And plesant was his absolution.
      CHAUCER.—*Canterbury Tales, Prol.* 221.

Oh laugh or mourn with me the rueful
  jest,
A cassocked huntsman, and a fiddling
  priest!
      COWPER.—*Progress of Error*, 110.

"A clergyman, lad," he used to say
to me, "should feel in himself a bit of
every class."
      GEO. ELIOT.—*Theophrastus Such,*
        Looking Backward.

The black earthly spirit of the priest
wounded my life.
      GEO. FOX.—*His Mission.*

I may attribute all changes of religion
in the world to one and the same cause,
and that is, unpleasing priests; and those
not only among the Catholics but even in
that Church that hath presumed most of
reformation. HOBBES.—*Leviathan,* 1, c. 12.

New Presbyter is but Old Priest writ large.
      MILTON.—*New Forcers of Conscience.*

Such as for their bellies' sake
Creep, and intrude, and climb into the
  fold.
Of other care they little reckoning make,
Than how to scramble at the shearers'
  feast.   MILTON.—*Lycidas*, 114.

Blind mouths! that scarce themselves
  know how to hold
A sheep-hook, or have learned aught else
  the least
That to the faithful herdman's art belongs!
      MILTON.—*Ib.*, 119.

The hungry sheep look up and are not
  fed,
But swollen with wind, and the rank mist
  they draw,
Rot inwardly, and foul contagion spread.
      MILTON.—*Ib.*, 125.

But first among the priests dissension
  springs—
Men who attend the altar and should most
Endeavour peace.
      MILTON.—*Paradise Lost, Bk.* 12, 353.

Clericalism ! That is our enemy !
 ALPHONSE PEYRAT.—*Speech*, 1859.

A wealthy priest, but rich without a
fault.   POPE.—*Iliad, Bk.* 5, 16.

So the priests hated him, and he
Repaid their hate with cheerful glee.
 SHELLEY.—*Rosalind.*

A little, round, fat, oily man of God.
 THOMSON.—*Castle of Indolence.*

Woe to the Crown that doth the Cowl
 obey !
WORDSWORTH.—*Eccles. Sonnets, Pt.* 1, 29.

If I were a Cassowary
 On the plains of Timbuctoo,
I would eat a missionary,
 Coat and bands and hymn-book too.
Attrib. to Bishop Wilberforce (1805-1873).

ECONOMY

Frugality is the science of avoiding
unnecessary expenditure, or the art of
managing our property with moderation.
 SENECA.—*De Beneficiis, Bk.* 2, 34.

ECSTASY

His voice grew faint and fixed was his eye,
As if gazing on visions of ecstasy :
The hue of his cheeks and lips decayed ;
Around his mouth a sweet smile played.
 EDMESTON.—*Which is the happiest death
 to die ?*

The young men well nigh wept, and e'en
 the wise
Thought they had reached the gate of
 Paradise.
 WM. MORRIS.—*Jason, Bk.* 13, 51.

EDIFICATION

Whoe'er was edified, themselves were not.
 COWPER.—*Time Piece.*

EDITORS

The dull duty of an editor.
 POPE.—*Pref. to Shakespeare.*

Ah me ! we wound where we never intended to strike ; we create anger where
we never meant harm ; and these thoughts
are the thorns in our Cushion.
 THACKERAY.—*Thorn in the Cushion.*

EDUCATION

Lord, they'd have taught me Latin in
 pure waste !   BROWNING.—*Fra Lippo.*

There's a new tribunal now,
Higher than God's—the educated man's.
 BROWNING.—*Ring and the Book,*
 10, 1976.

The languages, especially the dead,
 The sciences, and most of all the ab-
 struse,
The arts, at least all such as could be said
 To be the most remote from common
 use,
In all these she was much and deeply
 read. BYRON.—*Don Juan,* 1, 40.

A Burns is infinitely better educated
than a Byron.   CARLYLE.—*Note Book.*

What greater or better gift to the state
than to train up youth ?
 CICERO.—*De Divinatione.*

Better build schoolrooms for " the boy,"
Than cells and gibbets for " the man."
 ELIZA COOK.—*Ragged Schools.*

A teacher should be sparing of his smile.
 COWPER.—*Charity.*

With culture spoil what else would flourish
 wild,
And rock the cradle till they bruise the
 child.
 GEO. COX.—*Black Gowns and Red Coats.*

Women, in my observation, have little
or no difference in them, but as they are
or are not distinguished by education.
 DEFOE.—*Of Academies.*

A smattering of everything and a
knowledge of nothing.
 DICKENS.—*Sketches by Boz.*

The foundation of every state is the
education of its youth.
 DIOGENES (*According to Stobæus*).

By education most have been misled ;
So they believe because they so were
 bred.
The priest continues what the nurse began,
And thus the child imposes on the man.
 DRYDEN.—*Hind and the Panther,*
 Pt. 3, 389.

When want of learning kept the laymen
 low,
And none but priests were authorised to
 know ;
When what small knowledge was, in them
 did dwell ;
And he a god, who could but read and
 spell.   DRYDEN.—*Religio Laici.*

That's a bad sort of eddication as
makes folks unreasonable.
 GEO. ELIOT.—*Amos Barton.*

It is this wise mixture of good drill
in Latin grammar with good drill in
cricket, boating, and wrestling, that is
the boast of English education, and of
high importance to the matter in hand.
 EMERSON.—*Eloquence (Letters
 and Social Aims).*

Regular education is unfavourable to vigour or originality of understanding.
LORD JEFFREY.—*Edin. Review*, 1806.

Well may the bairn blesse that hym to book sette.
LANGLAND.—*Piers Plowman.*

A general State education is a mere contrivance for moulding people to be exactly like one another.
J. S. MILL.—*Liberty, ch.* 5.

What then is education? . . . Surely gymnastics for the body and music [i.e., literature and the arts] for the mind.
PLATO.—*Republic, Bk.* 2, 16.

The richest soil, if uncultivated, produces the rankest weeds.
PLUTARCH.—*Coriolanus.*

'Tis education forms the common mind; Just as the twig is bent, the tree's inclined.
POPE.—*Ep.* 1.

What is the most useful rule of all education? Not to gain time, but to lose it.
ROUSSEAU.—*Emile.*

The education of children is a business where one must know how to lose time in order to gain it.
ROUSSEAU.—*Ib.*

The great secret of education is to secure that bodily and mental exercises shall always serve to relax one another.
ROUSSEAU —*Ib.*

The book which, to my thinking, is the happiest treatise on natural education is " Robinson Crusoe."
ROUSSEAU.—*Ib.*

Children should be kept from all kinds of instruction that may make errors possible, until their sixteenth year—that is to say from philosophy, religion, and general views of all sorts.
SCHOPENHAUER.—*On Education.*

Thou hast most traitorously corrupted the youth of the realm in erecting a grammar school.
SHAKESPEARE.—*Henry VI., Pt.* 2, Act 4, 7.

To be a well-favoured man is the gift of fortune; but to write and read comes by nature.
SHAKESPEARE.—*Much Ado, Act* 3, 3.

Education has for its object the formation of character.
H. SPENCER.—*Social Statics, Pt.* 2, *ch.* 17, *sec.* 4.

An educated villain has all the more tools at command with which to do evil.
C. H. SPURGEON.—*" Salt-Cellars."*

The clothing of our minds certainly ought to be regarded before that of our bodies.
SIR R. STEELE.—*Spectator,* 75.

Delightful task! to rear the tender thought,
To teach the young idea how to shoot;
To pour the fresh instruction o'er the mind!
THOMSON.—*Seasons, Spring.*

The vices of the mind may be corrected, but when the heart is bad, nothing can change it.
VOLTAIRE.—*Charlot.*

Educate men without religion and you make them but clever devils.
DUKE OF WELLINGTON.—*Saying (attributed).*

Satan keeps school for neglected children.
Quoted as a saying in C. H. Spurgeon's " Salt-Cellars."

Education is a possession which cannot be taken away from men. *Greek saying.*

High learnt niggers ain't much use at rolling logs. *Negro prov.*

EFFEMINACY

None but those whose courage is unquestionable, can afford to be effeminate.
(1st) LORD LYTTON.—*Pelham, ch.* 44.

To waste undangered, on his mother's arm Youth without glory.
PINDAR.—*Pythian Odes,* 4, 327 (*Moore tr.*)

Elegance is not a manly ornament.
SENECA.—*Ep.* 115.

EFFICIENCY

And skill's a joy to any man.
J. MASEFIELD.—*Everlasting Mercy,* 600.

There are only two qualities in this world: efficiency and inefficiency; and only two sorts of people: the efficient and the inefficient.
G. B. SHAW.—*John Bull's Other Island, Act* 4.

EFFORT

For not on downy plumes, nor under shade Of canopy reposing, fame is won.
DANTE.—*Inferno* (tr. *H. F. Cary*), *c.* 24, 46.

The sum of wisdom is that the time is never lost that is devoted to work.
EMERSON.—*Success.*

Think not of rest; though dreams be sweet,
Start up, and ply your heavenward feet.
KEBLE.—*Christian Year, Second Sunday in Advent.*

Draw nigh, my friends, and let your
  thoughts be high ;
Great hearts are glad when it is time to
  give ;
Life is not life to him that dares not die,
  And death not death to him that dares
  to live.   SIR H. NEWBOLT.

After a bad crop you should sow.
                                SENECA.

If you can't be a lighthouse you can be
a night-light.
C. H. SPURGEON.—John Ploughman.

There is nothing which has not been
bitter before being ripe. PUBLILIUS SYRUS.

We must so strive that each man may
regard himself as the chief cause of the
victory.   XENOPHON.

Wherever nature does least, man does
most.   American saying.

It is easy to open a shop but hard to
keep it open.   Chinese prov.

Put a stout heart to a stey brae [a steep
hill].   Scottish prov.

You cannot do anything by doing
nothing.   Prov.

What you will have, quoth God, pay for
it and take it.
          Quoted as a prov. by Emerson.

EGOTISM

It is absurd for a man either to commend
or to disparage himself.
          CATO (According to Plutarch).

The surest way to be cheated is to think
oneself cleverer than other people.
LA ROCHEFOUCAULD.—Maxim 127.

You never say a word of yourself, dear
Lady Grey. You have that dreadful sin
of anti-egotism.
SYDNEY SMITH.—Letter to Countess Grey,
                      Nov. 29, 1840.

Yet egotism is good talk. Even dull
biographies are pleasant to read ; and if
to read, why not to hear ?
THACKERAY.—Adventures of Philip.

A reasoning, self-sufficing thing,
An intellectual All-in-all.
WORDSWORTH.—A Poet's Epitaph.

ELECTIONS, PARLIAMENTARY

The sacrifice septennial, when the sons
Of England meet, with watchful care to
  choose
Their delegates, wise, independent men,
Unbribing and unbribed.
SOUTHEY.—Maid of Orleans, Bk. 2.

ELECTRICITY

Knowledge hath clipped the lightning's
wings, and mewed it up for a purpose.
M. F. TUPPER.—Of Hidden Uses.

ELEVATION (OF CHARACTER)

As some tall cliff, that lifts its awful form,
Swells from the vale, and midway leaves
  the storm,
Though round its breast the rolling clouds
  are spread,
Eternal sunshine settles on its head.
GOLDSMITH.—Deserted Village.

There are in this loud stunning tide
  Of human care and crime,
With whom the melodies abide
  Of the everlasting chime :
Who carry music in their heart
Through dusky lane and wrangling mart,
Plying their daily task with busier feet,
Because their secret souls a holy strain
  repeat.   KEBLE.—Christian Year.

ELIZABETHAN AGE

The spacious times of great Elizabeth.
TENNYSON.—Dream of Fair Women.

ELOCUTION

He mouths a sentence as curs mouth a
bone.   CHURCHILL.—Rosciad, V. 322.

He would drown the stage with tears,
And cleave the general ear with horrid
  speech ;
Make mad the guilty, and appal the free ;
Confound the ignorant ; and amaze, in-
  deed,
The very faculties of eyes and ears.
SHAKESPEARE.—Hamlet, Act 2, 2.

Speak the speech, I pray you, as I pronounced it to you, trippingly on the
tongue : but if you mouth it, as many of
your players do, I had as lief the town
crier spoke my lines.
SHAKESPEARE.—Ib., Act 3, 2.

Nor do not saw the air too much with
your hand, thus ; but use all gently.
SHAKESPEARE.—Ib.

ELOQUENCE

Such is sweet eloquence, that does dispel
Envy and Hate, that thirst for human gore ;
And cause in sweet society to dwell
Vile savage minds that lurk in lonely
  cell.
WM. BLAKE.—Imitation of Spenser.

See how your words come from you in a
crowd !
BROWNING.—Soul's Tragedy, Act 1

Eloquence may exist without a propor-
tionable degree of wisdom.
BURKE.—Reflections on the Revolution.

None knew, nor how, nor why, but he en-
    twined
Himself perforce around the hearer's mind.
        BYRON.—*Lara, c. 1, st. 19.*

And of thy tonge the infinit gracious-
    nesse.   CHAUCER.—*Hypsipyle.*

I myself have heard a common blacksmith eloquent, when welding of iron has
been the theme. C. C. COLTON.—*Lacon.*

In addressing the multitude we must remember to follow the advice that Cromwell
gave his soldiers, " Fire low." This is the
great art of the Methodists. If our eloquence is directed above the heads of our
hearers we shall do no execution.
        C. C. COLTON.—*Ib.*

Though deep, yet clear ; though gentle,
    yet not dull ;
Strong without rage, without o'erflowing
full. SIR J. DENHAM.—*Cooper's Hill.*

Such was his force of eloquence, to make
The hearers more concerned than he that
    spake ;
Each seemed to act the part he came to
    see,
And none was more a looker-on than he.
SIR J. DENHAM.—*Lord Strafford's Trial.*

I grew intoxicated with my own eloquence.
        DISRAELI.—*Contarini Fleming, c. 7.*

The subtlest tempter has the smoothest
    style ;
Sirens sing sweetest when they would
    betray.
DRAYTON.—*England's Heroical Epistles.*

Eloquence is the power to translate
a truth into language perfectly intelligible
to the person to whom you speak.
    EMERSON.—*Eloquence (Letters
            and Social Aims).*

One of our statesmen said, " The curse
of this country [America] is eloquent men."
        EMERSON.—*Eloquence.*

On his lips persuasion hung,
And powerful reason ruled his tongue :
Thus he alone could boast the art
To charm at once and sting the heart.
    EUPOLIS.—*In praise of Pericles
            (quoted by Cicero).*

The applause of listening senates to
    command.   GRAY.—*Elegy.*

Thoughts that breathe and words that
    burn.
    GRAY.—*Progress of Poesy, 3, 110.*

His hearers could not cough or look
aside from him without loss. . . . The
fear of every man that heard him was
lest he should make an end.
        BEN JONSON.—*On Bacon.*

What pity 'tis, one that can speak so well,
Should, in his actions, be so ill.
MASSINGER.—*Parliament of Love, Act 3, 3.*

For eloquence the soul, song charms the
    sense.
        MILTON.—*Paradise Lost, Bk. 2, 556.*

The remark is just—but then you have
not been under the wand of the magician.
        WM. PITT.—*On Fox's Eloquence.*

Luxuriancy and pomp of style cheat
the ear, and disguise the weakness and
invalidity of an argument.
        PLUTARCH.—*Of Hearing.*

He ceased ; but left so charming on their
    ear
His voice, that listening still they seemed
    to hear.
        POPE.—*Odyssey, Bk. 11, 414.*

It is the heart which makes men
eloquent.   QUINTILIAN, 10, 7.

It is the province of a good man firstly
to think well, so that he may live rightly
for himself ; and next to speak well, so
that he may live for his country.
    J. C. SCALIGER.—*De Plantis, Bk. 1.*

When things have taken thorough
possession of the mind, words are plentiful.
        SENECA.—*Controvers., 3, Prem.*

But for your words, they rob the Hybla
    bees,
And leave them honeyless.
    SHAKESPEARE.—*Julius Cæsar, Act 5, 1.*

To make the weeper laugh, the laugher
    weep,
He had the dialect and different skill.
SHAKESPEARE.—*Lover's Complaint, st. 18.*

Runs not this speech like iron through
    your blood ?
    SHAKESPEARE.—*Much Ado, Act 5, 1.*

All that is spoke is marred.
    SHAKESPEARE.—*Othello, Act 5, 2.*

Was never eye did see that face,
    Was never ear did hear that tongue,
Was never mind did mind his grace
    That ever thought the travail long.
        SIR P. SIDNEY.—*Friend's Passion.*

Balaam's ass spoke well once, but
it never tried it again. Altogether it
differed greatly from its brethren.
        C. H. SPURGEON.—*" Salt-Cellars."*

Eloquence is the mistress of all the arts. TACITUS.—*De Oratoribus.*

A full-celled honeycomb of eloquence, Stored from all flowers. Poet-like he spoke. TENNYSON.—*Edwin Morris.*

Choice word, and measured phrase, above the reach
Of ordinary men. A stately speech.
WORDSWORTH.—*Resolution and Independence.*

ELYSIUM

And oh! if there be an elysium on earth,
It is this, it is this.
T. MOORE.—*Lalla Rookh, Fire Worshippers, Prol. 2.*

EMBRACE

Imparadised in one another's arms.
MILTON.—*Paradise Lost, Bk. 4, 506.*

EMINENCE

He above the rest
In shape and gesture proudly eminent,
Stood like a tower; his form had not yet lost
All her original brightness, nor appeared
Less than archangel ruined, and the excess
Of glory obscured.
MILTON.—*Paradise Lost, Bk. 1, 589.*

Satan exalted sat, by merit raised
To that bad eminence.
MILTON.—*Ib., Bk. 2, 5.*

The choice and master spirits of this age.
SHAKESPEARE.—*Julius Cæsar, Act 3, 1.*

I have somewhere heard it is a maxim that those to whom everybody allows the second place, have an undoubted title to the first.
SWIFT.—*Tale of a Tub, Booksellers' Dedication.*

Censure is the tax a man pays to the public for being eminent.
SWIFT.—*Thoughts on Various Subjects.*

EMOTION

And when the little heart is big, a little
" sets it off."
R. H. BARHAM.—*Misadventures at Margate.*

Nature has cast me in so soft a mould,
That but to hear a story feigned for pleasure,
Of some sad lover's death, moistens my eyes,
And robs me of my manhood.
DRYDEN.—*All for Love, Act 4, 1.*

Thrice he assayed, and thrice, in spite of scorn,
Tears, such as angels weep, burst forth. At last
Words interwove with sighs found out their way.
MILTON.—*Paradise Lost, Bk. 1, 613.*

And let me wring your heart: for so I shall,
If it be made of penetrable stuff.
SHAKESPEARE.—*Hamlet, Act 3, 4.*

I had to swallow suddenly, or my heart would have got out.
MARK TWAIN.—*Innocents at Home, ch. 33.*

Dull would he be of soul who could pass by
A sight so touching in its majesty.
WORDSWORTH.—*On Westminster Bridge.*

EMPIRE

Far as the breeze can bear, the billows foam,
Survey our empire, and behold our home!
BYRON.—*Corsair, c. 1, st. 1.*

Learn to think imperially.
JOSEPH CHAMBERLAIN.—*Speech, 1904.*

All empire is no more than power in trust.
DRYDEN.—*Absalom and Achitophel, Pt. 1, 411.*

An empire is an immense egotism.
EMERSON.—*The Young American (1844).*

Learn to think continentally.
ALEX. HAMILTON.

To them no bounds of Empire I assign,
Nor term of years to their immortal line.
VIRGIL.—*Æneid, Bk. 1 (Dryden).*

O weakness of the Great! O folly of the Wise!
Where now the haughty Empire that was spread
With such fond hope? Her very speech is dead.
WORDSWORTH.—*Pillar of Trajan (of the Roman Empire).*

The sun never sets on the Spanish dominions.
Spanish saying quoted by Capt. John Smith (1579-1631) and others.

EMPLOYERS AND SERVANTS

If they have a bad master, they keep quarrelling with him; if they have a good master, they keep quarrelling with one another.
GOLDSMITH.—*Good-Natured Man, Act 1.*

EMPLOYMENT

Nothing is so certain as that the vices of leisure are dispersed by occupation.
SENECA.—*Epist.*, 56.

The hand of little employment hath the daintier sense.
SHAKESPEARE.—*Hamlet*, Act 5, 1.

EMPTINESS

A beggarly account of empty boxes.
SHAKESPEARE.—*Romeo and Juliet*, Act 5, 1.

EMPTY-MINDEDNESS

Minds that have nothing to confer
Find little to perceive.
WORDSWORTH.—*Yes, thou art fair.*

EMULATION

Envy, to which the ignoble mind's a slave,
Is emulation in the learn'd or brave.
POPE.—*Essay on Man, Ep.* 2, 191.

Emulation is the whetstone of wits.
Latin prov.

ENCHANTMENT

'Tis wandering on enchanted ground
With dizzy brow and tottering feet.
KEBLE.—*4th Sun. in Advent.*

Enter these enchanted woods,
You who dare.
GEO. MEREDITH.—*The Woods of Westermain*, 1.

ENCOURAGEMENT

Not only hear, but patronise, befriend them,
And where ye justly can commend, commend them ;
And aiblins when they winna stand the test,
Wink hard and say the folks hae done their best ! BURNS.—*Prologue.*

Ye fearful saints, fresh courage take,
The clouds ye so much dread
Are big with mercy, and shall break
In blessings on your head.
COWPER.—*Hymn.*

In this country [England] it is considered a good thing to kill an admiral now and then, to encourage the others.
VOLTAIRE.—*Candide (referring to the execution of Admiral Byng).*

Fight on, my men, Sir Andrew said,
A little I'm hurt, but yet not slain ;
I'll but lie down and bleed awhile,
And then I'll rise and fight again.
Sir Andrew Barton (16th Century).

ENCROACHMENTS

The law doth punish man or woman,
That steals the goose from off the common,
But lets the greater felon loose
Who steals the common from the goose.
Anon.

ENDEAVOUR

For the cause that lacks assistance,
The wrong that needs resistance,
For the future in the distance
And the good that I can do.
G. LINNÆUS BANKS.—*What I live for.*

I will not cease from mental fight,
Nor shall my sword sleep in my hand
Till we have built Jerusalem
In England's green and pleasant land.
WM. BLAKE.—*Milton.*

Our best is bad, nor bears Thy test ;
Still, it should be our very best.
BROWNING.—*Christmas Eve.*

Life is probation, and the earth no goal,
But starting-point of man.
BROWNING.—*Ring and the Book,* 10, 1436.

When human power and failure are equalised for ever,
And the great Light that haloes all is the passionate bright endeavour.
R. BUCHANAN.—*David in Heaven.*

Wha does the utmost that he can,
Will whiles do mair.
BURNS.—*Epistle to Dr. Blacklock.*

Fail not for sorrow, falter not for sin,
But onward, upward, till the goal ye win !
FRANCES A. BUTLER.

The lyf so short, the craft so long to lerne,
Th' assay so hard, so sharp the conquering.
CHAUCER.—*Parliament of Fowls, v.* 1.

My creed is, he is safe that does his best,
And death's a doom sufficient for the rest.
COWPER.—*Hope,* 397.

He shoots higher, that threatens the moon, than he that aims at a tree.
GEO. HERBERT.—*Priest to the Temple.*

And sure th' Eternal Master found
The single talent well employed.
JOHNSON.—*On R. Levett.*

Be good, sweet maid, and let who can be clever ;
Do lovely things, not dream them, all day long ;
And so make Life, and Death, and that For Ever,
One grand sweet song.
C. KINGSLEY.—*Farewell.*

Attempt the end, and never stand to
    doubt ;
Nothing's so hard but search will find it
    out.   R. LOVELACE.—*Seek and Find.*

In the lexicon of youth, which fate reserves
For a bright manhood, there is no such
    word
As —*fail.*
    EDWARD 1st LORD LYTTON.—*Richelieu.*

Hard things are compassed oft by easy
    means.
    MASSINGER.—*New Way to Pay Old
              Debts,* Act 5, 1.

There are giants to slay and they call
    for their Jack.
    GEO. MEREDITH.—*Empty Purse.*

      The virtue lies
In the struggle, not the prize.
    R. M. MILNES (LORD HOUGHTON).
          —*World to the Soul.*

To do your best is to be one man picked
out of a thousand.   EDEN PHILLPOTTS.

Let fowk bide weel and strive to do their
    best ;
Nae mair's required—let Heaven make out
    the rest.
    A. RAMSAY.—*Gentle Shepherd,* Act 1, 2.

We always succeed when we only wish
to do well.   ROUSSEAU.—*Emile.*

      We fail !
But screw your courage to the sticking-
    place,
And we'll not fail.
    SHAKESPEARE.—*Macbeth,* Act 1, 7.

This thing is God ;
To be man with thy might,
To go straight in the strength of thy spirit
    and live out thy life in the light.
            SWINBURNE.

So many worlds, so much to do,
    So little done, such things to be.
    TENNYSON.—*In Memoriam, c.* 73.

Who is the happy Warrior ? Who is he
That every man in arms should wish to be ?
It is the generous Spirit, who, when
    brought
Among the tasks of real life, hath wrought
Upon the plan that pleased his boyish
    thought ;
Whose high endeavours are an inward
    light
That makes the path before him always
    bright ;
Who, with a natural instinct to discern
What knowledge can perform, is diligent
    to learn.
    WORDSWORTH.—*Character of the
            Happy Warrior.*

Yet a rich guerdon waits on minds that
    dare,
If aught be in them of immortal seed.
    WORDSWORTH.—*Sonnets, Pt.* 2, *No.* 4.

On him and on his high endeavour
The light of praise shall shine for ever.
    WORDSWORTH.—*White Doe of
            Rylstone, c.* 5.

Who does the best his circumstance allows,
Does well, acts nobly ; angels could no
    more.   YOUNG.—*Night Thoughts,* 2.

Do the likeliest and God will do the
best.   *Prov. (Scottish).*

ENDINGS

There is an endless merit in a man's
knowing when to have done.
      CARLYLE.—*Francia* (1843).

Som tyme an ende ther is of every dede.
      CHAUCER.—*Knight's Tale.*

Off with his head ! so much for Bucking-
    ham.
    C. CIBBER.—*Richard* III. (*Adapted*),
                Act 4, 3.

The bud may have a bitter taste,
    But sweet will be the flower.
    COWPER.—*Olney Hymns, Bk.* 3, 15.

" That's rayther a sudden pull up, ain't
it, Sammy ? " enquired Mr. Weller.
    DICKENS.—*Pickwick Papers, ch.* 33.

For though the day be never so longe,
At last the belles ringeth to evensonge.
STEPHEN HAWES.—*Pastime cf Pleasure.*

The first act's doubtful, but we say
It is the last commends the play.
      R. HERRICK.—*Hesperides,* 225.

But Scripture saith, an ending of all fine
    things must be.
    C. KINGSLEY.—*Last Buccaneer, st.* 6.

The end of a good thing is an evil ;
the end of an evil thing is a good thing
    LA ROCHEFOUCAULD.—*Maxim* 598.

Time is our tedious song should here have
    ending.   MILTON.—*Christmas Hymn.*

May the gods grant that this may be
the highest point of your glory !
           OVID.—*Heroides.*

It is much easier to begin than to finish.
      PLAUTUS.—*Pœnulus.*

The last of all the Romans, fare thee well.
    SHAKESPEARE.—*Julius Cæsar,* Act 5, 3.

    He makes a swan-like end,
    Fading in music.
    SHAKESPEARE.—*Merchant of Venice,*
                Act 3, 2.

Jack shall have Jill,
Nought shall go ill,
The man shall have his mare agaín, and
all shall be well.
SHAKESPEARE.—*Midsummer Night's
Dream*, Act 3, 2.

O most lame and impotent conclusion!
SHAKESPEARE.—*Othello*, Act 2, 1.

The end crowns all.
SHAKESPEARE.—*Troilus*, Act 4, 5.

Journeys end in lovers' meeting.
SHAKESPEARE.—*Twelfth Night*, Act 2, 3.

Then lullaby, the learned man hath got
the lady gay;
For now my song is ended.
Attrib. to SHAKESPEARE.—*Passionate
Pilgrim*, st. 14.

And, oh, how short are human schemes!
Here ended all our golden dreams.
SWIFT.—*On the death of Dr. Swift*.

There seems to be no part of knowledge
in fewer hands than that of discerning
when to be done. SWIFT.—*Tale of a Tub*.

From too much love of living,
From hope and fear set free,
We thank with brief thanksgiving
Whatever gods may be,
That no life lives for ever;
That dead men rise up never;
That even the weariest river
Winds somewhere safe to sea.
SWINBURNE.—*Garden of Proserpine*.

The end is come of pleasant places,
The end of tender words and faces,
The end of all, the poppied sleep.
SWINBURNE.—*Ilicet*.

Yet a few chapters more, and then the
last: after which, behold Finis itself
comes to an end, and the Infinite begun.
THACKERAY.—*De Finibus*.

At sunset the shadows are twice as long.
VIRGIL.—*Eclogue*, 3.

Whatsoever thou takest in hand, remember the end, and thou shalt never do amiss.
Ecclesiasticus vii, 36.

We bring our years to an end, as it were
a tale that is told. *Church Psalter* xc, 9.

Be the day weary, be the day long,
At length it ringeth to evensong.
Old Saying.

It's ill halting when the race is doun the
brae. *Scottish prov.*

ENDURANCE

Whatever happens, either you have
strength to bear it or you have not. If
you have, exert your strength and do not
murmur. If otherwise do not complain.
The weight will crush you and then destroy
itself. MARCUS AURELIUS.—*Bk.* 10, 3.

To bear is to conquer our fate.
CAMPBELL.—*On visiting Argyleshire*.

Wait, nor against the half-learned lesson
fret,
Nor chide at old belief as if it erred,
Because thou canst not reconcile as yet
The Worker and the Word.
JEAN INGELOW.—*Honours*, 2, *st.* 56.

But bear to-day whate'er To-day may
bring;
'Tis the one way to make To-morrow sing.
R. LE GALLIENNE.—*In her Diary*.

Sorrow and silence are strong, and patient
endurance is godlike.
LONGFELLOW.—*Evangeline, Pt.* 2, *c.* 1, 60.

Know how sublime a thing it is
To suffer and be strong.
LONGFELLOW.—*Light of Stars*.

Who best
Can suffer, best can do.
MILTON.—*Paradise Regained, Bk.* 3, 194.

So sung he joyously, nor knew that they
Must wander yet for many an evil day
Or ever the dread gods should let them
come
Back to the white walls of their long-left
home. W. MORRIS.—*Jason, Bk.* 9, 330.

One should try not to be distressed about
anything, and to take all that happens as
for the best. I believe this to be a duty,
and that not to fulfil it is a sin.
PASCAL.—*Pensées*.

He smarteth most who hides his smart,
And sues for no compassion.
SIR W. RALEGH.—*Silent Lover*.

Makes us rather bear those ills we have
Than fly to others, that we know not of.
SHAKESPEARE.—*Hamlet*, Act 3, 1.

For sufferance is the badge of all our tribe.
SHAKESPEARE.—*Merchant of Venice*,
Act 1, 3.

He's truly valiant that can wisely suffer
The worst that man can breathe.
SHAKESPEARE.—*Timon*, Act 3, 5.

To love, and bear; to hope till Hope
creates
From its own wreck the thing it contem-
plates;
Neither to change, nor falter, nor repent;
This, like thy glory, Titan, is to be
Good, great and joyous, beautiful and free;
This is alone Life, Joy, Empire, and Vic-
tory. SHELLEY.—*Prometheus*, Act 4.

By suffering well, our fortune we subdue ;
Fly when she frowns, and when she calls,
    pursue.
        VIRGIL.—*Æneid, Bk.* 5 (*Dryden tr.*).

Strange ! that a harp of thousand strings
Should keep in tune so long.
        I. WATTS.—*Hymns.*

Jouk (stoop) and let the jaw (wave) go
by.   *Scottish prov.*

He's worth nae weel that can bide nae wae,
As auld Eppie Orkney used to say.
           Scottish saying.

ENEMIES

The smyler with the knyf under the cloke.
        CHAUCER.—*Knight's Tale,* 1141.

The lovinge of oure enemy hath confounded the venim of the devel. For
right as the devel is discomfited by
humilitee, right so is he wounded to the
deeth by love of oure enemy.
        CHAUCER.—*Parson's Tale,* sec. 31.

It is impossible for any man not to
have some enemies.
    LORD CHESTERFIELD.—*Advice to his Son.*

He who has a thousand friends has not
    a friend to spare ;
And he who has one enemy will meet
    him everywhere.
        EMERSON.—*Translations.*

You may padlock the gate of a town,
But never the mouth of a foe.
        EMERSON.—*Tr. from Persian*
        (*Essay on Persian Poetry*).

When fails our dearest friend,
There may be refuge with our direst foe.
    J. S. KNOWLES.—*The Wife,* Act 5.

Reflect that a friend may be made out
of an enemy.   SENECA.

The gifts of enemies are not gifts, and
have no value.   SOPHOCLES.—*Ajax.*

        Never yet
Was noble man but made ignoble talk.
He makes no friend who never made a foe.
        TENNYSON.—*Lancelot.*

All cause of hate was ended in their death ;
Nor could he war with bodies void of
breath.
    VIRGIL.—*Æneid, Bk.* 11 (*Dryden tr.*).

His great heart rejoiced in having found,
on the field of honour, enemies worthy of
his valour.   VOLTAIRE.—*Henriade.*

A man can't be too careful in the choice
of his enemies.
    OSCAR WILDE.—*Dorian Gray.*

Abate their pride, assuage their malice,
and confound their devices.
    Common Prayer (*In Time of War*).

There is no worse pestilence than a
familiar foe.
    Prov. (*Chaucer's Merchant's Tale,* 549).

ENERGY

Genius is mainly an affair of energy.
        M. ARNOLD.

Languor is not in your heart,
Weakness is not in your word,
Weariness not on your brow.
    M. ARNOLD.—*Rugby Chapel.*

Energy is eternal delight.
    WM. BLAKE.—*Voice of the Devil.*

Time could not chill him, fortune sway,
Nor toil with all its burdens tire.
    O. W. HOLMES.—*F. W. C.*

Larikie, Larikie lee !
Wha'll gang up to the heaven wi' me ?
No the lout that lies in his bed,
No the doolfu' that dreeps (droops) his
    head.
    "*The Lark's Song,*" *Scottish rhyme.*

ENGLAND

The weary Titan [England].
    M. ARNOLD.—*Heine's Grave.*

England, England, England,
Girdled by ocean and skies,
And the power of a world and the heart
    of a race,
And a hope that never dies.
        WILFRID CAMPBELL.

Be England what she will,
With all her faults, she is my country still.
    CHURCHILL.—*The Farewell,* 27.

England, a happy land we know,
Where follies naturally grow.
    CHURCHILL.—*The Ghost, Bk.* 1, 112.

Bind her, grind her, burn her with fire,
Cast her ashes into the sea,—
She shall escape, she shall aspire,
She shall arise in a sacred scorn,
Lighting the lives that are yet unborn,
Spirit supernal, splendour eternal,
        England !
    HELEN GRAY CONE (New York).—
    Chant of Love for England (*c.* 1915).

    England be tearless ;
Rise, and with front serene
Answer, thou Spartan queen,
    " Still God is good to me :
    My sons are fearless."
    SIR A. QUILLER COUCH.—*Victoria.*

England, with all thy faults, I love thee
  still,
My country !   COWPER.—*Time Piece.*

England is unrivalled for two things—
sporting and politics.
          DISRAELI.—*Coningsby, Bk. 2, 1.*

  The Continent will not suffer England
to be the workshop of the world,
          DISRAELI.—*House of Commons,
                    March 15, 1838.*

If England's head and heart were one,
Where is that good beneath the sun
Her noble hands should leave undone ?
  S. DOBELL.—*Shower in War-Time.*

  A sea-shell should be the crest of England, not only because it represents a
power built on the waves, but also the
hard finish of the men.
          EMERSON.—*English Traits.
                    6, Manners.*

  Let who will fail, England will not.
These people have sat here a thousand
years, and here will continue to sit. They
will not break up or arrive at any desperate
revolution, like their neighbours ; for they
have as much energy, as much continence
of character, as they ever had.
          EMERSON.—*Ib.*

  There [in America] and not here [in
England] is the seat and centre of the
British race. . . . England, an old and
exhausted island, must one day be contented, like other parents, to be strong only
in her children.
          EMERSON.—*Ib., 16, Stonehenge.*

  England is the best of actual nations.
          EMERSON.—*Ib., 18, Result (1833).*

O England ! full of sin, but most of sloth,
Spit out thy phlegm, and fill thy breast
  with glory.
          GEO. HERBERT.—*Church Porch.*

Attend, all ye who list to hear our noble
  England's praise ;
I tell of the thrice famous deeds she
  wrought in ancient days.
          MACAULAY.—*Armada.*

Let the storm burst ! It will find the Old
  Land
Ready—ripe for a rough, red fray.
She will fight as she fought when she took
  her stand
For the Right in the olden day.
  G. MASSEY.—*Babe Christabel, Old
                    England, 4.*

Now victory to our England !
  And where'er she lifts her hand
In freedom's fight, to rescue Right,
  God bless the dear old Land.
  G. MASSEY.—*England goes to Battle.*

  Let not England forget her precedence
of teaching nations how to live.
          MILTON.—*Doctrine and Discipline of
                    Divorce.*

Land of the lordliest deeds and songs
Since Greece was great and wise.
          C. L. MOORE.—*To England.*

  The English people fancy that they are
free. They greatly deceive themselves.
It is only during the election of Members
of Parliament that they are so.
          ROUSSEAU.—*Contrat Social.*

Come the three corners of the world in
  arms,
  And we shall shock them ! Nought
    shall make us rue
If England to itself do rest but true.
  SHAKESPEARE.—*King John,* Act 5, 7.

This England never 'did, nor never shall,
Lie at the proud foot of a conqueror,
But when it first did help to wound itself.
          SHAKESPEARE.—*Ib.*

This royal throne of kings, this sceptred
  isle,
This earth of majesty, this seat of Mars,
This other Eden, demi-Paradise ;
This fortress built by Nature for herself,
Against infection and the hand of war ;
This happy breed of men, this little world ;
This precious stone, set in the silver sea,
Which serves it in the office of a wall,
Or as a moat defensive to a house,
Against the envy of less happier lands ;
This blessed plot, this earth, this realm,
  this England.
  SHAKESPEARE.—*Richard II.,* Act 2, 1.

England, bound in with the triumphant
  sea !   SHAKESPEARE.—*Ib.*

  Hector : And this ship we are all in ?
This soul's prison we call England ?
  Capt. Shotover : The captain is in his
bunk, drinking bottled ditchwater ; and
the crew is gambling in the forecastle.
She will strike and sink and split. Do
you think the laws of God will be suspended
in favour of England, because you were
born in it ?
  G. B. SHAW.—*Heartbreak House,* Act 3.

  There are only two classes in good society
in England : the equestrian classes and the
neurotic classes.   G. B. SHAW.—*Ib.*

All our past proclaims our future : Shakespeare's voice and Nelson's hand,
Milton's faith and Wordsworth's trust in
  this our chosen and chainless land,
Bear us witness : come the world against
  her, England yet shall stand.
  SWINBURNE.—*England, 2, st. 5.*

No man ever spake as he that bade our
    England be but true,
Keep but faith with England fast and
    firm, and none should bid her rue ;
None may speak as he : but all may know
    the sign that Shakespeare knew.
      SWINBURNE.—*England, 2, st. 7.*

Hope knows not if fear speaks truth, nor
    fear whether hope be not blind as she,
But the sun is in heaven that beholds
    her immortal, and girdled with life
    by the sea.
      SWINBURNE.—*Ib.*, 3, *st. 7.*

Bind fast her homeborn foes with links
    of shame
More strong than iron and more keen
    than flame :
Seal up their lips for shame's sake.
      SWINBURNE.—*New Year's Day.*

O, how good should we be found
Who live on England's happy ground !
    JANE TAYLOR.—*The English Girl.*

O Statesmen, guard us, guard the eye,
    the soul
Of Europe, keep our noble England whole,
    TENNYSON.—*On Wellington.*

We are not cotton-spinners all,
But some love England and her honour
    yet.
    TENNYSON.—*Third of February.*

It has cost much to establish liberty in
England. It has needed seas of blood
to drown the idol of despotic power, but
the English do not think that they have
bought their laws too dearly. Other
nations have not had less troubles, have
not shed less blood, but in their case the
blood they have sacrificed has only
cemented their servitude.
    VOLTAIRE.—*Letters on the English.*

Britons and Romans, Saxons and then
    Danes,
So many conquerors have taken it,
I somdel marvel any land is left.
Yet oak-trees grow, and daisies star the
    grass,
And blissful birds sing blithely as of yore ;
Sheep bleateth, and the mild-eyed cattle
    chaw
Their peaceful cud. Men waggon up the
    hay
And ear the soil and breed the olden way,
As if the conquerors had never passed.
    JAMES F. WAIGHT.—*Harold.*

Time, and the ocean, and some fostering
    star,
In high cabal have made us what we are !
    SIR W. WATSON.—*Ode, Coronation of
                 Edward VII.*

There's never a wave of ocean
The wind can set in motion
That shall not own our England—own
    our England queen.
    T. WATTS-DUNTON.—*Christmas at the
                   Mermaid, 1.*

Freedom's impregnable redoubt,
The wide earth's store-house, fenced about
With breakers roaring to the gales
That stretch a thousand thousand sails.
    WORDSWORTH.—*To Enterprise.*

In our halls is hung
Armoury of the invincible knights of old.
    WORDSWORTH.—*Poems to Nat. Indep.,
                   Pt. 1, 16.*

England is a prison for men, a paradise
for women, a purgatory for servants, a
hell for horses.
    *Proverb (Italian ?) quoted in Fuller's
        " Holy State " (1642).*

ENGLISH LANGUAGE

Praise enough
To fill the ambition of a private man,
That Chatham's language was his mother-
    tongue.   COWPER.—*Time Piece, 235.*

I like the Anglo-Saxon speech,
    With its direct revealings ;
It takes a hold, and seems to reach
    Way down into your feelings.
    EUGENE FIELD.—*Good-Bye ! God
                   Bless You !*

I like our language, as our men and coast ;
Who cannot dress it well, want wit, not
    words.   GEO. HERBERT.—*The Sun.*

ENGLISHMEN

In spite of their hats being very ugly,
Goddam ! I love the English.
    BÉRANGER.—*Les Boxeurs* (1814).

There is a peculiarity in the countenance, as everybody knows, which, though
it cannot be described, is sure to betray
the Englishman.
    BORROW.—*Bible in Spain.*

Cool and quite English, imperturbable.
    BYRON.—*Don Juan, c. 13, st. 14.*

I hope we English will long maintain
our " grand talent pour le silence."
    CARLYLE.—*Heroes, 6.*

Of all the nations in the world, at
present, the English are the stupidest in
speech, the wisest in action.
    CARLYLE.—*Past and Present.*

The English are a dumb people.
    CARLYLE.—*Sartor.*

Liberty is the idol of the English, under
whose banner all the nation lists.
    MRS. CENTLIVRE.—*The Wonder, Act 1, 1.*

An Englishman,
Being flattered, is a lamb ; threatened, a
lion.   CHAPMAN.—*Alphonsus*, Act 1.

A glorious charter, deny it who can,
Is breathed in the words, " I'm an
Englishman."
    ELIZA COOK.—*The Englishman.*

That vain, ill-natured thing, an Englishman.
DEFOE.—*True-born Englishman, Pt.* 1, 133.

No panegyric needs their praise record ;
An Englishman ne'er wants his own good
word.   DEFOE.—*Ib.*, Pt. 2, 152.

For Englishmen are ne'er contented long.
    DEFOE.—*Ib.*, Pt. 2, 244.

But English gratitude is always such,
To hate the hand which doth oblige too
much.   DEFOE.—*Ib.*, Pt. 2, 409.

Of all the nations in the world there is
none that I know of so entirely governed
by their humour as the English.
    DEFOE (*c.* 1690).

I find the Englishman to be him of all
men who stands firmest in his shoes.
    EMERSON.—*English Traits.*

The English composite character betrays a mixed origin. Everything English is a fusion of distant and antagon-
istic elements. . . . Nothing can be praised
in it without damning exceptions ; and
nothing denounced without salvoes of
cordial praise.
    EMERSON.—*Ib.*, 4, *Race.*

The one thing the English value is
pluck.   EMERSON.—*Ib.*, 6, *Manners.*

England produces under favourable
conditions of ease and culture the finest
women in the world.   EMERSON.—*Ib.*

In short, I am afraid that English
nature is so rank and aggressive as to be
a little incompatible with every other.
The world is not wide enough for two.
    EMERSON.—*Ib.*, 9, *Cockayne.*

The habit of brag runs through all
classes [in England].   EMERSON.—*Ib.*

Add to this . . . the peculiarity which
is alleged of the Englishman, that his
virtues do not come out until he quarrels.
    EMERSON.—*Walter Savage Landor*
                    (*Oct.*, 1841).

For he might have been a Roosian,
A French, or Turk, or Proosian,
Or perhaps I-ta-li-an !

But in spite of all temptations
To belong to other nations,
He remains an Englishman.
    SIR W. S. GILBERT.—*Pinafore.*

Then who is he who would deface
The scutcheon of his country's fame ?
. . . .
One wretch alone on earth you'll meet
Though all the universe you scan,
So steeped in treason and deceit—
The anti-English Englishman.
C. L. GRAVES.—*Anti-English Englishman.*

The English in a foreign land are the
gods of boredom . . . and leave everywhere a grey dark cloud of mournfulness
behind them. Their curiosity without
interest, their dressed-up awkwardness,
their insolent timidity, their angular
egotism, and their empty joy at all
melancholy objects, aid in this impression.
    HEINE.—*Florentine Nights.*

Heavy eaters, hard thinkers, often
given up to a peculiar melancholy of our
own, with a climate that for months together would frown away mirth if it could
—many of us with very gloomy thoughts
about our hereafter—if ever there were a
people who should avoid increasing their
dulness by all work and no play, we are
that people.
    SIR A. HELPS.—*Friends in Council,*
                   Bk. 1, ch. 4.

They [Englishmen] are resolute, en-
during, grave, modest, humorous. I lay
great stress upon the last of these qualifications. Nothing corrects theories better
than this sense of humour, which we have
in a greater degree than is to be met with,
I believe, in any other people.
    SIR A. HELPS.—*Ib.*, Bk. 2, ch. 5.

John [Bull] likes a bit of petty larceny
as well as anybody in the world. He
likes it, however, with this difference—the
iniquity must be made legal.
    D. JERROLD.—*Heads of the People.*

Of all the sarse that I can call to mind,
England *doos* make the most onpleasant
kind :
It's you're the sinner ollers, she's the saint ;
Wut's good's all English, all thet isn't ain't.
    J. R. LOWELL.—*Biglow Papers,* 2nd
                    Series, 2.

No people have true common sense
but those who are born in England.
    MONTESQUIEU.—*As cited by Emerson,*
                   English Traits, 5.

The people of England are never so
happy as when you tell them they are
ruined.   A. MURPHY.—*Upholsterer.*

But Lord! to see the absurd nature of Englishmen, that cannot forbear laughing and jeering at everything that looks strange! PEPYS.—*Diary, Nov.* 28, 1662.

It may be said of the English that neither in war are they brave nor in peace are they faithful. As the Spaniard says, " England is a good land with bad people."
STEPHEN PERLIN (*French writer*).—
Description of England and Scotland (Paris, 1558).

These villains [the English] hate all sorts of foreigners. Though they have a good land and a good soil, they are all constantly wicked and moved by every gust of wind. STEPHEN PERLIN.—*Ib.*

We Englishmen, trim, correct,
All minted in the self-same mould,
Warm hearted but of semblance cold,
All-courteous out of self-respect.
CHRISTINA ROSSETTI.—*Enrica.*

Their hearts were made of English oak,
their swords of Sheffield steel.
SCOTT.—*Bold Dragoon.*

John Bull was in his very worst of moods,
Raving of sterile farms and unsold goods.
SCOTT.—*Search after Happiness.*

It was alway yet the trick of our English nation, if they have a good thing to make it too common.
SHAKESPEARE.—*Henry IV.*, Pt. 2, Act 1, 2.

We have in England a curious belief in first-rate people, meaning all the people we do not know; and this consoles us for the undeniable second-rateness of the people we do know.
G. B. SHAW.—*Irrational Knot, Pref.* (1905).

No Englishman has any common sense, or ever had, or ever will.
G. B. SHAW.—*John Bull's Other Island,* Act 1.

There is nothing so bad or so good that you will not find Englishmen doing it; but you will never find an Englishman in the wrong. He does everything on principle. He fights you on patriotic principles; he robs you on business principles; he enslaves you on imperial principles.
G. B. SHAW.—*Man of Destiny.*

The English take their pleasures sadly.
DUC DE SULLY.—*Memoirs. (Wrongly attrib. to Froissart.)*

For the English nation, the best of them are in the centre of all Christians, because they have interior intellectual light. . . . This light they derive from the liberty of speaking and writing, and thereby of thinking.
SWEDENBORG.—*As cited by Emerson, English Traits, No. 3.*

I thank the goodness and the grace,
Which on my birth have smiled,
And made me, in these Christian days,
A happy English child.
ANN AND JANE TAYLOR.—*Child's Hymn of Praise.*

The last great Englishman is low.
TENNYSON.—*On the Duke of Wellington.*

No little lily-handed Baronet he,
A great broad-shouldered, genial Englishman.
TENNYSON.—*Princess, Conclusion.*

How hard it is to make an Englishman acknowledge that he is happy!
THACKERAY.—*Pendennis,* Bk. 2, ch. 31.

The English people are people who defend themselves.
VOLTAIRE.—*La Pucelle.*

When a Frenchman and an Englishman think the same, you may be pretty sure that they are right.
VOLTAIRE.—*Letters on the English.*

We are old in war, and if in guile we are young,
Young also is the spirit that evermore
Burns in our bosom even as heretofore.
SIR W. WATSON.—*To the Troubler of the World,* Aug. 5, 1914.

After a', I maun confess that I like the Englishers, if they wadna be sae pernicketty about what they eat.
JOHN WILSON.—*Noctes.*

Minds like ours, my dear James, must always be above national prejudices, and in all companies it gives me pleasure to declare that, as a people, the English are very little indeed inferior to the Scotch. JOHN WILSON.—*Noctes.*

A right Englishman knows not when a thing is well. *Prov. (Ray's collection).*

ENGRAVERS

Wherein the graver had a strife
With Nature, to out-do the life.
BEN JONSON.—*Shakespeare's Portrait.*

Or where the pictures for the page atone,
And Quarles is saved by beauties not his own. POPE.—*Dunciad,* Bk. 1, 139.

ENJOYMENT

An hour is long if lost in care;
They only live who life enjoy.
JOHN DALTON, D.D.—*Adaptation of Milton's " Comus "* (1738).

Never ending, still beginning,
Fighting still, and still destroying,
If the world be worth thy winning,
Think, O think it worth enjoying!
DRYDEN.—*Alexander's Feast,* st. 5.

A day in such serene enjoyment spent
Is worth an age of splendid discontent.
  Jas. Montgomery.—*Greenland*, 2.

Contented if he might enjoy
The things that others understand.
  Wordsworth.—*A Poet's Epitaph*, st. 14.

Let us start a new religion with one commandment, " Enjoy thyself."
  I. Zangwill.—*Children of the Ghetto,*
      Bk. 2, ch. 6.

ENLIGHTENMENT

Enable with perpetual light
The dulness of our blinded sight.
  John Cosin (Bishop of Durham).—
   Tr. of " Veni, Creator."

Ought one to rest idle amongst the
shadows [of doubt] ? Or ought one to light
a beacon at which calumny and envy
may re-light their torches ? For myself, I
believe that truth should no more hide
before these monsters than that one
should abstain from food for fear of being
poisoned.
  Voltaire.—*The Ignorant Philosopher.*

The shining light, that shineth more and
more unto the perfect day. *Proverbs* iv, 18.

ENMITY

What mark is so fair as the breast of a
foe ?
  Byron.—*Childe Harold, c. 2, st. 72.*

Enmities always keep pace and are
interwoven with friendships.
  Plutarch.—*On Friendships.*

ENTERPRISE

Are there not, dear Michal,
Two points in the adventure of the diver,
One,—when, a beggar, he prepares to
  plunge ;
One,—when, a prince, he rises with the
  pearl ?
Festus, I plunge.
  Browning.—*Paracelsus, Pt. 2.*

Some enterprise
That hath a stomach in 't.
  Shakespeare.—*Hamlet*, Act 1, 1.

The blood more stirs
To rouse a lion, than to start a hare.
  Shakespeare.—*Henry IV., Pt. 1, Act 1, 2.*

But thou, O Goddess ! in thy favourite Isle,
Quicken the slothful and exalt the vile !
Thy impulse is the life of Fame ;
Glad Hope would almost cease to be
If torn from thy society.
  Wordsworth.—*To Enterprise.*

ENTERTAINMENT

A friendly swarry, consisting of a boiled
leg of mutton with the usual trimmings.
  Dickens.—*Pickwick, c. 37.*

For one of the pleasures of having a rout
Is the pleasure of having it over.
  Hood.—*Miss Kilmansegg.*

Our true intent is—all for your delight.
  Shakespeare.—*Midsummer Night's
      Dream, Act 5, 1.*

ENTHUSIASM

It is unfortunate, considering that
enthusiasm moves the world, that so
few enthusiasts can be trusted to speak
the truth.
  A. J. Balfour.—*Letter to Mrs. Drew.*

A cause is like champagne and high
heels—one must be prepared to suffer
for it. Arnold Bennett.—*The Title.*

The sallow, virgin-minded, studious
Martyr to mild enthusiasm.
  Browning.—*Christmas Eve, c. 11.*

I do not blame such women, though for
love
They pick much oakum ; earth's fanatics
make
Too frequently heaven's saints.
  E. B. Browning.—*Aurora Leigh, Bk. 2.*

Never have a mission, my dear child.
[*Mr. Jellyby.*]
  Dickens.—*Bleak House, c. 30.*

Nothing great was ever achieved without
enthusiasm. Emerson.—*Circles.*

Every man—even the most cynical—
has one enthusiasm. He is in earnest
about some one thing. The all-round
trifler does not exist.
  John Oliver Hobbes.—*The
    Ambassador, Act 2.*

I am not going to let you talk like this.
You are doing me an ill turn ; you are
robbing me of my enthusiasm. [*Stensgaard.*] Ibsen.—*League of Youth,
      Act 1 (1869).*

Enthusiasm is the genius of sincerity,
and truth accomplishes no victories without it. Lord Lytton.—*Last Days of
     Pompeii, Bk. 1, c. 8.*

The prudent man may direct a state ;
but it is the enthusiast who regenerates
it, or ruins.
  Lord Lytton.—*Rienzi, Bk. 1, c. 8.*

National enthusiasm is the great nursery
of genius.
  H. T. Tuckerman.—*Defence of
     Enthusiasm.*

Those things which the English public never forgives—youth, power, and enthusiasm.
OSCAR WILDE.—*English Renaissance.*

ENTREATY

He did entreat me past all saying nay.
SHAKESPEARE.—*Merchant of Venice,*
Act 3, 2.

ENUNCIATION

Speak clearly, if you speak at all ;
Carve every word before you let it fall.
O. W. HOLMES.—*Rhymed Lesson.*

ENVY

Envy is hatred of other people's happiness. ST. AUGUSTINE.—*On Psalm,* 104, 25.

Envy has no holidays.
BACON.—*Instauratio, Pt.* 1, *Bk.* 6 (*Prov. ?*).

[His creed resulted] less from love to the many than from hatred of the few.
J. BENTHAM.—*Of James Mill.*

For wel unnethe [scarcely] is there any sinne that it hath not some delight in itself save only Envye, that ever hath in itself anguish and sorrow.
CHAUCER.—*Parson's Tale, sec.* 30.

He sickened at all triumphs but his own.
CHURCHILL.—*Rosciad, v.* 64.

For one man who sincerely pities our misfortunes, there are a thousand who sincerely hate our success.
C. C. COLTON.—*Lacon.*

The hate which we all bear with the most Christian patience is the hate of those who envy us.   C. C. COLTON.—*Ib.*

There is this frequent vice in great and free states, that envy is companion of glory. CORNELIUS NEPOS.—*Chabrias.*

He most is hated when he most is praised.   DRYDEN.—*Rival Ladies.*

Envy is a kind of praise.
GAY.—*Fables,* 44

Lo ! ill-rejoicing Envy, winged with lies,
Scattering calumnious rumours as she flies.
HESIOD.—*Works and Days* (*Elton tr.*).

The Sicilian tyrants have not invented a worse torment than envy.
HORACE.—*Ep., Bk.* 1.

This is the discharge of the black cuttlefish ; this is very envy.
HORACE.—*Sat., Bk.* 1.

Envy the living, not the dead, doth bite ;
For after death all men receive their right.   R. LOVELACE.—*On Sanazar.*

That most anti-social and odious of all passions, envy. J. S. MILL.—*Liberty, ch.* 4.

Can't I another's face commend,
And to her virtues be a friend,
But instantly your forehead lowers,
As if her merit lessened yours ?
EDWARD MOORE.—*Fables.*

The crop is more abundant in other people's fields ; our neighbour's herd has more milk than our own.
OVID.—*Ars Amat., Bk.* 1.

He, the Artificer of this universe, was good ; and in the good envy is never engendered concerning anything whatever.
PLATO.—*Timæus,* 10.

I would rather that my enemies envy me than that I should envy my enemies ; for it is misery to be envious because it is well with another and ill with yourself.
PLAUTUS.—*Truculentus, Act* 4, 2.

Spleen to mankind his envious heart possessed,
And much he hated all, but most the best.
POPE.—*Iliad, Bk.* 2, 267.

Whoso reaps above the rest,
With heaps of hate shall surely be oppressed.
SIR W. RALEGH.—*Commendation of the Steele Glas.*

Such men as he be never at heart's ease,
Whiles they behold a greater than themselves.
SHAKESPEARE.—*Julius Cæsar, Act* 1, 2.

'Tis eminence makes envy rise,
As fairest fruits attract the flies.
SWIFT.—*To Dr. Delany,* 1729.

If with such talents Heaven has blessed them,
Have I not reason to detest them ?
SWIFT.—*On the death of Dr. Swift.*

It is natural to mortals to look with sick eyes on the recent good fortune of others.   TACITUS.—*Hist., Bk.* 2.

Base Envy withers at another's joy,
And hates the excellence it cannot reach.
THOMSON.—*Seasons, Spring.*

Envy is a necessary evil ; it is a little goad which forces us to do yet better.
VOLTAIRE.

I laugh not at another's losse,
I grudge not at another's gaine.
Anon.—" *My Mind to me a Kingdom is.*"

Envy is better worth having than pity.
Greek prov.

The potter is envious of the potter, the smith of the smith.   *Latin prov.*

Envy, eldest born of hell!
Cease in human heart to dwell!
*Handel's "Saul" (1738), attr. to Chas.
Jennings.*

EPICURES

For he was Epicurus owne sone.
CHAUCER.—*Cant. Tales, Prol.*

Although they say, "Come, let us eat and
  drink;
Our life is but a spark, which quickly
  dies":
Though thus they say, they know not
  what to think;
But in their minds ten thousand doubts
  arise.
SIR J. DAVIES.—*Nosce Teipsum,
sec. 30, st. 14.*

He hath a fair sepulchre in the grateful stomach of the judicious epicure—and
for such a tomb might be content to die.
LAMB.—*Roast Pig.*

The fattest hog in Epicurus' sty.
W. MASON.—*Heroic Epistle.*

Serenely full, the epicure would say,
"Fate cannot harm me, I have dined
to-day."
SYDNEY SMITH.—*Recipe for Salad.*

EPILOGUES

If it be true that, "good wine needs no
bush," 'tis true that a good play needs no
epilogue.   SHAKESPEARE.—*Epilogue to
As you Like It.*

EPITAPHS

Stranger, to Lacedæmon go, and tell
That here, obedient to her words, we fell.
GEO. BURGES.—*Tr. of the famous Greek
epitaph by Simonides, on the Greeks
who fell at Thermopylæ.*

Believe a woman or an epitaph,
Or any other thing that's false.
BYRON.—*English Bards, 78.*

And here the precious dust is laid,
Whose purely-tempered clay was made
So fine that it the guest betrayed.
Else the soul grew so fast within,
It broke the outward shell of sin,
And so was hatched a Cherubin.
T. CAREW.—*On Maria Wentworth.*

Ere sin could blight or sorrow fade,
  Death came with friendly care;
The opening bud to Heaven conveyed,
  And bade it blossom there.
COLERIDGE.—*Epitaph on an Infant.*

Yet the work itself shall not be lost, for
it will (as he believed) appear once more
in a new and more beautiful edition, corrected and amended by THE AUTHOR.
B. FRANKLIN.—*Epitaph on Himself.*

If genius fire thee, reader, stay;
If nature move thee, drop a tear;
If neither touch thee, pass away,
For Hogarth's honoured dust lies here.
GARRICK.—*On Hogarth.*

The scene is changed, I am no more;
Death's the last act,—now all is o'er.
GARRICK.—*Epitaph on Quin, the Actor.*

And many a holy text around she strews,
That teach the rustic moralist to die.
GRAY.—*Elegy in a Country Churchyard.*

Here rests his head upon the lap of earth,
A youth to fortune and to fame unknown.   GRAY.—*Ib.*

Calm on the bosom of thy God,
  Fair spirit, rest thee now:
Even while with us thy footstep trod,
  His seal was on thy brow.
Dust, to its narrow house beneath!
  Soul, to its place on high!
They that have seen thy look in death
  No more may fear to die.
MRS. HEMANS.—*A Dirge (Inscribed
on her tomb at Dublin).*

"As I am now, so you must be;
Therefore prepare to follow me."
To follow you I'm not intent,
Till I can learn which way you went.
REV. WM. S. S. HUNTINGTON.—*On an
epitaph in St. Pancras Churchyard.*

The hand of Art here torpid lies,
That traced the essential form of Grace;
Here death has closed the attentive eyes
That saw the manners in the face.
JOHNSON.—*Epitaph for Mr. Hogarth.*

In lapidary inscriptions a man is not
upon oath.
JOHNSON.—*Remark to Dr. Burney, 1775.*

Underneath this stone doth lie
As much beauty as could die;
Which in life did harbour give
To more virtue than doth live.
BEN JONSON.—*Epitaph.*

Few tears, nor these too warm, are shed
By poet over poet dead.
Without premeditated lay
To catch the crowd, I only say,
As over Southey's tomb I bend,
The best of mortals was my friend.
W. S. LANDOR.—*For Southey's Tomb.*

Barring drink and the girls, I ne'er heard
  of a sin;
Many worse, better few, than poor broken
  Maginn.
J. G. LOCKHART.—*Epitaph on Dr. Wm.
Maginn (original of Thackeray's "Cap-
tain Shandon").*

Just to her lips the cup of life she pressed,
Found the taste bitter, and refused the rest;

She felt averse to life's returning day
And softly sighed her little soul away.
    ROBT. LOWTH, D.D.—*Epitaph on an
        Infant.*

      For that dear Name,
Through every form of danger, death, and
    shame,
Onward he journeyed to a happier shore,
Where danger, death, and shame assault
    no more.
    MACAULAY.—*On Henry Martin, ob. (in
        Persia),* 1812.

Gently, where lies our Sophocles in sleep,
Gently, green ivy, with light tendrils
    creep :
There may the roseleaf too and clustered
    vine
Climb round his honoured tomb in grace-
    ful twine :
Sweet were his lays, with sense and feeling
    fraught,
Alike by Muses and by Graces taught.
    MACGREGOR.—*Anthol., tr. of Greek
        epigram.*

    Gentle Lady, may thy grave
    Peace and quiet ever have.
      MILTON.—*Lady Winchester.*

So may some gentle Muse
With lucky words favour my destined urn,
And as he passes, turn
And bid fair Peace be to my sable shroud.
    MILTON.—*Lycidas,* 19.

Teach me like thee to think, and give,
    oh give
That harder happier task, like thee to
    live.
    POPE.—*Epitaph on his Mother.*

Here rests a woman, good without
    pretence,
Blest with plain reason and with sober
    sense ;
No conquests she, but o'er herself, desired ;
No arts essayed, but not to be admired.
    POPE.—*On Mrs. Corbet.*

Fear no more the heat o' the sun,
    Nor the furious winter's rages ;
Thou thy worldly task hast done,
    Home art gone and ta'en thy wages :
Golden lads and girls all must,
As chimney sweepers, come to dust.
    SHAKESPEARE.—*Cymbeline,* Act 4, 2.

    Quiet consummation have ;
    And renownèd be thy grave !
      SHAKESPEARE.—*Ib.*

Cruel is Death ? Nay, kind. He that
    is ta'en
Was old in wisdom, though his years
    were few ;

Life's pleasure hath he lost—escaped
    life's pain,
Nor wedded joys, nor wedded sorrows
    knew.
    GOLDWIN SMITH.—*Tr. of Greek epitaph
      by Julianus, " On a Youth."*

Under the wide and starry sky
Dig my grave and let me lie,
    And I lay me down with a will ;
This be the verse you grave for me—
" Here he lies where he longed to be,
Home is the sailor, home from the sea,
    And the hunter home from the hill."
    R. L. STEVENSON.—*Epitaph.*

Of this blest man let this just praise be
    given :
Heaven was in him before he was in heaven.
    I. WALTON.—*Written in R. Sibbes'
      " Returning Backslider."*

Earth is less fragrant now, and heaven
    more sweet.
    SIR W. WATSON.—*Maiden's Epitaph.*

If innocents are favourites of Heaven,
And God but little asks where little's
    given,
Thy just Creator has for thee in store
Eternal joys ;—can wisest men have
    more ?
    A. A. WATTS.—*On an Idiot Child.*

He first deceased ; she for a little tried
To live without him ; liked it not, and died.
    SIR H. WOTTON.—*Death of Sir A.
      Morton's Wife.*

Under this stone there lieth at rest
    A friendly man, a worthy knight ;
Whose heart and mind was ever prest
    To favour truth, to further right.
    SIR T. WYATT.—*On Sir T. Gravener.*

" Who gathered this flower ? " The
gardener answered, " The Master." And
his fellow-servant held his peace.
    Budock Churchyard and elsewhere.

Rest, gentle Shade, await thy Maker's
    will ;
Then rise unchanged and be an angel still.
    *Epitaph, at Chirk Church (N. Wales), in
      memory of Richard Jebb, who died
      Sept.* 10, 1845, *aged* 8. *(Erected by
      Viscount and Viscountess Dungannon.)*

Past is the fear of future doubt ;
    The sun is from the dial gone ;
The sands are sunk, the glass is out,
    The folly of the farce is done.
    Dirge.—Wit and Mirth (Reprinted 1719).

    Lie heavy on him, earth ! for he
    Laid many heavy loads on thee.
    *On Sir J. Vanbrugh, architect (by Dr.
      Evans).*

And if there be no meeting past the grave,
If all is darkness, silence, yet 'tis rest.
Be not afraid, ye waiting hearts that weep,
For still He giveth His beloved sleep,
And if an endless sleep He wills, 'tis best.
*Huxley's epitaph (1895), said to be by
Mrs. Huxley. Only the first three
lines are over his grave.*

Here lies Tom Hyde ;
It's a pity that he died ;
We had rather
It had been his father ;
If it had been his sister,
We had not missed her ;
If the whole generation,
It had been better for the nation.
*Quoted in letter July 9, 1667, as an epitaph
composed on the death of a son of Lord
Chancellor Hyde.*

Here lies Fred,
Who was alive and is dead.
Had it been his father
I had much rather ;
Had it been his brother,
Still better than the other ;
Had it been his sister,
No one would have missed her ;
Had it been the whole generation,
All the better for the nation ;
But since 'tis only Fred,
That was alive and is dead,
Why, there's no more to be said.
*Jacobite Epitaph on Frederick, Prince of
Wales (died 1751).*

Here lies one whose name was writ in
water.   *Keats's Epitaph, 1820.*

When life is past and death is come,
Then well are they who well have done.
Epitaph in Kilpeck Church.

Beneath this stone old Abra'm lies ;
Nobody laughs and nobody cries ;
Where he's gone or how he fares,
Nobody knows and no one cares.
*On Abraham Newland, Chief Cashier of
Bank of England (d. 1807).*

In heart a Lydia, and in tongue a Hanna,
In zeale a Ruth, in wedlock a Susanna,
Prudently simple, providently wary,
To the world a Martha, and to Heaven a
Mary. *On Dame Dorothy Selby (1641).*

Good frend, for Jesus sake forbear
To digg the Dust encloased here.
Bleste be the Man that spares thes stones,
And curst be he that moves my bones.
Shakespeare's Epitaph, Stratford-on-Avon.

Here am I laid, my life of misery done ;
Ask not my name ; I curse you every one.
*Epitaph of Timon of Athens, as recorded
by Plutarch (Life of Antony).*

Here lies a poor woman who always was
tired
She lived in a house where help was not
hired.
Her last words on earth were : " Dear
friends, I am going
Where washing ain't done, nor sweeping,
nor sewing ;
But everything there is exact to my wishes,
For where they don't eat there's no washing
of dishes ;
I'll be where loud anthems will always be
ringing,
But having no voice, I'll be clear of the
singing.
Don't mourn for me now, don't mourn
for me never,
I'm going to do nothing for ever and ever."
Tired Woman's Epitaph, c. 1850 ? Anon.

His throat they cut from ear to ear,
His brains they battered in :
His name was Mr. William Weare,
He lived in Lyon's Inn.
*Lines (by " Hoppy Webb " ?) on the
murder of William Weare, 1823.*

Here rests a man who never rested here.
*Latin Epitaph on a bishop in Ravenna
Cathedral.*

Between the stirrup and the ground
Mercy I asked, mercy I found.
Quoted in Camden's " Remaines," 1636.

EPITHETS

Adjectives are the greatest enemies of
substantives, though they agree in number,
gender and case.   VOLTAIRE.

EPITOMES

Epitomes have been called the moths of
just history ; they eat out the poetry of
it. SHELLEY.—*Defence of Poetry (1821).*

EQUALITY

The time will come when men
Will be as free and equal as the waves,
That seem to jostle, but that never jar.
ALFRED AUSTIN.—*Tower of Babel,
Act 2.*

Cousin Hastings, we cannot all be top
branches of the tree, though we all spring
from the same root.
FULLER.—*Worthies, Art of Shire Reeves
(Remark of the Earl of Huntingdon).*

And one man is as good as another—
and a great dale betther, as the Irish
philosopher said.
THACKERAY.—*Roundabout Papers,
On Ribbons.*

EQUITY

There is but one law for all, namely
that law which governs all law, the law

of our Creator, the law of humanity, justice, equity—the law of nature and of nations.
BURKE.—*Impeachment of Hastings.*

A good judge judges according to what is right and good, and prefers equity to strict law.   COKE.

EQUIVOCATION

The great sophism of all sophisms being equivocation or ambiguity of words or phrase.
BACON.—*Adv. of Learning, Bk. 2.*

God bless the king, I mean the faith's defender ;
God bless—no harm in blessing—the pretender ;
Who that pretender is—and who is king—
God bless us all,—that's quite another thing.   JOHN BYROM (1691-1753).

He sowed doubtful speeches, and reaped plain, unequivocal hatred.
LAMB.—*Last Essays.*

To doubt the equivocation of the fiend, That lies like truth.
SHAKESPEARE.—*Macbeth*, Act 5, 5.

And be these juggling fiends no more believed,
That palter with us in a double sense ;
That keep the word of promise to our ear,
And break it to our hope.
SHAKESPEARE.—*Ib.*, Act 5, 7.

I moralise two meanings in one word.
SHAKESPEARE.—*Richard III.*, Act 3, 1.

The cruellest lies are often told in silence.
R. L. STEVENSON.—*Virginibus*, Pt. 4.

ERROR

The best may err.
ADDISON.—*Cato*, Act 5, 4.

To err is human, to persist in error is devilish. ST. AUGUSTINE.—*Sermon* 164.

A double error sometimes sets us right.
P. J. BAILEY.—*Festus.*

Truth lies within a little and certain compass, but error is immense.
BOLINGBROKE.—*Reflections upon Exile.*

They defend their errors as if they were defending their inheritance.
BURKE.—*Speech on Economical Reform* (Feb. 1780).

The poor inhabitant below
Was quick to learn, and wise to know,
And keenly felt the friendly glow,
And softer flame ;

But thoughtless follies laid him low,
And stained his name !
BURNS.—*A Bard's Epitaph.*

O think not of his errors now ; remember
His greatness, his munificence, think on all
The lovely features of his character,
On all the noble exploits of his life,
And let them, like an angel's arm, unseen,
Arrest the lifted sword.
COLERIDGE.—*Wallenstein.*

The cottage is sure to suffer for every error of the court, the cabinet, or the camp.
C. C. COLTON.—*Reflections, No.* 5.

Reasoning at every step he treads,
Man yet mistakes his way,
Whilst meaner things, whom instinct leads,
Are rarely known to stray.
COWPER.—*The Doves.*

Faults in the life breed errors in the brain.
COWPER.—*Progress of Error,* 563.

The individual is always mistaken.
EMERSON.—*Experience.*

No vehement error can exist in this world with impunity.
J. A. FROUDE.—*Spinoza.*

Brother, brother, we are both in the wrong.
GAY.—*Beggar's Opera*, Act 2, 2.

The mixture of those things by speech, which by nature are divided, is the mother of all error.   HOOKER.

Error cannot be defended but by error. Untruth cannot be shielded but by untruth.
BISHOP JEWELL.—*Defence of the Apology for the Church of England.*

There is no anguish like an error of which we feel ashamed.
(1st) LORD LYTTON.—*Ernest Maltravers, Bk. 2, c. 3.*

Delusion may triumph, but the triumphs of delusion are but for a day.
MACAULAY.—*Speech*, 1839.

Alas ! how easily things go wrong !
A sigh too deep, or a kiss too long ;
And then comes a mist and a weeping rain,
And life is never the same again.
G. MACDONALD.—*Phantastes.*

The fatal tendency of mankind to leave off thinking about a thing, when it is no longer doubtful, is the cause of half their errors.   J. S. MILL.—*Liberty, c.* 2.

Error by his own arms is best evinced.
MILTON.—*Paradise Regained, Bk.* 4, 235.

For his was the error of head, not of heart.   MOORE.—*The Sloss.*

I see and I approve the better course ;
I follow the worse.   OVID.—*Metam, 7, 20.*

O hateful error, melancholy's child !
Why dost thou show to the apt thoughts
    of men,
The things that are not ?
    SHAKESPEARE.—*Julius Cæsar,* Act 5, 3.

A man finds he has been wrong at every
preceding stage of his career, only to
deduce the astonishing conclusion that
he is at last entirely right.
    R. L. STEVENSON.—*Crabbed Age.*

A man should never be ashamed to
own that he has been in the wrong, which
is but saying, in other words, that he is
wiser to-day than he was yesterday.
    SWIFT.—*Thoughts on Various Subjects*
        (also attrib. to Pope).

Someone had blundered.
    TENNYSON.—*Charge of Light Brigade.*

O purblind race of miserable men !
How many among us at this very hour
Do forge a lifelong trouble for ourselves
By taking true for false, or false for true !
    TENNYSON.—*Geraint and Enid,* 1.

O my princess ! true she errs,
    But in her own grand way.
        TENNYSON.—*Princess, c.* 3, 91.

Error is a hardy plant ; it flourisheth in
every soil.
    M. F. TUPPER.—*Proverbial Philosophy.*

For they are blest that have not much
    to rue—
That have not oft misheard the prompter's
    cue,
Stammered and stumbled, and the wrong
    parts played,
And life a Tragedy of Errors made.
    SIR W. WATSON.—*To a Friend.*

When the learned man errs, he errs in
a learned way.   *Arabic prov.*

It is the nature of men to err, of fools
to persist in error.   *Latin prov.*

ESQUIRE

Now 'Squire 's a title of much reputation—
    Belongs to people of *no*—occupation.
J. WOLCOT.—*Rights of Kings, To the Public.*

ESSEX

England has greater counties—
    Their peace to hers is small ;
Low hills, rich fields, calm rivers,—
    In Essex seek them all
        A. S. CRIPPS.—*Essex.*

ESTIMATES

There is usually less money, less wisdom
and less good faith than men do account
upon.   *Bacon's tr. of Italian prov.*

Maidens' tochers and ministers' stipends
are aye less than ca'd.   *Scottish prov.*

ESTRANGEMENT

I knew you once ; but in Paradise,
If we meet, I will pass nor turn my face.
    BROWNING.—*The Worst of it.*

Shake hands for ever, cancel all our vows,
    And when we meet at any time again,
    Be it not seen in either of our brows
That we one jot of former love retain.
    DRAYTON.—*Ideas, Sonnet* 61.

There must be now no passages of love
Betwixt us twain henceforward evermore.
    TENNYSON.—*Merlin and Vivien.*

ETERNITY

Eternity, thou pleasing, dreadful thought !
    ADDISON.—*Cato,* Act 5, 1.

Who can speak of Eternity without a
solecism ?
    SIR T. BROWNE.—*Religio Medici, Pt.* 1, 11.

He said, " What's time ? Leave Now
    for dogs and apes !
" Man has Forever."
    BROWNING.—*Grammarian's Funeral,* 83.

Nothing is there to come, and nothing past,
But an eternal now does always last.
    COWLEY.—*Davideis, Bk.* 1, 361.

Eternity for bubbles proves at last
A senseless bargain.
    COWPER.—*Garden,* 175.

And what a trifle is a moment's breath,
Laid in the scale with everlasting death !
    SIR J. DENHAM.—*Prudence,* 139.

Eternity be thou my refuge
    Epitaph on the tomb of Etienne
        Pivert de Sennacour.

ETHICS

Begin where we will, we are pretty sure
in a short space to be mumbling our ten
commandments.
        EMERSON.—*Prudence.*

Such a body of ethics, proved to be the
law of nature, from principles of reason,
and reaching all the duties of life, I think
nobody will say the world had before our
Saviour's time.
    LOCKE.—*Reasonableness of*
            Christianity.

I believe that other ethics than any which can be evolved from exclusively Christian sources, must exist, side by side with Christian ethics, to produce the moral regeneration of mankind.
J. S. MILL.—*Liberty, ch. 2.*

ETIQUETTE

But they couldn't chat together—they had not been introduced.
SIR W. S. GILBERT.—*Etiquette.*

Where etiquette prevents me from doing things disagreeable to myself, I am a perfect martinet.
SYDNEY SMITH.—*Letter to Lady Holland, Nov. 6, 1842.*

EUPHEMISM

It [Chinese Labour in South Africa] could not, in the opinion of His Majesty's Government, be classified as slavery in the extreme acceptance of the word without some risk of terminological inexactitude.
WINSTON CHURCHILL.—*Speech in House of Commons, Feb. 22, 1906.*

He had used the word in its Pickwickian sense. . . . He had merely considered him a humbug in a Pickwickian point of view,
DICKENS.—*Pickwick Papers, ch. 1.*

EVENING

At the close of the day, when the hamlet is still,
And mortals the sweets of forgetfulness prove.   BEATTIE.—*The Hermit.*

When the gloaming is, I never made the ghost of an endeavour
To discover—but whatever were the hour it would be sweet.
C. S. CALVERLEY.—*In the Gloaming.*

The dews of the evening most carefully shun,
Those tears of the sky for the loss of the sun.
EARL OF CHESTERFIELD.—*To a Lady in Autumn.*

The curfew tolls the knell of parting day,
The lowing herd winds slowly o'er the lea,
The ploughman homeward plods his weary way,
And leaves the world to darkness and to me.   GRAY.—*Elegy.*

Now fades the glimmering landscape on the sight,
And all the air a solemn stillness holds.
GRAY.—*Ib.*

The day is done, and the darkness
Falls from the wings of Night.
LONGFELLOW.—*Day is done.*

Now came still evening on, and twilight grey
Had in her sober livery all things clad.
MILTON.—*Paradise Lost, Bk. 4, 598.*

How dear to me the hour when daylight dies,
And sunbeams melt along the silent sea,
For then sweet dreams of other days arise,
And memory breathes her vesper sigh to me.   MOORE.—*Irish Melodies.*

The hills grow dark,
On purple peaks a deeper shade descending.
SCOTT.—*Lady of the Lake, Conclusion.*

As pensive evening deepens into night.
WORDSWORTH.—*To ———.*

EVENTS

There are moments in life worth purchasing with worlds.
FIELDING.—*Amelia, Bk. 3, c. 2.*

Oh ! what a crowded world one moment may contain !
MRS. HEMANS.—*The Last Constantine, 59.*

I claim not to have controlled events, but confess plainly that events have controlled me.
ABRAHAM LINCOLN.—*Speech, 1864.*

These most brisk and giddy-paced times.
SHAKESPEARE.—*Twelfth Night, Act. 2, 4.*

It is not an event ; it is a piece of news.
TALLEYRAND (*on the death of Napoleon*).

All the great events of this globe are like the globe itself, of which one half is in the full daylight and the other half is plunged in obscurity.
VOLTAIRE.—*Pyrrhonism of History.*

EVIDENCE

" You must not tell us what the soldier, or any other man said, sir," interposed the judge ; " it's not evidence."
DICKENS.—*Pickwick Papers, ch. 34.*

The ear is a less trustworthy witness than the eye.   HERODOTUS.

One eye-witness is better than ten hearsay witnesses.
PLAUTUS.—*Truculentus, Act 2.*

Give me six lines written by the hand of a most honourable man, and I will find in them something to cause him to be hanged.   RICHELIEU.

Some circumstantial evidence is very strong,—as when you find a trout in the milk.
H. D. THOREAU.—*Unpublished MSS.*

The eyes believe themselves, the ears believe other people.
Prov. (from the Greek).

One man's word is no man's word ;
Justice needs that both be heard.
Translation of Inscription in Frankfort Council Chamber.

EVIL

Evil, once manfully fronted, ceases to be evil.   CARLYLE.—*Chartism, ch.* 10.

The doing evil to avoid an evil cannot be good.   COLERIDGE.—*Piccolomini.*

To do evil to men differs in no respect from committing injustice.
PLATO.—*Crito*, 10 (*Cary tr.*).

Man, do not waste further time in searching for the author of evil ; that author is yourself.   ROUSSEAU.—*Emile.*

He was always for ill, and never for good.
SCOTT.—*Lay of the Last Minstrel, c.* 3, 12.

A thing
     Too bad for bad report.
SHAKESPEARE.—*Cymbeline,* Act 1, 1.

Evil perpetually tends to disappear.
HERBERT SPENCER.—*Social Statics, Pt.* 1, *ch.* 2.

The origin of evil has always been an abyss which no one can fathom.
VOLTAIRE.—*Dictionnaire Philosophique (Bien).*

Good and evil shall not be held equal.
Koran, ch. 41.

EVIL DEEDS

Some act
That has no relish of salvation in it.
SHAKESPEARE.—*Hamlet,* Act 3, 3.

EVILS

Of two evils the lesser is always to be chosen.   THOMAS À KEMPIS.—*De Imit.,* 3, 12, 2.

Of two evils choose neither.
C. H. SPURGEON.—*John Ploughman.*

On the right hand Scylla, on the left implacable Charybdis.
VIRGIL.—*Æneid,* 3, 420.

The twelve evils of the age : (1) A wise man without works ; (2) an old man without religion ; (3) a young man without obedience ; (4) a rich man without charity ; (5) a woman without modesty ; (6) a lord without valour ; (7) a quarrelsome Christian ; (8) a proud pauper ; (9) an unjust king ; (10) a negligent bishop ; (11) a lower class without discipline ; (12) a people without law.
Homily, c. 1200 (*E. E. T. S. No.* 34, *p.* 107).

EVOLUTION

There was an Ape in the days that were earlier ;
Centuries passed and his hair became curlier ;
Centuries more gave a thumb to his wrist,—
Then he was Man,—and a Positivist.
MORTIMER COLLINS.

Evolution is not a force but a process, not a cause but a law.
LORD MORLEY.—*Compromise.*

Yet I doubt not through the ages one increasing purpose runs,
And the thoughts of men are widened with the process of the suns.
TENNYSON.—*Locksley Hall.*

EXACTION

The pound of flesh, which I demand of him,
Is dearly bought, 'tis mine, and I will have it.
SHAKESPEARE.—*Merchant of Venice,* Act 4, 1.

EXAGGERATION

The speaking in perpetual hyperbole is comely in nothing but in love.
BACON.—*Essays, Love.*

A good speaker must be somewhat of a poet and therefore cannot adhere mathematically to the truth.   BISMARCK.

What you exaggerate you weaken.
LA HARPE.

O brother, speak with possibilities,
And do not break into these deep extremes.
SHAKESPEARE.—*Titus Andronicus,* 3, 1.

I am convinced that I cannot exaggerate enough even to lay the foundation of a true expression.
H. D. THOREAU.—*Walden, Conclusion.*

His statements was interesting but tough. MARK TWAIN.—*Huckleberry Finn.*

There was things which he stretched, but mainly he told the truth.
MARK TWAIN.—*Ib.*

EXAMINATIONS

Examinations are formidable even to the best prepared : for the greatest fool may ask more than the wisest man can answer.   C. C. COLTON.—*Lacon.*

EXAMPLE

Example is the school of mankind,
and they will learn at no other.
BURKE.—*Letters on a Regicide Peace.*

This noble ensample to his sheep he yaf,
That first he wroghte, and afterward
he taughte.
CHAUCER.—*Cant. Tales, Prol.*

Example does the whole. Whoever is
foremost
Still leads the herd.
COLERIDGE.—*Wallenstein.*

Himself a wanderer from the narrow way,
His silly sheep, what wonder if they stray ?
COWPER.—*Progress of Error,* 118.

Example is the greatest of all the seducers.
COLLIN D'HARLEVILLE.—*Les Mœurs
du Jour.*

Lives of great men all remind us
We can make our lives sublime,
And departing, leave behind us
Footprints in the sands of time.
LONGFELLOW.—*Psalm of Life.*

There taught us how to live, and (oh, too
high
The price for knowledge !) taught us how
to die.
TICKELL.—*Epitaph on Addison.*

Example is a lesson that all men can
read. GILBERT WEST.—*Education.*

O could we copy their mild virtues !
Then
What joy to live, what blessedness to die !
Methinks their very names shine still and
bright ;
Apart—like glow-worms on a summer's
night.
WORDSWORTH.—*Eccles. Sonnets, Pt.* 3, 5.

Thou hast left behind
Powers that will work for thee, air, earth,
and skies ;
There's not a breathing of the common
wind
That will forget thee. Thou hast great
allies ;
Thy friends are exultations, agonies,
And love, and man's unconquerable mind.
WORDSWORTH.—*Poems to National
Indep., Pt.* 1, *No.* 8 (*To Toussaint
l'Ouverture*).

He mourns the dead who lives as they
desire. YOUNG.—*Night Thoughts,* 2.

If the abbot sings well, the novice soon
gets in harmony with him. *French prov.*

A handful of good life is better than a
bushel of learning.
Prov. quoted by Geo. Herbert.

EXCELLENCE

Give me leave to make the excuse of
Boccace, who when he was upbraided that
some of his novels had not the spirit of
the rest, returned this answer, that Charle-
magne, who made the paladins, was never
able to raise an army of them.
DRYDEN.—*Dedic. of Æneid.*

All these I better in one general best.
SHAKESPEARE.—*Sonnet* 91.

EXCESS

The best things carried to excess are
wrong. CHURCHILL.—*Rosciad,* 1039.

The excesses of our youth are drafts
upon our old age, payable with interest
about thirty years after date.
C. C. COLTON.—*Lacon.*

Solid men of Boston, banish long potations;
Solid men of Boston, make no long
orations.
C. MORRIS.—*Founded on older lines.*

Something too much of this.
SHAKESPEARE.—*Hamlet,* Act 3, 2.

Ah ! No more of that, Hal, an thou lovest
me.
SHAKESPEARE.—*Henry IV., Pt.* 1, Act 2,3.

These violent delights have violent ends,
And in their triumph die.
SHAKESPEARE.—*Romeo and Juliet,*
Act 2, 6.

All owres [overs] are repute to be vyce,
Owre hich, owre low, owre rasch, owre nyce,
Owre het, or zit owre cauld.
Anon.—Cherry and the Slae.

He is like the devil's valet, he does more
than he is told. *French prov.*

All excess turns into vice. *Latin prov.*

EXCISE

Excise : A hateful tax levied upon
commodities. JOHNSON.—*Dictionary.*

EXCITABILITY

Heart of gunpowder, shun the candle
of temptation.
Given as a prov. by C. H. Spurgeon

EXCITEMENT

There was silence deep as death ;
And the boldest held his breath—
For a time.
CAMPBELL.—*Battle of the Baltic,* 2.

EXCLUSIVENESS

Their law of keeping out strangers is a
law of pusillanimity and fear.
BACON.—*New Atlantis.*

The rose that all are praising
Is not the rose for me.
T. H. BAYLY.—*Song.*

Farewell, farewell the heart that lives
alone,
Housed in a dream, at distance from the
. Kind !
Such happiness, wherever it be known,
Is to be pitied ; for 'tis surely blind.
WORDSWORTH.—*Elegiac Stanzas*, 1805.

EXCUSES

"Oh, surely ! surely !" said Mr. Spen-
low. . . . "I should be happy myself to
propose two months, . . . but I have a
partner, Mr. Jorkins."
DICKENS.—*Copperfield, c.* 23.

When you believe that you excuse yourself, you are accusing yourself.
ST. JEROME.—*Ep. 4, c.* 3, *Ad virginem
in exilium missam.*

Hence with denial vain and coy excuse !
MILTON.—*Lycidas*, 18.

In her face excuse
Came prologue, and apology too prompt.
MILTON.—*Paradise Lost, Bk.* 9, 853.

An excuse is worse and more terrible
than a lie ; for an excuse is a lie guarded.
POPE.—*Thoughts on Various Subjects.*

And, oftentimes, excusing of a fault
Doth make the fault the worse by the
excuse.
SHAKESPEARE.—*King John*, Act 4, 2.

A god's command he pleads,
And makes heaven accessory to his deeds.
VIRGIL —*Æneid, Bk.* 4 (*Dryden tr.*).

An excuse uncalled for becomes an obvious accusation.
*Law Maxim. Compare St. Jerome (supra)
and the French "Qui s'excuse s'accuse."*

EXECUTORS

Women be forgetful, children be unkind,
Executors be covetous, and take what they
find ;
If anybody ask where the dead's goods
became,
They answer, So God me help and holy
dome, he died a poor man.
*Quoted as " the old proverb " in Stowe's
" Survey of London,"* 1603.

EXERCISE

Better to hunt in fields for health un-
bought,
Than fee the doctor for a nauseous
draught.
The wise, for cure, on exercise depend ;
God never made his work for man to mend.
DRYDEN.—*To J. Driden.*

Diana is represented as the foe of love,
and the allegory is very correct ; the
languors of love are only born of a sweet
idleness.   ROUSSEAU.—*Emile.*

EXHAUSTION

These are among the effects of un-
remitted labour, when men exhaust their
attention, burn out their candles, and are
left in the dark.
BURKE.— *Letter to a member of
National Assembly* (1791).

The combat ceased for want of combatants.   CORNEILLE.—*Cid*, Act 4, 3.

Yet all the little that I got I spent,
And still returned as empty as I went.
DRYDEN.—*Virgil, Pastoral* 1.

EXILE

The deep unutterable woe
Which none save exiles feel.
W. E. AYTOUN.—*Island of the Scots.*

True patriots we ; for be it understood,
We left our country for our country's good.
G. BARRINGTON.—*Prologue.*

'Twas for the good of my country that I
should be abroad.
G. FARQUHAR.—*Beaux' Stratagem,*
Act 3, 2.

Oh thou, whom chance leads to this name-
less stone,
From that proud country which was once
my own,
By those white cliffs I never more must see,
By that dear language which I spake like
thee,
Forget all feuds and shed one English tear
O'er English dust ;—a broken heart lies
here. MACAULAY.—*On a Jacobite.*

By foreign hands thy dying eyes were
closed,
By foreign hands thy decent limbs composed,
By foreign hands thy humble grave
adorned,
By strangers honoured, and by strangers
mourned !   POPE.—*Elegy*, 51.

For exile hath more terror in his look,
Much more than death.
SHAKESPEARE.—*Romeo and Juliet,*
Act 3, 3.

Weep ye not for the dead, neither be-
moan him : but weep sore for him that
goeth away : for he shall return no more,
nor see his native country.
Jeremiah xxii, 10.

EXISTENCE

I came like Water, and like Wind I go.
FITZGERALD.—*Rubaiyat, st.* 28.

For who would lose,
Though full of pain, this intellectual being,
Those thoughts that wander through
    eternity,
To perish rather, swallowed up and lost
In the wide womb of uncreated night,
Devoid of sense and motion ?
    MILTON.—*Paradise Lost, Bk* 2, 146.

'Tis not the whole of life to live,
    Nor all of death to die.
    J. MONTGOMERY.—*Issues of Life.*

How good it is to live, even at the
    worst !
    STEPHEN PHILLIPS.—*Christ in Hades.*

To be or not to be, that is the question.
    SHAKESPEARE.—*Hamlet*, Act 3, 1.

We look before and after ;
    And pine for what is not ;
Our sincerest laughter
    With some pain is fraught.
    SHELLEY.—*To a Skylark.*

I 'spect I growed. Don't think nobody
never made me.
    MRS. H. B. STOWE.—*Uncle Tom's
        Cabin* (Topsy).

EXPECTANCY AND EXPECTATION

" In case anything turned up," which
was his [Mr. Micawber's] favourite expression. DICKENS.—*David Copperfield.*

Nothing is so good as it seems beforehand. GEO. ELIOT.—*Silas Marner, ch.* 18.

" Blessed is the man who expects
nothing for he shall never be disappointed," was the ninth beatitude which
a man of wit . . . added to the eighth.
    POPE.—*Letter to W. Fortescue, Sept.,*
        1725.

For now sits Expectation in the air.
    SHAKESPEARE.—*Henry V.,* Act 2,
        chorus.

He hath indeed better bettered expectation than you must expect me to tell you
how. SHAKESPEARE.—*Much Ado*, Act 1, 1.

'Tis expectation makes a blessing dear ;
Heaven were not heaven, if we knew what
    it were.
    SIR J. SUCKLING.—*Against Fruition, st.* 4.

Unhappy is he who trusts only to time
for his happiness. VOLTAIRE.—*Artèmire.*

" 'Tis expectation makes a blessing dear ;
Heaven were not heaven, if we knew what
    it were."
If 'twere not heaven, if we knew what it
    were,
'Twould not be heaven to those who now
    are there.
    WALLER.—*Answer to Sir J. Suckling.*

It is folly to expect men to do all that
they may reasonably be expected to do.
    ARCHBP. WHATELY.—*Apophthegms.*

" We'll wait a bit and see," as the puppy
said when he was a week old.   *Prov.*

EXPEDIENCY

If they, directed by Paul's holy pen,
Become discreetly all things to all men,
That all men may become all things to
    them,
Envy may hate, but Justice can't con-
    demn.
    CHURCHILL.—*Prophecy of Famine,* 211.

I [Thrasymachus] maintain that Justice
is merely that which is expedient for the
strongest. PLATO.—*Republic, Bk.* 1, 12.

Wrest once the law to your authority ;
To do a great right, do a little wrong.
    SHAKESPEARE.—*Merchant of Venice,*
        Act 4, 1.

As some affirm that we say, Let us do
evil, that good may come. *Romans* iii, 8.

EXPENDITURE

I see it is impossible for the King to have
things done as cheap as other men.
    PEPYS.—*Diary,* 1662.

Public money is like holy water—everyone helps himself.   *Italian prov.*

EXPERIENCE

By experience we find out a short way
by a long wandering. Learning teacheth
more in one year than experience in
twenty.   R. ASCHAM.—*Scholemaster.*

Difficulty is a severe instructor.
    BURKE.—*Reflections on the Revolution.*

Experience, slow preceptress, teaching oft
The way to glory by miscarriage foul.
    COWPER.—*Garden,* 566.

None know but they who feel the smart.
    SIR J. DENHAM.—*Friendship.*

Experience is the child of Thought, and
Thought is the child of Action. We cannot learn men from books.
    DISRAELI.—*Vivian Grey, Bk.* 5, ch. 1.

The years teach much which the days
never know. EMERSON.—*Experience.*

The Indian Red Jacket, when the young
braves were boasting their deeds, said :
But the sixties have all the twenties and
forties in them. EMERSON.—*Old Age.*

The knowledge which is most delightful
to others is not that which a man takes
out of his mind, as he would money out of

his pocket (both having the impress of another head), but what he gives you stamped with his own nature—his own knowledge.

> SIR A. HELPS.—*Friends in Council,
> Slavery, ch.* 1.

Trustfulness is silver ; experience of the world is golden. [Heire's " proverb of his own invention."]

> IBSEN.—*League of Youth*, Act 1 (1869).

We spend our lives in learning pilotage, And grow good steersmen when the vessel's crank.

> GEO. MEREDITH.—*Wisdom of Eld.*

It is well to be taught, even by an enemy.

> OVID.—*Metam., Bk.* 4.

Them as won't be ruled by the rudder, must be ruled by the rock.

> EDEN PHILLPOTTS.

Experience, that excellent master, has taught me many things.

> PLINY THE YOUNGER.—(*Adapted*).

He best can paint 'em who shall feel 'em most.   POPE.—*Eloisa*, 366.

Then Old Age and Experience, hand in hand, Lead him to Death, and make him understand, After a search so painful and so long, That all his life he has been in the wrong.

> EARL OF ROCHESTER.—*Satire.*

There are not words enough in all Shakespeare to express the merest fraction of a man's experience in an hour.

> R. L. STEVENSON.—*W. Whitman.*

The dirty nurse, Experience, in her kind Hath fouled me.

> TENNYSON.—*Last Tournament.*

Experience is a name everyone gives to their mistakes.

> OSCAR WILDE.—*Lady Windermere's Fan.*

Unless a serpent eats a serpent it will not become a dragon.
Latin (Mediæval) prov. [The meaning appears to be that unless a wise (or cunning) man avails himself of the wisdom (or cunning) of another, he will not be predominant.]

He wrongfully accuses Neptune who makes shipwreck a second time.
Latin prov. quoted by Gellius, Macrobius, Publilius Syrus, etc.

EXPERIMENT

In politics experiments mean revolutions.
> DISRAELI.—*Popanilla, c.* 4.

EXPLANATION

I wish he would explain his explanation.
> BYRON.—*Don Juan, c.* 1, *Dedication,* 2.

Glosyng [i.e., glossing, explaining] is a glorious thing, certeyn, For lettre sleeth [slayeth], so as we clerkes seyn.
> CHAUCER.—*Summoner's Tale,* 85.

The bearings of this observation lays in the application on it.
> DICKENS.—*Dombey, Bk.* 1, 23.

We only call it pretty Fanny's way.
> T. PARNELL.—*Elegy.*

Your defence, Socrates [said Protagoras], is more erroneous than the passage [in Simonides] which you defend.
> PLATO.—*Protagoras,* 76 (*Cary tr.*).

If reasons were as plenty as blackberries, I would give no man a reason upon compulsion, I.   SHAKESPEARE.—*Henry IV.,
Pt.* 1, Act 2, 4.

Egad, I think the interpreter is the hardest to be understood of the two.
> SHERIDAN.—*Critic,* Act 1, 2.

EXPLORATION

Take up the White Man's burden—
    Send forth the best ye breed—
Go, bind your sons to exile
    To serve your captives' need ;
To wait in heavy harness
    On fluttered folk and wild—
Your new-caught sullen peoples,
    Half devil and half child.
> KIPLING.—*White Man's Burden.*

Together let us beat this ample field, Try what the open, what the covert yield.
> POPE.—*Essay on Man.*

EXPLOSIVES

He [Captain Shotover] is trying to discover a psychic ray that will explode all the explosives at the will of a Mahatma.
> G. B. SHAW.—*Heartbreak House,* Act 1.

EXPRESSION

The silent rhetoric of a look.
> S. DANIEL.—*Queen's Arcadia.*

And leered like a love-sick pigeon.
> SOUTHEY.—*Devil's Walk.*

Barring that natural expression of villainy which we all have, the man looked honest enough.
> MARK TWAIN.—*Mysterious Visit.*

EXTENUATION

We must make allowances for a mind which has received a grievous wound.
> OVID.—*Ep. ex. Pont.*

EXTINCTION

Fate cropped him short—for be it understood,
He would have lived much longer, if he
could. W. B. RHODES.—*Bombastes*.

EXTORTION

God be wi' the gude laird o' Balmaghie,
for he ne'er took mair frae a poor man
than he had. *Scottish saying*.

EXTRAVAGANCE

What you do not want is dear at a
farthing. CATO (*Quoted by Seneca*).

Extravagance and good luck, by long
custom, go hand in hand.
MADAME D'ARBLAY.—*Camilla, Bk.* 10,
c. 13.

I never could teach the fools of this
age that the indigent world could be
clothed out of the trimmings of the vain.
GOLDSMITH.—*She Stoops to Conquer*,
Act 1.

Whose welth was want, whose plenty
made him poor.
SPENSER.—*Faerie Queene, Bk.* 1, 4, 29.

Far-fetched and dear bought is good for
ladies.
STUBBES.—*Anatomy of Abuses*, 1583
(*Prov.*).

As if a woman of education bought
things because she wanted them ! Quality
always distinguishes itself, and therefore
as the mechanic people buy things because
they have occasion for 'em, you see women
of rank always buy things because they
have not occasion for 'em.
SIR. J. VANBRUGH.—*Confederacy*,
Act 2, 1.

EXTREMES

Excess of sorrow laughs, excess of joy
weeps. WM. BLAKE.—*Proverbs of Hell*.

So men, who one extravagance would
shun,
Into the contrary extreme have run.
BUTLER.—*Satire on Age of Charles* II.

For blindness is the first-born of excess.
BYRON.—*Heaven and Earth*, 1, 1.

Avoid extremes.
CLEOBULUS OF LINDOS.—(*c. B.C.* 550).

I have seen gross intolerance shown in
support of toleration ; sectarian antipathy
most obtrusively displayed in the promotion of an undistinguishing comprehension of sects ; and acts of cruelty, I had
almost said of treachery, committed in
furtherance of an object vitally important

to the cause of humanity ; and all this
by men too of naturally kind dispositions
and exemplary conduct. COLERIDGE.—
Biographia Literaria, ch. 10.

An Englishman sees easily the absurdity
which lurks in any extreme proposition.
SIR A. HELPS.—*Friends on Council,
Bk.* 2, *ch.* 5.

And feel by turns the bitter change
Of fierce extremes, extremes by change
more fierce,
From beds of raging fire to starve in ice
Their soft ethereal warmth.
MILTON.—*Paradise Lost, Bk.* 2, 598.

Who love too much, hate in the like
extreme. POPE.—*Odyssey, Bk.* 15, 79.

Too far East is West. Your nice man
is nasty, your severely righteous man is
unfair, your ultra-democrat is a tyrant,
and your liberal thinker is a bigot.
C. H. SPURGEON.—"*Salt-Cellars.*"

The falsehood of extremes.
TENNYSON.—*Of Old sat Freedom*.

He that roars for liberty
Faster binds a tyrant's power ;
And the tyrant's cruel glee
Forces on the freer hour.
TENNYSON.—*Vision of Sin., st.* 17.

EXULTATION

Unholy is the voice
Of loud thanksgiving over slaughtered
men. COWPER.—*Odyssey*, 22, 412.

Soothed with the sound the King grew
vain ;
Fought all his battles o'er again ;
And thrice he routed all his foes and thrice
he slew the slain.
DRYDEN.—*Alexander's Feast, st.* 4.

True courage scorns
To vent her prowess in a storm of words ;
And, to the valiant, actions speak alone.
SMOLLETT.—*Regicide*, Act 1, 7.

Why these insulting words, this waste
of breath,
To souls undaunted and secure of death ?
'Tis no dishonour for the brave to die,
Nor came I here with hope of victory.
VIRGIL.—*Æneid, Bk.* 10 (*Dryden tr.*)

EYES

Those eyes of deep, soft, lucent hue—
Eyes too expressive to be blue,
Too lovely to be grey.
M. ARNOLD.—*Faded Leaves* (*On the
Rhine*), 4.

Those eyes, affectionate and glad,
That seemed to love whate'er they looked
upon. CAMPBELL.—*Gertrude, Pt.* 2, 4.

Sweet, silent rhetoric of persuading eyes,
Dumb eloquence, whose power doth move
the blood.
   S. DANIEL.—*Rosamond, st. 19.*

He [Mr. Squeers] had but one eye, and
the popular prejudice runs in favour of
two. DICKENS.—*Nickleby, c. 4.*

His smiling eyes with simple truth were
stored. PHINEAS FLETCHER (?).—
       Britain's Ida, c. 1.

His eyes had a godlike stedfastness,
for it is, generally speaking, the distinctive
mark of a god that his look is unmoved.
. . . Napoleon's eyes possessed this peculiarity, and hence I am convinced that he
also was a god.
  HEINE.—*The Romantic School.*

The lovers, interchanging words and sighs,
Lost in the heaven of one another's eyes.
  LEIGH HUNT.—*Rimini.*

Eyes of most unholy blue.
MOORE.—*Irish Melodies, By That Lake.*

Silence that spoke, and eloquence of
eyes. POPE.—*Iliad, Bk. 14, 252.*

The dew that on the violet lies
Mocks the dark lustre of thine eyes.
  SCOTT.—*Lord of the Isles, 1, 3.*

Those doves' eyes,
Which can make gods forsworn.
SHAKESPEARE.—*Coriolanus, Act 5, 3.*

From women's eyes this doctrine I derive:
They are the ground, the books, the
 academes,
From whence doth spring the true Prome-
 thean fire.
SHAKESPEARE.—*Love's Labour's Lost,*
      Act 4, 3.

For where is any author in the world
Teaches such beauty as a woman's eye?
  SHAKESPEARE.—*Ib.*

The heavenly rhetoric of thine eye.
  SHAKESPEARE.—*Ib.*

In silent wonder of still-gazing eyes.
  SHAKESPEARE.—*Lucrece, 12.*

Thy bones are marrowless, thy blood is
 cold;
Thou hast no speculation in those eyes
Which thou dost glare with.
SHAKESPEARE.—*Macbeth, Act 3, 4.*

Those eyes which burn through smiles that
 fade in tears,
Like stars half quenched in mists of silver
 dew.
  SHELLEY.—*Prometheus, Act 2, 1.*

His soul seemed hovering in his eyes.
  SHELLEY.—*Rosalind.*

An eye full of gentle salutations and soft
responses . . . whispering soft, like the
last low accents of an expiring saint. . . .
It did my Uncle Toby's business.
  STERNE.—*Tristram Shandy, vol. 7, 25.*

Those eyes, the greenest of things blue,
The bluest of things grey.
  SWINBURNE.—*Félise.*

Her eyes are homes of silent prayer.
  TENNYSON.—*In Memoriam, c. 32.*

For it is said by man expert
That the eye is traitor to the heart.
  SIR T. WYATT.—*The Eye Bewrayeth.*

Blue eyes go to the skies,
Grey eyes to Paradise,
Green eyes to hell are bound,
In Purgatory black are found.
  Tr. of old French rhyme.

Grey-eyed, greedy;
Brown-eyed, needy;
Black-eyed, never blin'
Till it shames a' its kin'.
   Scottish saying.

Jest not with the eye or with religion.
  Prov. (Geo. Herbert).

You should never touch your eye but
with your elbow.   *Prov.*

F

FABLES

Young persons are not able to judge
what is allegory and what is not, but
whatever opinions they receive at such an
age are wont to be obliterated with difficulty or immovable.
  PLATO.—*Republic, Bk. 2, 17 (Davis tr.).*

This fable, Glaucon, has been preserved
and is not lost; and it will preserve us
too if we accept its teaching, for thus we
shall happily pass over the river Lethe,
and shall not pollute our souls.
  PLATO.—*Ib., Bk. 10, 16 (of the fable*
       of Lethe).

The applycation most divinely true,
but the discourse itselfe fayned.
  SIR PHILIP SIDNEY.—*Apologie for*
       Poetrie.

Admiration, child of Ignorance, sang
of vain exploits (in reference to Greek
mythology).
  VOLTAIRE.—*To the Academy of Sciences.*

Beware of mixing up the doubtful and
the certain, the chimerical and the true.

We have enough proofs of the great revolutions of the world without searching for new. VOLTAIRE.—*Essay on the Manners of Nations (Introd.).*

The public loves fables best, and so fables are given it.
VOLTAIRE.—*Pyrrhonism of History.*

Fables and endless genealogies.
1 *Timothy* i, 4.

FACE

Thou hast a serious face,
A betting, bargaining, and saving face,
A rich face; pawn it to the usurer.
BEAUMONT AND FLETCHER.—*Scornful Lady*, Act 3.

His face,
The tablet of unutterable thoughts.
BYRON.—*The Dream*, st. 6.

And o'er that fair, broad brow were wrought
The intersected lines of thought.
BYRON.—*Parisina*, st. 17.

That had a fyr-reed cherubinnes face.
CHAUCER.—*Canterbury Tales, Prol.*

Of his visage children were aferd.
CHAUCER.—*Ib.*

And leered like a love-sick pigeon.
COLERIDGE.—*Devil's Thoughts*, st. 13.

Human face divine.
MILTON.—*Paradise Lost*, Bk. 3, 44.

The sweet expression of that face,
For ever changing, yet the same.
ROGERS.—*Farewell.*

The outward indications of the human feelings, however similar amongst all men, have national differences whereby one may easily be deceived. Nationalities have different languages in facial expression as well as in lingual expression.
ROUSSEAU.—*Emile*, Bk. 5.

It is pleasant to know that Pallas had blue eyes; but I think Homer might have also told us something about her lips and chin.
RUSKIN.—*Modern Painters*, Vol. 2, Pt. 3, ch. 3, 6 (*Note*, 1882, to Revised Ed.).

His face was of the doubtful kind
That wins the eye, but not the mind.
SCOTT.—*Rokeby*, c. 5, st. 16.

The tartness of his face sours ripe grapes.
SHAKESPEARE.—*Henry VIII.*, Act 5, 4.

There's no art
To find the mind's construction in the face.
SHAKESPEARE.—*Macbeth*, Act 1, 4.

I saw Othello's visage in his mind.
SHAKESPEARE.—*Othello*, Act 1, 3.

A picturesque countenance rather than one that is esteemed of regular features.
SHENSTONE.—*Humourist.*

If nature has made such a language of looks, it is only vernacular in each particular country. It is not the language of the whole world. SYDNEY SMITH.—*Lectures on Moral Philosophy, No. 22.*

Her face is like the milky way i' the sky,
A meeting of gentle lights without a name.
SIR J. SUCKLING.—*Brenneralt.*

FACTION

What dire effects from civil discord flow!
ADDISON.—*Cato*, Act 5, 4.

Faction, Disappointment's restless child.
SOAME JENYNS.—*On an attempt on His Majesty's Life.*

As we wax hot in faction,
In battle we wax cold;
Wherefore men fight not as they fought
In the brave days of old.
MACAULAY.—*Horatius*, st. 33.

Party is the madness of many for the gain of a few. POPE.—*Miscellanies.*

No men are so disposed to anger as those who are ambitious of honour and affect to carry on a faction in a city, which (according to Pindar) is but a splendid vexation. PLUTARCH.—*Morals*, Bk. 1.

For he will never follow anything
That other men begin.
SHAKESPEARE.—*Julius Cæsar*, Act 2, 1.

What though our danger is not really great?
'Tis brave to oppose a government we hate.
Poison the nation with your jealous fears,
And set the fools together by the ears.
SWIFT.—*Swan Tripe Club.*

The grateful work is done,
The seeds of discord sowed, the war begun;
Frauds, fears, and fury have possessed the state,
And fixed the causes of a lasting hate.
VIRGIL.—*Æneid*, Bk. 7 (*Dryden tr.*).

Nor can we expect that men of factious, peevish, and perverse spirits should be satisfied with anything that can be done in this kind by any other than themselves.
Book of Common Prayer. Pref.

FACTS

But facts are facts and flinch not.
BROWNING.—*Ring and the Book*, 2, 1049.

But facts are chiels that winna ding,
And downa be disputed.
BURNS.—*A Dream.*

Now what I want is, Facts. Facts alone
are wanted in life.
DICKENS.—*Hard Times, c. 1.*

Get your facts first, and then you can
distort them as you please.
MARK TWAIN.—*Interview.*

FAILINGS

True it is she had one failing—
Had a woman ever less?
BURNS.—*Lines under picture of Miss
Burns.*

And even his failings leaned to virtue's
side. GOLDSMITH.—*Deserted Village.*

When you know the failing of a man
whom you wish to please, you must indeed
be very clumsy if you do not succeed.
LE SAGE.—*Gil Blas, Bk. 8, ch. 2.*

Confess the failings as we must,
The lion's mark is always there.
F. T. PALGRAVE.—*Wordsworth.*

FAILURE

If this be then success
'Tis dismaller than any failure.
E. B. BROWNING.—*Aurora Leigh.*

On the earth the broken arcs; in the
heaven, a perfect round.
BROWNING.—*Abt. Vogler, st. 9.*

The best-laid schemes o' mice and men
Gang aft a-gley,
And leave us naught but grief and pain
For promised joy. BURNS.—*To a Mouse.*

Where he falls short, 'tis Nature's fault
alone;
Where he succeeds, the merit's all his own.
CHURCHILL.—*Rosciad,* 1025.

Invention flags, his brain grows muddy,
And black despair succeeds brown study.
CONGREVE.—*An Impossible Thing.*

Our enemies will tell the rest with
pleasure. BISHOP FLEETWOOD.—*Preface
to Sermons,* 1712.

Like ships that sailed for sunny isles
But never came to shore!
T. K. HERVEY.—*Devil's Progress.*

There is not a fiercer hell than the failure
in a great object.
KEATS.—*Pref. to Endymion.*

Boanerges Blitzen, servant of the queen,
Is a dismal failure—is a Might-have-been.
KIPLING.—*Departmental Ditties,
Man who could write.*

We might have been—these are but
common words,
And yet they make the sum of life's
bewailing.
L. E. LANDON.—*Diary of a Week.*

Each man makes his own shipwreck.
LUCANUS.—*Pharsalia.*

The man who loses his opportunity
loses himself. GEO. MOORE.—*Bending of
the Bough,* Act 5.

Born to fail,
A name without an echo.
SIR H. NEWBOLT.—*Non-Combatant.*

In beauty's cause illustriously he fails.
POPE.—*Odyssey,* 11, 358.

The painful warrior, famousèd for fight,
After a thousand victories, once foiled,
Is from the book of honour razèd quite,
And all the rest forgot for which he toiled.
SHAKESPEARE.—*Sonnet* 25.

We learn wisdom from failure much
more than from success. We often discover what *will* do, by finding out what
will not do. SMILES.—*Self-Help, c.* 11.

What though success will not attend on all?
Who bravely dares must sometimes risk a
fall. SMOLLETT.—*Advice.*

This proverb flashes through his head,
The many fail: the one succeeds.
TENNYSON.—*Day-dream, Arrival,* 2.

The King of France went up the hill
With twenty thousand men;
The King of France came down the hill
And ne'er went up again.
Old Tarlton's Song (16th Cent. ?).

The fish which we did not catch is a
very large one. *Prov.*

FAINT-HEARTEDNESS

Faint heart fair lady ne'er could win.
PHINEAS FLETCHER (?).—*Britain's
Ida, c.* 5, 1.

Fain would I climb but that I fear to fall.
SIR W. RALEGH.—*Written on a Glass
Window.* (*Queen Elizabeth is said to have
added:* "*If thy heart fail thee, do not
climb at all.*")

FAIR-DEALING

Fair and honest John o' the Bank,
Has aye the right gully [pocket-knife] by
the shank. *Scottish prov.*

FAIRIES

And now they throng the moonlight glade,
Above, below, on every side,
Their little minim forms arrayed,
In all the tricksy pomp of fairy pride.
J. R. DRAKE.—*Culprit Fay.*

Oh, then, I see, Queen Mab hath been with
    you.
She is the fairies' midwife ; and she comes
In shape no bigger than an agate-stone
On the forefinger of an alderman,
Drawn with a team of little atomies
Athwart men's noses as they lie asleep.
        SHAKESPEARE.—*Romeo and Juliet*,
                                Act 1, 4.

FAITH

Who once has doubted never quite be-
    lieves.
        . . . .
Who once believed will never wholly doubt.
        A. AUSTIN.—*Prince Lucifer*,
                                Act 6, 3.

The faith that Wordsworth had ;
The faith of Hugo, Dante, and of all
Great deep-souled poets—a great faith in
    God,
Apart from creeds and churches.
        G. BARLOW.—*Dawn to Sunset*, Bk. 2,
                        Poet's Letter, l. 237.

You must believe in good in order to
do it.   DE BONALD (1753–1840).

Methinks there be not impossibilities
enough in Religion for an active faith.
SIR T. BROWNE.—*Religio Medici*, Pt. 1, 9.

To believe only possibilities is not Faith,
but mere Philosophy
        SIR T. BROWNE.—*Ib.*, Pt. 1, 48.

'Tis well averred,
A scientific faith's absurd.
        BROWNING.—*Easter Day*, c. 6.

Believing hath a core of unbelieving.
        R. BUCHANAN.—*Book of Orm*.

For as implicit faith is far more stiff
Than that which understands its own
    belief,
So those that think, and do but think
    they know,
Are far more obstinate than those who do.
        S. BUTLER.—*On the Licentiousness of
                                the Age*.

He that will believe only what he can
fully comprehend must have a very long
head, or a very short creed.
        C. C. COLTON.—*Lacon*.

Each man's belief is right in his own eyes.
        COWPER.—*Hope*, 285.

The faith that stands on authority is
not faith.   EMERSON.—*The Over-Soul*.

I hear the message but I want the faith.
        GOETHE.

In Faith everything depends on the fact
of believing ; what is believed is a matter
of indifference. GOETHE.—*Autob.*, Bk. 14.

Much knowledge of things divine es-
capes us through want of faith.
        HERACLITUS (*according to Plutarch*).

A peasant may believe as much
As a great clerk, and reach the highest
    stature.   HERBERT.—*Faith*.

An opinion hath spread itself very far
in the world, as if the way to be ripe in
faith were to be raw in wit and judgment.
        HOOKER.—*Eccles. Pol.*, 3, 8, 4.

The ear of wheat laid low by a hailstorm
can never rear its head again ; nor can our
faith.
        IBSEN.—*Love's Comedy*, Act 3 (1862).

And Wisdom cries, " I know not any-
    thing ; "
And only Faith beholds that all is well.
        S. R. LYSAGHT.—*A Lesson*, l. 102.

Courage, brother ! do not stumble,
    Though thy path be dark as night :
There's a star to guide the humble ;
    Trust in God, and do the right.
        NORMAN MACLEOD.—*Trust in God*.

Unfaith clamouring to be coined
To faith by proof.
GEO. MEREDITH.—*Earth and Man*, st. 41.

O welcome, pure-eyed Faith !
        MILTON.—*Comus*, l. 213.

Who brought me hither
Will bring me hence : no other guide I
    seek.
        MILTON.—*Paradise Regained*, Bk. 1, 335.

Call no faith false which e'er hath brought
    Relief to any laden life,
Cessation from the pain of thought,
    Refreshment 'mid the dust of strife.
        SIR L. MORRIS.—*Tolerance*.

Beautiful Faith, surrendering unto Time.
        STEPHEN PHILLIPS.—*Marpessa*, 62.

Faith in something is an absolute and
vital essential to the life of every woman.
        EDEN PHILLPOTTS.

The talk is of perishing faith, and reason
answers that sooner will the principles of
gravitation and evolution perish than
faith. Faith is a permanent and vital
endowment of the human mind—a part of
reason itself. The insane alone are without it. E. PHILLPOTTS.—*A Shadow Passes*.

It is all very well to adjure me, " Put
your reason in subjection." Any man
who wishes to deceive me might say that,
but I require reasons why I should put
my reason in subjection.
        ROUSSEAU.—*Emile*, Bk. 4.

Faith . . . in the sense of adherence to resolution, obedience to law, regardfulness of promise, in which from all time it has been the test, as the shield, of the true being and life of man. RUSKIN.—*Modern Painters, vol. 2, sec. 2, ch. 3, 4.*

He wears his faith but as the fashion of his hat.
SHAKESPEARE.—*Much Ado, Act 1, 1.*

And bloody Faith, the foulest birth of time.
SHELLEY.—*Feelings of a Republican.*

What we do not believe is of no importance. The secret of life is to discover what we believe. EDITH SICHEL.—*Thoughts.*

Want of belief is a defect that ought to be concealed when it cannot be overcome.
SWIFT.—*Thoughts on Religion.*

Faith, haggard as fear that has borne her.
SWINBURNE.—*Autumn Vision, 7, 9.*

Believing where we cannot prove.
TENNYSON.—*In Memoriam, Introd.*

Whose faith has centre everywhere,
Nor cares to fix itself to form.
TENNYSON.—*Ib., c. 33.*

One in whom persuasion and belief
Had ripened into faith, and faith become
A passionate intuition.
WORDSWORTH.—*Excursion, Bk. 4.*

Faith is the assurance of things hoped for, the proving of things not seen.
Hebrews xi, 1 (*Rev. Ver.*).

Faith apart from works is barren.
James ii, 20 (*Rev. Ver.*).

FAITHFULNESS

The deepest hunger of a faithful heart
Is faithfulness.
GEO. ELIOT.—*Spanish Gypsy, 5.*

This is the famous stone
That turneth all to gold.
HERBERT.—*The Elixir.*

FAITHLESSNESS

Who should be trusted, when one's own right hand
Is perjured to the bosom ?
SHAKESPEARE.—*Two Gent. of Verona, Act 5, 4.*

There's no trust,
No faith, no honesty in men ; all perjured,
All forsworn, all naught, all dissemblers.
SHAKESPEARE.—*Romeo and Juliet, Act 3, 2.*

FALL

Fallen from his high estate,
And weltering in his blood.
DRYDEN.—*Alexander's Feast, st. 4.*

Of Man's first disobedience and the fruit
Of that forbidden tree, whose mortal taste
Brought death into the world, and all our woe,
With loss of Eden.
MILTON.—*Paradise Lost, Bk. 1, 1.*

Dropped from the zenith like a fallen star.
MILTON.—*Ib., Bk. 1, 745.*

Among the prime in splendour, now deposed,
Ejected, emptied, gazed, unpitied, shunned,
A spectacle of ruin or of scorn.
MILTON.—*Paradise Regained, Bk. 1, 413.*

Though they fell, they fell like stars,
Streaming splendour through the sky.
J. MONTGOMERY.—*Battle of Alexandria.*

The vulgar falls, and none laments his fate.
Sorrow has hardly leisure for the great.
N. ROWE.—*Pharsalia, Bk. 4.*

O Hamlet, what a falling off was there !
SHAKESPEARE.—*Hamlet, Act 1, 5.*

And when he falls, he falls like Lucifer,
Never to hope again.
SHAKESPEARE.—*Henry VIII., Act 3, 2.*

O, what a fall was there, my countrymen !
SHAKESPEARE.—*Julius Cæsar, Act 3, 2.*

He that climbs highest has the greatest fall.
C. TOURNEUR.—*Revenger's Tragedy, Act 5.*

There to thy fellow-ghosts with glory tell,
'Twas by the great Æneas' hand I fell.
VIRGIL.—*Æneid, Bk. 10 (Dryden tr.).*

How are the mighty fallen ! Tell it not in Gath, publish it not in the streets of Askelon. *2 Samuel* i, 19, 20.

How art thou fallen from heaven, O day star, son of the morning !
Isaiah xiv, 12 (*Rev. Ver.*).

Let the drunkard alone and he will fall of himself. *Hebrew prov.*

FALLACIES

There is always less money, less wisdom, and less honesty than people imagine.
Italian prov., as quoted by Bacon.

FALLEN IN BATTLE

With proud thanksgiving, a mother for her children,
England mourns for her dead across the sea.
Flesh of her flesh they were, spirit of her spirit,
Fallen in the cause of the free.
LAURENCE BINYON.—*For the Fallen.*

These laid the world away ; poured out the
   red
Sweet wine of youth ; gave up the years
   to be
Of work and joy, and that unhoped
   serene,
That men call age ; and those who
   would have been,
Their sons, they gave, their immortality.
   RUPERT BROOKE.—*The Dead.*

How sleep the brave, who sink to rest
By all their country's wishes blest !
   WM. COLLINS.—*Ode.*

Shout not, be still ! Unholy is the voice
Of loud thanksgiving over slaughtered
   men. HOMER.—*Odyssey, Bk.* 22, 411
                            (*Cowper tr.*).

FALLIBILITY

I beseech you, in the bowels of Christ,
think it possible you may be mistaken.
   CROMWELL.—*Letter to General
                     Assembly,* 1650.

We are none of us infallible, not even
the youngest.   W. H. THOMPSON.

FALSE REPORTS

The world is naturally averse
To all the truth it sees or hears,
But swallows nonsense and a lie
With greediness and gluttony.
   BUTLER.—*Hudibras, Pt.* 3, *c.* 2.

The feeblest vermin can destroy,
As sure as stoutest beasts of prey ;
And only with their eyes and breath
Infect, and poison men to death.
   BUTLER.—*Ode on Critics.*

Nothing gives such a blow to friendship
as the detecting another in an untruth.
It strikes at the root of our confidence ever
after.   HAZLITT.—*Characteristics.*

FALSEHOOD

Falsehood and fraud shoot up on every
   soil,
The product of all climes.
   ADDISON.—*Cato,* Act 4, 4.

There's a real love of a lie,
Liars find ready made for lies they make.
   BROWNING.—*Mr. Sludge.*

There is truth in falsehood, falsehood in
   untruth.
   BROWNING.—*Soul's Tragedy,* Act 2.

Falsehood has a perennial spring.
   BURKE.—*Speech on American Taxation.*

'Twas a most notorious flam.
   BUTLER.—*Hudibras, Pt.* 2, *c.* 3.

For things said false and never meant,
Do oft prove right by accident.
   BUTLER.—*Weakness of Man.*

Agree to a short armistice with truth.
   BYRON.—*Don Juan, c.* 3, 83.

The beginning of all is to have done with
Falsity.   CARLYLE.—*Journal.*

Ever to that truth,
Which but the semblance of a falsehood
   wears,
A man, if possible, should bar his lip.
H. F. CARY.—*Dante's " Hell," c.* 16, 147.

I know a maiden fair to see ;
   Take care !
She can both false and friendly be ;
   Beware ! Beware !
   Trust her not,
She is fooling thee !
   LONGFELLOW.—*Beware.*

Some falsehood mingles with all truth.
   LONGFELLOW.—*Golden Legend.*

Him thus intent Ithuriel with his spear
Touched lightly ; for no falsehood can
   endure
Touch of celestial temper, but returns
Of force to its own likeness.
   MILTON.—*Paradise Lost, Bk.* 4, 810.

A goodly apple, rotten at the heart.
O, what a goodly outside falsehood hath !
   SHAKESPEARE.—*Merchant of Venice,*
                            Act 1, 3.

For know, my heart stands armèd in mine
   ear,
And will not let a false sound enter there.
   SHAKESPEARE.—*Venus and Adonis,*
                            st. 130.

Falsehood flies and truth comes limping
after it, so that when men come to be un-
deceived it is too late.
   SWIFT.—*Examiner, No.* 15.

Man is ice to truth, fire to falsehood.
   VOLTAIRE (?).

FAME

And o'er the plain, where the dead age
Did its now silent warfare wage,
 . . . .
The one or two immortal lights
Rise slowly up into the sky
To shine there everlastingly.
   MATTHEW ARNOLD.—*Bacchanalia.*

Fame and her less fair followers, envy,
   strife,
Stupid detraction, jealousy, cabal,
Insincere praises.
   M. ARNOLD.—*Early Death and Fame.*

Here's an acre sown indeed
With the richest, royalest seed.
   F. BEAUMONT.—*Westminster Abbey.*

Strong towers decay,
But a great name shall never pass away.
   PARK BENJAMIN.—*A Great Name.*

High and adventurous actions, which
. . . leaveth their names canonised in
Fame's Eternal Calendar.
> JOHN BOURCHIER (BARON BERNERS)
> *Huon of Bordeaux*, Pref. (Printed c.
> 1534).

The eagle am I, with my fame in the
world ;
The wren is he, with his maiden face.
> BROWNING.—*A Light Woman.*

Sure of the Fortieth spare Arm-chair,
When gout and glory seat me there.
> BROWNING.—*Dis aliter visum.*

The glory dies not, and the grief is past.
> SIR S. E. BRYDGES.—*Death of Sir Walter
> Scott.*

Passion for fame ; a passion which is
the instinct of all great souls.
> BURKE.—*Speech on American Taxation.*

But these are deeds which should not pass
away,
And names that must not wither.
> BYRON.—*Childe Harold, c.* 3, 67.

Mortals, who sought and found, by dangerous roads,
A path to perpetuity of fame.
> BYRON.—*Ib., c.* 3, 105.

Fame is the thirst of youth,—but I am
not so young as to regard men's frown or
smile.   BYRON.—*Ib., c.* 3, 112.

I awoke one morning and found myself
famous.
> BYRON.—*Memorandum on the instanta-
> neous success of " Childe Harold "* (1812).

And Folly loves the martyrdom of Fame.
> BYRON.—*Death of Sheridan.*

What is the end of Fame ? 'tis but to fill
A certain portion of uncertain paper.
> BYRON.—*Don Juan, c.* 1, 218.

Renown's all hit or miss ;
There's fortune even in fame, we must
allow.   BYRON.—*Ib., c.* 7, 33.

Yet what is all that fires a hero's scorn
Of death ?—the hope to live in hearts unborn.
> CAMPBELL.—*Lines in " La Perouse."*

Victorious names, who made the world
obey ;
Who, while they lived, in deeds of arms
excelled,
And, after death for deities were held.
> DRYDEN.—*Flower and Leaf,* 518.

As such a one that ever strives to give
A blessed memory to after-time.
> J. FLETCHER.—*Faithful Shepherdess,
> Act* 5.

For whoso reaps renown above the rest,
With heaps of hate shall surely be oppressed.
> GASCOIGNE.—*Steel Glass* (1576).

The deed is everything ; the fame is
nothing.   GOETHE.

Beyond the limits of a vulgar fate,
Beneath the good how far—but far above
the great.
> GRAY.—*Progress of Poesy,* 3, 122.

For thou art Freedom's now, and Fame's,
One of the few, the immortal names,
That were not born to die.
> FITZ-GREENE HALLECK.—*Marco Bozzaris.*

Amongst whom Jove's ambassadress,
Fame, in her virtue shined,
Exciting greediness to hear
> HOMER.—*Iliad, Bk.* 2 (*Chapman tr.*).

Here if I stay, before the Trojan town,
Short is my date but deathless my re-
nown ;
If I return, I quit immortal praise,
For years on years and long extended days.
> HOMER.—*Ib., Bk.* 9, 410 (*Pope tr.*).

He left the name, at which the world grew
pale,
To point a moral or adorn a tale.
> JOHNSON—*Vanity of Human Wishes.*

According to eternal laws
('Tis useless to inquire the cause),
The gates of fame and of the grave
Stand under the same architrave.
> W. S. LANDOR.—*Miscell., No.* 39.

So, when a great man dies,
For years beyond our ken,
The light he leaves behind him lies
Upon the paths of men.
> LONGFELLOW.—*Birds of Passage,
> Flight* 3.

Deep, wondrous deep below,
How poor mistaken mortals wandering go,
Seeking the path to Happiness.   Some aim
At Learning, Wit, Nobility, or Fame ;
Others with cares and dangers vex each
hour
To reach the top of Wealth and sovereign
Power. LUCRETIUS, 2, 10 (*Creech tr.*).

Happy is the man who hath never
known what it is to taste of fame—to have
it is a purgatory, to want it is a Hell !
> EDWD. (1ST) LORD LYTTON.—*Last of
> the Barons, Bk.* 5, ch. 1.

Not till the fire is dying in the grate
Look we for any kinship with the stars.
> GEO. MEREDITH.—*Modern Love, st.* 4.

By labour and intent study . . . I
might perhaps leave something so written
to after-times, as they should not willingly
let it die. MILTON.—*Church Government.*

Fame is the spur that the clear spirit doth
    raise
(That last infirmity of noble mind)
To scorn delights, and live laborious days,
But the fair guerdon when we hope to find,
And seek to burst out into sudden blaze,
Comes the blind Fury with the abhorrèd
    shears,
And slits the thin-spun life.
        MILTON.—*Lycidas*, 70.

Fame is no plant that grows on mortal
    soil.   MILTON.—*Ib.*, 78.

As he pronounces lastly on each deed,
Of so much fame in Heaven expect thy
    meed.   MILTON.—*Ib.*, 83.

Not to know me argues yourselves un-
    known.
    MILTON.—*Paradise Lost, Bk.* 4, 830.

Life is too short for any distant aim ;
And cold the dull reward of future fame.
    LADY M. WORTLEY MONTAGU.—*To
    Lord Burlington.*

And like to one he seemed whose better
    day
Is over to himself, though foolish fame
Shouts louder year by year his empty name.
    W. MORRIS.—*Wanderers*, 466.

Unless what we do is useful, fame is
    folly.   PHÆDRUS.—*Fables.*

Immortal heirs of universal praise !
Whose honours with increase of ages grow,
As streams roll down, enlarging as they
    flow. POPE.—*Essay on Criticism*, 190.

Nations unborn your mighty names shall
    sound.   POPE.—*Ib.*, 193.

Above all Greek, above all Roman fame.
    POPE.—*Satires, Bk.* 2, 26.

Their pleas were different, their request the
    same,
For good and bad alike are fond of fame.
    POPE.—*Temple of Fame*, 292.

Fame's but a hollow echo ; Gold, pure
    clay ;
Honour, the darling but of one short day
    SIR W. RALEGH.—*A Farewell.*

Why do you ask how long he has lived ?
He has lived to posterity.
        SENECA.—*Ep.* 93.

Our names,
Familiar in his mouth as household words.
    SHAKESPEARE.—*Henry V.*, Act 4, 3.

The evil that men do lives after them ;
The good is often interred with their bones.
    SHAKESPEARE.—*Julius Cæsar*, Act 3, 2.

He lives in fame, that died in virtue's cause.
    SHAKESPEARE.—*Titus Andronicus*,
        Act 1, 2.

Fame's loudest trump upon the ear of Time
Leaves but a dying echo ; they alone
Are held in everlasting memory,
Whose deeds partake of heaven.
        SOUTHEY.—*Verses at Oxford.*

They have their passing paragraphs of
    praise
And are forgotten. SOUTHEY.—*Victory.*

Death opens the gate of Fame, and
shuts the gate of Envy after it.
    STERNE.—*Tristram Shandy, Vol.* 5, 3.

Many valiant chiefs of old
    Greatly lived and died before
Agamemnon, Grecian bold,
    Waged the ten years' famous war.
But their names, unsung, unwept,
    Unrecorded, lost and gone,
Long in endless night have slept,
    And shall now no more be known.
        SWIFT.—*Horace, Odes* 4, 19.

Thy works and mine are ripples on the sea.
Take heart, I say : we know not yet their
    end.   SWINBURNE.—*Locrine.*

    Their noonday never knows
      What names immortal are ;
    'Tis night alone that shows
      How star surpasseth star.
    J. B. TABB.—*Fame.*

The desire for fame is the last desire that
is laid aside even by the wise.
    TACITUS.—*Hist., Bk.* 4, 6.

To such a name for ages long,
    To such a name,
Preserve a broad approach of fame.
    TENNYSON.—*Duke of Wellington, st.* 5.

Man dreams of fame, while woman wakes
    to love.
    TENNYSON.—*Merlin and Vivien*, 458.

And what is fame in life but half-disfame,
And counterchanged with darkness ?
        TENNYSON.—*Ib.*, 463.

Sweet were the days when I was all un-
    known.   TENNYSON.—*Ib.*, 499.

Fame, like water, bears up the lighter
    things,
And lets the weighty sink.
    SIR S. TUKE.—*Adventures of Five Hours*,
        Act 2.

Advance, illustrious youth ! increase in
    fame,
And wide from east to west extend thy
    name.
    VIRGIL.—*Æneid, Bk.* 9, (*Apollo to
        Ascanius*) (*Dryden tr.*).

It is hard, I must confess, not to obtain, from one's contemporaries and compatriots, that which one may hope for from
strangers and from posterity.
    VOLTAIRE.—*Alzire, Prelim. Discourse*

A name famous too soon is a very heavy
burden.   VOLTAIRE.—*Henriade.*

One desires to be unknown, but only
when it is too late. As soon as the
trumpets of fame have sounded the name
of an unfortunate man, farewell for ever to
its repose.   VOLTAIRE.—*Letter to
M. Caperonnier, June 1, 1768.*

What sharks we mortals are for fame !
How poacher-like we hunt the game !
          J. WOLCOT.—*Odes for 1783, No. 7.*

What rage for fame attends both great and
small !
Better be damned than mentioned not at
all.   J. WOLCOT.—*Ib., No. 9.*

Great is the world's inconstancy, God
knows ;
Fame, like the ocean, ebbs as well as
flows.
          J. WOLCOT.—*Odes for 1785, No. 13.*

I am no cormorant of fame, d'ye see ?
I ask not all the laurel, but a sprig.
          J. WOLCOT.—*Ep. to Reviewers.*

Others are fond of Fame, but Fame of
you.   YOUNG.—*Love of Fame, sat. 1.*

And what so foolish as the chase of fame ?
          YOUNG.—*Ib., sat. 2.*

The melancholy ghosts of dead renown,
Whispering faint echoes of the world's
applause.
          YOUNG.—*Night Thoughts, 9.*

Let us now praise famous men.
          Ecclesiasticus xliv, 1.

All these were honoured in their generations, and were the glory of their times.
          Ecclesiasticus xliv, 7.

We fools accounted his life madness,
and his end without honour ; How was
he numbered among the sons of God ?
And how is his lot among saints ?
          Wisdom of Solomon v, 4, 5 (*R.V.*).

FAMILIARITY

The man that hails you Tom or Jack,
And proves by thumps upon your back
  How he esteems your merit,
Is such a friend, that one had need
Be very much his friend indeed
  To pardon or to bear it.
          COWPER.—*Friendship, st. 29.*

I hold he loves me best that calls me
Tom.   TOM HEYWOOD.—*Hierarchies
          of the Blessed Angels.*

To those who walk beside them, great men
  seem
Mere common earth ; but distance makes
  them stars. G. MASSEY.—*Hood, 11.*

The terrible gift of familiarity.
          MIRABEAU.

FAMILY

For still in every house,
That loves the right, their fate for evermore
Rejoiceth in an issue fair and good.
          ÆSCHYLUS.—*Agamemnon,* 750
          (*Plumptre tr.*).

But he, poor fellow, had a wife and
children
Two things for dying people quite be-
wildering.
          BYRON.—*Don Juan, c. 2, 43.*

A lady with her daughter or her nieces,
Shine like a guinea and seven-shilling
pieces.
          BYRON.—*Ib., c. 3, 60.*

Kill a man's family, and he may brook it,
But keep your hand out of his breeches'
pocket.   BYRON.—*Ib., c. 10, 79.*

Wronged me ! in the nicest point—
The honour of our house !
          T. OTWAY.—*Venice Preserved, Act 1, 1.*

A family is but too often a commonwealth of malignants.
          POPE.—*Thoughts on Various Subjects.*

He that loves not his wife and children
. . . blessing itself cannot make him
happy.
          JEREMY TAYLOR.—*Married Love.*

FAMINE

For great towns, like to crocodiles, are
found
In the belly aptest to receive a mortal
wound.
          S. BUTLER.—*To the Memory of Du Val,
          st. 7.*

Famine ends famine.
          BEN JONSON.—*Discoveries.*

And the niggardness of Nature makes the
misery of man.
          SIR W. WATSON.—*Ireland.*

FANATICISM

Earth's fanatics make
Too frequently heaven's saints.
          E. B. BROWNING.—*Aurora Leigh, Bk. 2.*

The aspiring youth that fired the Ephesian
dome
Outlives in fame the pious fool that raised
it.   C. CIBBER.—*Richard III.
          (adapted), Act 2, 1.*

But Faith, fanatic Faith, once wedded
fast
To some dear falsehood, hugs it to the last.
          MOORE.—*Lalla Rookh.*

FANCY

And visions, as poetic eyes avow,
Cling to each leaf and hang on every bough.
GRAY.—*Letter to H. Walpole* (*Tr. of
Virgil, Æneid*, 6, 282*).

In a good poem, whether it be epic or
dramatic, as also in sonnets, epigrams,
and other pieces, both judgment and
fancy are required ; but the fancy must be
more eminent. HOBBES.—*Leviathan, ch.* 8.

The truant Fancy was a wanderer ever.
CHAS. LAMB.—*Fancy Employed on Divine
Subjects.*

If but a beam of sober Reason play,
Lo, Fancy's fairy frost-work melts away.
ROGERS.—*Pleasures of Memory, Pt.* 2.

Old Homer's theme
Was but a dream,
Himself a fiction too.
SCOTT.—*Monastery. Answer to Introd.
Epistle.*

Chewing the food ["cud" in some
editions] of sweet and bitter fancy.
SHAKESPEARE.—*As You Like It*, Act 4, 3

Tell me where is fancy bred,
Or in the heart, or in the head ?
SHAKESPEARE.—*Merchant of Venice*,
Act 3, 2.

FARCE

What dear delight to Britons farce affords !
Ever the taste of mobs, but now of lords.
POPE.—*Ep. of Horace, Ep.* 1, 310.

FAREWELL

Once more farewell !
If e'er we meet hereafter, we shall meet
In happier climes and on a safer shore.
ADDISON.—*Cato*, Act 4.

Life ! we've been long together,
Through pleasant and through cloudy
weather ;
'Tis hard to part when friends are dear ;
Perhaps 'twill cost a sigh, a tear ;
Then steal away, give little warning ;
Choose thine own time ;
Say not "Good-night" ; but in some
brighter clime
Bid me "Good morning."
ANNA L. BARBAULD.—*Life.*

Ae fond kiss and then we sever.
BURNS.—*Farewell to Nancy.*

Had we never loved sae kindly,
Had we never loved sae blindly,
Never met—and never parted,
We had ne'er been broken-hearted.
BURNS.—*Ib.*

Farewell !
For in that word—that fatal word—howe'er

We promise — hope — believe — there
breathes despair.
BYRON.—*Corsair*, 2, 15.

Farewell ! a word that must be, and hath
been,
A sound which makes us linger ;—yet—
farewell !
BYRON.—*Childe Harold*, c. 5, st. 186.

Fare thee well ! and if for ever,
Still for ever, fare *thee well.*
BYRON.—*Fare thee well.*

I only know we loved in vain—
I only feel—Farewell !—Farewell !
BYRON.—*Farewell, if ever Fondest Prayer.*

Drew
A long, long sigh, and wept a last
adieu.
COWPER.—*His Mother's Picture.*

One fond kiss before we part,
Drop a tear and bid adieu.
R. DODSLEY.—*Parting Kiss.*

Only a little more
I have to write,
Then I'll give o'er
And bid the world Good-night.
HERRICK.—*Hesperides*, 211.

Good-bye ; no tears nor cries
Are fitting here, and long lament
were vain.
Only the last low words be softly said,
And the last greeting given above the
dead ;
For soul more pure and beautiful our eyes
Never shall see again.
J. W. MACKAIL.—*Death of Arnold
Toynbee.*

For ever and for ever farewell, Cassius !
If we do meet again, why, we shall smile ;
If not, why then this parting was well
made.
SHAKESPEARE.—*Julius Cæsar*, Act 5, 1.

Good night, good night ! Parting is such
sweet sorrow
That I shall say Good-night, till it be
morrow.   SHAKESPEARE.—*Romeo
and Juliet*, Act 2, 2.

So sweetly she bade me adieu,
I thought that she bade me return.
SHENSTONE.—*Absence.*

Come, then, I leave this isle,
And speak my parting words :
Farewell, O roof, long time
My one true guard and friend.
SOPHOCLES.—*Philoctetes*, 1146
(*Plumptre tr.*), (*Farewell to Lemnos*).

Good night, good sleep, good rest from
sorrow,
To these that shall not have good morrow ;
The gods be gentle to all these !
SWINBURNE.—*To Proserpine.*

I now bid you a welcome adoo.
ARTEMUS WARD.—*His Book, The
Shakers.*

We don't want to lose you,
But we think you ought to go.
Recruiting Song (1915).

FARMERS

The glory of the farmer is that in the
division of labours it is his part to create.
EMERSON.—*Farming.*

The farmer times himself to Nature,
and acquires that livelong patience which
belongs to her.   EMERSON.—*Ib.*

And farmers fatten most when famine
reigns.   SIR S. GARTH.—*Dispensary.*

Yet thou dost know
That the best compost for the lands
Is the wise master's feet and hands.
HERRICK.—*Country Life.*

I believe the first receipt to farm well is
to be rich.   SYDNEY SMITH.—*Letter to
J. Whishaw, April* 13, 1818.

He was a very inferior farmer when he
first begun, . . . and he is now fast rising
from affluence to poverty.
MARK TWAIN.—*Rev. H. W. Beecher's
Farm.*

His fields seemed to know what their
master was doing ;
And turnips and corn-land and meadow
and lea
All caught the infection—as generous as he.
WORDSWORTH.—*Farmer of Tilsbury Vale.*

FASCINATION

With fascination in his very bow.
BYRON.—*Don Juan, c.* 12, 84.

How like a moth, the simple maid
Still plays about the flame !
GAY.—*Beggar's Opera,* Act 1.

I shook my head perhaps,—but quite
Forgot to quite forget her.
F. LOCKER LAMPSON.—*St. James's
Street.*

He speaks the kindest words, and looks
such things,
Vows with such passion, swears with so
much grace.
That it is heaven to be deluded by him.
N. LEE.—*Rival Queens,* Act 1, 1.

We cannot choose ; our faces madden
men.
STEPHEN PHILLIPS.—*Paolo and Fran-
cesca,* Act 2, 1.

If the rascal have not given me medi-
cines to make me love him, I'll be hanged ;
it could not be else.
SHAKESPEARE.—*Henry IV., Pt.* 1, Act 2, 2.

He hath a person and a smooth dispose
To be suspected ; framed to make women
false.
SHAKESPEARE.—*Othello,* Act 1, 3.

Yes, I am a fatal man, Madame Fribsbi.
To inspire hopeless passion is my destiny
[*Mirobolant*].   THACKERAY.—*Pendennis.*

FASHION

There is not so variable a thing in
Nature as a lady's head-dress.
ADDISON.—*Spectator, vol.* 2, 98.

Two things, completely opposite to
each other, captivate us equally—habit
and novelty.
LA BRUYÈRE.—*Des Jugements, No.* 4.

For nothing can be bad or good
But as 'tis in or out of mode.
S. BUTLER.—*On our Ridiculous
Imitation of the French.*

A man of fashion never has recourse to
proverbs and vulgar aphorisms.
LORD CHESTERFIELD.—*Advice to his Son.*

Fashion, leader of a chattering train,
Whom man, for his own hurt, permits to
reign. COWPER.—*Conversation,* 457.

While the world lasts, fashion will
continue to lead it by the nose.
COWPER.

With other fashionable topics, such as
pictures, taste, Shakespeare, and the
musical glasses.
GOLDSMITH.—*Vicar of Wakefield, ch.* 9.

We praise and blame most things
simply because it is the fashion to praise
or blame them.
LA ROCHEFOUCAULD.—*Maxim* 612.

Be not the first by whom the new are
tried,
Nor yet the last to lay the old aside.
POPE.—*Criticism,* 333.

In almost every age, whether in literature or art, if a thoroughly wrong idea or
fashion or manner becomes in vogue, it is
admired. SCHOPENHAUER.—*On Authorship.*

This is our chief bane, that we live
not according to the light of reason, but
after the fashion of others.
SENECA.—*Octavia,* Act 2, 454.

What used to be vices are become
fashions.   SENECA.

He was the mark and glass, copy and book,
That fashioned others. And him—O
wondrous him !
O miracle of men !   SHAKESPEARE.—
Henry IV., Pt. 2, Act 2, 3.

The fashion wears out more apparel than the man.
SHAKESPEARE.—*Much Ado*, Act 3, 3.

Britons ever will be slaves when fashion is in the case.
C. H. SPURGEON.—" *Salt-Cellars.*"

In tea-cup times of hood and hoop,
Or while the patch was worn.
TENNYSON.—*Talking Oak.*

And Custom, which is God to gentlemen,
Says, " So it has been, therefore let it be ";
And we obey.   J. L. WARREN (LORD DE TABLEY).—*Soldier of Fortune*, Act 1.

FASTIDIOUSNESS

False taste may be known by its fastidiousness, by its demands of pomp, splendour, and unusual combination, by its enjoyment only of particular styles and modes of things, and by its pride also. RUSKIN.—*Modern Painters, Vol.* 2, sec. 1, ch. 3, 11.

He is a poor smith who cannot bear smoke. *Prov. as quoted by C. H. Spurgeon.*

FASTING

Is this a fast, to keep
    The larder lean
          And clean ?
No, 'tis a fast to dole
    Thy sheaf of wheat
          And meat
Unto the hungry soul.
It is to fast from strife,
    From old debate
          And hate;
To circumcise thy life.
To show a heart grief-rent;
    To starve thy sin,
          Not bin;
And that's to keep thy Lent.
HERRICK.—*Noble Numbers*, 228.

Fasting is all very well for those
Who have to contend with invisible foes ;
But I am quite sure it does not agree
With a quiet, peaceable man like me.
LONGFELLOW.—*Golden Legend*, 4.

FATALISM

What argufies pride and ambition ?
Soon or late death will take us in tow :
Each bullet has got its commission,
    And when our time's come we must
          go.   C. DIBDIN.—*Each Bullet.*

We moralise when it is too late ; nor is there anything more silly than to regret. One event makes another ; what we anticipate seldom occurs ; what we least expected generally happens.
DISRAELI.—*Henrietta Temple, Bk.* 2, c. 4,

Yet some must swim when others sink,
And some must sink when others swim ;
Make merry, comrades, eat and drink—
The lights are growing dim.
A. L. GORDON.—*Sunlight on the Sea.*

FATALITY

All human things are subject to decay,
And when fate summons, monarchs must obey.   DRYDEN.—*Mac Flecknoe, l.* 1.

As killing as the canker to the rose.
MILTON.—*Lycidas*, 45.

There's a divinity that shapes our ends,
Rough-hew them how we will.
SHAKESPEARE.—*Hamlet*, Act 5, 2.

From this ill-omened hour, in time, arose
Debate and death and all succeeding woes.
VIRGIL.—*Æneid, Bk.* 4 (*Dryden tr.*).

FATE

Can Fancy's fairy hands no veil create
To hide the sad realities of fate ?
CAMPBELL.—*Pleasures of Hope*, Pt. 2.

The best of men cannot suspend their fate ;
The good die early, and the bad die late.
DEFOE.—*Character of Dr. Annesley.*

'Tis Fate that flings the dice, and as she flings,
Of kings makes peasants and of peasants kings.   DRYDEN.

With equal pace impartial fate
Knocks at the palace as the cottage gate.
P. FRANCIS.—*Horace*, Ode 4.

Yet, ah ! why should they know their fate,
Since sorrow never comes too late,
And happiness too swiftly flies ?
GRAY.—*Distant Prospect of Eton College.*

'Tis writ on Paradise's gate,
" Woe to the dupe that yields to Fate."
HAFIZ.—*As given by Emerson, Essay on Persian Poetry.*

              So let it be !
Portents and prodigies are lost on me.
I know my fate,—to die and see no more
My much-loved parents and my native shore.
Enough—when heaven ordains I sink in night ;
Now perish Troy !—He said and rushed to fight.
HOMER.—*Iliad, Bk.* 19, 404 (*Pope tr.*).

Alas, how prone are humankind to blame
The Powers of Heaven ! From us, they say, proceed
The ills which they endure ; yet more than Fate
Herself inflicts, by their own crimes incur.
HOMER.—*Odyssey, Bk.* 1, 32 (*Cowper tr.*).

It lies not in our power to love or hate,
For will in us is over-ruled by fate.
  MARLOWE.—*Hero and Leander.*

But wisest Fate says No,
This must not yet be so.
  MILTON.—*Christmas Hymn.*

The fatal key,
Sad instrument of all our woe.
  MILTON.—*Paradise Lost, Bk.* 2, 871.

Big with the fate of Rome.
  T. OTWAY.—*Venice Preserved,* Act 3, 1.

Not you, but Fate, has vanquished me.
  SCOTT.—*Lay of the Last Minstrel, c.* 5, 26.

Let Hercules himself do what he may,
The cat will mew, and dog will have his
  day. SHAKESPEARE.—*Hamlet,*
           Act 5, 1.

Come what come may,
Time and the hour run through the
  roughest day.
  SHAKESPEARE.—*Macbeth,* Act 1, 3.

Who can control his fate ?
  SHAKESPEARE.—*Othello,* Act 5, 2.

As the old hermit of Prague [Jerome,
hermit of Camaldoli] said, " That that is,
is."
  SHAKESPEARE.—*Twelfth Night,* Act 4, 2.

The glories of our blood and state
  Are shadows, not substantial things ;
There is no armour against fate,
  Death lays his icy hand on kings.
    Sceptre and crown
      Must tumble down,
And in the dust be equal made
With the poor crooked scythe and spade.
  JAS. SHIRLEY.—*Ajax and Ulysses.*

The blackest ink of Fate was sure my lot,
And, when she writ my name, she made a
  blot [*Prince Pretty-man*].
  GEO. VILLIERS (DUKE OF BUCKING-
      HAM).—*Rehearsal.*

With patience bear, with prudence push,
your fate.
  VIRGIL.—*Æneid, Bk.* 5 (*Dryden tr.*),

For now the Fates prepared the sharpened
  shears,
And lifted high the flaming sword appears.
  VIRGIL.—*Ib., Bk.* 10 (*Dryden tr.*).

The stars in their courses fought against
Sisera.   *Judges* v, 20.

There, but for the grace of God, goes
John Bradford.
  *Ascribed to John Bradford (burnt at
  Smithfield,* 1555) *on seeing some
  criminals going to execution. (See
  " Nat. Dict. Biog.")*

FATHERS

I'll meet the raging of the skies,
  But not an angry father.
  CAMPBELL.—*Lord Ullin's Daughter.*

We think our fathers fools, so wise we grow;
Our wiser sons, no doubt, will think us so.
  POPE.—*Essay on Criticism,* 2, 238.

O heavens, this is my true-begotten
  father !
  SHAKESPEARE.—*Merchant of Venice,*
           Act 2, 2.

It is a wise father that knows his own
child.   SHAKESPEARE.—*Ib.*

Father !—to God Himself we cannot give
A holier name.
  WORDSWORTH.—*Borderers,* Act 1.

A father is a banker given by nature.
         French prov.

FATNESS

Who drives fat oxen should himself be
fat. JOHNSON.—*Boswell's Life,* 1784.

A bard here dwelt, more fat than bard
  beseems.
  JAS. THOMSON.—*Castle of Indolence,*
           c. 1, 68.

FAULT-FINDERS

In other men we faults can spy,
And blame the mote that dims their eye ;
Each little speck and blemish find,
To our own stronger errors blind.
        GAY.—*Fables.*

I believe that more breaches of friendship and love have been created, and
more hatred cemented, by needless
criticism, than by any other thing.
  SIR A. HELPS.—*Friends in Council,*
          Bk. 2, *ch.* 2.

Mankind praise against their will,
And mix as much detraction as they can.
  YOUNG.—*Night Thoughts.*

FAULT-FINDING

The reason why it is so easy to believe
that other people have faults is that it is
so easy to believe what one wishes.
  LA ROCHEFOUCAULD.—*Maxim* 592.

If I can catch him once upon the hip,
I will feed fat the ancient grudge I bear
him. SHAKESPEARE.—*Merchant of
         Venice,* Act 1, 3.

A man sooner finds out his own foibles
in a stranger than any other foibles.
  SHENSTONE.—*Men and Manners.*

However mean your life is, meet it and
live it ; do not shun it and call it hard
names. It is not so bad as you are. It

looks poorest when you are richest. The fault-finder will find faults even in paradise.
H. D. THOREAU.—*Walden, Conclusion.*

There is so much good in the worst of us,
And so much bad in the best of us,
That ill behoves any one of us
To find any fault with the rest of us.
ANON.

Enquire not too curiously into other men's failings, neither let the one of you speak ill of another in his absence. Would any of you desire to eat the flesh of his dead brother ?   *Koran, ch.* 49.

FAULTLESSNESS

Faultless to a fault.
BROWNING.—*Ring and the Book,*
9, 1177

Whoever thinks a faultless piece to see,
Thinks what ne'er was, nor is, not e'er shall be.   POPE.—*Criticism,* 253.

There's no such thing in nature, and you'll draw
A faultless monster, which the world ne'er saw.
J. SHEFFIELD.—*On Poetry,* 231.

Faultily faultless, icily regular, splendidly null,
Dead perfection, no more.
TENNYSON.—*Maud,* 1, 2.

FAULTS

It is great folly not to part with your own faults, which is always possible, but instead to try to escape from other people's faults, which is impossible.
MARCUS AURELIUS.—*Meditations,*
Bk. 7, 71.

It is the nature of folly to see the faults of others and forget its own.
CICERO.—*Tunc. Quæst.*

He is over-good who has nothing of evil.   ENNIUS (*quoted by Cicero*).

We should never speak, publicly at least, of our own faults, nor of the faults of others, unless we hope to effect some useful purpose by it.
GOETHE.—*Autob., Bk.* 10.

There are a hundred faults in this thing, and a hundred things might be said to prove them beauties.
GOLDSMITH.—*Pref. to Vicar of Wakefield.*

Such stains there are—as when a Grace
Sprinkles another's laughing face
With nectar, and runs on.
W. S. LANDOR.—*Catullus.*

Quarrels would not last long if the fault was only on one side. LA ROCHEFOUCAULD.

If we had no faults, we should not take so much pleasure in noticing them in others.   LA ROCHEFOUCAULD, 31.

We never admit our faults, excepting through vanity.
LA ROCHEFOUCAULD.—*Maxim* 551.

We are very apt in blaming the faults of others, but very slow in making use of them to correct our own.
LA ROCHEFOUCAULD.—*Maxim* 605.

When some great misfortune comes to you, say one of the Popes, examine yourself well and you will see that it has always been your own fault.
LE SAGE.—*Gil Blas, Bk.* 7, *ch.* 16.

It is no doubt an evil to be full of faults, but it is a still greater evil to be full of them and not to wish to know them.   PASCAL.—*Pensées.*

Trust not yourself ; but, your defects to know,
Make use of every friend—and every foe.
POPE.—*Essay on Criticism,* 213.

The chief fault of man is that he has so many small ones.   RICHTER.

I do not write to excuse my faults, but to prevent my readers from imitating them.   ROUSSEAU.—*Emile.*

You, gods, will give us
Some faults to make us men.
SHAKESPEARE.—*Antony and Cleopatra,*
Act 5, 1.

Condemn the fault and not the actor of it.
SHAKESPEARE.—*Measure for Measure,*
Act 2, 2

They say best men are moulded out of faults ;
And, for the most, become mv ch more than better
For being a little bad.
SHAKESPEARE.—*Ib.,* Act 5, 1.

When you have done a fault, be always pert and insolent and behave yourself as if you were the injured person.
SWIFT.—*Rules that concern all Servants.*

He is all fault who hath no fault at all,
For who loves me must have a touch of earth.   TENNYSON.—*Lancelot.*

He (Marlborough) was so great a man, said Bolingbroke, that I have forgotten his vices.
VOLTAIRE.—*Letters on the English.*

Whoever does not know how to recognise the faults of great men is incapable of estimating their perfections.
VOLTAIRE.—*Prefatory Letter to Œdipus.*

His greatness, not his littleness, concerns
mankind.   SIR WM. WATSON.—*On Burns.*

Men have many faults ;
    Poor women have but two :
There's nothing right they say,
And nothing right they do.
                            Anon.

Faults are thick when love is thin.
                            Prov. (Ray).

FAVOURITES

We may concede any man a right, without doing any man a wrong ; but we can
favour no one without injuring someone.
                C. C. COLTON.—*Lacon.*

A favourite has no friend.
        GRAY.—*On the death of a Cat.*

Favouritism governed kissage
Even as it does in this age.
        KIPLING.—*Departmental Ditties.*

'Tis the curse of service ;
Preferment goes by letter and affection,
Not by the old gradation, where each
second
Stood heir to the first.
        SHAKESPEARE.—*Othello,* Act 1, 1.

FAVOURS

Thy favours are but like the wind,
    That kisseth everything it meets.
        SIR R. AYTON.—*I do confess.*

Extreme eagerness to return an obligation is a kind of ingratitude.
                LA ROCHEFOUCAULD.

Lesbia hath a beaming eye,
But no one knows for whom it beameth.
                MOORE.—*Lesbia hath.*

If you do a favour to a bad man, the
favour is lost ; if you do ill to a good man,
it lasts for a length of time.
        PLAUTUS.—*Poenulus,* Act 3, 3.

Pelt a dog with a bone and you will not
offend him.   *Italian prov.*

FEAR

Better die once for all than live in continual terror.   ÆSOP.

Nothing is terrible except fear itself.
                BACON.—*Fortitudo.*

Fear is an ague, that forsakes
And haunts, by fits, those whom it takes.
        BUTLER.—*Hudibras,* Pt. 1, c. 3.

Fear has many eyes.
        CERVANTES.—*Don Quixote (Prov)*

Fear that makes faith may break faith.
        SWINBURNE.—*Bothwell,* Act 1, 3.

Despair and confidence both banish fear.
        EARL OF STIRLING.—*Doomsday.*

How wretched a thing it is to become
old through fear !   PUBLILIUS SYRUS.

Nothing is so much to be feared as fear.
Atheism may be comparatively popular
with God himself.
        H. D. THOREAU.—*Unpublished MSS.*

Fear follows crime and is its chastise-
ment.   VOLTAIRE.—*Sémiramis.*

Fear hath a hundred eyes, that all agree
To plague her beating heart.
    WORDSWORTH.—*Eccles. Sonnets, Pt. 2, 42.*

Full twenty times was Peter feared,
For once that Peter was respected.
        WORDSWORTH.—*Peter Bell,* Pt. 1.

Fear shakes the pencil ; Fancy loves ex-
cess ;
Dark Ignorance is lavish of her shades ;
And these the formidable picture drew.
        YOUNG.—*Night Thoughts,* 6.

Perfect love casteth out fear.
        1 *St. John* iv, 18.

FEASTS

Now to the banquet we press ;
    Now for the eggs and the ham !
Now for the mustard and cress !
    Now for the strawberry jam !
Now for the tea of our host !
    Now for the rollicking bun !
Now for the muffin and toast !
    And now for the gay Sally Lunn !
        SIR W. S. GILBERT.—*Sorcerer.*

The true essentials of a feast are only fun
and feed.
        O. W. HOLMES.—*Nux Postcœnatica.*

I will eat exceedingly, and prophesy.
        BEN JONSON.—*Barth. Fair.*

What neat repast shall feast us, light and
choice,
Of Attic taste ?
        MILTON.—*To Mr. Lawrence.*

A good dinner, and company that
pleased me mightily, being all eminent
men in their way.   PEPYS.—*Diary,* 1668.

Here let us feast, and to the feast be joined
Discourse, the sweeter banquet of the mind.
        POPE.—*Odyssey, Bk.* 15, 432.

Now good digestion wait on appetite,
And health on both !
        SHAKESPEARE.—*Macbeth,* Act 3, 4.

We have a trifling foolish banquet towards.
        SHAKESPEARE.—*Romeo and Juliet,*
                            Act 1, 5.

The farmer to full bowls invites his friends,
And what he got with pains with pleasure
  spends.
    VIRGIL.—*Georgics, Bk.* 1 (*Dryden tr.*).

Spots in your feasts of charity.
                              Jude, 12.

Spread the table and contention will
cease.   *Hebrew prov.* (*Ben Syra*).

FELLOWSHIP

And, certeinly, he was a good felawe.
    CHAUCER.—*Cant. Tales, Prol.*

I laugh not at another's loss ;
I grudge not at another's pain.
    SIR E. DYER.—*My mind to me.*

Write me as one that loves his fellow men.
    LEIGH HUNT.—*Abou Ben Adhem.*

Fellowship is heaven, and lack of fellowship is hell ; fellowship is life, and lack of
fellowship is death ; and the deeds that
ye do upon the earth, it is for fellowship's
sake that ye do them.
    W. MORRIS.—*John Ball.*

By mutual confidence and mutual aid
Great deeds are done and great discoveries
  made.   POPE.—*Iliad, Bk.* 10, 265.

If he be not fellow with the best king,
thou shalt find the best king of good
fellows.
    SHAKESPEARE.—*Henry V.*, Act 5, 2.

I like to think that there is no man but
has had kindly feelings for some other,
and he for his neighbour, until we bind
together the whole family of Adam.
    THACKERAY.—*From Cornhill to Grand
                                    Cairo.*

FEBRUARY

Snow in February is a pledge of a fine
summer.   *French prov.*

All the months in the year
Curse a fair Februeer.
                          Old Saying.

February fill dyke,
Be it black or be it white ;
But if it be white it's the better to like.
    Prov. (*Ray's Collection*).

February the short is the worst of the
lot.   *Gascon prov.*

FEELINGS

There are some feelings time cannot benumb.
    BYRON.—*Childe Harold, c.* 4, 19.

Not good it is to harp on the frayed
  string. W. MORRIS.—*Earthly Paradise.*

He who has felt nothing does not know
how to learn anything. ROUSSEAU.—*Julie.*

Some feelings are to mortals given,
With less of earth in them than heaven.
    SCOTT.—*Lady of the Lake*, 2, 22.

FEES

My learned profession I'll never disgrace,
By taking a fee with a grin on my face,
When I haven't been there to attend to
  the case.
    SIR W. S. GILBERT.—*Iolanthe.*

If money go before, all ways do lie open.
SHAKESPEARE.—*Merry Wives of Windsor*,
                              Act 2, 2.

FEET

The many twinkling feet so small and
  sylph-like,
Suggesting the more perfect symmetry
Of the fair forms which terminate so well.
    BYRON.—*Marino Faliero*, 4, 1.

O, so light a foot
Will ne'er wear out the everlasting flint.
    SHAKESPEARE.—*Romeo and Juliet*,
                              Act 2, 6.

A foot more light, a step more true,
Ne'er from the heath-flower dashed the
  dew.
    SCOTT.—*Lady of the Lake*, 1, 18.

FEMININITY

And femininely meaneth furiously,
Because all passions in excess are female.
    BYRON.—*Sardanapalus*, Act 3, 1.

What female heart can gold despise ?
GRAY.—*Ode on Death of a Favourite Cat.*

The female of the species is more deadly
  than the male.   KIPLING.—*The
                              Female.*

FERVOUR

I preached as never sure to preach again,
And as a dying man to dying men.
    R. BAXTER.—*Love breathing Thanks.*

No wild enthusiast ever yet could rest
Till half mankind were like himself possessed.
    COWPER.—*Progress of Error*, 470.

FESTIVITIES

Uprouse ye then, my merry men,
It is our opening day.
    JOANNA BAILLIE.—*Orra*, Act 3.

Then top and maintop crowd the sail,
  Heave Care owre side !
And large, before Enjoyment's gale,
  Let's tak' the tide.
    BURNS.—*Epistle to James Smith.*

The lamps shone o'er fair women and
  brave men ;
A thousand hearts beat happily ; and
  when

Music arose with its voluptuous swell,
Soft eyes looked love to eyes which spake
again,
And all went merry as a marriage bell.
BYRON.—*Childe Harold, c.* 3, 21.

If ever a people required to be amused
it is we sad-hearted Anglo-Saxons.
SIR A. HELPS.—*Friends in Council,*
Bk. 1, *ch.* 4.

And the flags were all a-flutter and the
bells were all a-chime.
SIR H. NEWBOLT.—*San Stefano.*

Power laid his rod and rule aside,
And Ceremony doffed her pride.
SCOTT.—*Marmion, c.* 6, *Intro.*

In frolics dispose
Your pounds, shillings and pence ;
For we shall be nothing
A hundred years hence.
ANON.—*Given by Ritson, and marked*
by him as "Old" in English Songs,
Vol. 2, *No.* 16.

FEUDS

Their ineffectual feuds and feeble hates—
Shadows of hates, but they distress them
still.   M. ARNOLD.—*Balder Dead.*

The feud between us was but of the house,
Not of the heart.
SOUTHEY.—*Roderick, sec.* 12.

FICKLENESS

" Yes," I answered you last night ;
" No," this morning, sir, I say ;
Colours seen by candlelight
Will not look the same by day.
E. B. BROWNING.—*The Lady's Yes.*

The fault was Nature's fault, not thine,
Which made thee fickle as thou art.
BYRON.—*To a Youthful Friend.*

You cannot eat breakfast all day,
Nor is it the act of a sinner,
When breakfast is taken away,
To turn your attention to dinner.
SIR W. S. GILBERT.—*Trial by Jury.*

Wert thou more fickle than the restless sea,
Still should I love thee, knowing thee for
such. W. MORRIS.—*Jason, Bk.* 9, 22.

For, boy, however we do praise ourselves,
Our fancies are more giddy and unfirm,
More longing, wavering, sooner lost and
worn*
Than women's are.
SHAKESPEARE.—*Twelfth Night,* Act 2, 4.

FICTION

A mixture of a lie doth ever add pleasure.
BACON.—*Of Truth.*

* "Won" in most modern editions; "worn" in
the folio.

Your poet who sings how Greeks
That never were, in Troy that never was,
Did this or the other impossible great
thing.   BROWNING.—*Mr. Sludge.*

Scrofulous novels of the age.
R. BUCHANAN.—*St. Abe.*

Literature is a luxury ; fiction is a
necessity.
G. K. CHESTERTON.—*The Defendant.*

Why should a poet doubt in story to
mend the intrigues of fortune by more delightful conveyances of probable fictions,
because austere historians have entered
into a bond to truth ?
SIR W. DAVENANT.—*Pref. Letter to Hobbes.*

Whate'er the story be, the moral's true.
DRYDEN.—*Univ. of Oxford Prol.*

The tragic poet who deceived was juster
than he who failed to deceive ; and he that
was deceived was wiser than he who was
not deceived.
GORGIAS.—*As cited by Plutarch.*

And Truth severe, by fairy Fiction drest.
GRAY.—*Bard, c.* 3.

We must remember, however, that
fiction is not falsehood.
SIR A. HELPS.—*Friends in Council,*
Bk. 1, *ch.* 6.

Let fictions meant to please be very
near the truth. HORACE.—*De Arte Poet.*

I am always at a loss to know how much
to believe of my own stories.
WASHINGTON IRVING.—*Tales of a*
Traveller, Pref.

Men who have had no time or opportunity to read novels in their youth, such
as those men who work with their hands,
have a decided advantage.
SCHOPENHAUER.—*On Education.*

O wondrous power of genius ! Field-
ing's men and women are alive, though
History's are not.
THACKERAY.—*Lithography in Paris*

Novels are sweets. All people with
healthy literary appetites love them—
almost all women ; a vast number of clever,
hard-headed men.
THACKERAY.—*Roundabout Papers, On*
a Lazy, Idle Boy

I grant it's a gey lee-like [very lie-like]
story, but it's as sure as death.
J. WILSON.—*Noctes,* 34. (*Ettrick Shepherd.*)

FIDELITY

For True and Faithful's sure to lose
Which way soever the game goes.
BUTLER.—*Hudibras, Pt.* 3, c. 2.

So spake the Seraph Abdiel, faithful found
Among the faithless, faithful only he ;
Among innumerable false, unmoved,
Unshaken, unseduced, unterrified,
His loyalty he kept, his love, his zeal.
    MILTON.—*Paradise Lost, Bk.* 5, 896.

        I will follow thee
To the last gasp with truth and loyalty.
    SHAKESPEARE.—*As You Like It,* Act 2, 3.

FIGHTING

    What can alone ennoble fight ?
    A noble cause !
        CAMPBELL.—*Hallowed Ground.*

    For of thy slaying nowise are we fain,
    If we may pass unfoughten.
        W. MORRIS.—*Jason, Bk.* 9, 368.

    For bragging time was over and fighting
       time was come.
        H. NEWBOLT.—*Hawke.*

Which spills the foremost foeman's life.
That party conquers in the strife.
    SCOTT.—*Lady of the Lake, c.* 6, 1.

    He never counted him a man
    Would strike below the knee.
    SCOTT.—*Lay of the Last Minstrel.*

There is such a thing as a man being too
proud to fight.
    PRESIDENT WILSON, U.S.A.—*(Speech,*
                     1915).

FIGURES OF SPEECH

    For rhetoric he could not ope
    His mouth but out there flew a trope.
        BUTLER—*Hudibras, Pt.* 1, *c.* 1.

A foolish figure,
But farewell it, for I will use no art.
    SHAKESPEARE.—*Hamlet,* Act 2, 2.

Which things are an allegory.
        Galatians iv, 24.

FINALITY

        Their fatal hands
    No second stroke intend.
    MILTON.—*Paradise Lost, Bk.* 2, 712.

What's done is done.
    SHAKESPEARE.—*Macbeth,* Act 3, 2.

        The end crowns all ;
And that old common arbitrator, Time,
Will one day end it.
    SHAKESPEARE.—*Troilus and Cressida,*
                     Act 4, 5.

FINANCE

    The plain high-road of finance.
    BURKE.—*Speech on American Taxation.*

Where are those martyred saints, the
    Five per Cents. ?
And where—oh, where the devil are the
    Rents ?
        BYRON.—*Don Juan, c.* 11, 77.

Public credit means the contracting
of debts which a nation never can pay.
    W. COBBETT.—*Advice to Young Men.*

Blest paper-credit ! last and best supply !
That lends corruption lighter wings to fly.
    POPE.—*Moral Essays, Ep.* 3

The tempter saw his time ; the work he
    plied ;
Stocks and subscriptions poured on every
    side,
Till all the demon makes his full descent
In one abundant shower of cent. per cent.
Sinks deep within him, and possesses whole,
Then dubs director, and secures his soul.
    POPE.—*Ib.*

Borrowers are nearly always ill-spenders,
and it is with lent money that all evil
is mainly done and all unjust war protracted.   RUSKIN.—*Crown of Wild Olive*
                     (1865-6).

The elegant simplicity of the three per
cents.   LORD STOWELL.—*Saying.*

He touched the dead corpse of Public
Credit and it sprung upon its feet.
    DANIEL WEBSTER.—*Speech,* 1831.

Of Augustus and Rome the poets yet
    warble,
That he found it of brick and he left it oi
    marble ;
So of Pitt and of England they say withou,
    vapour,
That he found it of gold and he left it of
    paper.
    ANON.—*Epigram, c.* 1806, *in reference*
                to British paper currency.

FIRMNESS

Tender-hearted stroke a nettle,
    And it stings you for your pains ;
Grasp it like a man of mettle,
    And it soft as silk remains.
    AARON HILL.—*Written on a Window.*

It is only those who possess firmness who
can possess true gentleness.
    LA ROCHEFOUCAULD.—*Maxims,* 479.

He hath a tear for pity, and a hand
Open as day for melting charity :
Yet, notwithstanding, being incensed,
    he's flint.   SHAKESPEARE.—*Henry*
                IV., Pt. 2, Act 4, 4.

A little fire is quickly trodden out,
Which, being suffered, rivers cannot
    quench.   SHAKESPEARE.—*Henry VI.,*
                Pt. 3, Act 4, 8.

Do not, for one repulse, forgo the purpose
That you resolv'd to effect.
> SHAKESPEARE.—*Tempest*, Act 3, 3.

FISH AND FISHING

That great fishpond, the sea.
> T. DEKKER.—*Honest Whore*, Act 1.

Three fishers went sailing away to the West,
Away to the West as the sun went down ;
Each thought on the woman who loved
him the best.
> C. KINGSLEY.—*Three Fishers.*

It is not fish, it is man : you are devouring man, Calliodorus.
> MARTIAL (*in allusion to the high price of
> fish paid by Roman Epicures*).

No fisher,
But a well-wisher
To the game.
> SIR WALTER SCOTT.

The herrings are na gude
,Till they smell the new hay.
> *Northumberland saying.*

Of a' fish i' the sea herring is king.
> *Scottish prov.*

The herring loves the merry moonlight,
The mackerel loves the wind,
But the oyster loves the dredging song,
For they come o' a gentle kind.
> *Scottish rhyme.*

He is an honest man and eats no fish.
> *Prov., 16th cent., meaning that a man
> was no Papist.*

When the wind is in the east,
Then the fishes do bite the least ;
When the wind is in the west,
Then the fishes bite the best ;
When the wind is in the north,
Then the fishes do come forth ;
When the wind is in the south,
It blows the bait in the fish's mouth.
> J. O. *Halliwell's " Popular Rhymes " Found
> in a variety of versions throughout
> Great Britain*).

FISHMONGERS

Hamlet : You are a fishmonger.—
Polonius : Not I, my lord.—
Hamlet : Then I would you were so
honest a man.
> SHAKESPEARE.—*Hamlet*, Act 2, 2.

FLAGS

There's a flag that waves o'er every sea,
No matter when or where.
> ELIZA COOK.—*The Englishman.*

Flag of the free heart's hope and home !
By angel hands to valour given ;
Thy stars have lit the welkin dome,
And all thy hues were born in heaven.
> J. R. DRAKE.—*American Flag*, st. 5.

For ever float that standard sheet !
Where breathes the foe but falls before
us ?—
With Freedom's soil beneath our feet,
And Freedom's banner streaming o'er
us.   J. R. DRAKE.—*Ib. st.* 5.

A moth-eaten rag on a worm-eaten pole,
It doesn't look likely to stir a man's soul ;
'Tis the deeds that were done 'neath the
moth-eaten rag,
When the pole was a staff and the rag was
a flag.
> SIR E. B. HAMLEY.—*Monmouth Church.*

Ay, tear her tattered ensign down !
Long has it waved on high,
And many an eye has danced to see
That banner in the sky.
> O. W. HOLMES.—*Old Ironsides.*

'Tis the star-spangled banner, O ! long may
it wave
O'er the land of the free and the home of
the brave !
> F. S. KEY.—*Star-Spangled Banner.*

Then conquer we must, when our cause it
is just,
And this be our motto—" In God is our
trust " :
And the star-spangled banner in triumph
shall wave
O'er the land of the free and the home of
the brave.   F. S. KEY.—*Ib.*

Never was isle so little, never was sea so
lone,
But over the scud and the palm-trees an
English flag was flown.
> KIPLING.—*English Flag.*

Take thy banner ! May it wave
Proudly o'er the good and brave.
> LONGFELLOW.—*Hymn of Moravian Nuns.*

The imperial ensign, which, full high
advanced,
Shone like a meteor, streaming to the
wind.
> MILTON.—*Paradise Lost*, Bk. 1, 536.

FLAT COUNTRIES

Some signal exceptions there are undoubtedly—though I forget them just
the noo,—but folk in general are a' flat-
souled as weel's flat-soled, in a flat kintra.
> J. WILSON.—*Noctes*, 24. (*Ettrick Shepherd.*)

FLATTERY

People generally despise where they
flatter and cringe to those whom they
desire to supersede.
> MARCUS AURELIUS, *Bk.* 11, 14.

O Adulation, canker-worme of Truth ;
The flattring glasse of Pride and Self-
conceit.

Pittie it is that thou art so rewarded,
Whilst Truth and Honestie goe unregarded.
   R. BARNFIELD.—*Complaint of Poetrie*
                    (1598).

It is always self-interest which makes
flatterers. That is why Judas, whom the
demon of self-interest had seduced, be-
took him to flattery.
   BOSSUET.—*Sermon, Good Friday.*

Flattery corrupts both the receiver and
the giver.
   BURKE.—*Reflections on the Revolution.*

     You've supped full of flattery ;
They say you like it too—'tis no great
   wonder.
   BYRON.—*Don Juan, c.* 9, 5 (*alluding to
              Wellington*).

Flatterers look like friends, as wolves like
dogs.   CHAPMAN.—*Byron's Conspiracy,
               Act* 3, 1.

Flatterers been [are] the develes
chapelleyns, that singen ever, " Placebo."*
   CHAUCER.—*Parson's Tale, sec.* 40.

A man shal winne us best with flaterye.
   CHAUCER.—*Wife of Bath's Tale.*

Every woman is infallibly to be gained
by every sort of flattery, and every man
by one sort or another.
   LORD CHESTERFIELD.—*Letter* (1752).

What cannot praise effect in mighty minds,
When flattery soothes, and when ambition
   blinds ?   DRYDEN.—*Absalom*, 301.

When flattery does not succeed, it is
not the fault of flattery, but of the flatterer.
   PIERRE GASTON (DUC DE LÉVIS) (1764–
             1830).—*Maxims.*

Learn to contemn all praise betimes ;
For flattery's the nurse of crimes.
   GAY.—*Fables, Pt.* 1, 1.

A flattering painter, who made it his care
To draw men as they ought to be, not as
   they are.   GOLDSMITH.—*Retaliation.*

Of all wild beasts preserve me from a
   tyrant ;
And of all tame, a flatterer.
   BEN JONSON.—*Sejanus, Act* 1.

Three sorts of personages cannot be
praised too highly—the gods, one's mistress, and one's king.   LA FONTAINE.

If we did not flatter ourselves, the
flattery of other people would not harm us.
   LA ROCHEFOUCAULD.

---

*Alluding to the anthem " Placebo Domino"
(Ps. cxvi, 9) used in the Burial Office. To "sing
Placebo" meant to be complaisant.

   A flatterer can risk everything with
great personages.
   LE SAGE.—*Gil Blas, Bk.* 4, *ch.* 7.

The firmest purpose of a woman's heart
To well-timed, artful flattery may yield.
   G. LILLO.—*Elmerick.*

   It is possible to be below flattery, as
well as above it.
   MACAULAY.—*Hist. of England, c.* 2.

And what, in a mean man, I should call
   folly,
Is in your majesty remarkable wisdom.
   MASSINGER.—*Great Duke.*

     Minds,
By nature great, are conscious of their
   greatness,
And hold it mean to borrow aught from
flattery.   N. ROWE.—*Royal Convert.*

'Tis the most pleasing flattery to like what
   other men like. J. SELDEN.—*Pleasure.*

How similar flattery is to friendship !
   SENECA.—*Ep.* 45.

     Nay, do not think I flatter :
For what advancement may I hope from
   thee,
That no revenue hast, but thy good
   spirits ?
   SHAKESPEARE.—*Hamlet, Act* 3, 2.

But when I tell him he hates flatterers,
He says he does, being then most flattered.
   SHAKESPEARE.—*Julius Cæsar, Act* 2, 1.

Flatter and praise, commend, extol their
   graces ;
Though ne'er so black, say they have
   angels' faces.
   SHAKESPEARE.—*Two Gentlemen of
             Verona, Act* 2, 7.

Cram us with praise and make us
As fat as tame things.
   SHAKESPEARE.—*Winter's Tale, Act* 1, 2.

What really flatters a man is that you
think him worth flattering.
   G. B. SHAW.—*Bull's Other Island.*

'Tis an old maxim in the schools
That flattery's the food of fools ;
Yet now and then your men of wit
Will condescend to take a bit.
   SWIFT.—*Cadenus.*

Face-flatterer and back-biter are the
   same.
   TENNYSON.—*Merlin and Vivien*, 822.

I am not formed, by flattery and praise,
By sighs and tears, and all the whining
   trade
Of love, to feed a fond one's vanity,
To charm at once and spoil her.
   THOMSON.—*Tancred and Sigismunda.*

If men did not flatter one another there
would be scarcely any society.
VAUVENARGUES.—*Maxim* 921.

Coquettes, kings, and poets are accustomed to be flattered.
VOLTAIRE.—*Letter.*

Flattery is like bad money, it im-
poverishes those who receive it.
MME. WOILLEZ (1785–1859).

Flattery's the turnpike road to fortune's
door :
Truth is a narrow lane and full of quags,
Leading to broken heads, abuse, and rags.
J. WOLCOT.—*Odes for 1785, No. 9.*

A man that flattereth his neighbour
spreadeth a net for his feet.
Proverbs xxix, 5.

FLESH

The freilé flesh, whose nature is
Ay ready for to spurn and fall,
The firsté foman is of all.

.   .   .   .   .

Forthy [therefore] is thilke [that] knight
the best,
Through might and grace of Goddès
sonde [gifts],
Which that batailé may withstonde.
GOWER.—*Confessio Amantis, Bk.* 5.

O! that this too too solid flesh would melt,
Thaw, and resolve itself into a dew !
SHAKESPEARE.—*Hamlet,* Act 1, 2.

FLIGHT

For those that fly may fight again,
Which he can never do that's slain.
BUTLER.—*Hudibras, Pt.* 3, c. 3.

It is an olde saw, he fighteth wele (well)
that fleith faste.
Gesta Romanorum ("*Wolf and the Hare*"),
15th *cent. MS.*

FLIRTATION

And so she flirted, like a true
Good woman, till we bade adieu.
CAMPBELL.—*My Child Sweetheart.*

He decreed in words succinct
That all who flirted, leered, or winked,
Unless connubially linked,
Should forthwith be beheaded.
SIR W. S. GILBERT.—*Mikado.*

What we find the least of in flirtation
is love.
LA ROCHEFOUCAULD.—*Maxim* 402.

FLOOD

The rising world of waters, dark and
deep.
MILTON.—*Paradise Lost, Bk.* 3, 11.

FLOWERS

Flowers of remarkable size and hue,
Flowers such as Eden never knew.
R. H. BARHAM.—*Ingoldsby Legends.*
Nurse's Story.

Wee, modest, crimson-tippèd flower.
BURNS.—*To a Mountain Daisy.*

When daisies and buttercups gladdened
my sight,
Like treasures of silver and gold.
CAMPBELL.—*Field Flowers.*

Of al the floures in the mede,
Than love I most these floures whyte and
rede,
Swiche as men callen daysies in our town.
CHAUCER.—*Legend of Good Women.*

Shine by the side of every path we tread
With such a lustre he that runs may read.
COWPER.—*Tirocinium,* 79.

The Frenchman's darling [mignonette].
COWPER.—*Winter Evening.*

Daisies smell-less, yet most quaint,
And sweet thyme true,
Primrose, first-born child of Ver,
Merry spring-time's harbinger.
J. FLETCHER.—*Two Noble Kinsmen,*
Act 1, 1.

The flowers that bloom in the spring,
tra la,
Have nothing to do with the case.
SIR W. S. GILBERT.—*Mikado.*

The cowslip is a country wench,
The violet is a nun ;
But I will woo the dainty rose,
The queen of every one.
HOOD.—*Flowers.*

Those veilèd nuns, meek violets.
HOOD.—*Midsummer Fairies.*

The tulip is a flower without a soul, but
the rose and the lily seem to possess one.
JOSEPH JOUBERT (1754–1824).

Spake full well, in language quaint and
olden,
One who dwelleth by the castled Rhine,
When he called the flowers, so blue and
golden,
Stars, that in earth's firmament do
shine.   LONGFELLOW.—*Flowers.*

Flowers, that their gay wardrobe wear.
MILTON.—*Lycidas,* 47.

Throw hither all your quaint enamelled
eyes,
That on the green turf suck the honied
showers.   MILTON.—*Ib.,* 139.

The rathe primrose that forsaken dies.
MILTON.—*Ib.,* 142.

The pansy freaked with jet.
> MILTON.—*Lycidas*, 145.

Cowslips wan, that hang the pensive head,
And every flower that sad embroidery
    wears.   MILTON.—*Ib.*, 146.

Flowers of all hue, and without thorn the
  rose.
> MILTON.—*Paradise Lost, Bk.* 4, 256.

In Eastern lands they talk in flowers,
    And they tell in a garland their loves
      and cares ;
Each blossom that blooms in their garden
  bowers
On its leaves a mystic language wears.
> J. G. PERCIVAL.

You pretty daughters of the Earth and
  Sun.
> SIR W. RALEGH.—*Shepherd to the
> Flowers.*

There's rosemary, that's for remembrance ; pray, love, remember ; and there is
pansies, that's for thoughts.
> SHAKESPEARE.—*Hamlet*, Act 4, 5.

When daisies pied and violets blue
And lady-smocks, all silver white,
And cuckoo-buds of yellow hue
  Do paint the meadows with delight.
> SHAKESPEARE.—*Love's Labour's Lost.*
> Act 5, 2.

I know a bank, whereon the wild thyme
  blows,
Where ox-lips and the nodding violet
  grows ;
Quite over-canopied with luscious wood-
  bine,
With sweet musk roses and with eglantine.
> SHAKESPEARE.—*Midsummer Night's
> Dream*, Act 2, 2.

Where the bee sucks, there suck I ;
In a cowslip's bell I lie.
> SHAKESPEARE.—*Tempest*, Act 5, 1.

    Violets dim,
But sweeter than the lids of Juno's eyes,
Or Cytherea's breath.
> SHAKESPEARE.—*Winter's Tale*, Act 4, 3.

And the jessamine faint, and the sweet
  tuberose,
The sweetest flower for scent that blows.
> SHELLEY.—*Sensitive Plant*, 10.

The tufted basil, pun-provoking thyme,
Fresh baum, and marigold of cheerful
  hue.   SHENSTONE.—*Schoolmistress.*

Were I, O God, in churchless lands re-
  maining,
    Far from all voice of teachers or divines,
My soul would find, in flowers of thy
  ordaining,
    Priests, sermons, shrines !
> HORACE SMITH.—*Hymn to the Flowers.*

Flowers of all heavens, and lovelier than
  their names.
> TENNYSON.—*Princess, Prologue*, 12.

A flower when offered in the bud
Is no vain sacrifice.
> I. WATTS.—*Early Religion.*

And 'tis my faith that every flower
Enjoys the air it breathes.
> WORDSWORTH.—*In Early Spring.*

Thanks to the human heart by which we
  live,
Thanks to its tenderness, its joys, and
  fears,
To me the meanest flower that blows can
  give
Thoughts that do often lie too deep for
  tears.
> WORDSWORTH.—*Intimations of Im-
> mortality* (1803-6).

So fair, so sweet, withal, so sensitive,
Would that the little Flowers were born
  to live,
Conscious of half the pleasure which they
  give ;
That to this mountain-daisy's self were
  known
The beauty of its star-shaped shadow,
  thrown
On the smooth surface of this naked stone !
> WORDSWORTH.—*Poems of Sentiment*, 40.

There's a flower that shall be mine ;
'Tis the little celandine.
> WORDSWORTH.—*To the Small Celandine.*

Pleasures newly found are sweet,
When they lie about our feet.
> WORDSWORTH.—*To the same Flower
> (The Small Celandine).*

Thou art indeed, by many a claim,
The poet's darling.
> WORDSWORTH.—*To the Daisy* (1802).

Thou unassuming Common-place
Of Nature, with that homely face,
And yet with something of a grace
Which Love makes for thee !
> WORDSWORTH.—*To the same Flower
> (The Daisy).*

Through storm and wind, sunshine and
  shower,
Still will ye find groundsel in flower.
> *Scottish rhyme (Dr. Robert Chambers's
> collection*, 1826).

The rose is red, the violet's blue,
Pinks are sweet, and so are you.
> *For St. Valentine's Day (Halliwell).*

FOG

    This is a London particular, . . . a fog,
miss.   DICKENS.—*Bleak House, ch.* 3.

O heavenly colour ! London town
Has blurred it from her skies,
And hooded in an earthly brown
Unheavened the city lies.
ALICE MEYNELL.—*November Blue.*

A grey fog in the early prime,
A blue fog by the breakfast hour,
A saffron fog at luncheon time,
At dinner a persistent shower
Of smut, and then a dismal power
Of choking darkness and despair,
Thickening and soddening all the air.
WALTER C. SMITH.—*Olrig Grange, Bk.* 3.

FOLLY AND FOOLS

Lulled by the same old baby-prattle,
With intermixture of the rattle.
BROWNING.—*Christmas Eve, c.* 11.

Which made some take him for a tool
That knaves do work with, called a Fool.
BUTLER.—*Hudibras, Pt.* 1, *c.* 1.

There is a greatest Fool, as a superlative
in every kind ; and *the* most Foolish man
in the Earth is now indubitably living and
breathing, and did this morning, or lately,
eat breakfast. CARLYLE.—*On Biography.*

Wise men learn more from fools than
fools from wise men.
CATO (*according to* Plutarch).

The picture placed the busts between,
Gives satire all its strength ;
Wisdom and wit are little seen,
But folly's at full length.
LORD CHESTERFIELD (attrib.).—*On
Richard Nash's picture, between the
busts of Newton and Pope, at Bath.*

Cou'd it be worth thy wondrous waste of
pains
To publish to the world thy lack of brains ?
CHURCHILL.—*Rosciad.*

Examinations are formidable even to
the best prepared, for the greatest fool
may ask more than the wisest man can
answer. C. C. COLTON.—*Lacon.*

A knave when tried on honesty's plain
rule,
And when by that of reason a mere fool.
COWPER.—*Hope,* 568.

Designed by Nature wise, but self-made
fools. COWPER.—*Tirocinium,* 837.

His ambition is to sink,
To reach a depth profounder still, and still
Profounder, in the fathomless abyss
Of folly.
COWPER.—*Winter Morning Walk.*

Folly in youth is sin, in age 'tis madness.
S. DANIEL.—*Cleopatra.*

An ass may do more adventitious ill
Than twenty tigers.
J. DAVIDSON.—*Godfrida,* Act 2.

True fops help nature's work, and go to
school
To file and finish God Almighty's fool.
DRYDEN.—*Man of Mode, Ep.*

The folly of others is ever most ridiculous to those who are themselves most
foolish.
GOLDSMITH.—*Citizen of the World,* 43.

None but a fool is always right.
J. C. HARE.—*Guesses at Truth, vol.* 2.

It is the folly of the world constantly
which confounds its wisdom.
O. W. HOLMES.—*Professor at Breakfast Table.*

All the world's a mass of folly,
Youth is gay, age melancholy :
Youth is spending, age is thrifty,
Mad at twenty, cold at fifty ;
Man is nought but folly's slave,
From the cradle to the grave.
W. H. IRELAND.—*Modern Ship of
Fools.* (*Of the Folly of all the World.*)

You look wise. Pray correct that error.
. . . He who hath not a dram of folly in
his mixture, hath pounds of much worse
matter in his composition.
LAMB.—*All Fools' Day.*

Who lives without folly is not so wise
as he thinks. LA ROCHEFOUCAULD.

A man of wit would often be very much
at a loss without the company of fools.
LA ROCHEFOUCAULD.

The event is the schoolmaster of fools.
LIVY.—*20,* 39.

The right to be a cussed fool
Is safe from all devices human ;
It's common (ez a gin'l rule)
To every critter born o' woman.
J. R. LOWELL.—*Biglow Papers,* 2, 7.

A wise fool is a worse fool than an ignorant fool.
MOLIÈRE.—*Femmes savantes,* Act 4.

But a' the fules' foolish sangs
That e'er cam' frae the moon,
Were naething to a sang I heard,
To a very foolish tune,
That a fule sang to me.
G. OUTRAM.—*The Fule's Song.*

Where lives the man that has not tried
How mirth can into folly glide,
And folly into sin ?
SCOTT.—*Bridal of Triermain.*

Motley's the only wear.
SHAKESPEARE.—*As You Like It,* Act 2, 7.

Let the doors be shut upon him, that he may play the fool nowhere but in 's own house. SHAKESPEARE.—*Hamlet*, Act 3, 1.

They fool me to the top of my bent.
SHAKESPEARE.—*Hamlet*, Act 3, 2.

Thus hath the candle singed the moth. O, these deliberate fools !
SHAKESPEARE.—*Merchant of Venice*, Act 2, 9.

Lord, what fools these mortals be !
SHAKESPEARE.—*Midsummer Night's Dream*, Act 3, 2.

That scorn of fools, by fools mistook for pride. SWIFT.—*On Sir W. Temple's Illness*, 1693.

'Tis fools we want, and of the largest size. SWIFT.—*Swan Tripe Club*.

Hated by fools, and fools to hate, Be that my motto and my fate.
SWIFT.—*To Dr. Delany*, 1729.

If thou hast never been a fool, be sure thou wilt never be a wise man.
THACKERAY.—*Lovel the Widower*.

Hain't we got all the fools in town on our side ? And ain't that a big enough majority in any town ?
MARK TWAIN.—*Huckleberry Finn, c.* 26.

O fruitful Britain ! doubtless thou wast meant
A nurse of fools, to stock the continent.
YOUNG.—*Love of Fame*.

Men may live fools, but fools they cannot die.   YOUNG.—*Night Thoughts*, 4.

Suffering more from folly than from fate.
YOUNG.—*Ib.*, 8.

For as the crackling of thorns under a pot, so is the laughter of the fool.
Ecclesiastes vii, 6.

Answer not a fool according to his folly, lest thou also be like unto him. Answer a fool according to his folly, lest he be wise in his own conceit. *Proverbs* xxvi, 4, 5.

Though thou shouldest bray a fool in a mortar among wheat with a pestle, yet will not his foolishness depart from him.
Proverbs xxvii, 22.

O Love, Love, on thy sowle God have mercye !
For as Peter is *princeps apostolorum*,
So to the[e] may be said clerlye,
Of all foolys that ever was, *stultus stultorum*.
The Epitaphe of Love, the Kinge's Foole.
Bodl. MSS., c. temp. Henry VIII.

A barber learns to shave by shaving fools.   *Old prov.*

The chief disease that reigns this year is folly.   *Prov. (Geo. Herbert).*

Fools will not part with their bauble for all Lombard Street.   *Prov.*

FOOD

A plate of turtle, green and glutinous.
BROWNING.—*Pied Piper, c.* 4.

The halesome parritch, chief of Scotia's food.
BURNS.—*Cotter's Saturday Night.*

Pasthry thot aggravates a mon 'stead of pacifying him. [*John Browdie.*]
DICKENS.—*Nickleby, c.* 42.

Give me barley meal and water and I will rival Jove in happiness.
EPICURUS.—(*Quoted by Seneca.*)

Ef dey's [there's] sump'n what I 'spizes hit's col' vittles.
J. C. HARRIS.—*Nights with Uncle Remus, ch.* 15.

Lazy fokes' stummicks don't git tired.
J. C. HARRIS.—*Plantation Proverbs.*

Cornwall squab-pie, and Devon whitepot brings ;
And Leicester beans and bacon, food of kings.
DR. W. KING.—*Art of Cookery.*

There is a physiognomical character in the tastes for food. C—— holds that a man cannot have a pure mind who refuses apple dumplings. I am not certain but he is right.   CHARLES LAMB.

Fame is at best an unperforming cheat, But 'tis substantial happiness to eat.
POPE.—*Prol., Durfey's Last Play.*

Salad, and eggs, and lighter fare, Tune the Italian spark's guitar ;
And, if I take Dan Congreve right,
Pudding and beef make Britons fight.
PRIOR.—*Alma*, 3, 246.

But mice and rats and such small deer Have been Tom's food for seven long year.
SHAKESPEARE.—*Lear*, Act 3, 4.

There is no love sincerer than the love of food.
G. B. SHAW.—*Man and Superman.*

I found that between ten and seventy years of age, I had eaten and drunk 44 waggon-loads of meat and drink more than would have preserved me in life and health. The value of this mass of nourishment I considered to be worth £7,000 sterling. It occurred to me that I must, by my voracity, have starved to death fully a hundred persons.   SYDNEY SMITH.—
Letter to Lord Murray, Sept. 29, 1843.

I am convinced digestion is the great secret of life ; and that character, talents, virtues, and qualities are powerfully affected by beef, mutton, pie-crust, and rich soups.
SYDNEY SMITH.—*Letter, Sept.* 30, 1837.

Let onion atoms lurk within the bowl,
And half-suspected animate the whole.
SYDNEY SMITH.—*Recipe for a Salad*.

A son of pudding and eternal beef.
SWIFT.—*Swan Tripe Club*.

Surfeit has killed more than famine.
THEOGNIS.—(*Greek*.)

It is a pleasant fact that thought depends entirely on the stomach, and that in spite of that the best stomachs are not the best thinkers.
VOLTAIRE.—*Letter to D'Alembert, Aug.* 20, 1770.

After a', I maun confess that I like the Englishers, if they wadna be sae pernicketty about what they eat.
JOHN WILSON.—*Noctes,* 9 (*Ettrick Shepherd*).

More pleased when knives and forks in concert join,
Than all the tinkling cymbals of the Nine *f*muses].
J. WOLCOT.—*Lousiad, c.* 3, 9.

All goeth down Gutter Lane.
Old London Saying (Ray).

It's by the mouth o' the cow that the milk comes.
Scottish prov.

FOOL'S PARADISE

A fool's paradise is better than a wiseacre's purgatory.
G. COLMAN, SEN.—*Deuce is in him*.

In this fool's paradise he drank delight.
CRABBE.—*The Borough, Letter* 12.

Into a Limbo large and broad, since called
The Paradise of Fools, to few unknown.
MILTON.—*Paradise Lost, Bk.* 3, 495.

FOOTBALL

Ye contented your souls
With the flannelled fools at the wickets, or the muddied oafs at the goals.
KIPLING.—*The Islanders*.

Yet, in a hundred scenes, all much the same,
I know that weekly half a million men
Who never actually played the game,
Hustling like cattle herded in a pen,
Look on and shout,
While two-and-twenty hirelings hack a ball about.
SIR OWEN SEAMAN.—*People's Sport.*

FOPPERY

There's Bardus, a six-foot column of fop,
A lighthouse without any light atop.
HOOD.—*Miss Kilmansegg*.

A pretty man is a paltry man.
MARTIAL.—I, 10.

Sir Plume, of amber snuff-box justly vain,
And the nice conduct of a clouded cane.
POPE.—*Rape of the Lock, c.* 4, 123.

The wealthy curlèd darlings of our nation.
SHAKESPEARE.—*Othello,* Act 1, 2.

FORBEARANCE

There is, however, a limit at which forbearance ceases to be a virtue.
BURKE.—*Observations on " Present State of the Nation."*

Woe to the purblind crew who fill
The heart with each day's care ;
Nor gain, from past or future, skill
To bear and to forbear.
WORDSWORTH.—*Poems of Sentiment,* 34.

Fifty years and three
Together in love lived we :
Angry both at once none ever did us see.
This was the fashion
God taught us, and not fear :
When one was in a passion
The other could forbear.
Ascribed to Mr. Shelly, a Cambridge parson (16th century), on being asked how long he had been married.

FORBIDDEN FRUIT

Forbede us thing, and that desyren we.
CHAUCER.—*Wife of Bath's Prologue*.

FORCE

Force is not a remedy.
JOHN BRIGHT.—*Speech, Nov.* 16, 1880.

Force is a rugged way of making love.
S. BUTLER.—*Cat and Puss*.

Might,
That makes a title where there is no right.
S. DANIEL.—*Civil Wars, st.* 36.

Who overcomes
By force, hath overcome but half his foe.
MILTON.—*Paradise Lost, Bk.* 1, 648.

This [constitutional pressure] may be force ; but it is force without injury, and therefore without blame. SYDNEY SMITH.
—*Peter Plymley's Letters,* No. 4.

The blind wild beast of force.
TENNYSON.—*Princess, c.* 5, 256.

FOREBODING

Knowing how Nature threatens ere she springs. R. BUCHANAN.—*Meg Blane.*

He [Grenville] was the raven of the House of Commons, always croaking defeat in the midst of triumphs.
MACAULAY.—*Earl of Chatham.*

Beware the Ides of March !
SHAKESPEARE.—*Julius Cæsar*, Act 1, 2.

By the pricking of my thumbs
Something wicked this way comes.
SHAKESPEARE.—*Macbeth*, Act 4, 1.

The weather is beautiful, but, as Noodle says,—with his eyes beaming with delight—" We shall suffer for this, Sir, by-and-by."
SYDNEY SMITH.—*Letter to Sir G. Phillips*, Dec. 22, 1836.

FORECAST

'Tis the sunset of life gives me mystical lore,
And coming events cast their shadows before. CAMPBELL.—*Theodric.*

  So often do the spirits
Of great events stride on before the events,
And in to-day already walks to-morrow.
COLERIDGE.—*Wallenstein*, Act 5.

O that a man might know
The end of this day's business ere it come !
SHAKESPEARE.—*Julius Cæsar*, Act 5, 1.

  The baby figure of the giant mass
  Of things to come at large.
SHAKESPEARE.—*Troilus*, Act 1, 3.

FOREIGN LANDS

Admire whate'er they find abroad,
But nothing here, though e'er so good ;
Be natives wheresoe'er they come,
And only foreigners at home.
S. BUTLER.—*On our Ridiculous Imitation of the French.*

  From Greenland's icy mountains,
  From India's coral strand,
  Where Afric's sunny fountains
  Roll down their golden sand.
BISHOP HEBER.—*Hymn.*

I am a barbarian here, because I am not understood by anyone.
OVID.—*Tristia*, Bk. 5, 10.

FORESIGHT

Never mind to-morrow, Hetty. Be like the sun and the meadow, which are not in the least concerned about the coming winter.
G. B. SHAW.—*Unsocial Socialist*, ch. 5.

Rainy days will surely come ;
Take your friend's umbrella home. ANON.

FORGETFULNESS

But each day brings its petty dust
Our soon-choked souls to fill,

And we forget because we must,
And not because we will.
MATTHEW ARNOLD.—*Absence.*

I feel assured there is no such thing as ultimate forgetting ; traces once impressed upon the memory are indestructible.
DE QUINCEY.—*Opium Eater*, Pt. 3.

With life's best balm—forgetfulness.
MRS. HEMANS.—*The Caravan in the Desert.*

Of all affliction taught a lover yet,
'Tis sure the hardest science to forget.
POPE.—*Eloisa to Abelard*, 189.

But men are men ; the best sometimes forget.
SHAKESPEARE.—*Othello*, Act 2, 3.

FORGIVENESS

But Thou art good ; and goodness still
Delighteth to forgive.
BURNS.—*Prayer in Prospect of Death.*

Forgiveness to the injured does belong ;
But they ne'er pardon who have done the wrong.
DRYDEN.—*Conquest of Granada*, Pt. 2, Act 1, 2.

To love is human ; it is also human to forgive. PLAUTUS.—*Mercator.*

To err is human ; to forgive, divine.
POPE.—*Criticism*, 525.

A brave man thinks no one his superior who does him an injury, for he has it then in his power to make himself superior to the other by forgiving it.
POPE.—*Thoughts on Various Subjects.*

Pardon's the word to all.
SHAKESPEARE.—*Cymbeline*, Act 5, 5.

To understand is to forgive.
MADAME DE STAËL.

The brave only know how to forgive.
. . . A coward never forgave ; it is not in his nature. STERNE.—*Sermon.*

Sleep ; and if life was bitter to thee,
 pardon ;
If sweet, give thanks ; thou hast no more
 to live ;
And to give thanks is good, and to forgive.
  SWINBURNE.—*Ave atque Vale.*

'Tis easier for the generous to forgive
Than for offence to ask it.
THOMSON.—*Edward and Eleonora.*

Love scarce is love that never knows
The sweetness of forgiving.
WHITTIER.—*Among the Hills.*

And unforgiving, unforgiven dies.
Anon. (On the Death of Queen, Caroline).

FORMALITY

In general, the more completely cased with formulas a man may be, the safer, happier is it for him.
CARLYLE.—*Past and Present*, Bk. 2, c. 17.

You are too senseless-obstinate, my lord,
Too ceremonious and traditional.
SHAKESPEARE.—*Richard III.*, Act 3, 1.

FORTUNE

Nothing more certaine than incertainties ;
Fortune is full of fresh varietie :
Constant in nothing but inconstancie.
R. BARNFIELD.—*Shepherd's Content* (1594).

There is a nick in Fortune's restless wheel
For each man's good.
CHAPMAN.—*Revenge of Bussy d'Ambois.*

The amiable fortune deceyveth folk ;
the contrarie Fortune techeth.
CHAUCER.—*Boethius.*

Gifts of fortune,
That passen as a shadow on the wall.
CHAUCER.—*Merchant's Tale.*

Let not one look of fortune cast you down ;
She were not fortune if she did not frown.
EARL OF CORK.—*Imit. of Horace.*

Extremes of fortune are true wisdom's test.
And he's of men most wise who bears them best.
R. CUMBERLAND.—*Philemon.*

How easy 'tis, when destiny proves kind,
With full-spread sails to run before the wind. DRYDEN.—*Astræa Redux*, 63.

Dame Nature gave him comeliness and health,
And Fortune (for a passport) gave him wealth. W. HARTE.—*Eulogius*, 411.

England's high Chancellor, the destined heir,
In his soft cradle, to his father's chair,
Whose even thread the Fates spin round and full,
Out of their choicest and their whitest wool.
BEN JONSON.—*On Francis Bacon.*

" After sharpest shoures," quath Peers,
" most sheene is the sonne ;
Ys no weder warmer than after watery cloudes." LANGLAND.—*Piers Plowman, Passus* 21.

Happiness or misery generally go to those who have most of either the one or the other.
LA ROCHEFOUCAULD.—*Maxims, Suppl.*, 3, 18.

Fortune gives too much to many, enough to none. MARTIAL.—*Bk.* 12.

If you count up the sunny and cloudy days in a complete year, you will find that the fine day has come more often.
OVID.—*Trist.*, 5, 8, 31.

Fortune is more treacherous and dangerous when she caresses than when she dismays. Experience has taught me this, not books or arguments.
PETRARCH.—*On the Remedies of Good and Bad Fortune.*

To a good man nothing is evil, neither while living nor when dead ; nor are his concerns neglected by the gods.
PLATO.—*Apol. of Socrates*, 33 (*Cary tr.*).

O Fortune, unkind to men of talent, how unequally do you distribute your rewards ! SENECA.—*Hercules Furens.*

On Fortune's cap we are not the very button.
SHAKESPEARE.—*Hamlet*, Act 2, 2.

For who would bear the whips and scorns of time,
The oppressor's wrong, the proud man's contumely,
The pangs of despised love, the law's delay,
The insolence of office, and the spurns
Which patient merit of the unworthy takes,
When he himself might his quietus make
With a bare bodkin ?
SHAKESPEARE.—*Ib.*, Act 3, 1.

Why let the strucken deer go weep,
The hart ungallèd play ;
For some must watch, while some must sleep :
So runs the world away.
SHAKESPEARE.—*Ib.*, Act 3, 2.

When Fortune means to men most good,
She looks upon them with a threatening eye.
SHAKESPEARE.—*King John*, Act 3, 4.

For herein Fortune shows herself more kind
Than is her custom.
SHAKESPEARE.—*Merch. of Venice*, Act 4, 1.

And turn the giddy round of Fortune's wheel. SHAKESPEARE.—*Lucrece*, st. 136.

Fortune makes a fool of the man whom she favours over much.
PUBLILIUS SYRUS.

O mortals ! blind in fate, who never know
To bear high fortune or endure the low.
VIRGIL.—*Æneid, Bk.* 10 (*Dryden tr.*).

Either let us fall or reign ! The lucky man is honoured. The conqueror becomes dear to posterity, which condemns the unfortunate.
VOLTAIRE.—*Don Pèdre.*

When the lady is not cruel you treat her as a nymph and a divinity ; if you are repulsed by her you make songs against her.   VOLTAIRE.—*Les Deux Tonneaux.*

When we do not act, the gods abandon us.   VOLTAIRE.—*Les Pélopides.*

One man, says the auld proverb, is born wi' a silver spoon in his mouth, and another wi' a wudden ladle.
J. WILSON.—*Noctes Ambrosianæ, Nov., 1831.*

It seems to me harder to find a man who bears good fortune well, than one who bears evil.   XENOPHON.

The lines are fallen unto me in pleasant places.   *Psalm* xvi, 6.

Fortune is glass ; just when it is bright it is broken.
Latin prov. (attrib. to Seneca).

What said Pluck ?
" The greater knave the greater luck."
Scottish rhyme.

FORTUNE TELLING

She knew the future, for the past she knew.
J. LANGHORNE.—*Country Justice, 214.*

With the fond maids in palmistry he deals ;
They tell the secret first which he reveals.
PRIOR.—*Henry and Emma.*

There is a history in all men's lives,
Figuring the nature of the times deceased ;
The which observed, a man may prophesy,
With a near aim, of the main chance of things
As yet not come to life ; which in their seeds,
And weak beginnings, lie intreasured.
SHAKESPEARE.—*Henry IV., Pt. 2, Act 3, 1.*

FOX-HUNTING

He thought at heart like courtly Chesterfield,
Who, after a long chase o'er hills, dales, bushes,
And what not, though he rode beyond all price,
Ask'd next day, " if men ever hunted *twice* ? "
BYRON.—*Don Juan, c. 14, 35.*

And though the fox he follows may be tamed,
A mere fox-follower never is reclaimed.
COWPER.—*Conversation, 409.*

FRANCE

France, famed in all great arts, in none supreme.
M. ARNOLD.—*Sonnet (Continued), 1848.*

They [the French] better understand the management of a war than our islanders ; but we know we are superior to them in the day of battle. They value themselves on their generals ; we on our soldiers.
DRYDEN.—*Dedication of Æneid.*

So it is with nearly all French things. There is a clever showy surface, but no Holy of Holies, far withdrawn ; conceived in the depth of a mind, and only to be received into the depth of ours after much attention.
E. FITZGERALD.—*Letter to F. Tennyson.*

Gay sprightly land of mirth and social ease,
Pleased with thyself, whom all the world can please.   GOLDSMITH.—*Traveller.*

France beloved of every soul that loves or serves its kind.
KIPLING.—*France (June, 1913).*

Yet who can help loving the land that has taught us
Six hundred and eighty-five ways to dress eggs.   MOORE.—*Fudge Family.*

All that is noble in Europe in sentiment, taste, and manners has been invented in France.
NIETZSCHE.—*As quoted by M. Poincaré, Speech, 1917.*

The vine-covered hills and gay regions of France.
W. ROSCOE.—*Lines written in 1788.*

A Parisian thinks he knows men, and he knows only Frenchmen.
ROUSSEAU.—*Emile.*

For the apparel oft proclaims the man ;
And they in France, of the best rank and station,
Are most select and generous chief in that.
SHAKESPEARE.—*Hamlet, Act 1, 3.*

That sweet enemy, France.
SIR P. SIDNEY.—*Astrophel.*

I find the [French] people now, as I did before, most delightful. Compared to them we are perfect barbarians.
SYDNEY SMITH.—*Letter from Rouen, Oct. 6, 1835.*

" They order," said I, " this matter better in France."
STERNE.—*Sent. Journey, ch. 1.*

If they [the French] have a fault, they are too serious.
STERNE.—*Sent. Journey : The Address, Versailles.*

Give us a name to fill the mind
With the shining thoughts that lead man-
    kind,
The glory of learning, the joy of art,—
A name that tells of a splendid part
In the long, long toil and the strenuous
    fight
Of the human race to win its way
From the ancient darkness into the day
Of Freedom, Brotherhood, Equal Right,—
A name like a star, a name of light,—
I give you *France*!
        DR. VAN DYKE (U.S.A.).—*Lines on
                        France* (1917).

Every Frenchwoman, as I imagine,
knows more or less something about the
art of cooking.
        VOLTAIRE.—*Origine des Métiers*.

FRANKNESS

'Tis not my talent to conceal my thoughts,
Or carry smiles and sunshine in my face,
When discontent sits heavy at my heart,
        ADDISON.—*Cato*, Act 1, 4.

There is no wisdom like frankness.
        DISRAELI.—*Sybil, Bk.* 4, *ch.* 9.

To be frank and sincere is my greatest
talent of all. I do not know how to trick
men in talking to them; and the man who
has not the gift of hiding what he thinks
should cut short his stay in this country.
        MOLIÈRE.—*Le Misanthrope*, Act 3, 7.
        (*Alceste, the "misanthrope."*)

I think there's never man in Christendom
Can lesser hide his hate or love than he.
        SHAKESPEARE.—*Richard III.*, Act 3, 4.

FRATERNITY

Good God! What a blissful age when
man says to man : "Let us be brothers or
I will cut your throat!"
        E. LEBRUN (1729–1807).—*Fraternity or
                        Death.*

FRAUDS, PIOUS

Well stored with pious frauds, and, like
most discourses of the sort, much better
calculated for the private advantage of
the preacher than the edification of the
hearers. BURKE.—*Observations on " The
        Present State of the Nation."*

The outworn rite, the old abuse,
    The pious fraud transparent grown.
        WHITTIER.—*The Reformer.*

FREEDOM

Within yourselves deliverance must be
    sought ;
Each man his prison makes.
        SIR E. ARNOLD.—*Light of Asia, Bk.* 8.

Ah! freedom is a noble thing!
Freedom makes man to have likeing !

Freedom all solace to man gives !
He lives at ease who freely lives !
        JOHN BARBOUR.—*The Bruce.*

The cause of Freedom is the cause of God.
        W. L. BOWLES.—*To E. Burke.*

Whilst freedom is true to itself, everything becomes subject to it.
        BURKE.—*Speech at Bristol.* 1780.

Slaves cannot breathe in England ; if
    their lungs
Receive our air, that moment they are
    free.   COWPER.—*Time Piece.*

He is the freeman whom the truth makes
    free. COWPER.—*Winter Morning Walk.*

" I think I know the delights of freedom," I [Pip] answered.—" Ah," said he
[Provis], shaking his head gravely, " But
you don't know it equal to me. You
must have been under lock and key, dear
boy, to know it equal to me ! "
        DICKENS.—*Great Expectations, c.* 54.

More liberty begets desire of more ;
The hunger still increases with the store.
        DRYDEN.—*Hind and the Panther,
                        Pt.* 1, 519.

Freedom! which in no other land will
    thrive—
Freedom! an English subject's sole
    prerogative.
        DRYDEN.—*Threnodia Augustalis, st.* 10.

I found that riches in general were, in
every country, another name for freedom,
and that no man is so fond of liberty
himself as not to be desirous of subjecting
the will of some individuals in society to
his own. GOLDSMITH.—*Vicar of Wakefield.*

The greatest glory of a freeborn people
Is to transmit that freedom to their
    children. WM. HAVARD.—*Regulus.*

Freedom is a new religion, the religion
of our age. If Christ is not the God of this
religion, he is still one of its high-priests.
        HEINE.—*The Liberation.*

Ay, call it holy ground,
    The soil where first they trod !
They have left unstained what there they
    found—
    Freedom to worship God !
        MRS. HEMANS.—*Pilgrim Fathers.*

All we have of freedom—all we use or
    know—
This our fathers bought for us, long and
    long ago.   KIPLING.—*The Old Issue.*

If I have freedom in my love,
    And in my soul am free,—
Angels alone, that soar above,
    Enjoy such liberty.
        LOVELACE.—*To Althea.*

Neither one person, nor any number of persons, is warranted in saying to another human creature of ripe years, that he shall not do with his life, for his own benefit, what he chooses to do with it.

J. S. MILL.—*Liberty, ch.* 4.

None can love freedom heartily but good men ; the rest love not freedom, but licence. MILTON.—*Tenure of Kings* (1649).

Oh ! remember life can be
No charm for him who lives not free !
MOORE.—*Before the Battle.*

O Freedom ! once thy flame hath fled,
It never lights again.
MOORE.—*Weep on.*

Service and freedom, when excessive, are each an evil ; but when moderate are altogether a good. PLATO.—*Epistle* 8.

No human being, however great, or powerful, was ever so free as a fish.
RUSKIN.—*Two Faiths.*

And, best beloved of best men, liberty,
Free lives and lips, free hands of men freeborn. SWINBURNE.—*Atalanta.*

Whatever harmonies of law
  The growing world assume,
Thy work is thine—The single note
From that deep chord which Hampden smote
  Will vibrate to the doom.
TENNYSON.—*England and America
in* 1782.

The thrall in person may be free in soul.
TENNYSON.—*Gareth.*

It is the land that freemen till,
  That sober-suited Freedom chose ;
The land, where girt with friends or foes
A man may speak the thing he will ;
A land of settled government,
A land of just and old renown,
Where Freedom slowly broadens down
From precedent to precedent.
TENNYSON.—*You ask me why.*

Ne'er yet by Force was Freedom overcome. THOMSON.—*Liberty.*

Man is free the moment he wishes to be.
VOLTAIRE.—*Brutus.*

You reasoners and fine wits, and you who think yourselves such, would you live happy, live always without a master.
VOLTAIRE.—*Discours* 4.

It is the freedom to think which has made such excellent books blossom forth amongst the English. It is because their minds are enlightened that they are hardy.
. . . It is this freedom which has made all the arts flourish in England and has covered the ocean with her vessels.
VOLTAIRE.—*Reflections for Fools.*

Good, which they dared not hope for, we
  have seen ;
A State whose generous will through earth
  is dealt ;
A State, which, balancing herself between
Licence and slavish order, dares be free.
WORDSWORTH.—*Eccles. Sonnets, Pt.* 3, 37.

The good man only is free ; all bad men are slaves.
Stoic Maxim quoted by Plutarch.

FREEMASONRY

For in heaven there's a lodge, and St.
  Peter keeps the door,
And none can enter in but those that are
  pure. *The Masonic Hymn.*

FREE SPEECH

No more need men keep in silence
Tongues fast bound ; for now the people
May with freedom speak at pleasure ;
For the yoke of power is broken.
ÆSCHYLUS.—*Persæ,* 395
(Plumptre tr.).

In the present age—which has been described as " destitute of faith but terrified at scepticism "— . . . the claims of an opinion to be protected from public attack are rested not so much on its truth as on its importance to society.
J. S. MILL.—*Liberty, ch.* 2
(1859).

This is true liberty, when freeborn men,
Having to advise the public, may speak
  free. MILTON.—*Translation,
Euripides.*

To speak his thought is every freeman's
  right,
In peace and war, in council and in fight
POPE.—*Iliad, Bk.* 12, 249.

FREE TRADE

Free Trade is not a principle ; it is an expedient.
DISRAELI.—*Speech, April* 25, 1843.

Free trade, one of the greatest blessings which a government can confer on a people, is in almost every country unpopular.
MACAULAY.—*Mitford's Greece.*

FREE WILL

Everywhere the human soul stands between a hemisphere of light and another of darkness ; on the confines of two ever-lasting hostile empires, Necessity and Free Will. CARLYLE.—*Essays ; Goethe's Works.*

Sufficient to have stood, though free to fall.
MILTON.—*Paradise Lost, Bk.* 3, 99.

Heaven wills our happiness, allows our doom. YOUNG.—*Night Thoughts,* 7.

FRENCH LEAVE

If you wish to depart before the rest of the company . . . take what they call a French leave, and which our polite neighbours, the French, have instructed us in, that is, to steal off as unnoticed as possible. ' REV. J. TRUSLER.—*System of Etiquette* (1804).

FRETFULNESS

You are so fretful, you cannot live long.
SHAKESPEARE.—*Henry IV.*, Pt. 1, Act 3, 3.

FRIDAY

Selde is the Friday al the wyke alike,
[" Fridays in the week are seldom alike,"
—i.e. Fridays are unlike each other. Compare the French prov. below.]
CHAUCER.—*Knight's Tale*, 681.

And on a Friday fil [fell] al this meschaunce.   CHAUCER.—*Nun's Priest's Tale.*

Friday is perhaps the best day of the week. . . . Friday's greatest merit is perhaps that it paves the way to Saturday and the cessation of work. That it ever was really unlucky I greatly doubt.
E. V. LUCAS.—*Fireside and Sunshine.*

Friday is always the best or the worst day in the week.
Old French prov. (*Recueil des Contes*, by A. Jubinal).

Friday's moon,
Come when it will,
It comes too soon.
Prov. (*Halliwell's " Popular Rhymes,"—in reference to the new moon*).

FRIENDSHIP

Thy bounteous hand with worldly bliss
Has made my cup run o'er,
And in a kind and faithful friend
Has doubled all my store.
ADDISON.—*Spectator*, 453.

Friendship is a poor adviser; politicians deep and wise
Many times are forced to learn a lesson from their enemies.
ARISTOPHANES.—*The Birds* (*Frere tr.*).

There is little friendship in the world and least of all between equals.
BACON.—*Of Followers.*

A crowd is not company and faces are but a gallery of pictures.
BACON.—*Of Friendship.*

It [friendship] redoubleth joys and cutteth griefs in half.   BACON.—*Ib.*

The worst solitude is to have no true friendships.
BACON.—*Instauratio*, Pt. 1, Bk. 6, 37.

But if Fortune once doe frowne,
Then farewell his great renowne :
They that fawnd on him before
Use his company no more.
R. BARNFIELD.—*Ode, As it fell upon a day.*

Every man will be thy friend,
Whilst thou hast wherewith to spend.
R. BARNFIELD.—*Ode.*

He that is thy friend indeed,
He will help thee in thy need.
R. BARNFIELD.—*Ib.*

Friendship ! mysterious cement of the soul !
Sweet'ner of life and solder of society !
R. BLAIR.—*The Grave*, 88.

You're my friend—
What a thing friendship is, world without end !   BROWNING.—*Flight of the Duchess, c.* 17.

Luitolfo was the proper
Friend-making, everywhere friend-finding soul,
Fit for the sunshine, so, it followed him.
BROWNING.—*Soul's Tragedy*, Act 1.

His honest, sonsie, baws'nt face
Aye gat him friends in ilka place.
BURNS.—*Twa Dogs.*

Friendship can smooth the front of rude despair.
R. CAMBRIDGE.—*Scribleriad*, 1, 196.

'Twas sung how they were lovely in their lives,
And in their deaths had not divided been.
CAMPBELL.—*Gertrude*, 33.

Friendship's a noble name, 'tis love refined.
MRS. CENTLIVRE.—*Stolen Heiress*, Act 2.

My sone, keep wel thy tonge and keep thy friend.
CHAUCER.—*Manciple's Tale*, 215.

Friendship excels kinship.   CICERO.

True friendships are very rarely found in such as are occupied in the pursuit of honours or public affairs.
CICERO.—*De Amicitia.*

Friends are as dangerous as enemies.
DE QUINCEY.—*Schlosser's Literary History.*

Codlin's the friend, not Short.
DICKENS.—*Old Curiosity Shop, ch.* 19.

A day for toil, an hour for sport,
But for a friend life is too short.
EMERSON.—*Considerations by the Way.*

The only way to have a friend is to be one.   EMERSON.—*Friendship.*

He who has a thousand friends, has not
    a friend to spare,
And he who has one enemy, will meet him
    everywhere.
        EMERSON.—*From Omar.*

These are called the pious frauds of
friendship.
    FIELDING.—*Amelia*, Bk. 6, c. 6.

A woman-friend! He that believes that
    weakness
Steers in a stormy night without a compass.
J. FLETCHER.—*Women Pleased*, Act 2, 1.

An open foe may prove a curse,
But a pretended friend is worse.
    GAY.—*Fables*, Pt. 1, 17.

Friendship, like love, is but a name.
    GAY.—*Ib.*, Pt. 1, 50.

And what is friendship but a name?
    GOLDSMITH.—*Hermit.*

He cast off his friends as a huntsman his
    pack,
For he knew, when he pleased, he could
    whistle them back.
    GOLDSMITH.—*Retaliation.*

Women do not have friends,—they only
have rivals. E. GONDINET.—*Jonathan.*

Of all the heavenly gifts that mortal men
    commend,
What trusty treasure in the world can
    countervail a friend?
    N. GRIMOALD.—*Friendship.*

Friends are not so easily made as kept.
    LORD HALIFAX (1630-95).—*Maxims
        of State.*

The wicked may have accomplices, but
heaven has ordained that here below only
honest folk can be friends.
    COLLIN D'HARLEVILLE.—*Vieux Céli-
        bataire*, Act 5.

But love is lost; the way of friendship's
    gone;
Though David had his Jonathan, Christ his
    John.   HERBERT.—*Church Porch.*

Like summer friends,
Flies of estate and sunshine.
    HERBERT.—*The Temble: The Answer.*

While in my senses I shall find nothing
preferable to a pleasant friend.
    HORACE.—*Sat.*, Bk. 1.

A man, sir, should keep his friendship in
constant repair.   JOHNSON.—*Remark to
        Sir Joshua Reynolds.*

True happiness
Consists not in the multitude of friends,
But in the worth and choice.
BEN JONSON.—*Cynthia's Revels*, Act 3, 4.

It is more common to find excess in
love than thoroughness in friendship.
    LA BRUYÈRE.—*Du Cœur*, 6.

Nothing so dangerous as an ignorant
friend; it is better to have a wise enemy.
    LA FONTAINE.

I have had playmates, I have had com-
    panions,
In my days of childhood, in my joyful
    schooldays,
All, all are gone, the old familiar faces.
    LAMB.—*Old Familiar Faces.*

Women, like princes, find few real friends
All who approach them their own ends
    pursue;
Lovers and ministers are seldom true.
    GEO. LORD LYTTELTON.—*Advice to
        a Lady.*

Farewell, uncivil man! let's meet no more;
Here our long web of friendship I untwist.
    MASSINGER.—*Fatal Dowry*, Act 3, 1.

O summer-friendship,
Whose flattering leaves, that shadowed us
    in our
Prosperity, with the least gust drop off
In the autumn of adversity.
    MASSINGER.—*Maid of Honour*, Act 3, 2.

Friend after friend departs:
    Who hath not lost a friend?
There is no union here of hearts
    That finds not here an end.
JAS. MONTGOMERY.—*Friends.*

If I speak to thee in Friendship's name,
    Thou think'st I speak too coldly;
If I mention Love's devoted flame,
    Thou say'st I speak too boldly.
    MOORE.—*How shall I woo?*

The thread of our life would be dark,
    Heaven knows,
If it were not with friendship and love
    intertwined. MOORE.—*Irish Melodies*

But oh, if grief thy steps attend,
    If want, if sickness, be thy lot,
And thou require a soothing friend,
    Forget me not, forget me not!
    MRS. OPIE.—*Forget me not.*

Few friendships would continue to
exist if each man knew what his friend
says of him in his absence, even though
it is said in all sincerity and without
vindictiveness.   PASCAL.—*Pensées.*

The name of friend is common, but truth
in friendship is rare.
    PHÆDRUS.—*Fables*, 3, 9.

Menander counted every man wonderfully honest and happy who has found
even the very shadow of a friend.
    PLUTARCH.—*Of the Folly of too many
        Friends.*

Many men, prejudiced early in disfavour of mankind by bad maxims, never aim at making friendships ; and while they only think of avoiding the evil, miss of the good that would meet them.
POPE.—*Thoughts on Various Subjects.*

Of all the gifts the gods afford,
(If we may take old Tully's word),
The greatest is a friend, whose love
Knows how to praise and when reprove.
PRIOR.—*Conversation*, 71.

Most friendship is feigning, most love mere folly. SHAKESPEARE.—*As You Like It*, Act 2, 7.

The friends thou hast, and their adoption tried,
Grapple them to thy soul with hoops of steel ;
But do not dull thy palm with entertainment
Of each new-hatched, unfledged comrade.
SHAKESPEARE.—*Hamlet*, Act 1, 3.

He was my friend, faithful and just to me.
SHAKESPEARE.—*Julius Cæsar*, Act 3, 2.

A friend should bear his friend's infirmities. SHAKESPEARE.—*Ib.*, Act 4, 3.

Alas, I then have chid away my friend :
He hath a stern look, but a gentle heart.
SHAKESPEARE.—*King John*, Act 4, 1.

I count myself in nothing else so happy
As in a soul remembering my good friends.
SHAKESPEARE.—*Richard II.*, Act 2, 3.

I do not know that Englishman alive,
With whom my soul is any jot at odds.
SHAKESPEARE.—*Richard III.*, Act 2, 1.

Let me not to the marriage of true minds
Admit impediments.
SHAKESPEARE.—*Sonnets*, 116.

There is a profound difference between the friendships of men and those of women. Men's friendships are linked by their pleasures, women's by their griefs.
EDITH SICHEL.—*Thoughts.*

Having some friends, whom he loves dearly,
And no lack of foes, whom he laughs at sincerely.
SOUTHEY.—*Robert the Rhymer.*

I am weary of friends, and friendships are all monsters. SWIFT.—*Letter*, 1710.

Some great misfortune to portend,
No enemy can match a friend.
SWIFT.—*On the death of Dr. Swift.*

So vanish friendships only made in wine.
TENNYSON.—*Geraint and Enid*, 481.

Were I to choose a friend, I'd rather have
An honest blockhead than a clever knave.
D. W. THOMPSON.—*Sales Attici.*

Friendship's an empty name, made to deceive
Those whose good nature tempts them to believe :
There's no such thing on earth ; the best that we
Can hope for here is faint neutrality.
SIR S. TUKE.—*Five Hours.*

His only crime (if friendship can offend)
Is too much love to his unhappy friend.
VIRGIL.—*Æneid*, Bk. 9 (*Dryden tr.*).

O divine friendship, perfect felicity !
the only motion of the soul in which excess is allowable. VOLTAIRE.—*Discours* 4.

Friendship, gift of heaven, pleasure of great souls ! Friendship, which kings, those illustrious practisers of ingratitude, are so unhappy as not to know.
VOLTAIRE.—*Henriade.*

Change your pleasures, but do not change your friends.
VOLTAIRE.—*Le Dépositaire* (*Ninon's advice*).

Flattery . . . is the natural language o' freenship. JOHN WILSON.—*Noctes*, 16 (*Ettrick Shepherd*).

All like the purchase ; few the price will pay ;
And this makes friends such miracles below. YOUNG.—*Night Thoughts*, 2.

But since friends grow not thick on every bough,
Nor every friend unrotten at the core,
First on thy friend deliberate with thyself.
YOUNG.—*Ib.*

A friend is worth all hazards we can run.
YOUNG.—*Ib.*

Friendship's the wine of life.
YOUNG.—*Ib.*

Even thou, my companion, my guide, and mine own familiar friend.
Church Psalter lv, 14.

A man that hath friends must show himself friendly. *Proverbs* xviii, 24.

A faithful friend is the medicine of life.
Ecclesiasticus vi, 16.

Forsake not an old friend ; for the new is not comparable to him : a new friend is as new wine ; when it is old, thou shalt drink it with pleasure.
Ecclesiasticus ix, 10.

Wounded in the house of my friends.
Zechariah xiii, 6.

O my friends, there is no friend.
Saying of Cato, as quoted by Diogenes
Laertus.

Friendship, love and brotherhood,
Of themselves are understood.
Quoted by Goethe, Autob., Bk. 11.

His friendships are so warm that he no
sooner takes them up than he puts them
down again.   *Attrib. to Douglas Jerrold*
by C. H. Spurgeon.

A good friend is worth a hundred relations. *French prov., quoted by Montaigne.*

Friendship is love without its wings.
French prov.

Friends are like fiddlestrings, they must
not be screwed too tight.   *Prov.*

They ranted, drank, and merrye made,
Till all his golde it waxed thinne,
And then his friends they slunk away,
They left the unthrifty Heir of Linne.
Old ballad, Heir of Linne.

FROWNS

Her very frowns are fairer far
Than smiles of other maidens are.
HARTLEY COLERIDGE.—*She is not fair to*
outward view.

Full well the busy whisper, circling round,
Conveyed the dismal tidings when he
frowned.
GOLDSMITH.—*Deserted Village.*

If she do frown, 'tis not in hate of you,
But rather to beget more love in you.
SHAKESPEARE.—*Two Gent. of Verona,*
Act 3, 1.

Convey a libel in a frown,
And wink a reputation down.
SWIFT.—*Journal of a Modern Lady.*

FRUGALITY

O'erjoyed was he to find
That though she was on pleasure bent,
She had a frugal mind.
COWPER.—*John Gilpin, st.* 8.

When the goodman's from home the
goodwife's table is soon spread.
Prov. (Ray).

Ken when to spend and when to spare,
And ye needna be busy and ye ne'er 'll be
bare.   *Scottish saying.*

FRUIT

Brer Fox he lif' up he han's, he did,
en holler : " Oh, hush, Brer Tarrypin !
You makes me dribble ! Wharbouts dat
Pimmerly Plum ? "
J. C. HARRIS.—*Nights with Uncle*
Remus, ch. 38.

Give cherries at time of year, or apricots;
and say they were sent you out of the
country, though you bought them in
Cheapside.
BEN JONSON.—*Silent Woman,* Act 4, 1.

Hunger and thirst at once
Powerful persuaders, quicken'd at the
scent
Of that alluring fruit.
MILTON.—*Paradise Lost, Bk.* 9, 586.

Though other things grow fair against the
sun,
Yet fruits that blossom first will first be
ripe.
SHAKESPEARE.—*Othello.* Act 2, 3.

Peel a fig for your friend, a peach for
your enemy.   *Prov. (Ray).*

After melon wine is a felon.
Prov. (Spanish).

FRUITION

The thorns which I have reap'd are of the
tree
I planted,—they have torn me, and I
bleed :
I should have known what fruit would
spring from such a seed.
BYRON.—*Childe Harold, c.* 4, 10.

The bud may have a bitter taste,
But sweet will be the flower.
COWPER.—*Hymn.*

FUNERALS

And fancy paints the muffled drum
And plaintive fife,
And the loud volley o'er the grave
That sounds sad requiems to the brave.
C. DIBDIN.—*Farewell.*

I've a notion [said Sir Condy Rackrent]
I shall not be long for this world any how,
and I've a great fancy to see my own
funeral afore I die.
MISS EDGEWORTH.—*Castle Rackrent, ch.* 2.

" Ay, Sir Condy has been a fool all his
days," said he [Sir Condy Rackrent] ; and
there was the last word he spoke. He had
but a very poor funeral after all.
MISS EDGEWORTH.—*Ib.*

Funeral pomp has more regard for the
vanity of the living than for the honour of
the dead.
LA ROCHEFOUCAULD.—*Maxim* 554.

FURNITURE

A Persian carpet, or piece of Sheraton
makes a distinguished end and bears
itself with dignity to the last—as aristo-
crats before the guillotine.
EDEN PHILLPOTTS.—*A Shadow Passes.*

FUSSINESS

Benevolent people are very apt to be one-sided and fussy, and not of the sweetest temper if others will not be good and happy in their way.

SIR A. HELPS.—*Friends in Council, Bk. 1, ch. 5.*

FUTILITY

Still we persist ; plough the light sand and sow
Seed after seed, where none can ever grow.
W. GIFFORD.—*Juvenal, Sat. 7.*

Wheresoe'er I turn my view,
All is strange, yet nothing new ;
Endless labour all along,
Endless labour to be wrong ;
Phrase that Time has flung away,
Uncouth words in disarray,
Tricked in antique ruff and bonnet,
Ode and elegy and sonnet.
JOHNSON.—*In ridicule of " a well-known author " (1777).*

'Tis no good planting boiled potatoes.
C. H. SPURGEON.—*John Ploughman.*

The King of France, with twenty thousand men,
Went up the hill, and then came down again.   *Old Tarlton's Song (16th cent.).*

FUTURE

But for our future fate
Since help for it is none,
Good-bye to it before it comes.—
ÆSCHYLUS.—*Agamemnon, 250 (Plumptre tr.).*

Years hence, perhaps, may dawn an age,
More fortunate, alas ! than we,
Which without hardness will be sage,
And gay without frivolity.
M. ARNOLD.—*Grande Chartreuse.*

Ignorance of future ills is a more useful thing than knowledge.
CICERO.—*De Div., 2, 9.*

" The present interests me more than the past," said the lady [Theodora Campian], " and the future more than the present."
DISRAELI.—*Lothair.*

England, like Greece, shall fall despoiled, defaced,
And weep, the Tadmor of the lonely waste ;
The wave shall mock her lone and manless shore ;
The deep shall know her freighted wealth no more ;
And unborn wanderers, in the future wood,
Where London stands, shall ask where London stood.
EBENEZER ELLIOTT.—*Love, Bk. 2.*

But truly these things rest on the knees of the gods.   HOMER.—*Iliad, 17,514 ; etc.*

Oh, earlier shall the rosebuds blow
In after years, those happier years ;
And children weep, when we lie low,
Far fewer tears, far softer tears.
ARMINE THOS. KENT.—*Otiis Addenda (1905), A song.*

Life, life we wish, still greedy to live on ;
And yet what Fortune with the following sun
Will rise, what chance will bring, is all unknown.
LUCRETIUS.—*De Rerum Natura, 3, 1099.*

She [the Roman Catholic Church] may still exist in undiminished vigour, when some traveller from New Zealand shall, in the midst of a vast solitude, take his stand on a broken arch of London Bridge to sketch the ruins of St. Paul's.
MACAULAY.—*Ranke's History.*

Full lasting is the song, though he,
The singer, passes : lasting too,
For souls not lent in usury,
The rapture of the forward view.
GEO. MEREDITH.—*Reading of Earth.*

Besides what hope the never-ending flight
Of future days may bring.
MILTON.—*Paradise Lost, Bk. 2, 221.*

Heaven from all creatures hides the book of fate.
POPE.—*Essay on Man, Ep. 1, 77.*

We know what we are, but know not what we may be.
SHAKESPEARE.—*Hamlet, Act 4, 5*

Happy those
Who in the after-days shall live, when Time
Hath spoken, and the multitude of years
Taught wisdom to mankind !
SOUTHEY.—*Joan of Arc, Bk. 1.*

For I dipped into the Future, far as human eye could see,
Saw the Vision of the world, and all the wonder that would be.
TENNYSON.—*Locksley Hall.*

In the Parliament of man, the Federation of the world.   TENNYSON.—*Ib.*

We see by the glad light
And breathe the sweet air of futurity ;
And so we live, or else we have no life.
WORDSWORTH.—*Excursion, Bk. 9, 24.*

FUTURE EXISTENCE

There was the Door to which I found no Key ;
There was the Veil through which I might not see.
E. FITZGERALD.—*Rubáiyát.*

Nor dies the Spirit, but new Life repeats
In other forms, and only changes seats.
OVID.—*Metam 15, 158 (Dryden tr.).*

Is there no bright reversion in the sky
For those who greatly think, or bravely
    die ?   POPE.—*Elegy to the memory of
        an Unfortunate Lady*, 9.

I go to seek for a great perhaps. Draw
the curtain ; the farce is played.
        RABELAIS.—*Attributed.*

What becomes of man so wise
    When he dies ?
    None can tell
Whether he goes to heaven or hell.
      SIR C. SEDLEY.—*Lycophron.*

Do you wish to know where you will
go when you are dead ? To the same place
where the unborn are.
      SENECA.—*Troades*, Act 2.

The undiscovered country, from whose
    bourn
No traveller returns.
    SHAKESPEARE.—*Hamlet*, Act 3, 1.

Ah Christ, that it were possible
For one short hour to see
The souls we loved, that they might tell
    us
What and where they be.
    TENNYSON.—*Maud, Pt.* 2, 4, 3.

A truth it is few doubt, but fewer trust :
" He sins against this life who slights the
    next."
    YOUNG.—*Night Thoughts, Night* 3.

G

GAIN

Whatsoever is somewhere gotten is
somewhere lost. BACON.—*Of Seditions.*

Gain cannot be made without some other
person's loss.   PUBLILIUS SYRUS.

God keep ill gear oot o' my hands, for
if my hands ance get it, my heart winna
part wi 't.
    Prayer of the " good Earl of Eglinton."

Gude Sir James Douglas
Who wise,wight (brave), and worthy was,
Was ne'er owre glad for no winning,
Nor yet owre sad for no tining (loss) ;
Good fortune and evil chance,
He weighed them both in one balance.
  *Contemporary Scottish Lines on the " good
    Sir James Douglas " (14th cent.).*

A' I got by him I may put in my eye,
and see nothing the worse for it.
    Scottish prov. (Jas. Kelly, 1721).

Fair winds may drive a ship too fast,
And gains may turn out loss at last.
    Tr. of Greek saying.

GALLANTRY

The ladies' hearts he did trepan.
      BURNS.—*Jolly Beggars.*

Is this that haughty, gallant, gay
Lothario ?
    ROWE.—*Fair Penitent*, Act, 5, 1.

And oh ! he had that merry glance
    That seldom lady's heart resists.
Lightly from fair to fair he flew,
And loved to plead, lament and sue.
      SCOTT.—*Marmion, c.* 5, 9.

So faithful in love and so dauntless in war,
There never was knight like the young
Lochinvar.   SCOTT.—*Ib., c.* 5, 12.

I do not think a braver gentleman,
More active-valiant, nor more valiant-
    young,
More daring, or more bold, is now alive.
  SHAKESPEARE.—*Henry IV., Pt.* 1, Act 5, 1.

GAMBLING

The winner's shout, the loser's curse,
Shall dance before dead England's hearse.
      WM. BLAKE.—*Proverbs.*

Gaming is a principle inherent in human
nature. It belongs to us all.
    BURKE.—*Speech on Economical Reform.*

And men spend freelier what they win,
Than what they've freely coming in.
    S. BUTLER.—*Upon Plagiarism.*

For most men (till by losing rendered sager)
Will back their own opinions with a wager.
    BYRON.—*Beppo*, st. 27.

Good at all things, but better at a bet.
    BYRON.—*Don Juan, c.* 13, st. 87.

In play there are two pleasures for your
    choosing—
The one is winning, and the other losing.
    BYRON.—*Ib., c.* 14, st. 12.

One hopeless dark idolater of Chance.
    CAMPBELL.—*Pleasures of Hope*, 2.

Gaming is the child of avarice but the
parent of prodigality.
    C. C. COLTON.—*Lacon.*

Who games is felon of his wealth,
His time, his liberty, his health.
    N. COTTON.—*Visions in Verse.*

Death and dice level all distinctions.
    S. FOOTE.—*The Minor*, Act 1, 1.

Play not for gain but sport. Who plays for
    more
Than he can lose with pleasure, stakes his
    heart—
Perhaps his wife's too, and whom she hath
    bore.   HERBERT.—*Church Porch.*

Who strive to sit out losing hands are lost.
> HERBERT.—*Church Porch.*

Man is a gaming animal.
> LAMB.—*Mrs. Battle.*

Swearing and supperless the hero sate,
Blasphemed his gods, the dice, and damned
his fate.
> POPE.—*Dunciad, Bk. 1, 115.*

Gaming is the mother of lies and
perjuries.
> JOHN OF SALISBURY (*Bishop of Chartres
> —d. 1180*).—*Polycraticus, Bk. 1.*

Their sinfulness is greater than their
use. [Referring to wine and gambling].
> *Koran, ch. 2.*

GAMES

There are two classes of men : those
who are content to yield to circumstances,
and who play whist ; those who aim to
control circumstances, and who play chess.
> MORTIMER COLLINS.—*Frances, 3, 14.*

It is not shameful to have played games,
but it is shameful not to have left off
playing them.   HORACE.—*Ep. Bk. 1.*

The only athletic sport I ever mastered
was backgammon.
> DOUGLAS JERROLD.—*(Attributed).*

Even our sports are dangers !
> BEN JONSON.—*Underwoods.*

What ? You do not play at whist, sir !
Alas, what a sad old age you are preparing
for yourself !   TALLEYRAND.

GARDENS

God Almighty first planted a garden :
and indeed it is the purest of human
pleasures.   BACON.—*Of Gardens.*

My garden is a lovesome thing, God wot !
> Rose plot,
> Fringed pool,
> Fern grot,
> The veriest school
> Of peace.
> T. E. BROWN.—*My Garden.*

God the first garden made, and the first
city Cain.   COWLEY.—*The Garden.*

Who loves a garden loves a greenhouse too.
> COWPER.—*The Garden, 566.*

A touch of the sun for pardon,
The song of a bird for mirth ;
We are nearer God's heart in the garden
Than anywhere else on the earth.
> D. F. GURNEY.

And add to these retirèd Leisure,
That in trim gardens takes his pleasure.
> MILTON.—*Il Penseroso, 49.*

You strove to cultivate a barren court in
vain,
Your garden's better worth your nobler
pain,
Here mankind fell, and hence must rise
again.   SWIFT.—*To Sir W. Temple.*

Cultivate your garden.
> VOLTAIRE.—*His favourite advice—in
> favour of a private or retired life.*

GENERALITIES

It being the nature of the mind of man,
to the extreme prejudice of knowledge, to
delight in the spacious liberty of generalities.   BACON.—*Adv. of Learning.*

The glittering and sounding generalities
of natural right which make up the
Declaration of Independence.
> R. CHOATE.—*Letter,* 1856.

Glittering generalities ! They are blazing
ubiquities.
> EMERSON.—*On someone characteris-
> ing the Declaration of Independence as
> " glittering generalities."*

Generalities always admit of exceptions.
> VICTOR HUGO.—*Pref. to Ruy Blas.*

Nothing is so useless as a general maxim.
> MACAULAY.—*Macchiavelli.*

General notions are generally wrong.
> LADY M. WORTLEY MONTAGU.—*Letter.*

General and abstract ideas are the source
of the greatest of men's errors.
> ROUSSEAU.—*Emile.*

GENEROSITY

If riches increase let thy mind hold pace
with them, and think it not enough to be
Liberal, but Munificent.
> SIR T. BROWNE.—*Christian Morals,
> Pt. 1, 5.*

There was a man, though some did think
him mad,
The more he cast away the more he had.
> BUNYAN.—*Pilgrim's Progress, Pt. 2.*

He who bestows his goods upon the poor
Shall have as much again and ten times
more.   BUNYAN.—*Ib.*

So that the more she [Largesse] gave away,
The more, y-wis, she hadde alwey.
> CHAUCER.—*Romaunt of the Rose.*

Friend to the friendless, to the sick man
health,
With generous joy he viewed his modest
wealth. COLERIDGE.—*Lines written at
> King's Arms, Ross.*

A hand as liberal as the light of day.
> COWPER.—*Hope,* 410.

One must be poor to know the luxury of giving.
GEO. ELIOT.—*Middlemarch, Bk. 2, ch. 17.*

We have heads to get money, and hearts to spend it.
FARQUHAR.—*Beaux' Stratagem, Act 1.*

Who shuts his hand, hath lost his gold ;
Who opens it, hath it twice told.
HERBERT.—*Charms and Knots.*

The truly generous is the truly wise.
J. HOME.—*Douglas, Act 3, 1.*

Sure the duke is
In the giving vein.
MASSINGER.—*Great Duke, Act 5, 3.*

And chiefly for the weaker by the wall,
You bore that lamp of sane benevolence.
GEO. MEREDITH.—*To a Friend Lost.*

Many men have been capable of doing a wise thing, more a cunning thing, but very few a generous thing.
POPE.—*Thoughts on Various Subjects.*

For his bounty,
There was no winter in 't ; an autumn
'twas.   SHAKESPEARE.—*Antony and Cleopatra, Act 5, 2.*

My bounty is as boundless as the sea,
My love as deep.
SHAKESPEARE.—*Romeo and Juliet, Act 2, 2.*

Give all thou canst ; high Heaven rejects the lore
Of nicely-calculated less or more.
WORDSWORTH.—*Eccles. Sonnets, Pt. 3, 43.*

But the liberal deviseth liberal things ;
and by liberal things shall he stand.
Isaiah xxxii, 8.

Fill a pot, fill a pan,
Fill a blind man's hand ;
He that has and winna gie,
An ill death may he dee,
And be buried in the sea.
Scottish saying.

GENIUS

No great genius is without an admixture of madness.
ARISTOTLE (*According to Seneca, " De Tranquillitate "*).

All men of genius are naturally melancholic.   ARISTOTLE.—*Probl., 30.*

Do not quarrel with genius. We have none ourselves, and yet are so constituted that we cannot live without it.
A. BIRRELL.—*Obiter Dicta, Carlyle.*

Improvement makes straight roads, but the crooked roads without improvement are roads of genius.
WM. BLAKE.—*Proverbs of Hell.*

Since when was genius found respectable ?
E. B. BROWNING.—*Aurora Leigh, Bk. 5.*

Genius has somewhat of the infantine :
But of/ the childish not a touch or taint.
BROWNING.—*Prince Hohenstiel-Schwangau.*

Genius is nothing but a great aptitude for patience.   BUFFON.

Misled by Fancy's meteor-ray,
By passion driven ;
But yet the light that led astray
Was light from Heaven.
BURNS.—*The Vision.*

When all of Genius which can perish dies.
BYRON.—*Death of Sheridan.*

Sighing that Nature formed but one such man,
And broke the die—in moulding Sheridan.
BYRON.—*Ib.*

But on the whole, " genius is ever a secret to itself."
CARLYLE.—*Characteristics.*

Genius, which means transcendent capacity of taking trouble, first of all.
CARLYLE.—*Frederick.*

Genius is of no country.
CHURCHILL.—*Rosciad, v. 207*

Great wits are sure to madness near allied,
And thin partitions do their bounds divide.
DRYDEN.—*Absalom and Achitophel, Pt. 1, 163.*

Hands that the rod of empire might have swayed,
Or waked to ecstasy the living lyre.
GRAY.—*Elegy.*

The few, whom genius gave to shine
Through every unborn age and undiscovered clime.
GRAY.—*Ode for Music, 15.*

He passed the flaming bounds of space and time ;
The living throne, the sapphire-blaze,
Where angels tremble as they gaze,
He saw ; but, blasted with excess of light,
Closed his eyes in endless night.
GRAY.—*On Milton.*

Only a narrow shopkeeper mind will attempt to weigh genius in its miserable cheese-scales.   HEINE.—*Don Quixote.*

Adverse fortune reveals genius ; prosperity hides it.   HORACE.—*Sat., Bk. 2.*

Each change of many-coloured life he drew ;
Exhausted worlds, and then imagined new ;
Existence saw him spurn her bounded reign,
And panting Time toiled after him in vain.
JOHNSON.—*Prologue.*

Genius does what it must, and talent does what it can.
(2nd) LORD LYTTON.—*Last Words.*

Genius can only breathe freely in an atmosphere of freedom.
J. S. MILL.—*Liberty, ch. 3.*

We are not called upon to place great men of his stamp as if they were collegians in a class-list.
LORD MORLEY.—*Introd. to Wordsworth.*

Ill-fortune is often an incentive to genius.
OVID.—*Ars. Amat.*

If you have genius, industry will improve it ; if you have none, industry will supply its place.
SIR JOSHUA REYNOLDS.—*Saying.*

Gone like a star that through the firmament
Shot and was lost, in its eccentric course
Dazzling, perplexing.
ROGERS.—*Italy (on Byron).*

Trefusis warmly replied that genius costs its possessor nothing ; that it was the inheritance of the whole race incidentally vested in a single individual, and that if that individual employed his monopoly of it to extort money from others, he deserved nothing better than hanging.
G. B. SHAW.—*Unsocial Socialist, ch. 10.*

A pard-like spirit, beautiful and swift.
SHELLEY.—*Adonais, st. 32.*

Them as has genius has no common-sense.
SAM SLICK.

Genius is the introduction of a new element in the intellectual universe.
WORDSWORTH.—*Essay, supplementary to Pref. to Poems.*

A genius bright, and base,
Of towering talents, and terrestrial aims.
YOUNG.—*Night Thoughts, 6.*

A Mercury is not made out of any block of wood.
Latin prov., quoted as a saying of Pythagoras.

GENTILITY

He saw a cottage with a double coach-house,
A cottage of gentility ;
And the Devil did grin, for his darling sin
Is pride that apes humility.
COLERIDGE AND SOUTHEY.—*Devil's Thoughts.*

He passed a cottage with a double coach-house,
A cottage of gentility ;
And he owned with a grin
That his favourite sin
Is pride that apes humility.
SOUTHEY'S *version of the above.*

When Adam dolve and Eve span,
Where was then the gentleman ?
Saying quoted by John Ball, insurrectionist, c. 1381

GENTLEMEN

He is the best bred man and the truest gentleman who takes leave of the world without a stain upon his scutcheon, and with nothing of falsehood and dissimulation, of luxury or pride, to tarnish his reputation. MARCUS AURELIUS.—*Bk.* 9, 2.

He is a Gentleman, because his nature
Is kinde and affable to everie creature.
R. BARNFIELD.—*Shepherd's Content* (1594).

I am a gentleman, though spoiled i' the breeding. The Buzzards are all gentlemen. We came in with the Conqueror.
R. BROME.—*English Moor.*

Somebody has said that a king may make a nobleman, but he cannot make a gentleman. BURKE.—*Letter to Wm. Smith* (1795).

Though modest, on his unembarrassed brow
Nature had written " gentleman."
BYRON.—*Don Juan, c.* 9, *st.* 83.

A finished gentleman from top to toe.
BYRON.—*Ib., c.* 12, *st.* 84.

He was a verray parfit gentil knight.
CHAUCER.—*Cant. Tales, Prol.*

For gentil herte kytheth [displayeth] gentillesse.
CHAUCER.—*Squire's Tale,* 475.

Loke who that is most vertuous alway,
Privee and apert, and most entendeth ay
To do the gentil dedes that he can,
And tak him for the grettest gentil man.
CHAUCER.—*Wife of Bath's Tale, v.* 6695.

I shall be a gen'l'm'n myself one of these days, perhaps, with a pipe in my mouth, and a summer-house in the back garden.
DICKENS.—*Pickwick, c.* 16.

His tribe were God Almighty's gentlemen.
DRYDEN.—*Absalom and Achitophel, Pt.* 1, 645.

He [Lord Spencer] satisfied that great description of what constitutes a gentleman. " He never hurt any man's feelings."
LORD FISHER.—*Memories.*

Gentlemanliness, being another word for intense humanity.
RUSKIN.—*Modern Painters, 5, Pt.* 9, 7, 23.

A kinder gentleman treads not the earth.
SHAKESPEARE.—*Merchant of Venice, Act* 2, 8

A gentleman ain't a man—leastways not a common man—the common man bein' but the slave wot feeds and clothes the gentleman beyond the common.
G. B. SHAW.—*Unsocial Socialist, ch.* 4 (*Jeff Smilash*).

And thus he bore without abuse
The grand old name of gentleman,
Defamed by every charlatan,
And soiled with all ignoble use.
TENNYSON.—*In Memoriam, c.* III.

O selfless man and stainless gentleman !
TENNYSON.—*Merlin and Vivien,* 790.

There is no character which a low-minded man so much mistrusts as that of a gentleman.
THACKERAY.—*Vanity Fair.*

You will always be fools ! We shall never be gentlemen.
Quoted by Lord Fisher (Times, June 16, 1919) *as " a classic " and as " the apposite words spoken by a German naval officer to his English confrère." " On the whole I think I prefer to be the fool—even as a matter of business ! "* (*Lord Fisher's comment.*)

GENTLENESS

Inwardness, mildness and self- renouncement do make for man's happiness.
M. ARNOLD.—*Literature and Dogma, c.* 3.

He is gentil that doth gentil dedis.
CHAUCER.—*Wife of Bath's Tale, v.* 6752.

Your gentleness shall force
More than your force move us to gentleness. SHAKESPEARE.—*As You Like It,* Act 2, 7.

Who can wrestle against Sleep ?—yet is that giant very gentleness.
M. F. TUPPER.—*Proverbial Philosophy.*

GEOMETRY

Geometry . . . is the only science that it hath pleased God to bestow on mankind.
HOBBES.—*Leviathan, ch.* 4.

Geometry . . is the mother of all natural science. HOBBES.—*Ib., ch.* 46.

God is a geometrician. PLATO (*Attributed*).

Let no one enter who is not a geometer.
Inscription said to have been on Plato's door.

GHOSTS

It is easy to raise ghosts, but it is difficult to send them back again to their dark night ; they look at us then so beseechingly, our own hearts lend them such power in pleading.
HEINE.—*Florentine Nights.*

O'er all there hung a shadow and a fear ;
A sense of mystery the spirit daunted,

And said as plain as whisper in the ear,
The place is Haunted.
HOOD.—*Haunted House*

All argument is against it but all belief is for it.
JOHNSON.—*On the appearance of men's spirits after death.*

What beckoning ghost, along the moonlight shade,
Invites my steps and points to yonder glade ?
POPE.—*Elegy to the Memory of an Unfortunate Lady.*

It is an honest ghost, that let me tell you.
SHAKESPEARE.—*Hamlet,* Act 1, 5.

Hence, horrible shadow !
Unreal mockery, hence !
SHAKESPEARE.—*Macbeth,* Act 3, 4.

GIFTS

That gift of his from God descended,
Ah, friend, what gift of man's does not ?
BROWNING.—*Christmas Eve, c.* 16.

For gifts are scorned where givers are despised.
DRYDEN.—*Hind and Panther,* Pt. 3, 64.

We do not quite forgive a giver.
EMERSON.—*Gifts.*

It is the one base thing, to receive and not to give. EMERSON.—*Saying.*

It is said that gifts persuade even the gods. EURIPIDES.—*Medea.*

The only present love demands is love.
GRAY.—*The Espousal.*

Presents, I often say, endear Absents.
LAMB.—*Roast Pig.*

He gives nothing but worthless gold,
Who gives from a sense of duty.
J. R. LOWELL.—*Sir Launfal,* Pt. 1, 6.

A small present may be the testimony of a great love.
PETRARCH.—*On the Remedies of Good and Bad Fortune.*

I think you must have heard at banquets men singing that song in which the singers enumerate that the best thing is Health, the second Beauty, and the third Riches gained without fraud.
PLATO.—*Gorgias,* 14 (*Cary tr.*).

For to the noble mind
Rich gifts wax poor, when givers prove unkind.
SHAKESPEARE.—*Hamlet,* Act 3, 1.

Let him learn to know when maidens sue,
Men give like gods.
SHAKESPEARE.—*Measure for Measure, Act* 1, 5.

I am not in the giving vein to-day
SHAKESPEARE.—*Richard III.*, Act 4, 2.

Give strength, give thought, give deeds,
        give pelf,
Give love, give tears, and give thyself ;
Give, give, be always giving ;
Who gives not, is not living.
        C. H. SPURGEON.—" *Salt-Cellars.*"

Whatever it be, I fear the Greeks, even
when they bring gifts.
                VIRGIL.—*Æneid*, 2.

Behold, I do not give lectures, or charity ;
When I give, I give myself.
        WALT WHITMAN.—*Song of Myself*, 40.

Give a thing and take again,
And you shall ride in hell's wain.
                Prov. (*Ray*).

GIPSIES

Gipsies, who every ill can cure,
Except the ill of being poor,
Who charms 'gainst love and agues sell,
Who can in hen-roost set a spell,
Prepared by arts, to them best known,
To catch all feet except their own,
Who, as to fortune, can unlock it,
As easily as pick a pocket.
        CHURCHILL.—*The Ghost*, Bk. 1.

A people still, whose common ties are
        gone ;
Who, mixed with every race, are lost in
        none.   CRABBE.—*The Borough*,
                        Letter 4.

GIRLHOOD

The de'il he couldna skaith thee,
        Nor aught that wad belang thee ;
He'd look into thy bonny face
        And say, " I canna wrang thee."
                BURNS.—*Bonny Lesley*.

Can any wind blow rough upon a blossom
So fair and tender ?
FLETCHER.—*The Pilgrim* (1621), Act 1, 1.

Be good, sweet maid, and let who will be
        clever ;
Do noble things, not dream them all
        day long ;
And so make life, death, and that vast for
        ever
        One grand sweet song.
        C. KINGSLEY.—*Farewell* (1882 ed.).

A human maid's more precious far,
In her sublime mortality,
Than faun, or nymph, or evening star,
Or moon upon the midnight sea.
Earth thrills to nothing half so sweet
As the caress of her young feet.
                EDEN PHILLPOTTS.

An unlessoned girl, unschooled, unpractised. SHAKESPEARE.—*Merchant of Venice*,
                        Act 3, 2.

GLORY
                But the pure soul
Shall . . . cut a path into the heaven of
        glory,
Leaving a track of light for men to wonder
        at.   WM. BLAKE.—*Edward III.*

And leaving in battle no blot on his name,
Look proudly to Heaven from the death-
bed of fame.
        CAMPBELL.—*Lochiel's Warning.*

Glory to them that die in this great
cause.   CAMPBELL.—*Spanish Patriots.*

Glory follows virtue like its shadow.
                CICERO.—*Tusc. Quæst.*

You told me, I remember, glory built
On selfish principles, is shame and guilt.
                COWPER.—*Table Talk*, 1.

War, he sung, is toil and trouble ;
Honour, but an empty bubble.
        DRYDEN.—*Alexander's Feast*, st. 5.

No path of flowers leads to glory.
                LA FONTAINE.—*Fables.*

'Tis Beauty calls and Glory shows the
        way. N. LEE.—*Rival Queens*, Act 4, 2.

He will have true glory who despises
glory.   LIVY.—*Bk.* 22.

Our aim is glory and to leave our names
To after time.
        MASSINGER.—*Roman Actor*, Act 1, 1.

And so sepulchred in such pomp dost lie,
That kings for such a tomb would wish
to die.   MILTON.—*On Shakspere.*

I'll make thee glorious by my pen,
        And famous by my sword.
        MARQUIS OF MONTROSE.—*My dear
                        and only Love.*

Go where glory waits thee,
        But while fame elates thee,
        Oh ! still remember me !
        MOORE.—*Irish Melodies.*

Not till earth be sunless, not till death
        strike blind the skies,
May the deathless love that waits on
        deathless deeds be dead.
        SWINBURNE.—*Grace Darling.*

Even from wise men the passion for
glory is the last surviving desire to be
eradicated.   TACITUS.—*Hist.* 4, 6.

When can their glory fade ?
TENNYSON.—*Charge of Light Brigade.*

Yet shall thy name, conspicuous and sub-
        lime,
Stand in the spacious firmament of time,
Fixed as a star : such glory is thy right.
        WORDSWORTH.—*Poems to National
                Independence*, Pt. 2, No. 19.

That man greatly lives,
Whate'er his fate or fame, who greatly
    dies.   YOUNG.—*Night Thoughts*, 8.

Their bodies are buried in peace ; but
their name liveth for evermore.
    Ecclesiasticus xliv, 14.

For they loved the glory of men more
than the glory of God.
    St. John xii, 43 (*R.V.*).

GLORY, VANITY OF

A little rule, a little sway,
A sunbeam in a winter's day,
Is all the proud and mighty have,
Between the cradle and the grave.
    JOHN DYER.—*Grongar Hill*.

Ah, take the Cash, and let the Credit go,
Nor heed the rumble of a distant Drum !
    E. FITZGERALD.—*Rubaiyat, st.* 13.

The paths of glory lead but to the grave.
    GRAY.—*Elegy*.

O the fierce wretchedness that glory
    brings us !
    SHAKESPEARE.—*Timon*, Act 4, 2.

Avoid shame, but do not seek glory—
nothing so expensive as glory.
    SYDNEY SMITH.—*Sayings*.

Glories, like glow-worms, afar off shine
    bright,
But looked too near, have neither heat nor
    light.   WEBSTER.—*Duchess of
                                    Malfi*.

GLOVES

Thou knowest the maiden who ventures
to kiss a sleeping man, wins of him a
pair of gloves.
    SCOTT.—*Fair Maid of Perth, ch.* 5.

Gie the Lord's leather to the Lord's
weather.
    Scottish prov. (against the use of gloves).

GLUTTONY

Swinish gluttony
Ne'er looks to Heaven amidst his gorgeous
    feast,
But with besotted, base ingratitude
Crams, and blasphemes his Feeder.
    MILTON.—*Comus*, 776.

Gluttony kills more than the sword, and
is the fomenter of all evils.
    FR. PATRICIUS, *Bishop of Gaeta*.

Gluttons dig their graves with their
teeth   *French prov.*

GOD

O Zeus !—whate'er He be,
If that name please him well,
By that on Him I call.

Weighing all other names, I fail to guess
Aught else but Zeus, if I would cast aside
    Clearly, in very deed,
From off my soul this idle weight of
    care.
    ÆSCHYLUS.—*Agamemnon*, 155
                        (*Plumptre tr.*).

God is more truly imagined than expressed, and he exists more truly than he
is imagined.
    ST. AUGUSTINE.—*De Trinitate*.

It is not profane to deny the gods of the
common people, but to apply the notions
of the common people to the gods is profane.   EPICURUS.

He was a wise man who originated the
idea of God.   EURIPIDES.—*Sisyphus*.

General, natural religion requires no
faith. The persuasion that a great
creating, regulating, and guiding Being
conceals himself, as it were, behind Nature,
to make himself comprehensible to us—
such a conviction forces itself on us all.
    GOETHE.—*Autob., Bk.* 4.

Dangerous as it were for the feeble
brain of man to wade far into the doings of
the Most High, whom although to know
be life, and joy to make mention of his
name ; yet our soundest knowledge is to
know that we know him not as indeed he
is, neither can know him ; and our safest
eloquence concerning him is our silence,
when we confess without confession that
his glory is inexplicable, his greatness
above our capacity and reach.
    HOOKER.—*Ecclesiastical Polity, Bk.* 1, *c.* 2.

If all the light of the world were to be
extinguished, still we should know what
light is—for it is God.
    IBSEN.—*Love's Comedy*, Act 3 (1862).

From thee, great God, we spring, to thee
    we tend,
Path, motive, guide, original, and end.
    JOHNSON.—*Rambler, No.* 7
    (*Translated from Boethius*).

No man can in sorrow charge God with
being unjust or hostile to him, so long as
he has at hand but one blade of grass
or one bud upon the trees.
    JOHN KEBLE.—*Lectures on Poetry,
                        No.* 26 (*E. K. Francis tr.*).

Man proposes but God disposes.
    THOMAS À KEMPIS.—*De Imit., Bk.* 1, 19.

Just are the ways of God,
And justifiable to men ;
Unless there be who think not God at all.
    MILTON.—*Samson Agonistes*, 293.

God is the brave man's hope, and not
the coward's excuse.
    PLUTARCH.—*Morals, Bk.* 1.

Father of all ! in every age,
In every clime adored,
By saint, by savage, and by sage,
Jehovah, Jove, or Lord !
Thou First Great Cause, least understood,
Who all my sense confined
To know but this, that thou art good
And that myself am blind.
        POPE.—*Universal Prayer.*

Would God I knew there were a God to
    thank,
When thanks rise in me.
      ROSSETTI.—*Versicles and Fragments.*

Faith is made sure and firm by understanding. The best of all religions is
infallibly the clearest. That which loads
with mysteries, with contradictions, the
worship which it preaches, prompts me
by that very fact to distrust it. The God
whom I adore is not a God of shadows.
           ROUSSEAU.—*Emile.*

What is an offence against the Divinity
is not to have no opinion about it, but to
have an evil opinion. ROUSSEAU.—*Ib.*

But O ! th' exceeding grace
Of highest God, that loves his creatures
    so,
And all his workes with mercy doth
    embrace.
   SPENSER.—*Faerie Queene, Bk. 2, c. 8, 1.*

He who truly loves God must not desire
God to love him in return.
    SPINOZA (*Quoted by Goethe as "that
                wonderful sentiment"*).

Small praise man gets dispraising the
   high gods. SWINBURNE.—*Atalanta.*

When all is done, learn this, my son,
Not friend, nor skill, nor wit at will,
Nor ship nor clod, but only God
    Doth all in all.
      T. TUSSER.—*The Author's Life.*

What better thought than think on God
and daily him to serve ?
What better gift than to the poor that
   ready be to sterve ?
      T. TUSSER.—*Posies for thine own
                 Bedchamber.*

If God did not exist it would be necessary
to invent Him.
      VOLTAIRE.—*To the Author of
  "Les trois imposteurs,"* 1771.

If God is not in us, He never existed.
         VOLTAIRE.—*Loi naturelle.*

Man in his prejudices, amorous of his
own foolish slavery, makes God in his
own image. We have made Him unjust,
wrongheaded, vain, jealous, a seducer,
inconstant, barbarous like ourselves.
               VOLTAIRE.—*Ib.*

And the infinite pathos of human trust
In a god whom no man knows.
    SIR WM. WATSON.—*Churchyard in the
                          Wold.*

The God I know of, I shall ne'er
   Know, though he dwells exceeding nigh.
" Raise thou the stone and find me there,
   Cleave thou the wood and there am I."
Yea, in my flesh his spirit doth flow,
Too near, too far, for me to know.
     SIR WM. WATSON.—*The Unknown God.*

Who worship God shall find him. Humble
   love,
And not proud reason, keeps the door of
   Heaven ;
Love finds admission where proud science
   fails.   YOUNG.—*Night Thoughts,* 9.

God is with those who persevere.
               Koran, ch. 8.

GOLD

How widely its agencies vary—
To save—to ruin—to curse—to bless—
As even its minted coins express,
Now stamped with the image of good
   Queen Bess,
And now of a Bloody Mary.
        HOOD.—*Miss Kilmansegg.*

Thou gaudy gold,
Hard food for Midas.
    SHAKESPEARE.—*Merchant of Venice,
                      Act* 3, 2.

GOOD DEEDS

Once in a century springs forth a deed,
From the dark bonds of forgetfulness
   freed,
Destined to shine and to help and to lead.
   H. ALFORD.—*Filiolæ Dulcissimæ,* 11

Not all the noblest songs are worth
   One noble deed.
      A. AUSTIN.—*Off Mesolongi,* 18.

Should heaven turn hell
For deeds well done, I would do ever well.
    CHAPMAN.—*Tears of Peace, Inductio.*

A short life is given us by nature, but
the memory of a well-spent life is eternal.
        CICERO.—*Phil.* 14, 12.

The reward of a thing well done is to
have done it.
    EMERSON.—*New England Reformers.*

I defy the wisest man in the world to
turn a truly good action into ridicule.
      FIELDING.—*Joseph Andrews,
                    Bk.* 3, *ch.* 6.

And learn the luxury of doing good.
         GOLDSMITH.—*Traveller.*

In working well, if travail you sustain,
Into the wind shall lightly pass the pain ;
But of the deed the glory shall remain,

And cause your name with worthy wights
　　to reign.
In working wrong, if pleasure you attain,
The pleasure soon shall fade, and void
　as vain ;
But of the deed throughout the life the
　shame
Endures, defacing you with foul defame.
　　　　　N. GRIMOALD.—*Musonius.*

If thou do ill, the joy fades, not the pains ;
If well, the pain doth fade, the joy remains.
　　　　　HERBERT.—*Church Porch.*

Thy works, and alms, and all thy good
　　endeavour,
　Stayed not behind, nor in the grave were
　　trod ;
　But, as Faith pointed with her golden
　　rod,
Followed thee up to joy and bliss for ever.
MILTON.—*To the Memory of Mrs. Thomson.*

Let humble Allen, with an awkward
　shame,
Do good by stealth, and blush to find it
　fame.
POPE.—*Satires, Epilogue, Dialogue* I, 135.

Do you believe that there is upon the
whole earth one man so depraved as
never to have allowed his heart to yield
to the temptation of doing well ?
　　　　　ROUSSEAU.—*Emile.*

I never did repent for doing good,
Nor shall not now.
　　SHAKESPEARE.—*Merchant of Venice,*
　　　　　　　　　　Act 3, 4.

How far that little candle throws his
　beams !
So shines a good deed in a naughty world.
　　SHAKESPEARE.—*Ib.,* Act 5, 1.

'Tis a lucky day, boy, and we'll do good
deeds on 't.
　　SHAKESPEARE.—*Winter's Tale,* Act 3, 3.

Tis well said again ;
And 'tis a kind of good deed to say well :
And yet words are no deeds.
　　SHAKESPEARE.—*Henry VIII.,* Act 3, 2.

As for doing good that is one of the professions that are full.
　　H. D. THOREAU.—*Economy.*

While we have time, let us do good unto
all men.
　Galatians vi, 10 (*Prayer Book Version*).

Whatsoever ye would that men should
do unto you, even so do unto them.
St. Matthew vii, 12 (*Prayer Book Version*).

For the Lord Jesus Christ's sake,
　Do all the good you can,
　　To all the people you can,

In all the ways you can,
　As long as ever you can.
*Said to be from a tombstone at Shrews-
　bury.* (*Quoted by D. L. Moody,
　American Evangelist.*)

Do good whilst you live, if you wish to
live after death.
Mediæval Inscription (Tamworth Church).
　Also found in Lambeth MS., No. 853,
　　　　　　　　　　circa 1450.

Good words make us laugh ; good deeds
make us silent.　　　　*French prov.*

GOODNESS

The friend of man, to vice alone a foe.
　　BURNS.—*Epitaph on his Father.*

So young, so fair,
Good without effort, great without a foe.
　　BYRON.—*Childe Harold c.* 4, 172.

That mighty truth—how happy are the
good !　　　　　CAMPBELL.—*Theodric.*

He was a good man, in the worst sense
of the word.
　Ascribed to DISRAELI (*in reference to
　　　　　　　　　W. E. Gladstone*).

Oft have I heard, and deem the witness
　true,
Whom man delights in, God delights in
　too.　　EMERSON.—*Tr. of " the old
　trouveur, Pons Capdeuil." Essay on
　　　　　　　　　　" Success."*

The art of arts, the art of being good,
Not saintly sad.
　NORMAN GALE.—*To a Nest of Young
　　　　　　　　　　Thrushes.*

Oh ! might we all our lineage prove,
Give and forgive, do good and love !
　　　　　KEBLE.—*Christian Year,* 2nd
　　　　　　　　　　Sunday after Trinity.

There are in this loud stunning tide
　Of human care and crime,
With whom the melodies abide
　Of the everlasting chime ;
Who carry music in their heart
Through dusky lane and wrangling mart,
Plying their daily task with busier feet,
Because their secret souls a holy strain
　repeat. KEBLE.—*St. Matthew's Day.*

A good heart is better than all the heads
in the world.
　(1st) LORD LYTTON.—*Disowned, c.* 33

For princes never more make known their
　wisdom,
Than when they cherish goodness where
　they find it.
　MASSINGER.—*Great Duke of Florence,*
　　　　　　　　　　Act I, I.

　　Abashed the devil stood,
And felt how awful goodness is.
　MILTON.—*Paradise Lost, Bk.* 4, 846.

Good and evil we know in the field of
this world grow up together almost
inseparably.   MILTON.—*Areopagitica.*

Oh ! she was good as she was fair ;
None—none on earth above her !
As pure in thought as angels are ;
To know her was to love her.
        ROGERS.—*Jacqueline, Pt.* 1.

People be dood. If you are dood
Dod will love you ; if you are not dood
Dod will not love you. People be dood.
     RUSKIN.—*Sermon preached, accord-
ing to his own statement, before he was
four years old.*

Hold thou the good : define it well :
For fear Divine Philosophy
Should push beyond her mark and be
Procuress to the Lords of Hell.
     TENNYSON.—*In Memoriam, c.* 53.

Pray God make all bad people good,
and all good people nice.
     A Child's Prayer (Attributed).

GOOD NIGHT

Here's a body—there's a bed ;
There's a pillow—here's a head ;
There's a curtain—here's a light ;
There's a puff—and so Goodnight !
THOS. HOOD.—*Sketches on the Road,* 1837.

To all, to each, a fair good-night
And pleasing dreams, and slumbers light !
     SCOTT.—*Marmion, c.* 6, *L'Envoi.*

Sleep dwell upon thine eyes, peace in thy
   breast !
Would I were sleep and peace, so sweet to
   rest !   SHAKESPEARE.—*Romeo and
            Juliet,* Act 2, 2.

GOSSIP

What the king has whispered into the
queen's ear, they know ; what Juno
chattered to Jove they know ; and things
which never will happen and never have
happened, they know them none the less.
     PLAUTUS.—*Trinummus.*

Pitchers have ears, and I have many
servants.
     SHAKESPEARE.—*Taming of the Shrew,*
            Act 4, 4.

How hard soe'er it be to bridle wit,
Yet memory oft no less requires the bit.
How many, hurried by its force away,
For ever in the land of gossips stray.
     B. STILLINGFLEET.—*Conversation.*

It is the folly of too many to mistake the
echo of a London Coffee-house for the
voice of the Kingdom.
     SWIFT.—*Conduct of the Allies.*

Believe not every tale.
     Ecclesiasticus xix, 15.

GOUT

Some haue left incomiums of the Gout
and think they extenuat the anguish of
it when they tell what famous men, what
Emperours and Learned Persons haue
been severe examples of that disease, and
that it is not a disease of fooles, but of
men of Parts and sences.
     SIR T. BROWNE.—*Of Consumptions
            (Fragment).*

Pangs arthritic that infest the toe
Of libertine excess.
     COWPER.—*Task,* 105.

The French have taste in all they do,
   Which we are quite without ;
For nature, which to them gave *goût*,
   To us gave only gout.
     THOS. ERSKINE (LORD ERSKINE).—
            Epigram.

What a very singular disease gout is !
It seems as if the stomach fell down into
the feet.
     SYDNEY SMITH.—*Letter to Lady Carlisle,
           Sept.* 5, 1840.

When I have the gout I feel as if I were
walking on my eyeballs.
     SYDNEY SMITH.—*Saying.*

GOVERNMENT

The greatest happiness of the greatest
number is the foundation of morals and
legislation.
     JEREMY BENTHAM.—*Works, vol.* 10.

Universal suffrage is the government
of a house by its nursery.—BISMARCK.

Brute force shall not rule Florence !
   Intellect
May rule her, bad or good as chance
   supplies,—
But intellect it shall be.
     BROWNING.—*Luria.*

If they ask me what a free government
is, I answer that for any practical purpose
it is what the people think so.
     BURKE.—*Letter.*

Government is a contrivance of human
wisdom to provide for human wants.
Men have a right that these wants should
be provided for by this wisdom.
     BURKE.—*Reflections on the
            Revolution.*

All Governments are pretty much alike,
with a tendency on the part of the last
to be the worst.
     AUSTEN CHAMBERLAIN, M.P.—*House of
           Commons,* 1919.

Arms are of little avail abroad unless
there is good counsel at home.
     CICERO.—*De Officiis.*

Of governments that of the mob is the most sanguinary, that of soldiers the most expensive, and that of civilians the most vexatious.   C. C. COLTON.—*Lacon.*

No government is safe unless buttressed by goodwill.   CORNELIUS NEPOS.—*Dion.*

You can only govern men by serving them.   The rule is without exception.
V. COUSIN.

For justice is the end of government.
DEFOE.—*True-born Englishman.*
Pt. 2, 368.

A Government of statesmen or of clerks ? Of Humbug or of Humdrum ?
DISRAELI.—*Coningsby, Bk.* 2, c. 4.

The divine right of kings may have been a plea for feeble tyrants, but the divine right of government is the keystone of human progress, and without it governments sink into police, and a nation is degraded into a mob.
DISRAELI.—*Lothair, Preface* (1870).

That fatal drollery called a representative government.
DISRAELI.—*Tancred, Bk.* 2, *ch.* 13.

Applaud the justice of well-governed states,
And Peace triumphant, with her open gates.
P. FRANCIS.—*Horace, Art of Poetry.*

For just experience tells, in every soil,
That those who think must govern those that toil,
And all that freedom's highest aims can reach,
Is but to lay proportioned loads on each.
GOLDSMITH.—*Traveller.*

I found that monarchy was the best government for the poor to live in, and commonwealths for the rich.
GOLDSMITH.—*Vicar of Wakefield.*

The great danger, as it appears to me, of representative government, is lest it should slide down from representative government to delegate government.
SIR A. HELPS.—*Friends in Council, Bk.* 1, *ch.* 6.

That action is best which procures the greatest Happiness for the greatest Numbers.
FR. HUTCHESON, SEN.—*Beauty and Virtue* (1725).

There is no state in Europe where the least wise have not governed the most wise.
W. S. LANDOR.—*Rousseau.*

Alike were they free from
Fear, that reigns with the tyrant, and envy, the vice of republics.
LONGFELLOW.—*Evangeline, Pt.* 1, 34,

Nothing is so galling to a people, not broken in from the birth, as a paternal, or, in other words, a meddling government, a government which tells them what to read, and say, and eat, and drink, and wear.
MACAULAY.—*Southey's Colloquies.*

Every nation has the government it deserves.   DE MAISTRE, *Letter,* 1811.

For Britain, to speak a truth not often spoken, as it is a land fruitful enough of men stout and courageous in war, so it is naturally not over-fertile of men able to govern justly and prudently in peace.
MILTON.—*History of England, Bk.* 3.

Local self-government is the life-blood of liberty.
J. L. MOTLEY.—*Rise of Dutch Republic, Pt.* 6, *ch.* 1.

To a wise man it is indifferent what card is trumps.   The game may be played as fair under clubs as diamonds.   If we are to be fettered, it is folly to be troubled whether our fetters consist of many links or but one.
FRANCIS OSBORNE.—*Advice to a Son* (1656).

Spare the spurs, boy, and hold the reins more firmly.   OVID.—*Metam.,* 2.

You do not know, my son, with how little wisdom men are governed.
COUNT AXEL OXENSTIERNA OF SWEDEN.
—*To his Son* (1583-1654).

In a change of rule among the citizens, the poor change nothing beyond the name of their master.
PHÆDRUS.—*Fables, Bk.* 1, 15.

There the golden Sisters reign,
From Themis sprung,—Eunomia pure,
Safe Justice, and congenial Peace,
Basis of states, whose counsels sure
With wealth and wisdom bless the world's increase.
PINDAR.—*Olympian Odes,* 13, 6
(*Moore tr.*).

The axiom of power united to philosophy is in every way true :   That neither a state nor a man can ever be happy unless by leading a life of prudence in subjection always to justice.
PLATO.—*Epistle 7 (Referring to the Errors of Dionysius the Younger of Syracuse).*

O Syracusans, above all things turn your regard to laws not designed merely for money-making and wealth.   There are three things, soul, body, and worldly prosperity.   Put the worth of the soul first ; that of the body second ; but third and last that of wealth, as being the servant of both body and soul.
PLATO.—*Epistle,* 8

One person calls it [the Greek government] a democracy, another by another name, as he pleases. But it is in truth a government by the best, combined with a good opinion of the people.
PLATO.—*Menexenus*, 8.

When it was said that Sparta was preserved because the kings knew how to govern, Theopompus replied : " No, but because the citizens knew how to be governed."
PLUTARCH.—*Laconic Apophthegms.*

For forms of government let fools contest ; Whate'er is best administered is best.
POPE.—*Essay on Man, Ep.* 3, 303.

The Pope says . . . Thou little thinkest what a little Foolery governs the whole world.   J. SELDEN.—*Pope.*

Governments which are hated never hold out long.   SENECA.—*Phœnissæ.*

No one has long maintained violent government ; temperate rule endures.
SENECA.—*Troades*, Act 2.

Where there is not modesty, nor regard for law, nor religion, reverence, good faith, the kingdom is insecure.
SENECA.—*Thyestes*, Act 2, 215.

Down with Governments by the Greyhaired. G. B. SHAW.—*Man and Superman.*

Fear not the tyrants shall rule for ever,
Or the priests of the bloody faith ;
They stand on the brink of that mighty river,
Whose waves they have tainted with death.   SHELLEY.—*Rosalind.*

— and —, who have every other qualification for governing, want that legion of devils in the interior, without whose aid mankind cannot be ruled.
SYDNEY SMITH.—*Letter to Countess Grey, Feb.* 4, 1835.

He seemed greater than a private. citizen while he was one, and by the consent of all would have been considered capable of government, if he had not governed.   TACITUS.—*History*, 1.

Where Fate and smiling Fortune show the way,
Pursue the ready path to sovereign sway.
VIRGIL.—*Æneid, Bk.* 8 (*Dryden tr.*).

The world is governed too much.
Motto of "Globe" newspaper (*U.S.A.*).

GRACE

Such easy greatness, such a graceful port,
So turned and finished for the camp or court !   ADDISON.—*Campaign.*

Who hath not own'd, with rapture-smitten frame,
The power of grace ?
CAMPBELL.—*Pleasures of Hope*, 2, 5.

Whate'er he did was done with so much ease,
In him alone 'twas natural to please.
DRYDEN.—*Absalom and Achitophel, Pt.* 1, 27.

He touched nothing which he did not adorn.   JOHNSON.—*Epitaph* (*Latin*) *on Goldsmith.*

Good Xenocrates, sacrifice to the Graces.
PLATO (*according to Plutarch*).

A foot more light, a step more true,
Ne'er from the heath-flower dashed the dew.
SCOTT.—*Lady of the Lake, c.* 1, *st.* 18.

These graces challenge grace.
SHAKESPEARE.—*Henry VI., Pt.* 3, Act 4, 8.

GRACE BEFORE MEAT

Some hae meat and canna eat,
   And some wad eat that want it ;
But we hae meat and we can eat,
   And sae the Lord be thankit.
BURNS.—*Selkirk Grace* (*founded on. traditional lines*).

Some have meat and cannot eat ;
Some can eat and have no meat ;
We have appetite and food :
Bless the Giver of all good.
C. H. SPURGEON's *version of the "Selkirk Grace."*

We thank thee, Lord, for this our food,
A happy home, and all things good ;
May thy rich blessings wide be spread,
And all thy little ones be fed.   Amen.
ANON.

GRACE (SPIRITUAL)

Prevenient grace descending had removed
The stony from their hearts.
MILTON.—*Paradise Lost, Bk.* 11, 3.

GRAMMAR

Priscian a little scratched ; 'twill serve.
SHAKESPEARE.—*Love's Labour's Lost.* Act 5, 1.

Here will be an old abusing of God's patience, and the King's English.
SHAKESPEARE.—*Merry Wives*, Act 1, 4.

I am the King of Rome, and above grammar.
SIGISMUND (*at the Council of Constance*).

Why care for grammar as long as we are good ? ARTEMUS WARD.—*Pyrotechny*, 5.

GRANDEUR

All flesh is grass, and all its glory fades
Like the fair flower, dishevell'd in the wind;
Riches have wings, and grandeur is a dream.   COWPER.—*Task*, 3, 259.

Let's do it after the high Roman fashion.
SHAKESPEARE.—*Antony and Cleopatra,*
Act 4, 13.

She looked as grand as doomsday and as
grave. TENNYSON.—*Princess, c. 1, 186.*

GRATITUDE

When our perils are past, shall our gratitude sleep ?
No—here's to the pilot that weathered
the storm.
GEO. CANNING.—*The Pilot (Pitt).*

No metaphysician ever felt the defici-
ency of language so much as the grateful.
C. C. COLTON.—*Lacon.*

Let others hail the rising sun ;
I bow to that whose course is run.
GARRICK.—*On Mr. H. Pelham.*

Only fools are unable to support that
crushing load which we call gratitude.
LABICHE.—*Perrichon.*

Wherever I find a great deal of gratitude
in a poor man, I take it for granted there
would be as much generosity if he were a
rich man.
POPE.—*Thoughts on Various Subjects.*

Evermore thanks, the exchequer of the
poor.
SHAKESPEARE.—*Richard II.,* Act 2, 3.

I've heard of hearts unkind, kind deeds
With coldness still returning ;
Alas ! the gratitude of man
Hath oftener left me mourning.
WORDSWORTH.—*Simon Lee.*

Gratitude is the least of virtues ; ingratitude is the worst of vices.   *Prov.*

GRAVE, THE

Each in his narrow cell for ever laid,
The rude forefathers of the hamlet sleep.
GRAY.—*Elegy.*

Yet even these bones from insult to pro-
tect,
Some frail memorial still erected nigh,
With uncouth rhymes and shapeless
sculpture decked,
Implores the passing tribute of a sigh.
GRAY.—*Ib.*

I like that ancient Saxon phrase which calls
The burial-ground God's-Acre !
LONGFELLOW.—*God's-Acre.*

And my large kingdom for a little grave,
A little little grave, an obscure grave.
SHAKESPEARE.—*Richard II.,* Act 3, 3.

Rest from all bitter thoughts and things !
How many a poor one's blessing went
With thee beneath the low green tent
Whose curtain never outward swings.
WHITTIER.—*Snowbound.*

The knell, the shroud, the mattock, and
the grave ;
The deep damp vault, the darkness, and
the worm :
These are the bugbears of a winter's eve,
The terrors of the living, not the dead.
YOUNG.—*Night Thoughts, 4.*

GREATNESS

He was a great man, and I have for-
gotten all his faults.
LORD BOLINGBROKE (HENRY ST. JOHN).
—*Of Marlborough.*

None are completely wretched but the
great.
W. BROOME.—*Ep. to Mr. Fenton.*

That pompous misery of being great.
W. BROOME.—*On the Seat of the War.*

All women love great men,
If young or old ; it is in all the tales.
BROWNING.—*In a Balcony.*

More compassionate than woman,
Lordly more than man
CAMPBELL.—*A Dream.*

From great folks great favours are expected.   CERVANTES.—*Don Quixote.*

Greatness and goodness are not means, but
ends !   COLERIDGE.—*Job's Luck.*

For he was great ere fortune made him
so.   DRYDEN.—*Death of Cromwell, st. 6.*

The great man makes the great thing.
Wherever Macdonald sits, there is the head
of the table.
EMERSON.—*The American Scholar.*

To be great is to be misunderstood.
EMERSON.—*Self-Reliance.*

Every great man is a unique.
EMERSON.—*Ib.*

Indeed while greatness consists in
power, pride, insolence, and doing mischief to mankind ;—to speak out, while
a great man and a great rogue are synonymous terms, so long shall Wild stand unrivalled on the pinnacle of greatness.
FIELDING.—*Jonathan Wild*

What is grandeur, what is power ?
Heavier toil, superior pain.
GRAY.—*Ode for Music.*

In honour dies he to whom the great
seems ever wonderful.
HAFIZ.—*As given by Emerson, Essay on
Persian Poetry.*

Oh, my friend !
(For with delight thy vigorous growth I
view,
And just proportion), be thou also bold,
And merit praise from ages yet to come !
HOMER.—*Odyssey, Bk. 1, 300 (Cowper tr.).*

Great honours are great burdens.
B. JONSON.—*Catiline.*

Greatness, which private men
Esteemed a blessing, is to me a curse ;
And we who, for our high births, they
    conclude
The only freemen, are the only slaves.
Happy the golden mean.
MASSINGER.—*Great Duke*, Act 1, 1.

It is always interesting, in the case of
a great man, to know how he affected the
women of his acquaintance.
LORD MORLEY.—*Burke.*

'Tis but the pastime, not the pain
Of Genius his unfailing word to give,
    That bravery shall not strive in vain,
That virtue, raised by him, in Fame's
    bright heaven shall live.
PINDAR.—*Isthmian Odes*, 1, 62 (*Moore tr.*).

If parts allure thee, think how Bacon
    shined,
The wisest, brightest, meanest of mankind ;
Or, ravished with the whistling of a
    name,
See Cromwell, damned to everlasting fame.
POPE.—*Essay on Man*, 4, 281.

These are imperial works, and worthy
    kings.
POPE.—*Moral Essays, Ep.* 4, 204.

It is the nature of a great mind to be
calm and undisturbed, and ever to despise
injuries and misfortunes.
SENECA.—*De Clementia*, 1, 5.

Farewell, a long farewell to all my great-
    ness !
SHAKESPEARE.—*Henry VIII.*, Act 3, 2.

The world hath noted, and your name is
    great
In mouths of wisest censure.
SHAKESPEARE.—*Othello*, Act 2, 3.

Be not afraid of greatness. Some men are
born great, some achieve greatness, and
some have greatness thrust upon them.
SHAKESPEARE.—*Twelfth Night*, Act 2, 5.

Nothing she does, or seems,
But smacks of something greater than
    herself ;
Too noble for this place.
SHAKESPEARE.—*Winter's Tale*, Act 4, 3.

The world knows nothing of its greatest
    men.
SIR H. TAYLOR.—*Philip von Artevelde.*

Great deeds cannot die ;
They, with the sun and moon, renew their
    light
For ever, blessing those that look on them.
TENNYSON.—*Princess, c.* 3, 237.

In the eyes of the immortals, and before
their splendour, there is no lowness, there
is no highness. The vilest of human beings,
the most august king, all are equal for
them ; nothing is great but the just.
VOLTAIRE.—*Eryphile*, Act 1, 1.

Man and his littleness perish, erased like
    an error and cancelled ;
Man and his greatness survive, lost in
    the greatness of God.
SIR WM. WATSON.—*Hymn to the Sea.*

Were I so tall to reach the pole,
    Or grasp the ocean in my span,
I must be measured by my soul :
    The mind's the standard of the man.
I. WATTS.—*False Greatness.*

And now he rests ; his greatness and his
    sweetness
No more shall seem at strife ;
And death has moulded into calm complete-
    ness
The statue of his life.
WHITTIER.—*On Joseph Sturge.*

Through love, through hope, and faith's
    transcendent dower,
We feel that we are greater than we know.
WORDSWORTH.—*River Duddon.*

O weakness of the Great ! O folly of the
    Wise !
WORDSWORTH.—*Tour in Italy*, 28.

Thou hast left behind
Powers that will work for thee, air, earth,
    and skies :
There's not a breathing of the common
    wind
That will forget thee ; thou hast great
    allies ;
Thy friends are exultations, agonies,
And love, and man's unconquerable mind.
WORDSWORTH.—*Toussaint L'Ouverture.*

None think the great unhappy, but the
    great. YOUNG.—*Love of Fame, Sat.* 1.

GREECE

Know ye the land where the cypress and
    myrtle
Are emblems of deeds that are done in
    their clime,
Where the rage of the vulture, the love
    of the turtle,
Now melt into sorrow, now madden to
    crime ?
BYRON.—*Bride of Abydos, c.* 1, *st.* 1.

Fair Greece ! Sad relic of departed worth !
Immortal, though no more ; though fallen,
    great !
BYRON.—*Childe Harold, c.* 2, *st.* 73.

The isles of Greece, the isles of Greece
    Where burning Sappho loved and sung,
    Where grew the arts of war and peace—

Where Delos rose, and Phœbus sprung !
Eternal summer gilds them yet,
But all except their sun is set.
          BYRON.—*Don Juan, c.* 3, 86.

Clime of the unforgotten brave.
          BYRON.—*The Giaour,* 103.

Make the Greek authors your supreme
     delight ;
Read them by day and study them by
     night.
     P. FRANCIS.—*Horace, Art of Poetry.*

     The olive grove of Academe,
Plato's retirement, where the Attic bird
Trills her thick-warbled notes the summer
     long.
     MILTON.—*Paradise Regained, Bk.* 4, 244.

Thence to the famous orators repair,
Those ancient, whose resistless eloquence
Wielded at will that fierce democratie,
Shook th' arsenal, and fulmined over
     Greece.   MILTON.—*Ib., Bk.* 4, 267.

All the world is sweeter, if the Athenian
     violet quicken :
All the world is brighter, if the Athenian
     sun return :
All things foul on earth wax fainter, by
     that sun's light stricken :
All ill growths are withered, where those
     fragrant flower-lights burn. . . .
Ours the lightning was that cleared the
     north and lit the nations,
But the light that gave the whole world
     light of old was she :
Ours an age or twain, but hers are endless
     generations :
All the world is hers at heart, and most of
     all are we.
          SWINBURNE.—*Ode to Athens.*

     The Greeks only tell the truth once a
year.   *Russian prov.*

GREED

Supine amidst our flowing store,
We slept securely, and we dreamt of more.
     DRYDEN.—*Threnodia Augustalis, st.* 1.

But somehow, when the dogs hed gut
     asleep,
Their love o' mutton beat their love o'
     sheep.
     J. R. LOWELL.—*Biglow Papers,* 2nd
               Series, No. 11.

I eat well, drink well, and sleep well,
but that's all, Tom, that's all.
     T. MORTON.—*Roland for an Oliver.*

Lazy folks' stomachs don't get tired.
     Uncle Remus (Negro Saying ?).

Greed is envy's eldest brither ;
Scraggy wark they mak' thegither.
                    Scottish prov.

GREETING

Good morrow, gentle child, and then
Again good morrow, and again
Good morrow following still good morrow
Without one cloud of strife or sorrow.
          MACAULAY.—*Valentine.*

     Welcome ever smiles,
And farewell goes out sighing.
     SHAKESPEARE.—*Troilus,* Act 3, 3.

GRIEF

And thus the heart will break, yet
     brokenly live on.
     BYRON.—*Childe Harold, c.* 3, 32.

What deep wounds ever closed without
     a scar ?   BYRON.—*Ib., c.* 3, 84.

But grief should be the instructor of the
     wise ;
Sorrow is knowledge.
          BYRON.—*Manfred,* 1, 1.

And long she pined—for broken hearts
     die slow.   CAMPBELL.—*Theodric.*

The ocean has her ebbings—so has grief.
          CAMPBELL.—*Ib.*

The waters wild went o'er his child,
And he was left lamenting.
     CAMPBELL.—*Lord Ullin's Daughter.*

It is foolish to tear one's hair, as though
sorrow would be made less by baldness.
          CICERO.

I shall grieve down this blow, of that I'm
     conscious :
What does not man grieve down ?
     COLERIDGE.—*Wallenstein,* Act 5, 1.

     Grief is itself a medicine.
          COWPER.—*Charity,* 159.

The path of sorrow, and that path alone,
Leads to the land where sorrow is unknown,
     COWPER.—*To a Protestant Lady.*

     Nothing speaks our grief so well
     As to speak nothing.
     RICHARD CRASHAW.—*Upon the Death
               of a Gentleman.*

A great sorrow is a great repose, and you
will come out from your grief stronger
than when you entered it.
     A. DUMAS.—*Mme. de Chamblay.*

In all the silent manliness of grief.
     GOLDSMITH.—*Deserted Village.*

A wanton widow may wear darkest weeds.
     C. G. LELAND.—*Story of a Lie.*

Indeed the tears live in an onion that
should water this sorrow.
     SHAKESPEARE.—*Antony and Cleopatra,*
               Act 1, 2.

O, woe is me !
To see what I have seen, see what I see !
SHAKESPEARE.—*Hamlet*, Act 3, 1.

You must wear your rue with a difference.
SHAKESPEARE.—*Ib.*, Act 4, 5.

What private griefs they have, alas! I
know not.
SHAKESPEARE.—*Julius Cæsar*, Act 3, 2.

Grief best is pleased with grief's society.
SHAKESPEARE.—*Lucrece*, 159.

What, man ! ne'er pull your hat upon your
brows ;
Give sorrow words.
SHAKESPEARE.—*Macbeth*, Act 4, 3.

No sighs but o' my breathing ; no tears
but o' my shedding.
SHAKESPEARE.—*Merchant of Venice*,
Act 3, 1.

For my particular grief
Is of so floodgate and o'erbearing nature,
That it engluts and swallows other sorrows.
SHAKESPEARE.—*Othello*, Act 1, 3.

People will pretend to grieve more than
they really do, and that takes off from their
true grief.   SWIFT.—*To Mrs. Dingley*,
Jan. 14, 1712-3.

Let Love clasp Grief lest both be
drowned.
TENNYSON.—*In Memoriam, c.* 1.

Never morning wore
To evening, but some heart did break.
TENNYSON.—*Ib., c.* 6.

'Tis held that sorrow makes us wise.
TENNYSON.—*Ib., c.* 108.

He gave a groan, and then another,
Of that which went before the brother,
And then he gave a third.
WORDSWORTH.—*Peter Bell, Pt.* 1, *st*, 51.

GRUMBLERS

It is a general popular error to suppose
the loudest complainers for the public
to be the most anxious for its welfare.
BURKE.—*Observation on Present*
State of the Nation.

But human bodies are sic fools,
For a' their colleges and schools,
That when nae real ills perplex them,
They mak enow themsels to vex them.
BURNS.—*Twa Dogs.*

Grousing, grousing, grousing,
Always blooming well grousing,
Roll on till my time is up,
And I shall grouse no more.
Popular Soldier Song.

Better be a grumph than a sumph (*i.e.*
a croaker than a fool).   *Scottish prov.*

Growling will not make the kettle boil.
Prov.

GUESSING

Depend upon it a lucky guess is never
merely luck—there is always some talent
in it.   JANE AUSTEN.—*Emma, ch.* 1.

Once I guessed right,
And I got credit by't ;
Thrice I guessed wrong,
And I kept my credit on.
Saying quoted by Dean Swift, 1710.

GUESTS

A pretty woman is a welcome guest.
BYRON.—*Beppo, st.* 23.

Light is the dance and doubly sweet the
lays,
When, for the dear delight, another pays.
POPE.—*Odyssey, Bk.* 1, 205.

True friendship's laws are by this rule
expressed,
Welcome the coming, speed the parting
guest.   POPE.—*Ib., Bk.* 15, 83.

For I who hold sage Homer's rule the best,
Welcome the coming, speed the parting
guest. POPE.—*Satires, Bk.* 2, 1, 158.

Must you stay ? Can't you go ?
Punch, under cartoon, Jan. 18, 1905.

Let the guests at table be three or four—
at most five.   *Old Greek prov.*

GUIDANCE

A fool may eke a wise man often guide.
CHAUCER.—*Troilus.*

The greatest cleverness of the least
clever people is to know how to submit to
the good guidance of other people.
LA ROCHEFOUCAULD.—*Maxim* 580.

What pilot so expert but needs must
wreck
Imbarked with such a steersmate at the
helm ?
MILTON.—*Samson Agonistes*, 1044.

Thou wert my guide, philosopher and
friend. POPE.—*Essay on Man*, 4, 390.

But chancing to espy a path
That promised to cut short the way,
As many a wiser man hath done,
He left a trusty guide for one
That might his steps betray.
WORDSWORTH.—*Peter Bell, Pt.* 1, *st.* 30.

GUILE

It afforded no small amusement to the
Rhegians that Phœnicians should com-
plain of anything accomplished by guile.
PLUTARCH.—*Timoleon.*

His heart doth think on many a wile,
How to deceive the poore.
Old Ballad, Jew of Venice.

Behold an Israelite indeed, in whom is
no guile.   *St. John i, 47.*

GUILT

God hath yoked to guilt
Her pale tormentor, misery.
W. C. BRYANT.—*Inscription for entrance
to a wood.*

Men that are greatly guilty are never
wise.
BURKE.—*Impeachment of Hastings,
May, 1794.*

Thank God, guilt was never a rational
thing.   BURKE.—*Ib.*

To what gulfs
A single deviation from the track
Of human duties leads !
BYRON.—*Sardanapalus, Act 4, 1.*

Crime makes the shame and not the
scaffold.   CORNEILLE.—*Comte d'Essex.*

Every man carries the bundle of his
sins
Upon his own back.
JOHN FLETCHER.—*Rule a Wife.*

But Guilt was my grim chamberlain
That lighted me to bed.
HOOD.—*Eugene Aram.*

How guilt, once harboured in the conscious
breast,
Intimidates the brave, degrades the great !
JOHNSON.—*Irene.*

Terror haunts the guilty mind.
N. LEE.—*Rival Queens, Act 5, 1.*

We mourn the guilty while the guilt we
blame.   D. MALLET.—*Prologue.*

Some undone widow sits upon my arm
And takes away the use of 't ; and my
sword,
Glued to my scabbard with wronged
orphans' tears,
Will not be drawn.
MASSINGER.—*New Way to Pay Old Debts,
Act 5, 1.*

I am in,
And must go on ; and since I have put off
From the shore of innocence, guilt be
thou my pilot.
MASSINGER.—*Duke of Milan, Act 2, 1.*

Guilt is the source of sorrow, 'tis the fiend,
Th' avenging fiend, that follows us behind
With whips and stings.
N. ROWE.—*Fair Penitent, Act 3, 1.*

And then it started, like a guilty thing,
Upon a fearful summons.
SHAKESPEARE.—*Hamlet, Act 1, 1.*

Suspicion always haunts the guilty mind ;
The thief doth fear each bush an officer.
SHAKESPEARE.—*Henry VI., Pt. 3, Act 5, 6.*

All the perfumes of Arabia
Will not sweeten this little hand.
SHAKESPEARE.—*Macbeth, Act 2, 2.*

Will all great Neptune's ocean wash this
blood
Clean from my hand ?   No ; this my hand
will rather
The multitudinous seas incarnadine,
Making the green—one red.
SHAKESPEARE.—*Ib.*

Tis now my bitter banishment I feel :
This is a wound too deep for time to heal.
My guilt thy growing virtues did defame ;
My blackness blotted thy unblemished
name.   VIRGIL.—*Æneid, Bk. 10 (Dry-
den tr.) (Mezentius to his slain son, Lausus).*

The guilty conscience fears, when there's
no fear
And thinks that every bush contains a
bear.
R. WATKYNS.—*Flamma sine Fumo.*

What heavy guilt upon him lies !
How cursed is his name !
The ravens shall pick out his eyes,
And eagles eat the same.
I. WATTS.—*Obedience.*

Let no man trust the first false step
Of guilt ; it hangs upon a precipice,
Whose steep descent in lost perdition ends.
YOUNG.—*Busiris.*

H

HABEAS CORPUS

The Habeas Corpus Act . . . the most
stringent curb that ever legislation imposed on tyranny.
MACAULAY.—*Hist.of England, c. 6.*

HABIT

My very chains and I grew friends,
So much a long communion tends
To make us what we are.
BYRON.—*Prisoner of Chillon.*

Great is the force of habit ; it teaches
us to bear labour and to scorn injury and
pain.
CICERO (*Adapted from Tusc. 2, 15 and 17*).

Ill habits gather by unseen degrees,
As brooks make rivers, rivers run to seas.
DRYDEN.—*Tr. Ovid, Metam., Bk. 15.*

Ill customs by degrees to habits rise,
Ill habits soon become exalted vice.
DRYDEN.—*Ib.*

Long customs are not easily broken ; he that attempts to change the course of his own life very often labours in vain.
JOHNSON.—*Rasselas, ch.* 29.

For use almost can change the stamp of nature.
SHAKESPEARE.—*Hamlet,* Act 3, 4.

Habits are at first cobwebs, at last cables.   *Prov.*

HAILSTORM

Rain, rain, rattle stanes,
Dinna rain on me,
But rain on Johnnie Groat's house,
Far owre the sea.
Old Scottish rhyme.

HAIR

My hair is grey, but not with years,
Nor grew it white
In a single night,
As men's have grown by sudden fears.
BYRON.—*Prisoner of Chillon.*

HANDS

There is no better sign of a brave mind than a hard hand.
SHAKESPEARE.—*Henry VI., Pt.* 2, 4, 2.

She has certainly the finest Hand of any woman in the world. STEELE.—*Spectator.*

HANDWRITING

O wretched the debtor who's signing a deed !
And wretched the letter that no one can read !
SIR W. S. GILBERT.—*Ruddigore.*

There's something unco affectionate in manuscripp.
J. WILSON.—*Noctes (Ettrick Shepherd).*

HAPPENINGS

Yet somtyme it shal fallen on a day
That falleth not oft within a thousand yere.
CHAUCER.—*Knight's Tale,* 810 (*a prov.*).

It chanceth in an hour that comes not in seven years.   *Prov. (Ray Collection)*

HAPPINESS

Time, so complained of,
Who to no one man
Shows partiality,
Brings round to all men
Some undimmed hours.
M. ARNOLD.—*Consolation.*

To be happy, give no cause for envy. The secret of happiness is to hide one's life.   DE LA BOUISSE.

O make us happy and you make us good·
BROWNING.—*Ring and the Book,* 4, 302

What is the worth of anything
But for the happiness 'twill bring ?
R. CAMBRIDGE.—*Learning,* 23.

We ne'er can be
Made happy by compulsion.
COLERIDGE.—*Three Graves.*

There is this difference between happiness and wisdom : he that thinks himself the happiest man really is so ; but he that thinks himself the wisest is generally the greatest fool.   C. C. COLTON.—*Lacon.*

All indistinctly apprehend a bliss,
On which the soul may rest; the hearts of all
Yearn after it.
DANTE.—*Purgatorio (tr. H. F. Cary), c.* 17, 124.

I've touched the height of human happiness,
And here I fix *nil ultra.*
FLETCHER AND MASSINGER.—*Prophetess* (1622), Act 4, 6.

How wide the limits stand
Between a splendid and a happy land !
GOLDSMITH.—*Deserted Village.*

And there is even a happiness
That makes the heart afraid.
HOOD.—*To Melancholy.*

Our own felicity we make or find.
JOHNSON.—*Lines added to Goldsmith's Traveller.*

One is never so happy or so unhappy as one imagines.
LA ROCHEFOUCAULD.—*Maxim* 49.

One is never so unhappy as one believes, nor so happy as one had hoped to be.
LA ROCHEFOUCAULD.—*Maxim* 514.

Best trust the happy moments. What they gave
Makes man less fearful of the certain grave,
And gives his work compassion and new eyes ;
The days that make us happy make us wise. JOHN MASEFIELD.—*Biography.*

In them is plainest taught, and easiest learnt,
What makes a nation happy, and keeps it so.
MILTON.—*Paradise Regained, Bk.* 4, 361.

Oh, think not my spirits are always as light
And as free from a pang as they seem to you now.
MOORE.—*Irish Melodies.*

Lights by mere chance upon some happy thought.   J. OLDHAM.—*St. Cecilia.*

There is this in common between the lives of ordinary men and of saints, that they all aspire to happiness; they differ only in the object where they place it.
PASCAL.—*Pensées*.

Two things alone, with wealth combined,
Feed life's fair flower, and thus bestow
Joy's purest blessings on mankind.
These are fair fortune and recording fame.
Aspire not to be Jove! All things are thine
If these great gifts thy destiny may claim:
To mortal hopes thy mortal means confine.
PINDAR.—*Isthmian Odes*, 5, 14 (*Moore tr.*).

Oh happiness! our being's end and aim!
Good, pleasure, ease, content, whate'er thy name:
That something still which prompts the eternal sigh,
For which we bear to live, or dare to die.
POPE.—*Essay on Man, Ep.* 4, 1.

Fixed to no spot is happiness sincere,
'Tis nowhere to be found, or everywhere:
'Tis never to be bought, but always free.
POPE.—*Ib., Ep.* 4, 15.

Reason's whole pleasure, all the joys of sense,
Lie in three words, health, peace, and competence.   POPE.—*Ib.*, 79.

I call any creature " happy " that can love, or that can exult in its sense of life.
RUSKIN.—*Pref.* (1882) *Revised Edition of " Modern Painters."*

No man is happy. Man strives all his life through for imaginary happiness, which he seldom attains, and if he does, it is only to be disillusioned.
SCHOPENHAUER.—*Emptiness of Existence.*

What a pity that a man of such exquisite genius will not be contented to be happy on the ordinary terms!
SCOTT.—*Letter to J. Murray, Dec.* 1816 (*referring to Byron*).

Mankind are always happier for having been happy, so that if you make them happy now, you make them happy twenty years hence by the memory of it.
SYDNEY SMITH.—*Lectures on Moral Philosophy*, 22.

Call no man happy before his death.
SOLON (*according to Aristotle*).

Happiness is added Life and the giver of Life.
HERBERT SPENCER.—*Representative Government.*

There is no duty we so much underrate, as the duty of being happy.
R. L. STEVENSON.—*Idlers.*

What thing so good which not some harm may bring?
Even to be happy is a dangerous thing.
EARL OF STIRLING.—*Darius, Chorus* 1.

Never yet
Had heaven appeared so blue, nor earth so green.
TENNYSON.—*Holy Grail*, 364.

Every mortal has for his share his own happiness near at hand to him.
VOLTAIRE.—*Sur l'Usage de la Vie*.

The little-known art of being happy.
VOLTAIRE.—*Ib.*

Macare (Happiness), it is thou whom I desire; we love thee and we lose thee; I believe that I have found you in my home, but I beware of saying so. When we boast of having thee we are deprived of thee by envy. To keep thee one must know how to hide thee—and to hide one's life.   VOLTAIRE.—*Thélème et Macare.*

Happiness is no laughing matter.
ARCHBISHOP WHATELY.—*Apophthegms.*

Compassed round by pleasure, sighed
For independent happiness.
WORDSWORTH.—*Excursion, Bk.* 3.

The happy only are the truly great.
YOUNG.—*Love of Fame, Sat.* 6.

How sad a sight is human happiness
To those whose thought can pierce beyond an hour.
YOUNG.—*Night Thoughts*, 1.

Beware what earth calls happiness; beware
All joys but joys that never can expire.
YOUNG.—*Ib.*

HARD-HEARTEDNESS

A stony adversary, an inhuman wretch,
Uncapable of pity, void and empty
From any dram of mercy.
SHAKESPEARE.—*Merchant of Venice, Act* 4, 1.

Worse than a bloody hand is a hard heart. SHELLEY.—*Cenci, Act* 5, 2.

And though she saw all heaven in flower above,
She would not love.
SWINBURNE.—*Leave-Taking.*

HARDNESS

Plenty and peace breeds cowards; hardness ever
Of hardiness is mother.
SHAKESPEARE.—*Cymbeline, Act* 3. 6.

The tyrant custom, most grave senators,
Hath made the flinty and steel couch of war,
My thrice-driven bed of down.
SHAKESPEARE.—*Othello, Act* 1, 3.

HARMONY

There's no music when a woman is in
the concert.
DEKKER.—*Honest Whore, Pt. 2*, Act 4, 3.

From harmony, from heavenly harmony
    This universal frame began :
    From harmony to harmony,
Through all the compass of the notes it ran,
The diapason closing full in Man.
DRYDEN.—*St. Cecilia's Day*, 1687.

Heard melodies are sweet, but those
    unheard are sweeter.
KEATS.—*A Grecian Urn.*

By harmony our souls are swayed ;
By harmony the world was made.
LORD LANSDOWNE.—*British
Enchanters*, Act I.

    Lifted on the breeze
Of harmony, beyond all earthly care.
WORDSWORTH.—*The fairest, brightest
hues.*

HARSHNESS

Now there will be an outbreak of new
    laws : . . .
This deed will prompt forthwith
All mortal men to callous recklessness. . .
For since no wrath on evil deeds will creep
Henceforth from those who watch
With wild, fierce souls the evil deeds of
    men,
I will let loose all crime.*
ÆSCHYLUS.—*Eumenides*, 727
(*Plumptre tr.*).

HARVEST

How good the God of Harvest is to you,
Who pours abundance o'er your flowing
    fields. THOMSON.—*Autumn*, 170.

If weather be fair and tidy thy grain,
Make speedy carriage, for fear of rain :
For tempest and showers deceiveth a
    many,
And lingering lubbers lose many a penny.
T. TUSSER.—*August's Husbandry.*

Mist in May and heat in June
Make the harvest richt lune.
Scottish prov.

Good harvests make men prodigal ; bad
ones, provident. *Prov. (Ray's Collection).*

HASTE

A man of sense may be in haste, but
can never be in a hurry, because he
knows that whatever he does in a hurry he
must necessarily do very ill.
LORD CHESTERFIELD.—*Advice to his
Son.*

---

* This is a faithfully-drawn picture of that over-
rigid severity with which men of sterner nature
generally meet the advocates of mercy and
indulgence. KEBLE.—*Lectures on Poetry.* No. 22
(*E. K. Francis tr.*).

Hurry is the mark of a weak mind ;
dispatch, of a strong one.
C. C. COLTON.—*Lacon.*

I find this proverb true,
That haste makes waste.
G. GASCOIGNE.—*Memories*, 3, 7.

Heyo dar ! don't kick 'fo' you er
spurred, honey !
J. C. HARRIS.—*Nights with Uncle Remus,
ch.* 22.

Bloody with spurring, fiery-red with
    haste.
SHAKESPEARE.—*Richard II.*, Act 2, 3.

Haste administers all things badly.
STATIUS.—*Thebaidos Libri.*

But who in heat of blood was ever wise ?
YOUNG.—*Love of Fame, Sat.* 3.

Man is created of haste. *Koran, ch.* 21.

A hasty man drinks his tea with a fork.
Chinese prov.

Hurry is of the devil, but slow advancing
comes from God. *Eastern prov.*

Dress slowly when you are in a hurry.
French prov.

HATE, HATRED

Dante, who loved well because he hated,
Hated wickedness that hinders loving.
BROWNING.—*One Word More.*

And when his frown of hatred darkly fell,
Hope withering fled—and Mercy sighed
    farewell. BYRON.—*Corsair, c.* 1, 9.

These two hated with a hate
Found only on the stage.
BYRON.—*Don Juan, c.* 4, 93.

Now rose the unleavened hatred of his
    heart. BYRON.—*Lara, c.* 2, 4.

The ruling principle of Hate,
Which for its pleasure doth create
The things it may annihilate.
BYRON.—*Prometheus.*

I do not hate him near as much as I fear
I ought to do.
CARLYLE.—*In reference to Bishop of
Oxford.*

Love, as though some day you would
have to hate ; hate, as though some day
you would have to love.
CHILO (*c.* 550 B.C.).

Heaven has no rage like love to hatred
    turned,
Nor hell a fury like a woman scorned.
CONGREVE.—*Mourning Bride*, Act 3, 2.

We can hardly hate anyone that we
know. HAZLITT.—*Distant Objects.*

A good hater.
> JOHNSON.—*Mrs. Piozzi's*
> "*Johnsoniana*."

Dear Bathurst was a man to my very heart's content. He hated a fool, and he hated a rogue, and he hated a whig. He was a very good hater.
> JOHNSON.—*Of Richard Bathurst*
> (*d.* 1762)

We never will forgo our hate ;
We have all but a single hate ;
We love as one, we hate as one,
We have one foe and one alone,
> England !
ERNST LISSAUER.—" *Song of Hate* " (1914) *as tr. by Barbara Henderson.*

There's nothing in this world so sweet as love,
And next to love the sweetest thing is hate.
LONGFELLOW.—*Spanish Student*, Act 2, 5.

Folks never understand the folks they hate.
> J. R. LOWELL.—*Biglow Papers*,
> 2*nd Series*, 2.

A true man hates no one. NAPOLEON.

As if thou hadst unlearned the power to hate. J. OLDHAM.—*On C. Morwent.*

There is no good result when hatred is returned for hatred. SCHILLER.

Honey from silkworms who can gather,
Or silk from the yellow bee ?
The grass may grow in winter weather
As soon as hate in me.
> SHELLEY.—*To a Critic.*

I would find grievous ways to have thee slain,
Intense device and superflux of pain.
> SWINBURNE.—*Anactoria.*

Who cannot hate, can love not.
> SWINBURNE.—*In the Bay.*

It is not so easy as people suppose to hate continuously.
> TALLEYRAND.—*Memoir read before the*
> *French Institute.*

There is no enmity can mate
With what was love and now is hate.
D. W. THOMPSON.—*From Euripides.*

To instruct the human race need one discard humanity ? Is the torch of Hatred indispensable to show us the Truth ?
> VOLTAIRE.—*Fanaticism.*

Hate and mistrust are the children of blindness ;
Could we but see one another, 'twere well !
Knowledge is sympathy, charity, kindness ;
Ignorance only is maker of hell.
SIR W. WATSON.—*England to Ireland.*

We hold our hate too choice a thing
For light and careless lavishing.
> SIR W. WATSON.—*Hate.*

And man is hate, but God is love.
> WHITTIER.—*Chapel of the Hermits.*

O, woman wronged can cherish hate
More dark and deep than manhood may.
> WHITTIER.—*Mogg Megone.*

HATS

In spite of their hats being very ugly, Goddam ! I love the English. BÉRANGER.

If he be not in love with some woman, there is no believing old signs : a' brushes his hat o' mornings ; what should that bode ? SHAKESPEARE.—*Much Ado,*
Act 3, 2.

HEALTH

To gather riches, do not hazard health, For truth to say, health is the wealth
of wealth. SIR RICHARD BAKER.

The healthy know not of their health, but only the sick : this is the Physician's Aphorism. CARLYLE.—*Characteristics.*

Good or bad health makes our philosophy. CHAULIEU.

What a searching preacher of self-command is the varying phenomenon of Health ! EMERSON.—*Discipline.*

I honour health as the first muse, and sleep as the condition of health.
> EMERSON.—*Inspiration.*

Give me health and a day and I will make the pomp of emperors ridiculous.
> EMERSON.—*Nature.*

Rich, from the very want of wealth,
In heaven's best treasures, peace and health. GRAY.—*Ode.*

We er sorter po'ly [sort of poorly], Sis Tempy, I'm 'blige ter you. You know w'at de jay-bird say ter der squinch-owl, " I'm sickly but sassy."
J. C. HARRIS.—*Nights with Uncle Remus,*
ch. 50.

A sound mind in a sound body is a thing to pray for. JUVENAL.—*Sat.* 4.

Life is not to be alive, but to be well.
> MARTIAL.—*Bk.* 6.

Perfect health and spirits . . . is an enjoyment [which] probably constitutes, in a great measure, the happiness of infants and brutes, especially of the lower and sedentary orders of animals, as of oysters, periwinkles, and the like, for which I have sometimes been at a loss to find out amusement. PALEY.—*Moral and Political*
Philosophy. Bk. 1, *ch.* 6

Grant me but health, thou great Be-
stower of it, and give me but this fair
goddess as my companion, and shower
down thy mitres, if it seem good unto thy
Divine Providence, upon those heads
which are aching for them.
> STERNE.—*Sentimental Journey.*

Look to your health ; and if you have it,
praise God, and value it next to a good
conscience ; for health is the second
blessing that we mortals are capable of ;
a blessing that money cannot buy.
> I. WALTON.—*Complete Angler, ch.* 21.

The health (or safety) of the people is
the highest law.
> *Derived (by tradition) from the* 12 *Law
> Tables at Rome.*

HEARTLESSNESS

He hath the sore which no man heleth,
The which is clepèd lacke of herte.
> GOWER.—*Conf. Amantis.*

One that would peep and botanize
Upon his mother's grave.
> WORDSWORTH.—*A Poet's Epitaph.*

HEARTS

With women the heart argues, not the
mind.   M. ARNOLD.—*Merope.*

All people have their blind side—their
superstitions ; and I have heard her declare, under the rose, that hearts was her
favourite suit.
> LAMB.—*Mrs. Battle on Whist.*

HEAVEN

I hear thee speak of the better land,
Thou callest its children a happy band ;
Mother, oh ! where is that radiant shore ;
Shall we not seek it and weep no more ?
> MRS. HEMANS.—*The Better Land.*

God, to remove His ways from human
sense,
Placed heaven from earth so far, that
earthly sight
If it presume, might err in things too
high,
And no advantage gain.
> MILTON.—*Paradise Lost, Bk.* 8, 119.

That Prophet ill sustains his holy call,
Who finds not heavens to suit the tastes
of all.   ☹   MOORE.—*Lalla Rookh.*

A Persian's heaven is easily made,
'Tis but black eyes and lemonade.
> MOORE.—*Twopenny Postbag,* 6.

For all we know
Of what the blessed do above
Is that they sing and that they love.
> WALLER.—*While I listen to thy Voice.*

HEIRESSES

All heiresses are beautiful.
> DRYDEN.—*King Arthur.*

HELL

The fear o' hell's a hangman's whip
To haud the wretch in order.
> BURNS.—*To a young friend.*

Grisly drede that evere shal laste.
> CHAUCER.—*Parson's Tale, sec.* 10 (*Part
> of a description of Hell*).

So that their joyis shal be without
measure ;
They shal rejoyce to see the great dolour
Of dampnit folk in hell, and thare torment.
> SIR D. LYNDESAY.—*Monarche.*

The most frightful idea that has ever
corroded human nature, the idea of eternal
punishment.
> LORD MORLEY.—*Vauvenargues.*

I see a brimstone sea of boiling fire,
And fiends, with knotted whips of flaming
wire,
Torturing poor souls, that gnash their
teeth in vain,
And gnaw their flame-tormented tongues
for pain.
> F. QUARLES.—*Emblems, Bk.* 3, 14.

To preach loud, long, and Damnation, is
the way to be cried up. We love a man that
Damns us, and we run after him to save us.
> J. SELDEN.—*Damnation.*

But always recollect, my dear,
That wicked people go to hell.
> ANN AND JANE TAYLOR.—*About
> Dying.*

How I shall admire, laugh, rejoice, exult, to see so many great Kings consigned
with Jove himself and his followers, to
groan in the lowest depths of darkness.
> TERTULLIAN.—*De Spectaculis.*

The loss of heaven's the greatest pain in
hell.
> SIR S. TUKE.—*Adv. of Five Hours,
> Act* 5.

The gates of hell are open night and day ;
Smooth the descent, and easy is the way.
> VIRGIL.—*Æneid, Bk.* 6 (*Dryden tr.*).

There is a dreadful hell,
And everlasting pains ;
Where sinners must with devils dwell
In darkness, fire, and chains.
> I. WATTS.—*Heaven and Hell.*

HELP

May Might and Right,
And sovran Zeus as third, my helpers be !
> ÆSCHYLUS.—*Choephoræ,* 244 (*Plumptre
> tr.*).

Sweet the help
Of one we have helped.
E. B. BROWNING.—*Aurora Leigh, Bk.* 7.

In man's most dark extremity
Oft succour dawns from Heaven.
SCOTT.—*Lord of the Isles, c.* 1, 20.

'Tis not enough to help the feeble up,
But to support him after.
SHAKESPEARE.—*Timon,* Act 1, 1.

Angels and ministers of grace defend
us! SHAKESPEARE.—*Hamlet,* Act 1, 4.

HEREDITY

Rarely into the branches of the tree
Doth human worth mount up.
DANTE.—*Purgatorio (Cary's tr.), c.* 7, 122.

Ah me! how seldom see we sons succeed
Their fathers' praise!
BISHOP JOS. HALL.—*Satire* 3 (*2nd series*).

Few sons attain the praise
Of their great sires, and most their sires
disgrace.
POPE.—*Odyssey, Bk.* 2, 315.

He's all the mother's, from the top to toe.
SHAKESPEARE.—*Richard III.,* Act 3, 1.

Those transparent swindles—transmissible nobility and kingship.
MARK TWAIN.—*Yankee at Court, c.* 28.

Be mindful of the race from whence you
came,
And emulate in arms your fathers' fame.
Fortune befriends the bold.
VIRGIL.—*Æneid, Bk.* 10 (*Dryden tr.*).

The fathers have eaten sour grapes and
the children's teeth are set on edge.
Jeremiah xxxi, 29 (*R.V.*) *and
Ezekiel* x, 10 (*A.V.*).

HERESY

I smelle a loller in the wind, quod he.
CHAUCER.—*Shipman's Tale.*

They that approve a private opinion
call it opinion; but they that mislike it,
heresy: and yet heresy signifies no more
than private opinion.
HOBBES.—*Leviathan, ch.* 11.

A man may be a heretic in the truth;
and if he believe things only because his
pastor says so, or the assembly so determines, without knowing other reason,
though his belief be true, yet the very
truth he holds becomes his heresy.
MILTON.—*Areopagitica.*

Better heresy of doctrine than heresy
of heart. WHITTIER.—*Mary Garvin*

HEROES

How sleep the brave who sink to rest,
By all their country's wishes blest?
. . . .
By fairy hands their knell is rung,
By forms unseen their dirge is sung.
W. COLLINS.—*Ode.*

All actual heroes are essential men,
And all men possible heroes.
E. B. BROWNING.—*Aurora Leigh, Bk.* 5.

In short, he was a perfect cavaliero,
And to his very valet seemed a hero.
BYRON.—*Beppo,* 33.

Heroes have trod this spot—'tis on their
dust ye tread.
BYRON.—*Childe Harold, c.* 4, 144.

Lights of the world and demi-gods of
Fame.
CAMPBELL.—*Pleasures of Hope,* 2.

Thou and I, my friend, can, in the most
flunky world, make, each of us, *one* non-flunky, one hero, if we like; that will be
two heroes to begin with.
CARLYLE.—*Past and Present, Bk.* 1, ch. 6.

That subject for an angel's song,
The hero, and the saint.
COWPER.—*On "Sir C. Grandison."*

Nurture your mind with great thoughts.
To believe in the heroic makes heroes.
DISRAELI.—*Coningsby, Bk.* 3, *c.* 1
(*Sidonia*).

Every hero becomes a bore at last.
EMERSON.—*Great Men.*

But to the hero, when his sword
Has won the battle of the free,
Thy voice sounds like a prophet's word
And in its hollow tones are heard
The thanks of millions yet to be.
F. HALLECK.—*Marco Bozzaris.*

Heroic virtues are the bons mots of life.
They do not appear often, and when they
do appear are too much prized, I think;
like the aloe-tree which shoots and flowers
once in a hundred years.
JOHNSON.—*Remark recorded by Mrs.
Piozzi.*

Brave men and worthy patriots, dear to
God, and famous to all ages.
MILTON.—*Of Education.*

Samson hath quit himself
Like Samson, and heroically hath finished
A life heroic.
MILTON.—*Samson Agonistes,* 1709.

Like the day-star in the wave,
Sinks a hero in his grave,
'Midst the dew-fall of a nation's tears.
MOORE.—*Before the Battle.*

Still, though death's wave without distinc-
tion roll
O'er all alike, the nameless and the great,
For warriors yet, that reach the eternal
goal,
Approved of heaven, conspicuous
honours wait.   PINDAR.—*Pythian
Odes*, 3, 137 (*Moore tr.*).

Hero-worship is strongest where there is
least regard for human freedom.
H. SPENCER.—*Social Statics, Pt.* 3.

Strange fate of heroes, who like comets
blaze,
And with a sudden light the world amaze ;
But when, with fading beams, they quit
the skies,
No more to shine the wonder of our eyes,
Their glories spent and all their fiery
store,
We scorn the omens which we feared
before.   SWIFT.—*Swan Tripe Club.*

One brave deed makes no hero.
WHITTIER.—*Hero.*

HESITATION

For if it be but half-denied,
'Tis half as good as justified.
BUTLER.—*Hudibras, Pt.* 2, *c.* 2.

Was none who would be foremost
To lead such dire attack ;
But those behind cried " Forward,"
And those before cried " Back."
MACAULAY.—*Horatius.*

And yet another yet.
SHAKESPEARE.—*Two Gentlemen of Verona,*
Act 2, 1.

When you are in doubt whether an
action is good or bad, abstain from it.
ZOROASTER (*Maxim*).

HINTS

Therefore use thy discretion ; I had as
lief thou didst break his neck as his finger.
SHAKESPEARE.—*As You Like It,* Act 1, 1.

Upon this hint I spake.
SHAKESPEARE.—*Othello,* Act 1, 3.

HISTORY

Histories make men wise.
BACON.—*Of Studies.*

But e'en when at college, I fairly acknow-
ledge I
Never was very precise at chronology.
R. H. BARHAM.—*Aunt Fanny.*

I have read somewhere or other—in
Dionysius of Halicarnassus, I think—
that History is Philosophy teaching by
examples.   BOLINGBROKE.—*Letter.**

* Found in Dionysius of Halicarnassus, who,
however, was quoting from Thucydides.

History is the essence of innumerable
biographies.   BOLINGBROKE.—*On History.*

The love of history seems inseparable
from human nature because it seems
inseparable from self-love.
BOLINGBROKE.—*Ib.*

These gentle historians, on the contrary,
dip their pens in nothing but the milk
of human kindness.
BURKE.—*Letter to a Noble Lord* (1796).

People will not look forward to posterity,
who never look backward to their ancestors.   BURKE.—*Reflections on the
Revolution.*

History after all is the true poetry.
CARLYLE.—*Boswell's Johnson.*

History, a distillation of Rumour.
CARLYLE.—*French Revolution.*

All History . . . is an inarticulate
Bible.   CARLYLE.—*Latter-Day Pamphlets.*

The first law of history is that it shall
not dare to state anything which is false,
and consequently that it shall not shrink
from stating anything that is true.
CICERO.—*De Oratore, Bk.* 2, 15.

Some write a narrative of wars, and feats
Of heroes little known, and call the rant
A history.   COWPER.—*Garden,* 139.

The use of history is to give value to
the present hour and its duty.
EMERSON.—*Works and Days.*

History, which is indeed little more than
the register of the crimes, follies, and
misfortunes of mankind.
GIBBON.—*Decline and Fall, ch.* 3 (1776).

On whatever side we regard the history
of Europe, we shall perceive it to be a
tissue of crimes, follies, and misfortunes.
GOLDSMITH.—*Citizen of the World,* 42
(1762).

History is the chart and compass for
national endeavour.
SIR A. HELPS.—*Friends in Council,
Bk.* 1, *ch.* 11.

Happy are the people whose annals are
tedious.   MONTESQUIEU.

The worst historians for a young man to
read are those who pronounce judgment.
Facts ! Facts ! Let him judge for himself !
ROUSSEAU.—*Emile.*

Alas ! Hegel was right when he said
that we learn from history that men never
learn anything from history.
G. B. SHAW.—*Heartbreak House, Pref.,
The Next Phase.*

Poetrie ever setteth forth virtue in her best colours. . . . But the Historian, being captived to the truth of a foolish world, is many times a terror from well doing and an encouragement to unbridled wickedness.
SIR P. SIDNEY.—*Apologie for Poetrie.*

The history of the great events of the world is little more than the history of crimes. VOLTAIRE.—*Essay on Manners, c. 23 (c. 1750).*

In effect history is only a picture of crimes and misfortunes.
VOLTAIRE.—*L'Ingénu* (1767).

How history makes one shudder and laugh by turns !
HORACE WALPOLE.—*Letter, 1786.*

Oh, do not read history, for that I know must be false. SIR R. WALPOLE.—*Saying.*

Deal not in history, often have I said ; 'Twill prove a most unprofitable trade.
J. WOLCOT.—*Ep. to Sylvanus Urban.*

HOLIDAYS

I care not a fig for the cares of business ; Politics fill me with doubt and dizziness.
R. BUCHANAN.—*Fine Weather.*

What is this life if, full of care, We have no time to stand and stare ?
W. H. DAVIES.—*Leisure.*

Who first invented work, and bound the free
And holiday-rejoicing spirit down ?
LAMB.—*Work.*

HOLLAND

A country that draws fifty feet of water ; In which men live as in the hold of nature ;
.   .   .   .
A land that rides at anchor and is moored ; In which they do not live, but go aboard.
S. BUTLER.—*Description of Holland.*

Embosomed in the deep where Holland lies,
Methinks her patient sons before me stand, Where the broad ocean leans against the land.   GOLDSMITH.—*Traveller.*

Holland, that scarce deserves the name of land,
As but the off-scouring of the British sand.
MARVELL.—*Character of Holland.*

HOME

His wee bit ingle, blinking bonnily.
BURNS.—*Cotter's Saturday Night.*

To make a happy fire-side clime
For weans and wife ;
That's the true pathos and sublime
Of human life.
BURNS.—*Epistle to Dr. Blacklock.*

My whinstone house my castle is,
I have my own four walls.
CARLYLE.—*My own Four Walls.*

The house of everyone is to him as his castle and fortress.
SIR E. COKE.—*Semayne's Case, 5 Rep. 91.*

None love their country but who love their home. COLERIDGE.—*Zapolya, Pt. 2.*

But wheresoe'er I'm doomed to roam, I still shall say—that home is home.
W. COMBE.—*Dr. Syntax, c. 26.*

The world has nothing to bestow ;
From our own selves our joys must flow, And that dear hut—our home.
N. COTTON.—*Fireside.*

Forced from home and all its pleasures.
COWPER.—*Negro's Complaint.*

The language of a ruder age has given to common law the maxim that every man's house is his castle. The progress of truth will make every house a shrine.
EMERSON.—*Domestic Life.*

Where'er I roam, whatever realms to see, My heart, untravelled, fondly turns to thee.   GOLDSMITH.—*Traveller.*

The stately homes of England !
How beautiful they stand,
Amidst their tall ancestral trees,
O'er all the pleasant land.
MRS. HEMANS.—*Homes of England.*

Awful Divinity ! be not incensed.
I know that my Penelope in form
And stature altogether yields to thee,
For she is mortal, and immortal thou,
From age exempt. Yet not the less I wish
My home, and languish daily to return.
HOMER.—*Odyssey, Bk. 5, 215 (Cowper tr.).*

The fairyest of fairy land.
The land of home.
JEAN INGELOW.—*Letter L. Absent, st. 34.*

It is this sweet home-feeling, this settled repose of affection in the domestic scene, that is, after all, the parent of the steadiest virtues and purest enjoyments.
WASHINGTON IRVING.—*Sketch Book (c. 1820).*

A man's best things are nearest him, Lie close about his feet.
R. M. MILNES.—*Men of Old.*

But O, my babies on the floor ;
My wife's blithe welcome at the door ;
My bread well earned with sweat of brows ;
My garden flowerful, green of boughs ;

Friends, books ;—I would not change ye
   for
      Ten thousand pounds.
   COSMO MONKHOUSE.—*Rondel, " Ten
            Thousand Pounds."*

There is a spot of earth supremely blest,
A dearer, sweeter spot than all the rest.
      JAS. MONTGOMERY.—*Home.*

I knew by the smoke that so gracefully
   curled
Above the green elms, that a cottage was
   near,
And I said, " If there's peace to be found
   in the world,
A heart that was humble might hope
   for it here."
      MOORE.—*Ballad Stanzas.*

Who has not felt how sadly sweet
   The dream of home, the dream of home,
Steals o'er the heart, too soon to fleet,
   When far o'er sea or land we roam ?
      MOORE.—*Dream of Home.*

Round the hearth-stone of home, in the
   land of our birth,
The holiest spot on the face of the earth.
      GEO. P. MORRIS.—*Land Ho !*

Mid pleasures and palaces though we may
   roam,
Be it never so humble, there's no place
   like home.   J. H. PAYNE.—*Clari.*

Home-keeping youth have ever homely
   wits.
      SHAKESPEARE.—*Two Gentlemen of
            Verona*, Act I, I.

A comfortable house is a great source
of happiness. It ranks immediately after
health and a good conscience.
SYDNEY SMITH.—*Letter to Lord Murray,
            Sept.* 29, 1843.

" There's no place like home." It's a
great pity when either husband or wife is
forced to answer, " I'm glad there isn't."
C. H. SPURGEON.—*'Salt-Cellars."*

That unconquerable love of home,
That burns even in the hearts of evil men.
      F. TENNYSON.—*Andros.*

      Seek home for rest,
      For home is best,
T. TUSSER.—*Instructions to Housewifery.*

Though home be but homely, yet housewife is taught
That home hath no fellow to such as have
   aught.   T. TUSSER.—*Ib.*

God looks down well pleased to mark
In earth's dusk gloom each rosy spark,
Lights of home and lights of love,
And the child, the heart thereof.
      K. TYNAN.—*Night Thought.*

O ! what's a table richly spread
Without a woman at its head ?
THOS. WARTON.—*Progress of Discontent.*

Whatever brawls disturb the street,
There should be peace at home.
      I. WATTS.—*Love.*

And a single small cottage, a nest like a
   dove's,
The one only dwelling on earth that she
   loves.
   WORDSWORTH.—*Reverie of Poor Susan.*

Type of the wise who soar, but never
   roam ;
True to the kindred points of heaven and
   home !
      WORDSWORTH.—*To a Skylark.*

HOMER

The blind old man of Scio's rocky isle.
   BYRON.—*Bride of Abydos, c.* 2, 2.

That blind bard, who on the Chian
   strand,
By those deep sounds possessed with
   inward light,
Beheld the Iliad and the Odyssee
   Rise to the swelling of the voiceful sea.
      COLERIDGE.—*Fancy in Nubibus.*

Read Homer once, and you can read no
   more ;
For all books else appear so mean, so
   poor,
Verse will seem prose ; but still persist to
   read,
And Homer will be all the books you need.
      J. SHEFFIELD.—*On Poetry*, 322.

HONESTY

In a word, to appear an honest man it
is necessary to be one.   BOILEAU.

'Tis my opinion every man cheats in
his way, and he is only honest who is
not discovered.
   MRS. CENTLIVRE.—*Artifice*, Act 5.

The modest front of this small floor,
Believe me, reader, can say more
Than many a braver marble can,—
" Here lies a truly honest man ! "
      R. CRASHAW.—*On Mr. Ashton.*

Honesty is really only the art of appearing honest.   GUARINI.—*Of the honesty or
            virtue of women.*

He that loseth his honestie hath nothing else to lose.   J. LYLY.—*Euphues.*

Ay, sir, to be honest, as this world
goes, is to be one man picked out of ten
thousand.
      SHAKESPEARE.—*Hamlet*, Act 2, 2.

Hamlet : What news ?—*Rosencrantz :*
None, my lord, but that the world's
grown honest.—*Hamlet :*   Then is doomsday near.   SHAKESPEARE.—*Ib.*

I am as honest as any man living, that
is an old man, and no honester than I.
SHAKESPEARE.—*Much Ado*, Act 3, 5.

Whip me such honest knaves.
SHAKESPEARE.—*Othello*, Act 1, 1.

Every man has his fault, and honesty
is his. SHAKESPEARE.—*Timon*, Act 3, 1.

Though I am not naturally honest, I
am so sometimes by chance.
SHAKESPEARE.—*Winter's Tale*, Act 4, 3.

Honesty is the best policy, but he who
acts on that principle is not an honest
man.
ARCHBISHOP WHATELY.—*Apophthegms.*

Th' Almighty, from his throne, on Earth
    surveys
Nought greater than an honest, humble
    heart. YOUNG.—*Night Thoughts*, 8.

Pope boldly states (some think his maxim
    odd),
" An honest man's the noblest work of
    God."
If this assertion is from error clear,
One of the noblest works of God lies
    here.   *Epitaph, Said to be in
Wingfield Churchyard, Suffolk.*

HONEYMOON

The moon—the moon, so silver and cold,
Her fickle temper has oft been told,
Now shady—now bright and sunny—
But of all the lunar things that change,
The one that shows most fickle and strange,
Is the moon—so called—of honey !
        HOOD.—*Miss Kilmansegg.*

Eat up the moon and keep the honey.
Some eat all the honey and have nothing
left but the moon.
C. H. SPURGEON.—*" Salt-Cellars."*

HONOUR

When vice prevails, and impious men
    bear sway,
The post of honour is a private station.
        ADDISON.—*Cato*, Act 4, 4.

It is gone, that sensibility of principle,
that chastity of honour, which felt a
stain like a wound.
BURKE.—*Reflections on French
Revolution.*

Honour is like a widow, won
With brisk attempt and putting on.
BUTLER.—*Hudibras, Pt. 1, c. 1.*

Quoth Ralpho, Honour's but a word
To swear by only in a Lord.
BUTLER.—*Ib., Pt. 2, c. 2.*

What is fitting is honourable ; what is
honourable is fitting.
        CICERO.—*De Officiis.*

By fairy hands their knell is rung,
By forms unseen their dirge is sung ;
There Honour comes, a pilgrim grey,
To bless the turf that wraps their clay.
        W. COLLINS.—*Ode.*

War, he sung, is toil and trouble ;
    Honour but an empty bubble.
        DRYDEN.—*Alexander's Feast.*

Costar : Pray now, what may be that
same bed of honour ?—*Kite :* Oh, a
mighty large bed ; bigger by half than the
great bed at Ware—ten thousand people
may lie in it together, and never feel one
another.
FARQUHAR.—*Recruiting Officer*, Act 1.

What can't be done with honour can't
be done at all.
HENRY FOX (LORD HOLLAND).—*Letter
to the Duke of Richmond*, 1756.

When honour's lost, 'tis a relief to die ;
Death's but a sure retreat from infamy.
SIR S. GARTH.—*Dispensary*, 5, 321.

Life is ended when our honour ends.
        GOLDSMITH.—*Prologue.*

Purity is the feminine, Truth the masculine, of Honour.
J. C. HARE.—*Guesses at Truth, vol. 1.*

Yet this inconstancy is such
    As you shall too adore ;
I could not love thee, dear, so much,
    Loved I not honour more.
        R. LOVELACE.—*To Lucasta.*

Once to every man and nation comes the
    moment to decide
In the strife of Truth with Falsehood, for
    the good or evil side.
        J. R. LOWELL.—*Present Crisis.*

I account more strength in a true heart
than in a walled citie.
        J. LYLY.—*Endymion.*

Let others write for glory or reward ;
Truth is well paid when she is sung and
    heard.
SIR THOS. OVERBURY.—*Elegy on Lord
Effingham.*

For honour is the guerdon of the brave.
PINDAR.—*Isthmian Odes*, 6, 31
(*Moore tr.*).

    Rightly to be great
Is not to stir without great argument,
But greatly to find quarrel in a straw,
When honour's at the stake.
SHAKESPEARE.—*Hamlet*, Act 4, 4.

I am more an antique Roman than a
Dane. SHAKESPEARE.—*Ib.*, Act 5, 2.

By heaven, methinks, it were an easy
    leap,
To pluck bright honour from the pale-
    faced moon ;

I*

Or dive into the bottom of the deep
Where fathom-line could never touch the
   ground,
And pluck up drownèd honour by the
   locks.
   SHAKESPEARE.—*Henry IV.*, *Pt.* 1, Act 1,2.

Honour pricks me on. Yea, but how
if honour prick me off, when I come on ?
how then ? Can honour set to a leg ?
No. Or an arm ? No. Or take away
the grief of a wound ? No. Honour hath
no skill in surgery, then ? No. What is
honour ? A word. . . . Who hath it ?
He that died o' Wednesday. Doth he
feel it ? No. Doth he hear it ? No.
Is it insensible, then ? Yea, to the dead.
But will it not live with the living ? No.
Why ? Detraction will not suffer it—
therefore, I'll none of it : honour is a mere
scutcheon :—and so ends my catechism.
   SHAKESPEARE.—*Ib.*, *Pt.* 1, Act 5, 1.

But if it be a sin to covet honour,
I am the most offending soul alive.
   SHAKESPEARE.—*Henry V.*, Act 4, 3.

For Brutus is an honourable man ;
So are they all, all honourable men.
   SHAKESPEARE.—*Julius Cæsar*, Act 3, 2.

Mine honour is my life ; both grow in one :
Take honour from me, and my life is done.
   SHAKESPEARE.—*Richard II.*, Act 1, 1.

Life every man holds dear ; but the brave
   man
Holds honour far more precious-dear than
   life.
   SHAKESPEARE.—*Troilus*, Act 5, 3.

Honour should be concerned in honour's
cause. T. SOUTHERN.—*Oroonoko*, Act 3.

Dearer is love than life, and fame than
   gold ;
But dearer than them both your faith once
   plighted hold.
   SPENSER.—*Faerie Queene*, *Bk.* 5, 11, 63.

Lo, one who loved true honour more than
   fame,
A real goodness, not a studied name.
   EARL OF STIRLING.—*Doomsday*, *8th hour*,
                       109.

As natural life the body warms,
And, scholars teach, the soul informs,
So honour animates the whole,
And is the spirit of the soul.
Those numerous virtues which the tribe
Of tedious moralists describe,
And by such various titles call,
True honour comprehends them all.
   SWIFT.—*To Stella*, 1720.

A true man, pure as faith's own vow,
Whose honour knows not rust.
   SWINBURNE.—*Balen*, 3, 18.

But this thing is God,
  To be man with thy might,
To grow straight in the strength of thy
   spirit,
  And live out thy life as the light.
   SWINBURNE.—*Hertha*, 15.

Man's word is God in man :
Let chance what will, I trust thee to the
   death.
   TENNYSON.—*Coming of Arthur*, 132.

Upon this fatal quest
Of honour, where no honour can be gained.
   TENNYSON.—*Geraint and Enid*, 704.

I would strangle you with my own hands
rather than allow an affront to your
honour, for mark you, I love you enough
for that.
   VOLTAIRE.—*L'Exchange* (*Baron de la
                   Canardière*).

Honour's a mistress all mankind pursue ;
Yet most mistake the false one for the
   true ;
Lured by the trappings, dazzled by the
   paint,
We worship oft the idol for the saint.
   P. WHITEHEAD.—*Honour*.

Honour that knows the path, and will
   not swerve.
   WORDSWORTH.—*Poems to National
     Independence*, *Pt.* 2, *No.* 28.

HONOURS (REWARDS)

Examine the honours list and you will
know exactly how the government feels
in its inside.
   A. BENNETT.—*The Title* (1918), Act 1.

I had rather it should be asked why I
had not a statue, than why I had one.
   CATO (*according to Plutarch*).

Fortune, the great commandress of the
   world,
Hath divers ways to advance her followers ;
To some she gives honour without deserv-
   ing ;
To other some, deserving without honour.
   CHAPMAN.—*All Fools*, Act 5.

Be not with honour's gilded baits beguiled,
  Nor think ambition wise because 'tis
   brave ;
For though we like it, as a forward child,
  'Tis so unsound her cradle is her grave.
   SIR W. DAVENANT.—*Gondibert*,
                 Bk. 1, *c.* 5, *st.* 75.

Honours and great employments are great
burthens.
   MASSINGER.—*Bondman*, Act 1, 3.

Honours never fail to purchase silence.
   MASSINGER.—*Duke of Milan*, Act 2, 1.

This man ought to have a statue of
gold.   PLAUTUS.—*Bacchides.*

Theopompus said : " Moderate honours time augments, but defaces the immoderate." PLUTARCH.—*Laconic Apophthegms.*

This is the state of man : to-day he puts forth
The tender leaves of hope ; to-morrow blossoms,
And bears his blushing honours thick upon him :
The third day comes a frost, a killing frost.
SHAKESPEARE.—*Henry VIII.*, Act 3, 2.

And, to add greater honours to his age
Than man could give him, he died fearing God.   SHAKESPEARE.—*Ib.*, Act 4, 2.

I would rather win honour than honours.
I would rather have genius than wealth,
I would rather make my name than inherit it.   THACKERAY.—*The Virginians.*

HOPE

With the faint glimmering of a doubtful hope.   ADDISON.—*Cato*, Act 3, 2.

Hope is a good breakfast, but it is a bad supper.   BACON.—*Apophthegms*, 95.

Were it not then for Hope the hart were slaine. R. BARNFIELD.—*Complaint of Poetrie* (1598).

Hope never leaves a wretched man that seeks her.
BEAUMONT AND FLETCHER.—*The Captain*, Act 2, 1.

Hope, thou nurse of young desire !
I. BICKERSTAFFE.—*Love in a Village*, Act 1,1.

What is man's hope, good friend ?
Is't not a beggar in the land of doubt ?
R. BRIDGES.—*Return of Ulysses*, Act 4.

One who never turned his back, but marched breast forward,
Never doubted clouds would break,
Never dreamed, though right were worsted wrong would triumph,
Held we fall to rise, are baffled to fight better, sleep to wake.
BROWNING.—*Asolando.*

Far greater numbers have been lost by hopes
Than all the magazines of daggers, ropes,
And other ammunitions of despair.
S. BUTLER.—*Miscellaneous Thoughts.*

Be thou the rainbow to the storms of life !
The evening beam that smiles the clouds away,
And tints to-morrow with prophetic ray.
BYRON.—*Bride of Abydos*, c. 2, st. 20.

But hope, the charmer lingered still behind.
CAMPBELL.—*Pleasures of Hope*, Pt. 1.

Cease, every joy, to glimmer on my mind,
But leave—oh ! leave the light of Hope behind !   CAMPBELL.—*Ib.*, P. 2.

Thou, undismayed, shalt o'er the ruins smile,
And light thy torch at Nature's funeral pile.   CAMPBELL.—*Ib., Conclusion.*

It has been well said : " Man is based on Hope, he has properly no other possession but Hope ; this habitation of his is named the Place of Hope."
CARLYLE.—*French Revolution*, Pt. 1, Bk. 2, ch. 3.

And Hope enchanted smiled, and waved her golden hair.
W. COLLINS.—*The Passions.*

I have been disappointed of my only hope ; and he that loses hope may part with anything.
CONGREVE.—*Love for Love*, Act 5, 2.

If things then from their end we happy call,
'Tis Hope is the most hopeless thing of all.
COWLEY.—*Against Hope.*

Hope ! of all ills that men endure
The only cheap and universal cure !
COWLEY.—*For Hope.*

Though hope be dying, yet it is not dead.
DRYDEN.—*Rival Ladies*, Act 4, 1.

Hope is a poor salad
To dine and sup with.
FLETCHER AND MASSINGER.—*Custom of the Country.*

All men are guests where Hope doth hold the feast.
G. GASCOIGNE.—*Fruits of War.*

Hope, like the glimmering taper's light,
Adorns and cheers the way,
And still, as darker grows the night,
Emits a brighter ray.
GOLDSMITH.—*Song.*

Gay Hope is theirs, by Fancy fed,
Less pleasing when possessed.
GRAY.—*Eton College.*

Hope is not yet taxed.
SIR ANTHONY HOPE HAWKINS.—*Dolly Dialogues*, 18.

Reflected on the lake, I love
To see the stars of evening glow ;
So tranquil in the heavens above,
So restless in the wave below.
Thus heavenly hope is all serene,
But earthly hope, how bright soe'er,
Still fluctuates o'er this changing scene,
As false and fleeting as 'tis fair.
BISHOP HEBER.—*On Heavenly and Earthly Hope.*

Hope, that with honey blends the cup of pain. SIR W. JONES.—*Sereswaty.*

Hope and fear are inseparable. There is no hope without fear and no fear without hope. LA ROCHEFOUCAULD.—*Maxim* 594.

None without hope e'er loved the brightest fair,
But love can hope where reason would despair. GEO. LORD LYTTELTON.—*Epigram.*

O welcome pure-eyed Faith, white-handed Hope,
Thou hovering angel, girt with golden wings! MILTON.—*Comus,* 213.

Was I deceived, or did a sable cloud
Turn forth her silver lining on the night? MILTON.—*Ib.,* 221.

Chase
Anguish, and doubt, and fear, and sorrow, and pain,
From mortal or immortal minds. MILTON.—*Paradise Lost, Bk.* 1, 557.

Hope elevates, and joy
Brightens his crest. MILTON.—*Ib., Bk.* 9, 633.

The Gods are kind, and hope to men they give
That they their little span on earth may live,
Nor yet faint utterly. W. MORRIS.—*Bellerophon,* 1617.

Hope it is which makes the shipwrecked sailor strike out with his arms in the midst of the sea, even though on all sides he can see no land. OVID.—*Ep. ex Pont., Bk.* 1, 6.

Hope springs eternal in the human breast;
Man never is, but always to be blest. POPE.—*Essay on Man,* 95.

For hope is but the dream of those that wake. PRIOR.—*Solomon, Bk.* 3, 102.

Hope told a flattering tale,
Much longer than my arm. W. B. RHODES.—*Bombastes.*

It may be said of man in general that befooled by hope he dances into the arms of death. SCHOPENHAUER.—*Emptiness of Existence.*

And thus Hope me deceived, as she deceiveth all. SCOTT.—*Harold,* 3, 1.

The miserable have
No other medicine but only hope. SHAKESPEARE.—*Measure for Measure,* Act 3, 1.

The worst is not,
So long as we can say, " This is the worst." SHAKESPEARE.—*Lear,* Act 4, 1.

Cozening hope; he is a flatterer,
A parasite, a keeper-back of death. SHAKESPEARE.—*Richard II.,* Act 2, 2.

True hope is swift and flies with swallow's wings;
Kings it makes gods, and meaner creatures kings. SHAKESPEARE.—*Richard III.,* Act 5, 2.

The essential truth of life remains,
Its goodness and its beauty too,
Pure love's unutterable gains,
And hope which thrills us through and through;
God has not fled;
Souls are not dead. J. L. SPALDING.—*Believe and Take Heart.*

Hope knows not if fear speaks truth, nor fear whether hope be not blind as she. SWINBURNE.—*England.*

Oh yet we trust that somehow good
Will be the final goal of ill. TENNYSON.—*In Memoriam, c.* 54.

So lives inveterate Hope, on her own hardihood. SIR W. WATSON.—*Hope of the World.*

Hope, the paramount duty that Heaven lays
For its own honour, on man's suffering heart. WORDSWORTH.—*Poems to National Independence, Pt.* 2, 33.

Hope rules a land for ever green:
All powers that serve the bright-eyed Queen
Are confident and gay;
Clouds at her bidding disappear;
Points she to aught? The bliss draws near,
And Fancy smooths the way. WORDSWORTH.—*The Wishing-Gate.*

Hope tells a flattering tale,
Delusive, vain, and hollow;
Ah, let not Hope prevail,
Lest disappointment follow! MISS WROTHER.—*Universal Songster.*

Restless hope, for ever on the wing. YOUNG.—*Night Thoughts,* 7.

Hope, of all passions, most befriends us here. YOUNG.—*Ib.*

Hope deferred maketh the heart sick. *Proverbs* xiii, 12.

Who against hope believed in hope. *Romans* iv, 18.

Be sober, and hope to the end. 1 *St. Peter* i, 13.

Yf hope were not, herte shulde breke.
Gesta Romanorum (15th cent. *MS.*).

Hope told a flattering tale
That joy would soon return.
                ANON.—*Song* (*c.* 1800).

In the wedding cake hope is the sweetest
of the plums.
Quoted as a proverb by C. H. Spurgeon.

HOPELESSNESS

A low, hopeless spirit puts out the eyes ;
scepticism is slow suicide.
                EMERSON.—*Resources.*

For where no hope is left, is left no fear.
MILTON.—*Paradise Regained, Bk.* 3, 206.

Regions of sorrow, doleful shades, where
    peace
And rest can never dwell : hope never
    comes,
That comes to all.
        MILTON.—*Paradise Lost, Bk.* 1, 62.

Alas ! I speak of heaven who am in hell.
I speak of change of days, who know full
    well
How hopeless now is change from misery.
WM. MORRIS.—*Earthly Paradise, Lovers
                of Gudrun,* 45.

I cultivate hope and I see it wither daily.
Alas, what does it serve to water the leaves
when the tree is cut off at its foot ?
                ROUSSEAU.—*Julie.*

HORRORS

        Tiger, tiger, burning bright
        In the forests of the night,
What immortal hand or eye
Dare frame thy fearful symmetry ?
        WM. BLAKE.—*The Tiger.*

Wi' mair o' horrible and awfu',
Which even to name wad be unlawfu'.
        BURNS.—*Tam o' Shanter.*

        Farewell happy fields,
Where joy for ever dwells ! Hail, horrors,
    hail !
    MILTON.—*Paradise Lost, Bk.* 1, 249.

        But that I am forbid
To tell the secrets of my prison house,
I could a tale unfold, whose lightest word
Would harrow up thy soul ; freeze thy
    young blood ;
Make thy two eyes like stars, start from
    their spheres ;
Thy knotted and combined locks to part,
Like quills upon the fretful porcupine.
    SHAKESPEARE.—*Hamlet, Act* 1, 5.

O horrible ! O horrible ! most horrible !
If thou hast nature in thee, bear it not.
        SHAKESPEARE.—*Ib.*

I have supped full with horrors.
    SHAKESPEARE.—*Macbeth, Act* 5, 5.

On horror's head horrors accumulate.
    SHAKESPEARE.—*Othello, Act* 3, 3.

HORSES

A true Philip—a lover of horses [*i.e.*
Phil-hippos].
    DR. J. BROWN.—*Horæ Subsecivæ,
                Agchinoia.*

So that his horse, or charger, hunter,
    hack,
Knew that he had a rider on his back.
        BYRON.—*Don Juan,* 14, 32.

Whose only fit companion is his horse.
        COWPER.—*Conversation,* 412.

His horse, who never in that sort
    Had handled been before,
What thing upon his back had got
    Did wonder more and more.
        COWPER.—*John Gilpin.*

A canter is the cure for every evil.
    DISRAELI.—*Young Duke, Bk.* 2, c. 5.

He made him turn and stop and bound,
To gallop and to trot the round,
He scarce could stand on any ground,
    He was so full of mettle.
            DRAYTON.—*Nymphidia.*

She was iron-sinewed and satin-skinned,
    Ribbed like a drum and limbed like
        a deer,
Fierce as the fire and fleet as the wind,
    There was nothing she couldn't climb
        or clear.
            A. L. GORDON.—*Britomarte.*

If man, of all the Creator planned,
    His noblest work is reckoned,
Of the works of His hand, by sea or land,
    The horse may at least rank second.
        A. L. GORDON.—*Hippodromania.*

Where folks that ride a bit of blood
    May break a bit of bone.
            HOOD.—*Epping Hunt.*

He [the horsedealer] dealeth not in
detraction, and would not disparage the
character even of a brute. Like unto
Love, he is blind to all blemishes.
        HOOD.—*A Horsedealer,* 1832.

There's nothing like a rattling ride
For curing melancholy.
        W. M. PRAED.—*Troubadour.*

        He grew into his seat ;
And to such wondrous doing brought his
        horse,
As he had been incorpsed and demi-natured
With the brave beast.
        SHAKESPEARE.—*Hamlet, Act* 4, 7.

I saw young Harry, with his beaver on,
His cuisses on his thighs, gallantly armed,
Rise from the ground like feathered Mer-
cury,
And vaulted with such ease into his seat,
As if an angel dropped down from the
clouds,
To turn and wind a fiery Pegasus,
And witch the world with noble horseman-
ship.
SHAKESPEARE.—*Henry IV., Pt.* 1, Act 4, 1.

A horse ! a horse ! my kingdom for a horse !
SHAKESPEARE.—*Richard III.*, Act 5, 4.

Look what a horse should have, he did
not lack,
Save a proud rider on so proud a back.
SHAKESPEARE.—*Venus and Adonis*, 50.

Go anywhere in England where there
are natural, wholesome, contented, and
really nice English people ; and what do
you find ? That the stables are the real
centre of the household.
G. B. SHAW.—*Heartbreak House*, Act 3.

Philip of Macedon reckoned a horse-
race, won at Olympus, among his three
fearful felicities.
SIR P. SIDNEY.—*Apology for Poetry.*

Horse-racing is supposed to improve
the breed of horses, but it sadly deterior-
ates the breed of men.
C. H. SPURGEON.—*" Salt-Cellars."*

A horse thou knowest, a man thou dost
not know.
TENNYSON.—*Gareth and Lynette*, 454.

A horse is counted but a vain thing to
save a man.
Psalter (Book of Common Prayer) 14, 6.

HOSPITALITY

The courteous host, and all-approving
guest.   BYRON.—*Lara, c.* 1, 29.

To do the honours of a table gracefully
is one of the outlines of a well-bred man.
LORD CHESTERFIELD.—*Letter to his Son.*

On hospitable thoughts intent.
MILTON.—*Paradise Lost, Bk.* 5, 332.

Be thou familiar, but by no means vulgar.
The friends thou hast, and their adoption
tried,
Grapple them to thy soul with hoops of
steel ;
But do not dull thy palm with entertain-
ment
Of each new-hatched, unfledged comrade.
SHAKESPEARE.—*Hamlet*, Act 1, 3.

Profusion is the charm of hospitality.
Have plenty, if it be only beer.
THACKERAY.—*Barmecide Banquets.*

Given to hospitality.   *Romans* xii, 13.

Thereby some have entertained angels
unawares.   *Hebrews* xiii, 2.

A drap and a bite's but a sma' requite.
Scottish prov.

HOSPITALS

I think it frets the saints in heaven to see
How many desolate creatures on the earth
Have learnt the simple dues of fellowship
And social comfort, in a hospital.
E. B. BROWNING.—*Aurora Leigh, Bk.* 3.

The atmosphere
Suggests the trail of a ghostly druggist.
Dressings and lint on the long, lean table—
Whom are they for ?
W. E. HENLEY.—*In Hospital*, 3.

Behold me waiting—waiting for the knife.
A little while, and at a leap I storm
The thick, sweet mystery of chloroform,
The drunken dark, the little death-in-life.
W. E. HENLEY.—*Ib.*, 4.

HOUSEKEEPING

Dreading that climax of all human ills,
The inflammation of his weekly bills.
BYRON.—*Don Juan, c.* 3, 35.

My sister manages the house for me and
does not leave me much to do as regards
the management of myself.
SIR A. HELPS.—*Friends in Council,
Bk.* 2, *ch.* 3.

Some respite to husbands the weather may
send,
But housewives' affairs have never an end.
T. TUSSER.—*Book of Housewifery.*

Man's work lasts till set of sun ;
Woman's work is never done.
Proverbial saying.

HOUSES

Houses are built to live in and not to
look on.   BACON.—*Of Building.*

A man's house is his castle.
COKE.—*On Littleton.*

Every English family, though it consist
of only two persons, must still have a
house to itself for its own castle.
HEINE.—*London.*

I in my own house am an emperor,
And will defend what's mine.
MASSINGER.—*Roman Actor*, Act 1, 2,

Thanks, sir, cried I, 'tis very fine,
But where d'ye sleep or where d'ye dine ?
I find by all you have been telling
That 'tis a house but not a dwelling.
SWIFT.—*Verses on Blenheim.*

HUMAN NATURE

Pity and need
Make all flesh kin. There is no caste in
    blood,
Which runneth of one hue ; nor caste in
    tears,
Which trickle salt with all.
    SIR E. ARNOLD.—*Light of Asia, Bk.* 6.

We are much beholden to Machiavel
and others, that write what men do, and
not what they ought to do.
BACON.—*Advancement of Learning, Bk.* 2.

Would you have your songs endure ?
Build on the human heart.
    BROWNING.—*Sordello, Bk.* 2.

We have hearts within
Warm, live, improvident, indecent hearts.
    E. B. BROWNING.—*Aurora Leigh, Bk.* 3.

But don't you go and make mistakes, like
    many durned fools I've known,
For dirt is dirt, and snakes is snakes, but
    an Injin's flesh and bone.
    R. BUCHANAN.—*Phil Blood's Leap.*

A fool and knave are plants of every
    soil.   BURNS.—*Prologue.*

Our actions often contradict each other
so amazingly that it seems impossible
that they can have come from the same
shop. CHARRON.—*De la Sagesse, Bk.* 1, 38.

What we all love is good touched up with
    evil—
Religion's self must have a spice of devil.
    A. H. CLOUGH.—*Dipsychus.*

All argument will vanish before one
touch of nature.
    G. COLMAN, JR.—*Poor Gentleman,*
                 Act 5, 1.

Would you know the qualities in which
a man is wanting ? Examine those of
which he boasts.   DE SÉGUR.

Even from the tomb the voice of Nature
    cries,
Even in our ashes live their wonted
    fires.   GRAY.—*Elegy.*

A thorough conviction of the difference
of men is the great thing to be assured of
in social knowledge.
    SIR A. HELPS.—*Friends in Council,*
                Bk. 1, *ch.* 7.

We praise him not for gifts divine,—
    His muse was born of woman,—
His manhood breathes in every line,—
    Was ever heart more human ?
    O. W. HOLMES.—*Burns Centennial.*

Truth is for ever truth, and love is love.
    LEIGH HUNT.—*Hero and Leander,*
                  c. 1, 13.

I have only two comforts to live upon.
The one is in the Perfections of Christ ;
the other is in the Imperfections of all
Christians.
    INCREASE MATHER.—*Saying (attrib.).*

Human nature is not a machine to be
built after a model and set to do exactly
the work prescribed for it, but a tree,
which requires to grow and develop itself
on all sides, according to the tendency
of the inward forces which make it a
living thing. J. S. MILL.—*Liberty, ch.* 3.

Our soul is full of a thousand internal
contrarieties. PLATO.—*Republic, Bk.* 10, 5.

Chaos of thought and passion, all confused ;
Still by himself abused, or disabused ;
Created half to rise, and half to fall ;
Great lord of all things, yet a prey to all ;
Sole judge of truth, in endless error hurled :
The glory, jest, and riddle of the world !
    POPE.—*Essay on Man, Ep.* 2, 13.

Virtuous and vicious every man must be,
Few in the extreme, but all in the degree.
    POPE.—*Ib., Ep.* 2, 231.

How hard it is to hide the sparks of nature !
    SHAKESPEARE.—*Cymbeline, Act* 3, 3.

Virtue ! a fig ! 'tis in ourselves that we
are thus or thus.
    SHAKESPEARE.—*Othello, Act* 1, 3.

You cannot slander human nature ; it
is worse than words can paint it.
    C. H. SPURGEON.—*" Salt-Cellars."*

I thought I could not breathe in that fine
    air,
That pure severity of perfect light—
I wanted warmth and colour, which I
    found
In Lancelot. TENNYSON.—*Guinevere,* 626.

E'en here the tear of pity springs,
And hearts are touched by human things.
    VIRGIL.—*Æneid,* 1, 462 (*Conington tr.*).

Heaven's Sovereign saves all beings, but
    himself,
That hideous sight, a naked human heart.
    YOUNG.—*Night Thoughts,* 3.

HUMANENESS

Mankind will not be reasoned out of the
feelings of humanity.
    BLACKSTONE.—*Commentaries,* 1, 5.

I'm truly sorry man's dominion
Has broken nature's social union,
And justifies the ill opinion,
    Which makes thee startle
At me, thy poor earth-born companion
    And fellow-mortal !
          BURNS.—*To a Mouse.*

Humanely glorious! Men will weep for
him
When many a guilty martial fame is
    dim. CAMPBELL.—*In " La Pérouse's
Voyages."*

He prayeth well who loveth well
Both man and bird and beast.
He prayeth best who loveth best
All things both great and small;
For the dear God, who loveth us,
He made and loveth all.
    COLERIDGE.—*Ancient Mariner, Pt. 7.*

I would not enter on my list of friends
(Though graced with polished manners and
    fine sense,
Yet wanting sensibility) the man
Who needlessly sets foot upon a worm.
    COWPER.—*Winter Morning Walk.*

Take not away the life you cannot give,
For all things have an equal right to live.
    DRYDEN.—*Tr. Ovid, Metam., Bk. 15.*

The behaviour of men to the lower
animals, and their behaviour to each other,
bear a constant relationship.
    HERBERT SPENCER.—*Social Statics, c. 30.*

The Animosities are mortal, but the
Humanities live for ever.
            JOHN WILSON.—*Noctes.*

Never to blend our pleasure or our pride
With sorrow of the meanest thing that
    feels.
    WORDSWORTH.—*Hart-leap Well, Pt. 2.*

Thou shalt not seethe a kid in his
mother's milk.   *Exodus* xxiii, 19.

Thou shalt not muzzle the ox when he
treadeth out the corn. *Deuteronomy* xxv, 4.

HUMBLE ORIGIN

Here rests his head upon the lap of Earth,
A youth to Fortune and to Fame un-
    known,
Fair Science frowned not on his humble
    birth,
And Melancholy marked him for her
    own.   GRAY.—*Elegy.*

I made all my generals out of mud.
                NAPOLEON.

As some divinely-gifted man
Whose life in low estate began,
And on a simple village green;
Who breaks his birth's invidious bar,
And grasps the skirts of happy chance,
And breasts the blows of circumstance,
And grapples with his evil star.
    TENNYSON.—*In Memoriam, c. 64.*

HUMILITY

Soaring you'll sink and sinking you will
    rise;

Let humble thoughts thy wary footsteps
    guide!
Regain by meekness what you lost by
    pride. ARBUTHNOT.—*Gnothi Seauton.*

Nothing is more scandalous than a man
that is proud of his humility.
    MARCUS AURELIUS.—*Bk. 12, 27.*

Life is a long lesson in humility.
SIR J. M. BARRIE.—*Little Minister, c. 3.*

He that is down need fear no fall,
He that is low, no pride.
    BUNYAN.—*Pilgrim's Progress, Pt. 2.*

Humility is the foundation of all virtues.
                CONFUCIUS.

A man should be a guest in his own
house, and a guest in his own thought.
    EMERSON.—*Sovereignty of Ethics.*

In the Christian graces humility stands
highest of all, in the form of the Madonna;
and in life this is the secret of the wise.
    EMERSON.—*Works and Days.*

Humility is the true cure for many a
needless heartache.
    SIR A. HELPS.—*Friends in Council,
Bk. 1, ch. 9.*

A great many people want to be devout,
but no one wants to be humble.
    LA ROCHEFOUCAULD.—*Maxim 613.*

Humility is the altar from which God
would receive sacrifices.
    LA ROCHEFOUCAULD.—*Maxim 616.*

Be lowly wise;
Think only what concerns thee and thy
    being;
Dream not of other worlds.
    MILTON.—*Paradise Lost, Bk. 8, 173.*

Humility, that low, sweet root,
From which all heavenly virtues shoot.
    MOORE.—*Loves of the Angels. Third
Angel's Story.*

Thy sum of duty let two words contain;
(O may they graven in thy heart remain!)
Be humble, and be just.
    PRIOR.—*Solomon, Bk. 3, 873 (The
angel's final advice to Solomon).*

I sing a Man, amid his sufferings here,
Who watched and served with humbleness
    and fear;
Gentle to others, to himself severe.
    ROGERS.—*Voyage of Columbus, c. 6.*

Humility is a virtue all preach, none
practise, and yet everybody is content
to hear.   SELDEN.—*Table Talk.*

I thank my God for my humility.
    SHAKESPEARE.—*Richard III.*, Act 2, 1.

Humility is to have a just idea of yourself.
C. H. Spurgeon.—"*Salt-Cellars.*"

True humility,
The highest virtue, mother of them all.
Tennyson.—*Holy Grail*, 445.

The lowly heart doth win the love of all.
G. Turberville.—*To Piero.*

Set not your mind on high things, but condescend to things that are lowly. Be not wise in your own conceits.
Romans xii, 16 (*R.V.*).

Better eat humble-pie than no pie at all.
Prov.

The vale best discovereth the hills.
Prov. (*quoted by Bacon*).

The meekness of Moses is better than the strength of Samson.
Prov.

HUMOUR

I hasten to laugh at everything, for fear of being obliged to weep.
Beaumarchais.—*Barbier de Séville.*

And if I laugh at any mortal thing,
'Tis that I may not weep.
Byron.—*Don Juan, c.* 44.

A joke's a very serious thing.
C. Churchill.—*The Ghost.*

A rogue alive to the ludicrous is still convertible. If that sense is lost his fellow-men can do little for him.
Emerson.—*Resources.*

Nothing corrects theories better than this sense of humour, which we [Englishmen] have in a greater degree than is to be met with, I believe, in any other people.
Sir A. Helps.—*Friends in Council, Bk.* 2, ch. 5.

All things are big with jest : nothing that's plain
But may be witty, if thou hast the vein.
Herbert.—*Church Porch.*

And since, I never dare to write
As funny as I can.
O. W. Holmes.—*Height of the Ridiculous.*

Is he gone to a land of no laughter,
This man who made mirth for us all?
Jas. Rhoades.—*On the death of Artemus Ward.*

Alas, poor Yorick ! I knew him, Horatio : a fellow of infinite jest, of most excellent fancy. Shakespeare.—*Hamlet*, Act 5, 1.

Argument for a week, laughter for a month, and a good jest for ever.
Shakespeare.—*Henry IV.*, Pt. 1, Act 2, 2.

A merrier man,
Within the limit of becoming mirth,
I never spent an hour's talk withal ;
His eye begets occasion for his wit ;
For every object that the one doth catch
The other turns to a mirth-moving jest.
Shakespeare.—*Love's Labour's Lost,*
Act 1, 1.

A jest's prosperity lies in the ear
Of him that hears it, never in the tongue
Of him that makes it.
Shakespeare.—*Ib.*, Act 5, 2.

Nature hath framed strange fellows in her time ;
Some that will evermore peep through their eyes
And laugh, like parrots, at a bagpiper ;
And other of such vinegar aspect,
That they'll not show their teeth in way of smile
Though Nestor swear the jest be laughable.
Shakespeare.—*Merchant of Venice,*
Act 1, 1.

This fellow's wise enough to play the fool,
And to do that well craves a kind of wit.
Shakespeare.—*Twelfth Night*, Act 3, 1.

It requires a surgical operation to get a joke well into a Scotch understanding.
Sydney Smith.—*Saying.*

Humour is odd, grotesque, and wild,
Only by affectation spoiled ;
'Tis never by invention got,
Men have it when they know it not.
Swift.—*To Mr. Delany*, 1718

I tried him with mild jokes ; then with severe ones. Mark Twain.—*A Deception.*

HUNGER

No one is so laughable as when he is hungry. Plautus.—*Stichus*, Act 2.

Hunger is insolent and will be fed.
Pope.—*Odyssey, Bk.* 7, 380.

It's ill speaking between a fou (full) man and a fasting *Scottish prov.*

HUNTING

If once we efface the joys of the chase
From the land and outroot the Stud,
Goodbye to the Anglo-Saxon race !
Farewell to the Norman blood.
A. L. Gordon.—*Wearie Wayfarer*, 7.

The field kept getting more select,
Each thicket served to thin it !
Hood.—*Epping Hunt.*

It is very strange and very melancholy that the paucity of human pleasures should persuade us ever to call hunting one of them.
Johnson.—*Remark as recorded by Mrs. Piozzi.*

Half the hurry and hubbub and horn-blowing in the world is provided by things invisible till caught and worthless afterwards. But . . . a brush is often won by manlier work than a peerage.
EDEN PHILLPOTTS.—*A Shadow Passes.*

A mighty hunter, and his prey was man.
POPE.—*Windsor Forest*, 62.

Huntsman, rest ! thy chase is done.
SCOTT.—*Lady of the Lake, c.* 1, 32.

The chase I follow far,
'Tis mimicry of noble war.
SCOTT.—*Ib., c.* 2, 26.

Hunting he loved, but love he laughed to scorn.
SHAKESPEARE.—*Venus and Adonis*, 1.

It isn't mere convention. Everyone can see that the people who hunt are the right people, and the people who don't are the wrong ones.
G. B. SHAW.—*Heartbreak House*, Act 3
(*Lady Utterford*).

Invites thee to the Chase, the sport of kings ;
Image of war without its guilt.
W. SOMERVILLE.—*The Chase*, Bk. 1.

Hunting has now an idea of quality joined to it, and is become the most important business in the life of a gentleman. Anciently it was quite otherwise. M. Fleury has severely remarked that this extravagant passion for hunting is a strong proof of our Gothic extraction, and shows an affinity of humour with the savage Americans.
WM. WALSH.—*Pref. to the Pastorals*
(*by Dryden*) (1697).

HUSBANDS

You're not married ; if you were, you would know that being a husband is a whole-time job.
ARNOLD BENNETT.—*The Title.*

Ah, gentle dames ! it gars me greet
To think how mony counsels sweet,
How mony lengthened sage advices
The husband frae the wife despises.
BURNS.—*Tam o' Shanter.*

But oh ! ye lords of ladies intellectual,
Inform us truly, have they not henpecked you all ?
BYRON.—*Don Juan, c.* 1, 22.

" Father to me thou art and mother dear,
And brother too, kind husband of my heart."
KEBLE.—*Christian Year. Monday before Easter.*

A man who admires a fine woman has yet no more reason to wish himself her husband than one, who admired the Hesperian fruit, would have had to wish himself the dragon that kept it.
POPE.—*Thoughts on Various Subjects.*

No woman should marry a teetotaller or a man who does not smoke.
R. L. STEVENSON.—*Virginibus, Pt.* 1.

I am thine husband—not a smaller soul,
Nor Lancelot, nor another.
TENNYSON.—*Guinevere*, 562.

I want to know how it is that women do not find out their husbands to be humbugs. Nature has so provided it.
THACKERAY.—*Ravenswing.*

The husband who wishes to surprise is often badly surprised himself.
VOLTAIRE.—*La Femme qui a Raison.*

Husbands, love your wives, and be not bitter against them.   *Colossians* iii, 19.

HYPERCRITICISM

At every trifle scorn to take offence ;
That always shows great pride, or little sense.   POPE.—*Criticism*, 386.

'Twere to consider too curiously to consider so.
SHAKESPEARE.—*Hamlet*, Act 5, 1.

All his faults observed,
Set in a notebook, learned and conned by rote,
To cast into my teeth.
SHAKESPEARE.—*Julius Cæsar*, Act 4, 3.

But optics sharp it needs, I ween,
To see what is not to be seen.
J. TRUMBULL.—*McFingal.*

HYPOCHONDRIA

Some men employ their health, an ugly trick,
In making known how oft they have been sick.   COWPER.—*Conversation*, 311.

I eat well, drink well and sleep well ; but that's all, Tom, that's all !
C. MORTON.—*Roland for an Oliver*
(*Sir Mark Chase*).

We con ailments, which makes us very fond of each other. SWIFT.—*Letter*, 1711.

She is very much interested in her own health.
OSCAR WILDE.—*Woman of no Importance.*

It's lang ere " like to dee " fills the kirkyard.   *Scottish prov.*

HYPOCRISY

Your cold hypocrisy's a state device,
A worn-out trick.
ADDISON.—*Cato*, Act 1, 3.

Great hypocrites are the real atheists.
BACON.—*Instauratio, Pt.* 1, *Bk.* 6.

It is the wisdom of the crocodiles, that
shed tears when they would devour.
BACON.—*Of Wisdom for a Man's Self.*

God knows I'm no the thing I should be,
Nor am I even the thing I could be,
But twenty times I rather would be
   An atheist clean,
Than under gospel colours hid be,
   Just for a screen.
BURNS.—*Epistle to J. M'Math.*

Compound for sins they are inclined to
By damning those they have no mind to.
BUTLER.—*Hudibras, Pt.* 1, *c.* 1.

As if hypocrisy and nonsense
Had got the advowson of his conscience.
BUTLER.—*Ib.*

Hypocrisy will serve as well
To propagate a church as zeal.
S. BUTLER.—*Miscellaneous Thoughts.*

There's nothing so absurd, or vain,
Or barbarous, or inhumane,
But if it lay the least pretence
To piety and godliness,
Or tender-hearted conscience,
And zeal for gospel-truths profess,
Does sacred instantly commence.
   S. BUTLER.—*On a Hypocritical*
             Nonconformist.

Oh, for a *forty-Parson power* to chant
Thy praise, Hypocrisy.
BYRON.—*Don Juan, c.* 10, 34.

The prayers of Abel linked to deeds of
Cain. BYRON.—*The Island, c.* 2, 4.

If the devil ever laughs it must be at
hypocrites. They are the greatest dupes
he has. C. C. COLTON.—*Lacon.*

My friends, I remember a duty unfulfilled yesterday. It is right that I
should be chastened in some penalty.
DICKENS.—*Bleak House, c.* 19 (*Chadband*).

Art thou a statesman,
And canst not be a hypocrite? Impos-
   sible!
Do not distrust thy virtues.
DRYDEN.—*Don Sebastian*, Act 2, 1.

All uneducated people are hypocrites.
HAZLITT.—*Knowledge of Character.*

I lie, I cheat, do anything for pelf,
But who on earth can say I am not pious?
HOOD.—*Ode to R. Wilson.*

Vice deceives, under the appearance
and shadow of virtue, when sad in its
appearance, and austere in countenance
and dress. JUVENAL.—*Sat.* 14, 109.

Hypocrisy is the homage which vice pays
to virtue.
   LA ROCHEFOUCAULD.—*Maxim* 218.

For neither man nor angel can discern
Hypocrisy, the only evil that walks
Invisible, except to God above.
MILTON.—*Paradise Lost, Bk.* 3, 682.

He was a man
Who stole the livery of the court of Heaven
To serve the Devil in.
R. POLLOK.—*Course of Time, Bk.* 8, 616.

O what a crocodilian world is this!
   F. QUARLES.—*Emblems, Bk.* 1, 4.

'Tis too much proved,—that with devo-
   tion's visage
And pious action, we do sugar o'er
The devil himself.
SHAKESPEARE.—*Hamlet*, Act 3, 1.

Now step I forth to whip hypocrisy.
SHAKESPEARE.—*Love's Labour's Lost*,
            Act 4, 3.

And thus I clothe my naked villainy
With odd old ends stol'n forth of holy writ.
SHAKESPEARE.—*Richard III.*, Act 1, 3.

There is as much folly in hypocrisy as
in vice. It is just as easy to be an honourable man as to seem one. MME. DE STAËL.

A man is at his worst when he pretends
to be good. PUBLILIUS SYRUS.

Are we bound, out of respect for society,
to speak of humbug only in a circumlo-
cutory way—to call it something else, as
they say some Indian people do their devil?
THACKERAY.—*On Men and Pictures.*

To speak like Paul and live like Epicurus.
VOLTAIRE.—*Hypocrisy.*

Indifference and hypocrisy between
them keep orthodoxy alive.
I. ZANGWILL.—*Children of the Ghetto*,
            ch. 15.

Religion is a stalking-horse to shoot
other fowl. *Prov.* (Geo. Herbert).

HYPOTHESIS

For of all sad words of tongue or pen,
The saddest are these: "It might have
   been." WHITTIER.—*Maud Muller.*

If all the world were paper
And all the sea were inke,
If all the trees were bread and cheese,
   How showld we do for drinke?
Wit's Recreations (1640). *Interrogation*
            Cantilena.

May-be's are no aye honey-bees.
Scottish prov.

I

IDEALISM AND IDEALS

But still the heart doth need a language, still
Doth the old instinct bring back the old names.
COLERIDGE.—*Piccolomini*, Act 2, 5.

Whence comes solace ? Not from seeing
What is doing, suffering, being ;
Not from noting life's conditions,
Not from heeding Time's monitions ;
  But in cleaving to the Dream
And in gazing at the gleam
Whereby grey things golden seem.
    T. HARDY.—*On a Fine Morning.*

She's all my fancy painted her,
She's lovely, she's divine.
    WM. MEE.—*Song.*

Wert thou all that I wish thee,—great, glorious, and free—
First flower of the earth, and first gem of the sea.   MOORE.—*Remember thee !*

Swift-footed to uphold the right
And to uproot the wrong.
CHRISTINA ROSSETTI.—*Noble Sisters.*

He is the greatest artist who has embodied, in the sum of his works, the greatest number of the greatest ideas.
    RUSKIN.—*Modern Painters*, 1, Pt. 1,
                  sect. 1.

The idea of her life shall sweetly creep
Into his study of imagination.
    SHAKESPEARE.—*Much Ado*, Act 4, 1.

To unpathed waters, undreamed shores.
    SHAKESPEARE.—*Winter's Tale*, Act 4, 3.

      Ah, my God,
What might I not have made of thy fair world
Had I but loved thy highest creature here ?
It was my duty to have loved the highest :
It surely was my profit had I known :
It would have been my pleasure had I seen.   TENNYSON.—*Guinevere*, 648.

We needs must love the highest when we see it,
Not Lancelot, nor another.
    TENNYSON.—*Ib.*, 654.

To nurse a blind ideal like a girl.
    TENNYSON.—*Princess*, c. 3, 201.

'Tis a thing impossible, to frame
Conceptions equal to the soul's desires.
    WORDSWORTH.—*Excursion*, Bk. 4.

Of all that is most beauteous—imaged there
In happier beauty ; more pellucid streams,
An ampler ether, a diviner air,
And fields invested in purpureal gleams.
    WORDSWORTH.—*Laodamia.*

Ah then, if mine had been the painter's hand,
To express what then I saw, and add the gleam,
The light that never was, on sea or land,
The consecration, and the Poet's dream.
    WORDSWORTH.—*On a picture of*
                  Peele Castle.

IDENTITY

    The real Simon Pure.
MRS. CENTLIVRE.—*Bold Stroke for a Wife.*

I am the true Amphitryon.
    DRYDEN.—*Amphitryon*, Act 5.

I am he, that unfortunate he.
SHAKESPEARE.—*As You Like It*, Act 3, 2.

If it be not Bran (Fingal's dog) it is Bran's brother.   *Highland prov.*

IDLENESS

  He slept beneath the moon,
  He basked beneath the sun ;
  He lived a life of going-to-do,
  And died with nothing done.
    JAS. ALBERY.—*Epitaph.*

An idle life is the life for me—
Idleness spiced with philosophy.
    R. BUCHANAN.—*Fine Weather on the*
                  Digentia, 4.

There is no greater cause of melancholy than idleness.
    BURTON.—*Anatomy of Melancholy.*
    Democritus to the Reader.

    Idleness overthrows all.
    BURTON.—*Ib.*, Pt. 3, sec. 2.

Then cometh Idleness, that is the gate of all harms. . . . Heaven is given to them that will labour, and not to idle folk.   CHAUCER.—*Parson's Tale*, sec. 57
                  (*de Accidia*)

Idleness is only the refuge of weak minds.
EARL OF CHESTERFIELD.—*Letter to his Son.*

Absence of occupation is not rest ;
A mind quite vacant is a mind distressed.
    COWPER.—*Retirement*, 623.

A life of ease, a difficult pursuit.
    COWPER.—*Ib.*, 634.

An idler is a watch that wants both hands,
As useless if it goes as when it stands.
    COWPER.—*Ib.*, 681.

Firm friends to peace, to pleasure, and good pay. COWPER.—*Table Talk*, 194.

Business was his aversion; pleasure was his business.
MISS EDGEWORTH.—*The Contrast, ch.* 1 (*of Philip Folingsby*).

Ye curious carpet knights, that spend the time in sport and play,
Abroad, and see new sights, your country's cause calls you away.
HUMPHREY GIFFORD.—*For Soldiers* (*A Posie of Gilloflowers*, 1580).

Sloth bringeth in all woe.
GOWER.—*Conf. Am.*

Slackness breeds worms.
HERBERT.—*Church Porch.*

Sloth, that shameful siren, is to be shunned. HORACE.—*Sat., Bk.* 2, 3.

It is impossible to enjoy idling thoroughly unless one has plenty of work to do.
J. K. JEROME.—*Idle Thoughts.*

Let the devil never find thee unemployed. ST. JEROME.

Every man is, or hopes to be, an Idler.
JOHNSON.—*Idler.*

Of all our passions the one we are least cognizant of is idleness.
LA ROCHEFOUCAULD.—*Maxim* 572.

It seems as though it must be the devil who has carefully placed idleness across the approach to several virtues.
LA ROCHEFOUCAULD.—*Maxim* 591.

A glorious lazy drone, grown fat with feeding
On others' toil.
MASSINGER.—*Great Duke*, Act 1, 2.

Thus Belial, with words clothed in reason's garb,
Counselled ignoble ease, and peaceful sloth,
Not peace.
MILTON.—*Paradise Lost, Bk.* 2, 226.

Remove idleness, and Cupid's artillery is silenced. OVID.—*Rem. Amoris.*

Stretched on the rack of a too easy chair. POPE.—*Dunciad, Bk.* 4, 342.

No father can transmit to his son the right of being useless to his fellow creatures.
ROUSSEAU.—*Emile.*

Rich or poor, powerful or weak, every idle citizen is a rogue. ROUSSEAU.—*Ib.*

Incapable of doing aught
Yet ill at ease with nought to do.
SCOTT.—*Triermain, c.* 2, 28.

They laboriously do nothing.
SENECA.—*De Brevitate Vitæ.*

If all the year were playing holidays,
To sport would be as tedious as to work.
SHAKESPEARE.—*Henry IV., Pt.* 1, Act 1, 2.

That ghostliest of all unrealities, the non-working man.
G. B. SHAW.—*Irrational Knot, ch.* 17.

For thee, O Idleness! the woes
Of life we patiently endure;
Thou art the source whence Labour flows,
We shun thee but to make thee sure.
CHRISTOPHER SMART.—*To Idleness.*

Sluggish idleness, the nourse of sin.
SPENSER.—*Faerie Queene, Bk.* 1, *c.* 4, 18.

The insupportable labour of doing nothing. STEELE.—*Spectator.*

A pleasing land of drowsy-head it was,
Of dreams that wave before the half-shut eye,
And of gay castles in the clouds that pass.
THOMSON.—*Castle of Indolence, c.* 1, 6.

Their only labour was to kill the time;
And labour dire it is, and heavy woe.
THOMSON.—*Ib., c.* 1, 72.

For sluggard's brow the laurel never grows;
Renown is not the child of indolent repose.
THOMSON.—*Ib., c.* 2, 50.

My profession is the profession of having none. VOLTAIRE.—*Les Originaux* (*Le Chevalier du Hasard*).

But when dread Sloth, the Mother of Doom, steals in,
And reigns where Labour's glory was to serve,
Then is the day of crumbling not far off.
SIR W. WATSON.—*The Mother of Doom* (*August* 28, 1919).

For Satan finds some mischief still
For idle hands to do.
I. WATTS.—*Against Idleness.*

'Tis the voice of the sluggard, I heard him complain
"You have waked me too soon, I must slumber again;"
As the door on its hinges, so he on his bed
Turns his sides and his shoulders and his heavy head. I. WATTS.—*Sluggard.*

For who does nothing with a better grace? YOUNG.—*Love of Fame, Sat.* 4.

"What are you doing, Joe?" said I,
"Nothing, sir," was his reply;
"And your job, Tom, I'd like to know?"
"I'm busy, sir—I'm helping Joe." ANON.

Blame is the lazy man's wages.
Danish prov.

He lives unworthily through whom no other person lives. *Latin prov.*

As lazy as Ludlam's dog, that leaned his head against the wall to bark.
Prov. (Ray).

He that does nothing finds helpers.
Prov.

Idle bodies are generally busybodies.
Prov.

Idleness is the devil's bolster. *Prov.*

Katie Sweerock, frae where she sat,
Cried " Reik (reach) me this and reik me
that." *Scottish saying.*

IF

Your " if " is the only peace-maker ; much virtue in " if."
SHAKESPEARE.—*As You Like It*, Act 5, 4.

With an " if " you might put Paris in a bottle. *French prov.*

If my aunt had wheels she would be an omnibus. *German prov.*

If my aunt had been a man, she'd have been my uncle. *Prov. (Ray's collection).*

IGNORANCE

'Tis ignorance makes the child sublime.
G. BARLOW.—*Poetry and Science*, 17.

Be ignorance thy choice, where knowledge leads to woe.
BEATTIE.—*The Minstrel*, Bk. 2, 30.

Ignorance is not innocence, but sin.
BROWNING.—*Inn Album*, c. 5.

The truest characters of ignorance
Are vanity and pride and arrogance.
S. BUTLER.—*Miscellaneous Thoughts.*

For men are grown above all knowledge
now,
And what they're ignorant of disdain to
know.
S. BUTLER.—*On the Licentiousness of the
Age.*

Until you understand a writer's ignorance, presume yourself ignorant of his
understanding.
COLERIDGE.—*Biog. Literaria, ch.* 12
(*his " golden rule* ")

Ignorance lies at the bottom of all
human knowledge, and the deeper we
penetrate, the nearer we arrive unto it.
C. C. COLTON.—*Lacon.*

General ignorance—in which accomplishment I excelled.
DE QUINCEY.—*Opium Eater.*

Some minds seem well glazed by nature
against the admission of knowledge.
GEO. ELIOT.—*Theophrastus Such. A
Political Molecule.*

The man in the street does not know a
star in the sky. EMERSON.—*Self-Reliance.*

Thought would destroy their Paradise.
No more :—where ignorance is bliss
'Tis folly to be wise.
GRAY.—*Eton College.*

Like Montanus [in Holberg's comedy
' Erasmus Montanus '] I assert that the
earth is flat, my friends. My eyes de-
ceived me ; it is flat,—flat as a pancake !
Now are you satisfied ?
IBSEN.—*Love's Comedy*, Act 3 (1862).

He that voluntarily continues ignorance
is guilty of all the crimes which ignorance
produces.
JOHNSON.—*Letter to W. Drummond,
Aug.* 30, 1766.

Art hath an enemy called ignorance.
BEN JONSON.—*Every Man Out of his
Humour.*

The only useful conquests, the only
conquests which leave no sort of regret
behind, are the conquests one makes over
ignorance. NAPOLEON I.

Fools grant whate'er ambition craves,
And men, once ignorant, are slaves.
POPE.—*Choruses to " Brutus,"* 26.

From ignorance our comfort flows,
The only wretched are the wise.
PRIOR.—*To C. Montague.*

For when I dinna clearly see,
I always own I dinna ken,
And that's the way with wisest men.
ALLAN RAMSAY.—*Eclogue.*

Let me not burst in ignorance !
SHAKESPEARE.—*Hamlet*, Act 1, 4.

Ignorance is the curse of God,
Knowledge the wing wherewith we fly to
heaven.
SHAKESPEARE.—*Henry VI.*, Pt. 2,
Act 4, 7.

A very superficial, ignorant unweighing
fellow. SHAKESPEARE.—*Measure for
Measure*, Act 3, 2.

There is no darkness but ignorance.
SHAKESPEARE.—*Twelfth Night*, Act 4, 2.

In knowing nothing is the sweetest life.
SOPHOCLES.—*Ajax.*

Our lives are usually shortened by our
ignorance.
HERBERT SPENCER,—*Principles of Biology,
Pt.* 6, *c.* 12, 372.

For as of old mathematicians
Were by the vulgar thought magicians,
So academic dull ale-drinkers
Pronounce all men of wit free-thinkers.
    SWIFT.—*To Dr. Delany*, 1729.

Where blind and naked ignorance
Delivers brawling judgments, unashamed,
On all things all day long.
    TENNYSON.—*Merlin and Vivien*, 662.

ILL-NATURE

Set not thy foot to make the blind to fall,
    Nor wilfully offend thy weaker brother,
Nor wound the dead with thy tongue's
        bitter gall ;
    Neither rejoice thou in the fall of
        other.   R. BURTON.—*From
            " Pybrac, Quadraint,"* 37.

In working evils for another a man
works evils for himself.
    HESIOD.—*Works and Days*, 265.

For pointed satire, I would Buckhurst
    choose,
The best good man with the worst-natured
    Muse.   EARL OF ROCHESTER.—
        Allusion to Horace.

ILLITERACY

He can't write nor rade writing from
his cradle, plase your honour ; but he can
make his mark equal to another, sir.
    MISS EDGEWORTH.—*Love and Law*, Act
    3, 1 (*Catty Rooney, of Ulick Rooney*).

For there be women fair as she
Whose verbs and nouns do more agree.
    BRET HARTE.—*Mrs. Judge Jenkins.*

He hath never fed of the dainties that
are bred in a book ; he hath not eat paper,
as it were ; he hath not drunk ink ; his
intellect is not replenished ; he is only an
animal, only sensible in the duller parts.
    SHAKESPEARE.—*Love's Labour's Lost,*
        4. 2.

ILLNESS

The surest way to health, say what they
    will,
Is never to suppose we shall be ill.
    C. CHURCHILL.—*Night*, 69.

Is there no hope ? the sick man said ;
The silent doctor shook his head.
    GAY.—*Fables*, Pt. 1, 27.

Now I am past all comforts here but
    prayers.   SHAKESPEARE.—*Henry
        VIII.*, Act 4, 2.

Be lang sick that ye may be sune hale.
        Scottish prov.

ILLUSION

What youth deemed crystal, age finds out
    was dew.
    BROWNING.—*Jochanan Hakkadosh.*

Half our daylight faith's a fable ;
Sleep disports with shadows too.
    CAMPBELL.—*A Dream.*

    Beauty's witching sway
Is now to me a star that's fallen—a dream
    that's passed away.
    CAMPBELL.—*Farewell to Love.*

Why should we strive, with cynic frown,
To knock their fairy castles down ?
    ELIZA COOK.—*Dear to Memory.*

The restless throbbings and burnings,
    That hope unsatisfied brings,
The weary longings and yearnings,
    For the mystical better things,
Are the sands on which is reflected
    The pitiless moving lake,
Where the wanderer falls dejected
    By a thirst he can never slake.
    A. L. GORDON.—*Wormwood and
            Nightshade.*

Dream on ! there's nothing but illusion
    true. O. W. HOLMES.—*The Old Player.*

So does the glory depart, and so dangerous and disillusioning is it to grow up.
    E. V. LUCAS.—*One Day and Another.*

Like Dead Sea fruits, that tempt the eye,
    But turn to ashes on the lips.
        MOORE.—*Lalla Rookh.*

O futile fires ! the counterpart are ye
Of most that we
Heap for our prizes, gather for our goal ;
While overhead the steadfast stars still
    burn,
And shine their challenge to the human
    soul.
    EDEN PHILLPOTTS.—*Dance of the Months,
            Jack o' Lantern (July).*

When all the illusions of his Youth were
    fled,
Indulged perhaps too much, cherished too
    long.   ROGERS.—*Italy, Arquà.*

O, who can hold a fire in his hand
By thinking on the frosty Caucasus ?
Or cloy the hungry edge of appetite
By bare imagination of a feast ?
Or wallow naked in December snow
By thinking on fantastic summer's heat ?
    SHAKESPEARE.—*Richard II.*, Act 1, 3.

Ah ! whither now are fled
Those dreams of greatness ? those un-
    solid hopes
Of happiness ? Those longings after
    fame ?
Those restless cares ? those busy, bustling
    days ?
Those gay-spent, festive nights ?
    THOMSON.—*Winter*, 1033.

IMAGINATION

Rub out the colours of imagination.
    MARCUS AURELIUS.—*Bk. 7, 29.*

Supposition is greater than truth.
BACON (*Given as a quotation in a letter to Lord Essex*).

To see the world in a grain of sand,
And a heaven in a wild flower.
WM. BLAKE.—*Auguries of Innocence.*

I know of no other Christianity and of no other gospel than the liberty both of body and mind to exercise the divine arts of imagination. WM. BLAKE.—*Jerusalem.*

What is now proved was once only imagined. WM. BLAKE.—*Proverbs of Hell.*

Imagination hath a grasp of joy
Finer than sense.
R. BRIDGES.—*Return of Ulysses*, Act 2.

One does see somewhat when one shuts one's eyes. BROWNING.—*Mr. Sludge.*

Thou wert a beautiful thought, and softly bodied forth.
BYRON.—*Childe Harold*, c. 4, 115.

Or wallow naked in December's snow,
By bare remembrance of the summer's heat.
C. CIBBER.—*Richard III.* (*Shakespeare adapted*) Act 1, 1.

Good sense is the Body of poetic genius, Fancy its drapery, Motion its Life, and Imagination the Soul that is everywhere and in each, and forms all into one graceful and intelligent whole.
COLERIDGE.—*Biog. Literaria*, ch. 14.

Some of your griefs you have cured,
And the sharpest you still have survived ;
But what torments of pain you endured
From evils that never arrived !
EMERSON.—*From " an old French verse "* (*Conduct of Life. Considerations by the way*).

Don't let us make imaginary evils, when you know we have so many real ones to encounter.
GOLDSMITH.—*Good-natured Man*, Act 1.

Imagination and memory are but one thing, which for divers considerations hath divers names.
HOBBES.—*Leviathan, Bk.* 1, *ch.* 2.

Imagination's paper kite,
Unless the string is held in tight,
Whatever fits and starts it takes,
Soon bounces on the ground and breaks.
W. S. LANDOR.—*Miscell.*, 306. *To Barry Cornwall.*

It is imagination which rules the human race. NAPOLEON.

The faculty of degrading God's works which man calls his " imagination."
RUSKIN.—*Modern Painters, Pref.*

The essence of the Imaginative faculty is utterly mysterious and inexplicable, and to be recognized in its results only.
RUSKIN.—*Ib., Vol.* 2 *Pt.* 3, *ch.* 1, 2.

This is the very coinage of your brain :
This bodiless creation ecstasy
Is very cunning in.
SHAKESPEARE.—*Hamlet*, Act 3, 4.

Give me an ounce of civet, good apothecary, to sweeten my imagination.
SHAKESPEARE.—*Lear*, Act 4, 6.

Poetry, in a general sense, may be defined to be " the expression of the imagination."
SHELLEY.—*Defence of Poetry* (1821).

Reason is to imagination as the instrument to the agent, as the body to the spirits, as the shadow to the substance.
SHELLEY.—*Ib.*

Imagination is the faculty which " images " within the mind the phenomena of sensation.
WM. TAYLOR.—*English Synonyms Described* (1813).

For any man with half an eye
What stands before him may espy ;
But optics sharp it needs, I ween,
To see what is not to be seen.
J. TRUMBULL.—*McFingal.*

We cannot reproach our author for having invented what he states ; nothing would be more unjust than to attribute imagination to him.
VOLTAIRE.—*On the Memoirs of Dangeau.*

Then blame not those who, by the mightiest lever
Known to the moral world, Imagination,
Upheave, so seems it, from her natural station,
All Christendom.
WORDSWORTH.—*Eccles. Sonnets, Pt.* 1, 34 (*Crusades*).

Imagination wanders far afield.
YOUNG.—*Night Thoughts*, 8.

A powerful imagination brings about the event.
Latin saying quoted by Montaigne.

IMITATION

No, not a good imitation of Johnson. It has all his pomp, without his force ; it has all the nodosities of the oak without its strength ; it has all the contortions of the sibyl, without the inspiration.
BURKE.—*See Prior's " Life of Burke."*

Imitation is the sincerest of flattery.
C. C. COLTON.—*Lacon.*

No man was ever great by imitation.
JOHNSON.—*Rasselas.*

We are all quick to imitate what is base
and depraved.   JUVENAL.—*Sat.* 14.

Wherever a poet of the first order has
appeared, before long a rank crop of
wretched imitators follows.
　　KEBLE.—*Lectures on Poetry, No.* 16
　　　　　　　　(E. K. Francis, tr.).

Most can raise the flowers now,
For all have got the seed.
　　　　　TENNYSON.—*The Flower*.

As if his whole vocation
Were endless imitation.
　　WORDSWORTH.—*Intimations of
　　　　　　　　Immortality*.

IMMORTALITY

It must be so,—Plato, thou reasonest
well !—
Else whence this pleasing hope, this fond
desire,
This longing after immortality ?
　　　　　ADDISON.—*Cato*, Act 5.

They shall not grow old, as we that are
left grow old ;
Age shall not weary them, nor the years
condemn.
At the going down of the sun, and in the
morning
We will remember them.
　　LAURENCE BINYON.—*For the Fallen*.

The graves of those that cannot die.
　　　　　BYRON.—*Giaour*, 140.

If I err in this, that I believe the souls
of men to be immortal, I err of my own
free will ; nor do I wish this error, in which
I find delight, to be wrested from me as
long as I live. CICERO.—*Of old age*, 23, 86.

To things immortal, Time can do no wrong,
And that which never is to die, for ever
must be young.
　　COWLEY.—*To Dr. Scarborough*.

If death do quench us quite, we have
great wrong.
　　SIR J. DAVIES.—*Nosce Teipsum*.

If then all souls, both good and bad do
teach
　With general voice, that souls can never
die ;
'Tis not man's flattering gloss, but Nature's
speech,
　Which, like God's oracles, can never lie.
　　SIR J. DAVIES.—*Ib., sec.* 30.

Immortality will come to such as are
fit for it, and he who would be a great
soul in future must be a great soul now.
　　EMERSON.—*Conduct of Life, Worship*.

Let no one honour me with tears or bury
me with lamentation. Why ? Because
I fly hither and thither, living in the
mouths of men. ENNIUS (*quoted by Cicero*).

For thou art Freedom's now, and Fame's :
One of the few immortal names
　That were not born to die.
　FITZ-GREENE HALLECK.—*Marco Bozzaris*.

I saw a dead man's finer part
Shining within each faithful heart
Of those bereft.　Then said I, " This must
be
His Immortality."
　　　　　T. HARDY.—*His Immortality*.

On wing sublime eternal valour soars,
And scorning human haunts and earthly
shores,
To those, whom Godlike deeds forbid to
die,
Unbars the gate of immortality.
　　HORACE.—*Odes, Bk.* 3, 2 (*tr. by
　　　　　　　　Wm. Pitt, jun.*).

In the wreck of noble lives
Something immortal still survives !
　　LONGFELLOW.—*Building of the Ship*.

Yet some there be that by due steps
aspire
To lay their just hands on that golden
key
That opes the palace of Eternity.
　　　　　MILTON.—*Comus*, 12.

We have nothing about us immortal
except the good qualities of our hearts and
intellects.　　OVID.—*Trist.*, 3, 7.

Then, as it seems, we shall obtain that
which we desire and which we profess
ourselves to be lovers of,—wisdom, when
we are dead, as reason shows, but not
while we are alive.
　　PLATO—*Phædo*, 30 (*Cary tr.*).

Ye are but poor philosophers, ye who do
say we must
Wane with the years in grief and tears
and turn again to the dust ;
Our Souls are ourselves—(though our dust
be dust, and our body sinks to the sod)
Coeval with all Eternity—and part of the
Very God.
　　LT.-COL. DUDLEY SAMPSON.—*Songs
　　　　　　　　of Love and Life*.

Age cannot wither her, nor custom stale
Her infinite variety.
　　SHAKESPEARE.—*Antony and
　　　　　　　　Cleopatra*, Act 2, 2.

But thy eternal summer shall not fade.
　　SHAKESPEARE.—*Sonnet* 18.

You still shall live—such virtue hath my
pen—
Where breath most breathes, even in the
mouths of men.
　　SHAKESPEARE.—*Sonnet* 81.

The shadow stayed not, but the splendour
stays,
Our brother, till the last of English days.
　　SWINBURNE.—*In the Bay*.

All outward wisdom yields to that within,
Whereof nor creed nor canon holds the
   key ;
We only feel that we have ever been,
   And evermore shall be.
        B. TAYLOR.—*Metempsychosis.*

I will give them an everlasting name,
that shall not be cut off.   *Isaiah* lvi, 5.

One thing is certain, when this life is o'er,
We die to live, and live to die no more.
        Epitaph at Brighton.

IMPENITENCE

No power can the impenitent absolve.
    DANTE.—*Inferno (Cary's tr.), c.* 27,
                     114.

May one be pardoned and retain th'
   offence ?
    SHAKESPEARE.—*Hamlet,* Act 3, 3.

He dies and makes no sign : O God, forgive him !   SHAKESPEARE.—*Henry
         VI., Pt.* 2, Act 3, 3.

IMPERFECTION

What does Man see or feel or apprehend,
Here, there, and everywhere, but faults
   to mend,
Omissions to supply,—one wide disease
Of things that are, which Man at once
   would ease,
Had will but power and knowledge?
    BROWNING.—*Francis Furini.*

Skill comes so slow, and life so fast doth
   fly,
We learn so little and forget so much.
    SIR J. DAVIES.—*Nosce Teipsum.*

   The best of what we do and are,
     Just God, forgive.
WORDSWORTH.—*On the Banks of Nith.*

Let other bards of angels sing,
   Bright suns without a spot ;
But thou art no such perfect thing ;
   Rejoice that thou art not !
    WORDSWORTH.—*To Mrs. —*

The flawed pot lasts longest.—*Prov.*

IMPETUOUSNESS

The tigers of wrath are wiser than the
horses of instruction.
    WM. BLAKE.—*Proverbs of Hell.*

And though he stumbles in a full career,
Yet rashness is a better fault than fear.
    DRYDEN.—*Tyrannic Love, Prol.*

His rash fierce blaze of riot cannot last,
For violent fires soon burn out themselves ;
Small showers last long, but sudden
   storms are short.
    SHAKESPEARE.—*Richard II.,* 2, 1.

IMPORTUNITY

Oliver Twist has asked for more.
    DICKENS.—*Oliver Twist, ch.* 2.

Hold the fleet angel fast until he bless thee.
    LONGFELLOW.—*Kavanagh.*

Antigonus the Elder, wearied of the
importunity of Bias, said to his servants,
" Give one talent to Bias, because it must
be so."   PLUTARCH.—*Morals, Bk.* 1.

Ask me no more, the moon may draw the
   sea.
    TENNYSON.—*Princess, c.* 7, *Song.*

The horseleach hath two daughters
crying, Give, give.   *Proverbs* xxx, 15.

IMPOSSIBILITY

It is not a lucky word this same *impossible :* no good comes of those that have
it so often in their mouth.
    CARLYLE.—*Chartism, ch.* 10.

And what's impossible can't be,
And never, never comes to pass.
    G. COLMAN.—*Maid of the Moor.*

Impossible is a word I never say.
    COLLIN D'HARLEVILLE.—*Malice pour
                 Malice* (1793).

    A wise man never
Attempts impossibilities.
    MASSINGER.—*Renegado,* Act 1, 1.

Impossible ! Never say that foolish
word to me !
    MIRABEAU.—*(as quoted by Carlyle).*

You write " It is not possible." That
is not French.
    NAPOLEON.—*Letter,* July 9, 1813.

IMPOTENCE

Thou canst hurt no man's fame with thy
   ill word ;
Thy pen is full as harmless as thy sword.
    SIR C. SCROPE.—*On Lord Rochester.*

And as, when heavy sleep has closed the
   sight,
The sickly fancy labours in the night ;
We seem to run, and destitute of force,
Our sinking limbs forsake us in the course :
In vain we heave for breath ; in vain we
   cry ;
The nerves unbraced their usual strength
   deny.
    VIRGIL.—*Æneid, Bk.* 12 *(Dryden tr.).*

IMPRESSIONABILITY

His heart was one of those which most
   enamour us,
Wax to receive, and marble to retain.
    BYRON.—*Beppo,* 34.

And when she ceased, we sighing saw
The floor lay paved with broken hearts.
  R. LOVELACE.—*Gratiana Dancing.*

No; life is a waste of wearisome hours,
 Which seldom the rose of enjoyment
  adorns;
And the heart that is soonest awake to the
  flowers,
 Is always the first to be touched by the
  thorns. MOORE.—*O Think Not.*

You are not wood, you are not stones, but
  men.
 SHAKESPEARE.—*Julius Cæsar*, Act 3, 2.

I am a part of all that I have met.
   TENNYSON.—*Ulysses.*

Thanks to the human heart by which we
  live,
Thanks to its tenderness, its joys, its
  fears,
To me the meanest flower that blows can
  give
Thoughts that do often lie too deep for
  tears.
  WORDSWORTH.—*Intimations of
    Immortality, c.* 11.

IMPRESSIVENESS

He, above the rest
In shape and gesture proudly eminent,
Stood like a tower.
  MILTON.—*Paradise Lost*, 1, 589.

Earth has not anything to show more
  fair:
Dull would he be of soul who could pass
  by
A sight so touching in its majesty.
  WORDSWORTH.—*Miscell. Sonnets*, 36.

IMPROMPTU

Impromptu is truly the touchstone of
wit.
MOLIÈRE.—*Les précieuses ridicules, sc.* 10.

Poured forth his unpremeditated strain.
 THOMSON.—*Castle of Indolence, c.* 1, 68.

IMPROVEMENT

Nothing is clearer to me than that the
present period of your life is as good for
philosophy and for improvement as any
other. MARCUS AURELIUS.—*Bk.* 11, 7.

The spirit of improvement is not always
a spirit of liberty, for it may aim at forcing
improvements on an unwilling people.
  J. S. MILL.—*Liberty, ch.* 3.

IMPROVIDENCE

Buy what thou hast no need of, and
ere long thou shalt sell thy necessaries.
 B. FRANKLIN.—*Poor Richard's Almanac.*

Who cannot live on twenty pounds a year
Cannot on forty; he's a man of pleasure,
A kind of thing that's for itself too dear.
  HERBERT.—*Church Porch.*

If people take no care for the future they
will soon have to sorrow for the present.
   Chinese prov.

He who reckons without his host,
May chance to find his labour lost.
   Old Saying.

IMPUDENCE

You have the gift of impudence; be thank-
 ful;
Every man has not the like talent.
 BEAUMONT AND FLETCHER.—*Wild
    Goose Chase.*

For he that has but impudence,
To all things has a just pretence.
 S. BUTLER.—*Miscellaneous Thoughts.*

"You don't happen to know why they
killed the pig, do you?" retorts Mr.
Bucket. ... "Why, they killed him...
on account of his having so much cheek."
  DICKENS.—*Bleak House, c.* 53.

Bold knaves thrive, without one grain of
 sense,
But good men starve for want of impudence. DRYDEN.—*Constantine, Ep.*

Nae wut without a portion o' impertinence. JOHN WILSON.—*Noctes,* 30.

When facts were weak, his native cheek
 Brought him serenely through.
"*Said of an eminent lawyer*" (*according
   to C. H. Spurgeon*).

IMPULSIVENESS

A thing of impulse and a child of song.
  BYRON.—*Don Juan*, 8, 24.

"Halloa! here's a church... Let's go
in!"... "Halloa!" said Wemmick,
"here's Miss Skiffins! Let's have a
wedding!"
 DICKENS.—*Great Expectations, ch.* 55.

A fiery soul, which, working out its way,
Fretted the pigmy body to decay.
 DRYDEN.—*Absalom and Achitophel,
    Pt.* 1, 156.

The pupil of impulse, it forced him along,
His conduct still right, with his argument
wrong. GOLDSMITH.—*Retaliation.*

Hasty impulse (impetus) manages all
things badly. STATIUS.—*Thebais.*

Ah, well! the world is discreet;
 There are plenty to pause and wait;
But here was a man who set his feet
 Sometimes in advance of fate.
  J. G. WHITTIER.—*On G. L. Smith.*

A youth to whom was given
So much of earth, so much of heaven,
And such impetuous blood.
     WORDSWORTH.—*Ruth.*

INACTION

As idle as a painted ship
Upon a painted ocean.
  COLERIDGE.—*Ancient Mariner, Pt. 2.*

Admirals, extolled for standing still,
And doing nothing with a deal of skill.
    COWPER.—*Table Talk,* 191.

A Book of Verses underneath the Bough,
A Jug of Wine, a Loaf of Bread—and
 Thou
Beside me singing in the Wilderness—
Oh, Wilderness were Paradise enow!
   E. FITZGERALD.—*Rubaiyat, st.* 12.

The Commons, faithful to their system,
remained in a wise and masterly inactivity.
  SIR J. MACKINTOSH.—*Vindiciæ Gallicæ.*

INAPPROPRIATENESS

When a dog is drowning everyone offers
him drink.   *Prov.* (Geo. Herbert).

You mustn't tie up a dog with a string
of sausages.   *Prov.*

INCLINATION

She is far too clever to understand anything she does not like.
   A. BENNETT.—*The Title* (1918), Act 1.

Men, as well as women, are much oftener
led by their hearts than by their understandings.
 LORD CHESTERFIELD.—*Advice to his Son.*

For though with judgment we on things
 reflect,
Our will determines, not our intellect.
    WALLER.—*Divine Love, c.* 1.

INCOHERENCE

These are but wild and whirling words,
 my lord.
   SHAKESPEARE.—*Hamlet,* Act 1, 5.

Put your discourse into some frame,
and start not so wildly from my affair.
    SHAKESPEARE.—*Ib.,* Act 3, 2.

It is a tale
Told by an idiot, full of sound and fury,
Signifying nothing.
   SHAKESPEARE.—*Macbeth,* Act 5, 5.

I understand a fury in your words,
But not the words.
   SHAKESPEARE.—*Othello,* Act 4, 2.

INCOME TAX

Taxing is an easy business. Any pro-
jector can contrive new impositions, any
bungler can add to the old; but is it altogether wise to have no other bounds to
your impositions than the patience of
those who are to bear them? BURKE.

Robin: On Tuesday I made a false income tax return. *All:* Ha! ha! 1st
Ghost: That's nothing. *2nd Ghost:*
Nothing at all. *3rd Ghost:* Everybody
does that. *4th Ghost:* It's expected of
you. SIR W. S. GILBERT.—*Ruddigore.*

These exactions,
Whereof my sovereign would have note,
 they are
Most pestilent to the hearing; and, to bear
 'em
The back is sacrifice to the load.
  SHAKESPEARE.—*Henry VIII.,* 1, 2.

INCOMPLETENESS

Never the time and the place
And the loved one all together!
  BROWNING.—*Never the Time.*

Inscribe all human effort with one word,
Artistry's haunting curse, the Incomplete!
BROWNING.—*Ring and the Book,* 11, 1560.

INCONGRUITY

Did He smile His work to see?
Did He who made the lamb make thee?
   WM. BLAKE.—*The Tiger.*

The offspring of ill-mated things is disagreement. OVID.—*Metam.,* 1.

Those who make the shoe do not feel it
pinch, and those who feel it pinch do not
know how shoes are made.
   SIR F. POLLOCK.—*Land Laws, ch.* 1.

Pretty in amber to observe the forms
Of hairs, or straws, or dirt, or grubs or
 worms!
The things, we know, are neither rich nor
 rare,
But wonder how the devil they get there.
    POPE.—*Prol. to Satires.*

If you choose to represent the various
parts in life by holes upon a table, of
different shapes,—some circular, some
triangular, some square, some oblong—
and the persons acting those parts by bits
of wood of similar shapes, we shall generally find that the triangular person has
got into the square hole, the oblong into
the triangular, and a square person has
squeezed himself into the round hole.
  SYDNEY SMITH.—*Lectures on Moral
     Philosophy, No.* 9.

In half the affairs of this busy life
(As that same day I said to my wife),
Our troubles come from trying to put
The left-hand shoe on the right-hand foot.
Saying quoted or invented by C. H. Spurgeon.

How agree the kettle and the earthen pot
together ?   *Ecclesiasticus* xiii, 2.

You cannot make a sparrow-hawk out
of a buzzard.   *French prov. (Roman de
la Rose).*

He that has teeth has not bread ; he
that has bread has not teeth.   *Italian prov.*

INCONSISTENCY

A marciful Providunce fashioned us holler,
O' purpose thet we might our principles
swaller.
J. R. LOWELL.—*Biglow Papers, series* 1, 4.

INCONSTANCY

Thy favours are but like the wind
That kisseth everything it meets.
SIR R. AYTON.—*I do confess.*

Of her scorn the maid repented,
And the shepherd of his love.
ANNA L. BARBAULD.—*Leave me, simple
shepherd.*

Maidens' hearts are always soft :
Would that men's were truer !
W. CULLEN BRYANT.—*Song.*

Let not woman e'er complain,
Fickle man is apt to rove :
Look abroad through nature's range,
Nature's mighty law is change.
BURNS.—*Let not woman e'er complain.*

Had sighed to many, though he loved but
one.   BYRON.—*Childe Harold, c.* 1, 5.

As Juan mused on mutability,
Or on his mistress—terms synonymous.
BYRON.—*Don Juan,* 15, 20.

The sea-green Incorruptible [Robespierre].
CARLYLE.—*French Revolution.*

The miracle to-day is that we find
A lover true : not that a woman's kind.
CONGREVE.—*Love for Love,* Act 5, 2.

The world's a scene of changes ; and to be
Constant, in Nature were inconstancy.
COWLEY.—*Inconstancy.*

Your Cleopatra, Dolabella's Cleopatra,
every man's Cleopatra !
DRYDEN.—*All for Love,* Act 4, 1.

Fool, not to know that love endures no tie,
And Jove but laughs at lovers' perjury.
DRYDEN.—*Palamon, Bk.* 2, 148.

How happy could I be with either,
Were t'other dear charmer away !

But while ye thus tease me together,
To neither a word will I say.
GAY.—*Beggar's Opera,* Act 2, 2.

Pretty Polly, say,
When I was away,
Did your fancy never stray
To some newer lover ?
GAY.—*Ib.*

Campaspe : Were women never so fair
men would be false.—*Apelles :* Were
women never so false, men would be fond.
LYLY.—*Alexander and Campaspe,*
Act 3, 3.

They that do change old love for new,
Pray gods they change for worse.
PEELE.—*Arraignment of Paris, Act* 1, 2.

Too dear I prized a fair enchanting face :
Beauty unchaste is beauty in disgrace.
POPE.—*Odyssey, Bk.* 8, 359.

Since 'tis Nature's law to change,
Constancy alone is strange.
EARL OF ROCHESTER.—*Dialogue.*

Murderous darts, blindness, and wings
are Cupid's attributes. The wings signify
inconstancy, which, as a rule, comes with
the disillusion following possession.
SCHOPENHAUER.—*Metaphysics of Love.*

Credit me, friend, it hath been ever thus,
Since the ark rested on Mount Ararat :
False man hath sworn, and woman hath
believed—
Repented and reproached, and then be-
lieved once more.
SCOTT.—*Fortunes of Nigel, ch.* 20.

Sigh no more ladies, sigh no more,
Men were deceivers ever.
SHAKESPEARE.—*Much Ado,* Act 2, 3.

Were man
But constant, he were perfect.
SHAKESPEARE.—*Two Gentlemen of
Verona,* Act 5, 4.

There is nothing in this world constant,
but inconstancy.
SWIFT.—*Faculties of the Mind.*

Who never sold the truth to serve the
hour,
Nor paltered with Eternal God for power.
TENNYSON.—*Duke of Wellington.*

With men and women 'tis alike the way,
To hate to-morrow what they love to-day.
D. W. THOMPSON.—*Sales Attici.*

I have somewhat against thee, because
thou hast left thy first love.
Revelation ii, 4.

Woman changeable we find,
As a feather in the wind.
Tr. of Italian prov.

INDECISION

Half the failures in life arise from pulling in one's horse as he is leaping.
J. C. HARE.—*Guesses at Truth, vol.* 1.

Like a man to double business bound,
I stand in pause where I shall first begin.
SHAKESPEARE.—*Hamlet,* Act 3, 3.

Lord Chatham, with his sword drawn,
Is waiting for Sir Richard Strachan ;
Sir Richard, longing to be at 'em,
Is waiting for the Earl of Chatham.
Epigram (1809), *referring to failure of the Earl of Chatham's military operations.*

INDEPENDENCE

I care for nobody, not I,
If no one cares for me.
I. BICKERSTAFFE.—*Love in a Village.*

For body-killing tyrants cannot kill
The public soul—the hereditary will,
That downward as from sire to son it goes,
By shifting bosoms more intensely grows.
CAMPBELL.—*On Poland.*

Heaven never meant him for that passive thing
That can be struck and hammered out to suit
Another's taste and fancy. He'll not dance
To every tune of every minister.
It goes against his nature—he can't do it.
COLERIDGE.—*Piccolomini, Act* 1, 4.

When independence of principle consists in having no principle to depend upon.
C. C. COLTON.—*Lacon.*

Nelson was nothing if he was not insubordinate. LORD FISHER.—*Memories.*

Give me, kind Heaven, a private station,
A mind serene for contemplation ;
Title and profit I resign ;
The post of honour shall be mine.
GAY.—*Fables, Pt.* 2, 2.

That independence Britons prize too high,
Keeps man from man, and breaks the social tie. GOLDSMITH.—*Traveller.*

Too poor for a bribe, and too proud to importune,
He had not the method of making a fortune. GRAY.—*His own Character.*

He earns whate'er he can,
And looks the whole world in the face,
For he owes not any man.
LONGFELLOW.—*Village Blacksmith.*

We've a war, an' a debt, an' a flag ; an' ef this
Ain't to be inderpendunt, why, wut on airth is ?
J. R. LOWELL.—*Biglow Papers, 2nd ser.,* 4.

Independence, like honour, is a rocky island without a beach. NAPOLEON.

I cannot tell what you and other men
Think of this life ; but, for my single self,
I had as lief not be, as live to be
In awe of such a thing as I myself.
SHAKESPEARE.—*Julius Cæsar, Act* 1, 2.

Thy spirit, Independence, let me share !
Lord of the lion-heart and eagle-eye,
Thy steps I follow with my bosom bare,
Nor heed the storm that howls along the sky. SMOLLETT.—*Independence.*

There are persons who are so independent that you cannot depend upon them.
C. H. SPURGEON.—" *Salt-Cellars.*"

In the end injustice produces independence. VOLTAIRE.

It is easier to control a hundred thousand men in battle than to subjugate the mind of one thoroughly convinced individual.
VOLTAIRE.—*Essay on Manners, Remarks,* 16.

His march is a go-as-you-please ;
He most keeps step with hisself.
E. WALLACE.—*Naval Brigade, st.* 2.

Happy is he who, caring not for Pope,
Consul or King, can sound himself to know
The destiny of man, and live in hope.
WORDSWORTH.—*Poems to National Indep., Pt.* 1, 5.

How happy is he born and taught,
That serveth not another's will,
Whose armour is his honest thought,
And simple truth his utmost skill.
SIR H. WOTTON.—*Character of a Happy Life.*

This man is freed of servile bands,
Of hope to rise, or fear to fall ;
Lord of himself, though not of lands,
And, having nothing, yet hath all.
SIR H. WOTTON.—*Ib.*

INDESCRIBABLE, THE

Not all the lip can speak is worth
The silence of the heart.
J. Q. ADAMS.—*Lip and Heart.*

A sight to dream of, not to tell.
COLERIDGE.—*Christabel, Pt.* 1.

INDEXES

The man who publishes a book without an index ought to be damned ten miles beyond hell, where the Devil himself cannot get, for stinging nettles.
JOHN BAYNES.

So essential did I consider an Index to be in every book, that I proposed to bring a Bill into Parliament to deprive an author, who publishes a book without an index, of the privilege of copyright, and moreover to subject him, for his offence, to a pecuniary penalty.

LORD CAMPBELL.—*Pref. to Lives of the Chief Justices* (1857).

One writer, for instance, excels at a plan or title-page, another works away at the book, and a third is a dab at an index.

GOLDSMITH.—*The Bee*, 1.

INDIA

Dominions of the Sun.

CAMPBELL.—*Pleasures of Hope*, 1.

India knelt at her feet and felt her sway more fruitful of life than spring.

SWINBURNE.—*England*.

INDIFFERENCE

A mild indifferentism.

BROWNING.—*Christmas Eve*.

He hated the bad world that loved not him.

R. BUCHANAN.—*Barbara Gray*.

Full of a sweet indifference.

R. BUCHANAN.—*Charmian*.

And I must say, I ne'er could see the very Great happiness of the " Nil Admirari."

BYRON.—*Don Juan, c.* 5, 100.

Here's a sigh for those who love me,
   And a smile to those who hate;
And whatever sky's above me
Here's a heart for every fate.

BYRON.—*To T. Moore*.

Nor fame I slight, nor for her favours call ; She comes unlooked for, if she comes at all.

POPE.—*Temple of Fame, l.* 513.

The worst sin towards our fellow-creatures is not to hate them, but to be indifferent to them. That's the essence of inhumanity.

G. B. SHAW.—*Devil's Disciple*, Act 2.

The noblest answer unto such,
Is kindly silence when they bawl.

TENNYSON.—*The After Thought*.

Charlotte, having seen his body
Borne before her on a shutter,
Like a well-conducted person,
Went on cutting bread and butter.

THACKERAY.—*Sorrows of Werther*.

And Gallio cared for none of those things.

Acts xviii, 17.

If ye winna come ye'll bide,
Quoth Rory to his bride.

Scottish saying.

INDIGNITIES

By indignities men come to dignities.

BACON.—*Essays of Great Place*.

It can never be
They will digest this harsh indignity.

SHAKESPEARE.—*Love's Labour's Lost*,
Act 5, 2.

INDISPENSABILITY

They love, they hate, but cannot do without him.

ARISTOPHANES (434 B.C.).—*As quoted by Plutarch*.

INDIVIDUALISM

The apple tree never asks the beech how he shall grow, nor the lion the horse how he shall take his prey.

WM. BLAKE.—*Proverbs of Hell*.

Use what language you will, you can never say anything but what you are. What I am, and what I think, is conveyed to you, in spite of my efforts to hold it back.

EMERSON.—*Conduct of Life, Worship*.

Literary history and all history is a record of the power of minorities, and of minorities of one.

EMERSON.—*Progress of Culture*.

You see the fact is that the strongest man upon earth is he who stands most alone.   IBSEN.—*An Enemy of Society*
(*Dr. Stockmann's " Great Discovery "*).

O, let me be myself ! But where, oh where
   Under this heap of precedent, this mound
Of customs, modes, and maxims, cumbrance rare,
   Shall the Myself be found ?

JEAN INGELOW.—*Honours, Pt.* 2, 30.

There is a limit to the legitimate interference of collective opinion with individual independence ; and to find that limit and maintain it against encroachment, is as indispensable to a good condition of human affairs as protection against political despotism.

J. S. MILL.—*Liberty, Introd.*

Whatever crushes individuality is despotism, by whatever name it may be called.   J. S. MILL.—*Ib.*

Only in the world I fill up a place, which may be better supplied when I have made it empty.

SHAKESPEARE.—*As You Like It*, Act 1, 2.

God is no respecter of persons.

Acts x, 34.

What is not good for the hive is not good for the bee.   *Greek prov.*

INDULGENCE

How sad and bad and mad it was—
But then, how it was sweet !

BROWNING.—*Confessions*.

Be to her virtues very kind,
Be to her faults a little blind.
PRIOR.—*English Padlock.*

The land of Egypt, when we sat by the flesh-pots, and when we did eat bread to the full.   *Exodus* xvi, 3.

INDUSTRY

There is nothing truly valuable which can be purchased without pains and labour.   ADDISON.—*Tatler, No.* 97.

Industry is a loadstone to draw all good things.
BURTON.—*Anatomy of Melancholy, Democritus to the Reader.*

Since what by Nature was denied
By art and industry's supplied.
S. BUTLER.—*Upon Plagiaries (written satirically).*

He was never less at leisure than when at leisure ; he was never less alone than when alone.
CICERO.—*(Quoted as a saying of Scipio Africanus).*

Chase brave employments with a naked sword
Throughout the world. Fool not, for all may have
If they dare try, a glorious life or grave.
HERBERT.—*Church Porch.*

Temperance and industry are the two real physicians of mankind.
ROUSSEAU.—*Emile.*

Abroad in arms, at home in studious kynd,
Who seekes with painfull toile, shall
Honor soonest fynd.
SPENSER.—*Faerie Queene, Bk.* 2, *c.* 3, 40.

Go to the ant—but don't go to your uncle's. C. H. SPURGEON.—*" Salt-Cellars."*

Riches consist in the great number of industrious men.
VOLTAIRE.—*Dialogues, No.* 4.

How doth the little busy bee
Improve each shining hour,
And gather honey all the day
From every opening flower !
I. WATTS.—*Against Idleness.*

Ease from this noble miser of his time
No moment steals ; pain narrows not his cares.
WORDSWORTH.—*Eccles. Sonnets, pt.* 1, 23.

Diligence is the mother of good fortune.
Prov. quoted by Cervantes.

INEQUALITY

But why should ae man better fare,
And a' men brithers ?
BURNS.—*To Dr. Blacklock.*

It's hardly in a body's power
To keep at times frae being sour,
To see how things are shared ;
How best o' chiels are whiles in want,
While coofs on countless thousands rant,
And ken na how to wair't.
BURNS.—*Epistle to Davie.*

Oh, there are moments for us here, when seeing
Life's inequalities, and woe, and care,
The burdens laid upon our mortal being
Seem heavier than the human heart can
bear.   W. G. CLARK.—*A Song of May.*

Order is Heaven's first law, and thus confessed,
Some are, and must be, greater than the rest. POPE.—*Essay on Man, Ep.* 4, 49.

He would not believe that Providence had sent a few men into the world, ready booted and spurred to ride, and millions ready saddled and bridled to be ridden.
R. RUMBOLD.—*At his execution,* 1685.
Macaulay's England, ch. 5.

Immortal gods ! How one man excels another ! What a difference between a man of sense and a fool !
TERENCE.—*Eunuchus.*

How unequal things are, that those who have very little should be always adding something to the possessions of the more wealthy.   TERENCE.—*Phormio, Act* 1.

What are we ? How unequal ! Now we soar
And now we sink.
YOUNG.—*Night Thoughts,* 5.

The Ox does the work, but the man eats the grain ;
One does the work, and another gets the gain.   *Chinese saying.*

INEXPERIENCE

My salad days,
When I was green in judgment.
SHAKESPEARE.—*Antony and Cleopatra, Act* 1, 5.

You speak like a green girl,
Unsifted in such perilous circumstance.
SHAKESPEARE.—*Hamlet, Act* 1, 3.

INFAMY

Infamy was never incurred for nothing.
BURKE.—*Impeachment of Hastings.*

Leaving behind them horrible dispraise.
DANTE.—*Inferno (Cary's tr.), c.* 8, 50.

Cancelled from Heaven, and sacred memory,
Nameless in dark oblivion let them dwell.
MILTON.—*Paradise Lost, Bk.* 6, 379.

Hate cannot wish thee worse
Than guilt and shame have made thee.
    MOORE.—*When First I Met.*

Shame and dishonour sit
By his grave ever ;
Blessing shall hallow it,—
  Never, O never !
    SCOTT.—*Marmion*, 3, 11.

INFANCY

The god in babe's disguise,
  BROWNING.—*Jas. Lee's Wife.*

O, hush thee, my baby, thy sire was a
  knight,
Thy mother a lady, both lovely and bright ;
The woods and the glens, from the towers
  which we see,
They all are belonging, dear baby, to thee.
    SCOTT.—*Lullaby.*

INFATUATION

She for him had given
Her all on earth, and more than all in
Heaven. BYRON.—*Corsair, c.* 3, 17.

She was his life,
The ocean to the river of his thoughts,
Which terminated all.
    BYRON.—*The Dream, st.* 2.

Why she would hang on him
As if increase of appetite had grown
By what it fed on.
    SHAKESPEARE.—*Hamlet*, Act 1, 2.

INFIDELITY

Mock on, mock on, Voltaire, Rousseau ;
 Mock on, mock on ; 'tis all in vain ;
You throw the dust against the wind,
 And the wind blows it back again.
    WM. BLAKE.—*Scoffers.*

If Christians would teach infidels to be
just to Christianity, they should themselves be just to infidelity.
    J. S. MILL.—*Liberty, ch.* 2.

INFINITY

But how can finite grasp infinity ?
DRYDEN.—*Hind and Panther, Pt.* 1, 105.

The infinity of God is not mysterious,
it is only unfathomable, not concealed, but
incomprehensible : it is a clear infinity,
the darkness of the pure, unsearchable sea.
RUSKIN.—*Modern Painters, Pt.* 3, sec. 1,
     ch. 5, 19.

INFLUENCE

Writers, especially when they act in a
body and with one direction, have great
influence on the public mind.
  BURKE.—*Reflections on French
    Revolution.*

Thoughts sublime that pierce the night
 like stars,
And with their mild persistence urge man's
 search
To vaster issues.
  GEO. ELIOT.—*O May I Join the Choir
     Invisible.*

Like moonlight on the troubled sea,
 Brightening the storm it cannot calm.
  MOORE.—*Loves of the Angels.*

The greatest efforts of the race have
always been traceable to the love of praise,
as its greatest catastrophes to the love of
pleasure.
  RUSKIN.—*Sesame and Lilies, Sec.* 1.

Whose powers shed round him in the com-
 mon strife,
Or mild concerns of ordinary life,
A constant influence, a peculiar grace.
  WORDSWORTH.—*Happy Warrior.*

A little leaven leaveneth the whole lump.
    Galatians v, 9.

INGRATITUDE

Men remember
When they're forgotten. When remem-
 bered, they
Themselves forget.
  A. AUSTIN.—*Fortunatus*, Act 2, 8.

    Much I muse,
How bitter can spring up, when sweet is
 sown.
H. F. CARY.—*Dante's "Paradise," c.* 8, 99.

The good received, the giver is forgot.
  CONGREVE.—*To Ld. Halifax.*

On adamant our wrongs we all engrave,
But write our benefits upon the wave.
  DR. W. KING.—*Art of Love.*

Ah, how have I deserved, inhuman maid,
To have my faithful service thus repaid ?
GEO. LORD LYTTELTON.—*Progress of Love.*

For vicious natures, when they once begin
To take distaste, and purpose no requital,
The greater debt they owe, the more they
 hate. T. MAY.—*Agrippina.*

Blow, blow, thou winter wind !
Thou art not so unkind
As man's ingratitude ;
Thy tooth is not so keen,
Because thou art not seen,
Although thy breath be rude.
SHAKESPEARE.—*As You Like It*, Act 2, 7.

Ingratitude, thou marble-hearted fiend,
More hideous when thou show'st thee in a
 child,
Than the sea-monster !
  SHAKESPEARE.—*Lear*, Act 1, 4.

J

I hate ingratitude more in a man
Than lying, vainness, babbling, drunken-
ness.
SHAKESPEARE.—*Twelfth Night*, Act 3, 4.

Ingratitude he often found,
And pitied those who meant the wound.
SWIFT.—*On the Death of Dr. Swift.*

Kindness is very indigestible. It dis-
agrees with very proud stomachs.
THACKERAY.—*Philip*, Bk. 2, ch. 6.

Injuries we write in marble; kindnesses in dust. *Prov.*

Do a man a gude turn and he'll ne'er
forgie ye. *Shetland prov.*

INHUMANITY

Blow, blow, ye winds, with heavier gusts!
And freeze, thou bitter, biting frost!
Descend, ye chilly, smothering snows!
Not all your rage, as now united, shows
More hard unkindness, unrelenting,
Vengeful malice, unrepenting,
Than heaven-illumined man on brother
man bestows. BURNS.—*A Winter Night.*

Man's inhumanity to man
Makes countless thousands mourn.
BURNS.—*Man was Made to Mourn.*

Where the virgins are soft as the roses they
twine,
And all, save the spirit of man, is divine.
BYRON.—*Bride of Abydos, c.* 1, *st.* 1.

Butchered to make a Roman holiday.
BYRON.—*Childe Harold, c.* 4, 141.

So young and so untender.
SHAKESPEARE.—*Lear*, Act 1, 1.

In nature there's no blemish but the mind.
None can be called deformed but the un-
kind.
SHAKESPEARE.—*Twelfth Night*, Act 3, 5.

No greater shame to man than inhu-
manitie.
SPENSER.—*Faerie Queene, Bk.* 6, *c.* 1,
st. 26.

INJURIES

For injuries are writ in brass, kind Graccho,
And not to be forgotten.
MASSINGER.—*Duke of Milan*, Act 5, 1.

A wound, though cured, yet leaves behind
a scar. J. OLDHAM.—*Lydia's Will.*

Oblivion is the remedy for injuries.
SENECA.—(*Quoted as from " an old poet."*)

Kindnesses are easily forgotten, but
Injuries!——what worthy man does not
keep those in mind?
THACKERAY.—*Lovel the Widower.*

A wounded spirit who can bear?
Proverbs xviii, 14.

INJUSTICE

Injustice is no less than high treason
against Heaven.
MARCUS AURELIUS.—*Bk.* 9, 1.

Omissions, no less than commissions, are
often a part of injustice.
MARCUS AURELIUS.—*Bk.* 9, 5.

"A book," I observed, "might be
written on the Injustice of the Just."
SIR A. HOPE HAWKINS.—*Dolly
Dialogues*, 15.

The injustice done to an individual is
sometimes of service to the public.
JUNIUS.—*Letter* 41.

Truth for ever on the scaffold, Wrong
for ever on the throne.
J. R. LOWELL.—*Present Crisis.*

It makes me very angry indeed to be in
the wrong when I am right.
MOLIÈRE.—(*George Dandin.*)

I should wish neither, but had I of
necessity to choose, I would rather suffer
unjustly than act unjustly.
PLATO.—*Gorgias*, 55. (*Remark attrib.
to Socrates.*)

The most complete injustice is to seem
just, when not so.
PLATO.—*Republic, Bk.* 2, 4.

Unjust rule never endures perpetually.
SENECA.—*Medea.*

In all time, in every place, the public
is unjust. Horace complained of it in the
empire of Augustus. Malice, pride, an
unworthy desire to disparage the talents
which form our delight, to blight the fine
arts which solace life, that is the heart of
man; it is born for envy.
VOLTAIRE.—*To Mdlle. Clairon.*

But Truth inspired the bards of old
When of an iron age they told,
Which to unequal laws gave birth
And drove Astræa [Justice] from the
earth. WORDSWORTH.—*The Italian
Itinerant, Pt.* 2, 2.

Jeddart (or Jedburgh) justice: first
hang a man and syne try him.—*Scottish
prov. founded on a wholesale hanging of
political prisoners at Jedburgh in* 1574.
(*A similar prov. attaches to Lidford, Devon.*)

INNOCENCE
Modesty does not long survive innocence.
BURKE.—*Impeachment of Hastings*
(*Feb.* 17, 1788).

Oh, Mirth and Innocence! Oh, Milk and
Water!
Ye happy mixtures of more happy days!
BYRON.—*Beppo, st.* 80.

Life is fullest of content,
Where delight is innocent.
T. Campion.—*Tell me, gentle hour of night.*

Folly and Innocence are so alike,
The difference, though essential, fails to strike.
Cowper.—*Progress of Error*, 203.

However few of the other good things of life are thy lot, the best of all things, which is innocence, is always within thy own power.
Fielding.—*Amelia, Bk.* 8, *c.* 3.

I dare (for what is that which innocence dares not ?).
Fletcher and Massinger.—*Little French Lawyer*, Act 3, 1.

The smile that was childlike and bland.
Bret Harte.—*Plain Language.*

He's armed without that's innocent within.
Pope.—*Satires, Bk.* 1, 94.

Not proven ! I hate that Caledonian *medium quid.* One who is not proved guilty is innocent in the eyes of the law.
Scott.—*Diary, Feb.* 20, 1827.

We that have free souls, it touches us not. Let the galled jade wince; our withers are unwrung.
Shakespeare.—*Hamlet*, Act 3, 2.

When my love swears that she is made of truth,
I do believe her, though I know she lies,
That she might think me some untutored youth,
Unlearnèd in the world's false subtleties.
Shakespeare.—*Sonnet* 138.

The silence often of pure innocence
Persuades, when speaking fails.
Shakespeare.—*Winter's Tale*, Act 2, 2.

There is no courage but in innocence,
No constancy but in an honest cause.
T. Southern.—*Fate of Capua.*

INNOVATIONS

Striving to better, oft we mar what's well.
Shakespeare.—*Lear*, Act 1, 4.

All with one consent praise new-born gauds.
Shakespeare.—*Troilus and Cressida*, 3, 3.

All great truths begin as blasphemies.
G. B. Shaw.—*Annajanska.*

They wha put plough into new land must look to have it hank on a stane now and then.
Scottish prov.

INNS

A novel.... should always be kept moving on. Nobody knew this better than Field-

ing, whose novels, like most good ones, are full of inns.
A. Birrell.—*Office of Literature.*

He knew the tavernes wel in every toun.
Chaucer.—*Cant. Tales, Prol.*

Along the varying road of life,
In calm content, in toil or strife,
At morn or noon, by night or day,
As time conducts him on his way,
How oft doth man, by care oppressed,
Find in an inn a place of rest.
W. Coombe.—*Dr. Syntax, c.* 9.

There is no private house in which people can enjoy themselves so well as in a capital tavern. Johnson.—*Remark*, 1776.

There is nothing which has yet been contrived by man by which so much happiness is produced, as by a good tavern or inn.
Johnson.—*Remark.*

Shall I not take mine ease in mine inn ?
Shakespeare.—*Henry IV.*, Pt. 1, Act 3, 3.

Whoe'er has travelled life's dull round,
Where'er his stages may have been,
May sigh to think he still hath found
The warmest welcome at an inn.
Shenstone.—*At Henley.*

INNUENDO

'Tis not the wholesome sharp morality,
Or modest anger of a satiric spirit,
That hurts or wounds the body of a state,
But the sinister application
Of the malicious, ignorant, and base
Interpreter. Ben Jonson.—*Poetaster*, 5, 1.

Nor do they trust their tongues alone,
But speak a language of their own ;
Can read a nod, a shrug, a look,
Far better than a printed book ;
Convey a libel in a frown,
And wink a reputation down.
Swift.—*Journal of a Modern Lady*, 1728.

INQUISITIVENESS

Seek not the wherefore, race of human kind. H. F. Cary.—*Dante's "Purgatory," c.* 3, 35.

Avoid a person who asks questions, for such a man is a talker ; nor will open ears keep faithfully the things entrusted to them.
Horace.—*Ep., Bk.* 1, 18.

Inquisitive people are all ill-natured.
Plautus.—*Stichus.*

I hope I don't intrude.
Poole.—*Paul Pry.*

You would play upon me ; you would seem to know my stops ; you would pluck out the heart of my mystery ; you would sound me from my lowest note to the top of my compass.
Shakespeare.—*Hamlet*, Act 3, 2.

INSANITY

Babylon in all its desolation is a sight not so awful as that of the human mind in ruins.   SCROPE DAVIES.—*Letter*, 1835.

All power of fancy over reason is a degree of insanity.
JOHNSON.—*Rasselas, ch.* 44.

Demoniac frenzy, moping melancholy,
And moon-struck madness.
MILTON.—*Paradise Lost, Bk.* 11, 485.

INSCRUTABILITY

Not a thought to be seen
On his steady brow and quiet mouth.
BROWNING.—*Statue and the Bust.*

His face,
The tablet of unutterable thoughts.
BYRON.—*The Dream,* 6.

High and inscrutable the old man stood,
Calm in his voice, and calm within his eye.   BYRON.—*Don Juan,* 4, 39.

INSECTS

Or great ugly things, All legs and wings,
With nasty long tails, Armed with nasty long stings.
R. H. BARHAM.—*The Knight and the Lady.*

Kill not the moth nor butterfly,
For the last judgment draweth nigh.
WM. BLAKE.—*Proverbs.*

Of all the plagues that Heaven has sent,
A wasp is most impertinent.
GAY.—*Fables.*

If you wish to live and thrive,
Let the spider run alive. *Old Saying.*

INSENSIBILITY

A stoic of the woods—a man without a tear.   CAMPBELL.—*Gertrude.*

If the man who turnips cries,
Cry not when his father dies,
'Tis a proof that he had rather
Have a turnip than his father.
JOHNSON.—*Burlesque of Lopez de Vega.*

INSIGNIFICANCE

'Tis not to die we fear, but to die poorly,
To fall forgotten, in a multitude.
FLETCHER.—*Humorous Lieutenant,* Act 2,2.

Willows are weak, yet they bind other wood.   *Prov. (Italian ?)*

INSINCERITY

Our hands have met but not our hearts.
HOOD.—*To a False Friend.*

I, under fair pretence of friendly ends,
And well-placed words of glozing courtesy
Baited with reasons not unplausible,
Wind me into the easy-hearted man,
And hug him into snares.
MILTON.—*Comus,* 160.

It is vile to say one thing and to think another. How much more base to write one thing and think another !
SENECA.—*Ep.* 24.

The hearts of old gave hands :
But our new heraldry is—hands not hearts.
SHAKESPEARE.—*Othello.* Act 3, 4.

INSPIRATION

And doubtless this too, comes from grace of Gods,
Seated in might upon their awful thrones.
ÆSCHYLUS.—*Agamemnon,* 170
(*Plumptre tr.*).

My soul within me burning with hot thoughts.
ÆSCHYLUS.—*Ib.* 1030 (*Plumptre tr.*).

Stung by the splendour of a sudden thought. BROWNING.—*Death in the Desert.*

There's a melody born of melody,
Which melts the world into a sea ;
Toil could never compass it ;
Art its height could never hit ;
It never came out of wit ;
But a music music-born
Well may Jove and Juno scorn.
EMERSON.—*Fate.*

Yet his look with the reach of past ages was wise,
And the soul of eternity thought through his eyes.
LEIGH HUNT.—*Feast of Poets.*

He ne'er is crowned
With immortality who fears to follow
Where airy voices lead.
KEATS.—*Endymion. Bk.* 2.

Great thoughts, great feelings came to him,
Like instincts, unawares.
R. M. MILNES (LORD HOUGHTON).—*Men of Old.*

And looks commercing with the skies,
Thy rapt soul sitting in thine eyes.
MILTON.—*Il Penseroso,* 39.

What in me is dark
Illumine ; what is low raise and support ;
That to the height of this great argument
I may assert eternal Providence,
And justify the ways of God to man.
MILTON.—*Paradise Lost, Bk.* 1, *l.* 27.

He who receives
Light from above, from the fountain of light,
No other doctrine needs, though granted true.
MILTON.—*Paradise Regained, Bk.* 4, 288.

There is a God within us, and we glow
when he stirs us. OVID.—*Fast., Bk.* 6.

From nature all perfections flow;
And though from tasked attention slow
  Taught excellence will sometimes strain
And struggle to renown; if Heaven
Has not the inspiring impulse given,
  'Tis silence best rewards the pain.
      PINDAR.—*Olympian Odes,* 9, 151
          (*Moore tr.*).

Some feelings are to mortals given,
With less of earth in them than Heaven.
      SCOTT.—*Lady of the Lake,* 2, 22.

The feather whence the pen
Was shaped, that traced the lives of these
      good men,
Dropped from an angel's wing.
WORDSWORTH.—*Eccles. Sonnets, Pt.* 3, 5.

        We are laid asleep
In body, and become a living soul:
While with an eye made quiet by the power
Of harmony, and the deep power of joy,
We see into the life of things.
      WORDSWORTH.—*Tintern Abbey.*

INSTABILITY

Nothing is fixed that mortals see or know,
Unless perhaps some stars be so.
      SWIFT.—*Ode to Sancroft.*

INSTINCT

    Instinct is untaught ability.
DR. A. BAIN.—*Senses and Intellect* (1855).

Reasoning at every step he treads,
  Man yet mistakes his way,
Whilst meaner things, whom instinct leads,
  Are rarely known to stray.
      COWPER.—*The Doves.*

  Armed men have gladly made
Him their guide, and him obeyed
.. ..
And to all this fame he rose,
Only following his nose.
      COWPER.—*On a Pointer Dog.*

    Instinct preceded wisdom
Even in the wisest men, and may some-
      times
Be much the better guide.
      G. LILLO.—*Fatal Curiosity.*

Instinct and reason how can we divide?
'Tis the fool's ignorance and the pedant's
  pride. PRIOR.—*Solomon, Bk.* 1, 235.

An instinct call it, a blind sense,
A happy, genial influence,
Coming one knows not how nor whence,
  Nor whither going.
      WORDSWORTH.—*To the Daisy.*

A few strong instincts and a few plain rules.
WORDSWORTH.—*Poems of the Imagination,
          Pt.* 2, 12.

Swift Instinct leaps; slow Reason feebly
  climbs. YOUNG.—*Night Thoughts,* 7.

For a man's mind is sometime wont to
tell him more than seven watchmen, that
sit above in an high tower.
      Ecclesiasticus xxxvii, 14.

INSTRUCTION

He that shortens the road to knowledge
lengthens life. C. C. COLTON.—*Lacon.*

It is always safe to learn, even from our
enemies; seldom safe to venture to instruct, even our friends. C. C. COLTON—*Ib.*

If wisdom were offered me on condition
that I should keep it close and not communicate it, I would refuse the gift.
                  SENECA

Lord teach **my** teacher that he may
teach me.   C. H. SPURGEON.

A nod for a wise man and a rod for a fool.
                  Hebrew prov.

INSUBORDINATION

Jellicoe has all the Nelsonic attributes
except *one*—he is totally wanting in the
great gift of insubordination.
LORD FISHER.—*Letter to a Privy Councillor,
          Dec.* 27, 1916.

INSUFFICIENCY

Oh, the little more, and how much it is!
And the little less, and what worlds away!
      BROWNING.—*By the Fireside.*

INSULTS

      Insects
Have made the lion mad ere now; a shaft
I' the heel o'erthrew the bravest of the
      brave.
      BYRON.—*Marino Faliero,* Act 5, 1.

An injury is much sooner forgotten than
an insult.
      LORD CHESTERFIELD.—*Letter,* 1746.

Fate never wounds more deep the generous
      heart,
Than when a blockhead's insult points the
      dart.   JOHNSON.—*London.*

Insults are like bad coins; we cannot
help their being offered to us, but we need
not take them.
      C. H. SPURGEON.—" *Salt-Cellars.*"

INTEGRITY
                  He had kept
The whiteness of his soul, and thus men
o'er him wept.
      BYRON.—*Childe Harold, c.* 3, 57.

Hath he not always treasures, always
      friends,
The good great man?—three treasures,
      love and light,

And calm thoughts, regular as infant's
    breath,
And three firm friends, more sure than
    day and night—
Himself, his Maker, and the angel Death.
            COLERIDGE.—*Job's Luck.*

His faith, perhaps, in some nice tenets,
    might
Be wrong; his life, I'm sure, was in the
    right.   COWLEY.—*On Mr. Crashaw.*

Nor holds this earth a more deserving
    knight,
For virtue, valour, and for noble blood,
Truth, honour, all that is comprised in
    good.
        DRYDEN.—*Palamon, Bk. 3, l. 823.*

Integrity is praised and starves.
            JUVENAL.—*Sat.* 1.

Free from self-seeking, envy, low design,
I have not found a whiter soul than thine.
            LAMB.—*To M. C. Burney.*

For he that is trewe of his tonge, and of his
    two handes,
And doth the werkes therewith, and willeth
    no man ille,
He is a god by the gospel.
            LANGLAND.—*Piers Plowman,
                        Passus 2, 82.*

He that has light, within his own clear
    breast
May sit i' th' centre, and enjoy bright day.
            MILTON.—*Comus,* 381.

Men whose life, learning, faith, and pure
    intent
Would have been held in high esteem with
    Paul.   MILTON.—*Sonnet.*

Teach me through life truth's simple path
    to find,
    That my sons blush not for their sire.
Some showers of gold from heaven
    require;
Others for boundless wealth have pined;
    Grant me my country's smiles to meet!
PINDAR.—*Nemean Odes,* 8, 60 *(Moore tr.).*

Preserve me, O my integrity, since I
    have diligently preserved thee.
            PLAUTUS.—*Curculio,* Act 5.

An honest man's the noblest work of God.
        POPE.—*Essay on Man, Ep.* 4, 248.

Statesman, yet friend to truth! of soul
    sincere,
In action faithful, and in honour clear;
Who broke no promise, served no private
    end,
Who gained no title, and who lost no
    friend.   POPE.—*Moral Essays, Ep.* 5.

Just of thy word, in every thought sincere,
Who knew no wish but what the world
    might hear.   POPE.—*On R. Digby.*

Horatio, thou art e'en as just a man
As e'er my conversation coped withal.
        SHAKESPEARE.—*Hamlet,* Act 3, 2.

Be just and fear not.
Let all the ends thou aim'st at be thy
    country's,
Thy God's and truth's.
        SHAKESPEARE.—*Henry VIII.,* Act 3, 2.

He was not born for shame:
Upon his brow shame is ashamed to sit.
    SHAKESPEARE.—*Romeo and Juliet,* Act 3, 2.

Villain and he be many miles asunder.
            SHAKESPEARE.—*Ib.,* Act 3, 5.

Though our works
Find righteous or unrighteous judgment,
    this
At least is ours, to make them righteous.
    SWINBURNE.—*Marino Faliero,* Act 3, 1.

Live pure, speak true, right wrong, follow
    the King—
Else, wherefore born?
            TENNYSON.—*Gareth.*

Who reverenced his conscience as his king;
Whose glory was, redressing human wrong;
Who spake no slander, no, nor listened to
    it.   TENNYSON.—*Idylls, Dedication.*

Who never sold the truth to serve the hour,
Nor paltered with Eternal God for power.
    TENNYSON.—*Duke of Wellington, st.* 7.

To God, thy country and thy friend be
    true. H. VAUGHAN.—*Rules and Lessons.*

Customs, interests, forms of worship,
laws,—all differ. Let a man be true, that
is enough. The rest does not matter.
            VOLTAIRE.—*La Loi naturelle.*

Suffice it that he never brought
    His conscience to the public mart;
But lived himself the truth he taught,
    White-souled, clean-handed, pure of
    heart.   WHITTIER.—*Sumner.*

Him only pleasure leads and peace attends,
Him, only him, the shield of Jove defends,
Whose means are fair and spotless as his
    ends.   WORDSWORTH.—*Laodamia.*

INTELLECT

Go put off holiness and put on intellect.
            WM. BLAKE.—*Jerusalem.*

The dome of Thought, the palace of the
    Soul. BYRON.—*Childe Harold, c.* 2, 6.

The true way to render age vigorous is
to prolong the youth of the mind.
            MORTIMER COLLINS.—*Village Comedy,*
                                1, 56.

My mind to me a kingdom is ;
  Such perfect joys therein I find,
That it excels all other bliss
  That earth affords, or grows by kind.
                          SIR E. DYER.

Though never nurtured in the lap
  Of luxury, yet I admonish you,
I am an intellectual chap,
  And think of things that would as-
    tonish you.
        SIR W. S. GILBERT.—*Iolanthe*.

All the wise—therein really extolling
themselves—agree that Mind is to us a
king of heaven and of earth.
              PLATO.—*Philebus*, 50.

The true and the pure pleasures, associated with health and sobriety and virtue,
these partake of. But those which accompany folly and depravity it is an absurdity
to mix with Intellect. PLATO.—*Ib.*, 152.

The feast of reason and the flow of soul.
        POPE.—*Satires*, Bk. 2, Sat. 1, 128.

The power least prized is that which
thinks and feels
        WORDSWORTH.—*Humanity*, 1, 94.

Intellect obscures more than it illumines.
  I. ZANGWILL.—*Children of the Ghetto,
                        Bk.* 2, *ch.* 15.

INTENTION

I praise the heart and pity the head of
  him.   BROWNING.—*Christmas Eve*.

I do believe you think what now you speak;
But what we do determine oft we break.
Purpose is but the slave to memory.
        SHAKESPEARE.—*Hamlet*, Act 3, 2.

        The attempt, and not the deed,
Confounds us.
        SHAKESPEARE.—*Macbeth*, Act 2, 2.

It has been more wittily than charit-
ably said that hell is paved with good intentions. They have their place in heaven
also.   SOUTHEY.—*Colloquies*.

If wrong our hearts, our heads are right
in vain.   YOUNG.—*Night Thoughts*, 6.

But the olde proverbe is exceeding true,
That these great wishers, and these com-
      mon woulders,
Are never, for the most part, good house-
  holders. *The Times' Whistle* (1614).

Heaven favours good intentions.
                        Spanish prov.

INTERRUPTION

The most intelligent of all the European nations has called "Never Interrupt" the eleventh commandment.
        SCHOPENHAUER.—*On Noise*.

You have displaced the mirth, broke the
  good meeting,
With most admired disorder.
        SHAKESPEARE.—*Macbeth*, Act 3, 4.

INTERVENTION

Those who in quarrels interpose,
Must often wipe a bloody nose.
              GAY.—*Fables*, Pt. 1, 34.

Come not between the dragon and his
wrath. SHAKESPEARE.—*Lear*, Act 1, 1.

INTERVIEWERS

With much communication will he
tempt thee, and smiling upon thee will get
out thy secrets. *Ecclesiasticus* xiii, 11.

INTOLERANCE

Religious persecution may shield itself
under the guise of a mistaken and over-
zealous piety. BURKE.—*Impeachment of
                  Hastings*, Feb. 17, 1788.

The soberest saints are more stiff-neckèd
Than th' hottest-headed of the wicked.
        S. BUTLER.—*Miscell. Thoughts*.

Christians have burnt each other, quite
  persuaded
That all the Apostles would have done as
  they did. BYRON.—*Don Juan, c.* 1, 83.

Bigotry murders Religion, to frighten
fools with her ghost.
        C. C. COLTON.—*Lacon*, No. 101.

For both were bigots—fateful souls that
  plague
The gentle world.
      J. DAVIDSON.—*A Woman and her Son*.

Where it is a duty to worship the sun it
is pretty sure to be a crime to examine the
laws of heat. LORD MORLEY.—*Voltaire*.

The Athenians, as it appears to me
[Socrates], do not care very much whether
they think a man is clever, so long as he
does not communicate his wisdom. When
they think a man makes others wise, they
are angry, either through envy, as you say,
or from some other cause.
              PLATO.—*Euthyphron*, 3.

To say a man is bound to believe is
neither truth nor sense.
        SWIFT.—*Thoughts on Religion*.

They [Luther and Calvin] condemned
the Pope and yet wished to imitate him.
      VOLTAIRE.—*To the Author of the Three
                              Impostors.*

INTROSPECTION

Yet we shall one day gain, life past,
  Clear prospect o'er our being's whole ;
Shall see ourselves, and learn at last
  Our true affinities of soul.
        MATTHEW ARNOLD.—*Farewell.*

Look then into thine heart and write.
LONGFELLOW.—*Voices of the Night, Prelude.*

True dignity abides with him alone
Who, in the silent hour of inward thought,
Can still suspect and still revere himself
In lowliness of heart.
WORDSWORTH.—*Lines,* 1795.

That inward eye
Which is the bliss of solitude.
WORDSWORTH.—*I Wandered Lonely.*

INTUITION

But God has a few of us, whom he whispers
in the ear ;
The rest may reason and welcome : 'tis we
musicians know.
BROWNING.—*Abt Vogler,* 11.

Thought is deeper than all speech ;
Feeling deeper than all thought ;
Souls to souls can never teach
What unto themselves was taught.
C. P. CRANCH.—*Stanzas.*

That you are fair or wise is vain,
Or strong, or rich, or generous ;
You must have also the untangled strain
That sheds the beauty on the rose.
EMERSON.—*Fate.*

Heroism feels and never reasons, and
therefore is always right.
EMERSON.—*Heroism.*

INVENTORS AND INVENTIONS

He shall have chariots easier than air,
That I will have invented ; . . . And thy-
self,
That art the messenger, shalt ride before
him
On a horse cut out of an entire diamond.
That shall be made to go with golden
wheels,
I know not how yet.
BEAUMONT AND FLETCHER.—*A King and
No King* (1611), Act 5.

For though some meaner artist's skill were
shown,
In mingling colours, or in placing light,
Yet still the fair designment was his own.
DRYDEN.—*Death of Cromwell,* st. 24.

The inventions of the last fifty years
counterpoise those of the fifty centuries
before them. EMERSON.—*Works and Days.*

Invention breeds invention. No sooner
is the electric telegraph devised than gutta-
percha, the very material it requires, is
found. EMERSON.—*Ib.*

Deduct all that men of the humbler
classes have done for England in the way
of inventions only, and see where she
would have been but for them.
SIR A. HELPS.—*Friends in Council,
Slavery, ch.* 3.

" I am Ymaginatyf," quath he, " ydel
was I nevere."
LANGLAND.—*Piers Plowman,
Passus* 15.

Th' invention all admir'd, and each how
he
To be th' inventor miss'd ; so easy it
seem'd,
Once found, which yet unfound most
would have thought
Impossible.
MILTON.—*Paradise Lost,* 6, 498.

Invention is the most expensive thing
in the world. It takes no end of time and
no end of money.
G. B. SHAW.—*Irrational Knot, ch.* 3.

In the arts of life man invents nothing ;
but in the arts of death he outdoes Nature
herself, and produces by chemistry and
machinery all the slaughter of plague, pestilence and famine.
G. B. SHAW.—*Man and Superman.*

The devil has a very inventive mind.
VOLTAIRE.—*La Pucelle.*

It is easy to add to inventions.
Latin prov.

INVISIBILITY

I could not see my little friend because
he was not there.
R. H. BARHAM.—*Misadventures at Margate.*

The Spanish fleet thou canst not see—
because
It is not yet in sight.
SHERIDAN.—*Critic,* Act 2, 2.

But optics sharp it needs, I ween,
To see what is not to be seen.
J. TRUMBULL.—*McFingal.*

INVITATION

" Will you walk into my parlour ? " said
a spider to a fly ;
" It's the prettiest little parlour that ever
you did spy."
MARY HOWITT.—*Spider and Fly.*

Come live with me and be my love.
MARLOWE.—*Jew of Malta, Song.*

Whether they give or refuse, it delights
women equally to have been asked.
OVID.—*Ars Amat., Bk.* 1.

Look, with what courteous action
It waves you to a more removèd ground.
SHAKESPEARE.—*Hamlet,* Act 1, 4.

IRELAND

There came to the beach a poor exile of
Erin. CAMPBELL.—*Exile of Erin.*

He sang the bold anthem of Erin-go-bragh
[" Ireland for Ever "]. CAMPBELL.—*Ib.*

That domestic Irish Giant, named of Despair.
CARLYLE.—*Latter Day Pamphlets*, 3.

Our Irish blunders are never blunders of the heart.
MISS EDGEWORTH.—*Essay on Irish Bulls,*
ch. 5.

There is one distinguishing peculiarity of the Irish Bull—its horns are tipped with brass [i.e. impudence or self-possession].
MISS EDGEWORTH.—*Ib., ch.* 7.

There is no harm, but sometimes a great deal of good done by laughing, especially in Ireland.   MISS EDGEWORTH.—*Rose,*
Thistle, and Shamrock, Act 1, 1.

I never met anyone in Ireland who understood the Irish question, except one Englishman who had only been there a week.
SIR K. FRASER, M.P., *House of Commons,*
May, 1919.

Oh, while a man may dream awake,
On gentle Irish ground,
'Tis Paradise without the snake—
That's easy to be found.
F. LANGBRIDGE.—*Dedicatory Poem.*

The Irish are a fair people ; they never speak well of one another.
JOHNSON.—*Remark.*

For 'tis the capital o' the finest nation,
Wid charming pisintry upon a fruitful
sod,
Fightin' like divils for conciliation,
An' hatin' each other for the love of
God.
C. LEVER.—*Founded on old Irish Ballad.*

And now the Irish are ashamed
To see themselves in one year tamed :
So much one man can do,
That does both act and know.
MARVELL.—*Ode on Cromwell,* 75.

An Irishman's heart is nothing but his imagination.
G. B. SHAW.—*John Bull's Other Island,*
Act 1.

Erin go bragh! A far better anthem would be, Erin go bread and cheese.
SYDNEY SMITH.—*On the Irish Roman*
Catholic Church.

Glorious Ireland, sword and song
Gird and crown thee : none may wrong,
Save thy sons alone.
The sea that laughs around us
Hath sundered not but bound us ;
The sun's first rising found us
Throned on its equal throne.
SWINBURNE.—*The Union.*

The lovely and the lonely bride,
Whom we have wedded but have never
won. W. WATSON.—*Coronation Ode.*

The cup of Ireland's miseries has long been overflowing, and even yet it is not full.   "*An Irish Patriot*" (*as quoted by*
C. H. Spurgeon).

He that would England win,
Must with Ireland first begin.
Old Saying (*Ray*).

IRRESOLUTION

Thus conscience doth make cowards of us
all ;
And thus the native hue of resolution
Is sicklied o'er with the pale cast of
thought ;
And enterprises of great pith and moment,
With this regard, their currents turn awry
And lose the name of action.
SHAKESPEARE.—*Hamlet,* Act 3, 1.

Now hear what I revolve :
A thought unripe, and scarcely yet resolve.
VIRGIL.—*Æneid, Bk.* 9 (*Dryden tr.*).

IRRESPONSIBILITY

The hare-brained chatter of irresponsible frivolity.   DISRAELI.—*Speech,* 1878.

A dark horse in a loose box.
LORD MORLEY.—*Referring to Lord*
Rosebery.

Blame not my lute ! for he must sound
Of this or that as liketh me.
SIR T. WYATT.—*The Lover's Lute.*

IRRESPONSIVENESS

Which refuseth to hear the voice of the charmer, charm he never so wisely.
Church Psalter lviii, 5.

We have piped unto you, and ye have not danced.   *St. Matthew* xi, 17.

IRRETRIEVABLE, THE

Ole Brer Rabbit, he lean fum out de steeple en 'pollygize de bes' he kin, but no 'pollygy aint gwine ter make ha'r come back whar de b'iling water hit.
J. C. HARRIS.—*Nights with Uncle*
Remus, ch. 45.

IRRITATION

There is a common saying that when a horse is rubbed on the gall, he will kick.
BISHOP LATIMER.—*Sermon,* 1552.

A' things anger you, and the cat breaks your heart.   *Scottish prov.*

ISOLATION

I have made a great discovery. . . .
The strongest man upon earth is he who stands most alone (Dr. Stockmann).
IBSEN.—*An Enemy of Society.*

One and none is all one.
Spanish prov. (*Ray*).

ITALY

Open my heart and you will see
Graved inside of it, " Italy."
BROWNING.—*De Gustibus.*

I love the language, that soft bastard Latin,
Which melts like kisses from a female
    mouth,
And sounds as if it should be writ on satin,
With syllables which breathe of the
    sweet south.
BYRON.—*Beppo, st.* 44.

A man who has not been in Italy is
always conscious of an inferiority.
JOHNSON.—*Remark,* 1776.

Subtle, discerning, eloquent, the slave
Of Love, of Hate, for ever in extremes ;
Gentle when unprovoked, easily won,
But quick in quarrel—through a thousand
    shades
His spirit flits, chameleon-like ; and mocks
The eye of the observer. [Sketch of
Italian character.]
ROGERS.—*Italy, Venice.*

They spell it Vinci and pronounce it
Vinchy ; foreigners always spell better
than they pronounce.
MARK TWAIN.—*Innocents Abroad,
                                            ch.* 19.

Lump the whole thing ! Say that the
Creator made Italy from designs by
Michael Angelo !
MARK TWAIN.—*Ib., ch.* 27.

Fair Land ! Thee all men greet with joy ;
    how few,
Whose souls take pride in freedom, virtue,
    fame,
Part from thee without pity dyed in shame !
WORDSWORTH.—*Tour in Italy,* 25.

J

JANUARY

If the grass grows in Janiveer,
It grows the worse for 't all the year.
Prov. (Ray).

JEALOUSY

There is more jealousy between rival
wits than rival beauties, for vanity has
no sex.   C. C. COLTON.—*Lacon.*

The wise too jealous are, fools too secure.
CONGREVE.—*Way of the World,
                                            Act* 3, 3.

Thou tyrant, tyrant Jealousy,
Thou tyrant of the mind !
DRYDEN.—*Love Triumphant.*

A jealous woman believes everything
her passion suggests.
GAY.—*Beggar's Opera, Act* 2, 2.

What frenzy dictates jealousy believes.
GAY.—*Dione.*

Jealousy is always born with love, but
does not always die with it.
LA ROCHEFOUCAULD.—*Maxim* 361.

In jealousy there is more self-love than
love. LA ROCHEFOUCAULD.—*Maxim* 361.

            Nor jealousy
Was understood, the injured lover's hell.
MILTON.—*Paradise Lost, Bk.* 5, 449.

For story and experience tell us
That man grows old and woman jealous.
PRIOR.—*Alma, c.* 2, 65.

            Rash-embraced despair,
And shuddering fear, and green-eyed
    jealousy. SHAKESPEARE.—*Merchant
                                of Venice, Act* 3, 2.

How many fools serve mad jealousy !
SHAKESPEARE.—*Much Ado, Act* 2, 1.

O beware, my lord, of jealousy ;
It is the green-eyed monster, which doth
    mock
The meat it feeds on.
SHAKESPEARE.—*Othello, Act* 3, 3.

    Trifles, light as air,
Are to the jealous confirmations strong
As proofs of holy writ.
SHAKESPEARE.—*Ib.*

For where Love reigns, disturbing Jealousy
Doth call himself Affection's sentinel ;
Gives false alarms, suggesteth mutiny.
SHAKESPEARE.—*Venus and Adonis, st.* 109.

This carry-tale dissentious Jealousy,
That sometimes true news, sometimes
    false doth bring.
SHAKESPEARE.—*Ib., st.* 110.

Jealousy's a city passion ; 'tis a thing
unknown among people of quality.
SIR J. VANBRUGH.—*Confederacy.*

And even mother earth had loved him
    more
Than me ; his wide sun-flooded meadows
    bore
A golden host that numbered mine thrice
    o'er.
AUGUSTA WEBSTER.—*The Snow Waste.*

    It is the hydra of calamities,
    The seven-fold death.
YOUNG.—*The Revenge.*

Love is strong as death ; jealousy is
cruel as the grave. *Song of Solomon* ii, 2.

JESTING

Beware of jokes ! Too much temperance
cannot be used—inestimable for sauce,
but corrupting for food ; we go away
hollow and ashamed.
EMERSON.—*Social Aims.*

Nor dare I rally with such dangerous folk,
Lest I be torn in pieces for a joke.
P. FRANCIS.—*Horace, Epistles, Bk.* 1, 19.

He makes a foe who makes a jest.
GAY.—*Fables*, 46.

Full well they laughed, with counter-
feited glee,
At all his jokes, for many a joke had he.
GOLDSMITH.—*Deserted Village.*

The jests of the rich are ever successful.
GOLDSMITH.—*Vicar of Wakefield, ch.* 7.

May there be no ill-natured interpreter
to put false constructions on the honest
meaning of my jests.
MARTIAL.—*Epig., Bk.* 1, *Preface.*

I suppose the chief bar to the action of
imagination, and stop to all greatness in
this present age of ours, is its mean and
shallow love of jest.   RUSKIN.—*Modern
Painters, vol.* 2, *Pt.* 3, *ch.* 3, 10.

For the love of laughter, hinder not the
humour of his design.
SHAKESPEARE.—*All's Well, Act* 3, 6.

No, no, they do but jest, poison in jest :
no offence i' the world.
SHAKESPEARE.—*Hamlet, Act* 3, 2.

A jest unseen, inscrutable, invisible
As a nose on a man's face, or a weather-
cock on a steeple !
SHAKESPEARE.—*Two Gentlemen of Verona,*
Act 2, 1.

My way of joking is to tell the truth.
It's the funniest joke in the world.
G. B. SHAW.—*John Bull's Other Island,*
Act 2.

Guides cannot master the subtleties of
the American joke.   MARK TWAIN.—
Innocents Abroad, ch. 27.

Better lose a joke than a friend.
French prov.

Affront your friend in daffin [in joke],
and tine [lose] him in earnest.
Scottish prov.

The wise make jests and fools repeat them.
Prov. (Ray).

JEWELS

Jewels, orators of Love.
S. DANIEL.—*Rosamond, st.* 52.

Rich and rare were the gems she wore,
And a bright gold ring on her hand she
bore.   MOORE.—*Irish Melodies.*

They marveyle that any men be so
folyshe as to have delite and pleasure in
the doubteful glisteringe of a lytil try-
fellynge stone, which maye beholde annye
of the starres or elles the sonne it selfe.
SIR T. MORE.—*Utopia (Ralph Robinson
tr.), Bk.* 2.

On her white breast a sparkling cross she
bore,
Which Jews might kiss, and infidels adore.
POPE.—*Rape of the Lock, c.* 2, 7.

Win her with gifts, if she respect not
words :
Dumb jewels often, in their silent kind,
More quick than words, do move a
woman's mind.
SHAKESPEARE.—*Two Gentlemen of Verona,*
Act, 3, 1.

JEWS

One of the most remarkable phenomena
in the history of this scattered people,
made for ages " a scorn and a hissing,"
is that . . . they have come out of it (in any
estimate which allows for numerical proportion) rivalling the nations of all
European countries in healthiness and
beauty of physique, in practical ability,
in scientific and artistic aptitude, and in
some forms of ethical value.
GEORGE ELIOT.—*Theophrastus Such.
The Modern Hep ! Hep ! Hep !*

A hopeless faith, a homeless race,
Yet seeking the most holy place,
And owning the true bliss.
KEBLE.—*5th Sun. in Lent.*

Hath not a Jew eyes ? Hath not a Jew
hands, organs, dimensions, senses, affections, passions ?
SHAKESPEARE.—*Merchant of Venice,*
Act 3, 1.

And Israel shall be a proverb and a
byword among all peoples.
1 *Kings* iv, 25 (*R.V.*).

JILTED

Better be courted and jilted
Than never be courted at all.
CAMPBELL.—*Jilted Nymph.*

Say what you will, 'tis better to be left,
than never to have been loved.
CONGREVE.—*Way of the World, Act* 2, 1.

Alas, she married another. They frequently do. I hope she is happy—because
I am.   ARTEMUS WARD.—*Lecture.*

JOHN BULL

The world is a bundle of hay,
Mankind are the asses who pull ;
Each tugs it a different way,
And the greatest of all is John Bull.
BYRON.—*Epigram.*

JOURNALISM

Nor ever once ashamed,
So we be named—
Press-men ; Slaves of the Lamp ; Servants
of Light.
SIR E. ARNOLD.—*Tenth Muse.*

Journalists always say what they know is untrue, in the hope that if they go on saying it long enough it will come true.
A. BENNETT.—*The Title* (1918), Act 2.

Great is Journalism. Is not every able Editor a Ruler of the World, being a persuader of it ?   CARLYLE.—*French Revolution, Pt. 2, Bk.* 1, 14.

The crimes I commit are not all kept out of the newspapers.
PETT RIDGE.—*Mr. Frank Cardwell (who " wrote for the press ").*

For a slashing article, sir, there's nobody like the Capting.
THACKERAY.—*Pendennis, Bk.* 1, ch. 32.

Ah, ye Knights of the pen ! May honour be your shield, and truth tip your lances ! Be gentle to all gentle people. Be modest to women. Be tender to children. And as for the Ogre Humbug, out sword and have at him !
THACKERAY.—*Roundabout Papers, Ogres.*

JOY

Full from the fount of Joy's delicious springs,
Some bitter o'er the flowers its bubbling venom flings.
BYRON.—*Childe Harold,* 82.

Earth's sweetest joy is but disguisèd woe.
W. DRUMMOND.—*Song.*

And Joy, whose hand is ever at his lips,
Bidding adieu.
KEATS.—*Ode to Melancholy.*

Great joys, like griefs, are silent.
S. MARMION.—*Holland's Leaguer, Act* 5, 1.

But headlong joy is ever on the wing.
MILTON.—*The Passion,* 5.

In folly's cup still laughs the bubble joy.
POPE.—*Essay on Man, Ep.* 2, 288.

For when the power of imparting joy
Is equal to the will, the human soul
Requires no other heaven.
SHELLEY.—*Queen Mab, c.* 3.

Though grief be a more violent passion than joy—as indeed all uneasy sensations seem naturally more pungent than the opposite agreeable ones—yet of the two, surprises of joy are still more insupportable than surprises of grief.
ADAM SMITH.—*History of Astronomy.*

JUDGES

A great judge and a little judge,
The judges of Assize.
HOOD.—*Tim Turpin.*

A Daniel come to judgment !
SHAKESPEARE.—*Merchant of Venice,* Act 4, 1.

If thou be a severe, sour-complexioned man, then I here disallow thee to be a competent judge.
IZAAK WALTON.—*Complete Angler, Pref.*

JUDGMENT

Virtuous and wise he was, but not severe ;
He still remembered that he once was young.
DR. J. ARMSTRONG.—*Art of Preserving Health, Bk.* 4.

Then at the balance let's be mute,
We never can adjust it ;
What's done we partly may compute,
We know not what's resisted.
BURNS.—*To the Unco Guid.*

Then gently scan your brother man,
Still gentlier sister woman ;
Though they may go a kennin wrang,
To step aside is human. BURNS.—*Ib.*

Affection bends the judgment to her ply.
H. F. CARY.—*Dante's Paradise, c.* 13, 115.

Why is it that we so constantly hear men complaining of their memory, but none of their judgment ?
C. C. COLTON.—*Lacon.*

And judgment at the helm was set,
But judgment was a child as yet,
And lack-a-day ! was all unfit,
    To guide the boat aright.
G. P. R. JAMES.—*The Voyage of Life.*

Still mark if vice or nature prompts the deed ;
Still mark the strong temptation, and the need.   J. LANGHORNE.—*Country Justice, Intro.,* 143.

In men whom men deem ill,
I find so much of goodness still ;
In men whom men pronounce divine,
I find so much of sin and blot,
I hesitate to draw the line
    Between the two, where God has not.
JOAQUIN MILLER.

The greatest and most beautiful example of intellect is when it is effective in the well-ordering of cities and of private dwellings, and which is given the name of judgment and justice.
PLATO.—*Banquet,* 33 (*Statement of Diotima*).

To perceive is to feel ; to compare is to judge. Judging and feeling are not the same thing.   ROUSSEAU.—*Emile.*

Commonly we say a Judgment falls upon a man for something in them we cannot abide.   SELDEN.—*Judgment.*

O judgment, thou art fled to brutish beasts,
And men have lost their reason !
SHAKESPEARE.—*Julius Cæsar,* Act 3, 2.

Before you answer ' Yea ' or ' Nay ,'
Hear what both sides shall have to say.
D. W. THOMPSON.—*Sales Attici.*

From all rash censure be the mind kept
free !
He only judges right who weighs, com-
pares,
And in the sternest sentence which his
voice
Pronounces, ne'er abandons Charity.
WORDSWORTH.—*Eccles. Sonnets, Pt.* 2, 1.

I speak as to wise men ; judge ye what
I say.   1 *Corinthians* x, 15.

The vials of the wrath of God.
Revelation xvi, 1.

JUNE

And what is so rare as a day in June ?
Then if ever come perfect days ;
Then heaven tries earth if it be in tune,
And over it softly her warm ear lays.
J. R. LOWELL.—*Sir Launfal.*

The roses make the world so sweet,
The bees, the birds have such a tune,
There's such a light and such a heat
And such a joy in June.
G. MACDONALD.—*To ———.*

Oh, to go back to the days of June,
Just to be young and alive again,
Hearken again to the mad sweet tune
Birds were singing with might and
main.
LOUISE C. MOULTON.—*Ballade of Winter.*

JURIES

The whole machinery of the State, all
the apparatus of the System and its varied
workings, end simply in bringing twelve
good men into a box.
LORD BROUGHAM.—*Present State of
the Law.*

Thou that goest upon Middlesex juries,
and will make haste to give up thy verdict
because thou will not lose thy dinner.
MIDDLETON.—*Trick to Catch the Old One,*
Act 4, 5.

Twelve good honest men shall decide in
our cause,
And be judges of fact, though not judges
of laws.
WM. PULTENEY (EARL OF BATH).—*Song
in " The Craftsman."*

The jury, passing on the prisoner's life,
May, in a sworn twelve, have a thief or two
Guiltier than him they try.
SHAKESPEARE.—*Measure for Measure,*
Act 2, 1.

JUSTICE

There are in nature certain fountains
of justice, whence all civil laws are derived
but as streams.
BACON.—*Adv. of Learning, Bk.* 2.

This world would be more just if truth
and lies,
And right and wrong, did bear an equal
price ;
But since impostures are so highly raised,
And faith and justice equally debased,
Few men have tempers for such paltry
gains
To undo themselves with drudgery and
pains.
S. BUTLER.—*Miscellaneous Thoughts.*

When justice on offenders is not done,
Law, government, and commerce are o'er-
thrown.
SIR J. DENHAM.—*Of Justice,* 85.

Justice is blind, he knows nobody.
DRYDEN.—*Wild Gallant,* Act 5, 1.

Stainless soldier on the walls,
Knowing this,—and knows no more,—
Whoever fights, whoever falls
Justice conquers evermore.
EMERSON.—*Voluntaries, No.* 4.

To honour justice and to love the right,
Which friends to friends and state to state
unite,
Be ours.   We honour equal aims and ends.
But still the greater with the less contends,
And evil times begin.
EURIPIDES.—*Phœn.,* 5, 545.

The rule of right and the eternal fitness
of things.
FIELDING.—*Tom Jones, Bk.* 4, *ch.* 4.

Justice is only a lively apprehension
lest we should be deprived of what belongs
to us. LA ROCHEFOUCAULD.—*Maxim* 520.

Justice is so fine a thing that one cannot
buy it too dear.   LE SAGE.—*Crispin.*

Where justice reigns, 'tis freedom to obey.
JAS. MONTGOMERY.—*Greenland.*

Justice is lame, as well as blind amongst
us.
T. OTWAY.—*Venice Preserved,* Act 1, 1.

Nothing becomes a king so much as the
distribution of justice. War is a tyrant,
as Timotheus (*c.* B.C. 500) expresses it,
but Pindar (B.C. 518-439) says, Justice is
the rightful sovereign of the world.
PLUTARCH.—*Life of Demetrius.*

Poetic justice, with her lifted scale,
Where, in nice balance, truth with gold
she weighs,
And solid pudding against empty praise.
POPE.—*Dunciad,* 52.

Strict justice is the sovereign guide
That o'er our actions should preside.
This queen of virtues is confessed
To regulate and bind the rest.
Thrice happy if you once can find
Her equal balance poise your mind :

All different graces soon will enter,
Like lines concurrent to their centre.
    PRIOR.—*Conversation*, 29.

The love of men, derived from self-love,
is the principle of human justice.
    ROUSSEAU.—*Emile.*

What stronger breastplate than a heart
untainted ?
Thrice is he armed that hath his quarrel
just.
SHAKESPEARE.—*Henry VI.*, *Pt.* 2, Act 3, 2.

Justice is pleasant even when she destroys.   SYDNEY SMITH.—*Lectures on
Moral Philosophy, No.* 12.

Justice is fled and truth is now no more.
    VIRGIL.—*Æneid, Bk.* 4 (*Dryden tr.*).

Extreme justice is an extreme injury.
VOLTAIRE.—*Œdipus*, Act 3. (*A variant of
the " trite saying " quoted by Cicero. See
" Law."*).

K

KENT

Kent, sir—everybody knows Kent—
apples, cherries, hops, and women.
    DICKENS.—*Pickwick Papers, ch.* 2.

For a yeoman of Kent, with his yearly
rent,
There never was a widow could say him
nay.   SCOTT.—*Ivanhoe*, 40.

Kent, in the commentaries of Cæsar writ,
Is termed the civillest place of all this isle.
SHAKESPEARE.—*Henry VI.*, *Pt.* 2, Act 4, 7.

KINDNESS

Thy Godlike crime was to be kind,
To render with thy precepts less
The sum of human wretchedness.
    BYRON.—*Prometheus.*

Little deeds of kindness, little words of
love,
Help to make earth happy, like the heaven
above.
    JULIA A. CARNEY.—*Little Things.*

Nothing is so popular as kindness.
    CICERO.—*Pro Ligario.*
And kind as kings upon their coronation
day.
DRYDEN.—*Hind and the Panther, Pt.* 1, 271.

A heart as soft, a heart as kind,
A heart as sound and free
As in the whole world thou canst find,
That heart I'll give to thee.
    HERRICK.—*Hesperides*, 268.

Give, if thou canst, an alms : if not, afford,
Instead of that, a sweet and gentle word.
HERRICK.—*Noble Numbers, No.* 71.

Men love us, or they need our love.
    KEBLE.—*Christian Year*, 7th *Sunday
after Trinity.*

Kindness, nobler ever than revenge.
SHAKESPEARE.—*As You Like It*, Act 4, 3.

Is she kind as she is fair ?
SHAKESPEARE.—*Two Gentlemen of Verona*,
    Act 4, 2.

Surely never did there live on earth
A man of kindlier nature.
    WORDSWORTH.—*Excursion, Bk.* 1.

That best portion of a good man's life,
His little, nameless, unremembered acts
Of kindness and of love.
    WORDSWORTH.—*Tintern Abbey.*

KINDRED

A little more than kin, and less than kind.
    SHAKESPEARE.—*Hamlet*, Act 1, 2.

KINGS

For this is the true strength of guilty kings,
When they corrupt the souls of those they
    rule.   M. ARNOLD.—*Merope.*

Alexander, Julius Cæsar, and Pompey,
what were they compared with Diogenes,
Heraclitus, and Socrates ?
    MARCUS AURELIUS, 8, 3

Kings will be tyrants from policy, when
subjects are rebels from principle.
    BURKE.—*Appeal from New to Old
Whigs.*

Whilst doubts assailed him, o'er and o'er
again,
If men were made for kings, or kings for
    men.   CAMPBELL.—*Pilgrim of Glencoe.*

Drede God, do law, love truth and wor-
thinesse,
And wed thy folk agein to stedfastnesse.
    CHAUCER.—*To K. Richard II.*

Power on an ancient consecrated throne,
Strong in possession, founded in old
    custom ;
Power by a thousand tough and stringy
    roots
Fixed to the people's pious nursery-faith.
    COLERIDGE.—*Piccolomini*, Act 4, 4.

A sovereign's ear ill brooks a subject's
questioning.
    COLERIDGE.—*Zapolya, Pt.* 1, 1.

We love
The king who loves the law.
COWPER.—*Winter Morning Walk*, 336.

I would not be a king to be beloved
Causeless, and daubed with undiscerning
    praise.   COWPER.—*Ib.*, 364.

When kings the sword of justice first lay
down,
They are no kings, though they possess
the crown.
DEFOE.—*True-Born Englishman, Pt.* 2, 313.

Titles are shadows, crowns are empty
things,
The good of subjects is the end of kings.
DEFOE.—*Ib., Pt.* 2, 315.

A patient man's a pattern for a king.
DEKKER.—*Honest Whore, Pt.* 2, Act 5, 2.

Thus Kings, by grasping more than they
could hold,
First made their subjects by oppression
bold ;
And popular sway, by forcing Kings to
give
More than was fit for subjects to receive,
Ran to the same extremes ; and one excess
Made both, by striving to be greater, less.
SIR J. DENHAM.—*Cooper's Hill,* 343.

Kings' titles commonly begin by force,
Which time wears off and mellows into
right ;
And power, which in one age is tyranny,
Is ripened in the next to true succession.
DRYDEN.—*Spanish Friar,* Act 4, 2.

'Tis hard for kings to steer an equal course,
And they who banish one oft gain a worse.
DRYDEN.—*Tarquin and Tullia.*

The fortune which made you a king, forbade you to have a friend. It is a law of
nature, which cannot be violated with
impunity.   JUNIUS.—*Letter* 35.

For therein stands the office of a king,
His honour, virtue, merit, and chief praise,
That for the public all this weight he bears.
MILTON.—*Paradise Regained, Bk.* 2, 463.

The Right Divine of kings to govern
wrong.   POPE.—*Dunciad, Bk.* 4, 188.

Here lies our sovereign lord the king,
Whose word no man relies on ;
He never says a foolish thing,
Nor ever does a wise one.
EARL OF ROCHESTER.—*On Charles II.*

A merry monarch, scandalous and poor.
EARL OF ROCHESTER.—*On the King.*

A King of shreds and patches.
SHAKESPEARE.—*Hamlet,* Act 3, 4.

There's such divinity doth hedge a king,
That treason can but peep to what it
would.   SHAKESPEARE.—*Ib.,* Act 4, 5.

Nice customs court'sey to great kings.
SHAKESPEARE.—*Henry V.,* Act 5, 2.

There was a Brutus once, that would have
brooked
The eternal devil to keep his state in Rome,
As easily as a king.
SHAKESPEARE.—*Julius Cæsar,* Act 1, 2.

Ay, every inch a King.
SHAKESPEARE.—*Lear,* Act 4, 6.

Not all the water in the rough, rude sea,
Can wash the balm from an anointed king.
SHAKESPEARE.—*Richard II.,* Act 3, 2.

Besides, the king's name is a tower of
strength.
SHAKESPEARE.—*Richard III.,* Act 5, 3.

What care these roarers for the name of
king ?
SHAKESPEARE.—*Tempest,* Act 1, 1.

Kings are like stars—they rise, they set,
they have
The worship of the world, but no repose.
SHELLEY.—*Hellas.*

Death lays his icy hand on kings :
     Sceptre and crown
     Must tumble down,
And in the dust be equal made
With the poor crooked scythe and spade.
JAS. SHIRLEY.—*Ajax and Ulysses.*

The power of kings (if rightly understood)
Is but a grant from Heaven of doing good.
W. SOMERVILLE.—*Fables, No.* 12.

Our great King [Cromwell] came from
Huntingdon, not Hanover.
THACKERAY.—*Esmond, Bk.* 3, *ch.* 5.
                   (*St. John*).

The universe distrusts the friendship of
kings.   VOLTAIRE.—*Don Pèdre.*

Heaven, in its vengeance, often bestows
kings.   VOLTAIRE.—*Sémiramis.*

Hail to the crown by Freedom shaped—
to gird
An English Sovereign's brow, and to the
throne
Whereon he sits ! whose deep foundations
lie
In veneration and the people's love.
WORDSWORTH.—*Excursion, Bk.* 6, 1.

The Crown alone can legally create that
which does not actually exist.
           Ancient law maxim (Lat.).

KISSES

A long, long kiss, a kiss of youth, and love.
BYRON.—*Don Juan, c.* 2, 186.

My wish is quite as wide, but not so bad,
. . . . . .
That womankind had but one rosy mouth,
To kiss them all at once from North to
South.   BYRON.—*Ib.,* 6, 27.

Being used but sisterly salutes to feel,
Insipid things—like sandwiches of veal.
           HOOD.—*Bianca's Dream.*

      O, a kiss,
Long as my exile, sweet as my revenge !
      SHAKESPEARE.—*Coriolanus,* Act 5, 3.

The woman that cries hush bids kiss : I learnt
So much of her that taught me kissing.
      SWINBURNE.—*Marino Faliero,* Act 1.

And sweet red splendid kissing mouth.
      SWINBURNE.—*Tr. of Villon.*

O Love, O fire ! once he drew
With one long kiss my whole soul through
My lips, as sunlight drinketh dew.
      TENNYSON.—*Fatima.*

A man had given all other bliss
And all his worldly worth for this,
To waste his whole heart in a kiss
      Upon her perfect lips.
    TENNYSON.—*Launcelot and Guinevere.*

And our spirits rushed together at the touching of the lips.
      TENNYSON.—*Locksley Hall.*

Dear as remembered kisses, after death,
And sweet as those by hopeless fancy feigned
On lips that are for others.
      TENNYSON.—*Princess, c.* 4, 36.

KNIGHTS

He was a verray parfit gentil knight.
    CHAUCER.—*Canterbury Tales, Prol.,* 72.

For lady's suit, and minstrel's strain,
By knight should ne'er be heard in vain.
      SCOTT.—*Marmion,* 1, 13.

He then that is not furnished in this sort
Doth but usurp the sacred name of knight.
SHAKESPEARE.—*Henry VI.,* Pt. 1, Act 4, 1.

KNOWLEDGE

For knowledge itself is power.
      BACON.—*De Hæresibus.*

A man is but what he knoweth.
      BACON.—*In Praise of Knowledge.*

Is it not knowledge which doth alone
clear the mind of all perturbations ?
      BACON.—*Ib.*

The sovereignty of man lieth hid in knowledge.   BACON.—*Ib.*

It is no less true in this human kingdom
of knowledge, than in God's kingdom of
heaven, that no man shall enter unto it,
" except he become first as a little child."
      BACON.—*Valerius Terminus.*

How small is our knowledge in comparison of our ignorance !
      BAXTER.—*Saints' Everlasting Rest.*

Be ignorance thy choice, when knowledge leads to woe.
      BEATTIE.—*Minstrel, Bk.* 2, st. 30.

Can you think at all and not pronounce
heartily that to labour in knowledge is to
build up Jerusalem, and to despise knowledge is to despise Jerusalem and her
builders ?   WM. BLAKE.—*Jerusalem.*

There is no knowledge which is not valuable.
    BURKE.—*Speech on American Taxation.*

Sorrow is knowledge : they who know the most
Must mourn the deepest o'er the fatal truth :
The tree of knowledge is not that of life.
      BYRON.—*Manfred,* Act 1, 1.

What a man *kens* he *cans.*
      CARLYLE.—*French Revolution.*

Grace is given of God, but knowledge
is bought in the market.
      A. H. CLOUGH.—*Tober-na-Vuolich.*

Knowledge and wisdom, far from being one,
Have oft-times no connection.
      COWPER.—*Winter Morning Walk.*

Knowledge is the antidote to fear.
      EMERSON.—*Courage.*

And still they gazed, and still the wonder grew,
That one small head could carry all he
knew.   GOLDSMITH.—*Deserted Village.*

Time and industry produce every day new knowledge.
      HOBBES.—*Leviathan, ch.* 30.

It is the province of knowledge to speak,
and it is the privilege of wisdom to listen.
O. W. HOLMES.—*Poet at Breakfast Table.*

If a little knowledge is dangerous, where
is the man who has so much as to be out
of danger ?
      T. H. HUXLEY.—*Science and Culture.*

What sages would have died to learn,
Now taught by cottage dames.
      KEBLE.—*Catechism.*

We are afflicted by what we can prove ;
We are distracted by what we know.
    KIPLING.—*Rewards and Fairies, Our
                Fathers of Old.*

To know is not to know, unless someone
else has known that I know.
      LUCULLUS.—*Fragments.*

The first and wisest of them all professed
To know this only, that he nothing knew.
MILTON.—*Paradise Regained* (*of Socrates*),
Bk. 4, 293.

Knowledge, when wisdom is too weak to
guide her,
Is like a headstrong horse, that throws the
rider.   QUARLES.—*Miscellanies.*

The more men know, the more they
deceive themselves. The only way to
avoid error is ignorance.
ROUSSEAU.—*Emile.*

The only thing we do not know is how
to be ignorant of that which we cannot
know.   ROUSSEAU.—*Ib.*

Most men want knowledge, not for
itself, but for the superiority which knowledge confers.
SYDNEY SMITH.—*Lectures on Moral
Philosophy, No.* 9.

A man who dedicates his life to knowledge becomes habituated to pleasure
which carries with it no reproach.
SYDNEY SMITH.—*Ib., No.* 19.

One eminent man of our time has said
of another that "science was his forte
and omniscience his foible." But that
instance was not an extreme one . . .
The universalist, who handles everything
and embraces nothing, has been seen to
pass into a pursuer of the mere vanities
and frivolities of intellectual display.
SIR H. TAYLOR.—*Notes from Life.*

Knowledge comes, but wisdom lingers.
TENNYSON.—*Locksley Hall.*

Woe to every mind which wishes to be
over-wise!   VOLTAIRE.—*Le Dépositaire.*

He who knows not and knows not that
he knows not is a fool—avoid him!
He who knows not and knows not that he
knows is asleep—awake him!
He who knows not and knows that he
knows not wants beating—beat him!
But he who knows and knows that he
knows is a wise man—know him!
Oriental prov.

L

LABELS

Don't rely too much on labels,
For too often they are fables.
C. H. SPURGEON.—" *Salt-Cellars.*"

LABOUR

Tools were made and born were hands,
Every farmer understands.
WM. BLAKE.—*Proverbs.*

They who always labour can have no
true judgment.   BURKE.—*Letter to Member
of National Assembly* (1791).

Such hath it been—shall be—beneath the
sun—
The many still must labour for the one.
BYRON.—*Corsair, c.* 1, 8.

Till toil grows cheaper than the trodden
weed,
And man competes with man, like foe
with foe.   CAMPBELL.—*On Re-visiting
a Scotch River.*

Labour makes us insensible to sorrow.
CICERO.—*Tusc. Quæst.*

I have found out, I repeat, the true
secret of happiness, Labour with Independence. [*Mr. Belfield.*]
MME. D'ARBLAY.—*Cecilia, Bk.* 8, *c.* 5.

Honest labour bears a lovely face.
DEKKER.—*Patient Grissell.*

Pay ransom to the owner,
And fill the bag to the brim.
Who is the owner ? The slave is owner
And ever was. Pay him.
EMERSON.—*Boston Hymn, Jan.* 1, 1863.

Life gives nothing to mortals except
with great labour. HORACE.—*Sat., Bk.* 1.

Never is work without reward, or reward
without work.   LIVY.—*Hist.,* 5.

Toiling—rejoicing—sorrowing,
Onward through life he goes ;
LONGFELLOW.—*Village Blacksmith.*

Labour is but refreshment from repose.
JAS. MONTGOMERY.—*Greenland.*

Another lean, unwashed artificer.
SHAKESPEARE.—*King John,* Act 4, 2.

Many faint with toil,
That few may know the cares and woes
of sloth. SHELLEY.—*Queen Mab, c.* 3.

He toiled, and toiled, of toil no end to
know,
But endless toil and never-ending woe.
SOUTHEY.—*Maid of Orleans, Bk.* 2.

I was not born a little slave,
To labour in the sun,
And wish I were but in my grave
And all my labour done.
ANN AND JANE TAYLOR.—*Child's
Hymn of Praise.*

O mortal man, who livest here by toil,
Do not complain of this thy hard estate.
THOMSON.—*Castle of Indolence, c.* 1, 1.

" All events are linked together for good
in this best of all worlds," said Pangloss.
" That is well said," replied Candide, " but
at the same time we must cultivate our
garden."   VOLTAIRE.—*Candide.*

Labour is often the father of pleasure.
VOLTAIRE.—*Discours*, 4.

Too long, that some may rest,
Tired millions toil unblest.
SIR W. WATSON.—*New National Anthem.*

Freedom, hand in hand with labour,
walketh strong and brave.
WHITTIER.—*Lumbermen.*

All things are full of labour ; man cannot
utter it : the eye is not satisfied with seeing, nor the ear filled with hearing.
Ecclesiastes i, 8.

Masters, give unto your servants that
which is just and equal. *Colossians* iv, 1.

Eight hours' work, and eight hours' play,
Eight hours' sleep, and eight bob a day.
Australian (?) saying (19th Century).

Many times has even a labouring man
spoken to the purpose.
*Ancient Greek prov. (quoted by Aulus
Gellius).*

Naething is got without pains, but an
ill name and long nails. *Scottish prov.*

Labour has a bitter root but a sweet
taste. *Prov.*

LAND AND LANDOWNERS

No, down with everything and up with
rent ! BYRON.—*Age of Bronze*, st. 14.

The trade of owning land.
CARLYLE.—*Downing Street.*

The first farmer was the first man, and
all historic nobility rests on possession and
use of land. EMERSON.—*Farming.*

Praise great estates ; cultivate a small
one. VIRGIL.—*Georgics*, 2, 413.

It [land] gives one position, and pre-
vents one from keeping it up.
OSCAR WILDE.—*Importance of being
Earnest*, Act 1.

LANGUAGES

And Frensh she spak ful faire and fetisly,
After the scole of Stratford atte Bowe.
CHAUCER.—*Cant. Tales, Prol.*

The basis of poetry is language, which
is material only on one side. It is a demi-
god. EMERSON.—*Art.*

I like to be beholden [i.e. in translations]
to the great metropolitan English speech,
which receives tributaries from every
region under heaven. EMERSON.—*Books.*

Writing is an abuse of language ; reading silently to oneself is a pitiful substitute
for speech. GOETHE.—*Autob., Bk.* 10.

His language is painful and free.
BRET HARTE.—*His Answer.*

Language is but a poor bull's-eye lantern
wherewith to show off the vast cathedral
of the world.
R. L. STEVENSON.—*Walt Whitman.*

Language is the amber on which a
thousand precious and subtle thoughts
have been safely embedded and preserved.
ARCHBP. TRENCH.

Music is the universal language.
JOHN WILSON.—*Noctes*, 8.

Where Nature's end of language is de-
clined,
And men talk only to conceal the mind.
YOUNG.—*Love of Fame, Sat.* 2.

You are worth as many men as you know
languages. *Attrib. to Charles V.*

LARK, THE

But the lark is so brimful of gladness and
love,
The green fields below him, the blue sky
above,
That he sings, and he sings ; and for ever
sings he—
" I love my Love, and my Love loves me ! "
COLERIDGE.—*Answer to a Child's
Question.*

Not loftiest bard of mightiest mind
Shall ever chant a note so pure,
Till he can cast the earth behind,
And breathe in heaven secure.
SIR W. WATSON.—*First Skylark of Spring.*

LATENESS

From youth to age, whate'er the game,
The unvarying practice is the same,—
The devil takes the hindmost, O !
A. H. CLOUGH.—*In the Great Metropolis.*

Brer Wolf fetcht a grab at 'im, but he
wuz des [just] in time fer ter be too late.
J. C. HARRIS.—*Nights with Uncle Remus,
ch.* 18.

Too late, too late ! ye cannot enter now.
TENNYSON.—*Guinevere.*

It is in vain to look for yesterday's fish
in the house of the otter. *Hindoo prov.*

LAUGHTER

Nothing is more foolish than foolish
laughter. CATULLUS.—*Carmen*, 39.

Ill may a sad mind forge a merry face ;
Nor hath constrainèd laughter any grace.
CHAPMAN.—*Hero and Leander
(Continuation of Marlowe's Poem)*, st. 5.

In my mind there is nothing so illiberal
and so ill-bred as audible laughter . . . not
to mention the disagreeable noise it makes

and the shocking distortion of the face
that it occasions.
LORD CHESTERFIELD.—*Advice to his Son.*

And laughter oft is but an art
To drown the outcry of the heart.
HARTLEY COLERIDGE.—*To Gold Fishes.*

There is nothing more unbecoming a
man of quality than to laugh.
CONGREVE.—*Double Dealer,* Act 1, 2.

And the loud laugh that spoke the vacant
mind.   GOLDSMITH.—*Deserted Village.*

I cannot say whether we had more wit
amongst us now than usual, but I am
certain we had more laughing, which
answered the end as well.
GOLDSMITH.—*Vicar of Wakefield, ch.* 32.

Laugh not too much : the witty man
laughs least. HERBERT.—*Church Porch.*

The giggler is a milkmaid.
HERBERT.—*Ib.*

You hear that boy laughing ?—You think
he's all fun ;
But the angels laugh, too, at the good he
has done ;
The children laugh loud as they troop at
his call,
And the poor man that knows him laughs
loudest of all !
O. W. HOLMES.—*The Boys.*

Sport that wrinkled Care derides,
And Laughter holding both his sides.
MILTON.—*L'Allegro,* 31.

Smiles from reason flow,
To brute denied, and are of love the food.
MILTON.—*Paradise Lost, Bk.* 9, 239.

Theirs was the glee of martial breast,
And laughter theirs at little jest.
SCOTT.—*Marmion, c.* 3, *st.* 4.

The heaving of my lungs provokes me
to ridiculous smiling.
SHAKESPEARE.—*Love's Labour's Lost,*
Act 3, 1.

O, I am stabbed with laughter.
SHAKESPEARE.—*Ib.,* Act 5, 2.

Laugh with a vast and inextinguishable
laughter. SHELLEY.—*Prometheus,* Act 4.

Gaiety without eclipse,
Wearieth me, May Lilian.
TENNYSON.—*Lilian.*

A sight to shake
The midriff of despair with laughter.
TENNYSON.—*Princess, c.* 1, 196.

Laugh while you can. Everything has
its time.   VOLTAIRE.—*Charlot.*

Laughter does not prove a man at ease.
French prov.

LAW

Law is king of all.
DEAN ALFORD.—*School of the Heart,* 6.

Law is a bottomless Pit.
J. ARBUTHNOT.—*Title of Pamphlet.*

One of the Seven was wont to say that
laws were like cobwebs, where the small
flies were caught and the great brake
through.   BACON.—*Apophthegms,* 291.

It is oppression to torture laws so that
they torture men.
BACON.—*Instauratio, Pt.* 1, *Bk.* 8, 3.

Laws are generally found to be nets of
such a texture, as the little creep through,
the great break through, and the middle-
sized alone are entangled in.
BACON.—*On Politics.*

What is a law if those who make it
Become the forwardest to break it ?
J. BEATTIE.—*Wolf and the Shepherds.*

All laws creative of liberty are, as far as
they go, abrogative of liberty.
J. BENTHAM.—*Theory of Legislation.*

People crushed by law have no hopes
but from power. If laws are their enemies
they will be enemies to laws ; and those
who have much to hope and nothing to
lose will always be dangerous, more or less.
BURKE.—*Letter to Fox* (Oct., 1777).

There is but one law for all, namely,
that law which governs all law, the law of
our Creator, the law of humanity, justice,
equity—the law of nature and of nations.
BURKE.—*Impeachment of Hastings*
(*May* 28, 1794).

Laws, like houses, lean on one another.
BURKE.—*On the Popery Laws, ch.* 3,
Pt. 1.

There are two, and only two, foundations of law . . . equity and utility.
BURKE.—*Ib.*

A good parson once said that where
mystery begins religion ends. Cannot I
say, as truly at least, of human laws, that
where mystery begins, justice ends ?
BURKE.—*Vindication of Natural Society.*

The law of England is the greatest
grievance of the nation, very expensive
and dilatory.
BURNET.—*Hist. of his own Times.*

That which is a law to-day is none to-
morrow.
BURTON.—*Anatomy of Melancholy.
Democritus to the Reader.*

So Justice, while she winks at crimes,
Stumbles on innocence sometimes.
S. BUTLER.—*Hudibras, Pt.* 1, *c.* 2.

The law can take a purse in open court,
Whilst it condemns a less delinquent for 't.
          S. BUTLER.—*Miscellaneous Thoughts.*

Law does not put the least restraint
Upon our freedom, but maintain 't. . . .
For wholesome laws preserve us free
By stinting of our liberty.
                    S. BUTLER.—*Ib.*

Where law ends, tyranny begins.
          LORD CHATHAM.—*Speech, 1770.*

Extreme law is extreme injustice.
     CICERO.—*De Off.* (quoted as a " *trite
                              +roverb* ").

But in every matter the consensus of
opinion among all nations is to be regarded
as the law of nature.
     CICERO.—*Tusc. Quæst.,* 1, 13, 30.

Laws are so framed that they shall speak
in all matters always with one and the
same voice.   CICERO.

The gladsome light of jurisprudence.
  COKE.—*On Littleton. Institutes,* No. 1.

The Law which is the perfection of
reason.   COKE.—*Ib.*

How long soever it hath continued, if
it be against reason, it is of no force in law.
          COKE.—*Ib.,* No. 1, 80.

Custom is the best interpreter of the
laws.   COKE.

The laws sleep sometimes, but never die.
                         COKE.

Law and equity are two things which
God hath joined, but which man hath put
asunder.   C. C. COLTON.—*Lacon.*

The mere repetition of the *Cantilena* of
the lawyers cannot make it law.
LORD CHIEF JUSTICE DENMAN.—*O'Connell
                        v. the Queen.*

" If the law supposes that," said Mr.
Bumble, . . . " the law is a ass,—a idiot."
     DICKENS.—*Oliver Twist, ch.* 51.

No written laws can be so plain, so pure,
But wit may gloss, and malice may
obscure.
DRYDEN.—*Hind and the Panther, Pt.* 2,318.

The law's made to take care of raskills.
GEO. ELIOT.—*Mill on the Floss, Bk.* 3, *ch.* 4.

Their law [English law] is a network of
fictions ; their property, a scrip or cer-
tificate of right to interest on money that
no man ever saw.   EMERSON.—*English
                       Traits,* 5, *Ability.*

A law or statute is to him [Hafiz] what
a fence is to the nimble schoolboy,—a
temptation for a jump.
     EMERSON.—*Essay on Persian Poetry.*

What natural reason has established
among all men we call the law of nations.
          GALUS.—*Inst. Jur. Civ.*

Do lawe away, what is a king ?
Where is the right of anything
If that there be no lawe in land ?
This ought a king well understand.
     GOWER.—*Confessio Amantis, Bk.* 7.

You chuckled over those people who
could see beauty only in pictures ; but
you cannot imagine the beauty of an intricate, mazy law process, embodying the
doubts and subtleties of generations of
men. I say looked at in that way there is
something picturesque in an Act of Parliament.
     SIR A. HELPS.—*Friends in Council.
                        Slavery, ch.* 1.

Unnecessary laws are not good laws, but
traps for money.
          HOBBES.—*Leviathan, ch.* 30.

Of law there can be no less acknowledged
than that her seat is the bosom of God,
her voice the harmony of the world.
     HOOKER.—*Ecclesiastical Polity,* 1, 16.

Let us hear no general abuse [of law].
The law is the last result of human wisdom
acting upon human experience for the
benefit of the public.
     JOHNSON.—*Remark as recorded by
                        Mrs. Piozzi.*

The law is so lordlich and loth to maken
ende.
     LANGLAND.—*Piers Plowman, Passus
                              4,* 199.

The law is a sort of hocus-pocus science
that smiles in yer face while it picks yer
pocket ; and the glorious uncertainty of
it is of mair use to the professors than the
justice of it.
          C. MACKLIN.—*Love à la Mode.*

Good laws are produced by bad customs.   MACROBIUS.—*Sat.* 2.

Litigious terms, fat contentions, and
flowing fees.   MILTON.—*Education.*

The law of England is, at best, but the
reason of parliament.
          MILTON.—*Eikonoclastes.*

Against the law of nature, law of nations.
     MILTON.—*Samson Agonistes,* 889.

It is the rule of rules, the law of laws,
that everyone should observe that of the
place where he is.   MONTAIGNE.—*Bk.* 1.

The atrocity of laws prevents their
execution.   MONTESQUIEU.

There is no worse tyranny than that
which is exercised under cover of the law.
                    MONTESQUIEU.

Law should be clear, precise, consistent.
To interpret it is to corrupt it. NAPOLEON.

Law, being a tyrant over men, compels
many things to be done contrary to nature.
PLATO.—*Protagoras*, 69 (*Remark
assigned to Hippias the Wise*) (*Cary tr.*).

Laws are subservient to custom.
PLAUTUS.—*Trinummus*.

The first Almighty Cause
Acts not by partial, but by general laws.
POPE.—*Essay on Man, Ep.* 1, 145.

" There take," says Justice, " take you
each a shell.
We thrive at Westminster on fools like
you.
'Twas a fat oyster—Live in peace—
Adieu !" POPE.—*Tr. from Boileau*.

The hungry judges soon the sentence sign,
And wretches hang that jurymen may dine.
POPE.—*Rape of the Lock, c.* 3, 21.

The spirit of the laws is like the Nile—
wide, immense, fruitful in its course ;
feeble and obscure in its source.
A. DE RIVAROL.

The universal spirit of the laws of all
countries is to put always the strong
against the weak, and him who has against
him who has nothing. This disadvantage
is inevitable and it is without exception.
ROUSSEAU.—*Emile*.

" That sounds like nonsense, my dear."
" May be so, my dear ; but it may be
very good law for all that."
SCOTT.—*Guy Mannering, ch.* 9.

The law's delay.
SHAKESPEARE.—*Hamlet*, Act 3, 1.

Old father antic, the law.
SHAKESPEARE.—*Henry IV., Pt.* 1, Act 1, 2.

But in these nice sharp quillets of the law,
Good faith, I am no wiser than a daw.
SHAKESPEARE.—*Henry VI., Pt.* 1, Act 2, 4.

We must not make a scarecrow of the law,
Setting it up to fear the birds of prey.
SHAKESPEARE.—*Measure for Measure,*
Act 2, 1.

In law what plea so tainted and corrupt
But, being seasoned with a gracious voice,
Obscures the show of evil ?
SHAKESPEARE.—*Merchant of Venice,*
Act 3, 2.

Still keep you o' the windy side of the law.
SHAKESPEARE.—*Twelfth Night*, Act 3, 4.

Who ever knew an honest brute
At law his neighbour prosecute,

Bring action for assault and battery,
Or friend beguile with lies and flattery ?
SWIFT.—*Logicians Refuted*.

A people can be strong where the laws
are strong. PUBLILIUS SYRUS.

Mercy loosens the law.
PUBLILIUS SYRUS.

In the most corrupt state there are the
most laws. TACITUS.—*Annals*.

Mastering the lawless science of our law,
That codeless myriad of precedent,
That wilderness of single instances,
Through which a few, by wit or fortune
led,
May beat a pathway out to wealth and
fame. TENNYSON.—*Aylmer's Field*.

The highest law is often the greatest
roguery. TERENCE.—*Heaut.*, Act 4.

No man e'er felt the halter draw,
With good opinion of the law.
J. TRUMBULL.—*McFingal*.

Your laws are your tyrants.
VOLTAIRE.—*Brutus*;

Would you have good laws ? Burn
those that exist and make new ones.
VOLTAIRE.—*Dictionnaire Philosophique
(Lois)*.

He (Zadig) believed that the laws were
intended to help citizens as much as to
intimidate them. VOLTAIRE.—*Zadig*.

The stars of heaven are free because
In amplitude of liberty
Their joy is to obey the laws.
SIR W. WATSON.—*Things that are more
excellent, st.* 4.

Laws were made to be broken.
JOHN WILSON.—*Noctes*.

When the law shows her teeth, but dares
not bite.
YOUNG.—*Love of Fame, Sat.* 1.

According to the law of the Medes and
Persians, which altereth not. *Daniel* vi, 8.

Let it be written among the laws of the
Persians and the Medes, that it be not
altered. *Esther* i, 19.

The law is good, if a man use it lawfully.
1 *Timothy* i, 8.

The law is King (Lex Rex).
Covenanters' saying.

Lawsuits consume time and money and
rest and friends. *Prov.* (*Geo. Herbert*).

Better a lean agreement than a fat
judgment. *Italian prov.*

Abundance o' law breaks nae law.
Scottish prov.

There is no law without a loophole.
Prov.

In law there's many a loss without a gain, but never a gain without a loss.
Saying.

LAWYERS

A lawyer is a gentleman who rescues your estate from your enemies and keeps it to himself. LORD BROUGHAM.—*Saying.*

But what his common sense cam short, He ekèd out wi' law, man.
BURNS.—*Extempore: On Two Lawyers*, 1.

'Tis boldness, boldness, does the deed in the Court. CHAPMAN.—*Monsieur d'Olive*, Act 3 (*Alluding to the King's Court*).

He saw a Lawyer killing a viper
On a dunghill hard by his own stable ;
And the Devil smiled, for it put him in mind
Of Cain and his brother Abel.
COLERIDGE.—*Devil's Thoughts.*

If there were no bad people, there would be no good lawyers.
DICKENS.—*Old Curiosity Shop*, ch. 56.

Battledore and shuttlecock's a wery good game, vhen you a'n't the shuttlecock and two lawyers the battledores, in wich case it gets too excitin' to be pleasant. [*Sam Weller.*]   DICKENS.—*Pickwick Papers, c.* 20.

I know you lawyers can with ease
Twist words and meanings as you please ;
That language, by your skill made pliant,
Will bend to favour every client.
GAY.—*Fables, Pt.* 2, 1.

Lawyers are always more ready to get a man into troubles than out of them.
GOLDSMITH.—*Good-natured Man.*

Yet one fault he had, and that was a thumper—
He was, could he help it ? a special attorney. GOLDSMITH.—*Retaliation.*

Do you know the lawyer's story. . . . " Many times when I have had a good case," he said, " I have failed ; but then I have often succeeded in bad cases. And so justice is done." SIR A. HELPS.— *Friends in Council, Bk.* 1, ch. 11.

I cannot exactly tell you, sir, who he is, and I would be loth to speak ill of any person who I do not know deserves it, but I am afraid he is an attorney.
JOHNSON.—*Remark as recorded by Mrs. Piozzi.*

The man of law, that never saw
The ways to buy and sell,
Wenyng to rise by merchandise,
I pray God spede him well !
SIR T. MORE.—*A Merry Jest.*

All lawyers, be they knaves or fools,
Know that a seat is worth the earning,
Since Parliament's astounding rules
Vouch for their honour and their learning.
J. E. THOROLD ROGERS.—*On the Eagerness of Lawyers to obtain Seats in the House.*

Where be his quiddits now, his quillets, his cases, his tenures and his tricks ?
SHAKESPEARE.—*Hamlet*, Act 5, 1.

The first thing we do, let's kill all the lawyers.
SHAKESPEARE.—*Henry VI., Pt.* 2, Act 4, 2.

And do as adversaries do in law,
Strive mightily, but eat and drink as friends.
SHAKESPEARE.—*Taming of the Shrew,* Act 1, 2.

No doubt the good people who are called lawyers are as honest as others ; though I once knew a gentleman who used to sigh for a day's shooting in Lincoln's Inn Fields.
C. H. SPURGEON.—" *Salt-Cellars.*"

Woe unto you, lawyers ! for ye have taken away the key of knowledge.
St. Luke xi, 52.

There was a young lady of Cirencester,
Who went to consult her solicitor,
When he asked for his fee
She said " Fiddle-de-dee !
I only looked in as a visitor."   *Anon.*

Our Civill Law doth seeme a royall thing,
It hath more titles than the *Spanish* King ;
But yet the Common Law quite puts it downe,
In getting, like the Pope, so many a Crowne.
The Sophister, Act 1, sc. 4 (*c.* 1650) (*Authorship uncertain*).

Every house which a man not a lawyer builds out of Edinburgh enables a man, who is a lawyer, to build one equally comfortable in Edinburgh.   *Scottish prov.*

Fools and obstinate men make rich lawyers.   *Spanish prov.*

" Virtue in the middle," said the devil when seated between two lawyers.
Said to be " a very old proverb."

Fools and perverse
Fill the lawyer's purse.   *Prov.*

LEADERSHIP

Rides in the whirlwind and directs the storm. ADDISON.—*The Campaign.*

We that had loved him so, followed him, honoured him,
Lived in his mild and magnificent eye,

Learned his great language, caught his clear
accents,
Made him our pattern to live and to die.
    BROWNING.—*The Lost Leader.*

Great men are the guide-posts and landmarks in the State.
    BURKE.—*Speech on American Taxation.*

The men of England—the men, I mean,
of light and leading in England.
    BURKE.—*Thoughts on French Revolution.*

Still sways their souls with that commanding art
That dazzles, leads, yet chills the vulgar
    heart.   BYRON.—*Corsair, c. 1, 8.*

And when we think we lead we most are
    led.   BYRON.—*Two Foscari, Act 2, 1.*

Here's to the pilot that weathered the
    storm.   G. CANNING.—*The Pilot.*

Surely of all " rights of man," this right
of the ignorant man to be guided by the
wiser, to be, gently or forcibly, held in the
true course by him, is the indisputablest.
    CARLYLE.—*Chartism, 6.*

A daring pilot in extremity,
Pleased with the danger when the waves
ran high.
    DRYDEN.—*Absalom and Achitophel,*
        Pt. 1, 159.

He led his regiment from behind
(He found it less exciting).
    SIR W. S. GILBERT.—*Gondoliers.*

When I rush on, sure none will dare to
    stay ;
'Tis Beauty calls and Glory shows the way.
    N. LEE.—*Rival Queens, Act 4, 2.*

The time is in want of a leader.
    LUCANUS.
A man, a man ! My Kingdom for a man !
    MARSTON.—*Scourge of Villainy.*

O for a living man to lead !
That will not babble when we bleed ;
O for the silent doer of the deed !
    STEPHEN PHILLIPS.—*A Man.*

The man within the coach that sits,
And to another's skill submits,
Is safer much, whate'er arrives,
And warmer too, than he that drives.
    PRIOR.—*Alma, c. 3, 137.*

Where, where was Roderick then ?
One blast upon his bugle horn
Were worth a thousand men.
    SCOTT.—*Lady of the Lake, c. 6, 18.*

A rarer spirit never,
Did steer humanity ; but you, gods, will
    give us
Some faults to make us men.
    SHAKESPEARE.—*Antony and Cleopatra,*
        Act 5, 1.

Go on, I'll follow thee.
    SHAKESPEARE.—*Hamlet, Act 1, 4.*

An two men ride of a horse, one must
ride behind.
    SHAKESPEARE.—*Much Ado, Act 3, 5.*

The fire of God
Fills him : I never saw his like : there
    lives
No greater leader.
    TENNYSON.—*Lancelot and Elaine, 314.*

Ten good soldiers, wisely led,
Will beat a hundred without a head.
    D. W. THOMPSON.—*Paraphr. of Euripides.*

When winds are steady and skies are clear,
Every hand the ship would steer ;
But soon as ever the wild winds blow,
Every hand would go below.
    D. W. THOMPSON.—*Ib.*

Oh, for a single hour of that Dundee,
Who on that day the word of onset gave !
    WORDSWORTH.—*Pass of Killiecrankie.*

An army of stags led by a lion would be
more formidable than an army of lions led
by a stag.   *Latin prov.*

Ah, John, by me thou setst no store.
And that I fairly finde ;
How ofte send I my men before,
And tarrye myself behinde ?
    Old Ballad. Robin Hood.

LEANNESS

Let me have men about me that are fat,
Sleek-headed men, and such as sleep o'
    nights ;
Yond' Cassius has a lean and hungry look ;
He thinks too much : such men are dan-
gerous.
    SHAKESPEARE.—*Julius Cæsar, Act 1, 2.*

LEARNING

All men naturally desire to know.
    ARISTOTLE.—*Metaph., 1, 1.*

There is no power on earth which setteth
up a throne or chair of state in the spirits
and souls of men, and in their cogitations,
imaginations, opinions, and beliefs, but
knowledge and learning.
    BACON.—*Adv. of Learning.*

The learned eye is still the loving one.
    BROWNING.—*Red Cotton Night Cap*
        Country, Bk. 1.

Learning, that cobweb of the brain,
Profane, erroneous, and vain.
    S. BUTLER.—*Hudibras, Pt. 1, c. 3.*

Man has a natural desire to know,
But th' one half is for interest, th' other
show.
    S. BUTLER.—*Human Learning, 151.*

Learn, but learn from the learned.   CATO.

For out of olde feldes, as men seith,
Cometh al this newe corn fro yere to yere ;
And out of olde bokes, in good feith,
Cometh al this newe science that men lere.
     CHAUCER.—*Parliament of Foules.*

To them the sounding jargon of the schools
Seems what it is—a cap and bells for fools.
     COWPER.—*Progress of Error*, 368.

Truths that the learn'd pursue with eager
thought
Are not important always as dear-bought.
     COWPER.—*Tirocinium*, 73.

Knowledge is proud that he has learned so
much,
Wisdom is humble that he knows no more.
     COWPER.—*Winter Walk at Noon*, 96.

And yet, alas ! when all our lamps are
burned,
Our bodies wasted, and our spirits spent,
When we have all the learned volumes
turned,
Which yield men's wits both help and
ornament,
What can we know or what can we discern ?
     SIR J. DAVIES.—*Nosce Teipsum. Intro.*

When land is gone and money's spent,
Then learning is most excellent.
Though house and land be never got,
Learning will give what they cannot.
DICKENS. — *Who, according to C. H.
Spurgeon, added the last two lines to the
old saying.*

Hated not learning worse than toad or
asp.   MILTON.—*Sonnet.*

Learning alone, of all things in our
possession, is immortal and divine.
     PLUTARCH.—*Morals.*

A little learning is a dangerous thing ;
Drink deep, or taste not the Pierian spring.
There shallow draughts intoxicate the
brain,
And drinking largely sobers us again.
     POPE.—*Criticism.*

Take from the learned the pleasure of
making their learning heard, and their
learning will be worth nothing to them.
     ROUSSEAU.—*Julie.*

Learning makes most men more stupid
and foolish than they are by nature.
     SCHOPENHAUER.—*Thinking for Oneself.*

No man is wiser for his learning. Wit
and wisdom are born with a man.
     SELDEN.—*Learning.*

The mind is slow in unlearning what it
has been long in learning.
     SENECA.—*Troades.*

A progeny of learning.
     SHERIDAN.—*The Rivals*, Act 1, 2.
         (*Mrs. Malaprop*).

Wearing all that weight
Of learning lightly, like a flower.
     TENNYSON.—*In Memoriam, Conclusion,
st.* 10.

Much learning shows how little mortals
know.   YOUNG.—*Night Thoughts*, 6.

For it is precept upon precept, precept
upon precept ; line upon line, line upon
line ; here a little, there a little.
     Isaiah xxviii, 10 (*R.V.*).

Much learning doth make thee mad.
     Acts xxvi, 24.

Learned fools are the greatest fools.
     Prov.

Learning makes the wise wiser, but
the fool more foolish.   *Prov.*

LEGENDS

So simple were those times, when a grave
sage
Could with an old wife's tale instruct the
age ; . . .
Make a dull sentence and a moral fable
Do more than all our holdings-forth are
able.   S. BUTLER.—*On the
Licentiousness of the Age.*

Most men of unusual power have
peculiarities which the vulgar folk cannot
understand : whence there rises round
them a rank growth of myth.
     MORTIMER COLLINS.—*Thoughts in my
Garden*, 2, 287.

These and a thousand more of doubtful
fame,
To whom old fables give a lasting name.
     POPE.—*Temple of Fame*, 129.

And twenty more such names and men as
these,
Which never were, nor no man ever saw.
     SHAKESPEARE.—*Taming of Shrew,
Induction, sc.* 2.

Fable is the elder sister of history.
     VOLTAIRE.—*Dictionnaire philosophique
(Zoroastre).*

There are no ancient histories—except
fables.   VOLTAIRE.—*Origin of Fables.*

I grant it's a gey lee-like story [a very
lie-like story].   JOHN WILSON.—*Noctes.*

LEGISLATION

Bad laws are the worst sort of tyranny.
     BURKE.—*Speech* (1780).

Moderation should be the guiding spirit
of the legislator.   MONTESQUIEU.

Poets are the unacknowledged legislators of the world.
     SHELLEY.—*Defence of Poetry* (1821).

No laws, however stringent, can make
the idle industrious, the thriftless provident, or the drunken sober.
S. SMILES.—*Self-Help, ch.* I.

As though conduct could be made right
or wrong by the votes of some men sitting
in a room at Westminster.
HERBT. SPENCER.—*Social Statics.*

LEISURE

What shelter to grow ripe is ours ?
What leisure to grow wise ?
M. ARNOLD.—*Obermann.*

When a man's busy, why, leisure
Strikes him as wonderful pleasure ;
'Faith, and at leisure once is he ?
Straightway he wants to be busy.
BROWNING.—*The Glove.*

How various his employments, whom the
world
Calls idle.   COWPER.—*Garden,* 352.

He who does not know how to use
leisure makes more business of it than there
is business in business itself.
ENNIUS.—*(quoted by Aulus Gellius).*

" Leisure " is the mother of " philosophy," and " Commonwealth " the
mother of " peace " and " leisure."
HOBBES.—*Leviathan, ch.* 46.

Leisure is time for doing something
useful.   DR. N. HOWE.—*Proverbs.*

And add to these retiréd leisure,
That in trim gardens takes his pleasure.
MILTON.—*Il Penseroso,* 49.

Leisure without books is death, burial
alive.   SENECA.—*Ep.,* 82.

He hath no leisure that useth it not.
Prov. (Geo. Herbert).

LENIENCY

Curse on his virtues ! They've undone his
country :
Such popular humanity is treason.
ADDISON.—*Cato,* Act 4, 4.

Forbear to judge, for we are sinners all.
Close up his eyes, and draw the curtain
close,
And let us all to meditation.
SHAKESPEARE.—*Henry VI., Pt.* 2, Act 3, 3.

He harms the good that doth the evil
spare.
" *Times Whistle* " (c. 1614), *A prov.*

LESSONS

" That's the reason they're called
lessons," the Gryphon remarked ; " because
they lessen from day to day."
C. L. DODGSON.—*Alice in Wonderland,
c.* 10.

Thus may we gather honey from the weed,
And make a moral of the devil himself.
SHAKESPEARE.—*Henry V.,* Act 4, 1.

Happy in this, she is not yet so old
But she may learn ; happier than this,
She is not bred so dull but she can learn.
SHAKESPEARE.—*Merchant of Venice,*
Act 3, 2.

LETTERS (ALPHABETICAL)

The invention of printing, though ingenious, compared with the invention of
letters, is no great matter.
HOBBES.—*Leviathan, ch.* 4.

LETTERS (CORRESPONDENCE)

The earth has nothing like a she epistle.
BYRON.—*Don Juan,* 13, 105.

Love is the life of friendship : letters are
The life of love.
J. HOWELL.—*Familiar Letters, Bk.* 1.

Love is the marrow of friendship, and
letters are the Elixir of love.
J. HOWELL.—*Ib.*

As keys do open chests,
So letters open breasts.
J. HOWELL.—*To the Sagacious Reader.*

Letter-writing, that most delightful
way of wasting time.
VISCOUNT MORLEY.—*Life of Geo. Eliot,
p.* 96.

For God's sake, Madam, let not my
correspondence [with you] be like a traffic
with the grave, from whence there is no
return.
POPE.—*Letter to Lady M. W. Montagu,
Oct.,* 1716 (?).

I dread letter writing, and envy the old
hermit of Prague, who never saw pen or
ink.   SCOTT.—*Diary,* 1826.

His letters, say they, are weighty and
powerful ; but his bodily presence is weak,
and his speech contemptible.
2 Corinthians x, 10.

LEVELLERS

Levelling is comfortable, as we often
say, levelling, yet only down to oneself.
CARLYLE.—*French Revolution, Pt.* 2,
Bk. 5, ch. 4.

Your levellers wish to level down as far
as themselves ; but they cannot bear
levelling up to themselves.
JOHNSON.—*Remark.*

LEVITY

Scoffing cometh not of wisdom.
SIR P. SIDNEY.—*Apologie for Poetrie.*

I think the immortal servants of mankind,
Who, from their graves watch by how slow
degrees

The World-Soul greatens with the centuries,
Mourn most man's barren levity of mind.
               SIR W. WATSON.—*Sonnet.*

LIBEL

For oh, it was nuts to the Father of Lies,
  (As this wily fiend is named in the Bible),
To find it was settled by laws so wise
    That the greater the truth, the worse
      the libel.   MOORE.—*Case of Libel.*

He evaded accusation for libel by speaking in humorous fables.
             PHÆDRUS.—*Bk. 3, Prol.*

It often happens that if a lie be believed
only for an hour, it has done its work and
there is no further occasion for it.
        SWIFT.—*Examiner, No.* 15.

LIBERAL, THE

But the liberal deviseth liberal things ;
and in liberal things shall he continue.
         Isaiah xxxii, 8. (*R.V.*).

LIBERTY

A day, an hour of virtuous liberty
Is worth a whole eternity in bondage.
        ADDISON.—*Cato,* Act 2, 1,

    When liberty is gone,
Life grows insipid and has lost its relish.
        ADDISON.—*Ib.,* Act 2, 3.

Chains or conquest, liberty or death.
        ADDISON.—*Ib.,* Act 2, 4.

Liberty of speech inviteth and pro-
voketh liberty to be used again, and so
bringeth much to a man's knowledge.
      BACON.—*Adv. of Learning.*

Liberty too must be limited in order to
be possessed.   BURKE.—*Letter.*

Abstract liberty, like other mere
abstractions, is not to be found.
     BURKE.—*Speech on Conciliation.*

The only liberty I mean, is a liberty
connected with order ; that not only exists
along with order and virtue, but which
cannot exist at all without them.
     BURKE.—*Speech at his arrival at*
                      Bristol.

    Liberty's in every blow !
    Let us do or die !
      BURNS.—*Bruce's Address.*

Hereditary bondsmen ! know ye not
Who would be free, themselves must strike
  the blow ?
   BYRON.—*Childe Harold, c.* 2, *st.* 76.

For Freedom's battle once begun,
Bequeathed by bleeding sire to son,
Though baffled oft, is ever won.
      BYRON.—*The Giaour,* 123.

Our land, the first garden of Liberty's
  tree—
It has been, and yet shall be, the land of
  the free.
     CAMPBELL.—*Song of the Greeks.*

Liberty will not descend to a people ;
a people must raise themselves to liberty.
It is a blessing that must be earned before
it can be enjoyed.
      C. C. COLTON.—*Lacon.*

Let my name perish so long as France is
free !   DANTON.—*March,* 1793.

The love of liberty with life is given,
And life itself the inferior gift of Heaven.
        DRYDEN.—*Palamon.*

In a perfect community liberty would
be complete. Every one would do as he
pleased. Human nature is for the present
unequal to the realisation of the ideal.
   FROUDE.—*Short Studies, Party Politics.*

There are two kinds of liberty—the
liberty of anarchy, which is death, and the
true liberty, which alone is worth a wise
man's caring for, the liberty which is made
possible by obedience to rational authority.
              FROUDE.—*Ib.*

The love of liberty is the love of others ;
the love of power is the love of ourselves.
      HAZLITT.—*Toad-Eaters.*

I know not what course others may take;
but as for me, give me liberty or give me
death !   PHILIP HENRY.—*Speech,* 1775.

As He died to make men holy, let us live
  to make men free,
While God is marching on !
    JULIA WARD HOWE.—*Battle Hymn.*

God who gave us life gave us liberty at
the same time.
T. JEFFERSON.—*Rights of British America.*

    There is but one task for all—
      For each one life to give.
    Who stands if freedom fall ?
    Who dies if England live ?
      KIPLING.—*For all we have.*

But libbaty's a kind o' thing
That don't agree with niggers.
   J. R. LOWELL.—*Biglow Papers, Series*
                     1, 6.

At length a mighty one of Greece began
To assert the natural liberty of man,
By senseless terrors and vain fancies led
To slavery. Straight the conquered phan-
  toms fled.
    LUCRETIUS.—*De Rerum Natura,* 1, 67
                   (*Creech tr.*).

  Pray you use your freedom,
And so far, if you please, allow me mine.
   MASSINGER.—*Duke of Milan,* Act 4, 3.

Liberty, as a principle, has no application to any state of things anterior to the time when mankind have become capable of being improved by free and equal discussion.   J. S. MILL.—*Liberty, Introd.*

The liberty of the individual must be thus far limited : he must not make himself a nuisance to other people.
J. S. MILL.—*Ib., ch. 3.*

None can love freedom heartily but good men ; the rest love not freedom, but licence.   MILTON.—*Tenure of Kings.*

To have a really free people, the governed must be virtuous and the governors must be gods.   NAPOLEON.

Yet well brave hearts, I ween,
Wounds deep as ours, with Freedom blest,
May bear ; and for success to come
On hope's assurance rest.
PINDAR.—*Isthmian Odes*, 8, 17 (*Moore tr.*).

Liberty is not in any form of government. It is in the heart of the free man ; he carries it with him everywhere.
ROUSSEAU.—*Emile.*

The more the State extends itself, the more liberty diminishes.
ROUSSEAU.—*Ib.*

That treacherous phantom which men call Liberty.
RUSKIN.—*Seven Lamps, c. 7, 1.*

And liberty plucks justice by the nose.
SHAKESPEARE.—*Measure for Measure,*
Act 1, 4.

So loving-jealous of his liberty.
SHAKESPEARE.—*Romeo and Juliet,*
Act 2, 2.

Englishmen never will be slaves ; they are free to do whatever the Government and public opinion allow them to do.
G. B. SHAW.—*Man and Superman.*

Fair liberty was all his cry ;
For her he stood prepared to die ;
For her he boldly stood alone ;
For her he oft exposed his own.
SWIFT.—*On the Death of Dr. Swift.*

If man is created free, he ought to govern himself. If man has tyrants, he ought to dethrone them. It is known only too well that these tyrants are the vices.
VOLTAIRE.—*Discours. De l'Envie.*

Liberty, when it begins to take root, is a plant of rapid growth.
GEO. WASHINGTON.—*Saying.*

Liberty and Union, now and for ever, one and inseparable.
D. WEBSTER.—*Speech on Foot's Resolution.*

We must be free or die, who speak the tongue
That Shakespeare spake ; the faith and morals hold
Which Milton held. In everything we are sprung
Of Earth's first blood, have titles manifold.
WORDSWORTH.—*Poems to National*
Independence.

O Liberty ! how many crimes are committed in thy name !
Attr. to Madame Roland, on the Scaffold.

If you love liberty don't keep it all for yourself.
Given as a prov. by C. H. Spurgeon.

Men rattle their chains to show that they are free.   *Prov.*

LIBRARY

A library is but the soul's burial ground ;
It is the land of shadows.
H. W. BEECHER.—*Oxford : Bodleian*
Library.

With awe, around these silent walks I tread ;
These are the lasting mansions of the dead:
" The dead," methinks a thousand tongues reply,
" These are the tombs of such as cannot die."
Crowned with eternal fame they sit sublime,
And laugh at all the little strife of time.
CRABBE.—*The Library.*

Athens lives here more than in Plutarch's lives.
VAUGHAN.—*Sir T. Bodley's Library.*

LICENCE

Poets and painters, as all artists know,
May shoot a little with a lengthened bow.
BYRON.—*Hints from Horace, l. 15.*

In all pointed sentences some degree of accuracy must be sacrificed to conciseness.
JOHNSON.—*On English Soldiers.*

Let the wild falcon soar her swing,
She'll stoop when she has tired her wing.
SCOTT.—*Marmion, c. 1, st. 17.*

LIFE

We are the voices of the wandering wind,
Which moan for rest, and rest can never find ;
Lo, as the wind is, so is mortal life,
A moan, a sigh, a sob, a storm, a strife.
SIR E. ARNOLD.—*Light of Asia : Deva's*
Song.

Joy comes and goes, hope ebbs and flows
Like the wave ;
Change doth unknit the tranquil strength of men.

Love lends life a little grace,
A few sad smiles; and then,
Both are laid in one cold place,
In the grave.
M. ARNOLD.—*A Question.*

Too fast we live, too much are tried,
Too harassed, to attain
Wordsworth's sweet calm, or Goethe's wide
And luminous view to gain.
M. ARNOLD.—*Obermann.*

Whose mind hath known all arts of governing,
Mused much, loved life a little, loathed it more.
M. ARNOLD.—*To a Gipsy Child.*

O born in days when wits were fresh and clear,
And life ran gaily as the sparkling Thames:
Before this strange disease of modern life,
With its sick hurry, its divided aims,
Its heads o'ertaxed, its palsied hearts, was rife.
M. ARNOLD.—*Scholar-Gipsy.*

Live every day as if thy last.
MARCUS AURELIUS.—7, 69.

He most lives
Who thinks most, feels the noblest, acts the best.   P. J. BAILEY.—*Festus.*

It is misery to be born, pain to live, grief to die.   ST. BERNARD.—*Chap.* 3.

Everything that lives is holy.
WM. BLAKE.—*Vala.*

How time runs away! and we meet with death almost ere we have time to think ourselves alive. One doth but breakfast here, another dines, he that liveth longest doth but sup; we must all go to bed in another world.
DR. JOHN BROWN.—*Horæ Subsecivæ.*

Thus we are men, and we know not how. There is something in us that can be without us, and will be after us, though it is strange that it hath no history what it was before us.
SIR T. BROWNE.—*Religio Medici, Pt.* I, 36.

Life treads on life, and heart on heart,
We press too close, in church and mart,
To keep a dream or grave apart.
E. B. BROWNING.—*Vision of Poets.*

A quiet life, which was not life at all.
E. B. BROWNING.—*Aurora Leigh.*

This world's no blot for us,
Nor blank: it means intensely, and means good.
To find its meaning is my meat and drink.
BROWNING.—*Fra Lippo Lippi.*

Life is probation, and the earth no goal,
But starting point of man.
BROWNING.—*Ring and the Book,* 10, 1436.

You never know what life means till you die;
Even throughout life, 'tis death that makes life live;
Give it whatever the significance.
BROWNING.—*Ib.,* 11, 2375.

O life! thou art a galling load,
Along a rough, a weary road,
To wretches such as I!
BURNS.—*Despondency.*

Life is but a day at most,
Sprung from night, in darkness lost.
BURNS.—*Lines in Friars-Carse Hermitage.*

Well—well, the world must turn upon its axis,
And all mankind turn with it, heads or tails,
And live and die, make love and pay our taxes,
And as the veering wind shifts, shift our sails.   BYRON.—*Don Juan,* 2, 4.

We live and die,
But which is best, you know no more than I.   BYRON.—*Ib.,* 7, 4.

The life even of the meanest man, it were good to remember, is a Poem.
CARLYLE.—*Cagliostro.*

" I must live, sir," say many. To which I answer, " No, sir, you need not live."
CARLYLE.*—*Letter Dec.* 20, 1831.

This world nis but a thurghfare ful of wo,
And we ben pilgrimes, passinge to and fro.
CHAUCER.—*Knightes Tale.*

No wish profaned my overwhelmèd heart.
Blest hour! it was a luxury,—to be!
COLERIDGE.—*On having left a place of Retirement.*

You promise heavens free from strife,
Pure truth, and perfect change of will;
But sweet, sweet is this human life,
So sweet I fain would breathe it still.
Your chilly stars I can forego;
This warm kind world is all I know.
WM. CORY.—*Mimnermus in Church.*

Life is an incurable disease.
COWLEY.—*To Dr. Scarborough.*

" Sairey," says Mrs. Harris, " sech is life.
Vich likewise is the hend of all things."
DICKENS.—*Martin Chuzzlewit, ch.* 29.

Youth is a blunder; Manhood is a struggle; Old age a regret.
DISRAELI.—*Coningsby, Bk.* 3, *ch.* 1.

* *Cf.* ROUSSEAU, page 286.

Live while you live, the epicure would say,
And seize the pleasures of the present day ;
Live while you live, the sacred preacher
    cries,
And give to God each moment as it flies.
Lord, in my view let both united be ;
I live in pleasure when I live to thee.
    REV. P. DODDRIDGE.—*On his family
        motto, " Dum vivimus vivamus."*

To view the light of life
To mortals is most sweet, but all beneath
Is nothing. Of his senses is he reft
Who hath a wish to die ; for life, though
    ill,
Excels whate'er there is of good in death.
    EURIPIDES.—*Andromeda*, 147
        (*Woodhull tr.*).

Think, in this battered Caravanserai,
Whose Portals are alternate Night and
    Day,
How Sultán after Sultán with his Pomp
Abode his destined Hour, and went his
    way.   FITZGERALD.—*Rubáiyát, st.* 17.

Into this Universe, and *Why* not knowing,
Nor *Whence*, like Water willy-nilly flowing;
    And out of it, as Wind along the Waste
I know not *Whither*, willy-nilly blowing.
    FITZGERALD.—*Ib., st.* 29.

A Moment's Halt—a momentary taste
Of BEING from the Well amid the waste—
    And Lo !—the phantom caravan has
        reached
The NOTHING it set out from—Oh, make
    haste.   FITZGERALD.—*Ib., st.* 48.

Glory is bought at the cost of happiness ;
pleasure at the cost of health ; favour at
the cost of independence.
    PIERRE GASTON (DUC DE LÉVIS).
        Maxims.

Life is a jest and all things show it ;
I thought so once and now I know it.
    GAY.—*My own Epitaph.*

A little season of love and laughter,
    Of light and life and pleasure and pain,
And a horror of outer darkness after,
    And dust returneth to dust again.
Then the lesser life shall be as the greater,
And the lover of life shall join the hater,
And the one thing cometh sooner or later,
    And no one knoweth the loss or gain.
    A. L. GORDON.—*The Swimmer.*

Life's little ironies.
THOS. HARDY.—*Title of Book* (1894).

Life is the greatest good, and death the
worst evil.   HEINE.—*Reisebilder, c.* 3.

Death is still working like a mole,
And digs my grave at each remove.
    HERBERT.—*Grace.*

Life is a fatal complaint and an
eminently contagious one.
    O. W. HOLMES.—*Poet at Breakfast Table.*

" To him that lives well," answered the
hermit, " every form of life is good."
    JOHNSON.—*Rasselas.*

Teach me to live that I may dread
The grave as little as my bed.
    BP. KEN.—*Evening Hymn.*

I strove with none, for none was worth
    my strife ;
Nature I loved, and next to Nature, Art;
I warmed both hands before the fire of
    life ;
It sinks, and I am ready to depart.
    W. S. LANDOR.—*Finis.*

For you the To-come,
    But for me the Gone-by ;
You are panting to live,
    I am waiting to die.
    R. LE GALLIENNE.—*Old Man's Song.*

Is Love a lie, and fame indeed a breath ;
And is there no sure thing in life—but
    death ?
    R. LE GALLIENNE.—*On Stevenson.*

Oh thou child of many prayers,
Life hath quicksands, life hath snares.
    LONGFELLOW.—*Maidenhood.*

Life is real ! life is earnest !
    And the grave is not its goal.
    LONGFELLOW.—*Psalm of Life.*

Our life must once have end ; in vain we
    fly
From following Fate ; e'en now, e'en now,
    we die.
    LUCRETIUS.—*De Rerum Natura*, 3, 1093
        (*Creech tr.*).

Nor love thy life, nor hate ; but what
    thou liv'st
Live well, how long or short permit to
    Heaven.
    MILTON.—*Paradise Lost, Bk.* 11, 553.

Who that hath ever been
    Could bear to be no more ?
Yet who would tread again the scene
    He trod through life before ?
    J. MONTGOMERY.—*Falling Leaf.*

This life is all chequered with pleasures
    and woes. MOORE.—*Irish Melodies.*

Still as death approaches nearer,
The joys of life are sweeter, dearer.
    MOORE.—*Odes of Anacreon.*

They may rail at this life—from the hour
    I began it,
I've found it a life full of kindness and
    bliss ·

And until they can show me some happier
   planet,
   More social and bright, I'll content me
      with this.   MOORE.—*They may rail.*

The great business of life is to be, to do,
to do without, and to depart.
   LORD MORLEY.—*Address, Nov.*, 1887.

Death have we hated, knowing not what
      it meant ;
Life have we loved, through green leaf
      and through sere,
Though still the less we knew of its intent.
   W. MORRIS.—*Earthly Paradise,*
                        L'Envoi, 13.

Make the most of life you may—
Life is short and wears away.
   W. OLDYS.—*Busy, curious, thirsty fly.*

      Alas ! Hope's rays
Die in the distance, and Life's sadness
      stays ;
Why, but because our task is yet undone.
   JOHN PAYNE.—*Ballad, " What do we here ? "*

In laments and in rejoicings, not merely
in dramas but in the whole tragedy and
comedy of life, and in ten thousand other
matters, pains and pleasures are mingled.
   PLATO.—*Philebus,* 112.

Crantor tells us that very wise men have
esteemed life a punishment, and to be
born a man the highest pitch of calamity.
   PLUTARCH.—*Consol. to Apollonius.*

The vanity of human life is like a river,
constantly passing away, and yet constantly coming on.
   POPE.—*Thoughts on Various Subjects.*

All covet life, yet call it pain,
And feel the ill, yet shun the cure.
   PRIOR.—*Written in Mezeray's History.*

Who breathes must suffer, and who thinks
      must mourn ;
And he alone is blest who ne'er was born.
   PRIOR.—*Solomon.*

" My lord, I must live," said an unfortunate satirical author to a minister who
reproached him with the infamy of his
calling. " I do not see the necessity," replied the man of office coldly. This reply,
excellent for a minister, would have been
barbarous and false in every other mouth.
It is necessary that every man should live.
   ROUSSEAU.—*Emile.* *

There is no wealth but Life—Life, including all its powers of love, of joy, and
of admiration.
   RUSKIN.—*Unto this Last, ch.* 4.

---

* VOLTAIRE (*Prelim. Discourse to " Alzire,"*
c. 1736), says that this reply was by the Comte
d'Argenson to the Abbé Guyot Desfontaines, who
had excused himself for writing scurrilous at-
tacks, on the ground that " he must live."

Life is a game, at which everybody loses.
   SARKADI-SCHULLER.—*Within Four Walls.*

In the world of human beings and in
that of animals [life] is sustained and kept
going by two simple impulses—hunger
and the instinct of sex, helped perhaps a
little by boredom.   SCHOPENHAUER.—
                        Emptiness of Existence.

Life is a difficult question. I have decided to spend my life in thinking about it.
   SCHOPENHAUER.—*Remark to Wieland*
                        (1809).

Twist ye, twine ye ! even so
Mingle shades of joy and woe,
Hope and fear, and peace and strife,
In the thread of human life.
   SCOTT.—*Guy Mannering, ch.* 4.

Life is long if you know how to use it.
   SENECA.—*De Brev. Vitæ.*

Life is like a tale ; what makes it of
value is not its length but its goodness.
   SENECA.—*Ep.* 87.

To live is to do battle.
   SENECA.—*Ep.* 96.

It matters not how long you have lived
but how well.
   SENECA.—(*Adapted*) *Ep.* 101 *and* 77.

The web of our life is of a mingled yarn,
good and ill together.
   SHAKESPEARE.—*All's Well,* Act 4, 3.

I do not set my life at a pin's fee.
   SHAKESPEARE.—*Hamlet,* Act 1, 4.

To-morrow, and to-morrow, and to-
      morrow,
Creeps in this petty pace from day to day,
To the last syllable of recorded time ;
And all our yesterdays have lighted fools
The way to dusty death. Out, out, brief
      candle !
Life's but a walking shadow ; a poor
      player,
That struts and frets his hour upon the
      stage,
And then is heard no more.
   SHAKESPEARE.—*Macbeth,* Act 5, 5.

Put out the light, and then—put out the
      light ?
If I quench thee, thou flaming minister,
I can again thy former light restore,
Should I repent me ;—but once put out
      thy light,
Thou cunningest pattern of excelling
      nature,
I know not where is that Promethean heat
That can thy light relume.
   SHAKESPEARE.—*Othello,* Act 5, 2.

We are such stuff
As dreams are made of, and our little life
Is rounded with a sleep.
   SHAKESPEARE.—*Tempest,* Act 4, 1.

We have passed Age's icy caves,
And Manhood's dark and tossing waves,
And Youth's smooth ocean, smiling to
    betray :
Beyond the glassy gulfs we flee
Of shadow-peopled Infancy
Through Death and Birth, to a diviner day.
        SHELLEY.—*Prometheus*, Act 2, 5.

Life's cup is nectar at the brink,
Midway a palatable drink,
        And wormwood at the bottom.
        JAS. SMITH.—*Chigwell Revisited.*

What is the life of man ? Is it not to
shift from side to side, from sorrow to
sorrow ?—to button up one cause of vexation and unbutton another.
STERNE.—*Tristram Shandy, Vol.* 4, *ch.* 31.

Old and young, we are all on our last
cruise. R. L. STEVENSON.—*Crabbed Age.*

For life and death are but indifferent
    things,
And of themselves not to be be shunned
    nor sought,
But for the good or ill that either brings.
        EARL OF STIRLING.—*Darius.*

His life is a watch or a vision,
    Between a sleep and a sleep.
        SWINBURNE.—*Atalanta.*

Sleep ; and if life was bitter to thee,
    pardon ;
If sweet, give thanks ; thou hast no more
    to live ;
And to give thanks is good, and to forgive.
        SWINBURNE.—*Ave atque Vale.*

A loving little life of sweet small works.
    SWINBURNE.—*Bothwell*, Act 1, 1.

A little sorrow, a little pleasure
Fate metes us out from the dusty measure
    That holds the date of all of us.
        ! SWINBURNE.—*Ilicet.*

No life that breathes with human breath
Has ever truly longed for death.
        TENNYSON.—*Two Voices.*

Were all things certain, nothing would
    be sure ;
    Joy would be joyless, of misfortune
    free ;
Were we all wealthy, then we all were poor;
And death not being, life would cease
    to be.
        D. W. THOMPSON.—*From Euripides.*

    Some come, some go ;
    This life is so.
    T. TUSSER.—*August's Abstract.*

In youth alone unhappy mortals live,
But ah ! the mighty bliss is fugitive.
    VIRGIL.—*Georgics· Bk.* 3 (*Dryden tr.*).

I see them walking in an air of glory,
    Whose light doth trample on my days ;
My days, which are at best but dull and
    hoary,
Mere glimmering and decays.
        H. VAUGHAN.—*Resolutions.*

Life is but a day. What does it matter
whether it finishes towards evening or
towards the morning ?
    VOLTAIRE.—*To the Prince de Ligne.*

Desire not to live long, but to live well ;
How long we live not years, but actions,
    tell.   R. WATKYNS.—*Hour Glass.*

        The petty joys
Of fleeting life indignantly it spurned,
And rested on the bosom of its God.
        H. K. WHITE.—*Time.*

Pleasure that most enchants us
    Seems the soonest done ;
What is life with all it grants us
    But a hunting run ?
    G. J. WHYTE-MELVILLE.—*Ranston
                    Bloodhounds.*

Somehow the grace, the bloom of things
    has flown,
And of all men we are most wretched
    who
Must live each other's lives and not our
    own,
For very pity's sake, and then undo
All that we lived for.
        OSCAR WILDE.—*Humanitad.*

One's real life is so often the life that
one does not lead.
OSCAR WILDE.—*L'Envoi to Rose-Leaf and
                    Apple-Leaf.*

Bliss was it in that dawn to be alive,
But to be young was very heaven !
        WORDSWORTH.—*Prelude.*

We live by admiration, hope, and love ;
And even as these are well and wisely
    fixed,
In dignity of being we ascend.
        WORDSWORTH.—*Excursion, Bk.* 4.

Life I repeat, is energy of love,
Divine or human.
        WORDSWORTH.—*Ib., Bk.* 5.

Each night we die,
Each morn are born anew : each day, a
    life ! YOUNG.—*Night Thoughts,* 2.

Death but entombs the body ; life, the
    soul.   YOUNG.—*Ib.,* 3.

Life is much flattered ; Death is much
    traduced.   YOUNG.—*Ib.,* 3.

That life is long which answers life's
    great end.   YOUNG.—*Ib.,* 5.

Our life is but a chain of many deaths.
        YOUNG.—*The Revenge,* Act 4, 1.

Fear less, hope more ; eat less, chew more ; whine less, breathe more ; talk less, say more ; hate less, love more ; and all good things are yours.
Quoted by Lord Fisher in " Records,"
Nov. 25, 1919.

The changes and chances of this mortal life.   *Common Prayer. Collect.*

The days of our age are threescore years and ten ; and though men be so strong that they come to fourscore years, yet is their strength then but labour and sorrow ; so soon passeth it away, and we are gone.
Psalter (Book of Common Prayer), 90, 10.

This world's a city with many a crooked street,
And Death the Market place where all men meet ;
If Life were merchandise that men could buy,
The rich would live and none but poor would die.
Henry Devall's Epitaph (1860), Nutfield Churchyard.

Man's life is like unto a summer's day :
Some break their fast and so away ;
Others stay dinner and depart full fed ;
The longest age but sups and goes to bed.
Old Epitaph. A prose version is in Dr. Brown's Horæ Subsecivæ (1858). (Vide p. 284.)

The life of love is better than the love of life.   *Prov.*

Round and round the unseen hand
Turns the fate o' mortal man ;
A screech at birth, a grane (groan) at even,
The flesh to earth, the soul to Heaven.
Scottish rhyme.

We scream when we are born,
We groan when we are dying ;
And all that is between
Is laughter and crying.
Old Rhyme.

LIGHT

God's first creature, which was light.
BACON.—*New Atlantis.*

Casting a dim religious light.
MILTON.—*Il Penseroso*, 161.

Hail, holy Light, offspring of Heaven first-born,
Or of th' Eternal co-eternal beam,
May I express thee unblamed ?
MILTON.—*Paradise Lost, Bk.* 3, 1.

Dark with excessive bright.
MILTON.—*Ib., Bk.* 3, 380.

Light, seeking light, doth light of light beguile.
SHAKESPEARE.—*Love's Labour's Lost, Act* 1, 1.

LIMITATIONS

Whether you fill it from the sea or from a tiny stream, the vessel will not contain a single drop more.
E. AUGIER.—*Joueur de Flûte.*

What you see, yet cannot see over, is as good as infinite.
CARLYLE.—*Sartor Resartus, Bk.* 2, *c.* 1.

Seek not to go beyond your tether
But cut your thongs unto your leather.
CHAPMAN.—*Eastward Hoe* (1605).

Feels himself spent, and fumbles for his brains.   COWPER.—*Table Talk*, 536.

Remember, cobbler, to keep to your last.   MARTIAL.—3, 16.

Each might his several province well command,
Would all but stoop to what they understand.   POPE.—*Essay on Criticism*, 66.

Such harmony is in immortal souls ;
But, whilst this muddy vesture of decay
Doth grossly close it in, we cannot hear it.
SHAKESPEARE.—*Merch. of Venice*, Act 5, 1.

My nature is subdued
To what it works in, like the dyer's hand ;
Pity me then, and wish I were renewed.
SHAKESPEARE.—*Sonnet* 111.

Hitherto shalt thou come, but no further : and here shall thy proud waves be stayed.   *Job* xxxviii, 11.

LIONS

A lion among ladies is a most dreadful thing, for there is not a more fearful wildfowl than your lion, living.
SHAKESPEARE.—*Midsummer Night's Dream*, Act 3, 1.

LISTENERS

Were we as eloquent as angels yet we should please some men, some women, and some children, much more by listening, than by talking.   C. C. COLTON.—*Lacon.*

Give us grace to listen well.
KEBLE.—*Palm Sunday.*

It takes two to speak the truth—one to speak, and another to hear.
H. D. THOREAU.—*A Week on the Concord.*

LITERATURE

Literature is always a good card to play for honours. It makes people think that Cabinet Ministers are educated.
ARNOLD BENNETT.—*The Title* (1917).

Let us be Catholics in this great matter [modern poetry] and burn our candles at many shrines.   A. BIRRELL.—*Obiter Dicta, Browning's Poetry.*

Literature and fiction are two entirely different things. Literature is a luxury, fiction is a necessity.
G. K. CHESTERTON.—*The Defendant. Defence of Penny Dreadfuls.*

No prince fares like him ; he breaks his fast with Aristotle, dines with Tully, drinks tea at Helicon, sups with Seneca.
COLLEY CIBBER.—*Love Makes the Man,* Act I, I.

Learn to write well or not to write at all.
DRYDEN.—*Upon Satire,* 281.

Beneath the rule of men entirely great The pen is mightier than the sword.
(1st) LORD LYTTON.—*Richelieu.*

Literature—the most seductive, the most deceiving, the most dangerous of professions.   LORD MORLEY.—*Burke.*

The Sibyl, uttering sentences all full of serious thought and meaning, continues her voice a thousand years, through the favour of the divinity that speaks within her.   PLUTARCH.—*Of the Pythian Oracle.*

Who lasts a century can have no flaw ; I hold that wit a classic, good in law.
POPE.—*Ep. of Horace, Ep.* I, 55.

You must not suppose, because I am a man of letters, that I never tried to earn an honest living.
G. B. SHAW.—*Preface* (1905) *to "The Irrational Knot."*

Captains and conquerors leave a little dust,
And Kings a dubious legend of their reign ;
The swords of Cæsars, they are less than rust ;
The poet doth remain.
SIR W. WATSON.—*Lachrymæ Musarum,* 114.

Communities are lost, and empires die, And things of holy use unhallowed lie ; They perish,—but the intellect can raise, From airy words alone, a pile that ne'er decays.   WORDSWORTH.—*Inscription for a seat at Coleorton.*

Dreams, books, are each a world ; and books, we know,
Are a substantial world, both pure and good. WORDSWORTH.—*Personal Talk.*

LITTLENESS

What dwarfs men are, when I come to think of it !   PLAUTUS.—*Capteivei, Prol.*

Fine by degrees and beautifully less.
PRIOR.—*Henry and Emma.*

Pygmies are pygmies still, though perched on Alps ;
And pyramids are pyramids in vales.
Each man makes his own stature, builds himself. YOUNG.—*Night Thoughts,* 6.

K

Small people love to talk of great people.
Prov.

LITURGY

It is an armoury of light ;
Let constant use but keep it bright,
    You'll find it yields
To holy hands and humble hearts,
    More swords and shields
Than sin hath snares, or hell hath darts.
CRASHAW.—*On a Prayer Book.*

The monk with unavailing cares,
Exhausted all the Church's prayers.
SCOTT.—*Marmion, c.* 6, 32.

LOCALISM

Poetic fields encompass me around,
And still I seem to tread on classic ground.
ADDISON.—*Letter from Italy.*

The genuine spirit of localism.
BORROW.—*Bible in Spain.*

My heart's in the Highlands, my heart is not here,
My heart's in the Highlands, a-chasing the deer ;
A-chasing the wild deer and following the roe—
My heart's in the Highlands, wherever I go.   BURNS.—*Song.*

Be useful where thou livèst.
HERBERT.—*Church Porch.*

God gave all men all earth to love,
But since our hearts are small,
Ordained for each one spot should prove Beloved over all.
RUDYARD KIPLING.—*Sussex.*

They take the rustic murmur of their bourg For the great wave that echoes round the world.
TENNYSON.—*Marriage of Geraint,* 419.

LOGIC

Logical consequences are the scarecrows of fools and the beacons of wise men.
T. H. HUXLEY.—*Science and Culture.*

Those points indeed you quaintly prove, But logic is no friend to love.
PRIOR.—*Turtle and Sparrow,* 263.

He owns her logic of the heart,
And reason of unreason.
WHITTIER.—*Among the Hills.*

Prove all things ; hold fast that which is good.   I *Thessalonians* v, 21.

LONDON

Lo, where huge London, huger day by day,
O'er six fair counties spreads its hideous sway.   A. AUSTIN.—*Golden Age.*

Why should I care for the men of Thames,
And the cheating waters of chartered
  streams ?
    WM. BLAKE.—*Thames and Ohio.*

Thou art in London—in that pleasant
  place
Where every kind of mischief's daily
  brewing. BYRON.—*Don Juan, 12, 23.*

That monstrous tuberosity of civilised
life, the capital of England.
    CARLYLE.—*Sartor.*

Let but thy wicked men from out thee go,
And all the fools that crowd thee so,
  Even thou who dost thy millions boast,
A village less than Islington wilt grow,
  A solitude almost.
    COWLEY.—*Of Solitude.*

The crowd, the buzz, and murmurings
Of this great hive, the city.
    COWLEY.—*The Wish.*

Oh thou, resort and mart of all the earth,
Chequered with all complexions of man-
  kind,
And spotted with all crimes ; in which I
  see
Much that I love, and more that I admire,
And all that I abhor ; thou freckled fair,
That pleases and yet shocks me.
    COWPER.—*Garden,* 835.

The centre of a thousand trades.
    COWPER.—*Hope,* 248.

Where has commerce such a mart,
So rich, so thronged, so drained, and so
  supplied,
As London, opulent, enlarged, and still
Increasing London ?
    COWPER.—*The Sofa.*

Mr. Weller's knowledge of London was
extensive and peculiar.
  DICKENS.—*Pickwick Papers, ch.* 20.

London is a roost for every bird.
    DISRAELI.—*Lothair, ch.* 11.

London—a nation, not a city.
    DISRAELI.—*Ib., ch.* 27.

I belong to the " Nation of London."
  GEORGE ELIOT.—*Theophrastus Such :
    Looking Backward.*

London is the epitome of our times and
the Rome of to-day.
  EMERSON.—*English Traits,* 18,
    Result (1833).

Ye towers of Julius, London's lasting
  shame,
With many a foul and midnight murder
  fed.   GRAY.—*Bard.*

I do not think there is anything deserving the name of society to be found out of

London. . . . You can pick your society
nowhere but in London.
  HAZLITT.—*On Coffee-House Politicians.*

London is the only place in which the
child grows completely up into the man.
    HAZLITT.—*Londoners.*

London ! the needy villain's general home,
The common-sewer of Paris and of Rome.
    JOHNSON.—*London.*

Prepare for death if here at night you roam,
And sign your will before you sup from
  home.   JOHNSON.—*Ib.*

When a man is tired of London he is
tired of life ; for there is in London all
that life can afford.
    JOHNSON.—*Remark to Boswell.*

Whoever has once experienced the full
flow of London talk, when he retires to
country friendships and rural sports, must
either be contented to turn baby again
and play with the rattle, or he will pine
away like a great fish in a little pond, and
die for want of his usual food.
  JOHNSON.—*Remark as recorded by
    Mrs. Piozzi.*

The noble spirit of the metropolis is the
lifeblood of the State, collected at the
heart.   JUNIUS.—*Letter,* 1770.

I'm sick for London again ; sick for the
sounds of 'er, an' the sights of 'er, and the
stinks of 'er ; orange peel and hasphalte
an' gas comin' in over Vauxhall Bridge . . .
That an' the Stran' lights, where you
knows ev'ry one.
    KIPLING.—*Stanley Ortheris.*

I love the halls of old Cockaigne,
  Where wit and wealth were squandered,
The halls that tell of hoop and train,
  Where grace and rank have wandered.
  F. LOCKER LAMPSON.—*St. James's
    Street.*

And London Town, of all towns, I'm
  glad to leave behind.
    J. MASEFIELD.—*London Town.*

London's the dining-room of Christendom.
  T. MIDDLETON.—*City Pageant* 1617.

There, London's voice : " Get money,
  money still !
And then let virtue follow if she will."
    POPE.—*Ep. of Horace, Ep.* 1, 79.

Where London's column, pointing to the
  skies,
Like a tall bully, lifts the head and lies.
    POPE.—*Moral Essays, Ep.* 3.

That great foul city of London—rattling,
growling, smoking, stinking—a ghastly
heap of fermenting brickwork, pouring out
poison at every pore—a cricket ground

without the turf, a huge billiard table without the cloth, and with pockets as deep as the bottomless pit.
RUSKIN.—*Crown of Wild Olive.*

In London, that great sea, whose ebb and flow
At once is deaf and loud.
SHELLEY.—*To Maria Gisborne.*

Fly, Honesty, fly to some safer retreat,
For there's craft in the river—and craft in the street.
JAMES SMITH.—*Epigram made at a dinner at his home in Craven Street.*

A few yards in London dissolve or cement friendship.   SYDNEY SMITH.—*Letter to Countess Grey, Feb. 9, 1821.*

To mery London, my most kyndly nurse,
That to me gave this life's first native source.   SPENSER.—*Prothalamion.*

Under the cross of gold
That shines over city and river.
TENNYSON.—*On Wellington.*

It is worth while living in London, surely, to enjoy the country when you get to it.   THACKERAY.—*Letter.*

Fleet Street ! Fleet Street ! Fleet Street in the evening,
Darkness set with golden lamps down Ludgate Hill a-row ;
Oh, hark the voice o' the city, that breaks our hearts with pity,
That crazes us with shame and wrath, and makes us love her so !
ALICE WERNER.—*Song of Fleet Street.*

LONELINESS

Alone !—that worn-out word,
So idly spoken, and so coldly heard,
Yet all that poets sing, and grief hath known,
Of hopes laid waste, knells in that word
ALONE !
(1st) LORD LYTTON.—*New Timon, Pt. 2, 7.*

When musing on companions gone,
We doubly feel ourselves alone.
SCOTT.—*Marmion, c. 2, Intro.*

LONGEVITY

His eye was not dim, nor his natural force abated.   *Deut.* xxxiv, 7.

Thou shalt come to thy grave in a full age, like as a shock of corn cometh in in his season.   *Job* v, 26.

LORD MAYORS

By the lord of Ludgate it's a fine life to be a lord mayor ; it's a stirring life, a fine life, a velvet life, a careful life.
T. DEKKER.—*Shoemaker's Holiday, Act 5, 2.*

LORDS

But let a lord once own the happy lines,
How the art brightens ! how the style refines !
Before his sacred name flies every fault,
And each exalted stanza teems with thought !
POPE.—*Essay on Criticism,* 419.

The court affords
Much food for satire ;—It abounds in lords.
YOUNG.—*Love of Fame,* 1

LOSS

Every mortal loss is an immortal gain. The ruins of time build mansions in eternity.   WM. BLAKE.—*Letter.*

Lose who may—I still can say,
Those who win heaven, blest are they.
BROWNING.—*One Way of Love,* 3.

For 'tis a truth well known to most,
That whatsoever thing is lost,
We seek it, ere it come to light,
In every cranny but the right.
COWPER.—*The Retired Cat.*

The loss of wealth is loss of dirt,
As sages in all times assert.
J. HEYWOOD.—*Be Merry.*

Measure thy life by loss instead of gain ;
Not by the wine drunk but by the wine poured forth.
H. E. HAMILTON KING.—*The Disciples.*

Better is a littel losse than a long sorrow.
LANGLAND.—*Piers Plowman, Passus* 1, 195

Then many a lad I liked is dead,
And many a lass grown old,
And as the lesson strikes my head,
My weary heart grows cold.
CHAS. MORRIS.—*Toper's Apology.*

I would rather have lost honourably than gained basely.   PUBLILIUS SYRUS.

Poor Jack, farewell !
I could have better spared a better man.
SHAKESPEARE.—*Henry IV., Pt. 1, Act 5,4.*

A fellow that hath had losses.
SHAKESPEARE.—*Much Ado, Act 4, 2*

O you gods !
Why do you make us love your goodly gifts,
And snatch them straight away ?
SHAKESPEARE.—*Pericles, Act 3, 1.*

Varus, give me back my legions !
SUETONIUS.—*Augustus.*

My loss may shine yet goodlier than your gain,
When time and God give judgment.
SWINBURNE.—*Marino Faliero.*

The shadow of his loss drew like eclipse,
Darkening the world.
TENNYSON.—*Idylls, Dedication.*

'Tis better to have loved and lost
Than never to have loved at all.
TENNYSON.—*In Memoriam, c.* 27.

The feeling of my loss will ne'er be old :
This, which I know, I speak with mind
serene.
WORDSWORTH.—*Elegiac Stanzas,* 1805.

Men are we, and must grieve when even
the shade
Of that which once was great is passed
away.
WORDSWORTH.—*On the Venetian Republic.*

How blessings brighten as they take
their flight !
YOUNG.—*Night Thoughts,* 2.

Good things are never good till they are
lost.   *Prov.*

Sometimes the best gain is to lose.
Prov. (Geo. Herbert).

LOVE

Love is not to be reasoned down, or lost
In high ambition and a thirst of greatness.
ADDISON.—*Cato,* Act 1, 1.

There is no worldly pleasure here below,
    Which by experience doth not folly
    prove ;
But amongst all the follies that I know
    The sweetest folly in the world is love.
SIR R. AYTON.—*On Love.*

Love is a fiend, a fire, a heaven, a hell,
Where pleasure, paine, and sad repentance
dwell.
R. BARNFIELD.—*Content* (1594).

Love and sorrow twins were born
On a shining showery morn.
DR. T. BLACKLOCK.—*The Graham.*

He caught me in his silken net
And shut me in his golden cage.
WM. BLAKE.—*Song.*

Love seeketh only Self to please,
To bind another to its delight,
Joys in another's loss of ease,
    And builds a Hell in Heaven's despite.
WM. BLAKE.—*The Clod and the Pebble.*

The moon returns, and the spring, birds
warble, trees burst into leaf,
But Love once gone goes for ever, and all
that endures is the grief.
MATHILDE BLIND.—*Love Trilogy,* 3.

Much ado there was, God wot :
He would love, and she would not.
N. BRETON.—*Phyllida and Corydon.*

Two human loves make one divine.
E. B. BROWNING.—*Isobel's Child.*

Whoso loves
Believes the impossible.
E. B. BROWNING.—*Aurora Leigh, Bk.* 5.

Love shut our eyes and all seemed right.
BROWNING.—*Christmas Eve, c.* 11.

What's the earth
With all its art, verse, music, worth—
Compared with love, found, gained, and
kept ? BROWNING.—*Dis aliter visum.*

So down the flowery path of love we
went.   R. BUCHANAN.—*Sigurd.*

But to see her was to love her,
Love but her, and love for ever.
BURNS.—*Farewell to Nancy.*

Let those love now who never loved before,
And those who always loved now love the
more.
BURTON.—(*Tr. of Pervigilium Veneris.*)

Love is too great a happiness
For wretched mortals to possess.
S. BUTLER.—*Miscellaneous Thoughts.*

Man's love is of man's life a thing apart,
'Tis woman's whole existence.
BYRON.—*Don Juan, c.* 1, 194.

Alas ! the love of women ! it is known
To be a lovely and a fearful thing.
BYRON.—*Ib., c.* 2, 199.

In her first passion woman loves her lover,
In all the others all she loves is love.
BYRON.—*Ib., c.* 3, 3.

And all because a lady fell in love.
BYRON.—*Ib.,* 4, 12.

For soon or late Love is his own avenger.
BYRON.—*Ib.,* 4, 73.

Love will find its way
Through paths where wolves would fear
'to prey.   BYRON.—*Giaour,* 1047.

A loving heart is the beginning of all
knowledge.   CARLYLE.—*On Biography.*

The god of love, a ! benedicite !
How mighty and how great a lord is he !
CHAUCER.—*Knight's Tale.*

Love and I be fer a-sonder.
CHAUCER.—*Troilus, Bk.* 5, 983 (*Cressid
to Diomed*).

Such maner folk, I gesse,
Defamen love, as no-thing of him knowe,
They spoken, but they bente never his
bowe.   CHAUCER.—*Troilus.*

What a recreation it is to be in love !
It sets the heart aching so delicately there's
no taking a wink of sleep for the pleasure
of the pain.
G. COLMAN, JR.—*Mountaineers,* Act 1, 1.

Life without love is load ; and time
    stands still :
What we refuse to him, to death we give,
And then, then only, when we love, we
    live.
  CONGREVE.—*Mourning Bride*, Act 2, 3.

Love's but a frailty of the mind,
When 'tis not with ambition joined.
  CONGREVE.—*Way of the World*, Act 3, 3.

If there's delight in love, 'tis when I see
That heart, which others bleed for, bleed
  for me.   CONGREVE.—*Ib.*

How wise are they that are but fools in
  love !
JOSHUA COOKE.—*How a man may choose*,
               Act 1, 1.

  A mighty pain to love it is,
  And 'tis a pain that pain to miss ;
  But of all pains the greatest pain
  It is to love, but love in vain.
             COWLEY.—*Gold.*

Better to love amiss than nothing to
  have loved.
  CRABBE.—*The Struggles of Conscience.*

To love is to know the sacrifices which
eternity exacts from life.
MRS. CRAIGIE (" JOHN OLIVER HOBBES ")
  —*School for Saints*, ch. 25.

Poor love is lost in men's capacious minds,
In ours, it fills up all the room it finds.
         J. CROWNE.—*Thyestes.*

Love most concealed doth most itself
  discover. W. DAVISON.—*Sonnet*, 14.

O what a heaven is love ! O what a hell !
      T. DEKKER.—*Honest Whore.*

The magic of first love is our ignorance
that it can ever end.
  DISRAELI.—*Henrietta Temple*, Bk. 2, c. 4.

See the couples advance,—
  Oh ! Love's but a dance !
A whisper, a glance,—
  " Shall we twirl down the middle ? "
Oh, Love's but a dance,
  Where time plays the fiddle.
  AUSTIN DOBSON.—*Triolet. Oh, Love's
               but a dance.*

That reason of all unreasonable actions.
      DRYDEN.—*Assignation.*

But she ne'er loved who durst not venture
  all. DRYDEN.—*Aureng-Zebe*, Act 5, 1.

Love's the noblest frailty of the mind.
  DRYDEN.—*Indian Emperor*, Act 2, 2.

To cure the pains of love no plant avails ;
And his own physic the physician fails.
  DRYDEN.—*Tr. Ovid, Metam.*, Bk. 1.

The proverb holds, that to be wise and love
Is hardly granted to the gods above.
  DRYDEN.—*Palamon*, Bk. 2, 364.

And Antony, who lost the world for love.
    DRYDEN.—*Ib.*, Bk. 2, 607.

In hell and earth and seas and heaven
  above,
Love conquers all ; and we must yield to
  Love.
    DRYDEN.—*Virgil, Pastoral*, 10.

All the young ladies said that to be sure
a love match was the only thing for happiness, where the parties could any way
afford it.
MISS EDGEWORTH.—*Castle Rackrent*, ch. 2.

If with love thy heart has burned,
If thy love is unreturned,
Hide thy grief within thy breast.
      EMERSON.—*To Rhea.*

The affirmative of affirmatives is love.
As much love, so much perception.
      EMERSON.—*Success.*

  Cupid is a blind gunner.
  FARQUHAR.—*Love and a Bottle*, Act 1, 1.

    I love you ;
I'll cut your throat for your own sake.
FLETCHER AND MASSINGER.—*Little French
              Lawyer*, Act 4, 1.

Only in love they happy prove.
Who love what most deserves their love.
  PHINEAS FLETCHER.—*Sicelides*, Act 3, 6.

Again new tumults fire my breast ;
Ah, spare me, Venus, let thy suppliant rest.
  P. FRANCIS.—*Horace, Odes* Bk. 4, 1.

Sorry her lot who loves too well,
Heavy the heart that hopes but vainly.
    SIR W. S. GILBERT.—*Pinafore.*

Time was when Love and I were well
  acquainted,
Time was when we walked ever hand in
  hand. SIR W. S. GILBERT.—*Sorcerer.*

To love for money all the world is prone ;
Some love themselves, and live all lonely ;
Give me the love that loves for love alone,
I love that love—I love it only.
      SIR W. S. GILBERT.—*Ib.*

Or love me less, or love me more ;
  And play not with my liberty :
Either take all, or all restore ;
  Bind me at least, or set me free !
    S. GODOLPHIN.—*Song.*

The bashful virgin's sidelong looks of love.
  GOLDSMITH.—*Deserted Village.*

Foolish loves make foolish people.
    E. GONDINET.—*The Club.*

Among the holy bookés wise,
I findé write in suche wise,
Who loveth nought is here as dede.
                GOWER.—*Confessio Amantis.*

For love's law is out of reule.
                        GOWER.—*Ib.*

But ah ! in vain from Fate I fly,
For first, or last, as all must die,
So 'tis as much decreed above,
That first, or last, we all must love.
G. GRANVILLE (LORD LANSDOWNE).—
                        To Myra.

Whoe'er thou art, thy lord and master
    see ;
Thou wast my slave, thou art, or thou shalt
    be. G. GRANVILLE (LORD LANSDOWNE).
        —*God of Love* (*Tr. of Voltaire*).

Love in extremes can never long endure.
                HERRICK.—*Hesperides*, 495.

Love of itself's too sweet.   The best of all
Is when love's honey has a dash of gall.
            HERRICK.—*Ib.*, No. 1085.

Pray love me little so you love me long.
HERRICK.—*Love me Little, Love me Long.*

Truth is for ever truth and love is love.
    LEIGH HUNT.—*Hero and Leander.*

Love is like the measles ; we all have to
go through it.
            J. K. JEROME.—*Idle Thoughts.*

Love in a hut, with water and a crust,
Is—Love, forgive us !—cinders, ashes, dust ;
Love in a palace is, perhaps, at last
More grievous torment than a hermit's
    fast.   KEATS.—*Lamia, Pt. 2.*

Love at fifty !—why look you, it is like
rheumatism, nothing can cure it.
LABICHE.—*Le Commandant Mathieu in
        " Le Voyage de M. Perrichon."*

I loved him too as woman loves—
Reckless of sorrow, sin, or scorn.
        L. E. LANDON.—*Indian Bride.*

Oh if thou lovest
And art a woman, hide thy love from him
Whom thou dost worship ; never let him
    know
How dear he is.   L. E. LANDON.

" I'm half in love," he who with smiles
        hath said,
In love will never be.
Whoe'er, " I'm not in love," and shakes
        his head,
In love too sure is he.
        W. S. LANDOR.—*Miscell.*, No. 258.

Like these cool lilies may our loves remain,
Perfect and pure, and know not any stain.
        A. LANG.—*To Heavenly Venus.*

True love is like the apparition of spirits;
everyone speaks of it but few have seen it.
    LA ROCHEFOUCAULD.—*Maxim 76.*

In their first passions women **love** the
lover ; in others they love love.
    LA ROCHEFOUCAULD.—*Maxim 471.*

Like Dian's kiss, unasked, unsought
Love gives itself, but is not bought.
        LONGFELLOW.—*Endymion.*

Luife (love) bene the ladder quhilk (which)
hes bot steppis twa (has but two steps),
Be quhilk we may clim up to lyfe againe
Out of this vaill of miserie and wa.
    SIR D. LYNDSAY.—*The Three Estates*
(*The two steps being* 1, *Love of God ;* 2, *Love
                of one's Neighbours*).

Tell me my heart, if this be love.
    GEO. LORD LYTTELTON.—*Song.*

Whoever loved that loved not at first
    sight ?   MARLOWE.—*Hero and
                Leander, Sestiad,* 1.

Love always makes those eloquent that
    have it.   MARLOWE.—*Ib., Sestiad,* 2.

Love not, love not, ye hapless sons of clay.
    LADY STIRLING MAXWELL.—*Rosalie.*

No, there's nothing half so sweet in life
As love's young dream.
        MOORE.—*Irish Melodies.*

Is it, in heaven, a crime to love too well ?
    POPE.—*Elegy to the Memory of an
                Unfortunate Lady,* 6.

Curse on all laws but those which love has
    made !   POPE.—*Eloisa, l.* 74.

Love, free as air, at sight of human ties
Spreads his light wings, and in a moment
    flies.   POPE.—*Ib.,* 75.

In her soft breast consenting passions
    move,
And the warm maid confessed a mutual
    love.
    POPE.—*Vertumnus and Pomona,* 122.

There is no pleasure like the pain
Of being loved, and loving.
W. M. PRAED.—*Legend of the Haunted Tree.*

A dish of married love right soon grows
    cauld.
ALLAN RAMSAY.—*Gentle Shepherd,* Act 1.

And where are you going with your love-
locks flowing ?
    CHRISTINA ROSSETTI.—*Amor Mundi.*

Knowledge is strong, but love is sweet ;
Yea all the progress he had made
Was but to learn that all is small
Save love, for love is all in all.
CHRISTINA ROSSETTI.—*Convent Threshold.*

Friendship is prodigal but love is avaricious.   ROUSSEAU.—*Julie.*

Love rules the court, the camp, the grove,
And men below, and saints above,
For love is heaven, and heaven is love.
SCOTT.—*Lay of the Last Minstrel* 3, 2.

True love's the gift which God has given
To man alone beneath the heaven.
SCOTT.—*Ib.*, 5, 13.

For love will still be lord of all.
SCOTT.—*Ib.*, 6, 11.

There's beggary in the love that can be reckoned.   SHAKESPEARE.—
Antony and Cleopatra, Act 1, 1.

Down on your knees,
And thank heaven, fasting, for a good man's love.
SHAKESPEARE.—*As You Like It*, Act 3, 5.

He that will divide a minute into a thousand parts, and break but a part of the thousandth part of a minute in the affairs of love, it may be said of him, that Cupid hath clapped him on the shoulder, but I'll warrant him heart-whole.
SHAKESPEARE.—*Ib.*, Act 4, 1.

Men have died from time to time, and worms have eaten them, but not for love.
SHAKESPEARE.—*Ib.*

No sooner met, but they looked; no sooner looked, but they loved; no sooner loved, but they sighed; no sooner sighed, but they asked one another the reason.
SHAKESPEARE.—*Ib.*, Act 5, 2.

From me, whose love was of that dignity,
That it went hand in hand even with the vow
I made to her in marriage.
SHAKESPEARE.—*Hamlet*, Act 1, 5.

This is the very ecstasy of love.
SHAKESPEARE.—*Ib.*, Act 2, 1.

This whimpled, whining, purblind, way-ward boy,
This senior-junior, giant-dwarf, Dan Cupid.
SHAKESPEARE.—*Love's Labour's Lost*, Act 3, 1.

Love like a shadow flies when substance love pursues,
Pursuing that that flies, and flying what pursues.
SHAKESPEARE.—*Merry Wives*, Act 2, 2.

O powerful love! that in some respects makes a beast a man; in some other, a man a beast.
SHAKESPEARE.—*Ib.*, Act 5, 5.

Love looks not with the eyes, but with the mind;
And therefore is winged Cupid painted blind.
SHAKESPEARE.—*Midsummer Night's 'Dream*, Act 1, 1.

The course of true love never did run smooth.   SHAKESPEARE.—*Ib.*

To say the truth, reason and love keep little company together now-a-days.
SHAKESPEARE.—*Ib.*, Act 3, 1.

Cupid is a knavish lad
Thus to make poor females mad.
SHAKESPEARE.—*Ib.*, Act 3, 2.

He brushes his hat o' mornings; what should that bode?
SHAKESPEARE.—*Much Ado*, Act 3, 2.

Excellent wretch! Perdition catch my soul,
But I do love thee! And when I love thee not,
Chaos is come again.
SHAKESPEARE.—*Othello*, Act 3, 3.

This bud of love, by summer's ripening breath,
May prove a beauteous flower when next we meet.
SHAKESPEARE.—*Romeo and Juliet*, Act 2, 2.

Love in Idleness.
SHAKESPEARE.—*Taming of the Shrew*, Act 1, 1.

Was not this love indeed?
We men may say more, swear more; but, indeed,
Our shows are more than will; for still we prove
Much in our vows, but little in our love.
SHAKESPEARE.—*Twelfth Night*, Act 2, 4.

Love sought is good, but given unsought is better.
SHAKESPEARE.—*Ib.*, Act 3, 1.

I have done penance for contemning love.
SHAKESPEARE.—*Two Gentlemen of Verona*, Act 2, 4.

Didst thou but know the inly touch of love,
Thou wouldst as soon go kindle fire with snow,
As seek to quench the fire of love with words.
SHAKESPEARE.—*Ib.*, Act 2, 7.

I hold him but a fool that will endanger
His body for a girl that loves him not.
SHAKESPEARE.—*Ib.*, Act 5, 4.

Love is a spirit, all compact of fire,
Not gross to sink, but light, and will aspire.
SHAKESPEARE.—*Venus and Adonis*, 25.

Were beauty under twenty locks kept fast,
Yet love breaks through and picks them
  all at last.   SHAKESPEARE.—
             Venus and Adonis, 96.

     Gone already !
Inch-thick, knee-deep, o'er head and ears,
  a forked one !
SHAKESPEARE.—*Winter's Tale*, Act 1, 2.

First love is only a little foolishness and
a lot of curiosity : no really self-respecting
woman would take advantage of it.
     G. B. SHAW.—*Bull's Other Island*.

Love did nothing but prove the soundness of La Rochefoucauld's saying that very
few people would fall in love if they had
never read about it.
     G. B. SHAW.—*Heartbreak House, Pref.*

     All love is sweet
Given or returned. Common as light is
  love,
And its familiar voice wearies not ever.
     SHELLEY.—*Prometheus*, Act 2, 5.

They who inspire it are most fortunate,
As I am now ; but those who feel it most
Are happier still.   SHELLEY.—*Ib.*

An oyster may be crossed in love.
     SHERIDAN.—*Critic*, Act 3, 1.

True be it said, whatever man it sayd,
That love with gall and hony doth abound.
     SPENSER.—*Faerie Queene*, c. 10, 1.

To love her is a liberal education.
     SIR R. STEELE.—*Spectator (of Lady
             Elizabeth Hastings)*.

" I thought *love* had been a joyous
thing," quoth my uncle Toby.—" 'Tis
the most serious thing, an' please your
Honour (sometimes) that is in the world."
     STERNE.—*Tristram Shandy*, vol. 7, 20.

Love, an' please your Honour, is exactly
like war, in this, that a soldier, though he
has escaped three weeks complete o'
Saturday night, may nevertheless be shot
through his heart on Sunday morning.
     STERNE.—*Ib.*, vol. 5, ch. 21.

God gives us love. Something to love
He lends us.   TENNYSON.—*To J. S.*

For the man's love once gone never returns.
     TENNYSON.—*Geraint and Enid*, 335.

I know not if I know what true love is,
But if I know, then, if I love not him,
I know there is none other I can love.
     TENNYSON.—*Lancelot and Elaine*, 672.

Sweet is true love, though given in vain.
     TENNYSON.—*Ib.*, 949.

Love took up the harp of Life, and smote
  on all the chords with might,

Smote the chord of Self, that, trembling,
  passed in music out of sight.
     TENNYSON.—*Locksley Hall.*

Love is love for evermore.
     TENNYSON.—*Ib.*

For in a wink the false love turns to hate.
     TENNYSON.—*Merlin and Vivien*, 850.

O God, that I had loved a smaller man !
I should have found in him a greater heart.
     TENNYSON.—*Ib.*, 860.

And he that shuts out love in turn shall be
Shut out from love, and on the threshold
  lie,
Howling in utter darkness.
TENNYSON.—*To——*(" *I send you here a
             sort of Allegory* ").

We love being in love, that's the truth
on't.   THACKERAY.—*Esmond, c.* 15.

Who does not know how to love has but
a faithless heart.
     VOLTAIRE.—*Fête de Bellébat.*

Love not each other too much, I beseech
you. It is the surest way to love each
other always. It is better to be friends
all your life than to be lovers for a few days.
VOLTAIRE.—*To Mdlle. de Guise on her im-
pending marriage with the Duc de Richelieu.*

Love is the breath and life of a godlike
and blessed man.
     JOHN WESSEL OF GRONINGEN.

O, rank is good, and gold is fair,
  And high and low mate ill ;
But love has never known a law
  Beyond its own sweet will.
     WHITTIER.—*Amy Wentworth.*

One should always be in love. That is
the reason one should never marry.
OSCAR WILDE.—*Woman of no Importance,*
                    Act 3.

When one is in love one begins to deceive
oneself. And one ends by deceiving others.
     OSCAR WILDE.—*Ib.*

Shall I, wasting in despair,
  Die because a woman's fair ?
     G. WITHER.—*Shepherd's Resolution.*

A Briton, even in love, should be
  A subject, not a slave !
WORDSWORTH.—*Ere with cold beads of
             midnight dew.*

He spake of love, such love as Spirits feel
In worlds whose course is equable and
  pure ;
No fears to beat away—no strife to heal—
The past unsighed for and the future
  sure.   WORDSWORTH.—*Laodamia.*

'Tis sense, unbridled will, and not true love
  That kills the soul. Love betters what
  is best,
Even here below, but more in heaven
  above.
> WORDSWORTH.—*Sonnets, No. 25.*

What easy, tame, suffering, trampled
things does that little god of talking
cowards make of us !
> WYCHERLEY.—*Plain Dealer.*

Ryches be unstable
  And beauty will dekay
But faithful love will ever last
  Till death dryve it away.
> *Old Rhyme.*

LOVERS

Thrice happy's the wooing that's not long
  a doing,
So much time is saved in the billing and
  cooing.   R. H. BARHAM.—*Sir Rupert.*

Affection chained her to that heart ;
Ambition tore the links apart.
> BYRON.—*Bride of Abydos,* 1, 6.

The miracle to-day is that we find
A lover true, not that a woman's kind.
> CONGREVE.—*Love for Love,* Act 5, 2.

All mankind love a lover.
> EMERSON.—*Love.*

Nor could the Fates this faithful pair
  divide ;
They lived united and united died.
> F. FAWKES.—*Hero and Leander,* 494.
> (*Tr. of Musæus.*)

A lover without indiscretion is no lover
at all.
> T. HARDY.—*Hand of Ethelberta, c. 20.*

The old, old story,—fair and young,
And fond,—and not too wise.
> O. W. HOLMES.—*Agnes.*

The lovers, interchanging words and sighs,
Lost in the heaven of one another's eyes.
> LEIGH HUNT.—*Rimini, c. 4.*

How strange a thing a lover seems
To animals that do not love.
> C. PATMORE.—*Angel in the House.*

The lover is a more godlike thing than
the beloved, as being inspired by a divinity.
> PLATO.—*Banquet, 7.*

Ye gods ! annihilate but space and time,
And make two lovers happy !
> POPE AND SWIFT.—*Art of Sinking, ch. 9.*
> *A quotation, the source not being
> indicated.*

No woman hates a man for being in love
with her ; but many a woman hates a man
for being a friend to her.
> POPE.—*Thoughts on Various Subjects.*

For love is blind and lovers cannot see
The pretty follies they themselves commit.
> SHAKESPEARE.—*Merchant of Venice,*
> Act 2, 6.

Then must you speak
Of one that loved not wisely, but too well ;
Of one not easily jealous, but, being
  wrought,
Perplexed in the extreme.
> SHAKESPEARE.—*Othello,* Act 5, 2.

I think there is not half a kiss to choose
Who loves another best.
> SHAKESPEARE.—*Winter's Tale,* Act 4, 3.

Why so pale and wan, fond lover ?
Prithee, why so pale ?
> SIR J. SUCKLING.—*Aglaura.*

The shackles of an old love straitened him,
His honour rooted in dishonour stood,
And faith unfaithful kept him falsely true.
> TENNYSON.—*Lancelot, 870.*

Our bond is not the bond of man and wife.
> TENNYSON.—*Ib., 1198.*

Perhaps all early love affairs ought to
be strangled or drowned, like so many
blind kittens.   THACKERAY.—*Pendennis.*

And sadly reflecting
  That a lover forsaken
A new love may get,
But a neck, when once broken,
  Can never be set.
> W. WALSH.—*Despairing Lover.*

LOYALTY

True as the dial to the sun,
Although it be not shined upon.
> BUTLER.—*Hudibras,* Pt. 3, 2.

I will never desert Mr. Micawber. [*Mrs.
Micawber.*]
> DICKENS.—*D. Copperfield, c. 12.*

The obligation of subjects to the
sovereign is understood to last as long,
and no longer, than the power lasteth by
which he is able to protect them.
> HOBBES.—*Leviathan, ch. 21.*

Devotion to princes is a second self-love.
> LA ROCHEFOUCAULD.—*Maxim 597.*

A jewel in a ten times barred up chest
Is a bold spirit in a loyal breast.
> SHAKESPEARE.—*Richard II.,* Act 1, 1.

Every subject's duty is the king's ; but
every subject's soul is his own.
> SHAKESPEARE.—*Henry V.,* 4, 1.

To reverence the King as if he were
Their conscience, and their conscience as
  their King.
> TENNYSON.—*Guinevere, 464.*

K*

LUCK

Renown's all hit or miss ;
There's fortune even in fame, we must
allow. BYRON.—*Don Juan*, 7, 33.

Shallow men believe in luck, believe in
circumstances ... Strong men believe in
cause and effect. EMERSON.—
Conduct of Life. Worship.

"Luck," continued the gambler [Oak-
shott] reflectively, "is a mighty queer
thing. All you know about it for certain
is that it's bound to change."
BRET HARTE.—*Outcasts of Poker Flat.*

Happiness or misery generally go to
those who have most of the one or the
other. LA ROCHEFOUCAULD.—*Maxim* 360.

"Then here goes another," says he, "to
make sure,
"For there's luck in odd numbers," says
Rory O'More.
S. LOVER.—*Rory O'More.*

For there's nae luck about the house;
There's nae luck at aw :
There's little pleasure in the house,
When our gude man's awa'.
W. J. MICKLE.—*Song.*

Call me not fool till heaven hath sent
me fortune.
SHAKESPEARE.—*As You Like It*, Act 2, 7.

I bear a charmèd life.
SHAKESPEARE.—*Macbeth*, Act 5, 7.

Fortune, which is imagined to be so
sovereign, can do scarcely anything without Nature.
VAUVENARGUES.—*Maxim* 579.

A chip of chance weigheth more than
a pound of wit.
SIR T. WYATT.—*Courtier's Life* (c. 1530).

LUKEWARMNESS

In doing good, we are generally cold,
and languid, and sluggish ; and of all
things afraid of being too much in the right.
But the works of malice and injustice are
quite in another style. They are finished
with a bold, masterly hand.
BURKE.—*Speech at Bristol* (1780).

Lukewarmness I account a sin,
As great in love as in religion.
COWLEY.—*The Mistress.—Love Verses ;
The Request.*

I know thy works, that thou art neither
cold nor hot ; I would thou wert cold or
hot. *Revelation* iii, 15.

LUXURY

What will not Luxury taste ? Earth, sea,
and air,
Are daily ransacked for the bill of fare !
GAY.—*Trivia, Bk.* 3, *l.* 199.

Such dainties to them, their health it
might hurt ;
It's like sending them ruffles, when wanting
a shirt.
GOLDSMITH.—*Haunch of Venison.*

Nature is free to all, and none were foes
Till partial luxury began the strife.
JAS. HAMMOND.—*Elegy, No.* 11.

Impatient of a scene whose luxuries stole,
Spite of himself, too deep into his soul.
MOORE.—*Lalla Rookh.*

The superfluous—a very necessary thing.
VOLTAIRE.—*Le Mondain.*

LYING

Behold him there ! He stands before your
eyes,
To bear you down with a superior frown,
A fiercer stare,
And more incessant, more exhaustless lies.
ARISTOPHANES.—*The Knights
(Frere tr.).*

It is not the lie that passeth through the
mind, but the lie that sinketh in and
settleth in it, that doth the hurt.
BACON.—*Of Truth.*

It isn' every fool that's fit
To make a real good lie, that'll sit
On her keel, and answer the helm.
T. E. BROWN.—*The Doctor.*

And after all, what is a lie ? 'Tis but
The truth in masquerade.
BYRON.—*Don Juan, c.* 11, *st.* 37.

Man everywhere is the born enemy of
lies. CARLYLE.—*Heroes, sec.* 1.

The talent of lying in a way that cannot
be laid hold of.
CARLYLE.—*Latter Day Pamphlets,* 7.

Thou liar of the first magnitude !
CONGREVE.—*Love for Love*, Act 4, 2.

A liar is always prodigal of oaths.
CORNEILLE.—*Le Menteur.*

"There's one thing you may be sure of,
Pip," said Joe, "namely that lies is lies.
However they come, they didn't ought to
come, and they come from the father of
lies, and work round to the same."
DICKENS.—*Gt. Expectations, ch.* 9.

The art of speaking well consists largely
in lying skilfully.
ERASMUS.—*Philetymus.*

" I am Ymaginatyf," quath he, " ydel
was I nevere."
LANGLAND.—*Piers Plowman, Passus* 15.

An innocent truth can never stand in need
Of a guilty lie.
MASSINGER.—*Emperor of East,*
Act 5, 3.

I have heard that a warm lie is the best.
Whatever the gods put into your mind is
the best thing to say.
PLAUTUS.—*Mostellaria,* Act 3.

He who tells a lie is not sensible how
great a task he undertakes ; for he must
be forced to invent twenty more to maintain that one.
POPE.—*Thoughts on Various Subjects.*

A very honest woman, but something
given to lie.
SHAKESPEARE.—*Antony and Cleopatra,*
Act 5, 2.

Lord, lord, how the world is given to
lying !
SHAKESPEARE.—*Henry IV., Pt.* 1,
Act 5, 4.

Let me have no lying ; it becomes none
but tradesmen.
SHAKESPEARE.—*Winter's Tale,* Act 4, 3.

Lying's a certain mark of cowardice.
T. SOUTHERN.—*Oroonoko,* Act 5.

A lie travels round the world while
Truth is putting on her boots.
C. H. SPURGEON.

If a man had the art of the second sight
for seeing lies, as they have in Scotland
for seeing spirits, how admirably he might
entertain himself in this town [London],
by observing the different shapes, sizes,
and colours of those swarms of lies which
buzz about the heads of some people.
SWIFT.—*Examiner, No.* 15.

An experienced, industrious, ambitious,
and often quite picturesque liar.
MARK TWAIN.—*Military Campaign.*

But liars we can never trust,
    Though they should speak the thing
        that's true ;
And he that does one fault at first,
    And lies to hide it, makes it two.
I. WATTS.—*Against Lying.*

There is such a thing as robbing a story
of its reality by trying to make it too
true. OSCAR WILDE.—*The Decay of
Lying.*

Truth never was indebted to a lie.
YOUNG.—*Night Thoughts,* 8.

Whosoever loveth and maketh a lie.
Revelation xxii, 15.

M

MADNESS

Out of my course I'm borne
By the wild spirit of fierce agony,
    And cannot curb my lips ;
And turbid speech at random dashes on
Upon the waves of dread calamity.
ÆSCHYLUS.—*Prometheus,* 877
(*Plumptre tr.*).

There is a pleasure sure
In being mad, which none but madmen
    know.
DRYDEN.—*Spanish Friar,* Act 2, 1.

O greater madman, pray have mercy
on a lesser one ! HORACE.—*Sat., Bk.* 2.

It is a common calamity ; at some time
or other we have all been mad.
JOH. BAPTISTA MANTUANUS.

That he is mad 'tis true ; 'tis true 'tis pity,
And pity 'tis 'tis true.
SHAKESPEARE.—*Hamlet,* Act 2, 2.

Though this be madness, yet there is
    method in it.
SHAKESPEARE.—*Ib.,* Act 2, 2.

I am but mad north-north-west. When
the wind is southerly, I know a hawk from
a handsaw. SHAKESPEARE.—*Ib.,* Act 2, 2.

Madness in great ones must not un-
    watched go.
SHAKESPEARE.—*Ib.,* Act 3, 1.

O, that way madness lies ; let me shun
    that ! SHAKESPEARE.—*Lear,* Act 3, 4.

Why, this is very midsummer madness.
SHAKESPEARE.—*Twelfth Night,* Act 3, 4.

I think for my part one half of the
Nation is mad—and the other not very
sound. SMOLLETT.—*Sir L. Greaves.*

He gave the little wealth he had
To build a house for fools and mad ;
To show, by one satiric touch,
No nation wanted it so much.
SWIFT.—*On the death of Dr. Swift.*

'Tis a mad world, my masters. *Prov.*

MAGIC

Charmes for woundes or maladye of
men or of bestes (beasts), if they taken any
effect, it may be peraventure that God
suffreth it, for [so that] folk sholden yeve
[should give] the more feith and reverence
to his name.
CHAUCER.—*Parson's Tale, sec.* 38.

Wizards that peep, and that mutter.
Isaiah viii, 19.

MAGISTRATES

Authority intoxicates
And makes mere sots of magistrates ;
The fumes of it invade the brain,
And make men giddy, proud, and vain.
S. BUTLER.—*Miscellaneous Thoughts.*

Be this, ye rural magistrates, your plan,
Firm be your justice, but be friends to
man.
J. LANGHORNE.—*Country Justice,* 133.

Fear God, and offend not the Prince and
his laws,
And keep thyself out of the magistrate's
claws. T. TUSSER.—*Good Husbandry.*

MAGNANIMITY

England and Ireland may flourish together. The world is large enough for us
both. Let it be our care not to make ourselves too little for it.
BURKE.—*Letter to Samuel Span.*

Magnanimity in politics is not seldom the
truest wisdom ; and a great empire and
little minds go ill together.
BURKE.—*Speech on Conciliation.*

His [Abraham Lincoln's] heart was as
great as the world, but there was no room
in it to hold the memory of a wrong.
EMERSON.—*Greatness.*

The eagle suffers little birds to sing,
And is not careful what they mean
thereby.
SHAKESPEARE.—*Titus Andronicus,* Act 4, 4.

Dowered with the hate of hate, the scorn
of scorn,
The love of love.   TENNYSON.—*The Poet.*

Praises to the vanquished are an addi-
tional laurel to the victors.
VOLTAIRE.—*Prelim. Discourse, Poème de
Fontenoi.*

MAGNIFICENCE

For wheresoe'er I turn my ravished eyes
Gay gilded scenes and shining prospects
rise.   ADDISON.—*Letter from Italy.*

Thought in gold and dreamed in silver.
STEPHEN PHILLIPS.—*Herod.*

MAHOMETANS

One of that saintly murderous brood,
To carnage and the Koran given.
MOORE.—*Lalla Rookh.*

MAJORITIES

A majority is always the best repartee.
DISRAELI.—*Tancred, Bk. 2, c.* 14.

Decision by majorities is as much an
expedient as lighting by gas.
W. E. GLADSTONE.—*Speech,* 1858.

The majority is never right ... Who
are they that make up the majority in a
country ? Is it the wise men or the foolish ?
... The minority is always right.
IBSEN.—*An Enemy of Society.*

Safer with multitudes to stray,
Than tread alone a fairer way :
To mingle with the erring throng,
Than boldly speak ten millions wrong.
EARL NUGENT.—*Ep. to a Lady.*

I believe it to be a great truth that to
carry a point in your house [Irish House
of Commons], the two following circumstances are of great advantage : first, to
have an ill cause ; and secondly, to be in
a minority ... Whereas on the contrary
a majority with a good cause are negligent
and supine.
SWIFT.—*Letter to an M.P. in Ireland* (1708).

Hain't we got all the fools in town on
our side ? And ain't that a big enough
majority in any town ?
MARK TWAIN.—*Huckleberry Finn, ch.* 26.

MALEVOLENCE AND MALICE

A truth that's told with bad intent
Beats all the lies you can invent.
WM. BLAKE.—*Proverbs.*

A bitter heart that bides its time and bites.
BROWNING.—*Caliban.*

Let those who have betrayed him [Lord
Chatham] by their adulation, insult him
with their malevolence. But what I do
not presume to censure, I may have leave
to lament.
BURKE.—*Speech on American Taxation.*

An honest man may like a glass,
An honest man may like a lass,
But mean revenge, an' malice fause,
He'll still disdain.
BURNS.—*Epistle to J. M'Math.*

Much malice mingled with a little wit.
DRYDEN.—*Hind and the Panther, Pt.* 3, 1.

Malice feeds on the living ; after life is
over, it rests.   OVID.—*Amores, Bk.* 1.

Willing to wound and yet afraid to strike.
POPE.—*Prol. to Satires.*

Let us taste the unique pleasure of unhappy souls—let us not be the only ones
to be miserable. QUINAULT.—*Theseus,* 3, 7.

Malice is the ordinary vice of those who
live in the mode of religion, without the
spirit of it.
STEELE.—*The Guardian, No.* 65
(*May* 26, 1713).

Shipwrecked, kindles on the coast
False fires, that others may be lost.
WORDSWORTH.—*To Lady Fleming.*

All malice is but little to the malice of a woman.   *Ecclesiasticus* xxv, 19
(R.V.).

MANKIND

Strong is the Soul, and wise, and beautiful ;
The seeds of godlike power are in us still :
Gods are we, Bards, Saints, Heroes, if we will.
   M. ARNOLD.—*In Emerson's Essays.*

The human comedy.
Title given to his works by H. DE BALZAC.

Nature has placed mankind under the governance of two sovereign masters, pain and pleasure . . . They govern us in all we do.   J. BENTHAM.—*Introd. to Principles of Morals.*

Most men are bad.
   BIAS OF PRIENE.—(c. B.C. 560.)

Man is a noble animal, splendid in ashes, and pompous in the grave.
   SIR T. BROWNE.—*Hydriotaphia.*

Men are not angels, neither are they brutes ;
Something we may see, all we cannot see.
   BROWNING.—*Bp. Blougram.*

Man seeks his own good at the whole world's cost.   BROWNING.—*Luria.*

Good Lord, what is man ? for as simple he looks,
Do but try to develop his hooks and his crooks ;
With his depths and his shallows, his good and his evil,
All in all he's a problem must puzzle the devil.   BURNS.—*To C. J. Fox.*

A man's a man for a' that.
   BURNS.—*Is there, for Honest Poverty ?*

Let us then praise their good, forget their ill !
Men must be men and women women still.
   CAMPION.—*Vain Men.*

For ours is a most fictile world, and man is the most fingent plastic of creatures.
CARLYLE.—*French Revolution, Pt. 1, Bk. 1.*

Ye were not formed to live the life of brutes,
But virtue to pursue, and knowledge high.
H. F. CARY.—*Dante's "Hell," c. 26, 116.*

Man is an embodied paradox, a bundle of contradictions. C. C. COLTON.—*Lacon.*

'Tis pleasant through the loopholes of retreat
To peep at such a world ; to see the stir
Of the great Babel, and not feel the crowd.
   COWPER.—*Winter Evening, 88.*

Men are but children of a larger growth,
Our appetites as apt to change as theirs,
And full as craving too, and full as vain.
   DRYDEN.—*All for Love, Act 4, 1.*

How dull, and how insensible a beast
Is man, who yet would lord it o'er the rest !
   DRYDEN.—*On Satire, l. 1.*

Men's men : gentle or simple, they're much of a muchness.
GEO. ELIOT.—*Daniel Deronda, Bk. 4, ch. 31.*

Men in all ways are better than they seem.
   EMERSON.—*New England Reformers.*

So nigh is grandeur to our dust
So near is God to man.
   EMERSON.—*Voluntaries.*

Oh Thou, who Man of baser Earth didst make,
And ev'n with Paradise devise the Snake ;
For all the Sin wherewith the Face of Man
Is blackened—Man's forgiveness give—and take !
   FITZGERALD.—*Rubáiyát, st. 81.*

Man is Nature's sole mistake.
   SIR W. S. GILBERT.—*Princess Ida*

Man will swear and man will storm ;
Man is not at all good form ;
Man is of no kind of use ;
Man's a donkey, man's a goose.
   SIR W. S. GILBERT.—*Ib.*

Man's not worth a moment's pain,
Base, ungrateful, fickle, vain.
   J. GRAINGER.—*Ode to Solitude.*

Though every prospect pleases,
And only man is vile.
   BISHOP HEBER.—*Hymn.*

Man is one world, and hath
Another to attend him.
   HERBERT.—*Man.*

Thou'lt find thy Manhood all too fast—
Soon come, soon gone ! and age at last
A sorry *breaking-up !*
   HOOD.—*Clapham Academy.*

If there is one beast in all the loathsome fauna of civilization I hate and despise, it is a man of the world.
   HENRY ARTHUR JONES.—*The Liars, Act 1.*

Hard fate of man, on whom the heavens bestow
A drop of pleasure for a sea of woe.
   SIR W. JONES.—*Laura.*

We fear all things as mortals, and we desire all things as if we were immortals.
   LA ROCHEFOUCAULD.—*Maxim 590.*

Man, false man, smiling, destructive man.
   N. LEE.—*Theodosius, Act 3, 2.*

Before Man made us citizens, great Nature
made us men.
J. R. LOWELL.—*Capture of Fugitive Slaves.*

I've studied men from my topsy-turvy
Close, and, I reckon, rather true.
Some are fine fellows : some, right scurvy :
Most, a dash between the two.
GEO. MEREDITH.—*Juggling Jerry, st. 7.*

Once in the flight of ages past,
There lived a man :—and who was he ?
Mortal ! howe'er thy lot be cast,
That man resembled thee.
J. MONTGOMERY.—*The Common Lot.*

Why hast thou made me so,
My Maker ? I would know
Wherefore Thou gav'st me such a mourn-
ful dower ;—
Toil that is oft in vain,
Knowledge that deepens pain,
And longing to be pure without the power.
J. J. MURPHY.—*Eternity.*

In short what is man in nature ?
Nothing in regard to the infinite, everything in regard to nothing, something in
between nothing and all.
PASCAL.—*Pensées.*

Child of a day, what's man ? What is
he not ?
His life a shadow's dream.
PINDAR.—*Pythian Odes, 8, 131.*

Let us (since life can little more supply
Than just to look about us and to die),
Expatiate free o'er all this scene of man ;
A mighty maze ! but not without a plan !
POPE.—*Essay on Man, Ep. 1, 3.*

All are but parts of one stupendous whole,
Whose body nature is, and God the soul.
POPE.—*Ib., 268.*

Know then thyself ; presume not God to
scan :
The proper study of mankind is man.
POPE.—*Ib., Ep. 2, 1.*

Placed on this isthmus of a middle state,
A being darkly wise and rudely great.
POPE.—*Ib., Ep. 2, 3.*

The glory, jest, and riddle of the world.
POPE.—*Ib., Ep. 2, 18.*

Man is man's A.B.C. There is none can
Read God aright, unless he first spell man.
QUARLES.—*Hieroglyphics.*

Once it came into my heart and whelmed
me like a flood,
That these too are men and women, human
flesh and blood ;
Men with hearts and men with souls,
though trodden down like mud.
CHRISTINA ROSSETTI.—*Royal Princess.*

Men, be human ; that is your first duty.
ROUSSEAU.—*Emile.*

Ah, let us for a little while abate
The outward roving eye, and seek within
Where spirit unto spirit is allied ;
There, in our inmost being, we may win
The joyful vision of the heavenly wise
To see the beauty in each other's eyes.
GEO. RUSSELL.—*Shadows and Lights.*

The doctor sees mankind in all its weaknesses ; the lawyer in all its wickedness ;
the theologian in all its stupidity.
SCHOPENHAUER.—*Psychological
Observations.*

What a piece of work is man ! How
noble in reason ! How infinite in faculty !
In form and moving how express and
admirable ! In action, how like an angel ; in
apprehension, how like a god ! The beauty
of the world, the paragon of animals !
And yet to me what is this quintessence
of dust ? Man delights not me, no nor
woman neither, though by your smiling
you seem to say so.
SHAKESPEARE.—*Hamlet,* Act 2, 2.

What should such fellows as I do,
crawling between heaven and earth ? We
are arrant knaves, all.
SHAKESPEARE.—*Ib.,* Act 3, 1.

Ay, in the catalogue ye go for men.
SHAKESPEARE.—*Macbeth,* Act 3, 1.

God made him, and therefore let him
pass for a man.
SHAKESPEARE.—*Merchant of Venice,*
Act 1, 2.

When I am grown to man's estate
I shall be very proud and great,
And tell the other girls and boys
Not to meddle with my toys.
R. L. STEVENSON.—*Looking Forward.*

I cannot but conclude the bulk of your
natives to be the most pernicious race of
odious little vermin that nature ever suffered to crawl upon the surface of the earth.
SWIFT.—*Brobdingnag.*

Vain humankind ! fantastic race !
Thy various follies who can trace ?
Self-love, ambition, envy, pride,
Their empire in our hearts divide.
SWIFT.—*On the death of Dr. Swift.*

For good ye are and bad, and like to coins,
Some true, some light, but every one of
you
Stamped with the image of the king.
TENNYSON.—*Holy Grail, 25.*

Thou madest man, he knows not why ;
He thinks he was not made to die.
TENNYSON.—*In Memoriam, Introd.*

I, the heir of all the ages, in the foremost
files of time.
TENNYSON.—*Locksley Hall.*

But what am I ?
An infant crying in the night :
An infant crying for the light :
And with no language but a cry.
TENNYSON.—*In Memoriam, c.* 54.

For man is man, and master of his fate.
TENNYSON.—*Marriage of Geraint, l.* 355.

Man is the hunter ; woman is his game.
TENNYSON.—*Princess, c.* 5, 147.

This truth within thy mind rehearse,
That in a boundless universe
Is boundless better, boundless worse.
TENNYSON.—*Two Voices.*

Every moment dies a man,
Every moment one is born.
TENNYSON.—*Vision of Sin, st.* 9 *and* 15.

Fill the can and fill the cup ;
All the windy ways of men
Are but dust that rises up
And is lightly laid again.
TENNYSON.—*Ib., st.* 18 *and* 27.

Oh, vanity of vanities !
How wayward the decrees of Fate are !
How very weak the very wise,
How very small the very great are !
THACKERAY.—*Vanitas Vanitatum.*

The mice inhabiting small holes in some immense building, do not know whether that building is eternal, nor who is the architect, nor why he built it. They try to preserve their lives, to people their holes, and to escape the preying animals which pursue them. We are the mice, and the Divine Architect, as far as I know, has not yet told his secret to any one of us.
VOLTAIRE.—*Letter to Frederick the Great, Aug.* 26,1736.

He that in sight diminishes mankind,
Does no addition to his stature find ;
But he that does a noble nature show,
Obliging others, still does higher grow.
WALLER.—*On the Fear of God, c.* 3, 7.

We are children of splendour and fame,
Of shuddering also, and tears ;
Magnificent out of the dust we came,
And abject from the spheres.
SIR W. WATSON.—*Ode in May.*

Good are life and laughter, though we look
    before and after,
And good to love the race of men a little
    ere we go.
ALICE WERNER.—*Song of Fleet Street.*

Here are we in a bright and breathing
    world :
Our origin, what matters it ?
WORDSWORTH.—*Excursion, Bk.* 3.

All creatures and all objects in degree
Are friends and patrons of humanity.

These are to whom the garden, grove, and
    field
Perpetual lessons of forbearance yield.
WORDSWORTH —*Humanity, l.* 103.

Much it grieved my heart to think
What man has made of man.
WORDSWORTH.—*In Early Spring.*

The still, sad music of humanity,
Nor harsh, nor grating, though of ample
    power,
To chasten and subdue.
WORDSWORTH.—*Lines, nr. Tintern Abbey.*

How poor, how rich, how abject, how
    august,
How complicate, how wonderful, is man !
YOUNG.—*Night Thoughts,* 1.

O what a miracle to man is man !
YOUNG.—*Ib.,* 1.

So great, so mean is man.
YOUNG.—*Ib.,* 6.

Fond man ! the vision of a moment made !
Dream of a dream, and shadow of a shade.
YOUNG.—*Book of Job,* 187.

There's nought so queer as folk.
North Country prov.

Man to man is either a god or a wolf.
Quoted as a Latin prov. by Erasmus.

MANLINESS

Do all things like a man, not sneakingly :
Think the King sees thee still, for his King
    doth.   HERBERT.—*Church Porch.*

Far may we search before we find
A heart so manly and so kind.
SCOTT.—*Marmion, c.* 4, *Intro.*

He only, in a general honest thought,
And common good to all, made one of
    them.
His life was gentle ; and the elements
So mixed in him that Nature might stand
    up
And say to all the world, " This was a
    man ! "
SHAKESPEARE.—*Julius Cæsar,* Act 5, 5.

MANNERISMS

And then in the fulness of joy and hope,
Seemed washing his hands with invisible
    soap,
In imperceptible water.
HOOD.—*Miss Kilmansegg.*

And rubbed his hands, and smiled aloud,
And bowed, and bowed, and bowed, and
    bowed,
Like a man who is sawing marble.
HOOD.—*Ib.*

And with a sweeping of the arm,
And a lack-lustre dead-blue eye,
Devolved his rounded periods.
TENNYSON.—*A Character.*

And slight Sir Robert, with his watery
smile
And educated whisker.
TENNYSON.—*Edwin Morris.*

MANNERS

He was the mildest mannered man
   That ever scuttled ship or cut a throat ;
With such true breeding of a gentleman
   You never could divine his real thought.
BYRON.—*Don Juan, c.* 3, 41.

Everyone's manners make his fortune.
CORNELIUS NEPOS.—*Vita Attici.*

The basis of good manners is self-
reliance . . . Those who are not self-possessed obtrude, and pain us.
EMERSON.—*Conduct of Life,
Behaviour.*

Who does not delight in fine manners ?
Their charm cannot be predicted or over-
stated.   EMERSON.—*Social Aims.*

Religious, moral, generous, and humane
He was,—but self-sufficient, rude and
   vain ;
Ill-bred and overbearing in dispute,
A scholar and a Christian,—yet a brute.
SOAME JENYNS.—*On Dr. S. Johnson.*

True is, that whilome that good poet sayd,
The gentle mind by gentle deeds is knowne;
For a man by nothing is so well bewrayd
As by his manners.
SPENSER.—*Faerie Queene, Bk.* 6, *c.* 3, 1.

Gentle bloud will gentle manners breed.
SPENSER.—*Ib., Bk.* 6, *c.* 3, 2.

There is an oblique way of reproof,
which takes off from the sharpness of it ;
and an address in flattery, which makes it
agreeable, though never so gross.
STEELE.—*The Guardian, No.* 10 (*March*
18, 1713).

Few are qualified to shine in company,
but it is in most men's power to be agreeable.
SWIFT.—*Thoughts on Various Subjects.*

How rude are the boys that throw pebbles
and mire !   I. WATTS.—*Innocent Play.*

The mainners o' a' nations are equally
bad.
JOHN WILSON.—*Noctes,* 39 (*Ettrick
Shepherd*).

Leave off first for manners' sake.
Ecclesiasticus xxxi, 17.

And this he truly taught, and this we know,
A man's own manners gild or soil his name.
F. E. W.—*In memory of Dr. Warre,
Jan.* 28, 1920.

Come when you're called,
And do as you're bid ;
Shut the door after you ;
And you'll never be chid.
*Old Rhyme.   Quoted by Miss Edgeworth in
" The Contrast," ch.* 1.

MAN'S AGES

At twenty years of age, the will reigns ;
at thirty, the wit ; and at forty, the judgment.   H. GRATTAN.

MARCH

When that the month in which the world
   bigan,
That highte [is called] March, when God
   first maked man.
CHAUCER.—*Nun Priest's Tale,* 367.

Slayer of the winter, art thou here again?
W. MORRIS.—*Earthly Paradise. March, l.* 1.

But when the wreath of March has
   blossomed,
Crocus, anemone, violet.
TENNYSON.—*To the Rev. F. D. Maurice.*

When March comes in with an adder's
head, it goes out with a peacock's tail ;
when March comes in with a peacock's
tail, it goes out with an adder's head.
Scottish saying.

MARRIAGE

Marriage is a tie which hope makes beautiful, which happiness preserves, and which
misfortune strengthens.
ALIBERT (1767–1837).

He was reputed one of the wise men,
[Thales] that made answer to the question
when a man should marry ?   " A young
man not yet ; an elder man not at all."
BACON.—*Of Marriage.*

They gied him my hand, though my heart
   was at sea.
LADY ANN BARNARD.—*Auld Robin Gray.*

We should marry to please ourselves,
not other people.
I. BICKERSTAFF.—*Maid of the Mill,* Act 3,4.

Youth means love ;
Vows can't change nature ; priests are
   only men.
BROWNING.—*Ring and the Book,* 1056.

Oh, gie me the lass that has acres o' charms,
Oh, gie me the lass wi' the weel-stockit
   farms.
BURNS.—*Hey for a Lass wi' a Tocher.*

One was never married, and that's his
hell ; another is, and that's his plague.
BURTON.—*Anatomy of Melancholy, Pt.* 1,
sec. 2, *mem.* 4, 7.

'Tis pity learned virgins ever wed
With persons of no sort of education.
BYRON.—*Don Juan, c.* 1, 22.

Yet 'tis "so nominated in the bond,"
That both are tied till one shall have ex-
pired.   BYRON.—*Ib., c.* 3, 7.

Why don't they knead two virtuous souls
for life
Into that moral centaur, man and wife ?
BYRON.—*Ib.,* 5, 158.

Though women are angels, yet wedlock's
the devil. BYRON.—*Hours of Idleness.*

Since first he called her his before the holy
man.
CAMPBELL.—*Pleasures of Hope, Pt.* 2.

It [marriage] is an action of life like to
a stratagem of war, wherein a man can err
but once. If thy estate be good, match
near home and at leisure ; if weak, far off
and quickly.
WM. CECIL (LORD BURGHLEY).—
Precepts to his Son.

Ther as myn herte is set, ther wol I wyve.
CHAUCER.—*Clerk's Tale.*

And such a bliss is there betwixt them
two,
That, save the Joye that lasteth evermo,
There is none like.
CHAUCER.—*Tale of the Man of Law,* 977.

Oh ! how many torments be in the small
circle of a wedding ring !
CIBBER.—*Double Gallant, Act* 1, 2.

Marriage is a feast where the grace is
sometimes better than the dinner.
C. C. COLTON.—*Lacon.*

Valentine : The two greatest monsters
in the world are a man and a woman.
Sir Sampson Legend : Why, my opinion
is that those two monsters, joined together, make a yet greater, that's a man
and his wife.
CONGREVE.—*Love for Love, Act* 4, 2.

Sharper : Thus grief still treads upon the
heels of pleasure ;
Married in haste, we may repent at leisure.
Setter : Some by experience find those
words misplaced ;
At leisure married, they repent in haste.
CONGREVE.—*Old Bachelor, Act* 5, 3.

Choose not alone a proper mate,
But proper time to marry.
COWPER.—*Pairing-Time.*

Wedlock, indeed, hath oft compared been
To public feasts, where meet a public
rout ;
Where they that are without would fain
go in,
And they that are within would fain
go out.
SIR JOHN DAVIES.—*Contention.*

Wen you're a married man, Samivel,
you'll understand a good many things as
you don't understand now ; but vether
it is worth while goin' through so much to
learn so little, as the charity boy said ven
he got to the end of the alphabet, is a
matter o' taste.
DICKENS.—*Pickwick, ch.* 27.

His designs were strictly honourable, as
the phrase is, that is to rob a lady of her
fortune by way of marriage.
FIELDING.—*Tom Jones, Bk.* 11, *ch.* 4.

They that marry ancient people, merely
in expectation to bury them, hang themselves, in hope that one will come and cut
the halter.
FULLER.—*Holy and Profane State of
Marriage.*

You are of the society of the wits and
railers ; . . . the surest sign is, you are an
enemy to marriage, the common butt of
every railer.
GARRICK.—*Country Girl, Act* 2.

I sit all day
Giving agreeable girls away,
With one for him, and one for he,
And one for you, and one for ye,
And one for them, and one for thee ;
But never, oh, never a one for me !
SIR W. S. GILBERT.—*Iolanthe.*

Husband twice as old as wife
Argues ill for married life.
SIR W. S. GILBERT.—*Princess Ida.*

Marriage is the great civiliser of the
world. ROBT. HALL.—*Modern Infidelity.*

Holy and pure are the drops that fall
When the young bride goes from her
father's hall.
MRS. HEMANS.—*Bride of Greek Isle.*

He loves his bonds, who, when the first
are broke,
Submits his neck unto a second yoke.
HERRICK.—*Hesperides,* 42.

Yet Wedlock's a very awful thing !
'Tis something like that feat in the ring,
Which requires good nerve to do it—
When one of a " Grand Equestrian Troop "
Makes a jump at a gilded hoop,
Not certain at all
Of what may befall
After his getting through it !
HOOD.—*Miss Kilmansegg.*

Nobody can define precisely what love is, or the reason for that delightful persuasion that bliss is only to be found in double harness.
IBSEN.—*Love's Comedy*, Act 3 (1862).

At length he stretches out his foolish head to the conjugal halter.
JUVENAL.—*Sat.*, 6, 43.

The lover in the husband may be lost.
GEO. LORD LYTTELTON.—*Advice to a Lady.*

How much the wife is dearer than the bride !
GEO. LORD LYTTELTON.—*Irregular Ode.*

The sum of all that makes a just man happy
Consists in the well choosing of a wife.
MASSINGER.—*New Way to pay Old Debts*, Act 4, 1.

For any man to match above his rank
Is but to sell his liberty.
MASSINGER.—*Virgin Martyr*, Act 1, 1.

As the birds do, so do we,
Bill our mate, and choose our tree.
GEO. MEREDITH.—*Three Singers.*

Hail wedded love, mysterious law, true source
Of human offspring, sole propriety
In Paradise of all things common else.
MILTON.—*Paradise Lost*, Bk. 4, 750.

It happens as one sees in cages. The birds outside despair of ever getting in ; those inside are equally desirous of getting out.
MONTAIGNE.—*Bk.* 3.

Where I love I must not marry ;
Where I marry, cannot love.
MOORE.—*Love and Marriage.*

People say that May is the month in which to marry bad wives.
OVID.—*Fast.* 5.

Strange to say what delight we married people have to see these poor folks decoyed into our condition.
PEPYS.—*Diary*, 1665.

There swims no goose so grey but soon or late
She finds some honest gander for her mate.
POPE.—*Wife of Bath.*

A dish o' married love right soon grows cauld,
And douzens doun (settles down) to nane, as folks grow auld.   A. RAMSAY.

Marry too soon, and you'll repent too late.
A sentence worth my meditation ;
For marriage is a serious thing.
T. RANDOLPH.—*Jealous Lovers*, Act 5, 1.

Wooed, and married, and a',
Married, and wooed, and a' !
And was she nae very weel off
That was wooed, and married, and a' ?
ALEX. ROSS.—*Song.*

I have often thought that if only one could prolong the joy of love in marriage, we should have paradise on earth. That is a thing which has never been seen hitherto.   ROUSSEAU.—*Emile*, Bk. 5.

In our part of the world, where monogamy rules, to marry means to halve one's rights and to double one's duties.
SCHOPENHAUER.—*On Women.*

Marriage itself is nothing but a civil contract.   SELDEN.—*Marriage.*

A young man married is a man that's marred.
SHAKESPEARE.—*All's Well*, Act 2, 3.

Men are April when they woo, December when they wed.
SHAKESPEARE.—*As You Like It*, Act 4, 1.

The funeral baked meats
Did coldly furnish forth the marriage tables.
SHAKESPEARE.—*Hamlet*, Act 1, 2.

Hasty marriage seldom proveth well.
SHAKESPEARE.—*Henry VI., Pt.* 3, Act 4, 1.

If there be no great love in the beginning, yet heaven may decrease it upon better acquaintance, when we are married, and have more occasion to know one another ; I hope upon familiarity will grow more contempt.
SHAKESPEARE.—*Merry Wives*, Act 1, 1.

But earthly happier is the rose distilled,
Than that which, withering on the virgin thorn,
Grows, lives, and dies, in single blessedness.   SHAKESPEARE.—*Midsummer Night's Dream*, Act 1, 1.

When I said I would die a bachelor, I did not think I should live till I were married.
SHAKESPEARE.—*Much Ado*, Act 2, 3.

For this alliance may so happy prove,
To turn your household's rancour to pure love.
SHAKESPEARE.—*Romeo and Juliet*, Act 2, 3.

Let still the woman take
An elder than herself : so wears she to him,
So sways she level in her husband's heart.
SHAKESPEARE.—*Twelfth Night*, Act 2, 4.

Every woman who hasn't any money is a matrimonial adventurer.
G. B. SHAW.—*Heartbreak House*, Act 2.

It is a woman's business to get married as soon as possible, and a man's to keep unmarried as long as he can.
G. B. Shaw.—*Man and Superman.*

When a man marries or turns Hindoo, His best friends hear no more of him.
Shelley.—*To Maria Gisborne.*

Whichever you do you will repent.
Socrates.—*Advice attributed to him when he was asked if it was better to marry or not.*

If marriages
Are made in Heaven, they should be happier.   T. Southern.—*Isabella.*

And other hopes and other fears
Effaced the thoughts of happier years.
Southey.—*To Mary.*

The marriage state, with and without the affection suitable to it, is the completest image of Heaven and Hell we are capable of receiving in this life.
Steele.—*Spectator.*

Even if we take matrimony at its lowest, even if we regard it as no more than a sort of friendship recognised by the police.
R. L. Stevenson.—*Virginibus.*

Cupid and Hymen thou hast set at odds, And bred such feuds between those kindred gods,
That Venus cannot reconcile her sons ; When one appears, away the other runs.
Swift.—*To Love.*

Marriage hath in it less of beauty and more of safety than the single life ; it hath more care but less danger ; it is more merry and more sad ; it is fuller of sorrows and fuller of joys.
Jeremy Taylor.—*25 Sermons* (*No. 17*).

Him
That was a god, and is a lawyer's clerk, The rentroll Cupid of our rainy isles.
Tennyson.—*Edwin Morris.*

Either sex alone
Is half itself, and in true marriage lies Nor equal nor unequal.
Tennyson.—*Princess, c. 7, 283.*

Remember, it's as easy to marry a rich woman as a poor woman.
Thackeray.—*Pendennis, Bk. 1, 28.*

If truth were truly bolted out, As touching thrift, I stand in doubt If men were best to wive.
T. Tusser.—*Wiving and Thriving.*

Design, or chance, makes others wive ; But Nature did this match contrive.
Waller.—*Marriage of the Dwarfs.*

He is dreadfully married. He is the most married man I ever saw in my life.
Artemus Ward.—*Moses the Sassy.*

For every marriage then is best in tune, When that the wife is May, the husband June.
R. Watkyns.—*To Mrs. E. Williams.*

'Tis just like a summer bird-cage in a garden ; the birds that are without despair to get in, and the birds that are within despair and are in a consumption, for fear they shall never get out.
Webster.—*White Devil*, Act 1, 2 (*from Montaigne*).

In married life three is company and two none.
Oscar Wilde.—*Importance of being Earnest.*

I wish I could make her agree with me in the church.
Wycherley.—*Plain Dealer*, Act 1, 1.

Marriage is honourable in all.
2 Timothy xiii, 4.

Needles and pins, needles and pins ! When a man marries his trouble begins.
Old Nursery Rhyme.

Then the little maid she said, " Your fire may warm the bed,
But what shall we do for to eat ?
Will the flames you're only rich in make a fire in the kitchen,
And the little God of Love turn the spit ? "
Version of Nursery Rhyme (printed at Strawberry Hill, 18th cent.).

Who marries between the sickle and scythe will never thrive.   *Prov.* (*Ray.*)

Gude Enough has got a wife and Fare Better wants.   *Scottish prov.*

Marriage is a creel where ye catch an adder or an eel.   *Scottish prov.*

Who marries for love must live in sorrow.
Spanish prov.

A friend married is a friend lost.
Prov. quoted by Ibsen in " Love's Comedy," Act 2 (1862).

Advice to persons about to marry.— Don't. *Punch's Almanac*, 1845. (*Attrib. to H. Mayhew.*)

MARTYRDOM

He that dies a martyr proves that he was not a knave, but by no means that he was not a fool.
C. C. Colton.—*Lacon.*

For all have not the gift of martyrdom.
Dryden.—*Hind and Panther, Pt.* 2, 59.

The torments of martyrdoms are probably most keenly felt by the bystanders.
EMERSON.—*Courage.*

I look on martyrs as mistakes,
But still they burned for it at stakes.
J. MASEFIELD.—*Everlasting Mercy*, 933.

It is the cause, not the death, which makes the martyr.   NAPOLEON.

Like a pale martyr in his shirt of fire.
ALEXANDER SMITH.—*Life Drama,
Sc. 2.*

I love truth very much, but I do not love martyrs at all.
VOLTAIRE.—*Letter to D'Alembert, Feb. 8,
1776.*

Unbounded is the might
Of martyrdom and fortitude and right.
WORDSWORTH.—*Poems to National
Independence, Pt. 2, 23.*

Who perisheth in needless danger is the devil's martyr.   *Prov. (Ray).*

MASTERS

More have been ruined by their servants than by their masters.
C. C. COLTON.—*Lacon.*

And, strange to tell, among that Earthen Lot
Some could articulate, while others not :
And suddenly one more impatient cried—
" Who *is* the Potter, pray, and who the Pot ? "
FITZGERALD.—*Rubáiyát, st. 69 (1st Ed.).*

The master who fears his servant is less than a servant.   PUBLILIUS SYRUS.

MATHEMATICS

Scarcely any person seems to have studied this science ardently without success.
CICERO.—*De Oratore, Bk. 1, 3
(Of Mathematics).*

MATTER

When Bishop Berkeley said " there was no matter,"
And proved it—'twas no matter what he said.   BYRON.—*Don Juan, c. 11, 1.*

MAXIMS

Don't you go believing in sayings, Picotee ; they are all made by men, for their own advantage.
T. HARDY.—*Hand of Ethelberta, ch. 20.*

Many men, prejudiced early in disfavour of mankind by bad maxims, never aim at making friendships.
POPE.—*Thoughts on Various Subjects.*

As Rochefoucauld his maxims drew
From nature, I believe them true ;
They argue no corrupted mind
In him ; the fault is in mankind.
SWIFT.—*On the Death of Dr. Swift.*

With a little hoard of maxims preaching down a daughter's heart.
TENNYSON.—*Locksley Hall.*

Faithful is the saying and worthy of all acceptation.   1 *Timothy* i, 15 (*R.V.*).

MAY

As it fell upon a day,
In the merry month of May.
R. BARNFIELD.—*Ode.*

He was as fresh as is the month of May.
CHAUCER.—*Cant. Tales, Prol.*

May, that moder is of monthes glade.
CHAUCER.—*Troilus and Cressid,
Bk. 2, 50.*

But winter lingering chills the lap of May.
GOLDSMITH.—*Traveller.*

O ! that we two were Maying !
C. KINGSLEY.—*Saints' Tragedy,* Act 2, 9.

May is a pious fraud of the Almanac.
J. R. LOWELL.—*Under the Willows.*

Hail bounteous May, that dost inspire
Mirth and youth and warm desire.
MILTON.—*On May Morning.*

Rough winds do shake the darling buds of May ;
And summer's lease hath all too short a date.   SHAKESPEARE.—*Sonnet 18.*

You must wake and call me early, call me early, mother dear ;
To-morrow 'ill be the happiest time of all the glad New Year ;
Of all the glad New Year, mother, the maddest, merriest day ;
For I'm to be Queen o' the May, mother, I'm to be Queen o' the May.
TENNYSON.—*May Queen.*

For Flora in her clene array,
New washen with a showir o' May,
Lookit full sweet and fair.
ANON.—*The Vision (c.* 1715 ?—*printed
1783).*

Button to chin
Till May be in ;
Cast not a clout
Till May be out.   *Old Saying.*

A hot May makes a full churchyard.
Prov.

MEANING

Where more is meant than meets the ear.
MILTON.—*Il Penseroso, 120.*

Oft has good nature been the fool's defence,
And honest meaning gilded want of sense.
SHENSTONE.—To a Lady.

MEANNESS

With one hand he put
A penny in the urn of poverty,
And with the other took a shilling out.
R. POLLOK.—Course of Time, Bk. 8.

It's just like Duncan McGirdie's mare;
he wanted to use her by degrees to live
without food, and she died just when he
had put her on a straw a day.
SCOTT.—Waverley.

There are some meannesses which are
too mean even for men—woman, lovely
woman alone, can venture to commit them.
THACKERAY.—Shabby Genteel Story, ch. 3.

" A penny savèd is a penny got ; "
Firm to this scoundrel maxim keepeth he.
THOMSON.—Castle of Indolence, c. 1, 50.

MEAT

Oh ! the roast beef of old England !
And oh ! the old English roast beef !
H. FIELDING.—Song.

The fat was so white and the lean was so
ruddy.
GOLDSMITH.—Haunch of Venison.

I am a great eater of beef, and I believe
that does harm to my wit.
SHAKESPEARE.—Twelfth Night, Act 1, 3.

MEDDLING

It may be true, it may be true,
But has it aught to do with you ?
C. H. SPURGEON.—" Salt-Cellars."

Do not stir up Lake Camarina [the lake
which caused pestilence through a futile
attempt to drain it].   <i>Greek prov.</i>

MEDICINE

Medicine is a science which hath been
more professed than laboured, and more
laboured than advanced ; the labour
having been, in my judgment, rather in
circle than in progression.
BACON.—Adv. of Learning, Bk. 2.

Better to hunt in fields for health unbought,
Than fee the doctor for a nauseous draught.
DRYDEN.—To J. Driden.

Some fell by laudanum, and some by
steel,
And death in ambush lay in every pill.
S. GARTH.—Dispensary, 4, 62.

Zinzis Khan, when he was most crim-
soned with blood, never slaughtered the
human race as they have been slaughtered
by rash and erroneous theories of medicine.
SYDNEY SMITH.—Lectures on Moral
Philosophy. Introductory (1804).

MEDIOCRITY

This miserable fate
Suffer the wretched souls of those who
lived
Without or praise or blame.
H. F. CARY.—Dante's " Hell," c. 3, 60.

Who like the hindmost chariot-wheels
art curst
Still to be near, but ne'er to reach the
first.   DRYDEN.—<i>Persius, Sat.</i> 5, 103.

Oh, mediocrity,
Thou priceless jewel, only mean men have,
But cannot value.
FLETCHER (AND MASSINGER ?).—
Queen of Corinth, Act 3, 1.

Yet still he fills affection's eye,
Obscurely wise, and coarsely kind.
JOHNSON.—On R. Levett.

Old Andrew Fairservice used to say that
" There were many things ower bad for
blessing and ower gude for banning, like
Rob Roy."
SCOTT.—Rob Roy, ch. 39 (Conclusion).

Too bad for a blessing, too good for a curse,
I wish from my soul they were better or
worse. SWIFT.—<i>On his Country House.</i>

Let us thank Heaven, my dear sir, for
according to us the power to taste and
appreciate the pleasures of mediocrity.
THACKERAY.—On the French School of
Painting.

With several others of ignobler name,
Whom time has not delivered o'er to fame.
VIRGIL.—Æneid, Bk. 5 (Dryden tr.).

A fool amongst philosophers, but a
philosopher amongst fools.
Greek saying referring to Critias, a
wealthy friend of Socrates, afterwards
his bitter enemy.

MEEKNESS

Now the man Moses was very meek,
above all the men which were upon the
face of the earth.   <i>Numbers</i> xii, 3.

The ornament of a meek and quiet spirit.
1 St. Peter iii, 4.

MELANCHOLY

It is a very dreadful melancholy when
it is a case of melancholy without any
cause.   PIERRE BALLANCHE (1786–1847).

Ah, what is mirth but turbulence unholy,
When with the charm compared of
heavenly melancholy ?
J. BEATTIE.—Minstrel, Bk. 1, st. 55.

309

All my joys to this are folly,
Nought so sweet as melancholy.
> BURTON.—*Anatomy of Melancholy.*

Heigho! now I'll be melancholy, as
melancholy as a watchlight.
> CONGREVE.—*Way of the World.*

Did it ever strike you on such a morning
as this, that drowning would be happiness
and peace? DICKENS.—*Pickwick, ch.* 5.

There is a kindly mood of melancholy
That wings the soul, and points her to the
skies. J. DYER.—*Ruins of Rome,* 346.

There's nought in this life sweet,
If men were wise to see't,
But only melancholy;
Oh, sweetest melancholy!
> FLETCHER.—*Nice Valour,* Act 3, 1.

Remote, unfriended, melancholy, slow.
> GOLDSMITH.—*Traveller.*

And Melancholy marked him for her own.
> GRAY.—*Elegy.*

Come let us sit and watch the sky,
And fancy clouds, where no clouds be.
> HOOD.—*To Melancholy.*

There's not a string attuned to Mirth
But has its chord in Melancholy.
> HOOD.—*Ib.*

There are times
When simplest things put on a sombre cast.
> KEATS.—*Otho,* Act 4, 1.

Hence, loathèd Melancholy,
Of Cerberus and blackest Midnight born,
In Stygian cave forlorn,
Mongst horrid shapes, and shrieks, and
sights unholy. MILTON.—*L'Allegro,* 1.

Hail, divinest Melancholy!
> MILTON.—*Il Penseroso,* 12.

I can suck melancholy out of a song as
a weasel sucks eggs.
> SHAKESPEARE.—*As You Like It,* Act 2, 5.

My cue is villainous melancholy, with
a sigh like Tom o' Bedlam.
> SHAKESPEARE.—*Lear,* Act 1, 2.

I am not merry, but I do beguile
The thing I am, by seeming otherwise.
> SHAKESPEARE.—*Othello,* Act 2, 1.

We should have shone at a wake, but
not at anything more festive.
> MARK TWAIN.—*Innocents Abroad, ch.* 2.

I have learned
To look on Nature, not as in the hour
Of thoughtless youth; but hearing often-
times
The still, sad music of humanity.
> WORDSWORTH.—*Lines, nr. Tintern Abbey*
> (1798).

Some folks like to sigh,
Some folks do;
Some folks like to die,
But that's not me nor you.
> *Song (c.* 1865).

Let him be wretched who thinks himself
so.   *Spanish prov.*

MELODRAMA

Some jealousy of someone's heir,
Some hopes of dying broken-hearted,
A miniature, a lock of hair,
The usual vows—and then we parted.
> W. M. PRAED.—*Belle of the Ball, st.* 12.

No, no, I'll love no more; let him who
can
Fancy the maid who fancies every man;
In some lone place I'll find a gloomy cave,
There my own hands shall dig a spacious
grave:
Then all unseen I'll lay me down and die,
Since woman's constancy is—all my eye.
> W. B. RHODES.—*Bombastes.*

MEMENTOES

So let it rest! And time will come
When here the tender-hearted
May heave a gentle sigh for him
As one of the departed.
> WORDSWORTH.—*Inscriptions,* 10 (1830).

MEMORY

O memory! thou fond deceiver,
Still importunate and vain.
> GOLDSMITH.—*Song.*

Much memory, or memory of many
things is called "experience."
> HOBBES.—*Leviathan, ch.* 2.

Ah tell me not that memory
Sheds gladness o'er the past;
What is recalled by faded flowers,
Save that they did not last?
Were it not better to forget,
Than but remember and regret?
> L. E. LANDON.—*Despondency.*

The other kind of pleasures, namely
those peculiar to the soul, are all produced
through memory. PLATO.—*Philebus,* 65.

Sorrows remembered sweeten present joy.
> POLLOK.—*Course of Time, Bk.* 1, 464.

The memory strengthens as you lay
burdens upon it.
> DE QUINCEY.—*Opium Eater, Pt.* 1.

Of this at least I feel assured, that there
is no such thing as ultimate forgetting.
Traces once impressed upon the memory
are indestructible.
> DE QUINCEY.—*Ib., Pt.* 3.

Sweet Memory, wafted by thy gentle gale,
Oft up the stream of Time I turn my sail.
> ROGERS.—*Pleasures of Memory, Pt.* 2.

Better by far you should forget and smile,
Than that you should remember and be
sad.
    CHRISTINA ROSSETTI.—*Remember.*

Memory, the warder of the brain.
    SHAKESPEARE.—*Macbeth,* Act 1, 7.

Memories, images, and precious thoughts,
That shall not die and cannot be destroyed.
    WORDSWORTH.—*Excursion, Bk.* 7.

My eyes are dim with childish tears,
  My heart is idly stirred,
For the same sound is in my ears
  Which in those days I heard.
    WORDSWORTH.—*Fountain.*

The music in my heart I bore,
Long after it was heard no more.
    WORDSWORTH.—*Solitary Reaper.*

MERCHANDISE

Good honest merchandise easily finds
a customer. PLAUTUS.—*Pœnulus,* Act 1.

Whose merchants are princes.
    Isaiah xxiii, 8.

MERCY

For soothly, our swete Lord Iesu Crist
hath spared us so debonairly [merci-
fully] in our 'folies, that if he ne hadde
pitee of mannes soule, a sory song we
mighten alle singe.
    CHAUCER.—*Parson's Tale, sec.* 15.

We hand folks over to God's mercy,
and show none ourselves.
    GEO. ELIOT.—*Adam Bede, ch.* 42.

    Yet shall I temper so
Justice with mercy, as may illustrate most
Them fully satisfied, and thee appease.
    MILTON.—*Paradise Lost, Bk.* 10, 77.

    He that's merciful
Unto the bad, is cruel to the good.
    T. RANDOLPH.—*Muses' Looking Glass.*

No ceremony that to great ones longs,
Not the King's crown, nor the deputed
  sword,
The Marshal's truncheon, nor the judge's
  robe,
Become them with one half so good a
  grace
As mercy does. SHAKESPEARE.—*Measure
    for Measure,* Act 2, 2.

The quality of mercy is not strained,
It droppeth as the gentle rain from heaven
Upon the place beneath ; it is twice blessed,
It blesseth him that gives and him that
  takes :
'Tis mightiest in the mightiest : it becomes
The crownèd monarch better than his
  crown.
SHAKESPEARE.—*Mercht. of Venice,* Act 4, 1.

It is an attribute to God Himself ;
And earthly power doth then 'show likest
  God's
When mercy seasons justice.
    SHAKESPEARE.—*Ib.*

    We do pray for mercy,
And that same prayer doth teach us all
  to render
The deeds of mercy. SHAKESPEARE.—*Ib.*

Sweet mercy is nobility's true badge.
SHAKESPEARE.—*Titus Andronicus,* Act 1, 2.

Brother, you have a vice of mercy in you,
Which better fits a lion than a man.
    SHAKESPEARE.—*Troilus,* Act 5, 3.

Yet think, oh, think ! if mercy may be
  shown—
Thou hadst a father once and hast a son.
    VIRGIL.—*Æneid, Bk.* 12 (*Dryden tr.*)
        (*Turnus to Æneas*).

For the man of low estate may be pardoned in mercy, but mighty men shall be
searched out mightily.
    Wisdom of Solomon vi, 6. (*R. V.*).

MERIT

I rejoice that we can of our own free
will love him, whom it was our duty to
love, whatever sort of man he might have
been.   CICERO.

It sounds like stories from the land of
  spirits,
If any man obtain that which he merits,
Or any merit that which he obtains.
    COLERIDGE.—*Complaint.*

It stung me to the quick that birth and
  title
Should have more weight than merit has
  in th' army. COLERIDGE.—*Piccolomini.*

What is merit ? The opinion one man
entertains of another.
VISCOUNT PALMERSTON. — *Speech* (*quoted
  by Carlyle in " Shooting Niagara ").*

Honour and shame from no condition rise ;
Act well your part ; there all the honour
  lies. POPE.—*Essay on Man, Ep.* 4, 193.

MESSENGERS

    Gently hast thou told
Thy message, which might else in telling
  wound.
    MILTON.—*Paradise Lost, Bk.* 11, 298.

God best knoweth whom he will appoint
for his messenger.   *Koran, ch.* 6.

METAPHOR

I hate to hunt down a tired metaphor.
    BYRON.—*Don Juan,* 13, 36.

It [imagery] is a wonderful aid to the memory, which carries away the image and never loses it. EMERSON.—*Eloquence.*

A symbol always stimulates the intellect ; therefore is poetry ever the best reading.   EMERSON.—*Poetry and Imagination.*

In all the mazes of metaphorical confusion.   JUNIUS.—*Letter*, 1769.

METAPHYSICS

Undoubtedly the study of the more abstruse regions of philosophy, which we now call Metaphysics, and wherein Lucretius took special delight, always seems to have included an element not very much removed from a sort of insanity.
KEBLE.—*Lectures on Poetry, No.* 34
(*E. K. Francis tr.*).

And reasoned high
Of providence, foreknowledge, will and fate,
Fixed fate, free will, foreknowledge absolute,
And found no end, in wandering mazes lost.
MILTON.—*Paradise Lost, Bk.* 2, 558.

For wit's false mirror held up nature's light ;
Showed erring pride, whatever is, is right ;
That reason, passion, answer one great aim ;
That true self-love and social are the same ;
That virtue only makes our bliss below ;
And all our knowledge is, ourselves to know.
POPE.—*Essay on Man, Ep.* 4, 393.

Abstracted metaphysical notions, beat out upon the anvil of the schools, can never support natural religion, or make any part of it.
BISHOP THOS. SHERLOCK.—*Immortality of the Soul.*

There is a word of dire sound and horrible import which I would fain have kept concealed if I possibly could. The word to which I allude is that very tremendous one of Metaphysics.
SYDNEY SMITH.—*Lectures on Moral Philosophy, Introductory* (1804).

In Scotland every man is a metaphysician.   SYDNEY SMITH.—*Lectures on Moral Philosophy, No.* 3.

He that has never doubted the existence of matter may be assured that he has no aptitude for metaphysical enquiries.
TURGOT.—*As cited by Emerson, Idealism.*

When the man to whom you speak does not understand, and when the man who speaks does not understand himself, that is metaphysics.   VOLTAIRE.

All metaphysic contains, as it seems to me, two things :—the first, all that men of good sense know ; the second, that which they will never know.
VOLTAIRE.—*Letter to Frederick*, 1737.

METHOD

Of method this may be said,—if we make it our slave, it is well ; but it is bad if we are slaves to method.
C. C. COLTON.—*Lacon.*

Let all things be done decently, and in order.   1 *Corinthians* xiv, 40.

METRES

And the rolling anapæstic
Curled like a vapour over shrines.
E. B. BROWNING.—*Wine of Cyprus.*

Strongly it bears us along in swelling and limitless billows,
Nothing before and nothing behind but the sky and the ocean.
COLERIDGE.—*Homeric Hexameter (from Schiller).*

In the hexameter rises the fountain's silvery column ;
In the pentameter aye falling in melody back.   COLERIDGE.—*Metrical Feet.*

Iambics march from short to long ;—
With a leap and a bound the swift anapæsts throng.   COLERIDGE.—*Ib.*

Trochee trips from long to short.
COLERIDGE.—*Ib.*

And ten low words oft creep in one dull line.   POPE.—*Criticism*, 347.

A needless Alexandrine ends the song,
Which, like a wounded snake, drags its slow length along.   POPE.—*Ib.*, 356.

MIDDLE AGE

She was not old, nor young, nor at the years
Which certain people call a "*certain age*,"
Which yet the most uncertain age appears.
BYRON.—*Beppo, st.* 22.

Laura was blooming still, had made the best
Of time, and time returned the compliment.   BYRON.—*Ib., st.* 23.

Of all the barbarous middle ages, that
Which is most barbarous, is the middle age
Of man ; it is—I really scarce know what,
But when we hover between fool and sage.   BYRON.—*Don Juan*, 12, 1.

A lady of a "certain age," which means
Certainly aged.   BYRON.—*Ib., c.* 6, 69.

Fat old women, fat and five and fifty.
FLETCHER AND BEAUMONT.—*Women
Pleased*, Act 3, 2.

Life declines from thirty-five.
JOHNSON.—*To Mrs. Thrale.*

Our youth began with tears and sighs,
  With seeking what we could not
    find ; . . .
We sought and knew not what we sought ;
We marvel, now we look behind :
Life's more amusing than we thought.
A. LANG.—*Ballade of Middle Age.*

For ah ! my heart, how very soon
  The glittering dreams of youth are
    passed !
And long before it reach its noon
  The sun of life is overcast.
MOORE.—*Elegiac Stanzas.*

A man not old, but mellow, like good
  wine. STEPHEN PHILLIPS.—*Ulysses,
3, 2.*

On his bold visage middle age
Had slightly pressed its signet sage,
Yet had not quenched the open truth
And fiery vehemence of youth.
SCOTT.—*Lady of the Lake, c.* 1, 21.

      At your age,
The hey-day in the blood is tame, it's
  humble,
And waits upon the judgment.
SHAKESPEARE.—*Hamlet*, Act 3, 4.

Your lordship, though not clean past
your youth, hath yet some smack of age
in you, some relish of the saltness of time.
SHAKESPEARE.—*Henry IV.*, Pt. 2, Act 1, 2.

    He is more than half way
On the road from Grizzle to Grey.
SOUTHEY.—*Robert the Rhymer.*

A' men begin to get into a kind o' dotage
after five-and-twunty. They think their-
sels wiser, but they're only stupider.
JOHN WILSON.—*Noctes,* 19 *(Ettrick
Shepherd).*

A fool at forty is a fool indeed.
YOUNG.—*Love of Fame, Sat.* 2.

MIDDLE CLASSES

    Tenants of life's middle state,
Securely placed between the small and
    great,
Whose character, yet undebauched, re-
  tains
Two-thirds of all the virtue that remains.
COWPER.—*Tirocinium,* 807.

All great men come out of the middle
classes. 'Tis better for the head ; 'tis
better for the heart.
EMERSON.—*Conduct of Life :
Considerations by the Way.*

" Bourgeois," I observed, " is an epithet
which the riff-raff apply to what is respectable, and the aristocracy to what is decent."
SIR ANTHONY HOPE HAWKINS.—*Dolly
Dialogues.*

Froth at top, dregs at bottom, but the
middle excellent.
VOLTAIRE.—*Description of the English
Nation.*

MIDNIGHT

The hour, o' night's black arch the key-
  stane. BURNS.—*Tam o' Shanter.*

Is it for work ? There comes no fool to
  bore us.
Midnight intoxicates the human swine ;
I, pen in hand, with all the gods for chorus,
  Write then my clearest thought, my
    noblest line.
Midnight is mine.
MORTIMER COLLINS.—*Midnight is Mine.*

But wouldst thou hear the melodies of
  time,
Listen when sleep and drowsy darkness
  roll
Over hushed cities, and the midnight chime
Sounds from their hundred clocks, and
  deep bells toll,
Like a last knell over the dead world's souL
HOOD.—*Plea of Midsummer Fairies*

There is a budding sorrow in midnight
KEATS.—*Sonnet to Homer.*

Soon as midnight brought on the dusky
  hour
Friendliest to sleep and silence.
MILTON.—*Paradise Lost, Bk.* 5, 667.

We have heard the chimes at midnight.
SHAKESPEARE.—*Henry IV.*, Pt. 2, Act 3, 2.

The iron tongue of midnight hath told
  twelve ;
Lovers, to bed ; 'tis almost fairy time.
SHAKESPEARE.—*Mid. Night's Dream,*
Act 5, 1.

Not to be abed after midnight is to be
up betimes.
SHAKESPEARE.—*Twelfth Night*, Act 2, 3.

MILITARISM

Such as do build their faith upon
The holy text of pike and gun.
BUTLER.—*Hudibras, Pt.* 1, *c.* 1.

The flames of Moscow were the aurora
of the liberty of the world.
BENJ. CONSTANT.—*Esprit de Conquête,
Pref.* (1813).

The good orator is despised ; the fierce
soldier is loved.
ENNIUS.—*Quoted by Aulus Gellius,
Bk.* 20, 10.

Brutes never meet in bloody fray,
Nor cut each other's throats for pay.
       GOLDSMITH.—*Logicians Refuted.*

MILITARY MUSIC

The trumpets' round clangour
     Excites us to arms.
       DRYDEN.—*St. Cecilia's Day, st.* 3.

For the rum-tum-tum
     Of the military drum,
And the guns that go boom ! boom !
       SIR W. S. GILBERT.—*Princess Ida.*

And nearer yet, and yet more near,
     The martial chorus strikes the ear.
BISHOP HEBER.—*Lines written to a March.*

MILTON

Milton's the prince of poets—so we say,
     A little heavy, but no less divine.
       BYRON.—*Don Juan, c.* 3, 91.

MIND

The mind is invincible when it turns to
itself and relies upon its own courage. If
this is so when only obstinacy is your
defence, what must the strength of a mind
be when fortified with reason ?
       MARCUS AURELIUS.—*Bk.* 8, 48.

The mind is the man.
     BACON.—*In Praise of Knowledge.*

The power of thought—the magic of the
Mind.   BYRON.—*Corsair, c.* 1, 8.

The mind itself does not know what the
mind is.   CICERO.—Founded on *Pro
Milone, c.* 31.

The mind is free, whate'er afflict the
man. DRAYTON.—*Baron's Wars, Bk.* 5,
                         st. 36.

A mind not to be changed by place or time,
The mind is its own place, and in itself
Can make a heaven of hell, a hell of
     heaven.
       MILTON.—*Paradise Lost, Bk.* 1, 253.

Mind is ever the ruler of the universe.
       PLATO.—*Philebus,* 57 (*see also under
                  " Intellect "*).

O what a noble mind is here o'erthrown !
     SHAKESPEARE.—*Hamlet, Act* 3, 1.

He who seeks the mind's improvement,
     Aids the world in aiding mind.
       CHAS. SWAIN.—*What is Noble ?*

Straining breaks the bow, relaxation
breaks the mind.   PUBLILIUS SYRUS.

My mind to me a kingdom is ;
     Such perfect joy therein I find
As far exceeds all earthly bliss
     That God or Nature hath assigned.
       Byrd's Collection (c. 1585).

MINISTRIES

To be acquainted with the merit of a
ministry, we need only observe the condition of the people.
       JUNIUS.—*Letter* 1, *Jan.* 21, 1769.

MINORITIES

To be in the weakest camp is to be in
the strongest school.
       G. K. CHESTERTON.—*Heretics.*

Minority is no disproof :
Wisdom is not so strong and fleet
As never to have known defeat.
       L. HOUSMAN.—*Advocatus Diaboli.*

The minority is always right.
       IBSEN.—*An Enemy of Society.*

They are slaves who dare not be
In the right with two or three.
       J. R. LOWELL.—*Freedom.*

The fewer men the greater share of
honour.
       SHAKESPEARE.—*Henry V.,* Act 4, 3.

MIRACLES

There never was miracle wrought by
God to convert an atheist, because the
light of nature might have led him to confess a God.
       BACON.—*Adv. of Learning, Bk.* 2.

The one miracle which God works evermore is in Nature, and imparting himself to
the mind.
       EMERSON.—*Sovereignty of Ethics.*

For myself I believe too much in God
to be able to believe in so many miracles
which are so little worthy of Him.
       ROUSSEAU.—*Emile, Bk.* 4.

Miracles are to those who believe in them.
                            Prov.

MIRTH

For wicked mirth never true pleasure
     brings,
But honest minds are pleased with honest
     things.
       BEAUMONT AND FLETCHER.—*Knight
           of the Burning Pestle, Prol.*

Flower o' the rose !
If I've been merry, what matter who
knows ?   BROWNING.—*Fra Lippo.*

The mirth and fun grew fast and furious.
       BURNS.—*Tam o' Shanter.*

And all went merry as a marriage bell.
       BYRON.—*Childe Harold, c.* 3, 21.

Mirth makes the banquet sweet.
       CHAPMAN.—*Blind Beggar.*

A merry fellow was never yet a respectable man.
LORD CHESTERFIELD.—*Advice to his Son.*

Nothing but mirth can conquer fortune's spite ;
No sky is heavy if the heart be light.
CHURCHILL.—*Prophecy of Famine,*
v. 360.

Nothing is more hopeless than a scheme of merriment. JOHNSON.—*Rambler, 74.*

Laugh, for the time is brief, a thread the length of a span.
Laugh, and be proud to belong to the old proud pageant of man.
JOHN MASEFIELD.—*Laugh and be Merry.*

Haste thee, Nymph, and bring with thee
Jest and youthful Jollity,
Quips, and Cranks, and wanton Wiles,
Nods, and Becks, and wreathèd Smiles.
MILTON.—*L'Allegro, 25.*

I had rather have a fool to make me merry, than experience to make me sad.
SHAKESPEARE.—*As You Like It,* Act 4, 1.

Where be your gibes now ? your gambols ? your songs ? your flashes of merriment that were wont to set the table on a roar ?
SHAKESPEARE.—*Hamlet,* Act 5, 1.

Woe to philosophers who do not know how to unbend ! I regard austerity as a disease. I would prefer a thousand times to languish and be subject to fever —as I am—than to think dismally. It seems to me that Virtue, Study and Gaiety are three sisters who should never be separated.
VOLTAIRE.—*Letter to Frederick,* 1737.

Hang sorrow ! care will kill a cat,
And therefore let's be merry.
G. WITHER.—*Christmas.*

MISANTHROPY

He that can please nobody is not so much to be pitied as he whom nobody can please. C. C. COLTON.—*Lacon.*

To be the friend of the human race is not at all in my line.
MOLIÈRE.—*Misanthrope.*

How weary, stale, flat and unprofitable
Seem to me all the uses of this world !
Fie on't ! O fie ! 'tis an unweeded garden,
That grows to seed ! Things rank and gross in nature
Possess it merely.
SHAKESPEARE.—*Hamlet,* Act 1, 2.

I hate and detest that animal called man, although I heartily love John, Peter, Thomas, and so forth.
SWIFT.—*Letter to Pope, Sept.,* 1725.

Alas, poor dear ! his only scope
Was to be held a misanthrope.
This into general odium drew him,
Which, if he liked, much good may't do him.
SWIFT.—*On the Death of Dr. Swift.*

MISCHIEF

He wolde sowen som difficultee
Or springen cokkel in our clene corn.
CHAUCER.—*Shipman's Prologue.*

The devil is diligent at his plough.
BISHOP LATIMER.—*Sermon.*

Marry, this is miching mallecho ; it means mischief.
SHAKESPEARE.—*Hamlet,* Act 3, 2.

Now let it work ; mischief thou art afoot ;
Take thou what course thou wilt !
SHAKESPEARE.—*Julius Cæsar,* Act 3, 2.

Nay, whether he kill Cassio,
Or Cassio him, or each do kill the other,
Every way makes my game.
SHAKESPEARE —*Othello,* Act 5, 1.

Factious and rich, bold at the councilboard,
But cautious in the field, he shunned the sword,—
A close caballer and tongue-valiant lord.
VIRGIL.—*Æneid, Bk.* II *(Dryden tr.)*
(Of Drances).

MISERY

He felt as if he ne'er should cease to feel—
A wretch live-broken on misfortune's wheel. CAMPBELL.—*Theodric.*

Who calls that wretched thing that was Alphonso ?
CONGREVE.—*Mourning Bride,* Act 2, 2.

O Misery ! where once thou art possessed,
See but how quickly thou canst alter kind,
And, like a Circe, metamorphosest
The man that hath not a most godlike mind.
DRAYTON.—*Baron's Wars, Bk.* 6, *st.* 77.

The big drops mingling with the milk he drew,
Gave the sad presage of his future years,
The child of misery, baptised in tears !
J. LANGHORNE.—*Country Justice,*
Intro. 164.

A wretched man is a sacred thing.
SENECA.

Meagre were his looks,
Sharp misery had worn him to the bones.
SHAKESPEARE.—*Romeo and Juliet,* Act 5, 1.

Famine is in thy cheeks,
Need and oppression starveth in thine eyes,
Contempt and beggary hang upon thy back. SHAKESPEARE.—*Ib.*

Misery acquaints a man with strange bedfellows.
SHAKESPEARE.—*Tempest*, Act 2, 1.

Preach to the storm, and reason with
despair,
But tell not Misery's son that life is fair.
H. K. WHITE.—*On reading Pref. to
N. Bloomfield's Poems.*

MISFORTUNE

When anything brings trouble, remember this maxim : This accident is not a disaster, but bearing it well may turn it into an advantage.
MARCUS AURELIUS.—*Meditations,
Bk. 4, 49.*

The amiable Fortune deceyveth folk ;
the contrarie Fortune techeth.
CHAUCER.—*Boethius, Bk. 2, 8.*

For of Fortunis sharp adversite
The worst kinde of infortune is this,
A man to have been in prosperite,
And it remembren, whan it passed is.
CHAUCER.—*Troilus, Bk. 3, v. 1625.*

This is the worst of all worst worsts that
hell could have devised.
BEN JONSON.—*Epicœne.*

It is a kind of happiness to know exactly
how far one ought to be unhappy.
LA ROCHEFOUCAULD.—*Maxim 512.*

The good are better made by Ill,
As odours crushed are sweeter still.
ROGERS.—*Jacqueline, Pt. 3.*

I do not read unavoidable evils into the
future, but I cultivate hope, and I see it
within day by day. Alas ! what serves
it to water the leaves when the tree is cut
off at the foot ?   ROUSSEAU.—*Julie.*

Would I had met my dearest foe in heaven,
Ere I had ever seen that day, Horatio !
SHAKESPEARE.—*Hamlet*, Act 1, 2.

I am a man
More sinned against than sinning.
SHAKESPEARE.—*Lear*, Act 3, 2.

O, no ! the apprehension of the good
Gives but the greater feeling to the worse.
SHAKESPEARE.—*Richard II.*, Act 1, 3.

The world is not thy friend, nor the
world's law.
SHAKESPEARE.—*Romeo and Juliet*, Act 5, 1.

Meseemes the world is runne quite out of
square
From the first point of his appointed
sourse ;
And being once amisse growes daily wourse
and wourse.
SPENSER.—*Faerie Queene, Bk. 5,
Intro. 1.*

These [Lutherans and Calvinists] had
lived in much friendship and agreement
. . . as it is the talent of fellow sufferers
to do, men in misfortune being like men in
the dark, to whom all colours are the same.
SWIFT.—*Tale of a Tub.*

Fortune is not satisfied with injuring
a man only once.   PUBLILIUS SYRUS.

If our hard fortune no compassion draws,
Nor hospitable rights nor human laws,
The gods are just, and will revenge our
cause.
VIRGIL.—*Æneid, Bk.* 1 *(Dryden).*

My flocks feed not,
My ewes breed not,
My rams speed not,
All is amiss.
*From Thos. Weelkes's Madrigals
(1597).—Adapted.*

For every ill beneath the sun
There is some remedy or none ;
If there be one, resolve to find it ;
If not, submit, and never mind it.
ANON (*c.* 1843).

MISGIVINGS

Something is rotten in the state of
Denmark.
SHAKESPEARE.—*Hamlet*, Act 1, 4.

MISOGYNY

No, you were too stern for an amorous
turn,
For Venus and Cupid too stern and too
stupid.   (*Of Æschylus.*)
ARISTOPHANES.—*Frogs,* 1039 (*Frere tr.*).

He seldom errs
Who thinks the worst he can of womankind.   J. HOME.—*Douglas, Act* 2, 3.

MISREPRESENTATION

And charge
His mind with meanings that he never
had.   COWPER.—*Garden,* 148.

He cannot 'scape their censures, who delight
To misapply whatever he shall write.
MASSINGER.—*Emperor of East, Prol*

There is nothing which cannot be perverted by being told badly.
TERENCE.—*Phormio,* Act 4.

Woe unto them that call evil good, and
good evil !   *Isaiah v,* 20.

MISTAKES

The man who makes no mistakes does
not usually make anything.
E. J. PHELPS.—*Speech,* 1889.

The best may slip, and the most cautious
    fall ;
He's more than mortal that ne'er erred at
    all.
    J. POMFRET.—*Love Triumphant over
                Reason*, 145.

Probably he who never made a mistake
never made a discovery.
    S. SMILES.—*Self-Help.*

For God's sake give me the young man
who has brains enough to make a fool of
himself.
    R. L. STEVENSON.—*Crabbed Age.*

To make mistakes as we are on the way
to knowledge is far more honourable than
to escape making them through never
having set out to seek knowledge.
    ARCHBP. TRENCH.—*Study of Words.*

With skill she vibrates her eternal tongue,
For ever most divinely in the wrong.
    YOUNG.—*Love of Fame, Sat.* 6.

MISUNDERSTANDING

All battle is well said to be *Misunderstanding.*
    CARLYLE.—*French Revolution, Pt.* 3,
                Bk. 3, *ch.* 2.

Alas ! they had been friends in youth :
But whispering tongues can poison truth ;
And constancy lives in realms above :
    And life is thorny ; and youth is vain ;
And to be wroth with one we love
    Doth work like madness in the brain.
    COLERIDGE.—*Christabel.*

Mal-information is more hopeless than
no information.   C. C. COLTON.—*Lacon.*

Pale famine and frightful pestilence
cannot equal the evils and diversity of
troubles which misunderstandings scatter
throughout the universe.
    DE RULHIÈRES.—*Disputes.*

MOB

A mob is a compound mass of human
beings in which each one has for the moment
all the follies and evil passions of the rest,
in addition to his own.
    SIR A. HELPS.—*Friends in Council :
                Slavery, ch.* 4.

MODERATION

Nothing which is moderate pleases the
crowd.
    BACON.—*Instauratio, Pt.* 1, *Bk.* 6.

A good cause needs not to be patroned
by passion, but can sustain itself upon
a temperate dispute.
    SIR T. BROWNE.—*Religio Medici,
                Pt.* 1, 5.

I know many have been taught to think
that moderation, in a case like this, is a
sort of treason.
    BURKE.—*Letter to Sheriffs of Bristol.*

This only grant me that my means may lie
Too low for envy, for contempt too high.
    COWLEY.—*Of Myself.*

To find the medium asks some share of
    wit
And therefore 'tis a mark fools never hit.
    COWPER.—*Conversation*, 884.

To be content with moderate fortune is
the best proof of philosophy. All others
seem to me doubtful.
    FRANÇOIS DROZ (1773-1851).—*The Art
                of being Happy.*

His best companions, innocence and health ;
And his best riches, ignorance of wealth.
    GOLDSMITH.—*Deserted Village.*

The flaming patriot, who so lately
scorched us in the meridian, sinks temperately to the west, and is hardly felt
as he descends.
    JUNIUS.—*Letter,* 1771.

    Mesure is medecyne.
    LANGLAND.—*Piers Plowman,
                Passus* 2, 33.

Joy and Temperance and Repose
Slam the door on the doctor's nose.
    LONGFELLOW.—*From the German.*

    If thou well observe
The rule of not too much, by temperance
    taught.
    MILTON.—*Paradise Lost, Bk.* 11, 530.

    By moderation doubling victory.
    F. T. PALGRAVE.—*Alfred the Great,
                Sonnet,* 3.

Give me again my hollow tree,
A crust of bread and liberty.
POPE.—*Imit. of Horace, Bk.* 2, *Sat.* 6, 220.

In moderation placing all my glory,
While Tories call me Whig, and Whigs a
    Tory.
    POPE.—*Satires of Horace, Bk.* 2, 67.

Over the doors of every school of Art
I would have this one word, relieved out
in deep letters of pure gold—Moderation.
    RUSKIN.—*Modern Painters, vol.* 2,
                sec. 2, *ch.* 6, 8.

I swear 'tis better to be lowly born,
And range with humble livers in content,
Than to be perked up, in a glist'ring grief,
And wear a golden sorrow.
    SHAKESPEARE.—*Henry VIII.,* Act 2, 3.

The moderation of the feeble man is
only idleness and vanity.
    VAUVENARGUES.—*Maxim* 73.

Ye sumph, I'm a hee-flyer mysel,—one
o' the wild men ; o' a' things whatsomever,
be it in sacred matters or profane, I detest
moderation.
JOHN WILSON.—*Noctes (Ettrick Shepherd).*

Man's rich with little, were his judgment
true ;
Nature is frugal, and her wants are few.
YOUNG.—*Love of Fame, Sat.* 5.

Give me neither poverty nor riches ;
feed me with food convenient for me.
Proverbs xxx, 8.

A little house well filled,
A little land well tilled,
A little wife well willed.
Old Saying.

MODERNITY

But we, brought forth and reared in hours
Of change, alarm, surprise—
What shelter to grow ripe is ours ?
What leisure to grow wise ?
M. ARNOLD.—*Memory of " Obermann."*

I am indignant when I hear something
abused, not because rudely or ungrace-
fully framed, but simply because it is
modern.   HORACE.—*Ep., Bk.* 2, 1, 75.

Motions and Means, on land and sea at
war
With old poetic feeling, not for this
Shall ye, by poets even, be judged amiss !
Nor shall your presence, howsoe'er it mar
The loveliness of Nature, prove a bar
To the mind's gaining that prophetic
sense
Of future change, that point of vision
whence
May be discovered what in soul ye are.
WORDSWORTH.—*Poems during a Summer
Tour,* 1833, *No.* 42. (*Steamboats, Viaducts
and Railways.*)

MODESTY

Ever with the best desert goes diffidence.
BROWNING.—*Blot in the 'Scutcheon.*

Modesty does not long survive innocence.
BURKE.—*Impeachment of Hastings
(Feb.,* 1788).

And though that he were worthy, he was
wise
And of his port as meek as is a maid.
CHAUCER.—*Cant. Tales, Prol.*

On their own merits modest men are
dumb. G. COLMAN, JR.—*Heir-at-Law.*

William was such a bashful youth ;
His modesty was such,
That one might say (to say the truth)
He rather had too much.
COWPER.—*Of Himself.*

He [Capt. John Brown] held the belief
that courage and chastity are silent concerning themselves. EMERSON.—*Courage.*

Wherever valour true is found
True modesty will there abound.
SIR W. S. GILBERT.—*Yeomen of the Guard.*

All men have their faults : too much
modesty is his.
GOLDSMITH.—*Good-Natured Man, Act* 2.

The maid who modestly conceals
Her beauties, while she hides, reveals.
E. MOORE.—*Fables, No.* 10.

Greediness is rich and shame poor.
PHÆDRUS.—*Bk.* 2.

I have marked
A thousand blushing apparitions start
Into her face ; a thousand innocent
shames
In angel whiteness bear away those
blushes.
SHAKESPEARE.—*Much Ado, Act* 4, 1.

A maiden never bold ;
Of spirit so still and quiet, that her motion
Blushed at herself.
SHAKESPEARE.—*Othello, Act* 1, 3.

No man can ever end with being superior
who will not begin with being inferior.
SYDNEY SMITH.—*Lectures on Moral
Philosophy, No.* 9.

We see him as he moved,
How modest, kindly, all-accomplished,
wise,
With what sublime repression of himself,
And in what limits, and how tenderly.
TENNYSON.—*Idylls, Dedication, l.* 16.

In me there dwells
No greatness, save it be some far-off touch
Of greatness to know well I am not great.
TENNYSON.—*Lancelot and Elaine,* 447.

It is easy, but it is a fine thing nevertheless, to be modest when one is great.
VOLTAIRE.—*La Pucelle.*

Methinks
Wisdom is oft-times nearer when we stoop,
Than when we soar.
WORDSWORTH.—*Excursion, Bk.* 3.

Modesty is a very good thing, but a man
in this country may get on very well without it.
*Motto said to have been inscribed on a banner
in a Western State.*

Bashful dogs get little meat :
Bravely take thy proper seat.
Old Saying.

MONARCHY

Never does liberty appear more pleasing
than under a righteous King.
CLAUDIAN.—24, 113.

All human things are subject to decay,
And when fate summons, monarchs must
   obey.   DRYDEN.—*MacFlecknoe, l. 1.*

The Prince exists for the sake of the
State, not the State for the sake of the
Prince.   ERASMUS.—*Fam. Coll.*

The trappings of a monarchy would set
up an ordinary commonwealth.
      JOHNSON.—*Quoted (paraphrastically)*
            as from Milton.

The prince is not above the laws, but
the laws above the prince.
      PLINY THE YOUNGER.—*Paneg. Traj.*

A King may be a tool, a thing of straw ;
but if he serves to frighten our enemies
and secure our property, it is well enough ;
a scarecrow is a thing of straw, but it protects the corn.
      POPE.—*Thoughts on Various Subjects.*

For a King to make an amiable character
he needs only to be a man of common
honesty, well advised.   POPE.—*Ib.*

Entire and sure the monarch's rule must
      prove,
Who founds her greatness on her sub-
      jects' love.   PRIOR.—*Prologue.*

For monarchs seldom sigh in vain.
      SCOTT.—*Marmion, c. 5, 9.*

No worthier victim and none more
acceptable can be sacrificed to Jove than
an evil-minded King.
      SENECA.—*Hercules Furens.*

And what so fair has the world beholden,
And what so firm has withstood the
      years,
As Monarchy bound in chains all golden,
And Freedom guarded about with peers ?
      SWINBURNE.—*Midsummer Holiday.*
            A Word from the Psalmist.

Princes are mortal, the commonwealth
is immortal.   TACITUS.—*Annals, Bk. 3.*

A doubtful throne is ice on summer sea.
      TENNYSON.—*Coming of Arthur.*

In that fierce light which beats upon a
      throne,
And blackens every blot.
      TENNYSON.—*Idylls, Dedication.*

Her court was pure ; her life serene ;
   God gave her peace ; her land reposed ;
A thousand claims to reverence closed
In her as Mother, Wife, and Queen.
      TENNYSON.—*To the Queen.*

That sober freedom out of which there
      springs
Our loyal passion for our temperate
      Kings.
      TENNYSON.—*On Wellington, st. 7.*

The passing poor magnificence of Kings.
      THOMSON.—*Liberty.*

Hail to the crown by Freedom shaped—to
      gird
An English sovereign's brow ! and to the
      throne
Whereon he sits ! whose deep foundations
      lie
In veneration and the people's love.
      WORDSWORTH.—*Excursion, Bk. 6.*

The King reigns but does not govern.
      JAN ZAMOISKI (*of Poland ; d.* 1605).

MONASTICISM

I cannot praise a fugitive and cloistered
virtue, unexercised and unbreathed, that
never sallies out and sees her adversary,
but slinks out of the race, where that immortal garland is to be run for, not without dust and heat.
      MILTON.—*Areopagitica.*

Embryos and idiots, eremites and friars,
White, black, and grey, with all their
      trumpery.
      MILTON.—*Paradise Lost, Bk.* 3, 474.

Here Man more purely lives, less oft doth
      fall,
More promptly rises, walks with stricter
      heed,
More safely rests, dies happier, is freed
Earlier from cleansing fires, and gains
      withal
A brighter crown.
      WORDSWORTH.—*Eccles. Sonnets, Pt.* 2, 3.

MONDAY

Monday is parson's holiday.
      SWIFT.—*Letter,* 1712.

Monday is the key of all the week. *Prov.*

Monday religion is better than Sunday
profession.   *Prov.*

MONEY

No man's fortune can be an end worthy
of his being.
      BACON.—*Adv. of Learning, Bk.* 2.

Wealth is a good servant ; a very bad
mistress.
      BACON.—*Instauratio, Pt.* 1, *Bk.* 6.

Money is like muck, not good except it
be spread.   BACON.—*Of Seditions.*

She is the Soveraigne Queene of all
      Delightes :
For her the Lawyer pleades ; the Souldier
      fights.
      R. BARNFIELD.—*Pecunia* (1598).

He may love riches that wanteth them,
as much as he that hath them.
      R. BAXTER.—*Christian Ethics.*

Money is honey, my little sonny,
And a rich man's joke is allis funny.
T. E. BROWN.—*The Doctor.*

Then hey for the lass wi' a tocher,
The nice yellow guineas for me!
BURNS.—*Song.*

What makes all doctrines plain and
clear? ——
About two hundred pounds a year.
BUTLER.—*Hudibras, Pt. 3, c. 1.*

Maidens, like moths, are ever caught by
glare,
And Mammon wins his way, where seraphs
might despair.
BYRON.—*Childe Harold, c. 1, 9.*

Kill a man's family and he may brook it,
But keep your hands out of his breeches
pocket!
BYRON.—*Don Juan, c. 10, 79.*

Yes, ready money *is* Aladdin's lamp.
BYRON.—*Ib., c. 12, 12.*

Money, which is of very uncertain value,
and sometimes has no value at all and even
less.   CARLYLE.—*Frederick the Great,
Bk. 4, 13.*

But one thing is, ye know it well enow,
Of chapmen, that their money is their
plough.
CHAUCER.—*Shopman's Tale, 287.*

Mirabeau was capable of everything for
money, even of a good action.
A. DE RIVAROL.

It is not the longest sword but the longest purse that conquers.
DEFOE.—(*A " favourite maxim "
several times repeated by him.*)

He [Sir Condy Rackrent] could never—
God bless him again! I say,—bring himself to ask a gentleman for money, despising such sort of conversation himself.
MISS EDGEWORTH.—*Castle Rackrent,
ch. 2.*

Gold is the touchstone whereby to try
men.   FULLER.—*The Good Judge.*

And gold can make of hate love,
And werre of pees, and right of wrong,
And long to short, and short to long,
Without gold may be no fest;
Gold is the lord of man and best.
GOWER.—*Conf. Amantis, Bk. 5, 238.*

Money, thou bane of bliss and source of
woe!   HERBERT.—*Avarice.*

Use alone
Makes money not a contemptible stone.
HERBERT.—*Church Porch.*

Fight thou with shafts of silver and o'er-
come,
When no force else can get the masterdom.
HERRICK.—*Money gets Mastery.*

Spurned by the young, but hugged by the
old
To the very verge of the churchyard
mould,
Price of many a crime untold;
Gold! Gold! Gold! Gold!
Good or bad a thousand-fold!
How widely its agencies vary!
HOOD.—*Miss Kilmansegg.*

Make Money! If you can, make money
honestly; if not, by whatever means you
can, make money. HORACE.—*Ep., Bk. 1.*

O citizens, citizens! Money is the first
thing; cash first, and virtue afterwards.
HORACE.—*Ib.*

Wealth sanctions folly.
HORACE.—*Ep. 1, 16.*

The Almighty Dollar, that great object
of universal devotion throughout our land.
WASHINGTON IRVING.—*Creole Village.*

There are few ways in which a man can
be more innocently employed than in
getting money.   JOHNSON.—*Remark.*

Get money, still get money, boy;
No matter by what means; money will do.
BEN JONSON.—*Every Man in his
Humour, Act 2, 5.*

" I wish the good old times would come
again," she said, " when we were not quite
so rich. I do not mean that I want to be
poor; but there was a middle state."
LAMB.—*Last Essays of Elia: Old China.*

Men who make money rarely saunter;
men who save money rarely swagger.
(1st) LORD LYTTON.—*My Novel, Bk. 11, 2.*

The picklock
That never fails.
MASSINGER.—*Unnatural Combat, Act 1, 1.*

Mammon led them on;
Mammon, the least erected Spirit that fell
From heaven; for e'en in heaven his
looks and thoughts
Were always downwards bent.
MILTON.—*Paradise Lost, Bk. 1, 678.*

Worth now means what a man is worth;
property gives honours; property brings
friendship: the poor man is everywhere
at a discount.   OVID.—*Fast.*

Happy the man who, void of cares and
strife,
In silken or in leathern purse retains
A Splendid Shilling.
J. PHILIPS.—*Splendid Shilling.*

The wealthy and the poverty-stricken are in like case : both are too preoccupied with finance to use time to better purpose. Perhaps that is a sound argument for sweeping both classes away.
EDEN PHILLPOTTS.—*A Shadow Passes.*

Even wisdom surrenders to desire of gain. PINDAR.

He must expend money who wants to make it. PLAUTUS.

More passionately fond of money than of glory, in order to live in abundance they die in obscurity, and leave to their children as their only example the love of the treasures they have amassed for their benefit. ROUSSEAU.—*Julie.*

To few is good faith dearer than money.
SALLUST.—*Jugurtha.*

He that wants money, means, and content, is without three good friends.
SHAKESPEARE.—*As You Like It*, Act 3, 2.

Seven hundred pounds, and possibilities, is good gifts.
SHAKESPEARE.—*Merry Wives*, Act 1, 1.

If money go before, all ways do lie open.
SHAKESPEARE.—*Ib.*, Act 2, 2.

O, what a world of vile, ill-favoured faults Looks handsome in three hundred pounds a year ! SHAKESPEARE.—*Ib.*, Act 3, 4.

Put money in thy purse.
SHAKESPEARE.—*Othello*, Act 1, 3.

Nothing comes amiss, so money comes withal.
SHAKESPEARE.—*Taming of Shrew*, Act 1, 2.

Money is indeed the most important thing in the world, and all sound and successful personal and national morality should have this fact for its basis. Every teacher or twaddler who denies it or suppresses it, is an enemy of life. Money controls morality.
G. B. SHAW.—*Irrational Knot, Pref.*(1905).

In losing fortune, many a lucky elf Has found himself.
HORACE SMITH.—*Moral Alchemy.*

A toiling man
Intent on worldly gains, one in whose heart
Affection had no root.
SOUTHEY.—*Joan of Arc*, Bk. 1.

There is nothing an honest man should fear more timorously than getting and spending more than he deserves.
R. L. STEVENSON.—*Profession of Letters.*

The world's chief idol, nurse of fretting cares,
Dumb trafficker, yet understood o'er all.
EARL OF STIRLING.—*Doomsday.*

Every door is barred with gold and opens but to golden keys.
TENNYSON.—*Locksley Hall.*

But the jingling of the guinea helps the hurt that Honour feels. TENNYSON.—*Ib.*

Or that eternal want of pence
Which vexes public men.
TENNYSON.—*Will Waterproof.*

The great rule is to be frugal in great matters and liberal in small ones.
J. TRUSLER.—*System of Etiquette* (1804).

There was worlds of reputation in it, but no money.
MARK TWAIN.—*A Yankee at Court of King Arthur, ch.* 9.

O love of Gold ! thou meanest of amours !
YOUNG.—*Night Thoughts*, 4.

The strongest castle, tower, and town,
The golden bullet beats it down.
No. 17 *in* "*The Passionate Pilgrim*" (1599), *Adapted from Thos. Weelkes's* "*Madrigals*" (1597).

Wine maketh merry ; but money answereth all things. *Ecclesiastes* x, 19.

A good name is rather to be chosen than great riches. *Proverbs* xxii, 1.

He that maketh haste to be rich shall not be innocent. *Proverbs* xxviii, 20.

Not greedy of filthy lucre.
1 *Timothy* iii, 3.
For the love of money is a root of all kinds of evil.
1 *Timothy* vi, 10 (*R.V.*).

God send us siller, for they're ill-thought o' that want it.
Prayer of the "*good Earl of Eglinton.*"

Earn all you can ; save all you can ; give all you can.
Attrib. by C. H. Spurgeon to John Wesley.

Put not your trust in money, put your money in trust. *American saying.*

If a little cash does not go out, much cash will not come in. *Chinese prov.*

Nothing more eloquent than ready money. *French prov.*

A guinea it will sink, and a note it will float,
But I'd rather have a guinea than a one-pound note.
Popular Song, c. 1830-1840.

Money is flat and meant to be piled up.
Scottish prov. (The English prov. is said to be " Money is round, and meant to roll.")

The best foundation in the world is money.
Spanish prov. found in " Don Quixote."

Honour and money are not found in the same purse.   *Spanish prov.*

Money is often lost for want of money.
Prov.

Hard got, soon gone.
Prov. (quoted by T. Carlyle).

When money's taken
Freedom's forsaken.
Old Saying.

MONOPOLISTS

Bone and Skin, two millers thin,
Would starve us all, or near it :
But be it known to Skin and Bone
That Flesh and Blood can't bear it.
J. BYROM.—*On Two Monopolists.*

MONSTERS

Worse
Than fables yet have feigned, or fear conceived,
Gorgons and Hydras and Chimæras dire.
MILTON.—*Paradise Lost, Bk. 2, 626.*

MONUMENTS

Death comes even to monumental stones, and the names inscribed thereon.
AUSONIUS.—*Ep. xxxv, 9.*

And, talking of epitaphs, much I admire his,
" Circumspice, si monumentum requiris,"
Which an erudite verger translated to me,
" If you ask for his monument, Sir—come—spy—see ! "
R. H. BARHAM.—*In allusion to Sir C. Wren's epitaph in St. Paul's Cathedral.*

No—marble and recording brass decay,
And, like the graver's memory, pass away.
COWPER.—*Conversation, 551.*

Toils much to earn a monumental pile,
That may record the mischiefs he hath done.   COWPER.—*Task, 276.*

Nothing can cover his high fame but Heaven ;
No pyramids set off his memories,
But the eternal substance of his greatness :
To which I leave him.
FLETCHER AND MASSINGER.—*The False One*, Act 2, 1.

The pyramids themselves, doting with age, have forgotten the names of their founders.
FULLER.—*Holy and Profane State : Of Tombs.*

Can storied urn or animated bust
Back to its mansion call the fleeting breath ?
Can Honour's voice provoke the silent dust,
Or Flattery soothe the dull, cold ear of Death ?   GRAY.—*Elegy.*

In lapidary inscriptions a man is not upon his oath.   JOHNSON.—*Remark.*

Protect his memory, and preserve his story
Remain a lasting monument of his glory.
QUARLES.—*Drayton's Monument.*

Vanity dies hard ; in some obstinate cases it outlives the man.
R. L. STEVENSON.—*Prince Otto.*

A warrior with his shield of pride
Cleaving humbly to his side,
And hands in resignation pressed,
Palm to palm, on his tranquil breast.
WORDSWORTH.—*White Doe of Rylstone, c. 1.*

MOON

What is there in thee, Moon ! that thou should'st move
My heart so potently ?
KEATS.—*Endymion, Bk. 2.*

Till the Moon,
Rising in clouded majesty, at length
Apparent queen, unveiled her peerless light,
And o'er the dark her silver mantle threw.
MILTON.—*Paradise Lost, Bk. 4, 606.*

Sing, minstrel, sing us now a tender song
Of meeting and parting, with the moon in it.
STEPHEN PHILLIPS.—*Ulysses*, Act 1, 1.

If thou would'st view fair Melrose aright,
Go visit it by the pale moonlight.
SCOTT.—*Lay of the Last Minstrel, c. 2, 1.*

That orbèd maiden, with white fire laden,
Whom mortals call the moon.
SHELLEY.—*The Cloud.*

With how sad steps, O Moon, thou climb'st the skies !
How silently and with how wan a face !
SIR P. SIDNEY.—*Astrophel, 31.*

Late, late yestreen, I saw the new moone,
Wi' the auld moone in hir arme ;
And, if we gang to sea, master,
I fear we'll come to harm.
Ballad, " Sir Patrick Spens " (circa 15th century).

MORALISING AND MORALISTS

Thou art an endless moralist.
WM. BLAKE.—*Edward III.*

A moral (like all morals) melancholy.
BYRON.—*Don Juan, c. 5, 63.*

Though sages may pour out their wisdom's
    treasure,
There is no sterner moralist than Pleasure.
            BYRON.—*Don Juan*, 3, 65.

Let us be moral. Let us contemplate
existence. (*Mr. Pecksniff.*)
    DICKENS.—*Martin Chuzzlewit, ch.* 10.

"Tut, tut, child," said the Duchess.
"Everything's got a moral if only you can
find it."
C. L. DODGSON.—*Alice in Wonderland, c.* 9.

Neckband pedants, dismal critics of
pleasures which they do not possess.
                    VOLTAIRE.

MORALITY

Men talk of "mere morality"—which
is much as if one should say, "Poor God,
with nobody to help Him!"
    EMERSON.—*Conduct of Life-Worship.*

The end of all political struggle is to
establish morality as the basis of legislation . . . Morality is the object of government. EMERSON.—*Fortune of the Republic.*

We know of no spectacle so ridiculous
as the British public in one of its periodical
fits of morality.
    MACAULAY.—*Moore's Byron.*

The plain good man, whose actions teach
More virtue than a sect can preach.
            MOORE.—*Morality.*

An Englishman thinks he is moral when
he is really only uncomfortable.
    G. B. SHAW.—*Man and Superman.*

Morality knows nothing of geographical
boundaries or distinctions of race.
H. SPENCER.—*Study of Sociology, ch.* 23

Morality was made for man, and not
man for morality.
I. ZANGWILL.—*Children of the Ghetto, Bk.* 2,
                    ch. 6.

MORNING

Now had the poore man's clock,—shrill
    chaunticleare—
Twice given notice of the Morne's approach,
That then began in glorie to appeare,
Drawne in her stately coloured saffron
    coach. R. BARNFIELD.—*Cassandra.*

The morn is up again, the dewy morn,
With breath all incense, and with cheek
    all bloom.
BYRON.—*Childe Harold, c.* 3, *st.* 98.

When genial Morn appears,
Like pensive Beauty, smiling in her tears.
    CAMPBELL.—*Pleasures of Hope,* 2.

Each matin bell, the Baron saith,
Knells us back to a world of death.
    COLERIDGE.—*Christabel,* Pt. 2.

The lark now leaves his watery nest,
And climbing, shakes his dewy wings.
    SIR W. D'AVENANT.—*Song.*

Awake, awake, the morn will never rise
Till she can dress her beauty at your eyes.
    SIR W. D'AVENANT.—*Ib.*

The rosy-fingered morn appears,
And from her mantle shakes her tears
In promise of a glorious day
            DRYDEN.—*Albion.*

None can tell how sweet,
How virtuous the morning air.
    EMERSON.—*May-Day.*

The breezy call of incense-breathing
Morn.   GRAY.—*Elegy.*

Beloved, it is morn!
A redder berry on the thorn,
A deeper yellow on the corn,
For this good day new-born.
EMILY H. HICKEY.—*Beloved, it is morn.*

A poet's face asleep is this grey morn.
    ALICE MEYNELL.—*In February.*

Under the opening eyelids of the morn.
    MILTON.—*Lycidas,* 26.

Sweet is the breath of morn, her rising
    sweet,
With charm of earliest birds; pleasant
    the Sun,
When first on this delightful land he
    spreads
His orient beams.
    MILTON.—*Paradise Lost, Bk.* 4, 641.

Now morn her rosy steps in th' eastern
    clime
Advancing, sowed the earth with orient
    pearl.   MILTON.—*Ib., Bk.* 5, 1.

Till morn,
Waked by the circling hours, with rosy
    hand
Unbarred the gates of light.
            MILTON.—*Ib., Bk.* 6, 2.

Till morning fair
Came forth with pilgrim steps in amice
    grey.
MILTON.—*Paradise Regained, Bk.* 4, 426.

Hark! hark! the lark at heaven's gate
    sings,
And Phœbus 'gins arise,
His steeds to water at those springs
    On chaliced flowers that lies;
And winking Mary-buds begin
    To ope their golden eyes;
With everything that pretty is,
    My lady sweet, arise!
    SHAKESPEARE.—*Cymbeline,* Act 2, 3.

But look the morn, in russet mantle clad,
Walks o'er the dew of yon high eastern hill.
    SHAKESPEARE.—*Hamlet,* Act 1, 1.

Night's candles are burnt out, and jocund
    day
Stands tiptoe on the misty mountain's tops.
SHAKESPEARE.—*Romeo and Juliet*, Act 3, 5.

Come into the garden, Maud,
For the black bat, night, hath flown.
    TENNYSON.—*Maud, Pt.* 1, 1, 22.

Mornings are mysteries ; the first world's
    youth,
Man's resurrection, and the future's bud,
Shroud in their births.
    H. VAUGHAN.—*Rules and Lessons.*

Few folk hae seen oftener than me
Natur gettin' up i' the mornin' . . . Never
see ye *her* hair in papers.
    JOHN WILSON.—*Noctes*, 19 (*Ettrick
                    Shepherd*).

All the speed is in the morning.
Saying attrib. by Gabriel Harvey (c. 1600)
        to his mother, Alice Harvey.

The morning hour has gold in its mouth.
                                    Prov.

MORTALITY

The earth is a host who murders his
guests.
    HAFIZ.—*As given by Emerson, Essay on
                    Persian Poetry.*

How gladly would I meet
Mortality my sentence, and be earth
Insensible ! how glad would lay me down
As in my mother's lap ! There should I
    rest
And sleep secure.
    MILTON.—*Paradise Lost, Bk.* 10, 775.

War its thousands slays ; Peace, its ten
    thousands.   BISHOP PORTEUS.—*Death.*

The form remains, the Function never
    dies
While we, the brave, the mighty, and the
    wise,
We men, who in our morn of life defied
The elements, must vanish. Be it so !
    WORDSWORTH.—*River Duddon*, 34.

All men think all men mortal but them-
    selves.   YOUNG.—*Night Thoughts*, 1.

MOTHERS

A mother is a mother still,
The holiest thing alive.
    COLERIDGE.—*Three Graves.*

Many men, my lord,
Of hardihood sufficient, have been known
To hold the memories of their mothers
dear. J. DAVIDSON.—*The Ordeal*, 241.

In the first days
Of my distracting grief, I found myself
As women wish to be, who love their lords.
    J. HOME.—*Douglas.*

Beer will grow " mothery," and ladies fair
Will grow like beer.
    HOOD.—*Stag-Eyed Lady.*

In the heavens above
The angels, whispering to one another,
Can find, amid their burning terms of love,
None so devotional as that of " mother."
    E. A. POE.—*To my Mother.*

Thou art thy mother's glass, and she in
    thee
Calls back the lovely April of her prime.
    SHAKESPEARE.—*Sonnet*, 3.

Who ran to help me when I fell,
And would some pretty story tell,
Or kiss the place to make it well ?
    My Mother !
    ANN TAYLOR.—*My Mother.*

Happy he
With such a mother ! Faith in womankind
Beats with his blood, and trust in all things
    high
Comes easy to him, and though he trip
    and fall,
He shall not blind his soul with clay.
    TENNYSON.—*Princess, c.* 7, 308.

Is not a young mother one of the
sweetest sights which life shows us ?
    THACKERAY.—*Newcomes, Bk.* 2, *c.* 13.

Mother is the name for God in the lips
and hearts of little children.
    THACKERAY.—*Vanity Fair, vol.* 2, *ch.* 12.

They say that man is mighty,
    He governs land and sea,
He wields a mighty sceptre
    O'er lesser powers that be ;
But a mightier power and stronger
    Man from his throne has hurled,
And the hand that rocks the cradle
    Is the hand that rules the world.
W. R. WALLACE.—*What rules the World ?*

All women become like their mothers.
That is their tragedy. No man does.
That is his.   OSCAR WILDE.—*Importance
                        of being Earnest.*

Thou, while thy babes around thee cling,
Shalt show us how divine a thing
A woman may be made.
    WORDSWORTH.—*To a young Lady.*

One good mother is worth a hundred
schoolmasters.   *Prov.*

There is no mother like my mother.
                                    Prov.

MOTHERS-IN-LAW

While thy wife's mother lives, expect no
    peace.   GIFFORD.—*Juvenal*, 6, 332.

There is no good mother-in-law but she that wears a green gown [*i.e.* who is under the turf]. *Old Prov.*

MOTIVES

It was a favourite remark of the late Mr. Whitbread's, that no man does anything from a single motive.
COLERIDGE.—*Biog. Literaria, ch.* 11.

And set his heart upon the goal,
Not on the prize.
SIR W. WATSON.—*Laleham Churchyard.*

And rare is noble impulse, rare
The impassioned aim.
SIR W. WATSON.—*Shelley's Centenary.*

MOUNTAINS

I live not in myself, but I become,
Portion of that around me ; and to me
High mountains are a feeling, but the hum
Of human cities, torture.
BYRON.—*Childe Harold, c.* 3, 72.

Mont Blanc is the monarch of mountains ;
They crowned him long ago
On a throne of rocks, in a robe of clouds,
With a diadem of snow.
BYRON.—*Manfred,* I, 1.

The nodding horror of whose shady brows
Threats the forlorn and wand'ring passenger. MILTON.—*Comus,* 38.

Two voices are there ; one is of the sea,
One of the mountains, each a mighty voice :
In both from age to age thou didst rejoice ;
They were thy chosen music, Liberty !
WORDSWORTH.—*On the Subjugation of Switzerland.*

Thou wear'st upon thy forehead clear
The freedom of a mountaineer.
WORDSWORTH.—*To a Highland Girl.*

MOURNING

Nature's law
That man was made to mourn.
BURNS.—*Man was made to Mourn.*

Happy long life, with honour at the close,
Friends' painless tears, the softened thought of foes !
J. R. LOWELL.—*Memoriæ Positum, R. G. S.,* 2.

Whom universal Nature did lament.
MILTON.—*Lycidas,* 60.

Weep not for her ! Her memory is the shrine
Of pleasant thoughts, soft as the scent of flowers,
Calm as on windless eve the sun's decline,

Sweet as the song of birds among the bowers,
Rich as a rainbow with its hues of light,
Pure as the moonshine of an autumn night ;
Weep not for her !
D. M. MOIR.—*A Dirge.*

He who general tears can shed
For folks that happen to be dead,
May e'en with equal justice mourn
For those who never yet were born.
PRIOR.—*The Turtle and the Sparrow.*

'Tis not alone my inky cloak, good mother,
Nor customary suits of solemn black, . . .
Nor the dejected 'haviour of the visage,
Together with all forms, modes, shows of grief,
That can denote me truly.
SHAKESPEARE.—*Hamlet,* Act I, 2.

I have that within which passeth show,
These but the trappings and the suits of woe.   SHAKESPEARE.—*Ib.*

Hung be the heavens with black, yield day to night.
SHAKESPEARE.—*Henry VI., Pt.* I, Act I, I.

Come not, when I am dead,
To drop thy foolish tears upon my grave,
To trample round my fallen head,
And vex the unhappy dust thou wouldst not save. TENNYSON.—*Come Not.*

Peace ; come away : the song of woe
Is after all an earthly song ;
Peace ; come away, we do him wrong
To sing so wildly : let us go.
TENNYSON.—*In Memoriam, c.* 57.

I count it crime
To mourn for any overmuch.
TENNYSON.—*Ib., c.* 85.

All gentle things that live will moan thee,
All fond regrets for ever wake ;
For earth is happier having known thee,
And heaven is sweeter for thy sake !
WM. WINTER.—*(New York). Vagrant Memories. On Henry Irving.*

Few and short were the prayers we said,
And we spoke not a word of sorrow ;
But we steadfastly gazed on the face that was dead,
And we bitterly thought of the morrow.
WOLFE.—*Burial of Sir J. Moore.*

Not without hope we suffer or we mourn.
WORDSWORTH.—*Elegiac Stanzas,* 1805.

He mourns the dead who lives as they desire. YOUNG.—*Night Thoughts,* 2.

How wretched is the man who never mourned !   YOUNG.—*Ib.,* 5.

It is better to go to the house of mourning, than to go to the house of feasting.
Ecclesiastes vii, 2.

MULTITUDE, THE

That great enemy of reason, virtue, and religion, the Multitude.
Sir T. Browne.—*Religio Medici, Pt.* 2, 1.

Learning will be cast into the mire and trodden down under the hoofs of a swinish multitude. Burke.—*Reflections on French Revolution.*

Serves and fears
The fury of the many-headed monster,
The giddy multitude.
Massinger.—*Unnatural Combat*, Act 3, 2.

Who o'er the herd would wish to reign,
Fantastic, fickle, fierce and vain ?
Vain as the leaf upon the stream,
And fickle as a changeful dream.
Scott.—*Lady of the Lake,* 5, 30.

MURDER

I come fairly to kill him honestly.
Fletcher and Massinger.—*Little French Lawyer,* Act 4, 1.

Murder most foul, as in the best it is,
But this most foul, strange, and unnatural.
Shakespeare.—*Hamlet,* Act 1, 5.

For murder, though it have no tongue, will speak
With most miraculous organ.
Shakespeare.—*Ib.,* Act 2, 2.

Simple, plain Clarence, I do love thee so,
That I will shortly send thy soul to heaven.
Shakespeare.—*Richard III.,* Act 1, 1.

They cut his throat from ear to ear,
His brains they battered in.
His name was Mr. William Weare,
He dwelt in Lyons Inn.
Anon.—*Alluding to the murder of Wm. Weare by John Thurtell* (1823).

MUSIC

Music, the greatest good that mortals know,
And all of heaven we have below.
Addison.—*St. Cecilia's Day.*

Nothing is capable of being well set to music that is not nonsense.
Addison.—*Spectator, vol.* 1, 18.

Rugged the breast that music cannot tame. J. C. Bampfylde.—*Sonnet.*

If musique and sweet poetrie agree,
As they must needes, the Sister and the Brother.
R. Barnfield.—*Poems in Divers Humors, Sonnet* 1.

His harp the sole companion of his way.
Beattie.—*The Minstrel, Bk.* 1, 3.

Is there a heart that music cannot melt ?
Alas ! how is that rugged heart forlorn.
Beattie.—*Ib., Bk.* 1, 56.

'Tis a sure sign work goes on merrily,
when folks sing at it.
I. Bickerstaff.—*Maid of the Mill,*Act 1, 1.

There is a music wherever there is harmony, order, or proportion : and thus far we may maintain the music of the Spheres ; for those well-ordered motions and regular paces, though they give no sound to the ear, yet to the understanding they strike a note most full of harmony.
Sir T. Browne.—*Religio Medici, Pt.* 2, sec. 9.

There are few such swains as he
Now-a-days for harmonie.
William Browne.—*Shepherd's Pipe.*

Who hears music, feels his solitude
Peopled at once.
Browning.—*Balaustion's Adventure.*

There is no truer truth obtainable
By man, than comes of music.
Browning.—*Chas. Avison.*

Such sweet,
Soft notes as yet musician's cunning
Never gave the enraptured air.
Browning.—*Pied Piper,* c. 12.

For this did Paganini comb the fierce
Electric sparks, or to tenuity
Pull forth the inmost wailing of the wire—
No cat-gut could swoon out so much of soul. Browning.—*Red Cotton Nightcap Country.*

In fact he had no singing education,
An ignorant, noteless, timeless, tuneless fellow.
Byron.—*Don Juan, c.* 4, 87.

There's music in the sighing of a reed ;
There's music in the gushing of a rill ;
There's music in all things, if men had ears,
Their earth is but an echo of the spheres.
Byron.—*Ib.,* 15, 5.

Her fingers witched the chords they passed along,
And her lips seemed to kiss the soul in song. Campbell.—*Theodric.*

When music, heavenly maid, was young,
While yet in early Greece she sung.
Collins.—*The Passions.*

A solemn, strange and mingled air,
'Twas sad by fits, by starts 'twas wild.
Collins.—*Ib.*

O Music ! sphere-descended maid,
Friend of Pleasure, Wisdom's aid.
Collins.—*Ib*

As if an angel's harp had sung of bliss
In some bright world beyond the tears of this. Rev. W. Colton.—*Byron.*

Music hath charms to soothe a savage breast,
To soften rocks, or bend a knotted oak.
CONGREVE.—*Mourning Bride*, Act I, I.

Music is the stalk
And flower of health, and most remedial.
J. DAVIDSON.—*Self's the Man*, Act 4.

No dinner goes off well without him
[Apollo]. [*Jupiter.*]
DISRAELI.—*Ixion*, c. I.

Sound the trumpets ; beat the drums !
Flushed with a purple grace
He shows his honest face ;
Now give the hautboys breath ; he comes, he comes !
DRYDEN.—*Alexander's Feast*, st. 3.

Softly sweet, in Lydian measures,
Soon he soothed his soul to pleasures.
DRYDEN.—*Ib.*, st. 5.

Could swell the soul to rage, or kindle soft desire.   DRYDEN.—*Ib.*, st. 6.

What passion cannot Music raise or quell ?
DRYDEN.—*St. Cecilia's Day*, st. 2.

The soft, complaining flute.
DRYDEN.—*Ib.*, st. 4.

Music is the poor man's Parnassus.
EMERSON.—*Poetry and Imagination.*

Where through the long drawn aisle and fretted vault
The pealing anthem swells the note of praise.   GRAY.—*Elegy.*

There is no music in Nature, neither melody or harmony. Music is the creation of man.   H. R. HAWEIS.—*Music and Morals*, Bk. I, I.

Emotion, not thought, is the sphere of music.   H. R. HAWEIS.—*Ib.*

Their discords sting through Burns and Moore,
Like hedgehogs dressed in lace.
O. W. HOLMES.—*Music Grinders.*

Of all noises I think music the least disagreeable.
JOHNSON.—*Reply to an enquiry whether he was fond of music.*

Music is the only sensual pleasure without vice.
JOHNSON.—*Remark recorded by Sir John Hawkins.*

Fair Melody ! kind Siren ! I've no choice ;
I must be thy sad servant evermore ;
I cannot choose but kneel here and adore.
KEATS.—*Endymion*, Bk. 4.

Let me have music dying, and I seek
No more delight.   KEATS.—*Ib.*

Popular favourites, I apprehend, please by the sequence rather than by the combination of sounds. Only a few highly trained experts can appreciate the masters of intricate Harmony.
KEBLE.—*Lectures on Poetry*, No. 3 (*E. K. Francis tr.*).

I even think that sentimentally I am disposed to harmony. But organically I am incapable of a tune.
LAMB.—*A Chapter on Ears.*

Though cheerfulness and I have long been strangers,
Harmonious sounds are still delightful to me :
There's sure no passion in the human soul
But finds its food in music.
G. LILLO.—*Fatal Curiosity.*

Music's the medicine of the mind.
J. LOGAN.—*Danish Ode.*

The sound of singing and the gurgling throb
Of lute and viol,—meant for many things,
But most for misery.
ERIC MACKAY.—*Lover's Litanies*, 8.

Lap me in soft Lydian airs,
Married to immortal Verse,
Such as the meeting soul may pierce,
In notes with many a winding bout
Of linkèd sweetness long drawn out.
MILTON.—*L'Allegro*, 135.

Such sweet compulsion doth in music lie.
MILTON.—*Arcades*, Song, I.

Musical as is Apollo's lute.
MILTON.—*Comus*, 478.

I was all ear,
And took in strains that might create a soul
Under the ribs of Death.
MILTON.—*Ib.*, 560.

Such notes as warbled to the string,
Drew iron tears down Pluto's cheek.
MILTON.—*Il Penseroso*, 104.

Sphere-born harmonious sisters, Voice and Verse.   MILTON.—*At a Solemn Music.*

None knew whether
The voice or lute was most divine,
So wondrously they went together.
MOORE.—*Lalla Rookh.*

Music doth all our joys refine,
And gives the relish to our wine.
J. OLDHAM.—*St. Cecilia.*

Music's the cordial of a troubled breast,
The softest remedy that grief can find ;
The gentle spell that charms our care to rest
And calms the ruffled passions of the mind.
J. OLDHAM.—*Ode.*

The half of music, I have heard men say,
Is to have grieved ; when comes the lonely
    wail
Over the mind.
    STEPHEN PHILLIPS.—*Marpessa*, 244.

Dealt to the wise, delight they bring ;
To vulgar ears unmeaning ring.
    PINDAR.—*Ol.*, 2, 154 (*Moore tr.*).

Philosophy is the highest music.
    PLATO.—*Phædo*, 12 (*Cary tr.*).

I know not what I was playing,
    Or what I was dreaming then,
But I struck one chord of music
    Like the sound of a great Amen.
    A. A. PROCTER.—*Lost Chord*.

The soul of music slumbers in the shell,
Till waked and kindled by the master's
    spell.   ROGERS.—*Human Life*.

The only universal tongue.
    ROGERS.—*Italy*.

It [music] is either the vain noise of
a language you do not understand, or it
is a vehemence of sentiment, which forces
you along with it and which it is impossible
for the soul to resist. ROUSSEAU.—*Julie*.

Music is the nearest at hand, the most
orderly, the most delicate, and the most
perfect of all bodily pleasures. It is the only
one which is equally helpful to all the ages
of man—helpful from the nurse's song to
her infant, to the music, unheard of others,
which so often haunts the deathbed of
pure and innocent spirits.
    RUSKIN.—*Letter XI.*, 1867.

So sweet, so soft, so faint,
    It seemed an angel's whispered call
To an expiring saint.
    SCOTT.—*Bridal of Triermain*, 1, 4.

As sweet and musical
As bright Apollo's lute, strung with his
    hair.
    SHAKESPEARE.—*Love's Labour's Lost*,
        Act 4, 1.
And the vile squeaking of the wry-necked
    fife.
    SHAKESPEARE.—*Merchant of Venice*,
        Act 2, 5.

Here will we sit and let the sounds of music
Creep in our ears.
    SHAKESPEARE.—*Ib.*, Act 4, 1.

I am never merry when I hear sweet
    music. SHAKESPEARE.—*Ib.*, Act 5, 1.

Since nought so stockish, hard, and full of
    rage,
But music for the time doth change his
    nature.   SHAKESPEARE.—*Ib.*

The man that hath no music in himself,
Nor is not moved with concord of sweet
    sounds,
Is fit for treasons, stratagems, and spoils :
The motions of his spirit are dull as night,
And his affections dark as Erebus ;
Let no such man be trusted !
    SHAKESPEARE.—*Ib.*

O she will sing the savageness out of a
    bear !
    SHAKESPEARE.—*Othello*, Act 4, 1.

" Music with her silver sound," because
musicians have no gold for sounding.
    SHAKESPEARE.—*Romeo and Juliet*,
        Act 4, 5.

That strain again—it had a dying fall ;
O, it came o'er my ear like the sweet south,
That breathes upon a bank of violets,
Stealing, and giving odour.
    SHAKESPEARE.—*Twelfth Night*, Act 1, 1.

True concord of well-tunèd sounds.
    SHAKESPEARE.—*Sonnet*, 8.

At every one of those concerts in England you will find rows of weary people who
are there, not because they really like
classical music, but because they think
they ought to like it.
    G. B. SHAW.—*Man and Superman*.

Hell is full of musical amateurs. Music
is the brandy of the damned.
    G. B. SHAW.—*Ib.*

If I were to begin life again, I would
dedicate it to music. It is the only cheap
and unpunished rapture upon earth.
    SYDNEY SMITH.—*Letter to Lady Carlisle*,
        Aug., 1844.

Discord ofte in music makes the sweeter
    lay.
    SPENSER.—*Faerie Queene*, 3, 2, 15.

Music bright as the soul of light, for
    wings an eagle, for notes a dove.
    SWINBURNE.—*Astrophel*.

Some dead lute-player,
That in dead years had done delicious
    things. SWINBURNE.—*Ballad of Life*.

The city is built
To music, therefore never built at all,
And therefore built for ever.
    TENNYSON.—*Gareth, l.* 272.

Music that gentlier on the spirit lies
Than tir'd eyelids upon tir'd eyes.
    TENNYSON.—*Lotos Eaters*.

Blow, bugle, blow ! set the wild echoes
    flying.
    TENNYSON.—*Princess, c.* 4, *Song*.

Music is the real universal speech of
    mankind.   C. F. WEBER.

Music is the universal language.
JOHN WILSON.—*Noctes (July,* 1826).

MUTABILITY

For this and that way swings
The flux of mortal things.
M. ARNOLD.—*Westminster Abbey.*

Our revels now are ended. These our
    actors,
As I foretold you, were all spirits, and
Are melted into air, into thin air ;
And like the baseless fabric of this vision,
The cloud-capped towers, the gorgeous
    palaces,
The solemn temples, the great globe itself,
Yea, all which it inherit, shall dissolve,
And like this unsubstantial pageant faded,
Leave not a rack behind.
SHAKESPEARE.—*Tempest,* Act 4, 1.

MUTINY

        But were I Brutus,
And Brutus Antony, there were an Antony
Would ruffle up your spirits, and put a
    tongue
In every wound of Cæsar, that should move
The very stones of Rome to rise and
    mutiny.
SHAKESPEARE.—*Julius Cæsar,* Act 3, 2.

MYSTERY

Veil after veil will lift—but there
    must be
Veil upon veil behind.
SIR E. ARNOLD.—*Light of Asia, Bk.* 8.

I love the doubt, the dark, the fear,
That still surroundeth all things here.
A. AUSTIN.—*Hymn to Death.*

Plain truth will influence half a score men
at most in a nation, while mystery will lead
millions by the nose.
BOLINGBROKE.—*Letter,* 1721.

The lucrative business of mystery.
BURKE.—*Vindication of Natural Society.*

Things that do almost mock the grasp of
    thought.
H. F. CARY.—*Dante's "Purgatory,"* c. 29, 41.

Take care never to seem dark and mysterious, which is not only a very unamiable
character, but a very suspicious one too.
LORD CHESTERFIELD.—*Advice to his Son.*

Mystery magnifies danger as the fog the
sun.   C. C. COLTON.—*Lacon.*

There was the Door to which I found no
    key :
There was the Veil through which I might
    not see.
FITZGERALD.—*Rubáiyát, st.* 32.

Deep into that darkness peering, long I
    stood there, wondering, fearing,
Doubting ; dreaming dreams no mortal
    ever dared to dream before.
E. A. POE.—*Raven.*

Everything unknown [i.e. mysterious]
is taken for something transcendent.
TACITUS.—*Agricola.*

So now I am in for Hobbes's Voyage ; a
great Leap in the Dark.
SIR J. VANBRUGH.—*Provoked Wife,*
                  Act 5, 5.

MYSTICISM

Myself when young did eagerly frequent
Doctor and Saint, and heard great Argu-
    ment
About it and about ; but evermore
Came out by the same door wherein I went.
FITZGERALD.—*Rubáiyát, st.* 27.

Where I am not understood, it shall be
concluded that something very useful and
profound is couched underneath.
SWIFT.—*Tale of a Tub: Author's Preface.*

N

NAMES

The glory and the Nothing of a Name.
BYRON.—*Churchill's Grave.*

Oh, Amos Cottle ! Phœbus ! what a name
To fill the speaking trump of future fame !
BYRON.—*English Bards.*

Who hath not owned, with rapture-smitten
    frame,
The power of grace, the magic of a name ?
CAMPBELL.—*Pleasures of Hope, Pt.* 2.

Giving a name, indeed, is a poetic art ;
all poetry, if we go to that with it, is but a
giving of names.   CARLYLE.—*Journal.*

It is not names which give confidence in
things, but things which give confidence in
names.   CHRYSOSTOM.

Charmed with the foolish whistlings of a
    name.   COWLEY.—*Of Agriculture.*

Some to the fascination of a name
Surrender judgment hoodwinked.
COWPER.—*Winter Morning Walk.*

Pride lives with all ; strange names our
    rustics give
To helpless infants, that their own may live.
CRABBE.—*Parish Register, Pt.* 1

I am not a man scrupulous about words
or names or such things.
OLIVER CROMWELL.—*Speech,* 1657.

L*

A man's name is not like a mantle, which merely hangs about him, and which perhaps may be safely twitched and pulled. It is a perfectly fitting garment, which has grown to him like his very skin, and one cannot scratch and scrape it without wounding the man himself.
GOETHE.—*Autob., Bk.* 10.

Fate tried to conceal him by naming him Smith.   O. W. HOLMES.—*The Boys.*

A name ?—if the party had a choice,
What mortal would be a Bugg by choice ?
As a Hogg, a Grubb, or a Chubb rejoice ?
  Or any such nauseous blazon ?
HOOD.—*Miss Kilmansegg.*

What's in a name ? as the white blackbird said when 'e sat on a wooden milestone eating a red blackberry.
H. G. HUTCHINSON.—*A Fine Ear for the Haspirate. Punch (Jan.* 29, 1919).

Indeed there is a woundy luck in names, sir,
And a main mystery an' a man knew where To vind it. BEN JONSON.—*Tale of a Tub.*

  A name and also an omen.
        PLAUTUS.—*Persa,* Act 4.

    Smith's no name at all.
        POPE.—*Epitaph.*

What's in a name ?   That which we call a rose
By any other name would smell as sweet.
SHAKESPEARE.—*Romeo and Juliet,* Act 2, 2.

    Human pride
Is skilful to invent most serious names,
To hide its ignorance.
        SHELLEY.—*Queen Mab, c.* 7.

A name which you all know by sight very well,
But which no one can speak, and no one can spell.
SOUTHEY.—*March to Moscow, c.* 8.

    The superstition of a name.
        TACITUS.—*Hist., Ch.* 3.

Let be my name until I make my name.
        TENNYSON.—*Gareth, l.* 563.

I cannot love my lord and not his name.
        TENNYSON.—*Marriage of Geraint,* 92.

And a wee bit name—canna it carry in it a wecht o' love !
        JOHN WILSON.—*Noctes (Ettrick Shepherd).*

A good name endureth for ever.
        Ecclesiasticus xli, 1, 3.

It is not fair to tell names.
Given as " a saying " in Mrs. Centlivre's " Beau's Ideal " (1702).

NAPLES

    Naples, the paradise of Italy,
    As that is of the earth.
    FLETCHER AND MASSINGER.—*Double Marriage,* Act 1.

NATIONS

Look to life in every part ; in all they practise, all they know,
Every nation has derived the best instruction from the foe.
ARISTOPHANES.—*The Birds (Frere tr.).*

A people is but the attempt of many
To rise to the completer life of one ;
And those who live as models for the mass
Are singly of more value than they all.
        BROWNING.—*Luria,* Act 5.

It is with nations as with men,—
One must be first.   We are the mightiest,
The heirs of Rome.
        J. DAVIDSON.—*Self's the Man,* Act 3.

Some people may be Rooshans and others may be Prooshans ; they are born so and will please themselves. Them which is of other naturs thinks different. [*Mrs. Gamp.*]
DICKENS.—*M. Chuzzlewit, c.* 19.

Our backs is easy ris. We must be cracked-up, or they rises and we snarls. You'd better crack us up, you had !
DICKENS.—*Ib., c.* 33.

Each nation grows after its own genius and has a civilization of its own.
        EMERSON.—*Civilization.*

If there be one test of national genius universally accepted, it is success.   And if there be one successful country in the universe for the last millennium, that country is England.
EMERSON.—*English Traits,* 3, *Land.*

A nation with whom sentiment is nothing is on the way to cease to be a nation at all.
        FROUDE.—*The Premier.*

Nations are but enlarged schoolboys.
        FROUDE.—*Exceptional Conditions.*

Strike—for your altars and your fires ;
Strike—for the green graves of your sires ;
  God—and your native land !
FITZ-GREENE HALLECK.—*Marco Bozzaris.*

The celebrated apophthegm that nations never profit by experience, becomes yearly more and more untrue.
SIR J. HERSCHEL.—*Influence of Science.*

There is no extremity of distress, which, of itself, ought to reduce a great nation to despair.   JUNIUS.—*Letter* 1.

Oh, East is East, and West is West, and never the twain shall meet.
        KIPLING.—*East and West.*

Nations are long results, by ruder ways
Gathering the might that warrants length
  of days.
    J. R. LOWELL.—*Under the Old Elm*, 4, 2.

It is better to remain a nation capable of
displaying the virtues of a nation, than
even to be free.   MAINE.

The world in all doth but two nations bear,
The good, the bad, and these mixed everywhere.   A. MARVELL.—*Loyal Scot.*

The worth of a State in the long run is
the worth of the individuals composing it.
    J. S. MILL.—*Liberty, ch.* 5.

Methinks I see in my mind a noble and
puissant nation rousing herself like a strong
man after sleep, and shaking her invincible
locks. Methinks I see her as an eagle
mewing her mighty youth, and kindling
her undazzled eyes at the full mid-day
beam.   MILTON.—*Areopagitica.*

An old and haughty nation, proud in arms.
    MILTON.—*Comus*, 33.

To a brave man every country is a native
land.   OVID.—*Fast.*, 1.

England has saved herself by her own
energy ; I hope that she will save Europe
by her example.
WILLIAM PITT.—*Speech*, 1805 (*afterwards compressed into the Latin inscription
on a medal, " Seipsum virtute, Europam
        exemplo "*).

Study a people apart from its cities ; it
is only thus that you can know it.
      ROUSSEAU.—*Emile, Bk.* 5.

That country is the richest which nourishes the greatest number of noble and
happy human beings.
    RUSKIN.—*Unto this Last, Essay* 4.

A nation's institutions and beliefs are
determined by its character.
HERBT. SPENCER.—*Social Statics, ch.* 16, 5.

Not with dreams, but with blood and
  with iron,
Shall a nation be moulded at last.
    SWINBURNE.—*Word for the Country.*

      If a state submit
At once, she may be blotted out at once,
And swallowed in the conqueror's chron-
  icle.   TENNYSON.—*The Cup.*

He was probably fond of them, but he
was always able to conceal it.
[*Referring to Thomas Carlyle and Americans.*]   MARK TWAIN.—*My First Lie.*

A people rude in peace, and rough in war.
VIRGIL.—*Æneid, Bk.* 1 (*Dryden*) (*Of the
        people of Libya*).

This was the race that sure portents fore-
  shew,
To sway the world and land and sea subdue.
    VIRGIL.—*Ib.*, *Bk.* 7 (*Dryden tr.*).

O citizens ! we wage unequal war
With men, not only heaven's peculiar care,
But heaven's own race,—unconquered in
  the field,
Or conquered, yet unknowing how to
  yield.
    VIRGIL.—*Ib.*, *Bk.* 11 (*Dryden tr.*).

Just pride is no mean factor in a State ;
The sense of greatness keeps a nation great.
    SIR W. WATSON.—*Ver Tenebrosum.*

The mainners o' a' nations are equally
bad.   JOHN WILSON.—*Noctes*, 39 (*Ettrick
        Shepherd*).

Minds like ours, my dear James, must
always be above national prejudices, and
in all companies it gives me true pleasure
to declare that, as a people, the English
are very little indeed inferior to the Scotch.
    JOHN WILSON.—*Noctes.*

The Land we from our fathers had in trust,
And to our children will transmit or die :
This is our maxim, this our piety.
    WORDSWORTH.—*Feelings of the Tyrolese.*

Once did she hold the gorgeous East in fee,
And was the safeguard of the West.
    WORDSWORTH.—*On the Venetian Republic.*

A fatherland focuses a people.
I. ZANGWILL.—*Children of the Ghetto, c.* 15.

She that was great among the nations,
and princess among the provinces, how is
she become tributary !   *Lamentations* i, 1.

Righteousness exalteth a nation.
        Proverbs xiv, 34.

The land that feeds me is my fatherland.
      Paraphr. of Euripides.

Every land is his native land to a brave
man.   *Greek prov.*

The Italians are wise before the deed ;
the Germans in the deed ; the French after
the deed.   *Italian prov.*

NATIVE LAND

Because all earth, except his native land,
To him is one wide prison, and each breath
Of foreign air he draws seems a slow poison,
Consuming but not killing.
    BYRON.—*Two Foscari*, 1, 1.

Nothing is more discreditable than to be
ignorant of one's own native land.
    GABRIEL HARVEY.—*Note in Lluyd's
        " Breviary of Britayne."*

We have learned the lesson of time, and we
 know three things of worth :
Only to sow and sing and reap in the land
 of our birth.   R. Le Gallienne.—
                        Cry of the Little Peoples.

My foot is on my native heath, and my
name is McGregor.
                Scott.—*Rob Roy, ch.* 24.

NATURALNESS

To me more dear, congenial to my heart,
One native charm, than all the gloss of art.
        Goldsmith.—*Deserted Village.*

Nothing so much hinders being natural
as the longing to appear so.
            La Rochefoucauld.

Ah, no ! the conquest was obtained with
 ease ;
He pleased you by not studying to please.
    Geo. Lord Lyttelton.—*Progress
                            of Love,* 3.

Various arts mankind delight,
 But he that tempts the field of fame
Must march with Nature to the fight.
    Pindar.—*Nemean Odes,* 1, 26
                        (*Moore tr.*).

Let your precept be, " Be Easy."
    Sir R. Steele.—*Spectator, vol.* 3, 196.

Then Nature said, " A lovelier flower
On earth was never sown ;
This child I to myself will take,
She shall be mine, and I will make
A lady of my own."
        Wordsworth.—*Three Years.*

NATURE

If Nature built by rule and square,
 Than man what wiser would she be ?
What wins us is her careless care,
 And sweet unpunctuality.
            A. Austin.—*Nature.*

There never was miracle wrought by God
to convert an atheist, because the light of
nature might have led him to confess a God.
    Bacon.—*Adv. of Learning, Bk.* 2.

Nature is not governed, except by obey-
ing her.   Bacon.—*Aphorism,* 129.

I beseech you that next after the Scriptures you study that great volume, the
works and created objects of God, strenu-
ously and before all books, which should
only be regarded as commentaries.
        Bacon.—*Epistolæ,* 6.

About Nature consult nature herself.
        Bacon.—*Instauratio, Pt.* 3, *Introd.*
[Described by Bacon as " the only way in
which the foundations of true and active
philosophy can be established."]

There's the wind on the heath, brother ;
if I could only feel that I would gladly live
for ever.   Borrow.—*Lavengro.*

Nature is the Art of God.
    Sir T. Browne.—*Religio Medici, Pt.* 1, 16.

Earth's crammed with heaven,
And every common bush afire with God ;
But only he who sees, takes off his shoes,
The rest sit round it and pluck blackberries,
And daub their natural faces unaware
More and more from the first similitude.
    E. B. Browning.—*Aurora Leigh, Bk.* 7.

God's gifts put man's best dreams to
 shame.
    E. B. Browning.—*Sonnets from the
                        Portuguese,* 26.

God is the perfect poet,
Who in His person acts His own creation.
    Browning.—*Paracelsus, pt.* 2.

Now is the time for those who wisdom love,
 Who love to walk in virtue's flowery
 road,
Along the lovely paths of Spring to rove,
 And follow Nature up to Nature's God.
    Michael Bruce.—*Elegy : To Spring.*

To him who in the love of Nature holds
Communion with her visible forms, she
 speaks
A various language.
    W. Cullen Bryant.—*Thanatopsis,* 1.

Go forth under the open sky and list
To Nature's teaching.
        W. C. Bryant.—*Ib.,* 14

Set him before a hedgerow in a lane,
And he was happy all alone for hours.
    R. Buchanan.—*E. Crowhurst.*

Never, no never, did Nature say one
thing and wisdom say another.
    Burke.—*Letters on a Regicide Peace*
        (*Borrowed from Juvenal, Sat.* 14).

Yet nature's charms—the hills and woods,
The sweeping vales and foaming floods,
 Are free alike to all.
        Burns.—*Epistle to Davie.*

Dear Nature is the kindest mother still,
Though always changing, in her aspect
 mild.
    Byron.—*Childe Harold, c.* 2, 37.

Art, Glory, Freedom fail, but Nature still
 is fair.   Byron.—*Ib., c.* 2, 87.

There is a pleasure in the pathless woods,
There is a rapture in the lonely shore,
There is society, where none intrudes,
By the deep sea, and music in its roar ;
I love not man the less, but Nature more,

From these our interviews, in which I steal
From all I may be, or have been before,
To mingle with the Universe, and feel
What I can ne'er express, yet cannot all
    conceal.   BYRON.—*Ib., c. 4, 178.*

Nature admits no lie.
    CARLYLE.—*Latter Day Pamphlets,* 5.

Nature, the vicar of the Almightie Lord.
    CHAUCER.—*Assembly of Foules.*

Habit can never conquer Nature ; she is
for ever unconquered.
    CICERO.—*Tusc. Quæst.,* 5, 27.

In nature there is nothing melancholy.
    COLERIDGE.—*The Nightingale.*

Full often too
Our wayward intellect, the more we learn
Of nature, overlooks her Author more.
    COWPER.—*Garden,* 235.

Nature is but a name for an effect,
Whose cause is God.
    COWPER.—*Winter Morning Walk.*

Time is as young as ever now,
Nature as fresh and sweet.
    J. DAVIDSON.—*Ballad of Euthanasia.*

For Nature in man's heart her laws doth
pen.
SIR J. DAVIES.—*Nosce Teipsum, sec.* 26, 2.

Nature is more powerful than education ;
time will develop everything.
    DISRAELI.—*Contarini Fleming, c.* 13.

For Art may err, but Nature cannot miss.
    DRYDEN.—*Cock and Fox, l.* 452.

Ever charming, ever new,
When will the landscape tire the view ?
    JOHN DYER.—*Grongar Hill.*

The ancient precept, " Know Thyself,"
and the modern precept, " Study Nature,"
become at last one maxim.
    EMERSON.—*The American Scholar*
                  (1837).

Nature never hurries. Atom by atom,
little by little, she achieves her work.
    EMERSON.—*Farming.*

For what are they all in their high conceit
When man in the bush with God may meet?
    EMERSON.—*Good-bye, Proud World.*

And in the vaunted works of Art
The master-stroke is still her part.
    EMERSON.—*Nature.*

The lover of nature is he whose inward
and outward senses are still truly adjusted
to each other ; who has retained the spirit
of infancy even into the era of manhood.
    EMERSON.—*Ib.*

Nothing is great but the inexhaustible
wealth of Nature.
    EMERSON.—*Resources.*

Nature paints the best part of the picture,
carves the best part of the statue, builds
the best part of the house, and speaks the
best part of the oration.
    EMERSON.—*Society and Solitude.*

Keep Nature's great original in view,
And thence the living images pursue.
    P. FRANCIS.—*Horace, Art of Poetry*

The meanest floweret of the vale,
The simplest note that swells the gale,
The common sun, the air, the skies,
To him are opening paradise.
    GRAY.—*Ode on Pleasure from Vicissitude,*
                      l. 53.

The house is a prison, the schoolroom's a
    cell ;
Leave study and books for the upland and
    dell.
    J. H. GREEN.—*Morning Invitation.*

He would adore my gifts instead of me,
And rest in Nature, not the God of Nature.
    HERBERT.—*The Pulley.*

You may drive out nature with a fork,
but she will ever return.
    HORACE.—*Ep., Bk.* 1, 10, 24.

I am tired of four walls and a ceiling ;
    I have need of the grass.
    R. HOVEY.—*Spring.*

A plant, a leaf, a blossom,—but contains
A folio volume. We may read and read,
And read again, and still find something
    new.
    JAMES HURDIS, D.D.—*Village Curate* (1788).

Nature never says one thing, and wisdom
another.   JUVENAL.—*Sat.* 14, 321.

The poetry of earth is never dead.
    KEATS.—*Grasshopper and Cricket.*

Tracing out wisdom, power, and love,
In earth or sky, in stream or grove.
    KEBLE.—*Evening*

Thou, who hast given me eyes to see
    And love this sight so fair,
Give me a heart to find out Thee
    And read Thee everywhere.
    KEBLE.—*Septuagesima.*

I am in love with this green earth.
    LAMB.—*New Year's Eve.*

As one awaked out of sleep, I saw the
Lord passing by—eternal, infinite, omni-
scient, omnipotent, and I stood as in a
trance.
    LINNÆUS.—*Systema Naturæ, ad init.*
          (*as translated by Ruskin*).

And Nature, the old nurse, took
The child upon her knee,
Saying, " Here is a story-book
Thy Father has written for thee."
LONGFELLOW.—*Fiftieth Birthday of
Agassiz.*

In those vernal seasons of the year, when
the air is calm and pleasant, it were an injury and sullenness against Nature not to
go out and see her riches, and partake in
her rejoicing.   MILTON.—*Of Education.*

Unspeakable desire to see and know
All these His wondrous works, but chiefly
man.
     MILTON.—*Paradise Lost, Bk.* 3, 663.

Thy desire which tends to know
The works of God, thereby to glorify
The great Work Master, leads to no excess
That reaches blame, but rather merits
praise
The more it seems excess.
         MILTON.—*Ib., Bk.* 3, 694.

But neither breath of Morn, when she as-
cends
With charm of earliest birds ; nor rising
Sun
On this delightful land ; nor herb, fruit,
flower,
Glist'ring with dew ; nor fragrance after
showers ;
Nor grateful evening mild ; nor silent
Night,
With this her solemn bird, nor walk by
Moon,
Or glittering starlight, without thee is
sweet.   MILTON.—*Ib., Bk.* 4, 650.

These are thy glorious works, Parent of
Good,
Almighty, thine this universal frame,
Thus wondrous fair ; thyself how wondrous
then !   MILTON.—*Ib., Bk.* 5, 153.

Nature hath need of what she asks.
MILTON.—*Paradise Regained, Bk.* 2, 253.

Nature's cult is above all things reasonable and thus fulfils the conditions of a good
working faith.   Much is hidden ; much is
lucid and practical.   Mystery does not
lack, for there are many holies where no
foot has trodden.
     EDEN PHILLPOTTS.—*A Shadow Passes.*

From Nature's chain, whatever link you
strike,
Tenth, or ten thousandth, breaks the chain
alike. POPE.—*Essay on Man,* 1, 245.

Slave to no sect, who takes no private road,
But looks through Nature up to Nature's
God.   POPE.—*Ib., Ep.* 4, 331.

Never does nature deceive us ; it is we
who deceive Nature.   ROUSSEAU.—*Emile.*

Clouds and mountains have been life to
me.   RUSKIN.—*Præterita.*

The saddest heart might pleasure take
To see all nature gay.
     SCOTT.—*Marmion,* 4, 15.

New Art would better Nature's best,
But Nature knows a thing or two.
     SIR OWEN SEAMAN.—*Ars Postera.*

O Nature ! how we worship thee, even
against our wills !   SENECA.—*Hippolytus.*

And this our life, exempt from public haunt,
Finds tongues in trees, books in the run-
ning brooks,
Sermons in stones, and good in everything.
SHAKESPEARE.—*As You Like It,* Act 2, 1.

One touch of nature makes the whole
world kin.
     SHAKESPEARE.—*Troilus,* Act 3, 3.

Nature's rules have no exceptions.
HERBT. SPENCER.—*Social Statics, Intro.*

What more felicitie can fall to creature
Than to enjoy delight with libertie,
And to be lord of all the workes of Nature ;
To raigne in th' aire from th' earth to
highest skie ;
To feed on flowres and weeds of glorious
feature ?
     SPENSER.—*Muiopotmos, st.* 26.

But any man that walks the mead,
In bud or blade, or bloom, may find,
According as his humours lead,
A meaning suited to his mind.
     TENNYSON.—*Day-Dream, Moral,* 2.

So careful of the type she seems,
So careless of the single life.
     TENNYSON.—*In Memoriam, c.* 55.

I care not, Fortune ! what you me deny ;
You cannot rob me of free Nature's grace ;
You cannot shut the windows of the sky,
Through which Aurora shows her brighten-
ing face ;
You cannot bar my constant feet to trace
The woods and lawns, by living stream, at
eve :
     THOMSON.—*Castle of Ignorance, c.* 2.

When on some gilded cloud or flower
My gazing soul would dwell an hour,
And in those weaker glories spy
Some shadows of eternity.
         VAUGHAN.—*The Retreat.*

Happy is he who has known the rural
divinities.   VIRGIL.—*Georgics,* 2.

Happy the man, who, studying Nature's
laws,
Through known effects can trace the secret
cause.
     VIRGIL.—*Georgics,* 2, 490 (*Dryden tr.*).

" Is this," I cried,
" The end of prayer, and preaching ?
Then down with pulpit, down with priest,
And give us Nature's teaching ! "
    WHITTIER.—*A Sabbath Scene.*

I never knew a Naturalist who was not a
good man.   JOHN WILSON.—*Noctes*, 11.

Few folk hae seen oftener than me Natur
gettin' up i' the mornin'. . . . She sleeps a'
nicht in her claes, yet they're never run-
kled. Never see ye *her* hair in papers.
    JOHN WILSON.—*Noctes*, 19 (*Ettrick
                Shepherd*).

As in the eye of Nature he has lived,
So in the eye of Nature let him die.
   WORDSWORTH.—*Old Cumberland Beggar.*

Vain is the glory of the sky,
  The beauty vain of field and grove,
Unless, while with admiring eye
  We gaze, we also learn to love.
   WORDSWORTH.—*Poems of Fancy*, 20.

Come forth into the light of things ;
Let nature be your teacher.
   WORDSWORTH.—*Tables Turned, st.* 4.

One impulse from a vernal wood
May teach you more of man,
Of moral evil, and of good,
Than all the sages can.
   WORDSWORTH.—*Ib., st.* 6.

Sweet is the love which Nature brings.
   WORDSWORTH.—*Ib.*

I have learned
To look on nature, not as in the hour
Of thoughtless youth ; but hearing often-
   times
The still, sad music of humanity,
Nor harsh, nor grating, though of ample
   power
To chasten and subdue.
   WORDSWORTH.—*Tintern Abbey.*

Nature never did betray
  The heart that loved her.
   WORDSWORTH.—*Ib.*

The sounding cataract
Haunted me like a passion. The tall rock,
The mountain, and the deep and gloomy
  wood,
Their colours and their forms, were then to
  me
An appetite ; a feeling and a love.
  WORDSWORTH.—*Lines, nr. Tintern Abbey*
                   (1798).

Read Nature ; Nature is a friend to truth ;
Nature is Christian ; preaches to mankind :
And bids dead matter aid us in our creed.
   YOUNG.—*Night Thoughts*, 4.

The course of Nature is the art of God.
   YOUNG.—*Ib.*, 9, *ad fin.*

Take God from Nature, nothing great is
  left.   YOUNG.—*Ib.*, 9.

Nature does nothing in vain.
               Latin prov.

It's merrye walkyng in the fayre forest,
To heare the smalle birdes song.
       Old Ballad, Robin Hood.

NAVY

Britain's best bulwarks are her wooden
  walls.   T. A. ARNE.—*Britain's Best
                    Bulwarks.*

Not all the legions of the land
Shall ever wrest from England's hand
  The Sceptre of the Sea.
   A. AUSTIN.—*Look Seaward.*

He that commands the sea is at great
liberty, and may take as much and as little
of the war as he will.
       BACON.—*Of Expense.*

Let us think of them that sleep,
  Full many a fathom deep,
By thy wild and stormy steep
Elsinore !
   CAMPBELL.—*Battle of the Baltic.*

While the battle rages loud and long,
And the stormy winds do blow.
   CAMPBELL.—*Ye Mariners.*

Naval matters involve great expenditure.
                 CICERO.

It was the opinion of Themistocles that
whoso can hold the sea has command of
the situation.   CICERO.—*Ep. ad At.*

Toll for the brave !
  The brave that are no more !
All sunk beneath the wave,
  Fast by their native shore.
   COWPER.—*Loss of "Royal George."*

With the submitted fasces of the main.
   DRYDEN.—*Astræa Redux*, 249.

Heart of oak are our ships,
Heart of oak are our men,
  We always are ready,
  Steady, boys, steady !
We'll fight and we'll conquer again and
  again.   GARRICK.—*Hearts of Oak.*

The British army should be a projectile
to be fired by the British navy.
   VISCOUNT GREY.—*Quoted by Lord
    Fisher, in " Memories," as " the
    splendid words of Sir Edward Grey."*

The trident of Neptune is the sceptre of
the world   LEMIERRE.—*Commerce.*

But on the sea be terrible, untamed,
Unconquerable still.
           THOMSON.—*Britannia.*

They that the whole world's monarchy
designed
Are to their ports by our bold fleet confined.
 WALLER.—*Of a War with Spain.*

Thus did England fight :
And shall not England smite
With Drake's strong stroke in battles yet
 to be ?
 T. WATTS-DUNTON.—*Christmas at the
   Mermaid. Chorus.*

NECESSITY

Thanne is it wisdom, as it thinketh me,
To maken vertu of necessitee.
 CHAUCER.—*Knight's Tale, v.* 3043.

Necessity hath no law. Feigned necessities, imaginary necessities, are the greatest cozenage men can put upon the Providence of God, and make pretences to
break known rules by.
 CROMWELL.—*Speech, Sept.* 12, 1654.

Necessity makes an honest man a knave.
 DEFOE.—*Robinson Crusoe.*

So spake the fiend, and with necessity,
The tyrant's plea, excused his devilish
 deeds.
 MILTON.—*Paradise Lost, Bk.* 4, 393.

Necessity is the plea for every infringe-
ment of human freedom. It is the argument of tyrants ; it is the creed of slaves.
 WM. PITT.—*Speech,* 1783.

There is no necessity to live in necessity.
 SENECA.—*Ep.* 58.

There is no virtue like necessity.
 SHAKESPEARE.—*Richard II.,* Act 1, 3.

Necessity, thou mother of the world !
 SHELLEY.—*Queen Mab, c.* 6.

Necessity, thou tyrant conscience of the
 great ! SWIFT.—*Ode to Sancroft.*

Wit's whetstone, Want, there made us
 quickly learn.
JOHN TAYLOR.—*Penniless Pilgrimage.*

NEGLECT

On Butler who can think without just rage?
The glory and the scandal of the age !
 J. OLDHAM.—*A Satire,* 175.

The wretch, at summing up his misspent
 days,
Found nothing left but poverty and praise.
 J. OLDHAM.—*Ib.,* 182.

O negligence,
Fit for a fool to fall by !
SHAKESPEARE.—*Henry VIII.,* Act 3, 2.

Ah me ! how sorely is my heart forlorn,
To think how modest worth neglected
 lies. SHENSTONE.—*Schoolmistress.*

NEGROES

Our Captain counts the image of God,
nevertheless his image, cut in ebony, as if
done in ivory.
 FULLER.—*The Good Sea-Captain.*

NEIGHBOURS

A bad neighbour is as great an evil as a
good neighbour is an advantage. HESIOD.

Surely it is your concern when the wall
of your neighbour's house is burning ; fire
neglected is apt to gain in power.
 HORACE.—*Ep., Bk.* 1, 18, 84.

There is no being alone but in a metropolis. The worst place in the world to find
solitude is the country. Questions grow
there, and that unpleasant Christian com-
modity, neighbours.
 HORACE WALPOLE.—*Letter.*

A hedge between keeps friendship green.
 Prov.

Love your neighbour, yet pull not down
your hedge. *Prov.* (Geo. Herbert).

NEMESIS

The sword of heaven is not in haste to
 smite,
Nor yet doth linger.
 H. F. CARY.—*Dante's " Paradise,"
   c.* 22, 16.

No less he knows
The day fast comes when all men must de-
 part
And pay for present pride in future woes.
The deeds that frantic mortals do
In this disordered nook of Jove's domain
All meet their meed.
 PINDAR.—*Olympian Odes,* 2, 105
   (Moore tr.).

NEUTRALITY

Here I am between two fires. Shall I be
an honest man or a rogue ? I think it is
most prudent to remain neutral.
 E. SCRIBE.—*Cascaro in " Les Frères
   invisibles."*

Something between a hindrance and a
 help. WORDSWORTH.—*Michael.*

NEVERMORE

" Take thy beak from out my heart, and
 take thy form from off my door ! "
Quoth the Raven, " Nevermore."
 E. A. POE.—*Raven.*

NEW YEAR

A towmont, sirs, is gane to wreck !
O Eighty-eight, in thy sma' space,
What dire events hae taken place !
Of what enjoyments thou hast reft us !
In what a pickle thou hast left us !
 BURNS.—*Elegy on* 1788.

For hark ! the last chime of the dial has
  ceased,
And Old Time, who, his leisure to cozen,
Has finished the Months, like the flasks at
  a feast,
Is preparing to tap a fresh dozen !
              HOOD.—*The New Year.*

Each age has deemed the new-born year
The fittest time for festal cheer.
        SCOTT.—*Marmion, c.* 6, *Intro.*

Ring out the old, ring in the new,
  Ring, happy bells, across the snow ;
The year is going ; let him go ;
Ring out the false, ring in the true.
     TENNYSON.—*In Memoriam, c.* 106.

NEWS

Ill news hath wings, and with the wind doth
  go ;
Comfort's a cripple, and comes ever slow.
    DRAYTON.—*Barons' Wars, Bk.* 2, 28.

Where village statesmen talked with looks
  profound,
And news, much older than their ale, went
  round. GOLDSMITH.—*Deserted Village.*

And are ye sure the news is true ?
And are ye sure he's weel ?
       W. J. MICKLE.—*Song.*
For evil news rides post, while good news
  baits.   MILTON.—*Samson Agonistes,*
                        l. 1538.

Even such a man, so faint, so spiritless,
So dull, so dead in look, so woe-begone,
Drew Priam's curtain in the dead of night,
And would have told him half his Troy was
  burned.
SHAKESPEARE.—*Henry IV., Pt.* 2, Act 1, 1.

Yet the first bringer of unwelcome news
Hath but a losing office ; and his tongue
Sounds ever after as a sullen bell,
Remembered knolling a departed friend.
           SHAKESPEARE.—*Ib.*

Here are a few of the unpleasant'st words
That ever blotted paper.
SHAKESPEARE.—*Mercht. of Venice,* Act 3, 2.

The messenger of good news is always
an object of benevolence . . . No one envies
his reward, though no one pretends to say
that he has deserved it.
    SYDNEY SMITH.—*Lectures on Moral
             Philosophy, No.* 22.

The times are big with tidings.
        SOUTHEY.—*Roderick.*

How beautiful upon the mountains are
the feet of him that bringeth good tidings,
that publisheth peace.   *Isaiah* lii, 7.

As cold waters to a thirsty soul, so is
good news from a far country.
             Proverbs xxv, 25.

NEWSPAPERS

If there's a hole in a' your coats,
  I rede you tent it ;
A chiel's amang you takin' notes,
  And, faith, he'll prent it !
BURNS.—*On Capt. Grose's Peregrinations.*

The true Church of England, at this moment, lies in the Editors of its newspapers.
    CARLYLE.—*Signs of the Times.*

This folio of four pages, happy work !
Which not even critics criticise.
    COWPER.—*Winter Evening.*

The tyrant on the throne
Is the morning and evening press.
    J. DAVIDSON.—*New Year's Day.*

Then hail to the Press ! chosen guardian of
  freedom !
Strong sword-arm of justice ! bright sunbeam of truth !
    HORACE GREELEY.—*The Press.*

News, the manna of a day.
  MATTHEW GREEN.—*Spleen,* 169.

A reply to a newspaper attack resembles
very much the attempt of Hercules to crop
the Hydra, without the slightest chance of
his ultimate success.
THEOD. HOOK.—*Gilbert Gurney, vol.* 2, *ch.* 1.

The liberty of the press is the palladium
of all the civil, political, and religious rights
of an Englishman.   JUNIUS.—*Dedication.*

He hath sold his heart to the old Black Art,
We call the daily Press.
        KIPLING.—*The Press.*

Newspapers always excite curiosity. No
one ever lays one down without a feeling
of disappointment.
    LAMB.—*Thoughts on Books.*

The gallery in which the reporters sit has
become a fourth estate of the realm.
    MACAULAY.—*On Hallam.*

Can it be maintained that a person of
any education can learn anything worth
knowing from a penny paper ?
MARQUIS OF SALISBURY.—*Speech,* 1861.

Newspapers are the Bibles of worldlings.
How diligently they read them ! Here they
find their law and profits, their judges and
chronicles, their epistles and revelations.
    C. H. SPURGEON.—*" Salt-Cellars."*

Here shall the Press the People's right
  maintain,
Unawed by influence and unbribed by gain.
    JOSEPH STORY.—*Salem Register.*

The *Pall Mall Gazette* is written by gentlemen for gentlemen.
    THACKERAY.—*Pendennis, Bk.* 1, *ch.* 32.

It [yellow journalism] means, according to my belief, a newspaper which glows with the colour of sunshine and throws light into dark places.
ELLA WHEELER WILCOX.—*The Worlds and I.*

In old days men had the rack. Now they have the press.
OSCAR WILDE.—*Soul of Man under Socialism.*

NICKNAMES

His intimate friends called him " Candle-ends,"
And his enemies, " Toasted-cheese."
C. L. DODGSON.—*Hunting of the Snark.*

Of all eloquence a nickname is the most concise ; of all arguments the most unanswerable.   HAZLITT.—*Nicknames.*

Nicknames and whippings, when they are once laid on, no one has discovered how to take off.
W. S. LANDOR.—*Imag. Conversations, Du Paty.*

Then you can call me " Timbertoes,"— thet's wut the people likes ;
Sutthin' combinin' morril truth with phrases sech ez strikes.
J. R. LOWELL.—*Biglow Papers,* No. 8.

A nickname is the hardest stone that the devil can throw at a man.
Quoted by Hazlitt in " Essay on Nicknames."

Sticks an' stanes may break my banes,
But names will never hurt me.
Scottish prov.

NIGGARDLINESS

That man may last, but never lives,
Who much receives but nothing gives ;
Whom none can love, whom none can thank,
Creation's blot, creation's blank.
THOS. GIBBONS.—*When Jesus dwelt.*

Never was scraper brave man. Get to live ;
Then live and use it.
HERBERT.—*Church Porch.*

Thou shalt not muzzle the ox when he treadeth out the corn.   *Deut.* xxv, 4.

NIGHT

And the sentinel stars set their watch in the sky.
CAMPBELL.—*Soldier's Dream.*

Night, with her train of stars,
And her great gift of sleep.
W. E. HENLEY.—*Margaritæ Sorori.*

And all the little birds had laid their heads
Under their wings, sleeping in feather-beds.
HOOD.—*Bianca's Dream.*

God makes sech nights, all white and still
Fur 'z you can look or listen.
J. R. LOWELL.—*Biglow Papers,* 2nd Series, *The Courtin'.*

Sable-vested Night, eldest of things.
MILTON.—*Paradise Lost, Bk.* 2, 962.

'Tis never too late for delight, my dear,
And the best of all ways
To lengthen our days
Is to steal a few hours from the night, my dear.   MOORE.—*Irish Melodies.*

Oft in the stilly night
Ere slumber's chain has bound me.
MOORE.—*Song.*

In complete steel,
Revisit'st thus the glimpses of the moon,
Making night hideous.
SHAKESPEARE.—*Hamlet,* Act 1, 4.

'Tis now the very witching time of night,
When churchyards yawn, and hell itself breathes out
Contagion.   SHAKESPEARE—*Ib.,* Act 3, 2.

Let us be Diana's foresters, gentlemen of the shade, minions of the moon.
SHAKESPEARE.—*Henry IV.,* Pt. 1, Act 1, 2.

Soft stillness and the night
Become the touches of sweet harmony.
SHAKESPEARE.—*Mercht. of Venice,* Act 5, 1.

O comfort-killing night, image of hell !
Dim register and notary of shame !
Black stage for tragedies and murders fell !
Vast sin-concealing chaos ! nurse of blame !
SHAKESPEARE.—*Lucrece,* 110.

Ne'er saw I, never felt, a calm so deep !
The river glideth at his own sweet will ;
Dear God ! the very houses seem asleep,
And all that mighty heart is lying still.
WORDSWORTH.—*Westminster Bridge.*

Creation sleeps.   'Tis, as the general pulse
Of life stood still, and Nature made a pause ;
An awful pause ! prophetic of her end.
YOUNG.—*Night Thoughts,* 1.

By night an atheist half believes in God.
YOUNG.—*Ib.,* 5.

Night is a good herdsman : she brings all creatures home.   *Gaelic prov.*

NIGHTINGALE

Like to that tawny one,
Insatiate in her wail,
The nightingale, who still with sorrowing soul
And " Itys, Itys " cry,
Bemoans a life o'erflourishing in ills.
ÆSCHYLUS.—*Agamemnon,* 1141 (*Plumptre tr.*).

Ah, for the doom of clear-voiced nightin-
    gale !
The Gods gave her a body bearing wings,
    And life of pleasant days
    With no fresh cause to weep.
    ÆSCHYLUS.—*Ib.*, 1146 (*Plumptre tr.*).

The nightingale among the thick-leaved
    spring
That sits alone in sorrow, and doth sing
Whole nights away in mourning.
    FLETCHER.—*Faithful Shepherdess*, Act 5.

Sweet bird that shunn'st the noise of folly,
Most musical, most melancholy.
    MILTON.—*Il Penseroso*, b. 61.

    All but the wakeful nightingale ;
She all night long her amorous descant
    sung ;
Silence was pleased.
    MILTON.—*Paradise Lost, Bk.* 4, 602.

But she [the " mother nightingale "] sup-
    plies the night with mournful strains,
And melancholy music fills the plains.
    VIRGIL.—*Georgics, Bk.* 4, 511 (*Dryden tr.*).

NOBILITY

Nobility of birth commonly abateth industry.   BACON.—*Of Nobility.*

Nobility is a graceful ornament to the
civil order. It is the Corinthian capital of
polished society.
    BURKE.—*Reflections on French
                    Revolution.*

It becomes noblemen to do nothing well.
    CHAPMAN.—*Gentleman Usher.*

    The nose of nice nobility.
    COWPER.—*Time Piece,* 259.

Great families of yesterday we show,
And lords, whose parents were the Lord
    knows who.
DEFOE.—*True-Born Englishman, Pt.* 1, 374.

Princes and lords may flourish, or may
    fade ;
A breath can make them, as a breath has
made. GOLDSMITH.—*Deserted Village.*

Virtue is the one and only nobility.
    JUVENAL.—*Sat.* 8.

As one lamp lights another, nor grows less,
So nobleness enkindleth nobleness.
    J. R. LOWELL.—*Yussouf,* 3.

Let wealth and commerce, laws and learn-
    ing die,
But give us still our old nobility.
    LORD J. MANNERS.—*England's Trust.*

" My nobility," said Iphicrates to Har-
modius, " begins with me ; yours ends with
you."   PLUTARCH.—*Morals, Bk.* 1.

This was the noblest Roman of them all.
    SHAKESPEARE.—*Julius Cæsar*, Act 5, 5.

Howe'er it be, it seems to me
    'Tis only noble to be good.
Kind hearts are more than coronets,
    And simple faith than Norman blood.
    TENNYSON.—*Clara Vere de Vere.*

Without fear and without reproach.
Description of the Chevalier Bayard (d. 1524).

NOISE

The blast that blows loudest is soon over-
blown. SMOLLETT.— *Reprisal*, Act 2.

Music is the sound which one's own
children make as they romp through the
house. Noise is the sound which other
people's children make under the same circumstances.
    *Given as a Quotation by C. H. Spurgeon,
                    in " Salt-Cellars."*

NONAGENARIANS

Fate seemed to wind him up for fourscore
    years,
Yet freshly ran he on ten winters more :
Till, like a clock worn out with eating time,
The wheels of weary life at last stood still.
    DRYDEN.-*Œdipus*, Act 4, 1.

NONCONFORMITY

Whoso would be a man must be a
Nonconformist.
    EMERSON.—*Self-Reliance.*

When we talk of non-conformity it may
only be that we non-conform to the immediate sect of thought or action about us,
to conform to a much wider thing in human
nature.
    SIR A. HELPS.—*Friends in Council,
                    Bk.* 1, *ch.* 2.

NONENTITIES

But Tom's no more—and so no more of
    Tom.   BYRON.—*Don Juan,* 11, 20.

Some men were born for great things ;
    Some were born for small ;
Some—it is not recorded
    Why they were born at all.
    W. CARLETON.—*Uncle Sammy.*

For three-score years this life Cleora led ;
At morn she rose, at night she went to bed.
    COWPER.—*On a Worthless Old Maid.*

Lord of oneself, uncumbered with a name.
    DRYDEN.—*Ep. to John Driden,* 18.

To do nothing is the way to be nothing.
    DR. N. HOWE.—*Proverbs.*

Unwept, unnoted, and for ever dead.
    POPE.—*Odyssey, Bk.* 5, 401.

It is a terrible advantage to have done nothing at all, but it is not right to abuse such an advantage.   DE RIVAROL.

The earth's high places who attain to fill
By most indomitably sitting still.
SIR W. WATSON.—*A Political Character.*

Find in the golden mean their proper bliss,
And doing nothing, never do amiss;
But lapt in men's good graces live, and die
By all regretted, nobody knows why.
SIR W. WATSON.—*Ib.*

'Tis infamy to die and not be missed.
C. WILCOX.—*Religion of Taste.*

NONSENSE

For learned nonsense has a deeper sound
Than easy sense, and goes for more profound.
S. BUTLER.—*Upon the Abuse of Human Learning.*

For daring nonsense seldom fails to hit,
Like scattered shot, and pass with some for wit.   S. BUTLER.—*Modern Critics.*

The rest to some faint meaning make pretence,
But Shadwell never deviates into sense.
DRYDEN.—*MacFlecknoe,* 19.

And such a deal of skimble-skamble stuff
As puts me from my faith.
SHAKESPEARE.—*Henry IV., Pt.* 1, Act 3, 1.

Gratiano speaks an infinite deal of nothing, more than any man in all Venice. His reasons are as two grains of wheat, hid in two bushels of chaff. You shall seek all day ere you find them; and when you have found them, they are not worth the search.
SHAKESPEARE.—*Merchant of Venice,* Act 1, 1.

NOON

With twelve great shocks of sound, the shameless noon
Was clashed and hammered from a hundred towers.   TENNYSON.—*Godiva.*

NORTH, THE

The pale unripened beauties of the North.
ADDISON.—*Cato,* Act 1, 4.

And dark and true and tender is the North.
TENNYSON.—*Princess, c.* 4, 80.

Out of the North
All ill comes forth.
Quoted as an old English prov. in 1588.

NOSES

When I want good headwork, I always choose a man, if otherwise suitable, with a long nose.   NAPOLEON.

If Cleopatra's nose had been shorter the whole face of the world would have been changed.   PASCAL.—*Pensées, Pt.* 1, 9, 46.

And lightly was her slender nose
Tip-tilted like the petal of a flower.
TENNYSON.—*Gareth,* 577.

Folks wi' lang noses aye tak' till themselves.   *Scottish prov.*

NOTHING

From nothing nothing can proceed, and nothing can be resolved into nothing.
PERSIUS.—*Sat.* 3.

Nothing! thou elder brother even to shade.
EARL OF ROCHESTER.—*On Nothing.*

NOTORIETY

Sir, if they should cease to talk of me I must starve.   JOHNSON.—*Remark,* 1784.

There are such as fain would be the worst
Amongst all men, since best they cannot be,
So strong is that wild lie that men call pride.
W. MORRIS.—*Hill of Venus, st.* 184.

It is a fine thing to be pointed at with the finger, and to hear people saying, "That's he!"   PERSIUS.—*Sat.* 1, 28.

As industry has brought others to fame, so knavery has brought this man.
TACITUS.—*Annals, Bk.* 16, 18.

Peregrinus is content as long as people talk of Peregrinus. Jean Jacques [Rousseau] would be charmed to be hanged, provided that they put his name in the sentence.   VOLTAIRE.—*Letter to d'Alembert, Jan.* 15, 1765.

NOVELTY

To innovate is not to reform.
BURKE.—*Letter to a Noble Lord.*

There is no new thing under the sun. Perhaps that sun himself, which now beams so impressively, is only an old warmed-up jest.   HEINE.—*Confessions.*

It is the customary fate of new truths, to begin as heresies, and to end as superstitions.   T. H. HUXLEY.—*Science and Culture.*

New opinions are always suspected, and usually opposed, without any other reason but because they are not already common.
LOCKE.—*Human Understanding: Dedicatory Epistle.*

It is the nature of man to be greedy for novelty.   PLINY THE ELDER.

New faces and new ties
Wash away old memories.
D. W. THOMPSON.—*Sales Attici.*

The one thing that the public dislike is novelty.   OSCAR WILDE.—*Soul of Man under Socialism.*

> Under the sun
>   There's nothing new ;
> Poem or pun,
> Under the sun,
> Said Solomon,
>   And he said true
> Under the sun
> There's nothing new.
> ANON.—*Triolet (Love in Idleness).*

NOVEMBER

> Oh ! for a day of a burning noon,
>   And a sun like a glowing ember,
> Oh ! for one hour of golden June
> In the heart of this chill November !
> LORD ALFRED DOUGLAS.—*In Winter.*

> No warmth, no cheerfulness, no healthful
>   ease—
> No comfortable feel in any member—
> No shade, no shine, no butterflies, no bees,
> No fruits, no flowers, no leaves, no birds,
>   No-vember !
> HOOD.—*No!* (1844).

> The month was November,
> And the weather a subject for prayer.
> E. NESBIT.—*Unofficial.*

> November's sky is chill and drear,
> November's leaf is red and sear.
> SCOTT.—*Marmion, Introd.*

NUMBER

A few honest men are better than numbers.   CROMWELL.—*Letter,* 1643.

And if you want it he makes a reduction on taking a quantity.
        SIR W. S. GILBERT.—*Sorcerer.*

> As thick and numberless
> As the gay motes that people the sunbeams.
> MILTON.—*Il Penseroso.*

> Thick as autumnal leaves that strew the
>   brooks
> In Vallombrosa.
> MILTON.—*Paradise Lost, Bk.* 1, 302.

> But Hercules himself must yield to odds ;
> And many strokes, though with a little axe,
> Hew down and fell the hardest timbered
>   oak.
> SHAKESPEARE.—*Henry VI., Pt.* 3, Act 2, 1.

They say that God is always for the big battalions.   VOLTAIRE.—*Letter,* 1770.

My name is Legion : for we are many.
        St. Mark v, 9.

NUMISMATICS

To have a relish for ancient coins it is necessary to have a contempt for the modern.   ADDISON.—*Ancient Medals.*

NUNS

> Her hopes, her fears, her joys were all
> Bounded within the cloister wall.
> SCOTT.—*Marmion,* 2, 3.

O

OAK

The builder oake, sole king of forests all.
SPENSER.—*Faerie Queene, Bk.* 1, 1, 8.

OATHS

Some fresh new othe that is not stale, but will rin round in the mouth.
        R. ASCHAM.—*Scholemaster.*

Oaths are but words, and words but wind.
        BUTLER.—*Hudibras, Pt.* 2, c. 2.

You may depend upon it, the more oath-taking, the more lying generally among the people.   COLERIDGE.—*Table Talk* (1830).

> Oaths terminate, as Paul observes, all
>   strife ;
> Some men have surely then a peaceful life.
> COWPER.—*Conversation,* 55.

I'm Gormed—and I can't say no fairer than that !   DICKENS.—*David Copperfield (Mr. Peggotty), ch.* 63.

"I'll take my world-without-end ever-lasting Alfred David," answered Riderhood.
DICKENS.—*Our Mutual Friend, Bk.* 2, ch.12.

A woman's oaths are wafers, break with making.
        FLETCHER.—*Chances* (1625), Act 2, 1.

When thou dost tell another's jest, therein Omit the oaths, which true wit cannot need.
        HERBERT.—*Church Porch.*

> A good mouth-filling oath.
> SHAKESPEARE.—*Henry IV., Pt.* 1, Act 3, 1.

That in the captain 's but a choleric word, Which in the soldier is flat blasphemy.
        SHAKESPEARE.—*Measure for Measure,* Act 2, 2.

> Do not swear at all ;
> Or, if thou wilt, swear by thy gracious self,
> Which is the god of my idolatry.
> SHAKESPEARE.—*Romeo and Juliet,* Act 2, 2.

Rather too close an imitation of that language which is used in the apostolic occupation of trafficking in fish.
SYDNEY SMITH.—*Third Letter to Arch-deacon Singleton.*

OBEDIENCE

Obedience is the mother of success, the wife of safety.   ÆSCHYLUS.—*Septem Duces.*

Only obedience can be great ;
It brings the golden age again.
J. DAVIDSON.—*Ballad of a Workman.*

For who is bounden, he must bowe ;
So will I bowe unto your hest.
GOWER.—*Confessio Amantis, Bk.* 2.

OBLIVION

Therefore eternal silence be their doom !
MILTON.—*Paradise Lost, Bk.* 6, 385.

But when the prosperous hour returns,
O'er woes long wept Oblivion softly lays
Her shadowy veil.
PINDAR.—*Olympian Odes,* 2, 34
(*Moore tr.*).

You'll be forgotten, as old debts
By persons who are used to borrow.
W. M. PRAED.—*Portrait of a Lady.*

A name to be washed out with all men's
tears. SWINBURNE.—*Atalanta.*

Out of the world's way, out of the light,
Out of the ages of worldly weather,
Forgotten of all men altogether.
SWINBURNE.—*Triumph of Time.*

Oblivion, the cold shadow of dead hope.
F. TENNYSON.—*Anaktoria,* 2, 184.

One Cæsar lives : a thousand are forgot.
YOUNG.—*Night Thoughts,* 8.

OBSCURITY (OF LANGUAGE OR THOUGHT)

In the natural fog of the good man's mind.
BROWNING.—*Christmas Eve, c.* 4.

Obscurity illustrated by further obscurity. BURKE.—*Impeachment of
Hastings, May,* 1798.

Darkness is more productive of sublime
ideas than light.
BURKE.—*Vindication of Natural Society.*

What is clear is wise, but what is not
clear is not wise. EURIPIDES.—*Orestes,* 397.

Labouring to be brief, I become obscure.
HORACE.—*De Arte Poetica.*

Whoever wrote it could, if he chose,
make himself understood ; but 'tis the
letter of an embarrassed man, sir.
JOHNSON.—*Remark (to Mrs. Piozzi)
concerning a letter difficult to interpret.*

A great interpreter of life ought not himself to need interpretation.
LORD MORLEY.—*Miscellanies : Emerson.*

Where I am not understood, it shall be
concluded that something very useful and
profound is couched underneath.
SWIFT.—*Tale of a Tub, Preface.*

Abstruse questions must have abstruse
answers.
*Philosopher's reply to Alexander (according
to Plutarch).*

That must be fine, for I cannot understand a word of it.
*French prov., see Molière, " Médecin
malgré lui,"* Act 2, 5.

OBSCURITY (OF LIFE, ETC.)

While glory crowns so many a meaner crest,
What hadst thou done to sink so peace-
fully to rest ?
BYRON.—*Childe Harold, c.* 1, 91.

Ah, reader, ere you turn the page,
I leave you this for Moral,—
Remember those who tread Life's stage
With weary feet and scantest wage,
And ne'er a leaf for laurel.
AUSTIN DOBSON.—*Before the Curtain.*

But knowledge to their eyes her ample
page,
Rich with the spoils of time, did ne'er
unroll ;
Chill penury repressed their noble rage,
And froze the genial current of the soul.
GRAY.—*Elegy.*

Let not ambition mock their useful toil,
Their homely joys and destiny obscure ;
Nor grandeur hear, with a disdainful
smile,
The short and simple annals of the poor.
GRAY.—*Ib.*

Full many a gem of purest ray serene
The dark, unfathomed caves of ocean
bear ;
Full many a flower is born to blush unseen
And waste its sweetness on the desert
air. GRAY.—*Ib.*

Some village Hampden, that with dauntless breast
The little tyrant of his fields withstood ;
Some mute, inglorious Milton here may
rest,
Some Cromwell, guiltless of his country's
blood. GRAY.—*Ib.*

Deeds
Above heroic, though in secret done,
And unrecorded left in many an age.
MILTON.—*Paradise Regained, Bk.* 1, 14.

And passed content, leaving to us the
pride
Of lives obscurely great.
SIR H. NEWBOLT.—*Minora Sidera.*

Thus let me live, unseen, unknown,
Thus unlamented let me die,
Steal from the world, and not a stone
Tell where I lie.
POPE.—*Ode on Solitude.*

Men who lived and died without a name,
Are the chief heroes in the sacred list of
fame.
> SWIFT.—*To the Athenian Society.*

Others too,
There are among the walks of homely life,
Still higher, men for contemplation framed,
Shy, and unpractised in the strife of phrase,

.   .   .   .   .

Words are but under-agents in their souls.
> WORDSWORTH.—*Postscript (to Preface)*
> (1835).

God, who feeds our hearts
For his own service, knoweth, loveth us,
When we are unregarded by the world.
> WORDSWORTH.—*Ib.*

OBSERVATION

Not deep the poet sees, but wide.
> M. ARNOLD.—*Resignation.*

He learns the look of things, and none the
less
For admonition from the hunger-pinch.
> BROWNING.—*Fra Lippo Lippi.*

I'm eyes, ears, mouth of me, one gaze and
gape,
Nothing eludes me, everything's a hint,
Handle, and help.
> BROWNING.—*Mr. Sludge.*

Still he beheld, nor mingled with the throng,
But viewed them not with misanthropic
hate.
> BYRON.—*Childe Harold, c. 1, st. 84.*

He had the skill, when Cunning's gaze
would seek
To probe his heart and watch his changing
cheek,
At once the observer's purpose to espy,
And on himself roll back the scrutiny.
> BYRON.—*Corsair, c. 1, 9.*

Stolen glances, sweeter for the theft.
> BYRON.—*Don Juan, c. 1, st. 74.*

Men are born with two eyes, but with
one tongue, in order that they should see
twice as much as they say.
> C. C. COLTON.—*Lacon.*

Here the heart
May give a useful lesson to the head,
And learning wiser grow without his books.
> COWPER.—*Winter Walk at Noon, 85.*

He listens to good purpose who takes
note.
> DANTE.—*Hell, c. 15, 100*
> *(Cary tr.).*

" He's got his eyes on me ! " cried Stagg.
" I feel 'em, though I can't see 'em. Take
'em off, noble captain. Remove 'em, for
they pierce like gimlets."
> DICKENS.—*Barnaby Rudge, c. 8.*

When found, make a note of.   [*Captain
Cuttle.*]
> DICKENS.—*Dombey and Son, ch. 15.*

" Yes, I have a pair of eyes," replied
Sam, " and that's just it. If they wos a
pair of patent double million magnifyin'
gas microscopes of hextra power, p'raps
I might be able to see through a flight o'
stairs and a deal door ; but bein' only eyes,
you see, my wision's limited."
> DICKENS.—*Pickwick, c. 34.*

The difference between landscape and
landscape is small ; but there is a great
difference between the beholders.
> EMERSON.—*Nature.*

If you would learn to write, 'tis in the
street you must learn it.
> EMERSON.—*Society and Solitude.*

One man does not see everything.
> EURIPIDES.—*Phœnissæ.*

Without doubt beauty is to be found
everywhere : but it needs an artist to see
it, and to understand it.
> IBSEN.—*Love's Comedy,* Act 3 (1862).

I describe not men, but manners ; not
an individual, but a species.
> FIELDING.—*Joseph Andrews, Bk. 3, c. 1.*

Let observation, with extensive view,
Survey mankind from China to Peru.
> JOHNSON.—*Vanity of Human
> Wishes*

Some are more strongly affected by the
facts of human life ; others by the beauty
of earth and sky.
> KEBLE.—*Lectures on Poetry, No. 31
> (E. K. Francis tr.).*

His vigorous and active mind was hurled
Beyond the flaming limits of this world,
Into the mighty space, and there did see
How things begin, what can, what cannot
be.
> LUCRETIUS.—*De Rerum Natura,* 1, 73
> *(Creech tr.) (Of Epicurus).*

From such like thoughts I mighty pleasure
find,
And silently admire thy strength of mind,
By whose one single force, to curious eyes,
All naked and exposed whole Nature lies.
> LUCRETIUS.—*Ib., 3, 28.*

He who has looked upon earth
Deeper than flower and fruit,
Losing some hue of his mirth,
As the tree striking rock at the root.
> GEO. MEREDITH.—*Day of the Daughter of
> Hades.*

For him there's a story in every breeze,
And a picture in every wave.
> MOORE.—*Boat Glee (from " M.P. ; or the
> Blue-Stocking ").*

And yet the fate of all extremes is such,
Men may be read, as well as books, too
much. POPE.—*Moral Essays, Ep.* 1, 9.

For he is but a bastard to the time,
That doth not smack of observation.
SHAKESPEARE.—*K. John,* Act 1, 1.

The harvest of a quiet eye
That broods and sleeps on his own heart.
WORDSWORTH.—*A Poet's Epitaph.*

Vain is the glory of the sky,
The beauty vain of field and grove,
Unless, while with admiring eye
We gaze, we also learn to love.
WORDSWORTH.—*Poems of the Fancy,*
No. 20.

O let me gaze! Of gazing there's no end.
YOUNG.—*Night Thoughts,* 9.

Seeing many things, but thou observest
not. *Isaiah* xlii, 20.

Where I look I like, and where I like I
love.
Saying quoted by R. BURTON, *Anat. Melan.*

OBSESSION

Mr. Dick had been for upwards of ten
years endeavouring to keep King Charles
the First out of the Memorial; but he had
been constantly getting into it, and was
there now. DICKENS.—*Copperfield, ch.* 15.

His name in my ear was ever ringing;
His form to my brain was ever clinging.
SHELLEY.—*Rosalind.*

OBSTINACY

The man who never alters his opinion
is like standing water, and breeds reptiles
of the mind.
W. BLAKE.—*Marriage of Heaven and Hell.*

And obstinacy's ne'er so stiff
As when 'tis in a wrong belief.
BUTLER.—*Hudibras, Pt.* 3, *c.* 2.

Wilful will do't, that's the word.
CONGREVE.—*Way of the World,* Act 4, 2
(*Sir Wilfull Witwould*).

Where Obstinacy takes his sturdy stand
To disconcert what Policy has planned.
COWPER.—*Expostulation,* 298.

The gods that unrelenting breast have
steeled
And cursed thee with a mind that cannot
yield. POPE.—*Iliad, Bk.* 9, 749.

As headstrong as an allegory on the
banks of the Nile.
SHERIDAN.—*Rivals,* Act 5, 3 (*Mrs.*
Malaprop).

There is nothing gained by arguing with
an enthusiast. It is no good trying to tell
a man the faults of his mistress, or to convince a litigant of the weakness of his case,
or to give reasons to a devotee.
VOLTAIRE.—*Letters on the English.*

The crest of the southern English is a
hog, and their motto is "We won't be
druv." *Saying (quoted by* C. H. SPURGEON).

OBVIOUS, THE

What need of books these truths to tell,
Which folks perceive who cannot spell?
And must we spectacles apply,
To view what hurts our naked eye?
PRIOR.—*Alma, c.* 3, 590.

There needs no ghost, my lord, come from
the grave
To tell us this.
SHAKESPEARE.—*Hamlet,* Act 1, 5.

An obvious case carries its own decision.
PUBLILIUS SYRUS.

OCCUPATIONS

I hold every man a debtor to his profession.
BACON.—*Elements of Common Law.*

Business whets the appetite and gives
a taste to pleasures, as exercise does to
food.
LORD CHESTERFIELD.—*Advice to his Son.*

For this of old is sure,
That change of toil is toil's sufficient cure.
SIR L. MORRIS.—*Love in Death.*

Hath this fellow no feeling of his business?
SHAKESPEARE.—*Hamlet,* Act 5, 1.

Farewell! Othello's occupation's gone!
SHAKESPEARE.—*Othello,* Act 3, 3.

A man who has no office to go to—I
don't care who he is—is a trial of which
you can have no conception.
G. B. SHAW.—*Irrational Knot, ch.* 18.

Did I not give you ten, then fifteen, now
twenty shillings a week to be sorrowful?
And the more I give you, I think the
gladder you are.
STEELE.—*Funeral,* Act 1, *sc.* 1 [*Sable,*
the undertaker, to his man].

There is no need for a sculptor to be himself made of marble. *French saying.*

OCTOBER

Hail, old October, bright and chill,
First freedman from the summer sun!
Spice high the bowl and drink your fill!
Thank heaven, at last the summer's done!
REV. THOS. CONSTABLE.—*Old October.*

Then came October, full of merry glee,
For yet his noule was totty of the must.
[his head was unsteady from the wine-
juice.]
SPENSER.—*Of Mutabilitie, c. 7,* 39 (*October was anciently called " Wine-month"*).

ODD NUMBERS

They say there is divinity in odd numbers, either in nativity, chance, or death.
SHAKESPEARE.—*Merry Wives,* Act 5, 1.

Unequal numbers please the gods.
VIRGIL.—*Pastoral* 8 (*Dryden tr.*).

ODOURS

Virtue is like precious odours, most fragrant when they are incensed and crushed.
BACON.—*Of Adversity.*

Sabean odours from the spicy shore
Of Araby the blest.
MILTON.—*Paradise Lost, Bk.* 4, 162.

The good are better made by ill,
As odours crushed are sweeter still.
ROGERS.—*Jacqueline, Pt.* 3.

OFFENCES

O! my offence is rank, it smells to heaven.
SHAKESPEARE.—*Hamlet,* Act 3, 3.

And where the offence is let the great axe
fall. SHAKESPEARE.—*Ib.,* Act 4, 5.

Raise no more spirits than you are able
to lay. *Prov.* (*Ray.*)

OFFICE (PUBLIC)

O Athenians, what toil do I undergo to
please you !
ALEXANDER THE GREAT.—(*Quoted by
Carlyle.*)

Men in great place are thrice servants.
BACON.—*Of Great Place.*

All countries are a wise man's home,
And so are governments to some.
BUTLER.—*Hudibras, Pt.* 3, *c.* 2.

Upon my soul, you mustn't come into
this place saying you want to know, you
know.
DICKENS.—*Little Dorrit, Pt.* 1, *ch.* 10.

Taper and Tadpole were great friends.
Neither of them ever despaired of the
Commonwealth.
DISRAELI.—*Coningsby, Bk.* 1, *ch* 1.

Stick close to your desks, and never go to
sea,
And you all may be rulers of the Queen's
Navee.
SIR W. S. GILBERT.—*H.M.S. Pinafore.*

Great positions render great men still
greater ; small positions make little men
smaller. LA BRUYÈRE.—*De l'Homme,* 95.

The proverb says true : " Leave the court
and the court will leave you." So is it
with me.
MALORY.— *Morte d'Arthur (Sir Gawain to
Merlin).*

The insolence of office, and the spurns
Which patient merit of the unworthy
takes.
SHAKESPEARE.—*Hamlet,* Act 3, 1.

But man, proud man !
Drest in a little brief authority,
Most ignorant of what he's most assured,—
His glassy essence,—like an angry ape,
Plays such fantastic tricks before high
heaven
As make the angels weep.
SHAKESPEARE.—*Measure for Measure,*
Act 2, 2.

We shall generally find that the triangular person has got into the square hole,
the oblong into the triangular, and a square
person has squeezed himself into the round
hole. SYDNEY SMITH.—*Lectures on
Moral Philosophy, No.* 9.

OFFICIOUSNESS

O fate of fools ! officious in contriving ;
In executing puzzled, lame and lost.
CONGREVE.—*Mourning Bride,* Act 5, 1.

Who can tell the mischief which the
very virtuous do ?
THACKERAY.—*Newcomes, Bk.* 1, *ch.* 20.

OLD ACQUAINTANCE

Should auld acquaintance be forgot,
And never brought to min' ?
Should auld acquaintance be forgot,
And auld lang syne ?
BURNS.—*Song (founded on older songs).*

Old wood, old friends, and old wine are
best. *Prov.*

Old loves and old brands rekindle suddenly at any moment. *French prov.*

OLD AGE

Old age is charming, but what a misfortune that it lasts so short a time !
EMILE AUGIER.

Men of age object too much, consult too
long, adventure too little, repent too soon.
BACON.—*Essays, Youth and Age.*

John Anderson, my jo, John,
We clamb the hill thegither,
And mony a canty day, John,
We've had wi' one anither ;

Now we maun totter down, John,
  But hand in hand we'll go,
And sleep thegither at the foot,
  John Anderson, my jo.
    BURNS.—*John Anderson.*

I've seen sae mony changefu' years,
  On earth I am a stranger grown ;
I wander in the ways of men,
  Alike unknowing and unknown.
    BURNS.—*Lament for James, Earl of
        Glencairn.*

'Tis the defect of age to rail at the
pleasures of youth.
    MRS. CENTLIVRE.—*Basset Table*, Act I.

As sooth is sayd, elde hath great avantage ;
In elde is bothe wisdom and usage [experience] ;
Men may the olde at-renne [out-run], and
  noght at-rede [surpass in counsel].
    CHAUCER.—*Knight's Tale, l.* 1589.

Yet in our asshen olde is fyr y-reke.
    CHAUCER.—*Reeve's Prologue*, 28.

No one is so old that he does not think
he has a year to live.
    CICERO.—*De Senectute*, 7.

I am very thankful to old age, which has
increased my eager desire for information.
    CICERO.—*Ib.*, 14.

But age is froward, uneasy, scrutinous,
Hard to be pleased, and parsimonious.
    SIR J. DENHAM.—*Old Age, Pt.* 3.

These are the effects of doting age,
Vain doubts and idle cares and over-
  caution.   DRYDEN.—*Sebastian.*

Few envy the consideration enjoyed by
the oldest inhabitant.
    EMERSON.—*Old Age.*

The creed of the street is, Old age is
not disgraceful, but immensely disadvan-
tageous.   EMERSON.—*Ib.*

It is time to be old,
  To take in sail.
    EMERSON.—*Terminus.*

His head was silvered o'er with age,
And long experience made him sage.
    GAY.—*Fables : Introduction.*

There is beauty in extreme old age :
Do you fancy you are elderly enough ?
    SIR W. S. GILBERT.—*Mikado.*

As newer comers crowd the fore,
  We drop behind,—
We who have laboured long and sore
  Times out of mind,
And keen are yet, must not regret
  To drop behind.
    THOS. HARDY.—*Superseded.*

W'en folks get old en stricken wid the
palsy, dey mus 'speck ter be laff'd at.
Goodness knows I bin used ter dat sence
de day my whiskers 'gun to bleach.
    J. C. HARRIS.—*Nights with Uncle Remus,
        ch.* 23.

And a crook is in his back,
  And a melancholy crack
    In his laugh.
    O. W. HOLMES.—*Last Leaf.*

Call him not old whose visionary brain
Holds o'er the past its undivided reign :
For him in vain the envious seasons roll,
Who bears eternal summer in his soul.
    O. W. HOLMES.—*Old Player.*

When he is forsaken,
  Withered and shaken,
What can an old man do but die ?
    HOOD.—*Ballad.*

Superfluous lags the veteran on the stage.
    JOHNSON.—*Vanity of Human Wishes.*

Life protracted is protracted woe.
Time hovers o'er, impatient to destroy,
And shuts up all the passages of joy.
    JOHNSON.—*Ib.*

On parent knees, a naked new-born child,
Weeping, thou sat'st whilst all around thee
  smiled ;
So live, that, sinking in thy last long sleep,
Calm thou mayst smile, while all around
  thee weep.
    SIR W. JONES.—*From the Persian.*

When our vices leave us, we flatter ourselves with the idea that we are leaving
them. LA ROCHEFOUCAULD.—*Maxim* 192.

Few people know how to be old.
    LA ROCHEFOUCAULD.—*Maxim* 423.

For you the To-come,
  But for me the Gone-by ;
You are panting to live,
  I am waiting to die.
    R. LE GALLIENNE.—*An Old Man's Song.*

Time hath laid his hand
Upon my heart, gently, not smiting it,
But as a harper lays his open palm
Upon his harp, to deaden its vibrations.
    LONGFELLOW.—*Golden Legend.*

So mayst thou live, till, like ripe fruit, thou
  drop
Into thy mother's lap, or be with ease
Gathered, not harshly plucked, for death
  mature.
This is old age.
    MILTON.—*Paradise Lost, Bk.* II, 535.

Old age plants more wrinkles in the
mind than in the face.   MONTAIGNE.

His golden locks time hath to silver
  turned ;
O time too swift ! O swiftness never
  ceasing ! G. PEELE.—*Polyhymnia.*

A man not old, but mellow, like good wine.
STEPHEN PHILLIPS.—*Ulysses,* Act 3.

The tree of deepest root is found
Least willing still to quit the ground ;
'Twas therefore said by ancient sages
That love of life increased with years.
MRS. PIOZZI.—*Three Warnings.*

In life's cool evening, satiate of applause.
POPE.—*Ep. of Horace, Ep.* 1, *l.* 9.

Old men for the most part are like old
chronicles, that give you dull but true
accounts of time past, and are worth knowing only on that score.
POPE.—*Thoughts on Various Subjects.*

When men grow virtuous in their old age
they only make a sacrifice to God of the
devil's leavings. POPE.—*Ib.*

Age sits with decent grace upon his visage,
And worthily becomes his silver locks ;
He wears the marks of many years well
  spent,
Of virtue, truth well tried, and wise ex-
  perience.   ROWE.—*Jane Shore.*

His withered fist still knocking at death's
  door.
T. SACKVILLE (LORD DORSET).—*Mirrour
              for Magistrates.*

Doubts, horrors, superstitious fears
Saddened and dimmed descending years.
SCOTT.—*Rokeby,* 1, 17.

Let me not live, quoth he,
After my flame lacks oil, to be the snuff
Of younger spirits.
SHAKESPEARE.—*All's Well,* Act 1, 2.

The satirical rogue says here, that old
men have grey beards ; that their faces are
wrinkled ; their eyes purging thick amber
and plum-tree gum ; and that they have a
plentiful lack of wit, together with most
weak hams.
SHAKESPEARE.—*Hamlet,* Act 2, 2.

You yourself, sir, should be as old as I
am, if, like a crab, you could go backward.
SHAKESPEARE.—*Ib.*

How subject we old men are to this
vice of lying !
SHAKESPEARE.—*Henry IV.,* Act 3, 2.

How ill white hairs become a fool and
jester. SHAKESPEARE.—*Ib.,* Act 5, 3.

An old man, broken with the storms of
state,
Is come to lay his weary bones among'ye.
Give him a little earth for charity.
SHAKESPEARE.—*Henry VIII.,* Act 4, 2.

O, sir, you are old !
Nature in you stands on the very verge
Of her confine.
SHAKESPEARE.—*Lear,* Act 2, 4.

I confess that I am old ;
Age is unnecessary.   SHAKESPEARE.—*Ib.*

A poor, infirm, weak and despised old man.
SHAKESPEARE.—*Ib.,* Act 3, 2.

I am a very foolish, fond old man.
SHAKESPEARE.—*Ib.,* Act 4, 7.

Vex not his ghost ! Oh, let him pass ! He
  hates him,
That would upon the rack of this tough
  world
Stretch him out longer.
SHAKESPEARE.—*Ib.,* Act 5, 3.

The wine of life is drawn, and the mere lees
Is left this vault to brag of.
SHAKESPEARE.—*Macbeth,* Act 2, 3.

I have lived long enough, my way of life
Is fall'n into the sear, the yellow leaf ;
And that which should accompany old age,
As honour, love, obedience, troops of
  friends,
I must not look to have.
SHAKESPEARE.—*Ib.,* Act 5, 3.

I am declined :
Into the vale of years.
SHAKESPEARE.—*Othello,* Act 3, 3.

To me, fair friend, you never can be old,
For as you were when first your eye I eyed,
Such seems your beauty still.
SHAKESPEARE.—*Sonnet* 104.

But spite of Heaven's fell rage,
Some beauty peeped through lattice of
  seared age.   SHAKESPEARE (?).—
              Lover's Complaint, st. 2.

Old men are testy, and will have their
  way.   SHELLEY.—*Cenci,* Act 1, 2.

You are old, Father William, the young
  man cried,
And pleasures with youth pass away ;
And yet you lament not the days that are
  gone :
Now tell me the reason I pray.
SOUTHEY.—*Old Man's Comforts.*

O ! why do wretched men so much desire
To draw their dayes unto the utmost date ?
SPENSER.—*Faerie Queene, Bk.* 4, *c.* 3, 1.

Age may have one side, but assuredly
Youth has the other. There is nothing
more certain than that both are right,
except perhaps that both are wrong.
R. L. STEVENSON.—*Crabbed Age.*

When an old gentleman waggles his head and says : " Ah, so I thought when I was your age," it is not thought an answer at all, if the young man retorts : " My venerable sir, so I shall most probably think when I am yours." And yet the one is as good as the other.   R. L. STEVENSON.—
Crabbed Age.

Let life burn down, and dream it is not death. SWINBURNE.—*Anactoria.*

Ah ! there's no fool like the old one.
  TENNYSON.—*The Grandmother.*

O good grey head which all men knew.
  TENNYSON.—*On Wellington.*

For Age, with stealing steps,
 Hath clawed me with his crutch.
 THOS. LORD VAUX.—*Aged Lover.*

Old age is reputed to be incorrigible ; for myself, I believe one ought to think of correcting one's errors even when a hundred years old.
 VOLTAIRE.—*Irène (Pref. Letter,* 1778).

The soul's dark cottage, battered and decayed,
Lets in new light through chinks that time has made ;
Stronger by weakness, wiser men become
As they draw near to their eternal home.
 WALLER.—*On the " Divine Poems."*

How strange it seems, with so much gone
Of life and love, to still live on !
  WHITTIER.—*Snowbound.*

Thus fares it still in our decay,
And yet the wiser mind
Mourns less for what age takes away
Than what it leaves behind.
 WORDSWORTH.—*The Fountain* (1799).

The Clouds that gather round the setting sun
Do take a sober colouring from an eye
That hath kept watch o'er man's mortality.
 WORDSWORTH.—*Intimations of Immortality, c.* 11.

The oldest man he seemed that ever wore grey hairs.
 WORDSWORTH.—*Resolution and Independence.*

But an old age, serene and bright,
And lovely as a Lapland night,
Shall lead thee to thy grave.
 WORDSWORTH.—*To a Young Lady.*

We see Time's furrows on another's brow,
And Death entrenched, preparing his assault.
How few themselves in that just mirror see ! YOUNG.—*Night Thoughts,* 5.

And gently slope our passage to the grave.   YOUNG.—*Ib.*

The man of wisdom is the man of years.
   YOUNG.—*Ib.*

With the ancient is wisdom ; and in length of days understanding. *Job* xii, 12.

Crabbed age and youth
 Cannot live together.
ANON.—*Song in " Passionate Pilgrim "*
   (*pub.* 1599).

Fear old age, for it does not come alone.
   Greek prov.

No Greek was ever an old man.
Greek prov. (implying that the ancient Greeks remained children all their lives).

I'm ower auld a dog to learn new tricks.
   Scottish prov.

Little may an old horse do if he mauna nicher (neigh). *Scottish prov.*

The feet are slow when the head wears snow.   *Prov.*

OLD FASHIONS

I know it is a sin
 For me to sit and grin
  At him here ;
But the old three-cornered hat,
And the breeches and all that,
  Are so queer !
  O. W. HOLMES.—*Last Leaf.*

O good old man, how well in thee appears
The constant service of the antique world,
When service sweat for duty, not for need !
SHAKESPEARE.—*As You Like It,* Act 2, 3.

Thou art not for the fashion of these times,
Where none will sweat but for promotion,
And having that, do choke their service up.
  SHAKESPEARE.—*Ib.*

OMENS

" A jolly place," said he, " in times of old,
But something ails it now ; the spot is cursed."
  WORDSWORTH.—*Heart-leap Well.*

A House,—but under some prodigious ban
Of excommunication.
 HOOD.—*The Haunted House.*

OMISSION

Poets lose half the praise they should have got,
Could it be known what they discreetly blot.
 WALLER.—*On Roscommon's " Horace."*

ONIONS

Let onion atoms lurk within the bowl,
And, half-suspected, animate the whole.
 SYDNEY SMITH.—*Recipe for Salad Dressing.*

For this is every cook's opinion,
No savoury dish without an onion ;
But lest your kissing should be spoiled,
Your onions must be thoroughly boiled.
                              SWIFT.—*Onions.*

ONLOOKERS

As many more
Crowd round the door,
To see them going to see it.
                      HOOD.—*Miss Kilmansegg.*

The little pleasure of the game
Is from afar to view the flight.
                      PRIOR.—*To C. Montague.*

OPEN-MINDEDNESS

A person who derives all his instruction
from teachers or books ... is under no
compulsion to hear both sides. Accordingly it is far from a frequent accomplishment, even among thinkers, to know both
sides.   J. S. MILL.—*Liberty, ch. 2.*

He who knows only his own side of the
case knows little of that.
                              J. S. MILL.—*Ib.*

One man's speech
Is no man's speech ;
Let a man give ear to each.
                              German saying.

OPINION

Remember that **all things are** only
opinion and that it is in your power to
think as you please.
          MARCUS AURELIUS.—*Bk. 12, 22.*

The absurd man is he who never changes
his opinions.   BARTHÉLEMY.

An illogical opinion only requires rope
enough to hang itself.
                      A. BIRRELL.—*Via Media.*

Who doth not know with what fierce rage
Opinions, true or false, engage ?
          S. BUTLER.—*Miscellaneous Thoughts.*

And nothing's so perverse in nature
As a profound opiniator.
                      S. BUTLER.—*Ib.*

It is opinion governs all mankind,—
As wisely as the blind that leads the blind.
          S. BUTLER.—*Upon the Abuse of Human
                      Learning, Pt. 2 (Fragment).*

We are more inclined to hate one another
for points on which we differ, than to love
one another on points on which we agree.
                      C. C. COLTON.—*Lacon.*

His sole opinion, whatsoe'er befall,
Centering at last in having none at all.
          COWPER.—*Conversation,* 133.

Mr. Podsnap settled that whatever he put
behind him he put out of existence. . . .
He had even acquired a peculiar flourish
of his right arm in often clearing the world

of its most difficult problems, by sweeping
them behind him.
          DICKENS.—*Our Mutual Friend, Bk.* 1,
                              ch. 11.

Stiff in opinions, always in the wrong,
Was everything by starts and nothing long.
          DRYDEN.—*Absalom and Achitophel,
                      Pt.* 1, 545.

As long as words a different sense will bear,
And each may be his own interpreter,
Our airy faith will no foundation find ;
The word's a weathercock for every wind.
          DRYDEN.—*Hind and Panther,* 462.

A heap er sayins en a heap er doins in
dis roun' worl' got to be tuck on trus'. You
got yo' sayins, en I got mine.
          J. C. HARRIS.—*Nights with Uncle Remus,
                              ch.* 42.

We are all of us more or less the slaves
of opinion.   HAZLITT.—*Court Influence.*

Men fear public opinion now as they did
in former times the Star Chamber : and
those awful goddesses, Appearances, are
to us what the Fates were to the Greeks.
          SIR A. HELPS.—*Friends in Council, Bk.* 1,
                              ch. 5.

Opinions are a great care and a great
trouble ; but still they are acquisitions.
          SIR A. HELPS.—*Ib., Bk.* 2, *ch.* 2.

Opinion is that high and mighty Dame
Which rules the world.
J. HOWELL.—*Before " The Vocal Forest."*

Opinions are like fashions, beautiful
when we first assume them—ugly when we
discard them.
          THEODORE JOUFFROY (1796–1842).

We scarcely ever find any people of good
sense, excepting those who are of our own
opinion.
          LA ROCHEFOUCAULD.—*Maxim* 347.

Men are never so good or so bad as their
opinions.
          SIR J. MACKINTOSH.—*Ethical Philosophy.*

Sir, though I would persuade, I'll not con-
strain :
Each man's opinion freely is his own
Concerning anything, or anybody.
          MASSINGER.—*Fatal Dowry,* Act 2, 2.

We can never be sure that the opinion
we are endeavouring to stifle is a false
opinion ; and if we were sure, stifling
would be an evil still.
          J. S. MILL.—*Liberty, ch.* 2.

Opinion in good men is but knowledge
in the making.   MILTON.—*Areopagitica.*

My opinion, my conviction, gains infinitely in strength and success, the
moment a second mind has adopted it.
          NOVALIS (*as tr. by Carlyle*).

349

He who does not know the truth, but hunts after opinions, will, as it appears, produce but a ridiculous and inartistic art of speaking.
PLATO.—*Phædrus*, 99 (*Cary tr.*).

'Tis with our judgments, as our watches, none
Go just alike, yet each believes his own.
POPE.—*Criticism*, 6.

Some praise at morning what they blame at night,
But always think the last opinion right.
POPE.—*Ib.*, 431.

Whenever opposite views are held with warmth by religious-minded men, we may take it for granted there is some higher truth which embraces both. All high truth is the union of contradictions.
F. W. ROBERTSON.

Opinion obeys the same law as the pendulum. If it goes beyond the centre of gravity on one side, it must go as far beyond on the other. It is only after a time that it finds its true resting-place and becomes settled.
SCHOPENHAUER.—*Psychological Observations.*

Human nature causes us to be dependent on other people's opinion in a way completely out of proportion to its value.
SCHOPENHAUER.—*On Women.*

Hear you this Triton of the minnows? mark you
His absolute *shall?*
SHAKESPEARE.—*Coriolanus*, Act 3, 1.

Hath there been such a time, I'd fain know that,
When I have positively said, " 'Tis so,"
And it proved otherwise?
SHAKESPEARE.—*Hamlet*, Act 2, 2.

There is nothing either good or bad, but thinking makes it so.
SHAKESPEARE.—*Ib.*, Act 2, 2.

His own opinion was his law.
SHAKESPEARE.—*Henry VIII.*, Act 4, 2.

I have bought
Golden opinions from all sorts of people.
SHAKESPEARE.—*Macbeth*, Act 1, 7.

A plague of opinion ! A man may wear it on both sides like a leather jerkin.
SHAKESPEARE.—*Troilus*, Act 3, 3.

Opinion is ultimately determined by the feelings, and not by the intellect.
H. SPENCER.—*Social Statics*, Pt. 3, sec. 8.

In war, opinion is nine parts in ten.
SWIFT.—*Letter*, 1711.

But foolish man still judges what is best
In his own balance, false and light,
Following opinion, dark and blind,
That vagrant leader of the mind,
Till honesty and conscience are clear out of sight.
SWIFT.—*Ode to Sancroft.*

So many men, so many opinions.
TERENCE.—*Phormio*, 2.

" So many heads, so many opinions "—fie !
Is't not a shame for Proverbs thus to lie
I've known, though my acquaintance be but small,
Heads which have no opinion at all.
Epigram. Founded on lines in Camden's " Remains " (1657).

OPPORTUNISM

" It's always best on these occasions to do what the mob do."—" But suppose there are two mobs ? " suggested Mr. Snodgrass.—" Shout with the largest," replied Mr. Pickwick.
DICKENS.—*Pickwick Papers.*

Let fools the name of loyalty divide !
Wise men and gods are on the strongest side. SIR C. SEDLEY.—*Marc Antony.*

An thou canst not smile as the wind sits, thou'lt catch cold shortly.
SHAKESPEARE.—*Lear*, Act 1, 4.

There is a right way and a wrong ;
You cannot travel both along.
Choose this or that without delay,
But don't pretend a middle way.
C. H. SPURGEON.—" *Salt-Cellars.*"

OPPORTUNITY

Give me a standing place, and I will move the earth. ARCHIMEDES (*traditional*).

Time, so complained of,
Who to one man
Shows partiality,
Brings round to all men
Some undimmed hours.
M. ARNOLD.—*Consolation.*

A wise man will make more opportunities than he finds.
BACON.—*Of Ceremonies.*

'Tis clear if we refuse
The means so limited, the tools so rude
To execute our purpose, life will fleet,
And we shall fade, and nothing will be done;
BROWNING.—*Paracelsus.*

Youth, once gone, is gone :
Deeds, let escape, are never to be done.
BROWNING.—*Sordello*, Bk. 3.

Any nose
May ravage with impunity a rose.
BROWNING.—*Ib.*, Bk. 6

Never had mortal man such opportunity,
Except Napoleon, or abused it more.
      BYRON.—*Don Juan, c. 9, 9.*

We must beat the iron while it is hot ;
but we may polish it at leisure.
      DRYDEN. —*Dedication of Æneid.*

Thou strong seducer, opportunity !
      DRYDEN.—*Conquest of Granada, Pt. 2,*
      Act 4, 3.

Use May, while that you may,
  For May hath but his time ;
When all the fruit is gone, it is
  Too late the tree to climb.
      R. EDWARDS.—*May.*

There is an hour in each man's life ap-
    pointed
To make his happiness, if then he seize it.
      FLETCHER AND MASSINGER.—*Custom of*
      the Country, Act 2, 1.

    Her case may any day
      Be yours, my dear, or mine.
    Let her make her hay
      While the sun doth shine.
SIR W. S. GILBERT.—*Pirates of Penzance.*

Give ample room and verge enough.
      GRAY.—*Bard.*

Here is the sum,—that when one door
opens, another shuts.
      HAFIZ.—*As given by Emerson, Essay on*
      Persian Poetry.

Gather ye rosebuds while ye may,
  Old Time is still a-flying ;
And this same flower, that smiles to-day,
  To-morrow will be dying.
      HERRICK.—*To the Virgins.*

The man who loses his opportunity,
loses himself.
      G. MOORE.—*Bending of the Bough, Act 5.*

Every French soldier carries in his knap-
sack the baton of a French field-marshal.
      NAPOLEON.—*Saying.*

Jupiter himself cannot bring back lost
opportunity.   PHÆDRUS.—*Bk. 5.*

Know the proper season.
      PITTACUS OF MITYLENE (*c.* B.C. 550).

Oh how bitter a thing it is to look into
happiness through another man's eyes !
      SHAKESPEARE.—*As You Like It, Act 5, 2.*

For courage mounteth with occasion.
      SHAKESPEARE.—*King John, Act 2, 1.*

How oft the sight of means to do ill deeds
Makes ill deeds done !
      SHAKESPEARE.—*Ib., Act 4, 2.*

There is a tide in the affairs of men,
  Which, taken at the flood, leads on to
  fortune ;

Omitted, all the voyage of their life
Is bound in shallows and in miseries.
      SHAKESPEARE.—*Julius Cæsar, Act 4, 3.*

O Opportunity, thy guilt is great !
'Tis thou that execut'st the traitor's
  treason.
      SHAKESPEARE.—*Lucrece, 126.*

Turning, for them who pass, the common
    dust
Of servile opportunity to gold.
      WORDSWORTH.—*Desultory Stanzas.*

I do but wait a time and fortune's chance ;
Oft many things do happen in one houre.
      SIR T. WYATT.—(*Tottel,* 1557.)

Let us crown ourselves with rosebuds,
before they be withered.
      Wisdom of Solomon ii, 8.

Be in time at the hedge if you would dry
your linen.   *Prov. quoted by Goethe.*

The open door tempts a saint.
      Spanish prov.

OPPOSITION

Without contraries is no progression.
      WM. BLAKE.—*Book of Thel.*

No Government can be long secure without a formidable Opposition.
      DISRAELI.—*Coningsby, Bk. 2, c. 1.*

Dame Partington, who lived upon the
beach, was seen at the door of her house,
with mop and pattens, trundling her mop,
squeezing out the sea water, and vigor-
ously pushing away the Atlantic Ocean.
The Atlantic was aroused. Mrs. Partington's spirit was up ; but I need not tell
you that the contest was unequal. The
Atlantic Ocean beat Mrs. Partington.
She was excellent at a slop or a puddle,
but she should not have meddled with
a tempest.
      SYDNEY SMITH.—*Speech at Taunton,*1831.

When I first came into Parliament, Mr.
Tierney, a great Whig authority, used
always to say that the duty of an Opposition was very simple—it was to oppose
everything and propose nothing.
      LORD STANLEY.—*Speech, June 4,* 1841.

The tiny-trumpeting gnat can break our
    dream
When sweetest ; and the vermin voices
    here
May buzz so loud—we scorn them, but
    they sting.
      TENNYSON.—*Lancelot and Elaine,* 137.

OPPRESSION

Oppression makes the wise man mad.
      BROWNING.—*Luria, Act 4.*

All oppressors . . . attribute the frustration of their desires to the want of sufficient rigour. Then they redouble the efforts of their impotent cruelty.
BURKE.—*Impeachment of Hastings.*

Hope, for a season, bade the world farewell,
And freedom shrieked—as Kosciusko fell.
CAMPBELL.—*Pleasures of Hope.*

3rd Fisher. Master, I marvel how the fishes live in the sea.—*1st Fisher.* Why, as men do a-land—the great ones eat up the little ones.
SHAKESPEARE.—*Pericles*, Act 2, 1.

It is the duty of a good shepherd to shear the sheep, not to flay them.
SUETONIUS.—*Given as a saying of Tiberius Cæsar.*

Mastiffs on whom their master has placed collars of iron can strangle dogs who have none.
VOLTAIRE.—*Historical Fragments on India, etc.*

My little finger shall be thicker than my father's loins.
1 *Kings* xii, 10. (*Also* 2 *Chron.* x, 10.)

My father hath chastised you with whips, but I will chastise you with scorpions.
1 *Kings* xii, 11. (*Also* 2 *Chron.* x, 14.)

And he looked for judgment, but behold oppression ; for righteousness, but behold a cry.   *Isaiah* v, 7.

Then has not the gude cause to grumble
That's forst to be a slave ?
Oppression does the judgment jumble,
And gars a wise man rave.
May chains then and pains then
Infernal be thair hyre,
Wha dang us and flang us,
Into this ugsum myre !
ANON.—*The Vision* (c. 1715 ?—*printed* 1783).

OPTIMISM

The barren optimistic sophistries
Of comfortable moles.
M. ARNOLD.—*To a Republican Friend.*

I find earth not grey but rosy,
Heaven not grim, but fair of hue.
BROWNING.—*At the Mermaid.*

O world as God has made it ! All is beauty.
BROWNING.—*Guardian Angel.*

God's in His heaven—
All's right with the world !
BROWNING.—*Pippa Passes.*

Seeing only what is fair,
Sipping only what is sweet,
Thou dost mock at fate and care.
EMERSON.—*To the Humble Bee.*

For some there are who say the ills which wait
On man exceed his joys ; but I maintain
The contrary opinion, that our lives
More bliss than woe experience.
EURIPIDES.—*Suppliants*, 198 (*Woodhull tr.*).

And I am right,
And you are right,
And all is right as right can be.
SIR W. S. GILBERT.—*Mikado*, Act 1.

By happy alchymy of mind
They turn to pleasure all they find.
MATTHEW GREEN.—*Spleen.* 630.

'Tis always morning somewhere, and above
The awakening continents, from shore to shore,
Somewhere the birds are singing evermore.
LONGFELLOW.—*Birds of Killingworth.*

Youth goes ; childhood need never be lost.   EDITH SICHEL.—*Thoughts.*

The world is a looking-glass, and gives back to every man the reflection of his own face. Frown at it and it will in turn look sourly upon you ; laugh at it and with it, and it is a jolly kind companion.
THACKERAY.—*Vanity Fair* (1847).

Heed not the folk who sing or say
In sonnet sad or sermon chill,
" Alas, alack, and well-a-day !
This round world's but a bitter pill."
We too are sad and careful ; still
We'd rather be alive than not.
GRAHAM R. TOMSON.—*Ballade of the Optimist.*

" What is optimism ? " said Cacambo. " Alas," said Candide, " it is the passion for saying that everything is well when it is evil."   VOLTAIRE.—*Candide.*

Age brought him no despairing
Of the world's future faring ;
In human nature still
He found more good than ill.
WHITTIER.—*An Autograph.*

Love lights more fire than hate extinguishes,
And men grow better as the world grows old.   ELLA W. WILCOX.—*Optimism.*

ORACLES

The oracles are dumb.
MILTON.—*Christmas Hymn.*

There is no truth at all i' the oracle.
SHAKESPEARE.—*Winter's Tale*, Act 3, 2.

ORATORY

Their discourses are as the stars, which give little light because they are so high.
BACON.—*Adv. of Learning.*

The clear harangue, and cold as it is clear,
Falls soporific on the listless ear.
        COWPER.—*Progress of Error*, 19.

The Chadband style of oratory is widely
received and much admired.
        DICKENS.—*Bleak House, ch.* 19.

A man may speak very well in the house
of Commons, and fail very completely in
the House of Lords. There are two distinct styles requisite ; I intend in the
course of my career, if I have time, to give
a specimen of both.
        DISRAELI.—*Young Duke, Bk.* **5, c. 7.**

I will sit down now, but the time will
come when you will hear me.
        DISRAELI.—*Maiden Speech in House of
Commons*, 1837.

The orator must be, to a certain extent,
a poet.   EMERSON.—*Eloquence.*

The finest eloquence is that which gets
things done ; the worst is that which
delays them.
D. LLOYD GEORGE.—*Conference of Paris,
Jan.*, 1919.

Sheridan once said of some speech . . .
that it contained a great deal of what was
new, and what was true ; but that what
was new was not true, and what was true
was not new.   HAZLITT.

In orations of praise, and in invectives,
the fancy is predominant ; because the
design is not truth, but to honour or dishonour.   HOBBES.—*Leviathan, ch.* 8.

See how he throws his baited lines about,
And plays his men as anglers play their
trout.   O. W. HOLMES.—*Banker's
Dinner.*

Ha ! my friend, rescue me from my
danger. You can deliver your speech
afterwards.   LA FONTAINE.—*Fables.*

Begin low, speak slow ;
Take fire, rise higher ;
When most impressed,
Be self-possessed ;
At the end wax warm
And sit down in a storm.
    DR. LEIFCHILD (?)—(18*th Century*).

Knowin' the ears long speeches suit air
mostly made to match.
    J. R. LOWELL.—*Biglow Papers, 2nd
Series*, 3.

He has one gift most dangerous to a
speculator, a vast command of a kind of
language, grave and majestic, but of vague
and uncertain import.
        MACAULAY.—(*On Gladstone*).

What orators lack in depth, they make
up in length.   MONTESQUIEU.

He who would be a good orator ought
to be just, and skilled in the knowledge of
things just.   PLATO.—*Gorgias*, 136
        (*Cary tr.*).

Cicero used to ridicule loud speakers,
saying that they shouted because they
could not speak, like lame men who get on
horseback because they cannot walk.
        PLUTARCH.—*Life of Cicero.*

"Young man," he [Phocion] said [to
Leosthenes], "your speeches are like
cypress-trees, stately and tall, but no fruit
to come of them."
        PLUTARCH.—*Life of Phocion.*

There are three qualities which an orator
ought to display, namely, that he should
instruct, he should move, and he should
delight.   QUINTILIAN.

There is not less eloquence in the tone
of the voice, in the eyes, and in the de-
meanour, than in the choice of words.
    LA ROCHEFOUCAULD.—*Maxim* 249
        (1678 *ed.*).

Few speeches which have produced an
electrical effect on an audience can bear
the colourless photography of a printed
record.
    LORD ROSEBERY.—*Life of Pitt, ch.* 13.

If you look for a good speech now, you
undo me.
SHAKESPEARE.—*Henry IV., Pt.* 2, *Epilogue.*

I am no orator, as Brutus is ;
But, as you know me all, a plain blunt
man,
That love my friend.
    SHAKESPEARE.—*Julius Cæsar*, Act 3, 2.

The right honourable gentleman is indebted to his memory for his jests, and to
his imagination for his facts.
SHERIDAN.—*Speech (reply to Mr. Dundas,
but borrowed from "Gil Blas")*.

Ye may say I am hot ;
I say I am not ;
Only warm, as the subject in which I am
got.   SWIFT.—*Famous Speech-maker.*

On the day of the dinner of the Oyster-
mongers' Company, what a noble speech I
thought of in the cab !
    THACKERAY.—*Roundabout Papers.*

It is with men as with asses ; whoever
would keep them fast must find a very good
hold at their ears.   *Slavonian prov.*

ORDER

Good order is the foundation of all good
things.
    BURKE.—*Reflections on Fr. Revolution.*

If God had laid all common, certainly
  Man would have been th' incloser ; but
    since now
God hath impaled us, on the contrary
  Man breaks the fence, and every ground
    will plough.
        HERBERT.—*Church Porch.*

Method is good in all things. Order
governs the world. The devil is the author
of confusion.   SWIFT.—*Letter*, 1710.

ORGANS

There let the pealing organ blow
To the full-voiced choir below,
In service high and anthems clear,
As may, with sweetness, through mine ear,
Dissolve me into ecstasies
And bring all heaven before mine eyes.
      MILTON.—*Il Penseroso*, 162.

While in more lengthened notes and slow
The deep, majestic, solemn organs blow.
      POPE.—*St. Cecilia's Day.*

ORIENTALISM

The East bowed low before the blast,
  In patient deep disdain ;
She let the legions thunder past,
  And plunged in thought again.
  MATTHEW ARNOLD.—*Obermann once
             more.*

The practice of politics in the East may
be defined by one word—dissimulation.
  DISRAELI.—*Contarini Fleming, Pt.* 5,
              ch. 10.

ORIGINALITY

You must not pump spring-water un-
  awares
Upon a gracious public full of nerves.
  E. B. BROWNING.—*Aurora Leigh, Bk.* 3.

Originality is the one thing which un-
original minds cannot feel the use of. They
cannot see what it is to do for them. How
should they ?   J. S. MILL.—*Freedom, ch.* 3.

All good things which exist are the fruits
of originality.   J. S. MILL.—*Ib.*

That virtue of originality that men so
strain after is not *newness*, as they vainly
think,—there is nothing new. It is only
genuineness.
RUSKIN.—*Modern Painters, vol.* 2, *Pt.* 3,
              ch. 3, 6.

ORNAMENT

His lockèd, lettered, braw brass collar
Showed him the gentleman and scholar.
      BURNS.—*The Twa Dogs.*

Often in the case of weighty enterprises
and great objects professed, one or two
purple patches are sewn on to make a fine
show in the distance.
      HORACE.—*De Arte Poetica.*

A carelessness about personal appearance becomes men.
      OVID.—*Ars Amat., Bk.* 1.

Ornament cannot be overcharged if it
is good, and is always overcharged when
it is bad.
    RUSKIN.—*Seven Lamps: Lamp of
                Sacrifice.*

The world is still deceived with ornament.
  SHAKESPEARE.—*Merchant of Venice,
                  Act* 3, 3.

For Loveliness
Needs not the foreign aid of ornament,
But is, when unadorned, adorned the most.
      THOMSON.—*Seasons : Autumn.*

OSTENTATION

Rich windows that exclude the light,
And passages that lead to nothing.
      GRAY.—*Long Story.*

Does it come to this, that your knowledge is nothing to you unless some other
person knows that you know it ?
      PERSIUS.—*Sat.* 1, 27.

Who builds a church to God, and not to
  fame,
Will never mark the marble with his name.
      POPE.—*Moral Essays, Ep.* 3, 285.

One who paraded with a certain amount
of art all that he said or did.
      TACITUS.—*Hist., Bk.* 2, 80.

That jewelled mass of millinery,
That oiled and curled Assyrian Bull.
      TENNYSON.—*Maud, Pt.* 1, 6.

But all their works they do for to be seen
of men : they make broad their phylac-
teries, and enlarge the borders of their
garments, And love the uppermost rooms
at feasts, and the chief seats in the syna-
gogues.   *St. Matthew* xxiii, 5, 6.

Prudent the man who builds his habitation,
Mansion or hall or villa as preferred ;
Yet let him curb his pride with modera-
  tion,
" Fine cage feeds not the bird."
  ANON.—*Tr. of Old French Inscription
    on a Manor House in Normandy.*

OUTCASTS

Whom the heart of man shuts out,
Sometimes the heart of God takes in.
      J. R. LOWELL.—*The Forlorn.*

His hand will be against every man, and
every man's hand against him.
      Genesis xvi, 12.

OUTLAWS

A famous man is Robin Hood,
  The English ballad-singer's joy !
  And Scotland has a thief as good,

An outlaw of as daring mood ;
She has her brave Rob Roy.
WORDSWORTH.—*Memorials of a Tour in
Scotland*, 11. (*Rob Roy's Grave*.)

OUTLOOK

Two men look out through the same bars :
One sees the mud, and one the stars.
F. LANGBRIDGE.—*Quiet Thoughts*.

The man who sees both sides of a question is the man who sees absolutely nothing
at all.   OSCAR WILDE.—*Intentions*.

OUTSPOKENNESS

To a poure man men sholde his vyces telle,
But nat to a lord, thogh he sholde go to
helle.   CHAUCER.—*Somnour's Tale*,
370.

" Not to put too fine a point upon it "—
a favourite apology for plain-speaking
with Mr. Snagsby.
DICKENS.—*Bleak House, ch.* 11.

Like a rough orator, that brings more
truth
Than rhetoric, to make good his accusation.
MASSINGER.—*Gt. Duke of Florence*, Act 5, 3.

We drank the pure daylight of honest
speech.
GEO. MEREDITH.—*Modern Love*, st. 48.

For I have neither wit, nor words, nor
worth,
Action, nor utterance, nor power of speech
To stir men's blood ; I only speak right on.
I tell you that which you yourselves do
know.
SHAKESPEARE.—*Julius Cæsar*, Act 3, 2.

Plain dealing is the best when all is
done.
WM. PRYNNE.—*Histrio-Mastix*, Act 3, 1.

Speak thy purpose out ;
I love not mystery or doubt.
SCOTT.—*Rokeby, c.* 3, 11.

Do you not know I am a woman ?
What I think I speak.
SHAKESPEARE.—*As You Like It*, Act 3, 2.

His heart's his mouth :
What his breast forges that his tongue
must vent.
SHAKESPEARE.—*Coriolanus*, Act 3, 1.

I will a round unvarnished tale deliver.
SHAKESPEARE.—*Othello*, Act 1, 3.

On an occasion of this kind it becomes
more than a moral duty to speak one's
mind. It becomes a pleasure.
OSCAR WILDE.—*Importance of being
Earnest.*

OXFORD

Oxford, of whom the poet said
That one of your unwritten laws is
To back the weaker side, and wed
Your gallant heart to wobbling causes.
SIR OWEN SEAMAN.—*Scholar Farmer*.

OYSTERS

" It's a wery remarkable circumstance,
sir," said Sam, " that poverty and oysters
always seem to go together."
DICKENS.—*Pickwick Papers, ch.* 22.

He had often eaten oysters, but had
never had enough.
SIR W. S. GILBERT.—*Etiquette*.

He was a bold man that first ate an
oyster.   SWIFT.—*Polite Conversation*.

A month without an R has nae richt
being in the year.
JOHN WILSON.—*Noctes*, 13.

What desperate breedy beasts eisters
maun be !
JOHN WILSON.—*Noctes*, 16 (*Ettrick
Shepherd*).

Eisters dinna interrupt talkin'.
JOHN WILSON.—*Ib.*

There's really no end in natur' to the
eatin' o' eisters.
JOHN WILSON.—*Ib.,* 17 (*Ettrick Shepherd*).

Hech, sirs ! but the month o' September's the month after my ain heart—
and worth ony ither twa in the year—
comin' upon you, as it does, after May,
June, July, and August, wi' its R and its
Eisters.
JOHN WILSON.—*Ib.,* 17 (*Oct.*, 1828).

The oyster is a gentle thing,
And will not come unless you sing.
Old Rhyme.

P

PACIFICATION

When the victors show themselves more
regardful of justice and equal laws than
the vanquished, then all things will be full
of security and felicity, and there will be
an escape from every ill.
PLATO.—*Epistle* 7 (*After the assassination
of Dion of Syracuse*).

PAGEANTRY

And pomp and feast and revelry
With mask, and antique pageantry.
MILTON.—*L'Allegro*, 127.

Thrones, Dominations, Princedoms, Virtues, Powers.
MILTON.—*Paradise Lost, Bk.* 5, 601.

PAIN

All that the proud can feel of pain.
BYRON.—*Prometheus.*

For all the happiness mankind can gain
Is not in pleasure, but in rest from pain.
DRYDEN.—*Indian Emperor*, Act 4, 1.

There are two things to be sanctified—
pains and pleasures.   PASCAL.—*Pensées*,
Pt. 2, 17, 28.

He loves to make parade of pain.
TENNYSON.—*In Memoriam, c.* 21.

Nothing begins and nothing ends
That is not paid with moan ;
For we are born in other's pain,
And perish in our own.
F. THOMPSON.—*Daisy.*

The mark of rank in nature is capacity for
pain,
And the anguish of the singer marks the
sweetness of the strain.
SARAH WILLIAMS.—*Twilight Hours.*

PAINTING

And Painting, mute and motionless,
Steals but a glance of time.
CAMPBELL.—*To J. P. Kemble.*

The violently increasing number of extremely foolish persons who now concern
themselves about pictures, may be
counted among the meanest calamities of
modern society.
RUSKIN.—*Note* (1882) *to Rev. Ed. of
Modern Painters, Vol.* 2, sec. 1, ch. 1.

The essential difference between painting
and daubing is that a *painter* lays not a
grain more colour than is needed.
RUSKIN.—*Ib., Vol.* 2, sec. 2, ch. 5.

No author can live by his work and be
as empty-headed as an average successful
painter.
G. B. SHAW.—*Unsocial Socialist, ch.* 12.
(*Sidney Trefusis.*)

Whate'er their errors, they no more remain,
For Time, like fuller's earth, takes out each
stain :
Nay more, on faults that modern works
would tarnish,
Time spreads a sacred coat of varnish.
J. WOLCOT.—*Odes for* 1786, *No.* 7.

PALESTINE

In those holy fields,
Over whose acres walked those blessed
feet,
Which, fourteen hundred years ago, were
nailed,
For our advantage, on the bitter cross.
SHAKESPEARE.—*Henry IV., Pt.* 1, Act 1, 1.

PARADISE

One universal smile it seemed of all things ;
Joy past compare.
DANTE.—*Paradise, c.* 27, 6 (*Cary tr.*)

If God hath made this world so fair,
Where sin and death abound,
How beautiful, beyond compare,
Will paradise be found !
J. MONTGOMERY.—*The Earth full of God's
Goodness.*

I have been there, and still would go ;
'Tis like a little heaven below.
I. WATTS.—*Lord's Day.*

PARADOX

Perhaps 'tis pretty to force together
Thoughts so all unlike each other.
S. T. COLERIDGE.—*Christabel, Pt.* 2
(*Conclusion*).

This will be found contrary to all experience, yet it is true.
LEONARD EULER (1707–1783).—*On his
law of Arches.*

Virtue itself turns vice, being misapplied,
And vice sometime's by action dignified.
SHAKESPEARE.—*Romeo and Juliet*,
Act 2, 3.

PARASITES

So, naturalists observe, a flea
Hath smaller fleas that on him prey :
And these have smaller still to bite 'em,
And so proceed *ad infinitum.*
SWIFT.—*On Poetry.*

Great fleas have little fleas upon their backs
to bite 'em,
And little fleas have lesser fleas, and so *ad
infinitum.*
And the great fleas themselves in turn have
greater fleas to go on,
While these again have greater still, and
greater still, and so on.
*Quoted in Prof. De Morgan's " Budget of
Paradoxes " (c.* 1850).

PARENTS

Lovers grow cold, men learn to hate their
wives,
And only parents' love can last our lives.
BROWNING.—*Pippa Passes.*

A great distinction, and among mankind
The most conspicuous, is to spring from
sires
Renowned for virtue. Generous souls
hence raise
To heights sublimer an ennobled name.
EURIPIDES.—*Hecuba*, 379 (*Woodhull tr.*).

The virtue of parents is a great dowry.
HORACE.—*Odes, Bk.* 3.

PARIS

Nothing is more excellent than the
legend that the Parisian women come into
this world with all possible failings, but

that a kind fairy has mercy on them and
lends to each fault a spell by which it works
as a charm.   That kind fairy is Grace.
HEINE.—*Florentine Nights.*

Paris is the New Jerusalem, and the
Rhine is the Jordan which separates the
land of Freedom from the land of the
Philistines.   HEINE.—*The Liberation.*

Adieu, Paris ! Famous city, city of noise,
of smoke, of mud, where the women have
ceased to believe in virtue, and the men in
honour.   ROUSSEAU.—*Emile.*

I think every wife has a right to insist
upon seeing Paris.
SYDNEY SMITH.—*Letter to Countess Grey,
Sept.* 11, 1835.

When good Americans die they go to
Paris.   *Ascribed to Thos. Gold Appleton.*

PARKS

Public money is scarcely ever so well
employed as in securing bits of waste
ground and keeping them as open spaces.
SIR A. HELPS.—*Friends in Council, Bk.* 1,
ch. 10.

PARLIAMENT

England, the mother of Parliaments.
JOHN BRIGHT.—*Speech, Jan.* 18,
1865.

I like a parliamentary debate,
Particularly when it's not too late.
BYRON.—*Beppo, st.* 47.

Beautiful talk is by no means the most
pressing want in Parliament.
CARLYLE.—*Latter Day Pamphlets,* 5.

A Parliament speaking through reporters
to Buncombe and the twenty-seven millions, mostly fools.   CARLYLE.—*Ib.,* 6.

Liberty to send your fifty-thousandth
part of a new Tongue-fencer into the
National Debating Club.
CARLYLE.—*French Revolution.*

The notion that a man's liberty consists
in giving his vote at election-hustings, and
saying, " Behold, now I too have my
twenty-thousandth part of a Talker in our
National Palaver."
CARLYLE.—*Past and Present, ch.* 13.

" You have not imparted to me," remarks Veneering, " what you think of
my entering the House of Commons."
—" I think," rejoins Twemlow feelingly,
" that it is the best club in London."
DICKENS.—*Our Mutual Friend, Bk.* 2,
ch. 3.

Only through the accident of being a
hereditary peer can anyone, in these days of
Votes for Everybody, get into parliament,
if handicapped by a serious modern cul-
tural equipment.
G. B. SHAW.—*Heartbreak House, Pref.
The Cherry Orchard.*

PAROCHIALISM

We never come to be citizens of the
world, but are still villagers, who think that
everything in their petty town is a little
superior to the same thing anywhere else.
EMERSON.—*Domestic Life.*

The parish makes the Constable, and
when the Constable is made he governs
the Parish.   SELDEN.—*People.*

Ye think the rustic cackle of your bourg
The murmur of the world.
TENNYSON.—*Marriage of Geraint, l.* 276.

O Lord, bless and be gracious to the
Greater and the Lesser Cumbrays, and in
thy mercy do not forget the adjacent
islands of Great Britain and Ireland.
*Prayer of the Minister of the Cumbrays,
" two miserable islands in the mouth of the
Clyde." (Sir W. Scott's Diary,* 1827.)

The sun and the moon may go wrong,
but the clock of St. Johnston (Perth) never
goes wrong.   *Scottish saying (Chambers).*

PARODY

It is not right to intrude the ludicrous
into what is not ludicrous.   To do so is to
spoil taste, to corrupt one's own judgment
and that of other people.
LA BRUYÈRE.—*Quoted by Geo. Eliot in
" Theophrastus Such " in support of a condemnation of burlesque and parody.*

PARTIES

Party divisions, whether on the whole
operating for good or evil, are things inseparable from free government.
BURKE.—*Observations on " Present State of
the Nation."*

The consequence is, being of no party,
I shall offend all parties.
BYRON.—*Don Juan, c.* 9, 26.

In a world which exists by the balance
of Antagonisms, the respective merit of
the Conservator or the Innovator must ever
remain debatable.
CARLYLE.—*On Boswell's Life of Johnson.*

I have never loved any parties, but with
my utmost zeal have sincerely espoused
the great and original interest of this nation, and of all nations—I mean truth and
liberty,—and whoever are of that party,
I desire to be with them.
DEFOE.—*History of the Union.*

The grand contention's plainly to be seen,
To get some men put out and some put in.
DEFOE.—*True-Born Englishman, Intro.*

I believe that without party, parliamentary government is impossible.
DISRAELI.—*Speech,* 1872.

At home the hateful names of parties cease,
And factious souls are wearied into peace.
DRYDEN.—*Astræa Redux,* 312.

Of the two great parties which, at this hour, almost share the nation between them, I should say that one has the best cause, and the other contains the best men.
EMERSON.—*Politics.*

Party Government—the crown and glory of the British constitution—is a peculiar structure, and involves a peculiar assumption.... Nature has created us with two eyes, but in matters of state, either of necessity or deliberately, we must extinguish one.
FROUDE.—*Short Studies: Party Politics.*

I often think it's comical
  How nature always does contrive
That every boy and every gal,
  That's born into this world alive,
Is either a little Liberal
  Or else a little Conservative.
SIR W. S. GILBERT.—*Iolanthe.*

I always voted at my party's call,
And I never thought of thinking for myself at all.
SIR W. S. GILBERT.—*H.M.S. Pinafore.*

He serves his party best who serves the country best.
R. B. HAYES.—*Address,* 1877.

[Government] is like an hour-glass; when one side's quite run out, we turn up the other and go on again.
D. JERROLD.—*Prisoner of War.*

A wise Tory and a wise Whig, I believe, will agree. Their principles are the same, though their modes of thinking are different.
JOHNSON.—*Written Memorandum,* 1783.

Ez to my princerples, I glory
  In havin' nothin' of the sort ;
I ain't a Wig, I ain't a Tory,
  I'm jest a candidate, in short.
J. R. LOWELL.—*Biglow Papers,* 1st *Series,* 7.

We're clean out o' money, an' 'most out o' lyin'.
J. R. LOWELL.—*Ib.,* 2nd *Series,* 4.

Then none was for a party ;
  Then all were for the State ;
Then the great man helped the poor,
  And the poor man loved the great.
MACAULAY.—*Horatius, st.* 32.

In politics, again, it is almost a commonplace that a party of order or stability and a party of progress or reform are both necessary elements of a healthy state of political life. J. S. MILL.—*Liberty, ch.* 2.

Party spirit, which, at best, is but the madness of many for the gain of a few.
POPE.—*Letter to E. Blount, Aug.* 27, 1714.

The three chief qualifications of a party writer are to stick at nothing, to delight in flinging dirt, and to slander in the dark by guess. POPE.—*Letter.*

There never was any party, faction, sect, or cabal whatsoever, in which the most ignorant were not the most violent.
POPE.—*Ib.*

When you have lived longer in this world and outlived the enthusiastic and pleasing illusions of youth, you will find your love and pity for the race increase tenfold, your admiration and attachment to any particular party or opinion fall away altogether. J. H. SHORTHOUSE.—
John Inglesant, Vol. 1, *ch.* 6.

I have never given way to that puritanical feeling of the Whigs against dining with the Tories—
Tory and Whig in turns shall be my host ;
I taste no politics in boiled and roast.
SYDNEY SMITH.—*Letter to John Murray*
(*c.* 1834).

The outs and the ins are as like as two pins : they both want to stick in good places. C. H. SPURGEON.—*"Salt-Cellars."*

Abundance of political lying is a sure sign of true English liberty.
SWIFT.—*Art of Political Lying.*

In this quarrel whole rivulets of ink have been exhausted, and the virulence of both parties enormously augmented.
SWIFT.—*Battle of the Books.*

He could not forbear taking me up in his right hand, and, stroking me gently with the other, after a hearty fit of laughing, asked me whether I was a Whig or Tory. SWIFT.—*Brobdingnag.*

It is alleged, indeed, that the high heels are most agreeable to our ancient constitution, but, however that may be, his majesty has determined to make use only of low heels in the administration.
SWIFT.—*Voyage to Lilliput.*

Ring out a slowly-dying cause,
  And ancient forms of party strife ;
Ring in the nobler modes of life,
  With sweeter manners, purer laws.
TENNYSON.—*In Memoriam, c.* 106.

Let Whig and Tory stir their blood ;
There must be stormy weather ;
But for some true result of good
All parties work together.
          TENNYSON.—*Will Waterproof.*

" Fancy a party all Mulligans ! "
thought I, with a secret terror.
          THACKERAY.—*Mrs. Perkins's Ball.*

The puzzling sons of Party next appeared,
In dark cabals and nightly juntos met.
          THOMSON.—*Castle of Indolence, c.* 1,
                              st. 54.

When two parties divide a kingdom, no
more pleasures, no more tranquillity, no
more tenderness, no more honesty !
          VOLTAIRE.—*Guerre civile de Genève.*

It is true that there are always two
parties amongst us [the English] which
fight with the pen and by intrigues ; but
it is also true that they always unite together when it is a question of taking arms
in defence of country and liberty. These
two parties watch over each other ; they
mutually prevent any violation of the
sacred depositary of the law ; they hate
each other, but they love the state ; they
are jealous lovers who serve with emulation the same mistress.
          VOLTAIRE.—*Princesse de Babylone.*

It is a pleasure to read the books of the
Whigs and the Tories : listen to the Whigs,
and the Tories have betrayed England ;
listen to the Tories, every Whig has sacrificed the state to self-interest. So that if
you believe both parties there is not a
single honest man in the nation.
          VOLTAIRE.—*Pyrrhonism of History.*

Toryism is an innate principle o' human
nature.—Whiggism but an evil habit.
          JOHN WILSON.—*Noctes,* 4 (*Ettrick
                              Shepherd*).

All political parties die at length of
swallowing their own lies.
          Attrib. to Dr. J. Arbuthnot.

PARTING

Maid of Athens, ere we part,
Give, oh, give me back my heart.
          BYRON.—*Maid of Athens.*

When we two parted
In silence and tears,
Half broken-hearted
To sever for years.
          BYRON.—*When we two parted.*

Weep not, she says, at Nature's transient
pain ;
Congenial spirits part to meet again.
          CAMPBELL.—*Pleasures of Hope.*

Since there's no help, come let us kiss and
part.   DRAYTON.—*Ideas, Sonnet* 61.

In every parting there is an image of
death.   GEO. ELIOT.—*Amos Barton.*

There's sma' sorrow at our pairting, as
the auld mear [mare] said to the broken
cart.
          SCOTT.—*Rob Roy* (*Andrew Fairservice*).

I remember the way we parted,
The day and the way we met ;
You hoped we were both broken-hearted,
And knew we should both forget.
          SWINBURNE.—*Interlude.*

But Fate ordains that dearest friends
must part.
          YOUNG.—*Love of Fame, Sat.* 2.

PASSIONS

And creeping things can tell the vehement
rage
Of whirling storms of winds.
But who man's temper overbold may tell,
Or daring passionate loves
Of women bold in heart
Passions close bound with man's calam-
ities ?
          ÆSCHYLUS.—*Choephorœ,* 585
                              (*Plumptre tr.*).

His madness was not of the head, but
heart.   BYRON.—*Lara, c.* 1, 18.

For the sword outwears its sheath,
And the soul wears out the breast.
          BYRON.—*So, we'll go no more a roving.*

In all disputes, so much as there is of
passion, so much there is of nothing to the
purpose.
          SIR T. BROWNE.—*Religio Medici,*
                              Pt. 2, 3.

Angry friendship is sometimes as bad
as calm enmity.
          BURKE.—*Appeal from New to Old Whigs.*

It was not strange ; for in the human
breast
Two master-passions cannot co-exist.
          CAMPBELL.—*Theodric.*

Nor can a man of passions judge aright,
Except his mind be from all passions free.
          SIR JOHN DAVIES.—*Nosce Teipsum.*

His passion cast a mist before his sense,
And either made, or magnified the offence.
          DRYDEN.—*Palamon and Arcite, Bk.* 2, 334.

But love the sense of right and wrong confounds,
Strong love and proud ambition have no
bounds.   DRYDEN.—*Ib., Bk.* 3, 808.

Where passion rules, how weak does
reason prove !
          DRYDEN.—*Rival Ladies.*

Sensuality, vanity, and avarice, these are the three things that destroy a man.
W. E. GLADSTONE.—*Remark as reported by Lord Morley ("Recollections)."*

Whatever wild desires have swelled the breast,
Whatever passions have the soul possessed,
Joy, Sorrow, Fear, Love, Hatred, Transport, Rage,
Shall form the motley subject of my page.
JUVENAL.—*Sat. 1, 86 (Gifford tr.).*

The passions are the only orators which always persuade.
LA ROCHEFOUCAULD.—*Maxim 8.*

A man might preserve himself from all the dangers and errors of vice, if, before yielding to the voice of imperious desire, he would consult the past and read a little of the future. LE SÉGUR.—*Galerie Morale.*

There's sure no passion in the human soul But finds its food in music.
G. LILLO.—*Fatal Curiosity*, Act 1, 2.

But all subsists by elemental strife,
And passions are the elements of life.
POPE.—*Essay on Man*, Ep. 1, 169.

What Reason weaves by Passion is undone. POPE.—*Ib.*, Ep. 2, 42.

And hence one master passion in the breast,
Like Aaron's serpent, swallows up the rest.
POPE.—*Ib.*, Ep. 2, 131.

Search then, the ruling passion: there alone
The wild are constant, and the cunning known;
The fool consistent, and the false sincere;
Priests, princes, women, no dissemblers here.
POPE.—*Moral Essays*, Ep. 1, 174.

And you, brave Cobham! to the latest breath,
Shall feel your ruling passion strong in death:
Such in those moments as in all the past,
"Oh, save my country, Heaven!" shall be your last.
POPE.—*Ib.*, Ep. 1, 262.

The ruling passion, be it what it will,
The ruling passion conquers reason still.
POPE.—*Ib.*, Ep. 3, 153.

Passions are likened best to floods and streams;
The shallow murmur, but the deep are dumb.
SIR W. RALEGH.—*Silent Lover.*

Conscience is the voice of the soul; passions are the voice of the body. Is it astonishing that these two languages are often contradictory? ROUSSEAU.—*Emile.*

His soul, like bark with rudder lost,
On passion's changeful tide was lost.
SCOTT.—*Rokeby.*

I never heard a passion so confused,
So strange, outrageous, and so variable.
SHAKESPEARE.—*Mercht. of Venice,*
Act 2, 8.

Is the devil to have all the passions as well as all the good tunes?
G. B. SHAW.—*Man and Superman.*

Of all the tyrants that the world affords,
Our own affections are the fiercest lords.
EARL OF STIRLING.—*Julius Cæsar.*

O daughter of Death and Priapus,
Our Lady of Pain.
SWINBURNE.—*Dolores.*

"Consider well," the voice replied,
"His face, that two hours since hath died;
Wilt thou find passion, pain, or pride?"
TENNYSON.—*Two Voices.*

Love, anguish, wrath, and grief, to madness wrought;
Despair and secret shame and conscious thought
Of inborn worth his labouring soul oppressed,
Rolled in his eyes and raged within his breast.
VIRGIL.—*Æneid, Bk.* 10 *(Dryden tr.).* (*Of Mezentius*).

As it were a ramping and a roaring lion.
Church Psalter xiv, 6.

We also are men of like passions with you. *Acts* xiv, 15.

PAST

The world but feels the present's spell,
The poet feels the past as well.
MATTHEW ARNOLD.—*Bacchanalia.*

The past is in its grave,
Though its ghost haunts us.
BROWNING.—*Pauline.*

The light of other days.
A. BUNN.—*Bohemian Girl.*

People will not look forward to posterity, who never look backward to their ancestors.
BURKE.—*Reflections on Fr. Revolution.*

The "good old times"—all times when old are good. BYRON.—*Age of Bronze.*

And learn the future by the past of man.
CAMPBELL.—*Pleasures of Hope,* Pt. 1;

While Memory watches o'er the sad review
Of joys that faded like the morning dew.
CAMPBELL.—*Ib.*, Pt. 2.

To be ignorant of what happened before you were born is to be ever a child. For what is man's lifetime unless the memory of past events is woven with those of earlier times? CICERO.—*Orator*, 34, 120.

The Knight's bones are dust,
And his good sword rust ;—
His soul is with the saints, I trust.
COLERIDGE.—*Knight's Tomb*.

Actions of the last age are like almanacs of the last year.
SIR J. DENHAM.—*The Sophy*.

A proverb haunts my mind,
As a spell is cast ;
" The mill cannot grind
With the water that is past,"
SARAH DOUDNEY.

Another symptom, therefore, in all noble peoples is to admire, and perhaps exaggerate the greatness of the past.
FROUDE.—*Short Studies : Party Politics*.

Our sympathy is cold to the relation of distant misery.
GIBBON.—*Decline and Fall*, ch. 49.

" Ah, Lord, Sis Tempy ! " he [Uncle Remus] exclaimed sorrowfully, " don't le's we all go foolin' roun' mungs' dem ole times. De bes' kinder bread gits sour."
J. C. HARRIS.—*Nights with Uncle Remus*, ch. 41.

Even men who have warmly espoused the cause of modernism, ever retain a secret sympathy with the heritages of olden time. Those ghostly voices of the past, no matter how faint their echo, stir our souls marvellously.
HEINE.—*The Romantic School*.

Hours of work and hours of play
Fade away
Into one immense Inane. . . .
Life goes crooning, faint and fain,
One refrain,
" If it could be always May ! "
W. E. HENLEY.—*Ballade of Truisms*.

Let's consider the past with a lingering gaze,
Like a peacock whose eyes are inclined to his tail. HOOD.—*Parthian Glance*.

Be fair or foul, or rain, or shine,
The joys I have possessed are mine ;
Not Heaven itself upon the past has power,
But what has been has been, and I have had my hour.
HORACE.—*Odes (Dryden tr.*).

Where is the heart that doth not keep
Within its inmost core
Some fond remembrance, hidden deep,
Of days that are no more.
ELLEN C. HOWARTH.—*'Tis but a little faded flower*.

Pindar blended passing events with ancient times in such wise that he does not seem to be praising the past, but rather fanning into flames the embers of a dying beauty.
KEBLE.—*Lectures on Poetry*, No. 24 (*E. K. Francis tr.*).

The best friend one can have is the past.
BARONESS DE KRUDENER.—(*Russian.*) (1766–1824.)

Hans Breitmann gife a barty—
Vhere is dat barty now ?
C. G. LELAND.—*Breitmann's Party*.

This is the place. Stand still, my steed,
Let me review the scene,
And summon from the shadowy Past
The forms that once have been.
LONGFELLOW.—*Gleam of Sunshine*.

For Time will teach thee soon the truth,
There are no birds in last year's nest.
LONGFELLOW.—*It is not always May*.

Old loves, old aspirations, and old dreams,
More beautiful for being old and gone.
J. R. LOWELL.—*Parting of the Ways*.

Time will run back and fetch the age of gold. MILTON.—*Christmas Hymn*.

Who ever saw old age which did not praise the past time, and blame the present ? MONTAIGNE.—*Bk.* 2, 13.

To joys too exquisite to last,
And yet more exquisite when past.
J. MONTGOMERY.—*The Little Cloud*.

The harp that once through Tara's halls
The soul of music shed,
Now hangs as mute on Tara's walls
As if that soul were fled.
MOORE.—*Irish Melodies*.

When Time, who steals our years away,
Shall steal our pleasures too,
The memory of the past will stay
And half our joys renew.
MOORE.—*Song*.

For hope shall brighten days to come,
And memory gild the past !
MOORE.—*Song*.

I am listening for the voices
Which I heard in days of old.
CAROLINE E. S. NORTON (LADY STIRLING MAXWELL).—*The Lonely Harp* (*Song*).

Prince, I counsel you, never say,
Alack for the years that are left behind !
Look you, keep love when your dreams decay ;
All else flits past on the wings of the wind.
JOHN PAYNE.—*Ballad of Past Delight*.

M*

The glory and the glow
Of the world's loveliness have passed away;
And Fate hath little to inflict to-day,
And nothing to bestow !
    W. M. PRAED.—*Stanzas.*

Where is the man whose soul has never
    waked
To sudden pity of the poor torn past ?
    ROSSETTI.—*Versicles.*

Where is the life that late I led ?
    SHAKESPEARE.—*Henry IV.*, Pt. 2,
                  Act 5, 3.

Let us not burden our remembrance with
An heaviness that's gone.
    SHAKESPEARE.—*Tempest*, Act 5, 1.

What's gone, and what's past help,
Should be past grief.
    SHAKESPEARE.—*Winter's Tale*, Act 3, 2.

So far as the contemplation of the past
does not go to put us out of conceit with
the future, it is wise : when it does, it is
the idleness of genius and feeling.
    SYDNEY SMITH.—*Lectures on Moral
        Philosophy, No.* 22.

The good of ancient times let others state ;
I think it lucky I was born so late.
    SYDNEY SMITH.—*Modern Changes.*

An intelligent man judges the present
by the past.
    SOPHOCLES.—*Œdipus Tyrannus.*

Man hath a weary pilgrimage
    As through the world he wends :
On every stage from youth to age
    Still discontent attends ;
With heaviness he casts his eye
    Upon the road before,
And still remembers with a sigh
    The days that are no more.
    SOUTHEY.—*Remembrance.*

Danger well past remembered work's
delight.
    EARL OF SURREY.—*Bonum est.*

I have put my days and dreams out of
    mind,
Days that are over, dreams that are done.
    SWINBURNE.—*Triumph of Time.*

We praise things which are ancient,
careless of those which are modern.
    TACITUS.—*Annals, Bk.* 2, 88.

Old things are always in good repute,
present things in disfavour.
    TACITUS.—*Dialogus de Oratoribus*, 18.

Let us alone. Time driveth onward fast,
    And in a little while our lips are dumb.
Let us alone. What is it that will last ?
    All things are taken from us and become
Portions and parcels of the dreadful Past.
    TENNYSON.—*Lotos Eaters.*

So sad, so strange, the days that are no
    more. TENNYSON.—*Princess, c.* 4, 35.

O Death in Life, the days that are no
    more ! TENNYSON.—*Ib., c.* 4, 40.

For it was in the golden prime
    Of good Haroun Alraschid.
TENNYSON.—*Recollections of Arabian
                Nights.*

The past, at least, is secure.
    D. WEBSTER.—*Speech.*

Old customs, habits, superstitions, fears,
All that lies buried under fifty years.
    WHITTIER.—*The Countess.*

What lies before me is my past. I have
got to make myself look on that with different eyes, to make God look on it with
different eyes. This I cannot do by ig-
noring it, or slighting it, or praising it, or
denying it. OSCAR WILDE.—*De Profundis.*

What are mony o' the pleasures o'
memory, sirs, but the pains o' the past
spiritualeezed ?
    JOHN WILSON.—*Noctes*, 31 (*Ettrick
               Shepherd*).

The thought of our past years in me doth
    breed
Perpetual benediction.
    WORDSWORTH.—*Intimations of
             Immortality, c.* 9.

'Tis greatly wise to talk with our past
    hours :
And ask them what report they bore to
    Heaven.
    YOUNG.—*Night Thoughts*, 2.

Say not thou, What is the cause that the
former days were better than these ? for
thou dost not enquire wisely concerning
this. *Ecclesiastes* vii, 10.

He praises al thing that es gon,
O present thing he praises non.
    Cursor Mundi (14th *Cent.*).

There are no birds in last year's nest.
    Spanish prov.

PATHOS

Some things are of that nature as to make
One's fancy chuckle, while his heart doth
ache.
    BUNYAN.—*Pilgrim's Progress, Pt.* 2, *Pref.*

Strains that sigh and words that weep.
    D. MALLET.—*Funeral Hymn.*

PATIENCE

With close-lipped patience for our only
    friend,
Sad patience, too near neighbour to
    despair.
    M. ARNOLD.—*Scholar Gipsy*, st. 20.

I worked with patience, which means
almost power.
E. B. BROWNING.—*Aurora Leigh, Bk.* 3.

O he is patient, and he will await
Century after century in peace,
So that he hears sweet songs of her he
seeks,
So that his guides do speak to him of her,
So that he thinks to clasp her in the end.
R. BUCHANAN.—*Titan and Avatar*, 2.

Our patience will achieve more than our
force.   BURKE.—*Reflections on the
Revolution.*

Hope and patience are two sovereign
remedies for all, the surest reposals, the
softest cushions to lean on in adversity.
BURTON.—*Anatomy of Melancholy,
Pt.* 2, 3, 3.

Pacience is an high vertu certeyn ;
For it vanquisheth, as these clerkes seyn,
Thinges that rigour [harshness] sholde
never atteyne.
CHAUCER.—*Franklin's Tale*, 45.

This vertu [Patience] maketh a man lyk
to God, and maketh him Goddes owene
dere child, as seith Crist.
CHAUCER.—*Parson's Tale, sec.* 50.

He hasteth wel that wysely can abide.
CHAUCER.—*Tale of Melibeus.*

Patience is sorrow's salve ; what can't be
cured,
So Donald right areads, must be endured.
CHURCHILL.—*Prophecy of Famine*, 360.

A patient man 's a pattern for a king.
DEKKER.—*Honest Whore, Pt.* 2, Act 5.

Great Prize Competition for Patience—
Hawkins, First Prize ; Job, Honourable
Mention.
MR. JUSTICE HAWKINS.—*At
Nottingham Assizes.*

For troubles wrought of men
Patience is hard—I tell you it is hard.
JEAN INGELOW.—*Brothers and a Sermon*,
503.

It may be well to wait a century for a
reader, as God has waited six thousand
years for an observer.
JOHN KEPLER (1571-1630).

We should be lowe and loveliche, and leel
eche man to other,
And pacient as pilgrimes, for pilgrimes are
we all.   LANGLAND.—*Piers Plowman,
Passus* 13, 129.

Patience is an important part of justice.
PLINY THE YOUNGER.

Patience is bitter, but its fruit is sweet.
ROUSSEAU.

Though patience be a tired mare, yet
she will plod.
SHAKESPEARE.—*Henry V.*, Act 2, 1.

'Tis all men's office to speak patience
To those that wring under the load of
sorrow.
SHAKESPEARE.—*Much Ado*, Act 5, 1.

How poor are they that have not patience !
What wound did ever heal, but by degrees?
SHAKESPEARE.—*Othello*, Act 2, 3.

Patience, thou young and rose-lipped
cherubim ! SHAKESPEARE.—*Ib.*, Act 4, 2.

She sat like patience on a monument,
Smiling at grief.
SHAKESPEARE.—*Twelfth Night*, Act 2, 4.

Keep a thing, its use will come.
TENNYSON.—*The Epic.*

Birdie, rest a little longer,
Till the little wings are stronger.
So she rests a little longer,
Then she flies away.
TENNYSON.—*Sea Dreams.*

God's ways seem dark, but soon or late
They touch the shining hills of day ;
The evil cannot brook delay,
The good can well afford to wait.
WHITTIER.—*Lines to Friends.*

Ye have heard of the patience of Job.
St. James v, 11.

The king himself must wait while his
beer is being drawn, and the queen cannot
eat honey till the bees have made it.
Given as a " saying " by C. H. Spurgeon.

Though God take the sun out of heaven,
yet we must have patience.
Prov. (Geo. Herbert).

Patience is a flower that grows not in
everyone's garden.   *Prov. (Ray).*

Patience is the greatest prayer.
Hindu prov. (a saying of Buddha).

Patience conquers the world.
Italian prov.

Patience ! and shuffle the cards !
Spanish prov. found in " Don Quixote."

Patience is the key of Paradise.
Turkish prov.

PATRIOTISM

These gentry are invariably saying all
they can in dispraise of their native land ;
and it is my opinion, grounded upon experience, that an individual who is capable
of such baseness would not hesitate at the
perpetration of any villainy, for next to the
love of God, the love of country is the best
preventive of crime.
BORROW.—*Bible in Spain.*

Here and here did England help me : how can I help England ?—say
Whoso turns as I, this evening, turn to God to praise and pray,
While Jove's planet rises yonder, silent over Africa.
BROWNING.—*Home Thoughts, from the Sea.*

One likes to die where his father before him
Died, with the same sky shinin' o'er him.
R. BUCHANAN.—*White Rose and Red.*

He who loves not his country can love nothing.   BYRON.—*Two Foscari.*

The patriot's blood 's the seed of Freedom's tree.
CAMPBELL.—*Spanish Patriots.*

" My country, right or wrong," is a thing that no patriot would think of saying except in a desperate case. It is like saying, " My mother, drunk or sober."
G. K. CHESTERTON.—*The Defendant.*

Who loves his country cannot hate mankind.   CHURCHILL.—*The Farewell*, 300.

Dear are our parents, dear are our children, our neighbours, our companions ; but all the affections of all men are bound up in their own native land.
CICERO.—*De Officiis, Bk.* 1, 17.

Our country ! In her intercourse with foreign nations may she always be in the right ; but our country, right or wrong.
S. DECATUR.—*Toast, April,* 1816.

Then, seized with fear, yet still affecting fame,
Usurped a patriot's all-atoning name.
DRYDEN.—*Absalom and Achitophel, Pt.* 1, 178.

Never was patriot yet, but was a fool.
DRYDEN.—*Ib., Pt.* 1, 969.

Is it an offence, is it a mistake, is it a crime to take a hopeful view of the prospects of your own country ? Why should it be ? Why should patriotism and pessimism be identical ? Hope is the mainspring of patriotism.
D. LLOYD GEORGE.—*House of Commons, Oct.* 30, 1919.

Strike—for your altars and your fires !
Strike—for the green graves of your sires !
God—and your native land !
FITZGREENE HALLECK.—*Marco Bozzaris.*

When shall the saner, softer polities,
Whereof we dream, have play in each proud land,
And patriotism, grown Godlike, scorn to stand
Bondslave to realms, but circle earth and seas ?   T. HARDY.—*Departure.*

Life is good and joy runs high
Between English earth and sky :
Death is death : but we shall die
To the Song on your bugles blown, England.
W. E. HENLEY.—*Rhymes.*

Patriotism is the last refuge of a scoundrel.   JOHNSON.—*Remark,* 1775.

Far dearer the grave or the prison,
Illumed by one patriot name,
Than the trophies of all who have risen
On liberty's ruins to fame !
MOORE.—*Forget not the field.*

A patriot is a fool in every age.
POPE.—*Satires, Epilogue.*

Where there is no longer such a thing as native-land there can be no citizens. Those two words *patrie* (native land) and *citoyens* (citizens) ought to be expunged from modern languages. I know the reason very well, but I do not choose to tell it.
ROUSSEAU.—*Emile.*

Breathes there the man, with soul so dead,
Who never to himself hath said,
This is my own, my native land ?
Whose heart hath ne'er within him burned,
As home his footsteps he hath turned,
From wandering on a foreign strand ?
SCOTT.—*Lay of the Last Minstrel, c.* 6, 1.

Where's the coward that would not dare
To fight for such a land ?
SCOTT.—*Ib., c.* 4, 30.

Stood for his country's glory fast,
And nailed her colours to the mast.
SCOTT.—*Marmion, c.* 1, *Intro.*

He died a gallant knight,
With sword in hand, for England's right.
SCOTT.—*Ib., c.* 6, 37.

Who is here so vile that will not love his country ? If any, speak ; for him I have offended.
SHAKESPEARE.—*Julius Cæsar,* Act 3, 2.

You 'll never have a quiet world till you knock the patriotism out of the human race.   G. B. SHAW.—*O'Flaherty, V.C.*

My country, 'tis of thee,
Sweet land of liberty—
Of thee I sing.
DR. S. F. SMITH.—*National Hymn.*

True patriotism is of no party.
SMOLLETT.—*Sir L. Greaves.*

" Libertas et natale solum ! "
Fine words, indeed ! I wonder where he stole 'em.
SWIFT.—*On Chief Justice Whitshed's Motto.*

None loves his king and country better,
Yet none was ever less their debtor.
Swift.—*Pastoral Dialogue*, 1727.

Yet all things good await
Him who cares not to be great,
But as he saves or serves the state.
Not once or twice in our rough island-story
The path of duty was the way to glory.
Tennyson.—*On Wellington.*

Yet in whose fiery love for their own land
No hatred of another's finds a place.
Sir W. Watson.—*Wales.*

Hands across the sea !
Feet on English ground !
The old blood is bold blood the whole
world round.
Byron Webber.—*Song.*

Go, tell the Spartans, thou that passest by,
That here obedient to their laws we lie.
Greek epitaph.

This have I done (quoth he)
For lovely England's sake.
Old Ballad. Honour of a London Prentice.

PATRONAGE

The mud of English patronage
Grows round his feet, and keeps him down.
R. Buchanan.—*Edward Crowhurst*, 1.

Is not a patron, my lord, one who looks
with unconcern on a man struggling for
life in the water, and when he has reached
ground encumbers him with help ?
Johnson.—*To Lord Chesterfield*, 1755.

Patron : Commonly a wretch who supports with insolence, and is paid with
flattery.   Johnson.—*Dictionary.*

Let there be Mæcenases and there will
not be wanting Virgils.
Martial.—*Bk.* 8, 56.

Getting Patronage is the whole art of
life. A man cannot have a career without
it.   G. B. Shaw.—*Capt. Brassbound.*

PATTER

This particularly rapid, unintelligible
patter
Isn't generally heard, and if it is it doesn't
matter !
Sir W. S. Gilbert.—*Ruddigore.*

PAUPERISM AND POOR LAWS

Parish pay is hush money.
H. Spencer.—*Social Statics*, Pt. 3.

The right of the state to require the
services of its members, even to the
jeoparding of their lives, in the common

defence, establishes a right in the people
. . . to public support, when, from any
cause, they may be unable to support
themselves.
Wordsworth.—*Postscript (to Preface)*
(1835).

PAYMENT

Alas ! how deeply painful is all payment !
Byron.—*Don Juan, c.* 10, 79.

Wise men aver it is the English way
Never to grumble till they come to pay.
Defoe.—*True-born Englishman. Britannia*,
84.

Base is the slave that pays.
Shakespeare.—*Henry V.*, Act 2, 1.

Pay beforehand and your work will be
behindhand.   *Prov.*

PEACE

Calm soul of all things ! make it mine
To feel, amid the city's jeer,
That there abides a peace of thine,
Man did not make, and cannot mar.
Matthew Arnold.—*In Kensington
Gardens.*

There's but the twinkling of a star
Between a man of peace and war.
Butler.—*Hudibras*, Pt. 2, *c.* 3.

Peace is to be produced by victory, not
by negotiation.   Cicero.

You [Meneclides] are counselling slavery
in the name of ease. For peace is produced by war.
Cornelius Nepos.—15, *Epaminondas.*

Peace itself is war in masquerade.
Dryden.—*Absalom and Achitophel*,
Pt. 1, 752.

Those who in quarrels interpose,
Must often wipe a bloody nose.
J. Gay.—*Fables*, Pt. 1, 34.

So were it good if at this tyde
That every man upon his syde
Besought and prayéd for the peace
Which is the cause of all increase,
Of worship, and of worldés wealth,
Of hertés rest, and soulés health.
Gower.—*Confessio Amantis*, Bk. 1.

Without peace stondeth nothing good.
Gower.—*Ib.*

Plenty breeds Pride ; Pride, Envy ; Envy
Warre ;
Warre, Poverty ; Poverty, humble Care.
Humility breeds Peace and Peace breeds
Plenty.
Thus rounde this world doth roale alter-
nately.
Robert Hayman.—*Quodlibets* (1628)
(*Founded on traditional sayings to this
effect*).

Ef you want peace, the thing you've gut
  to du
Is jes' to show you're up to fightin', tu.
        J. R. LOWELL.—*Biglow Papers,*
                             2nd Series, 2.

The inglorious arts of peace.
        A. MARVELL.—*Horatian Ode.*

Nor war nor battle's sound
  Was heard the world around ;
The idle spear and shield were high up
  hung.   MILTON.—*Nativity Hymn.*

The brazen throat of war had ceased to
    roar :
All now was turned to jollity and game,
To luxury and riot, feast and dance.
        MILTON.—*Paradise Lost, Bk.* 11, 713.

Peace to corrupt no less than war to waste.
        MILTON.—*Ib., Bk.* 11, 784.

    Peace hath her victories
    No less renowned than war.
        MILTON.—*Sonnet.*

No vain desire of unknown things
Shall vex you there, no hope or fear
Of that which never draweth near ;
But in that lovely land and still
Ye may remember what ye will,
And what ye will forget for aye.
        W. MORRIS.—*Jason, Bk.* 14, 368.

These honours Peace to happy Britain
    brings ;
These are imperial works and worthy
    kings.
        POPE.—*Moral Essays, Ep.* 4, *l.* 203.

Plenty is the child of peace.
        W. PRYNNE.—*Histrio-Mastix.*

    'Twere good
That kings would think withal,
When peace and wealth their land has
    blessed
'Tis better to sit still and rest,
Than rise, perchance to fall.
        SCOTT.—*Marmion,* 4, 29.

The cankers of a calm world and a long
peace. SHAKESPEARE.—*Henry IV., Pt.* 1,
                                   Act 4, 2.

A moth of peace.
        SHAKESPEARE.—*Othello,* Act 1, 3.

Our stern alarums changed for merry
    meetings,
Our dreadful marches to delightful
    measures.
        SHAKESPEARE.—*Richard III.,* Act 1, 1.

Grim-visaged war hath smoothed his
    wrinkled front,
And now,—instead of mounting barbèd
    steeds, . . .
He capers nimbly in a lady's chamber,
To the lascivious pleasing of a lute.
        SHAKESPEARE.—*Ib.*

Not thus doth Peace return.
A blessed visitant she comes ;
Honour in his right hand
Doth lead her like a bride.
        SOUTHEY—*Carmina Aulica* (1814).

Only the laurel got by peace
    No thunder e'er can blast,
And ever green and flourishing will last.
        SWIFT.—*To Sir W. Temple.*

It was rather a cessation of war than a
beginning of peace.   TACITUS.—*Hist*

Ah ! when shall all men's good
Be each man's rule, and universal Peace
Lie like a shaft of light across the land,
And like a lane of beams athwart the sea ?
        TENNYSON.—*Golden Year.*

Why do they prate of the blessings of
    Peace ? We have made them a curse,
Pickpockets, each hand lusting for all that
    is not its own.
        TENNYSON.—*Maud, Pt.* 1, 1, 6.

The surly murmurs of the people cease ;
And as the Fates required, they give the
    peace.
        VIRGIL.—*Æneid, Bk.* 1 (*Dryden*).

Sweet Mercy ! to the gates of Heaven
This minstrel lead, his sins forgiven ;
The rueful conflict, the heart riven
    With vain endeavour,
And memory of Earth's bitter leaven
    Effaced for ever.
        WORDSWORTH.—*On the Banks of Nith.*

Saying, Peace, peace ; when there is no
peace.   *Jeremiah* vi, 14.

Though peace be made, yet it 's interest
that keeps peace.
Quoted by Cromwell, Sept. 4, 1654, *as " a
    maxim not to be despised."*

Peace maketh Plenty, Plenty maketh
    Pride,
Pride maketh plee [pleasure], Plee maketh
    Poverty,
Poverty maketh peace.
        15*th Century saying* (*of older origin*)
                (*vide p.* 365), *Hayman.*

Where there is peace, God is.
        Prov. (*Geo. Herbert*).

PEASANTRY

The villager, born humbly and bred hard
Content his wealth, and poverty his guard,
    .   .   .   .   .   .
His means but scanty, and his wants but
    few,
Labour his business and his pleasure too,
Enjoys more comforts, in a single hour,
Than ages give the wretch condemned to
    power. CHURCHILL.—*Gotham, Bk.* 3.

Ill fares the land, to hastening ills a prey,
Where wealth accumulates, and men
decay ;
Princes and lords may flourish, or may
fade ;
A breath can make them as a breath has
made ;
But a bold peasantry, their country's
pride,
When once destroyed can never be supplied. GOLDSMITH.—*Deserted Village.*

PEDANTRY

A Babylonish dialect
Which learned pedants much affect.
BUTLER.—*Hudibras, Pt.* 1, *c.* 1.

He [Magis] is not a man at all—he 's
a lecture (une tirade).
LABICHE.—*Le Capitaine Tic.*

What's all the noisy jargon of the schools
But idle nonsense of laborious fools,
Who fetter reason with perplexing rules ?
JOHN POMFRET.—*Reason,* 57.

They purchase knowledge at the expense
Of common breeding, common sense,
And grow at once scholars and fools.
SWIFT.—*To Sir W. Temple.*

PEDIGREE

A degenerate nobleman, or one that is
proud of his birth, is like a turnip. There
is nothing good of him but what is underground. S. BUTLER.—*Characters.*

I can trace my ancestry back to a proto-
plasmal primordial atomic globule.
SIR W. S. GILBERT.—*Mikado.*

The fascination of pedigree-hunting no
doubt lies in its inscrutable conundrums.
FREDERIC HARRISON.—*John Ruskin*
(*Eng. Men of Letters Series*), *ch.* 1.

Nor stand so much on your gentility,
Which is an airy and mere borrowed thing,
From dead men's dust and bones, and
none of yours,
Unless you make or hold it.
BEN JONSON.—*Every Man in his Humour,*
Act 1, 1.

To have the feeling of gentility it is not
necessary to have been born gentle.
LAMB.

They talk about their Pilgrim blood,
Their birthright high and holy !
A mountain-stream that ends in mud
Methinks is melancholy.
J. R. LOWELL.—*Interview with Miles*
Standish.

A penniless lass wi' a lang pedigree.
BARONESS NAIRN.—*Laird of Cockpen.*

Better be the best of a bad family than
the worst of a good one.
GREGORIUS NAZIANZEN.—(*Greek.*)

Nobles and heralds, by your leave,
Here lies what once was Matthew Prior ;
The son of Adam and of Eve :
Can Bourbon or Nassau claim higher ?
PRIOR.—*Epitaph on himself.*

No tenth transmitter of a foolish face.
R. SAVAGE.—*Bastard.*

What can they see in the longest kingly
line in Europe, save that it runs back to
a successful soldier ?
SCOTT.—*Woodstock, Vol.* 2, *ch.* 37.

Each has his own tree of ancestors, but
at the top of all sits Probably Arboreal.
R. L. STEVENSON.—*Memories.*

From yon blue heavens above us bent
The gardener Adam and his wife
Smile at the claims of long descent.
TENNYSON.—*Clara Vere de Vere.*

From whence came Smith, albe he knight
or squire,
But from the smith that forgeth at the
fire ?
RICHD. VERSTEGAN.—*Restitution of*
Decayed Intelligence (*c.* 1630).

Who is born in the purple is seldom
worthy of it. VOLTAIRE.—*Brutus,* Act 2.

You should study the Peerage, Gerald.
. . . It is the best thing in fiction the
English have ever done.
OSCAR WILDE.—*Woman of No*
Importance, Act 3.

Mules boast much that their ancestors
were horses. *German prov.*

PENITENCE

Gloomy penitence is only madness
turned upside down.
JOHNSON.—*In Boswell's " Life."*

I do not shame
To tell you what I was, since my conversion
So sweetly tastes, being the thing I am.
SHAKESPEARE.—*As You Like It,*
Act 4, 3.

The lowliest garb of penitence and prayer.
S. J. STONE.—*Weary of Earth.*

Repentance is the May of the virtues.
Chinese prov.

PENSIONS

Pension : An allowance made to anyone
without an equivalent. In England it is
generally understood to mean pay given to
a state hireling for treason to his country.
JOHNSON.—*Dictionary.*

PEOPLE

A people is but the attempt of many
To rise to the completer life of one.
        BROWNING.—*Luria*, Act 5.

In all forms of government the people
is the true legislator.
        BURKE.—*Tracts on Popery Laws.*

But while we sing " God save the King,"
We'll ne'er forget the People.
        BURNS.—*Dumfries Volunteers.*

O stormy peple ! unsad [unsettled] and
        ever untrewe ;
Ay undiscreet and chaunging as a vane,
Delyting ever in rumbel [rumour] that is
newe.   CHAUCER.—*Clerk's Tale*, 939.

And what the people but a herd confused,
A miscellaneous rabble, who extol
Things vulgar ?
        MILTON.—*Paradise Regained, Bk.* 3, 49.

        O People keen
For change, to whom the new looks ever
        green !
WORDSWORTH.—*Eccles. Sonnets, Pt.* 2, 33.

PERCEPTION

Minds that have nothing to confer
Find little to perceive.
        WORDSWORTH.—*Poems on the
                Affections, No.* 16.

He that sits on the giant's shoulder sees
further than the giant.   *French prov.*

PERDITION

The gates of hell are open night and day ;
Smooth the descent, and easy is the way.
        DRYDEN.—*Æneid, Bk.* 6, 192.

PERFECTION

Nor was perfection made for man below.
        BEATTIE.—*The Minstrel, Bk.* 1, 6.

If you get simple beauty, and nought else,
You get about the best thing God invents.
        BROWNING.—*Fra Lippo.*

In virtues nothing earthly could surpass
        her,
Save thine " incomparable oil," Macassar !
        BYRON.—*Don Juan, c.* 1, *st.* 17.

What is better than wisdom ? Woman.
And what is better than a good woman ?
Nothing.   CHAUCER.—*Tale of Melibeus.*

Thou hast no faults, or I no faults can
        spy ;
Thou art all beauty, or all blindness I.
    C. CODRINGTON.—*Lines to Garth on his
                " Dispensary "* (1696).

Mind cannot follow it, nor words express
Her infinite sweetness.
        DANTE.—*Paradise,* 14, 75 (*Cary tr.*).

My natural instinct teaches me
        (And instinct is important O !)
You're everything you ought to be,
        And nothing that you oughtn't O !
        SIR W. S. GILBERT.—*Princess Ida.*

Death ere thou hast slain another,
Learn'd and fair and good as she,
Time shall throw a dart at thee.
        BEN JONSON.—*On Lady Pembroke.*

Take away the idea of perfection, and
you take away enthusiasm.
        ROUSSEAU.—*Julie.*

The nobler and more perfect a thing is,
the later and the slower it is in reaching
maturity.
        SCHOPENHAUER.—*On Women.*

        A maid
That paragons description and wild fame ;
One that excels the quirks of blazoning
        pens.
        SHAKESPEARE.—*Othello*, Act 2, 1.

No one can be perfectly free till all are
free ; no one can be perfectly moral till
all are moral ; no one can be perfectly
happy till all are happy.
        H. SPENCER.—*Social Statics, ch.* 28, 16.

Faultily faulty, icily regular, splendidly
        null,
Dead perfection, no more.
        TENNYSON.—*Maud, Pt.* 1, 2.

The Grecian artist gleaned from many
        faces,
And in a perfect whole the parts com-
        bined,
So have I counted o'er dear women's
        graces
To form the Mary of my ardent mind.
        H. T. TUCKERMAN.—*Mary.*

To keep in sight Perfection, and adore
The vision, is the artist's best delight.
        SIR W. WATSON.—*Epigrams.*

Let other bards of angels sing,
Bright suns without a spot ;
But thou art no such perfect thing :
Rejoice that thou art not !
        WORDSWORTH.—*Poems on the
                Affections, No.* 15.

Trust not a man ; we are by nature false,
Dissembling, subtle, cruel, and inconstant.
        OTWAY.—*The Orphan*, Act 2, 1.

Perfidious she is, but however perfidious
still she is dear.
        TIBULLUS.—*Bk.* 3, 7, 24.

PERFORMANCE

He made no answer ; but he took the city.
        BYRON.—*Don Juan, c.* 7, 53
                (*referring to Suwaroff*).

To fair request
Silent performance maketh best return.
DANTE.—*Hell (Cary's tr.), c.* 24, 74.

When thou dost purpose ought (within thy
    power),
Be sure to do it, though it be but small.
        HERBERT.—*Church Porch.*

And what he greatly thought he nobly
dared. POPE.—*Odyssey, Bk.* 2, 312.

I carena if the fire gae about the roast,
or the roast gae about the fire, if the meat
be ready.   *Scottish prov.*

PERFUME

I cannot talk with civet in the room,
A fine puss gentleman that's all perfume ;
The sight's enough—no need to smell a
beau ! COWPER.—*Conversation,* 283.

A woman smells best when she smells of
nothing.
        PLAUTUS.—*Mostellaria,* 1, 3, 116.

He was perfumèd like a milliner.
SHAKESPEARE.—*Henry IV., Pt.* 1, Act 1, 2.

PERIODS

These are the times that try men's souls.
        THOS. PAINE.—*American Crisis.*

For in the fatness of these pursy times
Virtue itself of vice must pardon beg.
        SHAKESPEARE.—*Hamlet,* Act 3, 4.

The splendid period of Louis XIV.—
that period our glory, our model, and our
despair.
        VOLTAIRE.—*Irène (Pref. Letter,* 1778).

PERJURY

For breaking of an oath and lying
Is but a kind of self-denying,
A saint-like virtue ; and from hence
Some have broke oaths by Providence.
        BUTLER.—*Hudibras, Pt.* 2, *c.* 2.

Perjury, that heaven-defying vice,
Sells oaths by tale, and at the lowest price,
Stamps God's own name upon a lie just
    made,
To turn a penny in the way of trade.
        COWPER.—*Table-Talk,* 419.

PERSECUTION

Religious persecution may shield itself
under the guise of a mistaken and over-
zealous piety.
        BURKE.—*Impeachment of Hastings
                (Feb.* 17, 1788).

They lived unknown,
Till Persecution dragged them into fame,
And chased them up to Heaven.
        COWPER.—*Winter Morning Walk.*

Ignorance and fear combined have made
the religious annals of mankind the most
hideous chapters in history.
        FROUDE.—*Short Studies, Party
                        Politics.*

Persecution produced its natural effect
on them. It found them a sect ; it made
them a faction.
        MACAULAY.—*Hist. of England, ch.* 1.

When men of ability are punished, their
authority spreads.
        TACITUS.—*Annals, Bk.* 4.

I ask who has most religion, the calumniator, who persecutes, or the calumniated,
who forgives.
        VOLTAIRE.—*Alzire, Prelim. Discourse.*

But who would force the soul, tilts with a
    straw
Against a champion cased in adamant.
        WORDSWORTH.—*Eccles. Sonnets, Pt.* 3, 7.

PERSISTENCE

If the fool would persist in his folly he
would become wise.
        WM. BLAKE.—*Proverbs of Hell.*

Obstinacy in a bad cause is but constancy in a good.
        SIR T. BROWNE.—*Religio Medici,
                        Pt.* 1, *sec.* 25.

Enter, but this warning hear :
He forth again departs who looks behind.
        DANTE.—*Purgatory (Cary's tr.), c.* 9.

Nor yet perceived the vital spirit fled,
But yet fought on, nor knew that he was
    dead.
        MISS EDGEWORTH.—*From the Italian
                (Essay on Irish Bulls, ch.* 6).

If goodness lead him not, yet weariness
May toss him to my breast.
        HERBERT.—*The Pulley.*

'Tis a lesson you should heed,
    Try, try, try again.
If at first you don't succeed,
    Try, try, try again.
W. E. HICKSON.—*Try and try again.*

The heights by great men reached and kept
Were not attained by sudden flight,
But they, while their companions slept,
Were toiling upward in the night.
        LONGFELLOW.—*St. Augustine.*

Let us then be up and doing,
    With a heart for any fate ;
Still achieving, still pursuing,
    Learn to labour and to wait.
        LONGFELLOW.—*Psalm of Life.*

What is harder than rock, what softer
than water ? Yet hard rocks are hollowed
out by soft water.   OVID.—*Ars Amat.*

369

A great devotee of the Gospel of Getting
On.
G. B. Shaw.—*Mrs. Warren's Profession,*
Act 4.

No rock so hard but that a little wave
May beat admission in a thousand years.
TENNYSON.—*Princess, c* 3, 138.

God is with those who persevere.
Koran, ch. 8;

For Witherington my heart is wo,
As one in doleful dumps ;
For when his legs were smitten off,
He fought upon his stumps.
Chevy Chase (15th century).

By perseverance the snail reached the
ark.   *Saying given by C. H. Spurgeon*
(" *Salt-Cellars* ").

PERSONALITIES

Do not attack persons but expose the
vices.   MARTIAL.—*Epig.* 10, 33.

Forgiving all things personal,
He hated only wrong to man.
J. G. WHITTIER.—*Sumner, st.* 20.

PERSUASION

You can do anything with children if
you only play with them.   BISMARCK.

The great mind knows the power of gen-
tleness,
Only tries force because persuasion fails.
BROWNING.—*Prince Hohenstiel-
Schwangau.*

Adding once more the music of her tongue
To the sweet speech of her alluring eyes.
SIR J. DAVIES.—*Orchestra, st.* 97.

But Dick put a couple of balls in his nob
And perwailed on him to stop.
DICKENS.—*Pickwick, c.* 43.
(*Sam Weller's Song.*)

Plutarch tells us that Thucydides, when
Archidamus, king of Sparta, asked him
which was the best wrestler, Pericles or
he,—replied, " When I throw him, he says
he was never down, and he persuades the
very spectators to believe him."
EMERSON.—*Eloquence.*

Truth from his lips prevailed with double
sway,
And fools, who came to scoff, remained to
pray.   GOLDSMITH.—*Deserted Village.*

By winning words to conquer willing
hearts,
And make persuasion do the work of fear.
MILTON.—*Paradise Regained, Bk.* 1, 231.

There are two levers for moving men—
interest and fear.   NAPOLEON.

I have often heard, Socrates, from
Gorgias, that the art of persuasion far
excels all other arts. For it would make
all things its slaves willingly and not by
violence, and so is of all arts the best.
PLATO.—*Philebus,* 136.

Men are more eloquent than women made,
But women are more powerful to persuade.
T. RANDOLPH.—*Amyntas.*

He who has the truth at his heart need
never fear the want of persuasion on his
tongue.
RUSKIN.—*Stones of Venice, c.* 6, 99.

Your gentleness shall force,
More than your force move us to gentle-
ness.
SHAKESPEARE.—*As You Like It,* Act 2, 7.

Ay, springes to catch woodcocks. I do
know
When the blood burns, how prodigal the
soul
Lends the tongue vows.
SHAKESPEARE.—*Hamlet,* Act 1, 3.

O, thou hast damnable iteration ; and
art, indeed, able to corrupt a saint.
SHAKESPEARE.—*Henry IV.,* Pt. 1, Act 1.

This is the only witchcraft I have used.
SHAKESPEARE.—*Othello,* Act 1, 3.

O for a falconer's voice,
To lure this tassel-gentle back again !
SHAKESPEARE.—*Romeo and Juliet,*
Act 2, 2.

There is no tongue that moves, none none
i' the world,
So soon as yours could win me.
SHAKESPEARE.—*Winter's Tale,* Act 1, 2.

For love will not be drawne, but must be
ledde. SPENSER.—*Colin Clout, l.* 129.

His gentle reason so persuasive stole,
That the charmed hearer thought it was
his own.
THOMSON.—*On Lord Talbot.*

Good manners and soft words have
brought many a difficult thing to pass.
SIR J. VANBRUGH.—*Æsop, Pt.* 1, Act 4, 2.

Who in his pocket hath no money,
In his mouth he must have honey.
R. WATKYNS.—*Flamma sine Fumo.*

PERVERSITY

In truth he was a strange and wayward
wight.   BEATTIE.—*The Minstrel.*

Ah, Genoese ! men perverse in every way,
With every foulness stained, why from the
earth
Are ye not cancelled ?
DANTE.—*Hell* (*Cary's tr.*), *c.* 33, 149.

Men take more pains to lose themselves than would be requisite to keep them in the right road.
K. H. DIGBY.—*Broadstone of Honour* (1822).

Look round the habitable world ! How few Know their own good, or, knowing it, pursue. DRYDEN.—*Juvenal, Sat.* 10, 1.

Fair moon, to thee I sing,
Bright regent of the heavens:
Say, why is everything
Either at sixes or at sevens ?
SIR W. S. GILBERT.—*H.M.S. Pinafore.*

Irrationally held truths may be more harmful than reasoned errors.
T. H. HUXLEY.—*Science and Culture.*

But was ever Pride contented,
Or would Folly e'er be taught ?
W. S. LANDOR.—*Arab to his Mistress.*

Fall'n Cherub, to be weak is miserable,
Doing or suffering : but of this be sure,
To do ought good never will be our task,
But ever to do ill our sole delight.
MILTON.—*Paradise Lost, Bk.* 1, 157.

If then his providence
Out of our evil seek to bring forth good,
Our labour must be to pervert that end,
And out of good still to find means of evil.
MILTON.—*Ib.*, 162.

Daphne knows, with equal ease,
How to vex and how to please ;
But the folly of her sex
Makes her sole delight to vex.
SWIFT.—*Daphne.*

PESSIMISM

Ay ! you're in love, I see, with difficulties And miseries.
ARISTOPHANES.—*The Birds* (Hoopoe to Euelpides) (*Frere tr.*).

Some people always sigh in thanking God.
E. B. BROWNING.—*Aurora Leigh, Bk.* 1.

One really lives nowhere ; one does but vegetate and wish it all at an end. [*Mr. Meadows.*]
MME. D'ARBLAY.—*Cecilia, Bk.* 7, c. 9.

Can anybody remember when the times were not hard, and money not scarce ?
EMERSON.—*Works and Days.*

Fools ! who fancy Christ mistaken ;
Man a tool to buy and sell ;
Earth a failure, God-forsaken,
Ante-room of Hell.
C. KINGSLEY.—*World's Age.*

What need a man forestall his date of grief,
And run to meet what he would most avoid ?   MILTON.—*Comus*, 362.

Polydore. Nay then,
Let us embrace, and from this very moment
Vow an eternal misery together.
Monimia. And wilt thou be a very faithful wretch,
Never grow fond of cheerful peace again ?
Wilt thou with me study to be unhappy,
And find out ways how to increase afflic-
tion ?
OTWAY.—*The Orphan*, Act 4, 2. *Original Ed.* 1685 (*omitted in some later Editions.*)

Weary waiting and weary striving,
Glad outsetting and sad arriving ;
What is it worth when the goal is won ?
All things must end that have begun.
JOHN H. PAYNE.—*Kyrielle.*

Who breathes must suffer, and who thinks must mourn,
And he alone is blessed who ne'er was born.
PRIOR.—*Solomon, Bk.* 3, 239.

I have the secret of extracting sadness from all things, instead of joy.
RUSKIN.—*Letter to his Mother*, 1867.

That human life must be a kind of mistake is clear from the fact that man is a compound of needs, which are difficult to satisfy ; and if they are satisfied, all that he attains is a state of painlessness, in which he can only give himself up to boredom.   SCHOPENHAUER.—*Emptiness of Existence.*

I was not always a man of woe.
SCOTT.—*Lay of the Last Minstrel*, 2, 12.

He grieves more than he needs who grieves before he needs.
SENECA.—*Ep.* 95.

It goes so heavily with my disposition, that this goodly frame, the earth, seems to me a sterile promontory ; this most excellent canopy, the air, look you,—this brave o'erhanging firmament, this majestical roof fretted with golden fire,—why, it appears no other thing to me but a foul and pestilent congregation of vapours.
SHAKESPEARE.—*Hamlet*, Act 2, 2.

Of comfort no man speak :
Let's talk of graves, of worms, and epi-
taphs.
SHAKESPEARE.—*Richard II.*, Act 3, 2.

Let's choose executors and talk of wills.
SHAKESPEARE.—*Ib.*

" Do you know what a pessimist is ? "
—" A man who thinks everybody as nasty as himself, and hates them for it."
G. B. SHAW.—*Unsocial Socialist, ch.* 5.

I shall never be friends again with roses.
SWINBURNE.—*Triumph of Time.*

I shall hate sweet music my whole life long.
SWINBURNE.—*Triumph of Time.*

Welcome, kindred glooms !
Congenial horrors, hail !
THOMSON.—*Seasons, Winter.*

Away with this cowardly and vulgar talk of man for ever degenerating, of everything exhausting itself, and coming to an end ! Nature is inexhaustible, and indefatigable toil is a god which rejuvenates her. VOLTAIRE.—*A. M* ⁂

Blessed be nothing.
Prov. quoted by Emerson as expressing " the transcendentalism of common life."

PETITIONS

From plots and treasons Heaven preserve my years,
But save me most from my petitioners !
DRYDEN.—*Absalom and Achitophel,*
Pt. **1,** 985.

Petition me no petitions.
FIELDING.—*Tom Thumb,* Act 1, 2.

Petitions not sweetened
With gold are but unsavoury ; oft refused ;
Or, if received, are pocketed, not read.
MASSINGER.—*Emperor of the East,*
Act 1, 2.

A short petition to a great man is not only a suit to him for his favour, but also a panegyric upon his parts.
R. SOUTH.—*Sermon* 16.

PETTINESS

The most disagreeable two-legged animal I know is a little great man ; and the next, a little great man's factotum and friend. C. C. COLTON.—*Lacon.*

Thou canst not mean so poorly as thou talk'st.
CONGREVE.—*Mourning Bride,* Act 2, 3.

These little things are great to little men.
GOLDSMITH.—*Traveller.*

Small things become a small man.
HORACE.—*Ep.,* Bk. 1.

Those who apply themselves too much to little things usually become incapable of great things.
LA ROCHEFOUCAULD.—*Maxim* 41.

In men this blunder still you find :
All think their little set mankind.
HANNAH MORE.—*Florio.*

The snail, say the Hindoos, sees nothing but his own shell, and thinks it the grandest palace in the universe.
SYDNEY SMITH.—*Peter Plymley's Letters,*
No. 10.

For who would be satirical
Upon a thing so very small ?
SWIFT.—*Dr. Delany's Villa.*

PHILANTHROPY

The drying up a single tear has more
Of honest fame, than shedding seas of gore.
BYRON.—*Don Juan,* c. 8, 3.

Thy Godlike crime was to be kind,
To render with thy precepts less
The sum of human wretchedness.
BYRON.—*Prometheus.*

Humanely glorious ! Men will weep for him,
When many a guilty martial fame is dim.
CAMPBELL.—*La Pérouse.*

Our noble society for providing the infant negroes in the West Indies with flannel waistcoats and moral pocket-hand-kerchiefs. DICKENS.—*Pickwick,* c. 27.

Their chat on various subjects ran,
But most what each had done for man.
GAY.—*Fables,* Pt. 2, 13.

Far other aims his heart had learned to prize ;
More bent to raise the wretched than to rise. GOLDSMITH.—*Deserted Village.*

Whose glory was, redressing human wrong.
TENNYSON.—*Idylls: Dedication.*

PHILOSOPHY

In the calm lights of mild philosophy.
ADDISON.—*Cato,* Act 1, 1.

What then is that which is able to guide a man ? One thing and only one,—philosophy. M. AURELIUS.

A little philosophy inclineth man's mind to atheism ; but depth in philosophy bringeth men's minds about to religion.
BACON.—*Of Atheism.*

All good moral philosophy, as was said, is but a handmaid to religion.
BACON.—*Adv. of Learning,* Bk. **2.**

Well, as I take it, all philosophy
Is questionable guessing, but the sense
A man grows up with bears the stamp of nature.
R. BRIDGES.—*First Part of Nero,*
Act 1, 1.

But as I said,
I *won't* philosophise, and *will* be read.
BYRON.—*Don Juan,* c. 10, 28.

It ill becomes a philosopher to be cast down in mind. CICERO.

There is nothing so absurd that it might not have been spoken by some one of the philosophers.
CICERO.—*De Divinatione,* 2, 58.

It is neither possible or necessary for all men, nor for many, to be philosophers.
COLERIDGE.—*Biog. Literaria, ch. 12.*

To them the sounding jargon of the schools
Seems what it is—a cap and bells for fools.
COWPER.—*Truth, 368.*

He [Plato] contains the future, as he came out of the past.
EMERSON.—*Books.*

Philosophers dwell in the moon.
FORD.—*Lovers' Melancholy,* Act 3, 3.

Divine philosophy, by whose pure light
We first distinguish, then pursue the right.
GIFFORD.—*Juvenal,* 13, 254.

There is nothing so ridiculous that has not at some time been said by some philosopher.
GOLDSMITH.—*Citizen of the World,* 16
(*from Cicero*).

This same philosophy is a good horse in the stable, but an arrant jade on a journey.
GOLDSMITH.—*Good-Natured Man,* Act 1.

Brer Rabbit des [just] put out fer home. W'en he git dar, wat do he do? Do he go off in a cornder by hisse'f, en wipe he weepin' eye? Dat he don't—dat he don't. He des tuck 'n wait he chance.
J. C. HARRIS.—*Nights with Uncle Remus,
ch. 30.*

Do not all charms fly
At the mere touch of cold philosophy?
KEATS.—*Lamia, Pt. 2.*

Philosophy will clip an angel's wings.
KEATS.—*Ib.*

Philosophy triumphs easily over ills past and ills to come; present ills triumph over philosophy.
LA ROCHEFOUCAULD.—*Maxim 22.*

Experience shows that the knowledge of morality, by mere natural light (how agreeable soever it be to it), makes but slow progress and little advance in the world.
LOCKE.—*Reasonableness of Christianity.*

But above all 'tis pleasantest to get
The top of high Philosophy, and sit
On the calm, peaceful, flourishing head of it,
Whence we may view, deep, wondrous deep below,
How poor mistaken mortals wandering go,
Seeking the path to Happiness.
LUCRETIUS.—*De Rerum Natura,* 2, 6
(*Creech tr.*).

Thou, parent of Philosophy, hast shown
The way to Truth by precepts of thy own.
LUCRETIUS.—*Ib.,* 3, 9. (*Of Epicurus*).

Thus from the Laureat fraternity of Poets riper years and the ceaseless round of study and reading led me to the shady spaces of philosophy; but chiefly to the divine volumes of Plato.
MILTON.—*Apology against a pamphlet
called Smectymnuus* (1642).

How charming is divine philosophy!
Not harsh and crabbèd, as dull fools suppose,
But musical as is Apollo's lute,
And a perpetual feast of nectared sweets,
Where no crude surfeit reigns.
MILTON.—*Comus,* 476.

To ridicule philosophy is to be truly a philosopher.
PASCAL.—*Pensées, Pt.* 1, 10, 36.

A man of business may talk of philosophy; a man who has none may practise it.
POPE.—*Thoughts on Various Subjects.*

It is the path of the passions which has led me to philosophy.   ROUSSEAU.

Hast any philosophy in thee, shepherd?
SHAKESPEARE.—*As You Like It,* Act 3, 2.

For there was never yet philosopher
That could endure the toothache patiently.
SHAKESPEARE.—*Much Ado,* Act 5, 1.

Adversity's sweet milk, philosophy.
SHAKESPEARE.—*Romeo and Juliet,*
Act 3, 3.

Hang up philosophy!
Unless philosophy can make a Juliet.
SHAKESPEARE.—*Ib.*

To suck the sweets of sweet philosophy.
SHAKESPEARE.—*Taming of the Shrew,*
Act 1, 1.

Bishop Berkeley destroyed this world in one volume octavo; and nothing remained after his time but mind; which experienced a similar fate from the hand of Mr. Hume in 1737.
SYDNEY SMITH.—*Lectures on Moral
Philosophy, Introductory* (1804).

Philosophy! the lumber of the schools.
SWIFT.—*To Sir W. Temple.*

What though the radiance, which was once so bright,
Be now for ever taken from my sight,
Though nothing can bring back the hour
Of splendour in the grass, of glory in the flower;
We will grieve not, rather find
Strength in what remains behind;

. . . .

In the faith that looks through death,
In years that bring the philosophic mind.
WORDSWORTH.—*Intimations of
Immortality.*

PHYSICIANS

Nor bring, to see me cease to live,
Some doctor full of phrase and fame,
To shake his sapient head, and give
The ill he cannot cure a name.
    MATTHEW ARNOLD.—*A Wish.*

A skilful leech is better far
Than half a hundred men of war.
    BUTLER.—*Hudibras, Pt.* 1, *c.* 2.

This is the way physicians mend or end us.
    BYRON.—*Don Juan, c.* 10, 42.

In nothing do men more nearly approach
the gods than in giving health to men.
    CICERO.—*Pro Ligario.*

When ill, indeed,
E'en dismissing the doctor don't always
succeed.
    G. COLMAN.—*Lodgings for Single
    Gentlemen.*

Every physician, almost, hath his
favourite disease.
    FIELDING.—*Tom Jones, Bk.* 2, *c.*9.

His wise, rare smile is sweet with certainties.
    W. E. HENLEY.—*In Hospital,* 15.

In fact he did not find M.D.'s
Worth one D——M.
    HOOD.—*Jack Hall.*

Murderers are mony leches (physicians).
Lord them amende !
    LANGLAND.—*Piers Plowman, Passus* 6.

For none but a clever dialectician
Can hope to become a great physician ;
That has been settled long ago ;
Logic makes an important part
Of the mystery of the healing art.
    LONGFELLOW.—*Golden Legend,* 6.

God and the Doctor we alike adore,
But only when in danger, not before ;
The danger o'er, both are alike requited :
God is forgotten and the Doctor slighted.
    ROBT. OWEN.—*Epigram (founded on
    Quarles, v. "Soldiers").*

A feeble body weakens the mind. Hence
the empire of medicine, an art more pernicious to men than all the ills it pretends
to cure.
    ROUSSEAU.—*Emile.*

Throw physic to the dogs, I'll none of it.
    SHAKESPEARE.—*Macbeth,* Act 5, 3.

Who knows his art but not his trade.
    SWIFT.—*In Sickness (of Dr. Arbuthnot,
    who attended him without fee).*

The learned leeches in despair depart,
And shake their heads, desponding of
their art.
    VIRGIL.—*Georgics, Bk.* 3 (*Dryden tr.*).

Honour a physician with the honour due
unto him.   *Ecclesiasticus* XXXVIII, 1.

And had suffered many things of many
physicians, and had spent all that she had
and was nothing bettered, but rather grew
worse.   *St. Mark* v, 6.

Physician, heal thyself.
    St. Luke iv, 23 (*Arabic prov.*).

Where there are three doctors there are
two atheists.   *Mediæval Latin prov.*

If the doctor cures, the sun sees it ; if
he kills, the earth hides it.
    Proverb (Scottish ?).

A physician is a man who pours drugs,
of which he knows little, into a body of
which he knows less.   *Attrib. to Voltaire.*

PICTURES

Everybody who has the least sensibility
or imagination derives a certain pleasure
from pictures.
    MACAULAY.—*On R. Montgomery's
    poems.*

A room hung with pictures is a room
hung with thoughts.
    SIR JOSHUA REYNOLDS.

Dost thou love pictures ? we will fetch
    thee straight
Adonis painted by a running brook,
And Cytherea all in sedges hid.
    SHAKESPEARE.—*Taming of the Shrew,
    Induction,* 2.

They are good furniture pictures, unworthy of praise and undeserving of blame.
    RUSKIN.—*Modern Painters,* 1, *Pt.* 2, *sec.* 5.

PIONEERS

Hail to the courage which gave voice to
its creed, ere the creed won consecration
from time !
    M. ARNOLD.—*Haworth Churchyard
    (Written of Harriet Martineau).*

We were the first that ever burst
Into that silent sea.
    COLERIDGE.—*Ancient Mariner.*

Sleep, ye shall sleep, but within you
Dwelleth the gift of the Lord :
Ye shall have sons for reward
And your seed upon earth shall continue.
    L. HOUSMAN.—*House-Builder.*

Then to side with Truth is noble when we
    share her wretched crust,
Ere her cause bring fame and profit, and
    'tis prosperous to be just ;
Then it is the brave man chooses, while
    the coward turns aside,
Doubting in his abject spirit, till his Lord
    is crucified.
    J. R. LOWELL.—*Present Crisis.*

To whatever height we may carry human knowledge, I hope we shall never forget those energetic and enterprising men who met the difficulty in its rudest shape.
SYDNEY SMITH.—*Lectures on Moral Philosophy*, 3.

You are our predecessors, but the servant who carries the torch and walks in front of his master, ought not to regard himself as superior to his master.
VOLTAIRE.—*Christian against Six Jews.*

If I had not lifted up the stone, you had not found the jewel. *Hebrew prov.*

PITY

Then cherish pity, lest you drive an angel from your door.
WM. BLAKE.—*Holy Thursday.*

Humblest of herte, hyest of reverence,
Benignè flour, coroune of vertues alle.
CHAUCER.—*Complaint unto Pity.*

For pitee renneth sone in gentil herte.
CHAUCER.—*Knight's Tale.*

Here pity most doth show herself alive,
When she is dead.
DANTE.—*Hell* (Cary's tr.), c. 20, 26 (*Virgil's reproach to Dante on his pitying Amphiraüs*).

Pity is sworn servant unto love ;
And thus be sure, wherever it begin
To make the way, it lets the master in.
S. DANIEL.—*Queen's Arcadia.*

But they that han't pity, why I pities they.
C. DIBDIN.—*True Courage.*

'Twas but a kindred sound to move,
For pity melts the heart to love.
DRYDEN.—*Alexander's Feast*, st. 5.

Can you pretend to love,
And have no pity ? Love and that are twins.
DRYDEN.—*Don Sebastian*, Act 3, 1.

Of all the paths that lead to a woman's love
Pity's the straightest.
FLETCHER AND MASSINGER.—*Knight of Malta*, Act 1, 1.

Taught by the power that pities me,
I learn to pity them.
GOLDSMITH.—*The Hermit.*

He that woll maister be
He mot [must] be servaunt to pite.
GOWER.—*Confessio Amantis*, Bk. 2.

Love gains the shrine when pity opes the door.
(1st) LORD LYTTON.—*New Timon*, Pt. 3, 1.

I have no longing for things great and fair,
Beauty and strength and grace of word or deed ;
For all sweet things my soul has ceased to care :
Infinite pity—that is all its need.
J. B. B. NICHOLS.—*During Music.*

"It is a hard thing," said Agesilaus, " to be pitiful and wise at the same time."
PLUTARCH.—*Morals*, Bk. 1.

A thing of pity.
SHAKESPEARE.—*Cymbeline*, Act 5, 4.

But yet the pity of it, Iago !—O, Iago, the pity of it, Iago !
SHAKESPEARE.—*Othello*, Act 4, 1.

Soft pity enters at an iron gate.
SHAKESPEARE.—*Lucrece*, st. 85.

Pity swells the tide of love.
YOUNG.—*Night Thoughts*, 3.

PLACE

Thou cam'st not to thy place by accident ;
It is the very place God meant for thee.
ARCHBISHOP TRENCH.—*Sonnets*, No. 2.

A ruler who appoints any man to an office, when there is in his dominions another man better qualified, sins against God and against the state. *Koran.*

PLACE-SEEKERS

I have never concealed from him that in order to serve my country I would accept the highest positions.
E. GONDINET.—*Pontdrisson in " La Panache,"* Act 1.

To place and power all public spirit tends ;
In place and power all public spirit ends.
MOORE.—*Irish Melodies : Corruption.*

But bees, on flowers alighting, cease their hum ;
So, settling upon places, Whigs grow dumb.
MOORE.—*Ib.*

PLAGIARISM

Why should the world be so severe
On every small-wit privateer ?
S. BUTLER.—*Upon Plagiaries* (*marginal emendation of opening lines*).

Who, to patch up his fame, or fill his purse,
Still pilfers wretched plans and makes them worse ;
Like gipsies, lest the stolen brat be known,
Defacing first, then claiming for his own.
CHURCHILL.—*Apology*, v. 233.

Perched on the eagle's towering wing
The lowly linnet loves to sing.
C. CIBBER.—*Birthday Ode.*

They will not let my play run and yet they steal my thunder.
JOHN DENNIS.—*Attributed.*

The poet who borrows nothing from others is yet to be born. He and the Jews' Messias will come together.
DRYDEN.—*Dedic. of Æneid.*

When a poor thief appears in rich garments, we immediately know they are none of his own.
POPE.—*Thoughts on Various Subjects.*

Most writers steal a good thing when they can. B. W. PROCTER.—*Diego*, 4.

Steal! to be sure they may, and egad, serve your best thoughts as gipsies do stolen children—disfigure them to make 'em pass for their own.
SHERIDAN.—*Critic,* Act 1, 1.

It is scarcely possible for anyone to write or say anything, in this late time of the world, to which, in the literature of the world, a parallel could not somewhere be found.
TENNYSON.—*Letter (cited in Sir Edwd. Cook's "More Literary Recollections").*

If ye had not plowed with my heifer, ye had not found out my riddle.
Judges xiv, 18.

PLEASING

Too much desire to please pleasure divorces.
CHAPMAN.—*Ovid's Banquet of Sense.*

Confidence in pleasing is often an infallible method of displeasing.
LA ROCHEFOUCAULD.—*Maxim* 564.

Who seeks to please all men each way,
And not himself offend,
He may begin his work to-day
But God knows when he'll end.
S. ROWLANDS.—*Epigrams.*

They who are pleased themselves must always please.
THOMSON.—*Castle of Indolence,* 1, 15.

PLEASURE

He made a feast, drank fierce and fast,
And crowned his head with flowers—
No easier nor no quicker passed
The impracticable hours.
M. ARNOLD.—*Obermann once More.*

Very sure it is,
Pleasure is not for him who pleasure serves.
R. BRIDGES.—*Achilles in Scyros,*
l. 1700.

Then top and maintop crowd the sail,
Heave Care owre side !
And large before Enjoyment's gale
Let's tak' the tide.
BURNS.—*To Jas. Smith.*

Chords that vibrate sweetest pleasure
Thrill the deepest notes of woe.
BURNS.—*On Sensibility.*

Our pains are real things, but all
Our pleasures but fantastical.
S. BUTLER.—*Satire.*

On with the dance ; let joy be unconfined ;
No sleep till morn, when Youth and Pleasure meet
To chase the glowing hours with flying feet.
BYRON.—*Childe Harold, c.* 3, 22.

Pleasure's a sin, and sometimes sin's a pleasure.
BYRON.—*Don Juan, c.* 1, 133.

Let us have wine and women, mirth and laughter,
Sermons and soda-water the day after.
BYRON.—*Ib., c.* 2, 178.

Pleasure (whene'er she sings at least)'s a siren,
That lures, to flay alive, the young beginner.   BYRON.—*Ib., c.* 3, 36.

Though sages may pour out their wisdom's treasure,
There is no sterner moralist than Pleasure.
BYRON.—*Ib., c.* 3, 65.

There is not a little generalship and strategy required in the managing and marshalling of our pleasures.
C. C. COLTON.—*Lacon.*

Thus grief still treads upon the heels of pleasure ;
Married in haste, we may repent at leisure.
CONGREVE.—*Old Bachelor,* Act 5, 3.

Where pleasure is adored,
That reeling goddess with the zoneless waist
And wandering eyes, still leaning on the arm
Of Novelty, her fickle frail support.
COWPER.—*Garden,* 51.

Pleasure is labour too, and tires as much.
COWPER.—*Hope,* 20.

No blinder bigot, I maintain it still,
Than he who must have pleasure, come what will.   COWPER.—*Ib.,* 595.

And pleasure brings as surely in her train,
Remorse, and Sorrow, and vindictive Pain.
COWPER.—*Progress of Error,* 43.

Mingle your cares with pleasures now and then.   DION.—*Cato.*

Sweet is pleasure after pain.
DRYDEN.—*Alexander's Feast, st.* 3.

A Book of Verses underneath the Bough,
A Jug of Wine, a Loaf of Bread—and Thou
Beside me singing in the Wilderness—
Oh, Wilderness were Paradise enow !
FITZGERALD.—*Rubáiyát, st.* 12.

All pleasure must be bought at the price of pain. The difference between false pleasure and true is just this : for the true, the price is paid before you enjoy it ; for the false, after you enjoy it.

JOHN FOSTER.

A life of pleasure is therefore the most unpleasing life in the world.

GOLDSMITH.—*Citizen of the World*, 44.

The heart distrusting asks if this be joy.

GOLDSMITH.—*Deserted Village*.

In gallant trim the gilded vessel goes,
Youth on the prow, and Pleasure at the helm.   GRAY.—*Bard*.

And feign, like truth, for one mad day,
That Earth is Paradise.

T. HARDY.—*To Life*.

Men may scoff and men may pray,
But they pay
Every pleasure with a pain.

W. E. HENLEY.—*Ballade of Truisms*.

Pleasure is very seldom found where it is sought.   JOHNSON.—*Rambler, No.* 58.

Life must be filled up, and the man who is not capable of intellectual pleasures must content himself with such as his senses can afford.

JOHNSON.—*Remark as recorded by Mrs. Piozzi.*

Rarity enhances pleasures.

JUVENAL.—*Sat.* 11.

Even bees, the little almsmen of spring-
bowers,
Know there is richest juice in poison-
flowers.   KEATS.—*Isabella*.

Hence, vain deluding joys,
The brood of Folly, without father bred.

MILTON.—*Il Penseroso*.

In mirth, that after no repenting draws.

MILTON.—*Sonnet*.

For other things [than study] mild
Heaven a time ordains,
And disapproves that care, though wise in show,
That with superfluous burden loads the day,
And when God sends a cheerful hour, refrains.   MILTON.—*Ib.*

Nothing gives pleasure but that which gives pain.   MONTAIGNE.—*Bk.* 3.

Till Florio with a sigh confessed
The simplest pleasures are the best.

HANNAH MORE.

There is no unalloyed pleasure; some tinge of anxiety is mixed with all our joys.

OVID.—*Metam., Bk.* 7.

There are two things to be sanctified—
pains and pleasures.

PASCAL.—*Pensées, Pt.* 2, 17, 28.

Wicked men, for the most part, delight in false pleasures, but good men in the true pleasures.   PLATO.—*Philebus*, 85.

Offered to us are two cups, one of pleasure, filled, as it were, with honey ; the other, that of intellect, simple and healthful, sober and wineless, like water. These let us be ready to blend in the best manner we can.   PLATO.—*Ib.*, 145.

Of all things pleasure is the greatest braggart ; . . . for pleasures like children possess very little intelligence.

PLATO.—*Ib.*, 157.

Pleasure, or wrong or rightly understood,
Our greatest evil or our greatest good.

POPE.—*Essay on Man, Ep.* 2, 91.

Behold the child, by Nature's kindly law,
Pleased with a rattle, tickled with a straw :
Some livelier plaything gives his youth delight,
A little louder, but as empty quite :
Scarfs, garters, gold, amuse his riper stage,
And beads and prayer-books are the toys of age :
Pleased with this bauble still, as that before ;
Till tired he sleeps, and life's poor play is o'er.   POPE.—*Ib., Ep.* 2, 275.

Pleasures the sex, as children birds, pursue,
Still out of reach, yet never out of view.

POPE.—*Moral Essays, Ep.* 2, 231.

To pleasure such as leaves no sting behind.

ROGERS.—*Human Life*.

Exclusive pleasures are the death of pleasure.   ROUSSEAU.—*Emile*.

Think you these are the gifts of Fortune ? Trust me they are her traps.

SENECA.—*Epistle* 8 (*Lodge's tr.*).

No profit grows where is no pleasure ta'en.   SHAKESPEARE.—*Taming of the Shrew*, Act 1, 1.

Learn thou, whate'er the motive they may call,
That Pleasure is the aim, and Self the spring of all.

SOUTHEY.—*Pilgrimage to Waterloo, Pt.* 2, *c.* 1.

Delight, the rootless flower,
And love, the bloomless bower ;
Delight that lives an hour,
And love that lives a day.

SWINBURNE.—*Before Dawn*.

Know that to really enjoy pleasures you must know how to leave them.

VOLTAIRE.—*Sur l'Usage de la Vie.*

He was of those
Whom Delight flies, because they give her
    chase.   SIR W. WATSON.—*Byron.*

And then my heart with pleasure fills
And dances with the daffodils.
    WORDSWORTH.—*I wandered lonely.*

That sweet taste of pleasure unpursued.
    WORDSWORTH.—*Old Cumberland Beggar.*

    Sure as night follows day,
Death treads in pleasure's footsteps round
    the world,
When pleasure treads the paths which
    reason shuns,
When, against reason, riot shuts the door.
    YOUNG.—*Night Thoughts*, 5.

A man of pleasure is a man of pains.
    YOUNG.—*Ib.*, 8.

Pleasure, we both agree, is man's chief
    good ;
Or only contest what deserves the name.
    YOUNG.—*Ib.*

Dogs, birds, arms, and amours ; for one
pleasure a thousand pains.   *French prov.*

PLENTY

Each extreme to equal danger tends,
Plenty, as well as want, can sep'rate
    friends.
    COWLEY.—*Davideis, Bk.* 3, 205.

I like the sentiment of the poor woman,
who, coming from a wretched garret in
an inland manufacturing town for the first
time to the sea shore, gazing at the ocean,
said " she was glad for once in her life to
see something which there was enough of."
    EMERSON.—*Resources.*

To scatter plenty o'er a smiling land.
    GRAY.—*Elegy.*

PLOTS

Plots, true or false, are necessary things,
To raise up commonwealths, and ruin
    kings.
    DRYDEN.—*Absalom and Achitophel,*
            Pt. 1, 83.

I have 't ; it is engendered ;—hell and
    night
Must bring this monstrous birth to the
    world's light.
    SHAKESPEARE.—*Othello,* Act 1, 3.

God is the best layer of plots.
    Koran, ch. 8.

POACHERS

Much given to all unluckiness in stealing
venison and rabbits.
RICHD. DAVIES (*vicar of Sapperton, Glos.*).
—*Notes made in reference to Shakespeare,*
    circa 1700.

He did not know that a keeper is only
a poacher turned inside out, and a poacher
a keeper turned outside in.
    C. KINGSLEY.—*Water Babies, ch.* 1.

We live by plunder and delight in prey.
    VIRGIL.—*Æneid, Bk.* 9 (*Dryden tr.*).

POETRY

I think nothing which is a phrase or
saying in common talk, should be admitted
into a serious poem.
    ADDISON.—*Essay on the Georgics.*

Poetry is the devil's wine.
    ST. AUGUSTINE.

One of the fathers [St. Augustine] in
great severity called poesy " vinum dæmo-
num " [the wine of devils].
    BACON.—*Essays, Truth.*

Reads verse, and thinks she understands.
    BROWNING.—*Dis aliter visum.*

Poetry, which has been defined as the
harmonious unison of man with nature.
    CARLYLE.—*Early German Literature.*

Poetry, therefore, we will call *Musical
Thought.*   CARLYLE.—*Heroes*, 3.

Good sense is the body of poetic genius,
fancy its drapery, motion its life, and
imagination the soul that is everywhere
and in each, and forms all into one graceful
and intelligent whole.
    COLERIDGE.—*Biog. Literaria, ch.* 14.

Prose = words in their best order; poetry
= the best words in the best order.
    COLERIDGE.—*Table Talk.*

A poet does not work by square or line.
    COWPER.—*Conversation,* 794.

For all these pretty knacks that you com-
    pose,
Alas, what are they but poems in prose ?
    SIR J. DENHAM.—*To the Five Members.*

Why then we should drop into poetry.
[*Silas Wegg.*]
    DICKENS.—*Mutual Friend, ch.* 5.

Poetry's unnat'ral ; no man ever talked
poetry 'cept a beadle on boxin' day, or
Warren's blackin' or Rowland's oil, or
some o' them low fellows [*Weller sen.*]
    DICKENS.—*Pickwick, ch.* 33.

In poetry, where every word is free,
every word is necessary. Good poetry
could not have been otherwise written than
it is.   EMERSON.—*Art.*

Charles James Fox thought " Poetry the
great refreshment of the human mind,—
the only thing, after all ; that men first
found out that they had minds by making
and tasting poetry."
    EMERSON.—*Poetry and Imagination.*

Poetry is the consolation of mortal men.
EMERSON.—*Poetry and Imagination.*

Something more than the lilt of the strain,
Something more than the touch of the
lute ;
For the voice of the minstrel is vain
If the heart of the minstrel is mute.
LUCIUS H. FOOTE.—*Poetry.*

Poems like pictures are : some charm
when nigh,
Others at distance more delight your eye ;
That gives us pleasure for a single view ;
And this, ten times repeated, still is new.
P. FRANCIS.—*Horace, Art of Poetry.*

Could a man live by it, it were not unpleasant employment to be a poet.
GOLDSMITH.—*Letter,* 1759.

Science sees signs ; poetry the thing
signified.
J. C. HARE.—*Guesses at Truth.*

Is poetry, perhaps, a disease of humanity, as the pearl is the morbid matter
of the diseased oyster ?
HEINE.—*The Romantic School.*

Like its colleague, the famous war-horse
Bayard, it [the Pegasus of Uhland] possesses all possible virtues, and only one
fault ; it is dead.   HEINE.—*Ib.*

A verse may find him who a sermon flies.
HERBERT.—*Church Porch.*

In a good poem both judgment and
fancy are required ; but the fancy must
be more eminent, because they please for
the extravagancy.   HOBBES.

Give me a theme that's great and new,
Untouched by any other Muse.
HORACE.—*Odes, Bk.* 3, 25 *(Francis tr.).*

Dreaming on nought but idle poetry,
That fruitless and unprofitable art,
Good unto none ; but least to the professors.   BEN JONSON.—*Every Man
in his Humour,* Act 1, 1.

In rhyme, fine tinkling rhyme and flowand
verse,
With now and then some sense.
BEN JONSON.—*Fortunate Isles, vol. 6,
p.* 192.

[In Poetry] to Nature, Exercise, Imitation and Study, Art must be added to
make all these perfect. . . . It is Art only
can lead him [the Poet] to perfection and
leave him there in possession.
BEN JONSON.—*Discoveries : What is a
Poet ?*

Its chief aim [i.e. the chief aim of
Poetry] is to recall, to renew, and bring
vividly before us pictures of absent objects.
KEBLE.—*Lectures on Poetry, No.* 1
(E. K. Francis tr.).

Poetry is the handmaid to Imagination
and Fancy.   KEBLE.—*Ib.*

Let us deem the glorious art of Poetry
a kind of medicine divinely bestowed upon
man.   KEBLE.—*Ib.*

Verse has more power to soothe than
prose.   KEBLE.—*Ib., No.* 6.

Whether sweetness or dignity be aimed
at, true and genuine poetry will be essentially distinguished by quietness and calm.
KEBLE.—*Ib., No.* 17.

Poetry,—native and true Poetry—is
nothing else than each poet's innermost
feeling issuing in rhythmic language.
KEBLE.—*Ib., No.* 22.

The essence of all poetry is to be found,
not in high-wrought subtlety of thought,
nor in pointed cleverness of phrase, but in
the depths of the heart and the most
sacred feelings of the men who write.
KEBLE.—*Ib., No.* 28.

The mysteries of divine Truth supplied
the place of poetry among our forefathers,
while now the present generation readily
foregoes that higher wisdom, satisfied as it
would seem with that poetry which is but
a shadow of it.   KEBLE.—*Ib., No.* 30.

It is a clear, or at least a probable
hypothesis, that . . . poetry was provi-
dentially destined to prepare the way for
Revealed Truth itself.
KEBLE.—*Ib., No.* 40.

As civilization advances, poetry almost
necessarily declines. MACAULAY.—*Milton.*

My unpremeditated verse.
MILTON.—*Paradise Lost, Bk.* 9, 24.

Rhyme brings, with honied tones, an ano-
dyne to pain.
SIR L. MORRIS.—*Rhyme the Consoler.*

There's no second-rate in poetry.
J. OLDHAM.—*St. Cecilia.*

Her everlasting word survives
The doer and the deed,
When graceful genius largely gives
From wisdom's deepest fount the living
meed.
PINDAR.—*Nemean Odes,* 4, 11 *(Moore tr.).*

Poetry therefore is a kind of popular
speaking, . . . a rhetorical method of
popular speaking.
PLATO.—*Gorgias,* 124 *(Remark attrib. to
Socrates) (Cary tr.).*

Hymns to the gods and the praises of
worthy actions are the only sort of poetry
to be admitted to our state. For if you
were to admit the pleasurable muse also,
in songs or verses, we should have pleasure
and pain reigning in our state instead of
law.   PLATO.—*Republic, Bk.* 10, 8.

The varying verse, the full resounding line,
The long majestic march and energy
divine.   POPE.—*On Dryden.*

But lived in Settle's numbers one day
more.   POPE.—*Dunciad, Bk.* 1, 90.

So sweetly mawkish, and so smoothly dull;
Heady, not strong; o'erflowing, though
not full.   POPE—*Ib.,* Bk. 3, 171.

It stands on record that in Richard's times
A man was hanged for very honest rhymes.
          POPE.—*Referring to John Ball.*

Oh! why did he write poetry,
     That hereto was so civil;
And sell his soul for vanity,
     To rhyming and the devil?
          POPE.—*Sandy's Ghost.*

And he whose fustian's so sublimely bad,
It is not poetry, but prose run mad.
          POPE.—*Prol. to Satires,* 188.

The lines are weak, another's pleased to
     say,
Lord Fanny spins a thousand such a day.
          POPE.—*Satires,* Bk. 2, Sat. 1, 5.

In poetry there is always fallacy, and
sometimes fiction.
     SCOTT.—*Bride of Lammermoor, ch.* 21.

The unpremeditated lay.
     SCOTT.—*Lay of the Last Minstrel, Intro.*

Small thought was his, in after-time,
E'er to be hitched into a rhyme.
          SCOTT.—*Marmion, c.* 6, *Intro.*

The truest poetry is the most feigning;
and lovers are given to poetry.
     SHAKESPEARE.—*As You Like It,* Act 3, 2.

Is this a prologue, or the posy of a ring?
     SHAKESPEARE.—*Hamlet,* Act 3, 2.

Mincing poetry,—
'Tis like the forced gait of a shuffling nag.
     SHAKESPEARE.—*Henry IV.,* Pt. 1, Act 3, 1.

Assist me, some extemporal god of
rhyme, for I am sure I shall turn sonneteer.
     SHAKESPEARE.—*Love's Labour's Lost,*
               Act 1, 2.

I was not born under a rhyming planet.
     SHAKESPEARE.—*Much Ado,* Act 5, 2.

Not marble, nor the gilded monuments
Of princes, shall outlive this powerful
     rhyme.   SHAKESPEARE.—*Sonnet* 55.

Much is the force of heaven-bred poesy.
     SHAKESPEARE.—*Two Gentlemen of Verona,*
                    Act 3, 2.

A poem is the very image of life expressed in its eternal truth.
     SHELLEY.—*Defence of Poetry* (1821).

Poetry ever communicates all the
pleasure which men are capable of receiving; it is ever still the light of life;
the source of whatever of beautiful or
generous or true can have place in an evil
time.   SHELLEY.—*Ib.*

All high poetry is infinite; it is as the
first acorn, which contained all oaks po-
tentially.   SHELLEY.—*Ib.*

A great poem is a fountain for ever overflowing with the waters of wisdom and
delight.   SHELLEY.—*Ib.*

The most glorious poetry that has ever
been communicated to the world is probably a feeble shadow of the original conceptions of the poet.   SHELLEY.—*Ib.*

Poetry is the record of the best and
happiest moments of the happiest and
best minds.   SHELLEY.—*Ib.*

          Most wretched men
Are cradled into poetry by wrong:
They learn in suffering what they teach in
     song.   SHELLEY.—*Julian.*

Poetry is of all humane learning the
most ancient and of most fatherly antiquity, as from whence all other learnings
have taken their beginnings.
     SIR P. SIDNEY.—*Apologie for Poetrie.*

But if anything be already said in the
defence of sweet Poetry, all concurreth to
the maintaining of the Heroical, which is
not only a kind, but the best, and most
accomplished kind of Poetry.
          SIR P. SIDNEY.—*Ib.*

Certainly, I must confess mine own
barbarousness. I never heard the old
song of Percy and Douglas that I found
not my heart moved more than with a
trumpet.   SIR P. SIDNEY.—*Ib.*

For indeed Poetry ever setteth virtue
out in her best colours, making Fortune
her well-waiting handmaid, that one must
needs be enamoured of her.
          SIR P. SIDNEY.—*Ib.*

You cannot hear the planet-like music
of poetry.   SIR P. SIDNEY.—*Ib.*

A poem, round and perfect as a star.
          ALEX. SMITH.—*Life Drama, Sc.* 2.

Realms yet unborn, in accents now un-
     known,
Thy song shall learn, and bless it for their
     own. C. SPRAGUE.—*Shakespeare Ode.*

But thought and faith are mightier things
     than time
          Can wrong,
Made splendid once with speech or made
     sublime
          With song.
          SWINBURNE.—*Interpreters.*

With scraps of thundrous Epic lilted out.
TENNYSON.—*Princess, c. 2, 353.*

And quoted odes, and jewels five-words
long,
That on the stretched forefinger of all
Time
Sparkle for ever.
TENNYSON.—*Ib., c. 2, 355.*

Old-fashioned poetry, but choicely good.
I. WALTON.—*Compleat Angler, ch. 4.*

Your metres that writhe, your rhythms
that sprawl.
SIR W. WATSON.—*Orgy on Parnassus.*

The Lake-poetry . . . is a' sound and
nae sense.
JOHN WILSON.—*Noctes (Ettrick Shepherd).*

Transitory as a prize poem.
J. WILSON.—*Ib.*

Wisdom married to immortal verse.
WORDSWORTH.—*Excursion, Bk. 7.*

All good poetry is the spontaneous over-
flow of powerful feelings.
WORDSWORTH.—*Pref. to Second Ed. of
Lyrical Ballads* (1800).

Poetry is the breath and finer spirit of
all knowledge ; it is the impassioned expression which is in the countenance of all
science.   WORDSWORTH.—*Ib.*

Poetry is the first and last of all knowledge—it is as immortal as the heart of
man.   WORDSWORTH.—*Ib.*

POETS

Beethoven, Raphael, cannot reach
The charm which Homer, Shakespeare,
teach.   M. ARNOLD.—
Epilogue to Lessing's Laocoon.
Time may restore us in his course
Goethe's sage mind and Byron's force ;
But where will Europe's latter hour
Again find Wordsworth's healing power ?
M. ARNOLD.—*Memorial Verses,* 1850.

Not deep the poet sees, but wide.
M. ARNOLD.—*Resignation,* 214.

Such a price
The Gods exact for song :
To become what we sing.
M. ARNOLD.—*Strayed Reveller.*

O World, for me ne'er care to weave a
crown,
Who hold your smile as lightly as your
frown !
Yet I grow sad to think upon my songs,
For which no man, nor even maiden, longs.
O my poor flowers, dead in the lap of
spring !
THOS. ASHE.—*Poems* (1885).

O souls, perplexed by hood and cowl,
Fain would you find a teacher :
Consult the lark and not the owl,
The poet, not the preacher.
A. AUSTIN.—*The Owl and the Lark.*

Renownèd Spenser, lie a thought more nigh
To learned Chaucer ; and rare Beaumont,
lie
A little nearer Spenser, to make room
For Shakespeare in your threefold, four-
fold tomb.
W. BASSE.—*On Shakespeare.*

Young men, ay and maids,
Too often sow their wild oats in tame verse.
E. B. BROWNING.—*Aurora Leigh, Bk.* I.

For poets (bear the word),
Half poets even, are still whole democrats.
E. B. BROWNING.—*Ib., Bk.* 4.

I do distrust the poet who discerns
No character or glory in his times.
E. B. BROWNING.—*Ib., Bk.* 5.

And poets evermore are scant of gold.
E. B. BROWNING.—*Ib.*

Ah, did you once see Shelley plain,
And did he stop and speak to you,
And did you speak to him again ?
How strange it seems, and new !
BROWNING.—*Memorabilia.*

The palfrey pace and the glittering grace
Of Spenser's magical song.
R. BUCHANAN.—*Cloudland.*

I am nae poet, in a sense,
But just a rhymer, like by chance,
And hae to learning no pretence,
But what's the matter ?
BURNS.—*Epistle to John Lapraik.*

Gie me ae spark o' Nature's fire !
That's a' the learning I desire ;
Then, though I trudge through dub an'
mire—
At plough or cart,
My Muse, though hamely in attire,
May touch the heart.
BURNS.—*Ib.*

Poverty is the muse's patrimony.
BURTON.—*Anat. of Melan., Pt.* I.

But those that write in verse still make
The one verse for the other's sake.
BUTLER.—*Hudibras, Pt.* 2, c. I.

It is not poetry that makes men poor,
For few do write that were not so before.
BUTLER.—*Miscellaneous Thoughts.*

When poets say, " I've written *fifty*
rhymes,"
They make you dread that they'll recite
them too.
BYRON.—*Don Juan, c.* I, 108.

He lied with such a fervour of intention—
There was no doubt he earned his laureate
    pension.
        BYRON.—*Don Juan, c.* 3, 80.

Milton's the prince of poets—so we say ;
  A little heavy, but no less divine.
        BYRON.—*Ib.*, 3, 91.

Let such forego the poet's sacred name,
Who rack their brains for lucre, not for
    fame.   BYRON.—*English Bards.*

The man who weds the sacred muse
Disdains all mercenary views.
    C. CHURCHILL.—*The Ghost, Bk.* 3.

No man was ever yet a great poet without being at the same time a profound
philosopher.
    COLERIDGE.—*Biog. Literaria, ch.* 15.

There is a pleasure in poetic pains
That only poets know.
        COWPER.—*Time Piece.*

Whoso picnics on Parnassus
  Need not look for cakes and ale.
COTSFORD DICK.—*Comin' thro' the Rhyme.*

He will not canter, walk, or trot,
  My Pegasus ; I spur, I beat
    In vain to-day. . . .
Alas ! 'tis all too clear I'm not
    In vein to-day.
  AUSTIN DOBSON.—*Rondel, " In Vain
              To-day."*
For that fine madness he did still retain,
Which rightly should possess a poet's
  brain. DRAYTON.—*To H. Reynolds.*

A poet is as much privileged to lie, as
an ambassador, for the honour and interest of his country.
    DRYDEN.—*Dedic. of Æneid.*

Nothing is to be called a fault in poetry
(says Aristotle) but what is against the
art. Therefore a man may be an admirable poet without being an exact chron-
ologer.   DRYDEN.—*Ib.*

Three poets in three distant ages born,
Greece, Italy, and England, did adorn ;
The first, in loftiness of thought surpassed ;
The next in majesty ; in both the last.
The force of nature could no further go ;
To make a third, she joined the other two.
DRYDEN.—*Under Milton's Picture (refer-
    ring to Homer, Virgil, and Milton).*

There was never poet who had not the
heart in the right place.
        EMERSON.—*Success.*

I stept into Bedlame, where I saw
several poore miserable creatures in
chaines ; one of them was mad with
making verses.
JOHN EVELYN.—*Diary, April* 21, 1657.

'Tis long disputed whether poets claim
From art or nature their best right to
    fame ;
But art, if not enriched by nature's vein,
And a rude genius of uncultured strain,
Are useless both ; but when in friendship
    joined
A mutual succour in each other find.
    P. FRANCIS.—*Horace, Art of Poetry.*

What are our poets, take them as they fall,
Good, bad, rich, poor, much read, not read
    at all ?
Them and their works in the same class
    you'll find—
They are the mere wastepaper of mankind.
        B. FRANKLIN.—*Paper.*

Poets have morals and manners of their
own.
THOS. HARDY.—*Hand of Ethelberta, ch.* 2.

The biography of poets must be sought
in their works ; there are to be found their
most confidential confessions.
        HEINE.—*Don Quixote.*

Beggar envies beggar, and poet poet.
        HESIOD.—*Works and Days.*

Poets are prosy in their common talk,
As the fast trotters, for the most part,
    walk.
  O. W. HOLMES.—*The Banker's Dinner.*

I sometimes sit beneath a tree
  And read my own sweet songs.
  O. W. HOLMES.—*The Last Reader.*

He, whose thoughts differing not in shape,
  but dress,
What others feel more fitly can express.
  O. W. HOLMES.—*Metrical Essay.*

Poetry and poverty both begin with
the same letter, and in more respects than
one are " as like each other as two P's."
    HOOD.—*Poems by a Poor Gentleman*
                    (1834).

Neither gods, nor men, nor the book-
shops allow the poets the favour of being
mediocre. HORACE.—*De Arte Poetica.*

The Muse that loves the woodland and
    the farm
To Virgil lends her gayest, tenderest
    charm.
  HORACE.—*Sat.* 1, 10, 43 *(Conington tr.).*

We poets are, in every age and nation,
A most absurd, wrong-headed generation.
        SOAME JENYNS.—*Horace.*

They swayed about upon a rocking-horse,
And thought it Pegasus.
    KEATS.—*Sleep and Poetry.*

And they shall be accounted poet-kings
Who simply tell the most heart-easing
things.   KEATS.—*Ib.*

William Wordsworth, true philosopher
and inspired poet, who, by the special gift
and calling of Almighty God, whether he
sang of man or of nature, failed not to
lift up men's hearts to holy things.
KEBLE.—*Dedic. of Lectures on Poetry
1832-41 (E. K. Francis tr.).*

The authors are like untrained boys
trying to sing : the one aim of each is to
sing as loud as he can. Whether they are
singing sweetly and in tune they neither
know nor care.   KEBLE.—*Ib., No. 1.*

The sentiment itself might have occurred
to many, but the expression in song to
none but a consummate poet.
          J. KEBLE.—*Ib., No. 2.*

We feel he [Dryden] never heartily and
sincerely praised any human being, or felt
any real enthusiasm for any subject he
took up.   KEBLE.—*Ib., No. 5.*

As fire is kindled by fire, so is a poet's
mind kindled by contact with a brother
poet.   KEBLE.—*Ib., No. 16.*

It is a great merit, I might almost call
it a divine gift, when any poet is seen to
retain throughout life traces of his youthful impressions and feelings.
          KEBLE.—*Ib., No. 26.*

Those who, from their very heart, either
burst into poetry, or seek the Deity in
prayer, must needs ever cherish with their
whole spirit the vision of something more
beautiful, greater and more lovable, than
all that mortal eye can see.
          KEBLE.—*Ib., No. 40.*

Ye whose hearts are beating high
With the pulse of Poesy,
Heirs of more than mortal race,
Framed by heaven's peculiar grace,
God's own work to do on earth.
          KEBLE.—*Palm Sunday.*

The bards sublime,
Whose distant footsteps echo
Through the corridors of Time.
          LONGFELLOW.—*Day is Done.*

He is the poet of the dawn.
          LONGFELLOW.—*(Sonnet, Chaucer.)*

God sent his Singers upon earth
With songs of sadness and of mirth.
          LONGFELLOW.—*Singers.*

Sithe of our language he was the lodesterre.
LYDGATE.—*Falls of Princes (Of Chaucer).*

Sith he in Englishmaking was the best,
Pray unto God to give his soul good rest.
          LYDGATE.—*Ib.*

He [Byron] had a head which statuaries
loved to copy, and a foot the deformity of
which the beggars in the street mimicked.
          MACAULAY.—*Byron.*

Perhaps no person can be a poet, or
even enjoy poetry, without a certain un-
soundness of mind.
          MACAULAY.—*Milton.*

He who would not be frustrate of his
hope to write well hereafter in laudable
things, ought himself to be a true poem.
          MILTON.—*Apology for Smectymnuus*

Such sights as youthful poets dream,
On summer eves by haunted stream.
          MILTON.—*L'Allegro, 129.*

He knew
Himself to sing, and build the lofty rhyme.
          MILTON.—*Lycidas, 10.*

A poet soaring in the high season of his
fancies, with his garland and singing-robes
about him.
          MILTON.—*The Reason of Church
Government, Bk. 2, Introd.*

Oh, blame not the bard !
MOORE.—*Irish Melodies : O, Blame not.*

Poverty ! thou source of human art,
Thou great inspirer of the poet's song !
          EDWD. MOORE.—*Hymn to Poverty.*

The idle singer of an empty day.
          W. MORRIS.—*Earthly Paradise, Intro.*

Lulled by the singer of an empty day.
          W. MORRIS.—*Ib.*

The true poet is all knowing ; he is an
actual world in miniature.
          NOVALIS.—*(As tr. by Carlyle.)*

To his own self not always just,
Bound in the bonds that all men share,—
Confess the failings as we must,
The lion's mark is always there !
Nor any song so pure so great,
Since his, who closed the sightless eyes,
Our Homer of the war in Heaven,
To wake in his own Paradise.
          F. T. PALGRAVE.—*Wordsworth.*

Poetry is "making," and they alone
who possess creative power are poets
[i.e. "makers" or "creators"].
PLATO.—*Banquet, 30 (Diotima to Socrates).*

A poet cannot compose unless he becomes inspired and is out of his sober
senses, with his imagination no longer
under his control. . . . On this account a
deity deprives poets of their senses, and
employs them as his ministers and oracle-
singers and divine prophets.
          PLATO (?).—*Ion, 5.*

Poets are allowed to lie.
          PLINY THE YOUNGER.—*Ep., Bk. 6.*

We poets are (upon a poet's word),
Of all mankind the creatures most absurd.
          POPE.—*Ep. of Horace, Ep. 1, 358.*

Cursed be the verse, how well soe'er it
flow,
That tends to make one worthy man my
foe.   POPE.—*Prol. to Satires*, 283.

True Poets are the guardians of a state,
And, when they fail, portend approaching
fate.
    ROSCOMMON.—*Essay on Translated
        Verse.*

Burns of all poets is most a Man.
    ROSSETTI.—*On Burns.*

A torturer of phrases into sonnets.
    SCOTT.—*Auchindrane*, Act 3, 1.

For ne'er
Was flattery lost on poet's ear.
A simple race, they waste their toil
For the vain tribute of a smile.
SCOTT.—*Lay of the Last Minstrel*, c. 4, 35.

Call it not vain :—they do not err,
    Who say that when the Poet dies,
Mute Nature mourns her worshipper
And celebrates his obsequies.
    SCOTT.—*Ib.*, c. 5, 1.

Profaned the God-given strength, and
marred the lofty line.
    SCOTT.—*Marmion*, c. 1, *Intro.*

The lunatic, the lover, and the poet
Are of imagination all compact
    . . . . . .
The poet's eye, in a fine frenzy rolling,
Doth glance from heaven to earth, from
    earth to heaven,
And, as imagination bodies forth
The forms of things unknown, the poet's
    pen
Turns them to shapes, and gives to airy
    nothing
A local habitation and a name.
    SHAKESPEARE.—*Midsummer Night's
        Dream*, Act 5, 1.

Poets . . . were called, in the earlier
epochs of the world, legislators or
prophets. A poet essentially comprises
and unites both these characters.
    SHELLEY.—*Defence of Poetry* (1821).

The poetry of Dante may be considered
as the bridge thrown over the stream of
time which unites the modern and ancient
world.   SHELLEY.—*Ib.*

Show me [said Sarona] one wicked man
who has written poetry, and I will show
you where his poetry is not poetry ; or
rather I will show you in his poetry no
poetry at all.
    MISS SHEPPARD.—*Counterparts, vol.* 1.

Among the Romans a poet was called a
Vates, which is as much a Diviner, Fore-
seer, or Prophet.
    SIR PHILIP SIDNEY.—*Apologie for Poetrie.*

One may be a Poet without versing
and a versifier without Poetry.
    SIR P. SIDNEY.—*Ib.*

Sir, I admit your general rule
That every poet is a fool ;
But you yourself may serve to show it,
That every fool is not a poet.
    SWIFT.—*Epigram from the French.*

Love reads out first, at head of all our
    choir,
Villon, our sad bad glad mad brother's
    name.
    SWINBURNE.—*François Villon.*

Prince of sweet songs, made out of tears
    and fire ;
A harlot was thy nurse, a God thy sire.
    SWINBURNE.—*Ib.*

Shame soiled thy song, and song assoiled
    thy shame.
But from thy feet now death hath washed
    the mire.   SWINBURNE.—*Ib.*

And those high songs of thine
That stung the sense like wine,
Or fell more soft than snow or dew by
    night ;
Or wailed as in some flooded cave
Sobs the strong broken spirit of a wave.
    SWINBURNE.—*To Victor Hugo.*

And round thee with the breeze of song
To stir a little dust of praise.
    TENNYSON.—*In Memoriam*, c. 75.

The passionate heart of the poet is whirled
into folly and vice.
    TENNYSON.—*Maud*, Pt. 1, 4, 7.

Vex not thou the poet's mind
    With thy shallow wit ;
Vex not thou the poet's mind,
    For thou canst not fathom it.
    TENNYSON.—*The Poet.*

And Creteus, whom the Muses held so
    dear :
He fought with courage and he sang the
    fight ;
Arms were his business, verses his delight.
    VIRGIL.—*Æneid*, Bk. 9 (*Dryden tr.*).

It is the great poets who have decided
the genius of languages.
    VOLTAIRE.—*Discourse to French Academy*,
        1746.

Illustrious acts high raptures do infuse,
And every conqueror creates a muse.
    WALLER.—*Cromwell.*

Shelley, the hectic, flamelike rose of verse,
All colour, and all odour, and all bloom,
Steeped in the moonlight, glutted with
    the sun,
But somewhat lacking root in homely
    earth.
    SIR W. WATSON.—*To E. Dowden.*

The poet's fate is here in emblem shown,
He asked for bread, and he received a
    stone.
            SAMUEL WESLEY.—*On Butler's*
                        Monument.

Poets (so unimpeached tradition says),
The sole historians were of ancient days,
Who helped their heroes Fame's high hill
    to clamber.
        J. WOLCOT.—*The Apple Dumpling.*

A great deal, my dear liege, depends
On having clever bards for friends.
What had Achilles been without his
    Homer ?
A tailor, woollen-draper, or a comber !
        J. WOLCOT.—*Moral Reflection.*

        That mighty orb of song,
The divine Milton.
        WORDSWORTH.—*Excursion, Bk.* 1.

I mourned with thousands, but as one
More deeply grieved, for he was gone
Whose light I hailed when first it shone,
        And showed my youth
How Verse may build a princely throne
        On humble truth.
    WORDSWORTH.—*Memorials of a Town in*
        Scotland, 2.   (Grave of Burns.)

The poets, who on earth have made us
    heirs
Of truth and pure delight, by heavenly
    lays.
        WORDSWORTH.—*Personal Talk.*

I thought of Chatterton, the marvellous
    boy,
The sleepless soul, that perished in his
    pride.
        WORDSWORTH.—*Resolution and*
                    Independence.

We poets in our youth begin in gladness,
But thereof come in the end despondency
    and madness.   WORDSWORTH.—*Ib.*

A cheerful life is what the Muses love ;
A soaring spirit is their prime delight.
        WORDSWORTH.—*Sonnets, Pt.* 2, *No.* 4.

A volant Tribe of Bards on earth are
    found, . . .
Dust for oblivion ! To the solid ground
Of nature trusts the mind that builds for
    aye.   WORDSWORTH.—*Ib., No.* 34.

In his breast the mighty Poet bore
A Patriot's heart, warm with undying fire.
        WORDSWORTH.—*Tour in Italy,* 19.

Those who err follow the poets.
Koran, ch. 26. (*Referring to the belief that*
    the devils prompt the poets with such in-
    coherent scraps of the angels' converse as
    they can hear by stealth.)

POISON

The coward's weapon, poison.
    PHINEAS FLETCHER.—*Sicelides,* Act 5, 3.

The wine is bright at the goblet's brim,
Though the poison lurk beneath.
        D. ROSSETTI.—*King's Tragedy.*

I speak from experience,—poison is
drunk out of gold.
        SENECA.—*Thyestes,* Act 3, 453.

POLICE

When constabulary duty's to be done,
A policeman's lot is not a happy one.
    SIR W. S. GILBERT.—*Pirates of Penzance.*

Policemen are soldiers who act alone ;
soldiers are policemen who act in unison.
        HERBT. SPENCER.—*Social Statics,*
                    Pt. 3, *ch.* 21, 8

Some staid guardian of the public peace
    WORDSWORTH.—*Excursion, Bk.* 7.

POLICY

I feel all the pride of power sink, and all
presumption in the wisdom of human con-
trivances melt and die away within me.
My rigour relents.   I pardon something to
the spirit of liberty.
        BURKE.—*Speech on Conciliation.*

And Policy regained what arms had lost.
        BYRON.—*Childe Harold, c.* 1, 25.

Incidents ought not to govern policy,
but policy, incidents.
        NAPOLEON.—*As quoted by Emerson,*
            " Representative Men."

The first advice I have to give the party
is that it should clean its slate.
        LORD ROSEBERY.—*Speech, Dec.,* 1901.

I speak against my present profit, but
my wish hath a preferment in 't.
        SHAKESPEARE.—*Cymbeline,* Act 5, 4.

Never did base and rotten policy
Colour her working with such deadly
    wounds.
    SHAKESPEARE.—*Henry IV., Pt.* 1, Act 1, 2.

Love thyself last : cherish those hearts
    that hate thee :
Corruption wins not more than honesty.
    SHAKESPEARE.—*Henry VIII.,* Act 3, 2.

Great God ! (said I) what have I seen !
    On what poor engines move
The thoughts of monarchs and designs of
    states,
    What petty motives rule their fates !
        SWIFT.—*To Sir W. Temple.*

POLITENESS

Sometimes politeness is only the varnish
of falsehood.
    PIERRE HYACINTHE AZAIS (1766-1845).

Politeness is to goodness what words are to thoughts.   JOUBERT.

Politeness has been well defined as benevolence in small things.
MACAULAY.—*Boswell.*

Politeness costs nothing and gains everything.
LADY M. WORTLEY MONTAGU.—*Letter.*

Politeness to those we do not respect is no more a breach of faith than " your humble Servant " at the bottom of a challenge ; they are universally understood to be things of course.
J. TRUSLER.—*Principles of Politeness.*

The first rule of education, in all lands, is never to say anything offensive to anyone.   VOLTAIRE.—*On Satire,* 1739.

As in smooth oil the razor best is whet,
So wit is by politeness sharpest set :
Their want of edge from their offence is seen ;
Both pain us least when exquisitely keen.
YOUNG.—*Love of Fame, Sat.* 2.

Politeness is excellent, but it does not pay the bill.
Saying. (C. H. Spurgeon, " Salt-Cellars.")

POLITICAL ECONOMY

What we might call, by way of eminence, the *dismal science.*
CARLYLE.—*Nigger Question.*

Respectable Professors of the Dismal Science.
CARLYLE.—*The Present Time* (1850).

To apply, in all their unmitigated authority, the principles of abstract political economy to the people and circumstances of Ireland, exactly as if he had been proposing to legislate for the inhabitants of Saturn or Jupiter.
GLADSTONE.—*House of Commons, April* 7, 1881.

The rich have become richer, and the poor have become poorer ; and the vessel of the state is driven between the Scylla and Charybdis of anarchy and despotism.
SHELLEY.—*Defence of Poetry* (1821).

POLITICIANS

These oracles hit my fancy ! Notwithstanding
I'm partly doubtful how I could contrive
To manage an administration altogether.
ARISTOPHANES.—*The Knights (The Sausage-Seller). (Frere tr.)*

Even in your tender years
And your early disposition
You betrayed an inward sense

Of the conscious impudence,
Which constitutes a politician.
ARISTOPHANES.—*Ib.*

It is as hard and severe a thing to be a true politician as to be truly moral.
BACON.—*Adv. of Learning, Bk.* 2.

A Politician who screams is never likely to occupy a commanding place in the House of Commons.
A. BIRRELL.—*E. Burke.*

Resolved to die in the last dyke of prevarication.
BURKE.—*Impeachment of Hastings, May,* 1789.

The quacks of government (who sate
At th' unregarded helm of State).
BUTLER.—*Hudibras, Pt.* 3, *c.* 2.

Well can ye mouth fair Freedom's classic line,
And talk of Constitutions o'er your wine.
CAMPBELL.—*Poland.*

But all your vows to break the tyrant's yoke
Expire in Bacchanalian song and smoke.
CAMPBELL.—*Ib.*

An upright minister asks, *what* recommends a man ; a corrupt minister, *who.*
C. C. COLTON.—*Reflections, No.* 9.

Patriots are grown too shrewd to be sincere,
And we too wise to trust them.
COWPER.—*Winter Morning Walk,* 500.

I lay my yoke on feeble folk,
And march across the neck of fools.
J. DAVIDSON.—*The Aristocrat.*

Though political troubles are hot,
They never disturb me a jot,
With language discursive and methods inversive
I easily settle the lot.
E. DE STEIN.—*(Russian Bolshevist's Statement.)*

For politicians neither love nor hate.
DRYDEN.—*Absalom and Achitophel, Pt.* 1, 223.

He [Sir Condy Rackrent] . . . was very ill used by the government about a place that was promised him and never given, after his supporting them against his conscience very honourably, and being greatly abused for it, which hurt him greatly, he having the name of a great patriot in the county before.
MISS EDGEWORTH.—*Castle Rackrent, ch.* 2.

Measures, not men, have always been my mark.
GOLDSMITH.—*Good-Natured Man,* Act 2.

Here lies our good Edmund, whose genius was such,
We scarcely can praise it or blame it too much ;

Who, born for the universe, narrowed his
    mind,
And to party gave up what was meant for
    mankind ;
Though fraught with all learning, yet
    straining his throat,
To persuade Tommy Townshend to lend
    him a vote.
          GOLDSMITH.—*Retaliation.*

D'ye think that statesmen's kindnesses
    proceed
From any principles but their own need ?
          SIR R. HOWARD.—*Vestal Virgin.*

Learn'd or unlearn'd, we all are politicians.
          S. JENYNS.—*Horace.*

We're the original friends o' the nation,
All the rest air a paltry an' base fabrica-
    tion.
J. R. LOWELL.—*Biglow Papers, 1st Series,
                              No. 5.*

It ain't by princerples nor men
    My preudunt course is steadied ;
I scent wich pays the best, an' then
    Go into it baldheaded.
          J. R. LOWELL.—*Ib., No. 6.*

Now warn't thet a system wuth pains in
    presarvin',
Where the people found jints an' their
    frien's done the carvin'.
J. R. LOWELL.—*Ib., 2nd Series, No.5.*

We have hundreds of ministers, who
press forward into office, without having
ever learned that art which is necessary
for every business, the art of thinking.
H. MACKENZIE.—*Man of Feeling, ch.* 20.

Some lie beneath the churchyard stone,
    And some before the Speaker.
          W. M. PRAED.—*School.*

Fools who think to make themselves
great men out of little by swaggering in
the rear of a party.
          SCOTT.—*Diary, Feb.,* 1826.

The pate of a politician, . . . one that
could circumvent God.
          SHAKESPEARE.—*Hamlet*, Act 5, 1.

Turn him to any cause of policy,
The Gordian knot of it he will unloose,
Familiar as his garter.
          SHAKESPEARE.—*Henry V.*, Act 1, 1.

To a member's wife, Nora, nobody is
common, provided he's on the register.
          G. B. SHAW.—*Bull's Other Island.*

On the other hand we have three Social-
Democrats amongst us. They are not on
speaking terms ; and they have put before
us three distinct and incompatible views of
Social-Democracy.
          G. B. SHAW.—*Man and Superman.*

Who makes the quartern loaf and Lud-
    dites rise ?
Who fills the butchers' shops with large
    blue flies ?
H. AND J. SMITH.—*Rejected Addresses,
                    No. 1, Loyal Effusion.*

Of all ingenious instruments of despotism I most commend a popular assembly,
where the majority are paid and hired,
and a few bold and able men, by their
brave speeches, make the people believe
they are free.
SYDNEY SMITH.—*Letter to Countess Grey,
                              Feb.* 9, 1821.

To talk of not acting from fear is mere
parliamentary cant. From what motive
but fear, I should be glad to know, have
all the improvements in our constitution
proceeded ?
SYDNEY SMITH.—*Peter Plymley's Letters,
                              No. 6.*

The Statesman tells you, with a sneer,
His fault is to be too sincere ;
And, having no sinister ends,
Is apt to disoblige his friends.
          SWIFT.—*Beasts' Confession.*

There is one essential point wherein a
political liar differs from others of the
faculty, that he ought to have but a short
memory.   SWIFT.—*Examiner, No.* 15.

Families, when a child is born,
Want it to be intelligent.
I, through intelligence,
Having wrecked my whole life,
Only hope the baby will prove
Ignorant and stupid.
Then he will crown a tranquil life
By becoming a Cabinet Minister.
SU TUNG-P'O.—(*Chinese poet, 11th century.*)
          (*Arthur Waley's translation.*)

Talk on, ye quaint haranguers of the
    crowd,
Declaim in praise of peace, when danger
    calls,
And the fierce foes in arms approach the
    walls.
          VIRGIL.—*Æneid, Bk.* 11 (*Dryden tr.*).

Some patriot fools to popular praise
    aspire,
Of public speeches, which worse fools
    admire.
          VIRGIL.—*Georgics, Bk.* 2 (*Dryden tr.*).

POLITICS

I have lived too long . . . to be of any
politics save gipsy politics ; and it is well
known that during elections the children
of Roma [gipsies] side with both parties

so long as the event is doubtful, promising success to each ; and when the fight is done and the battle won, invariably range themselves in the ranks of the victorious.
BORROW.—*Bible in Spain, ch.* 14.

Politics fill me with doubt and dizziness.
. . . .
Altogether they puzzle me quite ;
They all seem wrong and they all seem
    right. R. BUCHANAN.—*Fine Weather.*

A race that binds
Its body in chains, and calls them
    Liberty ;
And calls each fresh link Progress.
    R. BUCHANAN.—*Political Mystics.*

Of this stamp is the cant of " Not men but measures " ; a sort of charm by which many people get loose from every honourable engagement.
BURKE.—*Cause of Present Discontents.*

All the politics of the great
Are like the cunning of a cheat.
    BUTLER.—*Miscellaneous Thoughts.*

In politics what begins in fear usually ends in folly.
COLERIDGE.—*Table Talk, Oct.* 5, 1830.

Patriotism, Liberty, Reform, and many other good things have got a bad name by keeping bad company ; for those who have ill intentions cannot afford to work with tools that have ill sounds.
C. C. COLTON.—*Lacon.*

The age of virtuous politics is past.
COWPER.—*Winter Morning Walk,* 498.

Politics we bar ;
    They are not our bent ;
On the whole we are
    Not intelligent.
SIR W. S. GILBERT.—*Princess Ida.*

I always admired Mrs. Grote's saying that politics and theology were the only two really great subjects.
W. E. GLADSTONE.—*Letter* 1880
(*cf. O. W. Holmes, as quoted below*).

They politics like ours profess—
The greater prey upon the less.
    MATTHEW GREEN.—*Grotto.*

When shall the softer, saner politics Whereof we dream, have play in each proud land ?
THOS. HARDY.—*Departure,* 11.

With what a genius for administration
We rearrange the rumbling universe,
And map the course of man's regeneration,
    Over a pipe !
W. E. HENLEY.—*Inter Sodales.*

Religion and government appear to me the two subjects which, of all others, should belong to the common talk of people who enjoy the blessings of freedom.
O. W. HOLMES.—*Prof. at Breakfast Table.*

He that goeth about to persuade a multitude that they are not so well governed as they ought to be, shall never want attentive and favourable hearers.
HOOKER.—*Eccles. Pol.,* I, I.

There is a holy, mistaken zeal in politics, as well as religion. By persuading others we convince ourselves.
JUNIUS.—*Letter* 35.

In political discussion heat is in inverse proportion to knowledge.
J. G. COTTON MINCHIN.—*Growth
    of Freedom.*

Those who would treat politics and morality apart will never understand the one or the other.
LORD MORLEY.—*Rousseau.*

The body political, like the human body, begins to die from the date of its birth, and carries in itself the causes of its destruction.
ROUSSEAU.—*Contrat Social, Bk.* 3, *ch.* 11.

Not to th' ensanguined field of death alone
Is Valour limited ; she sits serene
In the deliberate council ; sagely scans
The source of action ; weighs, prevents,
    provides.
    SMOLLETT.—*The Regicide,* Act 1, 1.

Those two amusements for all fools of eminence, Politics or Poetry.
STEELE.—*Spectator, vol.* 1, 43.

Politics is perhaps the only profession for which no preparation is thought necessary.
R. L. STEVENSON.—*Yoshida-Torajiro.*

But after sage monitions from his friends,
His talents to employ for nobler ends ;
To better judgments willing to submit,
He turns to politics his dangerous wit.
SWIFT.—*The Author upon himself,* 1713.

In politics I am sure it is even a Machiavellian holy maxim, " That some men should be ruined for the good of others."
SWIFT.—*On English Bubbles* (1720).

My pollertics, like my religion, being of an exceedin' accommodatin' character.
ARTEMUS WARD.—*The Crisis.*

I am not a politician and my other habits are good.
ARTEMUS WARD.—*Fourth of July Oration.*

POLLUTION

The light, even though it passes through pollution, is unpolluted.
ST. AUGUSTINE.—*In Joannem.*

He that toucheth pitch shall be defiled therewith.　　　*Ecclesiasticus* xiii, 1.

Dirty water does not wash clean.
　　　　　　　　　　Italian prov.

POMP

Make not my path offensive to the Gods
By spreading it with carpets.　They alone
May claim that honour ; but for mortal men
To walk on fair embroidery, to me
Seems nowise without peril.　So I bid you
To honour me as man, and not as God.
ÆSCHYLUS.—*Agamemnon*, 893 (*Plumptre tr.*).

There's sic parade, sic pomp and art,
The joy can scarcely reach the heart.
　　　　　　　　BURNS.—*Twa Dogs*.

Vain pomp and glory of this world, I hate ye.
SHAKESPEARE.—*Henry VIII.*, Act 3, 2.

The pomps and vanity of this wicked world.　　　　*Church Catechism*.

POPULARITY

He more had pleased us had he pleased us less.　　ADDISON.—*English Poets*.

I hate the vulgar popular cattle.
　　　　R. BUCHANAN.—*Fine Weather*.

I have not loved the world, nor the world me ;
I have not flattered its rank breath, nor bowed
To its idolatries a patient knee.
　　BYRON.—*Childe Harold*, c. 3, 113.

What are the rank tongues
Of this vile herd, grown insolent with feeding,
That I should prize their noisy praise, or dread
Their noisome clamour ?
　　BYRON.—*Sardanapalus*, Act 1, 2.

Certes the commendacion of the peple
Is somtyme ful fals and ful brotel for to trist [very brittle to trust to] ; this day they preyse, tomorwe they blame.　God woot [God knows] desyr to have commendacion of the peple hath caused deeth to many a bisy [industrious] man.
　　CHAUCER.—*Parson's Tale, sec.* 28.

Vain men will speak well of him that does ill.
OLIVER CROMWELL.—*To Richard Mayor.*

Nor is the people's judgment always true :
The most may err as grossly as the few.
DRYDEN.—*Absalom and Achitophel*, Pt. 1, 779.

That truth once known, all else is worthless lumber ;

The greatest pleasure of the greatest number.
　　(1st) LORD LYTTON.—*King Arthur, Bk.* 8, 70.

Honour, glory, and popular praise,
Rocks whereon greatest men have oftest wrecked.
MILTON.—*Paradise Regained, Bk.* 2, 227.

The multitude is always in the wrong.
EARL OF ROSCOMMON.—*On Translated Verse.*

I thank you for your voices, thank you—
Your most sweet voices.
　　SHAKESPEARE.—*Coriolanus*, Act 2, 3.

You all did love him once, not without cause.
SHAKESPEARE.—*Julius Cæsar*, Act 3, 2.

That empty and ugly thing called popularity.
R. L. STEVENSON.—*To a Young Gentleman.*

His enemies, for want of charity,
Said he affected popularity.
　　SWIFT.—*Beasts' Confession.*

God will not love thee less, because men love thee more.
　　M. F. TUPPER.—*Of Tolerance.*

PORTRAITS

There are only two styles of portrait painting, the serious and the smirk. [*Miss La Creevy.*]
　　　　DICKENS.—*Nickleby, c.* 10.

I am all for a little flattery in portraits, —that is so far as, I think, the painter or sculptor should try at something more agreeable than anything he sees sitting to him.　　E. FITZGERALD.—*Letter to W. H. Thompson.*

Speak of me as I am ; nothing extenuate,
Nor set down aught in malice.
　　SHAKESPEARE.—*Othello*, Act 5, 2.

Alas ! how little can a moment show
Of an eye where feeling plays
In ten thousand dewy rays ;
A face o'er which a thousand shadows go !
　　WORDSWORTH.—*The Triad.*

POSIES

So let our love
As endless prove ;
And pure as gold for ever.
　　HERRICK.—*Hesperides*, 172.

Is this a prologue or the posy of a ring ?
SHAKESPEARE.—*Hamlet*, Act 3, 2.

I still rejoice
In my first choice.
　　　　Love Posies, c. 1596

I send to you a pair of Gloves :
  If you love me,
  Leave out the G,
And make a pair of Loves.
    Cupid's Posies (1674), *No.* 5.

Love itself discloses by Gifts with Posies.
    Ib., No. 43.

You and I will Lovers die.
    Ib., No. 54.
I wish that we two were a pair,
As these happy Gloves here are.
    Ib., No. 56.

There is no jewel I can see
Like love that's set in constancy.
    Ib., No. 64.

POSITION

For when a man is most above,
Him nedeth most to get him love.
    GOWER.—*Confessio Amantis, Bk.* 3.

Better to reign in Hell than serve in
  Heaven.
    MILTON.—*Paradise Lost, Bk.* 1, 263.

He that is below envieth him that riseth,
And he that is above, him that's below
  depiseth.
    ANON.—*" Hullo my fancy ! " (c.* 1600).

Better be the head of the yeomanry
than the tail of the gentry.
    Prov. (Ray).

POSITIVENESS

Where men of judgment creep and feel
  their way,
The positive pronounce without dismay.
    COWPER.—*Conversation,* 145.

Positiveness is a good quality for
preachers and teachers.
    SWIFT.—*Thoughts.*

I'm positive I'm in the right ; and if
you'll keep up the prerogative of a woman
you'll likewise be positive you are in the
right, whenever you do anything you have
a mind to.
    SIR J. VANBRUGH.—*Provoked Wife,*
    Act 1, 1.
It is only the charlatans who are certain.
We know nothing of first principles. . . .
Doubt is not a very agreeable condition,
but assurance is a ridiculous one.
    VOLTAIRE.—*To the Crown Prince of*
    Prussia, 1766.

POSSESSION

The thing possessed is not the thing it
seems.
    S. DANIEL.—*Civil Wars, st.* 104.

The pleasure of possessing,
  Surpasses all expressing,
But 'tis too short a blessing,
  And love too long a pain.
    DRYDEN.—*Spanish Friar,* Act 5, 1.

Hungry rooster don't cackle w'en he finc
a wum.
    J. C. HARRIS.—*Plantation Proverbs.*

Possession means to sit astride of the
  world,
Instead of having it astride of you.
    KINGSLEY.—*The Saint's Tragedy,* Act 1, 2.

Laws are always useful to those who
possess, and obnoxious to those who have
nothing.
    ROUSSEAU.—*Contrat Social, Bk.* 1,
    ch. 9 (*note*).

For it so falls out,
That what we have we prize not to the
  worth,
Whiles we enjoy it ; but being lacked and
  lost,
Why then we rack the value.
    SHAKESPEARE.—*Much Ado,* Act 4, 1.

They well deserve to have
That know the strong'st and surest way
  to get.
    SHAKESPEARE.—*Richard II.,* Act 3, 3.

Farewell ! thou art too dear for my possessing.   SHAKESPEARE.—*Sonnet* 87.

Possession, they say, is eleven parts of
the law.   SWIFT.

The want of a thing is perplexing
enough, but the possession of it is
intolerable.
    SIR J. VANBRUGH.—*Confederacy,* Act 1, 2.

The good old rule
Sufficeth them, the simple plan
That they should take who have the
  power,
  And they should keep who can.
    WORDSWORTH.—*Rob Roy's Grave.*

Who has but one lamb makes it fat.
    French prov.

We all have more than each man knows,
Of sins, of debts, of years, and foes.
    Said to be derived from the Persian.

POSSIBILITIES

Strong is the soul, and wise and beautiful ;
The seeds of godlike power are in us still ;
Gods are we, bards, saints, heroes, if we
  will.
    M. ARNOLD.—*Written in Emerson's Essays.*

Since that cannot be done which you
wish, wish what can be done.
    TERENCE.—*Andria,* 2.

These things are possible because they
seem to be possible.
    VIRGIL.—*Æneid. Bk.* 5.

May-be's fly na at this time o' year.
    Scottish prov. (see also *"Hypothesis"*).

POSTERITY

The seed ye sow, another reaps ;
The wealth ye find, another keeps ;
The robe ye weave, another wears ;
The arms ye forge, another bears.
SHELLEY.—*Men of England.*

Let no man write my epitaph ! Let my
  grave
Be uninscribed, and let my memory rest
Till other times are come, and other men,
Who then may do me justice.
SOUTHEY.—*On R. Emmet.*

We are always doing, says he, something
for Posterity, but I would fain see Posterity do something for us.
STEELE.—*Spectator, Vol.* 8, 583.

What has posterity done for us,
That we, lest they their rights should lose,
Should trust our necks to gripe of noose ?
J. TRUMBULL.—*McFingal.*

POSTHUMOUS FAME

Seldom comes Glory till a man be dead.
HERRICK.—*Glory.*

See nations, slowly wise and meanly just,
To buried merit raise the tardy bust.
JOHNSON.—*Vanity of Human Wishes.*

Ages to come and men unborn
Shall bless her name and sigh her fate.
PRIOR.—*Ode after Queen Mary's
                          Death,* 1795.
Seven wealthy towns contend for Homer
  dead,
Through which the living Homer begged
  his bread.   THOS. SEWARD (?).

Die two months ago, and not forgotten
yet ? Then there's hope a great man's
memory may outlive his life half a year ;
but, by'r lady, he must build churches
then.   SHAKESPEARE.—*Hamlet,* Act 3, 2.

Those glories come too late
That on our ashes wait.
ANON.—*Tr. of Martial, Bk.* 1, 26.

POSTPONEMENT

I give him three years and a day to match
  my Toledo,
And then we'll fight like dragons.
MASSINGER.—*The Maid of Honour,*
                                Act 2, 2.

Then do we sin against our own estate,
When we may profit meet, and come too
  late.
SHAKESPEARE.—*Timon of Athens,*
                                Act 5, 1.
That we would do,
We should do when we would, for this
" would " changes,

And hath abatements and delays as many
As there are tongues, are hands, are
  accidents.
SHAKESPEARE.—*Hamlet,* Act 4, 7.

By the street of By-and-By one comes
to the house of Never.
Span. prov. (Don Quixote).

POSTSCRIPTS

I knew one that when he wrote a letter
he would put that which was most material
in the postscript, as if it had been a bye
matter.   BACON.—*Of Cunning.*

Wit in the letter will prate, but wisdom
speaks in a postscript.
A. H. CLOUGH.—*Bothie of Tober-na-
                          Vuolich, Pt.* 9.

His sayings are generally like women's
letters : all the pith is in the postscript.
HAZLITT.—*Boswell Redivivus. Conv.
with Northcote (in allusion to Lamb).*

POVERTY

Poverty is the discoverer of all the arts.
APOLLONIUS.—*De Magia.*

For who sings commonly so merry a Noate
As he that cannot chop or change a groate ?
R. BARNFIELD.—*Content* (1594).

Poverty's unconquerable bar.
BEATTIE.—*The Minstrel, Bk.* 1, 1.

No one should praise poverty but he
who is poor.   ST. BERNARD.—*Sermon.*

The poor man's farthing is worth more
Than all the gold on Afric's shore.
WM. BLAKE.—*Proverbs.*

I wish my deadly foe no worse
Than want of friends and empty purse.
N. BRETON.—*Farewell to Town.*

The labouring people are only poor
because they are numerous.
BURKE.—*Thoughts on Scarcity.*

And what poor cot-folk pit their painch in,
I own it's past my comprehension.
BURNS.—*Twa Dogs.*

Poverty and eccentricity are very bad
bedfellows.   H. J. BYRON.—" *Mirth.*"

And rustic life and poverty
Grew beautiful beneath his touch.
CAMPBELL.—*On Burns.*

A poor fool indeed is a very scandalous
thing.
MRS. CENTLIVRE.—*The Wonder,* Act 1, 1.

But al be that he was a philosophre,
Yet hadde he but litel gold in cofre.
CHAUCER.—*Cant. Tales, Prol.*

Thilke that thou clepest [those whom thou callest] thy thralles been [are] goddes peple; for humble folk been Cristes freendes.
CHAUCER.—*Parson's Tale, sec.* 65.

Poverty, the reward of honest fools.
C. CIBBER.—*Richard III.*, Act 2, 2.

He found it inconvenient to be poor.
COWPER.—*Charity,* 189.

The poor, inured to drudgery and distress,
Act without aim, think little, and feel less,
And nowhere, but in feigned Arcadian scenes,
Taste happiness, or know what pleasure means.   COWPER.—*Hope,* 7.

Want is a bitter and a hateful good,
Because its virtues are not understood.
DRYDEN.

The greatest man in history was the poorest.   EMERSON.—*Domestic Life.*

Poverty consists in feeling poor.
EMERSON.—*Ib.*

There's no scandal like rags, nor any crime so shameful as poverty.
FARQUHAR.—*Beaux' Stratagem,* Act 1, 1.

Man is God's image: but a poor man is Christ's stamp to boot.
GEO. HERBERT.—*Church Porch.*

The poor man alone,
When he hears the poor moan,
From a morsel a morsel will give,
Welladay!
T. HOLCROFT.—*Gaffer Gray.*

For all the poor that are,
And all the strangers, are the care of Jove.
HOMER.—*Odyssey,* 6, 207 (*Cowper tr.*).

She had an idea from the very sound
That people with naught were naughty.
HOOD.—*Miss Kilmansegg.*

Oh, God, that bread should be so dear
And flesh and blood so cheap!
HOOD.—*Song of the Shirt.*

All crimes are safe but hated poverty.
JOHNSON.—*London.*

This mournful truth is everywhere confessed,
Slow rises worth by poverty depressed.
JOHNSON.—*Ib.*

A man guilty of poverty easily believes himself suspected.
JOHNSON.—*Rambler, No.* 26.

Few, save the poor, feel for the poor.
L. E. LANDON.—*The Poor.*

Poverty makes some humble, but more malignant.
LORD LYTTON.—*Eugene Aram, Bk.* 1, *c.* 7.

The Lady Poverty was fair,
But she has lost her looks of late,
With change of times and change of air.
Ah, slattern, she neglects her hair,
Her gown, her shoes. She keeps no state
As once, when her pure feet were bare.
ALICE MEYNELL.—*The Lady Poverty.*

Rattle his bones over the stones,
He's only a pauper whom nobody owns.
T. NOEL.—*Pauper's Drive.*

Poverty is a thorough instructress in all the arts.   PLAUTUS.—*Stichus.*

No wonder that his soul was sad,
When not one penny piece he had.
CHRISTINA ROSSETTI.—*Johnny.*

No one lives so poor as he is born.
SENECA.—*Quare bonis.*

A needy, hollow-eyed, sharp-looking wretch;
A living dead man.
SHAKESPEARE.—*Comedy of Errors,* Act 5, 1.

I am poor as Job, my lord, but not so patient. SHAKESPEARE.—*King Henry IV.,*
Pt. 2, Act 1, 2.

I am the friend of the unfriended poor.
SHELLEY.—*To Cambria.*

No society can surely be flourishing and happy, of which the far greater part of the members are poor and miserable.
ADAM SMITH.—*Wealth of Nations,*
Bk. 1, *ch.* 8.

Poverty is no disgrace to a man, but it is confoundedly inconvenient.
SYDNEY SMITH.—*Saying.*

'Tis infamous, I grant it, to be poor.
SMOLLETT.—*Advice,* 2.

Oh, holy is the patience of the poor!
F. TENNYSON.—*Alcœus,* 3, 61.

Our hoard is little, but our hearts are great.
TENNYSON.—*Marriage of Geraint.*

These two parties still divide the world
Of those that want, and those that have;
and still
The same old sore breaks out from age to age,
With much the same result.
TENNYSON.—*Walking to the Mail.*

Poverty is a hateful boon, mother of health, remover of cares, restorer of wisdom, a possession without loss.
VINCENT OF BEAUVAIS.—*Speculum Historiale, Bk.* 10, *c.* 71 (*an older saying*).

The poor is never free; he serves in every land.   VOLTAIRE.—*Les Guèbres.*

Whene'er I take my walks abroad,
How many poor I see!
I. WATTS.—*Praise for Mercies.*

The keen, the wholesome air of poverty.
WORDSWORTH.—*Excursion, Bk.* 1.

Splendid poverty.
YOUNG.—*Love of Fame, Sat.* 1.

For the poor ye have always with you.
St. John xii, 8 (*R.V.*).

The rich and poor meet together: the
Lord is the maker of them all.
Proverbs xxii, 2.

Never turn thy face from any poor man.
Tobit iv (*Prayer Book Version*).

God help the poor: the rich can make
shift.   *Motto in Dekker's " Worke for
Armourers "* (1609).

Poverty is the sixth sense.   *Prov.*

Poverty is no sin, but twice as bad.
Russian prov.

POWER

It is a strange desire, to seek power and
lose liberty.   BACON.—*Of Great Place.*

As wealth is power, so all power will
infallibly draw wealth to itself by some
means or other.   BURKE.—*Speech* (1780).

Power gradually extirpates from the
mind every humane and gentle virtue.
BURKE.—*Vindication of Natural Society.*

God is generally for the big battalions
against the little ones.
BUSSY-RABUTIN—.*Letter, Oct.* 18, 1677.

The depositary of power is always unpopular.
DISRAELI.—*Coningsby, Bk.* 4, *ch.* 13.

Little he loved, but power the most of all,
And that he seemed to scorn, as one who
knew
By what foul paths men choose to crawl
thereto.
J. R. LOWELL.—*Legend of Brittany,
st.* 17.

The more the state expands, the more
liberty diminishes.
ROUSSEAU.—*Contrat Social, Bk.* 3, *ch.* 1.

The Monarch drank, that happy hour,
The sweetest, holiest draught of Power.
SCOTT.—*Lady of the Lake, c.* 6, 28.

No pent-up Utica contracts your powers,
But the whole boundless continent is
yours.
J. M. SEWALL.—*Epilogue to Cato.*

Power, like a desolating pestilence,
Pollutes whate'er it touches.
SHELLEY.—*Queen Mab.*

PRACTICE

Constant practice often excels even talent.
CICERO.—*Pro Cornelio Balbo,* 20.

Practice is the best master.
CICERO.—*Pro Rabirio Postumo,* 4.

Practice is everything.
PERIANDER OF CORINTH (*c.* B.C. 550).

An ounce of practice is worth a pound
of preaching.   *Prov.*

PRAISE

It was his noble mind that movèd mee
To write his praise, and eeke his acts
commend.
R. BARNFIELD.—*Complaint of Poetrie*
(1598).

Good, strong, thick, stupefying incense-
smoke.
BROWNING.—*The Bishop orders
his Tomb.*

Praise is deeper than the lips.
BROWNING.—*Hervé Riel.*

On earth I confess an itch for the praise
of fools—that's Vanity.
BROWNING.—*Solomon and Balkis.*

For praise, that's due, does give no more
To worth than what it had before;
But to commend without desert
Requires a mastery of art,
That sets a gloss on what's amiss,
And writes what should be, not what is.
S. BUTLER.—*Miscellaneous Thoughts.*

But Shakespeare also says, 'tis very silly
" To gild refinèd gold, or paint the lily."
BYRON.—*Don Juan, c.* 3, 76.

Some man preyseth his neighbour by a
wikke entente [evil intention]; for he
maketh alwey a wikked knotte [difficulty]
at the last ende. Alwey he maketh a
" but " at the last ende.
CHAUCER.—*Parson's Tale, sec.* 30.

Praises of the unworthy are felt by
ardent minds as robberies of the deserving.
COLERIDGE.—*Biog. Literaria, ch.* 3.

Nothing so soon the drooping spirits can
raise
As praises from the men whom all men
praise.   COWLEY.—*Ode.*

Oh spare your idol! think him human
still;
Charms he may have, but he has frailties
too;
Dote not too much, nor spoil what ye
admire.   COWPER.—*Time Piece,* 496.

Daubed with undiscerning praise.
COWPER.—*Winter Morning Walk.*

Say not that she did well or ill,
Only, " She did her best."
DINAH M. CRAIK.—*Poems* (1852).

N*   393

Praise is devotion fit for mighty minds,
The differing world's agreeing sacrifice.
　　SIR W. D'AVENANT.—*See Oxford Book
　　　　　　　　of English Verse.*

Contemn the danger and the praise pursue.
　　DRYDEN.—*Tr. Ovid, Meleager and
　　　　　　　　Atalanta.*

For he who sings thy praise secures his
own.　DRYDEN.—*Virgil, Pastoral 6.*

Of praise a mere glutton, he swallowed
　　what came,
And the puff of a dunce he mistook it for
　　fame.　GOLDSMITH.—*Retaliation.*

Who peppered the highest was surest to
　　please.　　GOLDSMITH.—*Ib.*

Sweet is the scene where genial friendship
　　plays
The pleasing game of interchanging praise.
　　O. W. HOLMES.—*After Dinner Poem.*

　　　　Be silent, Praise,
Blind guide with siren voice, and blinding
　　all
　　　　That hear thy call.
　　KEBLE.—*Wednes. before Easter.*

As a rule we only praise in order to be
praised.
　　LA ROCHEFOUCAULD.—*Maxim 146.*

There are some censures which praise,
and some praises which condemn.
　　LA ROCHEFOUCAULD.—*Maxim 148.*

The refusal of praise is really the wish
to be praised twice.
　　LA ROCHEFOUCAULD.—*Maxim 149.*

　　When affection only speaks,
Truth is not always there.
　　MIDDLETON.—*Old Law*, Act 4, 2.

And hearts that once beat high for praise
　Now feel that pulse no more.
　　MOORE.—*The Harp that Once.*

To those who know thee not, no words
　　can paint ;
And those who know thee know all words
　　are faint.
　　HANNAH MOORE.—*Sensibility.*

Praise, the fine diet which we're apt to
　　love,
If given to excess doth hurtful prove.
　　J. OLDHAM.—*To a Friend.*

Do you wish people to speak well of
you ?　Don't yourself.
　　PASCAL.—*Pensées, Pt.* 1, 9, 59.

The bad, when praised, become still worse.
　　PHILOSTRATUS (*Greek*).

This feeling of self-importance [from
the praise of the public orator] remains
with me for more than three days.　In
fact so much do the speech and tone of
the orator ring in my ears and sink in my
heart, that even on the fourth or fifth day
I can hardly pull myself together or
realise where on earth I am.　For a while
I fancy myself in the isles of the blessed.
So clever are our orators !
　　PLATO.—*Menexenus,* 2 (*Spoken by
　　　Socrates in ridicule of the Grecian
　　　public orators*).

What would have been very honourable
if another had related it, becomes nothing
if the doer narrates it himself.
　　PLINY THE YOUNGER.—*Bk.* 1, *Ep.* 8.

Those who are greedy of praise prove
that they are poor in merit.
　　PLUTARCH.—*As quoted by La Harpe.*

When a sophister was declaiming the
praises of Hercules, Antalcidas asked :
" Who ever said anything against him ? "
　　PLUTARCH.—*Morals, Bk.* 1.

Avoid extremes ; and shun the fault of
　　such
Who still are pleased too little or too much.
　　POPE.—*Criticism,* 384.

I see no reason that because one man
is eminent, therefore another has a right
to be impertinent and throw praises in
his face.　POPE.—*The Guardian, No.* 4
　　　　　　　(*March* 16, 1713).

Fame impatient of extremes, decays
Not more by envy than excess of praise.
　　POPE.—*Temple of Fame,* 44.

Drive from my breast that wretched lust
　　of praise,
Unblemished let me live, or die unknown ;
Oh grant an honest fame, or grant me
　　none !　　POPE.—*Ib.,* 522.

Praise is like ambergris ; a little whiff
of it, and by snatches, is very agreeable,
but when a man holds a whole lump of it
to his nose, it is a stink and strikes you
down.
　　POPE.—*Thoughts on Various Subjects.*

Praise undeserved is scandal in disguise.
　　POPE.—(*Said to be quoted from an anon.
　　poem in Tonson's Miscellanies,* 1709.)

When all the world conspires to praise her
The woman's deaf and does not hear.
　　POPE.—*To a Lady at Court.*

Praise cannot wound his generous spirit
　　now.　ROGERS.—*Pleasures of Memory.*

When one is flagging, a little praise is
a cordial after all. . . . To-day I have
already written four pages with confi-

dence. **Thus** does flattery or praise oil the wheels. Scott.—*Diary, Feb.*, 1826.

Praising what is lost
Makes the remembrance dear.
Shakespeare.—*All's Well*, Act 5, 3.

I will praise any man that will praise me.
Shakespeare.—*Antony and Cleopatra*, Act 2, 6.

Well said! That was laid on with a trowel.
Shakespeare.—*As You Like It*, Act 1, 2.

I come to bury Cæsar, not to praise him.
Shakespeare.—*Julius Cæsar*, Act 3, 2.

This comes too near the praising of myself.
Shakespeare.—*Merchant of Venice*, Act 3, 4.

Who is Sylvia ? What is she
That all our swains commend her ?
Shakespeare.—*Two Gentlemen of Verona*, Act 4, 1.

Our praises are our wages.
Shakespeare.—*Winter's Tale*, Act 1, 2.

Such is the mode of these censorious days,
The art is lost of knowing how to praise.
J. Sheffield (Duke of Buckingham-shire).—*On Mr. Hobbes.*

We are not content with praise unless we deserve it, nor are we content with deserving it unless we obtain it.
Adam Smith.

Among the smaller duties of life I hardly know any one more important than that of not praising where praise is not due.
Sydney Smith.—*Lectures on Moral Philosophy, No.* 9.

Praise is the best diet for us, after all.
Sydney Smith.—*Saying.*

So double was his paines, so double be his praise.
Spenser.—*Faerie Queene, Bk.* 2, c. 2, 25.

And what is most commended at this time,
Succeeding ages may account a crime.
Earl of Stirling.—*Darius.*

Your panegyrics here provide ;
You cannot err on flattery's side.
Swift.—*On Poetry.*

The poor encomium, so thinly spread,
Lampoons the injured ashes of the dead ;
Though for the orator 'tis said withal,
He meant to praise him, if he meant at all.
Swift.—*Swan Tripe Club.*

That worst class of enemies, those who praise you. Tacitus.—*Agric.* 41.

The art of praising is the beginning of the art of pleasing.
Voltaire.—*La Pucelle.*

Who praises everything is only a flatterer. He only knows how to praise who praises with restraint.
Voltaire.—*Temple du Goût. Prelim. Letter.*

Why, praise is satire in these sinful days.
P. Whitehead.—*Manners.*

I had been nourished by the sickly food
Of popular applause. I now perceived
That we are praised, only as men in us
Do recognise some image of themselves,
An abject counterpart of what they are,
Or the empty thing that they would wish to be.
Wordsworth.—*Borderers*, Act 4.

With faint praises one another damn.
Wycherley.—*Plain Dealer* (1674), *Prol.*

The love of praise, howe'er concealed by art,
Reigns, more or less, and glows, in every heart.
Young.—*Love of Fame, Sat.* 1.

When most the world applauds you, most beware ;
'Tis often less a blessing than a snare.
Distrust mankind ; with your own heart confer ;
And dread even there to find a flatterer.
Young.—*Ib., Sat.* 6.

Woe unto you, when all men shall speak well of you ! *St. Luke* vi, 26.

Ye who would in aught excel,
Regard this simple maxim well :
A wise man's censure may appal,
But a fool's praise is worse than all.
Anon.—*Tr. of Yriarte, L'Oso y la Mona.*

Who praiseth St. Peter doth not blame St. Paul. *Prov.* (Geo. Herbert).

PRAYER

Long tarries destiny,
But comes to those who pray.
Æschylus.—*Choephoræ*, 462 (*Plumptre tr.*).

He who labours, prays.
St. Augustine.

He who prays and also works, lifts his heart to God with his hands.
St. Bernard.—*Ad sororem.*

Pray and work, said the mediæval saint.
Pray as though nothing were to be done by work ; work as though nothing were to be gained by prayer.
J. H. Bridges.—*Essays and Addresses, Pt.* 1, 1.

At my devotion I love to use the civility of my knee, my hat, and hand.
Sir T. Browne.—*Religio Medici, Pt.* 1, 3.

Sleep is in fine so like death, I dare not
trust it without my prayers.
SIR T. BROWNE.—*Religio Medici,*
Pt. 2, sec. 12.

A child may say amen
To a bishop's prayer, and feel the way it
goes.
E. B. BROWNING.—*Aurora Leigh, Bk. 2.*

They never sought in vain that sought
the Lord aright.
BURNS.—*Cotter's Saturday Night.*

I would not exchange the prayer of the
deceased [Mrs. John Sheppard] in my
behalf for the united glory of Homer,
Cæsar, and Napoleon, could such be accumulated upon a living head.
BYRON.—*Letter to John Sheppard of
Frome (No. 469 in Moore's " Life
of Byron ").*

He prayeth best who loveth best
All things both great and small ;
For the dear God who loveth us,
He made and loveth all.
COLERIDGE.—*Ancient Mariner.*

And Satan trembles when he sees
The weakest saint upon his knees.
COWPER.—*Hymn.*

I'm heard when answered, soon or late,
And heard when I no answer get ;
Yea, kindly answered when refused,
And treated well when harshly used.
R. ERSKINE.

Who their ill-tasted, home-brewed prayer
To the State's mellow forms prefer.
MATTHEW GREEN.—*Spleen, 306.*

And help us this, and every day,
To live more nearly as we pray.
KEBLE.—*Morning.*

If by prayer
Incessant I could hope to change the will
Of him who all things can, I would not
cease
To weary him with my assiduous cries ;
But prayer against his absolute decree
No more avails than breath against the
wind.
MILTON.—*Paradise Lost, 11, 307.*

Prayer is the soul's sincere desire,
Uttered or unexpressed ;
The motion of a hidden fire
That trembles in the breast.
JAS. MONTGOMERY.—*Praying always.*

Do you wish to find out the really
sublime ? Repeat the Lord's Prayer.
NAPOLEON.

The prayer to pray is the one that you
can answer yourself. EDEN PHILLPOTTS.

Nymph, in thy orisons
Be all my sins remembered.
SHAKESPEARE.—*Hamlet, Act 3, 1.*

Words without thoughts never to heaven
go. SHAKESPEARE.—*Ib.,* Act 3, 3.

Only righteous prayers are heard by the
gods. TACITUS.—*Annals, Bk. 3.*

More things are wrought by prayer
Than this world dreams of.
TENNYSON.—*Passing of Arthur.*

Battering the gates of heaven with storms
of prayer.
TENNYSON.—*Simeon Stylites.*

Work, as though work alone thine end
could gain ;
But pray to God as though all work were
vain.
D. W. THOMPSON.—*Tr. Euripides.*

Cease to hope that the gods' decrees
are to be changed by prayer.
VIRGIL.—*Æneid.*

The sure relief of prayer.
WORDSWORTH.—*During a Storm.*

In every storm that either frowns or falls,
What an asylum has the soul in prayer !
YOUNG.—*Night Thoughts, 9.*

Pray regularly morning and evening,
and in the early part of the evening, for
good works drive away evils.
Koran, ch. 11.

Prayer should be the key of the day
and the lock of the night.   *Prov.*

PREACHERS AND PREACHING

The pig-of-lead-like pressure
Of the preaching man's immense stupidity.
BROWNING.—*Christmas Eve, Canto 3.*

Who prove their doctrine orthodox
By apostolic blows and knocks.
BUTLER.—*Hudibras, I, 1, 199.*

Though language forms the preacher,
'Tis " good works " make the man.
ELIZA COOK.—*Good Works.*

Mean you to prophesy or but to preach ?
COWPER.—*Table Talk, 478.*

Reading what they never wrote,
Just fifteen minutes, huddle up their work,
And with a well-bred whisper close the
scene.
COWPER.—*The Time Piece, 411.*

Heard at conventicle, where worthy men,
Misled by custom, strain celestial themes
Through the pressed nostril.
COWPER.—*Ib., 437.*

How oft, when Paul has served us with a
text,
Has Epictetus, Plato, Tully, preached !
COWPER.—*Ib., 539.*

For public preaching indeed is the gift
of the Spirit, working as best seems to his
secret will.
      MILTON.—*Church Government, ch.* 1.

Truth and the text he labours to display,
Till both are quite interpreted away.
      CHRISTOPHER PITT.—*On Preaching.*

To rest the cushion and soft dean invite,
Who never mentions hell to ears polite.
      POPE.—*Moral Essays, Ep.* 4.

Preachers say, Do as I say, not as I do.
      SELDEN.—*Preaching.*

Do not, as some ungracious pastors do,
Show me the steep and thorny path to
   Heaven,
Whilst, like a puffed and reckless libertine
Himself the primrose path of dalliance
   treads,
And recks not his own rede.
      SHAKESPEARE.—*Hamlet*, Act 1, 3

And coughing drowns the parson's saw.
      SHAKESPEARE.—*Love's Labour's Lost,*
                            Act 5, 2.

Preaching is a good calling but a bad
trade.
      C. H. SPURGEON.—*John Ploughman.*

Don't go to hear Dr. Smoothaway. He
preaches down at St. Judas's church, and
a brother of his is minister at the Modern
Thought chapel.
      C. H. SPURGEON.—"*Salt-Cellars.*"

"Parson," said I, "you pitch the pipe too
   low."   TENNYSON.—*Edwin Morris.*

With mild heat of holy oratory.
      TENNYSON.—*Idylls of the King:*
             Geraint and Enid, 867.

Thou art no Sabbath-drawler of old saws,
Distilled from some worm-cankered
   homily.   TENNYSON.—*To J. M. K.*

Ah me! the doctor who preaches is only
taller than most of us by the height of the
pulpit.
      THACKERAY.—*Adventures of Philip.*

Preach not because you have to say
something, but because you have something to say.
      ARCHBP. WHATELY.—*Apophthegms.*

A sermon should never exceed twenty-
five minutes.
      JOHN WILSON.—*Noctes,* 15 (1827).

And from the pulpit zealously maintained
The cause of Christ and civil liberty
As one, and moving to one glorious end.
      WORDSWORTH.—*Excursion, Bk.* 2.

And hark! how blithe the throstle sings!
He too is no mean preacher:
Come forth into the light of things;
Let Nature be your Teacher.
      WORDSWORTH.—*Tables Turned,* 4.

The foolishness of preaching.
               1 *Corinthians* i, 21

A dreigh (dry) drink is better than a
dreigh sermon.   *Scottish prov.*

He who is short of grace thinks sermons
long. *Given as a saying by C. H. Spurgeon.*

PRECEDENT

Set it down to tnyself, as well to create
good precedents as to follow them.
      BACON.—*Of Great Place.*

To follow foolish precedents, and wink
With both our eyes, is easier than to
   think.   COWPER.—*Tirocinium,* 255.

A precedent embalms a principle.
      DISRAELI.—*Speech,* 1848.

All the sentences of precedent judges
that have ever been cannot all together
make a law contrary to natural equity.
      HOBBES.—*Leviathan, ch.* 26.

One precedent creates another. They
soon accumulate and become law.
      JUNIUS.—*Dedication.*

'Twill be recorded for a precedent;
And many an error, by the same example,
Will rush into the state.
      SHAKESPEARE.—*Merchant of Venice,*
                            Act 4, 1.

Is not Precedent indeed a King of men?
      SWINBURNE.—*Word from the Psalmist.*

PRECISENESS

      Her taste exact
      For faultless fact
      Amounts to a disease.
      SIR W. S. GILBERT.—*Mikado.*

The devil turned precisian!
      MASSINGER.—*New Way to pay Old Debts,*
                            Act 1, 1.

How absolute the knave is! we must
speak by the card, or equivocation will
undo us.
      SHAKESPEARE.—*Hamlet*, Act 5, 1.

In such a time as this, it is not meet
That every nice offence should bear his
   comment.
      SHAKESPEARE.—*Julius Cæsar*, Act 4, 3.

Let him look to his bond!
      SHAKESPEARE.—*Merchant of Venice,*
                            Act 3, 1.

Ye tithe mint and anise and cummin,
and have left undone the weightier matters
of the law, judgement, and mercy, and
faith.   *St. Matthew* xxiii, 23 (*R.V.*).

The letter killeth, but the spirit maketh alive.   2 *Corinthians* iii, 6.

PRECOCITY

Precocious youth is a sign of premature death.   PLINY.—7, 51.

I never knew so young a body with so old a head.
SHAKESPEARE.—*Merchant of Venice*, Act 4, 1.

So wise, so young, they say, do ne'er live long.
SHAKESPEARE.—*Richard III.*, Act 3, 1.

Soon tod [toothed], soon with God.
Northern saying.

PREFACES

I had long seen the uselessness of all prefaces, for the more pains a writer takes to render his views clear, the more occasion he gives for embarrassment.
GOETHE.—*Autob., Bk.* 13.

I have somewhere read or heard that the Preface before a book, like the portico before a house, should be contrived so as to catch, but not detain the attention of those who desire admission to the family within.
MRS. PIOZZI.—*Pref. to Anecdotes of S. Johnson, LL.D.*

Nor will I tire thy patience with a train Of preface, or what ancient poets feign.
VIRGIL.—*Georgics, Bk.* 2 (*Dryden tr.*).

It is a foolish thing to make a long prologue, and to be short in the story itself.   2 *Maccabees* ii, 32.

PREFERMENT

The parson knows enough who knows a Duke.   COWPER.—*Tirocinium*, 403.

Plough-hoss don't squeal en kick w'en dey puts n'er [another] hoss in he place.
J. C. HARRIS.—*Nights with Uncle Remus*, ch. 47.

Desert may make a sergeant to a colonel, And it may hinder him from rising higher.
MASSINGER.—*The Maid of Honour*, Act 3, 1.

A ruler who appoints any man to an office, when there is in his dominions another man better qualified for it, sins against God and against the State.
Koran. Cited by J. S. Mill, Liberty, ch. 2.

PREJUDICE

Mother is far too clever to understand anything she does not like.
ARNOLD BENNETT.—*The Title.*

But his eddication to his ruination had not been over nice,
And his stupid skull was choking full of vulgar prejudice.
R. BUCHANAN.—*Phil Blood's Leap.*

All kinds of vulgar prejudice I pray you set aside.
SIR W. S. GILBERT.—*Trial by Jury.*

To be prejudiced is always to be weak ; yet there are prejudices so near to laudable that they have been often praised and are always pardoned.
JOHNSON.—*Taxation no Tyranny.*

I am, in plainer words, a bundle of prejudices—made up of likings and dislikings.   LAMB.—*Imperfect Sympathies.*

Every man should let alone other's prejudices and examine his own.   LOCKE.

Remember when the judgment's weak, the prejudice is strong.
K. O'HARA.—*Midas.*

All seems infected that the infected spy, As all looks yellow to the jaundiced eye.
POPE.—*Criticism*, 558.

All manners take a tincture from our own, Or some discoloured through our passions shown,
Or fancy's beam enlarges, multiplies, Contracts, inverts, and gives ten thousand dyes.
POPE.—*Moral Essays, Ep.* 1, 33.

If ever from an English heart, O *here* let prejudice depart !
SCOTT.—*Marmion, Introd.*

Some men there are, love not a gaping pig, Some, that are mad if they behold a cat.
SHAKESPEARE.—*Merchant of Venice*, Act 4, 1.

We all decry prejudice, yet are all prejudiced.
HERBT. SPENCER.—*Social Statics*, Pt. 2, ch. 17, 2.

Are you going to hang him *anyhow*— and try him afterwards ?
MARK TWAIN.—*Innocents at Home, ch.* 5.

Custom and indolence combine together to keep ignorance in possession.
VOLTAIRE.—*Chinese Letters.*

Prejudices are the reasoning of fools.
VOLTAIRE.—*La Loi naturelle.*

Prejudice gets into the pulpit first ; reason does not arrive until later on. That is the ordinary march of the human mind.   VOLTAIRE.—*Letters on the English.*

Passion and prejudice govern the world ; only under the name of reason.
J. WESLEY.—*Letter to J. Benson, Oct.*, 1770.

PREMATURENESS

You are like the eels of Melun ; you cry out before you are skinned.
RABELAIS.—*Gargantua* (1534).

It's time enough to make my bed when I'm gaun to lie doun.   *Scottish prov.*

PREPARATION

Forewarned, forearmed ; to be prepared is half the victory.
CERVANTES.—*Don Quixote, II.,* 17.

When any great design thou dost intend, Think on the means, the manner, and the end. SIR J. DENHAM.—*Prudence,* 186.

Every one with one of his hands wrought in the work, and with the other hand held a weapon.   *Nehemiah* iv, 17.

Light your lamp before it becomes dark.
Arabic prov.

A beard well lathered is half shaved.
Italian prov.

PRESENCE OF MIND

Presence of mind and courage in distress Are more than armies to procure success.
DRYDEN.—*Aurengzebe,* Act 2.

PRESENT, THE

The present moment is our ain,
   The neist we never saw.
BEATTIE.—*Stanza added to " There's nae luck about the house."*

     Every age,
Through being beheld too close, is ill discerned.
E. B. BROWNING.—*Aurora Leigh, Bk.* 5.

     Every age
Appears to souls who live in it (ask Carlyle)
Most unheroic.   E. B. BROWNING.—*Ib.*

Shakespeare says, we are creatures that look before and after. The more surprising that we do not look round a little and see what is passing under our very eyes.
CARLYLE.—*Sartor Resartus, Bk.* 1, 1.

The present is the living sum-total of the whole past.
CARLYLE.—*Essays, Characteristics.*

To-morrow do thy worst, for I have lived to-day,
     DRYDEN.—*Tr. of Horace.*

Take time, while time doth serve ; 'tis time to-day,
For secret dangers will attend delay.
Do what thou canst ; to-day hath eagle's wings :
For who can tell what change to-morrow brings ?
     J. G. LOCKHART.—*His Epitaph.*

Consult the dead upon the things that were,
But the living only on things that are.
   LONGFELLOW.—*Golden Legend, Pt.* 1.

Trust no future, howe'er pleasant ;
Let the dead Past bury its dead ;
Act, act in the living Present,
   Heart within and God o'erhead.
     LONGFELLOW.—*Psalm of Life.*

These most brisk and giddy-pacèd times.
SHAKESPEARE.—*Twelfth Night,* Act 2, 4.

For we are Ancients of the earth,
   And in the morning of the times.
     TENNYSON.—*Locksley Hall.*

In what alone is ours, the living NOW.
   WORDSWORTH.—*Tour in Italy.*

Live to-day, forgetting the anxieties of the past.   *Epicurean Maxim.*

Can ye not discern the signs of the times ?   *St. Matthew* xvi, 3.

Give me to-day and take to-morrow.
Greek prov., condemned by St. Chrysostom.

PRESS, THE

Flee fro the prees* and dwelle with sothefastnesse.
   CHAUCER.—*Ballad of Good Counsel.*

Did Charity prevail, the press would prove A vehicle of virtue, truth, and love.
   COWPER.—*Charity,* 624.

Newspapers always excite curiosity. No one ever lays one down without a feeling of disappointment.
LAMB.—*Essays of Elia ; Detached Thoughts.*

Four hostile newspapers are more to be feared than a thousand bayonets.
     NAPOLEON.

Turn to the press—its teeming sheets survey,
Big with the wonders of each passing day ;
Births, deaths, and weddings, forgeries, fires, and wrecks,
Harangues and hailstones, brawls and broken necks.
   CHARLES SPRAGUE.—*Curiosity.*

They said the Press was the Arkymedian Leaver which moved the world.
ARTEMUS WARD.—*The Press.*

PRESUMPTION

Presumptuous hope, that fain would stretch
To heaven's high throne her daring view,
Is but the wingèd steed that threw
Bellerophon, what time his frenzied pride
Aspired to tread the eternal domes above,
And sit among the peers of Jove.
PINDAR.—*Isthmian Odes,* 6, 60 (*Moore tr.*).

* "Press" = crowd; it has been humourously taken to mean "press."

In pride, in reasoning pride our error lies ;
All quit their sphere, and rush into the
skies.
> POPE.—*Essay on Man, Ep.* 2, 123.

A twalpenny cat may look at a king.
> *Scottish prov.*

PRETENTIOUSNESS

His wit invites you by his looks to come,
But when you knock it never is at home.
> COWPER.—*Conversation*, 303.

Musical as the chime of tinkling rills,
Weak to perform, though mighty to
pretend.
> COWPER.—*Progress of Error*, 14.

He made me mad
To see him shine so brisk, and smell so
sweet,
And talk so like a waiting-gentlewoman,
Of guns, and drums, and wounds.
> SHAKESPEARE.—*Henry IV.*, Pt. 1, Act 1, 2.

Glendower. I can call spirits from the
vasty deep.
Hotspur. Why, so can I, and so can any
man,
But will they come when you do call for
them ?
> SHAKESPEARE.—*Ib.*, Pt. 1, Act 3, 1.

PREVARICATION

Resolved to die in the last dyke of prevarication.
> BURKE.—*Impeachment of Hastings*
> (May 7, 1789).

I love not a sophisticated truth with an
alloy of lie in it.
> DRYDEN.—*Assignation*, Act 5, 4.

O pardon me, my lord ; it oft falls out,
To have what we would have, we speak
not what we mean.
> SHAKESPEARE.—*Measure for Measure*,
> Act 2, 4.

A lie which is half a truth is ever the
blackest of lies.
> TENNYSON.—*The Grandmother.*

" Almost " and " very nigh "
Save the teller many a lie.
> *Old Saying.*

PREY

Hobbes clearly proves that every creature
Lives in a state of war by nature ;
The greater for the smaller watch,
But seldom meddle with their match.
> SWIFT.—*On Poetry.*

For wheresoever the carcase is, there will
the eagles be gathered together.
> *St. Matthew* xxiv, 28.

PRIDE

No mere mortal has a right
To carry that exalted air ;
Best people are not angels quite.
> BROWNING.—*Pippa Passes*, 9, 36.

The fient a pride, nae pride had he,
Nor sauce, nor state, that I could see,
Mair than an honest ploughman.
> BURNS.—*On meeting Lord Daer.*

But his heart was swollen and turned aside
By deep, interminable pride.
> BYRON.—*Siege of Corinth, st.* 21.

The proud will sooner lose than ask their
way.
> C. CHURCHILL.—*The Farewell*, 380.

The addition of pride contaminates the
best manners.   CLAUDIUS.

The proud are always most provoked by
pride.   COWPER.—*Conversation*, 160.

For Lucifer, with them that felle,
Bare pride with him into helle ;
There was pride of too great cost,
When he for pride hath heaven lost.
> GOWER.—*Conf. Amantis, Bk.* 1.

Pride is the cause of alle wo.
> GOWER.—*Ib.*, 1, 3006

A pride there is of rank,—a pride of birth,
A pride of learning, and a pride of purse,
A London pride,—in short, there be on
earth
A host of prides some better and some
worse ;
But of all prides, since Lucifer's attaint,
The proudest swells a self-elected saint.
> HOOD.—*Ode to R. Wilson.*

Hating that solemn vice of greatness,
pride.   BEN JONSON.—*Lady Bedford.*

Oh why should the spirit of mortal be
proud ?
Like a swift-fleeting meteor, a fast-flying
cloud,
A flash of the lightning, a break of the
wave,
He passes from life to his rest in the grave.
> WM. KNOX.—*Said to have been the
> favourite poem of Abraham Lincoln.*

Of all the garbs I ever saw Pride put
on, that of her humility is to me the most
disgusting.
> H. MACKENZIE.—*Man of Feeling, ch.* 33.

Pride, the never-failing vice of fools.
> POPE.—*Criticism*, 204.

We are sometimes apt to wonder to see
those people proud who have done the
meanest things ; whereas a consciousness
of having done poor things, and a shame
of hearing of them, often make the composition we call pride.
> POPE.—*Thoughts on Various Subjects.*

Pride is at the bottom of all great
mistakes.   RUSKIN.—*Modern Painters*, 4,
> Pt. 5, sec. 22.

But sure he's proud ; and yet his pride
  becomes him.
SHAKESPEARE.—*As You Like It*, Act 3, 5.

'Tis pride that pulls the country down.
SHAKESPEARE.—*Othello* (*quoted from old
                              ballad*), Act 2, 3.

Two curs shall tame each other ; pride
  alone
Must tarre the mastiffs on.
          SHAKESPEARE.—*Troilus*, Act 1, 3.

Some glory in their birth, some in their
  skill,
Some in their wealth, some in their body's
  force.   SHAKESPEARE.—*Sonnet* 91.

Was never in this world ought worthy
  tride,
Without some spark of such self-pleasing
  pride. SPENSER.—*Amoretti, Sonnet* 5.

But if they all should be denied,
Then you're too proud to own your pride.
      ANN and JANE TAYLOR.—*To find out
                                    Pride.*

There was as great a sin in His eyes as
that of the poor erring woman,—it was
the sin of pride.
      THACKERAY.—*Our Batch of Novels for
                        Christmas*, 1837.

Curst pride, that creeps securely in,
And swells a haughty worm.
          I. WATTS.—*Sincere Praise.*

      Pride,
Howe'er disguised in its own majesty,
Is littleness.
WORDSWORTH.—*Lines left upon a Seat.*

When pride cometh, then cometh shame.
                  Proverbs xi, 2.

Pride goeth before destruction, and an
haughty spirit before a fall.
                  Proverbs xvi, 18.

PRIMROSES

A primrose by a river's brim
A yellow primrose was to him,
And it was nothing more.
      WORDSWORTH.—*Peter Bell*, Pt. 1.

PRINCES

He may not, as unvalued persons do,
Carve for himself ; for on his choice
  depends
The safety and the health of the whole
  state.
      SHAKESPEARE.—*Hamlet*, Act 1, 3.

For princes are the glass, the school, the
  book,
Where subjects' eyes do learn, do read,
  do look.
      SHAKESPEARE.—*Lucrece*, st. 88.

A prince, born for the good of other men ;
Whose god-like office is to draw the sword
Against oppression, and set free mankind.
      T. SOUTHERN.—*Oroonoko*, Act 3, 3.

PRINCIPLE

  I *don't* believe in princerple,
    But oh, I *du* in interest.
J. R. LOWELL.—*Biglow Papers, No.* 6.

It was against my principles, but I find
that principles have no real force except
when one is well fed.
      MARK TWAIN.—*Adam's Diary.*

PRINTING

'Tis pleasant sure to see one's name in
  print ;
A book's a book, although there's nothing
  in't.   BYRON.—*English Bards*, 51.

He that cometh in print because he
would be known, is like the fool that
cometh into the market because he would
be seen.   LYLY.—*Euphues.*

Thou hast most traitorously corrupted
the youth of the realm in erecting a
grammar school ; and whereas, before,
our forefathers had no other books but
the score and the tally, thou hast caused
printing to be used ; and, contrary to the
King, his crown and dignity, thou hast
built a paper-mill.
      SHAKESPEARE.—*Henry VI., Pt.* 2,
                              Act 4, 7.

I love a ballad in print, a' life ; for then
we are sure they are true.
SHAKESPEARE.—*Winter's Tale*, Act 4, 3.

The art which is the conserver of all arts
(*i.e.* printing).   *Old Motto.*

PRISONS

    Stone walls do not a prison make,
      Nor iron bars a cage ;
    Minds innocent and quiet take
      That for an hermitage.
          LOVELACE.—*To Althea.*

As he passed through Cold Bath fields, he
    looked
  At a solitary cell ;
And he was well pleased, for it gave him
    a hint
  For improving the prisons in Hell.
      SOUTHEY.—*Devil's Walk.*

I know not whether Laws be right
  Or whether Laws be wrong ;
All that we know, who be in gaol,
  Is that the wall is strong ;
And that each day is like a year,
  A year whose days are long.
OSCAR WILDE.—*Ballad of Reading Gaol.*

The vilest deeds like poison-weeds
  Bloom well in prison-air ;
It is only what is good in Man
  That wastes and withers there :
Pale Anguish keeps the heavy gate,
  And the Warder is Despair.
  OSCAR WILDE.—*Ballad of Reading Gaol.*

Nightingales will not sing in a cage.
                                    Prov.

PRIVILEGE

By non-usage all privileges are lost, say
the clerks. RABELAIS.—*Pantagruel* (1533).

Privilege does not avail against the
commonwealth.   *Law Maxim.*

Privilege is, as it were, a private law.
                              Law Maxim.

PROBABILITY

But to Us probability is the very guide
of life. BISHOP BUTLER.—*Analogy, Intro.*

Fate laughs at probabilities.
(1st) LORD LYTTON.—*Eugene Aram, c.* 10.

Arguments which draw their demonstra-
tions from probabilities are idle ; and
unless one is on one's guard against them
they are very deceptive.
        PLATO.—*Phædo,* 94 (*Cary tr.*).

Almost all human life turns on probabilities.   VOLTAIRE.—*On Probabilities.*

PROBLEMS

There's somewhat in this world amiss
Shall be unriddled by and by.
        TENNYSON.—*Miller's Daughter.*

No question is ever settled
Until it is settled right.
ELLA W. WILCOX.—*Settle the Question.*

          Those obstinate questionings
Of sense and outward things,
Fallings from us, vanishings ;
Blank misgivings of a creature
Moving about in worlds not realised.
        WORDSWORTH.—*Intimations of
                      Immortality, c.* 9.

PROCRASTINATION

By and by never comes.
        ST. AUGUSTINE.—*Conf. Bk.* 8.

The rule is, jam to-morrow and jam
yesterday—but never jam to-day.
        L. CARROLL.—*Alice through the Looking
                      Glass.*

Ther is an old proverbe, quod she [Dame
Prudence] seith : that the goodnesse that
thou mayst do this day, do it ; and abyd
nat ne delaye it nat til to-morwe.
        CHAUCER.—*Tale of Melibeus.*

Defer not till to-morrow to be wise ;
To-morrow's sun to thee may never rise.
        CONGREVE.—*Letter to Cobham.*

Five minutes ! Zounds ! I have been
five minutes too late all my lifetime.
        MRS. H. COWLEY.—*Belle's Stratagem,*
                      Act 1, 1 [*Saville*].

Begin, be bold, and venture to be wise ;
He who defers this work from day to day,
Doth on a river's bank expecting stay,
Till the whole stream, which stopped him,
      should be gone,
That runs, and as it runs, for ever will
      run on.   COWLEY.—*Tr. of Horace.*

It's but little good you'll do, a-watering
the last year's crop.
        GEO. ELIOT.—*Adam Bede, ch.* 18.

And evermore he said, " To-morowe."
        GOWER.—*Conf. Amantis. Bk.* 4, 9.

How soon " not now " becomes " never."
                              LUTHER (?).

Who is not prepared to-day will be less
so to-morrow.   OVID.—*Rem. Amor.*

He that procrastinates in an affair
courts destruction.
        PLUTARCH.—*Consol. to Apollonius.*

My name is Might-have-been ;
I am also called No-more, Too-late, Farewell.   ROSSETTI.—*Sonnet* 97.

Nay dally not with time, the wise man's
      treasure,
Though fools are lavish on't—the fatal
      Fisher
Hooks souls, while we waste moments.
SCOTT (?).—*Monastery (Heading to ch.* 8,
        with words " Old Play " attached).

'Tis wisdom's use
Still to delay what we dare not refuse.
        SCOTT.—*Harold, c.* 4, 11.

Better late than never, but better never
late.
        C. H. SPURGEON.—*Version of old prov.*

Still last to come where thou art wanted
most.   WORDSWORTH.—*To Sleep.*

Be wise to-day ; 'tis madness to defer.
        YOUNG.—*Night Thoughts,* 1.

Procrastination is the thief of time.
                              YOUNG.—*Ib.*

At thirty man suspects himself a fool ;
Knows it at forty, and reforms his plan ;
At fifty chides his infamous delay,
Pushes his prudent purpose to resolve ;
In all the magnanimity of thought
Resolves, and re-resolves ; then dies the
      same.   YOUNG.—*Ib.*

When I have a convenient season, I will
call for thee.   *Acts* xxiv, 25.

I expect to pass through this world but
once. Any good therefore that I can do,
or any kindness that I can show to any

fellow creature, let me do it now. Let me not defer or neglect it, for I shall not pass this way again.
Attrib. by WM. C. GANNETT (*in slightly different form*), *in " Blessed be Drudgery," to " the old Quaker." All efforts to discover the authorship have been unavailing.*

Procrastination is the hinge of business.
Lawyers' Motto.

Be always in time ;
Too late is a crime.
Old Saying.

" To-morrow " is the day on which idle men work.   *Prov.*

PRODIGALS AND PROFLIGACY

Let friends of prodigals say what they will,
Spendthrifts at home, abroad are spend-
    thrifts still.
CHURCHILL.—*The Candidate.*

H'has been a dragon in his days.
FLETCHER.—*Chances*, Act 3, 4 (1625)

Only a herald, who that way doth pass
Finds his cracked name at length in the
    church glass.
HERBERT.—*Church Porch.*

A system in which the two great commandments were, to hate your neighbour,
and to love your neighbour's wife.
MACAULAY.—*Moore's Byron.*

With cards and dice and dress and friends,
My savings are complete ;
I light the candle at both ends,
And thus make both ends meet.
ANON.

PROFANITY

Bad language or abuse
I never, never use,
Whatever the emergency ;
    Though " Bother it ! " I may
Occasionally say,
I never use a big, big D.
SIR W. S. GILBERT.—*H.M.S. Pinafore.*

But the cheap swearer, through his open
    sluice,
Lets his soul run for nought, as little
    fearing ;
Were I an Epicure, I could bate swearing.
HERBERT.—*Church Porch.*

Seeing would certainly have led to D—ing.
HOOD.—*Legend of Navarre.*

"Our armies swore terribly in Flanders,"
cried my Uncle Toby, " but nothing to
this." STERNE.—*Tristram Shandy, Vol.* 2,
ch. 11.
The Accusing Spirit, which flew up to
Heaven's chancery with the oath, blushed
as he gave it in ; and the Recording Angel,

as he wrote it down, dropped a tear upon
the word, and blotted it out for ever.
STERNE.—*Ib., Vol.* 6, *ch.* 8

PROFIT

No profit grows where is no pleasure
    ta'en. SHAKESPEARE.—*Taming of
                    the Shrew*, Act 1, 1.

Better it is to have more of profit and
less honour. *Melusine (Eng. tr. c.* 1500).

No one was ever ruined by taking a
profit.   *Stock Exchange Saying.*

It is a wicked thing to make dearth one's
garner.   *Prov. (Geo. Herbert).*

PROFUNDITY

What a very singularly deep young man.
This deep young man must be !
SIR W. S. GILBERT.—*Patience.*

Always, when a proposition is incon-
ceivable, we must suspend our judgment.
PASCAL.—*Pensées, Pt.* 1, 2.

PROGRESS

While the eagle of Thought rides the
    tempest in scorn,
Who cares if the lightning is burning the
    corn ?
E. B. BROWNING.—*Rhapsody on Life's
                    Progress.*

Progress is
The law of life ; man is not man as yet.
BROWNING.—*Paracelsus, Pt.* 5.

Nothing in progression can rest on its
original plan. We might as well think of
rocking a grown man in the cradle of an
infant.
BURKE.—*Letter to Sheriffs of Bristol.*

The march of the human mind is slow.
BURKE.—*Speech on Conciliation.*

We see in the intellectual movements of
our times the tendency to expansion, to
universality ; and this must continue.
W. E. CHANNING, D.D.—*The Present Age.*

Progress is the development of order.
AUGUSTE COMTE.

So slow
The growth of what is excellent, so hard
To attain perfection in this nether world.
COWPER.—*Task*, 83.

Everything bears within itself an impulse to strive after a higher degree of
divinity, and that is the great law of
progress throughout all nature.
HEINE.—*The Romantic School.*

The progress of mankind is like the in-
coming of the tide, which for any given
moment is almost as much of a retreat as
an advance, but still the tide moves on.
SIR A. HELPS.—*Friends in Council,
                    Bk.* 2, *ch.* 4.

Impossibilities recede as experience advances; and men walk over many well-tilled fields which, in the childhood of their thought, were deserts or morasses, peopled with fabulous animals, the ends of the earth.
> SIR A. HELPS.—*Friends in Council, Slavery, ch.* 6.

All things, going upwards or downwards, are in a perpetual flux.
> HERACLITUS.—*Cited by Plato, " Philebus,"* 92.

The history of England is emphatically the history of progress.
> MACAULAY.—*On Mackintosh's Hist. of Revolution.*

We're driven back for our next fray
A newer strength to borrow ;
And where the vanguard camps to-day,
The rear shall rest to-morrow.
> G. MASSEY.—*'Tis weary watching.*

Virtue, if not in action, is a vice ;
And when we move not forward, we go backward.
> MASSINGER.—*The Maid of Honour, Act* I, I.

A people, it appears, may be progressive for a certain length of time and then stop. When does it stop ? When it ceases to possess individuality.
> J. S. MILL.—*Liberty, ch.* 3.

One must draw back in order to leap further.
> MONTAIGNE.—*Bk.* I, *ch.* 38 *A French prov.*

Push on, keep moving.
> C. MORTON.—*Cure for Heart-Ache (Young Rapid).*

The work of the world must still be done,
And minds are many though truth be one.
> SIR H. J. NEWBOLT.—*The Echo.*

The long succession of the generations of mankind should be regarded as a single man, ever living and ever learning.
> PASCAL.—*Traité sur la Vide. Pref.*

And still to-morrow's wiser than to-day.
We think our fathers fools, so wise we grow ;
Our wiser sons, no doubt, will think us so.
> POPE.—*Criticism,* 437.

Not to go back, is somewhat to advance,
And men must walk at least before they dance.
> POPE.—*Ep. of Horace, Ep.* I, 53.

Progress, therefore, is not an accident, but a necessity. . . . It is part of nature.
> H. SPENCER.—*Social Statics, Pt.* I, *c.* 2.

Ring out the darkness of the land,
Ring in the Christ that is to be.
> TENNYSON.—*In Memoriam, c.* 106.

Forward, forward, let us range,
Let the great world spin for ever down the ringing grooves of change.
> TENNYSON.—*Locksley Hall.*

Through the shadow of the globe we sweep into the younger day ;
Better fifty years of Europe than a cycle of Cathay.
> TENNYSON.—*Ib.*

Falsehoods which we spurn to-day
Were the truths of long ago.
> J. G. WHITTIER.—*Calef in Boston.*

Progress is the realisation of Utopias.
> OSCAR WILDE.—*Soul of Man under Socialism.*

In the unreasoning progress of the world
A wiser spirit is at work for us,
A better eye than ours.
> WORDSWORTH.—*Postscript (to Preface) (1835).*

Of old things all are over old,
Of good things none are good enough ;
We'll show them we can help to frame
A world of other stuff.
> WORDSWORTH.—*Rob Roy's Grave.*

Nature revolves but man advances.
> YOUNG.—*Night Thoughts,* 6.

Follow me ; and let the dead bury their dead.
> *St. Matthew* viii, 22.

PROHIBITION

Forbede us thing and that desyren we.
> CHAUCER.—*Wife of Bath, Prol.,* 519.

Forbidden wares sell twice as dear.
> SIR J. DENHAM.—*Natura Naturata.*

    If all the world
Should, in a pet of temperance, feed on pulse,
Drink the clear stream, and nothing wear but frieze,
The All-giver would be unthank'd, would be unprais'd ;
Not half his riches known, and yet despis'd;
And we should serve him as a grudging master,
As a penurious niggard of his wealth ;
And live like Nature's bastards, not her sons.
> MILTON.—*Comus,* 720.

Dost thou think because thou art virtuous there shall be no more cakes and ale ?
> SHAKESPEARE.—*Twelfth Night,* Act 2, 3.

PROLIXITY

There is nothing in Nature so irksome as general discourses.
> ADDISON.—*Spectator, Vol.* 2, 267.

And long petitions spoil the cause they plead.
> CAMPBELL.—*Pilgrim of Glencoe.*

And drags at each remove a lengthening chain.
> GOLDSMITH.—*Traveller.*

One half will never be believed,
The other never read.
> POPE.—*Epigram.*

Why then a final note prolong,
Or lengthen out a closing song?
> SCOTT.—*Marmion.*

What, will the line stretch out to the crack of doom?
> SHAKESPEARE.—*Macbeth*, Act 4, I.

Fond to begin, but still to finish loth.
> JAS. THOMSON.—*Castle of Indolence,*
> *c. 2, st. 4.*

Woe to the author who wishes always to instruct! The secret of boring is the attempt to say everything.
> VOLTAIRE.—*Discours,* 6.

PROMISES

Boldness is an ill keeper of promise.
> BACON.—*Essays, Boldness.*

If we've promised them aught, let us keep our promise.
> BROWNING.—*Pied Piper.*

Shake your rattle, here it is,
Listen to its merry noise;
And when you are tired of this,
I will bring you other toys.
> MISS M. L. DUNCAN.—*Rhymes.*

A vow you make
You must not break;
If you think you may, it's a great mistake.
> SIR W. S. GILBERT.—*Princess Ida.*

Promise is a promise, dough you make it in de dark er de moon.
> J. C. HARRIS.—*Nights with Uncle Remus,*
> *ch.* 39.

Promise, large promise, is the soul of an advertisement.
> JOHNSON.—*Idler, No.* 40.

He that raises false hopes to serve a present purpose, only makes a way for disappointment and discontent.
> JOHNSON.—*The Patriot.*

Great men
Till they have gained their ends, are giants in
Their promises, but those obtained, weak pigmies
In their performance.
> MASSINGER.—*Great Duke*, Act 2, 3.

Make a point of promising; for what harm can it do to promise? Anyone can be rich in promises.
> OVID.—*Ars Amat., Bk.* I.

And so obliging that he ne'er obliged.
> POPE.—*Prol. to Satires.*

He began to promise seas and mountains.
> SALLUST.—*Catilina.*

Thy promises are like Adonis' gardens,
That one day bloomed, and fruitful were the next.
> SHAKESPEARE.—*Henry VI., Pt.* I,
> Act I, 6.

He was ever precise in promise-keeping.
> SHAKESPEARE.—*Measure for Measure,*
> Act I, 2.

You put me off with limber vows.
> SHAKESPEARE.—*Winter's Tale*, Act I, 2.

I was promised on a time
To have reason for my rhyme;
From that time unto this season,
I received nor rhyme nor reason.
> SPENSER.—*Lines on his Pension.*

A boy at a crossing begged a copper of a gentleman who said he would give him something as he came back. The boy replied: "Your honour would be surprised if you knew the money I have lost by giving credit in that way."
> C. H. SPURGEON.—"*Salt-Cellars.*"

Promising mountains of gold.
> TERENCE.—*Phormio.*

Better is it that thou shouldest not vow, than that thou shouldest vow and not pay.
> *Ecclesiastes* v, 5.

O true believers, perform your contracts.
> *Koran, ch.* 5.

A long tongue is a sign of a short hand.
> *Prov. (Geo. Herbert).*

Promising is not giving, but it contents fools.
> *Prov. (Portuguese).*

Promises make debts and debts make promises.
> *Prov.*

PRONUNCIATION

"Fine ear for the haspirate"—that's what my darter Maria 'ave and what I, for one, 'ave not."
> H. G. HUTCHINSON.—*Fine Ear for the*
> *Haspirate. Punch (Jan.* 29, 1919).

Speak the speech, I pray you, as I pronounced it to you, trippingly on the tongue; but if you mouth it, as many of our players do, I had as lief the town-crier spoke my lines.
> SHAKESPEARE.—*Hamlet*, Act 3, 2.

PROPERTY

The essential, unalterable right, in nature, engrafted into the British constitution, as a fundamental law, and ever held sacred and irrevocable by the subjects within the realm, that what a man has honestly acquired is absolutely his own, which he may freely give, but cannot be taken from him without his consent.
> SAMUEL ADAMS.—*Massachusetts.*
> *Circular Letter,* 1768.

The magic of property turns sand to gold. JEREMY BENTHAM.—*Saying.*

That gentleman who sells an acre of land sells a pound of credit. For gentility is nothing else but ancient riches. So that if the foundation shall at any time sink, the building must need follow.
WM. CECIL (LORD BURGHLEY).—*Precepts to his son.*

Fye on possessioun,
But if a man be vertuous withal.
CHAUCER.—*Franklin's Tale.*

Property has its duties as well as its rights.
MARQUIS OF NORMANBY (CONSTANTINE H. PHIPPS).—*Letter when Lord-Lieutenant of Ireland* (1835–9). (*Others had a share in composing this letter.*)

Property is robbery.
PROUDHON.—*Principle of Right, ch.* 1.

I have found that empire and liberty being two incompatible words, I cannot be master of a cottage except by ceasing to be master of myself.
ROUSSEAU.—*Emile, Bk.* 5.

The demon of property infects everything it touches. The rich man wishes to be master everywhere, and is never at ease where he is not master.
ROUSSEAU.—*Ib.*

An ill-favoured thing, sir, but mine own.
SHAKESPEARE.—*As You Like It,* Act 5, 4.

Saw from his windows nothing save his own.
TENNYSON.—*Aylmer's Field,* 22.

"Liberty and Property" is the English motto. It is worth more than "St. George and my right," "St. Denys et Montjoie." It is the motto of Nature.
VOLTAIRE.—*Dictionnaire Philosophique (Propriété).*

The first thing the student has to do is to get rid of the idea of absolute ownership. Such an idea is quite unknown to the English law.
JOSHUA WILLIAMS.—*Real Property* (1845), *Pt.* 1, *ch.* 1.

The magic of property turns sand into gold.
ARTHUR YOUNG.—*Travels in France* (*v. supra, Jeremy Bentham*).

Woe unto them that join house to house, that lay field to field, till there be no place! *Isaiah* v, 8.

He that buys a house ready wrought, Hath many a pin and nail for nought.
Old Saying.

There are but two families in the world, the Haves and the Have-nots.
Spanish prov.

PROPHETS AND PROPHECY

Cato used to say that he wondered one soothsayer did not laugh when he saw another. CICERO.—*De Divinatione,* 2, 24.

You can scarcely answer a prophet; you can only disbelieve him.
COWPER.—*Of Pitt's predictions as to Ireland* (1800).

Sweet is the harp of prophecy; too sweet Not to be wronged by a mere mortal touch.
COWPER.—*Winter Walk at Noon,* 747.

Or Prophecy, which dreams a lie, That fools believe, and knaves apply.
MATTHEW GREEN.—*Grotto,* 97.

Till old experience do attain To something like prophetic strain.
MILTON.—*Il Penseroso,* 173.

It cannot be made, it shall not be made, it will not be made; but if it were made there would be a war between France and England for the possession of Egypt.
LORD PALMERSTON.—*Speech,* 1851, *referring to the Suez Canal (an example of an indiscreet and unfulfilled prophecy).*

Out of our reach the gods have laid Of time to come th' event, And laugh to see the fools afraid Of what the knaves invent.
SIR C. SEDLEY.—*Lycophron.*

The poet beholds the future in the present, and his thoughts are the germs of the flower and the fruit of latest time.
SHELLEY.—*Defence of Poetry* (1821).

I prophesied that, though I never told anybody.
H. AND J. SMITH.—*Rejected Addresses.*

If it rains to-day it will keep on till it leaves off.
C. H. SPURGEON.—*Given as an example of "safe prophecy."*

Some great misfortune to portend, No enemy can match a friend.
SWIFT.—*On the Death of Dr. Swift.*

He'd rather choose that I should die Than his predictions prove a lie.
SWIFT.—*Ib.*

You know I always feared the worst, And often told you so at first.
SWIFT.—*Ib.*

Cassandra cried, and cursed the unhappy hour;
Foretold our fate: but, by the gods' decree,
All heard and none believed the prophecy.
VIRGIL.—*Æneid, Bk.* 2 (*Dryden*).

Is Saul also among the prophets?
1 Samuel xix, 24.

The prophets prophesy falsely, and the priests bear rule by their means ; and my people love to have it so : and what will ye do in the end thereof ?
Jeremiah v, 31.

Beware of false prophets, which come to you in sheep's clothing, but inwardly they are ravening wolves.
St. Matthew vii, 15.

A prophet is not without honour, save in his own country, and in his own house.
St. Matthew xiii, 57. (*See Mark* vi, 4 ;
Luke iv, 24 ; *John* iv, 44.)

PROPORTION

How sour sweet music is,
When time is broke, and no proportion kept !
So is it in the music of men's lives.
SHAKESPEARE.—*Richard II.*, Act 5, 5.

Often our self-love extinguishes our good sense. Often we are like the frogs of Homer, who besought with loud cries the proud god of war and the god of hell and Bellona and Pallas and the lightnings of heaven, to avenge them on the rats.
VOLTAIRE.—*Satire, Vanity.*

PROSAIC, THE

O why do you walk through the fields in gloves,
Missing so much and so much ?
O fat white woman whom nobody loves,
Why do you walk through the fields in gloves ?
FRANCES CORNFORD.—*To a Lady
seen from the Train.*

The soft blue sky did never melt
Into his heart,—he never felt
The witchery of the soft blue sky.
WORDSWORTH.—*Peter Bell, Pt.* I.

PROSPERITY

And you shall find the greatest enemy
A man can have is his prosperity.
S. DANIEL.—*Philotas.*

Greater virtues are necessary in bearing good fortune than bad.
LA ROCHEFOUCAULD.—*Maxim* 25.

A Sultan consulted Solomon on the proper inscription for a signet ring, requiring that the maxim should be at once proper for moderating the presumption of prosperity and tempering the pressure of adversity. The apophthegm supplied by the Jewish sage was comprehended in the words, " And this also shall pass away."
SCOTT.—*Letter to Byron*, 1813.

Welcome the sour cup of prosperity !
Affliction may one day smile again ; and until then, sit down Sorrow.
SHAKESPEARE.—*Love's Labour's Lost,*
Act I, I.

Now is the winter of our discontent
Made glorious summer by this sun of York.
SHAKESPEARE.—*Richard III.*, Act I, I.

Now that I no longer need,
I can get full many a feed.
*Given as a saying in C. H. Spurgeon's
" Salt-Cellars."*

The ungodly . . . flourishing like a green bay tree. *Church Psalter* xxxvii, 36.

PROTESTANTISM

All Protestantism, even the most cold and passive, is a sort of dissent. But the religion most prevalent in our northern colonies is a refinement on the principle of resistance : it is the dissidence of dissent, and the Protestantism of the Protestant religion.
BURKE.—*Speech on Conciliation.*

A real Protestant is a person who has examined the evidences of religion for himself, and who accepts them because, after examination, he is satisfied of their genuineness and sufficiency.
J. A. HAMMERTON.—*Modern Frenchmen.*

Protestantism was very successful in bringing about that purity of morals and that strictness in fulfilment of duty, which is generally called morality.
HEINE.—*Religion and Philosophy.*

People who hold such absolute opinions
Should stay at home in Protestant dominions. HOOD.—*Ode to Rae Wilson.*

PROTESTATION

The lady doth protest too much, methinks.
SHAKESPEARE.—*Hamlet*, Act 3, 2.

PROVERBS

There are no proverbial sayings which are not true. CERVANTES.—*Don Quixote.*

Proverbs are short sentences, drawn from long experience. CERVANTES.—*Ib.*

A man of fashion never has recourse to proverbs and vulgar aphorisms.
LORD CHESTERFIELD.

A most remarkably long-headed flowing-bearded, and patriarchal proverb.
DICKENS.—*M. Chuzzlewit, ch.* 13.

Like all the world he doth repeat himself,
Making an adage stuff the holes of thought.
" MICHAEL FIELD "—*Calirrhöe* (1884).

[A proverb is] much matter decocted into few words. FULLER.—*Worthies.*

Even the best proverb . . . can be misapplied. . . . Its wisdom lies in the ear of the hearer.
SIR A. HELPS.—*Friends in Council,
Bk.* I, *ch.* II.

The People's Voice the voice of God we
  call;
And what are proverbs but the People's
  Voice?
J. Howell.—*Before a Volume of Proverbs.*

An old saying, sanctioned by time,
becomes like an ordinance.
                  Plautus.—*Pœnulus.*

The wit of one man, the wisdom of
many.   Lord J. Russell (1850).

          The justice,
In fair round belly, with good capon lined,
With eyes severe, and beard of formal cut,
Full of wise saws and modern instances.
Shakespeare.—*As You Like It*, Act 2, 7.

    The proverb is something musty.
      Shakespeare.—*Hamlet*, Act 3, 2.

Patch grief with proverbs.
    Shakespeare.—*Much Ado*, Act 5, 1.

He gave good heed, and sought out, and
set in order many proverbs.
                  Ecclesiastes xii, 9.

Wise sayings, dark sentences, and parables, and certain particular antient godly
stories of men that pleased God.
    Ecclesiasticus. (*Prologue attributed by
            some to Athanasius.*)

Wel short in wordes and wel lang in
witte.
    Mediæval definition of Lord's Prayer.

PROVIDENCE

And yet the will of Zeus is hard to scan;
  Through all it brightly gleams,
E'en in the darkness and the gloom of
      chance
  For us poor mortals wrapt.
Æschylus.—*Suppliants*, 86 (*Plumptre tr.*).

    Seated on holiest throne,
Thence, though we know not how,
He works His perfect will.
    Æschylus.—*Ib.*, 110 (*Plumptre tr.*).

Whatever may happen to thee, it was
prepared for thee from all eternity.
                  Marcus Aurelius.

Irony is the foundation of the character
of Providence. Balzac.—*Eugénie Grandet.*

But Heaven that brings out good from
  evil,
And loves to disappoint the Devil.
      Coleridge.—*Job's Luck.*

God moves in a mysterious way
    His wonders to perform.
                  Cowper.—*Hymn.*

Behind a frowning providence
He hides a smiling face.
                  Cowper.—*Ib.*

There's a sweet little cherub that sits up
    aloft
To keep watch for the life of poor Jack.
          C. Dibdin.—*Poor Jack.*

However great the uncertainty and
variety which appear to exist in this world,
one observes nevertheless a certain secret
inter-connection (enchaînement) and an
order ruled at all times by Providence,
which causes each thing to proceed in its
rank and follow the course of its destiny.
La Rochefoucauld.—*Maxim* 555. (*This
maxim, suppressed in the 2nd Edition, is
the only one in which " Providence " is mentioned, and is said to have been " a concession
            to the ideas of the time.*")

All nature is but art, unknown to thee;
All chance, direction which thou canst
    not see;
All discord, harmony not understood;
All partial evil, universal good;
And, spite of pride, in erring reason's spite,
One truth is clear, whatever is is right.
      Pope.—*Essay on Man*, Ep. 1, 289.

    Man's world is Pain and Terror;
      He found it pure and fair,
  And wove in nets of sorrow
      The golden summer air.
  Black, hideous, cold and dreary,
    Man's curse, not God's is there.
          A. A. Procter.—*Two Worlds.*

There's a divinity that shapes our ends,
Rough-hew them how we will.
      Shakespeare.—*Hamlet*, Act 5, 2.

There's a providence in the fall of a
sparrow.   Shakespeare.—*Ib.*

But He, that hath the steerage of my
    course,
Direct my sail.
Shakespeare.—*Romeo and Juliet*, Act 1, 4.

A greater Power than we can contradict
Hath thwarted our intents.
          Shakespeare.—*Ib.*, Act 5, 3.

God gives every bird its food but does
not cast it into the nest.   *Swedish prov.*

PRUDENCE

Prudence is of no service unless it be
prompt.
      Bacon.—*Instauratio*, Pt. 1, Bk. 6.

    Prudence is but conceit
    Hoodwinked by ignorance.
Geo. Eliot.—*Spanish Gipsy*, Bk. 2.

One virtue he had in perfection, which
was prudence—often the only one that is
left us at seventy-two.
Goldsmith.—*Vicar of Wakefield*, ch. 2.

A sad wise valour is the brave complexion.
      Herbert.—*Church Porch.*

Prudence is the first thing to desert the wretched. OVID.—*Ep. de. Pont.*, 4.

Have more than thou showest,
Speak less than thou knowest,
Lend less than thou owest.
SHAKESPEARE.—*Lear*, Act 1, 4.

I like, my dear Lord, the road you are travelling, but I don't like the pace you are driving ; too similar to that of the son of Nimshi. I always feel myself inclined to cry out, Gently, John—gently down hill. Put on the drag.
S. SMITH.—*Letter to Lord John Russell.*

But wise and wary was that noble pere.
SPENSER.—*Faerie Queene, Bk.* 1,
c. 6, 7.

Think not that Prudence dwells in dark abodes ;
She scans the future with the eye of gods.
WORDSWORTH.—*Sonnets to Liberty and Order*, 11.

If you are prudent, do not thrust your hand into the fire.
Latin prov., quoted by St. Jerome.

No divinity is absent if Prudence is present.
Latin prov. (see JUVENAL, *Sat.* 10, 365).

PRUDERY

" I am afraid," replied Elinor, " that the pleasantness of an employment does not always evince its propriety."
JANE AUSTEN.—*Sense and Sensibility,*
ch. 13.

This noble soul,
Worth thousand prudish clods of barren clay,
Who mope for heaven because earth's grapes are sour.
C. KINGSLEY.—*Saints' Tragedy*, Act 2.

Prudery is the hypocrisy of modesty.
BARON NICOLAS MASSIAS (1764–1848).

Always ding-dinging Dame Grundy into my ears—What will Mrs. Grundy say ? or, What will Mrs. Grundy think ?
T. MORTON.—*Speed the Plough.*

Prudery in a woman, where it outlives youth and beauty, reminds me of a scarecrow that has been left forgotten in the fields, after the harvest is over.
PETIT-SENN.—*(French.)*

What is prudery ? 'tis a beldam,
Seen with wit and beauty seldom.
POPE.—*To Mrs. Howe.*

Unbecoming things are unsafe things.
TACITUS.—*Hist., Bk.* 1.

PUBLIC OPINION

The coquetry of public opinion, which has her caprices, and must have her way.
BURKE.—*Letter to Thos. Burgh* (1779).

The individual is foolish ; the multitude, for the moment is foolish, when they act without deliberation ; but the species is wise, and, when time is given to it, as a species it always acts right.
BURKE.—*Speech in the House of Commons* (May 7, 1782).

The Public is an old woman. Let her maunder and mumble.
CARLYLE.—*Journal.*

The public ! why the public's nothing better than a great baby.
T. CHALMERS.—*Letter.*

When the people have no other tyrant, their own public opinion becomes one.
(1st) LORD LYTTON.—*Ernest Maltravers, Bk.* 6.

The Pythoness [of Delphi], when consulted by Cicero as to how he could best attain glory, replied, " By making your own genius, and not the opinion of the people, the guide of your life."
PLUTARCH.—*Life of Cicero.*

PUBLIC SERVICE

For if ye, with kindly welcome,
Honour these as kind protectors,
Then shall ye be famed as keeping,
Just and upright in all dealings,
Land and city evermore.
ÆSCHYLUS.—*Eumenides*, 990
(Plumptre tr.).

That grounded maxim,
So rife and celebrated in the mouths
Of wisest men, that to the public good
Private respects must yield.
MILTON.—*Samson Agonistes*, 865.

If you do anything well, gratitude is lighter than a feather ; if you have done anything wrong, the people's wrath is heavy as lead.   PLAUTUS.—*Pœnulus.*

Forced into virtue thus, by self-defence,
Ev'n kings learned justice and benevolence :
Self-love forsook the path it first pursued
And found the private in the public good.
POPE.—*Essay on Man, Ep.* 3, 279.

He husbands best his life that freely gives
It for the public good : he rightly lives
That nobly dies.
QUARLES.—*Esther, sec.* 15.

The noblest motive is the public good.
STEELE.—*Spectator, vol.* 3, 200.

PUBLICITY

In full, fair tide let information flow ;
That evil is half-cured whose cause we
know.
>   CHURCHILL.—*Gotham, Bk.* 3, 652.

Youk'n hide de fier, but w'at you gwine
do wid de smoke ?
>   J. C. HARRIS.—*Plantation Proverbs.*

It [the publication of his name in connection with the solution of an important
problem] would perhaps increase my
acquaintance, the thing which I chiefly
study to decline.
>   SIR I. NEWTON.—*Letter to Collins.*

This thing was not done in a corner.
>   *Acts* xxvi, 26.

PUNCTUALITY

" Punctuality," said Louis XIV., " is
the politeness of kings." It is also the
duty of gentlemen and the necessity of
men of business.   S. SMILES.—*Self-Help.*

He was always late on principle, his
principle being that punctuality is the
thief of time.
>   OSCAR WILDE.—*Dorian Gray.*

PUNCTUATION

Old laws have not been suffered to be
pointed,
To leave the sense at large the more dis-
jointed,
And furnish lawyers, with the greater
ease,
To turn and wind them any way they
please.
>   S. BUTLER.—*Miscellaneous Thoughts.*

PUNISHMENT

All punishment is mischief. All punishment in itself is evil. . . . It ought only
to be admitted in as far as it promises to
exclude some greater evil.
>   JEREMY BENTHAM.—*Morals and
>   Legislation, ch.* 15, *sec.* 1.

Hanging is too good for him, said Mr.
Cruelty.
>   BUNYAN.—*Pilgrim's Progress, Pt.* 1.

" I wol bete thee," quod [quoth] the
maister, " for thy correction." " Forsooth," quod the childe, " ye oughten firste
correcte yourself that have lost al your
pacience for the gilt of a child." " Forsooth," quod the maister al wepinge,
" thou seyst sooth [truth] ; have thou the
yerde [rod], my dere sone, and correct me
for myn impatience."
>   CHAUCER.—*Boethius.*

Anger is to be very specially avoided in
inflicting punishment.
>   CICERO.—*De Officiis.*

The hope of not being punished is the
greatest incitement to sin.
>   CICERO.—*Pro Milone.*

Lo, when two dogs are fighting in the
streets,
With a third dog one of the two dogs
meets ;
With angry teeth he bites him to the bone,
And this dog smarts for what that dog
has done.
>   FIELDING.—*Tom Thumb*, Act 1, 6.

He that will not use the rod on his
child, his child shall be used as a rod on
him.   FULLER.—*The Good Parent.*

My object all sublime
I shall achieve in time—
To make the punishment fit the crime.
>   SIR W. S. GILBERT.—*Mikado.*

Something lingering with boiling oil in
it. . . . something humorous but lingering.
>   SIR W. S. GILBERT.—*Ib.*

O heaven, that such companions thou'dst
unfold,
And put in every honest hand a whip,
To lash the rascals naked through the
world,
Even from the east to the west !
>   SHAKESPEARE.—*Othello*, Act 4, 1.

I would have him nine years a killing.
>   SHAKESPEARE.—*Ib.*

I will kill thee,
And love thee after.
>   SHAKESPEARE.—*Ib.*, Act 5, 2.

There needeth not the hell that bigots
frame
To punish those who err : earth in itself
Contains at once the evil and the cure ;
And all-sufficing Nature can chastise
Those who transgress her law,—she only
knows
How justly to proportion to the fault
The punishment it merits.
>   SHELLEY.—*Queen Mab*, 3.

Every unpunished delinquency has a
family of delinquencies.
>   HERBT. SPENCER.—*Sociology.*

Every great example of punishment has
something unequal in it, which is compen-
sated, so much as it is to the disadvantage
of individuals, by its public usefulness.
>   TACITUS.—*Annals, Bk.* 14, 44.

The stroke of the whip maketh marks
in the flesh ; but the stroke of the tongue
breaketh bones.   *Ecclesiasticus* xxviii, 17.

If you want a reason for whipping a
dog, say that he ate the frying-pan.
>   *Prov.*

Who spares the wicked does an injury
to the good.   *Ancient Greek prov.*

PUNNING

The seeds of punning are in the minds
of all men ... though they may be subdued
by reason, reflection, and good sense.
ADDISON.—*Spectator, 61.*

But still a pun I do detest,
'Tis such a paltry, humbug jest ;
They who've least wit can make them best.
W. COMBE.—*Syntax in Search of the
Picturesque, c. 26.*

Any man who could make such an
execrable pun would pick a pocket.
JOHN DENNIS.—*Attributed.*

A pun is a noble thing *per se.* O never
bring it in as an accessory ! . . . It fills
the mind ; it is as perfect as a sonnet ;
better.   LAMB.—*Letter.*

How every fool can play upon the word !
SHAKESPEARE.—*Merchant of Venice,
Act 3, 5.*

I am thankful that my name is
obnoxious to no pun.
SHENSTONE.—*Egotisms.*

Punning grows upon everybody, and
punning is the wit of words. . . . The wit
of language is so miserably inferior to the
wit of ideas that it is very deservedly
driven out of good company.
SYDNEY SMITH.—*Lectures on Moral
Philosophy, No. 10.*

PURITANISM

Religion, harsh, intolerant, austere,
Parent of manners, like herself, severe.
COWPER.—*Table Talk, 611 (of
Cromwellian Puritanism).*

The Puritan hated bearbaiting, not
because it gave pain to the bear, but
because it gave pleasure to the spectators.
MACAULAY.—*Hist. of England, ch. 2.*

They need their pious exercises less
Than schooling in the Pleasures.
GEO. MEREDITH.—*A Certain People.*

The bigots of the iron time
Had called his harmless art a crime.
SCOTT.—*Lay of the Last Minstrel, Intro.*

Those sombre puritans (rigoristes) who
imagine themselves good when they are
only dismal (tristes).
VOLTAIRE.—*Le Dépositaire.*

PURITY

The purest soul that e'er was sent
Into a clayey tenement.
T. CAREW.—*On Lady Mary Villiers.*

He who puts off impurity thereby puts
on purity.
EMERSON.—*Address, July 15, 1838.*

Blest are the pure in heart,
For they shall see our God.
KEBLE.—*Purification.*

Still to the lowly soul
He doth himself impart,
And for His cradle and His throne
Chooseth the pure in heart.
KEBLE.—*Ib.*

Wearing the white flower of a blameless
life. TENNYSON.—*Idylls, Dedication.*

Unto the pure all things are pure.
2 Timothy i, 15.

PURSUITS

Remember that the true worth of a
man is to be measured by the objects he
pursues. MARCUS AURELIUS.—*Bk. 7, 3.*

There is a passion for hunting something,
deeply implanted in the human breast.
DICKENS.—*Oliver Twist, ch. 10.*

PUSILLANIMITY

Nothing is so rash as fear ; and the
counsels of pusillanimity very rarely put
off, whilst they are always sure to aggravate, the evils from which they would fly.
BURKE.—*Letters on a Regicide Peace.*

I envy no mortal though ever so great,
Nor scorn I a wretch for his lowly estate ;
But what I abhor and esteem as a curse
Is poorness of Spirit, not poorness of Purse.
HENRY CAREY.—*Reply to the Libelling
Gentry.*

Thus Beliat, with words clothed in reason's
garb,
Counselled ignoble ease and peaceful sloth,
Not peace.
MILTON.—*Paradise-Lost, Bk. 2, 226.*

Refusing to accept as great a share
Of hazard as of honour.
MILTON.—*Ib., Bk. 2, 452.*

He that trusts to you,
Where he should find you lions, finds you
hares ;
Where foxes, geese.
SHAKESPEARE.—*Coriolanus, Act 1, 1.*

But I am pigeon-livered, and lack gall
To make oppression bitter.
SHAKESPEARE.—*Hamlet, Act 2, 2.*

Most forcible Feeble.
SHAKESPEARE.—*Henry IV., Act 3, 2.*

The fault, dear Brutus, is not in our stars,
But in ourselves, that we are underlings.
SHAKESPEARE.—*Julius Cæsar, Act 1, 2.*

What 'twas weak to do.
'Tis weaker to lament, once being done.
SHELLEY.—*Cenci, Act 5, 3.*

Great empires are not maintained by cowardice. TACITUS.—*Annals, Bk.* 15, 1.

Poor John was a gallant captain,
In battles much delighting ;
He fled full soon
On the first of June—
But he bade the rest keep fighting.
Anti-Jacobin, May 14, 1790.

Q

QUACKERY

An impudent mountebank who sold pills, which, as he told the country people, were very good against an earthquake.
ADDISON.—*Tatler, No.* 240.

Quackery gives birth to nothing ; gives death to all things.
CARLYLE.—*Heroes,* 1.

There's equal quackery in a' things alike.
JOHN WILSON.—*Noctes (Ettrick Shepherd).*

QUARRELS

Ay me ! what perils do environ
The man that meddles with cold iron.
BUTLER.—*Hudibras, Pt.* 1, *c.* 3.

Where there is strife 'twixt man and wife, 'tis hell ;
And mutual love may be compared to heaven.
JOSHUA COOKE.—*How a man may choose,* Act 1.

Who ever knew an honest brute
At law his neighbour persecute ?
GOLDSMITH.—*Logicians Refuted.*

Potter quarrels with potter, poet with poet, and beggar with beggar.
HESIOD.—*Nights and Days,* 5, 25.

I called for quarter, but alas !
It was not Quarter-Day.
HOOD.—*A Waterloo Ballad,* 1834.

Quarrels would not last long if the wrong were only on one side.
LA ROCHEFOUCAULD.—*Maxim* 496.

Only a goose would ever make attempt
To settle a dispute when foxes fight.
C. G. LELAND.—*Ballad of the Foxes,* 6.

Alas ! how light a cause may move
Dissension between hearts that love !
MOORE.—*Lalla Rookh.*

What dire offence from amorous causes springs !
What mighty contests rise from trivial things !
POPE.—*Rape of the Lock, c.* 1, 1.

Beware
Of entrance to a quarrel ; but, being in,
Bear't that th' opposèd may beware of thee.
SHAKESPEARE.—*Hamlet,* Act 1, 3.

Thy head is as full of quarrels as an egg is full of meat.
SHAKESPEARE.—*Romeo and Juliet,* Act 3, 1.

A plague o' both your houses.
SHAKESPEARE.—*Ib.*

A woman moved is like a fountain troubled,
Muddy, ill-seeming, thick, bereft of beauty. SHAKESPEARE.—*Taming of the Shrew,* Act 5, 2.

The quarrel is a very pretty quarrel as it stands ; we should only spoil it by trying to explain it.
SHERIDAN.—*Rivals,* Act 4, 3.

But what they fought each other for
I could not well make out.
SOUTHEY.—*Battle of Blenheim.*

It is the little rift within the lute,
That by and by will make the music mute,
And ever widening, slowly silence all.
TENNYSON.—*Merlin and Vivien.*

And blessings on the falling out
That all the more endears,
When we fall out with those we love,
And kiss again with tears.
TENNYSON.—*Princess, c.* 2, *Song.*

And musing on the little lives of men,
And how they mar this little by their feuds. TENNYSON.—*Sea Dreams.*

Let dogs delight to bark and bite,
For God hath made them so :
Let bears and lions growl and fight,
For 'tis their nature too.
I. WATTS.—*Against Quarrelling.*

Birds in their little nests agree,
And 'tis a shameful sight
When children of one family
Fall out, and chide, and fight.
I. WATTS.--*Love.*

I labour for peace, but when I speak unto them thereof, they make them ready to battle.
Psalter (Book of Common Prayer), 120, 6.

Quarrel and strife make short life.
Swedish prov.

When two quarrel both are in the wrong. *Prov.*

QUEENS

But she was lucky, and luck's all. Your queens
Are generally prosperous in reigning.
BYRON.—*Don Juan,* 10, 47.

Queens must be ridiculous when they would appear as women. The softer attractions of sex vanish on the throne.
THOS. WARTON.—*Hist. of Eng. Poetry* (1774–81). (*A fallacy—apropos of Queen Elizabeth—since disproved on many occasions.*)

QUESTIONS

Perchance my too much questioning offends.
DANTE.—*Purgatorio, c.* 18, 6. (*Cary tr.*).

" A man may *ask* a question, so he may," returned Kedgwick, strongly implying that another man might not answer a question, so he mightn't.
DICKENS.—*Chuzzlewit, ch.* 22.

" Anybody may ask," said Mr. Trumbull ; " anybody may interrogate ; any-one may give their remarks an inter-rogative turn."
GEO. ELIOT.—*Middlemarch, Bk.* 3, *ch.* 32.

The greatest men
May ask a foolish question, now and then.
JOHN WOLCOT.—*Apple Dumpling.*

What sent the messengers to hell
Was asking what they knew full well.
Scottish prov.

QUIET

Ah, Quiet, all things feel thy balm !
Those blue hills too, this river's flow,
Were restless once, but long ago.
Tamed is their turbulent youthful glow ;
Their joy is in their calm.
M. ARNOLD.—*On the Rhine.*

But quiet, to quick bosoms, is a hell.
BYRON.—*Childe Harold, c.* 3, 42.

Anythin' for a quiet life, as the man said wen he took the sitivation at the lighthouse. DICKENS.—*Pickwick, c.* 37.

Sometimes quiet is disquieting.
SENECA.—*Ep.* 56.

Passionless bride, divine Tranquillity.
TENNYSON.—*Lucretius.*

And that ye study to be quiet, and to do your own business.
Thessalonians iv, 11.

In quietness and in confidence shall be your strength. *Isaiah* xxx, 15.

QUOTATIONS

They serve to be recited upon occasion of themselves. They serve, if you take out the kernel of them and make them your own.
BACON.—*Apophthegms, Preface.*

Bright passages that strike your mind,
And which perhaps you may have reason
To think of at another season.
J. BYROM.—*Miscellaneous Poems.*

With just enough of learning to misquote.
BYRON.—*English Bards,* 66.

The art of quotation requires more delicacy in the practice than those conceive who can see nothing more in a quotation than an extract.
I. D'ISRAELI.—*Curiosities of Literature.*

The wisdom of the wise, and the experience of ages, may be preserved by quotations. I. D'ISRAELI.—*Ib.*

Next to the originator of a good sentence is the first quoter of it. Many will read the book before one thinks of quoting a passage.
EMERSON.—*Quotation and Originality.*

Nothing gives an author so much pleasure as to find his works respectfully quoted by other learned authors.
B. FRANKLIN.—*Pennsylvania Almanac,* 1758.

Pointed axioms and acute replies fly loose about the world, and are assigned successively to those whom it may be the fashion to celebrate.
JOHNSON.—*Life of Waller.*

He that has but ever so little examined the citations of writers cannot doubt how little credit the quotations deserve, where the originals are wanting ; and, consequently, how much less quotations of quotations can be relied on.
LOCKE.—*Human Understanding, Bk.* 4.

One might say of me that I have only made here a collection of other people's flowers, with nothing of my own but the cord to bind them. MONTAIGNE.—*Bk.* 3.

Always verify your references.
DR. ROUTH (1847).

The little honesty existing among authors is to be seen in the outrageous way in which they misquote from the writings of others.
SCHOPENHAUER.—*On Authorship.*

A forward critic often dupes us
With sham quotations *peri hupsos ;*
And if we have not read Longinus,
Will magisterially outshine us.
Then, lest with Greek he over-run ye,
Procure the book for love or money,
Translated from Boileau's translation,
And quote quotation on quotation.
SWIFT.—*On Poetry.*

Some for renown on scraps of learning dote,
And think they grow immortal as they quote.
YOUNG.—*Love of Fame, Sat.* 1.

R

RAILLERY

Raillery is a poison which if undiluted kills friendship and excites hatred, but which qualified by a mixture of wit and the flattery of praise, produces friendship or preserves it.
LA ROCHEFOUCAULD.—*Maxim 646.*

Raillery is a discourse in favour of one's wit, against one's good nature.
MONTESQUIEU.

You know how to scoff without abusing, and have the charming gift of never irritating though always contradicting.
VOLTAIRE.—*Fête de Bellébat.*

RAILWAYS

" I con-sider," said Mr. Weller, " that the rail is unconstitootional and an inwaser o' privileges."
DICKENS.—*Master Humphrey's Clock.*

Facility of communication begets "community of interests," which is the only treaty that is not a " scrap of paper."
LORD FISHER.—*Letter to Times,* Oct. 21, 1919. (*In support of more railways, steamers, and channel tubes.*)

The iron roads . . . of England . . . contracting all its various life, its rocky arms and rural heart, into a narrow, finite, calculating metropolis of manufactures.
RUSKIN.—*Modern Painters, vol. 2, sec. 1, ch. 1, 7 (1846).*

Going by railroad I do not consider as travelling at all ; it is merely being "sent" to a place, and very little different from becoming a parcel.
RUSKIN.—*Ib., vol. 3, pt. 4, ch. 17, 24.*

Your railroad, when you come to understand it, is only a device for making the world smaller. RUSKIN.—*Ib., sec. 35.*

It [the railway station] is the very temple of discomfort, and the only charity that the builder can extend to us is to show us, plainly as may be, how soonest to escape from it.
RUSKIN.—*Seven Lamps, ch. 4, 21.*

Steam is a tyrant.
JOHN WILSON.—*Noctes No.* 36 (*Nov.* 1834).

Collisions four or five she bore,
The signals were in vain ;
Grown old and rusted, her biler busted
And smashed the excursion train.
Her end was pieces.
Mock epitaph on a locomotive, c. 1860.

RAIN

How beautiful is the rain !
After the dust and heat,
In the broad and fiery street,
In the narrow lane,
How beautiful is the rain !
LONGFELLOW.—*Rain in Summer.*

Rain, rain, glistening rain !
Bidding us to hope again.
F. ROBERTSON.—*Rain, st.* 2.

The gentle rain from heaven.
SHAKESPEARE.—*Merchant of Venice,* Act 4, 1.

For the rain it raineth every day.
SHAKESPEARE.—*Twelfth Night,* Act 5, 1.

Since I was man,
Such sheets of fire, such bursts of horrid thunder,
Such groans of roaring wind and rain, I never
Remember to have heard.
SHAKESPEARE.—*Lear,* Act 3, 2.

Rain, rain, rattlestanes,
Dinna rain on me,
But rain on Johnnie Groat's house,
Far owre the sea.
Scottish saying.

RAINBOW

Triumphal arch, that fill'st the sky
When storms prepare to part,
I ask not proud Philosophy
To teach me what thou art.
CAMPBELL.—*To the Rainbow.*

My heart leaps up when I behold
A rainbow in the sky.
WORDSWORTH.—*My Heart Leaps Up.*

The rainbow in the morning
Is the shepherd's warning
To carry his coat on his back.
The rainbow at night
Is the shepherd's delight,
For then no coat will he lack.
Old Rhyme.

RALLYING CRY

Charge, Chester, charge ! On, Stanley, on !
Were the last words of Marmion.
SCOTT.—*Marmion, c.* 6, 32.

O for a blast of that dread horn
On Fontarabian echoes borne !
SCOTT.—*Ib.,* 33.

RANCOUR

Pryde . . . ay bloweth and encreaseth the fyr [of anger] by chydinge and wicked words. Then standeth Envye, and holdeth the hote iren [hot iron] upon the herte of man with a peire of long tonges of long rancour.
CHAUCER.—*Parson's Tale, sec.* 33.

Pray, goody, please to moderate the rancour of your tongue.
K. O'HARA.—*Midas.*

Rancour will out.
>   SHAKESPEARE.—*Henry VI., Pt. 2,*
>   *Act 1, 1.*

Anon is there then
Such rancour in the harts of mightie men ?
>   SPENSER.—*Muiopotmos.*

To revile your family, your church,
your trade, your country, is a very unsavoury thing.
>   C. H. SPURGEON.—" *Salt-Cellars.*"

RANK

I could sit at rich men's tables,—though
    the courtesies that raised me,
Still suggested clear between us the pale
    spectrum of the salt.
>   E. B. BROWNING.—*Lady Geraldine's
>   Courtship.*

Princes and lords are but the breath of
    kings,
"An honest man's the noblest work of
    God."
>   BURNS.—*Cotter's Saturday Night.*

The rank is but the guinea stamp ;
    The man's the gowd for a' that !
>   BURNS.—*Is there, for Honest Poverty ?*

A king can mak' a belted knight,
A marquis, duke, and a' that ;
But an honest man's aboon his might,
Guid faith he mauna fa' that.
>   BURNS.—*Ib.*

Also I prey yow to forgive it me
Al I have not set folk in their degree.
>   CHAUCER.—*Cant. Tales, Prol.,* 743.

Spurn not the nobly born with love
affected :
Nor treat with virtuous scorn the well-
    connected !
>   SIR W. S. GILBERT.—*Iolanthe.*

Rank is a great beautifier.
    (1st) LORD LYTTON.—*Lady of Lyons,*
                             Act 21.

Through tattered clothes small vices do
    appear ;
Robes and furred gowns hide all.
>   SHAKESPEARE.—*Lear,* Act 4, 6.

Let the nobility be free from vice, and
an example to others.
>   *The Twelve Tables at Rome.*

RANT

It out-herods Herod : pray you, avoid it.
>   SHAKESPEARE.—*Hamlet,* Act 3, 2.

Nay, an thou 'lt mouth,
I'll rant as well as thou.
>   SHAKESPEARE.—*Ib.,* Act 5, 1.

RASHNESS

He has no bearing on the prudent side.
>   COWPER.—*Progress of Error,* 548.

And though he stumbles in a full career
Yet rashness is a better fault than fear.
>   DRYDEN.—*Tyrannic Love, Prol.*

She opened ; but to shut
Excelled her power.
>   MILTON.—*Paradise Lost, Bk.* 2, 883.

And who would run, that's moderately
    wise,
A certain danger, for a doubtful prize ?
>   J. POMFRET.—*Love triumphant over
>   Reason,* 85.

For fools rush in where angels fear to
    tread.   POPE.—*Criticism,* 625.

It is too rash, too unadvised, too sudden.
>   SHAKESPEARE.—*Romeo and Juliet,* Act 2, 2.

At last she spyde at that rowme's upper
    end
Another yron dore, on which was writ,
Be not too bold.
>   SPENSER.—*Faerie Queene, Bk.* 3, *c.* 11, 54.

RATS

Anything like the sound of a rat
Makes my heart go pit-a-pat !
>   BROWNING.—*Pied Piper.*

Now, muse, let's sing of rats.
>   JAS. GRAINGER.—*Lines (expunged) in
>   " The Sugar Cane."*

REACTION

It is not in the storm, nor in the strife
    We feel benumbed, and wish to be no
    more,
But in the after-silence on the shore,
When all is lost, except a little life.
>   BYRON.—*On hearing Lady Byron was ill.*

Repeal the Union ?   Restore the Hept-
archy !   CANNING.—*Speech in the House
>   of Commons,* Feb. 3, 1812.

One always returns to one's first love.
>   ETIENNE.—*Joconde,* Act 3.

All that is human must retrograde if it
does not advance.
>   GIBBON.—*Decline and Fall, c.* 71.

At length the morn and cold indifference
    came.
>   N. ROWE.—*Fair Penitent,* Act 1, 1.

READINESS

Now's the day, and now's the hour ;
See the front o' battle lour.
>   BURNS.—*Bruce's Address.*

Abra was ready ere I called her name,
And, though I called another, Abra came.
>   PRIOR.—*Solomon, Bk.* 2, 364.

READING

Preserve proportion in your reading.
>   THOS. ARNOLD.

I wis, all their sport in the park is but a shadow to that pleasure that I find in Plato. Alas, good folk! they never felt what true pleasure meant.
R. ASCHAM.—*Scholemaster, Bk.* 1 (*Remark of Lady Jane Grey*).

Read not to contradict and confute; nor to believe and take for granted; nor to find talk and discourse; but to weigh and consider. BACON.—*Of Studies.*

Hobbes used to say " that if he had read as many books as other men, he should have been as ignorant as they," clearly implying that reading is sometimes an ingenious device for avoiding thought.
SIR A. HELPS.—*Friends in Council, Bk.* 2, *ch.* 1.

If I were to pray for a taste which should stand me in stead under every variety of circumstances, and be a source of happiness and cheerfulness to me through life, and a shield against its ills, it would be a taste for reading.
SIR J. HERSCHEL.—*Address to subscribers to Windsor Public Library* (1833).

To read in every spare moment, and to read constantly, is more paralysing to the mind than continual manual work, which at least allows a man to follow his own thoughts.
SCHOPENHAUER.—*On Reading.*

Reading is thinking with some one else's head instead of one's own.
SCHOPENHAUER.—*Thinking for Oneself.*

It [reading a book mentioned] is like washing bushels of sand for a grain of gold. It passes the time, however.
SCOTT.—*Diary, Feb.,* 1826.

Reading is to the mind what exercise is to the body. STEELE.—*Tatler,* 147.

Always read and think aloud.
TOLSTOY.—*Maxim in Diary.*

Learn to read slow: all other graces Will follow in their proper places.
W. WALKER.—*Art of Reading.*

REALISM

Stark-naked thought is in request enough.
BROWNING.—*Transcendentalism.*

Without or with offence to friend or foes, I sketch your world exactly as it goes.
BYRON.—*Don Juan, c.* 8, 89.

But now I'm going to be immoral; now I mean to show things really as they are, Not as they ought to be
BYRON.—*Ib., c.* 12, 40.

Paint me as I am. If you leave out the scars and the wrinkles, I will pay you not a shilling.
OLIVER CROMWELL.—*Remark to Lely, the Painter.*

Make bare the poor dead secrets of his heart,
Strip the stark-naked soul that all may peer,
Spy, smirk, sniff, snap, snort, snivel, snarl, and sneer.
SWINBURNE.—*In Sepulchretis,* 2.

REALITY

God Himself is the best Poet, And the Real is His song.
E. B. BROWNING.—*The Dead Pan.*

For present joys are more to flesh and blood
Than a dull prospect of a distant good.
DRYDEN.—*Hind and Panther, Pt.* 3, 364.

For the soul is dead that slumbers, And things are not what they seem.
LONGFELLOW.—*Psalm of Life.*

Not in Utopia, subterranean fields, Or some secreted island, Heaven knows where!
But in the very world, which is the world Of all of us,—the place where in the end We find our happiness, or not at all.
WORDSWORTH.—*Lines nr. Tintern Abbey* (1798).

Hips and haws are very good meat, But bread and butter is better to eat.
Scottish saying.

REASON AND REASONING

Whoever acts without reason may do a great deal of harm without knowing it.
WM. BLAKE.—*Edward III.*

If the truth must be told, reason is often the worst of all our ills.
BOILEAU.—*Sat.* 4, 114.

Every man's own reason is his best Œdipus. SIR T. BROWNE.—*Religio Medici, Pt.* 1, *sec.* 6.

For every why he had a wherefore.
BUTLER.—*Hudibras, Pt.* 1, *c.* 1.

Reason is a mirror given us by heaven. It becomes tarnished; we must wipe it. To correct other men we must correct ourselves. CONFUCIUS.—*Maxim (according to Voltaire).*

Reason, the power
To guess at right and wrong, the twinkling lamp
Of wandering life, that winks and wakes by turns,
Fooling the follower, betwixt shade and shining. CONGREVE.—*Mourning Bride,* Act 3, 1.

He that will not reason is a bigot ; he that cannot reason is a fool ; and he that dares not reason is a slave.
     SIR WM. DRUMMOND.

Never mind the why and wherefore.
   SIR W. S. GILBERT.—*H.M.S. Pinafore.*

Atter w'ile he [Brer Rabbit] 'low ter hisself, "Hit look lak sparrer-grass, hit feel like sparrer-grass, hit tas'e like sparrer-grass, en I bless ef 'taint sparrer-grass." J. C. HARRIS.—*Nights with Uncle Remus, ch.* 27.

We may take Fancy for a companion, but must follow Reason as our guide.
    JOHNSON.—*Letter,* 1774.

Endued
With sanctity of reason.
MILTON.—*Paradise Lost, Bk.* **7,** 507.

There is light enough for those who wish to see, and darkness enough for those who have the opposite disposition.
   PASCAL.—*Pensées, Part* 2, 13, 2.

The heart has reasons of which reason has no knowledge. PASCAL.—*Ib.,* 2, 17.

Let us beware [said Socrates] . . . that we do not become haters of reasoning. . . . For no greater evil can happen to anyone than to hate reasoning.
   PLATO.—*Phædo,* 88 (*Cary tr.*).

Reason's the rightful empress of the soul.
J. POMFRET.—*Love triumphant over Reason,* 400.

Two things are equally unaccountable to reason and not the object of reason—the wisdom of God and the madness of man.
   POPE.—*Thoughts on Various Subjects.*

Reason, an ignis fatuus of the mind.
   EARL OF ROCHESTER.—*Satire.*

If you wish to master all things, let reason be your master. SENECA.—*Ep.* 37.

Sure he, that made us with such large discourse,
Looking before and after, gave us not
That capability and godlike reason
To fust in us unused.
   SHAKESPEARE.—*Hamlet,* Act 4, 4.

By slow degrees his reason drove away
The mists of passion and resumed her sway. VIRGIL.—*Æneid, Bk.* 12
   (*Dryden tr.*) (*of Turnus*).

Beware of reliance on your own feeble reason. God has made you to love Him, not to understand Him
   VOLTAIRE.—*Henriade.*

If you will not hear Reason, she will surely rap your knuckles. *Poor Richard.*

At best thou'rt but a glimmering light,
 Which serves not to direct our way ;
But, like the moon, confounds our sight,
 And only shows it is not day.
 (*From* " *Miscellany Poems and Translations by Oxford Hands.*" *Printed* 1685.)

REBELLION

Kings will be tyrants from policy when subjects are rebels from principle.
   BURKE.—*Reflections on Rev. in France.*

The Devil was the first o' th' name
From whom the race of rebels came.
   S. BUTLER.—*Miscellaneous Thoughts.*

My chief, in his wine-cups, forgave twelve men,
And of these a dozen rebelled again.
   AUBREY DE VERE.—*From The Bard Ethell, st.* 10.

Rebels in Cork are patriots at Madrid.
   MOORE.—*Irish Melodies.*

Rebellion ! foul dishonouring word
 Whose wrongful blight so oft has stained
The holiest cause that tongue or sword
 Of mortal ever lost or gained.
How many a spirit, born to bless,
 Hath sunk beneath that withering name,
Whom but a day's, an hour's success,
 Had wafted to eternal fame.
   MOORE.—*Lalla Rookh.*

In civil strife nothing is safer than speed. TACITUS.—*Hist., Bk.* 1.

Rebel in all but opportunity,
Traitor in all but daring to rebel.
LORD DE TABLEY.—*Soldier of Fortune,* Act 1.

REBUKE

Open rebuke is better than secret love [" than love that is hidden "—R.V.].
   Proverbs xxvii, 5.

Rebuke should have a grain more of salt than of sugar. *Prov.*

RECIPROCITY

As I am true to thee and thine,
Do thou be true to me and mine !
   SCOTT.—*Lay of the Last Minstrel, c.* 5, 26.

I ne'er could any lustre see
In eyes that would not look on me ;
I ne'er saw nectar on a lip
But where my own did hope to sip.
   SHERIDAN.—*Duenna,* Act 1, 3.

And if you'll blow to me a kiss,
 I'll blow a kiss to you.
H. AND J. SMITH.—*Rejected Addresses.*

RECKLESSNESS

He was a care-defying blade
As ever Bacchus listed.
   BURNS.—*Jolly Beggars.*

Earth shakes beneath them, and heaven
  roars above ;
But nothing scares them from the course
  they love.
      COWPER.—*Table Talk*, 359.

He has no hope who never had a fear.
      COWPER.—*Truth*, 299.

More childish valorous than manly wise.
      MARLOWE.—*Tamburlaine, Pt. 2,*
                          Act 4, 1.

Every drunken skipper trusts to Providence. But one of the ways of Providence
with drunken skippers is to run them on
the rocks.
      G. B. SHAW.—*Heartbreak House,*
                          Act 3.

But how can he expect that others should
Build for him, sow for him, and at his call
Love him, who for himself will take no
  heed at all ?
      WORDSWORTH.—*Resolution and*
                          Independence.

The driving is like the driving of Jehu
the son of Nimshi ; for he driveth furiously.
      2 Kings ix, 20.

He that leaves certainty for chance,
When fools pipe, he may dance.
                          Old Saying.

RECKONING

So comes a reck'ning when the banquet's
  o'er,
The dreadful reck'ning, and men smile no
  more.   GAY.—*What d'ye call 't ?*

At the Captain's mess, in the Banquet-
  hall,
Sat feasting the officers, one and all—
Like a sabre-blow, like the swing of a sail,
One raised his glass, held high to hail,
Sharp snapped like the stroke of a rud-
  der's play,
Spoke three words only : " To the day ! "
      ERNEST LISSAUER (*German, b. 1882*).—
      Hassgesung gegen England (Song of
      Hate against England), (1914).

The feast is good until the reckoning
  comes. QUARLES.—*Feast for Worms,*
                      sec. 6, med. 6.

I am ill at reckoning ; it fitteth the
spirit of a tapster.
      SHAKESPEARE.—*Love's Labour's Lost,*
                          Act 1, 2.

RECONCILIATION

Reconciliation with our enemies is only
a desire to improve our own condition,
a weariness of combat, and a fear of some
unpleasant outcome.
      LA ROCHEFOUCAULD.—*Maxim 82.*

      Yet winds to seas
Are reconciled at length, and sea to shore.
      MILTON.—*Samson Agonistes,* 961.

Remember thy end, and let enmity
cease.   *Ecclesiasticus* xxviii, 6.

Cold broth hot again, that loved I never ;
Old love renewed again, that loved I ever.
                          Old Saying.

RECORDS

Vain was the chief's, the sage's pride ;
They had no poet, and they died.
      POPE.—*Tr. of Horace.*

Report me and my cause aright.
      SHAKESPEARE.—*Hamlet,* Act 5, 2.

      Horatio, what a wounded name,
Things standing thus unknown shall live
  behind me !
If thou didst ever hold me in thy heart,
Absent thee from felicity a while,
And in this harsh world draw thy breath
  in pain,
To tell my story.   SHAKESPEARE.—*Ib.*

Men's evil manners live in brass ; their
  virtues
We write in water.
      SHAKESPEARE.—*Henry VIII.,* Act 4, 2.

RECREATION

What Cato advises most certainly wise is,
  Not always to labour but sometimes to
    play,
To mingle sweet pleasure with search after
  treasure,
Indulging at night for the toils of the
    day. H. CAREY.—*Cato's Advice.*

My brain is dull, my sight is foul,
  I cannot write a verse or read ;
Then Pallas, take away thine Owl
  And let us have a Lark instead.
      HOOD.—*To Minerva.*

RECRIMINATION

This [reviling] is a ful grisly [horrible]
sin, as Crist seith in the gospel.
      CHAUCER.—*Parson's Tale, sec. 42*

Now I hold it is not decent for a scientific
  gent
To say another is an ass—at least, to all
  intent ;
Nor should the individual, who happens to
  be meant
Reply by heaving rocks at him to any
  great extent.
      BRET HARTE.—*Society upon the*
                          Stanislaus.

RECTITUDE

Would you never be sad ? Live rightly !
      ISIDORUS.—8, 13.

And so wherever Time shall speak your
  fame,
Truth will nail high this writ above your
  name :
He kept his soul unspotted of the mire

Wherein so many smirch their souls for
hire.
However fortune wavered, still all men
Revered the austere honour of his pen.
God made him of unpurchasable stuff :
Say this at last, and this will be enough !
  EDWIN MARKHAM.—*To Wm. Winter.*

REFLECTION

A sadder and a wiser man
He rose the morrow morn.
  COLERIDGE.—*Ancient Mariner.*

The wildest scorner of his Maker's laws
Finds in a sober moment time to pause.
  COWPER.—*Tirocinium*, 55.

With thy heart commune and be still.
  SCOTT.—*Marmion, c.* 6, *st.* 33.

Consideration, like an angel, came,
And whipped the offending Adam out of
him.
  SHAKESPEARE.—*Henry V.,* Act 1, 1.

REFORM AND REFORMATION

This world has been harsh and strange ;
Something is wrong : there needeth a
change.
  BROWNING.—*Holy-Cross Day.*

To innovate is not to reform.
  BURKE.—*Letter to a Noble Lord* (1796).

All reform except a moral one will prove
unavailing.
  CARLYLE.—*Essays : Corn Law Rhymes.*

Every reform, however necessary, will
by weak minds be carried to an excess
which will itself need reforming.
  COLERIDGE.—*Biog. Literaria, ch.* 1.

Is not every man sometimes a radical in
politics ? Men are conservative when
they are least vigorous, or when they are
most luxurious. They are conservatives
after dinner.
  EMERSON.—*New England Reformers.*

Moderate reformers always hate those
who go beyond them.
  FROUDE.—*Erasmus. Lecture* 20.

I've given up all my wild proceedings,
  My taste for a wandering life is waning ;
Now I'm a dab at penny readings ;
  They're not remarkably entertaining.
  SIR W. S. GILBERT.—*Ruddigore.*

I hope that we have reformed that indifferently. SHAKESPEARE.—*Hamlet,*
                              Act 3, 2.

Repent what's past ; avoid what is to
come. SHAKESPEARE.—*Ib.,* Act 3, 4.

Presume not that I am the thing I was.
  SHAKESPEARE.—*Henry IV., Pt.* 2,
                              Act 5, 3.

Every generation needs regeneration.
  C. H. SPURGEON.—*"Salt-Cellars."*

To ride abroad, redressing human wrongs.
  TENNYSON.—*Guinevere*

Ring out the want, the care, the sin,
The faithless coldness of the times.
  TENNYSON.—*In Memoriam, c.* 106.

Ring out old shapes of foul disease ;
Ring out the narrowing lust of gold ;
Ring out the thousand wars of old,
Ring in the thousand years of peace.
  TENNYSON.—*Ib.*

Ah for a man to arise in me,
That the man I am may cease to be !
  TENNYSON.—*Maud, Pt.* 1, 10.

Press bravely onward ! Not in vain
Your generous trust in human-kind ;
The good which bloodshed could not gain
Your peaceful zeal shall find.
  WHITTIER.—*To the Reformers of England.*

Alas ! with most who weigh futurity
Against time present, passion holds the
  scales :
Hence equal ignorance of both prevails,
And nations sink ; or, struggling to be
  free,
Are doomed to flounder on, like wounded
  whales
Tossed on the bosom of a stormy sea.
  WORDSWORTH.—*Sonnets to Liberty*
                    and Order, 12.

REFORMATION, THE

Thus this brook hath conveyed his
(Wickliffe's) ashes into Avon ; Avon into
Severn ; Severn into the narrow seas ;
they into the main ocean. And thus the
ashes of Wickliffe are the emblem of his
doctrine, which now is dispersed all the
world over.
  FULLER.—*Church History, Sec.* 2,
                              Bk. 4.

When love could teach a monarch to be
  wise,
And gospel-light first dawned from Bul-
  len's eyes.   GRAY.—*Education.*

The solitary monk that shook the world.
  ROBT. MONTGOMERY.—*Luther.*

Ere yet, in scorn of Peter's pence,
  And numbered bead, and shrift,
Bluff Harry broke into the spence
  And turned the cowls adrift.
  TENNYSON.—*The Talking Oak.*

Paternoster built churches, and Our
Father pulls them down.   *Prov.* (*Ray*).

REFUSAL

Then do not strike him dead with a denial.
  ADDISON.—*Cato,* Act 3, 2.

I give thee sixpence ? I will see thee
damned first.
         G. CANNING.—*Knife Grinder.*

But the snail replied, " Too far, too far ! "
   and gave a look askance—
Said he thanked the whiting kindly, but
   he would not join the dance.
     C. L. DODGSON.—*Alice in Wonderland,*
                            c. 11.

You would be entreated, and say
" *Nolo, nolo, nolo,*" three times, like any
bishop, when your mouth waters at the
diocese.   DRYDEN.—*Limberham,* Act 3.

The swain did woo ; she was nice ;
Following fashion, nayed him twice.
         GREENE.—*Shepherd's Ode*
                 (Ciceronis Amor).

When late I attempted your pity to move,
Why seemed you so deaf to my prayers ?
Perhaps it was right to dissemble your
   love,
But—why did you kick me downstairs ?
     J. P. KEMBLE.*—*The Panel,* Act 1, 1.

Not Hebrew, Arabic, Syriac, Coptic, nor
even the Chinese language, seems half so
difficult to me as the language of refusal.
         SHENSTONE.—*Egotisms.*

But they wavered not long, for conscience
   was strong,
And they thought they might get more,
And they refused the gold, but not
   So rudely as before.
         SOUTHEY.—*Surgeon's Warning.*

Above all things we advise young people
to learn to say " No." It will save them
from a thousand ills if they can clearly and
distinctly pronounce that monosyllable.
     C. H. SPURGEON.—" *Salt-Cellars.*"

A reason for refusing is never wanting
to an avaricious man. PUBLILIUS SYRUS.

From such a sharp and waspish word as
" No "
To pluck the sting.
     HENRY TAYLOR.—*Philip van Artevelde,*
                       1, 2 (1834).

Have you not heard it said full oft,
A woman's nay doth stand for nought ?
Passionate Pilgrim, No. 17 (*Adapted from
   Thos. Weelkes's* " *Madrigals,*" 1597).

Cut off the head and tail and throw the
rest away.   *Prov. (Ray).*

REGRET

Perhaps if we had never met,
I had been spared this vain regret,
This endless striving to forget.
         LADY CURRIE.—*Song.*

---

* In Kemble's adaptation of Bickerstaffe's
comedy "The Panel" (1778), but not in the
original (1770). Given in "Annual Register,"
1783, App., p. 201, among "Miscellaneous Poems,"
without author's name.

Weep no more, nor sigh nor groan,
Sorrow calls no time that's gone :
Violets plucked the sweetest rain
Makes not fresh nor grow again.
         FLETCHER (?).—*Queen of Corinth,*
         Act 3, 1 (*probably an addition*).

Oh days and years departed,
Vain hopes, vain fears that smarted,
I turn to you, sad-hearted—
     I turn to you in tears !
Your daily sun shone brightly,
Your happy dreams came nightly,
Flowers bloomed and birds sang lightly
   Through all your hopes and fears.
         A. L. GORDON.—*Ashtaroth*
                 (*Agatha's Song*).

In all our lamentations and regrets
pleasures have been mixed up with pains.
         PLATO.—*Philebus,* 105.

REJOICING

Men met each other with erected look,
The steps were higher that they took ;
Friends to congratulate their friends made
   haste,
And long inveterate foes saluted as they
   passed.
     DRYDEN.—*Threnodia Augustalis, st.* 4.

'Tis sometimes natural to be glad,
And no man can be always sad,
   Unless he wills to have it so.
         JEAN INGELOW.—*Scholar and
                 Carpenter,* 39.

And the flags were all a-flutter,
And the bells were all a-chime.
         SIR H. NEWBOLT.—*San Stefano.*

True joy is a serious matter.
         SENECA.—*Ep.* 23, 4.

As when a mighty people rejoice
With shawms and with cymbals and harps
   of gold,
And the tumult of their acclaim is rolled
Through the open gates of the city afar,
To the shepherd who watcheth the evening
   star. TENNYSON.—*The Dying Swan.*

Beauty for ashes, the oil of joy for
mourning, the garment of praise for the
spirit of heaviness.   *Isaiah* lxi, 3.

RELAPSE

Alas, from what high hope to what relapse
Unlooked for, are we fallen !
     MILTON.—*Paradise Regained,* Bk. **2**, 30.

RELATIONS

It is a melancholy truth, that even great
men have their poor relations.
     DICKENS.—*Bleak House, ch.* 28.

A Poor Relation is the most irrelevant
thing in nature. . . . He is known by his
knock—a rap, between familiarity and
respect.

     LAMB.—*Last Essays, Poor Relations.*

A little more than kin, and less than kind.
SHAKESPEARE.—*Hamlet*, Act 1, 2.

O my prophetic soul ! mine uncle !
SHAKESPEARE.—*Ib.*, Act 1, 5.

A man canna 'bear a' his ain kin aboot
on his back.   *Scottish prov.*

RELAXATION

There is one piece of advice, in a life of
study, which I think no one will object to ;
and that is every now and then to be
completely idle,—to do nothing at all.
Indeed this part of a life of study is
commonly considered so decidedly superior
to the rest that it has almost obtained an
exclusive preference.
     SYDNEY SMITH.—*Lectures on Moral
         Philosophy, No.* 19.

Up, up ! my friend, and quit your books,
   Or surely you'll grow double :
Up, up ! my friend, and clear your looks,
   Why all this toil and trouble ?
     WORDSWORTH.—*Tables Turned, st.* 1.

RELIGION

He is to be feared who fears the gods.
     ÆSCHYLUS.—*Septem Duces.*

For rigorous teachers seized my youth,
And purged its faith and trimmed its fire,
Showed me the high white star of Truth,
There bade me gaze and there aspire.
     M. ARNOLD.—*Grande Chartreuse.*

Children of men ! the Unseen Power,
   whose eye
For ever doth accompany mankind,
Hath looked on no religion scornfully,
   That man did ever find.
     M. ARNOLD.—*Progress.*

A religion that is jealous of the variety
of learning, discourse, opinions, and sects,
as misdoubting it may shake the foundations, or that cherisheth devotion upon
simplicity and ignorance, as ascribing ordinary effects to the immediate working of
God, is adverse to knowledge.
     BACON.—*Valerius Terminus*, 25.

The religions of all nations are derived
from each nation's different reception of
the poetic genius, which is everywhere
called the spirit of prophecy.
     WM. BLAKE.—*There is no Natural
         Religion.*

As all men are alike (though infinitely
various), so all religions, and as all similars
have one source.   WM. BLAKE.—*Ib.*

Nothing is so fatal to religion as indifference, which is, at least, half infidelity.
     BURKE.—*Letter to Wm. Smith*
                 (1795).

Man is by his constitution a religious
animal.   BURKE.—*Reflections on French
                 Revolution.*

And still be doing, never done ;
As if Religion were intended
For nothing else but to be mended.
     BUTLER.—*Hudibras, Pt.* 1, *c.* 1.

Why should not piety be made,
   As well as equity, a trade ?
     S. BUTLER.—*Miscellaneous Thoughts.*

The fair humanities of old religion.
     COLERIDGE.—*Piccolomini*, Act 2, 5.

Men will wrangle for religion ; write for
it ; fight for it ; die for it ; anything but
—live for it.   C. C. COLTON.—*Lacon.*

Religion harsh, intolerant, austere,
Parent of manners, like herself, severe.
     COWPER.—*Table Talk*, 611.

For my salvation must its doom receive,
Not from what others, but what I believe.
     DRYDEN.—*Religio Laici*, 304.

Men are better than their theology.
     EMERSON.—*Compensation.*

You say, there is no religion now. 'Tis
like saying, in rainy weather, there is no
sun, when at that moment we are witness-
ing one of his superlative effects.
     EMERSON.—*Conduct of Life : Worship.*

There is no age which religion does not
become.   ERASMUS.—*Fam. Coll.*

'Tis a strange thing, Sam, that among
us people can't agree the whole week,
because they go different ways on Sundays.
     G. FARQUHAR.—*Letter, Oct.*, 1700.

Religion is religion and business is
business, and you will succeed in neither
if you do not keep them properly apart.
. . . I have never neglected either, though
if I had introduced religion into my business relations, and business capacity into
my religious life, I should have been
neither the rich man nor the accredited
churchwarden that I am.
ELLEN THORNEYCROFT FOWLER.—(*Opinion
                 of a Lawyer.*)

The ecclesiastical writers, who, in the
heat of religious faction, are apt to despise the profane virtues of sincerity and
moderation.
     GIBBON.—*Decline and Fall, ch.* 26.

Man, without religion, is the creature of
circumstances.
     J. C. HARE.—*Guesses at Truth, Vol.* 1.

From the moment that religion seeks
assistance from philosophy her downfall
is inevitable. She strives to defend herself and always talks herself deeper into
ruin. Religion, like other absolutisms,
may not justify herself.
     HEINE.—*Religion and Philosophy.*

A daw's not reckoned a religious bird,
Because it keeps a-cawing from a steeple.
> HOOD.—*Ode to R. Wilson.*

A sparing and infrequent worshipper of
the gods, whilst I wander absorbed in
raving philosophy, now I am compelled to
turn sail, and follow once more the course
I had abandoned.
> HORACE.—*Odes, Bk.* 1, 34.

What excellent fools
Religion makes of men !
> BEN JONSON.—*Sejanus,* Act 5.

Next to a sound rule of faith, there is
nothing of so much consequence as a sober
standard of feeling in matters of practical
religion.   KEBLE.—*Christian Year, Pref.*

Men of loftiest piety are reserved and
reverent as regards holy things . . . and
only in the narrow circle of intimate
friends ever speak of God's forgiveness or
their hopes of heaven.
> KEBLE.—*Lectures on Poetry, No.* 5
> (*E. K. Francis tr.*).

To what extent will not men let themselves be carried away in the cause of
religion, of which they are so little convinced, and which they practise so badly ?
> LA BRUYÈRE.

Religion is the elder sister of Philosophy.
> W. S. LANDOR.—*David Hume.*

Perhaps those simple souls might teach,
Lessons as high as we could set them,
And if they're striving heaven to reach
Their own strange road—by all means
   let them !
R. MONCKTON MILNES (Lord HOUGHTON).
> —*Easter in Florence.*

To prayer, repentance, and obedience due.
> MILTON.—*Paradise Lost, Bk.* 3, 191.

I find no quality so easy to counterfeit
as religious devotion, if one does not conform one's manners and life to it.
> MONTAIGNE.—*Essays, Bk.* 3, 2.

There is no greater disagreement than
one about religion.
> MONTANUS.—*In Micah.*

A man who discovers the proofs of the
Christian religion is like an heir who finds
the title-deeds of his house. Will he declare that they are false, and will he
neglect to examine them ?
> PASCAL.—*Pensées, Pt.* 2, 17, 20.

To have deceived yourself in believing the
Christian religion would not involve any
great loss. But what a calamity to have
deceived yourself in believing it false !
> PASCAL.—*Ib.,* Pt. 2, 17, 36.

The humble, meek, merciful, just, pious
and devout souls, are everywhere of one
religion ; and when death has taken off
the mask they will know one another.
> PENN.—*Some Fruits of Solitude.*

Without Thy presence, wealth are bags of
   cares ;
Wisdom, but folly ; joy, disquiet, sadness ;
Friendship is treason and delights are
   snares ;
Pleasure's but pain and mirth but pleasing
   madness.
> QUARLES.—*Emblems, Bk.* 5, 6.

And hated all for love of Jesus Christ.
> CHRISTINA ROSSETTI.—*Portrait.*

Forgetfulness of all religion leads to the
forgetfulness of the duties of man.
> ROUSSEAU.—*Emile.*

Never let us confuse the ceremonial of
religion with religion. The worship God
demands is that of the heart, and this
worship, when it is sincere, is always
uniform.   ROUSSEAU.—*Ib.*

All false religion combats nature.
> ROUSSEAU.—*Julie.*

I believe in religion all that I can understand, and respect the rest without reject-
ing it.   ROUSSEAU.—*Ib.*

A knave's religion is always the rotten-
est thing about him.
> RUSKIN.—*Letter V.,* 1867.

I grew more sure that the peace of God
rested on all the dutiful and kindly hearts
of the laborious poor ; and that the only
constant form of pure religion was in useful
work, faithful love, and stintless charity.
> RUSKIN.—*Prœterita,* 3, 7.

Religion is like someone taking a blind
person's hand and leading him, because
he cannot see for himself. All the blind
person wants is to attain his destination ;
not to see everything as he passes along.
> SCHOPENHAUER.—*Demopheles in*
> *Dialogue on " Religion."*

Religions are like glow-worms ; before
they can give light it must be dark. A
certain degree of ignorance is necessary
in every religion—the only element in
which it can exist.
> SCHOPENHAUER.—*Philalethes in*
> *Dialogue on " Religion."*

Religion, like Janus, or rather like the
Brahman god of death, Yama, has two
faces, one very kindly and one very sullen.
Each of us has his eyes fixed on one only.
> SCHOPENHAUER.—*Dialogue on " Religion "*
> (*Demopheles*).

His worst fault is that he is given to prayer ; he is something peevish that way; but nobody but has his fault ; but let that pass.   SHAKESPEARE.—*Merry Wives*, Act 1, 4.

For the life to come, I sleep out the thought of it.
SHAKESPEARE.—*Winter's Tale*, Act 4, 2.

There is only one religion, though there are a hundred versions of it.
G. B. SHAW.—*Philanderer*.

Your northern religions, harsh and bitter as your skies.
J. H. SHORTHOUSE.—*John Inglesant*, Vol. 2, ch. 6.

The luxury of false religion is to be unhappy.
SYDNEY SMITH.—*Letter to F. Horner*, Nov. 25, 1816.

In the days of my youth I remembered my God,
And he hath not forgotten my age.
SOUTHEY.—*Old Man's Comforts*.

Fear first made gods in the world.
STATIUS.—*Thebais*, 3.

Ask not, my frighted sons, from whence I came,
But mark me well : Religion is my name ;
An angel once, but now a fury grown,
Too often talked of but too little known.
SWIFT.—*Swan Tripe Club*.

We have just enough religion to make us hate, but not enough to make us love one another.
SWIFT.—*Thoughts on Various Subjects*.

Leave thou thy sister, when she prays,
Her early Heaven, her happy views ;
Nor thou with shadowed hint confuse
A life that leads melodious days.
TENNYSON.—*In Memoriam*, st. 33.

In religion it is as in gaming. "One begins by being dupe, and ends by being rogue."   VOLTAIRE.—*Dialogues*, No. 26.

England is the land of sects. An Englishman, as a free man, goes to heaven by the road which pleases him.
VOLTAIRE.—*Letters on the English*.

If there were only one religion in England, its despotism would be a cause for alarm. If there were only two, they would cut each other's throats. But as there are thirty, they live at peace and are happy.   VOLTAIRE.—*Ib.*

We are all of the same religion without knowing it.
VOLTAIRE.—*Sermon by " Josias Rossette."*

Lord, I ascribe it to thy grace,
And not to chance, as others do,
That I was born of Christian race,
And not a Heathen or a Jew.
I. WATTS.

He worshipped as his fathers did,
And kept the faith of childish days,
And howsoe'er he strayed or slid,
He loved the good old ways.
WHITTIER.—*My Namesake*.

The Earl [Shaftesbury] said at last, . . . " Men of sense are really but of one religion." Upon which says the lady, of a sudden, " Pray, my lord, what religion is that which men of sense agree in ? " " Madam," says the earl, " men of sense never tell it."
Note by Speaker Onslow, to Burnet's notice of Lord Shaftesbury, " History of his own Times," Vol. 1.

The devil divides the world between atheism and superstition.
Prov. (Geo. Herbert).

Old churches have dark windows.
Prov. quoted by Goethe.

Let there be no violence in religion.
Koran, ch. 2.

REMEDIES

No men despise physic so much as physicians, because no men so thoroughly understand how little it can perform.
C. C. COLTON.—*Lacon*.

I touch on these things unwillingly, even as wounds, but wounds cannot be cured unless handled and dressed.
LIVY.—*Bk.* 28, *ch.* 27, *Speech of Scipio*.

It was a sign of health that he was willing to be cured.
SENECA.—*Hippolytus*.

By medicine life may be prolonged, yet death
Will seize the doctor too.
SHAKESPEARE.—*Cymbeline*, Act 5, 5.

The time is out of joint ; O cursed spite,
That ever I was born to set it right !
SHAKESPEARE.—*Hamlet*, Act 1, 5.

Diseases, desperate grown,
By desperate appliance are relieved,
Or not at all.
SHAKESPEARE.—*Ib.*, Act 4, 3.

The labour we delight in physics pain.
SHAKESPEARE.—*Macbeth*, Act 2, 3.

We have scotched the snake, not killed it.   SHAKESPEARE.—*Ib.*, Act 3, 2.

O mickle is the powerful grace that lies
In herbs, plants, stones, and their true qualities.
SHAKESPEARE.—*Romeo and Juliet*, Act 2, 3;

Remedies are slower than illnesses.
TACITUS.—*Agricola.*

In his remedies he was more grievous than the offences had been.
TACITUS.—*Annals, Bk. 3.*

Is there no balm in Gilead ; is there no physician there ? *Jeremiah* v, 31.

God heals, and the physician has the thanks. *Prov. (Geo. Herbert).*

It is a step towards health to know what the complaint is.
Latin prov. quoted by Erasmus.

This, with a jerk, will do your work,
And cure you o'er and o'er ;
Read, judge and try, and if you die,
Never believe me more.
Quoted by SWIFT (?), *under the name,* "*A. Tripe, M.D.,*" *as* "*that celebrated observation of one of our learned predecessors.*"

REMEMBRANCE

Soon you will have forgotten all ; soon all will have forgotten you.
MARCUS AURELIUS.—*7, 21.*

Oh ! scenes in strong remembrance set,
Scenes never, never to return !
BURNS.—*Lament.*

Still o'er these scenes my memory wakes
And fondly broods with miser care !
Time but the impression stronger makes,
As streams their channels deeper wear.
BURNS.—*To Mary in Heaven.*

To that loved land, where'er he goes,
His tenderest thoughts are cast ;
And dearer still, through absence, grows
The memory of the past.
REV. J. DRUMMOND BURNS.

To live in hearts we leave behind
Is not to die.
CAMPBELL.—*Hallowed Ground.*

Good fortune that is past does not vanish from our memories ; evil fortune we should not remember.
CICERO.—*De Finibus, Bk. 2, 32.*

The remembrance of past labours is agreeable. CICERO.—*Ib., 185.*

The strongest plume in wisdom's pinion
Is the memory of past folly.
COLERIDGE.—*To an Unfortunate Woman.*

Sweet is the remembrance of troubles when you are in safety.
EURIPIDES.—*Andromache.*

'Tis but a little faded flower,
But oh, how fondly dear !
'Twill bring me back one golden hour
Through many a weary year.
ELLEN C. HOWARTH.—'*Tis but a little faded flower.*

Ah tell me not that memory
Sheds gladness o'er the past ;
What is recalled by faded flowers
Save that they did not last ?
L. E. LANDON.—*Despondency.*

To live with them is far less sweet
Than to remember thee.
MOORE.—*I saw thy form.*

Fond memory brings the light
Of other days around me.
MOORE.—*Oft in the stilly night.*

Lulled in the countless chambers of the brain,
Our thoughts are linked by many a hidden chain.
ROGERS.—*Pleasures of Memory, Pt. 1.*

The hours I spent with thee, dear heart,
Are as a string of pearls to me ;
I count them over, every one apart,
My rosary.
R. C. ROGERS.—*The Rosary.*

Remember me when I am gone away,
Gone far away into the silent land.
CHRISTINA ROSSETTI.—*Remember.*

And if thou wilt, remember,
And if thou wilt, forget.
CHRISTINA ROSSETTI.—*When I am dead.*

Reminiscences make one feel so deliciously aged and sad.
G. B. SHAW.—*Irrational Knot, ch. 14.*

Music, when soft voices die,
Vibrates in the memory ;
Odours, when sweet violets sicken,
Live within the sense they quicken.
SHELLEY.—*Poems in 1821. To——.*

In the years fled
Lips that are dead
Sang me that song.
MRS. R. A. M. STEVENSON.

I shall remember while the light is yet,
And in the night-time I will not forget.
SWINBURNE.—*Erotion.*

The sweet remembrance of the just
Shall flourish when he sleeps in dust.
TATE AND BRADY.—*Ps. 112.*

But the tender grace of a day that is dead
Will never come back to me.
TENNYSON.—*Break, break.*

Tears, idle tears, I know not what they mean,
Tears from the depth of some divine despair

Rise in the heart, and gather in the eyes,
In looking on the happy Autumn fields,
And thinking of the days that are no more.
TENNYSON.—*Princess, c.* 6, 21.

Kindnesses are easily forgotten ; but
injuries ?—what worthy man does not
keep *those* in mind ?
THACKERAY.—*Lovel the Widower.*

Some day it may be a pleasure even to
remember these things.
VIRGIL.—*Æneid, Bk.* 1.

What are mony o' the pleasures o'
memory, sirs, but the pains o' the past
spiritualeezed ?   JOHN WILSON.—*Noctes,*
31 (*Ettrick Shepherd*).

What so fair
As blameless pleasure, not without some
tears,
Reviewed through Love's transparent veil
of years ?   WORDSWORTH.—*Ep. to
Sir G. Beaumont (Sequel).*

O joy ! that in our embers
Is something that doth live !
WORDSWORTH.—*Intimations of
Immortality, c.* 9.

Who loves well is slow to forget.
*Old French maxim, quoted by Chaucer,
Parlement of Foules,* 679.

REMORSE

Remorse, the fatal egg by Pleasure laid.
COWPER.—*Progress of Error,* 239.

Remorse does but add to the evil which
bred it, when it promotes not penitence
but despair.   SIR A. HELPS.—*Friends in
Council, Bk.* 1, *ch.* 3.

High minds, of native pride and force,
Most deeply feel thy pangs, Remorse !
SCOTT.—*Marmion,* 2, 13.

Consider it not so deeply.
SHAKESPEARE.—*Macbeth,* Act 2, 2.

Surely there was a time I might have trod
The sunlit heights, and from life's disso-
nance
Struck one clear note to reach the ears of
God.   OSCAR WILDE.—*Hélas !*

REMOTENESS

Remote, unfriended, melancholy, slow.
GOLDSMITH.—*Traveller.*

Remote from towns he ran his godly race,
Nor e'er had changed nor wished to change
his place.
GOLDSMITH.—*Deserted Village.*

As far removed from God and light of
heaven,
As from the centre thrice to th' utmost
pole.
MILTON.—*Paradise Lost, Bk.* 1, 73.

Far from the sweet society of men.
POPE.—*Odyssey, Bk.* 21, 394.

A maid whom there were none to praise,
And very few to love.
WORDSWORTH.—*She dwelt among the
untrodden ways.*

RENEGADES

Thus my first benefactor I o'erthrew ;
And how should I be to a second true ?
DEFOE.—*True-born Englishman :
Britannia,* 224.

Still violent, whatever cause he took,
But most against the party he forsook.
DRYDEN.—*Absalom and Achitophel,
Pt.* 2, 364.

RENEWAL

The mother, wi' her needle and her shears,
Gars auld claes look amaist as weel's the
new.
BURNS.—*Cotter's Saturday Night.*

So sinks the day-star in the ocean bed,
And yet anon repairs his drooping head,
And tricks his beams, and with new
spangled ore
Flames in the forehead of the morning sky.
MILTON.—*Lycidas,* 166.

RENOWN

Renown's all hit or miss ;
There's fortune even in fame, we must
allow.   BYRON.—*Don Juan, c.* 7,
st. 33.

And all the fair examples of renown
Out of distress and misery are grown.
S. DANIEL.—*On the Earl of Southampton.*

Many brave men lived before Agamemnon, but for want of a divine poet they
are lost in the distant night, unmourned
and unknown.   HORACE.—*Odes,* 4, 9.

Thus fame shall be achieved, renown on
earth,
And what most merits fame in silence hid.
MILTON.—*Paradise Lost, Bk.* 11, 698.

Wins for the work the brave man's crown,
The lofty lucre of renown,
His nation's pride, the world's delight.
PINDAR.—*Isthmian Odes,* 1, 62 (*Moore tr.*).

Speak no more of his renown,
Lay your earthly fancies down,
And in the vast cathedral leave him ;
God accept him, Christ receive him.
TENNYSON.—*On the Death of Wellington.*

RENT

The years of sorrow and want and toil,
And the murdering rent for the bit of soil.
R. BUCHANAN.—*O'Murtogh.*

The grand agrarian alchemy, light *rent.*
BYRON.—*Age of Bronze, st.* 14.

Year after year they voted cent. per cent.,
Blood, sweat, and tear-wrung millions—
 why? for rent!
 BYRON.—*Age of Bronze.*

Their good, ill, health, wealth, joy, or dis-
 content,
Being, end, aim, religion—rent, rent, rent.
 BYRON.—*Ib.*

REPENTANCE

The proper process of unsinning sin
Is to begin well doing.
 BROWNING.—*Ring and the Book*, 4, 285.

The weak alone repent.
 BYRON.—*Corsair, c.* 2, 10.

Repentance is the virtue of weak minds.
 DRYDEN.—*Indian Emperor,* Act 3, 1.

Repentance is but want of power to sin.
 DRYDEN.—*Palamon, Bk.* 3, 813.

I ne'er repented anything yet in my life,
And scorn to begin now.
 JOHN FLETCHER.—*Queen of Corinth,*
 Act 4, 1.

Death-bed repentance seldom reaches to
restitution. JUNIUS.—*Dedication.*

Our repentance is not so much regret
for the ill we have done as fear of that
which may come to us.
 LA ROCHEFOUCAULD.—*Maxim* 180.

Without any snivelling signs of contri-
tion or repentance.
 GEO. LORD LYTTELTON.—*Dialogues of
 the Dead.*

How shall I lose the sin, yet keep the
 sense,
And love the offender, yet detest the
 offence? POPE.—*Eloisa,* 189.

He who repents having sinned is almost
innocent. SENECA.—*Agamemnon.*

Try what repentance can; what can it
 not?
Yet what can it, when one can not repent?
 SHAKESPEARE.—*Hamlet,* Act 3, 3.

Repentance for past crimes is just and
 easy;
But Sin no more's a task too hard for
 mortals.
SIR J. VANBRUGH.—*The Relapse,* Act 5, 4.

Bring forth therefore fruits worthy of
repentance. *St. Luke* iii, 8.

Repentance is good, but innocence better.
 Prov.

REPETITION

That is never said too often which is
never learnt sufficiently. SENECA.

Repetition is the soul of journalism.
 *Maxim attrib. to Thos. Barnes, editor of
 " The Times,"* 1817-1841.

REPLY

At length the fateful answer came.
 SCOTT.—*Lady of the Lake, c.* 4, 6.

But answer made it none.
 SHAKESPEARE.—*Hamlet,* Act 1, 2.

REPORT

Such difference is there in an oft-told tale;
But Truth, by its own sinews, will prevail.
 DRYDEN.—*Religio Laici,* 348.

He's gone, and who knows how he may
 report
Thy words by adding fuel to the flame.
 MILTON.—*Samson Agonistes,* 1350.

When I did well, I heard it never;
When I did ill, I heard it ever.
 Old Saying.

REPOSE

When you cannot find your repose in
yourself, it is useless to look for it elsewhere.
 LA ROCHEFOUCAULD.—*Maxim* 513.

Repose is the especial and separating
characteristic of the eternal mind and
power.
 RUSKIN.—*Modern Painters, Vol.* 2,
 sec. 1, *ch.* 3, 1.

No work of art can be great without it
[repose]. RUSKIN.—*Ib., sec.* 2, *ch.* 3, 5.

The best of men have ever loved repose.
 THOMSON.—*Castle of Indolence,* 1, 17.

The universal instinct of repose,
The longing for confirmed tranquillity,
Inward and outward, humble yet sublime;
The life where hope and memory are as one.
 WORDSWORTH.—*Excursion, Bk.* 3 (*the
 fourth line is described by Ruskin as
 " the beautiful line which describes a
 perfectly happy life "*).

REPROACH AND REPROOF

Reproach cuts deeper than the keenest
 sword
And cleaves my heart.
 CONGREVE.—*Mourning Bride,* Act 4, 1.

Those best can bear reproof who merit
 praise. POPE.—*Criticism,* 583.

A countenance more
In sorrow than in anger.
 SHAKESPEARE.—*Hamlet,* Act 1, 2.

I will speak daggers to her, but use none.
 SHAKESPEARE.—*Ib.,* Act 3, 2.

I must be cruel, only to be kind.
 SHAKESPEARE.—*Ib.,* Act 3, 4.

Thou stick'st a dagger into me.
SHAKESPEARE.—*Merchant of Venice,*
Act 3, 1.

Speak not of my debts unless you mean
to pay them.   *Prov. (Geo. Herbert).*

REPUBLICS

The Republican form of government is
the highest form of government ; but because of this it requires the highest type
of human nature—a type nowhere at
present existing.
HERBT. SPENCER.—*The Americans.*

REPUDIATION

Thou canst not say I did it ; never shake
Thy gory locks at me.
SHAKESPEARE.—*Macbeth,* Act 3, 4.

Let him be Anathema.
1 *Corinthians* xvi, 22.

REPUTATION

For my name and memory I leave it
to men's charitable speeches, and to
foreign nations, and the next ages.
BACON.—*Will.*

It is a maxim with me that no man was
ever written out of reputation but by himself.   BENTLEY.—*Monk's " Life."*

Every man ought to do his diligence and
his business to get him a good name.
CHAUCER.—*Tale of Melibeus, sec.* 77.

Glasses that are cracked are soon
broken. Such is man's good name, once
tainted with just reproach. BISHOP HALL.

How many people live on the reputation
of the reputation they might have made !
O. W. HOLMES.—*Autocrat, ch.* 3.

I am now past the craggy paths of
study, and come to the flowery plains of
honour and reputation.
BEN JONSON.—*Volpone,* Act 2, 2.

If I can preserve my good name I shall
be rich enough. PLAUTUS.—*Mostellaria.*

I would thou and I knew where a com-
modity of good names were to be bought !
SHAKESPEARE.—*Henry IV.,* Pt. 1, Act 1, 2.

Reputation, reputation, reputation ! O,
I have lost my reputation ! I have lost
the immortal part of myself, and what
remains is bestial.
SHAKESPEARE.—*Othello,* Act 2, 3.

Good name in man or woman, dear my
lord,
Is the immediate jewel of their souls.
SHAKESPEARE.—*Ib.,* Act 3, 3.

Who steals my purse, steals trash ; 'tis
something, nothing ;
'Twas mine, 'tis his, and has been slave
to thousands ;

But he that filches from me my good name,
Robs me of that which not enriches him,
And makes me poor indeed.
SHAKESPEARE.—*Ib.,* Act 3, 3.

The purest treasure mortal times afford
Is spotless reputation ; that away,
Men are but gilded loam or painted clay.
SHAKESPEARE.—*Richard II.,* Act 1, 1.

Gain accompanied by ill report may be
called loss.   PUBLIIUS SYRUS.

To an upright man a good reputation
is the greatest inheritance.   *Ib.*

No one ever loses credit excepting he
who has it not.   *Ib.*

A good report
Makes men live long, although their life be
short.   R. WATKYNS.—*Flamma sine*
Fumo : A Good Report.

Who swerves from innocence, who makes
divorce
Of that serene companion, a good name,
Recovers not his loss ; but walks with
shame,
With doubt, with fear, and haply with
remorse.
WORDSWORTH.—*River Duddon,* 30.

A good name is better than precious
ointment.   *Ecclesiastes* vii, 1.

It is not as thy mother says, but as thy
neighbours say.   *Hebrew prov.*

RESEARCH

Those hateful persons called Original
Researchers.   SIR J. M. BARRIE.—*My*
Lady Nicotine, ch. 14.

As none by travelling over known lands
can find out the unknown, so from already
acquired knowledge man could not acquire
more.
WM. BLAKE.—*There is no Natural Religion.*

That like an intellectual magnet stone
Drew truth from judgments simpler than
his own.
CAMPBELL.—*Pilgrim of Glencoe.*

Under every deep a lower depth opens.
EMERSON.—*Circles.*

We are all richer for the measurement
of a degree of latitude on the earth's
surface.
EMERSON.—*Conduct of Life : Wealth.*

Nothing's so hard but search will find it
out.   HERRICK.—*(From Terence.)*

From such-like thoughts I mighty pleasure
find,
And silently admire thy strength of Mind ;
By whose one single force, to curious eyes,
All naked and exposed whole Nature lies.
LUCRETIUS.—*De Rerum Natura,* 3, 28
(Creech tr.).

The universe is full of magical things patiently waiting for our wits to grow sharper.
EDEN PHILPOTTS.—*A Shadow Passes.*

Science moves but slowly, slowly, creeping on from point to point.
TENNYSON.—*Locksley Hall.*

The intellectual power, through words and things,
Went sounding on, a dim and perilous way.
WORDSWORTH.—*Excursion, Bk. 3.*

Be mine to follow with no timid step
Where knowledge leads me ; it shall be my pride
That I have dared to tread this holy ground.
WORDSWORTH.—*Postscript (to Preface)* (1835).

RESEMBLANCE

Who drives fat oxen should himself be fat.   JOHNSON.—*Parody.*

For one of us was born a twin ;
And not a soul knew which.
H. S. LEIGH.—*Twins.*

Very like a whale.
SHAKESPEARE.—*Hamlet*, Act 3, 2.

Like—but oh, how different !
WORDSWORTH.—*Mountain Echo.*

RESENTMENTS

Resentment gratifies him who intended an injury, and pains him unjustly who did not intend it.
JOHNSON.—*Boswell's " Life."*

What a fool
An injury may make of a staid man !
KEATS.—*Otho*, Act 3, 1.

Men are grateful in the same degree as they are resentful.
POPE.—*Thoughts on Various Subjects.*

Nature seemed to have done with her resentments in him :—he showed none.
STERNE.—*Sent. Journey : The Monk.*

RESIGNATION

I needs must bear
My destiny as best I may, knowing well
The might resistless of Necessity.
ÆSCHYLUS.—*Prometheus*, 103 (*Plumptre tr.*).

Thy will be done, though in my own undoing.   SIR T. BROWNE.—*Religio Medici, Pt. 2, sec. 15.*

Not as we wanted it,
But as God granted it.
SIR A. T. QUILLER COUCH.—*To Bearers.*

Just as a bird, that flies about
And beats itself against the cage,
Finding at last no passage out,
It sits and sings and so o'ercomes its rage.
COWLEY.—*Friendship in Absence.*

That which cannot be repaired is not to be regretted.   JOHNSON.—*Rasselas, ch. 4.*

Let us be patient ! These severe afflictions
Not from the ground arise,
But oftentimes celestial benedictions
Assume this dark disguise.
LONGFELLOW.—*By the Fireside, Resignation.*

Come wealth or want, come good or ill,
Let young and old accept their part,
And bow before the awful Will,
And bear it with an honest heart.
THACKERAY.

RESOLUTION

Tender-handed stroke a nettle,
And it stings you for your pains ;
Grasp it like a man of mettle
And it soft as silk remains.
'Tis the same with common natures ;
Use 'em kindly, they rebel ;
But be rough as nutmeg-graters,
And the rogues obey you well.
AARON HILL.—*On a Window.*

My resolution's placed, and I have nothing
Of woman in me : now from head to foot
I am marble-constant.
SHAKESPEARE.—*Antony and Cleopatra,* Act 5, 2.

The native hue of resolution
Is sicklied o'er with the pale cast of thought ;
And enterprises of great pith and moment,
With this regard, their currents turn awry,
And lose the name of action.
SHAKESPEARE.—*Hamlet*, Act 3, 1.

We said on that first day, we said and swore
That self should be no more,
That we were risen, that we would wholly be
For love and liberty ;
And in the exhilaration of that oath
We cast off spite and sloth,
And laboured for an hour, till we began,
Man after piteous man,
To lose the splendour, to forget the dream.
EDWD. SHANKS.—*Meditation in June,* 1917.

Set thy sails warily,
Tempests will come ;
Steer thy course steadily ;
Christian, steer home !
MRS. SOUTHEY (*née* BOWLES).— *Mariner's Hymn.*

RESOURCEFULNESS

'Tis good in every case, you know,
To have two strings unto our bow.
CHURCHILL.—*The Ghost, Bk. 4, 1282.*

Presence of mind and courage in distress
Are more than armies to procure success.
    DRYDEN.—*Aurengzebe*, Act 2.

The mouse that always trusts to one poor
    hole,
Can never be a mouse of any soul.
    POPE.—*Wife of Bath, Prologue*, 298.

RESPECTABILITY

Since when was genius found respectable ?
    E. B. BROWNING.—*Aurora Leigh, Bk.* 6.

The devil's most devilish when respectable.
    E. B. BROWNING.—*Ib., Bk.* 7.

The honest witness who said, " I always
thought him a respectable man ; he kept
his gig," would probably not have admitted in direct terms that every man who
keeps a gig must be respectable.
    DE MORGAN.—*Formal Logic,*
        ch. 20.

And wheresoever he appeared,
Full twenty times was Peter feared
For once he was respected.
    WORDSWORTH.—*Peter Bell, Pt.* 1, 3.

Respect yourself, or no one else will.
    Prov. Founded on Greek precept of the
        Pythagoreans.

RESPITE

A short delay is all I ask him now—
A pause of grief, an interval of woe.
    VIRGIL.—*Æneid, Bk.* 4 (*Dryden tr.*).

RESPONSIBILITY

He who has been wont to pronounce
so fluently upon the defects of another's
rule and management, finds, when in power
himself, what a different thing it is to act
and to talk. His rash and heated judgment is all at once sobered by the weight
of responsibility.
    SIR A. HELPS.—*Friends in Council,*
        Bk. 2, *ch.* 2.

Whenever I met with a boy particularly
mischievous, I made him a monitor. I
never knew this to fail.
    J. LANCASTER.—*As quoted by Sydney*
        Smith, Lecture No. 22 (1805).

The plea of ignorance will never take
away our responsibilities.
    RUSKIN.—*Lectures on Architecture and*
        Painting.

I differ from my king in this alone—
He hath ten thousand masters ; I have
    one.
Paraphr. of Euripides (D. W. THOMPSON).

REST

The end and the reward of toil is rest.
    BEATTIE.—*The Minstrel, Bk.* 2, 16.

Of all the thoughts of God that are
Borne inward into souls afar,
Along the Psalmist's music deep,
Now tell me if that any is,
For gift or grace surpassing this,—
" He giveth His beloved sleep " ?
    E. B. BROWNING.—*Sleep.*

O earth, so full of dreary noises !
O men, with wailing in your voices !
O delvèd gold, the wailers heap !
O strife, O curse, that o'er it fall !
God strikes a silence through you all,
And giveth His beloved sleep.
    E. B. BROWNING.—*Ib.*

Rest comes at length, though life be long
    and dreary ;
The day must dawn and darksome night
    be passed.   F. W. FABER.—*Hymn.*

His listless length at noontide would he
    stretch,
And pore upon the brook that babbles
    by.
    GRAY.—*Elegy in a Country Churchyard.*

We wish him health : he sighs for rest,
And Heaven accepts the prayer.
    KEBLE.—*Restoration.*

Once long ago, as you, with hollow pursuit
    of fame,
We filled all the shaking world with the
    sound of our name ;
But now we are glad to rest, our battles
    and boasting done,
Glad just to sow and sing and reap in our
    share of the sun.
    R. LE GALLIENNE.—*The Little Peoples.*

Come rest in this bosom, my own stricken
    deer,
Though the herd have fled from thee, thy
    love is still here.
    MOORE.—*Come rest in this bosom.*

        Weariness
Can snore upon the flint, when resty sloth
Finds the down pillow hard.
    SHAKESPEARE.—*Cymbeline*, Act 3, 6.

Rest, rest, perturbèd spirit.
    SHAKESPEARE.—*Hamlet*, Act 1, 5.

So may he rest ! His faults lie gently on
    him !
    SHAKESPEARE.—*Henry VIII.*, Act 4, 2.

Some respite to its turbulence unresting
    ocean knows ;
Whatever moves, or toils, or grieves, hath
    its appointed sleep.
    SHELLEY.—*Stanzas*, 1814.

Sleepe after toyle, port after stormie seas,
Ease after warre, death after life, does
    greatly please.
    SPENSER.—*Faerie Queene, Bk.* 1, *c.* 9, 40.

If rest is sweet at shut of day
  For tirèd hands and tirèd feet,
How sweet at last to rest for aye,
  If rest is sweet.
    ARTHUR SYMONS.—*Roundel of Rest.*

And after toilsome days a soft repose
  at night.
    VIRGIL.—*Georgics, Bk.* 2 *(Dryden tr.).*

Repose is a good thing, but boredom is
its brother.   VOLTAIRE.

What hadst thou that could make such
    large amends
For all thou hadst not, and thy peers
    possessed,
Motion and fire, swift means to radiant
    ends ?
Thou hadst, for weary feet, the gift of
    rest.
    SIR W. WATSON.—*Wordsworth's Grave.*

To tired limbs and over-busy thoughts
Inviting sleep and soft forgetfulness.
    WORDSWORTH.—*Excursion, Bk.* 4.

O that I had wings like a dove, for then
would I flee away, and be at rest.
    Church Psalter, Ps. cv, 6.

They rest from their labours.
    Common Prayer, Burial Service.

RESTLESSNESS

Thus every man is troubled with unrest,
From rich to poor, from high to low
    degree.
    R. BARNFIELD.—*Shepherd's Complaint.*

He who dwells everywhere, never dwells
anywhere. MARTIAL.—*Epig., Bk.* 7, 72, 6.

So, when a raging fever burns,
We shift from side to side by turns ;
And 'tis a poor relief we gain,
To change the place, but keep the pain.
    ISAAC WATTS.—*Hymns, Bk.* 2, 146.

RESTRAINT

Restraint from ill is freedom to the wise ;
But Englishmen do all restraint despise.
    DEFOE.—*True-Born Englishman,*
                        Pt. 2, 206.

But now I am cabined, cribbed, confined, bound in.
    SHAKESPEARE.—*Macbeth,* Act 3, 4.

There are four things that keep us all
    from having our own way :
Money, Fortune, Mrs. Grundy, and
    Policeman A.
    D. W. THOMPSON.—*Paraphr. of*
                        Euripides.

RESULTS

O fate of fools ! officious in contriving ;
In executing puzzled, lame, and lost.
    CONGREVE.—*Mourning Bride,* Act 5, 1

It is the end that crowns us, not the
fight. HERRICK.—*Hesperides,* 309.

The mountains are in labour ; a ridiculous mouse is produced.
    HORACE.—*De Arte Poetica.*

The mountain was in labour, and Jove
was afraid, but it brought forth a mouse.
    TACHOS, KING OF EGYPT.—*Quoted by*
        Athenæus. Deipn., 14, 7.

The Fates are just : they give us but our
    own ;
Nemesis ripens what our hands have
    sown. WHITTIER.—*To a Southern*
                        Statesman, 1864.

And he looked that it should bring forth
grapes, and it brought forth wild grapes.
                        Isaiah v, 2.

He who sows thorns will not gather
grapes with them.   *Arabic proverb.*

One ploughs, another sows ;
Who will reap no-one knows.
                        Old Saying.

RETALIATION

For time at last sets all things even—
  And if we do but watch the hour,
There never yet was human power
  Which could evade, if unforgiven,
The patient search and vigil long
  Of him who treasures up a wrong.
    BYRON.—*Mazeppa, st.* 10.

Nor should the individual, who happens
    to be meant.
Reply by heaving rocks at him to any
    great extent.
    BRET HARTE.—*Society upon the Stanislaus.*

Wisdom has taught us to be calm and
    meek,
To take one blow, and turn the other
    cheek ;
It is not written what a man shall do,
If the rude caitiff smite the other too.
    O. W. HOLMES.—*Non-Resistance.*

" Now we are even," quoth Stephen,
when he gave his wife six blows for one.
    SWIFT.—*Letter, Jan.* 20, 1711.

RETICENCE

Oh ! no ! we never mention her,
  Her name is never heard ;
My lips are now forbid to speak
  That once familiar word.
    T. H. BAYLY.—*Song.*

All things to all men only fools will tell ;
Truth profits none but those that use it
well. J. S. BLACKIE.—*Wise Men of*
                        Greece.

The first of virtues is to restrain the
tongue ; he is nearest God who knows the
rule of silence. DION. CATO.—*Dist.,* 1, 3.

My son, keep wel thy tonge and keep thy
    friend.   CHAUCER.—*Manciple's Tale.*

The first vertu, sone, if thou wolt lere
    [learn],
Is to restreyne and kepè wel thy tonge.
                         CHAUCER.—*Ib.*

Be wary, and slow to give your confidence.   This is the backbone of the mind's
strength.
        EPICHARMUS.—*Ahreus de Dialecto
                     Dorica,* 119.

He [Klopstock] had another peculiarity
of men of the world—namely, not readily
to speak on subjects upon which he was
particularly desired and expected to discourse.   GOETHE.—*Autob., Bk.* 15.

No never say nothin' without you're com-
    pelled tu,
An' then don't say nothin' thet you can
    be held tu.   J. R. LOWELL.—*Biglow
          Papers, 2nd Series, No.* 5.

'Aig [F.-M. Sir Douglas Haig] 'e don't
say much ; 'e don't, so to say, say nothin' ;
but what 'e don't say don't mean nothin',
not 'arf.   But when 'e do say something
—my Gawd !
      E. V. LUCAS.—*Boswell of Baghdad.*

O have a care of natures that are mute !
    GEO. MEREDITH.—*Modern Love, st.* 35.

Slave is the open mouth beneath the
    closed.
    GEO. MEREDITH.—*Sage Enamoured,* 4.

Nature has given every man two ears
and but one tongue, as a secret intimation
that he ought to speak less than he hears.
    PLUTARCH.—*Of Hearing (quoted as
                   a saying).*

Simonides said that it never repented
him that he had held his tongue, but often
that he had spoken.
        PLUTARCH.—*Morals, Bk.* 1.

Forbear to mention what thou canst
not praise. PRIOR.—*Carmen Seculare,* 106.

Give every man thine ear, but few thy
    voice ;
Take each man's censure, but reserve thy
    judgment.
       SHAKESPEARE.—*Hamlet,* Act 1, 3.

But ye, keep ye on earth
Your lips from over-speech ;
Loud words and longing are so little
    worth,
And the end is hard to reach :
For silence after grievous things is good,
    And reverence, and the fear that makes
    men whole,
And shame, and righteous government of
    blood,
And lordship of the soul.
          SWINBURNE.—*Atalanta.*

Fear oftentimes restraineth words,
    But makes not thought to cease ;
And he speaks best that hath the skill
    When for to hold his peace.
    THOS. LORD VAUX.—*A Contented Mind.*

And I oft have heard defended,
    Little said is soonest mended.
      G. WITHER.—*Shepherd's Hunting.*

This modest charm of not too much,
Part seen, imagined part.
         WORDSWORTH.—*To May.*

God is in heaven, and thou upon earth :
therefore let thy words be few.
                Ecclesiastes v, 2.

Open not thine heart to every man.
          Ecclesiasticus viii, 19.

A man that hideth his foolishness is
better than a man that hideth his wisdom.
          Ecclesiasticus xli, 15.

Even a fool, when he holdeth his peace,
is counted wise.   *Proverbs* xvii, 28.

There's twa things in my mind and that's
the least of them.   *Scottish prov.*

RETIREMENT

For he that lives retired in mind and spirit
Is still in Paradise.
    BEAUMONT AND FLETCHER.—*Nice
                    Valour,* Act 5, 2.

A quiet life, which was not life at all.
  E. B. BROWNING.—*Aurora Leigh, Bk.* 1.

May I a small house and large garden
    have !
And a few friends, and many books, both
    true.   COWLEY.—*The Prophet.*

         A mind released
From anxious thoughts how wealth may
    be increased.
        COWPER.—*Retirement,* 139.

The disencumbered Atlas of the state.
          COWPER.—*Ib.,* 394.

Oh for a lodge in some vast wilderness,
Some boundless contiguity of shade !
        COWPER.—*Time Piece,* 1.

Where from all rude resort he happily doth
    dwell.
      DRAYTON.—*Polyolbion, Song* 13.

They saw the happiness of a private life,
but they deferred it. . . . Put them to the
necessity of a present choice and they preferred continuance in power ; like the
wretch who called Death to his assistance,
but refused him when he came.
      DRYDEN.—*Dedication to Georgics.*

A foundation of good sense and a cultivation of learning are required to give a seasoning to retirement and make us taste the blessing.
DRYDEN.—*Dedication to Georgics.*

How blessed is he who leads a country life,
Unvexed with anxious cares, and void of strife !
Who, studying peace, and shunning civil rage,
Enjoyed his youth, and now enjoys his age.   DRYDEN.—*To J. Dryden.*

How blest is he who crowns in shades like these
A youth of labour with an age of ease.
GOLDSMITH.—*Deserted Village.*

Far from the madding crowd's ignoble strife ;
Their sober wishes never learned to stray ;
Along the cool sequestered vale of life
They kept the noiseless tenour of their way.   GRAY.—*Elegy.*

There bounteous Nature makes supplies for ease ;
There minds enjoy an undisturbèd peace
LUCRETIUS.—3, 18 (*Creech tr.*).

Not, like a cloistered drone, to read and doze,
In undeserving, undeserved repose.
GEO. LORD LYTTELTON.—*To Dr. Ayscough.*

For solitude sometimes is best society,
And short retirement urges sweet return.
MILTON.—*Paradise Lost, Bk.* 9, 249.

His life,
Private, unactive, calm, contemplative.
MILTON.—*Paradise Regained, Bk.* 2, 80.

How happy is the blameless Vestal's lot !
The world forgetting, by the world forgot.
POPE.—*Eloisa,* 207.

Happy the man whose wish and care
A few paternal acres bound,
Content to breathe his native air
In his own ground.
POPE.—*Solitude.*

Farewell ! Othello's occupation's gone.
SHAKESPEARE.—*Othello,* Act 3, 3.

Thus in a sea of folly tossed,
My choicest hours of life are lost,
Yet always wishing to retreat—
O, could I see my country seat !
There, leaning near a gentle brook,
Sleep, or peruse some ancient book ;
And there in sweet oblivion drown
Those cares that haunt the court and town.   SWIFT.—*Imit. of Horace,
Sat., Bk.* 2, 6.

I built my soul a lordly pleasure-house,
Wherein at ease for aye to dwell.
TENNYSON.—*Palace of Art.*

How dull it is to pause, to make an end
To rust unburnished, not to shine in use !
TENNYSON.—*Ulysses.*

The best of men have ever loved repose ;
They hate to mingle in the filthy fray.
THOMSON.—*Castle of Indolence,
c.* 1, *st.* 17.

Nor pompous cares nor palaces he knew,
But wisely from the infectious world withdrew.
VIRGIL.—*Æneid, Bk.* 12 (*Dryden tr.*)
(*of Menœtes, the fisherman*).

One must cultivate letters or one's garden.
VOLTAIRE.—*Letter to D'Alembert,
July* 14, 1773.

It is good at last to live for one's self,
and to know how to leave the world which leaves us.   VOLTAIRE.—*To Mme. Denis.*

He is retired as noontide dew,
Or fountain in a noonday grove ;
And you must love him, ere to you
He will seem worthy of your love.
WORDSWORTH.—*A Poet's Epitaph.*

To you
The remnant of his days at least was true ;
You whom, though long deserted, he loved best ;
You,—muses, books, fields, liberty and rest !
WORDSWORTH.—*Liberty (of Cowley*).

And thou henceforth wilt have a good man's calm,
A great man's happiness. Thy zeal shall find
Repose at length, firm friend of human kind !
WORDSWORTH.—*Poems to National Indep.,
Pt.* 2, 3 (*to Thos. Clarkson*).

Where good men, disappointed in the quest
Of wealth and power and honours, long for rest ;
Or having known the splendours of success,
Sigh for the obscurities of happiness.
WORDSWORTH.—*Evening Voluntaries,* 10.

RETREAT

Our backward march,
After our wars unhurt, unsuffering led
Our prospering armies home.
ÆSCHYLUS.—*Persæ,* 868 (*Plumptre tr.*).

In all the trade of war no feat
Is nobler than a brave retreat ;
For those that run away and fly,
Take place at least o' the enemy.
BUTLER.—*Hudibras, Pt.* 1, *c.* 3.

For those that fly may fight again,
Which he can never do that's slain.
BUTLER.—*Ib., Pt.* 3, *c.* 3.

He who fights and runs away
May live to fight another day ;
But he who is in battle slain
Can never rise to fight again.
GOLDSMITH.—*Art of Poetry.*

We're driven back for our next fray
A newer strength to borrow,
And where the vanguard camps to-day,
The rear shall rest to-morrow.
GERALD MASSEY.—*Song.*

He that fights and runs away,
May turn and fight another day ;
But he that is in battle slain
Will never rise to fight again.
ANON.—*As quoted in Ray's Hist.
of the Rebellion* (1752).

The man who flies shall fight again.
Greek. Attrib. to Demosthenes.

RETRIBUTION

They therefore, having wrought
Deeds evil, now are suffering, and will
suffer
Evil not less ; and not as yet is seen
E'en the bare groundwork of the ills, but
still
They grow up to completeness.
ÆSCHYLUS.—*Persæ*, 817 (*Plumptre tr.*).

Take courage, then ;
In their own time, and at the appointed
day,
Whoever slights the Gods shall pay for it.
ÆSCHYLUS.—*Suppliants*, 732
(*Plumptre tr.*).

Long trains of ill may pass unheeded,
dumb,
But vengeance is behind and justice is to
come. CAMPBELL.—*Spanish Patriots.*

Justice conquers evermore,
Justice after as before,—
And he who battles on her side,
God, though he were ten times slain,
Crowns him victor glorified.
EMERSON.—*Voluntaries, No. 4.*

The man recovered of the bite,
The dog it was that died.
GOLDSMITH.—*Mad Dog.*

And well he merited the death he found ;
So perish all who shall like him offend !
HOMER.—*Odyssey, Bk.* 1, 44 (*Cowper tr.*)
(*Pallas, of the death of Ægisthus*).

For agony and spoil
Of nations beat to dust,
For poisoned air and tortured soil
And cold, commanded lust,
And every secret woe
The shuddering waters saw—
Willed and fulfilled by high and low—
Let them relearn the Law.
RUDYARD KIPLING.—*Justice
(Oct.* 24, 1918).

Though the mills of God grind slowly, yet
they grind exceeding small ;
Though with patience he stands waiting,
with exactness grinds he all.
LONGFELLOW.—*Fr. the German.*

The gods are just, and of our pleasant vices
Make instruments to plague us.*
SHAKESPEARE.—*King Lear*, Act 5, 3.

And though the villain 'scape awhile, he
feels
Slow vengeance, like a bloodhound, at his
heels. SWIFT.—*Horace, Bk.* 3, 2.

And though circuitous and obscure
The feet of Nemesis how sure !
SIR W. WATSON.—*Europe at the
Play*, 33.

The gathering blackness of the frown of
God.
SIR W. WATSON.—*Turk in Armenia.*

For they have sown the wind, and they
shall reap the whirlwind. *Hosea* viii, 7.

The good you will do by your death will
somewhat balance the evils of your life.
ANON.—*Pref. to "Killing no Murder,"
addressed to Cromwell.*

RETROSPECT

Ah ! happy years ! once more who would
not be a boy ?
BYRON.—*Childe Harold, c.* 2, 23.

What peaceful hours I once enjoyed !
How sweet their memory still !
But they have left an aching void,
The world can never fill.
COWPER.—*Hymn.*

The present scene, the future lot,
His toils, his wants, were all forgot.
SCOTT.—*Lay of the Last Minstrel, Intro.*

When to the sessions of sweet silent
thought
I summon up remembrance of things past,
I sigh the lack of many a thing I sought.
SHAKESPEARE.—*Sonnet* 30.

As one
Who sits and gazes on a faded fire,
When all the goodlier guests are passed
away.
TENNYSON.—*Last Tournament*, 158

O, that our lives, which flee so fast,
In purity were such,
That not an image of the past
Should fear that pencil's touch.
WORDSWORTH.—*Memory.*

RETURN

Will you no come back again ?
Will you no come back again ?
Better lo'ed you'll never be,
And will you no come back again ?
ANON.—*Jacobite Song.*

*"Scourge" instead of "plague" in the quarto
editions.

And now will I to home and household
   hearth
Move on, and first give thanks unto the
   Gods,
Who led me forth and brought me back
   again.   ÆSCHYLUS.—*Agamemnon*,
                        851 (*Plumptre tr.*).

The men will cheer, the boys will shout,
The ladies they will all turn out,
And we'll all feel gay when Johnny comes
   marching home.   ANON.—*Song.*

RE-UNION

O thou soul of my soul! I shall clasp
   thee again,
And with God be the rest.
              BROWNING.—*Prospice.*

And doth not a meeting like this make
   amends
For all the long years I've been wandering
   away?   MOORE.—*Irish Melodies.*

And with the morn those angel faces smile,
Which I have loved long since and lost
   awhile.
   CARD. NEWMAN.—*Pillar of Cloud.*

When shall we three meet again,
In thunder, lightning, or in rain?
   SHAKESPEARE.—*Macbeth*, Act 1, 1.

REVELRY

There was a sound of revelry by night.
   BYRON.—*Childe Harold, c.* 3, 21.

So no more we'll go a roving
   So late into the night.
              BYRON.—*Song.*

He lovèd bet [better] the taverne than the
   shop.   CHAUCER.—*Cook's Tale.* 12.

Midnight Shout and Revelry,
Tipsy Dance, and Jollity.
         MILTON.—*Comus*, 103.
              And when night
Darkens the streets, then wander forth
   the sons
Of Belial, flown with insolence and wine.
   MILTON.—*Paradise Lost, Bk.* 1, 500.

Fly not yet; 'tis just the hour
When pleasure, like the midnight flower,
That scorns the eye of vulgar light,
Begins to bloom for sons of night,
   And maids who love the moon.
              MOORE.—*Fly not yet.*

What were revel without wine?
What were wine without a song?
   STEPHEN PHILLIPS.—*Ulysses*, Act 3, 2.

REVENGE

The best way of revenge is to avoid
imitating the injury.
   MARCUS AURELIUS.—*Bk.* 6, 6.

Revenge is a kind of wild justice.
              BACON.—*Revenge.*

A man that studieth revenge keeps his
own wounds green.   BACON.—*Ib.*

No animal revenge,
No brute-like punishment of bad by worse.
              BROWNING.—*Luria.*

Sweet is revenge—especially to women.
   BYRON.—*Don Juan, c.* 1, 124.

And their revenge is as the tiger's spring,
Deadly and quick and crushing.
              BYRON.—*Ib.*, 2, 199.

Feeble spirits only vaunt
Of revenge, the poorest pride.
              CAMPION.—*Wise Men.*

At last a time for just revenge is given;
Revenge, the darling attribute of heaven!
   DRYDEN.—*Spanish Friar*, Act 4, 2.

Revenge proves its own executioner.
   FORD.—*Broken Heart*, Act 4, 1.

Revenge is profitable, gratitude is expensive.   GIBBON.—*Decline and Fall,*
                                   ch. 11.

Revenge, that thirsty dropsy of our souls,
Which makes us covet that which hurts
   us most.
   MASSINGER.—*Very Woman*, Act 4, 2.

Now Vengeance has a brood of eggs,
But Patience must be hen.
   GEO. MEREDITH.—*Archduchess Anne,*
                                   st. 12.

Which, if not victory, is yet revenge.
   MILTON.—*Paradise Lost, Bk.* 2, 105.

Revenge, at first, though sweet—
Bitter ere long, back on itself recoils.
   MILTON.—*Ib.*, Bk. 9, 179.

It is not right to return an injury or to
do evil to any man, however one may
have suffered from him.
   PLATO.—*Crito*, 10 (*Cary tr.*).

Where there is much pride or self-conceit there will be a great desire for revenge.
   SCHOPENHAUER.—*Psychological*
                                   Observations.

Vengeance, deep-brooding o'er the slain,
   Had locked the source of softer woe;
And burning pride, and high disdain
   Forbade the rising tear to flow.
   SCOTT.—*Lay of the Last Minstrel*, 1, 9.

Revenge is a confession of pain.
              SENECA.—*De Ira.*

If it will feed nothing else, it will feed
my revenge.
   SHAKESPEARE.—*Merchant of Venice,*
                                   Act 3, 1.

O that the slave had forty thousand lives !
One is too poor, too weak for my revenge.
SHAKESPEARE.—*Othello*, Act 3, 3.

Revenge is the naked idol of the worship
of a barbarous age.
SHELLEY.—*Defence of Poetry* (1821).

Thank God that I have lived to see the
time
When the great truth begins at last to
find
An utterance from the deep heart of
mankind,
Earnest and clear, that all Revenge is
Crime.   WHITTIER.—*Lines on the
Abolition of the Gallows*, 4, 1.

It costs more to revenge injuries than
to bear them.
BISHOP THOS. WILSON.—*Maxims*.

REVERENCE

Where'er we tread 'tis haunted holy
ground.
BYRON.—*Childe Harold*, c. 2, 88.

Kneeling ne'er spoilt silk stocking ; quit
thy state :
All equal are within the church's gate.
HERBERT.—*Church Porch*.

We English have many false ideas about
reverence : we should be shocked, for
instance, to see a market-woman come
into church with a basket of eggs on her
arm.   RUSKIN.—*Modern Painters*, 3,
Pt. 4, c. 10, 22.

Though mean and mighty, rotting
Together, have one dust ; yet reverence
(That angel of the world) doth make
distinction
Of place 'tween high and low.
SHAKESPEARE.—*Cymbeline*, Act 4, 2.

Let knowledge grow from more to more,
But more of reverence in us dwell ;
That mind and soul, according well,
May make one music as before.
TENNYSON.—*In Memoriam, Intro.*

All seem to feel the spirit of the place,
And by the general reverence God is
praised.
Profane Despoilers ! stand ye not re-
proved,
While thus these simple-hearted men are
moved ?
WORDSWORTH.—*Miscell. Sonnets*, 48.

REVERSES

Nay, list to me, and be not over-grieved,
Ye have not been defeated, but the cause
Came fairly to a tie. No shame to thee !
ÆSCHYLUS.—*Eumenides*, 794 (*Plumptre
tr.*) (*Minerva to the Furies, on the equal
division of the Gods respecting the punishment of Orestes*).

The fairest day must set in night ;
Summer in winter ends ;
So anguish still succeeds delight,
And grief our joy attends.
G. LILLO.—*Song from " Sylvia."*

Though fall'n on evil days,
On evil days though fall'n, and evil
tongues.
MILTON.—*Paradise Lost, Bk.* 7, 25.

Some natural tears they dropped, but
wiped them soon :
The world was all before them, where to
choose
Their place of rest, and Providence their
guide.   MILTON.—*Ib., Bk.* 12, 645.

In his own palace forced to ask his bread,
Scorned by those slaves his former bounties fed.   POPE.—*Argus*.

The way was long, the wind was cold,
The Minstrel was infirm and old ;
His withered cheek and tresses grey
Seemed to have known a better day.
SCOTT.—*Lay of the Last Minstrel, Intro.*

To what base uses we may return,
Horatio !
SHAKESPEARE.—*Hamlet*, Act 5, 1.

The third day comes a frost, a killing
frost ;
And—when he thinks, good easy man,
full surely
His greatness is a ripening,—nips his root,
And then he falls as I do.
SHAKESPEARE.—*Henry VIII.*, Act 3, 2.

But yesterday, the word of Cæsar might
Have stood against the world ; now, lies
he there,
And none so poor to do him reverence.
SHAKESPEARE.—*Julius Cæsar*, Act 3, 2.

Though his bark cannot be lost,
Yet it shall be tempest-tossed.
SHAKESPEARE.—*Macbeth*, Act 1, 3.

Take up this mangled matter at the best.
SHAKESPEARE.—*Othello*, Act 1, 3.

I see my glory, like a shooting star,
Fall to the base earth from the firmament.
SHAKESPEARE.—*Richard II.*, Act 2, 4.

All my merry jigs are quite forgot.
Attrib. to SHAKESPEARE.—*Passionate
Pilgrim, No.* 16.

And from the top of all my trust
Mishap hath thrown me in the dust.
Tottel's Collection (1557) (*attrib. to
John Harrington*).

REVOLT

Man is the genuine offspring of revolt.
COWPER.—*Hope*.

We'll cry both arts and learning down,
    And hey ! then up go we !
      QUARLES.—*Shepherd's Oracles.*

Ye gods, it doth amaze me,
A man of such a feeble temper should
So get the start of this majestic world,
And bear the palm alone.
    SHAKESPEARE.—*Julius Cæsar*, Act 1, 2.

What rights are his that dare not strike
    for them ?
    TENNYSON.—*Last Tournament*, 527.

REVOLUTION

Every revolution contains in it something of evil.
    BURKE.—*Appeal from New to Old Whigs.*

The first step to empire is revolution,
by which power is conferred.
    BURKE.—*Impeachment of Hastings*
                (*Feb.* 16, 1788).

Hope ushers in a Revolution,—as
earthquakes are preceded by bright
weather.   CARLYLE.—*French Revolution,*
                Pt. 1, Bk. 2, ch. 1.

They rose in dark and evil days
    To right their native land ;
They kindled here a living blaze
    That nothing shall withstand.
    J. K. INGRAM.—*Memory of the Dead.*

Who fears to speak of Ninety-Eight,
Who blushes at the name ?
When cowards mock the patriot's fate,
Who hangs his head for shame ?
    J. K. INGRAM.—*Song.*

It is not a revolt ; it is a revolution.
    DUC DE LIANCOURT.—*To Louis XVI.*
                (*July*, 1789).

Revolutions are not made with rose-
water.   (1st) LORD LYTTON.—*Parisians.*

One sharp, stern struggle, and the slaves
of centuries are free.
    G. MASSEY.—*Patriot, l.* 58.

Licence they mean when they cry Liberty ;
For who loves that, must first be wise and
good.
    MILTON.—*On the Detraction, etc.*

The children born of thee are sword and
    fire,
Red ruin, and the breaking up of laws.
    TENNYSON.—*Guinevere.*

Revolutions were always rapid.
    VOLTAIRE.—*Irène.*

    Alas ! of fearful things
'Tis the most fearful when the people's eye
Abuse hath cleared from vain imaginings,
And taught the general voice to prophesy
Of Justice armed, and Pride to be laid low.
WORDSWORTH.—*Eccles. Sonnets, Pt. 2,* 18.

And the more faithful were compelled to
    exclaim,
As Brutus did to Virtue, " Liberty,
I worshipped thee and find thee but a
    Shade."
    WORDSWORTH.—*Excursion, Bk.* 3
    (*referring to the French Revolution*).

REWARDS

'Tis an old lesson ; Time approves it true,
    And those who know it best deplore it
    most ;
When all is won that all desire to woo,
    The paltry prize is hardly worth the
    cost.
      BYRON.—*Childe Harold, c.* 2, 35.

The " wages " of every noble work do
yet lie in Heaven or else nowhere.
    CARLYLE.—*Past and Present, Bk.* 3, 12.

That is the ende why men should do
good works. For in the accomplissinge of
great good works lyeth the great guerdoun.
    CHAUCER.—*Parson's Tale, sec.* 61.

The consciousness of having done a
splendid action is itself a sufficient reward.
    CICERO.—*Phil.,* 2.

For blessings ever wait on virtuous deeds,
And though a late a sure reward succeeds.
    CONGREVE.—*Mourning Bride*, Act 5, 3.

What is vulgar, and the essence of all
vulgarity, but the avarice of reward ?
    EMERSON.—*Conduct of Life :*
                Worship.
The reward of a thing well done is to
have done it.
    EMERSON.—*New England Reformers.*

Since all must life resign,
    Those sweet rewards, which decorate
    the brave,
'Tis folly to decline,
    And steal inglorious to the silent grave.
    JOHNSON.—*Lines added to an Ode.*

The thirst for fame is greater than that
for virtue ; for who would embrace virtue
if you removed her rewards ?
    JUVENAL.—*Sat.*, 10, 140.

Ladies, whose bright eyes
Rain influence, and judge the prize
Of wit or arms.
    MILTON.—*L'Allegro*, 121.

Not easily will you find one man in many
thousands who considers that virtue is its
own reward.   OVID.—*Ep. ex Pont.*

No pain, no palm ; no thorns, no
throne ; no gall, no glory ; no cross, no
crown. WM. PENN.—*No Cross, No Crown.*

Solid pudding against empty praise.
    POPE.—*Dunciad, Bk.* 1, 54.

The champion then before Æneas came,
Proud of his prize, but prouder of his fame.
    VIRGIL.—*Æneid, Bk. 5 (Dryden tr.)*.

Be thou faithful unto death, and I will
give thee the crown of life.
    Revelation ii, 10 *(R.V.)*.

When the Captain comed for to hear on 't,
He werry much applauded her for what
    she'd done,
And quickly made her first lieutenant
Of the gallant Thunder-Bomb.
    Popular Song. Billy Taylor (c. 1824).

RHETORIC

Truth needs not the foil of rhetoric.
    MIDDLETON.—*Family of Love*,
    Act 5, 3.

Enjoy your dear wit and gay rhetoric,
That hath so well been taught her dazzling
fence.   MILTON.—*Comus*, 790.

These flowers of speech would be all
very well in a court of justice ; but in such
a conference as this why should you vainly
deck yourself with empty words ?
    PLATO.—*Laches, 26*.

Flowers of rhetoric, in sermons and
serious discourses, are like the blue and
red flowers in corn, pleasing to those who
come only for amusement, but prejudicial
to him who would reap the profit.
    POPE.—*Thoughts on Various Subjects*.

Touch. Truly, I would the gods had
made thee poetical.—*Aud.* I do not know
what poetical is : is it honest in deed and
word ? Is it a true thing ?
    SHAKESPEARE.—*As You Like It*, Act 3, 3.

I have always looked upon it as a high
point of indiscretion in monster-mongers
and other retailers of strange sights, to
hang out a fair large picture over the door,
drawn after the life, with a most eloquent
description underneath. This has saved
me many a threepence, for my curiosity
was fully satisfied.
    SWIFT.—*Tale of a Tub*.

RHINE

The wide and winding Rhine
Whose breast of waters broadly swells
    Between the banks which bear the vine,
And hills all rich with blossom'd trees,
    And fields which promise corn and wine,
And scatter'd cities crowning these,
    Whose far white walls along them shine.
    BYRON.—*Childe Harold, c. 3, st. 55*.

The river Rhine, it is well known,
Doth wash your city of Cologne ;
But tell me, Nymphs, what power divine
Shall henceforth wash the river Rhine ?
    COLERIDGE.—*Cologne*.

RHYME

For rhyme the rudder is of verses,
With which, like ships, they steer their
    courses.
    BUTLER.—*Hudibras, Pt. 1, c. 1*.

May he be damned who first found out
    that course
To imprison and confine his thoughts in
    verse ;
To hang so dull a clog upon his wit,
And make his reason to his rhyme submit.
    BUTLER.—*On Rhyme (tr. from Boileau)*.

He who can write well in rhyme may
write better in blank verse. Rhyme is
certainly a constraint even to the best
poets and those who make it with most
ease.   DRYDEN.—*Dedic. of Æneid*.

What it [rhyme] adds to sweetness it
takes away from sense.   DRYDEN.—*Ib*.

The troublesom and modern bondage
of Rimeing.
    MILTON.—*Pref. to Paradise Lost (1669)*

Rime being no necessary adjunct or true
ornament of Poem or good Verse, in longer
works especially, but the invention of a
barbarous age, to set off wretched matter
and lame Meeter.
    MILTON.—*Paradise Lost (Preface)*

He that writes in rhymes dances in
fetters.   PRIOR.—*Pref. to Solomon*.

I had rather be a kitten and cry mew,
Than one of these same metre ballad-
    mongers.
    SHAKESPEARE.—*Henry IV., Pt. 1, Act 3, 1*.

RIDICULE AND THE RIDICULOUS

    Nothing can confound
A wise man more than laughter from a
    dunce.
    BYRON.—*Don Juan, c. 16, st. 88*

On the day of resurrection, those who
have indulged in ridicule will be called to
the door of Paradise and have it shut in
their faces.   EMERSON.—*Social Aims*.

What provokes your risibility, sir ?
Have I said anything that you understand ? Then I ask the pardon of the
rest of the company.
    JOHNSON.—*Remark as recorded by*
    Rd. Cumberland.

From the sublime there is a descent
little by little to the ridiculous.
    LONGINUS.—*(Greek)*.

From the sublime to the ridiculous there
is only one step.
    NAPOLEON.—*Saying (attributed)*.

When we laugh at what is ridiculous in our friends, by mixing delight with envy we mingle pleasure and pain. For envy was long ago recognized as a pain to the soul, and laughter as a pleasure.
PLATO.—*Philebus*, 112.

All fools have still an itching to deride,
And still would be upon the laughing side.
POPE.—*Criticism*, 33.

The triumph of the mockers is of short duration. Truth endures, and their senseless laughter vanishes.
ROUSSEAU.—*Emile*.

There are very few who would not rather be hated than be laughed at.
SYDNEY SMITH.—*Lectures on Moral Philosophy, No.* 11.

I think there are not many things cheaper than supposing and laughing.
SWIFT.—*Sermon: On Sleeping in Church.*

As my method of reforming
Is by laughing, not by storming,
Would you have me change my style,
On your faults no longer smile,
But, to patch up all your quarrels,
Quote you texts from Plutarch's Morals ?
SWIFT.—*To a Lady.*

For still the world prevailed, and its dread laugh,
Which scarce the firm philosopher can scorn.
THOMSON.—*Seasons: Autumn*, 233.

I have always made one prayer to God, a very short one. Here it is : " My God, make our enemies very ridiculous ! " God has granted it to me.
VOLTAIRE.—*Letter to M. Damilaville, May* 16, 1767.

RIGHT

Be sure you are right. Then go ahead.
DAVID CROCKETT.
You may undo
Injustice by injustice, but the right
Can be established only by the right.
J. DAVIDSON.—*Self's the Man*, Act 3.

For aye Valerius loathed the wrong
And aye upheld the right.
MACAULAY.—*Battle of Lake Regillus*, st. 18.

England, on thy knees to-night,
Pray that God defend the right.
SIR H. NEWBOLT.—*Vigil.*

We find justice itself to be the best reward for the soul ; and that it ought to do what is just, whether or not it have Gyges' ring [which rendered him invisible and enabled him to kill the king of Lydia and marry the queen].
PLATO.—*Republic*, Bk. 10, 12.

If angels fight,
Weak men must fail ; for heaven still guards the right.
SHAKESPEARE.—*Richard II.*, Act 3, 2.

RIGHTEOUSNESS

Have all men hostile rather than the Gods.   ÆSCHYLUS.—*Choephoræ*, 901
(*Plumptre tr.*).

The rigid righteous is a fool,
The rigid wise another.
BURNS.—*To the Unco Guid.*

What is all righteousness that men devise ?
What, but a sordid bargain for the skies ?
COWPER.—*Truth*, 75.

" Oh let me die his death," all Nature cries.
" Then live his life."—All Nature falters there.   YOUNG.—*Night Thoughts*, 5.

I have been young, and now am old ; and yet saw I never the righteous forsaken, nor his seed begging their bread.
Psalter (Book of Common Prayer), 37, 25.

RIGHTS

" Natural rights " is simple nonsense ; " natural and imprescriptible rights," rhetorical nonsense,—nonsense upon stilts.
J. BENTHAM.—*Anarchical Fallacies* (*c.* 1791).

There is an Unconquerable in man, when he stands on his Rights of Man.
CARLYLE.—*French Revolution*, Pt. 3, Bk. 5, ch. 7.

RITUAL

Folly revived, refurbished sophistries,
And pullulating rites, externe and vain.
M. ARNOLD.—*Westminster Abbey.*

For me, I neither know nor care
Whether a parson ought to wear
A black dress or a white dress ;
I have a trouble of my own,
A wife who preaches in a gown
And lectures in a night-dress.
GEO. ROSE.

RIVALRY

Fool that I was ! upon my eagle's wings
I bore this wren, till I was tired with soaring,
And now he mounts above me.
DRYDEN.—*All for Love*, Act 2, 1.

Bombastes. So have I heard on Afric's burning shore
A hungry lion give a grievous roar ;
The grievous roar echoed along the shore.
King. So have I heard on Afric's burning shore
Another lion give a grievous roar,
And the first lion thought the last a bore !
W. B. RHODES.—*Bombastes.*

Two stars keep not their motion in one
  sphere.
SHAKESPEARE.—*Henry IV.*, Pt. 1, Act 5, 4.

RIVERS

And the thronged river toiling to the main.
  HARTLEY COLERIDGE.—*To a Friend.*
                              Sonnet.

Like thee, noble river, like thee,
Let our lives in beginning and ending,
  Fair in their gathering be,
And great in the time of their spending.
  ISA (CRAIG) KNOX.—*Thames.*

Rivers are roads which march, and carry
you where you wish to go.
  PASCAL.—*Pensées*, Pt. 1, 10, 38.

I chatter, chatter as I flow
  To join the brimming river,
For men may come and men may go,
  But I go on for ever.
          TENNYSON.—*The Brook.*

ROADS

This road is not passable.
  Not even jackassable.
  Attrib. to JESSE DOUGLASS (c.1840).

Had you seen these roads before they were
  made,
You'd lift up your eyes and bless General
  Wade.
  "*Inscription on a British Signpost,*"
    according to Miss Edgeworth, *Essay
    on Irish Bulls*, ch. 5.

The rule of the road is a paradox quite,
  Both in riding and driving along;
If you keep to the left, you are sure to be
  right,
If you keep to the right you are wrong;
But in walking the streets 'tis a different
  case,
To the right it is right you should bear,
Whereas to the left should be left enough
  space
For those whom you chance to meet
  there.   *Old Rhyme.*

ROBIN

Art thou the bird whom Man loves best,
The pious bird with the scarlet breast,
  Our little English Robin?
          .   .   .   .   .
The bird, who by some name or other ·
All men who know thee call their brother.
  WORDSWORTH.—*The Redbreast chasing
                      the Butterfly.*

ROCKS

The rocky summits, split and rent,
Formed turret, dome, or battlement,
Or seemed fantastically set
With cupola or minaret.
  SCOTT.—*Lady of the Lake*, 11.

ROGUES

"Ye're a vera clever chiel, man, but ye
wad be nane the waur o' a hanging."
  LORD BRAXFIELD.—"*To an eloquent
    culprit at the bar*" (*according to Sir
    W. Scott*).

For one rogue still suspects another,
Well knowing, by unerring rules,
Knaves starve not in the land of fools.
  CHURCHILL.—*The Ghost*, Bk. 2, 293.

A rogue is a roundabout fool.
  COLERIDGE.—*Table Talk.*

Such was the power of habit over these
illustrious persons that Mr. Wild could
not keep his hands out of the Count's
pockets, though he knew they were
empty; nor could the Count abstain from
palming a card, though he was well aware
Mr. Wild had no money to pay him.
  FIELDING.—*Jonathan Wild.*

I'll never assume that a rogue or a thief
Is a gentleman worthy implicit belief.
  SIR W. S. GILBERT.—*Iolanthe.*

We men of intrigues observe more rigorous faith to one another than honest folk
do. [*Labranche.*]   LE SAGE.—*Crispin.*

Yes, sir, we [Labranche and Crispin] are
so mortified at not having succeeded in
our scheme, that we renounce all roguery
in future.   LE SAGE.—*Ib.*

Are there any people in the world except
robbers? No, my friend, all men love to
appropriate the belongings of other men.
It is a universal sentiment; only the method
of carrying it into effect varies.
  LE SAGE.—*Gil Blas*, Bk. 1, ch. 5.

We attack no one, we assassinate no
one; we only seek to live at the expense
of others. And if stealing is an unjust
action, well the necessity for it corrects its
injustice. [*Don Raphael.*] LE SAGE.—*Ib.,*
                        Bk. 4, ch. 11.

A more præternotorious rogue than himself. MASSINGER (or FLETCHER?).—*Fair
                Maid of the Inn*, Act 4.

Honest men
Are the soft easy cushions on which knaves
Repose and fatten.
  OTWAY.—*Venice Preserved*, Act 1, 1.

When rich villains have need of poor ones,
Poor ones may make what price they will.
  SHAKESPEARE.—*Measure for Measure,*
                            Act 3, 3.

Masters, it is proved already that you
are little better than false knaves; and it
will go near to be thought so presently.
  SHAKESPEARE.—*Much Ado*, Act 4, 2.

Say what you like, the rogue is more
often than not only a fool.
> VOLTAIRE.—*Le Dépositaire.*

ROMANCE

And both were young, and one was
beautiful.
> BYRON.—*The Dream, st. 2.*

Romances paint at full length people's
wooings,
But only give a bust of marriages ;
For no one cares for matrimonial cooings,
There's nothing wrong in a connubial kiss.
Think you, if Laura had been Petrarch's
wife,
He would have written sonnets all his life ?
> BYRON.—*Don Juan, c. 3, 8.*

For feeble is Love's world, his home, his
birthplace ;
Delightedly dwells he 'mong fays and
talismans
And spirits ; and delightedly believes
Divinities, being himself divine.
> S. T. COLERIDGE.—*Piccolomini, Act 2, 5.*

Whether the charmer sinner it or saint it ;
If folly grow romantic, I must paint it.
> POPE.—*Moral Essays, Ep. 2, 15.*

If all the world and love were young,
And truth in every shepherd's tongue,
These pretty pleasures might me move
To live with thee, and be thy love.
> SIR W. RALEGH.—*The Nymph's Reply.*

Tradition wears a snowy beard, romance
is always young.
> WHITTIER.—*Mary Garvin.*

The worst of having a romance is that
it leaves you so unromantic.
> OSCAR WILDE.—*Dorian Gray, ch. 1.*

Lady Nancy she died out of pure, pure
grief,
Lord Lovel he died out of sorrow,
sorrow.   *Lord Lovel (Old Ballad).*

ROME

Everyone, soon or late, comes round by
Rome.   BROWNING.—*Ring and
the Book, 5, 296.*

The Niobe of nations ! there she stands,
Childless and crownless, in her voiceless
woe. BYRON.—*Childe Harold, c. 4, 79.*

While stands the Coliseum, Rome shall
stand ;
When falls the Coliseum, Rome shall fall ;
And when Rome falls—the World.
> BYRON.—*Ib., 145.*

Rome shall perish—write that word—
In the blood that she has spilt ;
Perish, hopeless and abhorred,
Deep in ruin as in guilt.
> COWPER.—*Boadicea.*

See the wild waste of all-devouring years !
How Rome her own sad Sepulchre appears,
With nodding arches, broken temples
spread !
The very Tombs now vanish'd like their
dead.
> POPE.—*Moral Essays, Ep. to Addison.*

The city which thou seest no other deem
Than great and glorious Rome, Queen of
the Earth
So far renowned, and with the spoils en-
riched
Of nations.
> MILTON.—*Paradise Regained, 4, 44.*

Go thou to Rome, at once the Paradise,
The grave, the city. and the wilderness.
> SHELLEY.—*Adonais, st. 49.*

Rome is no more : but if the shade of Rome
May of the body yield a seeming sight,
It's like a corse drawn forth out of the
tomb
By magic skill out of eternal night.
> SPENSER.—*Ruins of Rome, 5.*

The eternal city [Rome].
> *So called by Tibullus, 1st century.*

ROMISH CHURCH

The church of Rome,
Mixing two governments that ill assort,
Hath missed her footing, fallen into the
mire,
And there herself and burden much defiled.
> DANTE.—*Purgatory, c. 16, 129 (Cary tr.).*

A little skill in antiquity inclines a man
to Popery ; but depth in that study brings
him about again to our religion.
> FULLER.—*True Church Antiquary.*

If a man consider the original of this
great ecclesiastical dominion, he will easily
perceive, that the Papacy is no other than
the Ghost of the deceased Roman Empire,
sitting crowned upon the grave thereof :
for so did the Papacy start up on a sudden
out of the ruins of that heathen power.
> HOBBES.—*Leviathan, ch. 47.*

She [The Roman Catholic Church] may
still exist in undiminished vigour, when
some traveller from New Zealand shall,
in the midst of a vast solitude, take his
stand on a broken arch of London Bridge
to sketch the ruins of St. Paul's.
> MACAULAY.—*Essay on Ranke's History
of the Popes.*

The command to uncover the depths
of one's heart to one individual only is
one of the chief causes which have led a
great part of Europe to revolt against the
Church.   PASCAL.—*Pensées, Pt. 1, 5, 8.*

The [Catholic] Church has three sorts
of enemies : the Jews, who have never

been of her body ; the heretics, who have withdrawn from it ; the evil Christians who tear her from within.

PASCAL.—*Pensées, Pt. 2, 16, 9.*

Most of the players, who had very little faith before, were now desirous of having as much as they could, and therefore embraced the Roman Catholic religion.

SWIFT.—*True and Faithful Narrative (of panic caused by expectation of the Day of Judgment).*

ROSES

She wore a wreath of roses,
The night that first we met.
T. H. BAYLY.—*Song.*

Earth hath no princelier flowers
Than roses white and roses red.
CAMPION.—*Now hath Flora.*

Let princes princely flowers defend !
Roses, the garden's pride
Are flowers for love and flowers for kings.
CAMPION.—*Ib.*

Look to the blowing Rose about us—
" So,
Laughing," she says, " into the world I blow,
At once the silken tassel of my Purse
Tear, and its Treasure on the Garden throw." FITZGERALD.—*Rubáiyát, 14.*

Roses, their sharp spines being gone,
Not royal in their smells alone,
But in their hue.
JOHN FLETCHER (and SHAKESPEARE ?).—
Two Noble Kinsmen, Act 1, 1.

Sweet rose, whose hue angrie and brave
Bids the rash gazer wipe his eye :
Thy root is ever in its grave,
And thou must die.
HERBERT.—*The Temple, 63 (Vertue).*

Then in that Parly, all those flowers
Voted the Rose the Queen of flowers.
HERRICK.—*Hesperides, 11.*

You may break, you may shatter the vase,
if you will,
But the scent of the roses will hang round it still.   MOORE.—*Irish Melodies.*

Ah see, who so faire thing doest faine to see,
In springing flowre the image of thy day ;
Ah see the Virgin Rose, how sweetly shee
Doth first peepe forth with bashfull modestee,
That fairer seemes the lesse ye see her may;
So see soone after, how more bold and free
Her bared bosome she doth broad display;
Soe see soone after, how she fades and falles away.
SPENSER.—*Faerie Queene, 2, 12, 74.*

Go, lovely Rose !
Tell her that wastes her time and me,
That now she knows
When I resemble her to thee
How sweet and fair she seems to be.
WALLER.—*Go, Lovely Rose.*

Yet though thou fade,
From thy dead leaves let fragrance rise ;
And teach the maid
That Goodness Time's rude hand defies,
That Virtue lives when Beauty dies.
H. K. WHITE.—*Additional Stanza to the foregoing.*

Both roses flourish, red and white ;
In love and sisterly delight ;
The two that were at strife are blended,
And all old troubles now are ended.
WORDSWORTH.—*Song at Feast of Brougham Castle.*

ROUTINE

Night and day ! night and day !
Sound the song the hours rehearse !
Work and play ! work and play !
The order of the universe.
J. DAVIDSON.—*Piper, play.*

We all of us live too much in a circle.
DISRAELI.—*Sybil, Bk. 3, c. 7.*

ROYAL ACADEMY

A Royal Academy is a kind of hospital and infirmary for the obliquities of taste and ingenuity—a receptacle where enthusiasm and originality stop and stagnate.
WM. HAZLITT.—*Table Talk : On Corporate Bodies.*

An institution like this has often been recommended upon considerations merely mercantile ; but an Academy, founded upon such principles, can never effect even its own narrow purposes. If it has an origin no higher, no taste can ever be formed in manufactures ; but if the higher Arts of Design flourish, these inferior ends will be answered of course.
SIR JOSHUA REYNOLDS.—*Discourse at Opening of the Royal Academy.*

Paint and the men of canvas fire my lays,
Who show their work for profit and for praise ;
Whose pockets know most comfortable fillings,
Gaining two thousand pounds a year, by shillings.
J. WOLCOT.—*Odes to the Royal Academicians, 1792. Pref. to Ode 1.*

ROYALTY

Princes are like to heavenly bodies, which cause good or evil times ; and which have much veneration but no rest.
BACON.—*Of Empire.*

Kings are naturally lovers of low company.
BURKE.—*Speech on Economical Reform.*

A crown, what is it?
Is it to bear the miseries of a people,
To hear their murmurs, feel their discontents,
And sink beneath a load of splendid care?
      HANNAH MORE.—*Daniel.*

Uneasy lies the head that wears a crown.
 SHAKESPEARE.—*Henry IV., Pt. 2, Act 3, 1.*

For law and gospel both determine
All virtues lodge in royal ermine.
     SWIFT.—*On Poetry.*

O poor and short-lived glory and renown!
O false unenvied pleasures of a crown!
So soon are all thy shining honours fled,
Traduced while living, and defamed when
 dead. SWIFT.—*Swan Tripe Club.*

RUIN AND RUINS

Stern Ruin's ploughshare drives, elate,
 Full on thy bloom.
  BURNS.—*To a Mountain Daisy.*

Ruins yet beauteous in decay.
  BURNS.—*Lincluden Abbey.*

And chiefless castles, breathing stern farewells.
 BYRON.—*Childe Harold, c. 3, st. 46.*

The castled crag of Drachenfels
Frowns o'er the wide and winding Rhine.
  BYRON.—*Ib., st. 55.*

A ruin—yet what ruin! from its mass
Walls, palaces, half-cities, have been
 reared. BYRON.—*Ib., c. 4, st. 143.*

Ruin seize thee, ruthless king!
Confusion on thy banners wait!
     GRAY.—*Bard.*
The ruin of a neighbour pleases both
his friends and his enemies.
 LA ROCHEFOUCAULD.—*Maxim 600.*

And princely counsel in his face yet shone,
Majestic, though in ruin.
 MILTON.—*Paradise Lost, Bk. 2, 304.*

With ruin upon ruin, rout on rout,
Confusion worse confounded.
 f MILTON.—*Ib., 995.*

I do love these ancient ruins.
We never tread upon them but we set
Our foot upon some reverend history
 WEBSTER.—*Duchess of Mafy, Act 5, 3.*

To chant thy birth thou hast
No meaner poet than the whistling blast,
And Desolation is thy patron saint.
 WORDSWORTH.—*River Duddon, 2.*

Lovely in death the beauteous ruin lay.
  YOUNG.—*Night Thoughts, 3.*

Stars rush, and final Ruin fiercely drives
Her ploughshare o'er Creation.
     YOUNG.—*Ib., 9.*

RULERS

Still sways their souls with that commanding art
That dazzles, leads, yet chills the vulgar
 heart. BYRON.—*Corsair, 1, 8.*

He ruled them—man may rule the worst,
By ever daring to be first.
 BYRON.—*Siege of Corinth, st. 12.*

Pride in their port, defiance in their eye,
I see the lords of human kind pass by.
   GOLDSMITH.—*Traveller.*

We must not all be kings. The rule is
 most irregular
Where many rule.
  HOMER.—*Iliad, Bk. 2, 204*
      (*Chapman tr.*).

Seems it to thee a burden to be feared
By men above all others? Trust me, no.
There is no ill in royalty. The man,
So stationed, waits not long ere he obtain
Riches and honour.
  HOMER.—*Odyssey, Bk. 1, 391*
      (*Cowper tr.*).

For one restraint, lords of the world
 besides.
 MILTON.—*Paradise Lost, Bk. 1, 32.*

Better to reign in hell than serve in
 heaven. MILTON.—*Ib., 263.*

A crown
Golden in show, is but a wreath of thorns,
Brings dangers, troubles, cares, and sleepless nights.
 MILTON.—*Paradise Regained, Bk. 2, 458.*

They who grasp the world,
The Kingdom, and the power, and the
 glory,
Must pay with deepest misery of spirit,
Atoning unto God for a brief brightness.
 STEPHEN PHILLIPS.—*Herod, Act 3.*

It is folly for you to be sulky towards
him whose power is superior to yours.
 PLAUTUS.—*Casina, Act 2, 4, 4.*

Was never subject longed to be a king,
As I do long and wish to be a subject.
 SHAKESPEARE.—*Henry VI., Pt. 2,*
      Act 4, 9.

Why, man, he doth bestride the narrow
 world
Like a Colossus; and we petty men
Walk under his huge legs, and peep about
To find ourselves dishonourable graves.
 SHAKESPEARE.—*Julius Cæsar, Act 1, 2.*

Most potent, grave, and reverend signiors,
My very noble and approved good masters.
 SHAKESPEARE.—*Othello, Act 1, 3.*

The ruling passion is the passion for
ruling. TACITUS.—*Annals, Bk. 15, 53.*

Ah, God, for a man with heart, head, hand,
Like some of the simple great ones gone
For ever and ever by.
One still strong man in a blatant land,
Whatever they call him, what care I ?
Aristocrat, democrat, autocrat—one
Who can rule, and dare not lie.
    TENNYSON.—*Maud, Pt.* 1, 10, 5.

We shall exult if they who rule the land
Be men who hold its many blessings dear,
Wise, upright, valiant ; not a servile band,
Who are to judge of danger which they
    fear,
And honour which they do not understand.
    WORDSWORTH.—*Nov.,* 1806.

'Tis not in battles that from youth we
    train
The Governor who must be wise and good.
    WORDSWORTH.—*Sonnet,* 1801.

Now there arose up a new king over
Egypt, which knew not Joseph.
    Exodus i, 8.

Not afraid to speak evil of dignities.
    2 *St. Peter* ii, 10.

He shall rule them with a rod of iron.
    Revelation ii, 27, *and* xix, 15.

The emperor rules the empire, but the
empress rules the emperor.   *Prov.*

RUMOUR

The crowd values few things according
to truth, but many according to report.
    CICERO.—*Pro. Q. Roscio Com.,* 10, 29.

Let the ear despise nothing, nor believe
anything forthwith. PHÆDRUS.—*Fables.*

I believe there is nothing among mankind swifter than rumour.
    PLAUTUS.—*Fragm.*

Heraclitus said that a fool is startled
and shaken by everything he hears.
    PLUTARCH.—*Of Hearing.*

In hearing, as in war, there are many
false alarms.   PLUTARCH.—*Ib.*

If my gossip report be an honest woman
of her word.
    SHAKESPEARE.—*Merchant of Venice,*
    Act 3, 1.

A thing devised by the enemy.
    SHAKESPEARE.—*Richard III.,* Act 5, 3.

Fancies too weak for boys, too green and
    idle
For girls of nine !
    SHAKESPEARE.—*Winter's Tale,* Act 3, 2.

What some invent the rest enlarge.
    SWIFT.—*Journal of a Modern Lady.*

The rolling fictions grow in strength and
    size,
Each author adding to the former lies.
    SWIFT.—*Tr. of Ovid. (Examiner,*
    No. 15.)

In calamity any rumour is listened to.
    PUBLILIUS SYRUS.

" They say so " is half a lie.   *Prov.*

Truth is in the mouths of the people.
*Saying cited by Ibsen in " Lady Inger of
Ostraat,"* Act 1 (1854). *(Founded on
    Æschylus.)*

RURAL LIFE

In the country, in a long time, for want
of good conversation, one's understanding
and invention contract a moss on them,
like an old paling in an orchard.
    JOHN AUBREY.—*Minutes of Lives.*

Nor rural sights alone, but rural sounds
Exhilarate the spirit and restore
The tone of languid nature.
    COWPER.—*Task, The Sofa, l.* 181.

No more my song shall please the rural
    crew :
Adieu, my tuneful pipe, and all the world,
    adieu ! DRYDEN.—*Virgil, Pastoral,* 1.

In my time the follies of the town crept
slowly among us, but now they travel
faster than a stage-coach.
    GOLDSMITH.—*She Stoops to Conquer,*
    Act 1.

I began to think if there were no such
place as London it really would be very
desirable to live in the country.
    SIR A. HELPS.—*Friends in Council,*
    Bk. 1, *ch.* 3.

The fondness for rural life among the
higher classes of the English has had a
great and salutary effect upon the national
character. I do not know a finer race of
men than the English gentlemen.
    WASHINGTON IRVING.—*Sketch Book*
    (c. 1820).

It is the country which makes the land ;
it is the country-people who make the
nation.   ROUSSEAU.—*Emile.*

Hast any philosophy in thee, shepherd ?
    SHAKESPEARE.—*As You Like It,*
    Act 3, 2.

I have no relish for the country ; it is
a kind of healthy grave. I am afraid you
are not exempt from the delusions of
flowers, green turf, and birds ; they all
afford slight gratification, but not worth
an hour of rational conversation.
    SYDNEY SMITH.—*Letter to
    Miss G. Harcourt,* 1838.

You may laugh, dear G., but after all
the country is most dreadful ! The real
use of it is to find food for cities.
    SYDNEY SMITH.—*Letter to
    Mrs. Meynell, Dec.,* 1841.

I do all I can to love the country, and endeavour to believe those poetical lies which I read in Rogers and others on the subject : which said deviations from truth were, by Rogers, all written in St. James's Place.
SYDNEY SMITH.—*Letter to Lady Holland, Jan.* 3, 1841.

The moan of doves in immemorial elms, And murmuring of innumerable bees.
TENNYSON.—*Princess, c.* 7, 206.

When one thinks of country houses and country walks, one wonders that any man is left unmarried.
THACKERAY.—*Pendennis.*

Drinks the pure pleasures of the rural life. THOMPSON.—*Autumn, l.* 1236.

O you poor folk in cities,
A thousand thousand pities !
Heaping the fairy gold that withers and dies :
One field in the June weather
Is worth all the gold ye gather,
One field in June weather—one Paradise.
K. TYNAN.—*June Song.*

But easy quiet, a secure retreat,
A harmless life that knows not how to cheat,
With home-bred plenty, the rich owner bless,
And rural pleasures crown his happiness.
VIRGIL.—*Georgics, Bk.* 2 (*Dryden tr.*).

My next desire is, void of care and strife,
To lead a soft, secure, inglorious life—
A country cottage near a crystal flood,
A winding valley and a lofty wood.
VIRGIL.—*Ib.*

Unvexed with quarrels, undisturbed with noise,
The country king his peaceful realm enjoys. VIRGIL.—*Ib.*

Would you know why I like London so much ? Why, if the world must consist of so many fools as it does, I choose to take them in the gross, and not made in separate pills, as they are prepared in the country. HORACE WALPOLE.—*Letter.*

Anybody can be good in the country.
OSCAR WILDE.—*Dorian Gray, ch.* 13.

The common growth of Mother Earth
Suffices me—her tears, her mirth,
Her humblest mirth and tears.
WORDSWORTH.—*Peter Bell, Prol.*

Country folk are best when weeping and worst when rejoicing.
Quoted as a Latin saying by Gabriel Harvey, c. 1600.

It were better to hear the lark sing than the mouse cheep.
Scottish prov. of the Douglases (*Scott's "Fair Maid of Perth"*).

S

SACRAMENT

He was the Word that spake it ;
He took the bread and brake it ;
And what that Word did make it,
I do believe and take it.
J. DONNE.—*The Sacrament.*

SACRIFICE

But whether on the scaffold high,
Or in the battle's van,
The fittest place where man can die
Is where he dies for man.
M. J. BARRY.—*Dublin Nation.*

Blow out, you bugles, over the rich Dead !
There's none of these so lonely and poor of old,
But, dying, has made us rarer gifts than gold.
These laid the world away : poured out the red
Sweet wine of youth ; gave up the years to be
Of work and joy, and that unhoped serene
That men call age, and those who would have been
Their sons, they gave their immortality.
RUPERT BROOKE.—*The Dead* (1914).

If I should die, think only this of me :
That there's some corner of a foreign field,
That is for ever England.
RUPERT BROOKE.—*The Soldier.*

They never fail who die
In a great cause.
BYRON.—*Marino Faliero,* Act 2, 2.

There is a victory in dying well
For Freedom—and ye have not died in vain. CAMPBELL.—*Spanish Patriots.*

Was anything real ever gained without sacrifice of some kind ?
SIR A. HELPS.—*Friends in Council, Bk.* 2, *ch.* 1.

O willing hearts turned quick to clay,
Glad lovers holding death in scorn,
Out of the lives ye cast away
The coming race is born.
L. HOUSMAN.—*Settlers.*

To every man upon this earth
Death cometh soon or late ;
And how can man die better
Than facing fearful odds,
For the ashes of his fathers,
And the temples of his Gods ?
MACAULAY.—*Horatius, st.* 27.

He died the noblest death a man may die,
Fighting for God and Right and Liberty ;
And such a death is Immortality.
J. OXENHAM.

Ask me not whether he were friend or foe
  That lies beneath,
Nor whether in a worthy fight or no
  He came to death.
Pass on, and leave such reckonings un-
    moved,
  Remembering now
Here lieth one who gave for that he loved
  A greater gift than thou.
          MARGARET POSTGATE.

High sacrifice, and labour without pause,
Even to the death :—else wherefore should
    the eye
Of man converse with immortality.
      WORDSWORTH.—Feelings of the
                  Tyrolese (No. 14).

SADNESS

Beauty and sadness always go together.
Nature thought beauty too rich to go
    forth
Upon the earth without a meet alloy.
      GEO. MACDONALD.—Within and
                        Without.

In sooth I know not why I am so sad.
      SHAKESPEARE.—Merchant of Venice,
                          Act 1, 1.

A merry heart goes all the day,
  Your sad tires in a mile-a.
SHAKESPEARE.—Winter's Tale, Act 4, 3.

Fancy, who leads the pastimes of the glad,
Full oft is pleased a wayward dart to
    throw,
Sending sad shadows after things not sad,
Peopling the harmless fields with signs of
    woe.
      WORDSWORTH.—Morning Exercise.

'Tis impious in a good man to be sad.
      YOUNG.—Night Thoughts, 4.

SAFETY

Oh ! are they safe ?—we ask not of
  success.   BYRON.—Corsair, c. 1, 5.

Those who would give up essential
liberty to purchase a little temporary
safety deserve neither liberty nor safety.
                      B. FRANKLIN.

The strongest tower has not the highest
    wall.
Think well of this, when you sit safe at
    home.   W. MORRIS.—Earthly
      Paradise : Cupid and Psyche, 896.

Out of this nettle, danger, we pluck this
flower, safety.
      SHAKESPEARE.—Henry IV., Pt. 1,
                          Act 3, 2.

SAILORS

Those who go to sea are only four inches
from death.   ANACHARSIS (Greek).

And then he hitched his trousers up, as is,
  I'm told, their use.

It's very odd that sailor-men should wear
  those things so loose.
      R. H. BARHAM.—Misadventures at
                        Margate.

England his heart, his corpse the waters
    have,
And that which raised his fame became his
    grave.
      R. BARNFIELD.—Epitaph on Drake.

The waters were his winding-sheet, the
    sea was made his tomb,
Yet for his fame the Ocean sea was not
    sufficient room.
      R. BARNFIELD.—On Hawkins.

What furie or malicious hagge
Hath now let Loose the Aeolian bag ?
The waves swell high, the surges reare
As though each man a Jonas were.
      SIR T. BROWNE.—Tempest at Sea.

      The joys and sorrows sailors find,
Cooped in their wingèd sea-girt citadel.
      BYRON.—Childe Harold, c. 2, 28.

He loves to talk with mariners
  That come from a far countree.
      COLERIDGE.—Ancient Mariner, Pt. 7

I never was on the dull, tame shore,
But I loved the great sea more and more.
      BARRY CORNWALL.—The Sea.

For if bold tars are Fortune's sport,
  Still are they Fortune's care.
      C. DIBDIN.—Blind Sailor.

And the sign of a true-hearted sailor
  Is to give and to take a good joke.
      C. DIBDIN.—Jack at the Windlass.

In every mess I find a friend,
  In every port a wife.
      C. DIBDIN.—Jack in his Element.

And did you not hear of a jolly young
    waterman,
  Who at Blackfriars Bridge used for to
    ply ?
He feathered his oars with much skill and
    dexterity,
  Winning each heart and delighting each
    eye.
      C. DIBDIN.—Jolly Young Waterman.

For they say there's a Providence sits up
    aloft
To keep watch for the life of poor Jack.
      C. DIBDIN.—Poor Jack.

Faithful, below, he did his duty,
  But now he's gone aloft.
      C. DIBDIN.—Tom Bowling.

The wonder is always new that any sane
man can be a sailor.
      EMERSON.—English Traits,
              2, Voyage to England.

But his little daughter whispered
    As she took his icy hand,
" Isn't God upon the ocean,
    Just the same as on the land ? "
    JAMES T. FIELDS.—*The Tempest.*

For who are so free as the sons of the
    waves ?
    DAVID GARRICK.—*Hearts of Oak.*

    Sailors should never be shy.
    SIR W. S. GILBERT.—*H.M.S. Pinafore.*

I am never known to quail
    At the fury of a gale,
And I'm never, never sick at sea.
    SIR W. S. GILBERT.—*Ib.*

Did you voyage all unspoken, small and
    lonely ?
Or with fame, the happy portion of the
    few ?
So you win the Golden Harbour in the
    old way,
There's the old sea welcome waiting there
    for you.
    CAPT. RONALD HOPWOOD, R.N. (1916).

'E's a kind of a giddy harumfrodite—
    soldier an' sailor too !
    KIPLING.—*Soldier and Sailor.*

Every man thinks meanly of himself for
not having been a soldier, or not having
been at sea. JOHNSON.—*Remark, 1778.*

When men come to like a sea life they
are not fit to live on land.
    JOHNSON.—*Remark.*

Down, down beneath the deep,
That oft in triumph bore him,
He sleeps a sound and peaceful sleep,
With the salt waves dashing o'er him.
    H. F. LYTE.—*Sailor's Grave.*

Sleep on, sleep on, thou mighty dead !
A glorious tomb they've found thee ;
The broad blue sky above thee spread,
The boundless ocean round thee.
    H. F. LYTE.—*Ib.*

There were gentlemen and there were
seamen in the navy of Charles the Second.
But the seamen were not gentlemen ; and
the gentlemen were not seamen.
    MACAULAY.—*Hist. of Eng., c.* 3.

I must go down to the seas again, to the
    vagrant gipsy life,
To the gull's way and the whale's way,
    where the wind's like a whetted knife ;
And all I ask is a merry yarn from a
    laughing fellow rover,
And quiet sleep and a sweet dream when
    the long trick's over.
    JOHN MASEFIELD.—*Sea Fever.*

O Mother, think on us who think on
    thee !
Earth-home, birth-home, with love re-
    member yet
The sons in exile on the eternal sea.
    SIR H. NEWBOLT.—*Outward Bound.*

Ye gentlemen of England,
    Who live at home at ease,
Ah, little do you think upon
    The dangers of the seas !
MARTIN PARKER.—*Gentlemen of England.*

A strong nor'-wester's blowing, Bill,
    Hark ! don't ye hear it roar now ?
Lord help 'em, how I pities them
    Unhappy folk on shore now !
WM. PITT (*d.* 1840).—*Sailor's Confession.*

Ships are but boards, sailors but men ;
there be land rats and water rats.
    SHAKESPEARE.—*Merchant of Venice,*
    Act 1, 3.

I make good the old saying, we sailors
get money like horses, and spend it like
asses. SMOLLETT.—*Peregrine Pickle, ch.* 2.

A purer passion, a lordlier leisure,
    A peace more happy than lives on land,
Fulfils with pulse of diviner pleasure
    The dreaming head and the steering
    hand.
    SWINBURNE.—*Summer's Dream.*

The anger of the sea is on your lips,
The laughter of the sea is in your eye.
SIR W. WATSON.—*Sonnet. To Lord Fisher*
    (*Jan.* 12, 1920).

For his heart is like the sea,
    Ever open, brave, and free.
F. E. WEATHERLEY.—*They all love Jack.*

Why, Jack's the king of all,
    For they all love Jack.
    F. E. WEATHERLEY.—*Ib.*

Rocked in the cradle of the deep,
I calmly rest and soundly sleep.
EMMA HART WILLARD.—*Rocked in the*
    Cradle of the Deep.

He goes a great voyage that goes to the
bottom of the sea.   *Prov.*

ST. SWITHIN

O, here, St. Swithin's, the fifteenth day
[of July], " variable weather, for the most
part rain." Good !—" for the most part
rain." Why it should rain forty days
after, now, more or less; it was a rule
held afore I was able to hold a plough.
    BEN JONSON.—*Every man out of his*
    Humour, Act 1, 3.

St. Swithin's Day, if thou dost rain,
For forty days it will remain ;
St. Swithin's day, if thou be fair,
For forty days 'twill rain nae mair.
    Old Adage.

SAINTS

Many are worshipped at the altar who
are burning in the fire. ST. AUGUSTINE.

The scripture has lighted up excellent examples of holiness in the lives of the saints upon earth, for our direction and imitation.
WM. BATES, D.D.—*Sermons* (*published 1700*).

There are many (questionless) canonised on earth, that shall never be Saints in Heaven.
SIR T. BROWNE.—*Religio Medici, Pt. 1, sec. 26.*

Saints, to do us good,
Must be in heaven.
BROWNING.—*Ring and the Book, 6, 176.*

But this she knows, in joys and woes,
That saints will aid if men will call ;
For the blue sky bends over all.
COLERIDGE.—*Christabel : Conclusion to Pt. 1.*

A painter of saints must be a saint himself.
RUSKIN.—*Note* (1882) *to Revised Ed. of Modern Painters, Vol. 2, sec. 3, ch. 3.*

Be my soul with such saints, whatever their creed and communion !
GEO. TYRRELL.—*Of the wider "Communion of Saints."*

SARCASM

And that sarcastic levity of tongue,
The stinging of a heart the world hath stung.
BYRON.—*Lara, c. 1, 5.*

Sarcasm, I now see to be, in general, the language of the devil.
CARLYLE.—*Sartor, Bk. 2, ch. 4.*

A great master of gibes and flouts and jeers.
DISRAELI.—*Speech*, 1874.

Do not let us separate from each other with sarcasms.
SCHOPENHAUER.—*Dialogue on Religion.*

Surely there must be some meaning beneath all this terrible irony.
G. B. SHAW.—*Major Barbara.*

A true sarcasm is like a sword-stick,— it appears at first sight to be much more innocent than it really is, till all of a sudden there leaps something out of it— sharp, and deadly, and incisive—which makes you tremble and recoil.
SYDNEY SMITH.—*Lectures on Moral Philosophy, No. 10.*

N.B.—This is wrote sarkastikul.
ARTEMUS WARD.—*A Visit to Brigham Young.*

SATIETY

And she became a bore intense
Unto her lovesick boy.
SIR W. S. GILBERT—*Trial by Jury.*

It's curious, that falling off in things,
Just when one's taste is keenest.
R. MONCKTON MILNES (LORD HOUGHTON).—*Gone.*

The torment of all-things-compassed, the plague of naught-to-desire.
SIR W. WATSON.—*Dream of Man*, 105.

All sun makes the desert. *Arab. prov.*

That which is sweet if it be often repeated is no longer sweet. *Greek prov.*

SATIRE

Satire is a greater enemy to friendship than is anger. HENRY ATTWELL.

He that hath a satirical vein, as he maketh others afraid of his wit, so he had need be afraid of others' memory.
BACON.—*Of Discourse.*

The ordinary and over-worn trade of jesting
At lords, and courtiers, and citizens.
F. BEAUMONT.—*Woman Hater, Prol.* (1607).

I'll publish, right or wrong.
Fools are my theme, let satire be my song.
BYRON.—*English Bards*, 5.

When satire flies abroad on falsehood's wing,
Short is her life, and impotent her sting ;
But when to truth allied, the wound she gives
Sinks deep, and to remotest ages lives.
CHURCHILL.—*The Author*, 217.

Satire is always virtue's friend.
CHURCHILL.—*The Ghost, Bk.* 3, 936.

When scandal has new minted an old lie,
Or taxed invention for a fresh supply,
'Tis called a satire.
COWPER.—*Charity*, 513.

Crack the satiric thong.
COWPER.—*The Garden.*

Satire has always shone among the rest,
And is the boldest way, if not the best,
To tell men freely of their foulest faults ;
To laugh at their vain deeds and vainer thoughts. DRYDEN.—*On Satire*, 11.

It is difficult not to write satire.
JUVENAL.—*Satire*, 1.

Satire should, like a polished razor keen,
Wound with a touch that's scarcely felt or seen.
LADY M. W. MONTAGU.—*To Pope.*

And pointed satire runs him through and through.
J. OLDHAM.—*Upon a Printer.*

Formed to delight at once and lash the age. POPE.—*On Gay.*

Satire's my weapon, but I'm too discreet
To run amuck, and tilt at all I meet.
    Pope.—*Satires of Horace, Bk. 2*, 69.

The flash of that satiric rage,
Which, bursting on the early stage,
Branded the vices of the age,
And broke the keys of Rome.
    Scott.—*Marmion*, 4, 7.

Satire is a sort of glass wherein beholders
do generally discover every face but their
own.   Swift.—*Battle of the Books.*

Men are pleased enough if you expose
follies in general, always provided you
indicate no one in particular. Each one
applies to his neighbour the satire which
belongs to himself, and so all men laugh
at the expense of each other.
    Voltaire.—*Dialogues, No.* 9.

SAVAGES

Ere the base laws of servitude began,
When wild in woods the noble savage ran.
    Dryden.—*Conquest of Granada*, Act 1, 1.

Hunting their sport, and plundering was
their trade.
    Virgil.—*Æneid. Bk.* 7 (*Dryden tr.*).

SCANDAL

We had among us, not so much a spy,
As a recording chief-inquisitor.
    Browning.—*How it Strikes a
    Contemporary.*

The mair they talk I'm kenned the better ;
E'en let them clash !
    Burns.—*Welcome to his Illegitimate
    Child.*

Dead scandals form good subjects for dis-
section. Byron.—*Don Juan, c.* 1, 31.

And dye conjecture with a darker hue.
    Byron.—*Lara*, 2, 6.

In scandal, as in robbery, the receiver
is always thought as bad as the thief.
    Lord Chesterfield.—*Advice to his Son.*

Flavia, most tender of her own good name,
Is rather careless of her sister's fame.
    Cowper.—*Charity*, 453.

Love and scandal are the best sweeten-
ers of tea.
    Fielding.—*Love in Several Masques*,
    Act 4, 2.

'Tis the talk and not the intrigue that's
the crime.
    Lord Lansdowne.—*She Gallants.*

Her tea she sweetens, as she sips, with
scandal.
    Rogers.—*Written to be spoken by
    Mrs. Siddons.*

For greatest scandal waits on greatest
state.
    Shakespeare.—*Lucrece, st.* 144.

No scandal about Queen Elizabeth, I
hope ?   Sheridan.—*Critic*, Act 2, 1.

Scandal's the sweetener of a female feast.
    Young.—*Love of Fame, Sat.* 6.

Tattlers also and busybodies, speaking
things which they ought not.
    1 *Timothy* v, 13.

SCENERY

I say the world is lovely
And that loveliness is enough.
    R. Buchanan.—*Artist and Model.*

The mountains look on Marathon,
And Marathon looks on the sea.
    Byron.—*Don Juan, c.* 3, 86.

To disparage scenery as quite flat is, of
course, like disparaging a swan as quite
white, or an Italian sky as quite blue.
    G. K. Chesterton.—*R. Browning, ch.* 6.

The great charm, however, of English
scenery is the moral feeling that seems to
pervade it. It is associated with the ideas
of order, of quiet, of sober well-estab-
lished principles, of hoary usage and
reverend custom. Everything seems to
be the growth of ages.
    Washington Irving.—*Sketch Book
    (c.* 1820).

Which of us is not sometimes affected
almost to despair by the splendid vision of
earth and sky, when, wherever a man
casts his gaze, the lights and shadows of
hill, wood, and shore all appear charmingly
intermingled . . . and nevertheless he feels
himself unequal to true admiration or
appreciation ?
    Keble.—*Lectures on Poetry, No.* 31
    (*E. K. Francis tr.*).

As I have grown older, the aspects of
nature conducive to human life have
become hourly more dear to me ; and I
had rather now see a brown harvest field
than the brightest Aurora Borealis.
    Ruskin.—*Note* (1882) *to Revised Ed. of
    Modern Painters (referring to his
    youthful predilection for wild and
    mountainous scenery*).

First of earthly singers, the sun-loved rill.
    Geo. Meredith.—*Phœbus with Admetus,
    st.* 3.

There also is the Muse not loth to range,
Watching the twilight smoke of cot or
grange,
Skyward ascending from a woody dell.

Soft is the music that would charm for
ever ;
The flower of sweetest smell is shy and
lowly.
    Wordsworth.—*Sonnets, Pt.* 2, *No.* 9.

SCENT

There the sweet smells that do perfume
    the air,
Arising from the infinite repair
Of odoriferous buds and herbs of price,
(As if it were another Paradise)
So please the smelling sense, that you are
    fain
Where last you walk'd to turn and walk
    again.
    WM. BROWNE.—*Britannia's Pastorals.*

In Köln, a town of monks and bones,
And pavements fanged with murderous
    stones,
And rags, and hags, and hideous wenches,
I counted two and seventy stenches,
All well defined, and several stinks.
    COLERIDGE.—*Cologne.*

Who, that has reason, and his smell,
Would not among roses and jasmine dwell,
Rather than all his spirits choke
With exhalations of dirt and smoke ?
    COWLEY.—*Of Gardens.*

    Sweet scents
Are the swift vehicles of still sweeter
    thoughts,
And nurse and pillow the dull memory
That would let drop without them her best
    stores.
    W. SAVAGE LANDOR.—*A Fiesolan Idyl.*

A woman smells well when she smells of
nothing.   PLAUTUS.—*Mostellaria.*

A very ancient and fish-like smell.
    SHAKESPEARE.—*Tempest*, Act 2, 2.

SCEPTICISM

    It's just the proper way to baulk
These troublesome fellows—liars, one and
    all,
Are not these sceptics ? Well, to baffle
    them,
No use in being squeamish : lie yourself.
    BROWNING.—*Mr. Sludge.*

O Incredulity ! the wit of fools,
That slovenly will spit on all things fair.
    CHAPMAN.—*De Guiana*, 82.

It is the pert superficial thinker who is
generally strongest in every kind of unbelief.   SIR HUMPHRY DAVY.—*Salmonia.*

If he does really think that there is no
distinction between virtue and vice, why,
sir, when he leaves our houses let us count
our spoons.
    JOHNSON.—*Remark to Boswell*, 1763.

We talk of a credulous vulgar, without
always recollecting that there is a vulgar
incredulity, which, in historical matters
as well as in those of religion, finds it
easier to doubt than to examine.
    SCOTT.—*Fair Maid of Perth.*

Whilst the sceptic destroys gross superstitions, let him spare to deface, as some
of the French writers have defaced, the
eternal truths charactered upon the
imaginations of men.
    SHELLEY.—*Defence of Poetry* (1821).

SCEPTRE

A sceptre, snatched with an unruly hand,
Must be as boisterously maintained as
    gained.
    SHAKESPEARE.—*King John*, Act 3, 4.

His sceptre shows the force of temporal
    power,
The attribute to awe and majesty,
Wherein doth sit the dread and fear of
    kings.
    SHAKESPEARE.—*Merchant of Venice*,
        Act 4, 1.

SCHOLARSHIP

Besides, 'tis known he could speak Greek
As naturally as pigs squeak.
    BUTLER.—*Hudibras*, Pt. 1, c. 1.

The world's great man have not commonly been great scholars, nor its great
scholars great men.
    O. W. HOLMES.—*Autocrat.*

Mark what ills the scholar's life assail,
Toil, envy, want, the patron, and the gaol.
    JOHNSON.—*Vanity of Human Wishes.*

The scholar and the world ! The endless
    strife,
The discord in the harmonies of life !
The love of learning, the sequestered nooks,
And all the sweet serenity of books ;
The market-place, the eager love of gain,
Whose aim is vanity, and whose end is pain.
    LONGFELLOW.—*Morituri*
        Salutamus.

He was a scholar, and a ripe and good one ;
Exceeding wise, fair-spoken, and persuading.
    SHAKESPEARE.—*Henry VIII.*, Act 4, 2.

SCHOOLS AND SCHOOLBOYS

    The schoolboy spot
We ne'er forget, though there we are forgot.   BYRON.—*Don Juan*, c. 1, 130.

Would you your son should be a sot or
    dunce,
Lascivious, headstrong, or all these at
    once ;
That in good time, the stripling's finished
    taste
For loose expense and fashionable waste
Should prove your ruin, and his own at
    last,
Train him in public with a mob of boys.
    COWPER.—*Tirocinium*, 201.

The useful is exploded. The definition
of a public school is " a school which

excludes all that could fit a man for standing behind a counter."
EMERSON.—*English Traits*, 12, *Universities* (1833).

The microcosm of a public school.
DISRAELI.—*Vivian Grey, Bk.* 1, *ch.* 2.

All the Latin at that school might be comprised in one line, "Arma virumque cano,"—an arm, a man, and a cane.
HOOD.—*Health of the Dominie*, 1834.

The fiend hath much to do that keeps a school,
Or is the father of a family ;
Or governs but a country academy.
BEN JONSON.—*Sad Shepherd.*

Twelve years ago I was a boy,
A happy boy, at Drury's.
W. M. PRAED.—*School and Schoolfellows, st.* 1.

At home a boy learns only what is taught to him; at school he learns also from what is taught to others.   QUINTILIAN.

Public school education in England is the best which I have ever seen, and it is abominable. TALLEYRAND.—*Saying.*

As cruel as a schoolboy.
TENNYSON.—*Walking to the Mail.*

What money is better bestowed than that of a schoolboy's tip ?
THACKERAY.—*Newcomes, Bk.* 1, *ch.* 16

Boys who learn nothing else at our public schools learn at least good manners, —or what we consider to be such.
THACKERAY.—*Ib.*

We fought with amazing emulation for the last place in the class.
THACKERAY.—*A Gambler's Death.*

SCIENCE

To refuse the conduct of the light of nature (luminis naturalis) is not merely foolish but even impious.
ST. AUGUSTINE.—*De Trinitate, Bk.* 4, *ch.* 6 (*quoted by Hooker, Eccles. Pol.*, 3, 9, 1).

By the glare of false Science betrayed,
That leads to bewilder, and dazzles to blind.   BEATTIE.—*The Hermit.*

Geology, ethnology, what not ?—
(Greek endings, each the little passing bell
That signifies some faith's about to die.)
BROWNING.—*Bishop Blougram.*

Oh ! star-eyed Science, hast thou wandered there,
To waft us home the message of despair ?
CAMPBELL.—*Pleasures of Hope, Pt.* 2.

Science in England, in America, is jealous of theory, hates the name of moral purpose. There's a revenge for

this inhumanity. What manner of man does science make ?
EMERSON.—*Conduct of Life. Beauty.*

All science has one aim, namely, to find a theory of nature.
EMERSON.—*Nature. Introd.*

Science is a first-rate piece of furniture for a man's upper-chamber, if he has common-sense on the ground floor.
O. W. HOLMES.—*Poet at Breakfast Table, ch.* 5.

As children gathering pebbles on the shore.
MILTON.—*Paradise Regained, Bk.* 4, 330.

Science is nothing else but perception.
PLATO.—*Theœtetus*, 46 (*Remark ascribed to Theœtetus, and commended, but with reservations, by Socrates*).

Science is true judgment in conjunction with reason.
PLATO.—*Ib.*, 141 (*approved by Socrates*).

Yet holds the eel of science by the tail.
POPE.—*Dunciad, Bk.* 1, 280.

The learned is happy nature to explore ;
The fool is happy that he knows no more.
POPE.—*Essay on Man, Ep.* 2, 261.

Nature and nature's laws lay hid in night ;
God said, " Let Newton be ! " and all was light.   POPE.—*On Sir I. Newton.*

Forced by reflective reason, I confess
That human science is uncertain guess.
PRIOR.—*Solomon, Bk.* 1, 739.

Science is the great antidote to the poison of enthusiasm and superstition.
ADAM SMITH.—*Wealth of Nations, Bk.* 5

Only when genius is married to science can the highest results be attained.
HERBT. SPENCER.—*Education.*

Science is organized knowledge.
HERBT. SPENCER.—*Ib.*

Science moves but slowly, slowly, creeping on from point to point.
TENNYSON.—*Locksley Hall.*

All the ancients who have reasoned on physical science without having the torch of practical experiment to guide them, have been only like blind people explaining the nature of colours to other blind people.
VOLTAIRE.—*Physique, Pref.*

True is it Nature hides
Her treasures less and less. Man now presides
In power, where once he trembled in his weakness ;
Science advances with gigantic strides ;
But are we aught enriched in love and meekness ?
WORDSWORTH.—*Miscell, Sonnets, Pt.* 3, 41.

SCOFFERS

Morality was held a standing jest,
And faith a necessary fraud at best.
CHURCHILL.—*Gotham, Bk. 2.*

Truth from his lips prevailed with double
sway,
And fools, who came to scoff, remained to
pray. GOLDSMITH.—*Deserted Village.*

They ["shallow and cynical critics"]
are men who not merely jest themselves,
but worse than that, declare that everyone
treats everything as a jest; they cannot
conceive the possibility of serious treat-
ment of any subject.
KEBLE.—*Lectures on Poetry, No. 17*
(E. K. Francis, tr.).

Scoffing cometh not of wisdom.
SIR P. SIDNEY.—*Apology for Poetry.*
Objections stated.

He never mocks,
For mockery is the fume of little hearts.
TENNYSON.—*Guinevere.*

SCOLDING

Trust me, dear, good humour can prevail,
When airs, and flights, and screams, and
scolding fail.
POPE.—*Rape of the Lock, c. 5, 29.*

For she had a tongue with a tang.
SHAKESPEARE.—*Tempest, Act 2, 1.*

Thus I find it, by experiment,
Scolding moves you less than merriment.
SWIFT.—*To a Lady.*

SCORN

Of all the griefs that harass the distressed
Sure the most bitter is a scornful jest.
JOHNSON.—*London.*

Teach not thy lip such scorn; for it was
made
For kissing, lady, not for such contempt.
SHAKESPEARE.—*Richard III., Act 1, 2.*

O, what a deal of scorn looks beautiful
In the contempt and anger of her lip!
SHAKESPEARE.—*Twelfth Night, Act 3, 1.*

SCOTLAND

Nowhere beats the heart so kindly
As beneath the tartan plaid.
W. E. AYTOUN.—*Chas. Edward.*

Scots, wha hae wi' Wallace bled,
Scots, wham Bruce has often led.
BURNS.—*Bruce's Address.*

From scenes like this old Scotia's grandeur
springs
That makes her loved at home, revered
abroad.
BURNS.—*Cotter's Saturday Night.*

A land of meanness, sophistry and lust,
BYRON.—*English Bards.*

The Scots are steadfast—not their clime.
CAMPBELL.—*Pilgrim of Glencoe.*

Treacherous Scotland, to no interest true.
DRYDEN.—*Death of Cromwell, st. 17.*

Much may be made of a Scotchman, if
he be caught young.
JOHNSON.—*Remark.*

The noblest prospect which a Scotchman ever sees is the high road which leads
him to England. JOHNSON.—*Ib*

I have been trying all my life to like
Scotchmen, and am obliged to desist from
the experiment in despair.
LAMB.—*Imperfect Sympathies.*

In all my travels I never met with any
one Scotchman but what was a man
of sense. I believe everybody of that
country, that has any, leaves it as fast as
he can. F. LOCKIER.—*Scotchmen.*

Mutton old and claret good were Cale-
donia's forte,
Before the Southron taxed her drink and
poisoned her with port.
LORD NEAVES.—*Beef and*
Potatoes.

O Caledonia! stern and wild,
Meet nurse for a poetic child!
Land of brown heath and shaggy wood,
Land of the mountain and the flood,
Land of my sires!
SCOTT.—*Lay of the Last Minstrel, c. 6, st. 2.*

Stands Scotland where it did?
SHAKESPEARE.—*Macbeth, Act 4, 3.*

I look upon Switzerland as an inferior
sort of Scotland.
SYDNEY SMITH.—*Letter to Lord Holland,*
1815.

Scotland, that knuckle-end of England,
that land of Calvin, oatcakes and sulphur.
SYDNEY SMITH.—*Sayings.*

Edinburgh is a hot-bed of genius.
SMOLLETT.—*Humphrey Clinker.*

From the lone shieling of the misty island
Mountains divide us, and a waste of seas;
Yet still the blood is warm, the heart is
Highland,
And we in dreams behold the Hebrides.
JOHN WILSON.—*Noctes Ambrosianæ*
(1827). (Lines by Wilson or possibly
by Lockhart.)

Minds like ours, my dear James, must
always be above national prejudices, and
in all companies it gives me true pleasure
to declare that, as a people, the English are
very little indeed inferior to the Scotch.
JOHN WILSON.—*Noctes, 9.*

Scotsmen tak a' they can get, and a little more if they can.

> *Quoted as a saying by Lord Advocate Maitland, House of Commons, March 6, 1888.*

A Scotsman is one who keeps the Sabbath and every other darned thing he can lay his hands on.   *American saying.*

A Scotsman is aye wise ahint the hand. (i.e. after the event).
> *Scottish prov. (Scott, Fortunes of Nigel).*

The Scot will not fight till he sees his own blood.
> *North of England prov. (Scott.—Ib.).*

If the Scot likes a small pot, he pays a sure penny.   *Scottish prov.*

A Scotsman, a cow, and a Newcastle grindstone travel a' the world ower.   *Ib.*

The Englishman greets (weeps),
The Irishman sleeps,
But the Scotsman gangs till he gets it.
> *Scottish saying.*

The Scotsman is never at home but when he's abroad.   *Ib.*

The Scots wear short patience and long daggers.   *Ib.*

The Scotch are a nation of gentlemen.
> *Saying of George IV. (according to Sir W. Scott).*

A crook in the Forth
Is worth an earldom in North.
Scottish prov. (referring to the fertility of land on the banks of the Forth).

SCRUPULOUSNESS

Too fond of the right to pursue the expedient.   GOLDSMITH.—*Retaliation.*

Yet do I fear thy nature ;
It is too full o' the milk of human kindness
To catch the nearest way.
          SHAKESPEARE.—*Macbeth*, Act 1, 4.

Thou wouldst be great ;
Art not without ambition ; but without
The illness should attend it. What thou wouldst highly
That wouldst thou holily ; wouldst not play false,
And yet wouldst wrongly win.
          SHAKESPEARE.—*Ib.*, Act 1, 5.

Though in the trade of war I have slain men,
Yet do I hold it very stuff o' the conscience
To do no contrived murder. I lack iniquity
Sometime to do me service.
          SHAKESPEARE.—*Othello*, Act 1, 2.

SCULPTURE

The conscious stone to beauty grew.
          EMERSON.—*The Problem.*

Sculptures are far closer akin to Poetry than paintings are.
          KEBLE.—*Lectures on Poetry, No. 2 (E. K. Francis tr.).*

And the cold marble leapt to life a god.
          H. H. MILMAN.—*Apollo Belvedere.*

There is no instance of fine sculpture being produced by a nation either torpid, weak, or in decadence.
          RUSKIN.—*Aratra Pentelici*, 1870.

From many a garnished niche around
Stern saints and tortured martyrs frowned.
          SCOTT.—*Lay of the Last Minstrel*, 6, 29.

SEA

Now the great winds shoreward blow,
Now the salt tides seaward flow ;
Now the white wild horses play,
Champ and chafe and toss in the spray.
          M. ARNOLD.—*Forsaken Merman.*

The unplumbed, salt, estranging sea.
          M. ARNOLD.—*To Marguerite.*

Old ocean's grey and melancholy waste.
          W. C. BRYANT.—*Thanatopsis*, 43.

Once more upon the waters ! yet once more !
And the waves bound beneath me as a steed
That knows his rider.
          BYRON.—*Childe Harold*, c. 3, st. 2.

The hell of waters, where they howl and hiss,
And boil in endless torture.
          BYRON.—*Ib.*, c. 4, 69.

He sinks into thy depths with bubbling groan,
Without a grave, unknelled, uncoffined, and unknown. BYRON.—*Ib.*, st. 179.

Time writes no wrinkle on thine azure brow ;
Such as creation's dawn beheld, thou rollest now.   BYRON.—*Ib.*, st. 182.

Thou glorious mirror, where the Almighty's form
Glasses itself in tempests.
          BYRON.—*Ib.*, 183.

Dark, heaving ; —boundless, endless, and sublime—
The image of eternity. BYRON.—*Ib.*, 183.

O'er the glad waters of the dark blue sea,
Our thoughts as boundless, and our souls as free,
Far as the breeze can bear, the billows foam,
Survey our empire, and behold our home !
          BYRON.—*Corsair*, 1, 1.

Oh, who can tell, save he whose heart hath
tried,
And danced in triumph o'er the waters
wide,
The exulting sense—the pulse's maddening
play,
That thrills the wanderer of that trackless
way?   BYRON.—*Corsair*, 1, 1.

'Twas twilight, and the sunless day went
down
Over the waste of waters.
          BYRON.—*Don Juan, c.* 2, 49.

"Oh! darkly, deeply, beautifully blue,"
As some one somewhere sings about the sea.
BYRON.—*Ib., c.* 4, 110. (cf. *Southey, infra*).

Water, water, everywhere,
Nor any drop to drink.
COLERIDGE.—*Ancient Mariner*, Pt. 2.

Alone, alone, all, all alone,
Alone on a wide, wide sea!
          COLERIDGE.—*Ib., Pt.* 4.

The sea! the sea! the open sea!
The blue, the fresh, the ever free!
BARRY CORNWALL.—*The Sea.*

I'm on the sea! I'm on the sea!
I am where I would ever be,
With the blue above, and the blue below,
And silence wheresoe'er I go.
          BARRY CORNWALL.—*Ib.*

That great fishpond, the sea.
     DEKKER.—*Honest Whore, Pt.* 1,
                    Act 1, 2 (1604).
Women and cowards on the land may lie,
The sea's a tomb that's proper for the
brave.
     DRYDEN.—*Annus Mirabilis, st.* 101.

Sea, full of food, the nourisher of kinds,
Purger of earth and medicine of men.
          EMERSON.—*Sea-Shore.*

I once heard one blue-jacket say to
another the reason *he* believed in the Bible
was that in heaven there is "no more
sea."   LORD FISHER.—*Memories.*

Old Indefatigable,
Time's right hand man, the sea.
     W. E. HENLEY.—*To J. A. C.*

The bounding pinnace played a game
Of dreary pitch and toss ;
A game that, on the good dry land,
Is apt to bring a loss !
          HOOD.—*Sea Spell.*

The many-twinkling smile of ocean.
KEBLE.—*Christian Year*, 2 *Sun. after Trin.*

I must go down to the seas again, to the
lonely sea and the sky,
And all I ask is a tall ship and a star to
steer her by ;

And the wheel's kick and the wind's song
and the white sail's shaking,
And a grey mist on the sea's face, and a
grey dawn breaking.
     JOHN MASEFIELD.—*Sea Fever.*

O bitter sea, tumultuous sea !
Full many an ill is wrought by thee.
     W. MORRIS.—*Jason, Bk.* 4, 109.

For the Island's sons the word still runs,
"The King and the King's Highway."
     SIR H. NEWBOLT.—*King's Highway.*

The sea indeed is assuredly common to
all.   PLAUTUS.—*Rudens*, Act 4.

And seas but join the regions they
divide.   POPE.—*Windsor Forest*, 400.

I love the sea : she is my fellow-creature.
          QUARLES.—*Emblems.*

The sea hath no king but God alone.
          ROSSETTI.—*White Ship.*

What dreadful noise of water in mine ears !
What sights of ugly death within mine eyes !
Methought I saw a thousand fearful
wrecks ;
A thousand men that fishes gnawed upon ;
Wedges of gold, great anchors, heaps of
pearl,
Inestimable stones, unvalued jewels,
All scattered in the bottom of the sea ;
     SHAKESPEARE.—*Richard III.*, Act 1, 4.

Nothing of him that doth fade
But doth suffer a sea change
Into something rich and strange.
     SHAKESPEARE.—*Tempest*, Act 1, 2.

Thetis, bright image of eternity.
          SHELLEY.—*Prometheus.*

Day after day, day after day the same—
A weary waste of waters.
     SOUTHEY.—*Madoc, sec.* 4.

Blue, darkly, deeply, beautifully blue.
          SOUTHEY.—*Ib., sec.* 5.

Beneath thy spell, O radiant summer sea,
Lulled by thy voice, rocked on thy shining
breast,
Fanned by thy soft breath, by thy touch
caressed,
Let all thy treacheries forgotten be.
SUSAN MARR SPALDING.—*The Sea's Spell.*

I will go back to the great sweet mother,
Mother and lover of men, the sea.
     SWINBURNE.—*Triumph of Time.*

E'en utmost Thule shall thy power obey ;
And Neptune shall resign the fasces of the
sea.
     VIRGIL.—*Georgics, Bk.* 1 (*Dryden tr.*).

Others may use the ocean as their road ;
Only the English make it their abode.
          WALLER.—*Miscellanies.*

Sea, that breakest for ever, that breakest
and never art broken.
SIR W. WATSON.—*To the Sea.*

'Tis the broad and mighty sea
That has made us strong and free,
And will keep us what we are.
F. E. WEATHERLEY.—*The Sea.*

Calm and peaceful shall we sleep,
Rocked in the cradle of the deep.
EMMA WILLARD.—*Cradle of the Deep.*

Two Voices are there : one is of the Sea,
One of the Mountains,—each a mighty
voice :
In both from age to age thou didst rejoice ;
They were thy chosen music, Liberty !
WORDSWORTH.—*Poems to National*
Indep., Pt. I, 12.

SEA-SICKNESS

The best of remedies is a beef-steak
Against sea-sickness.
BYRON.—*Don Juan,* 2, 13.

I lay along the deck, wrapped in a cloak
... and reflected that as I had so little life
to lose, it was of little consequence whether
I was drowned, or died, like a resident
clergyman, from indigestion.
SYDNEY SMITH.—*Letter to Mrs. Holland,*
Oct. 6, 1835.

We all like to see people sea-sick when
we are not ourselves.
MARK TWAIN.—*Innocents Abroad, ch.* 3.

SEASONS

Summer is more wooing and seductive,
more versatile and human, appeals to the
affections and the sentiments, and fosters
inquiry and the art impulse.   Winter is of
a more heroic cast, and addresses the intellect.
JOHN BURROUGHS.—*The Snow Walkers.*

O, Winter ! Put away thy snowy pride ;
O, Spring ! Neglect the cowslip and the
bell ;
O, Summer ! Throw thy pears and plums
aside ;
O, Autumn ! Bid the grape with poison
swell.   CHATTERTON.—*February.*

Oh, Nature ! All thy seasons please the
eye
Of him who sees a Deity in all.
JAS. GRAHAME.—*The Birds of Scotland.*

The Seasons four,—
Green-kirtled Spring, flush Summer, golden
store
In Autumn's sickle, Winter frosty hoar,
Join dance with shadowy Hours.
KEATS.—*Endymion, Bk.* 4.

All seasons, and their change, all please
alike.
MILTON.—*Paradise Lost, Bk.* 4, 640.

The lusty spring smells well, but drooping autumn tastes well.
WEBSTER.—*Duchess of Malfi,* Act 2, 2.

To every thing there is a season, and a
time to every purpose under the heaven :
A time to be born, and a time to die.
Ecclesiastes iii, 1, 2.

SEAWEED

Call us not weeds—we are flowers of the
sea.   MRS. AVELINE.—*Tales and Fables.*

There arose
Tall stems, that, rooted in the depths
below,
Swing idly with the motions of the sea ;
And here were shrubberies in whose mazy
screen
The creatures of the deep made haunt.
WM. CULLEN BRYANT.—*Sella.*

The world below the brine,
Forests at the bottom of the sea, the
branches and the leaves,
Sea lettuce, vast lichens, strange flowers
and seeds.   WALT WHITMAN.

SECLUSION

Secret and self-contained and solitary as
an oyster.   DICKENS.—*Christmas Carol.*

Worth concealed differs little from
buried indolence.
HORACE.—*Odes, Bk.* 4, 9.

Far from gay cities, and the ways of
men.   POPE.—*Odyssey,* 14, 410.

By being seldom seen, I could not stir,
But, like a comet, I was wondered at.
SHAKESPEARE.—*Henry IV., Pt.* 1,
Act 3, 2.

SECRECY

There's a secret in his breast,
Which will never let him rest.
M. ARNOLD.—*Tristram, Pt.* 1.

These matters are always a secret till it
is found out that everybody knows them.
JANE AUSTEN.—*Emma, ch.* 53.

None are so fond of secrets as those who
do not mean to keep them.
C. C. COLTON.—*Lacon, No.* 40.

Some fools there are who prate of love
platonic,
Just like the secret famed of tribe masonic ;
A secret of such note that those who win it
Find for their pains that there is nothing
in it.
W. H. IRELAND.—*Modern Ship of Fools.*
Of Fools in Love.

But still remember that a prince's secrets
Are balm concealed ; but poison if dis-
covered.
MASSINGER.—*Duke of Milan,* Act 1, 3.

A free tongued woman,
And very excellent at telling secrets.
 MASSINGER.—*Old Law*, Act 4, 2.

Silence is the soul of war ;
Deliberate counsel must prepare
The mighty work, which valour must complete. PRIOR.—*Ode in Imit. of Horace*
     (1692), *l*. 34.

If you have hitherto concealed this sight,
Let it be tenable in your silence still ;
And whatsoever else shall hap to-night,
Give it an understanding, but no tongue.
 SHAKESPEARE.—*Hamlet*, Act 1, 2.

Above all, be always master of your own
secrets. Who tells another's secret ought
to be regarded as a traitor ; who tells his
own passes here for a fool.
   VOLTAIRE.—*L'Indiscret.*

Wisdom sometimes walks in clouted
shoes.   *Prov.*

If you cannot keep your own counsel,
how can you expect another person to
keep it ?
 *Latin prov., Martinus Dumiensis, De
Moribus, see Chaucer, " Melibeus," sec. 20.*

SECTS

There was never law, or sect, or opinion
did so much magnify goodness, as the
Christian religion doth.
  BACON.—*Essays ; Of Goodness.*

And though thou'rt of a different church,
I will not leave thee in the lurch.
  BUTLER.—*Hudibras*, Pt. 1, *c*. 3.

Religion spawned a various rout
Of petulant capricious sects,
The maggot of corrupted texts,
That first run all religion down,
And after every swarm its own.
  BUTLER.—*Ib.*, Pt. 3, *c*. 2.

All the sects are different, because they
come from men ; morality is everywhere
the same, because it comes from God.
 VOLTAIRE.—*Dictionnaire Philosophique
      (Théisme).*

Every sect seems to me the rallying-
place of error. Tell me, are there any
sects in geometry ?
   VOLTAIRE.—*L'Ingénu.*

In Christianity alone there are more than
two hundred different sects, all crying :
" Mortals, buy of me ; I am the only one
which deals in the truth ; all the others
are impostors."
 VOLTAIRE.—*Theists' Profession of Faith.*

SECURITY

And you all know, security
Is mortal's chiefest enemy.
 SHAKESPEARE.—*Macbeth*, Act 3, 5.

But yet I'll make assurance double sure,
And take a bond of fate.
  SHAKESPEARE.—*Ib.*, Act 4, 1.

SEDITION

The ancient politicians in popular estates were wont to compare the people
to the sea, and the orators to the winds,
because, as the sea would of itself be calm
and quiet if the winds did not move and
trouble it, so the people would be peaceable
and tractable if the seditious orators did
not set them in working and agitation.
  BACON.—*Adv. of Learning, Bk. 2.*

The surest way to prevent seditions, if
the times do bear it, is to take away the
matter of them.
  BACON.—*Essays, Seditions.*

The vile vulgar, ever discontent,
Their growing fears in secret murmurs
 vent ;
Still prone to change, though still the
 slaves of state,
And sure the monarch whom they have,
 to hate.
  POPE.—*Statius's Thebais, Bk.* 1.

SELF

Deliver me from the evil man, even from
myself.   ST. AUGUSTINE.

The arch-flatterer, with whom all the
petty flatterers have intelligence, is a man's
self.   BACON.—*Of Love.*

Because, however sad the truth may seem,
Sludge is of all-importance to himself.
  BROWNING.—*Mr. Sludge.*

Lord of himself ;—that heritage of woe.
  BYRON.—*Lara, c.* 1, *st.* 2.

Ful ofte tyme I rede [very often I
counsel], thet no man truste in his owene
perfeccioun, but [unless] he be stronger
than Sampson, and holier than Daniel,
and wyser than Solomon.
  CHAUCER.—*Parson's Tale, sec.* 83.

As for the largest-hearted of us, what
is the word we write most often in our
cheque-books ?—" Self."
 EDEN PHILLPOTTS.—*A Shadow Passes.*

Whate'er the passion, knowledge, fame, or
 pelf,
Not one will change his neighbour with
 himself.
  POPE.—*Essay on Man*, 3, 261.

As I walked by myself, I said to myself,
 And myself said again to me :
" Look to thyself, take care of thyself,
 For nobody cares for thee."
     Old Saying.

Self's allers (always) at home.
     Suffolk prov.

Self is the man. *German prov*

SELF-CONDEMNATION

Meantime I seek no sympathies, nor need ;
The thorns which I have reaped are of the tree
I planted,—they have torn me,—and I bleed ;
I should have known what fruit would spring from such a seed.
      Byron.—*Childe Harold, c.* 4, 10.

There is no future pang
Can deal that justice on the self-condemned
He deals on his own soul.
      Byron.—*Manfred,* Act 3, 1.

Absolved from guilt, but never self-for-given.   Campbell.—*Theodric.*

Good to the poor, to kindred dear,
To servants kind, to friendship clear,
To nothing but herself severe.
      T. Carew.—*On Maria Wentworth.*

Better to stand ten thousand sneers than one abiding pang, such as time could not abolish, of bitter self-reproach.
      De Quincey.—*Confessions.*

Trust me, no tortures which the poets feign
Can match the fierce, the unutterable pain,
He feels, who night and day, devoid of rest,
Carries his own accuser in his breast.
      W. Gifford.—*Juvenal,* 13, 267.

If there be
Among the auditors, one whose conscience tells him
He is of the same mould,—*We cannot help it.*
      Massinger.—*Roman Actor,* Act 1, 3.

Gentle to others, to himself severe.
      Rogers.—*Pleasures of Memory.*

Leave her to Heaven,
And to those thorns that in her bosom lodge,
To prick and sting her.
      Shakespeare.—*Hamlet,* Act 1, 5.

I had most need of blessing, and " Amen " Stuck in my throat.
      Shakespeare.—*Macbeth,* Act 2, 2.

My conscience hath a thousand several tongues,
And every tongue brings in a several tale,
And every tale condemns me for a villain.
      Shakespeare.—*Richard III.,* Act 5, 3.

Each one thinks his lot the worst : but he is mistaken. If he thought himself the worst of the lot he might be right.
      C. H. Spurgeon.—" *Salt-Cellars.*"

And I said, It is mine own infirmity.
      Church Psalter lxxvii, 10.

SELF-CONSCIOUSNESS

Self-contemplation is infallibly **the** symptom of disease, be it or be it not the cure.   Carlyle.—*Characteristics.*

Mr. Phunky, blushing into the very whites of his eyes, tried to look as if he didn't know that everybody was gazing at him : a thing which no man ever succeeded in doing yet, or, in all reasonable prob-ability, ever will.
      Dickens.—*Pickwick Papers, ch.* 34

I believe they talked of me, for they laughed consumedly.
      Farquhar.—*Beaux' Stratagem,* Act 3, 1.

At night, to his own sharp fancies a prey,
He lies like a hedgehog rolled up the wrong way,
Tormenting himself with his prickles.
      Hood.—*Miss Kilmansegg.*

SELF-CONTROL

Prudent, cautious self-control
Is wisdom's root.
      Burns.—*A Bard's Epitaph.*

Two principles in human nature reign :
Self-love to urge and reason to restrain.
      Pope.—*Essay on Man, Ep.* 2, 53

And mistress of herself, though china fall.   Pope.—*Moral Essays, Ep.* 2.

A man that fortune's buffets and rewards
Hath ta'en with equal thanks ; and blessed are those,
Whose blood and judgment are so well commingled,
That they are not a pipe for Fortune's finger
To sound what stop she please.
      Shakespeare.—*Hamlet,* Act 3, 2.

Give me that man
That is not passion's slave, and I will wear him
In my heart's core, ay, in my heart of heart.
      Shakespeare.—*Ib.*

My pulse, as yours, doth temperately keep time,
And makes as healthful music.
      Shakespeare.—*Ib.,* Act 3, 4.

Man, who man would be,
Must rule the empire of himself ; in **it** Must be supreme.
      Shelley.—*Political Greatness.*

In vain he seeketh others to suppresse
That hath not learnd himselfe first to subdew.
      Spenser.—*Faerie Queene, Bk.* 6, *c.* 1, 41

SELF-DECEPTION

This trade of mine—I don't know, can't
be sure
But there was something in it, tricks and
all !
Really, I want to light up my own mind.
BROWNING.—*Mr. Sludge.*

If a man proves too clearly and con-
vincingly to himself . . . that a tiger is an
optical illusion—well, he will find out he
is wrong.   The tiger will himself intervene
in the discussion, in a manner which will
be in every sense conclusive.
G. K. CHESTERTON.—*(April, 1917).*

Yet still we hug the dear deceit.
N. COTTON.—*Visions in Verse.*

First wish to be imposed on, and then
are.   COWPER.—*Progress of Error,* 290.

All other swindlers upon earth are nothing
to the self-swindlers, and with such pretences did I cheat myself.
DICKENS.—*Great Expectations, ch.* 28.

With how much ease believe we what
we wish !
DRYDEN.—*All for Love,* Act 4, 1.

The easiest person to deceive is one's
own self.   (1st) LORD LYTTON.—*Disowned.*

Our years, our debts, and our enemies
are always more numerous than we believe.
CHAS. NODIER (1783–1844).

Till their own dreams at length deceive
'em,
And oft, repeating, they believe 'em.
PRIOR.—*Alma, c.* 3, 13.

Made such a sinner of his memory,
To credit his own lie.
SHAKESPEARE.—*Tempest,* Act 1, 2.

SELF-DESTRUCTION

So the struck eagle, stretched upon the
plain,
No more through rolling clouds to soar
again,
Viewed his own feather on the fatal dart,
And winged the shaft that quivered in his
heart ;
Keen were his pangs, but keener far to feel
He nursed the pinion which impelled the
steel.   BYRON.—*English Bards,* 824.

So fond are mortal men
Fallen into wrath divine,
As their own ruin on themselves to invite.
MILTON.—*Samson Agonistes,* 1684.

SELF-HELP

Each person is the founder
Of his own fortune, good or bad.
BEAUMONT AND FLETCHER.—*Love's
Pilgrimage,* Act 1, 1.

The dog that trots about finds a bone.
BORROW.—*Bible in Spain, ch.* 47
(*Cited as a gipsy saying*).

Unless above himself he can
Erect himself, how poor a thing is man !
S. DANIEL.—*To Lady Cumberland.*

Our own felicity we make or find.
GOLDSMITH.—*Traveller.*

What merit to be dropped on fortune's
hill ?
The honour is to mount it.
J. S. KNOWLES.—*Hunchback,* Act 1, 1.

Accuse not Nature ; she hath done her
part ;
Do thou but thine, and be not diffident
Of wisdom.
MILTON.—*Paradise Lost, Bk.* 8, 561.

Every man is the author of his own
fortune.   SALLUST.—*De Republica.*

He lives to build, not boast, a generous
race ;
No tenth transmitter of a foolish face.
R. SAVAGE.—*Bastard,* 1.

Our remedies oft in ourselves do lie,
Which we ascribe to Heaven.
SHAKESPEARE.—*All's Well,* Act 1, 1.

You must scratch your own head with
your own nails.   *Arabic prov.*

Give orders, and do it, and you will be
free from anxiety.   *Portuguese prov.*

Pray to God, sailor, but pull to the shore.
Prov.

In smooth water, God help me ! In
rough water I will help myself.   *Prov.*

Pray devoutly, but hammer stoutly.
Prov.

SELF-KNOWLEDGE

Oh wad some power the giftie gie us
To see oursels as others see us !
It wad frae mony a blunder free us
And foolish notion.
BURNS.—*To a Louse.*

The first step to self-knowledge is self-
distrust.   J. C. HARE.—*Guesses at Truth.*

Self-reverence, self-knowledge, self-control,
These three alone lead life to sovereign
power.   TENNYSON.—*Œnone.*

Know thyself.   *Solon.*

The eye that sees all things else sees not
itself.   *Prov.*

SELF-LOVE (AMOUR PROPRE)

Self-love is the greatest of all flatterers.
LA ROCHEFOUCAULD.—*Maxim* 3.

P*

View yourselves
In the deceiving mirror of self-love.
MASSINGER.—*Parliament of Love*, Act 1, 5.

The only passion natural to man is self-love or "amour-propre" taken in an extended sense.
ROUSSEAU.—*Emile*.

Self-love (amour propre) makes more libertines than love.
ROUSSEAU.—*Ib*.

Self-love, my liege, is not so vile a sin
As self-neglecting.
SHAKESPEARE.—*Henry V.*, Act 2, 4.

O villainous! I have looked upon the world for four times seven years; and since I could distinguish betwixt a benefit and an injury, I never found man that knew how to love himself.
SHAKESPEARE.—*Othello*, Act 1, 3.

SELF-RELIANCE

Resolve to be thy self; and know that he,
Who finds himself, loses his misery!
MATTHEW ARNOLD.—*Self-Dependence*.

When is a man strong, until he feels alone?
BROWNING.—*Colombe's Birthday*, Act 3.

The basis of good manners is self-reliance.
EMERSON.—*Behaviour*.

There is no dependence that can be sure but a dependence upon one's self.
GAY.—*Letter*, 1729.

I am the master of my fate:
I am the captain of my soul.
W. E. HENLEY.—*Echoes*.

What weapons has the lion but himself?
KEATS.—*King Stephen, Scene* 3.

And all your fortune lies beneath your hat.   J. OLDHAM.—*To a Friend*.

I am myself my own commander.
PLAUTUS.—*Mercator*.

Men at some time are masters of their fates.
SHAKESPEARE.—*Julius Cæsar*, Act 1, 2.

Then where is truth if there be no self-trust?   SHAKESPEARE.—*Lucrece*, 23.

I believe he [Lord John Russell] would perform the operation for the stone, build St. Peter's, or assume, with or without ten minutes' notice, the command of the Channel Fleet.   SYDNEY SMITH.—*Letter*.

An ounce o' a man's wit is worth ten o' ither folk's.   *Scottish prov.*

SELF-RESPECT

The reverence of a man's self is, next religion, the chiefest bridle of all vices.
BACON.—*New Atlantis*.

Oft-times nothing profits more
Than self esteem, grounded on just and right.
MILTON.—*Paradise Lost, Bk.* 8, 571.

There is also a certain delight in having pleased one's self.   OVID.—*Medic. Faciei*.

It is rare that anyone reverences himself enough.   QUINTILIAN.—107.

This above all,—To thine own self be true,
And it must follow, as the night the day,
Thou canst not then be false to any man.
SHAKESPEARE.—*Hamlet*, Act 1, 3.

It is easy—terribly easy—to shake a man's faith in himself.   To take advantage of that to break a man's spirit is devil's work.   G. B. SHAW.—*Candida*.

If it be a duty to respect other men's claims, so also it is a duty to maintain our own.   H. SPENCER.—*Social Statics, Pt.* 3.

SELFISHNESS

It is the nature of extreme self-lovers, as they will set a house on fire an it were but to roast their eggs.
BACON.—*Of Wisdom for a Man's Self*.

There's lang-tochered Nancy
Maist fetches his fancy—
But the laddie's dear sel' he lo'es dearest of a'.
BURNS.—*There's a Youth in this City*.

The Golden Calf of self-love.
CARLYLE.—*Burns*.

And therefore at the Kinges court, my brother,
Each man for himself, ther is non other.
CHAUCER.—*Knight's Tale*, 323.

He asks what most in life is worth his care,
Looks in the glass, and finds the answer there.
COTSFORD DICK.—*Ways of the World* (1896). *New Narcissus*.

Selfishness is the greatest curse of the human race.   GLADSTONE.—*Speech*, 1890.

Selfishness, Love's cousin.
KEATS.—*Isabella*.

Self-interest sets in motion all sorts of virtues and vices.   LA ROCHEFOUCAULD, *Maxim* 253.

He'd been true to *one* party—an' thet is himself.
J. R. LOWELL.—*Biglow Papers, Series* 3.

You've got to choose in this world between being selfish and being a fool.
EDEN PHILLPOTTS.

I never knew any man in my life who
could not bear another's misfortunes perfectly like a Christian.
POPE.—*Thoughts on Various Subjects.*

No man is born unto himself alone ;
Who lives unto himself, he lives to none.
QUARLES.—*Esther.*

Despite those titles, power, and pelf,
The wretch concentred all in self
Living, shall forfeit fair renown,
And, doubly-dying, shall go down
To the vile dust from whence he sprung,
Unwept, unhonoured, and unsung.
SCOTT.—*Lay of the Last Minstrel, c. 6, 1.*

Twin-sister of religion, selfishness.
SHELLEY.—*Queen Mab, c. 5.*

'Tis myself, quoth he, I must mind most ;
So the Devil may take the hindmost.
SOUTHEY.—*March to Moscow, c. 8.*

Himself unto himself he sold ;
Upon himself himself did feed,
Quiet, dispassionate, and cold.
TENNYSON.—*A Character.*

We all wish things to go better with ourselves than with someone else.
TERENCE.—*Andria, 2, 5, 16.*

There's plenty of boys that will come
hankering and gruvvelling around when
you've got an apple, and beg the core off
you ; but when *they've* got one, and you
beg for the core, and remind them how
you give them a core one time, they make
a mouth at you, and say thank you 'most
to death, but there ain't a-going to be no
core.
MARK TWAIN.—*Tom Sawyer Abroad, c. 1.*

All the passions become extinguished
with age, except self-love, which never
dies.   VOLTAIRE.—*Stances ou Quatrains.*

The selfish heart deserves the pain it feels.
YOUNG.—*Night Thoughts, 1.*

Self is the man.   *German prov.*

SENILITY

Lord Tyrawley and I have been dead
these two years, but we don't choose to
have it known.
LORD CHESTERFIELD.—(*Saying—
according to Boswell.*)

Old Age, a second child, by nature curst
With more and greater evils than the first,
Weak, sickly, full of pains : in every
breath
Railing at life, and yet afraid of death.
CHURCHILL.—*Gotham.*

I would rather be dead than live dead,
CURIUS DENTATUS.—(*According to
Seneca.*)

I have not that alacrity of spirit
Nor cheer of mind, that I was wont to have.
SHAKESPEARE.—*Richard III., Act 5, 3.*

SENSATIONALISM

In darkness and in storm he took delight
BEATTIE.—*The Minstrel.*

'Tis strange but true ; for truth is always
strange ;
Stranger than fiction.
BYRON.—*Don Juan, 15, 101.*

And Katerfelto, with his hair on end,
At his own wonders, wondering for his
bread.   COWPER.—*Winter Evening.*

Something will come of this. I hope it
mayn't be human gore.
DICKENS.—*Barnaby Rudge, ch. 4.*

" I wants to make your flesh creep,"
replied the boy.
DICKENS.—*Pickwick Papers, ch. 8.*

Let not Medea, with unnatural rage,
Slaughter her mangled infants on the stage.
P. FRANCIS.—*Horace, Art of Poetry.*

The imitative poet [i.e. the dramatist
and epic poet] establishes a bad republic
in the soul of each individual, gratifying
the foolish part of it.
PLATO.—*Republic, Bk. 10, 7 (Davis tr.).*

She [Agatha Wylie] looked in again to
say in a low voice : " Prepare for something thrilling. I feel just in the humour
to say the most awful things."
G. B. SHAW.—*Unsocial Socialist, ch. 4.*

SENSE

Take care of the sense and the sounds
will take care of themselves.
C. L. DODGSON.—*Alice in Wonderland.*

It is hard to talk sense, but harder to
find listeners if you do.
Given as a saying by C. H. Spurgeon.

A' complain o' want o' siller ; nane o'
want o' sense.   *Scottish prov.*

SENSES, THE

And taste and touch and sight and sound
and smell,
That sing and dance round Reason's fine-
wrought throne,
Shall flee away and leave him all forlorn.
WM. BLAKE.—*Edward III.*

Sight has to do with the understanding ;
hearing with reason ; smell with memory.
Touch and taste are realistic and depend
on contact ; they have no ideal side.
SCHOPENHAUER.—*Psychological
Observations.*

SENSITIVENESS

Nor peace nor ease the heart can know,
    Which, like the needle true,
Turns at the touch of joy or woe,
    But, turning, trembles too.
MRS. GREVILLE.—*Prayer for Indifference.*

O Julie! what a fatal gift from heaven
is a sensitive soul! He who has received
it must expect to have nothing but suffering and sorrow on this earth.
                    ROUSSEAU.—*Julie.*

He that has a muckle nose thinks ilka
ane speaks o't.   *Scottish prov.*

SENSUALITY

Bred only and completed to the taste
Of lustful appetence, to sing, to dance,
To dress, and troll the tongue, and roll the
    eye.
    MILTON.—*Paradise Lost, Bk. 11, 618.*

SENTIMENT AND SENTIMENTALISM

There are some feelings time cannot
benumb.
    BYRON.—*Childe Harold, c. 4, 19.*

The barrenest of all mortals is the senti-
mentalist.   CARLYLE.—*Characteristics.*

Is not Sentimentalism twin-sister to
Cant, if not one and the same with it?
    CARLYLE.—*French Revolution.*

Words that weep and tears that speak.
    COWLEY.—*The Prophet.*

Sentiment cannot be defined; it would
always be more clear than any definition.
But it serves to define all the phenomena
of soul and body.
    DE RIVAROL.—*Of Language, sec. 2.*

" There are strings," said Mr. Tappertit,
" . . . in the human heart that had better
not be wibrated."
    DICKENS.—*Barnaby Rudge, c. 22.*

Blest if I don't think he's got a main in
his head, as is always turned on.
    DICKENS.—*Pickwick, c. 16.*

The understanding's copper coin
Counts not with the gold of love.
    HAFIZ.—*As given by Emerson, Essay
            on Persian Poetry.*

The mind is always the dupe of the heart.
    LA ROCHEFOUCAULD.—*Maxim 102.*

The heart has reasons of which reason
has no knowledge.
    PASCAL.—*Pensées, 2, 17, 5.*

What's Hecuba to him or he to Hecuba,
That he should weep for her?
    SHAKESPEARE.—*Hamlet, Act 2, 2.*

I never was a good son or a good brother
or a good patriot, in the sense of thinking
that my mother and my sister and my
native country were better than other
people's, because I happened to belong to
them.
    G. B. SHAW.—*Irrational Knot, ch. 6.*

SERENITY

A quiet conscience makes one so serene!
    BYRON.—*Don Juan, c. 1, st. 83.*

Serene, yet warm; humane, yet firm his
    mind;
As little touched as any man's with bad.
    THOMSON.—*Castle of Indolence, c. 1, 65.*

SERIOUSNESS

An event has happened on which it is
difficult to speak, and impossible to keep
silence.
    BURKE.—*Impeachment of Hastings,
                    May 5, 1789.*

There is something in the heart of everything, if we can reach it, that we shall not
be inclined to laugh at.
    RUSKIN.—*Modern Painters, vol. 2,
                    Pt. 3, ch. 3, 8.*

SERMONS

For the preacher's merit or demerit,
It were to be wished that the flaws were
    fewer,
In the earthen vessel, holding treasure,
But the main thing is, does it hold good
    measure?
Heaven soon sets right all other matters.
    BROWNING.—*Christmas Eve.*

I shook the sermon out of my mind.
    BUNYAN.—*Grace Abounding.*

Politics and the pulpit are terms that
have little agreement. No sound ought
to be heard in the church but the healing
voice of Christian charity.
    BURKE.—*Reflections on the Revolution.*

And pulpit, drum ecclesiastic,
Was beat with fist instead of a stick.
    BUTLER.—*Hudibras, Pt. 1, c. 1.*

Our old Divines will hereafter be considered our classics. EDWD. FITZGERALD.

One may prefer fresh eggs, though laid
by a fowl of the meanest understanding,
but why fresh sermons?
    GEO. ELIOT.—*Theophrastus Such.
                    Looking Backward.*

We have no official knowledge of hell.
That the poor souls who dwell there are
condemned to read all day long, the dreary
sermons preached here on earth I refuse
to believe. It is a calumny. Even in
hell it has not come to that.   HEINE.

Judge not the preacher ; for he is thy
    judge :
If thou mistake him, thou conceiv'st him
    not.
God calleth preaching folly. Do not
    grudge
To pick out treasures from an earthen pot.
The worst speaks something good : if all
    want sense,
God takes a text and preaches patience.
                HERBERT.—*Church Porch.*

The parson exceeds not an hour in preaching, because all ages have thought that a
competency.
        HERBERT.—*Priest to the Temple, c.* 7.

The excellence of this text is that it will
suit any sermon ; and of this sermon that
it will suit any text,
    STERNE.—*Tristram Shandy, vol.* 6, *ch.* 11.

By our pastor perplexed,
    How shall we determine ?
" Watch and pray," says the text ;
" Go to sleep," says the sermon.
ANON.—*Found in a Commonplace Book,*
                                c. 1820.

    Funeral sermon, lying sermon.
                            German prov.

SERVANTS

So many servants, so many enemies.
            CATO.—*(Quoted by Seneca.)*

Murmure eek [murmuring also] is ofte
amonges servants that grucchen [grudge]
when their sovereyns [masters] bidden
them do lawful things, whiche words men
clepen [call] the develes Paternoster.
        CHAUCER.—*Parson's Tale, sec.* 30.

In all the necessaries of life there is not
a greater plague than servants.
    C. CIBBER.—*She Would and She Would
                        Not, Act* 1, 1.

We ought not to treat living creatures
like shoes or household belongings, which
when worn with use we throw away.
            PLUTARCH.—*Life of Cato.*

Great folk's servants are aye more saucy
than themselves.
    SIR W. SCOTT.—*Heart of Midlothian.*

Lucky is the man whose servants speak
well of him.   THACKERAY.—*Newcomes.*

SERVICE

All service ranks the same with God—
With God, whose puppets, best and worst
Are we : there is no last nor first.
        BROWNING.—*Pippa Passes, Pt.* 4.

There never was a bad man that had
ability for good service.
        BURKE.—*Impeachment of Hastings,
                        Feb.,* 1788.

Serve and thou shalt be served. If you
love and serve men, you cannot, by any
hiding or stratagem, escape the remunera-
tion.   EMERSON.—*Sovereignty of Ethics.*

A servant with this clause
    Makes drudgery divine ;
Who sweeps a room, as for thy laws,
    Makes that and th'action fine.
                    HERBERT.—*Elixir.*

In all the faith my innocence could give
    me,
In the best language my true tongue could
    tell me,
And all the broken sighs my sick heart
    lend me,
I sued, and served ; long did I love this
    lady,
Long was my travail, long my trade to win
    her,
With all the duty of my soul I served her.
        MASSINGER.—*Very Woman, Act* 4, 3.

Servant of God, well done ! Well hast thou
    fought
The better fight who singly hast main-
    tained
Against revolted multitudes the cause
Of truth.
        MILTON.—*Paradise Lost, Bk.* 6, 29.

        God doth not need
Either man's work or his own gifts ;
    who best
Bear his mild yoke, they serve him best.
    His state
Is kingly ; thousands at his bidding speed
And post o'er land and ocean without
    rest ;
They also serve who only stand and wait.
                MILTON.—*Sonnet.*

To keep the house unharmed
    Their fathers built so fair,
Deeming endurance armed
    Better than brute despair,
They found the secret of the word that saith
" Service is sweet, for all true life is death."
    SIR H. NEWBOLT.—*Farewell* (1910).

Scanty goods have I to give,
    Scanty skill to woo ;
But¡I have a will to work,
    And a heart for you.
    CHRISTINA ROSSETTI.—*Maiden Song.*

Had I but served my God with half the
    zeal
I served my king, he would not in mine age
Have left me naked to mine enemies.
    SHAKESPEARE.—*Henry VIII., Act* 3, 2.

I have done the state some service, and
they know't.
        SHAKESPEARE.—*Othello, Act* 5, 2.

All spirits are enslaved which serve
    things evil.
        SHELLEY.—*Prometheus, Act* 2. 4

When God is to be served, the cost we weigh
In anxious balance, grudging the expense.
ARCHBP. TRENCH.—*Sonnet.*

Small service is true service while it lasts.   WORDSWORTH.—*In a Child's Album* (1834).

The Daisy, by the shadow that it casts,
Protects the lingering dew-drop from the sun.   WORDSWORTH.—*Ib.*

God for his service needeth not proud work of human skill ;
They please him best who labour most in peace to do his will.
WORDSWORTH.—*Poet's Dream.*

SERVILITY

By being commonplace and cringing one gets everything.
BEAUMARCHAIS.—*Barbier de Séville,*
Act 3, 7.

I live by pulling off the hat.
MATTHEW GREEN.—*Barclay's Apology.*

No slavery is more disgraceful than voluntary slavery.   SENECA.—*Ep.* 47.

A servile race, in folly nursed,
Who truckle most when treated worst.
SWIFT.—*On the Death of Dr. Swift,*
(*Alluding to Ireland*).

Where might is the right is ;
Long purses make strong swords.
Let weakness learn meekness :
God save the House of Lords !
SWINBURNE.—*Word for the Country.*

Rough to common men,
But honeying at the whisper of a lord.
TENNYSON.—*Princess, Prol.,* 114.

Grin when he laughs that beareth all the sway ;
Frown when he frowns, and groan when he is pale.
SIR T. WYATT.—*The Courtier's Life.*

SERVITUDE

Servitude that hugs her chain.
GRAY.—*Ode for Music.*

Slavery chains a few ; more chain themselves to slavery.   SENECA.—*Epist.* 22.

SEVERITY

He knows not how to wink at human frailty,
Or pardon weakness that he never felt.
ADDISON.—*Cato, Act* 5, 4.

Be not austere !
Outward austerity, as oft as not,
Is but the friar's serge, 'neath which there lurks
More taste for sack than sack-cloth.
A. AUSTIN.—*Savonarola, Act* 1, 1.

Severity breedeth fear, but roughness breedeth hate.   BACON.—*Of Great Place.*

He's just, your cousin, ay, abhorrently ;
He'd wash his hands in blood, to keep them clean.
E. B. BROWNING.—*Aurora Leigh, Bk.* 9.

The rigid righteous is a fool,
The rigid wise anither.
BURNS.—*To the Unco Guid.*

Laws that are too severe are temptations to plunder on the part of the criminal, and to perjury on the part of the prosecutor.   C. C. COLTON.—*Lacon.*

Thwackum was for doing justice, and leaving mercy to Heaven.
FIELDING.—*Tom Jones, Bk.* 3, *c.* 10.

A man severe he was, and stern to view,
I knew him well, and every truant knew.
GOLDSMITH.—*Deserted Village.*

Yet he was kind, or if severe in aught,
The love he bore to learning was at fault.
GOLDSMITH.—*Ib.*

An unforgiving eye and a damned disinheriting countenance.
SHERIDAN.—*School for Scandal, Act* 4, 1.

The vow that binds too strictly snaps itself.
TENNYSON.—*Last Tournament.*

SEX

Their tricks and craft hae put me daft,
They've ta'en me in and a' that,
But clear your decks, and —Here's the sex !
I like the jads for a' that.
BURNS.—*Jolly Beggars.*

As the man beholds the woman,
As the woman sees the man,
Curiously they note each other,
As each other only can.
Never can the man divest her
Of that wondrous charm of sex ;
Ever must she, dreaming of him
That same mystic charm annex.
BARRY CORNWALL.—*Sexes.*

For contemplation he and valour formed ;
For softness she and sweet attractive grace ;
He for God only, she for God in him.
MILTON.—*Paradise Lost, Bk.* 4, 297.

Each sex has what the other has not ; each completes the other, and is completed by the other.   They are in nothing alike, and the happiness and perfection of both depends on each asking and receiving from the other what the other only can give.
RUSKIN.—*Sesame and Lilies.*

Either sex alone
Is half itself, and in true marriage lies
Nor equal nor unequal.
    TENNYSON.—*Princess, 7, 283.*

She [Catherine de Médicis] possessed the
faults of her sex and few of its virtues.
    VOLTAIRE.—*Henriade, c. 2.*

SHADOWS

Strange to relate ; **but** wonderfully true,
That even shadows have their shadows.
  too.   CHURCHILL.—*Rosciad, v. 411.*

By the Apostle Paul, shadows to-night
Have struck more terror to the soul of
    Richard,
Than can the substance of ten thousand
    soldiers.
  SHAKESPEARE.—*Richard III.,* Act 5, 3.

SHAKESPEARE

Others abide our question. Thou art free.
We ask and ask : thou smilest and art still,
Out-topping knowledge.
    M. ARNOLD.—*Shakespeare.*

O eyes sublime
With tears and laughter for all time.
  E. B. BROWNING.—*Aurora Leigh, Bk. 9.*

A thousand poets pried at life,
  And only one amid the strife
Rose to be Shakespeare.
  BROWNING.—*Christmas Eve, c. 16.*

Our " myriad-minded " Shakespeare.
    COLERIDGE.—*Biog. Lit.*

Subtract from many modern poets all
that may be found in Shakespeare, and
trash will remain.
  C. C. COLTON.—*Lacon. Reflections,*
    568.

Heaven that but once was prodigal before,
To Shakespeare gave as much ; she could
  not give him more.
    DRYDEN.—*To Congreve.*

But Shakespeare's magic could not copied
  be ;
Within that circle none dare walk but he.
    DRYDEN.—*Prologue.*

I know the signs of an immortal man—
Nature's chief darling and illustrious mate.
    HOOD.—*Midsummer Fairies.*

    Soul of the age !
The applause, delight, and wonder of our
    stage !
My Shakespeare, rise ! I will not lodge
    thee by
Chaucer or Spenser, or bid Beaumont lie
A little further off, to make thee room ;
Thou art a monument, without a tomb.
  BEN JONSON.—*To the Memory of*
    Shakespeare.

He was not for an age, but for all time.
    BEN JONSON.—*Ib.*

I loved the man, and doe honour his
memory, on this side idolatry, as much as
any. Hee was indeed honest, and of an
open and free nature ; had an excellent
phantsie ; brave notions and gentle expressions ; wherein he flowed with that
facility that sometimes it was necessary
he should be stopped.
  BEN JONSON.—*Timber (c. 1630 ?)*

We may quote him [Shakespeare] . .
as a splendid example of that consistent
inconsistency which . . . sometimes charac-
terises Primary Poets.
  KEBLE.—*Lectures on Poetry, No. 5*
    (E. K. Francis tr.).

We accord to Shakespeare as of pre-
eminent right, the high commendation of
holding nothing that is human alien to
himself, seeing that he was able to enter
into the mind, the character, the very
features of all classes of men in all parts of
the world. In this respect he may be
compared to Nature herself.
    KEBLE.—*Ib., 28.*

Or sweetest Shakespeare, Fancy's child,
Warble his native wood-notes wild.
    MILTON.—*L'Allegro, l. 133.*

Dear Son of Memory, great heir of Fame,
What need'st thou such weak witness of
    thy name ?
Thou in our wonder and astonishment
Hast built thyself a live-long monument.
    MILTON.—*On Shakespeare.*

What needs my Shakespeare for his
    honoured bones
The labour of an age in pilèd stones ?
    MILTON.—*Ib.*

And one wild Shakespeare, following
    Nature's lights,
Is worth whole planets filled with Stagy-
    rites.   MOORE.—*The Sceptic.*

He seems to have known the world by
intuition, to have looked through nature
at one glance.
  POPE.—*Pref. to Shakespeare.*

There is no getting round the fact that
Shakespeare was an aristocrat and what
we should nowadays call a bit of a snob.
  G. B. SHAW.—*Public Opinion, Dec. 29,*
    1905.

It is our misfortune that the sordid
misery and hopeless horror of his [Shake-
speare's] view of man's destiny is still so
appropriate to English society that we
even to-day regard him as not for an age,
but for all time.
  G. B. SHAW.—*Unsocial Socialist,*
    Appendix.

She*, with Æschylean music on her lips
  that laughed back fear,
In the face of Time's grey godhead shook
  the splendour of her spear.
                SWINBURNE.—*Athens, an Ode.*

The trivial and immoral works of Shakespeare and his imitators, aiming merely at
the recreation and amusement of the spectators, cannot possibly represent the
teaching of life.
        TOLSTOY.—*Shakespeare and the Drama.*

The sooner people free themselves from
the false glorification of Shakespeare, the
better it will be.   TOLSTOY.—*Ib.*

Shakespeare is the Corneille of London,
and a great clown to boot, and more often
resembling Gilles than Corneille. But he
has some admirable passages.
        VOLTAIRE.—*Letter to M. de Cideville,*
                                Nov. 3, 1735.

Shakespeare is hardly to be compared
with Molière either in respect of art or of
insight into manners.
        VOLTAIRE.—*Letter to M. de Champfort,*
                                Sept., 1769.

Shakespeare is a barbarian, with occasional sparks of genius which shine in a
horrible night.
        VOLTAIRE.—*Prefatory Letter to Irène*
                                (1778).

SHALLOWNESS

Many affecting wit beyond their power
Have got to be a dear fool for an hour.
                HERBERT.—*Church Porch.*

Some people will never learn anything,
for this reason, because they understand
everything too soon.
        POPE.—*Thoughts on Various Subjects.*

The art of being deep-learned and shal-
low-read.   SWIFT.—*Tale of a Tub.*

SHAME

We are ashamed of not being shameless.
        ST. AUGUSTINE.—*Conf. Bk. 2.*

Men the most infamous are fond of fame,
And those who fear not guilt, yet start at
  shame.
        CHURCHILL.—*The Author, 233.*

Shame leaves us by degrees.
        S. DANIEL.—*Complaint of Rosamond,*
                                st. 64.

I hold him to be dead in whom shame
is dead.   PLAUTUS.

        Such an act,
That blurs the grace and blush of modesty.
        SHAKESPEARE.—*Hamlet, Act 3, 4.*

No more ashamed of doing wrong,
  We are ashamed of feeling right,
Ashamed of any feeling strong,
  And of all shame ashamèd quite.
WALTER C. SMITH.—*Olrig Grange, Bk. 5.*

He is without the sense of shame or
glory, as some men are without the sense
of smelling ; and therefore a good name
to him is no more than a precious ointment would be to these.
        SWIFT.—*Character of Lord Wharton.*

Shame, that stings sharpest of the worms
in hell.
        SWINBURNE.—*Marino Faliero.*

Man is a beast when shame stands off
from him.
        SWINBURNE.—*Phædra : Hippolytus.*

There is a shame which is glory and
grace.   *Ecclesiasticus* iv, 21.

SHAVING

        Men for their sins
Have shaving too entailed upon their chins.
        BYRON.—*Don Juan, 14, 23.*

Fresh as a bridegroom ; and his chin new
  reaped,
Showed like a stubble-land at harvest
  home.
        SHAKESPEARE.—*Henry IV., Pt. 1,*
                                Act 1, 3.

The barber's man hath been seen with
him, and the old ornament of his cheek
hath already stuffed tennis balls.
        SHAKESPEARE.—*Much Ado, Act 3, 2.*

SHELLS

        From within were heard
Murmurings whereby the monitor ex-
  pressed
Mysterious union with its native sea.
        WORDSWORTH.—*Excursion, Bk. 4.*

SHEPHERDS

My name is Norval ; on the Grampian
  hills
My father feeds his flocks ; a frugal swain,
Whose constant cares were to increase his
  store.
        J. HOME.—*Douglas, Act 2, 1.*

And every shepherd tells his tale
Under the hawthorn in the dale.
        MILTON.—*L'Allegro, 67.*

SHIPS

What is a ship but a prison ?
        BURTON.—*Anatomy of Melancholy,*
                                Pt. 2, sec. 3, 4.

This quiet sail is as a noiseless wing.
To waft me from distraction.
        BYRON.—*Childe Harold, c. 3, st. 85.*

---
* *I.e.* Elizabethan England.

She walks the waters like a thing of life,
And seems to dare the elements to strife.
BYRON.—*Corsair, c.* 1, *st.* 3.

My boat is on the shore
And my bark is on the sea.
BYRON.—*To T. Moore.*

A wet sheet and a flowing sea,
A wind that follows fast,
And fills the white and rustling sail,
And bends the gallant mast.
A. CUNNINGHAM.—*A Wet Sheet.*

The most advanced nations are always
those who navigate the most.
EMERSON.—*Society and Solitude.
Civilization.*

Fair laughs the Morn and soft the Zephyr
blows,
While proudly riding o'er the azure realm,
In gallant trim the gilded vessel goes.
GRAY.—*Bard, c.* 2.

No man will be a sailor who has contrivance enough to get himself into a jail :
for being in a ship is being in jail with the
chance of being drowned. . . . A man in a
jail has more room, better food, and commonly better company.
JOHNSON.—*Remark,* 1759.

The Liner she's a lady.
KIPLING.—*Seven Seas.*

The gift of being near ships, of seeing each
day
A city of ships with great ships under weigh ;
The great street paved with water, filled
with shipping,
And all the world's flags flying and sea-
gulls dipping.
JOHN MASEFIELD.—*Biography.*

Those proud ones swaying home,
With mainyards backed and bows a cream
of foam,
Those bows so lovely-curving, cut so fine
Those coulters of the many-bubbled brine,
As once, long since, when all the docks
were filled
With that sea beauty man has ceased to
build.   JOHN MASEFIELD.—*Ships.*

It was that fatal and perfidious bark,
Built in th'eclipse, and rigged with curses
dark,
That sunk so low that sacred head of thine.
MILTON.—*Lycidas,* 100.

That mysterious forest below London
Bridge.
RUSKIN.—*Modern Painters,* 5, *c.* 9.

The Goodwins, I think they call the
place ; a very dangerous flat and fatal,
where the carcases of many a tall ship lie
buried, as they say.
SHAKESPEARE.—*Merchant of Venice,
Act* 3, 1.

An ocean steamer is the next worst
thing to the Palace of Truth.
G. B. SHAW.—*Irrational Knot, ch.* 18.

Build few and build fast,
Each one better than the last.
*Naval Maxim quoted by Lord Fisher,
" Records," Nov.* 25, 1919.

SHOEMAKERS

Ye tuneful cobblers ! still your notes pro-
long,
Compose at once a slipper and a song ;
So shall the fair your handiwork peruse,
Your sonnets sure shall please—perhaps
your shoes.
BYRON.—*English Bards and Scotch
Reviewers.*

A man cannot make a pair of shoes
rightly unless he do it in a devout manner.
CARLYLE.—*To T. Erskine.*

I am indeed, sir, a surgeon to old shoes ;
when they are in great danger I re-cover
them.
SHAKESPEARE.—*Julius Cæsar, Act* 1, 1.

SHOUTING

A shout that tore hell's concave, and be-
yond
Frightened the reign of Chaos and old
Night.
MILTON.—*Paradise Lost, Bk.* 1, 542.

SIGHING

Not suchè sorrowful sighès as men makè
For wo, or ellès when that folk ben sickè,
But easy sighès, such as been to likè.
CHAUCER.—*Troilus.*

Where's the use of sighing ?
Sorrow as you may,
Time is always flying—
Flying !—and defying
Men to say him nay.
Where's the use of sighing ?
W. E. HENLEY.—*Villanelle.*

Words may be false and full of art ;
Sighs are the natural language of the heart.
T. SHADWELL.—*Psyche.*

And easy sighs, such as folk drawe in
love.
EARL OF SURREY.—*Prisoner in Windsor.*

Or sighed and looked unutterable things.
THOMSON.—*Seasons : Summer.*

SILENCE

I feel as if an ox had trodden on my
tongue.
ÆSCHYLUS (*Greek prov. expression for
constrained silence*).

Her talents were of the more silent class.
BYRON.—*Don Juan, c.* 6, 49.

No speech ever uttered or utterable is worth comparison with silence.
CARLYLE.—*Lecture* (1838).

Speech is of time, silence is of eternity.
CARLYLE.—*Sartor Resartus, Bk.* 33, *ch.* 3.

Like the harmony of the spheres that is to be admired and never heard.
DRYDEN.—*Sir Martin Mar-all,* Act 6.

Silence is become his mother-tongue.
GOLDSMITH.—*Good-Natured Man,* Act 2.

There is the silent criticism of silence, worth all the rest.
SIR A. HELPS.—*Friends in Council, Bk.* 2, *ch.* 2.

We returned home not sorry to be mostly silent as we went, and glad that our friendship was so assured that we could be silent without the slightest danger of offence.
SIR A. HELPS.—*Ib.*

And Silence like a poultice comes
To heal the blows of sound.
O. W. HOLMES.—*Music Grinders.*

Alas for those who never sing,
But die with all their music in them.
O. W. HOLMES.—*The Voiceless.*

Adam, whiles he spak nat, had paradys at wille.
LANGLAND.—*Piers Plowman, Passus* 14.

O have a care of natures that are mute!
GEO. MEREDITH.—*Modern Love, st.* 35.

Demaratus, when asked whether he held his tongue because he was a fool or for want of words, replied, " A fool cannot hold his tongue."
PLUTARCH.—*Laconic Apophthegms.*

A prating barber asked Archelaus how he would be trimmed. He answered, " In silence." PLUTARCH.—*Morals, Bk.* 1.

Silence, says Euripides, is an answer to a wise man. PLUTARCH.—*Ib.*

When Dido found Æneas would not come,
She mourned in silence, and was Dido dumb.
PORSON.—*Facetiæ.*

Silence in love bewrays more woe
Than words, though ne'er so witty;
A beggar that is dumb, you know,
May challenge double pity.
SIR W. RALEGH.—*Silent Lover.*

The rest is silence.
SHAKESPEARE.—*Hamlet,* Act 5, 2.

O my Antonio, I do know of these,
That therefore only are reputed wise,
For saying nothing.
SHAKESPEARE.—*Merchant of Venice,* Act 1, 1.

Silence is the perfected herald of joy;
I were but little happy, if I could say how much.
SHAKESPEARE.—*Much Ado,* Act 2, 1.

They froze into silence.
SHAKESPEARE.—*Timon,* Act 2, 2.

Much I fear
Lest from such silence evil deeds burst out.
SOPHOCLES.—*Œdipus,* 1095 (*Plumptre tr.*).

Why creep'st thou off in silence? Know'st thou not
That silence but admits the accuser's charge. SOPHOCLES.—*Trachiniæ,* 826 (*Plumptre tr.*).

For words divide and rend,
But silence is most noble till the end.
SWINBURNE.—*Atalanta.*

Xenocrates said that he had often repented speaking, but never of holding his tongue. VALERIUS MAXIMUS.—*Bk.* 7.

What? Do you also possess the art of holding your tongue? Ah, you have all the talents for pleasing.
VOLTAIRE.—*La Prude.*

Not a drum was heard, not a funeral note. WOLFE.—*Burial of Sir John Moore.*

The silence that is in the starry sky,
The sleep that is among the lonely hills.
WORDSWORTH.—*Song at the Feast of Brougham Castle.*

I kept silence, yea even from good words; but it was pain and grief to me.
Church Psalter xxxix, 3.

A wise old owl lived in an oak;
The more he saw the less he spoke;
The less he spoke the more he heard:
Why can't we all be like that bird?
ANON.—(*American?*)

Silence is a friend that will never betray.
Attrib. to Confucius.

SIMILES

Indeed reasons are the pillars of the fabric of a sermon, but similitudes are the windows, which give the best lights.
FULLER.—*Holy State.*

Poetry lends Religion her wealth of symbols and similes: Religion restores these again to Poetry, clothed with so splendid a radiance that they appear to be no longer merely symbols, but to partake (I might almost say) of the nature of sacraments.
KEBLE.—*Lectures on Poetry, No.* 40. (*E. K. Francis tr.*)

Similes are like songs in love;
They much describe; they nothing prove.
PRIOR.—*Alma, c.* 3, 314.

Thou hast the most unsavoury similes.
SHAKESPEARE.—*Henry IV.*, *Pt.* 1, *Act* 1, 2.

    Oft on the dappled turf at ease
    I sit and play with similes.
    WORDSWORTH.—*To the Daisy* (1805).

SIMPLE LIFE

His drink, the running stream ; his cup,
    the bare
Of his palm closed ; his bed, the hard, cold
    ground.
    T. SACKVILLE.—*Mirrour for Magistrates.*

Plain living and high thinking are no more ;
The homely beauty of the good old cause
Is gone ; our peace, our fearful innocence,
And pure religion, breathing household
    laws.
    WORDSWORTH.—*In London*, 1802.

SIMPLICITY

    When the rich learned Pharisee
    Came to consult Him secretly,
    Upon his heart with iron pen
    He wrote, " Ye must be born again."
    WM. BLAKE.—*The Everlasting
    Gospel.*

    Though Devotion needs not Art,
Sometimes for the rich may borrow.
    CAMPION.—*Tune thy Music to thy
    Heart.*

Nothing is more simple than greatness ;
indeed, to be simple is to be great.
    EMERSON.—*Literary Ethics.*

For such a child I blesse God, in whose
bosom he is. May I and mine become as
this little child. EVELYN.—*Diary*, 1658.

The greatest thoughts are the simplest ;
and so are the greatest men.
    J. C. HARE.—*Guesses at Truth.*

Such sweet neglect more taketh me
Than all th' adulteries of art ;
They strike mine eyes, but not my heart.
    BEN JONSON.—*Epicæne*, Act 1.

Give true hearts but earth and sky,
And some flowers to bloom and die,—
Homely scenes and simple views
Lowly thoughts may best infuse.
    KEBLE.—*1st Sun. after Epiph.*

Lo, the poor Indian ! whose untutored
    mind
Sees God in clouds or hears him in the
    wind;
His soul proud science never taught to
    stray
Far as the solar walk or milky way ;
Yet simple nature to his hope has given
Behind the cloud-topped hill, an humbler
    heaven.
    POPE.—*Essay on Man, Ep.* 1, 99.

Of manners gentle, of affections mild ;
In wit, a man ; simplicity, a child.
    POPE.—*On Gay.*

Unlearn'd, he knew no schoolman's subtle
    art,
No language but the language of the heart.
    POPE.—*Prol. to Satires.*

The law of simplicity and naiveness
holds good in all fine art, for it is com-
patible with what is most sublime.
    SCHOPENHAUER.—*On Authorship.*

You speak like a green girl,
Unsifted in such perilous circumstance.
    SHAKESPEARE.—*Hamlet*, Act 1, 3.

I swear to thee . . .
By the simplicity of Venus' doves.
    SHAKESPEARE.—*Mid. Night's Dream*,
    Act 1, 1.

Never anything can be amiss
When simpleness and duty tender it.
    SHAKESPEARE.—*Ib.*, Act 5, 1.

But this good Sir did follow the plaine word,
Ne medled with their controversies vaine.
    SPENSER.—*Mother Hubberd, l.* 390.

A simple maiden in her flower
Is worth a hundred coats-of-arms.
    TENNYSON.—*Clara Vere de Vere.*

    Often ornateness
    Goes with greatness ;
    Oftener felicity
    Comes of simplicity.
    SIR W. WATSON.—*Art Maxims.*

Innocence is strong,
And an entire simplicity of mind
A thing most sacred in the eyes of Heaven.
    WORDSWORTH.—*Excursion, Bk.* 6.

The moving accident is not my trade ;
    To freeze the blood I have no ready arts :
'Tis my delight, alone in summer shade,
    To pipe a simple song for thinking hearts.
    WORDSWORTH.—*Hart-leap Well, Pt.* 2, *st.* 1.

Days undefiled by luxury or sloth,
Firm self-denial, manners grave and staid,
Rights equal, laws with cheerfulness
    obeyed,
Words that require no sanction from an
    oath,
And simple honesty a common growth.
    WORDSWORTH.—*Sonnets to Liberty*, 9.

SIN

Pleasure's a sin and sometimes sin's a
    pleasure. BYRON.—*Don Juan*, 1, 133.

But, sad as angels for the good man's sin,
Weep to record, and blush to give it in.
    CAMPBELL.—*Pleasures of Hope, Pt.* 2.

    The proverb seith that for to do sinne
is mannish, but certes for to persevere longe
in sinne is work of the devil.
    CHAUCER.—*Tale of Melibous, sec.* 29.

Little sins make room for great, and one brings in all.
 T. EDWARDS.—*Gangrene of Heresy.*

Oh, Thou, who Man of baser Earth didst make,
And ev'n with Paradise devise the Snake ;
For all the Sin wherewith the Face of Man
Is blackened—Man's forgiveness give— and take !
 FITZGERALD.—*Rubáiyát, st. 81.*

  The sin
Is in itself excusable ; to be taken
Is a crime.
 JOHN FLETCHER.—*Lover's Progress,*
    Act 4, 1.

Unto each man comes a day when his favourite sins all forsake him,
And he complacently thinks he has forsaken his sins.
 JOHN HAY.—*Pike County Ballads,*
    Distich 11.

Man may securely sin, but safely never.
 BEN JONSON.—*Forest (from Seneca).*

Even the inclination to sin brings its penalties. JUVENAL.—*Sat. 13.*

'Twas but one little drop of sin
We saw this morning enter in,
And lo ! at eventide the world was drowned. KEBLE.—*Sexagesima.*

Each man shall bear his own sin without doubt. W. MORRIS.—*Jason, 17, 122.*

He who does not forbid sin, when he can, encourages it. SENECA.—*Troades.*

The chief and greatest punishment of sinners is the fact of having sinned.
 SENECA.—*Ep. 97.*

From scalp to sole one slough and crust of sin. TENNYSON.—*Simeon Stylites.*

Hate me or pity me, as you will,
The Lord will have mercy on sinners still ;
And I, who am chiefest, say to all,
Watch and pray, lest ye also fall.
 WHITTIER.—*John Underhill, st. 19.*

He does not win who plays with sin
In the secret House of Shame.
 OSCAR WILDE.—*Ballad of Reading Gaol.*

Love covereth a multitude of sins.
 1 *St. Peter* iv., 8 (*R.V.*).

SINCERITY

The sincere alone can recognise sincerity.
 CARLYLE.—*Heroes.*

Let all thy converse be sincere.
 BISHOP KEN.—*Morning.*

A little sincerity is a dangerous thing, and a great deal of it is absolutely fatal.
 OSCAR WILDE.—*Intentions.*

Men who would blush at being thought sincere. YOUNG.—*Night Thoughts, 8.*

Kythe (appear) in your ain colours, that folks may ken you. *Scottish prov.*

That which cometh from the heart will go to the heart. *Prov.*

SINGERS AND SINGING

Come, sing now, sing ; for I know you sing well ;
I see you have a singing face.
 BEAUMONT AND FLETCHER.—*Wild*
    Goose Chase, Act 2, 2.

And her voice was the warble of a bird,
So soft, so sweet, so delicately clear.
The sort of sound we echo with a tear.
 BYRON.—*Don Juan, c. 2, 151.*

Let the singing singers,
With vocal voices, most vociferous,
In sweet vociferation, out-vociferise
Ev'n sound itself.
 H. CAREY.—*Chrononhotonthologos, 1, 1.*

Lamekes' sone [son] Tubal,
That fond [found] at first the art of songe ;
For, as his brothers hamers ronge [rung]
Upon his anvelt up and doun,
Therof he took the firsté soun.
 CHAUCER.—*Book of the Duchesse, 1162.*

With this one vice all songsters are possessed ;
Sing they can never at a friend's request,
Yet chant it forth, unasked, from morn to night.
 P. FRANCIS.—*Horace, Sat., Bk. 1, 3.*

Verse sweetens toil, however rude the sound ;
She feels no biting pang the while she sings ;
Nor, as she turns the giddy wheel around,
Revolves the sad vicissitudes of things.
 R. GIFFORD.—*Contemplation.*
(Dr. Johnson altered the second line to "All at her work the village maiden sings.")

W'en he [Brer Rabbit] chuned up fer ter sing he make dem yuther creeters hol' der breff. J. C. HARRIS.—*Nights with Uncle*
    Remus, ch. 3.

I would both sing thy praise and praise thy singing.
 HUGH HOLLAND.—*To G. Farnaby.*

The melting voice through mazes running,
Untwisting all the chains that tie
The hidden soul of harmony.
 MILTON.—*L'Allegro, 143.*

Who, as they sung, would take the prisoned
    soul,
And lap it in Elysium.
              MILTON.—*Comus*, 256.

She sang the tears into his eyes,
    The heart out of his breast.
CHRISTINA ROSSETTI.—*Maiden-Song.*

My soul is an enchanted boat,
Which, like a sleeping swan, doth float
Upon the silver waves of thy sweet singing.
    SHELLEY.—*Prometheus*, Act 2, 5.

And singing still dost soar, and soaring
    ever singest.   SHELLEY.—*Skylark.*

Knitting and withal singing, and it
seemed that her voice comforted her hands
to work.   SIR P. SIDNEY.—*Arcadia, Bk.* 1.

God giveth speech to all, song to the few.
    WALTER C. SMITH.—*Olrig Grange,*
                        Bk. 15.

I do but sing because I must,
    And pipe just as the linnets sing.
    TENNYSON.—*In Memoriam, c.* 21.

I can't sing. As a singist I am not a
success. I am saddest when I sing. So
are those who hear me. They are sadder
even than I am.
        ARTEMUS WARD.—*Lecture.*

SINGULARITY

Each the known track of sage philosophy
Deserts, and has a byway of his own ;
So much the restless eagerness to shine,
And love of singularity, prevail.
        DANTE.—*Paradise, c.* 29, 89
                  (*H. F. Cary tr.*).

The trick of singularity.
SHAKESPEARE.—*Twelfth Night*, Act 2, 5.

Woe to every mortal, and especially in
these days, who affects singularity in order
to be a personage.   VOLTAIRE.—*Vanity.*

SISTERS

My sister ! my sweet sister ! if a name
Dearer and purer were, it should be thine.
        BYRON.—*To Augusta.*

For there is no friend like a sister,
    In calm or stormy weather.
CHRISTINA ROSSETTI.—*Goblin Market.*

SKATING

Skating is a chilly pleasure, and therefore no sin.
    HEINE.—*Religion and Philosophy.*

SKITTLES

He's up to these grand games, but one
of these days I'll loore him on to skittles,
and astonish him.
    H. J. BYRON.—*Our Boys.*

SLANDER

Skilled by a touch to deepen scandal's
    tints,
With all the kind mendacity of hints,
While mingling truth with falsehood, sneers
    with smiles,
A thread of candour with a web of wiles,
A plain blunt show of briefly-spoken seem-
    ing
To hide her bloodless heart's soul-hardened
    scheming.   BYRON.—*A Sketch.*

Slander, the foulest whelp of sin.
    R. POLLOK.—*Course of Time.*

Slander,
Whose edge is sharper than the sword ;
    Whose tongue
Out-venoms all the worms of Nile.
    SHAKESPEARE.—*Cymbeline*, Act 3, 4.

Done to death by slanderous tongues.
    SHAKESPEARE.—*Much Ado*, Act 5, 3.

I will be hanged if some eternal villain,
Some busy and insinuating rogue,
Some cogging, cozening slave, to get some
    office,
Have not devised this slander.
        SHAKESPEARE.—*Othello*, Act 4, 2.

Slander,
Whose sting is sharper than the sword's.
    SHAKESPEARE.—*Winter's Tale*, Act 2, 3.

So thou be good, slander doth but approve
Thy worth the greater.
        SHAKESPEARE.—*Sonnets, No.* 70.

Who spake no slander, no, nor listened
to it. TENNYSON.—*Idylls : Dedication.*

Defaming and defacing, till she left
Not even Launcelot brave, nor Galahad
    clean.
        TENNYSON.—*Merlin and Vivien.*

SLANG

All slang is metaphor, and all metaphor
is poetry.
    G. K. CHESTERTON.—*The Defendant.*

Rabble-charming words, which carry so
much wild-fire with them.
    SOUTH.—(*Quoted on Title-page of " The
                  Slang Dictionary."*)

SLAUGHTER

The thundering guns are heard on every
    side,
The wounded coveys, reeling, scatter wide ;
The feathered field-mates, bound by
    Nature's tie,
Sires, mothers, children, in one carnage
    lie.   BURNS.—*Brigs of Ayr.*

Unholy is the voice
Of loud thanksgiving over slaughtered
    men.   COWPER—*Odyssey.*

Pity it is to slay the meanest thing.
> HOOD.—*Midsummer Fairies.*

How now! a rat!
Dead for a ducat, dead.
> SHAKESPEARE.—*Hamlet*, Act 3, 4.

SLAVERY

Born slaves, bred slaves,
Branded in the blood and bone slaves.
> BROWNING.—*Soul's Tragedy*, Act 1.

Slavery they can have anywhere; it is
a weed that grows in every soil.
> BURKE.—*Speech on Conciliation.*

I would not have a slave to till my ground,
To carry me, to fan me while I sleep,
And tremble when I wake, for all the
wealth
That sinews bought and sold have ever
earned.   COWPER.—*Time Piece*, 29.

For whom Jove dooms to servitude, he
takes
At once the half of that man's worth away.
> HOMER.—*Odyssey*, 17, 322 (*Cowper tr.*).

"Disguise thyself as thou wilt, still,
Slavery," said I,—"still thou art a bitter
draught."   STERNE.—*Sent. Journey.*

SLEEP

Death without dying—living, but not
Life.
> SIR E. ARNOLD.—*Light of the World,*
> *Bk.* 4.

Sleep is sweet to the labouring man.
> BUNYAN.—*Pilgrim's Progress.*

Death, so called, is a thing which makes
men weep,
And yet a third of life is passed in sleep.
> BYRON.—*Don Juan*, c. 14, 3.

Oh Sleep! it is a gentle thing,
Beloved from pole to pole.
> COLERIDGE.—*Ancient Mariner,*
> *Pt.* 5.

Care-charmer Sleep, son of the sable night,
Brother to Death, in silent darkness born.
> S. DANIEL.—*To Delia* (1592).

Indifferent host to shepherds and to kings,
Sole comforter of minds with grief oppressed.   W. DRUMMOND.—*Sonnet.*

Care-charming Sleep, thou easer of all woes,
Brother to Death.
> JOHN FLETCHER.—*Valentinian,*
> Act 5, 2 (*c.* 1615).

But sleep stole on me unawares,
Even on me at last,
Though drop by drop the minutes faint
Like hours at midnight passed.
> HARRIET E. HAMILTON-KING.—*Ballads*
> *of the North, No.* 1, *First of June.*

What blessed ignorance equals this,
To sleep—and not to know it?
> HOOD.—*Miss Kilmansegg.*

The cares that infest the day
Shall fold their tents, like the Arabs,
And as silently steal away.
> LONGFELLOW.—*Day is done.*

O sleep! O gentle sleep!
Nature's soft nurse, how have I frighted
thee,
That thou no more wilt weigh mine eyelids
down,
And steep my senses in forgetfulness?
> SHAKESPEARE.—*Henry IV.*, Pt. **2,**
> Act 3, 1.

Methought I heard a voice cry, "Sleep no
more!
Macbeth does murder sleep,"—the innocent sleep:
Sleep that knits up the ravelled sleave of
care,
The death of each day's life, sore labour's
bath,
Balm of hurt minds, great Nature's second
course,
Chief nourisher in life's feast.
> SHAKESPEARE.—*Macbeth*, Act 2, 2.

And sleep that sometimes shuts up sorrow's
eye.
> SHAKESPEARE.—*Midsummer Night's*
> *Dream*, Act 3, 2.

It argues a distempered head
So soon to bid good-morrow to thy bed:
Care keeps his watch in every old man's
eye,
And, where care lodges, sleep will never lie.
> SHAKESPEARE.—*Romeo and Juliet,*
> Act 2, 3.

Come Sleep, O Sleep! the certain knot of
peace,
The baiting place of wit, the balm of woe,
The poor man's wealth, the prisoner's
release,
The indifferent judge between the high
and low.   SIR P. SIDNEY.—*Astrophel.*

Thou hast been called, O Sleep! the friend
of Woe,
But 'tis the happy who have called thee so.
> SOUTHEY.—*Curse of Kehama.*

"God's blessing," said Sancho Panza,
"be upon the man who first invented this
self-same thing called sleep; it covers a
man all over like a cloak."
> STERNE.—*Tristram Shandy, vol.* 4, *ch.* 15.

How sweet, though lifeless, yet with life
to lie!
And, without dying, O how sweet to die!
> DR. WOLCOT.—*On Sleep.*

Perverse, self-willed to own and to disown,
Mere slave of them who never for thee
prayed,

Still last to come where thou art wanted
    most.
    WORDSWORTH.—*Sonnet No. 13, To Sleep.*

Without thee what is all the morning's
    wealth ?
Come, blessed barrier between day and
    day,
Dear mother of fresh thoughts and joyous
    health !
    WORDSWORTH.—*Sonnet No. 14, To Sleep.*

Tired Nature's sweet restorer, balmy
    sleep.   YOUNG.—*Night Thoughts,* 1.

For so he giveth unto his beloved sleep.
    Psalm cxxvii, 2 (*R.V.*).
Wakeful youth, drowsy age,—
Two things which death presage.
    Tr. of French prov.

To sleep seven hours is enough for either
a young man or an old one.
Health Precepts of University of Salerno.

A morning's sleep is worth a fauld o'
sheep to a hudderin' dudderin' daw.
    *Scottish prov., stated by James Kelly
    (1721) to be " a reflection upon lazy
    sleepy drabs, who prefer nothing to soak-
    ing in their beds in the morning."*

Nature requires five, custom takes seven,
Laziness takes nine, and wickedness
    eleven.   *Old Saying.*

SLOTH

Then cometh Sompnolence, that is
sluggy slombringe, that maketh a man
be hevy and dull, in body and in soule ;
and thus sinne cometh of Slouthe.
    CHAUCER.—*Parson's Tale, sec.* 58.

Sloth is a foe unto all virtuous deeds.
    A. MUNDAY.—*Sloth.*

Go to the ant, thou sluggard, consider
her ways, and be wise.   *Proverbs* vi, 6.

Drowsiness shall clothe a man with rags.
    Proverbs xxiii, 21.

SLOW AND SURE

Youer might peart, Brer Fox, yit somehow er nudder you ain't bin a-keepin' up
wid ole Slickum Slow-come.
    J. C. HARRIS.—*Nights with Uncle Remus,
        ch.* 38 (" *Brer Tarrypin* ").

Said Tweed to Till, " What gars ye rin sae
    still ? "
Said Till to Tweed, " Though ye rin with
    speed
    And I rin slaw,
For ae mon that ye droon,
    I droon twa."
*Old Rhyme. The river Till, a deep and slug-
gish stream, flows through part of North-
umberland and joins the Tweed between
Norham and Coldstream.*

SMATTERERS

All smatterers are more brisk and pert
Than those that understand an art.
    S. BUTLER.—*Miscellaneous Thoughts.*

His mind is furnished as hotels are, with
everything for occasional and transient
use.   GEO. ELIOT.—*Theophrastus Such :
            A Too Deferential Man.*

It is just being particular which makes
the difference between the scholar and the
sciolist.   OUIDA.—*Wanda, ch.* 23.

SMILES

Eternal smiles his emptiness betray,
As shallow streams run dimpling all the
    way.   POPE.—*Prol. to Satires,* 315.

One may smile, and smile, and be a
    villain.
    SHAKESPEARE.—*Hamlet,* Act 1, 5.

Send me hence ten thousand miles
From a face that always smiles.
    SWIFT.—*Daphne.*

SNEERING

Sapping a solemn creed with solemn sneer.
    BYRON.—*Childe Harold, c.* 3, 107.

There was a laughing devil in his sneer.
    BYRON.—*Corsair, c.* 1, 9.

Better to stand ten thousand sneers than
one abiding pang, such as time could not
abolish, of bitter self-reproach.
    DE QUINCEY.—*Opium Eater.*

Who can refute a sneer ?
    W. PALEY.—*Moral Philosophy.*

SNOBS

Of vanities and fopperies, to brag of
gentility is the greatest.
    BURTON.—*Anat. of Melan., Pt.* 2,
                sec. 3, 2.

It is impossible in our condition of
Society, not to be sometimes a snob.
    THACKERAY.—*Book of Snobs.*

You must not judge hastily or vulgarly
of Snobs. To do so shows that you are
yourself a Snob.   THACKERAY.—*Ib.*

He who meanly admires mean things is
a Snob.   THACKERAY.—*Ib.*

SNORING

I heard the cabin snoring
With universal nose.
    THACKERAY.—*White Squall.*

There ain't no way to find out why a
snorer can't hear himself snore.
    MARK TWAIN.—*Tom Sawyer Abroad,
                ch.* 10.

SOCIABILITY

In all thy humours, whether grave or
  mellow,
Thou'rt such a touchy, testy, pleasant
  fellow,
Hast so much wit and mirth and spleen
  about thee,
There is no living with thee or without
  thee. ADDISON.—*Trans. of Martial.*

The social hours, swift-winged, unnoticed
  fleet.
    BURNS.—*Cotter's Saturday Night.*

For thus the royal mandate ran,
When first the human race began,
The social, friendly, honest man,
  Whate'er he be,
'Tis he fulfils great Nature's plan,
  And none but he !
    BURNS.—*Epistle to J. Lapraik.*

He had twa fauts, or maybe three,
  Yet what remead ?
Ae honest social man want we :
  Tam Samson's dead !
    BURNS.—*Tam Samson's Elegy.*

What is the odds so long as the fire of
souls is kindled at the taper of conwivi-
ality, and the wing of friendship never
moults a feather ? [*Dick Swiveller.*]
    DICKENS.—*Old Curiosity Shop, ch.* 2.

A fresshe, a free, a frendly man.
    GOWER.—*Confessio Amantis, Bk.* 5.

      Society is no comfort
To one not sociable.
    SHAKESPEARE.—*Cymbeline,* Act 4, 2.

      As merry
As first, good company, good wine, good
  welcome,
Can make good people.
    SHAKESPEARE.—*Henry VIII.,* Act 1, 4.

That I have lived on good terms with
so many good people gives me more pleasure than any other reflection.
    SYDNEY SMITH.—*Letter to Countess
                        Grey,* 1830.

      Little we fear
      Weather without,
      Sheltered about
      The Mahogany Tree.
    THACKERAY.—*The Mahogany Tree.*

Certes, he was a most engaging wight,
Of social glee, and wit humane though
  keen,
Turning the night to day, and day to night.
    THOMSON.—*Castle of Indolence,
                        c.* 1, 63.

It's my earnest desire to see a' the haill
warld shakin hauns.
    JOHN WILSON.—*Noctes,* 34 (*Ettrick
                        Shepherd*).

Harmonious thoughts, a soul by truth refined,
Entire affection for all human kind.
    WORDSWORTH.—*Evening Walk.*

Iron sharpeneth iron ; so a man sharpeneth the countenance of his friend.
    Proverbs xxvii, 17.

Better is a dinner of herbs where love is,
than a stalled ox and hatred therewith.
    Proverbs xv, 17.

And he loved keeping companie.
    Old Ballad. Heir of Linne.

SOCIALISM

It is known that the bad workmen, who
form the majority of the operatives in
many branches of industry, are decidedly
of opinion that bad workmen ought to
receive the same wage as good, and that
no one ought to be allowed, through piece-
work or otherwise, to earn by superior
skill or industry more than others without
it.   J. S. MILL.—*Liberty, ch.* 4.

In economics all roads lead to Socialism,
though in nine cases out of ten, so far, the
economist does not recognise his destination.
    G. B. SHAW.—*Unsocial Socialist, ch.* 15

SOCIETY

Man seeketh in society comfort, use,
and protection.
    BACON.—*Adv. of Learning.*

Man was formed for society.
    SIR W. BLACKSTONE.—*Of the Nature of
                        Laws.*

      Solomon of saloons,
  And philosophic diner-out.
    BROWNING.—*Mr. Sludge.*

Society is now one polished horde,
Formed of two mighty tribes, the *Bores*
  and *Bored.*
    BYRON.—*Don Juan, c.* 13, 95.

      She that asks
Her dear five hundred friends.
    COWPER.—*Time Piece,* 652.

The people are to be taken in very small
doses. If solitude is proud, so is society
vulgar. EMERSON.—*Society and Solitude.*

Society in large towns is babyish, and
wealth is made a toy.
    EMERSON.—*Wealth.*

Crowds without company, and dissi-
pation without pleasure.
    GIBBON.—*Memoir,* 1, *p.* 116.

Hearts just as pure and fair,
May beat in Belgrave Square,
As in the lowly air
  Of Seven Dials.
    SIR W. S. GILBERT.—*Iolanthe.*

Billing. Society is like a ship ; every man must help in the steering.

Horster (ship's captain). That may be all right on shore, but at sea it would not do at all. IBSEN.—*An Enemy of Society.*

The greatest natural genius cannot subsist on its own stock. He who resolves never to ransack any mind but his own will be soon reduced from mere barrenness to the poorest of all imitations—he will be obliged to imitate himself and to repeat what he has before repeated.
SIR J. REYNOLDS.—*Lecture.*

Of all animals man is the least suited to live in flocks. ROUSSEAU.—*Emile.*

The Social Contract then is the basis of all civil society, and it is in the nature of this that we must seek the nature of the society it forms. ROUSSEAU.—*Ib.*

I am a woman of the world, Hector ; and I assure you that if you will only take the trouble to do the perfectly correct thing, and to say the perfectly correct thing, you can do just what you like.
G. B. SHAW.—*Heartbreak House*, Act 1.

Society is the best preservative of that equal and happy temper which is so necessary to self-satisfaction and enjoyment. Men of retirement and speculation . . . seldom possess that equality of temper.
ADAM SMITH.

The society exists for the benefit of its members ; not the members for the benefit of the society.
HERBT. SPENCER.—*Ethics.*

Only longed,
All else was well, for she-society.
TENNYSON.—*Princess.*

Society has this good at least, that it lessens our conceit by teaching us our insignificance, and making us acquainted with our betters.
THACKERAY.—*Virginians.*

She loves that round
Of treadmill ceremonies, mimic talks,
We make our women's lives—
Good heavens, what work
To set the creatures to, whom we declare
God purposed for companions to us men—
Companions to each other only now,
Their business but to waste each other's time.
AUGUSTA WEBSTER.—*Portraits* (1870)
1, *Tired.*

Gerald. I suppose Society is wonderfully delightful. *Lord Illingworth.* To be in it is merely a bore. But to be out of it is simply a tragedy.
OSCAR WILDE.—*Woman of No Importance*,
Act 3.

Nor greetings where no kindness is, nor all
The dreary intercourse of daily life.
WORDSWORTH.—*Tintern Abbey.*

SOLDIERS

He has no grave, no dirge, no mourning crowd,
He has no pall save the low-drifting cloud,
But Glory covers him as with a shroud.
F. W. D. BENDALL.—*Missing* (1918).

If I should die, think only this of me :
That there's some corner of a foreign field
That is for ever England.
RUPERT BROOKE.

Glory is the sodger's prize,
The sodger's wealth is honour.
BURNS.—*Song.*

Such great achievements cannot fail
To cast salt on a woman's tail.
BUTLER.—*Hudibras, Pt. 2, c. 1.*

And dim was that eye, once expressively beaming,
That melted in love, and kindled in war.
CAMPBELL.—*Wounded Hussar.*

I never knew a warrior yet, but thee,
From wine, tobacco, debts, dice, oaths, so free. T. CARLTON.—*To Capt. J. Smith.*

Counsel dwells not under the plumed hat.
CARLYLE.—*French Revolution, Pt. 1,
Bk. 5, ch. 4.*

And thus the soldier, armed with resolution,
Told his soft tale, and was a thriving wooer. CIBBER.—*Richard III.
(adapted)*, Act 2, 1.

A modern general has said that the best troops would be as follows :—an Irishman half drunk, a Scotchman half starved, and an Englishman with his belly full.
C. C. COLTON.—*Lacon.*

In the name of soldiership and sense.
COWPER.—*Time Piece.*

For a soldier I listed, to grow great in fame,
And be shot at for sixpence a day.
C. DIBDIN.—*Charity.*

Drinking is the soldier's pleasure.
DRYDEN.—*Alexander's Feast.*

He's a successful warrior
And has the soldiers' hearts.
DRYDEN.—*Spanish Friar*, Act 1, 1.

There are many soldiers and few brave men. J. ESPRIT.—*Fausseté des vertus.*

Captains are casual things.
JOHN FLETCHER.—*Rule a Wife*, Act 3.

An army, like a serpent, goes upon its belly.
FREDERICK THE GREAT.—*Attributed*

Cowards in scarlet pass for men of war.
G. GRANVILLE (LORD LANSDOWNE).—
She Gallants, Act 5, 1.

What of the faith and fire within us,
Men who march away
Ere the barncocks say,
Night is growing gray ?
THOS. HARDY.—*Song of the Soldiers.*

He seen his duty, a dead-sure thing—
And wend for it thar and then ;
And Christ ain't a-going to be too hard
On a man that died for men.
JOHN HAY.—*Jim Bludso.*

The love that loves a scarlet coat
Should be more uniform.
HOOD.—*Nelly Gray.*

They taught him how to turn his toes
And stand as stiff as starch ;
I thought that it was love and May,
But it was love and March.
HOOD.—*Waterloo Ballad*, 1834.

Let those that have no homes at all,
Go battle for a long one.
HOOD.—*The Volunteer.*

Every man thinks meanly of himself for
not having been a soldier, or not having
been at sea.   JOHNSON.—*Remark*, 1778.

Soldiers relish a speaker delivering himself a little unreservedly : they delight in
the freedom, not to say the audacity, in
which lyric poets, more than any others,
indulge.   KEBLE.—*Lectures on Poetry,
No. 25 (E. K. Francis tr.).*

The 'eathen in his blindness bows down to
wood an' stone ;
'E don't obey no orders unless they is 'is
own ;
The 'eathen in his blindness must end
where 'e began,
But the backbone of the Army is the non-
commissioned man !
KIPLING.—*The 'Eathen.*

O ! it's Tommy this, an' Tommy that, an'
" Tommy, go away " ;
But it's " Thank you, Mister Atkins,"
when the band begins to play.
KIPLING.—*Tommy.*

Then it's Tommy this, an' Tommy that,
an' " Tommy, 'ow's yer soul ? "
But it's " thin red line of 'eroes," when
the drum begins to roll.
KIPLING.—*Ib.*

We aren't no thin red 'eroes, an we aren't
no blackguards too,
But single men in barricks, most remarkable like you ;
An' if sometimes our conduck isn't all your
fancy paints,
Why, single men in barricks don't grow
into plaster saints.   KIPLING.—*Ib.*

A keen-edged sword, a soldier's heart
Is greater than a poet's art,
And greater than a poet's fame
A little grave that has no name.
FRANCIS LEDWIDGE.

Bad luck to this marching,
Pipe-claying and starching,
How neat one must be to be killed by the
French !
C. J. LEVER.—*Bad Luck to this Marching.*

The talents of the soldier and the ruler
are not the same.   LIVY.—*Bk. 25.*

Ninepunce a day fer killin' folks comes
kind o' low fer murder.
J. R. LOWELL.—*Biglow Papers*, 2.

A thousand leagues of ocean, a company
of kings,
You came across the watching world to
show how heroes die.
When the splendour of your story
Builds the halo of its glory,
'Twill belt the earth like Saturn's rings
And diadem the sky.
" M.R.C.S."—*In " Anzac " (On Colonial
Soldiers)* (1919).

Our swords shall play the orator for us.
MARLOWE.—*Tamburlaine.*

No soldier can fight unless he is properly
fed on beef and beer.
DUKE OF MARLBOROUGH.—*Attributed.*

Every French soldier carries in his knap-
sack the baton of a field-marshal.
NAPOLEON.

The worse the man, the better the
soldier. If soldiers are not corrupt they
ought to be made so.   NAPOLEON.

How happy's the soldier who lives on his
pay,
And spends half-a-crown out of sixpence
a day !
J. O'KEEFE.—*The Poor Soldier.*

Truly, it does appear, on some accounts,
to be very nearly a beautiful thing to fall
in battle. For such a person, though poor,
has a fine and gorgeous public funeral, and
though of no mark, is praised by men of
cleverness, not praising at random, for
their beautiful speeches have been prepared a long while beforehand.
PLATO.—*Menexenus 2 (said by Socrates
in satire).*

Our God and soldier we alike adore,
When at the brink of ruin, not before ;
After deliverance both alike requited,
Our God forgotten, and our soldiers
slighted.   QUARLES.—*Epigram*

Soldier, rest ! thy warfare o'er,
 Sleep the sleep that knows not breaking !
Dream of battled fields no more,
 Days of danger, nights of waking !
 SCOTT.—*Lady of the Lake, c.* 1, 31.

His square-turned joints and strength of
  limb
Showed him no carpet-knight so trim,
But in close fight a champion grim,
 In camps, a leader sage.
 SCOTT.—*Marmion, c.* 1, 5.

Yet, trained in camps, he knew the art
To win the soldiers' hardy heart :
They love a captain to obey,
Boisterous as March, yet fresh as May ;
With open hand, and brow as free,
Lover of wine and minstrelsy.
 SCOTT.—*Ib., c.* 3, 4

Fell as he was in act and mind,
He left no bolder heart behind :
Then give him, for a soldier meet,
A soldier's cloak for winding sheet.
 SCOTT.—*Rokeby, c.* 6, 33.

The chief bond of military service is
superstition, and the love of banners.
 SENECA.—*Ep.* 95.

To the wars, my boy, to the wars !
He wears his honour in a box unseen,
That hugs his kicksy-wicksy here at home.
 SHAKESPEARE.—*All's Well*, Act 2, 3.

A soldier,
Full of strange oaths, and bearded like the
  pard,
Seeking the bubble reputation
Even in the cannon's mouth.
 SHAKESPEARE.—*As You Like It*, Act 2, 7.

O farewell, honest soldier !
 SHAKESPEARE.—*Hamlet*, Act 1, 1.

If I be not ashamed of my soldiers, I am
a soused gurnet.
 SHAKESPEARE.—*Henry IV.*, Act 4, 2.

Food for powder, food for powder ;
they'll fill a pit as well as better.
 SHAKESPEARE.—*Ib.*, Act 4, 2.

Why then the world's mine oyster,
which I with sword will open.
 SHAKESPEARE.—*Merry Wives*, Act 2, 2.

He was wont to speak plain, and to the
purpose, like an honest man and a soldier ;
and now he is turned orthographer.
 SHAKESPEARE.—*Much Ado*, Act 2, 3.

Rude am I in my speech,
And little blessed with the soft phrase of
  peace.
 SHAKESPEARE.—*Othello*, Act 1, 3.

He speaks home, madam ; you may
relish him more in the soldier than in the
scholar.   SHAKESPEARE.—*Ib.*, Act 2, 1.

And let me the canakin clink !
 A soldier's a man,
 A life's but a span ;
Why, then, let a soldier drink.
 SHAKESPEARE.—*Ib.*, Act 2, 3.

And then dreams he of cutting foreign
  throats,
Of breaches, ambuscadoes, Spanish blades,
Of healths five fathom deep.
 SHAKESPEARE.—*Romeo and Juliet*,
  Act 1, 4.

And little of this great world can I speak,
More than pertains to feats of broil and
  battle ;
And therefore little shall I grace my cause,
In speaking for myself.
 SHAKESPEARE.—*Ib.*, Act 2.

I never expect a soldier to think.
 G. B. SHAW.—*Devil's Disciple*, Act 3.

The British soldier can stand up to anything—except the British War Office.
 G. B. SHAW.—*Ib.*

The soldier is an anachronism of which
we must get rid.
 G. B. SHAW.—*J. Bull's Other Island. Pref.*

When the military man approaches, the
world locks up its spoons and packs off its
womankind.
 G. B. SHAW.—*Man and Superman.*

Dost thou not know the fate of soldiers ?
They're but ambition's tools, to cut a way
To her unlawful ends : and when they're
  worn,
Hacked, hewn with constant service,
  thrown aside
To rust in peace and rot in hospitals.
 T. SOUTHERN.—*Loyal Brothers.*

True, quoth my Uncle Toby, thou didst
very right as a soldier—but certainly very
wrong as a man.
 STERNE.—*Tristram Shandy*, vol. 6, 8.

" A soldier," cried my Uncle Toby, in-
terrupting the Corporal, " is no more exempt
from saying a foolish thing, Trim, than
a man of letters." " But not so often, an'
please your Honour," replied the Corporal.
 STERNE.—*Ib.*, vol. 7, ch. 19.

Sidney, lord of the stainless sword.
 SWINBURNE.—*Astrophel*, 2, 4.

All in the Valley of Death
 Rode the Six Hundred.
 TENNYSON.—*Charge of the Light Brigade.*

Home they brought her warrior dead.
 TENNYSON.—*Princess, c.* 6. Song.

I wonder is it because men are cowards
in heart that they admire bravery so much,
and place military valour so far beyond
every other quality for reward and worship ?   THACKERAY.—*Vanity Fair.*

He lay like a warrior taking his rest,
  With his martial cloak around him.
      WOLFE.—*Burial of Sir J. Moore.*

Does this become a soldier, this become
Whom armies followed, and a people loved?
      YOUNG.—*The Revenge (Zanga).*

Tell them, O guns, that we have heard
    their call,
  That we have sworn, and will not turn
    aside,
That we will onward till we win or fall,
  That we will keep the faith for which
    they died.   ANON.—1918.

O little Force that in your agony
Stood fast while England girt her armour
    on,
Held high our honour in your wounded
    hands,
Carried our honour safe with bleeding
    feet—
We have no glory great enough for you,
The very soul of Britain keeps your day.
      ANON.—*Published in a London
                Newspaper, 1917.*

A man is known by the Company he joins.
Bad communication trenches corrupt good
    manners.
Never look a gift gun in the mouth.
A drop of oil in time saves time.
One swallow doesn't make a rum issue.
Where there's a war there's a way.
      Army proverbs (1917).

Persons maimed in the wars should be
maintained at the public charge.
      *One of the laws of Solon (according to
            Plutarch).*

The man-at-arms is the only man.
*Old Norse saying, as cited by Ibsen, in
"Lady Inger of Ostraat," Act* 1 (1854).

The more we work, the more we may,
It makes no difference to our pay.
" *We are the Royal Sappers," War Song
                (c.* 1915).

An old soldier, an old fool.
      French prov.

Old soldiers never die;
  They fade away!
      Popular Song, 1919.

Whoever fighteth for the religion of God,
whether he be slain or be victorious, we
will surely give him a great reward.
      Koran, ch. 4.

SOLEMNITY

We are growing serious, and let me tell
you that's the very next step to being dull.
      ADDISON.—*The Drummer,* Act 4.

Levity is often less foolish, and gravity
less wise, than each of them appears.
      C. C. COLTON.—*Lacon.*

Hence, avaunt ('tis holy ground),
Comus and his midnight crew!
      GRAY.—*Ode for Music*

Thou say'st an undisputed thing
In such a solemn way.
      O. W. HOLMES.—*To an Insect.*

The perpetual gravity of small minds,
which is only the mask of mediocrity.
      VOLTAIRE.—*Discourse to French
                  Academy,* 1746.

The gravest fish is an oyster,
  The gravest bird is an owl,
The gravest beast is an ass,
  An' the gravest man's a fule.
      Old Scottish rhyme.

SOLITUDE

'Midst the crowd, the hum, the shock of
    men,
To hear, to see, to feel, and to possess,
And roam along, the world's tired denizen,
With none who bless us, none whom we
    can bless:
Minions of splendour shrinking from dis-
    tress!
None that, with kindred consciousness
    endued,
If we were not, would seem to smile the
    less,
Of all that flattered, followed, sought,
    and sued,
This is to be alone; this, this is solitude!
      BYRON.—*Childe Harold, c.* 2, *st.* 26.

In solitude, where we are *least* alone.
      BYRON.—*Childe Harold, c.* 3, 90.

My life must linger on alone.
      BYRON.—*Parisina.*

The wise seyth, Woe to him that is allone,
Fore, and he falle, he hath noon help to rise.
      CHAUCER.—*Troilus, Bk.* 1, 694.

So lonely 'twas that God himself
Scarce seemèd there to be.
      COLERIDGE.—*Ancient Mariner,
                      Pt.* 7.

O solitude! where are the charms
That sages have seen in thy face?
      COWPER.—*Alex. Selkirk.*

I praise the Frenchman—his remark was
    shrewd,—
" How sweet, how passing sweet is soli-
    tude!
But grant me still a friend in my retreat,
Whom I may whisper—Solitude is sweet."
      COWPER.—*Retirement.*

Woe be to him that lust to be alone
For if he falle, helpé hath he none.
      THOS. HOCCLEVE.—*De Regimine.*

If you are idle, be not solitary; if you
are solitary, be not idle.
      JOHNSON.—*Letter,* 1779.

The solitary mortal is certainly luxurious, probably superstitious, and possibly mad. The mind stagnates for want of employment, grows morbid, and is extinguished like a candle in foul air.
JOHNSON.—*Remark as recorded by Mrs. Piozzi.*

In solitude
What happiness ? Who can enjoy alone,
Or all enjoying, what contentment find ?
MILTON.—*Paradise Lost, Bk.* 8, 364.

Solitude sometimes is best society.
MILTON.—*Paradise Lost, Bk.* 9, 249.

Overbearing austerity is always the companion of solitude.
PLATO.—(*According to Plutarch*).

Thus let me live, unseen, unknown,
Thus unlamented let me die ;
Steal from the world, and not a stone
Tell where I lie.
POPE.—*Ode on Solitude.*

But there are moments which he calls his own :
Then never less alone than when alone.
ROGERS.—*Human Life.*

I never found the companion that was so companionable as solitude.
H. D. THOREAU.—*Solitude.*

Other people are quite dreadful. The only possible society is oneself.
OSCAR WILDE.—*Ideal Husband.*

Impulses of deeper birth
Have come to him in solitude.
WORDSWORTH.—*A Poet's Epitaph.*

O lost to virtue, lost to manly thought,
Lost to the noble sallies of the soul,
Who think it solitude to be alone !
YOUNG.—*Night Thoughts*, 3.

But woe unto him that is alone when he falleth.
Ecclesiastes iv, 10.

SONG AND SONGS

That which is not worth saying is sung.
BEAUMARCHAIS.—*Barbier de Séville.*

In Highland sang,
Was made lang syne—Lord knows how lang.
BURNS.—*Twa Dogs.*

I knew a very wise man so much of Sir Christopher's [Musgrave's] sentiment, that he believed if a man were permitted to make all the ballads, he need not care who should make the laws of a nation.
ANDREW FLETCHER (1703).

Good people all, of every sort,
Give ear unto my song ;

And if you find it wondrous short,
It cannot hold you long.
GOLDSMITH.—*Elegy on the Death of a Mad Dog.*

For doth not Song
To the whole world belong ?
Is it not given where tears can fall,
Wherever hearts can melt, or blushes grow,
Or mirth and sadness mingle as they flow,
A heritage to all ?
ISA (CRAIG) KNOX.—*Ode on the Centenary of Burns.*

Why " words for music " are almost invariably trash now, though the words of Elizabethan songs are better than any music, is a gloomy and difficult question.
A. LANG.—*Essay on T. H. Bayly.*

Songs have immunity from death.
OVID.—*Amores.*

What will a child learn sooner than a song ?
POPE.—*Satires.*

Odds life ! must one swear to the truth of a song ?
PRIOR.—*Better Answer.*

If unmelodious was the song,
It was a hearty note and strong.
SCOTT.—*Marmion, c.* 6. *Intro.*

More solid things do not show the complexion of the times so well as Ballads and Libels [pamphlets].
SIR J. SELDEN.—*Libels.*

The world was very guilty of such a ballad some three ages since ; but I think now 'tis not to be found.
SHAKESPEARE.—*Love's Labour's Lost,* Act 1, 2.

Note this before my notes,
There's not a note of mine that's worth the noting.
SHAKESPEARE.—*Much Ado,* Act 2, 3.

And stretchèd metre of an antique song.
SHAKESPEARE.—*Sonnet* 17.

Our sweetest songs are those that tell of saddest thought.
SHELLEY.—*Skylark.*

Was there ever such stupid trash as these humorous songs ? If there is anything on earth makes me melancholy it is a humorous song.
SYDNEY SMITH.—*Letter to Miss G. Harcourt, March* 29, 1843.

The whole world sings my song, and I alone
Am silent : yet through tears I sometimes say,
" To which of us doth greater joy belong ? "
He hath his love ; but I,—I have my song.
SUSAN MARR SPALDING.—*A Song's Worth.*

A song is, as it were, a little image in enamel, that requires all the nice touches of the pencil, a gloss and a smoothness, with those delicate finishing strokes, which would be superfluous and thrown away upon larger figures.
  STEELE.—*The Guardian, No.* 16
    (*March* 30, 1713).

Songs with a lilt of words, that seem
To sing themselves. R. L. STEVENSON.

Your song
Tastes sharp of sea and the sea's bitterness.
  SWINBURNE.—*Chastelard*, Act 1, 1.

They sang of love, and not of fame ;
Forgot was Britain's glory ;
Each heart recalled a different name,
But all sang Annie Lawrie.
  BAYARD TAYLOR.—*Songs of the Camp.*

Short swallow-flights of song, that dip
Their wings in tears, and skim away.
  TENNYSON.—*In Memoriam, c.* 48.

Soft words, with nothing in them, make
a song. WALLER.—*To Mr. Creech.*

Empires dissolve, and peoples disappear ;
Song passes not away.
  SIR W. WATSON.—*Lacrimæ Musarum,* 112.

Old songs, the precious music of the
heart !
  WORDSWORTH.—*Feelings of the Tyrolese.*

When droops the boldest, when hope flies.
When hearts are coldest, dead songs rise ;
Young voices sound still, bright thoughts thrive,
Friends pass around still, so songs live.
       Harrow School Song

SONNETS

Happy the feeling from the bosom thrown'
In perfect shape, (whose beauty Time shall spare
Though a breath made it), like a bubble blown
For summer pastime into wanton air.
  WORDSWORTH.—*Miscell. Sonnets.*
    Dedication.

Scorn not the sonnet. Critic, you have frowned,
Mindless of its just honours ; with this key
Shakespeare unlocked his heart.
  WORDSWORTH.—*Scorn not the Sonnet.*

SONS

He was not all a father's heart could wish ;
But oh, he was my son ! —my only son.
My child.
  JOANNA BAILLIE.—*Orra*, Act 3, 2.

That unfeathered two-legged thing, a son.
DRYDEN.—*Absalom and Achitophel*, 1, 170.

O wonderful son, that can so astonish
a mother !
  SHAKESPEARE.—*Hamlet*, Act 3, 2.

Forget not, nor think shame ; I was thy son.
Time was I did not shame thee ; and time was
I thought to live and make thee honourable. SWINBURNE.—*Meleager.*

This is not the son of Achilles, but Achilles himself.
  Greek prov. (*Plutarch : Life of
    Alcibiades.*)

SOPHISTRY

The barren optimistic sophistries
Of comfortable moles.
  M. ARNOLD.—*To a Republican Friend.*

As creeping ivy clings to wood and stone,
And hides the ruin that it feeds upon,
So sophistry cleaves close to and protects
Sin's rotten trunk, concealing its defects.
  COWPER.—*Progress of Error,* 285.

Dark-browed sophist, come not anear,
All the place is holy ground.
  TENNYSON.—*The Poet.*

SORROW

Sorrow preys upon
Its solitude, and nothing more diverts it
From its sad visions of the other world
Than calling it at moments back to this.
  BYRON.—*The Two Foscari*, Act 4, 1.

But sorrow returned with the dawning of morn,
And the voice in my dreaming ear melted
away. CAMPBELL.—*Soldier's Dream.*

There is no grief which length of time
does not diminish and soften.
  CICERO.—*See De Fin., Bk.* 1, 12, 40.

Some ease it is hid sorrows to declare.
  F. DAVISON.—*A Complaint.*

To each his sufferings ; all are men
Condemned alike to groan ;
The tender for another's pain,
Th' unfeeling for his own.
  GRAY.—*Eton College.*

What sorrow was, thou bad'st her know,
And from her own, she learned to melt at
others' woe.
  GRAY.—*Hymn to Adversity.*

A solitary sorrow best befits
Thy lips, and antheming a lonely grief.
  KEATS.—*Hyperion, Bk.* 3, 5.

For sorrow, long-indulged and slow,
Is to Humanity a foe.
J. LANGHORNE.—*Hymn to Humanity, st.* 2.

Who ne'er his bread in sorrow ate,
Who ne'er the mournful midnight hours
Weeping upon his bed has sate,
He knows you not, ye Heavenly Powers.
  LONGFELLOW.—*From Goethe*

Earth has no sorrow that Heaven cannot heal.   MOORE.—*Sacred Songs.*

Much then I learned, and much can show,
Of human guilt and human woe,
Yet ne'er have, in my wanderings, known
A wretch whose sorrows matched my own.
            SCOTT.—*Rokeby, c. 4, st. 23.*

When sorrows come, they come not single
            spies,
But in battalions.
        SHAKESPEARE.—*Hamlet, Act 4, 5.*

One woe doth tread upon another's heel,
So fast they follow.
            SHAKESPEARE.—*Ib.*, Act 4, 7.

I have a silent sorrow here,
    A grief I'll ne'er impart.
            SHERIDAN.—*Stranger.*

When sorrow sleepeth, wake it not,
    But let it slumber on.
            M. A. STODART.—*Song.*

Never morning wore
To evening, but some heart did break.
        TENNYSON.—*In Memoriam, Pt. 6, 2.*

This is truth the poet sings,
That a sorrow's crown of sorrow is remembering happier things.
            TENNYSON.—*Locksley Hall.*

Past sorrows, let us moderately lament
    them ;
For those to come, seek wisely to prevent
    them.   WEBSTER.—*Duchess of Malfi.*

But each heart keeps its sorrow for its own,
    Nor bares its wound to the chill general
    gaze ;
Men laugh together—if they weep alone :
    But sorrow walks in all the wide world's
    ways.
    AUGUSTA WEBSTER.—*A Woman Sold,
                    3. To and Fro.*

Where there is sorrow, there is holy
    ground.
        OSCAR WILDE.—*De Profundis.*

A deep distress hath humanised my soul.
    WORDSWORTH.—*Elegiac Stanzas 1805.*

A man of sorrows, and acquainted with
grief.   *Isaiah liii, 3.*

Sorrow is good for nothing but sin.
                        Prov. (Ray).

SOUL

        Wander at will,
            Day after day,—
            Wander away,
            Wandering still—
        Soul that canst soar !
            Body may slumber :
            Body shall cumber
        Soul-flight no more.
    BROWNING.—*La Saisiaz, Prologue.*

But I have lived, and have not lived in
    vain :
My mind may lose its force, my blood its
    fire,
And my frame perish even in conquering
    pain ;
But there is that within me which shall
    tire
Torture and Time, and breathe when I
    expire ;
Something unearthly, which they deem
    not of.
        BYRON.—*Childe Harold, c. 4, 137.*

Soul is the Man ! For who will so
    The body name ?
        CAMPION.—*Are you what your fair
                    looks express ?*

There is in souls a sympathy with
    sounds,
And as the mind is pitched the ear is
    pleased
With melting airs or martial, brisk or
    grave.   COWPER.—*Task, Bk. 6, 1.*

But as Noah's pigeon, which returned no
    more,
Did show she footing found, for all the
    flood,
So when good souls, departed through
    death's door,
Come not again, it shows their dwelling
    good.
        SIR J. DAVIES.—*Nosce Teipsum.*

Of that ineffable substance which we
call Spirit he that thinks most will say
least.   EMERSON.—*Spirit.*

The soul's a sort of sentimental wife,
That prays and whimpers of the higher
    life.
    R. LE GALLIENNE.—*Decadent to his Soul.*

Hands of invisible spirits touch the strings
Of that mysterious instrument, the soul,
And play the prelude of our fate.
    LONGFELLOW.—*Spanish Student*, Act 1, 1.

The soul on earth is an immortal guest,
Compelled to starve at an unreal feast.
    HANNAH MORE.—*King Hezekiah, 125.*

If we are ever to know anything purely,
we must be separated from the body and
contemplate the things themselves by the
mere soul.
        PLATO.—*Phædo, 30 (Cary tr.).*

Vital spark of heavenly flame !
Quit, oh quit this mortal frame.
    POPE.—*The Dying Christian to his Soul.*

Stab at thee he that will,
No stab the soul can kill.
        SIR W. RALEGH.—*The Lie.*

If I had no other proof of the imma-
teriality of the soul, than the triumph of
the wicked and the oppression of justice
in this world, that alone would prevent
my doubting it.   ROUSSEAU.—*Emile.*

Ah, no ! it is not dead, ne can it die,
But lives for aie, in blissful Paradise :
Where like a new-borne babe it soft doth
        lie,
In bed of lilies wrapped in tender wise ;
And compast all about with roses sweet,
And daintie violets from head to feet.
              SPENSER.—*Clorinda, st.* 12.

So every spirit, as it is most pure,
And hath in it the more of heavenly light,
So it the fairer bodie doth procure
To habit in, and it more fairely dight,
With chearefull grace and amiable sight ;
For of the soule the bodie forme doth take,
For soule is forme, and doth the bodie
        make.
       SPENSER.—*Hymn in Honour of Beauty.*

Who tells me he denies his soul's immortal,
Whate'er his boast, has told me he's a
        knave.   YOUNG.—*Night Thoughts,*
                                      7, 1168.

SOUNDS

O, it came o'er my ear like the sweet south,
That breathes upon a bank of violets,
Stealing and giving odour.
         SHAKESPEARE.—*Twelfth Night,* Act 1, 1.

Low, sweet, faint sounds, like the fare-
        well of ghosts.
              SHELLEY.—*Prometheus,* Act 2, 1.

Sounds overflow the listener's brain,
So sweet, that joy is almost pain.
              SHELLEY.—*Ib.,* Act 2, 2.

SOUTH

O tell her, Swallow, thou that knowest each,
That bright and fierce and fickle is the
        South,
And dark and true and tender is the North.
              TENNYSON.—*Princess, c.* 4, 78.

SOVEREIGNTY

What all your sex desire is Sovereignty.
         DRYDEN.—*Wife of Bath's Tale,* 279.

We were not born to sue, but to com-
        mand.
         SHAKESPEARE.—*Richard II.,* Act 1, 1.

SPAIN

Not all the blood at Talavera shed,
Not all the marvels of Barossa's fight,
Not Albuera lavish of the dead,
Have won for Spain her well-asserted right.
When shall her olive-branch be free from
        blight ?
When shall she breathe her from the blush-
        ing toil ?
         BYRON.—*Childe Harold, c.* 1, *st.* 90.

The land of war and crimes.
         BYRON.—*Childe Harold, c.* 2, 16.

Her soil has felt the foot-prints, and her
        clime
Been winnowed by the wings of Liberty.
         CAMPBELL.—*Stanzas to the Memory of the
                                Spanish Patriots.*

Who has not seen Seville has seen
nothing.
         Spanish prov. (quoted by Le Sage, Gil Blas,
                                Bk. 10, ch. 10).

SPECULATION

The region of speculation is the region
of opinion, and a hazy, lazy, delightful
region it is ; good to talk in, good to
smoke in, peopled with pleasant fancies
and charming ideas.
         A. BIRRELL.—*Obiter Dicta : Truth
                                Hunting.*

No man should so act as to make a gain
out of another man's ignorance.
              CICERO.—*De Officiis.*

In my school-days, when I had lost one
        shaft,
I shot his fellow of the self-same flight
The self-same way, with more advisèd
        watch,
To find the other forth ; and by adven-
        turing both
I oft found both.
         SHAKESPEARE.—*Merch. of Venice,* Act 1, 1.

You must lose a fly to catch a trout.
                                      Prov.

SPEECH

And with your speech let mood not over-
        bold,
Nor vain nor wanton, shine from modest
        brow
And calm clear eye : and be not prompt
        to speak
Not full of words.
         ÆSCHYLUS.—*Suppliants,* 197
                                (Plumptre tr.).

Speak always according to your conscience, but do it in terms of good nature
and modesty and sincerity.
              MARCUS AURELIUS.—*Bk.* 8, 5.

There is no man but speaketh more
honestly than he can do or think.
              BACON.—*Adv. of Learning.*

Discretion of speech is more than eloquence.   BACON.—*Of Discourse.*

Now I'll say something to remember.
         BROWNING.—*Soul's Tragedy,* Act 1.

        He said
Little but to the purpose ; and his manner
Flung hovering graces o'er him like a
banner.   BYRON.—*Don Juan,* 9, 83.

Thing that is seyd is seyd, and forth it
gooth [goeth].
    CHAUCER.—*Manciple's Tale*, 251.

I am a womman, needès most [must] I
speke,
Or ellès swellè til myn hertè breke.
    CHAUCER.—*Marchantes Tale*, 1061.

Never hear the sweet music of speech.
    COWPER.—*Alex. Selkirk.*

When malefactors come to die
They claim uncommon liberty :
Freedom of speech gives no distaste ;
They let them talk at large, because they
talk their last.
    DEFOE.—*Elegy on the Author.*

This indeed is what speech is for—to
make the statement ; and all that is called
eloquence seems to me of little use, for the
most part, to those who have it, but inestimable to such as have something to say.
    EMERSON.—*Eloquence.*

Not able to speak, but unable to hold
his tongue.
    EPICHARMUS.—(*Greek : as quoted by
Aulus Gellius*).

The true use of speech is not so much
to express our wants as to conceal them.
    GOLDSMITH.—*The Bee, No.* 3.
(*Adapted from a French saying.*)

And, when you stick on conversation's
burrs,
Don't strew your pathway with those
dreadful *urs.*
    O. W. HOLMES.—*Rhymed Lesson.*

The mixture of those things by speech,
which by nature are divided, is the mother
of all error.
    HOOKER.—*Eccles. Pol.*, 3, 3, 1.

You may blot what is written, but the
spoken word can never be recalled.
    HORACE.—*De Art. Poet.*

Men will be ever to their errors blind,
Where woman's not allowed to speak her
mind.
    JOHNSON.—*Epilogue to Irene.*

That large utterance of the early Gods.
    KEATS.—*Hyperion, Bk.* 1, 50.

Trust on the dede and not in gaye
speechys.
    LYDGATE.—*Secreta Secretorum (c.* 1400).

The magic of the tongue is the most
dangerous of all spells.
(1st) LORD LYTTON.—*Eugene Aram, ch.* 7.

Men are never so likely to settle a question rightly as when they discuss it freely.
    MACAULAY.—*Southey's Colloquies.*

"But how divine is utterance ! " she
said, " as we to the brutes, poets are to us."
    GEO. MEREDITH.—*Diana, ch.* 16.

If you your lips would keep from slips,
Five things observe with care :
To whom you speak, of whom you speak,
And how, and when, and where.
    W. E. NORRIS.—*Thirlby Hall. Modern
version of old lines (see " Talk," p.* 500).

Speak properly and in as few words as
you can, but always plainly ; for the end
of speech is not ostentation but to be
understood.   PENN.—*Fruits of Solitude.*

Bias being desired by Amasis to send
him the best and the worst part of the
sacrificial offering sent the tongue, because
the greatest blessings and the worst curses
are derived to us thereby.
    PLUTARCH.—*Of Hearing.*

And the lady shall speak her mind freely,
or the blank verse shall halt for it.
    SHAKESPEARE.—*Hamlet*, Act 2, 2.

He gave man speech, and speech created
    thought,
Which is the measure of the universe.
    SHELLEY.—*Prometheus*, Act 2, 4.

I a'n't dead, but I'm speechless
    SMOLLETT.—*Count Fathom, ch.* 42.

The first duty of a man is to speak ; that
is his chief business in this world.
    R. L. STEVENSON.—*Memories.*

But oft the words come forth awrie of
him that loveth well.
    EARL OF SURREY.—*Fickle Affections.*

Peace and be wise ; no gods love idle
speech.   SWINBURNE.—*Atalanta.*

Let your speech be alway with grace,
seasoned with salt.   *Colossians* iv, 6.

The stroke of the tongue breaketh the
bones. Many have fallen by the edge of
the sword ; but not so many as have fallen
by the tongue. *Ecclesiasticus* xxviii, 17, 18.

The tongue can no man tame ; it is an
unruly evil, full of deadly poison.
    St. James iii, 8.

Let him now speak, or else hereafter for
ever hold his peace.
    Common Prayer : Marriage Service.

Some things that you have said are true,
And some things you have said are new ;
But what are true, alas ! they are not
    new,
And what are new, they are, alas ! not true.
    ANON.

The ear tires sooner than the tongue.
    Prov.

SPEED

Back to thy punishment
False fugitive, and to thy speed add wings.
MILTON.—*Paradise Lost, Bk.* 2, 699.

Out-fly the nimble sail, and leave the
lagging wind. POPE.—*Odyssey*, 11, 74.

The spirit of the time shall teach me
speed.
SHAKESPEARE.—*King John*, Act 4, 2.

I'll put a girdle round about the earth
In forty minutes.
SHAKESPEARE.—*Midsummer Night's
Dream*, Act 2, 2.

SPELLING

" Do you spell it with a ' V ' or a ' W ' ? "
inquired the judge. " That depends upon
the taste and fancy of the speller, my
Lord," replied Sam.
DICKENS.—*Pickwick, ch.* 34.

They spell it Vinci, and pronounce it
Vinchy ; foreigners always spell better
than they pronounce.
MARK TWAIN.—*Innocents Abroad, ch.* 9.

SPIDERS

Much like a subtle spider which doth sit
In middle of her web, which spreadeth
wide ;
If aught do touch the utmost thread of it,
She feels it instantly on every side.
SIR JOHN DAVIES.—*Immortality of the
Soul.*

" Will you walk into my parlour ? " said
the spider to the fly.
MARY HOWITT.—*The Spider and the
Fly.*

The spider's touch, how exquisitely fine !
Feels at each thread and lives along the
line. POPE.—*Essay on Man*, 1, 217.

SPIES

His was the subtle look and sly,
That, spying all, seems nought to spy.
SCOTT.—*Rokeby*, 5, 16.

The great thing in life is to be simple ;
and the perfectly simple thing is to look
through key-holes.
G. B. SHAW.—*Great Catherine, Sc.* 1.

SPIRITS

It is easier to call up an evil spirit than
to allay it.
ERASMUS.—*(Quoted as an old saying in
Conv. Poet.).*

The spirit world around this world of sense
Floats like an atmosphere, and every-
where
Wafts through these earthly mists and
vapours dense
A vital breath of more ethereal air.
LONGFELLOW.—*Haunted Houses.*

For spirits, when they please,
Can either sex assume, or both ; so soft
And uncompounded is their essence pure.
MILTON.—*Paradise Lost, Bk.* 1, 423.

Millions of spiritual creatures walk the
earth
Unseen, both when we wake and when we
sleep. MILTON.—*Ib., Bk.* 4, 677.

Thus all things are but altered ; nothing
dies :
And here and there the unbodied spirit
flies,
By Time, or Force, or Sickness dispossessed,
And lodges, where it lights, in man or beast.
OVID.—*Metam., Bk.* 15 *(Dryden tr.).*

Know then, unnumbered spirits round thee
fly,
The light Militia of the lower sky.
POPE.—*Rape of the Lock*, 1, 41.

SPITEFULNESS

And are you—since the world began,
All women are—a little spiteful ?
W. M. PRAED.—*Portrait of a Lady.*

SPLEEN

The spleen is seldom felt where Flora
reigns ;
The lowering eye, the petulance, the frown,
And sullen sadness, that o'ershade, distort,
And mar the face of beauty, when no cause
For such immeasurable woe appears ;
These Flora banishes, and gives the fair
Sweet smiles, and bloom less transient
than her own.
COWPER.—*The Task, Bk.* 1, 455.

Spleen, which only seizes on the lazy,
the luxurious, and the rich.
SWIFT.—*Houyhnhnms.*

SPORT AND SPORTSMEN

They [the English] are the most voracious
people of prey that ever existed. Every
season turns out the aristocracy into the
country to shoot and fish.
EMERSON.—*English Traits*, 4, *Race.*

It is a proverb in England that it is safer
to shoot a man than a hare.
EMERSON.—*Ib.*

Wild animals never kill for sport. Man
is the only one to whom the torture and
death of his fellow creatures is amusing in
itself. FROUDE.—*Oceana.*

No game was ever yet worth a rap
For a rational man to play,
Into which no accident, no mishap,
Could possibly find a way.
A. L. GORDON.—*Weary Wayfarer.*

Then ye returned to your trinkets ; then
  ye contented your souls
With the flannelled fools at the wicket or
  the muddied oafs at the goals.
              KIPLING.—*Islanders.*

Great manliness and love of sports,
A grave, wise thoughtfulness and truth,
A merry fun outlasting youth,
A courage terrible to see,
And mercy for his enemy.
      J. MASEFIELD.—*Reynard the Fox.*

The voice of the schoolboy rallies the
  ranks :
" Play up, play up ! and play the game ! "
      SIR H. NEWBOLT.—*Vitæ Lampada.*

A mighty spearsman and a seaman wise,
A hunter, and at need a lord of lies.
      STEPHEN PHILLIPS.—*Ulysses, Prol.
                        (Of Ulysses).*

A rider unequalled—a sportsman complete,
A rum one to follow, a bad one to beat.
  G. J. WHYTE-MELVILLE.—*Hunting Song.*

Without danger the game grows cold.
*Latin Maxim, quoted in Chapman's " All
                    Fools " (1605).*

SPRING

Sunlight runs a race with rain,
All the world grows young again.
      MATHILDE BLIND.—*Street-Children's
                        Dance.*

In fact, 'tis the season of billing and cooing,
Amorous flying and fond pursuing.
      R. BUCHANAN.—*Fine Weather on the
                  Digentia,* 1, st. 1.

Now Nature hangs her mantle green
  On every blooming tree,
And spreads her sheets o' daisies white
  Out o'er the grassy lea.
  BURNS.—*Lament of Mary Queen of Scots.*

Now spring begins her smiling round,
Lavish to paint the enamelled ground.
      WM. HAMILTON (1704-1754).—*Ode to
                        Mrs. A. R.*

I come, I come, ye have called me long,
I come o'er the mountains with light and
  song.   HEMANS.—*Voice of Spring.*

Sweet spring, full of sweet days and roses,
A box where sweets compacted lie.
              HERBERT.—*Virtue.*

Slayer of the winter, art thou here again ?
      W. MORRIS.—*March.*

There are as many Springs as there are
  years,
And glad or sad, we love this dear old
  earth.
  LOUISE C. MOULTON.—*The Birds and I.*

But Spring counts no seed and gleans
no treasure . . . Summer kisses her tired
eyes, and takes her crown and sceptre.
  EDEN PHILLPOTTS.—*Girl and the Faun.*

Why, then comes in the sweet o' the
  year.
      SHAKESPEARE.—*Winter's Tale,* Act 4, 2.

When proud-pied April, dressed in all his
  trim,
Hath put a spirit of youth in everything.
      SHAKESPEARE.—*Sonnet* 98.

The sootè [sweet] season, that bud and
  bloom forth brings.
      EARL OF SURREY.—*Spring.*

In hawthorn time the heart grows light.
      SWINBURNE.—*Tale of Balen.*

In the Spring a young man's fancy
  lightly turns to thoughts of love.
      TENNYSON.—*Locksley Hall.*

Come, gentle Spring ! ethereal mildness,
  come !   THOMSON.—*Seasons.*

For lo, the winter is past, the rain is over
and gone ; the flowers appear on the earth ;
the time of the singing of birds is come,
and the voice of the turtle is heard in our
land.   *Song of Solomon* ii, 11 *and* 12.

Spring has come when you can put your
foot on three daisies at once. *Old Saying.*

SQUIRES

For what were all these country patriots
  born ?
To hunt, and vote, and raise the price of
  corn ?   BYRON.—*Age of Bronze,* 14.

Yet was he but a squire of low degree.
      SPENSER.—*Faerie Queene,* Bk. 4, c. 7,
                        st. 15.

Sir Aylmer Aylmer, that almighty man,
The county God.
      TENNYSON.—*Aylmer's Field,* 13.

These old pheasant-lords,
These partridge-breeders of a thousand
  years,
Who had mildewed in their thousands,
  doing nothing
Since Egbert. TENNYSON.—*Ib.,* 382

STABILITY

If this fail,
The pillared firmament is rottenness,
And earth's base built on stubble.
      MILTON.—*Comus,* 597,

But this is fixed
As are the roots of earth and base of all.
      TENNYSON.—*Princess,* 5, 256.

STARS

Ah ! the lamps numberless,
The mystical jewels of God,
The luminous, wonderful,
  Beautiful Lights of the Veil !
      R. BUCHANAN.—*Book of Orm.*

And the sentinel stars set their watch
in the sky.
        CAMPBELL.—*Soldier's Dream.*

Its roof star-pictured Nature's ceiling,
Where tracing the rapt spirit's feeling,
And God Himself to man revealing,
        The harmonious spheres
Make music, though unheard their pealing
By mortal ears.   CAMPBELL.—*Ib.*

Soothing the home-bound navy's peaceful
        way,
And rocking e'en the fisher's little bark
As gently as a mother rocks her child.
        CAMPBELL.—*View from St. Leonards.*

When I gazed into those stars, have they
not looked down on me with pity from
their serene spaces, like eyes glistening
with heavenly tears over the little lot of
man ?
        CARLYLE.—*Sartor Resartus, Bk. 2, ch. 8.*

The stars that have most glory have no
        rest.   S. DANIEL.—*Civil War.*

Blossomed the lovely stars, the forget-
me-nots of the angels.
        LONGFELLOW.—*Evangeline, Pt. 1, c. 3.*

So may we read, and little find them cold :
Not frosty lamps illumining dead space,
Not distant aliens, not senseless Powers.
The fire is in them whereof we are born ;
The music of their motion may be ours.
GEO. MEREDITH.—*Meditation under Stars.*

Observe how system into system runs,
What other planets circle other suns,
What varied being peoples every star.
        POPE.—*Essay on Man, Ep. 1, 25.*

Thus some, who have the stars surveyed,
        Are ignorantly led
To think those glorious lamps were made
To light Tom Fool to bed.
        NICHOLAS ROWE.—*On a Fine Woman.*

This majestical roof fretted with golden
fire.   SHAKESPEARE.—*Hamlet*, Act 2, 2.

        Look how the floor of heaven
Is thick inlaid with patines of bright gold ;
There's not the smallest orb which thou
        behold'st
But in his motion like an angel sings,
Still quiring to the young-eyed cherubins ;
Such harmony is in immortal souls ;
But whilst this muddy vesture of decay
Doth grossly close it in, we cannot hear it.
        SHAKESPEARE.—*Merchant of Venice,*
                                Act 5, 1.

In this interminable wilderness
        Of worlds, at whose immensity
        Even soaring fancy staggers.
                SHELLEY.—*Queen Mab.*

Twinkle, twinkle, little star !
How I wonder what you are,
Up above the world so high,
Like a diamond in the sky.
        JANE TAYLOR.—*The Star.*

You meaner beauties of the night,
        That poorly satisfy our eyes
More by your number than your light—
        You common people of the skies !
What are you when the sun shall rise ?
        SIR H. WOTTON.—*To the Queen of
                                Bohemia.*

Eternity is written in the skies.
        YOUNG.—*Night Thoughts,* 9.

An undevout astronomer is mad.
                YOUNG.—*Ib.*

STATESMEN

Good statesmen, who pulled ruin on the
        state,
Good patriots, who for a theory risked a
        cause,
        .   .   .   .
Now may the good God pardon all good
        men !
        E. B. BROWNING.—*Aurora Leigh, Bk. 4.*

Refined policy has ever been the parent
of confusion, and ever will be so.
                BURKE.—*Speech* (1775).

Individuals pass like shadows ; but the
commonwealth is fixed and stable.
                BURKE.—*Speech* (1780).

His strength lay in his knowledge of
England.
        BISHOP BURNET.—*History of his own
        Times* (1713) (*Of Lord Shaftesbury*).

I prefer prudence which is not eloquent,
to folly which is talkative.
                CICERO.—*De Oratore.*

He [Burke] was a scientific statesman ;
and therefore a seer. For every principle
contains in itself the germs of a prophecy.
        COLERIDGE.—*Biog. Literaria, ch.* 10.

The disencumbered Atlas of the state
        COWPER.—*Retirement,* 394.

The lawyer has spoiled the statesman
[of Brougham].
        DISRAELI.—*Young Duke, Bk.* 5, *ch.* 6.

        Art thou a statesman,
And canst not be a hypocrite ? Impos-
        sible !
Do not distrust thy virtues !
        DRYDEN.—*Don Sebastian,* Act 2, 1.

        He who rules
Must humour full as much as he com-
        mands ;
Must let men vow impossibilities ;
Grant folly's prayers that hinder folly's
        wish,
And serve the ends of wisdom.
        GEO. ELIOT.—*Spanish Gipsy, Bk.* 4.

What constitutes a state ?
Not high-raised battlements or laboured
    mound,
Thick wall or moated gate.
No : men, high-minded men,
Men, who their duties know,
But know their rights, and knowing, dare
    maintain,
These constitute a State.
        SIR W. JONES.—*Ode in Imitation of
                                    Alcæus.*

Is this the wisdom of a great minister,
or is it the ominous vibration of a pendulum ?   JUNIUS.—*Letter* 12.

The immense and brooding spirit still
    Shall quicken and control.
Living he was the land, and dead
    His soul shall be her soul.
        KIPLING.—*C. J. Rhodes.*

It may be better to be a John Knox than
an Alcibiades [brilliant and debauched],
but it is better to be a Pericles [an enlightened statesman] than either.
        J. S. MILL.—*Liberty, ch.* 3.

In his rising seemed
A pillar of state : deep on his front en-
    graven
Deliberation sat and public care.
        MILTON.—*Paradise Lost, Bk.* 2, 301.

A statesman's heart should always be
in his head.   NAPOLEON.

One that is happy in his height ;
And one that, in a nation's night,
Hath solitary certitude of light.
        STEPHEN PHILLIPS.—*A Man.*

A brave man struggling in the storms of
    fate,
And greatly falling, with a falling state.
        POPE.—*Prologue to Cato.*

Notwithstanding the common complaint of the knavery of men in power, I
have known no great ministers or men of
parts and business so wicked as their in-
feriors.
        POPE.—*Thoughts on Various Subjects.*

The greatest things and the most praise-
worthy that can be done for the public
good are not what require great parts, but
great honesty.   POPE.—*Ib.*

'Tis true the people understood
That all he did was for their good ;
Their kind affections he has tried ;
No love is lost on either side.
        SWIFT.—*Beasts' Confession.*

Flimnap, the treasurer, is allowed to cut
a caper on the straight rope at least an
inch higher than any other lord in the empire. I have seen him do the summerset
several times together.
        SWIFT.—*Voyage to Lilliput.*

Who makes by force his merit known,
And lives to clutch the golden keys,
To mould a mighty state's decrees,
And shape the whisper of the throne.
        TENNYSON.—*In Memoriam, c.* 64.

The pillar of a people's hope,
The centre of a world's desire.
        TENNYSON.—*Ib.*

And statesmen at her council met
Who knew the seasons when to take
Occasion by the hand, and make
The bounds of freedom wider yet.
        TENNYSON.—*To the Queen.*

O true yoke-fellow of Time,
Duty's intrepid liegeman ! See, the palm
Is won, and by all Nations shall be worn !
        WORDSWORTH.—*Poems to National
                        Independence, Pt.* 2, 3.

STATISTICS

A judicious man looks at Statistics, not
to get knowledge but to save himself from
having ignorance foisted on him.
        CARLYLE.—*Chartism, 2.*

Nature hates calculators.
        EMERSON.—*Experience.*

You may prove anything by figures.
        *Quoted by Carlyle as the saying of " a
                        witty statesman."*

STATUARY

Neither can I, from my present knowledge, fix upon an ancient statue which
expresses by the countenance any one
elevated character of soul, or any single
enthusiastic self - abandoning affection,
much less any such majesty of feeling as
might mark the features for supernatural.
        RUSKIN.—*Modern Painters, Pt.* 3, ch. 5,
        19. (*On the " pernicious element " in
                                Greek art*).

I know not of anything in the range of
art more unspiritual than the Apollo
Belvedere. RUSKIN.—*Ib., ch.* 5, 20 (*Note*).

STATURE

Her stature tall—I hate a dumpy woman.
        BYRON.—*Don Juan, c.* 1, 61.

Often the cockloft is empty in those
which Nature hath built many stories high.
        FULLER.—*Andronicus.*

She was a dumpy woman, though
    Her family was high.
        HOOD.—*John Trot.*

In small proportion we just beauties see,
And in short measures life may perfect be.
        BEN JONSON.—*Good Life, Long Life.*

The shortest ladies love the longest men.
        MASSINGER (?) or FLETCHER.—*Love's
                                    Cure, Act* 3.

A daughter of the gods, divinely tall,
And most divinely fair.
TENNYSON.—*Dream of Fair Women.*

Thou art long, and lank, and brown,
As is the ribbed sea-sand.
WORDSWORTH.—*Lines added to the
Ancient Mariner.*

STEAM

Soon shall thy arm, unconquered steam,
afar
Drag the slow barge, or drive the rapid
car ;
Or on wide waving wings expanded bear
The flying chariot through the field of air.
ERASMUS DARWIN.—*Botanic Garden.*

Steam is a tyrant.
JOHN WILSON.—*Noctes.*

STEDFASTNESS

Thy mind, thy mind, thy brave, thy manly
mind,
(That, like a rock, stands all the storms of
fortune,
And beats 'em roaring back, they cannot
reach thee).
BEAUMONT AND FLETCHER.—*Double
Marriage, Act* 2.

STEP-MOTHERS AND STEP-FATHERS

Lost in the children of the present spouse,
They slight the pledges of the former vows.
POPE.—*Odyssey,* 15, 25.

Stepmothers mostly are a cruel race,
And like the spikèd aloe plant, they bear
A rose of love once in a hundred years.
F. TENNYSON.—*King Athamas, Pt.* 1,
3, 45.

Be a stepmother kindly as she will,
There's in her love some hint of winter's
chill.
D. W. THOMPSON.—*From Euripides.*

STEWARDSHIP

We are Goddes stewardes all, noughte of
our owne we bear.
CHATTERTON.—*Balade of Charitie.*

That old hereditary bore,
The steward.   ROGERS.—*Italy.*

STOCK EXCHANGE

If to the Stock Exchange you speed,
To try with bulls and bears your luck,
'Tis odds you soon from gold are freed
And waddle forth a limping duck.
W. H. IRELAND.—*Modern Ship of Fools :
Of Gambling Fools* (1807).

Exchange is no robbery ;
But on it there is jobbery.
C. H. SPURGEON.—*" Salt-Cellars."*

STONEHENGE

Ill did those mighty men to trust thee with
their story ;
That hast forgot their names who reared
thee for their glory.
DRAYTON.—*Polyolbion, Song* 3.

STORIES

I am always at a loss to know how much
to believe of my own stories.
WASHINGTON IRVING.—*Tales of a
Traveller, Pref.*

One of the signs of mediocrity of mind
is the habit of always telling stories.
LA BRUYÈRE.

Faith ! he must make his stories shorter
Or change his comrades once a quarter.
SWIFT.—*On the Death of Dr. Swift.*

STORM

O pilot ! 'tis a fearful night,
There's danger on the deep.
T. H. BAYLY.—*The Pilot*

The sky is changed !—and such a change !
O night,
And storm, and darkness, ye are wondrous
strong,
Yet lovely in your strength, as is the light
Of a dark eye in woman ! Far along,
From peak to peak the rattling crags
among,
Leaps the live thunder !
BYRON.—*Childe Harold, c.* 3, *st.* 92.

Without was Nature's elemental din.
CAMPBELL.—*Theodric.*

We often see, against some storm,
A silence in the heavens, the wrack stand
still,
The bold winds speechless, and the orb
below
As hush as death.
SHAKESPEARE.—*Hamlet,* Act 2, 2.

Blow, winds, and crack your cheeks ! rage !
blow !
You cataracts and hurricanoes, spout
Till you have drenched our steeples !
SHAKESPEARE.—*King Lear,* Act 3, 2.

STOUTNESS

Stouter than I used to be,
Still more corpulent grow I ;
There will be too much of me
In the coming by-and-by.
SIR W. S. GILBERT.—*Iolanthe.*

I see no objection to stoutness—in
moderation. SIR W. S. GILBERT.—*Ib.*

If you hear of sixteen or eighteen pounds
of human flesh, they belong to me. I look
as if a curate had been taken out of me.
SYDNEY SMITH.—*Letter Oct.* 21, 1844.

When Munckley walks the streets the
   paviors cry
" God bless you, Sir ! " and lay their
   rammers by.
      ANON.—*Of Dr. Nicholas Munckley.*

STRAIGHTFORWARDNESS

Never believe anything to be for your
interest which obliges you to break your
word, sacrifice your modesty, hate, suspect, or curse any person, or which inclines you to any practice which will not
bear the light.
      MARCUS AURELIUS.—*Meditations,*
                              Bk. 3, 7.

   Plain-dealing is a jewel.
   WYCHERLEY.—*Country Wife*, Act 4, 3.

Come give us your plain-dealing fellows,
   Who never from honesty shrink,
Not thinking of all they should tell us,
   But telling us all that they think.
                        Broderers' Song.

True, straight, open, he had nothing
about him of dissimulation or pretence.
Words used of a Pope of Rome. (*The
original Latin form is, " Verus, integer,
apertus, nil habuit ficti, nil simulati."*)

STRATAGEMS

Where the lion's skin falls short, eke it
out with the fox's.
      LYSANDER.—(*According to Plutarch.*)

By indirection find directions out.
      SHAKESPEARE.—*Hamlet*, Act 2, 1.

Your bait of falsehood takes this carp of
   truth.   SHAKESPEARE.—*Ib.*

Sweet innocent, the mother cried,
   And started from her nook,
That horrid fly is put to hide
   The sharpness of the hook.
   ANN AND JANE TAYLOR.—*The Little
                              Fish.*
On others practise thy Ligurian arts :
Thin stratagems and tricks of little hearts
Are lost on me.
   VIRGIL.—*Æneid, Bk. 11 (Dryden tr.)*
                  (*Camilla to Aunus*).

STRAWBERRIES

Really, these strawberries are ex-straw-
berry fine.
      H. J. BYRON.—*Burlesque (c. 1880).*

Doubtless God could have made a better
berry [than the strawberry], but doubtless God never did.
      *Attrib. in this form, by Izaak Walton,
                  to " Dr. Boteler."*

STRENGTH

Languor is not in your heart,
   Weakness is not in your word,
Weariness not on your brow.
      M. ARNOLD.—*Rugby Chapel.*

O fall'n at length that tower of strength
Which stood foursquare to all the winds
   that blew.
      TENNYSON.—*On Wellington.*

An antique stone he saw, the common
   bound
Of neighbouring fields, and barrier of
   the ground—
So vast that twelve strong men of modern
   days
The enormous weight from earth could
   hardly raise.
He heaved it at a lift, and poised on high,
Ran staggering on against the enemy.
   VIRGIL.—*Æneid, Bk. 12 (Dryden tr.)*
                        (*Of Turnus*).

STRIFE

When civil dudgeon first grew high,
And men fell out, they knew not why.
      BUTLER.—*Hudibras, Pt. 1, c. 1.*

   Know that relentless strife
   Remains by sea and land
   The holiest law of life.
      J. DAVIDSON.—*War Song.*

Achilles' wrath, to Greece the direful spring
Of woes unnumbered, heavenly goddess,
   sing !   POPE.—*Iliad, Bk. 1, 1.*

To strive with an equal is a doubtful
thing, with a superior, a mad thing, with
an inferior, a vulgar thing.
      SENECA.—*De Ira.*

And where two raging fires do meet together,
They do consume the thing that feeds their
   fury.
      SHAKESPEARE.—*Taming of the Shrew,*
                              Act 2, 1.

In tumults and dissensions the worst
man gets the most power ; peace and quiet
bring out the good qualities of men.
      TACITUS.—*Hist., Bk. 4.*

STRUGGLE

Only streams which fettered be
Fret their way at last to sea.
      L. HOUSMAN.—*Bonds.*

When Greeks joined Greeks, then was
the tug of war.
      N. LEE.—*Rival Queens*, Act 4, 2.

STUARTS

If ever men had fidelity, 'twas they [the
Stuarts] ; if ever men squandered opportunity, 'twas they ; and, of all the enemies
they had, they themselves were the most
fatal. THACKERAY.—*Esmond, Bk. 2, ch. 4.*

Like almost all the Stuarts, James II.
was a mixture of greatness and feebleness,
and did too much and too little.
      VOLTAIRE.—*Letters on the English.*

STUDY

But so many books thou readest,
But so many schemes thou breedest,
But so many wishes feedest
   That thy poor head almost turns.
        M. ARNOLD.—*Second Best.*

Reading maketh a full man ; conference
a ready man ; and writing an exact man.
        BACON.—*Of Studies.*

Studies serve for delight, for ornament,
and for ability. BACON.—*Essays, Studies.*

To spend too much time in studies is
sloth.   BACON.—*Ib.*

Oh, what a noble heart was here undone,
When science' self destroyed her favourite
   son !   BYRON.—*English Bards.*

'Twas thine own genius gave the final blow,
And helped to plant the wound that laid
   thee low.   BYRON.—*Ib.*

With curious art the brain, too finely
   wrought,
Preys on herself, and is destroyed by
   thought. CHURCHILL.—*To Hogarth.*

Through seas of knowledge we our course
   advance,
Discovering still new worlds of ignorance.
   SIR J. DENHAM.—*Progress of Learning,*
              195.

Some people study all their life ; at their
death they have learnt everything except
to think. FRANÇOIS URBAIN DOMERGUE
                 (1745–1810).

There is no satiety in study.
        ERASMUS.—*Fam. Coll.*

Learning by study must be won ;
'Twas ne'er entailed from son to son.
       GAY.—*Fables, Pt. 2, 11.*

If you decide for the intellectual life,
you will incur a definite loss to set against
your gain. . . . Severed from the vanities
of the Illusory, you will live with the
realities of knowledge as one who has
quitted the painted scenery of the theatre
to listen by the eternal ocean, or gaze at
the granite hills.
   P. G. HAMERTON.—*The Intellectual Life,*
             9, 4.

Much study had made him very lean,
   And pale, and leaden eyed.
       HOOD.—*Eugene Aram.*

What is twice read is commonly better
remembered than what is transcribed.
       JOHNSON.—*Rambler, 74.*

Knowledge is of two kinds. We know
a subject ourselves, or we know where we
can find information upon it.
       JOHNSON.—*Remark, 1775.*

Reading furnishes the mind only with
materials of knowledge ; it is thinking
makes what we read ours.   JOHN LOCKE.

Keep your consciences clear, your curiosity fresh, and embrace every opportunity
of cultivating your minds.
   HUGH MILLER.—*The Old Red Sandstone.*

Alas ! what boots it with incessant care
To tend the homely slighted shepherd's
   trade,
And strictly meditate the thankless Muse ?
Were it not better done as others use,
To sport with Amaryllis in the shade,
Or with the tangles of Neæra's hair ?
       MILTON.—*Lycidas, 64.*

To scorn delights, and live laborious
   days.   MILTON.—*Ib., 72.*

Deeper, deeper let us toil
In the mines of knowledge.
   JAS. MONTGOMERY.—*Aspirations.*

For sure no minutes bring us more content
Than those in pleasing, useful studies spent.
       J. POMFRET.—*The Choice.*

One science only will one genius fit ;
So vast is art, so narrow human wit.
       POPE.—*Criticism, 60.*

We spend our midday sweat, our midnight oil ;
We tire the night in thought, the day in
   toil.   QUARLES.—*Emblems, Bk. 2, 2.*

Books bear him up awhile, and make him
   try
To swim with bladders of philosophy.
   EARL OF ROCHESTER.—*Satire against*
             Mankind, 20.

Study is like the heaven's glorious sun,
   That will not be deep-searched by saucy
     looks,
Small have continual plodders ever won
   Save base authority from others' books.
   SHAKESPEARE.—*Love's Labour's Lost,*
             Act 1, 1.

I thus neglecting worldly ends, all dedi-
   cated
To closeness and the bettering of my mind.
   SHAKESPEARE.—*Tempest, Act 1, 2.*

There is nothing so horrible as languid
study . . . The only way to read with any
efficacy is to read so heartily that dinner
time comes two hours before you expected
it.   SYDNEY SMITH.—*Lectures on Moral*
           Philosophy, No. 19.

When a man's knowledge is not in order,
the more of it he has the greater will be
his confusion.
       HERBT. SPENCER.—*Sociology.*

But thanks to my friends for their care in
   my breeding,
Who taught me betimes to love working
   and reading.   I. WATTS.—*Sluggard.*

Time not given to study is time lost.
  Latin. The motto of Budæus.

STUPIDITY

Now your rater and debater
Is baulked by a mere spectator
Who simply stares and listens.
  BROWNING.—*Of Pacchiarotto.*

Such as take lodgings in a head
That's to be let unfurnishèd.
  BUTLER.—*Hudibras, Pt.* 1, *c.* 1.

There is a Stupidest of London men,
actually resident, with bed and board of
some kind, in London.
  CARLYLE.—*On Biography.*

Oh that he were here to write me down
an ass !—but, masters, remember that I
am an ass ; though it be not written down,
yet forget not that I am an ass.
  SHAKESPEARE.—*Much Ado,* Act 4, 2.

There is no sin but stupidity.
  OSCAR WILDE.—*Intentions.*

STYLE (LITERARY)

Of all those arts in which the wise excel,
Nature's chief masterpiece is writing well.
  DUKE OF BUCKINGHAM (JOHN
  SHEFFIELD).—*Essay on Poetry,* 1.

Facts are external to a man. Style is
the man himself.
  COMTE DE BUFFON.—*Remarques,* 1753.

May I not write in such a style as this ?
In such a method, too, and yet not miss
My end—thy good ?
  BUNYAN.—*Pilgrim's Progress, Pt.* 1.

How strong an influence works in well-
placed words !
  CHAPMAN.—*Gentleman Usher,* Act 4, 2.

Telle us som mery thing of aventures ;—
Your termes, your colours, and your
 figures,
Kepe hem in stoor [keep them in store]
 til so be ye endyte
Heigh style, as whan that men to kinges
 wryte. CHAUCER.—*Clerk's Prol.,* 15.

Intense study of the Bible will keep any
writer from being vulgar in point of style.
  COLERIDGE.—*Table Talk.*

Whoever wishes to attain an English
style, familiar but not coarse, and elegant
but not ostentatious, must give his days
and nights to the volumes of Addison.
  JOHNSON.—*Life of Addison.*

A good writer does not write as *people*
write but as *he* writes. MONTESQUIEU.

Who that heard [Agatho's] persuasion
could fail to be impressed by the beauty
of the nouns and the verbs.
PLATO.—*Banquet* 24. (*Remark of Socrates
 Satirizing a mere rhetorician or stylist.*)

True ease in writing comes from art, not
 chance,
As those move easiest who have learned to
 dance. POPE.—*Criticism,* 362.

'Tis not enough no harshness gives offence ;
The sound must seem an echo to the sense.
  POPE.—*Ib.,* 364.

Style is merely the silhouette of thought.
To write in a vague or bad style means a
stupid or confused mind.
  SCHOPENHAUER.—*On Authorship.*

I do not much dislike the matter, but
The manner of his speech.
  SHAKESPEARE.—*Antony and Cleopatra,*
         Act 2, 2.

Base is the style and matter meane
withall. SPENSER.—*Mother Hubberd.*

Proper words in proper places.
  SWIFT.—*Definition of a Good Style.*

What is easy to read has been difficult
to write. . . . A limpid style is invariably
the result of hard labour.
  G. M. TREVELYAN.—*Clio, A Muse.*

Would you repeat that again, sir, for
it soun's sae sonorous that the words
droon the ideas ?
  JOHN WILSON.—*Noctes,* 27.

SUBLIME, THE

The beautiful is the most useful in art ;
but the sublime in art is the most helpful
to morals, for it elevates the mind.
  JOUBERT.—*Pensée,* 326.

As for the sublime, it is, even among the
greatest geniuses, only the most elevated
that can reach it.
  LA BRUYÈRE.—*Characters.*

The sublime and the ridiculous are so
often nearly related that it is difficult to
class them separately. One step above
the sublime makes the ridiculous, and one
step above the ridiculous makes the sublime
again. TOM PAINE.—*Age of Reason.*

SUBMARINES

Hence . . . the remark of the highly-
trained sailorman in these latitudes [the
northern ice regions], who, on being told
by his superior officer in the execution of
his duty to go to Hell, did insubordinately
and enviously reply, " D'you think I'd be
here if I could ? " whereby he caused the
entire personnel, beginning with the commander, to say " Amen," or words to that
effect. KIPLING.—*Tales of " The Trade "*
            (1916).

Their feats, their fortunes and their fames
Are hidden from their nearest kin ;
No eager public backs or blames,
No journal prints the yarns they spin ;

. . . . . .

Unheard they work, unseen they win,
That is the custom of " The Trade."
KIPLING.—*Tales of " The Trade,"*
I (1916). *" No one knows how the title
of 'The Trade' came to be applied to
the Submarine Service."*

SUBMISSION

Ay, do despise me. I'm the prouder
for it ; I likes to be despised.
I. BICKERSTAFFE.—*Hypocrite.*

Thy will be done, though in my own
undoing.
SIR T. BROWNE.—*Religio Medici*, Pt. 2, 15.

Soft ! Ask no questions ! Give no vent to
thought !
Such is the custom of the Powers divine.
HOMER.—*Odyssey, Bk.* 7, 200. *(Cowper tr.).*

Yet I argue not
Against Heaven's hand or will, nor bate
a jot
Of heart or hope : but still bear up and
steer
Right onward.   MILTON.—*Sonnet.*

O calm, dishonourable, vile submission !
SHAKESPEARE.—*Romeo and Juliet*, Act 3, 1.

One by whom
All effort seems forgotten ; one to whom
Long patience hath such mild composure
given,
That patience now doth seem a thing of
which
He hath no need.
WORDSWORTH.—*Animal Tranquillity.*

Ills that God blesses are my good ;
All unblest good is ill ;
And all is right that seems most wrong,
If it be God's dear will.
*Quoted by C. H. Spurgeon as " a fine distich
which deserves to be made proverbial."*

Jouk [duck] and let the jaw [storm]
gae o'er.
Allan Ramsay's Scottish Proverbs (1737).

Better bow to my faes than beg frae my
friends.   *Scottish prov.*

SUBSERVIENCE

Oh, let us love our occupations,
Bless the squire and his relations,
Live upon our daily rations,
And always know our proper stations.
DICKENS.—*Chimes.*

I am now no more than a mere lodger in
my own house.
GOLDSMITH.—*Good-Natured Man*, Act 1.

I am his Highness's dog at Kew ;
Pray tell me, sir, whose dog are you ?
POPE.—*Epigram.*

As for you, modern peoples, you have
no slaves ; but you are slaves. You pay
for their liberty with your own. You
have boasted much of this choice ; I find
in it more cowardice than humanity.
ROUSSEAU.—*Contrat Social, Bk.* 3, *ch.* 15.

It needs more skill than I can tell
To play the second fiddle well.
C. H. SPURGEON.—*" Salt-Cellars."*

SUCCESS

'Tis not in mortals to command success
But we'll do more, Sempronius, we'll
deserve it. ADDISON.—*Cato*, Act 1, 2.

Fame in excess is but a perilous thing ;

. . . . . .

I praise the good success
That rouses not God's wrath.
ÆSCHYLUS.—*Agamemnon*, 466
(Plumptre tr.).

Success is full of promise till men get it ;
then it is a last year's nest, from which the
bird has flown.   H. W. BEECHER.

God will estimate
Success some day.
BROWNING.—*Prince Hohenstiel-
Schwangau.*

If this be then success, 'tis dismaller
Than any failure.
E. B. BROWNING.—*Aurora Leigh, Bk.* 5.

The only infallible criterion of wisdom
to vulgar judgments—success.
BURKE.—*Letter to Member of National
Assembly* (1791).

Success, the mark no mortal wit,
Or surest hand, can always hit.
BUTLER.—*Hudibras, Pt.* 1, *c.* 1.

Well, if I don't succeed, I *have* succeeded,
And that's enough.
BYRON.—*Don Juan, c.* 12, 17.

But try the Cæsar, or the Catiline,
By the true touchstone of desert—success.
BYRON.—*Marino Faliero.*

He builded better than he knew.
EMERSON.—*The Problem.*

Still to new heights his restless wishes
tower,
Claim leads to claim, and power advances
power ;
Till conquest unresisted ceased to please,
And rights submitted left him none to
seize.   JOHNSON.—*London.*

Fate holds the strings, and men like
children move
But as they're led : Success is from above.
LORD LANSDOWNE.—*Heroic Love.*

Surer to prosper than prosperity
Could have assured us.
  MILTON.—*Paradise Lost, Bk.* 2, 39.

Success has brought many to destruction.   PHÆDRUS.—*Fables, Bk.* 3.

A hit, a very palpable hit.
  SHAKESPEARE.—*Hamlet,* Act 5, 2.

In the race
He equalled all the promise of his form
In those his rounds, and so with noblest prize
Of conquest left the ground.
  SOPHOCLES.—*Electra,* 687 (*Plumptre tr.*).

SUCCESSORS

And Tom the second reigns like Tom the first.   DRYDEN.—*To Congreve.*

Not Amurath an Amurath succeeds,
But Harry, Harry.
  SHAKESPEARE.—*Henry IV., Pt.* 2, Act 3, 2.

SUFFERING

Justice turns the scale
For those to whom through pain
At last comes wisdom's gain.
  ÆSCHYLUS.—*Agamemnon,* 239
                  (*Plumptre tr.*).

Knowledge by suffering entereth,
And life is perfected by death.
  E. B. BROWNING.—*Vision of Poets.*

The best of men
That e'er wore earth about him, was a sufferer ;
A soft, meek, patient, humble, tranquil spirit,
The first true gentleman that ever breathed.
  DEKKER.—*Honest Whore, Pt.* 1, Act 1, 1.

Measure thy life by loss instead of gain ;
Not by the wine drunk, but the wine poured forth ;
For love's strength standeth in love's sacrifice,
And whoso suffers most hath most to give.
  HARRIET ELEANOR HAMILTON-KING.—
                  The Disciples.

But if Himself He come to thee, and stand,
Pallid and royal, saying " Drink with Me,"
Wilt thou refuse ? Nay, not for Paradise !
The pale brow will compel thee, the pure hands
Will minister unto thee.
  HARRIET ELEANOR HAMILTON-KING.—*Ib.*

Our present joys are sweeter for past pain ;
To Love and Heaven by suffering we attain.
  LORD LANSDOWNE.—*British Enchanters,*
                  Act 5, 2.

What deaths we suffer ere we die !
  J. LOGAN.—*On the Death of a Young Lady.*

There is nothing the body suffers that
the soul may not profit by.
  GEO. MEREDITH.—*Diana of the Crossways.*

Can it be, O Christ in heaven, that the
holiest suffer most,
That the strongest wander furthest, and
more hopelessly are lost ?
  SARAH WILLIAMS.—*Twilight Hours.*

SUFFICIENCY

" Little to do ; and plenty to get, I suppose ? " said Sergeant Buzfuz, with jocularity. " Oh, quite enough to get, sir, as the soldier said ven they ordered him three hundred and fifty lashes," replied Sam.   DICKENS.—*Pickwick, ch.* 34.

No, 'tis not so deep as a well, nor so wide as a church door ; but 'tis enough ; 'twill serve.
  SHAKESPEARE.—*Romeo and Juliet,* Act 3, 1.

Enough's as good as a feast
To one that's not a beast.
                  Prov. (*Ray*).

SUICIDE

Self-destruction is the effect of cowardice
in the highest extreme.
  DEFOE.—*Hist. of Projects.*

One more unfortunate,
  Weary of breath,
Rashly importunate,
  Gone to her death !
  HOOD.—*Bridge of Sighs.*

Yet we should not,
Howe'er besieged, deliver up our fort
Of life, till it be forced.
  MASSINGER.—*Guardian,* Act 2, 4.

If you like not hanging, drown yourself ;
Take some course for your reputation.
  MASSINGER.—*New Way to pay Old Debts,*
                  Act 2, 1.

When all the blandishments of life are gone,
The coward sneaks to death ; the brave live on.
  G. SEWELL.—*Suicide* (*fr. Martial*).

Against self-slaughter
There is a prohibition so divine,
That cravens my weak hand.
  SHAKESPEARE.—*Cymbeline,* Act 3, 4.

When you have demonstrated, in verse
or otherwise, why so many men cut their
throats in this best of all possible worlds,
I shall be greatly obliged to you.
  VOLTAIRE.—*To Martin Kahle* (*c.* 1752).

Less base the fear of death than fear of life.
O Britain, infamous for suicide !
  YOUNG.—*Night Thoughts,* 5.

SUITORS

Suit lightly won and short-lived pain,
For monarchs seldom sue in vain.
              SCOTT.—*Marmion, c.* 5, 9.

Full little knowest thou, that hast not
tride,
What hell it is, in suing long to bide.
              SPENSER.—*Mother Hubberd.*

SUMMER

All the live murmur of a summer's day.
              M. ARNOLD.—*Scholar Gipsy.*

Summer is gone on swallow's wings.
              HOOD.—*Departure of Summer.*

Worshippe, ye that lovers bene, this May!
For of your bliss the calends are begun;
And sing with us, "Away! winter, away!
Come, summer, come, the sweet season
      and sun!"
JAMES I. (*of Scotland*).—*King's Quair,*
                              st. 15.

Summer, as my friend Coleridge wag-
gishly remarks, has set in with its usual
severity.   LAMB.—(*Letter,* 1826.)

On the bat's back I do fly
After summer, merrily.
  SHAKESPEARE.—*Tempest,* Act 5, 1.

Then came the jolly Summer, being dight
In a thin silken cassock, coloured green,
That was unlinèd all, to be more light.
      SPENSER.—*Faerie Queene, Bk.* 7. *c.* 7,
                              st. 89.

In linden-time the heart is high,
For pride of summer passing by
With lordly laughter in her eye.
              SWINBURNE.—*Tale of Balen.*

Summer looks out from her brazen tower,
Through the flashing bars of July.
      FRANCIS THOMPSON.—*A Corymbus for*
                              Autumn.

From brightening fields of ether fair dis-
      closed,
Child of the Sun, refulgent Summer comes,
In pride of youth, and felt through
      nature's depth;
He comes attended by the sultry hours
And ever-fanning breezes.
      THOMSON.—*The Seasons : Summer,* 1.

That muddy and mizzly misnomer,
summer.   JOHN WILSON.—*Noctes,* 25.

A dry summer ne'er made a dear peck.
                              Scottish prov.

Summer is y-comen in;
Loude sing cuckoo!
              Song (13*th Century*).

SUNDAY

Sunday clears away the rust of the whole
week.   ADDISON.—*Spectator, vol.* 2, 112.

And beer undrawn, and beards unmown,
      display
Your holy reverence for the Sabbath-day.
      BYRON.—*English Bards and Scotch*
                              Reviewers, 636.

Of all the days that's in the week,
  I dearly love but one day;
And that's the day that comes betwixt
  A Saturday and Monday.
              H. CAREY.—*Sally.*

O Italy!—thy sabbaths will be soon
Our sabbaths.
      COWPER.—*Progress of Error,* 152.

Hail, Sabbath! thee I hail, the poor
      man's friend.
      JAS. GRAHAME.—*Sabbath.*

O day most calm, most bright,
The fruit of this, the next world's bud;
Th'endorsement of supreme delight,
Writ by a friend, and with his blood.
              HERBERT.—*Sunday.*

The other days and thou
Make up one man; whose face thou art,
Knocking at heaven with thy brow:
The worky-days are the back-part;
The burden of the week lies there.
              HERBERT.—*Ib.*

The Sundays of man's life
Threaded together on Time's string,
Make bracelets to adorn the wife
Of the eternal glorious King.
On Sunday heaven's gate stands ope,
Blessings are plentiful and rife,
      More plentiful than hope.
              HERBERT.—*Ib.*

Yes, child of suffering, thou mayst well be
      sure
He who ordained the Sabbath loves the
      poor.
      O. W. HOLMES.—*Rhymed Lesson.*

Who backs his rigid Sabbath, so to speak,
Against the wicked remnant of the week.
              HOOD.—*Ode to R. Wilson.*

The only ground, therefore, on which
restrictions on Sunday amusements can be
defended, must be that they are religiously
wrong; a motive of legislation which can
never be too earnestly protested against.
      J. S. MILL.—*Liberty, ch.* 4.

But at least to begin the week well,
Let us all be unhappy on Sunday.
LORD NEAVES.—*Songs and Verses* (1868
ed.): *Let us all be unhappy on Sunday.*

Whose sore task
Does not divide the Sunday from the week.
      SHAKESPEARE.—*Hamlet,* Act 1, 1.

Go thou and seek the House of Prayer!
I to the woodlands wend, and there,
In lovely Nature see the God of Love.
      SOUTHEY.—*Sunday Morning.*

A Sabbath well spent brings a week of content,
And health for the toils of the morrow ;
But a Sabbath profaned, whate'er may be gained,
Is a certain forerunner of sorrow.
Known as " Sir Matthew Hale's Golden Maxim."

SUN-DIALS

Milverton had put up a sundial in the centre of the lawn, with the motto, " Horas non numero nisi serenas," which, I remember, gave occasion to Ellesmere to say that for men the dial was either totally useless or utterly false.
SIR A. HELPS.—*Friends in Council, Bk. 2, ch. 1.*

SUNRISE

And like a lobster boiled, the morn
From black to red began to turn.
BUTLER.—*Hudibras, c. 2.*

The heavenly-harnessed team
Begins his golden progress in the East.
SHAKESPEARE.—*Henry IV., Pt. 1, Act 3, 1.*

Yonder comes the powerful king of day
Rejoicing in the East. The lessening cloud,
The kindling azure, and the mountain's brow,
Illumed with fluid gold, his near approach
Betoken glad.
THOMSON.—*The Seasons : Summer, 81.*

SUNSET

Call for the grandest of all earthly spectacles, what is that ? It is the sun going to his rest.   DE QUINCEY.—*Opium Eater.*

The gilded car of day
His glowing axle doth allay
In the steep Atlantic stream.
MILTON.—*Comus.*

The weary sun hath made a golden set,
And, by the bright track of his fiery car,
Gives token of a goodly day to-morrow.
SHAKESPEARE.—*Richard III., Act 5, 3.*

Sunsets are quite old-fashioned. They belong to the time when Turner was the last note in art. To admire them is a distinct sign of provincialism of temperament.
OSCAR WILDE.—*Intentions : Decay of Lying.*

How pleasant, as the sun declines, to view
The spacious landscape change in form and hue !
WORDSWORTH.—*Evening Walk.*

Objects all for the eye
Of silent rapture ! But we felt the while
We should forget them ; they are of the sky
And from our earthly memory fade away.
WORDSWORTH.—*Sonnets, Pt. 2, 11.*

SUPERFICIALITY

With too much quickness ever to be taught;
With too much thinking to have common thought.
POPE.—*Moral Essays, Ep. 2, 97.*

Like a Corsehill shop, a' in the window.
Scottish prov.

SUPERFLUITIES

All our wants, beyond those which a very moderate income will supply, are purely imaginary.
LORD BOLINGBROKE.—*Letter, 1719.*

Embarrassment of riches.
D'ALLAINVAL.

To gild refinèd gold, to paint the lily,
To throw a perfume on the violet,
To smooth the ice, or add another hue
Unto the rainbow, or with taper light
To seek the beauteous eye of heaven to garnish,
Is wasteful and ridiculous excess.
SHAKESPEARE.—*King John, Act 4, 2.*

So geographers, in Afric maps,
With savage pictures fill their gaps,
And o'er unhabitable downs
Place elephants for want of towns.
SWIFT.—*On Poetry.*

The superfluous, a highly necessary thing.   VOLTAIRE.—*Le Mondain, 22.*

A' owers are ill, but ower the water and ower the hill.   *Scottish prov.*
(*See " All owres " under " Excess."*)

It's needless pouring water on a drowned mouse.   *Scottish prov.*

SUPERIORITY

And yet thou art the nobler of us two :
What dare I dream of, that thou canst not do,
Outstripping my ten small steps with thy stride ?   BROWNING.—*Any Wife to any Husband, 148.*

Never seem wiser or more learned than your company.
LORD CHESTERFIELD.—*Advice to his Son.*

Behold, this is the world ! Everyone thinks himself a little above his neighbour.
LE SAGE.—*Gil Blas, Bk. 5, ch. 1.*

Painful pre-eminence ! yourself to view
Above life's weakness, and its comforts too.
POPE.—*Essay on Man, Ep. 4, 267.*

I know nothing more inept than that expression, " I told you so."
ROUSSEAU.—*Emile.*

And all the courses of my life do show
I am not in the roll of common men.
SHAKESPEARE.—*Henry IV., Pt. 1, Act 3, 1.*

I hold you as a thing ensky'd and sainted.
SHAKESPEARE.—*Measure for Measure*,
Act 1, 5.

As in a theatre, the eyes of men,
After a well-graced actor leaves the stage,
Are idly bent on him that enters next,
Thinking his prattle to be tedious.
SHAKESPEARE.—*Richard II.*, Act 5, 2.

How blessed are we that are not simple
men,
Yet nature might have made me as these
are,
Therefore, I'll not disdain.
SHAKESPEARE.—*Winter's Tale*, Act 4, 3.

Others may be all very well ; but *we*
live at Nonsuch House, in the parish of
Nonpareil.   C. H. SPURGEON.—
"*Salt-Cellars.*"

SUPERNATURAL, THE

Some have mistaken blocks and posts
For spectres, apparitions, ghosts,
With saucer-eyes and horns ; and some
Have heard the devil beat a drum.
BUTLER.—*Hudibras, Pt. 2, 1, 129.*

No doubt the bravest cowers
When he can't tell what 'tis that doth
appal.
How odd a single hobgoblin's nonentity
Should cause more fear than a whole host's
identity !
BYRON.—*Don Juan, c. 16, st. 120.*

Millions of spiritual creatures walk the
earth
Unseen, both when we wake, and when we
sleep.
MILTON.—*Paradise Lost, Bk. 4, l. 678.*

There is something in this more than
natural, if philosophy could find it out.
SHAKESPEARE.—*Hamlet*, Act 2, 2.

And often times to win us to our harm,
The instruments of darkness tell us truths,
Win us with honest trifles, to betray us
In deepest consequence.
SHAKESPEARE.—*Macbeth*, Act 1, 3.

Look how the world's poor people are
amazed
At apparitions, signs, and prodigies.
SHAKESPEARE.—*Venus and Adonis, st. 155.*

SUPERSTITION

There is a superstition in avoiding superstition.   BACON.—*Of Superstition.*

Superstition is the religion of feeble
minds.
BURKE.—*Thoughts on French Revolution.*

Shallow men believe in luck.
EMERSON.—*Worship.*

Superstition is the poetry of life.
GOETHE.

Superstition is godless religion, devout
impiety.
BISHOP HALL.—*Of the Superstitious.*

All power of fancy over reason is a degree of insanity.   JOHNSON.—*Rasselas.*

Superstition is the only religion of which
base souls are capable.
JOUBERT.—*Pensée, 27.*

No itch is more infectious than superstition.   JOVIAN.—*Pont. Ant. Dial.*

Long time men lay oppressed with slavish
fear ;
Religion's tyranny did domineer.
LUCRETIUS.—*De Rerum Natura*, 1, 63
(*Creech tr.*).

The greatest burden in the world is
superstition, not only of ceremonies in the
church, but of imaginary and scarecrow
sins at home.
MILTON.—*Doctrine and Discipline of
Divorce.*

Force first made conquest, and that con-
quest law,
Till Superstition taught the tyrant awe,
Then shared the tyranny, then lent it aid,
And gods of conquerors, slaves of subjects
made.
POPE.—*Essay on Man, Ep. 3, l. 245.*

Superstition is the spleen of the soul.
POPE.—*Thoughts on Various Subjects.*

Giant error, darkly grand,
Grasped the globe with iron hand.
ROGERS.—*Ode to Superstition, 2, 1.*

For not to rank or sex confined
Is this vain ague of the mind.
SCOTT.—*Rokeby, c. 2, 11.*

Superstition obeys vanity just like a
father.
SOCRATES.—(*According to Stobæus*).

How foolishly and miserably superstitious all we women are !
TERENCE.—*Heaut.*, Act 4.

It was necessary for me (Hermogides,
prince of Argos) to succumb before superstitions, which are, much more than we,
the kings of the nations.
VOLTAIRE.—*Eryphile*, Act 3, 1.

Superstitious people in society are like
cowards in an army.   They are possessed
by panic and they produce it.
VOLTAIRE.—*Letters on the English.*

Superstition is to religion what astrology
is to astronomy, the very foolish daughter
of a very wise mother.
VOLTAIRE.—*On Tolerance.*

When was there ever religion without
superstition, worship without idolatry ?
JOHN WILSON.—*Noctes, 26.*

In all things I perceive that ye are some-what superstitious.   *Acts* xvii, 22 (*R.V.*).

SUPERVISION

Where the eye of the master has been most continually, there the fruit will ripen most profusely.   COLUMELLA.—*Bk.* 3.

One eye of the master doth more than both his hands.   *Prov.*

SUPPER

Women should talk an hour
After supper. 'Tis their exercise.
BEAUMONT AND FLETCHER.—*Philaster*,
Act 2.

And men sit down to that nourishment which is called supper.
SHAKESPEARE.—*Love's Labour's Lost*,
Act 1, 1.

SUPPRESSION

All which, though I most potently be-lieve, yet I hold it not honesty to have it thus set down.
SHAKESPEARE.—*Hamlet*, Act 2, 2.

Bondage is hoarse, and may not speak
    aloud ;
Else would I tear the cave where Echo
    lies.
SHAKESPEARE.—*Romeo and Juliet*, Act 2, 2.

SUPREMACY

Divine right of kings means the divine right of anyone who can get uppermost.
HERBT. SPENCER.—*Social Statics.*

SURETYSHIP

He that is surety for a stranger shall smart for it.   *Proverbs* xi, 15.

SURGERY

For want of timely care
Millions have died of medicable wounds.
ARMSTRONG.—*Art of Preserving
Health, Bk.* 3.

Whatever part of a human being could be cut out, without necessarily killing him, they cut out ; and he often died (un-necessarily of course) in consequence. From such trifles as uvulas and tonsils, they [the doctors and surgeons] went on to ovaries and appendices, until at last no one's inside was safe.
G. B. SHAW.—*Heartbreak House: Pref.,
Hypochondria.*

A good surgeon must have an eagle's eye, a lion's heart, and a lady's hand.
Italian prov.

SURNAMES

For as those surnames are esteemed the
    best
That signify in all things else the least,
So men pass fairest in the world's opinion,

That have the least of truth and reason
    in 'em.
BUTLER.—*Upon the Abuse of Human
Learning.*

Fate tried to conceal him by naming him
    Smith.   O. W. HOLMES.—*The Boys.*

SURPRISE

Life is a series of surprises.
EMERSON.—*Circles.*

It is the part of a fool to say, " I should not have thought it." SCIPIO AFRICANUS.

Can such things be,
And overcome us like a summer's cloud,
Without our special wonder ?
SHAKESPEARE.—*Macbeth*, Act 3, 4.

Why is this thus ? What is the reason of this thusness ?
ARTEMUS WARD.—*Moses, the Sassy.*

Where we least think, there goeth the hare away.   *Prov.* (*Ray*).

SURVIVAL

One rose of the wilderness left on its stalk
To mark where a garden had been.
CAMPBELL.—*Lines on Visiting Argyleshire.*

Some they have died, and some they
    have left me,
And some are taken from me ; all are de-
    parted ;
All, all are gone, the old familiar faces.
LAMB.—*The Old Familiar Faces.*

'Tis the last rose of summer
    Left blooming alone ;
All her lovely companions
    Are faded and gone.
MOORE.—*Irish Melodies.*

I feel like one
    Who treads alone
Some banquet-hall deserted,
    Whose lights are fled,
    Whose garlands dead,
And all but he departed.
MOORE.—*Song.*

All of me that remains appears in sight ;
I live, if living be to loathe the light.
VIRGIL.—*Æneid, Bk.* 3 (*Dryden.*)

SUSPICION

Old age is more suspicious than the free
And valiant heart of youth, or manhood's
    firm
Unclouded reason. M. ARNOLD.—*Merope.*

Over-suspicion is a kind of public mad-ness. BACON.—*Instauratio, Pt.* 1, *Bk.* 6, 45.

And when his first suspicions dimly stole,
Rebuked them back like phantoms from
    his soul.   CAMPBELL.—*Theodric.*

It was a maxim with Foxey—our revered father, gentlemen—" Always suspect everybody." [*Sampson Brass.*]
DICKENS.—*Barnaby Rudge, ch.* 66.

" Bother Mrs. Harris ! " said Betsy Prig. " I don't believe there's no sich a person ! "
DICKENS.—*Martin Chuzzlewit, ch.* 49.

Suspicion will make fools of nations as of citizens.
EMERSON.—*English Traits, 7 : Truth.*

Men do not suspect faults which they do not commit. JOHNSON.—*Letter,* 1755.

It is more shameful to mistrust your friends than to be deceived by them.
LA ROCHEFOUCAULD.—*Maxim* 84.

Suspicion's but at best a coward's virtue.
T. OTWAY.—*Venice Preserved,* Act 3, 1.

Julius Cæsar divorced his wife Pompeia, but declared at the trial that he knew nothing of what was alleged against her and Clodius. When asked why, in that case, he had divorced her, he replied : " Because I must have the chastity of my wife clear even of suspicion."
PLUTARCH.—*Life of Julius Cæsar.*

All seems infected that the infected spy, As all looks yellow to a jaundiced eye.
POPE.—*Essay on Criticism,* 568.

Man's of a jealous and mistaking kind.
POPE.—*Odyssey, Bk.* 7, 394.

See what a ready tongue suspicion hath !
SHAKESPEARE.—*Henry IV., Pt.* 2, Act 1, 1.

Who finds the heifer dead, and bleeding fresh, And sees fast by a butcher with an axe, But will suspect 'twas he that made the slaughter ?
SHAKESPEARE.—*Henry VI., Pt.* 2, Act 3, 2.

Suspicion always haunts the guilty mind ; The thief doth fear each bush an officer.
SHAKESPEARE.—*Henry VI., Pt.* 3, Act 5, 6.

But, O, what damnèd minutes tells he o'er, Who dotes, yet doubts ; suspects, yet fondly loves.
SHAKESPEARE.—*Othello,* Act 3, 3.

All men of poor condition are somehow or other suspicious and ready to take offence. TERENCE.—*Adelphi,* 4.

Some might suspect the nymph not over-good— Nor would they be mistaken, if they should.
YOUNG.—*Love of Fame, Sat.* 6.

The virtue of a coward is suspicion.
Prov. (*Geo. Herbert*).

SWANS

There's a double beauty whenever a swan Swims on a lake with her double thereon.
HOOD.—*Miss Kilmansegg.*

The swan, with archèd neck Between her white wings mantling proudly, rows Her state with oary feet.
MILTON.—*Paradise Lost, Bk.* 7, *l.* 438.

All the water in the ocean Can never turn the swan's black legs to white, Although she lave them hourly.
SHAKESPEARE.—*Titus Andron.,* Act 4, 2.

The silver swanne doth sing before her dying day As shee that feeles the deepe delight that is in death.
SPENSER.—*Shep. Cal., October* (*Glosse*).

The eye that marks the gliding creatures sees How graceful pride can be, and how majestic ease.
WORDSWORTH.—*Evening Walk.*

SWEARING

Gret swering is a thing abhominable, And false swering is yet more reprovable. The heighe god forbad swering at al, Witnesse on Mathewe ; but in special Of swering seith the holy Jeremye, " Thou shalt seye sooth thyn othes, and nat lye, And swere in dome, and eke in rightwisnesse " ; But ydel swering is a cursednesse.
CHAUCER.—*Pardoner's Tale,* 631.*

Since we are civilized Englishmen, let us not be naked savages in our talk.
FULLER.—*Holy and Profane State.*

Take not His name, who made thy mouth, in vain ; It gets thee nothing, and has no excuse.
HERBERT.—*Church Porch.*

When a gentleman is disposed to swear, it is not for any bystanders to curtail his oaths.
SHAKESPEARE.—*Cymbeline,* Act 2, 1.

It [swearing] is not so easy an acquirement as a few ignorant pretenders may imagine. A footman may swear, but he cannot swear like a lord. He can swear as often ; but can he swear with equal delicacy, propriety, and judgment ?
SWIFT.—*Intro. to Polite Conversation.*

Some of his words were not Sunday School words.
MARK TWAIN.—*Tramp Abroad.*

" Witnesse on Mathewe "—" Take the evidence of Matthew" (v. 36). The other reference is to Jeremiah iv. 2, and means : "Thou shalt speak truly thine oaths, and not lie, and swear in judgment and also in righteousness."

Her grace she turned her round about,
And like a royall queene she swore.
Old Ballad. Rising in the North.

SWEETNESS

To pile up honey upon sugar, and sugar
upon honey, to an interminable tedious
sweetness.   LAMB.—*On Ears.*

Sweets to the sweet : farewell !
SHAKESPEARE.—*Hamlet, Act 5, 1.*

SWIMMING

He could, perhaps, have passed the Helles-
pont
As once (a feat on which ourselves we
prided)
Leander, Mr. Ekenhead, and I did.
BYRON.—*Don Juan, c. 2, 105.*

This is the purest exercise of health,
The kind refresher of the summer heats ;
Nor, when cold Winter keens the brighten-
ing flood
Would I, weak-shivering, linger on the
brink.   THOMSON.—*The Seasons :
Summer.*

SWITZERLAND

All Switzerland is, so to speak, only one
large town, whose wide and long streets,
more so than that of Saint-Antoine, are
sown with forests, divided by mountains,
and whose rare and isolated houses are
joined only by " English gardens."
ROUSSEAU.—*Rêveries d'un Promeneur
solitaire, 7.*

SYLLOGISMS

Syllogisms do breed, or rather are, all
the variety of man's life. They are the
steps by which we walk in all our busi-
nesses. Man, as he is man, doth nothing
else but weave such chains.
SIR KENELM DIGBY.—*Of Bodies and
Souls (1644).*

Syllogism at best is but the art of fen-
cing with the little knowledge we have,
without making any addition to it.
LOCKE.—*Essay 4, 17.*

SYMPATHY

Those who want friends to open themselves unto, are cannibals of their own
hearts.   BACON.—*Of Friendship.*

Sweet the help
Of one we have helped.
E. B. BROWNING.—*Aurora Leigh, Bk. 7.*

Needs there groan a world in anguish,
Just to teach us sympathy ?
BROWNING.—*La Saisiaz.*

The learned eye is still the loving one.
BROWNING.—*Red Cotton Nightcap
Country.*

All who joy would win
Must share it—Happiness was born a twin.
BYRON.—*Don Juan, c. 2, 172.*

For 'tis some ease our sorrows to reveal,
If they to whom we shall impart our woes.
Seem but to feel a part of what we feel,
And meet us with a sigh, but at the close.
S. DANIEL.—*Cleopatra, Act 4, 1.*

Everything is my cousin.
EMERSON.—*Eloquence.*

A fellow-feeling makes us wondrous kind.
GARRICK.—*Prologue, 1776.*

The sigh that rends thy constant heart,
Shall break thy Edwin's too.
GOLDSMITH.—*The Hermit*

So sorrow is cheered by being poured
From one vessel into another.
HOOD.—*Miss Kilmansegg.*

Our hearts, our hopes, are all with thee,
Our hearts, our hopes, our prayers, our
tears,
Our faith, triumphant o'er our fears,
Are all with thee,—are all with thee !
LONGFELLOW.—*Building of the Ship.*

No one is so accurs'd by fate,
No one so utterly desolate,
But some heart, though unknown,
Responds unto his own.
LONGFELLOW.—*Endymion.*

Two souls with but a single thought,
Two hearts that beat as one.
MARIA A. LOVELL.—*Tr. from German.*

The sad relief
That misery loves—the fellowship of grief.
J. MONTGOMERY.—*West Indies, Pt. 3.*

Yet, taught by time, my heart has learned
to glow
For others' good, and melt at others' woe.
POPE.—*Odyssey, Bk. 18, 279.*

It is man's weakness which makes him
sociable ; it is our common miseries which
draw our hearts to humanity.
ROUSSEAU.—*Emile.*

It is the secret sympathy,
The silver link, the silken tie,
Which heart to heart, and mind to mind,
In body and in soul can bind.
SCOTT.—*Lay of the Last Minstrel, 5, 13.*

She loved me for the dangers I had passed,
And I loved her that she did pity them.
SHAKESPEARE.—*Othello, Act 1, 3.*

He oft finds med'cine who his griefe imparts.
SPENSER.—*Faerie Queene, Bk. 1, c. 2, 34.*

Feel for others—in your pocket.
C. H. SPURGEON.—*" Salt-Cellars."*

How patiently you hear him groan !
How glad the case is not your own !
SWIFT.—*On the Death of Dr. Swift.*

For nothing human foreign was to him.
THOMSON.—*On Lord Talbot* (tr. of
*Terence's " Humani nihil a me alienum
puto "*).

Ever in the New rejoicing,
  Kindly beckoning back the Old,
Turning, with the gift of Midas,
  All things into gold.
WHITTIER.—*To* ——

Yet tears to human suffering are due.
WORDSWORTH.—*Laodamia.*

A sorrow shared is but half a trouble,
But a joy that's shared is a joy made
  double.   *Old Saying.*

T

TABLE-TALK

But still his tongue ran on, the less
Of weight it bore, with greater ease ;
And with its everlasting clack
Set all men's ears upon the rack.
BUTLER.—*Hudibras, Pt.* 3, *c.* 2, 443.

Talk often, but never long ; in that case,
if you do not please, at least you are sure
not to tire your hearers.
LORD CHESTERFIELD.—*Letters to His Son*
(*Oct.* 19, 1748).

A table-talker rich in sense,
And witty without wit's pretence.
C. MATHER.—*Tr. of Epitaph.*

A good talker, even more than a good
orator, implies a good audience.
LESLIE STEPHEN.—*Samuel Johnson*
(*Eng. Men of Letters*), *ch.* 3.

TALENTS

What we acquire by pains and art
Is only due to our own desert ;
While all the endowments she [Nature]
  confers
Are not so much our own as hers.
BUTLER.—*Upon Plagiaries.*

That one talent which is death to hide.
MILTON.—*Sonnet.*

Now this is how I define talent : it is
a gift God has given us in secret, which
we reveal without knowing it.
MONTESQUIEU.

Let the pathway be open to talent.
NAPOLEON.

Talent is talent and mind is mind, in all
its branches . . . We must despise no sort
of talent ; they all have their separate
duties and uses ; all, the happiness of man
for their object : they all improve, exalt,
and gladden life.
SYDNEY SMITH.—*Lectures on Moral
Philosophy, No.* 19.

Creatures of every kind but ours
Well comprehend their natural powers,
While we, whom reason ought to sway,
Mistake our talents every day.
SWIFT.—*Beasts' Confession.*

A sinful soul possessed of many gifts,
A spacious garden full of flowering weeds.
TENNYSON.—*To* ——

Talents angel-bright,
If wanting worth, are shining instruments
In false ambition's hand, to finish faults
Illustrious, and give infamy renown.
YOUNG.—*Night Thoughts,* 6, 273.

TALES

Tell me the tales that to me were so dear,
Long, long ago, long, long ago.
T. H. BAYLY.—*Long Ago.*

Various and strange was the long-
  winded tale.
BEATTIE.—*The Minstrel, Bk.* 1, 44.

'Tis old to you
As the story of Adam and Eve, and pos-
  sibly quite as true.
BROWNING.—*Iván Ivánovitch,* 16.

The Souter told his queerest stories,
The landlord's laugh was ready chorus.
BURNS.—*Tam o' Shanter.*

Of all tales 'tis the saddest—and more sad,
Because it makes us smile.
BYRON.—*Don Juan,* 13, 9 (*Of " Don
Quixote "*).

Story ! God bless you ! I have none to tell,
  sir.   G. CANNING.—*Knife Grinder.*

Whoso shal telle a tale after a man,
He moot reherce, as ny as ever he can,
Everich a word, if it be in his charge,
Al speke he never so rudeliche and large ;
Or elles he moot telle his tale untrewe,
Or feyne thing, or finde wordes newe.
CHAUCER.—*Cant. Tales, Prol.*

Let every felawe telle his tale aboute.
CHAUCER.—*Knight's Tale.*

Sey forth thy tale, and tarie nat the
  tyme. CHAUCER.—*Reeve's Prologue.*

A tale should be judicious, clear, succinct,
The language plain, the incidents well
  linked ;
Tell not as old what everybody knows
And, new or old, still hasten to a close.
COWPER.—*Conversation,* 235.

" I'll tell you an excellent story "—an
exordium ever to be avoided by all prudent
wits. MISS EDGEWORTH.—*Essay on Irish
Bulls, ch.* 5.

" I'm bad ez de chillun 'bout dem ole
tales " [said Aunt Tempy], " kase I kin
des [just] set up yer [here] un lissen at um

de whole blessid night, on a good part er de day.   Yass, Lord ! "
J. C. HARRIS.—*Nights with Uncle Remus,
ch. 27.*

" I 'clar' ter goodness, honey," he [Uncle Remus] exclaimed, " ef you hol's on ter yo' pra'rs lak you does ter deze yer tales, youer doin' mighty well."
J. C. HARRIS.—*Ib., ch. 47.*

But stories and sayings they will well remember.
HERBERT.—*Priest to the Temple, ch. 7.*

And what so tedious as a twice-told tale ?
POPE.—*Odyssey, Bk. 12, 522.*

And all who told it added something new, And all who heard it, made enlargements too.   POPE.—*Temple of Fame, 470.*

Examples draw when precept fails, And sermons are less read than tales.
PRIOR.—*Turtle and Sparrow.*

I cannot tell how the truth may be ; I tell the tale as 'twas said to me.
SCOTT.—*Lay of the Last Minstrel, c. 2, 22.*

I love such holy ramblers ; still They know to charm a weary hill With song, romance, or lay ; Some jovial tale, or glee, or jest, Some lying legend at the least, They bring to cheer the way.
SCOTT.—*Marmion, c. 1, 25.*

'Tis an old tale, and often told.
SCOTT.—*Ib., c. 2, 27.*

And so, from hour to hour, we ripe and ripe
And then from hour to hour, we rot and rot ;
And thereby hangs a tale.
SHAKESPEARE.—*As You Like It,* Act 2, 7.

Delivers in such apt and gracious words, That aged ears play truant at his tales, And younger hearings are quite ravishèd ; So sweet and voluble is his discourse.
SHAKESPEARE.—*Love's Labour's Lost,
Act 2, 1.*
I ran it through, even from my boyish days
To the very moment that he bade me tell it.   SHAKESPEARE.—*Othello,* Act 1, 3.

An honest tale speeds best, being plainly told.
SHAKESPEARE.—*Richard III.,* Act 4, 4.

Your tale, sir, would cure deafness.
SHAKESPEARE.—*Tempest,* Act 1, 2.

A sad tale's best for winter ; I have one of sprites and goblins.
SHAKESPEARE.—*Winter's Tale,* Act 2, 1.

Come listen to my mournful tale, Ye tender hearts and lovers dear ; Not will you scorn to heave a sigh, Nor need you blush to shed a tear.
SHENSTONE.—*Jemmy Dawson.*

For seldom shall she hear a tale, So sad, so tender, and so true.
SHENSTONE.—*Ib.*

With a tale, forsooth, he cometh unto you, with a tale which holdeth children from play, and old men from the chimney-corner.
SIR P. SIDNEY.—*Apology for Poetry.*

So it is in man (most of which are childish in the best things, till they be cradled in their graves), glad they will be to hear the tales of Hercules, Achilles, Cyrus, and Æneas.   SIR P. SIDNEY.—*Ib.*

" Now tell us what 'twas all about," Young Peterkin he cries ; And little Wilhelmine looks up With wonder-waiting eyes.
SOUTHEY.—*Battle of Blenheim.*

Such wondrous tales as childhood loves to hear.   SOUTHEY.—*Joan of Arc.*

The first law of story-telling—" Every man is bound to leave a story better than he found it."
MRS. HUMPHRY WARD.—*Robert Elsmere,
Bk. 1, ch. 3.*
It's a gey lee-like story, but it's as sure as death.
JOHN WILSON.—*Noctes (Ettrick Shepherd).*

O Reader ! had you in your mind Such stores as silent thought can bring, O gentle Reader ! you would find A tale in every thing.
WORDSWORTH.—*Simon Lee.*

And their words seemed to them as idle tales.   *St. Luke* xxiv, 11.

If it is not true, it is very well invented.
*Italian prov. found in Doni's " Marmi "
(1552).*

TALK
Those who talk much never say anything.   BOILEAU.

The mair they talk I'm kenned the better, E'en let them clash !
BURNS.—*To his Illegitimate Child.*

Talk that does not end in any kind of action is better suppressed altogether.
CARLYLE.—*Address (1866).*

Avoid argument with the verbose ; power of speech is given to all ; wisdom of mind to few.   CATO.

O lady! we shall never know the truth,—
What man, what love, what God is,—till
  we cease
To talk of them,—which all do in the grave.
        J. DAVIDSON.—*Smith*, Act 3.

But fools to talking ever prone,
Are sure to make their follies known.
        GAY.—*Fables*, 44.

Though I'm anything but clever,
I could talk like that for ever.
        SIR W. S. GILBERT.—*H.M.S. Pinafore.*

To talk without effort is, after all, the
great charm of talking.
        J. C. HARE.—*Guesses at Truth.*

" I'll do de talkin'," sez Brer Rabbit,
sezee, "'en you kin set back and say *yea*,"
sezee.
        J. C. HARRIS.—*Nights with Uncle Remus,*
                                    ch. 19.

The most fluent talkers or most plaus-
ible reasoners are not always the justest
thinkers.   W. HAZLITT.—*On Prejudice.*

The worst of Warburton is that he has
a rage for saying something when there is
nothing to be said.   JOHNSON.—*Remark.*

We talk little when vanity does not
make us talk.
        LA ROCHEFOUCAULD.—*Maxim* 137.

Then he will talk—good gods, how he will
talk! N. LEE.—*Rival Queens*, Act 1, 1.

I am a maker of war and not a maker of
phrases.
        LONGFELLOW.—*Courtship of Miles
                                    Standish*, 2.

But as they hedn't no gret things to say,
An' sed 'em often, I come right away.
J. R. LOWELL.—*Biglow Papers*, 2nd Ser., 2.

Woord is but wynd; leave woord and
take the dede. J. LYDGATE.—*Secreta.*

With patient inattention hear him prate.
GEO. MEREDITH.—*Bellerophon*, st. 4.

Say-all-you-know shall go with clouted
  head,
Say-nought-at-all is beaten.
        W. MORRIS.—*The Lovers of Gudrun.*

Strange the difference of men's talk!
        S. PEPYS.—*Diary*, 1660.

And boasting youth, and narrative old
  age.   POPE.—*Eloisa.*

And 'tis remarkable that they
Talk most who have the least to say.
        PRIOR.—*Alma, c.* 2, 345.

They never taste who always drink;
They always talk who never think.
        PRIOR.—*On a Passage in the Scaligera.*

Man says what he knows; woman says
what will please.   ROUSSEAU.—*Emile.*

This bald, unjointed chat of his.
SHAKESPEARE.—*Henry IV.*, Pt. 1, Act 1, 2.

Let it serve for table talk.
SHAKESPEARE.—*Merch. of Venice*, Act 3, 5.

For the watch to babble and talk, is
most tolerable and not to be endured.
        SHAKESPEARE.—*Much Ado*, Act 3, 3.

A good old man, sir, he will be talking;
as they say, " When the age is in, the wit
is out."   SHAKESPEARE.—*Ib.*, Act 3, 5.

    Mere prattle without practice
    Is all his scholarship.
        SHAKESPEARE.—*Othello*, Act 1, 1.

A gentleman, nurse, that loves to hear
himself talk, and will speak more in a
minute than he will stand to in a month.
SHAKESPEARE.—*Romeo and Juliet*, Act 2, 4.

A fool and his words are soon parted.
        SHENSTONE.—*On Reserve.*

How can his fluent tongue and thought
  keep touch,
Who thinks too little but who talks too
  much?   SWIFT.—*Swan Tripe Club.*

Two great talkers will not travel far
together. *Quoted by Borrow (" Lavengro ")
                as a Spanish prov.*

Yf that thow wolte speke aryght,
Syx thynggys thow moste (must) ob-
  serve then:
What thow spekyst, and of what wyght,
Whare, to wham, whye and whenne.
        MS. Trin. Coll., Cambridge (c. 1530)
                        (see p. 481, *Norris).*

Glib i' the tongue is aye glaiket (foolish
or trifling) at the heart.   *Scottish prov.*

TARDINESS

'Tis cruel to prolong a pain and to defer
  a joy.   SIR C. SEDLEY.—*Song.*

The favour which sticks too long in the
hands of the donor is not thankfully received.   SENECA.—*De Beneficiis.*

To be slow in granting a favour is to
show unwillingness; even to be slow in
desiring to grant it is evidence of unwillingness.   SENECA.

Why, one that rode to his execution, man,
Could never go so slow.
        SHAKESPEARE.—*Cymbeline*, Act 3, 2.

When the dog comes, a stone cannot be
found; when the stone is found, the dog
does not come.   *Prov. (Telegu).*

TASTE

Good native Taste, though rude, is seldom
    wrong,
Be it in music, painting, or in song :
But this, as well as other faculties,
Improves with age and ripens by degrees.
        ARMSTRONG.—*Taste*, 26.

Wealth had done wonders—taste not
    much. BYRON.—*Don Juan, c.* 5, 94.

The wild vicissitudes of taste.
        JOHNSON.—*Prologue.*

How many a thing which we cast to the
    ground
When others pick it up becomes a gem !
    GEO. MEREDITH.—*Modern Love, st.* 41.

A person's taste is as much his own
peculiar concern as his opinion or his purse.
        J. S. MILL.—*Liberty, ch.* 4.

Talk as you will of taste, my friend, you'll
    find
Two of a face, as soon as of a mind.
        POPE.—*Moral Essays.*

Perfect taste is the faculty of receiving
the greatest possible pleasure from these
material sources which are attractive to
our moral nature in its purity and perfection.
    RUSKIN.—*Mod. Painters, Pt.* I, *Sec.* I,
        ch. 6, §2.

I have always suspected public taste to
be a mongrel product, out of affectation
by dogmatism.
    R. L. STEVENSON.—*Virginibus, Pt.* I.

Because you and I are epicures or dainty
feeders, it does not follow that Hodge is
miserable with his homely meal of bread
and bacon.
    THACKERAY.—*The Virginians.*

Simple was the noble architecture [of the
Temple of Taste]. Each ornament, fixed
in its place, seemed there of necessity.
Art hid itself under the air of nature. The
eye satisfied embraced the structure, never
surprised and always enchanted.
    VOLTAIRE.—*Temple du Goût.*

The ear to no grave harmonies inclined,
The witless thirst for false wit's worthless
    lees,
The laugh mistimed in tragic presences,
The eye to all majestic meanings blind.
    SIR W. WATSON.—*Sonnet.*

The word Taste has been stretched to
the sense which it bears in modern Europe
by habits of self-conceit, inducing that in-
version in the order of things whereby a
passive faculty is made paramount among
the faculties conversant with the fine arts.
    WORDSWORTH.—*Essay, supplementary
        to Pref. to Poems.*

TAXATION

No people overcharged with tribute is
fit for empire.
    BACON.—*Essays : Of Expense.*

To tax and to please, no more than to
love and be wise, is not given to men.
    BURKE.—*Speech on American Taxation.*

What is't to us if taxes rise or fall ?
Thanks to our fortune, we pay none at all.
    CHURCHILL.—*Apology.*

" It was as true," said Mr. Barkis, " as
taxes is. And nothing's truer than them."
    DICKENS.—*David Copperfield, ch.* 21.

Was it Napoleon who said that he found
vices very good patriots ?—" he got five
millions from the love of brandy, and he
should be glad to know which of the virtues
could pay him as much."
    EMERSON.—*Civilization.*

Of all debts men are least willing to pay
the taxes. What a satire this on Government ! EMERSON.—*Politics.*

Taxes are indeed very heavy . . . We
are taxed twice as much by our idleness,
three times as much by our pride, and four
times as much by our folly.
    B. FRANKLIN.—*Way to Wealth.*

All men are by nature provided of no-
table multiplying glasses,—that is their
passions and self-love, through which
every little payment appeareth a great
grievance ; but are destitute of those pros-
pective glasses,—namely moral and civil
science—to see afar off the miseries that
hang over them and cannot, without such
payments, be avoided.
    HOBBES.—*Leviathan, ch.* 18.

Taxes milks dry, but, neighbour, you'll
    allow
Thet havin' things onsettled kills the cow.
    J. R. LOWELL.—*Biglow Papers,* 2nd
        Ser., 2.

Men who prefer any load of infamy,
however great, to any pressure of taxation, however light.
    SYDNEY SMITH.—*Petition to the House
        of Congress at Washington.*

Folly taxes us four times as much as
Parliament.
    C. H. SPURGEON.—" *Salt-Cellars.*"
        (*V. supra, Franklin.*)

The peace of nations cannot be secured
without arms, nor arms without pay, nor
pay without taxes.
    TACITUS.—*Hist., Bk.* 4.

What the church leaves, the exchequer
takes. *Spanish prov.*

TEA

Tea, thou soft, thou sober, sage and venerable liquid !
C. CIBBER.—*Lady's Last Stake*, Act 1, 1.

The bubbling and loud-hissing urn
Throws up a steamy column, and the cups
That cheer but not inebriate wait on each.*
COWPER.—*The Task : Winter Evening.*

This here old lady next to me is a drowndin' herself in tea. . . . There's a young 'ooman on the next form but two as has drunk nine breakfast cups and a half ; and she's a swellin' wisibly before my wery eyes. [*Samuel Weller, sen.*]
DICKENS.—*Pickwick Papers, ch.* 33.

My constant drink is tea, or a little wine and water ; 'tis prescribed by the physicians for a remedy against the spleen.
FARQUHAR.—*Beaux' Stratagem*, 3.

Thank God for tea ! What would the world do without tea ! How did it exist ? I am glad I was not born before tea !
SYDNEY SMITH.—*Memoir.*

Indeed Madam, your ladyship is very sparing of your tea : I protest the last I took was no more than water bewitched.
SWIFT.—*Polite Conversations*, 1.

When a body has had an early denner, what a glorious meal's the " Fowre-oors " !
JOHN WILSON.—*Noctes*, 27.

TEACHING

'Tis the taught already that profits by teaching.
BROWNING.—*Christmas Eve.*

And gladly wolde he lerne and gladly teche. CHAUCER.—*Cant. Tales, Prol.*

We loved the doctrine for the teacher's sake.
DEFOE.—*Character of Dr. Annesley* (*c.* 1700).

We love the precept for the teacher's sake. FARQUHAR.—
Constant Couple, Act 5, 3 (1700).

Men must be taught as if you taught them not,
And things unknown proposed as things forgot.
POPE.—*Essay on Criticism*, 574.

Long is the way (to learning) by rules ; short and effective by examples.
SENECA.—*Ep.* 6.

⁾ Probably founded on a passage in Bishop Berkeley's *Siris* (pubd. 20 years previously), in which he says that tar-water is so " proportioned to the human constitution, as to warm without heating, *to cheer but not inebriate.*"

It is a good divine that follows his own instructions ; I can easier teach twenty what were good to be done, than to be one of the twenty to follow mine own teachings.
SHAKESPEARE.—*Merch. of Venice*, Act 1, 2.

TEARS

There are worse plagues on earth than tears. M. ARNOLD.—*A Wish.*

For where Teares cannot, nothing can prevaile. R. BARNFIELD.—
Affectionate Shepheard (1594).

A lady's tears are silent orators.
BEAUMONT AND FLETCHER.—*Love's Cure*, Act 3, 3.

For a tear is an intellectual thing,
And a sigh is the sword of an angel-king.
BLAKE.—*Grey Monk.*

Every tear from every eye
Becomes a babe in eternity.
BLAKE.—*Proverbs.*

Oh ! too convincing—dangerously dear—
In woman's eye the unanswerable tear !
BYRON.—*Corsair*, 2, 15.

What lost a world, and bade a hero fly ?
The timid tear in Cleopatra's eye.
BYRON.—*Ib.*

He bids me dry the last, the first,
The only tears that ever burst
From Outalissi's soul.
CAMPBELL.—*Gertrude.*

For Beauty's tears are lovelier than her smile.
CAMPBELL.—*Pleasures of Hope*, 1;

Nothing dries quicker than a tear.
CICERO.—*Ad Herennium.*

And the tear that is wiped with a little address,
May be followed perhaps by a smile.
COWPER.—*The Rose.*

He doubted, but God said " Even so ;
Nothing is lost that's wrought with tears."
J. DAVIDSON.—*Ballad of Heaven.*

What argufies snivelling and piping your eye ? C. DIBDIN.—*Poor Jack.*

They [the critics] make Æneas little better than a kind of St. Swithin-hero, always raining.
DRYDEN.—*Dedic. of Æneid.*

Had I, my father, the persuasive voice
Of Orpheus, and his skill to charm the rocks
To follow me, and soothe whome'er I please
With winning words, I would make trial of it ;
But I have nothing to present thee now
Save tears, my only eloquence.
EURIPIDES.—*Iphigenia in Aul.*, 1222 (*R. Potter tr.*).

Oh, would I were dead now,
Or up in my bed now,
To cover my head now
And have a good cry !
  Hood.—*Table of Errata.*

For men must work, and women must
 weep
And the sooner it's over, the sooner to
 sleep. C. Kingsley.—*Three Fishers.*

It is only to the happy that tears are
a luxury. Moore.—*Lalla Rookh.*

Sometimes tears have the weight of
words. Ovid.—*Ep. ex Pont.*

Weep no more, lady, weep no more ;
Thy sorrow is in vain,
For violets plucked the sweetest showers
Will ne'er make grow again.
  Bishop Percy.—*Friar of Orders Grey.*

The tribute of a tear is all I crave,
And the possession of a peaceful grave.
  Pope.—*Odyssey*, 11, 89.

When the big lip and watery eye
Tell me the rising storm is nigh.
  Prior.—*The Lady's Looking Glass.*

That very law which moulds a tear,
And bids it trickle from its source,
That law preserves the earth a sphere,
And guides the planets in their course.
  Rogers.—*On a Tear.*

But woe awaits a country when
She sees the tears of bearded men.
  Scott.—*Marmion, c.* 5, 16.

All things are cause for either laughter
or tears. Seneca.—*De Ira, Bk.* 2, 10.

The big round tears
Coursed one another down his innocent
 nose,
In piteous chase.
 Shakespeare.—*As You Like It,* Act 2, 1.

Like Niobe, all tears.
  Shakespeare.—*Hamlet,* Act 1, 2.

Too much of water hadst thou, poor
 Ophelia,
And therefore I forbid my tears ; but yet
It is our trick, nature her custom holds,
Let shame say what it will.
  Shakespeare.—*Ib.,* Act 4, 7.

And all my mother came into mine eyes,
And gave me up to tears.
  Shakespeare.—*Henry V.,* Act 4, 6.

If you have tears, prepare to shed them
 now.
Shakespeare.—*Julius Cæsar,* Act 3, 2.

These foolish drops do somewhat drown
 my manly spirit.
  Shakespeare.—*Merchant of Venice,*
    Act 2, 3.

O father, what a hell of witchcraft lies
In the small orb of one particular tear !
 Shakespeare (?).—*Lover's Complaint,*
    st. 42.

I loved thee for the tear thou couldst
 not hide. Tennyson.—*Bridesmaid.*

Tears, idle tears, I know not what they
 mean,
Tears from the depths of some divine
 despair
Rise in the heart, and gather in the eyes.
  Tennyson.—*Princess, c.* 4, 21.

One small pretended tear, which, with
much dismal rubbing of the eye, she could
scarcely squeeze out by force.
  Terence.—*Eunuchus,* 1.

You cannot cleanse your heart with
tears.
  Archbp. Trench.—*Justin Martyr.*

Why these weeps ?
  Artemus Ward.—*Lecture.*

Grief is the unhappy charter of our sex :
The gods who gave us readier tears to shed,
Gave us more cause to shed them.
  W. Whitehead.—*Creusa.*

And what are sighs and tears but wind and
 water,
That show the leakiness of mortal nature ?
  J. Wolcot.—*Instructions to a late*
    celebrated Laureate.

Yet tears to human suffering are due ;
And mortal hopes, defeated and o'erthrown,
Are mourned by man, and not by man
 alone. Wordsworth.—*Laodamia.*

Scorn the proud man that is ashamed to
 weep. Young.—*Night Thoughts,* 3.

Our funeral tears from different causes
 rise. Young.—*Ib.,* 5.

Men given to tears are good men.
    Greek prov.

TEDIOUSNESS

Like some poor nigh-related guest,
That may not rudely be dismissed ;
He hath outstayed his welcome while,
And tells the jest without the smile.
  Coleridge.—*Youth and Age.*

If in dull length your moral is expressed,
The tedious wisdom overflows the breast.
  P. Francis.—*Horace, Art of Poetry.*

Sometimes even the excellent Homer
grows drowsy. Horace.—*De Arte Poet.*

A man whose eloquence has power
To clear the fullest house in half an hour.
  Soame Jenyns.—*Horace.*

These tedious old fools !
  Shakespeare.—*Hamlet,* Act 2, 2

O, he's as tedious
As a tired horse, a railing wife ;
Worse than a smoky house :—I had rather
    live
With cheese and garlic in a windmill.
        SHAKESPEARE.—*Henry IV., Pt. 1,*
                            Act 3, 1.

Life is as tedious as a twice-told tale,
Vexing the dull ear of a drowsy man.
    SHAKESPEARE.—*King John, Act 3, 4.*

Faith ! he must make his stories shorter,
Or change his comrades once a quarter.
    SWIFT.—*On the Death of Dr. Swift.*

TEETH

Some asked how pearls did grow, and
    where ?
Then spoke I to my Girl
To part her lips, and showed them there
The quarrelets of Pearl.
        HERRICK.—*Rock of Rubies.*

The best of friends fall out, and so
His teeth had done some years ago.
        HOOD.—*True Story.*

For her teeth, where there is one of ivory,
its neighbour is pure ebony, black and
white alternately, just like the keys of a
harpsichord.
    SHERIDAN.—*The Duenna, Act 2, 3.*

Those cherries fairly do enclose
Of orient pearl a double row,
Which, when her lovely laughter shows,
    They look like rosebuds filled with snow.
    Elizabethan Song (set to music by
                    Richard Alison).

TEMPER

You know a saying attributed to the
Bishop of —— about temper. No ? Somebody, I suppose, was excusing something
on the score of temper, to which the Bishop
replied, " Temper is nine-tenths of Christianity."
    SIR A. HELPS.—*Friends in Council,*
                        Bk. 1, ch. 7.

Your spirits kindle to a flame,
Moved with the lightest touch of blame ;
And when a friend in kindness tries
To show you where your error lies,
Conviction does but more incense ;
Perverseness is your whole defence.
        SWIFT.—*To Stella, 1720.*

TEMPERAMENT

We boil at different degrees.
        EMERSON.—*Eloquence.*

In every imaginable thing, that which
I cannot do with pleasure soon becomes
to me impossible to do.
    ROUSSEAU.—*Rêveries d'un Promeneur*
                        solitaire, 6.
These flashes on the surface are not he ;
He has a solid base of temperament.
        TENNYSON.—*Princess, c. 4, 234.*

TEMPERANCE

Temperance is a bridle of gold.
        BURTON.—*Anatomy of Melancholy,*
                    Pt. 2, sec. 2, 1, 2.

Temp'rate in every place—abroad, at home,
Thence will applause, and hence will profit
    come ;
And health from either.
        CRABBE.—*The Borough, Letter 17.*

Be not a beast in courtesy, but stay,
Stay at the third cup, or forego the place.
Wine above all things doth God's stamp
    deface.   HERBERT.—*Church Porch.*

Drink not the third glass, which thou
    canst not tame,
When once it is within thee.
        GEO. HERBERT.—*Ib.*

Abstinence is as easy to me as temperance would be difficult.
    JOHNSON.—*Johnsoniana (H. More).*

    She [Nature], good cateress,
Means her provision only to the good,
That live according to her sober laws,
And holy dictate of spare Temperance.
        MILTON.—*Comus, l. 764.*

" Know thyself " and " Be temperate "
are the same thing, as the writings assert,
and as I [Critias] maintain.
        PLATO.—*Charmides, 27.*

Temperance and labour are the two true
physicians of man.   ROUSSEAU.

Let's teach ourselves that honourable stop,
Not to outsport discretion.
        SHAKESPEARE.—*Othello, Act 2, 3.*

Temperance is reason's girdle and passion's bridle.   JEREMY TAYLOR.

He knew no beverage but the flowing
    stream.   THOMSON.—*Castle of*
                        Indolence, c. 2, 7.

TEMPORISING

The foul sluggard's comfort : " It will
last my time."
        CARLYLE.—*Cagliostro.*

Unskilful he to fawn or seek for power,
By doctrines fashioned to the varying
    hour. GOLDSMITH.—*Deserted Village.*

Some blamed him, some believed him
    good—
    The truth lay doubtless 'twixt the two,—
He reconciled as best he could
    Old faith and fancies new.
        WHITTIER.—*My Namesake.*

TEMPTATION

    A dear-loved lad, convenience snug,
    A treacherous inclination—
    But let me whisper i' your lug,
    Ye're aiblins nae temptation.
        BURNS.—*To the Unco Guid.*

The devil tempts us not, 'tis we tempt him,
Beckoning his skill with opportunity.
> GEO. ELIOT.

'Gainst the logic of the devil
Human logic strives in vain.
> A. L. GORDON.—*Ashtaroth.*

For he who tempts, though in vain, at
least asperses
The tempted with dishonour foul.
> MILTON.—*Paradise Lost, Bk.* 9, 296.

So glozed the Tempter.
> MILTON.—*Ib.,* 549.

The veriest hermit in the nation
May yield, God knows, to strong temptation.   POPE.—*Imit. of Horace,*
> *Bk.* 2, *Sat.* 6, *l.* 181.

'Tis one thing to be tempted, Escalus,
Another thing to fall.
> SHAKESPEARE.—*Measure for Measure,*
> Act 2, 1.

The tempter or the tempted, who sins
most ? SHAKESPEARE.—*Ib.,* Act 2, 2.

Ay me, how many perils doe enfold
The righteous man, to make him daily
fall,
Were not that heavenly grace doth him
uphold,
And stedfast Truth acquite him out of
all !
> SPENSER.—*Faerie Queene, Bk.* 1, *c.* 8, 1.

When a man is tempted to do a tempting
thing, he can find a hundred ingenious
reasons for gratifying his liking.
> THACKERAY.—*Pendennis.*

The gates of hell are open night and day ;
Smooth the descent, and easy is the way.
> VIRGIL.—*Æneid, Bk.* 6 (*Dryden tr.*).

The only way to get rid of a temptation
is to yield to it.
> OSCAR WILDE.—*Dorian Gray.*

TERROR

No divine terror will ever be found in the
work of the man who wastes a colossal
strength in elaborating toys ; for the first
lesson that terror is sent to teach us is, the
value of the human soul, and the shortness
of mortal time.
> RUSKIN.—*Stones of Venice, ch.* 3.

He that only rules by terror
Doeth grievous wrong.
> TENNYSON.—*The Captain.*

For all things are less dreadful than they
seem.
> WORDSWORTH.—*Eccles. Sonnets, Pt.* 1.

THANKSGIVING

For these things it is meet to give the Gods
Thank-offerings long-enduring.
> ÆSCHYLUS.—*Agamemnon,* 821
> (*Plumptre tr.*).

Such thanks
As fits a king's remembrance.
> SHAKESPEARE.—*Hamlet,* Act 2, 2.

Beggar that I am, I am poor even in
thanks.   SHAKESPEARE.—*Ib.*

And though I ebb in worth I'll flow in
thanks.   JOHN TAYLOR.—*Merry-*
> *Wherry-Ferry Voyage.*

I doubt whether that practice of piety,
. . . to be thankful because we are better off
than somebody else, be a very rational
religious exercise.
> THACKERAY.—*Vanity Fair, ch.* 66.

But whether we have less or more,
Alway thank we God therefor.
> *Sir Cleyes* (15*th Century*).

THEATRES

The stage I choose, a subject fair and free
'Tis yours—'tis mine—'tis public property.
All common exhibitions open lie,
For praise or censure, to the common eye.
> CHURCHILL.—*Apology.*

Like hungry guests a sitting audience looks;
Plays are like suppers ; poets are the cooks.
> PETER MOTTEUX.—*Prol. to Farquhar's*
> *" Inconstant."*

To wake the soul by tender strokes of art,
To raise the genius and to mend the heart,
To make mankind in conscious virtue bold,
Live o'er each scene, and be what they be-
hold ;
For this the tragic muse first trod the stage,
Commanding tears to stream through every
age. POPE.—*Prol. to Addison's Cato.*

I have heard
That guilty creatures sitting at a play
Have, by the very cunning of the scene,
Been struck so to the soul that presently
They have proclaimed their malefactions.
> SHAKESPEARE.—*Hamlet,* Act 2, 2.

Some come to take their ease,
And sleep an act or two.
> SHAKESPEARE.—*Henry VIII., Epilogue.*

In a theatre the eyes of men,
After a well-grac'd actor leaves the stage,
Are idly bent on him that enters next.
> SHAKESPEARE.—*Richard II.,* Act 5, 2.

THEOLOGY

Myself when young did eagerly frequent
Doctor and Saint, and heard great Argu-
ment,
About it and about : but evermore
Came out by the same door wherein I went.
> E. FITZGERALD.—*Rubáiyát, st.* 27.

The various modes of worship which
prevailed in the Roman world were all considered by the people as equally true ; by
the philosopher as equally false ; and by
the magistrate as equally useful.
> GIBBON.—*Decline and Fall.*

I always admired Mrs. Grote's saying that politics and theology were the only two really great subjects.
GLADSTONE.—*Letter*, 1880. (*Cf. O. W. Holmes, as quoted below.*)

Religion and government appear to me the two subjects which, of all others, should belong to the common talk of people who enjoy the blessings of freedom.
O. W. HOLMES.—*Prof. at Breakfast Table.*

The saying of the priest of Apollo to the Bishop of Magnum Bonum, " You have your theology, and let me have my-thology." HOOD.—*The Rope Dancer*, 1834.

Ac [but] theologie hath teened [grieved] me ten score tymes ;
The more I muse thereon, the mystiloker [mistier] it semeth,
And the deeper I devyne, the derker me thynketh it.
LANGLAND.—*Piers Plowman, Passus 12, 129.*

By what fatality does it happen that so many theologians are, of all men of letters, the most hardy calumniators, if indeed one may give the title of men of letters to these fanatics ?
VOLTAIRE.—*Pyrrhonism of History.*

Carried about with every wind of doc-trine.   *Ephesians* iv, 14.

There are no wild beasts in England except in the Theological Gardens.
Schoolgirl's essay, quoted in Chancery Court, Nov. 13, 1917.

THEORY

Good patriots, who for a theory risked a cause.
E. B. BROWNING.—*Aurora Leigh, Bk.* 4.

A thing may look specious in theory, and yet be ruinous in practice ; a thing may look evil in theory, and yet be in practice excellent. BURKE.—*Impeachment of Hastings (Feb.* 19, 1788).

'Tis mighty easy, o'er a glass of wine,
On vain refinements vainly to refine,
To laugh at poverty in plenty's reign,
To boast of apathy when out of pain.
CHURCHILL.—*The Farewell.*

O fate of fools ! officious in contriving ;
In executing puzzled, lame and lost.
CONGREVE.—*Mourning Bride, Act* 5, 1.

The frigid theories of a generalising age.
DISRAELI.—*Coningsby, Bk.* 9, *c.* 7.

Some man for lakke of occupacioún
Musethé ferther than his witte may strecche,
And all thurghe the fiendé's instigacioún
Dampnable erroure holdethe.
T. HOCCLEVE.—*La male règle.*

Every conjecture we can form with regard to the works of God, has as little probability as the conjectures of a child with regard to the works of a man.
DR. REID.—*Intellectual Powers, vol.* 1.

If to do were as easy as to know what were good to do, chapels had been churches, and poor men's cottages princes' palaces.
SHAKESPEARE.—*Merch. of Venice,* Act 1, 2.

She was crammed with theories out of books.
TENNYSON.—*Princess, Conclusion.*

THIRST

The panting thirst, which scorches in the breath
Of those that die the soldier's fiery death,
In vain impels the burning mouth to crave
One drop—the last—to cool it for the grave. BYRON.—*Lara, c.* 2, *st.* 16.

Hunger is bitter, but the worst
Of human pangs, the most accursed
Of Want's fell scorpions, is Thirst.
ELIZA COOK.—*Melaia.*

THOROUGHNESS

Only, do finish something !
BROWNING.—*Sordello, Bk.* 3.

What is worth doing at all is worth doing well. EARL OF CHESTERFIELD.— *Letter to his Son.*

Not from a vain or shallow thought
His awful Jove young Phidias brought.
EMERSON.—*The Problem.*

Build to-day, then, strong and sure,
With a firm and ample base ;
And ascending and secure
Shall to-morrow find its place.
LONGFELLOW.—*Builders.*

In the elder days of Art
Builders wrought with greatest care
Each minute and unseen part,
For the Gods see everywhere.
LONGFELLOW.—*Ib.*

And whatsoever ye do, do it heartily, as to the Lord, and not unto men.
Colossians iii, 23.

THOUGHT

The kings of modern thought are dumb.
M. ARNOLD.—*Grande Chartreuse, st.* 20.

Who can mistake great thoughts ?
P. J. BAILEY.—*Festus.*

And many a thought did I build up on thought,
As the wild bee hangs cell to cell.
BROWNING.—*Pauline.*

Ah thought which saddens while it soothes ! BROWNING.—*Pictor Ignotus.*

Thought is the soul of act.
BROWNING.—*Sordello, Bk. 5.*

Thou wert a beautiful thought, and softly
bodied forth.
BYRON.—*Childe Harold, c. 4, st. 115.*

To live is to think.
CICERO.—*Tusc. Quæst., 5.*

Why should I disparage my parts by
thinking what to say? None but dull
rogues think. CONGREVE.—*Double Dealer.*

Thought is deeper than all speech,
Feeling deeper than all thought;
Souls to souls can never teach
What unto themselves was taught.
C. P. CRANCH.—*Stanza from an Early
Poem.*

I think, therefore I am.
DESCARTES.—*Principles of Philosophy.*

Beware when the great God lets loose
a thinker on this planet.
EMERSON.—*Circles.*

Thought is the seed of action.
EMERSON.—*Society and Solitude.*

Evil is wrought by want of thought,
As well as want of heart.
HOOD.—*Lady's Dream.*

If young hearts were not so clever,
Oh, they would be young for ever.
Think no more! 'Tis only thinking
Lays lads underground.
A. E. HOUSMAN.—*A Shropshire Lad,
49, 2.*

Truth gains more even by the errors of
one who, with due study and preparation,
thinks for himself, than by the true
opinions of those who only hold them
because they do not suffer themselves to
think.   J. S. MILL.—*Liberty, ch. 2.*

If I have done the public any service,
it is due to patient thought.
SIR I. NEWTON.—*Remark to Dr. Bentley.*

Let every man examine his thought,
and he will find it always occupied with
the past and the future. We scarcely give
any thought to the present.
PASCAL.—*Pensées.*

What thin partitions sense from thought
divide!
POPE.—*Essay on Man, Ep. 1, 226.*

It is very difficult to think nobly when
one thinks only to get a living.
ROUSSEAU.—*Confessions, 2, 9.*

Man does not easily begin to think, but
when once he has begun he does not leave
off.   ROUSSEAU.—*Emile.*

Reverie is a recreation to me and an
amusement; reflection tires me and saddens me. Thinking has always been to

me an occupation painful and without
charm.
ROUSSEAU.—*Rêveries d'un Promeneur
solitaire, 7.*

With thoughts beyond the reaches of our
souls.
SHAKESPEARE.—*Hamlet, Act 1, 4.*

He thinks too much: such men are
dangerous.
SHAKESPEARE.—*Julius Cæsar, Act 1, 2.*

And the imperial votaress passèd on
In maiden meditation, fancy free.
SHAKESPEARE.—*Midsummer Night's
Dream, Act 2, 2.*

They are never alone that are accompanied with noble thoughts.
SIR P. SIDNEY.—*Arcadia.*

Thinking is but an idle waste of thought,
And naught is everything, and everything
is naught.
H. AND J. SMITH.—*Rejected Addresses.*

I have asked several men what passes
in their minds when they are thinking;
and I never could find any man who could
think for two minutes together.
SYDNEY SMITH.—*Lectures on Moral
Philosophy, No. 19.*

How few think justly of the thinking few!
How many never think, who think they do.
JANE TAYLOR.—*Stanzas.*

And Thought leapt out to wed with
Thought
Ere Thought could wed itself with Speech.
TENNYSON.—*In Memoriam, c. 23*

No one is punished for his thoughts.
ULPIAN.—*Ad Edictum.*

And yet, as angels in some brighter dreams
Call to the soul when man doth sleep,
So some strange thoughts transcend our
wonted themes,
And into glory peep.
H. VAUGHAN.—*Retreat.*

Thoughts too deep to be expressed,
And too strong to be suppressed.
G. WITHER.—*Mistress of Philarete.*

In that sweet mood when pleasant thoughts
Bring sad thoughts to the mind.
WORDSWORTH.—*In Early Spring.*

O reader! had you in your mind
Such stores as silent thought can bring,
O gentle reader! you would find
A tale in everything.
WORDSWORTH.—*Simon Lee.*

Thought, busy thought! too busy for my
peace! YOUNG.—*Night Thoughts, 1.*

It was an holy and good thought.
2 Maccabees xii, 45

THREATS

If it is not right to hurt, it is neither right nor wise to menace.
BURKE.—*Speech* (1773).

Get out of my sight or I'll knock you down.   W. B. RHODES.—*Bombastes*.

There is no terror, Cassius, in your threats ;
For I am armed so strong in honesty
That they pass by me as the idle wind.
SHAKESPEARE.—*Julius Cæsar*, Act 4, 3.

By gar, de herring is no dead, so as I will kill him !
SHAKESPEARE.—*Merry Wives*, Act 2, 3.

THREE, NUMBER

The third of all things, they say, is very critical.
FARQUHAR.—*Constant Couple*, Act 3.

Three merry boys, three merry boys,
And three merry boys are we.
FLETCHER AND BEAUMONT.—*Rollo*,
Act 3, 2 (*Chorus*).

Three is the most perfect number.
Mediæval Latin prov.

Of all the numbers arithmeticall
The number three is held for principall.
"*Times Whistle*" (c. 1614).

THRIFT

No one is aware of the advantage of frugality but those who have tried it.
LORD CHESTERFIELD.—*Letters to his Son*.

Men do not realise how great a revenue thrift is.   CICERO.—*Paradoxa*.

Annual income twenty pounds, annual expenditure nineteen nineteen six, result happiness ; annual income twenty pounds, annual expenditure twenty pound ought and six, result misery.
DICKENS.—*David Copperfield*, ch. 12.

If we take a farthing from a thousand pounds, it will be a thousand pounds no longer.   GOLDSMITH.—
Citizen of the World, No. 27.

Without frugality none can be rich, and with it very few would be poor.
JOHNSON.—*Rambler*.

It is saving, not getting, that is the mother of riches.
SIR W. SCOTT.—*Diary, April*, 1829.

Thrift is too late at the bottom of the purse.   SENECA.—*Ep.* 1.

There is more art in saving than in gaining.   *German Prov.*

Who heeds not a penny
Shall never have any.
Old Saying.

A' the wives o' Corncairn,
Drilling up their harn yarn,
They hae corn, they hae kye [cattle],
They hae webs o' claith forbye.
Scottish saying.

THRIFTLESSNESS

But poverty, with most who whimper forth
Their long complaints, is self-inflicted woe ;
The effect of laziness, or sottish waste.
COWPER.—*Winter Evening*, 429.

Good at a fight, but better at a play,
Godlike in giving, but the devil to pay.
MOORE.—*On Sheridan's Hand*.

TIDES

Nae man can tether time or tide.
BURNS.—*Tam O'Shanter*.

"People can't die, along the coast," said Mr. Peggotty, "except when the tide's pretty nigh out. They can't be born, unless it's pretty nigh in—not properly born, till flood. He's a-going out with the tide."
DICKENS.—*Copperfield*, ch. 30.

"What is the cause of tides, Pummel ? " "Well, sir, nobody rightly knows. Many gives their opinion, but if I was to give mine, it 'ud be different."
GEO. ELIOT.—*Theophrastus Such :
Watchdog of Knowledge.*

A' made a finer end and went away an it had been any christom child ; a' parted even just between twelve and one, even at the turning o' the tide.
SHAKESPEARE.—*Henry V.*, Act 2, 3.

TIME

Time
With the ceaseless stroke of his wings
Brushed off the bloom from their soul.
MATTHEW ARNOLD.—*Youth of Man*.

Time is the greatest innovator.
BACON.—*Of Innovation*.

Time, the author of authors, and so of full authority.
BACON.—*Instauratio, Pt.* 2, *Bk.* 1, 84.

What Horace says is,
" Eheu fugaces
Anni labuntur, Postume, Postume,"
Years glide away and are lost to me, lost to me.   R. H. BARHAM.—*Epigram*.

Time's noblest offspring is his last.
BISHOP BERKELEY.—*Planting Arts and
Learning in America.*

Here my master bids me stand,
And mark the time with faithful hand ;
What is his will is my delight,
To tell the hours by day, by night.
Master, be wise, and learn of me
To serve thy God as I serve thee.
REV. J. BERRIDGE.—*Lines Placed on
his Clock.*

Time may rage but rage in vain.
WM. BLAKE.—*For a Picture of the Last Judgment.*

Time was made for slaves.
J. B. BUCKSTONE.—*Billy Taylor.*

The grand instructor, Time.
BURKE.—*Letter* (1795).

The silent touches of Time.
BURKE.—*Letter.*

Oh Time! the beautifier of the dead,
Adorner of the ruin, comforter
And only healer when the heart hath bled—
Time! the corrector where our judgments
err. BYRON.—*Childe Harold, c.* 4, 130.

The poorest day that passes over us is
the conflux of two eternities.
CARLYLE.—*Signs of the Times.*

For los of catel may recovered be,
But los of tymè shendeth [ruineth] us,
quod he.
CHAUCER.—*Man of Law's Prologue.*

Wel may that man that no good work
ne dooth, sing thilke [that same] newe
Frenshe song: "Iay tout perdu mon
temps et mon labour."
CHAUCER.—*Parson's Tale, sec.* 11.

Time y-lost may not recovered be.
CHAUCER.—*Troilus and Cressid.*

Time consecrates,
And what is grey with age becomes
religion. COLERIDGE.—*Piccolomini.*

Touch us gently, gentle Time.
BARRY CORNWALL.—*The Sea.*

For who knows most, him loss of time
most grieves.
DANTE.—*Purgatory, c.* 3, *l.* 77 (*Cary tr.*).

Mere by-blows are the world and we,
And time, within eternity,
A sheer anachronism.
J. DAVIDSON.—*Queen Elizabeth's Day.*

Time goes, you say? Ah, no!
Alas, Time stays; *we* go.
AUSTIN DOBSON.—*After Ronsard.*

The surest poison is time.
EMERSON.—*Old Age.*

A poor Indian chief . . . made a wiser
reply than any philosopher, to someone
complaining that he had not enough time.
"Well," said Red Jacket, "I suppose you
have all there is."
EMERSON.—*Works and Days.*

Oh threats of Hell and Hopes of Paradise!
One thing at least is certain—*This* life
flies;
One thing is certain, and the rest is Lies;
The Flower that once has blown for ever
dies. FITZGERALD.—*Rubáiyát, st.* 63.

Dost thou love life? Then do not
squander time, for that is the stuff life is
made of. B. FRANKLIN.—
Pennsylvania Almanack, 1758.

Money is like time—lose none and you
will have plenty.
PIERRE GASTON (DUC DE LÉVIS) (1764-
1830).—*Maxims.*

The noiseless foot of Time steals swiftly
by,
And ere we dream of manhood, age is nigh.
W. GIFFORD.—*Juvenal, Sat.* 9, 182.

Men may recover loss of good,
But so wise man yet never stood
Which say recover time ilore [lost].
GOWER.—*Conf. Amantis.*

Fear not that I shall mar so fair an harvest
By putting in my sickle ere 'tis ripe.
J. HOME.—*Douglas,* Act 3, 1.

Seven hours to law, to soothing slumber
seven,
Ten to the world allot, and all to heaven.
SIR W. JONES.—*Lines in Substitution
for the old Latin Version.*

O, for an engine to keep back all clocks!
BEN JONSON.—*New Inn,* Act 4, 4.

Our to-days and yesterdays
Are the blocks with which we build.
LONGFELLOW.—*Builders.*

Art is long and Time is fleeting,
And our hearts, though stout and brave,
Still, like muffled drums, are beating
Funeral marches to the grave.
LONGFELLOW.—*Psalm of Life.*

From morn
To noon he fell, from noon to dewy eve.
MILTON.—*Paradise Lost, Bk.* 1, 742.

When Time who steals our years away,
Shall steal our pleasures too,
The memory of the past will stay
And half our joys renew.
MOORE.—*Song.*

Time hath a taming hand.
CARD. NEWMAN.—*Persecution.*

The greatest of all sacrifices, which is
the sacrifice of time.
PLUTARCH.—*Quoted from Antiphon.*

Instruct the planets in what orbs to run;
Correct old time and regulate the sun.
POPE.—*Essay on Man, Ep.* 2, 21.

Time conquers all, and we must time
obey. POPE.—*Pastorals, Winter,* 88.

Years following years steal something
every day;
At last they steal us from ourselves away.
POPE.—*Satires, Bk.* 2, *Ep.* 2, 73.

Now Time has fled—the world is strange,
Something there is of pain and change ;
My books lie closed upon my shelf ;
I miss the old heart in myself.
   A. A. Procter.—*A Student.*

Even such is Time, that takes on trust
Our youth, our joys, our all we have,
And pays us but with age and dust.
  Sir W. Ralegh.—*Written the night*
     before his Death.

" Knowest thou not me ? " the Deep
  Voice cried ;
 " So long enjoyed, so oft misused—
Alternate, in thy fickle pride,
Desired, neglected, and accused ?
Before my breath, like blazing flax,
Man and his marvels pass away ;
And changing empires wane and wax,
 Are founded, flourish, and decay."
 (Time.) Scott.—*Antiquary*

Happy is he who has well employed his
time, however brief it may have been.
      Seneca.

What reason has been unable to effect,
lapse of time has often cured.
   Seneca.—*Agamemnon.*

The inaudible and noiseless foot of time.
 Shakespeare.—*All's Well*, Act 5, 3.

And then he drew a dial from his poke,
And, looking on it with lack-lustre eye,
Says very wisely, " It is ten o'clock.
Thus may we see," quoth he, " how the
 world wags." Shakespeare.—
   As You Like It, Act 2, 7.

 The lazy foot of time.
  Shakespeare.—*Ib.*, Act 3, 2.

Spite of cormorant devouring Time.
 Shakespeare.—*Love's Labour's Lost*,
     Act 1, 1.
In the dark backward and abysm of time.
 Shakespeare.—*Tempest*, Act 1, 2.

And thus the whirligig of time brings in
his revenges.
 Shakespeare.—*Twelfth Night*, Act 5, 1.

Time is the nurse and breeder of all good.
 Shakespeare.—*Two Gentlemen of*
    Verona, Act 3, 1.

Time's glory is to calm contending kings,
To unmask falsehood, and bring truth to
 light.
 Shakespeare.—*Lucrece, st.* 135.

 Time is a gentle deity.
  Sophocles.—*Electra.*

Too late I stayed—forgive the crime ;
 Unheeded flew the hours :
How noiseless falls the foot of Time
 That only treads on flowers !
W. R. Spencer.—*To Lady A. Hamilton.*

What a foolish thing is time ! And how
foolish is man, who would be as angry if
time stopped, as if it passed !
  Swift.—*To Vanessa, Aug.* 7, 1722.

He put this engine [a watch] to our ears,
which made an incessant noise like that of
a water-mill : and we conjecture it is
either some unknown animal, or the god
that he worships, but we are more inclined
to the latter opinion.
  Swift.—*Voyage to Lilliput.*

The forward-flowing tide of time.
 Tennyson.—*Recollections of Arabian*
     Nights.

 What greater crime
 Than loss of time ?
 T. Tusser.—*January's Abstract.*

The unimaginable touch of time.
 Wordsworth.—*Eccles. Sonnets,*
     Pt. 3, 34.

Time elaborately thrown away.
   Young.—*Last Day.*

The bell strikes *one*. We take no note of
 time
But from its loss.
   Young.—*Night Thoughts,* 1.

And what its worth,* ask death beds ;
 they can tell. Young.—*Ib.,* 2.

Time wasted is existence, used, is life.
    Young.—*Ib.*

We push time from us and we wish him
 back.   Young.—*Ib.*

O how omnipotent is Time !
   Young.—*Ib.*

Time is the soul of the business.
    Law Maxim.

Keep a thing seven years and you'll find
a use for it. *Scottish prov.*

Mak' up for lost time, as the piper o'
Sligo did when he ate a haill side o'
mutton.
 Scottish prov. (Scott's " Woodstock ").

TIME-SERVERS

He was a man who had seen many changes,
And always changed as true as any needle.
 Byron.—*Don Juan, c.* 3, 80.

I mean a kin' o' hangin' roun' an' settin'
 on a fence,
Till Prov'dunce pinted how to jump an'
 save the most expense.
 J. R. Lowell.—*Biglow Papers,* 2nd
    Ser., No. 3.

Thou ever strong upon the stronger side !
Thou Fortune's champion, that dost never
 fight

---

    * A moment.

But when her humorous ladyship is by,
To teach thee safety !
    SHAKESPEARE.—*King John*, Act 3, 1.

That, sir, which serves and seeks for gain
And follows but for form,
Will pack, when it begins to rain,
And leave thee in the storm.
    SHAKESPEARE.—*King Lear*, Act 2, 4.

Men shut their doors against a setting
sun. SHAKESPEARE.—*Timon*, Act 1, 2.

More people admire the rising than the
setting sun.
    SYLLA.—(*According to Francis Bacon.*)

Waverings of every vane with every wind,
And wordy trucklings to the transient
    hour,
And fierce or careless looseners of the faith.
    TENNYSON.—*To the Queen*, 49.

TIMIDITY

The schoolboy with his satchel in his hand,
Whistling aloud to keep his courage up.
    BLAIR.—*The Grave.*

Wee sleekit, cowrin', tim'rous beestie !
Oh, what a panic's in thy breastie.
    BURNS.—*To a Mouse.*

Fear and Guilt
Are the same things, and when our actions
    are not,
Our fears are, crimes.
    SIR J. DENHAM.—*The Sophy.*

Still as they run they look behind,
They hear a voice in every wind,
    And snatch a fearful joy.
    GRAY.—*Eton College.*

When the sun sets, shadows, that showed
    at noon
But small, appear most long and terrible.
    N. LEE.—*Œdipus.*

The less there is of fear, so much the
less generally is there of danger.
    LIVY.—22, 5.

Be not afraid of every stranger ;
Start not aside at every danger.
    G. PEELE.—*Old Wives' Tale.*

He who asks faint-heartedly teaches
how to refuse. SENECA.—*Hippolytus.*

That which in mean men we entitle
    patience,
Is pale cold cowardice in noble breasts.
    SHAKESPEARE.—*Richard II.*, Act 1, 2.

Full of pale fancies and chimæras huge.
    THOMSON.—*Seasons, Autumn.*

One of the greatest misfortunes of
honest folk is that they are cowards.
    VOLTAIRE.

Happy occasions oft by self-mistrust
Are forfeited ; but infamy doth kill.
    WORDSWORTH —*Poems to National
        Independence*, Pt. 2, No. 17.

Woe be to fearful hearts, and faint hands
and the sinner that goeth two ways : Woe
unto him that is faint-hearted.
    Ecclesiasticus ii, 12, 13.

The slothful man saith, There is a lion
in the way ; a lion is in the streets.
    Proverbs xxvi, 13.

Who fears to suffer, suffers from fear.
    Prov.

He that counts all costs will never put
plough in the earth. *Scottish prov.* (*Ray.*)

TITHES

Tithes, which sure are Discord's torches.
    BYRON.—*Don Juan*, 16, 60.

Restore to God his due in tithe and time,
A tithe purloined cankers the whole estate.
    HERBERT.—*Church Porch*, st. 65.

'Tis ridiculous to say the Tythes are
God's part, and therefore the Clergy must
have them. Why, so they are if the lay-
man has them. SELDEN.—*Table Talk.*

TITLES

Somebody has said that the King may
make a nobleman, but he cannot make a
gentleman. BURKE.—*Letter to W. Smith.*

He shrunk into insignificancy and an
earldom.   EARL OF CHESTERFIELD.—
        Character of Pulteney.

Oh, fond attempt to give a deathless lot
To names ignoble, born to be forgot !
    COWPER.—*On observing some names of
        little note.*

Nature's first great title—mind.
    GEO. CROLY.—*Pericles.*

It was not the custom in England to
confer titles on men distinguished by
peaceful services, however good and great ;
unless occasionally, when they consisted
of the accumulation of some very large
amount of money.
    DICKENS.—*Bleak House*, ch. 35.

Proud o' the title, as the Living Skel-
lington said ven they showed him.
    DICKENS.—*Pickwick*, ch. 15.

Another stride that has been taken [in
England] appears in the perishing of
heraldry. Whilst the privileges of the
nobility are passing to the middle class,
the badge is discredited, and the titles of
lordship are getting musty and cumbersome. I wonder that sensible men have
not been already impatient of them.
    EMERSON.—*English Traits*, 11 : *Aristocracy.*

A studious decliner of honours and titles. EVELYN.—*Diary, Intro.*

It is patent to the mob,
That my being made a nob,
Was effected by a job.
SIR W. S. GILBERT.—*Trial by Jury.*

There's as much vanity in " Plain John " as in " John, Viscount."
LORD MORLEY.—*Recollections* (1917).

High though his titles, proud his name,
Boundless his wealth as wish can claim,
Despite those titles, power, and pelf,
The wretch, concentred all in self,
Living, shall forfeit fair renown,
And, doubly dying, shall go down
To the vile dust from whence he sprung,
Unwept, unhonoured, and unsung.
SCOTT.—*Lay of the Last Minstrel, c.* 6, *st.* 6.

For never title yet so mean could prove,
But there was eke a mind which did that title love.
SHENSTONE.—*Schoolmistress.*

Titles are abolished ; and the American Republic swarms with men claiming and bearing them. THACKERAY.—*On Ribbons.*

Those transparent swindles—transmissible nobility and kingship.
MARK TWAIN.—*Yankee at Court of King Arthur, ch.* 28.

I weigh the man, not his title ; 'tis not the King's stamp can make the metal heavier or better. WYCHERLEY.—*Plain Dealer* (1674), Act 1, 1.

Titles are marks of honest men and wise ;
The fool or knave that wears a title, lies.
YOUNG.—*Love of Fame*, 1, 137.

The label is bigger than the package.
Old Greek prov.

TOASTS

Then who need care a fig
Who's a tory or whig ?
Here's a health to all honest men !
TOM BROWN.—*Song : Every man take a glass in his hand.*

Drink ye to her that each loves best,
And if you nurse a flame
That's told but to her mutual breast,
We will not ask her name.
CAMPBELL.—*Drink ye to Her.*

But the standing toast that pleased the most,
Was—The wind that blows, the ship that goes,
And the lass that loves a sailor.
C. DIBDIN.—*Standing Toast.*

We drank Sir Condy's good health and the downfall of his enemies, till we could stand no longer ourselves.
MISS EDGEWORTH.—*Castle Rackrent, ch.* 12.

Drink to me only with thine eyes,
And I will pledge with mine ;
Or leave a kiss but in the cup,
And I'll not look for wine.
BEN JONSON.—*Forest.*

Drink ! to our father that begot us men,
To the dead voices that are never dumb,
Then to the land of all our loves, and then
To the long parting, and the age to come.
SIR H. NEWBOLT.—*Sacramentum Supremum* (1915).

Be in their flowing cups freshly remembered.
SHAKESPEARE.—*Henry V.*, Act 4, 3.

Here's to the maiden of bashful fifteen ;
Here's to the widow of fifty ;
Here's to the flaunting extravagant quean ;
And here's to the housewife that's thrifty !
Let the cup pass,
Drink to the lass,
I'll warrant she'll prove an excuse for the glass.
SHERIDAN.—*School for Scandal*, Act 3, 3.

Here's a health to you and yours,
Likewise to us and ours ;
And if ever you and yours
Need help that's in our powers,
We'll do as much for you and yours
As you have done for us and ours.
Old Saying.

Here's a health to all those that we love,
Here's a health to all those that love us,
Here's a health to all them that love them that love those
That love them that love those that love us.
Old Toast.

Here's to thee and me and aw'on us !
May we ne'er want nought, none of us !
Neither thee nor me nor anybody else,
Aw' on us—nawn on us ! *Old Toast.*

Here's to you in water ;
I wish was in the wine :
You drink to your true love,
An' I'll drink to mine.
Scottish toast.

TOBACCO

Little tube of mighty power,
Charmer of an idle hour.
ISAAC H. BROWNE.

The sweet post-prandial cigar.
R. BUCHANAN.—*London Poems.*

Tobacco, divine, rare, superexcellent tobacco, which goes far beyond all the panaceas, potable gold, and philosopher's stones, a sovereign remedy to all diseases.
BURTON.—*Anat. Melan., Pt.* 3.

Sublime tobacco ! which, from east to west,
Cheers the tar's labour or the Turk man's rest. BYRON.—*The Island*, 2 19.

Divine in hookas, glorious in a pipe !
    BYRON.—*The Island*, 2, 19.

Like other charmers, wooing the caress
More dazzlingly when daring in full dress;
Yet thy true lovers more admire by far
Thy naked beauties—give me a cigar.
    BYRON.—*Ib.*

Sweet, when the morn is grey,
  Sweet when they've cleared away
Lunch ; and at close of day
  Possibly sweetest.
    C. S. CALVERLEY.—*Ode to Tobacco.*

You abuse snuff ! Perhaps it is the final
cause of the human nose.
    COLERIDGE.—*Table Talk* (*Jan.* 4, 1823).

Pernicious weed ! whose scent the fair
  annoys,
Unfriendly to society's chief joys,
Thy worst effect is banishing for hours
The sex whose presence civilises ours.
    COWPER.—*Conversation.*

A custom loathsome to the eye, hateful
to the nose, harmful to the brain, dangerous to the lungs, and in the black, stinking
fume thereof nearest resembling the horrible Stygian smoke of the pit that is
bottomless.
    JAMES I. (OF ENGLAND).—*Counterblast
      to Tobacco* (1604).

Neither do thou lust after that tawny
weed tobacco.
    BEN JONSON.—*Bartholomew Fair.*

Ods me ! I marvel what pleasure or
felicity they have in taking their roguish
tobacco. It is good for nothing but to
choke a man, and fill him full of smoke
and embers. BEN JONSON.—*Every Man
    in his Humour*, Act 3, 3.

For thy sake, tobacco, I
  Would do anything but die.
    LAMB.—*Farewell to Tobacco.*

O thou weed,
Who art so lovely fair, and smell'st so
  sweet,
That the sense aches at thee, would thou
  hadst ne'er been born !
    SHAKESPEARE.—*Othello*, Act 4, 2 (*not
      so applied by Shakespeare*).

Yes, social friend, I love thee well,
  In learned doctor's spite ;
Thy clouds all other clouds dispel,
  And lap me in delight.
    C. SPRAGUE.—*Tony Cigar.*

James the First was a knave, a tyrant,
a fool, a liar, a coward ; but I love him,
I worship him, because he slit the throat
of that blackguard Ralegh, who invented
this filthy smoking.
    SWINBURNE.—*Spoken in the Arts Club.*

A cigarette is the perfect type of
pleasure. It is exquisite and it leaves
one unsatisfied. What more can you
want ? OSCAR WILDE.—*Dorian Gray.*

Tobacco is a filthy weed—
  I like it !
It satisfies no normal need—
  I like it !
It makes you grow both thin and lean,
It takes the hair right off your bean,
It's the worst darned stuff I've ever seen.
  I like it !
    ANON.—(*American College Magazine*,
      1919).

And when the pipe is foul within
Think how the soul's defiled with sin ;
To purge with fire it does require,
  Thus think and drink tobacco.
    Pills to Purge Melancholy (1699).

TO-DAY

There is an old proverb, quoth she
[Dame Prudence], that the goodness that
thou mayst do this day, do it ; and abyde
not ne delaye it not till to-morrow.
    CHAUCER.—*Tale of Melibeus, sec.* 71.

To-day is ours ; what do we fear ?
To-day is ours ; we have it here.
Let's treat it kindly, that it may
Wish, at least, with us to stay.
    COWLEY.—*The Epicure.*

Happy the man, and happy he alone,
He who can call to-day his own :
He who, secure within, can say,
To-morrow, do thy worst, for I have lived
  to-day.
    DRYDEN.—*Imit. of Horace, Bk.* 3, 29.

TOLERATION

Toleration is good for all or it is good
for none. BURKE.—*Speech*, 1773.

" Well, well, Brer Jack," said Uncle
Remus, soothingly, " in deze low groun's
er sorrer, you des [just] got ter lean back
en make 'lowances fer all sorts er folks.
You got ter 'low fer dem dat knows too
much same ez dem w'at knows too little."
    J. C. HARRIS.—*Nights with Uncle
      Remus, ch.* 42.

Not to be able to endure all the bad
characters of which the world is full, is
not the sign of a very good character ; in
commerce there must be gold and also
small change.
    LA BRUYÈRE.—*De la Société*, 37.

In essentials, unity ; in matters doubtful, liberty ; in all things, charity.
    " RUPERTUS MELDENIUS."—*Parænesis
      Votiva* (1622).

You all are right and all are wrong :
When next you talk of what you view,
Think others see as well as you.
    J. MERRICK.—*The Chameleon.*

Yet if all cannot be of one mind,—as who looks they should be ?—this doubtless is more wholesome, more prudent, and more christian, that many be tolerated rather than all compelled.
    MILTON.—*Liberty of Unlicensed Printing.*

And when religious sects ran mad,
    He held, in spite of all their learning,
That if a man's belief is bad,
    It will not be improved by burning.
        W. M. PRAED.—*Vicar*, st. 9.

Forgive me if, midst all Thy works,
    No hint I see of damning ;
And think there's faith among the Turks,
    And hope for e'en the Brahmin.
        THACKERAY.—*Jolly Jack.*

Of all superstitions is not the most dangerous that of hating your neighbour for his opinions ?
        VOLTAIRE.—*On Tolerance.*

The great principle of the Roman senate and people was : It is for the gods alone to trouble about offences against the gods.
        VOLTAIRE.—*Ib.*

For as by discipline of Time made wise,
We learn to tolerate the infirmities
And faults of others—gently as he may,
So with our own the mild Instructor deals,
Teaching us to forget them or forgive.
    WORDSWORTH.—*Eccles. Sonnets, Pt.* 3, 35.

TOMBS

Dear was our chief, and dear to us his tomb,
    For dear the life it hides ;
Aidoneus, O Aidoneus, send him forth ;
Thou who dost lead the dead to Earth again,
Yea, send Darius.
    ÆSCHYLUS.—*Persæ*, 650 (*Plumptre tr.*).

May no rude hand deface it,
    And its forlorn *hic jacet !*
        WORDSWORTH.—*Ellen Irwin.*

TO-MORROW

Defer not till to-morrow to be wise,
To-morrow's sun on thee may never rise ;
Or should to-morrow chance to cheer thy sight
With her enlivening and unlooked for light,
How grateful will appear her dawning rays,
As favours unexpected doubly please.
    CONGREVE.—*Letter to Cobham.*

To-morrow !—Why, To-morrow I may be Myself with Yesterday's Seven Thousand Years.
    FITZGERALD.—*Rubáiyát*, st. 21.

To-morrow to fresh woods and pastures new.   MILTON.—*Lycidas, ad fin.*

To-morrow shall be like
To-day, but much more sweet.
    CHRISTINA ROSSETTI.—*The Unseen World.*

To-morrow, and to-morrow, and to-morrow,
Creeps in this petty pace from day to day,
To the last syllable of recorded time.
    SHAKESPEARE.—*Macbeth*, Act 5, 5.

We were, fair queen,
Two lads that thought there was no more behind
But such a day to-morrow as to-day.
    SHAKESPEARE.—*Winter's Tale*, Act 1, 2.

To-morrow yet would reap to-day.
    TENNYSON.—*Love thou the Land.*

In human hearts what bolder thoughts can rise
Than man's presumption on to-morrow's dawn !
Where is to-morrow ?
    YOUNG.—*Night Thoughts, Bk.* 1, 374.

TOO LATE

Ah, " all things come to those who wait,"
    (I say these words to make me glad),
But something answers, soft and sad,
" They come, but often come too late."
    VIOLET FANE.—*Tout vient à qui sait attendre.*

A message late is a message lost.
    SIR H. NEWBOLT.—*The Last Word*, st. 5.

Love that comes too late,
Like a remorseful pardon slowly carried,
To the great sender turns a sour offence.
    SHAKESPEARE.—*All's Well*, Act 5, 3.

Late, late, so late ! and dark the night and chill !
Late, late, so late ! but we can enter still.
Too late, too late ! ye cannot enter now.
    TENNYSON.—*Guinevere*, 160.

TOOTHACHE

Of all our pains, since man was curst,
I mean of body, not the mental,
To name the worst among the worst,
The dental sure is transcendental.
    HOOD.—*True Story.*

For there was never yet philosopher
That could endure the toothache patiently.
    SHAKESPEARE.—*Much Ado About Nothing*, Act 5, 1.

TORIES

The rising hope of those stern and unbending Tories.   MACAULAY.—*Gladstone on Church and State.*

Toryism is an innate principle o' human nature—Whiggism but an evil habit.
    JOHN WILSON.—*Noctes (Ettrick Shepherd).*

TOWNS

Everyone for himself is the gospel of all the large towns.
BALZAC.—*César Birotteau.*

Her towns, where civic independence flings
The gauntlet down to senates, courts, and kings.   CAMPBELL.—*Theodric.*

He likes the country, but in truth
Most likes it when he studies it in town.
COWPER.—*Retirement*, 573.

The city is recruited from the country.
EMERSON —*Manners.*

Away in towns, where eyes have nought to see
But dead museums and miles of misery,
  .   .   .   .
And life made wretched out of human ken,
And miles of shopping women served by men. JOHN MASEFIELD.—*Biography.*

A house is much more to my taste than a tree,
And for groves, O ! a good grove of chimneys for me.
CHAS. MORRIS.—*The Contrast.*

All capitals are alike ; all races mix there, all manners are confused together ; it is not there one should go to study nations.   ROUSSEAU.—*Emile.*

Towns are the destructive whirlpool of the human race.   ROUSSEAU.—*Ib.*

TRADE

The buying and the selling, and the strife
Of little natures.
R. BUCHANAN.—*London Poems.*

Merchants, unimpeachable of sin
Against the charities of domestic life,
Incorporated, seem at once to lose
Their nature ; and, disclaiming all regard
For mercy and the common rights of man,
Build factories with blood, conducting trade
At the sword's point.
COWPER.—*The Task : Winter Evening*, 676.

A tradesman behind his counter must have no flesh and blood about him, no passions, no resentment ; he must never be angry—no, not so much as seem to be so.
DEFOE.—*Complete English Tradesman.*

We are indeed a nation of shopkeepers.
DISRAELI.—*Young Duke* (*saying found in earlier writers in Gt. Britain and the United States*).

Trade which, like blood, should circularly flow.
DRYDEN.—*Annus Mirabilis*, st. 2.

The philosopher and lover of man have much harm to say of trade ; but the historian will see that trade was the principle of Liberty ; that trade planted America and destroyed Feudalism ; that it makes peace and keeps peace.
EMERSON.—*The Young American* (1844).

Trade goes to make the governments insignificant and to bring every kind of faculty of every individual, that can in any manner serve any person, on sale.
EMERSON.—*Ib.*

The greatest meliorator of the world is selfish, huckstering trade.
EMERSON.—*Works and Days.*

In every age and clime we see
Two of a trade can ne'er agree.
GAY.—*Fables, Pt.* 1, 21.

Trade's proud empire hastes to swift decay.
JOHNSON.—*Line added to " The Deserted Village."*

We are not here to sell a parcel of boilers and vats, but the potentiality of growing rich beyond the dreams of avarice.
JOHNSON.—*Remark at Sale of Thrale's Brewery.*

It is of less importance to learn a trade in order to know a trade than to conquer the prejudices which despise it.
ROUSSEAU.—*Emile.*

Let us choose an honest trade ; but remember always that there is no honesty without utility.   ROUSSEAU.—*Ib.*

Mind your till and till your mind.
C. H. SPURGEON.—*" Salt-Cellars."*

Everyone lives by selling something.
R. L. STEVENSON.—*Beggars.*

I cannot sit still, James, and hear you abuse the shopocracy.
JOHN WILSON.—*Noctes.*

Who will sell the cow must say the word.
Prov. (Geo. Herbert).

There is a mystery in the meanest trade.
Prov. (Ray.)

Who buys has need of a hundred eyes ; who sells needs only one.   *Old Prov.*

Keep your shop and your shop will keep you.   *Quoted by Steele, Spectator*, 509.

TRADITION

The idols of the market-place are the most troublesome of all—those namely which have entwined themselves round the understanding from the associations of words and names.
BACON.—*Novum Organum, Bk.* 1, 59;

For how can that be false, which
    every tongue
Of every mortal man affirms for true ?
    SIR JOHN DAVIES.—*Nosce Teipsum.*

Tradition is the sigh
Of one who hath no hope ; and History
Bears, like a river deep, tumultuous,
    wide,
Gloom, guilt, and woe on his eternal tide.
    EBENEZER ELLIOTT.—*Love, Bk. 2.*

Say what you will against Tradition,
we know the significance of words by
nothing but Tradition.
    SELDEN.—*Table Talk.*

This story shall the good man teach his
    son.
    SHAKESPEARE.—*Henry V.*, Act 4, 3.

TRAGEDY

A perfect tragedy is the noblest production of human nature.
    ADDISON.—*Spectator*, 39.

The black and white literature of pain.
    G. K. CHESTERTON.—*The Defendant.*

That long drip of human tears
Which peoples old in tragedy
Have left upon the centuried years.
    T. HARDY.—*On an Invitation to the
    United States.*

Such is generally the case in real life :
Serious things and mere trifles, laughable
things and things that cause pain, are wont
to be mixed in strangest medley. It is
necessary then that Tragedy, as being a
mirror of life, must leave room for an
element of comic humour.
    KEBLE.—*Lectures on Poetry, No.* 28
    (*E. K. Francis tr.*).

Sometime let gorgeous Tragedy
In sceptred pall come sweeping by.
    MILTON.—*Il Penseroso*, 97.

It is observable that the ladies frequent
tragedies more than comedies. The reason
may be that in tragedy their sex is deified
and adored ; in comedy exposed and ridi-
culed.
    POPE.—*Thoughts on Various Subjects.*

Ah me, what act,
That roars so loud, and thunders in the
    index ?
    SHAKESPEARE.—*Hamlet*, Act 3, 4.

Between the acting of a dreadful thing
And the first motion, all the interim is
Like a phantasma, or a hideous dream.
    SHAKESPEARE.—*Julius Cæsar*, Act 2, 1.

Very tragical mirth.
    SHAKESPEARE.—*Midsummer Night's
    Dream.* Act 5, 1.

'Tis double death to drown in ken of
    shore. SHAKESPEARE.—*Lucrece*, 160.

Sorrow, terror, anguish, despair itself,
are often the chosen expressions of an
approximation to the highest good. . . .
Tragedy delights by affording a shadow
of the pleasure which exists in pain.
    SHELLEY.—*Defence of Poetry* (1821).

Tragedy openeth the greatest wounds,
and showeth forth the ulcers that are
covered with tissue.
    SIR P. SIDNEY.—*Apology for Poetry.*

I chanced to cast my eye upon a part
in the Tragedy of Richard the Third, which
filled my mind with a very agreeable
horror.
    Tatler, No. 90, *Nov.* 5, 1709.

She weaves and multiplies
Exceeding pleasure out of extreme pain.
    SWINBURNE.—*Laus Veneris.*

TRAINING

Train up a fig-tree in the way it should
go, and when you are old sit under the
shade of it. [*Capt. Cuttle.*]
    DICKENS.—*Dombey, ch.* 19.

This sort of thing takes a deal of training.
    SIR W. S. GILBERT.—*Ruddigore.*

Just as the twig is bent the tree's in-
    clined.
    POPE.—*Moral Essays, Ep.* 1, 150.

He amongst us who best knows how to
bear the good and the evil of this life is in
my view the best brought up.
    ROUSSEAU.—*Emile.*

The bearing and the training of a child
Is woman's wisdom.
    TENNYSON.—*Princess, c.* 5, 456.

TRAITORS

He's Judas to a tittle, that man is,
Just such a face !
    BROWNING.—*Fra Lippo..*

The smyler with the knyf under the cloke.
    CHAUCER.—*Knight's Tale*, 1141.

Princes in this case
Do hate the traitor, though they love the
    treason. S. DANIEL.—*Cleopatra.*

This principle is old, but true as fate,
Kings may love treason, but the traitor
    hate. DEKKER.—*Honest Whore,
    Pt.* 1, Act 4, 4.

Hast thou betrayed my credulous inno-
    cence
With vizored falsehood and base forgery ?
    MILTON.—*Comus*

The man was noble,
But with his last attempt he wiped it out :
Destroyed his country, and his name remains
To the ensuing age abhorred.
SHAKESPEARE.—*Coriolanus*, Act 5, 3.

To say the truth, so Judas kissed his master,
And cried " All hail ! " whereas he meant all harm.
SHAKESPEARE.—*Henry VI.*, Pt. 3,
Act 5, 7.

Traitors are hated even by those they have benefited. TACITUS.—*Annals*, Bk. I.

To call men traitors
May make men traitors.
TENNYSON.—*Sir J. Oldcastle*.

TRANSIENCY

What's not destroyed by Time's devouring hand ?
Where's Troy, and where's the Maypole in the Strand ?
J. BRAMSTON.—*Art of Politics*.

Loveliest of lovely things are they,
On earth that soonest pass away.
The rose that lives its little hour
Is prized beyond the sculptured flower.
W. C. BRYANT.—*The Banks of the Hudson*.

And like a passing thought she fled
In light away.
BURNS.—*Jolly Beggars*.

But pleasures are like poppies spread !
You seize the flower, its bloom is shed !
Or like the snowfall in the river,
A moment white—then melts for ever.
BURNS.—*Tam o' Shanter*.

The comet of a season.
BYRON.—*Churchill's Grave*.

Thus ever fade my fairy dreams of bliss.
BYRON.—*Corsair*, 1, 14.

Alas, the moral brings a tear !
'Tis all a transient hour below ;
And we that would detain thee here,
Ourselves as fleetly go !
CAMPBELL.—*To J. S. Kemble*.

Life's joy for us a moment lingers,
And death seems in that word—farewell.
CAMPBELL.—*Song*.

Some pleasures live a month and some a year,
But short the date of all we gather here.
COWPER.—*Retirement*, 459.

The bloom of a rose passes quickly away,
And the pride of a butterfly dies in a day.
J. CUNNINGHAM.—*Rose and Butterfly*.

You know how little while we have to stay,
And, once departed, may return no more.
FITZGERALD.—*Rubáiyát*, st. 3.

The Worldly Hope men set their Hearts upon
Turns Ashes—or it prospers ; and anon,
Like Snow upon the Desert's dusty Face
Lighting a little hour or two—is gone.
FITZGERALD.—*Ib.*, st. 16.

One Moment in Annihilation's Waste,
One Moment, of the Well of Life to taste—
The Stars are setting and the Caravan
Starts for the Dawn of Nothing—Oh, make haste !
FITZGERALD.—*Ib.*, st. 48 (1st Ed.).

Sweet day, so cool, so calm, so bright,
The bridal of the earth and sky,
The dew shall weep thy fall to-night,
For thou must die.
HERBERT.—*Vertue*.

Sweet rose, whose hue, angry and brave,
Bids the rash gazer wipe his eye,
Thy root is ever in the grave.
And thou must die. HERBERT.—*Ib.*

Catch then, O catch the transient hour ;
Improve each moment as it flies ;
Life's a short summer—man a flower :
He dies—alas, how soon he dies !
JOHNSON.—*Winter*.

All that's bright must fade,—
The brightest still the fleetest.
MOORE.—*All that's bright*.

May's flowers outlast not May ;
And when the hour has fled,
Around the roses dead
The mournful echoes say—
Summer has seen decay.
GEO. MOORE.—*Rondel, Summer has seen decay*.

A pilgrim panting for the rest to come ;
An exile, anxious for his native home ;
A drop dissevered from the boundless sea ;
A moment parted from eternity.
HANNAH MORE.—*King Hezekiah*, 129.

Yet ah ! how short the vernal hour
Allowed for mortal bliss to blow !
Fate from the storm soon shakes the fluttering flower,
That drops and dies below.
PINDAR.—*Pythian Odes*, 8, 131 (*Moore tr.*).

Before my breath, like blazing flax,
Man and his marvels pass away,
And changing empires wane and wax,
Are founded, flourish, and decay.
SCOTT.—*The Antiquary*.

Like the dew on the mountain,
Like the foam on the river,
Like the bubble on the fountain,
Thou art gone, and for ever.
SCOTT.—*Lady of the Lake, c.* 3, 16.

A violet in the youth of primy nature,
Forward, not permanent, sweet, not lasting.
The perfume and suppliance of a minute.
SHAKESPEARE.—*Hamlet*, Act 1, 3.

The earth hath bubbles, as the water hath,
And these are of them.
> SHAKESPEARE —*Macbeth*, Act 1, 3.

But thou art fled
Like some frail exhalation.
> SHELLEY.—*Queen Mab.*

O Kings, bethink ye then how vain
The pride and pomp of earthly things ;
A little pain, a little gain,
Then dust in dust are the bones of
Kings.
> ARTHUR SYMONS.—*Ballade of Kings.*

Our little systems have their day ;
They have their day and cease to be.
> TENNYSON.—*In Memoriam, Intro.*

Time, like an ever-rolling stream,
Bears all its sons away.
They fly forgotten, as a dream
Dies at the opening day.
> ISAAC WATTS.—*O God, our Help.*

What is this passing scene ?
A peevish April day !
A little sun—a little rain,
And then night sweeps along the plain,
And all things fade away.
> H. K. WHITE.—*On Disappointment.*

The Rainbow comes and goes,
And lovely is the Rose.
> WORDSWORTH.—*Intimations of
Immortality, c. 2.*

But garlands wither ; festal shows
depart,
Like dreams themselves ; and sweetest
sound—
(Albeit of effect profound)
It was—and it is gone !
> WORDSWORTH.—*Poems to National
Independence, Pt. 2, No. 39.*

Till another king arose, which knew not
Joseph.   *Acts* vii, 18.

TRANSITION

Wandering between two worlds, one dead,
The other powerless to be born.
> M. ARNOLD.—*Grande Chartreuse.*

TRANSLATORS

Nor ought a genius less than his that writ
Attempt translation.
> SIR J. DENHAM.—*To Sir R. Fanshaw.*

Some hold translations not unlike to be
The wrong side of a Turkey tapestry.
> J. HOWELL.—*Of Translations.*

Translations increase the faults of a
work and spoil its beauties.
> VOLTAIRE.—*Essay on Epic Poetry.*

TRAVEL

What singular emotions fill
Their bosoms who have been induced to
roam ! BYRON.—*Don Juan, c.* 3, 21.

How much a dunce that has been sent to
roam
Excels a dunce that has been left at home !
> COWPER.—*Progress of Error,* 414.

Travelling is the ruin of all happiness.
There's no looking at a building here after
seeing Italy. [*Mr. Meadows, " Man of
the Ton."*]
> MME. D'ARBLAY.—*Cecilia, Bk.* 2, *ch.* 6.

Fain would I travel to some foreign shore,
Never to see my native country more,
So might I to myself myself restore.
> DRYDEN.—*Tr. Ovid, Cinyras and Myrrha.*

The superstition of Travelling.
> EMERSON.—*Civilization.*

One use of travel is to recommend the
books and works of home. We go to
Europe to be Americanised.
> EMERSON.—*Conduct of Life: Culture.*

Travelling is a Fool's Paradise.
> EMERSON.—*Self-Reliance.*

Anxious through seas and land to search
for rest
Is but laborious idleness at best.
In desert Ulubræ the bliss you'll find,
If you preserve a firm and equal mind.
> P. FRANCIS.—*Horace, Epistles, Bk.* 1, 11.

A prudent traveller never disparages
his own country.   GOLDONI.

A man who leaves home to mend himself
and others is a philosopher ; but he who
goes from country to country, guided by
the blind impulse of curiosity, is a vagabond.
> GOLDSMITH.—*Citizen of the World, No.* 7.

Creation's heir, the world, the world is
mine.   GOLDSMITH.—*Traveller.*

To pass the seas some think a toil ;
Some think it strange abroad to roam ;
Some think it grief to leave their soil,
Their parents, kinsfolk and their home.
Think so who list, I like it not ;
I must abroad to try my lot.
> BARNABE GOOGE.—*In Praise of
Seafaring Men.*

Some minds improve by travel, others
rather
Resemble copper wire or brass,
Which gets the narrower by going farther.
> HOOD.—*Ode to R. Wilson.*

We come to this ; when all the world we
range,
'Tis but our climate, not our minds we
change. HORACE.—*Epistles,* 1, 11, 27
(Conington tr.)

Lord of the main ! direct aright,
With toils unvexed, their prosperous way.
PINDAR.—*Olympic Odes*, 6, 149.

Change of soil and climate has in it much
that is pleasurable.
PLINY THE YOUNGER.

Wandering from clime to clime, observant
strayed,
Their manners noted, and their states
surveyed, POPE.—*Odyssey, Bk.* 1, 5.

I hold it an indisputable maxim that he
who has only seen one race of people, instead of knowing men, merely knows the
people with whom he has lived.
ROUSSEAU.—*Emile.*

There is a great deal of difference
between travelling to see countries and
travelling to see peoples.
ROUSSEAU.—*Ib.*

A traveller ! By my faith, you have
reason to be sad. I fear you have sold
your own lands to see other men's.
SHAKESPEARE.—*As You Like It*, Act 4, 1.

And of the cannibals that each other eat,
The Anthropophagi, and men whose heads
Do grow beneath their shoulders.
SHAKESPEARE.—*Othello*, Act 1, 3.

Travellers ne'er did lie,
Though fools at home condemn 'em.
SHAKESPEARE.—*Tempest*, Act 3, 3.

If you want to see how selfish people are,
and how skin-deep fashionable politeness
is, take a voyage.
G. B. SHAW.—*Irrational Knot*, ch. 18.

A man is the happier for life for having
once made an agreeable tour.
SYDNEY SMITH.—*Lectures on Moral
Philosophy, No.* 22.

An Englishman does not travel to see
Englishmen.
STERNE.—*Sent. Journey, Preface.*

I pity the man who can travel from Dan
to Beersheba, and cry "'Tis all barren."
STERNE.—*Ib., In the Street, Calais.*

There's nothing under heaven so blue
That's fairly worth the travelling to.
R. L. STEVENSON.—*Song of the Road.*

A perfect Englishman, travelling without design, buying modern antiques at an
excessive price, regarding everything with
a haughty air, and despising the saints and
their relics. VOLTAIRE.—*La Pucelle.*

A book like Mandeville's, that yields de-
light,
And puts poor probability to flight.
J. WOLCOT.—*Ep. to James Bruce.*

He travelled here, he travelled there,
But not the value of a hair
Was head or heart the better.
WORDSWORTH.—*Peter Bell*, Pt. 1.

I travelled among unknown men
In lands beyond the sea ;
Nor, England, did I know till then
What love I bore to thee.
WORDSWORTH.—*Poems on the Affections,
No.* 9 (1799).

A Passage perillus makyth a Port
pleasaunt.
Inscription on a harbour at Lake Como.

TREACHERY AND TREASON

Ah me ! with what a foot doth treason
post,
While loyalty, with all her speed, is slow !
M. ARNOLD.—*Merope (Arcas).*

But treason is not owned when 'tis des-
cried ;
Successful crimes alone are justified.
DRYDEN.—*The Medal.*

Treason doth never prosper ; what's the
reason ?
For if it prosper, none dare call it treason.
SIR J. HARRINGTON.—*Epigram.*

O for a tongue to curse the slave
Whose treason, like a deadly blight,
Comes o'er the councils of the brave
And blasts them in their hour of might !
MOORE.—*Lalla Rookh : The Fire-
Worshippers.*

I love the treason, but I do not praise
the traitor. PLUTARCH.

Why, as a woodcock to mine own springe,
Osric :
I am justly killed with mine own treachery.
SHAKESPEARE.—*Hamlet*, Act 5, 2.

Treason is but tricked like the fox
Who, ne'er so tame, so cherished and
locked up,
Will have a wild trick of his ancestors.
SHAKESPEARE.—*Henry IV.*, Pt. 1,
Act 5, 2.

He is composed and framed of treachery.
SHAKESPEARE.—*Much Ado*, Act 5, 1.

TREES

Trees can smile in light at the sinking sun
Just as the storm comes, as a girl would
look
On a departing lover—most serene.
BROWNING.—*Pauline*, 726.

No tree in all the grove but has its charms,
Though each its hue peculiar.
COWPER.—*The Task, Bk.* 1, *l.* 307.

Good luck to dem w'at come and go,
W'at set in de shade er de sycamo'.
J. C. HARRIS.—*Nights with Uncle Remus,
ch.* 38.

And garnished with trees that a man might
    cut down,
Instead of his own expenses.
            HOOD.—*Miss Kilmansegg.*

Poems are made by fools like me,
But only God can make a tree.
            JOYCE KILMER.—*Trees.*

The birch, most shy and lady-like of trees.
            J. R. LOWELL.—*Indian Summer.*

Cedar, and pine, and fir, and branching
    palm,
A sylvan scene, and as the ranks ascend
Shade above shade, a woody theatre
Of stateliest view.
            MILTON.—*Paradise Lost, Bk. 4, 139.*

Welcome, ye shades ! ye bowery thickets,
    hail !
Ye lofty pines ! ye venerable oaks !
Ye ashes wild, resounding o'er the steep !
Delicious is your shelter to the soul.
            THOMSON.—*Seasons : Summer, 469.*

And he spake of trees, from the cedar
tree that is in Lebanon even unto the
hyssop that springeth out of the wall.
            1 Kings iv, 33.

TRIALS AND TRIBULATIONS

Restless Anxiety, forlorn Despair,
And all the faded family of Care.
            SIR S. GARTH.—*Dispensary.*

The weariness, the fever, and the fret,
Here, where men sit and hear each other
groan. KEATS.—*Ode to a Nightingale.*

Eye me, blest Providence, and square my
    trial
To my proportioned strength.
            MILTON.—*Comus, 329.*

Comfort's in heaven ; and we are on the
    earth,
Where nothing lives but crosses, care, and
    grief.
            SHAKESPEARE.—*Richard II., Act 2, 2.*

Till from the straw the flail the corn doth
    beat
Until the chaff be purgèd from the wheat,
Yea, till the mill the grain in pieces tear,
The richness of the flour will scarce appear.
            GEO. WITHER.

The finest diamond must be cut. *Prov.*

TRIFLES

Trifles make perfection, and perfection
is no trifle.
            MICHAEL ANGELO.—*Attributed.*

Small matters win great commendation.
    BACON.—*Essays : Of Ceremonies.*

He that shuns trifles must shun the
world. CHAPMAN.—*Dedication, Hero and
                                    Leander.*

It is a life of toys and trinkets. We are
too easily pleased.
            R. W. EMERSON.—*Domestic Life.*

Small things are best ;
    Grief and unrest
To rank and wealth are given ;
    But little things
    On little wings
Bear little souls to heaven.
            F. W. FABER.—*In a Child's Album.*

To a philosopher no circumstance, however trifling, is too minute.
            GOLDSMITH.—*Citizen of the World,
                                    No. 30.*

Not oaks alone are trees, nor roses flowers ;
Much humble wealth makes rich this
    world of ours.
            LEIGH HUNT.—*On reading Pomfret's
                                    " Choice."*

Those who apply themselves too much
to little things usually become incapable
of great things. LA ROCHEFOUCAULD.

These are small things, but it was by
not despising these small things that our
ancestors achieved this very great thing.
            LIVY.—*Hist., Bk. 6.*

The smallest effort is not lost ;
Each wavelet on the ocean tossed
Aids in the ebb-tide or the flow ;
Each raindrop makes some flow'ret blow ;
Each struggle lessens human woe.
            C. MACKAY.—*Old and New, 44.*

Since trifles make the sum of human things,
And half our misery from our foibles
    springs ;
Since life's best joys consist in peace and
    ease ;
And though but few can serve yet all may
    please ;
Oh, let the ungentle spirit learn from hence
A small unkindness is a great offence.
            HANNAH MORE.—*Sensibility.*

Little drops of water, little grains of sand,
Make the mighty ocean and the pleasant
    land ;
Thus the little minutes, humble though
    they be,
Make the mighty ages of eternity.
            FRANCES OSGOOD.—*Little Things.*

And trifles I alike pursue,
Because they're old, because they're new.
            PRIOR.—*Alma, 3, 362.*

Trifles, light as air,
Are to the jealous confirmation strong
As proofs of holy writ.
            SHAKESPEARE.—*Othello, Act 3, 3.*

Are there not little chapters in everybody's life that seem to be nothing, and yet affect all the rest of the history?
THACKERAY.—*Vanity Fair.*

The dangerous bar in the harbour's mouth is only grains of sand.
M. F. TUPPER.—*Proverbial Philosophy.*

Think nought a trifle, though it small appear;
Small sands the mountain, moments make the year,
And trifles life.
YOUNG.—*Love of Fame, Sat.* 6.

He that contemneth small things shall fall by little and little. *Ecclesiasticus* xix, 1.

Law does not concern itself about trifles.
Legal Maxim.

To know how cherries and berries taste, ask children and sparrows.
Prov. quoted by Goethe.

Despise not a small wound, a poor relation, or a humble enemy.   *Danish prov.*

The eagle does not catch flies.
Latin prov.

TRIUMPH

Joyous and bold as when feasting of old,
When his battles were ended, triumphant and splendid.
ARISTOPHANES.—*The Knights (Frere tr.).*

It was roses, roses, all the way.
BROWNING.—*The Patriot.*

Another hand thy sword shall wield,
Another hand the standard wave,
Till from the trumpet's mouth is pealed
The blast of triumph o'er thy grave.
W. CULLEN BRYANT.—*Battlefield.*

Unholy is the voice
Of loud thanksgiving over slaughtered men.   COWPER.—*Odyssey*, 22, 412.

And hast thou slain the Jabberwock?
Come to my arms, my beamish boy!
O frabjous day! Callooh! Callay!
He chortled in his joy.
C. L. DODGSON.—*Through the Looking-Glass.*

Hail to the chief who in triumph advances!
SCOTT.—*Lady of the Lake, c.* 2, 19.

Now, infidel, I have thee on the hip.
SHAKESPEARE.—*Merchant of Venice,* Act 4, 1.

Not simple conquest, triumph is his aim.
YOUNG.—*Night Thoughts,* 5.

TROUBLES

The greater part of your trouble lies in your own imagination, and so you may free yourself from it when you please.
MARCUS AURELIUS.—*Bk.* 9, 32.

Not such sorrowful sighès as men make
For woe, or ellès when that folk be sike
But easy sighès, such as been to like.
CHAUCER.—*Troilus and Cressida.*

There is this of good in real evils,—they deliver us, while they last, from the petty despotism of all that were imaginary.
C. C. COLTON.—*Lacon.*

In trouble to be troubled
Is to have your trouble doubled.
DEFOE.—*Robinson Crusoe.*

Life is mostly froth and bubble;
Two things stand like stone:
Kindness in another's trouble,
Courage in our own.
A. L. GORDON.—*Weary Wayfarer.*

" Law, Brer Tarrypin ! " sez Brer Fox, sezee, " you ain't see no trouble yit. Ef you wanter see sho' nuff [sure enough] trouble, you des [just] oughter go 'longer me; I'm de man w'at kin show you trouble," sezee.   J. C. HARRIS.—*Nights with Uncle Remus, ch.* 17.

Thus woe succeeds a woe, as wave a wave.
HERRICK.—*Sorrows Succeed.*

We all have sufficient strength to bear other people's troubles.
LA ROCHEFOUCAULD.

Of our troubles we must seek some other causes, and not God.
PLATO.—*Republic, Bk.* 2, 18 *(Davis tr.).*

If the just man happen to be in poverty, or in diseases, or in any other of those seeming evils, these things to him issue in something good, either whilst alive or after he is dead.   PLATO.—*Ib., Bk.* 10, 12.

Light troubles speak; immense troubles are silent.   SENECA.—*Hippolytus.*

I could lie down like a tired child,
And weep away the life of care
Which I have borne, and still must bear.
SHELLEY.—*In Dejection.*

'Gainst minor evils let him pray
Who fortune's favour curries,—
For one that big misfortunes slay,
Ten die of " little worries."
GEO. R. SIMS.

In all distresses of our friends
We first consult our private ends.
SWIFT.—*On the Death of Dr. Swift.*

Disasters, do the best we can,
Will reach both great and small;
And he is oft the wisest man
Who is not wise at all.
WORDSWORTH.—*Waterfall and Eglantine.*

Woes cluster.   Rare are solitary woes;
They love a train, they tread each other's heel.   YOUNG.—*Night Thoughts,* 3.

R*

A small evil is a great good.
Greek prov.

If there were no clouds, we should not enjoy the sun. *Prov.*

TRUST

But when I trust a wild fool, and a woman,
May I lend gratis, and build hospitals.
BEAUMONT AND FLETCHER.—*Scornful Lady*, Act 3.

When young, we trust ourselves too much ; and we trust others too little, when old. C. C. COLTON.—*Lacon.*

And oft, though Wisdom wake, Suspicion sleeps
At Wisdom's gate, and to Simplicity
Resigns her charge, while Goodness thinks no ill
Where no ill seems.
MILTON.—*Paradise Lost, Bk.* 3, 686.

Women and princes must trust somebody. SELDEN.—*Women.*

Trust none ;
For oaths are straw, men's faiths are wafer-cakes,
And hold-fast is the only dog.
SHAKESPEARE.—*Henry V.*, Act 2, 3.

He was a gentleman on whom I built
An absolute trust.
SHAKESPEARE.—*Macbeth*, Act 1, 4.

Ha, ha ! what a fool Honesty is ! and Trust, his sworn brother, a very simple gentleman !
SHAKESPEARE.—*Winter's Tale*, Act 4, 3.

Confidence, like the soul, never returns to whence it has departed.
PUBLILIUS SYRUS.

And trust me not at all or all in all.
TENNYSON.—*Merlin and Vivien.*

By trust I lost money ; by distrust I saved it. THEOGNIS.

Confidence is never safe.
VIRGIL.—*Æneid, Bk.* 4.

Words that require no sanction from an oath,
And simple honesty a common growth.
WORDSWORTH.—*Sonnets to Liberty and Order*, 9.

Since man to man is so unjust,
No man can tell what man to trust ;
I've trusted many to my sorrow :
Pay to-day, take trust to-morrow.
Lines in an Inn at Chichester.

TRUTH

Plato and truth are both dear to me, but it is my duty to prefer truth.
ARISTOTLE.

Yea, I take myself to witness,
That I have loved no darkness,
Sophisticated no truth,
Nursed no delusion,
Allowed no fear.
M. ARNOLD.—*Empedocles on Etna*, Act 2.

Ah, love, let us be true
To one another ! For the world, which seems
To lie before us like a land of dreams,
So various, so beautiful, so new,
Hath really neither joy, nor love, nor light,
Nor certitude, nor peace, nor help for pain.
M. ARNOLD.—*Dover Beach.*

There is only one thing here worth minding, and that is to be true and just, and to show charity, even to the untrue and the unjust.
MARCUS AURELIUS.—*Bk.* 6, 47.

The inseparable propriety of time, which is ever more and more to disclose truth.
BACON.—*Adv. of Learning.*

Is truth ever barren ?
BACON.—*In Praise of Knowledge.*

No pleasure is comparable to the standing upon the vantage ground of truth.
BACON.—*Of Truth.*

" What is truth ? " said jesting Pilate ; and would not stay for an answer.
BACON.—*Ib.*

Words, phrases, fashions pass away,
But truth and nature live through all.
B. BARTON.—*On Bloomfield.*

And much they grope for Truth, but never hit.
BEATTIE.—*The Minstrel, Bk.* 1, 49.

Truth can never be told so as to be understood and not be believed.
WM. BLAKE.—*Proverbs of Hell.*

Truth is the hardest taunt to bear.
R. BRIDGES.—*Return of Ulysses*, Act 4, 1688.

Truth never hurts the teller.
BROWNING.—*Fifine.*

Truth is the strong thing. Let man's life be true !
BROWNING.—*In a Balcony.*

There is an inmost centre in us all,
Where truth abides in fulness.
BROWNING.—*Paracelsus.*

Truth is within ourselves : it takes no rise
From outward things, whate'er you may believe. BROWNING.—*Pauline.*

Why with old truth needs new truth disagree ? BROWNING.—*Red Cotton Nightcap Country, Bk.* 2.

But here's the plague,
That all this trouble comes of telling truth,
Which truth, by when it reaches him, looks
    false,
Seems to be just the thing it would sup-
    plant.
    BROWNING.—*Ring and the Book*, 12, 852.

There is truth in falsehood, falsehood
    in truth.
    BROWNING.—*Soul's Tragedy*, Act 2.

Truth, crushed to earth, shall rise again ;
    The eternal years of God are hers ;
But Error, wounded, writhes with pain,
    And dies among his worshippers.
    W. CULLEN BRYANT.—*Battlefield.*

No one can tell whether any single truth
may not be so consequent on all truths,
for the most part in ways mysterious and
unseen, but so notwithstanding that on
denial of a single one all fall and dissolve.
    BISHOP BUTLER.—*Analogy of Religion,*
        Pt. 1, ch. 7.

For truth is precious and divine,
Too rich a pearl for carnal swine.
    BUTLER.—*Hudibras, Pt. 1, c. 3.*

'Tis strange, but true ; for truth is always
    strange ;
Stranger than fiction.
    BYRON.—*Don Juan*, 15, 101.

Truth, ever lovely,—since the world began,
The foe of tyrants and the friend of man.
    CAMPBELL.—*Pleasures of Hope, Pt. 2.*

Truth, fact, is the life of all things ;
falsity, "fiction" or whatever it may call
itself, is certain to be the death.
    CARLYLE.—*Latter-Day Pamphlets, No. 8.*

Trouthe is the hyeste thing that man
    may kepe.
    CHAUCER.—*Franklin's Tale*, 751.

Truth is bitter and disagreeable to fools ;
but falsehood is sweet and acceptable.
    St. Chrysostom.

Truth is truest poesy.
    COWLEY.—*Davideis.*

All truth is precious, if not all divine.
    COWPER.—*Charity.*

And differing judgments serve but to de-
    clare,
That Truth lies somewhere, if we knew but
    where.   COWPER.—*Hope*, 425.

Fear makes an enemy of truth itself.
    J. DAVIDSON.—*Godfrida*, Act 3.

"It is," says Chadband, "the ray of
rays, the sun of suns, the moon of moons,
the star of stars. It is the light of
Terewth." DICKENS.—*Bleak House, ch. 25.*

For truth has such a face and such a mien
As to be loved needs only to be seen.
    DRYDEN.—*Hind and the Panther, Pt. 1, 33.*

Truth is only falsehood well disguised.
    FARQUHAR.—*Constant Couple*, Act 3, 4.

The trouthe, how so it ever come,
    May for no time be overcome ;
It may wel suffre for a throwe,
    But atte last it shall be knowe.
        GOWER.—*Conf. Amantis.*

When false things are brought low,
    And swift things have grown slow,
Feigning like froth shall go,
        Faith be for aye.
      T. HARDY.—*Between us Now*, 3.

"Dat's so," exclaimed Aunt Tempy,
"dat's de Lord's trufe !"
    J. C. HARRIS.—*Nights with Uncle
        Remus, ch. 42.*

Dare to be true. Nothing can need a lie :
A fault, which needs it most, grows two
    thereby.   HERBERT.—*Church Porch.*

Truth is for ever truth, and love is love.
    LEIGH HUNT.—*Hero and Leander.*

It is always the best policy to speak the
truth, unless of course you are an ex-
ceptionally good liar.
    J. K. JEROME.—*Idler, Feb.,* 1892.

Truth is characterised by consistency ;
fraud, deceit and vainglory are shifting
and shifty.
    KEBLE.—*Lectures on Poetry, No. 5
        (E. K. Francis tr.).*

I reckon there's more things told than are
    true,
And more things true than are told.
    KIPLING.—*Ballad of Minepit Shaw.*

When alle tresours ben tryed, treuth y's
    the best.
    LANGLAND.—*Piers Plowman
        (c.* 1362), *Passus 2, 203.*

Seek ye Seint Trouthe.
    LANGLAND.—*Ib., Passus 6, 198.*

Truth is the foundation and the reason
of all perfection and beauty.
    LA ROCHEFOUCAULD.—*Maxim 568.*

Native and original truth is not so
easily wrought out of the mine as we, who
have it ready dug and fashioned into our
hands, are apt to imagine.
    LOCKE.—*Reasonableness of Christianity.*

He's true to God, who's true to man what-
    ever wrong is done,
To the humblest and the weakest 'neath
    the all-beholding sun.
    J. R. LOWELL.—*Interview with Miles
        Standish.*

Who speaks the truth stabs falsehood to
  the heart,
And his mere word makes despots tremble
  more
Than ever Brutus with his dagger could.
          J. R. LOWELL.—*L'Envoi.*

But O the truth, the truth ! the many eyes
That look on it ! the diverse things they
  see !
  GEO. MEREDITH.—*Ballad of Fair Ladies.*

It is a piece of idle sentimentality that
truth, merely as truth, has any inherent
power denied to error, of prevailing against
the dungeon and the stake.
          J. S. MILL.—*Liberty, ch.* 2.

The well-being of mankind may almost
be measured by the number and gravity
of the truths which have reached the point
of being uncontested.   J. S. MILL.—*Ib.*

Let her and Falsehood grapple! Who
ever knew truth put to the worse in a free
and open encounter ?
          MILTON.—*Areopagitica.*

Truth is as impossible to be soiled by
any outward touch as the sunbeam.
          MILTON.—*On Shakespeare.*

Hard are the ways of truth and rough
  to walk.
  MILTON.—*Paradise Regained, Bk.* 1, 478.

And with those few art eminently seen,
That labour up the hill of heavenly truth.
          MILTON.—*To a Virtuous Lady.*

Truth alone wounds.   NAPOLEON.

Truth in all states her fearless front may
  rear,
Whether proud kings or fierce democracies
Or sapient peers the public weal maintain.
PINDAR.—*Pythian Odes,* 2, 157 (*Moore tr.*).

The more I examine myself, the more
I consider, the more I read these words
written on my soul, " Be true (*juste*) and
you will be happy."   ROUSSEAU.—*Emile.*

General and abstract truth is the most
precious of all good things. Without it
man is blind ; it is the eye of reason.
ROUSSEAU.—*Rêveries d'un Promeneur
                              solitaire,* 4.

In the invention of fables I take every
care that I can that they shall not be falsehoods, that is to say that they shall not
wound either justice or truth.
          ROUSSEAU.—*Ib.*

Speaking truth is like writing fair, and
only comes by practice.
          RUSKIN.—*Seven Lamps, ch.* 2, 1.

Truth cannot appear naked before the
people. SCHOPENHAUER.—*World as Will
              and Idea, Supp. to Bk.* 1, 17.

'Tis true 'tis pity,
And pity 'tis 'tis true.
  SHAKESPEARE.—*Hamlet,* Act 2, 2.

O, while you live, tell truth and shame
the devil.
  SHAKESPEARE.—*Henry IV.,* Act 3, 1.

For truth is truth
  To th' end of the reckoning.
  SHAKESPEARE.—*Measure for Measure,*
                              Act 5, 1.

All great truths begin as blasphemies.
  G. B. SHAW.—*Annajanska* (1918).

My way of joking is to tell the truth.
It's the finest joke in the world.
  G. B. SHAW.—*John Bull's Other Island,*
                      Act 2 (*Keegan*).

Dark is the abyss of Time,
But light enough to guide your steps is
  given ;
Whatever weal or woe betide,
Turn never from the way of truth aside,
And leave the event, in holy hope, to
  Heaven.
          SOUTHEY.—*Curse of Kehama.*

Truth is eternal and the son of heaven.
          SWIFT.—*Ode to Sancroft.*

Change lays not her hand upon truth.
          SWINBURNE.—*Dedication,* 1865.

Truth is that which a man troweth.
          J. H. TOOKE.—*Diversions of Purley.*

It is one thing to wish to have truth on
our side, and another to wish sincerely to
be on the side of truth.
  ARCHBP. WHATELY.—*Essay on Truth.*

Truths that wake,
To perish never ;
Which neither listlessness, nor mad en-
deavour,
    Nor Man nor Boy,
Nor all that is at enmity with joy,
Can utterly abolish and destroy.
          WORDSWORTH.—*Intimations of
                              Immortality, c.* 9.

Women are strongest ; but above all
things Truth beareth away the victory.
                      1 *Esdras* iii, 12.

As for the truth, it endureth, and is
always strong ; it liveth and conquereth
for evermore.   1 *Esdras* iv, 38.

Great is truth, and mighty above all
things.   1 *Esdras* iv, 41.

TYRANNY AND TYRANTS

Take care that you have not too much
of a Cæsar in you, and that you are not
dyed with that dye.
          MARCUS AURELIUS.—*Bk.* 6, 30.

Power gradually extirpates from the mind every humane and gentle virtue.
BURKE.—*Vindication of Natural Society.*

A tyrant is the best sacrifice to Jupiter, as the ancients held.
BURTON.—*Anat. of Melan., Pt. 2.*

Their power is hated, their life is wretched, who prefer being feared to being loved. CORNELIUS NEPOS.

Nature has left this tincture in the blood, That all men would be tyrants if they could. DEFOE.—*Kentish Petition.*

Of all wild beasts preserve me from a tyrant. BEN JONSON.—*Sejanus, Act 1.*

Whatever crushes individuality is despotism, by whatever name it may be called, and whether it professes to be enforcing the will of God or the injunctions of men. J. S. MILL.—*Liberty, ch. 3.*

Tyranny must be,
Though to the tyrant thereby no excuse.
MILTON.—*Paradise Lost, Bk. 12, 95.*

Though sweet are our friendships, our hopes, our affections,
Revenge on a tyrant is sweetest of all.
MOORE.—*Irish Melodies.*

You thought to grasp the world ; but you shall keep
Its curses only crowned upon your brow.
You that have fouled the purple, broke your vow,
And sowed the wind of death, the whirlwind shall you reap.
EDEN PHILLPOTTS.—*Unto this Last.*

For liberty and true friendship the tyrant's nature has no relish whatever.
PLATO.—*Republic, Bk. 9, 3 (Davis tr.).*

The bigger a state becomes the more liberty diminishes.
ROUSSEAU.—*Contrat Social, Bk. 3, ch. 1.*

Now in the names of all the gods at once, Upon what meat doth this our Cæsar feed, That he is grown so great ?
SHAKESPEARE.—*Julius Cæsar, Act 1, 2.*

O ! it is excellent
To have a giant's strength ; but it is tyrannous
To use it like a giant. SHAKESPEARE.—
Measure for Measure, Act 2, 2.

'Tis time to fear when tyrants seem to kiss. SHAKESPEARE.—*Pericles, Act 1, 2.*

Mankind, it seems, is made for you alone, We but the slaves who mount you to the throne—
A base, ignoble crowd, without a name.
VIRGIL.—*Æneid, Bk. 11 (Dryden tr.).*
(Drances, inveighing against Turnus.)

Still have I found, where Tyranny prevails,
That virtue languishes and pleasure fails.
WORDSWORTH.—*Descriptive Sketches.*

Never may from our souls one truth depart—
That an accursed thing it is to gaze
On prosperous tyrants with a dazzled eye !
WORDSWORTH.—*Poems to National Independence, Pt. 2, 33.*

U

UGLINESS

The secret of ugliness consists not in irregularity, but in being uninteresting.
R. W. EMERSON.—*Conduct of Life : Beauty.*

If shape it might be called that shape had none.
MILTON.—*Paradise Lost, Bk. 2, 667.*

UNBELIEF

Be a Napoleon, and yet disbelieve !
Why the man's mad, friend, take his light away.
BROWNING.—*Bishop Blougram.*

O Incredulity ! the wit of fools,
That slovenly will spit on all things fair.
CHAPMAN.—*De Guiana, 82.*

The coward's castle and the sluggard's cradle [Incredulity]. CHAPMAN.—*Ib.*

Blind unbelief is sure to err,
And scan His work in vain.
COWPER.—*Hymn.*

There lives more faith in honest doubt, Believe me, than in half the creeds.
TENNYSON.—*In Memoriam, c. 96.*

It may be that we can no longer share The faith which from his fathers he received ;
It may be that our doom is to despair, Where he with joy believed.
SIR W. WATSON.—*To James Bromley.*

UNCERTAINTY

For we are all, like swimmers in the sea, Poised on the top of a huge wave of fate, Which hangs uncertain to which side to fall.
M. ARNOLD.—*Sohrab and Rustum.*

Ah, half in darkness on this earth we dwell, Not in the light, but shadow, of the truth ; Confounding good with evil, heaven with hell,
Misjudging rage and hate for love and ruth.
A. AUSTIN.—*Human Tragedy, Act 3.*

Certainty is the mother of Quietness and Repose ; and Incertainty the cause of variance and contentions.
SIR E. COKE.—*Institutes, No. 3, 302.*

Dreams that bring us little comfort, heavenly promises that lapse
Into some remote It-may-be, into some forlorn Perhaps.
S. R. LYSAGHT.—*Confession of Unfaith, st. 32.*

The only thing certain is that nothing is certain.
PLINY THE ELDER.—*Nat. Hist.*

Nothing is
But what is not.
SHAKESPEARE.—*Macbeth,* Act 1, 3.

This
I ever held worse than all certitude,
To know not what the worst ahead might be.
SWINBURNE.—*Marino Faliero,* Act 5.

Alternate hopes and fears their minds possess.   VIRGIL.—*Æneid, Bk. 1 (Dryden tr).*

Wandering stars, to whom is reserved the blackness of darkness for ever.
Jude 13.

UNCO GUID

Ye, wha are sae guid yoursel',
Sae pious and sae holy,
Ye've nought to do but mark and tell
Your neebour's fauts and folly.
BURNS.—*Address.*

A Godly man, that has served out his time
In holiness, may set up any crime ;
As scholars, when they've taken their degrees,
May set up any faculty they please.
S. BUTLER.—*Miscellaneous Thoughts.*

Several explanations of casuists to multiply the catalogue of sins may be called amendments to the ten commandments.
POPE.—*Thoughts on Various Subjects.*

A nice man is a man of nasty ideas.
SWIFT.—*Thoughts on Various Subjects.*

UNIFORMS

Such is the country maiden's fright,
When first a red-coat is in sight ;
Behind the door she hides her face ;
Next time at distance eyes the lace.
GAY.—*Fables, Pt. 1, 13.*

Apes are apes, though clothed in scarlet.
BEN JONSON.—*Poetaster,* Act 5, 3.

See now comes the captain all daubed in gold lace.
SWIFT.—*Grand Question Debated.*

Uniforms are often masks.
DUKE OF WELLINGTON.—*Saying (attributed).*

UNION AND UNITY

All colours will agree in the dark.
BACON.—*Of Uniformity (Prov.).*

One flag, one land, one heart, one hand,
One nation, evermore !
O. W. HOLMES.—*Voyage of the "Union."*

A song for our banner ? The watchword recall
Which gave the Republic her station :
United we stand—divided we fall !
It made and preserves us a nation.
G. P. MORRIS.—*Flag of Our Union.*

The union of hearts, the union of hands,
And the Flag of our Union for ever.
G. P. MORRIS.—*Ib.*

I would that we were all of one mind, and one mind good.
SHAKESPEARE.—*Cymbeline,* Act 5, 4.

So we grew together,
Like to a double cherry, seeming parted,
But yet a union in partition ;
Two lovely berries moulded on one stem.
SHAKESPEARE.—*Midsummer Night's Dream,* Act 3, 2.

There is always victory where there is unanimity.   PUBLILIUS SYRUS.

Foes in the forum in the field were friends,
By social danger bound.
THOMSON.—*Liberty,* Pt. 3, 218.

Behold how good and how pleasant it is for brethren to dwell together in unity !
Psalm cxxxiii, 1.

A threefold cord is not quickly broken.
Ecclesiastes iv, 12.

UNIVERSITIES

Granta, sweet Granta, where, studious of ease,
Seven years did I sleep, and then lost my degrees.   CHR. ANSTEY.—*Epilogue.*

Universities incline wits to sophistry and affectation.
BACON.—*Valerius Terminus.*

The King to Oxford sent a troop of horse,
For Tories own no argument but force ;
With equal care to Cambridge books hesent,
For Whigs allow no force but argument.
SIR WM. BROWNE.—*Epigram.*

The true university in these days is a collection of books.
CARLYLE.—*Miscellanies, 7.*

The next evil is the pedantical veneration that is maintained at the university, for the Greek and Latin, which puts the youth upon such exercises as many of them are incapable of performing with any tolerable success.
STEELE.—*The Guardian, No. 94 (June 29, 1713).*

The King observing with judicious eyes,
The state of both his universities,
To one he sent a regiment, for why ?
That learned body wanted loyalty ;
To the other he sent books, as well dis-
    cerning
How much that loyal body wanted learn-
    ing.
J. TRAPP —*On George I. giving a Library
        to Cambridge University.*

UNKINDNESS

A small unkindness is a great offence.
        HANNAH MORE.—*Sensibility.*

And so the cruel word was spoken,
And so it was two hearts were broken.
        J. G. SAXE.—*Way of the World.*

This was the most unkindest cut of all.
SHAKESPEARE.—*Julius Cæsar*, Act 3, 2.

In nature there's no blemish but the mind :
None can be called deformed but the un-
    kind.
SHAKESPEARE.—*Twelfth Night*, Act 3, 4.

" Ah me," quoth Venus, " young and so
    unkind."   SHAKESPEARE.—
        Venus and Adonis, st. 32.

And yet we cannot be kind to each other
    here for an hour ;
We whisper, and hint, and chuckle, and
    grin at a brother's shame ;
However we brave it out, we men are a
    little breed.   TENNYSON.—*Maud.*

UNPATRIOTIC

He disdaineth all things above his reach,
and preferreth all countries before his own.
SIR T. OVERBURY.—*Affectate Traveller.*

Bind fast her homeborn foes with links of
    shame,
More strong than iron and more keen than
    flame ;
Seal up their lips for shame's sake.
    SWINBURNE.—*New Year's Day* (1889).

UNPOPULARITY

To displease is my pleasure ; I love to
be hated.
        E. ROSTAND.—*Cyrano de Bergerac.*

The more he was with vulgar hate op-
    pressed,
The more his fury boiled within his breast.
    VIRGIL.—*Æneid, Bk.* 12 (*Dryden tr.*)
        (*Of Turnus*).

UNREALITY

His blissful soul was in Heaven, though
    a breathing man was he ;
He was out of time's dominion, so far as
    the living may be.
        W. ALLINGHAM.—*Poems.*

We wake in a dream, and we ache in a
    dream,
And we break in a dream, and die.
        R. BUCHANAN.—*Balder.*

What shadows we are and what shadows
we pursue !
    BURKE.—*Speech on Declining the Poll.*

UNREASONABLENESS

Do I carry the moon in my pocket ?
        BROWNING.—*Master Hughes.*

Oh we are querulous creatures ! Little less
Than all things can suffice to make us
    happy ;
And little more than nothing is enough
To discontent us.
        COLERIDGE.—*Zapolya, Pt.* 2,
            Act 1, 1.
    Women, giddy women !
In her the blemish of your sex you prove,
There is no reason for your hate or love.
    MASSINGER.—*Very Woman*, Act 5, 2.

It's idle to spur a hamshackled horse
(*i.e.* a horse with its head fastened to one
of its forelegs).   *Scottish prov.*

UNSEEN

Veil after veil will lift—but there must be
Veil upon veil behind.
        SIR E. ARNOLD.—*Light of Asia.*

Unseen by all but Heaven,
Like diamond blazing in the mine.
    KEBLE.—*3rd Sun. after Epiphany.*

What the eye views not, the heart craves
not as well as rues not.
        W. PENN.—*No Cross, No Crown.*

The things which are seen are temporal ;
but the things which are not seen are
eternal.   *2 Corinthians* iv, 18.

UNSELFISHNESS

Heaven doth with us as we with torches do,
Not light them for themselves.
    SHAKESPEARE.—*Measure for Measure*,
            Act 1, 1.

Selfishness is the only real atheism ;
aspiration, unselfishness, the only real
religion.
    I. ZANGWILL.—*Children of the Ghetto,*
            Bk. 2, ch. 16.

USELESSNESS

Once he [Mr. Albany] took the liberty
to ask me what service I was to the world.
. . . He really bores me to a degree.
[*Capt. Aresby.*]
    MME. D'ARBLAY.—*Cecilia, Bk.* 2, ch. 6.

Dim lights of life, that burn a length of
    years,
Useless, unseen, as lamps in sepulchres.
        POPE.—*Elegy.*

Remember that the most beautiful things in the world are the most useless; peacocks and lilies, for instance.
RUSKIN.—*Sesame and Lilies.*

USURPATION

Lord! how they chided with themselves,
  That they had let him in;
To see him grow so monstrous now,
  That came so small and thin!
HOOD.—*Wee Man.*

This dog is mine, said these poor children [lawless persons and thieves]; there is my place in the sun. There you have the beginning and the emblem of the usurpation of all the earth.
PASCAL.—*Pensées, Pt.* 1, 9, 53.

UTILITY AND UTILITARIANISM

I learnt to see that utility was the test and measure of all virtues.
J. BENTHAM.—*Fragment on Government.*

Man having enslaved the elements remains himself a slave.
SHELLEY.—*Defence of Poetry* (1821).

Keep a thing seven years and ye'll find a use for 't.
Scottish prov. (Scott's " Antiquary," xxi.)

UTOPIA

Things which are not practicable are not desirable.   BURKE.—*Speech* (1780).

Utopias are often only premature truths.
LAMARTINE.

Ah splendid Vision, golden time!
An end of hunger, cold, and crime,
An end of rent, an end of rank,
An end of balance at the bank,
An end of everything that's meant
To bring investors five per cent.
A. LANG.—*The New Millennium.*

An acre in Middlesex is better than a principality in Utopia.
MACAULAY.—*On Bacon.*

We are told that a people of true christians would form the most perfect society that can be imagined. I can only see one great difficulty in this supposition, and that is that a society of true christians would be no longer a society of men.
ROUSSEAU.—*Contrat Social, Bk.* 4, *ch.* 8.

V

VACILLATION

And still be doing, never done.
BUTLER.—*Hudibras, Pt.* 1, *c.* 1.

Enter, but this warning hear:
He forth again departs who looks behind.
DANTE.—*Purgatory, c.* 9, 124 (*Cary tr.*).

At Rome you long for the country; in the country you praise the absent town to the skies.   HORACE.—*Sat., Bk.* 2, 7, 28.

She [Madame Oronte] is always of the opinion of the person who last speaks to her.   LE SAGE.—*Crispin.*

I thought I'd go, I thought I'd not,
And then I thought I'd think about it.
F. LOCKER-LAMPSON.—*Invitation to Rome,* 9.

I tell ye wut, my jedgment is you're pooty sure to fail,
Ez lon' 'z the head keeps turnin' back tor counsel to the tail.
J. R. LOWELL.—*Biglow Papers, 2nd Series,* 3.

No mortle man can boast of perfic' vision,
But the one moleblin' thing is Indecision.
J. R. LOWELL.—*Ib.,* 11.

To the timid and hesitating everything is impossible because it seems so.
SCOTT.—*Rob Roy,* 16.

Letting "I dare not "wait upon "I would,"
Like the poor cat i' the adage.
SHAKESPEARE.—*Macbeth,* Act 1, 7.

Infirm of purpose.
SHAKESPEARE.—*Ib.,* Act 2, 2.

I am a feather for each wind that blows.
SHAKESPEARE.—*Winter's Tale,* Act 2, 3.

Unstable as water, thou shalt not excel.
Genesis xlix, 4.

How long halt ye between two opinions?
1 *Kings* xviii, 21.

VAGABONDS

Under the canopy, . . . i' the city of kites and crows.
SHAKESPEARE.—*Coriolanus,* Act 4, 5.

But rough, in open air, he chose to lie;
Earth was his couch, his covering was the sky;
On hills unshorn, or in a desert den,
He shunned the dire society of men.
VIRGIL.—*Æneid, Bk.* 11 (*Dryden tr.*). (*Of Metabus.*)

As in the eye of Nature he has lived,
So in the eye of Nature let him die!
WORDSWORTH.—*Old Cumberland Beggar.*

VALENTINE, ST.

Seint Valentyne! to you I renovele [renew]
My woful lyf, as I can, compleyninge;

Upon your day doth ech foul chese his make [doth each bird choose his mate.]
CHAUCER.—*Complaint to my Mortal Fos*

Oft have I heard both youths and virgins
   say,
Birds choose their mates and couple too
   this day ;
But by their flight I never can divine
When I shall couple with my valentine.
      HERRICK.—*To his Valentine, on St.*
                Valentine's Day.

Hail to thy returning festival, old
Bishop Valentine ! Great is thy name in
the rubric, thou venerable arch-flamen of
Hymen !
   LAMB.—*Essays on Elia, Valentine's Day.*

To-morrow is St. Valentine's Day,
   All in the morning betime,
And I a maid at your window,
   To be your Valentine.
      SHAKESPEARE.—*Hamlet,* Act 4, 5.

VALOUR

He whose valour scorns his sense,
Has changed it into impudence.
Man may to man his valour show,
And 'tis his virtue to do so ;
But who's of his Maker not afraid,
Is not courageous then, but mad.
      DEFOE.—*The Storm.*

Fear to do base unworthy things is valour ;
If they be done to us, to suffer them
Is valour too.
   BEN JONSON.—*The New Inn,* Act 4, 3.

In vain doth valour bleed
While Avarice and Rapine share the
   land. MILTON.—*Sonnet to Fairfax.*

When the cross [at Rome] had expelled
the eagle, all the Roman valour dis-
appeared.
   ROUSSEAU.—*Contrat Social, Bk.* 4, *ch.* 8.

Valour, destitute of other virtues, cannot render a man worthy of any true esteem. . . . A man may be very valiant, and
yet impious and vicious.
     J. R. DE SÉGRAIS.—(*As quoted and*
   translated by Dryden, Dedic. of Æneid.)

This earth, that bears thee dead,
Bears not alive so stout a gentleman.
SHAKESPEARE.—*Henry IV., Pt.* 1, Act 5, 4.

The better part of valour is discretion.
      SHAKESPEARE.—*Ib.*

Thou wilt be as valiant as the wrathful
dove, or most magnanimous mouse.
     SHAKESPEARE.—*Ib., Pt.* 2, Act 3.

He's truly valiant that can wisely suffer
The worst that man can breathe, and make
   his wrongs
His outsides, to wear them like his raiment,
   carelessly.
     SHAKESPEARE.—*Timon of Athens,*
                      Act 3, 5.

VALUE

What is of little value regard as dear ;
what is dear regard as of little value.
                CATO.

The good we never miss we rarely prize.
      COWPER.—*Retirement,* 406.

VANITY (CONCEIT)

On earth I confess an itch for the praise
   of fools—that's Vanity.
     BROWNING.—*Solomon and Balkis.*

The sixth insatiable Sense [Vanity].
     CARLYLE.—*French Revolution.*

Vanity, like murder, will out.
   MRS. H. COWLEY.—*Belle's Stratagem,*
                   Act 1, 4.

What dotage will not Vanity maintain ?
     COWPER.—*Expostulation,* 628.

Virtue would not go so far if vanity did
not keep her company.
   LA ROCHEFOUCAULD.—*Maxim* 200.

It is impossible to count all the varieties
of vanity.
   LA ROCHEFOUCAULD.—*Maxim* 585.

Every man has just as much vanity as
he wants understanding.
   POPE.—*Thoughts on Various Subjects.*

Let us thank God for imparting to us
poor, weak mortals the inestimable blessing of vanity. THACKERAY.—*The Artists.*

Vanity is an able machine if it operates
to benevolence.
   HORACE WALPOLE.—*Letter to Dr. W.*
              Robertson, 1759.

Vanity is one of the most amiable of the
large Family of Human Frailties.
     JOHN WILSON.—*Noctes,* 34.

VANITY (EMPTINESS)

All our pride is but a jest,
None are worst and none are best ;
Grief and joy and hope and fear
Play their Pageants everywhere :
Vain opinion all doth sway,
And the world is but a play.
   CAMPION.—*Whether Men do Laugh.*

How vain the ardour of the crowd,
How low, how little are the proud,
   How indigent the great !
      GRAY.—*Ode on Spring.*

In order not to hate men, it has been
necessary for me to flee from them.
   ROUSSEAU.—*Rêveries d'un Promeneur*
              solitaire, 7.

Vain is the world, but only to the vain.
   YOUNG.—*Night Thoughts,* 3.

Why all this toil for triumphs of an hour ?
What though we wade in wealth or soar in
    fame ?
Earth's highest station ends in " Here he
    lies,"
And " dust to dust " concludes her noblest
    song.   YOUNG.—*Night Thoughts*, 4.

Every man at his best state is altogether
vanity.   *Psalms* xxxix, 5.

Vanity of vanities, saith the Preacher,
vanity of vanities ; all is vanity.
            Ecclesiastes i, 2 ; xi, 8.

The present life is no other than a toy
and a plaything ; but the future abode of
paradise is life indeed.   *Koran, ch.* 29.

VARIETY

Such and so various are the tastes of
men.
    AKENSIDE.—*Pleasures of Imagination,*
                            Bk. 3, 567.
    Enchanting spirit, dear Variety.
        R. BLOOMFIELD.—*Farmer's Boy.*

The earth was made so various, that the
    mind
Of desultory man, studious of change,
And pleased with novelty, might be in-
    dulged.   COWPER.—*The Sofa.*

    Variety's the very spice of life,
    That gives it all its flavour.
            COWPER.—*Time Piece.*

Variety, which all the rest endears.
    SIR J. DENHAM.—*Cooper's Hill.*

Variety is the mother of enjoyment.
    DISRAELI.—*Vivian Grey, Bk.* 5, *ch.* 4.

The great source of pleasure is variety.
        JOHNSON.—*Life of Butler.*

They are the weakest-minded and the
hardest-hearted men, that most love
variety and change.
    RUSKIN.—*Modern Painters*, 2, *Pt.* 2, *ch.* 7.

Age cannot wither her, nor custom stale
Her infinite variety.
    SHAKESPEARE.—*Antony and Cleopatra,*
                            Act 2, 2.
    Vary everything, except your loves.
        VOLTAIRE.—*Sur l'usage de la Vie.*

    Variety is charming,
    And not at all alarming.
    Quoted (" *Essex Herald," Oct.* 12, 1830)
            as from an old song.

VENICE

I stood in Venice, on the Bridge of Sighs ;
A palace and a prison on each hand.
        BYRON.—*Childe Harold, c.* 41.

Where Venice sat in state, throned on
    her hundred isles.   BYRON.—*Ib.*

Thank God I am here [Venice].   It is
the Paradise of cities.
        RUSKIN.—*Letter, May* 6, 1841.

VERBOSITY

A sophistical rhetorician, intoxicated
with the exuberance of his own verbosity.
        DISRAELI.—*Speech*, 1878.

Avoid the barren exuberance of the
Abbé de Bernis (a verbose poet).
    FREDERICK THE GREAT.—(*Cited by*
                Voltaire in his Memoirs.)

As men abound in copiousness of language, so they become more wise or more
mad than ordinary.
        HOBBES.—*Leviathan, ch.* 4.

Copiousness of words, however ranged,
is always false eloquence, though it will
ever impose on some sort of understandings.
    LADY M. W. MONTAGU.—*Letter*, 1754.

A fonde olde manne is often as full of
woordes as a woman.   SIR T. MORE.

Such laboured nothings, in so strange a
style,
Amaze the unlearn'd, and make the learned
    smile.
        POPE.—*Essay on Criticism*, 327.

He that useth many words for the explaining any subject, doth, like the cuttle
fish, hide himself for the most part in his
own ink.   JOHN RAY.—*On Creation.*

For these fellows of infinite tongue, that
can rhyme themselves into ladies' favours,
they do always reason themselves out
again ! SHAKESPEARE.—*Henry V.*, Act 5, 2.

He draweth out the thread of his ver-
bosity finer than the staple of his argument.
    SHAKESPEARE.—*Love's Labour's Lost,*
                            Act 5, 1.
Taffeta phrases, silken terms precise,
Three-piled hyperboles, spruce affectation,
Figures pedantical.
        SHAKESPEARE.—*Ib.*, Act 5, 2.

You [Pindar] who possessed the talent
of speaking much without saying anything.
    VOLTAIRE.—*Sur la Carrousel de l'Im-
                    pératrice de Russie.*

Who is this that darkeneth counsel by
words without knowledge ? *Job* xxxviii, 2.

VERSATILITY

By different methods different men excel,
But where is he who can do all things well ?
    CHURCHILL.—*To W. Hogarth*, 573.

He was a man (then boldly dare to say)
In whose rich soul the virtues well did suit ;
In whom so mixed the elements all lay
That none to one could sovereignty impute,

As all did govern, yet all did obey :
He of a temper was so absolute
As that it seemed when Nature him began,
She meant to show all that might be in man.
    DRAYTON.—*Barons' Wars, Bk.* 3, *st.* 40.

A man so various that he seemed to be
Not one, but all mankind's epitome.
    DRYDEN.—*Absalom and Achitophel,*
        Pt. 1, 545.

Though equal to all things, for all things
    unfit,
Too nice for a statesman, too proud for a
    wit.   GOLDSMITH.—*Retaliation.*

None so happy as the versatile, provided
they have not their bread to make by it.
    C. READE.—*Cloister and the Hearth.*

You are not like Cerberus, three gentlemen at once, are you ?
    SHERIDAN.—*Rivals,* Act 4, 2.

A man who can do everything can do
nothing.   *Prov.*

VICE

Vice itself lost half its evil by losing all
its grossness.
BURKE.—*Reflections on French Revolution.*

If a man should unfortunately have any
vices, he ought at least to be content with
his own, and not adopt other people's.
    LORD CHESTERFIELD.—*Advice to his Son.*

The martyrs to vice far exceed the martyrs to virtue, both in endurance and in
number. So blinded are we by our passions that we suffer more to be damned
than to be saved.   C. C. COLTON.—*Lacon.*

Every vice hath a cloake and creepeth
in under the mask of a virtue.
    GABRIEL HARVEY.—*Commonplace Book*
        (c. 1600).

When our vices leave us, we flatter ourselves with the notion that it is we who
leave them.
    LA ROCHEFOUCAULD.—*Maxim* 192.

Saint Augustine ! well hast thou said,
    That of our vices we can frame
A ladder, if we will but tread
    Beneath our feet each deed of shame.
LONGFELLOW.—*Birds of Passage, Flight* 1.

Vice is a monster of so frightful mien,
As, to be hated, needs but to be seen ;
Yet, seen too oft, familiar with her face,
We first endure, then pity, then embrace.
    POPE.—*Essay on Man, Ep.* 2, 217.

The road to vices is not only smooth,
but steep.   SENECA.—*Ep.* 9.

No vice is complete by itself (*i.e.* one
vice leads to another). SENECA.—*Ep.* 95.

There is no vice so simple but assumes
Some mark of virtue on his outward parts.
    SHAKESPEARE.—*Merchant of Venice,*
        Act 3, 2.
Men touch them and change in a trice
The lilies and languors of virtue
For the raptures and roses of vice.
    SWINBURNE.—*Dolores.*

VICISSITUDE

Man was made for joy and woe,
And when this we rightly know,
Safely through the world we go.
    WM. BLAKE.—*Proverbs.*

Man !
Thou pendulum betwixt a smile and tear.
    BYRON.—*Childe Harold, c.* 4, 109.

O God, if you want a man to sense the pains
    of hell,
Before you pitch him in, just keep him in
    heaven a spell.
W. CARLETON.—*Gone with a Handsomer*
        Man.

" I find," said 'e, " things very much as
    'ow I've always found,
For mostly they goes up and down or else
    goes round and round."
P. R. CHALMERS.—*Roundabouts and*
        Swings.

O sodeyn wo ! that ever art successour
To worldly blisse !
    CHAUCER.—*Man of Law's Tale.*

Revolving in his altered soul
The various turns of chance below.
    DRYDEN.—*Alexander's Feast.*

Nations and empires flourish and decay,
By turns command and in their turns obey;
Time softens hardy people, time again
Hardens to war a soft unwarlike train.
    DRYDEN.—*Tr. Ovid, Metam., Bk.* 15.

For every worldes thing is vain,
And ever goth the whele about.
    GOWER.—*Conf. Amantis, Prol.* 560.

So goth the world ; now wo, now weal.
    GOWER.—*Ib., Bk.* 8.

The tumult and the shouting dies,
    The captains and the kings depart ;
Still stands thine ancient sacrifice,
    A humble and a contrite heart.
Lord God of hosts, be with us yet,
Lest we forget, lest we forget.
    KIPLING.—*Recessional.*

The years will pass, and hearts will range,
You conquer Time and Care and Change.
Time, Change, nor Care hath learned the
    art
To fleck your hair, to chill your heart,
To touch your tresses with the snow,
To mar your mirth of long ago.
    ANDREW LANG.—*Grass of Parnassus .*
        Dedication.

We've had some happy hours together,
But joy must often change its wing ;
And spring would be but gloomy weather,
If we had nothing else but spring.
　　　　MOORE.—*Juvenile Poems.*

Half my life is full of sorrow,
　Half of joy, still fresh and new ;
One of these lives is a fancy,
　But the other one is true.
　ADELAIDE A. PROCTER.—*Dream Life.*

The body politic, like the human body,
begins to die from the date of its birth,
and carries in itself the causes of its destruction.
ROUSSEAU.—*Contrat Social, Bk.* 3, *ch.* 11.

VICTORY

Hannibal knows how to gain a victory,
but not how to use it.
　BARCA.—(*To Hannibal : according to
　　　　　　　　Plutarch.*)

Woe to the conquering, not the conquered host.
　BYRON.—*Childe Harold, c.* 1, 25.

Ye are brothers ! ye are men !
And we conquer but to save.
　CAMPBELL.—*Battle of the Baltic,* 5.

For they can conquer who believe they
　can.　　DRYDEN.—*Æneid, Bk.* 5, 300.

Then conquer we must, for our cause it is
　just,
And this be our motto, " In God is our
　trust."
　　F. S. KEY.—*Star-spangled Banner.*

See the conquering hero comes
Sound the trumpets, beat the drums !
　N. LEE.—*Rival Queens* (*Stage Edition*),
　　　　　　　　　　Act 2, 1.

England, so strong to slay, be strong to
　spare ;
England, have courage even to forgive,
Give back the little nation leave to live.
　R. LE GALLIENNE.—*Christmas in War-
　　　　　　　　　　Time.*

It is more easy to conquer than to rule.
ROUSSEAU.—*Contrat Social, Bk.* 3, *ch.* 6.

" But what good came of it at last ? "
　Quoth little Peterkin.
" Why, that I cannot tell " said he,
" But 'twas a famous victory."
　　SOUTHEY.—*Battle of Blenheim.*

He is twice a conqueror who conquers
himself in the moment of victory.
　　　　PUBLILIUS SYRUS.

Most victories are like those of Cadmus
—enemies are born of them.
　　　　VOLTAIRE.—*Pensées.*

Friends strike at friends—the flying shall
　pursue—
And victory sickens, ignorant where to
　rest.
WORDSWORTH.—*Eccles. Sonnets, Pt.* 2, 36.

He came forth conquering, and to conquer.　　　*Revelation* vi, 2 (*R.V.*).

Another such victory and we are undone.
　*Pyrrhus after the " Pyrrhic victory " of
　　Asculum, where he lost* 3,500 *men.*

VILLAGE LIFE

The hawthorn bush, with seats beneath
　the shade,
For talking age and whispering lovers
　made ! GOLDSMITH.—*Deserted Village.*

In every village marked with little spire,
Embowered in trees, and hardly known to
fame. SHENSTONE.—*Schoolmistress.*

Below me there is the village, and looks
　how quiet and small !
And yet bubbles o'er like a city, with
　gossip, scandal, and spite.
　　　　TENNYSON.—*Maud.*

And villages embosomed soft in trees.
　　THOMSON.—*Seasons : Spring.*

A village is a hive of glass,
Where nothing unobserved can pass.
　*Quoted or invented by C. H. Spurgeon
　　　　　　　(" Salt-Cellars ").*

VILLAINY

O villain, villain, smiling, damnèd villain !
　SHAKESPEARE.—*Hamlet,* Act 1, 5.

My tables—meet it is I set it down,
That one may smile, and smile, and be a
　villain.　　SHAKESPEARE.—*Ib.*

A fellow by the hand of nature marked,
Quoted, and signed, to do a deed of shame.
　SHAKESPEARE.—*King John,* Act 4, 2.

A deed without a name.
　SHAKESPEARE.—*Macbeth,* Act 4, 1.

I would not be the villain that thou think'st
For the whole space that's in the tyrant's
　grasp,
And the rich East to boot.
　　SHAKESPEARE.—*Ib.,* Act 4, 3.

I like not fair terms and a villain's mind.
　SHAKESPEARE.—*Merchant of Venice,*
　　　　　　　　　　Act 1, 3.

The villainy you teach me I will execute ;
and it shall go hard but I will better the
instruction. SHAKESPEARE.—*Ib.,* Act 3, 1.

Fie, there is no such man ; it is impossible.
　SHAKESPEARE.—*Othello,* Act 4, 2.

I clothe my naked villainy
With old odd ends stolen out of holy writ,
And seem a saint, when most I play to
devil.
SHAKESPEARE.—*Richard III.*, Act 1, 3.

If one good deed in all my life I did,
I do repent it from my very soul.
SHAKESPEARE.—*Titus Andronicus*,
Act 5, 3.

A deadly snake once bit a Cappadocian,
but it died.   *Greek epigram.*

VILLAS

The woods we used to walk, my love,
Are woods no more,
But " villas " now with sounding names—
All name and door.
R. LE GALLIENNE.—*Love's Landmarks*, 1.

VINDICTIVENESS

During the late Irish rebellion there was
a banker to whom they had a peculiar dislike and on whom they vowed vengeance.
Accordingly they got possession of as many
of his banknotes as they could and made
a bonfire of them.
MISS EDGEWORTH.—*Essay on Irish
Bulls, ch. 7.*

I love you ;
I'll cut your throat for your own sake.
FLETCHER AND MASSINGER.—*Little
French Lawyer*, Act 4.

The dog, to gain his private ends,
Went mad and bit the man.
GOLDSMITH.—*Mad Dog.*

That no compunctious visitings of nature
Shake my fell purpose.
SHAKESPEARE.—*Macbeth*, Act 1, 5.

Each line shall stab, shall blast, like
daggers and a fire.
SWIFT.—*Ode to Sancroft.*

I would my love could kill thee ; I am
satiated
With seeing thee live, and fain would have
thee dead. SWINBURNE.—*Anactoria.*

The Animosities are mortal, but the
Humanities live for ever.
JOHN WILSON.—*Noctes*, 35.

My father hath chastised you with
whips, but I will chastise you with scorpions.   1 *Kings* xii, 11.

Is it necessary to add acid to the lemon ?
Hindu prov.

VIOLENCE

A kick that scarce would move a horse,
May kill a sound divine.
COWPER.—*Yearly Distress.*

An angel with a trumpet said,
" For ever more, for ever more,
The reign of violence is o'er ! "
LONGFELLOW.—*Occultation of Orion.*

For you'll ne'er mend your fortunes nor
help the just cause
By breaking of windows or breaking of
laws.
HANNAH MORE.—*Address to a Meeting*
(1817).

We do it wrong, being so majestical,
To offer it the show of violence.
SHAKESPEARE.—*Hamlet*, Act 1, 1.

What is violent is not lasting.
Latin prov.

VIRGIN MARY

Yet some, I ween,
Not unforgiven the suppliant knee might
bend,
As to a visible power, in which did blend
All that was mixed and reconciled in thee,
Of Mother's Love with Maiden Purity,
Of high with low, celestial with terrene.
WORDSWORTH.—*Eccles. Sonnets, Pt. 2,
25 (The Virgin).*

VIRTUE

Those are necessarily the greatest virtues
which are most useful to others (*e.g.* Justice, Courage, Moderation, Magnanimity,
Liberality, Gentleness, Reasonableness,
Wisdom). ARISTOTLE.—*Rhetor.*, 1, ch. 9.

Apply thy minde to be a vertuous man ;
Avoyd ill company, the spoyl of youth ;
To follow Vertue's lore doo what thou can,
Whereby great profit unto thee ensuth.
R. BARNFIELD.—*Affectionate Shepheard*
(1594).

Virtue must be the happiness, and vice
the misery, of every creature.
BISHOP BUTLER.—*Analogy of Religion,
Introduction.*

As beasts are hunted for their furs,
Men for their virtues fare the worse.
S. BUTLER.—*Miscellaneous Thoughts.*

" The good," said I, " are Heaven's
peculiar care,
" And such as honour Heaven shall
heavenly honour share."
DRYDEN.—*Tr. Ovid, Baucis and Philemon.*

Fooled thou must be, though wisest of
the wise,
Then be the fool of virtue, not of vice.
EMERSON.—*From the Persian
(Conduct of Life : Illusions).*

Men proclaim their own virtues, as shopkeepers expose their goods, in order to
profit by them.
FIELDING.—*Jonathan Wild (One of
his 15 Maxims).*

Be in general virtuous, and you will be
happy.
B. FRANKLIN.—*On Early Marriages.*

Hard was their lodging, homely was their
    food
For all their luxury was doing good.
        SIR S. GARTH.—*Claremont.*

Virtue alone is true nobility.
        W. GIFFORD.—*Juvenal.*

The greatest offence against virtue is to
speak ill of it.   HAZLITT.—*On Cant.*

Only a sweet and virtuous soul,
Like seasoned timber, never gives,
But though the whole world turn to coal
Then chiefly lives.
        HERBERT.—*Virtue.*

But Virtue dwells on high ; . . .
And at the first to that sublime abode
Long, steep, the ascent, and rough the
    rugged road.
      HESIOD.—*Works and Days*, 1, 287
               (*Elton tr.*).

Virtue is to flee from vice, and the first
wisdom is to be without folly.
      HORACE.—*Epist.*, Bk. 1, 41.

Often what we take for virtues are only
vices resembling them, and disguised to
us by self-love.
    LA ROCHEFOUCAULD.—*Maxim* 549.

Virtue would not go so far if vanity did
not keep her company.
    LA ROCHEFOUCAULD.—*Maxim* 200.

Virtue may be assailed, but never hurt,
Surprised by unjust force, but not enthralled.   MILTON.—*Comus*, 589.

  Love Virtue ; she alone is free,
  She can teach ye how to climb
  Higher than the sphery chime ;
  Or, if Virtue feeble were,
  Heaven itself would stoop to her.
        MILTON.—*Ib.*, 1019.

    Most men admire
Virtue, who follow not her lore.
MILTON.—*Paradise Regained*, Bk. 1, 482.

Beauty, strength, youth, are flowers but
  fading seen ;
Duty, faith, love, are roots, and ever green.
        G. PEELE.—*Polyhymnia.*

Virtue does not spring from riches ; but
riches and all other human blessings, both
private and public, from virtue.
    PLATO.—*Apol. of Socrates*, 17 (*Cary tr.*).

Virtue, then, as it seems, is a kind of
health, beauty, and good habit of the soul ;
and vice its disease, deformity, and infirmity.
    PLATO.—*Republic*, Bk. 2, 19 (*Davis tr.*).

Never at any time is that man neglected
by the gods, who inclines earnestly to
endeavour to become just, and practises
virtue as far as it is possible for man to
resemble God.   PLATO.—*Ib.*, Bk. 10, 12.

Know then this truth (enough for man to
  know),
" Virtue alone is happiness below."
    POPE.—*Essay on Man, Ep.* 4, 309.

Who ne'er knew joy but friendship might
  decide,
Or gave his father grief, but when he died.
      POPE.—*On S. Harcourt.*

And conscious virtue, still its own reward.   POPE.—*Statius*, Bk. 1, 758.

I know and I feel that to do good is the
truest happiness that the human heart can
taste.
    ROUSSEAU.—*Rêveries d'un Promeneur
               solitaire,* 6.

So clear in his great office, that his virtues
Will plead like angels, trumpet-tongued,
  against
The deep damnation of his taking off.
    SHAKESPEARE.—*Macbeth*, Act 1, 7.

He hath a daily beauty in his life.
    SHAKESPEARE.—*Othello*, Act 5, 1.

Only the actions of the just
Smell sweet and blossom in the dust.
    JAS. SHIRLEY.—*Ajax and Ulysses.*

Virtue concealed within our breast
Is inactivity at best.
    SWIFT.—*Horace*, Bk. 4, Ode 9.

A virtuous gentlewoman, deeply wronged.
    TENNYSON.—*Merlin and Vivien.*

But what is virtue but repose of mind ?
    THOMSON.—*Castle of Indolence,*
                  c. 1, 16.

Be virtuous and you will be eccentric.
    MARK TWAIN.—*Mental Photographs.*

I love virtue very much, but sensible
people know that those who talk about it
too much never have enough.
      VOLTAIRE.—*Le Dépositaire.*

Men and women are very frail ; beware
of reckoning upon virtue.
      VOLTAIRE.—*La Pucelle.*

  Yet though thou fade,
From thy dead leaves let fragrance rise,
  And teach the maid
That Goodness Time's rude hand defies,
That Virtue lives when Beauty dies.
  H. K. WHITE.—*Added to Waller's " Go,
                  lovely Rose."*

I hope you have not been leading a
double life, pretending to be wicked and
being really good all the time. That
would be hypocrisy.
    OSCAR WILDE.—*Importance of being
                Earnest.*

Men who can hear the decalogue, and feel
No self-reproach.
    WORDSWORTH.—*Old Cumberland Beggar.*

Virtue is the roughest way,
But proves at night a bed of down.
   Sir H. Wotton.—*On the Imprisonment
     of the Earl of Essex.*

Sinking in virtue as you rise in fame.
   Young.—*Night Thoughts,* 5.

Virtue alone outbuilds the pyramids;
Her monuments shall last, when Egypt's
  fall.   Young.—*Ib.,* 6.

Virtue now is in herbs and stones and
words only.   *Prov. (Geo. Herbert).*

There is no going to heaven in a sedan.
           Prov.

Purchase the next world with this; you
will win both.   *Arabic prov.*

It's gude to be gude in your time; ye
kenna how long it may last. *Scottish prov.*

VISIONS AND VISIONARIES

Still bent to make some port he knows not
  where,
Still standing for some false impossible
  shore. M. Arnold.—*Summer Night.*

Father, O father! what do we here,
In this land of unbelief and fear ?
The land of dreams is better far,
Above the light of the morning star.
   Wm. Blake.—*The Land of Dreams.*

What is now proved was once only
imagined. Wm. Blake.—*Proverbs of Hell.*

We are led to believe a lie
When we see *with* not *through* the eye.
         Wm. Blake.—*Ib.*

When I build castles in the air,
Void of sorrow, void of fear.
   Burton.—*Anat. of Melan., Author's
              Abstract.*

And what's impossible can't be,
And never, never comes to pass.
   G. Colman.—*Maid of the Moor.*

Sometimes he thinks that Heaven the
  vision sent,
And ordered all the pageants as they went;
Sometimes, that only 'twas wild Fancy's
  play,
The loose and scattered relics of the day.
   Cowley.—*Davideis, Bk.* 2, 789.

Dream after dream ensues,
And still they dream that they shall still
  succeed,
And still are disappointed.
       Cowper.—*The Garden.*

From reveries so airy, from the toil
Of dropping buckets into empty wells,
And growing old in drawing nothing up.
           Cowper.—*Ib.*

I strongly wish for what I faintly hope;
Like the day-dreams of melancholy men,
I think and think on things impossible,
Yet love to wander in that golden maze.
   Dryden.—*Rival Ladies,* Act 3, 1.

I seche [seek] that I may nought finde;
I haste and ever am behinde.
   Gower.—*Confessio Amantis, Bk.* 4, 289.

Do I sleep ? Do I dream ?
Do I wander and doubt ?
Are things what they seem ?
Or is visions about ?
   Bret Harte.—*Further Language.*

Was it a vision or a waking dream ?
Fled is that music :—Do I wake or sleep ?
   Keats.—*Ode to a Nightingale.*

Dreamer of dreams, born out of my due
  time,
Why should I strive to set the crooked
  straight ?
     W. Morris.—*Earthly Paradise.*

We are near awakening when we dream
that we dream.
    Novalis.—*(As tr. by Carlyle.)*

Suppose the chariot of the Sun were given
you, what would you do ?
   Ovid.—*Metam., Bk.* 2 (*Apollo's question
              to Phaeton*).

Love to his soul gave eyes; he knew things
  are not as they seem.
The dream is his real life: the world
  around him is the dream.
   F. T. Palgrave.—*Dream of Maxim
               Wledig.*

All that we see or seem
Is but a dream within a dream.
       E. A. Poe.—*A Dream.*

To see clearly is poetry, prophecy, and
religion,—all in one.
  Ruskin.—*Modern Painters,* 3, Pt. 4, c. 16.

Dark is the shadow of invisible things
On us who look not up, whose vision fails.
   Geo. Russell.—*Shadows and Lights.*

Youth is a fine carver and gilder.
   Sir W. Scott.—*Diary, Sept.,* 1826.

Is this a dagger which I see before me,
The handle towards my hand ? Come, let
  me clutch thee—
I have thee not and yet I see thee still.
   Shakespeare.—*Macbeth,* Act 2, 1.

A dagger of the mind, a false creation,
Proceeding from the heat-oppressèd brain.
         Shakespeare.—*Ib.*

He had been eight years upon a project
for extracting sunbeams out of cucumbers,
which were to be put into phials her-
metically sealed, and let out to warm the
air in raw inclement summers.
         Swift.—*Laputa.*

I seemed to move among a world of ghosts,
And feel myself the shadow of a dream.
TENNYSON.—*Princess, c.* 1, 17.

While poets dream by lamplight of the
morn,—
Dream that they feel what they have never
known.
F. TENNYSON.—*Isles of Greece, Alcæus,*
3, 78.

Ten thousand great ideas filled his mind;
But with the clouds they fled, and left no
trace behind.
THOMSON.—*Castle of Indolence, c.* 1, *st.* 59.

Do me eyes deceive me earsight? Is
it some dreams?
ARTEMUS WARD.—*Moses, the Sassy.*

Confiding, though confounded; hoping
on,
Untaught by trial, unconvinced by proof,
And ever looking for the never seen.
YOUNG.—*Night Thoughts,* 8.

Your old men shall dream dreams, your
young men shall see visions. *Joel* ii, 28.

Leave not the meat to gnaw the bones,
Nor break your teeth on worthless stones.
Old Saying.

VISITS
Its visits
Like those of angels, short and far between.
R. BLAIR.—*The Grave* (1743).

What though my wingèd hours of bliss
have been,
Like angel-visits, few and far between.
CAMPBELL.—*Pleasures of Hope, Pt.* 2
(1799).

A visit should never exceed three days—
the rest day, the drest day, and the
prest day.
MISS FERRIER.—*As quoted by Scott*
(*see Lockhart's Life, ch.* 64, *note*).

Visits are for the most part neither more
nor less than inventions for discharging
upon our neighbour somewhat of our own
unendurable weight. NICOLE.—*Thoughts.*

The real impediment to making visits is
that derangeable health which belongs to
old age. ... This made the wise man say
that a man should give over arguing at
thirty, riding at sixty, and visiting at
seventy.
SYDNEY SMITH.—*Letter, Dec.* 3, 1843.

VIVACITY
Of all fools the liveliest are the most intolerable.   DUCLOS.—*Considerations on
the Manners of the Age, c.* 13.

It is with narrow-souled people as with
narrow-necked bottles, the less they have
in them the more noise they make in pouring it out.
POPE.—*Thoughts on Various Subjects.*

VOCATION
It is the first of all problems for a man
to find out what kind of work he is to do
in this universe.
CARLYLE.—*Address at Edinburgh,*
1866.

Whether with reason, or with instinct
blest,
Know, all enjoy that power which suits
them best;
To bliss alike by that direction tend,
And find the means proportioned to their
end.
POPE.—*Essay on Man, Ep.* 2, 79.

Why, Hal, 'tis my vocation, Hal; 'tis
no sin for a man to labour in his vocation.
SHAKESPEARE.—*Henry IV., Pt.* 1, Act 1, 2.

VOICE
The devil hath not, in all his quiver's
choice,
An arrow for the heart like a sweet voice.
BYRON.—*Don Juan, c.* 15, 5.

Man was never meant to sing;
And all his mimic organs e'er expressed
Was but an imitative howl at best.
J. LANGHORNE.—*Country Justice, Pt.* 2,
223.

How sweetly sounds the voice of a good
woman!
It is so seldom heard that, when it speaks,
It ravishes all senses.
MASSINGER.—*The Old Law,* Act 4, 2.

Her voice was like the voice the stars
Had when they sang together.
ROSSETTI.—*The Blessed Damozel.*

Her voice was ever soft,
Gentle, and low; an excellent thing in
woman.
SHAKESPEARE.—*Lear,* Act 5, 3.

I will roar you as gently as any sucking
dove: I will roar you as 'twere any
nightingale.
SHAKESPEARE.—*Midsummer Night's
Dream,* Act 1, 2.

How silver-sweet sound lovers' tongues by
night,
Like softest music to attending ears.
SHAKESPEARE.—*Romeo and Juliet,*
Act 2, 2.

VOLTAIRE
Thou art so witty, profligate, and thin,
Thou seem'st a Milton with his Death and
Sin.   YOUNG.—*Epigram on Voltaire.*

VOTES
The freeman, casting with unpurchased
hand
The vote that shakes the turrets of the land.
O. W. HOLMES.—*Metrical Essay.*

The English people imagine that they are free ; they greatly deceive themselves. It is only during the election of members of parliament that they are so. As soon as these are elected the people are slaves ; they are nothing. In the brief moments of their liberty the use they make of it is such that they thoroughly deserve to lose it.   ROUSSEAU.—*Contrat Social*, Bk. 3, ch. 15.

The moment a people gives itself a representative system, it is no longer free ; it no longer exists.   ROUSSEAU.—*Ib.*

Is a vote a coat ? Will franchise feed you ?   SWINBURNE.—*Word from the Psalmist.*

The votes of veering crowds are not The things that are more excellent. SIR W. WATSON.—*Things that are more Excellent.*

VULGARITY

The vulgar of England are, without exception, the most barbarous and unknowing of any in Europe. GOLDSMITH.—*Bee, 7.*

I believe that vulgarity is generally as much opposed to wisdom as it is to good taste. SIR A. HELPS.—*Friends in Council, Bk. 2, ch. 5.*

Vulgarity is only in concealment of truth or affectation. RUSKIN.—*Modern Painters, 2, Pt. 2, c. 6.*

The higher a man stands, the more the word " vulgar " becomes unintelligible to him.   RUSKIN.—*Ib., 3, Pt. 4, c. 7.*

Highly fed and lowly taught. SHAKESPEARE.—*All's Well*, Act 2, 2.

To endeavour to work upon the vulgar with fine sense is like attempting to hew blocks with a razor. SWIFT.—*Thoughts on Various Subjects.*

W

WAGERS

Fools for arguments use wagers. BUTLER.—*Hudibras*, Pt. 2, c. 1.

For most men (till by losing rendered sager) Will back their own opinions with a wager. BYRON.—*Beppo*, st. 27.

Ducks lay eggs, geese lay wagers. *Prov.*

Lay no wagers. " *The Twelve Good Rules* " (No. 12) (ascribed to Charles I. See Goldsmith's " *Deserted Village*," l. 232).

WAGES

The labourer is worthy of his hire. *St. Luke* x, 7.

When wages are paid, work is over. *Prov. (from the Spanish ?).*

WAISTS

Her ringlets are in taste : What an arm ! and what a waist For an arm ! F. LOCKER-LAMPSON.—*London Lyrics : My Grandmother.*

A narrow compass, and yet there Dwelt all that's good, and all that's fair : Give me but what this riband bound, Take all the rest the sun goes round. WALLER.—*On a Girdle.*

WALKING

Never walk fast in the streets, which is a mark of vulgarity, ill befitting the character of a gentleman or a man of fashion, though it may be tolerable in a tradesman. LORD CHESTERFIELD.—*Advice to his Son.*

I nauseate walking ; 'tis a country diversion ; I loathe the country. CONGREVE.—*Way of the World*, Act 4, 1.

I am for the Peripatetics against all other philosophers. SIR A. HELPS.—*Friends in Council, Bk. 1, ch. 3 (Milverton).*

Who fastest walks, but walks astray, Is only furthest from his way. PRIOR.—*Alma, c. 3.*

WANDERERS

Here awa, there awa, wandering Willie, Here awa, there awa, haud awa hame ; Come to my bosom, my ain only dearie, Tell me thou bring'st me my Willie the same.   BURNS.—*Wandering Willie, Founded on old Scottish Song.*

He had the passion and the power to roam : The desert, forest, cavern, breaker's foam Were unto him companionship ; they spake A mutual language. BYRON.—*Childe Harold, c.* 3, 13.

I asked him where he lived—a stare Was all I got in answer, As on he trudged ; I rightly judged The stare said, " Where I can, sir." C. S. CALVERLEY.—*Wanderers.*

All pastors are alike To wandering sheep, resolved to follow none.   COWPER.—*The Task*, 890.

O canny sons of Jacob, to fret and toiling tied, We grudge you not the birthright for which your father lied ! We own the right of roaming, and the world is wide. BERTHA B. RUNKLE.—*Song of the Sons of Esau.*

Wealth I ask not, hope nor love,
Nor a friend to know me ;
All I ask, the heaven above,
And the road below me.
R. L. STEVENSON.—*Vagabond.*

Kind Nature's charities his steps attend ;
In every babbling brook he finds a friend :
While chastening thoughts of sweetest use,
bestowed
By wisdom, moralise his pensive road.
WORDSWORTH.—*Sketches during
Pedestrian Tour among the Alps.*

WANTS

Our real wants in a small compass lie.
CHURCHILL.—*Independence.*

Man wants but little here below,
Nor wants that little long.
GOLDSMITH.—*Hermit.*

How can you tell what you want in the
future, when you do not know what you
want in the present ?
LA ROCHEFOUCAULD.—*Maxim* 517.

Man wants but little ; nor that little long
YOUNG.—*Night Thoughts, 4*

WAR

My voice is still for war.
ADDISON.—*Cato, Act 2, 1.*

What rights the brave ?
The sword !
What frees the slave ?
The sword !
What cleaves in twain
The despot's chain,
And makes his gyves and dungeons vain ?
The sword !
M. J. BARRY.—*The Sword.*

Our wearisome pedantic art of war,
By which we prove retreat may be success,
Delay best speed, half-loss, at times,
whole gain.   BROWNING.—*Luria.*

A commonplace against war ; the easiest
of all topics.
BURKE.—*Observations on " Present
State of the Nation."*

It hath been said that an unjust peace
is to be preferred before a just war.
S. BUTLER.—*" Speeches in the Rump
Parliament."* (Founded on
Cicero, Epist. ad. Att. 7, 14.)

Ah, monarchs ! could ye taste the mirth
ye mar,
Not in toils of Glory would ye fret ;
The hoarse dull drum would sleep, and man
be happy yet.
BYRON.—*Childe Harold, c. 1, st. 47.*

War, war is still the cry, " War to the
knife ! "   BYRON.—*Ib., 86.*

The unreturning brave.
BYRON.—*Ib., c. 3, st. 27.*

Battle's magnificently stern array.
BYRON.—*Ib., st. 28.*

Rider and horse—friend, foe—in one red
burial blent.   BYRON.—*Ib.*

War's a brain-spattering, windpipe-slitting
art,
Unless her cause by right be sanctified.
BYRON.—*Don Juan, c. 9, 4.*

The combat deepens. On, ye brave,
Who rush to glory or the grave !
Wave, Munich, all thy banners wave,
And charge with all thy chivalry.
CAMPBELL.—*Hohenlinden.*

What millions died that Cæsar might be
great !
CAMPBELL.—*Pleasures of Hope.*

Wars are to be undertaken in order that
it may be possible to live in peace without
molestation.
CICERO.—*De Officiis, Bk. 1, 11.*

Any peace is better than civil war.
CICERO.—*Philippic, 2, 15.*

In the clamour of arms the laws are
dumb.   CICERO.—*Pro Milone.*

War in fact is becoming contemptible,
and ought to be put down by the great
nations of Europe, just as we put down a
vulgar mob.   MORTIMER COLLINS.—
Thoughts in my Garden, 2, 243.

War is a game in which princes seldom
win, the people never.
C. C. COLTON.—*Lacon.*

Nothing is to be despised in war.
CORNELIUS NEPOS.—*Thrasybulus.*

But war's a game, which, were their sub-
jects wise,
Kings would not play at.
COWPER.—*Winter Morning's Walk.*

From fear in every guise,
From sloth, from love of pelf,
By war's great sacrifice
The world redeems itself.
J. DAVIDSON.—*War Song.*

'Tis startin' a polis foorce to prevint
war . . . How'll they be ar-rmed ? What
a foolish question. They'll be ar-rmed
with love, if coorse. Who'll pay thim ?
That's a financyal detail that can be ar-
ranged later on. What'll happen if wan
iv th' rough-necks reaches f'r a gun ?
Don't bother me with thrifles.
MR. DOOLEY.—*On Making a Will, etc.
Speech attrib. to Mr. Bryan* (1920).

War is the trade of Kings.
DRYDEN.—*King Arthur.*

There never was a good war or a bad
peace.   B. FRANKLIN.

Force and fraud are in war the two cardinal virtues.
> HOBBES.—*Leviathan, ch.* 13.

And dearer to their hearts than thoughts
of home,
Or wished return, became the battle-field.
> HOMER.—*Iliad, Bk.* 10, 199 (*Lord
Derby tr.*).

The closeness of their intercourse [the
intercourse of nations] will assuredly render
war as absurd and impossible by-and-by,
as it would be for Manchester to fight with
Birmingham, or Holborn Hill with the
Strand.
> LEIGH HUNT.—*Pref. to Poems* (1849).

Art, thou hast many infamies,
But not an infamy like this.
O snap the fife and still the drum
And show the monster as she is.
> R. LE GALLIENNE.—*The Illusion of War.*

War is just, to those to whom war is
necessary.   LIVY.—*Hist., Bk.* 9.

Ez fer war, I call it murder—
  There you hev it plain an' flat ;
I don't want to go no furder
  Than my Testyment fer that ;
God hez sed so plump an' fairly,
  It's ez long ez it is broad,
An' you've gut to git up airly
  Ef you want to take in God.
> J. R. LOWELL.—*Biglow Papers,* 1st *Ser.,* 1.

Not but wut abstract war is horrid,
  I sign to thet with all my heart,—
But civilysation *doos* git forrid
  Sometimes, upon a powder-cart.
> J. R. LOWELL.—*Ib.,* 7.

My sentence is for open war : of wiles
More unexpert I boast not.
> MILTON.—*Paradise Lost, Bk.* 2, 51.

For what can war but endless war still
breed ?   MILTON.—*Sonnet.*

In warlike affairs the science of a general
looks ahead with fine foresight, and ac-
knowledges no service to the prophet's
art, but claims to rule it as knowing better
what does and will take place in war.
And indeed the law enjoins that the prophet shall not rule over the general, but
the general over the prophet.
> PLATO.—*Laches,* 30.

When Archidamus saw a dart shot out
of an engine brought from Sicily, he exclaimed, " Good God ! true valour is gone
for ever."
> PLUTARCH.—*Laconic Apophthegms.*

It is the province of kings to bring wars
about ; it is the province of God to end
them.
> CARDINAL POLE.—*To Henry VIII.*

Cursed is the man, and void of law and
  right,
Unworthy property, unworthy light,
Unfit for public rule, or private care ;
That wretch, that monster, who delights
  in war. POPE.—*Iliad, Bk.* 9, 87.

Silence is the soul of war.
> PRIOR.—*Ode.*

The right of war—*qui potest capere
capiat,* " let him take who can take."
> RABELAIS.—*Pantagruel.*

War, the needy bankrupt's last resort.
> N. ROWE.—*Pharsalia, Bk.* 1, 343.

Worse than war is the fear of war.
> SENECA.—*Thyestes.*

It was great pity, so it was,
That villainous saltpetre should be digged
Out of the bowels of the harmless earth,
Which many a good tall fellow had de-
  stroyed
So cowardly ; and but for these vile guns,
He would himself have been a soldier.
> SHAKESPEARE.—*Henry IV., Pt.* 1, Act 1, 2.

Cry " Havoc ! " and let slip the dogs of
  war.
> SHAKESPEARE.—*Julius Cæsar,* Act 3, 1.

Horribly stuffed with epithets of war.
> SHAKESPEARE.—*Othello,* Act 1, 1.

The tented field.
> SHAKESPEARE.—*Ib.,* Act 1, 3.

Farewell the plumed troops and the big
  wars,
That make ambition virtue ! O, farewell !
Farewell the neighing steed, and the shrill
  trump,
The spirit-stirring drum, the ear-piercing
  fife,
The royal banner and all quality,
Pride, pomp, and circumstance of glorious
  war ! SHAKESPEARE.—*Ib.,* Act 3, 3.

There was only one virtue, pugnacity ;
only one vice, pacifism. That is an essential condition of war.
> G. B. SHAW.—*Heartbreak House: Pref.,
Madness in Court.*

Blood will have blood, revenge beget revenge,
Evil must come of evil.
> SHELLEY.—*Madoc, Sec.* 7.

War is the statesman's game, the priest's
  delight,
The lawyer's jest, the hired assassin's
  trade. SHELLEY.—*Queen Mab, c.* 4.

War should be long in preparing in order
that you may conquer more quickly.
> PUBLILIUS SYRUS.

Wild War, who breaks the converse of
the wise.
TENNYSON.—*Third of February*, 1852.

And ever since historian writ,
And ever since a bard could sing,
Doth each exalt with all his wit
The noble art of murdering.
THACKERAY.—*Chronicle of the Drum.*

Your interest in the war should never cease;
But we have felt enough to wish the
peace.
VIRGIL.—*Æneid, Bk.* 11 (*Dryden tr.*).

We do not with God's name make wanton
play;
We are not on such easy terms with
Heaven;
But in Earth's hearing we can verily say,
"Our hands are pure; for peace, for
peace we have striven,"
And not by Earth shall he be soon for-
given
Who lit the fire accurst that flames to-day.
SIR W. WATSON.—*To the Troubler of the
World, Aug.* 5, 1914.

The whole art of war consists in getting
at what is on the other side of the hill.
DUKE OF WELLINGTON.—*Saying.*

As long as war is regarded as wicked it
will always have its fascinations. When
it is looked upon as vulgar, it will cease to
be popular.   OSCAR WILDE.—*Intentions.*

But thy most dreaded instrument,
In working out a pure intent,
Is Man—arrayed for mutual slaughter—
Yea, Carnage is thy daughter.
WORDSWORTH.—*Poems to National
Independence, Pt.* 2, *No.* 46.

But Man is thy most awful instrument
In working out a pure intent;
Thou cloth'st the wicked in their dazzling
mail,
And for thy righteous purpose they pre-
vail.
WORDSWORTH.—(*Later version sub-
stituted for the foregoing lines*).

One to destroy, is murder by the law;
And gibbets keep the lifted hand in awe;
To murder thousands, takes a specious
name,
War's glorious art, and gives immortal
fame.
YOUNG.—*Love of Fame, Sat.* 7.

It is magnificent, but it is not war.
*Attrib. to Marshal Canrobert, in reference
to the Charge of the Light Brigade at
Balaclava.*

If there were no fools there would be
no war.   *Prov.*
Stir not the fire with a sword.
Greek prov.

WARNING

I know the warning song is sung in vain,
That few will hear and fewer heed the
strain.   COWPER.—*Expostulation,* 724.

But he shall meet a hideous doom,
Prepared for him by—I know whom.
SIR W. S. GILBERT.—*Patience.*

Troy fell because Cassandra was not
believed.   PHÆDRUS.—*Fables.*

Hear it not, Duncan; for it is a knell
That summons thee to heaven or to hell!
SHAKESPEARE.—*Macbeth,* Act 2, 1.

WARWICKSHIRE

That shire which we the heart of England well may call.
M. DRAYTON.—*Polyolbion, Song* 13, *l.* 3.

WASTE

Waste is not grandeur.
WM. MASON.—*English Garden.*

If you throw crumbs on the fire you are
feeding the devil.   *Old prov.*

Haste makes waste, waste want, want
strife,
Betwixt the good man and his wife.
Prov. (*Ray*).

WATER

"You disliked the killibeate taste, perhaps?" "I don't know much about that
'ere," said Sam. "I thought they'd a
wery strong flavour o' warm flat-irons."
"That *is* the killibeate, Mr. Weller,"
observed Mr. John Smauker, contemp-
tuously.   DICKENS.—*Pickwick, ch.* 37.

I'm very fond of water:
It ever must delight
Each mother's son and daughter,—
When qualified aright.
LORD NEAVES.—*I'm very fond of Water*
(*June*, 1861).

Pure water is the best of gifts that man to
man can bring,
But who am I that I should have the best
of anything?
Let princes revel at the pump, let peers
with ponds make free,
Whisky, or wine, or even *beer* is good
enough for me.
ANON.—*See the "Spectator," July* 31,
1920, *Attrib. to Hon. G. W. E. Russell, also
to Lord Neaves, but not found in his "Songs
and Verses." Two versions were given in
"Notes and Queries," Oct.* 23, 1897.

WEAKNESSES

Very little indulgence for the most amiable weaknesses of human nature.
GIBBON.—*Decline and Fall, ch.* 14.

Some of our weaknesses are born in us ; others are the result of education. It is a question which of the two gives us most trouble.   GOETHE.

All wickedness is weakness.
MILTON.—*Samson Agonistes*, 834.

WEALTH

Fortunes ... come tumbling into some men's laps.   BACON.—*Adv. of Learning.*

When a man is rich he is always worth his price (*i.e.* he will always be worth consideration).   BOILEAU.—*Sat.* 5, 131.

If riches increase, let thy mind hold pace with them ; and think it not enough to be Liberal, but Munificent.
SIR T. BROWNE.—*Christian Morals.*

With loves and doves, at all events
With money in the Three per Cents.
BROWNING.—*Dis aliter visum.*

If we command our wealth, we shall be rich and free ; if our wealth commands us, we are poor indeed.
BURKE.—*Letters on a Regicide Peace.*

It is the interest of the commercial world that wealth should be found everywhere.
BURKE.—*Letter to Samuel Span.*

It is not the fact that a man has riches which keeps him from the kingdom of heaven, but the fact that riches have him.
DR. CAIRD.

Money, which is of very uncertain value and sometimes has no value at all and even less.
CARLYLE.—*Frederick the Great, Bk.* 4, 3.

Midas-eared Mammonism, double-barrelled Dilettantism, and their thousand adjuncts and corollaries, are *not* the Law by which God Almighty has appointed this His universe to go.
CARLYLE.—*Past and Present, ch.* 6.

Surplus wealth is a sacred trust which its possessor is bound to administer in his lifetime for the good of the community.
A. CARNEGIE.—*Gospel of Wealth* (1886).

Men seyn that the rich man hath seld [seldom] good counsel but if he have it of himself.
CHAUCER.—*Tale of Melibeus, sec.* 20.

Nothing is so characteristic of a narrow and small mind as to love riches.
CICERO.—*De Officiis, Bk.* 1.

Increase of power begets increase of wealth.   COWPER.—*Winter Evening*, 580.

Wealth, howsoever got, in England makes
Lords of mechanics, gentlemen of rakes ;
Antiquity and birth are needless here ;
'Tis impudence and money makes a peer.
DEFOE.—*True-born Englishman*, 300.

Endless follies follow endless wealth.
DEKKER.—*Old Fortunatus*, Act 2, 2.

The love of wealth seems to grow chiefly out of the root of the love of the Beautiful. The desire of gold is not for gold. . . It is the means of freedom, and benefit.
EMERSON.—*Domestic Life.*

There is no country in which so absolute a homage is paid to wealth. In America there is a touch of shame when a man exhibits the evidences of large property, as if, after all, it needed apology. But the Englishman has pure pride in his wealth.
EMERSON.—*English Traits*, 10 : *Wealth.*

I am not the least versed in the Chrematistic art (*i.e.* the art of acquiring wealth). FIELDING.—*Amelia, Bk.* 9, *ch.* 5.

For he that needs five thousand pound to live,
Is full as poor as he that needs but five.
HERBERT.—*Church Porch.*

Wealth is the conjuror's devil ;
Whom when he thinks he hath, the devil hath him.   HERBERT.—*Ib.*

Plutus, as sponsor, stood at her font,
And Midas rocked the cradle.
HOOD.—*Miss Kilmansegg.*

Our Lord commonly giveth riches to such gross asses to whom he affordeth nothing else that is good.   LUTHER.—*Colloquies.*

Wealth, and plenty, in a land where justice reigns not, is no argument of a flourishing state, but of a nearness rather to ruin and commotion. MILTON.—*Eikonoclastes.*

They whom I favour thrive in wealth amain,
While virtue, valour, wisdom, sit in want.
MILTON.—*Paradise Regained, Bk.* 2, 430.

If at great things thou would'st arrive.
Get riches first.
MILTON.—*Paradise Regained, Bk.* 4, 426.

I am rich beyond the dreams of avarice.
EDWD. MOORE.—*Gamester.*

And Wealth, more bright with Virtue joined,
Brings golden Opportunity,
The sparkling star, the sunbeam of mankind.
PINDAR.—*Olympian Odes*, 2, 96
(*Moore tr.*).

The language which calls the rich happy is itself unhappy, being indeed the senseless language of women and children, and it makes those who accept the precept senseless in like manner.
PLATO.—*Epistle* 8.

To heirs unknown descends the unguarded store,
Or wanders, heaven-directed, to the poor.
POPE.—*Moral Essays, Ep.* 2, 149.

Who sees pale Mammon pine amidst his store,
Sees but a backward steward for the poor ;
This year a reservoir, to keep and spare ;
The next, a fountain, spouting through his heir.   POPE.—*Ep.* 3, 171.

But Satan now is wiser than of yore,
And tempts by making rich, not making poor.   POPE.—*Ib.*, 331.

Joy is more the friend of half-pence than of sovereigns.
ROUSSEAU.—*Rêveries d'un Promeneur solitaire*, 9.

What is really desired, under the name of riches, is essentially power over men.
RUSKIN.—*Unto this Last, Essay* 2.

A great fortune is a great bondage.
SENECA.—*De Consol.*, 26.

He most enjoys riches who least needs riches.   SENECA.—*Ep.* 14.

Well, whiles I am a beggar, I will rail,
And say,—There is no sin, but to be rich ;
And, being rich, my virtue then shall be,
To say,—There is no vice, but beggary.
SHAKESPEARE.—*King John*, Act 2, 2.

The man is mechanically turned, and made for getting. . . It was very prettily said that we may learn the little value of fortune by the persons on whom Heaven is pleased to bestow it.
STEELE.—*Tatler, No.* 203.

They who know all the wealth they have are poor ;
He's only rich that cannot tell his store.
SIR J. SUCKLING.—*Against Fruition*, 5.

There is a limit to enjoyment, though the sources of wealth be boundless
M. F. TUPPER.—*Of Compensation.*

Riches are akin
To fear, to change, to cowardice and death.
WORDSWORTH.—*Poems to National Independence, Pt.* 1, 20.

Make to yourselves friends by means of the mammon of unrighteousness.
St. Luke xvi, 9 (*R.V.*).

Seek to attain by the means which God hath given thee the future abode of bliss.
Koran, ch. 29.

WEATHER

Melancholy . . . often conveys herself to us in an easterly wind.
ADDISON.—*Spectator, vol.* 5, *No.* 387.

A frosty winter, a dusty March, a rain about April,
Another about the Lammas time, when the corn begins to fill,
Is worth a pleuch o' gowd, and a' her pins theretill.
GEO. BUCHANAN.—*On being asked what would buy a Plough of Gold.*

I like the weather when it's not too rainy,
That is, I like two months of every year.
BYRON.—*Beppo, st.* 48.

And finds a changing clime a happy source
Of wise reflection and well-timed discourse.
COWPER.—*Conversation*, 387.

Liberal in all things else, yet Nature here
With stern severity deals out the year.
COWPER.—*Table Talk.*

Snowy, Flowy, Blowy,
Showery, Flowery, Bowery,
Hoppy, Croppy, Droppy,
Breezy, Sneezy, Freezy.
GEO. ELLIS.—*The Twelve Months.*

'Tis the hard grey weather
Breeds hard English men.
C. KINGSLEY.—*Ode to N.E. Wind.*

But methought it lessened my esteem of a king, that he should not be able to command the rain.
PEPYS.—*Diary, July* 19, 1662.

'Tis a naughty night to swim in.
SHAKESPEARE.—*Lear*, Act 3, 4.

Mine enemy's dog,
Though he had bit me, should have stood that night
Against my fire.
SHAKESPEARE.—*Ib.*, Act 4, 7.

The beauty of our English weather is that when it is bad we may hope it will soon change. Its fault is that when it is good we may be pretty sure it will soon alter.   C. H. SPURGEON.—"*Salt-Cellars.*"

We have no climate, but only weather.
C. H. SPURGEON.—*Ib.*

A coming shower your shooting corns presage.   SWIFT.—*City Shower.*

Commend me to the bold, bricht, blue, black, boisterous, and blusterin' beauty o' the British heavens !
JOHN WILSON.—*Noctes* 25.

First it rained, and then it snew,
Then it friz, and then it thew,
And then it friz again.   ANON.

If the oak's before the ash,
Then you'll only get a splash ;
If the ash is before the oak,
Then you may expect a soak.
Old Saying.

When the sand doth feed the clay [*i.e.* in a
wet summer],
England woe and well-a-day !
But when the clay doth feed the sand,
Then it is well with England.
Old Saying (Ray).

Winter's thunder and summer's flood
Never boded Englishman good.
Old Saying (Ray).

" When you are all agreed upon a time,"
quoth the vicar, " I'll make it rain."
Prov.

Little kens the wife, that sits by the fire,
How the wind blows cold in hurle burle
swyre.   *Scottish prov.* (Ray).

Mist in May and heat in June
Make the harvest richt sune.
Scottish prov.

Mony rains, mony rowans (fruit of ash
trees) ; mony rowans. mony yewns (refuse
of grain blown away by the fanners.)
Scottish prov.

When clouds appear like rocks and towers,
The earth's refreshed with frequent
showers.
Scottish prov. (*Andrew Cheviot Collection*).

Mony a frost and mony a thowe,
Soon maks mony a rotten yowe [ewe.]
Scottish saying.

To talk of the weather it's nothing but folly,
For when it's rain on the hills, it may be
sun in the valley.
Scottish saying (*Dr. Robt. Chambers's
Collection,* 1826).

'Tween Martinmas [Nov. 11] and Yule,
Water's wine in every pool.
Scottish saying.

If it rains on St. Médard's day [June 8],
it will rain for six weeks after, unless St.
Barnabas [June 11] has put everything
right.   *Swiss prov.* (*cp.* ST. SWITHIN).

As the Devil said to Noah, " It's bound
to clear up ! "
Prov. saying. (*A Yorkshire variant of
this saying attributes it to a Pudsey man, who
declined Noah's offer of a passage in the
ark because the fare was too high.*)

WEDDING RING

Oh, how many torments be in the small
circle of a wedding-ring !
C. CIBBER.—*Double Gallant,* Act 1, 2.

Let nothing break our bond but Death,
For in the world above
'Tis the breaker Death that soldereth
Our ring of Wedded Love.
GERALD MASSEY.—*On a Wedding Day.*

Constancy and Heaven are round,
And in this the emblem's found.
Wedding Ring Posy (*c.* 1620).

WELCOME

'Tis sweet to hear the honest watch-dog's
bark
Bay, deep-mouthed welcome, as we draw
near home ;
'Tis sweet to know there is an eye will mark
Our coming, and look brighter when we
come. BYRON.—*Don Juan, c.* 1, 123.

Sae true his heart, sae smooth his speech,
His breath like cauler air,
His very foot has music in't,
As he comes up the stair.
W. J. MICKLE.—*Song.*

Small cheer and great welcome makes a
merry feast.
SHAKESPEARE.—*Comedy of Errors,*
Act 3, 1.

Sir, you are very welcome to our house :
It must appear in other ways than words,
Therefore I scant this breathing courtesy.
SHAKESPEARE.—*Merch. of Venice,*
Act 5, 1.

Welcome ever smiles
And farewell goes out sighing.
SHAKESPEARE.—*Troilus and Cressida,*
Act 3, 3.

WEST, THE

'Tis inspiration
Expounds experience ; 'tis the west ex-
plains
The east.   BAILEY.—*Festus.*

Westward the course of empire takes its
way.
BP. BERKELEY.—*Planting Arts and
Learning in America.*

It's the white road westwards is the road
I must tread
To the green grass, the cool grass, and rest
for heart and head,
To the violets and the brown brooks and
the thrushes' song
In the fine land, the west land, the land
where I belong.
JOHN MASEFIELD.—*The West
Wind.*

Her blue eyes sought the west afar,
For lovers love the western star.
SCOTT.—*Lay of the Last Minstrel, c.* 3.

Olivia. There lies your way, due west.
Viola.   Then westward-ho !
SHAKESPEARE.—*Tewlfth Night,*
Act 3, 1.

I think it was Jekyll who used to say
that the further he went west, the more
convinced he felt that the wise men came
from the east. SYDNEY SMITH.—*Saying.*

WESTMINSTER ABBEY

Here's an acre sown indeed
With the richest, royalest seed.
FRANCIS BEAUMONT.—*On Westminster
Abbey.*

That temple of silence and reconciliation
where the enmities of twenty generations
lie buried, the Great Abbey which has
during many ages afforded a quiet resting-
place to those whose minds and bodies have
been shattered by the contentions of the
Great Hall.   MACAULAY.—*Warren
Hastings.*

Westminster Abbey, or Victory!
*Nelson's exclamation on boarding the " San
Josef" at the Battle of Cape St. Vincent.*

WICKEDNESS

There is a method in man's wickedness;
It grows up by degrees.
BEAUMONT AND FLETCHER.—*King and
No King, Act 5, 4.*

All wickedness comes of weakness.
ROUSSEAU.—*Emile.*

The life of a wicked or worldly man is
a very drudgery, infinitely more toilsome,
vexatious, and unpleasant than a godly
life is.   BISHOP ROBT. SANDERSON.

What rein can hold licentious wickedness
When down the hill he holds his fierce
career?
SHAKESPEARE.—*Henry V., Act 3, 3.*

I have seen the wicked in great power,
and spreading himself like a green bay
tree.   *Psalm xxxvii, 35.*

WIDOWS

These widows, sir, are the most perverse
creatures in the world.
ADDISON.—*Spectator, Vol. 5, No. 335.*

Your husband left you wealthy, ay, and
wise;
Continue so, sweet duck—continue so.
BEAUMONT AND FLETCHER.—*The
Scornful Lady, Act 1, 3.*

Take example by your father, my boy,
be wery careful o' widders all your life.
[*Sam Weller, sen.*]
DICKENS.—*Pickwick Papers, ch. 20.*

When widows exclaim loudly against
second marriages, I would always lay a
wager that the man, if not the wedding-
day, is absolutely fixed on.
FIELDING.—*Amelia, Bk. 6, ch. 8.*

Why are those tears? Why droops your
head?
Is then your other husband dead?
Or does a worse disgrace betide?
Hath no one since his death applied?
GAY.—*Fables, Pt. 1, 37.*

Why is a garden's wildered maze
Like a young widow, fresh and fair?
Because it wants some hand to raise
The weeds, which " have no business
there."
MOORE.—*To Lady H. (1805).*

Thus day by day, and month by month,
we passed;
It pleased the Lord to take my spouse at
last.
I tore my gown, I spoiled my locks with
dust,
And beat my breast—as wretched widows
must:
Before my face my handkerchief I spread,
To hide the flood of tears I did—not shed.
POPE.—*The Wife of Bath.*

He that woos a maid must come seldom
in her sight,
But he that woos a widow must woo her
day and night.   *Prov. (Ray).*

WIFE, *see* WIVES

WILFULNESS

Muse not that I thus suddenly proceed;
For what I will, I will, and there an end.
SHAKESPEARE.—*Two Gent. of Verona,
Act 1, 3.*

Will was his guide, and griefe led him
astray.
SPENSER.—*Faerie Queene, Bk. 1, 12.*

It has been said, and may be sae,
A wilfu' man wants never wae,
Thocht he gets little gains.
Cherry and the Slae.

Where is the man that hath the power and
skill,
To stem the torrent of a woman's will?
For if she will, she will, you may depend
on 't
And if she won't, she won't; so there's an
end on 't.   *Inscription at Canterbury.*

WILL

No man can rob us of our will.
MARCUS AURELIUS.—11, 36.

In idle wishes fools supinely stay,
Be there a will, and wisdom finds a way.
CRABBE.—*The Birth of Flattery.*

Everything in this world depends upon
will.   DISRAELI.—*Endymion, ch. 65.*

And binding nature fast in fate
Left free the human will.
POPE.—*The Universal Prayer.*

Will is the zealous slave of the passions
and the tyrant of reason.
DE RIVAROL.—*Of Language, sec. 4.*

God can, because he wills ; it is his will
which makes his power.
ROUSSEAU.—Emile.

What I will not, that I cannot do.
SHAKESPEARE.—Meas. for Meas., Act 2, 2.

O well for him whose will is strong !
He suffers, but he will not suffer long !
He suffers, but he cannot suffer wrong.
TENNYSON.—Will.

The Will is the Man.
JOHN WILSON.—Noctes.

WILLINGNESS

Oh, whistle, and I'll come to you, my
   lad.   BURNS.—Song.

Barkis is willin'.
DICKENS.—David Copperfield, ch. 5.

" When a man says he's willin'," said
Mr. Barkis, " it's as much as to say, that
man's a-waitin' for an answer."
DICKENS.—Ib., ch. 8.

The readiness of doing doth express
No other but the doer's willingness.
HERRICK.—Hesperides : Readiness.

WILLS

No customer brings so much grist to the
   mill,
As the wealthy old woman who makes her
   own Will.
LORD NEAVES.—The Jolly Testator who
makes his own Will.

The man who has not made his will at
forty is worse than a fool—almost a knave.
JOHN WILSON.—Noctes, 19.

WINDOWS

From a window richly peint
With lives of many divers seint.
CHAUCER.—Chaucer's Dream.

And storied windows richly dight,
Casting a dim religious light.
MILTON.—Il Penseroso.

WINDS

Perhaps the wind
Wails so in winter for the summer's dead,
And all sad sounds are nature's funeral
   cries
For what has been and is not.
GEO. ELIOT.—The Spanish Gypsy, Bk. I.

It's a warm wind, the west wind, full of
   birds' cries.
J. MASEFIELD.—West Wind.

So near to mute the zephyrs flute
   That only leaflets dance.
GEO. MEREDITH.—Outer and Inner, st. 19.

Take a straw and throw it up into the
air, and you may see by that which way the
wind is.   SELDEN.—Table Talk : Libels.

Cease, rude Boreas ! blustering railer !
G. A. STEVENS.—The Storm

Yet true it is as cow chews cud,
And trees at spring do yield forth bud,
Except wind stands as never it stood
It is an ill wind turns none to good.
T. TUSSER.—A Description of the
Properties of Winds (Ed. 1580).

The south wind brings wet weather ;
The north wind wet and cold together ;
The west wind always brings us rain ;
The east wind blows it back again.
Old Saying.

When the wind is in the east,
It's neither good for man nor beast ;
When the wind is in the west,
Then the fishes bite the best ;
When the wind is in the north,
Then it blows the fishes forth ;
When the wind is in the south,
It blows the bait in the fishes' mouth.
Old Saying.

East and Wast,
The sign o' a blast ;
North and South,
The sign o' a drouth.
Scottish saying.

WINE

I love good wine
As I love health and joy of heart, but tem-
   perately.
BEAUMONT AND FLETCHER.—Wit
without Money, Act 3.

" I rather like bad wine," said Mr.
Mountchesney : " one gets so bored with
good wine."   DISRAELI.—Sybil, ch. 1.

And much as Wine has played the Infidel,
And robbed me of my Robe of Honour,—
   Well,
I wonder often what the Vintners buy
One-half so precious as the stuff they sell.
FITZGERALD.—Rubáiyát, st. 95.

Claret is the liquor for boys ; port for
men ; but he who aspires to be a hero must
drink brandy.   JOHNSON.—Remark, 1779.

O for a beaker full of the warm South,
Full of the true, the blushful Hippocrene,
With beaded bubbles winking at the brim,
And purple stainèd mouth.
KEATS.—Ode to a Nightingale.

Note the superiority of wine over Venus
—I may say the magnanimity of wine !
Our jealousy turns on him that will not
share !   GEO. MEREDITH.—Egoist, ch. 19.

Come, come ! Good wine is a good
familiar creature, if it be well used.
SHAKESPEARE.—Othello, Act 2, 3.

Wines that, Heaven knows when,
Had sucked the fire of some forgotten sun,
And kept it through a hundred years of
   gloom.
TENNYSON.—Golden Supper, l. 192.

S

545

Look not thou upon the wine when it is red.   *Proverbs* xxiii, 31.

Drink no longer water, but use a little wine for thy stomach's sake.
                                                 1 *Timothy* v, 23.

Firm and erect the Caledonian stood ;
Sound was his mutton, and his claret good ;
" Let him drink port ! " the English states-
    man cried :
He drank the poison, and his spirit died.
        ANON.—(*Dodd's Epigrammatists*, 1870,
                    p. 423.—*See* "*Scotland*.")

WINTER

The tendinous part of the mind, so to speak, is more developed in winter ; the fleshy, in summer. I should say winter had given the bone and sinew to litera-ture, summer the tissues and the blood.
    JOHN BURROUGHS.—*The Snow-Walkers.*

On Linden when the sun was low,
All bloodless lay the untrodden snow,
And dark as winter was the flow
Of Iser, rolling rapidly.
            CAMPBELL.—*Hohenlinden.*

I crown thee king of intimate delights,
Fireside enjoyments, homeborn happiness.
        COWPER.—*Winter Evening*

In winter when the dismal rain
    Came down in slanting lines,
And wind, that grand old harper, smote
    His thunder-harp of pines
        ALEX. SMITH.—*Life Drama.*

We have had a superb summer, but I am glad it is over. I am never happy till the fires are lighted.
        SYDNEY SMITH.—*Letter to Mrs.
                            Meynell*, 1843.

See, Winter comes to rule the varied year,
Sullen and sad.   THOMSON.—*Winter*, 1.

An air [early] winter makes a sair [sore] winter.
        Scottish prov. (*The English version is :*
    "*An early winter, a surly winter.*")

Seagull, seagull, sit on the sand ;
It's never guid weather when you're on the
    land.   *Scottish saying.*

        Under snaw, bread ;
        Under water, dearth.
Scottish saying (*as to the respective effects of
            a snowy or a wet winter*).

WISDOM

He thought as a sage, though he felt as
    a man.   BEATTIE.—*The Hermit.*

Knowledge is proud that he has learned so
    much ;
Wisdom is humble that he knows no more.
        COWPER.—*Winter Morning Walk.*

Raphael paints wisdom, Handel sings it, Phidias carves it, Shakespeare writes it, Wren builds it, Columbus sails it, Luther preaches it, Washington arms it, Watt mechanizes it.   EMERSON.—*Civilization.*

They who travel in pursuit of wisdom walk only in a circle, and, after all their labour, at last return to their pristine ignorance.
        GOLDSMITH.—*Citizen of the World*, 37.

Yet his look with the reach of past ages
        was wise,
And the soul of eternity thought through
        his eyes.
            LEIGH HUNT.—*Feast of Poets.*

Wisdom is to the soul what health is to the body.   LA ROCHEFOUCAULD.—
                                Maxim 620.

For only by unlearning Wisdom comes.
    J. R. LOWELL.—*Parting of the Ways.*

People are never so near playing the fool as when they think themselves wise.
        LADY M. WORTLEY MONTAGU.—
                Letter, March 1, 1755.

Many agree with you [Hippias, a venal sophist] that the wise man should be wise for himself especially. The definition of such a wise man is, " He who can make most money." PLATO.—*Hippias Major*, 6.

Wisdom and knowledge are the most powerful of all human things.
        PLATO.—*Protagoras*, 104 (*Cary tr.*).
                (*Remark of Protagoras.*)

No mortal is wise at all times.
            PLINY THE ELDER.

We live and learn, but not the wiser
    grow.   J. POMFRET.—*Reason.*

Be wisely worldly, be not worldly wise.
            QUARLES.—*Emblems.*

        Unmuzzle your wisdom.
    SHAKESPEARE.—*As You Like It*, Act 1, 2.

Thou speakest wiser than thou art ware of.
        SHAKESPEARE.—*Ib.*, Act 2, 4.

Some folks are wise, and some are otherwise. SMOLLETT.—*Roderick Random, ch.* 6.

A good life is the best way to understand wisdom and religion.
            JEREMY TAYLOR.

Wearing his wisdom lightly.
        TENNYSON.—*Dedication.*

To the first (Pleasure), in a gallant fashion, he gave two kisses in passing ; to the second (Wisdom), he gave his heart.
        VOLTAIRE.—*Sésostris.*

Wisdom alone is true ambition's aim,
Wisdom the source of virtue, and of fame,
Obtained with labour, for mankind employed,
And then, when most you share it, best enjoyed.
    W. WHITEHEAD.—*On Nobility.*

Disasters, do the best we can,
  Will reach both great and small ;
And he is oft the wisest man
  Who is not wise at all.
    WORDSWORTH.—*Oak and Broom.*

Thy wisdom all can do, but—make thee
  wise.   YOUNG.—*Night Thoughts,* 8.

No doubt but ye are the people, and
wisdom shall die with you.   *Job* xii, 2.

Wisdom is better than rubies.
    Proverbs viii, 11.

In much wisdom is much grief.
    Ecclesiastes i, 18.

The words of the wise are as goads.
    Ecclesiastes xii, 11.

Do you not know with how little wisdom
the world is governed ?
Attrib. to Count Axel Oxenstierna of Sweden
  (1583–1654). See Government.

Some men are wise, and some are otherwise.   *Prov. (Ray).*

He is very wise who is not foolish for
long.   *Latin prov.*

WISHES

Time teaches us that oft One Higher,
Unasked, a happier lot bestows,
Than if each blighted dream-desire
Had blossomed like a rose.
  SIR F. H. C. DOYLE.—*Dedicatory*
    Stanzas, 8.

I have often had the fool's hectic of
wishing about the unalterable.
  GEO. ELIOT.—*Theophrastus Such :*
    Looking Backward.

I wish I knew the good of wishing.
  H. S. LEIGH.—*Wishing.*

Wishers were ever fools.
  SHAKESPEARE.—*Antony and Cleopatra,*
    Act 4, 13.

Thy wish was father, Harry, to that
thought.
  SHAKESPEARE.—*Henry IV., Pt.* 2,
    Act 4, 4.

In such a case they talk in tropes,
And by their fears express their hopes.
  SWIFT.—*On the Death of Dr. Swift.*

What most we wish, with ease we fancy
  near. YOUNG.—*Love of Fame, Sat.* 3.

Wishing of all employments, is the worst.
  YOUNG.—*Night Thoughts,* 4.

Wishing, that constant hectic of a fool.
    YOUNG.—*Ib.*

Like our shadows,
Our wishes lengthen, as our sun declines.
    YOUNG.—*Ib.,* 5.

What ardently we wish, we soon believe.
    YOUNG.—*Ib.,* 7.

WIT

What foolish people wits are !
  BEAUMARCHAIS.—*Barber of Seville.*

What things have we seen
Done at the Mermaid ! heard words that
  have been
So nimble, and so full of subtile flame,
As if that everyone from whence they came
Had meant to put his whole wit in a jest,
And had resolved to live a fool the rest
Of his dull life.
  F. BEAUMONT.—*Letter to B. Jonson.*

We grant although he had much wit,
He was very shy of using it.
    BUTLER.—*Hudibras, Pt.* 1, 1.

Wit is that which excites agreeable surprise in the mind by the strange assemblage
of related images presented to it.
  G. CAMPBELL.—*Philosophy of Rhetoric*
    (1771).

Wit will shine
Through the harsh cadence of a rugged
  line.
  DRYDEN.—*In Memory of Mr. Oldham.*

His wit is of the lambent and not of the
forked kind : it lights up every topic with
grace and variety, and it hurts nobody.
  SIR A. HELPS.—*Friends in Council,*
    Bk. 2, *ch.* 3.

Wit is the clash and reconcilement of
incongruities ; the meeting of extremes
round a corner.
  LEIGH HUNT.—*Wit and Humour.*

There are no fools so troublesome as
those who have wit.
  LA ROCHEFOUCAULD.—*Maxim* 451.

His wit burns at the expense of his
memory.   LE SAGE.—*Gil Blas, Bk.* 3,
ch. 11 *(Of Carlos Alonso de la Ventoleria).*

Whose wit, in the combat, as gentle as
  bright,
Ne'er carried a heart-stain away on its
  blade.   MOORE.—*On Sheridan.*

True wit is nature to advantage dressed,
What oft was thought, but ne'er so well
  expressed.   POPE.—*Criticism,* 297.

Some men's wit is like a dark lantern,
which serves their own turn and guides
them their own way, but is never known
(according to the Scripture phrase) either
to shine forth before men or to glorify
their Father in heaven.
  POPE.—*Thoughts on Various Subjects.*

Generally speaking there is more wit than talent in this world. Society swarms with witty people who lack talent.
DE RIVAROL.—*On Mme. de Stael.*

And wit that loved to play, not wound.
SCOTT.—*Marmion, Intro.*

Honesty sometimes keeps a man from growing rich, and civility from being witty.
J. SELDEN.—*Wit.*

You have a nimble wit; I think it was made of Atalanta's heels.
SHAKESPEARE.—*As You Like It,*
Act 3, 2.

I am not only witty in myself, but the cause that wit is in other men.
SHAKESPEARE.—*Henry IV., Pt.* 2,
Act 1, 2.

Your wit's too hot, it speeds too fast, 'twill tire.   SHAKESPEARE.—
Love's Labour's Lost, Act 2, 1.

Thy wit is a very bitter sweeting: it is most sharp sauce.
SHAKESPEARE.—*Romeo and Juliet,*
Act 2, 4.

Surprise is so essential an ingredient of wit that no wit will bear repetition; —at least the original electrical feeling produced by any piece of wit can never be renewed.   SYDNEY SMITH.—
Lectures on Moral Philosophy, No. 10.

It is with wits as with razors, which are never so apt to cut those they are employed on as when they have lost their edge.
SWIFT.—*Tale of a Tub: Author's Preface.*

And wit its honey lent, without the sting.
THOMSON.—*On Lord Talbot.*

Nae wut [wit] without a portion o' impertinence.
JOHN WILSON.—*Noctes Ambrosianæ.*

For though he is a *wit,* he is no *fool.*
YOUNG.—*Love of Fame, Sat.* 2.

May those perish who have said our good things before us !
Attrib. to Donatus; also to St. Augustine.

WITCHES

I have ever believed, and do now know, that there are Witches. They that are in doubt of these ... are obliquely and upon consequence a sort, not of Infidels, but of Atheists.   SIR T. BROWNE.—
Religio Medici, Pt. 1, 30.

What are these,
So withered and so wild in their attire ;
That look not like the inhabitants o' the earth,
And yet are on it ?
SHAKESPEARE.—*Macbeth,* Act 1, 3.

The Devil will fetch me now in fire,
My witchcrafts to atone ;
And I, who have rifled the dead man's grave,
Shall never have rest in my own.
SOUTHEY.—*Old Woman of Berkeley.*

WIVES

Nothing can match, where'er we roam,
An English wife in English home.
A. AUSTIN.—*On Returning to*
England, l. 148.

So bent on self-sanctifying,—
That she never thought of trying
To save her poor husband as well.
R. BUCHANAN.—*Fra Giacomo.*

Were such the wife had fallen to my part,
I'd break her spirit, or I'd break her heart.
BURNS.—*Henpecked Husband.*

I hae a wife o' my ain.
BURNS.—*I hae a Wife.*

Man's best possession is a loving wife.
BURTON.—*Tr. of Euripides.*

The flour of wyfly patience.
CHAUCER.—*Clerk's Tale.*

A wife is goddes gifte verily,
All other manner giftes hardily, [assuredly]
As londes, rentes, pasture, or commune,
Or moebles [moveable chattels], alle ben giftes of fortune,
That passen as a shadow upon a wall.
CHAUCER.—*Merchant's Tale,* 67.

Ther been ful good wyves many a one,
And ever a thousand good against one bad.
CHAUCER.—*Miller's Prol.,* 46.

Men seyn that three things dryven a man out of his house : that is to seyn, smoke, dropping of rain, and wicked wives.
CHAUCER.—*Tale of Melibeus, sec.* 15.

What rugged ways attend the noon of life !
Our sun declines, and with what anxious strife,
What pain, we tug that galling load, a wife !
CONGREVE.—*Old Bachelor,* Act 5, 5.

O Mrs. Higden, Mrs. Higden, you was a woman and a mother, and a mangler in a million million.
DICKENS.—*Mutual Friend, Bk.* 2, *ch.* 9.

There is no worse evil than a bad woman; and nothing has ever been produced better than a good one.
EURIPIDES.—*Melanippe.*

One wife is too much for most husbands to bear,
But two at a time there's no mortal can bear.
GAY.—*Beggar's Opera,* Act 2, 2

If you'll marry me, I'll scrub for you and
  bake for you ;
If you'll marry me, all others I'll forsake
  for you.
  Sir W. S. Gilbert.—*Sorcerer.*

She will tend him, nurse him, mend him,
  Air his linen, dry his tears ;
Bless the thoughtful fates that send him
  Such a wife to soothe his years !
  Sir W. S. Gilbert.—*Ib.*

Sure, I said, Heaven did not mean,
Where I reap thou shouldst but glean,
Lay thy sheaf a down and come,
Share my harvest and my home.
  Hood.—*Ruth.*

Alas ! another instance of the triumph
of hope over experience.
  Johnson.—*Remark in reference to the
second marriage of a friend who had been
unfortunate in his first wife.* (Sir J. Hawkins's Collective Ed. of Johnson, 1787.)

Being married to those sleepy-souled
women is just like playing at cards for
nothing : no passion is excited and the
time is filled up.   I do not, however, envy
a fellow one of those honeysuckle wives
for my part, as they are but creepers at
best and commonly destroy the tree they
so tenderly cling about.
  Johnson.—*Remark as Recorded by
Mrs. Piozzi.*

She is my own lawfully begotten wife,
In wedlock.
  Ben Jonson.—*New Inn,* Act 4, 3.

I fear that in the election of a wife,
As in a project of war, to err but once
Is to be undone for ever.
  Middleton.—*Anything for a Quiet
Life,* Act I, I.

God is thy law, thou mine ; to know no
  more
Is woman's happiest knowledge and her
  praise.
  Milton.—*Paradise Lost,* Bk. 4, 637.

My fairest, my espoused, my latest found,
Heaven's last best gift, my ever new
  delight.   Milton.—*Ib.,* Bk. 5, 18.

For nothing lovelier can be found
In woman, than to study household good,
And good works in her husband to pro-
  mote.   Milton.—*Ib.,* Bk. 9, 232.

The wife, where danger or dishonour lurks,
Safest and seemliest by her husband stays.
  Milton.—*Ib.,* 267.

This woman, whom thou mad'st to be my
  help,
And gav'st me as thy perfect gift, so good,
So fit, so acceptable, so divine.
  Milton.—*Ib.,* Bk. 10, 137.

Well-dowered wives bring evil and loss
to their husbands.
  Plautus.—*Aulularia, sc.* 17.

All other goods by Fortune's hand are
  given,
A wife is the peculiar gift of heaven.
  Pope.—*January and May,* 51.

She who ne'er answers till a husband cools,
Or, if she rules him, never shows she rules ;
Charms by accepting, by submitting
  sways,
Yet has her humour most when she obeys.
  Pope.—*Moral Essays, Ep.* 2, 261.

A guardian angel, o'er his life presiding,
Doubling his pleasures and his cares
  dividing.   Rogers.—*Human Life.*

      The partner of my soul,
My wife, the kindest, dearest, and the
  truest,
That ever wore the name.
  N. Rowe.—*Royal Convert,* Act 2, 1.

You are my true and honourable wife ;
As dear to me as are the ruddy drops
That visit my sad heart.
  Shakespeare.—*Julius Cæsar,* Act 2, 1.

A fellow almost damned in a fair wife,
That never set a squadron in the field
Nor the division of a battle knows,
More than a spinster.
  Shakespeare.—*Othello,* Act I, I.

My wife ! my wife ! what wife ?—I have
no wife.   Shakespeare.—*Ib.,* Act 5, 2.

Such duty as the subject owes the prince,
Even such a woman oweth to her husband.
  Shakespeare.—*Taming of the Shrew,*
                                  Act 5, 2.
      She is mine own ;
And I as rich in having such a jewel,
As twenty seas, if all their sand were pearl,
The water nectar, and the rocks pure gold.
  Shakespeare.—*Two Gentlemen of
                              Verona,* Act 2, 4.
Men may be bad, but still they like
A pious wife that lives for heaven.
  Walter C. Smith.—*Olrig Grange,* Bk. 3.

Richard Penlake was a cheerful man,
  Cheerful and frank and free,
But he led a sad life with Rebecca his wife,
  For a terrible shrew was she.
  Southey.—*St. Michael's Chair.*

He will hold thee, when his passion shall
  have spent its novel force,
Something better than his dog, a little
  dearer than his horse.
  Tennyson.—*Locksley Hall.*

When the man wants weight, the woman
  takes it up,
And topples down the scales.
  Tennyson.—*Princess, c.* 5, 434.

A good housewife is of necessity a humbug.
THACKERAY.—*Vanity Fair, Bk.* 1, *ch.* 17.

But when the closer view of wedded life
Hath shown that nothing human can be clear
From frailty, for that insight may the Wife
To her indulgent Lord become more dear !
WORDSWORTH.—*Sonnet, On the Eve of the marriage of a Friend,* 1812.

Giving honour unto the wife, as unto the weaker vessel. 1 *St. Peter* iii, 7.

The wife of every Englishman is counted blest. *Song (c.* 1596).

A good wife and health are a man's best wealth. *Prov.*

Better a fortune in a wife than with a wife. *Prov.*

Husbands can earn, but only wives can save. *Prov.*

If your wife be crust, mind that you are crumb. *Prov.*

It is a good horse that never stumbles,
And a good wife that never grumbles. *Prov.*

A diamond daughter turns to glass as a wife. *Dutch prov.*

Go down the ladder when thou choosest a wife, go up when thou choosest a friend. *Hebrew prov.*

Wae's the wife that wants the tongue, but weel's the man that gets her. *Scottish prov.*

Mony wyte [blame] their wife for their ain thriftless life. *Scottish prov.*

A' are guid lasses, but where do a' the ill wives come frae ? *Scottish prov.*

The foot at the cradle and the hand at the reel
Is a sign that a woman means to do weel. *Scottish saying.*

WOE

A woman's counsel brought us first to woe,
And made her man his paradise forgo.
DRYDEN.—*Cock and the Fox.*

In all the sad variety of woe.
W. GIFFORD.—*Baviad.*

And her woe began to run afresh,
As if she'd said Gee woe !
HOOD.—*Sally Brown.*

When our heads are bowed with woe,
When our bitter tears o'erflow.
DEAN MILMAN.—*Hymn.*

Weep on : and as thy sorrows flow,
I'll taste the luxury of woe.
MOORE.—*Anacreontic.*

Aghast I stood, a monument of woe.
POPE.—*Iliad, Bk.* 12, 311.

WOMAN

Woman's love is writ in water !
Woman's faith is traced in sand.
W. E. AYTOUN.—*Chas. Edwards.*

But woman, wakeful woman's never weary,
Above all, when she waits to thump her deary ! R. H. BARHAM.—*The Ghost.*

Man had a Conscience to obey his will,
And never would be tempted thereunto,
Untill the Woeman, shee, did worke *man woe.* R. BARNFIELD.—*Conscience and Covetousnesse* (1598).

Not she with trait'rous kiss her Saviour stung,
Not she denied Him with unholy tongue ;
She, while apostles shrank, could danger brave,
Last at His cross and earliest at His grave.
EATON S. BARRETT.—*Woman.*

Poets, beware ! Never compare
Women to aught in earth or in air.
T. H. BAYLY.—*Song.*

The fool that willingly provokes a woman
Has made himself another evil angel,
And a new hell, to which all other torments
Are but mere pastime.
BEAUMONT AND FLETCHER.—*Cupid's Revenge (c.* 1612), Act 3.

Tell me the cause ; I know there is a woman in 't.
BEAUMONT AND FLETCHER.—*Humorous Lieutenant,* Act 4, 3.

There is no other purgatory but a woman.
BEAUMONT AND FLETCHER.—*Scornful Lady,* Act 3.

Let men say what they will,
Woman, woman, rules them still.
1. BICKERSTAFFE.—*Sultan.*

Womanliness means only motherhood ;
All love begins and ends there.
BROWNING.—*Inn Album.*

Mothers, wives, and maids,
These be the tools wherewith priests manage men.
BROWNING.—*Ring and the Book,* 4, 503.

A woman's always younger than a man
At equal years.
E. B. BROWNING.—*Aurora Leigh, Bk.* 2.

Perhaps a better woman after all,
With chubby children hanging on my neck
To keep me low and wise.
E. B. BROWNING.—*Ib.*

There is no solace under heaven,
Of all that a man may neven,
That should a man so much glew,
As a good woman that loveth trew.
ROBERT DE BRUNNE.—*Handlyng of Sins.*

And farewell, dear, deluding woman,
  The joy of joys !
  BURNS.—*Epistle to Jas. Smith.*

Auld Nature swears the lovely dears
  Her noblest work she classes, O ;
Her prentice hand she tried on man,
  And then she made the lasses, O.
  BURNS.—*Green grow the rashes.*

The wisest man the warl' e'er saw,
  He dearly loved the lasses, O.
  BURNS.—*Ib.*

Their tricks and craft hae put me daft,
  They've ta'en me in, and a' that,
But clear your decks, and—Here's the
  sex !
I like the jads for a' that.
  BURNS.—*Jolly Beggars.*

'Twas a strange riddle of a lady.
  BUTLER.—*Hudibras, Pt. 1.*

For 'tis in vain to think or guess
At women by appearances.
  BUTLER.—*Ib., Pt. 3.*

The souls of women are so small
That some believe they've none at all.
  BUTLER.—*Miscellaneous Thoughts.*

Not much he kens, I ween, of woman's
  breast,
Who thinks that wanton thing is won by
  sighs.
  BYRON.—*Childe Harold, c. 2, 34.*

There is a tide in the affairs of women
Which, taken at the flood, leads—God
  knows where.
  BYRON.—*Don Juan, c. 6, 2.*

Believe a woman or an epitaph,
Or any other thing that's false.
  BYRON.—*English Bards.*

The world was sad ; the garden was a wild !
And man, the hermit, sighed—till woman
  smiled.
  CAMPBELL.—*Pleasures of Hope, 2.*

O sely womman, ful of innocence,
Ful of pitee, of trouthe, and conscience,
What maked yow to men to trusten so ?
  CHAUCER.—*Dido.*

For lakke of answer noon of [t]hem shall
  dyen.
  CHAUCER.—*Merchant's Tale, 1027.*

I am a wooman, needès most [must] I
  speke,
Or ellès [else] swellè til myn hertè breke.
  CHAUCER.—*Ib., 1061.*

For also siker [sure] as In principio
Mulier est hominis confusio ;
Madame, the sentence [meaning] of this
  Latin is—
Womman is mannes Ioye and al his blis.
  CHAUCER.—*Nun Priest's Tale, 343.*

There said once a clerk : " What is better
than gold ? Jasper. What is better than
Jasper ? Wisdom. And what is better
than Wisdom ? Woman. And what is
better than a good Woman ? Nothing."
  CHAUCER.—*Tale of Melibeus, sec. 15.*

What is woman ? Only one of Nature's
agreeable blunders.
  MRS. H. COWLEY.—*Who's the Dupe ?*
                          Act 2, 2.

While learning, once the man's exclusive
  pride,
Seems verging fast towards the female side.
  COWPER.—*Progress of Error, 428.*

Women may be whole oceans deeper
than we are, but they are also a whole
paradise better. She may have got us out
of Eden, but as a compensation she makes
the earth very pleasant.
  JOHN OLIVER HOBBES.
  —*The Ambassador, Act 3.*

Were there no women, men might live
  like gods.   DEKKER.—*Honest Whore,*
                          Pt. 1, Act 3, 1.

There's no music when a woman is in
the concert.
  DEKKER.—*Ib., Pt. 2, Act 4, 3.*

What all your sex desire is Sovereignty.
  DRYDEN.—*Wife of Bath.*

A woman should always stand by a
woman.   EURIPIDES.—*Helena.*

I hate a learned woman.
  EURIPIDES.—*Hip., 640.*

But sure among all those
Who have with breath and reason been
  endued,
We women are the most unhappy race.
  EURIPIDES.—*Medea, 230*
                  (Woodhull tr.).

How a little love and conversation improve a woman !
  FARQUHAR.—*Beaux' Stratagem, Act 4, 2.*

Our sex still strikes an awe upon the
  brave,
And only cowards dare affront a woman.
  FARQUHAR.—*Constant Couple, Act 5, 1.*

A woman friend ! He tnat believes that
  weakness,
Steers in a stormy night without a compass.
  FLETCHER.—*Woman Pleased, Act 2, 1.*

Yet when I hold her best, she's but a
woman,
As full of frailty as of faith ; a poor slight
woman,
And her best thoughts but weak forti-
fications.
    FLETCHER AND MASSINGER.—*Little
French Lawyer*, Act 3.

Woman, I tell you, is a microcosm :
and rightly to rule her, requires as great
talents as to govern a state.
    S. FOOTE.—*The Minor*.

'Tis woman that seduces all mankind.
    GAY.—*Beggar's Opera*.

And when a lady's in the case,
You know all other things give place.
    GAY.—*Fables*.

Man has his will,—but woman has her
way.
    O. W. HOLMES.—*Poems from the Auto-
crat of the Breakfast Table. Prologue.*

Still, for all slips of hers,
One of Eve's family.
    HOOD.—*Bridge of Sighs*.

Owning her weakness,
Her evil behaviour,
And leaving, with meekness,
Her sins to her Saviour !
    HOOD.—*Ib*.

Man, born of woman, must of woman die.
    HOOD.—*Valentine*.

O woman ! thou wert fashioned to beguile ;
So have all ages said, all poets sung.
    JEAN INGELOW.—*Four Bridges*, st. 68.

One woman reads another's character
Without the tedious trouble of deciphering.
    BEN JONSON.—*New Inn*, Act 4.

Of all the plagues with which the world is
curst,
Of every ill, a woman is the worst.
    LORD LANSDOWNE.—*British Enchanters*,
Act 2.

Standing with reluctant feet
Where the brook and river meet,
Womanhood and childhood fleet.
    LONGFELLOW.—*Maidenhood*.

Earth's noblest thing, a Woman perfected.   J. R. LOWELL.—*Irene*.

God's rarest blessing is, after all, a good
woman.
    GEO. MEREDITH.—*Richard Feverel*, ch. 34.

I always thought a tinge of blue
Improved a charming woman's stocking.
    R. MONCKTON MILNES (LORD HOUGHTON).
    —*Four Lovers*, 2 : *In Summer*.

What she wills to do or say
Seems wisest, virtuousest, discreetest,
best :
All higher knowledge in her presence falls
Degraded.
    MILTON.—*Paradise Lost, Bk.* 8, 549.

Thus it shall befall
Him, who to worth in women overtrusting,
Lets her will rule. Restraint she will not
brook ;
And left to herself, if evil thence ensue,
She first his weak indulgence will accuse.
    MILTON.—*Ib., Bk.* 9, 1182.

A bevy of fair women, richly gay
In gems and wanton dress.
    MILTON.—*Ib., Bk.* 11, 582.

Wisest men
Have erred, and by bad women been deceived,
And shall again, pretend they ne'er so
wise.   MILTON.—*Samson Agonistes*.

Feminine policy has a mysterious
method ; it is better to leave it to them.
    MONTAIGNE.—*Essays, Bk.* 3, 5.

Howe'er man rules in science and in art,
The sphere of woman's glories is the heart.
    MOORE.—*Epilogue to " Ina."*

My only books
Were women's looks,
And folly's all they've taught me.
    MOORE.—*Irish Melodies*.

Disguise our bondage as we will
'Tis woman, woman, rules us still.
    MOORE.—*Sovereign Woman*.

The light that lies
In woman's eyes,
Has been my heart's undoing.
    MOORE.—*The Time I've lost*.

We cannot tell what blessed forces move
And so transform the careless girlish heart
To bear so high a part.
We cannot tell : we can but praise.
    SIR L. MORRIS.—*Ode of Perfect Years*,
Pt. 2, 53.

So I wonder a woman, the Mistress of
Hearts,
Should descend to aspire to be Master of
Arts ;
A Ministering Angel in Woman we see,
And an Angel need covet no other Degree.
    LORD NEAVES.—*O why should a
Woman not get a Degree ?*

Destructive, damnable, deceitful woman !
    OTWAY.—*Orphan*.

What mighty ills have not been done by
woman ?

Who lost Mark Antony the world ? A
woman !   OTWAY.—*Ib*.

O woman, lovely woman, nature made thee
To temper man ; we had been brutes with-
   out you ;
Angels are painted fair to look like you.
  OTWAY.—*Venice Preserved*, Act 1, 1.

Forbear to distribute amongst all women
the guilt of a few.   OVID.—*Ars Amat.*

Woman's at best a contradiction still.
  POPE.—*Moral Essays, Ep.* 2.

Those who always speak well of women
do not know them sufficiently ; those who
always speak ill of them do not know them
at all.   GUILLAUME PIGAULT-LEBRUN
       (1753–1835).
Men, some to business, some to pleasure
   take ;
But every woman is at heart a rake.
  POPE.—*Ib.*

Nothing so true as what you once let fall,
" Most women have no characters at all."
  POPE.—*Ib.*

O woman, woman, when to ill thy mind
Is bent, all hell contains no fouler fiend.
  POPE.—*Iliad, Bk.* 11, 531.

Women, as they are like riddles in being
unintelligible, so generally resemble them
in this that they please us no longer when
once we know them.
  POPE.—*Thoughts on Various Subjects.*

Too far, I own, the girl was tried—
The women all were on my side.
  PRIOR.—*Conversation*, 59.

As for the women, though we scorn and
   flout' em,
We may live with, but cannot live without
   'em.   F. REYNOLDS.—*The Will.*

Every girl ought to have her mother's
religion, and every wife her husband's.
  ROUSSEAU.—*Emile.*

The more women wish to resemble men
the less they govern men ; and it is thus
that men will be truly the masters.
  ROUSSEAU.—*Ib.*

Woman has more wit and man has more
genius ; woman observes and man reasons.
  ROUSSEAU.—*Ib.*

Women in general love none of the arts,
are proficient in none, and have no genius.
  ROUSSEAU.—*Letter to D'Alembert.*

Such, Polly, are your sex—part truth, part
   fiction ;
Some thought, much whim, and all a contradiction.
  R. SAVAGE.—*To a Young Lady.*

Women in their hearts believe that men
are intended to earn money so that they

may spend it—if possible during the husband's lifetime, but at any rate after his
death.   SCHOPENHAUER.—*On Women.*

The fundamental fault in the character
of women is that they have no sense of
justice.   SCHOPENHAUER.—*Ib.*

A woman who is perfectly truthful and
does not dissemble at all, is perhaps an
impossibility.   SCHOPENHAUER.—*Ib.*

Women are and remain, taken altogether, most thorough and incurable
philistines.   SCHOPENHAUER.—*Ib.*

They would have all men bound and thrall
To them, and they for to be free.
  ALEX. SCOT.—*Womankind.*

Like all rogues he was a great calumniator
of the fair sex.
  SCOTT.—*Heart of Midlothian, ch.* 18.

We hold our greyhound in our hand,
 Our falcon on our glove ;
But where should we find leash or band
 For dame that loves to rove ?
  SCOTT.—*Marmion*, 1, 17.

With a smile on her lips and a tear in
 her eye.   SCOTT.—*Ib.*, 5, 12.

O woman ! in our hours of ease
Uncertain, coy, and hard to please,
And variable as the shade
By the light quivering aspen made,—
When pain and anguish wring the brow,
A ministering angel thou !
  SCOTT.—*Ib.*, 6, 30.

Who is 't can read a woman ?
  SHAKESPEARE.—*Cymbeline*, Act 5, 5.

Frailty, thy name is woman.
  SHAKESPEARE.—*Hamlet*, Act 1, 2.

I have heard of your paintings too, well
enough. God hath given you one face, and
you make yourselves another.
  SHAKESPEARE.—*Ib.*, Act 3, 1.

She's beautiful, and therefore to be wooed ;
She is a woman, therefore to be won.
  SHAKESPEARE.—*Henry VI.*, Act 5, 3.

A child of our grandmother Eve, a
female ; or, for thy more sweet understanding, a woman.
  SHAKESPEARE.—*Love's Labour's Lost*,
       Act 1, 1.

She is a woman, therefore may be wooed ;
She is a woman, therefore may be won ;
She is Lavinia, therefore must be loved.
  SHAKESPEARE.—*Titus Andronicus*,
       Act 2, 1.

Women are angels, wooing.
  SHAKESPEARE.—*Troilus*, Act 1, 2.

Woman reduces us all to the common denominator.
G. B. SHAW.—*Great Catherine*, sc. 1.

The fickleness of the woman I love is only equalled by the infernal constancy of the women who love me.
G. B. SHAW.—*Philanderer*, Act 2.

Woman's dearest delight is to wound Man's self-conceit, though Man's dearest delight is to gratify hers.
G. B. SHAW.—*Unsocial Socialist, ch.* 5. (*Sidney Trefusis.*)

You sometimes have to answer a woman according to her womanishness, just as you have to answer a fool according to his folly.
G. B. SHAW.—*Ib., ch.* 18.

Can man be free if woman be a slave?
SHELLEY.—*Islam.*

Lor', but women's rum cattle to deal with, the first man found that to his cost,
And I reckon it's just through a woman the last man on earth'll be lost.
G. R. SIMS.—*Moll Jarvis o' Morley.*

The weaker sex, to piety more prone.
EARL OF STIRLING.—*Doomsday,* 5*th Hour,* 55.

Lose no time to contradict her,
Nor endeavour to convict her;
Only take this rule along,
Always to advise her wrong,
And reprove her when she's right;
She may then grow wise for spite.
SWIFT.—*Daphne.*

The women were proposed to be taxed according to their beauty and skill in dressing ... but constancy, charity, good sense, and good nature were not to be rated, because they would not bear the charge of collecting.   SWIFT.—*Laputa.*

Your sweet faces make good fellows fools And traitors.
TENNYSON.—*Geraint and Enid,* 400.

Lo now, what hearts have men! they never mount
As high as woman in her selfless mood.
TENNYSON.—*Merlin and Vivien,* 440.

For men at most differ as Heaven and Earth,
But women, worst and best, as Heaven and Hell.   TENNYSON.—*Ib.,* 812.

O miracle of noble womanhood!
TENNYSON.—*Princess: Prologue,* 48.

With prudes for proctors, dowagers for deans,
And sweet girl-graduates in their golden hair.   TENNYSON.—*Ib.,* 141.

"They hunt old trails," said Cyril, "very well;
But when did women ever yet invent?"
TENNYSON.—*Ib., c.* 2, 368.

Man for the field, and woman for the hearth;
Man for the sword, and for the needle she;
Man with the head and woman with the heart;
Man in command and woman to obey.
All else confusion.
TENNYSON.—*Ib., c.* 5, 437.

The woman is so hard
Upon the woman.
TENNYSON.—*Ib., c.* 6, 205.

The woman's cause is man's; they rise or sink
Together.   TENNYSON.—*Ib., c.* 7, 243.

When I say that I know women, I mean that I know that I don't know them. Every single woman I ever knew is a puzzle to me, as I have no doubt she is to herself.
THACKERAY.—*Mr. Brown's Letters.*

How much finer a woman's nature than a man's!   THACKERAY.—*The Proser.*

The man that lays his hand upon a woman, Except in the way of kindness, is a wretch, Whom 'twere gross flattery to name a coward.   J. TOBIN.—*Honeymoon.*

Regard the society of women as a necessary unpleasantness of social life, and avoid it as far as possible.   TOLSTOY.—*Diary.*

Woman is more impressionable than man. Therefore in the Golden Age they were better than men; now they are worse.
TOLSTOY.—*Ib.*

He is a fool who thinks by force or skill To turn the current of a woman's will.
SIR S. TUKE.—*Five Hours.*

Let our weakness be what it will, mankind will still be weaker; and whilst ther is a world, 'tis woman that will govern it.
VANBRUGH.—*Provoked Wife,* Act 3 (*Lady Brute*).

Woman is man's confusion.
VINCENT OF BEAUVAIS.
(*In translating this from the Latin, in the "Nonne Prieste's Tale," Chaucer humorously "confused" it by rendering it: "Womann is mannes joye and all his blisse." See p.* 551.)

Here cease thy vaunts and own my victory;
A woman warrior was too strong for thee.
Yet if the ghosts demand the conqueror's name,
Confessing great Camilla, save thy shame.
VIRGIL.—*Æneid, Bk.* 11. (*Dryden tr.*).

The female woman is one of the greatest institooshuns of which this land can boast.
ARTEMUS WARD.

There are only two kinds of women, the plain and the coloured.
OSCAR WILDE.—*Dorian Gray, ch.* 3.

Gerald. There are many different kinds of women, aren't there ?
Lord Illingworth. Only two kinds in Society: the plain and the coloured.
OSCAR WILDE.—*Woman of No Importance,* Act 3.

Women are in churches, saints ; abroad, angels ; at home, devils.
G. WILKINS.—*Miseries of Enforced Marriage,* Act 1.

A spirit, yet a woman too !
Her household motions light and free,
And steps of virgin liberty ;
A countenance in which did meet
Sweet records, promises as sweet ;
A creature not too bright or good
For human nature's daily food.
WORDSWORTH.—*She was a Phantom of Delight.*

A perfect woman, nobly planned,
To warn, to comfort, and command.
WORDSWORTH.—*Ib.*

Thou, while thy babes around thee cling,
Shalt show us how divine a thing
A Woman may be made.
WORDSWORTH.—*To a Young Lady* (1803).

All wickedness is but little to the wickedness of a woman. *Ecclesiasticus* xxv, 19.

Between a woman's Yes and No
There is not room for a pin to go.
Old Saying (from the Spanish).

Women's chief weapon is their tongue, and they will not let it rust. *French prov.*

All women are good for something or nothing. *Old Saying.*

WOMEN'S LOGIC

With women the heart argues, not the mind.   M. ARNOLD.—*Merope.*

First, then, a woman will, or won't, depend on't ;
If she will do't, she will, and there's an end on't.
AARON HILL.—*Epilogue to Zara.*

The weakness of their reasoning faculty also explains why women show more sympathy for the unfortunate than men ; ... and why, on the contrary, they are inferior to men as regards justice, and less honourable and conscientious.
SCHOPENHAUER.—*On Women.*

I have no other but a woman's reason :
I think him so, because I think him so.
SHAKESPEARE.—*Two Gentlemen of Verona,* Act 1, 2.

WONDER AND WONDERS

How inexperienced is that man and how ludicrous does he appear, who makes a wonder of anything he meets with in this life !   MARCUS AURELIUS.—*Bk.* 12, 13.

My religion consists mainly of wonder and gratitude. This is the religion of paradise and of childhood.
DR. JOHN BROWN.

Amaze,
(Not long the inmate of a noble heart.)
DANTE.—*Purgatory, c.* 26, 65. (*Cary's tr.*).

" Never see ... a dead post-boy, did you ? " inquired Sam. ... " No," rejoined Bob, " I never did." " No ! " rejoined Sam triumphantly. " Nor never vill ; and there's another thing that no man never see, and that's a dead donkey."
DICKENS.—*Pickwick, ch.* 51.

Men love to wonder and that is the seed of our science.
EMERSON.—*Works and Days.*

Not to admire, is of all means the best,
The only means, to make and keep us blest.
P. FRANCIS.—*Horace, Epistles, Bk.* 1, 6.

For to admire an' for to see,
For to be'old this world so wide—
It never done no good to me,
But I can't drop it if I tried !
KIPLING.—*For to Admire : The Seven Seas.*

E'en what we now with greatest ease receive,
Seemed strange at first, and we could scarce believe ;
And what we wonder at, as years increase,
Will seem more plain, and all our wonder cease.
LUCRETIUS.—*De Rerum Natura,* 2, 1027 (*Creech tr.*).

Wonder [said Socrates] is very much the affection of a philosopher ; for there is no other beginning of philosophy than this.
PLATO.—*Theætetus,* 32 (*Cary tr.*).

O wonderful, wonderful, and most wonderful wonderful ! and yet again wonderful, and after that, out of all whooping.
SHAKESPEARE.—*As You Like It,* Act 3, 2.

There are more things in heaven and earth, Horatio,
Than are dreamt of in your philosophy.
SHAKESPEARE.—*Hamlet,* Act 1, 5.

" I have seen so many extraordinary things," said Martin, " that nothing is any longer extraordinary."
VOLTAIRE.—*Candide, ch.* 21.

The weight of sadness was in wonder lost. WORDSWORTH.—*Beloved Vale.*

For wonder is involuntary praise.
YOUNG.—*The Revenge.*

We nothing know, but what is marvellous ; Yet what is marvellous, we can't believe.
YOUNG.—*Night Thoughts,* 7.

Nothing but what astonishes is true.
YOUNG.—*Ib.,* 9.

Fools are aye seein' ferlies [wonders].
Scottish prov.

WORDS

Waste words addle questions.
BISHOP ANDREWES.

Words are but the current tokens or marks of popular notions of things.
BACON.—*Adv. of Learning, Bk.* 2.

They come home to men's business and bosoms. BACON.—*Preface to Essays.*

'Tis not Good wordes that can a man maintaine ;
Wordes are but winde ; and winde is all in vaine. R. BARNFIELD.—
Complaint of Poetrie (1598).

What so wild as words are ?
BROWNING.—*Woman's Last Word.*

A very great part of the mischiefs that vex this world arises from words.
BURKE.—*Letter (c.* 1795).

Words are but pictures, true or false designed,
To draw the lines and features of the mind.
BUTLER.—*Upon the Abuse of Human Learning.*

But words are things, and a small drop of ink,
Falling like dew upon a thought, produces
That which makes thousands, perhaps millions, think.
BYRON.—*Don Juan, c.* 3, 88.

Examine Language ; what, if you except some few primitive elements (of natural sound), what is it all but Metaphors, recognised as such, or no longer recognised ?
CARLYLE.—*Sartor Resartus, Bk.* 1, *ch.* 11.

How strong an influence works in well-placed words !
CHAPMAN.—*Gentleman Usher,* Act 4, 2.

Men's words are ever bolder than their deeds. COLERIDGE.—*Piccolomini.*

Words will not build walls.
CRATINUS (*according to Plutarch*).

With words we govern men.
DISRAELI.—*Contarini Fleming, ch.* 21.

I trade both with the living and the dead for the enrichment of our native language.
DRYDEN.—*Dedic. of Æneid (on the practice of coining words).*

And torture one poor word a thousand ways. DRYDEN.—*MacFlecknoe,* 208.

Though the origin of most of our words is forgotten, each word was at first a stroke of genius. EMERSON.—*The Poet.*

New words and lately made shall credit claim
If from a Grecian source they gently stream.
P. FRANCIS.—*Horace, Art of Poetry.*

An undisputed power
Of coining money from the rugged ore,
Nor less of coining words, is still confessed,
If with a legal public stamp impressed.
P. FRANCIS.—*Ib.*

While words of learned length and thundering sound
Amazed the gazing rustics ranged around.
GOLDSMITH.—*Deserted Village.*

Words are the only things that last for ever. W. HAZLITT.—*Thought and Action.*

Nowadays a word is a deed whose consequences cannot be measured.
HEINE.—*Reisebilder, Last Words.*

The arrow belongs not to the archer when it has once left the bow ; the word no longer belongs to the speaker when it has once passed his lips, especially when it has been multiplied by the press.
HEINE.—*Religion and Philosophy, Pref.* (1852).

Rolled under the tongue as a sweet morsel.
MATTHEW HENRY.—*Commentaries.*

Words are wise men's counters ; they do but reckon by them : but they are the money of fools.
HOBBES.—*Leviathan, Pt.* 1.

Words are the soul's ambassadors, who go Abroad upon her errands to and fro.
J. HOWELL.—*Of Words.*

I am not yet so lost in lexicography as to forget that *words are the daughters of earth, and that things are the sons of heaven.*
JOHNSON.—*Dictionary, Pref.* (*stated by Sir W. Jones to be an Indian saying*).

Words that may become alive and walk up and down in the hearts of the hearers.
KIPLING.—*Academy Banquet Speech.*

We should have a great many fewer disputes in the world if words were taken for what they are, the signs of our ideas only, and not for things themselves.
LOCKE.—*Essay*, 3, 10.

Cato's words were few, but they came from a heart full of truth.
LUCANUS.—*Pharsalia.*

Words die so soon when fit but to be said ; Words only live when worthy to be read.
E. R. BULWER-LYTTON, EARL OF LYTTON (1831-1891).—*The Orator.*

His words, like so many nimble and airy servitors, trip about him at command.
MILTON.—*Apology for Smectymnuus.*

With high words, that bore Semblance of worth, not substance.
MILTON.—*Paradise Lost, Bk.* 1, 528.

That would have made Quintilian stare and gasp.   MILTON.—*Sonnet.*

How many quarrels, and how important, has the doubt as to the meaning of this syllable " Hoc " produced for the world !
MONTAIGNE.—*Essays, Bk.* 2, 12.
(Referring to the controversies on transub-stantiation—" Hoc est corpus meum.")

So spake those wary foes, fair friends in look,
And so in words great gifts they gave and took,
And had small profit, and small loss there-by. W. MORRIS.—*Jason, Bk.* 8, 379.

This the just right of poets ever was,
And will be still, to coin what words they please. J. OLDHAM —*Imit. of Horace.*

Things were first made, then words.
SIR T. OVERBURY.—*A Wife.*

Grant me the power of saying things,
Too simple and too sweet for words.
C. PATMORE.—*Angel in the House, Bk.* 1, *c.* 1.

When things are small the terms should still be so,
For low words please us when the theme is low. C. PITT.—*Vida's Art of Poetry.*

Each word-catcher, that lives on syllables.
POPE.—*Prol. to Satires,* 166.

Words are like leaves ; and where they most abound,
Much fruit of sense beneath is rarely found. POPE.—*Criticism,* 309.

In words, as fashions, the same rule will hold :
Alike fantastic, if too new, or old :
Be not the first by whom the new are tried,
Nor yet the last to lay the old aside.
POPE.—*Ib.,* 333.

Every word man's lips have uttered Echoes in God's skies.
A. A. PROCTER.—*Words.*

O ! many a shaft, at random sent,
Finds mark the archer little meant !
And many a word, at random spoken,
May soothe or wound a heart that's broken.
SCOTT.—*Lord of the Isles.*

Men should use common words to say uncommon things ; but they do the re-verse. SCHOPENHAUER.—*On Authorship.*

Syllables govern the world.
J. SELDEN.—*Power.*

That's an ill phrase, a vile phrase ;
" beautified " is a vile phrase.
SHAKESPEARE.—*Hamlet,* Act 2, 2.

Words, words, words !
SHAKESPEARE.—*Ib.*

Suit the action to the word, the word to the action ; with this special observ-ance that you o'erstep not the modesty of nature. SHAKESPEARE.—*Ib.,* Act 3, 2.

Zounds ! I was never so bethumped with words.
SHAKESPEARE.—*King John,* Act 2, 2.

They have been at a great feast of lan-guages and stolen the scraps.
SHAKESPEARE.—*Love's Labour's Lost,* Act 5, 1.

The word is well culled, chose ; sweet, and apt,
I do assure you, sir, I do assure.
SHAKESPEARE.—*Ib.*

His words are a very fantastical ban-quet, just so many strange dishes.
SHAKESPEARE.—*Much Ado,* Act 2, 3.

So all my best is dressing old words new.
SHAKESPEARE.—*Sonnet* 76.

Words pay no debts.
SHAKESPEARE.—*Troilus,* Act 3, 2.

I am well aware that I do not express myself with exact ability. Ladies and gentlemen have that power over words that they can always say what they mean, but a common man like me can't.
G. B. SHAW.—*Unsocial Socialist, ch.* 4.

The arts Babblative and Scriblative.
SOUTHEY.—*Colloquies.*

Many a pang has been incurred,
Through a single hasty word.
C. H. SPURGEON.—*"Salt-Cellars."*

For words, like Nature, half reveal
And half conceal the soul within.
TENNYSON.—*In Memoriam, c.* 3

As shadows attend substances, so words
follow upon things.
ARCHBP. TRENCH.—*Study of Words.*

Some of those old American words have
a kind of bully swing to them.
MARK TWAIN.—*Tramp Abroad.*

You phrase-tormenting fantastic chorus,
With strangest words at your beck and
call.
SIR W. WATSON.—*Orgy on Parnassus.*

Would you repeat that again, sir, for it
soun's sae sonorous that the words droon
the ideas ?   JOHN WILSON.—*Noctes,* 27.

                    The Intellect can raise,
From airy words alone, a Pile that ne'er
decays.
WORDSWORTH.—*Inscriptions, No.* 4.

Say not you *love* a roasted fowl,
But you may love a screaming owl,
And, if you can, the unwieldy toad,
That crawls from his secure abode.
WORDSWORTH.—*Loving and Liking.*

From generation to generation men are
the dupes of words.
·WORDSWORTH.—*Postscript (to Preface)*
                    (1835).

Fair words enough a man shall find ;
They be good cheap ; they cost right
nought ;
Their substance is but only wind.
SIR T. WYATT.—*Dissembling Words.*

How forcible are right words !
                    Job vi, 25.

The words of his mouth were smoother
than butter, but war was in his heart ; his
words were softer than oil, yet were they
drawn swords.   *Psalm* lv, 21.

A word spoken in due season, how good
is it !   *Proverbs* xv, 23.

A word fitly spoken is like apples of gold
in pictures [" baskets " in *R.V.*] of silver.
                    Proverbs xxv, 11.

Let no man deceive you with vain
words.   *Ephesians* v, 6.

Hold fast the form of sound words.
                    2 *Timothy* i, 13.

A man of words and not of deeds
Is like a garden full of weeds.
                    Old Rhyme.

Whose words were half battles.
                    Saying in reference to Luther.

WORK

                    Work I may dispense
With talk about, since work in evidence,
Perhaps in history ; who knows or cares ?
                    BROWNING.—*A Forgiveness.*

A Man !—a right true man, however,
Whose work was worthy a man's endeavour.
                    BROWNING.—*Christmas Eve, c.* 15.

Man's work is to labour and leaven—
As best he may—earth here with heaven ;
'Tis work for work's sake he is needing.
                    BROWNING.—*Of Pacchiarotto.*

For work is a good investment, and
almost always pays.
                    W. CARLETON.—*Out o' the Fire.*

Work is the grand cure of all the maladies and miseries that ever beset mankind.
                    CARLYLE.—*Address,* 1886.

The *best* worship, however, is stout working.   CARLYLE.—*Letter to his wife* (1831).

All work, even cotton-spinning, is noble.
                    CARLYLE.—*Past and Present, Bk.* 3, *ch.* 4.

Blessed is he who has found his work ;
let him ask no other blessedness.
                    CARLYLE.—*Ib., ch.* 11.

The glory of a workman, still more of a
master-workman, that he does his work
well, ought to be his most precious possession ; like the " honour of a soldier,"
dearer to him than life.
                    CARLYLE.—*Shooting Niagara,* 7 (1867).

My life is one demd horrid grind !
                    DICKENS.—*Nicholas Nickleby, ch.* 64.

Work is victory. Wherever work is
done, victory is obtained. There is no
chance, and no blanks.
                    EMERSON.—*Conduct of Life :
                    Worship.*

" He can toil terribly," said Cecil of
Sir Walter Raleigh. These few words
sting and bite and lash us when we are
frivolous. Let us get out of the way of
their blows, by making them true of ourselves.   EMERSON.—*Greatness.*

The sum of wisdom is that the time is
never lost that is devoted to work.
                    EMERSON.—*Success.*

The gods sell us all good things for hard
work.   EPICHARMUS.—*(Greek.)*

Our best friend is ever work.
                    COLLIN D'HARLEVILLE.—*Mœurs du
                    Jour.*

Now God bless all true workers, let us pray :
The night-time cometh when we all must
rest.
Strive we and do, lest by and by we sit
In that blind life, to which all other fate
Is cause for envy ; with the naked souls
Who never lived, knowing nor praise nor
blame,
But kept themselves in mean neutrality,
Hateful alike to God and to his foes.
                    EMILY H. HICKEY.—*Michael Villiers.*

I like work ; it fascinates me. I can sit and look at it for hours. I love to keep it by me : the idea of getting rid of it nearly breaks my heart.
J. K. JEROME.—*Three Men in a Boat, ch. 15.*

He that will not live by toil
Has no right on English soil !
C. KINGSLEY.—*Alton Locke's Song.*

For men must work, and women must weep,
And there's little to earn, and many to keep,
Though the harbour bar be moaning.
C. KINGSLEY.—*Three Fishers.*

But till we are built like angels, with hammer and chisel and pen,
We will work for ourself and a woman, for ever and ever, Amen.
KIPLING.—*Imperial Rescript.*

And the Sons of Mary smile and are blessed
—they know the angels are on their side ;
They know in them is the Grace confessed, and for them are the Mercies multiplied ;
They sit at the Feet, they hear the Word, they see how truly the Promise runs ;
They have cast their burden upon the Lord, and—the Lord He lays it on Martha's Sons ! KIPLING.—*The Sons of Mary.*

And learne to labour with hands, for livelihood is swete.
LANGLAND.—*Piers Plowman, Passus 6.*

When I die, may I be taken in the midst of work. OVID.—*Amores, 2, 10, 36.*

Do not work for necessity ; work for the glory of working. ROUSSEAU.—*Emile.*

Dusting, darning, drudging, nothing is great or small,
Nothing is mean or irksome, love will hallow it all.
WALTER C. SMITH.—*Hilda, Bk. 2.*

O what an endlesse worke have I in hand.
SPENSER.—*Faerie Queene, c. 12, 1.*

Men that wrought by the grace of thought and toil things goodlier than praise dare trace.
SWINBURNE.—*On the South Coast.*

Men my brothers, men the workers, ever reaping something new ;
That which they have done but earnest of the things that they shall do.
TENNYSON.—*Locksley Hall.*

The Father of all did not will that the way of cultivating the soil should be easy.
VIRGIL.—*Georgic I.*

Their works do follow them.
Revelation xiv, 13.

Man is immortal till his work is done.
ANON.—*Fuller (Church History, Bk. 3) has : "God's children are immortal while their Father has anything for them to do on earth."*

The workman makes the work, but the work also makes the workman.
Old Saying.

WORLD, THE

It's a weary warld and nobody bides in it. SIR J. M. BARRIE.—*Little Minister, ch. 4.*

This world's no blot for us,
Nor blank ; it means intensely, and means good :
To find its meaning is my meat and drink.
BROWNING.—*Fra Lippo Lippi.*

Was it likelier, now,
That this our one out of all worlds beside,
The what-d'you-call-'em millions, should be just
Precisely chosen to make Adam for,
And the rest o' the tale ? Yet the tale's true, you know.
BROWNING.—*Mr. Sludge.*

If there's another world, he lives in bliss :
If there is none, he made the best of this.
BURNS.—*On a Friend.*

'Tis but a worthless world to win or lose.
BYRON.—*Childe Harold, c. 1.*

There's not a joy the world can give like that it takes away.
BYRON.—*Stanzas for Music.*

Courts and camps are the only places to learn the world in.
EARL OF CHESTERFIELD.—*Letter to his Son.*

The world is good in the lump.
G. COLMAN, JR.—*Torrent.*

Well then ; I now do plainly see
This busy world and I shall ne'er agree.
COWLEY.—*The Wish.*

Behold the world how it is whirlèd round,
And for it is so whirled is so namèd so.
SIR JOHN DAVIES.—*Orchestra*

This pendent world, in bigness as a star
Of smallest magnitude, close by the moon.
MILTON.—*Paradise Lost, Bk. 2, 1052.*

All the world's a stage,
And all the men and women merely players ;
They have their exits and their entrances,
And one man in his time plays many parts.
SHAKESPEARE.—*As You Like It, Act 2, 7.*

O, how full of briers is this working-day world ! SHAKESPEARE.—*Ib., Act 1, 3.*

I hold the world but as the world, Gratiano,
A stage, where every man must play a part,
And mine a sad one.
SHAKESPEARE.—*Merchant of Venice,*
Act 1, 1.

You have too much respect upon the world:
They lose it that do buy it with much care.
SHAKESPEARE.—*Ib.*

This fine old world of ours is but a child
Yet in the go-cart. Patience! give it time
To learn its limbs: there is a hand that guides.
TENNYSON.—*Princess : Conclusion.*

The world is a comedy to those that think; a tragedy to those who feel.
HORACE WALPOLE.—*Letter,* 1770.

The fretful stir
Unprofitable, and the fever of the world.
WORDSWORTH.—*Tintern Abbey, l.* 51.

The world is too much with us; late and soon,
Getting and spending, we lay waste our powers.
WORDSWORTH.—*The World is too much with us.*

Let not the cooings of the world allure thee!
Which of her lovers ever found her true?
YOUNG.—*Night Thoughts,* 8.

To know the world, not love her, is thy point.
She gives but little, nor that little long.
YOUNG.—*Ib.*

It's a very good world that we live in,
To lend or to spend or to give in;
But to borrow, or beg, or to come by your own,
It's the very worst world that ever was known.
ANON.—(*Traced back to* 1737.)

WORLDLY WISDOM

Worldly in this world,
I take and like its way of life.
BROWNING.—*Bp. Blougram.*

I may not be Meethoosalem, but I am not a child in arms.
DICKENS.—*Dombey, ch.* 44.

Stay, Worldling, stay; whither away so fast?
Hark, hark awhile to Virtue's counsels current! J. SYLVESTER.—*Spectacles.*

Man of the World (for such wouldst thou be called)—
And art thou proud of that inglorious style?
YOUNG.—*Night Thoughts,* 8.

WORSHIP

Compared with this, how poor religion's pride,
In all the pomp of method and of art!
BURNS.—*Cotter's Saturday Night.*

Devotion's every grace, except the heart.
BURNS.—*Ib.*

Here some are thinkin' on their sins,
And some upo' their claes.
BURNS.—*Holy Fair.*

Man always worships something; always he sees the Infinite shadowed forth in something finite; and indeed can and must so see it in any finite thing.
CARLYLE.—*Essays : Goethe's Works.*

Worship is transcendent wonder.
CARLYLE.—*Heroes, Sec.* 1

Wherever God erects a house of prayer,
The Devil always builds a chapel there;
And 'twill be found, upon examination,
The latter has the largest congregation.
DEFOE.—*True-Born Englishman, Pt.* 11.

Resort to sermons, but to prayers most,
Praying's the end of preaching.
HERBERT.—*Church Porch.*

One wishes worship freely given to God,
Another wants to make it statute-labour.
HOOD.—*Ode to Rae Wilson, Esquire.*

WORTH

For what is worth in anything
But so much money as 'twill bring?
BUTLER.—*Hudibras, Pt.* 2, *c.* 1.

Wisdom and worth were all he had,
But these were all to me.
GOLDSMITH.—*The Hermit.*

He has not left a wiser or better behind.
GOLDSMITH.—*Retaliation.*

The "value" or "worth" of a man is, as of all other things, his price; that is to say, so much as would be given for the use of his power.
HOBBES.—*Leviathan, ch.* 10.

Not oaks alone are trees, nor roses flowers,
Much humble wealth makes rich this world of ours.
LEIGH HUNT.—*On reading Pomfret's "Choice."*

This mournful truth is everywhere confessed,
So slow rises worth by poverty depressed.
JOHNSON.—*London.*

Worth makes the man, and want of it the fellow;
The rest is all but leather or prunella.
POPE.—*Essay on Man, Ep.* 4, 203.

What is aught but as 'tis valued?
SHAKESPEARE.—*Troilus*, Act 2, 2.

WRITING

Of all those arts in which the wise excel
Nature's chief masterpiece is writing well.
DUKE OF BUCKINGHAM.—*Essay on Poetry*.

Why did I write? what sin to me unknown
Dipped me in ink,—my parents', or my own?
POPE.—*Epistle to Arbuthnot*, 125.

True ease in writing comes from art, not chance,
As those more easiest who have learned to dance.
POPE.—*Essay on Criticism*, 361.

I once did hold it, as our statists do,
A baseness to write fair, and laboured much
How to forget that learning; but, sir, now
It did me yeoman's service.
SHAKESPEARE.—*Hamlet*, Act 5, 2.

Put not things in black and white,
If they will not bear the light.
C. H. SPURGEON.—"*Salt-Cellars*."

Pens are most dangerous tools, more sharp by odds
Than swords, and cut more keen than whips or rods.
JOHN TAYLOR.—*Three Satirical Lashes*.

Who can write so fast as men run mad?
YOUNG.—*Love of Fame, Sat.* 1.

WRONGS

Some kind of wrongs there are which flesh and blood
Cannot endure.
FLETCHER AND MASSINGER.—*Little French Lawyer*, Act 1, 1.

If of all words of tongue and pen,
The saddest are, " It might have been,"
More sad are these we daily see,
" It is, but it hadn't ought to be."
BRET HARTE.—*Mrs. Jenkins*.

Some grave their wrongs on marble ; He, more just,
Stooped down serene and wrote them on the dust.
DR. R. R. MADDEN.—*Poems*.

And Sorrow tracketh wrong,
As echo follows song.
H. MARTINEAU.—*Hymn*.

And simple truth miscalled simplicity,
And captive good attending captain ill.
SHAKESPEARE.—*Sonnet* 66.

It often falls, in course of common life,
That right long time is overborne of wrong.
SPENSER.—*Faerie Queene, Bk.* 5, *c.* 11.

Wrong and right
Are twain for ever : nor, though night kiss day,
Shall right kiss wrong and die not.
SWINBURNE.—*Marino Faliero*.

Y

YARNS

There are a set of heads that can credit the relations of Mariners.
SIR T. BROWNE.—*Religio Medici, Pt.* 121.

He loves to talk with mariners
That come from a far countree.
COLERIDGE.—*Ancient Mariner, Pt.* 7.

YEARS, THE

Years steal
Fire from the mind, as vigour from the limbs ;
And life's enchanted cup but sparkles near the brim.
BYRON.—*Childe Harold, c.* 3, *st.* 8.

The years, as they come, bring with them many things to our advantage ; as they leave, they take many away.
HORACE.—*De Arte Poetica*, 175.

Each year bears something from us as it flies ;
We only blow it farther with our sighs.
W. S. LANDOR.—*Miscell., No.* 274.

Our noisy years seem moments in the being
Of the eternal silence.
WORDSWORTH.—*Intimations of Immortality*, 9.

YESTERDAY

All our yesterdays have lighted fools
The way to dusty death.
SHAKESPEARE.—*Macbeth*, Act 5, 5.

O, call back yesterday, bid time return.
SHAKESPEARE.—*Richard II.*, Act 3, 2.

O for yesterdays to come !
YOUNG.—*Night Thoughts*, 2.

Whose yesterdays look backward with a smile.
YOUNG.—*Ib.*

YOUTH

Youth calls for Pleasure, Pleasure calls for love.
AKENSIDE.—*Love.*

A man that is young in years may be old in hours, if he have lost no time.
BACON.—*Of Youth.*

I was between
A man and a boy, A hobble-de-hoy,
A fat, little, punchy concern of sixteen
R. H. BARHAM.—*Aunt Fanny.*

You should not take a fellow eight years
old
And make him swear to never kiss the
girls.   BROWNING.—*Fra Lippo.*

O Life ! how pleasant is thy morning,
Young Fancy's rays the hills adorning !
        BURNS.—*Epistle to Jas. Smith.*

And still my delight is in proper young
    men.   BURNS.—*Jolly Beggars.*

What can a young lassie, what shall a
    young lassie,
What can a young lassie do wi' an auld
    man ?   BURNS.—*Song.*

Youth with swift feet walks onward in the
    way ;
The land of joy lies all before his eyes ;
Age, stumbling, lingers slowly day by day,
Still looking back, for it behind him lies.
        FRANCES BUTLER.

Alas, they were so young, so beautiful.
        BYRON.—*Don Juan, c.* 2, 192.

In life's morning march, when my bosom
    was young.
        CAMPBELL.—*Soldier's Dream.*

'Tis the defect of Age to rail at the
pleasures of Youth.
    MRS. CENTLIVRE.—*Basset Table,* Act 1.

Young men think old men are fools ;
but old men know young men are fools.
    CHAPMAN.—*All Fools,* Act 5, 1.

The atrocious crime of being a young
man. . . . I shall never attempt to
palliate or deny.
WILLIAM PITT (EARL OF CHATHAM).—
Speech, 1740. (*As reported by Dr. Johnson.*)

As I like a young man in whom there is
something of the old, so do I like an old
man in whom is something of the young.
    CICERO.—*De Senectute, ch.* 2.

A man whose youth has no follies, will
in his maturity have no power.
    MORTIMER COLLINS.—*Thoughts in my
                    Garden,* 2, 108.

A young Apollo, golden haired,
Stands dreaming on the verge of strife,
Magnificently unprepared
For the long littleness of life.
        MRS. CORNFORD.—*On Rupert
                    Brooke* (1915).

Our most important are our earliest years.
    COWPER.—*Progress of Error,* 353.

Almost everything that is great has been
done by youth. [*Sidonia.*]
    DISRAELI.—*Coningsby, Bk.* 3, *ch.* 1.

The blunders of youth are preferable to
the triumphs of manhood, or the success of
old age.   DISRAELI.—*Lothair, ch.* 31.

The Youth of a Nation are the Trustees
of Posterity.
        DISRAELI.—*Sybil, Bk.* 6, *ch.* 13.

In flower of youth, in beauty's pride.
    DRYDEN.—*Alexander's Feast, st.* 1.

There's a hope for every woe,
    And a balm for every pain,
But the first joys o' our heart
    Come never back again.
        R. GILFILLAN.—*Exile's Song.*

Youth should be allowed its own course.
It does not stick very long to false maxims;
life soon snatches or charms it away from
them.   GOETHE.—*Autob., Bk.* 6.

Youth on the prow, and pleasure at the
    helm.   GRAY.—*The Bard, c.* 2, 2.

Youth is unselfish in its thoughts and
feelings. On that account it feels truth
most deeply.   HEINE.—*Don Quixote.*

O Youth, alas, why wilt thou not incline
And unto rulèd reason bowè thee,
Syn Reason is the verray straightè line
That leadeth folk into felicitee ?
        HOCCLEVE.—*La male Règle.*

There are worse losses than the loss of
    youth.
        JEAN INGELOW.—*Star's Monument.*

Towering in the confidence of twenty-
one.   JOHNSON.—*Letter* (1758).

The imagination of a boy is healthy, and
the mature imagination of a man is healthy;
but there is a space of life between, in
which the soul is in a ferment, the character
undecided, the way of life uncertain, the
ambition thick-sighted : thence proceeds
mawkishness.
        KEATS.—*Pref. to Endymion.*

There is no need to say " forget," I know,
For youth is youth and time will have it so.
        A. LANG.—*Good-bye.*

A boy's will is the wind's will,
And the thoughts of youth are long, long
    thoughts.
        LONGFELLOW.—*Lost Youth.*

For ah, my heart ! how very soon
    The glittering dreams of youth are past !
And long before it reach its noon,
    The sun of life is overcast.
        MOORE.—*Elegiac Stanzas.*

I've wandered east, I've wandered west,
    Through mony a weary way ;
But never, never can forget
    The love of life's young day.
        W. MOTHERWELL.—*Jeanie Morrison.*

But never twice is a woman young.
LOUISE C. MOULTON.—*Song for Rosalys.*

When the brisk minor pants for twenty-one. POPE.—*Ep. of Horace, Ep.* 1, 38.

When all things pleased, for life itself was new,
And the heart promised what the fancy drew.
ROGERS.—*Pleasures of Memory, Pt.* 1.

Youth is the time to study wisdom;
old age is the time to practise it.
ROUSSEAU.—*Rêveries d'un Promeneur solitaire.*

Youth is a fine carver and gilder.
SCOTT.—*Diary,* 1826.

Just at the age 'twixt boy and youth,
When thought is speech, and speech is truth.
SCOTT.—*Marmion, c.* 2, *Intro.*

The canker galls the infants of the spring,
Too oft before their buttons be disclosed;
And in the morn and liquid dew of youth,
Contagious blastments are most imminent.
SHAKESPEARE.—*Hamlet,* Act 1, 3.

A very riband in the cap of youth.
SHAKESPEARE.—*Ib.,* Act 4, 7.

Two lads that thought there was no more behind,
But such a day to-morrow as to-day,
And to be boy eternal.
SHAKESPEARE.—*Winter's Tale,* Act 1, 2.

Small show of man was yet upon his chin.
SHAKESPEARE.—*Lover's Complaint,* 14.

When youth hath passed away,
With all its follies light,
What sorrow is not there?
What trouble then is absent from our lot?
SOPHOCLES.—*Oedipus Col.,* 1289
(*Plumptre tr.*).

Gather therefore the rose whilst yet is prime,
For soone comes age, that will her pride defloure.
SPENSER.—*Faerie Queene, Bk.* 2, *c.* 12, 75.

Youth is wholly experimental.
R. L. STEVENSON.—*To a Young Gentleman.*

They do their Maker wrong,
Who, in the pride of age,
Cry down youth's heritage,
And all the eager throng
Of thoughts and plans and schemes,
With which the young brain teems.
C. W. STUBBS.—*The Conscience: A Prayer of Age.*

Whose youth was full of foolish noise.
TENNYSON.—*In Memoriam, c.* 53.

Brave hearts and clean! and yet—God guide them—young!
TENNYSON.—*Merlin and Vivien,* 29.

Old the proverb,—old, but true—
Age should think and Youth should do.
D. W. THOMPSON.—*Sales Attici.*

In youth alone unhappy mortals live;
But ah! the mighty bliss is fugitive:
Discoloured sickness, anxious labour, come,
And age, and death's inexorable doom.
VIRGIL.—*Georgics,* 3, 66 (*Dryden tr.*).

Maidens withering on the stalk.
WORDSWORTH.—*Personal Talk.*

For him—a Youth to whom was given
So much of earth, so much of heaven,
And such impetuous blood.
WORDSWORTH.—*Ruth.*

It is good for a man that he bear the yoke in his youth. *Lamentations* iii, 27.

Life let us cherish, while yet the taper glows,
And the fresh flowret pluck ere it close.
Song (from Nägelis's " Volkslied "; words by Johan Martin Usteri).

Let no man despise thy youth.
1 *Timothy* iv, 12.

Age, I do abhor thee;
Youth, I do adore thee.
ANON.—*Passionate Pilgrim, No.* 10.

Happy is he that knows his follies in his youth. *Prov. (Ray.)*

Youth and white paper take any impression. *Prov. (Ray.)*

A young cowte (colt) will canter, be it uphill or down. *Scottish prov.*

Z

ZEAL

Religious persecution may shield itself under the guise of a mistaken and over-zealous piety.
BURKE.—*Impeachment of W. Hastings, Feb.,* 1788.

For zeal's a dreadful termagant,
That teaches Saints to tear and rant.
BUTLER.—*Hudibras, Pt.* 3, *c.* 2.

The soberest saints are more stiff-neckèd
Than the hottest-headed of the wicked.
BUTLER.—*Miscellaneous Thoughts.*

I do not love a man who is zealous for nothing.
GOLDSMITH.—*Vicar of Wakefield (expunged portion).*

For modes of faith let graceless zealots
fight ;
His can't be wrong whose life is in the
right.
> Pope.—*Essay on Man, Ep.* 3, 305.

But zeal is weak and ignorant, though
wondrous proud,
Though very turbulent and very loud.
> Swift.—*Ode to Sancroft.*

Violent zeal for truth has a hundred to
one odds to be either petulancy, ambition,
or pride.
> Swift.—*Thoughts on Religion.*

Is it not a shameful thing that the fanatics
have all the zeal and that the wise have
none ? It is right to be prudent, but one
should not be timid.
> Voltaire.—*Dialogues, No.* 26.

Crime has its heroes, error has its martyrs : of the true zeal and the false what
vain judges we are !
> Voltaire.—*Henriade.*

It is good to be zealously affected always
in a good thing.   *Galatians* iv, 18.

Zeal is like fire ; it needs both feeding
and watching.   *Prov.*

Zeal without knowledge is a runaway
horse.   *Prov.*

INDEX OF SUBJECT-HEADINGS

WITH

CROSS-REFERENCES

By the use of this Index the consulter will readily be able to find quotations on any subject treated in the book, no matter under what heading it is included. All the subject-headings are given in the Index; these are printed in **Clarendon** type. Other sections that deal with the same or similar subjects, to which the consulter is directed for further applicable extracts, are given immediately beneath the subject-heading in small type; while topics that are dealt with under various headings but that have not been treated under a separate heading of their own are shown in *Clarendon Italic.*

A

Abasement, 1
Humility
Meekness
Self-condemnation
Submission
Subservience
Ability, 1
Accomplishments
Cleverness
Distinction
Efficiency
Genius
Skill
Talents
Versatility
Abridgment
Books (Montaigne)
Absence, 1
Alibi
Departure
Dislike
Distance
Exile
Farewell
Forgetfulness
Poetry (Keble)
Return
Absent-mindedness
Detachment
Abstinence, 1
Alcohol
Asceticism
Drinking
Drunkenness
Moderation

Prohibition
Simple Life
Teetotallers
Temperance
Water
Wine
Abstruseness, 1
Argument
Depth
Metaphysics
Profundity
Reason
Theology
Absurdity, 2
Eccentricity
Extremes
Folly
Humour
Jesting
Laughter
Nonsense
Ridicule
Stupidity
Abundance, 2
Money
Number
Plenty
Sufficiency
Wealth
Abuse, 2
Affronts
Backbiting
Bitterness
Calumny
Disaster
Ill-will
Injuries

Insults
Libel
Malice
Quarrels
Raillery
Rancour
Recrimination
Revilers
Scolding
Slander
Abuses, 2
Evils
Accident
Adventures
Chance
Destiny
Luck
Accomplishments, 2
Ability
Action
Skill
Talents
Versatility
Accountancy, 2
Algebra
Arithmetic
Calculation
Figures
Mathematics
Accuracy
Criticism (Disraeli)
Preciseness
Accusation 2
Abuse
Bloodguiltiness
Calumny
Condemnation

INDEX OF SUBJECT-HEADINGS

INDEX OF SUBJECT-HEADINGS

INDEX OF SUBJECT-HEADINGS

T

INDEX OF SUBJECT-HEADINGS

INDEX OF SUBJECT-HEADINGS

INDEX OF SUBJECT-HEADINGS

Misunderstanding, 317
Commentators
Disclaimer
Disputes (q.v.)
Doubt
Envy
Greatness
  (Emerson)
Incredulity
Jesting
Misrepresentation
Quarrels
Trust
Unbelief
War
Mob, 317
Demagogues
Democracy
Multitude
People
Politicians
Popularity
Press (Chaucer)
Moderation, 317
Competence
Content
Controversy
Government (Seneca)
Greatness (Massinger)
Legislation
Mediocrity
Obscurity of Life
Submission
Temperance
Virtue
Wants
Modernity, 318
Innovation
Invention
Novelty
Realism
Modesty, 318
Ambition
Amenability
Beauty (Juvenal)
Blushes
Clothing
Conversation
Coyness
Diffidence
Epitaphs (Pope)
Fallibility
Gentleness
Greatness
Humility
Innocence
Meekness
Obscurity
Retirement
Self-Condemnation
Simplicity
Submission
Virtue
Monarchy, 318
Government (Goldsmith)
Kings
Queens

Monasticism, 319
Ecclesiasticism
Ecclesiastics
Reformation
Monday, 319
Days (q.v.)
Money, 319
Alternatives
Authorship (Johnson)
Avarice
Borrowers
Bribery
Business
Capital
Competence
Conduct
Estimates
Expenditure
Finance
Generosity
Gold
London (Pope)
Stock Exchange
Trade
Wealth
Wisdom
Worth (Plato)
World (ad fin.)
Monopolists, 322
Genius (Shaw)
Privilege
Profit
Months
April
Autumn
Days
February
January
June
March
May
New Year
November
October
Oysters
Spring
Weather (Ellis)
Winter
Monuments, 322
Burial
Dead
Epitaphs
Stonehenge
Tombs
Moon, 322
Astronomy
Moralising and Moralists, 322
Morality (q.v.)
Morality, 323
Cheerfulness (Voltaire)
Christianity
Dogma
Fiction
Money (Shaw)
Philosophy
Protestantism

Religion
Scoffers
Sects
Unco Guid
Virtue
Morning, 323
Breakfast
Dreams
Early Rising
Nature (Milton)
Sunrise
Mortality, 324
Dead
Death
Dying
Life
Mankind
Old Age
Transiency
Youth (Shakespeare)
Mothers, 324
Authors (Disraeli)
Beauty (Horace)
Birth
Children
Daughters
Heredity
Wives
Woman
Mothers-in-Law, 324
Brides
Motives, 325
Cause and Effect (q.v.)
Intention
Mountains, 325
Boundaries
Choice (Scottish saying)
Nature (Ruskin, Wordsworth, etc.)
Scenery
Spring
Mourning, 325
Bereavement (q.v.)
Cheerfulness (Scottish saying)
Dead
Epitaphs
Grief
Occupation (Steele)
Regret
Sadness
Sighing
Sorrow
Tears
Trial
Troubles
Multitude, The, 326
Democracy
Mob
People
Politicians
Popularity
Press (Chaucer)
Public Opinion
World
Municipality
Cities

U
609

INDEX OF SUBJECT-HEADINGS

INDEX OF SUBJECT-HEADINGS

LIST OF QUOTED AUTHORS

(Names without any Nationality Note are those of English Writers)

A

Adams, John Quincy	U.S.A.		1767–1848
Adams, Samuel	U.S.A.		1722–1803
Addison, Joseph			1672–1719
Æschylus	Greek	B.C.	525–456
Agesilaus	Greek	B.C.	398–c.360
Akenside, Mark			1721–1770
Albertano of Brescia	Ital.		fl. c. 1246
Albery, James			1838–1889
Alcuin, Archbishop of York, alias Ealwhine or Albinus			735–804
Aldrich, Henry, D.D., Dean of Christ Church, Oxford			1647–1710
Alexander the Great	Macedonian	B.C.	356–323
Alexander, Sir Wm., Earl of Stirling	Scot		1567?–1640
Alford, Henry, Dean of Canterbury			1810–1871
Alibert, Jean Louis, Baron	French		1766–1837
Alison, Richard			16th century
Allainval, Léonore Soulas	French		1700 ?–1753
Allingham, William	Irish		1824–1889
Allston, Washington	U.S.A.		1779–1843
Anacharsis	Greek		c. B.C. 600
Anstey, Christopher			1724–1805
Antisthenes	Greek		c.B.C.440–370
Apollonius (Apollonius Rhodius)	Greek		fl. B.C.222–181
Appleton, Thos. Gold	U.S.A.		1812–1884
Aquinas, St. Thos.	Ital.		c. 1227?–1274
Arblay, Madame D' (Fanny Burney)			1752–1840
Arbuthnot, John, M.D.	Scot		1667–1735
Archimedes	Greek		c. B.C. 287–212
Aristophanes	Greek		fl. c. B.C. 434

Aristotle	Greek	B.C.	384–322
Armstrong, John, M.D.	Scot		1709–1779
Arne, Thomas Augustine			1710–1778
Arnold, Sir Edwin			1832–1904
Arnold, Thomas			1795–1842
Arnold, Matthew			1822–1888
Ascham, Roger			1515–1568
Ashby-Sterry, Joseph			b. 1845
Ashe, Rev. Thomas			1836–1889
Athenæus	Greek		c. A.D. 230
Attwell, Henry			19th century
Aubrey, John			1626–1697
Aubrotas, see Miræus			
Augier, Guillaume Victor Émile	French		1820-1889
Augustine, St.	Numidian		354–430
Aulus Gellius	Roman		fl. c. 117–180
Aurelius, Marcus (Marcus Aurelius Antoninus), Emperor	Roman		121–180
Ausonius, Decimus Magnus	Roman		c. 310–394
Austen, Jane			1775–1817
Austin, Alfred			1835–1913
Avebury, Lord, see Lubbock, Sir John.			
Aveline, Mrs.			d.c. 1850
Aylmer, Mrs.			c. 1865
Ayton, Sir Robert.	Scot		1570–1638
Aytoun, Wm. Edmonstoune	Scot		1813–1865
Azaïs, Pierre Hyacinthe	French		1766–1845

B

Bacon, Francis Lord Verulam, Viscount St. Albans			1561–1626
Bailey, Philip J.			1816–1902
Baillie, Joanna	Scot		1762–1851
Bain, Alexander, LL.D.	Scot		1818–1903

Cary, Henry
Francis 1772–1844
Cary, Phœbe .. *U.S.A.*. . 1824–1871
Cato, Marcus
Portius (" The
Censor ") .. *Roman*.. B.C. 234–149
Cato, Marcus
Portius (" Uti-
censis ") .. *Roman*.. B.C. 95–46
Catullus, Caius
Valerius .. *Roman*.. B.C. 87–40
Cecil, Robert
Arthur Talbot
(3rd Marquis of
Salisbury) 1830–1903
Cecil, William
1st Baron
Burghley 1520–1598
Centlivre,
Susannah (née
Freeman) .. .. 1667?–1723
Cervantes (Miguel
Cervantes de
Saavedra) .. *Spanish*: 1547–1616
Chalmers,
Thomas, D.D.. *Scot* .. 1780–1847
Chamberlain, J.
Austen .. .. *b.* 1863
Chamberlain,
Joseph 1836–1914
Chambers,
Charles
Haddon .. *Austral-
ian* .. *b.* 1860
Channing,
William
Ellery, D.D... *U.S.A.*. . 1780–1842
Chapman, George .. 1559?–1634
Charles V.,
Emperor .. *Fleming*. 1500–1558
Chatham, Lord,
see Pitt.
Chatterton,
Thomas 1752–1770
Chaucer, Geof-
frey .. .. 1340?–1400
Chaulieu, Guil-
laume Amfrye
de .. *French*. 1639–1720
Ch'en Tzu-agig *Chinese*. 7th cent.
Chesterfield, [? B.C. or A.D.
Lord, *see* Stan-
hope.
Chesterton,
Gilbert Keith .. *b.* 1874
Cheviot, Andrew *Scot* .. *fl.* 1896
Chilo of Sparta *Greek* .. *fl.* B.C. 556
Choate, Rufus .. *U.S.A.*... 1799–1859
Chrysostom, St. *Syrian* . 347?–407
Churchill,
Charles 1731–1764
Churchill, John,
1st Duke of
Marlborough.. .. 1650–1722
Churchill, Lord
Randolph
Henry Spencer .. 1849–1895

Churchill, Win-
ston Leonard
Spencer .. .. *b.* 1874
Cibber, Colley.. .. 1671–1757
Cicero, Marcus
Tullius .. *Roman*.. B.C. 106–43
Clark, Willis
Gaylord .. *U.S.A.*. . 1810–1841
Claudianus,
Claudius .. *Roman*.. 365?–408?
Claudius (Ti-
berius Claudius
Drusus), Em-
peror .. *Roman*.. B.C. 10–A.D.54
Clemens,
Samuel Lang-
horne (Mark
Twain) . *U.S.A*... 1835–1910
Cleveland, John .. 1613–1658
Clough, Arthur
Hugh 1819–1861
Cobbett, Wil-
liam 1762–1835
Codrington,
Christopher 1668–1710
Coke, Sir
Edward 1552–1634
Coleridge, Hart-
ley 1796–1849
Coleridge, Sam-
uel Taylor 1772–1834
Collin, d'Harle-
ville, Jean
François .. *French*.. 1755–1806
Collins, Mor-
timer 1827–1876
Collins, Wil-
liam 1721–1759
Colman, George,
the Elder 1732–1794
Colman, George,
the Younger.. .. 1762–1836
Colton, Charles
Caleb (Rev.).. .. 1780–1832
Colton, Walter *U.S.A*... 1797–1851
Columella,
Lucius Junius
Moderatus .. *Roman*.. 1st cent. A.D.
Combe, Wil-
liam 1741–1823
Confucius .. *Chinese*. 551?–478
Congreve, Wil-
liam 1670–1729
Constable,
Thomas
Constant, de Re-
becque, Henri
Benjamin .. *French*.. 1767–1830
Cook, Eliza .. 1818–1889
Cooke, Jo. (?
Joshua) .. .. *fl.* 1614
Cooper, Anthony
Ashley, 3rd
Earl of Shaftes-
bury 1671–1713
Cooper, John
Gilbert 1723–1769

Corbet, Richard,
D.D., Bishop
of Oxford and
Norwich 1582–1635
Cork, Earl of, see
Boyle.
Corneille,
Pierre .. French.. 1606–1684
Cornelius Nepos Roman.. B.C. 99 ?–24
Cornford, Fran-
ces .. .. 20th century
Cornwall,
Barry, see
Procter, B. W.
Cory, William
Johnson 1823–1892
Cosin, John, D.D.,
Bishop of Dur-
ham 1594–1672
Cotton, Nath-
aniel 1705–1788
Couch, Sir
Arthur Thomas
Quiller- .. .. b. 1863
Cowley, Abraham .. 1618–1667
Cowley, Han-
nah (née Park-
house) 1743–1809
Cowper, William .. 1731–1800
Cox, George
Valentine 1786–1875
Crabbe, George .. 1754–1832
Craig, Isa, see
Knox.
Craigie, Pearl
Mary Teresa
(née Richards)
(" John Oliver
Hobbes ") .. U.S.A... 1867–1906
Craik, Dinah
Maria (née
Mulock) 1826–1887
Cranch, Chris-
topher Pearse U.S.A... 1813–1892
Crashaw, Rich-
ard 1613–1649
Cratinus .. Greek .. B.C. 520–423
Creech, Thomas,
B.D. 1659–1700
Cripps, A. S. .. 19th century
Crockett,
David .. U.S.A... 1786–1836
Croly, George Irish .. 1780–1860
Cromwell,
Oliver 1599–1658
Cross, Marian
(née Evans)
(" George Eliot ") .. 1819–1880
Crowne, John .. d. 1703 ?
Cruger, M.P. for
Bristol .. .. fl. 1774
Culpeper, Nich-
olas 1616–1654
Cumberland,
Richard 1732–1811
Cunningham,
Allan .. Scot .. 1784–1842

Curius Dentatus,
see Dentatus.
Currie, Lady
(née Mary
Montgomerie
Lamb)
(" Violet Fane") .. 1843–1905

D

Daigne, D. .. French.. 19th century
D'Allainval, see
Allainval.
Dalton, John,
D.D. 1709–1763
Daniel, Samuel .. 1562–1619
Dante, Alighieri Italian.. 1265–1321
Danton, Georges
Jacques .. French.. 1759–1794
Darwin, Eras-
mus 1731–1802
D'Avenant, Sir
William 1606–1668
Davidson, John Scot .. 1857–1909
Davies, Sir John .. 1569–1626
Davies, Richard Welsh .. 1635–1708
Davies, Scrope
Berdmore .. .. 1771 ?–1852
Davis, Henry,
M.A., transla-
tor of Plato .. .. b. 1849
Davison, Francis .. 1541–1608
Davison, Walter .. 1581–1608 ?
Davy, Sir Hum-
phry 1778–1829
Decatur,
Stephen .. U.S.A... 1779–1820
Defoe, Daniel .. 1661–1731
Dekker, Thomas .. 1570 ?–1641 ?
Delany, Patrick,
Dean of Down Irish .. 1685?–1768
De Maistre,
Xavier, see
Maistre.
De Morgan, Au-
gustus 1806–1871
Demosthenes, .. Greek .. B.C. 384–322
Denham, Sir
John 1615–1669
Denman, Thomas,
Lord Denman,
Lord Chief
Justice 1779–1854
Dennis, John .. 1657–1734
Dentatus, Marcus
Curius .. Roman.. d. B.C. 265
De Quincey,
Thomas 1785–1859
Destouches,
Philippe Néri-
cault .. French.. 1680–1754
De Vere, Sir Au-
brey .. Irish .. 1788–1846
Dibdin, Charles .. 1745–1814
Dibdin, Thomas .. 1771–1841

Hickson, William Edward..	..	1803–1870
Hill, Aaron ..	..	1685–1750
Hinkson, Katharine Tynan ..	*Irish* ..	*b.* 1861
Hippias	*Greek* ..	*fl.* B.C. 435 ?
Hippocrates ..	*Greek* ..	B.C. 460–357
Hobbes, John Oliver, *see* Craigie.		
Hobbes, Thomas	..	1588–1679
Hoccleve, Thomas	..	1370 ?–1450 ?
Hodgkin, Thomas, M.D.	..	1798–1866
Hogg, James, " The Ettrick Shepherd " ..	*Scot* ..	1770–1835
Holcroft, Thomas	..	1745–1809
Holland, 1st Baron, *see* Fox, Henry.		
Holland, Hugh	..	*d.* 1633
Holmes, Oliver Wendell	.. *U.S.A.* .	1809–1894
Home, John	.. *Scot* ..	1722–1808
Homer	.. *Greek fl.* B.C. 962–927 ?	
Hood, Thomas..	..	1799–1845
Hook, Theodore Edward	..	1788–1841
Hooker, Richard	..	1554 ?–1600
Hooper, Ellen (née Sturgis) ..	..	*fl.* 1840
Hope, Anthony, *see* Hawkins, Sir Anthony Hope.		
Hopkinson, Joseph	.. *U.S.A.* .	1770–1842
Hopwood, Ronald	..	20th century
Horace	.. *Roman*..	B.C. 65–B.C. 8
Houghton, Lord, *see* Milnes.		
Housman, Alfred Edward	..	*b.* 1859
Housman, Lawrence	..	*b.* 1867
Hovey, Richard,	*U.S.A.*.	1864–1900
Howard, Henry, Earl of Surrey	..	1517 ?–1547
Howard, Sir Robert	..	1626–1698
Howarth, Ellen Clementine (née Doran) ..	*U.S.A.*.	1827–1899
Howe, Julia (née Ward)	.. *U.S.A.* .	*b.* 1819–1910
Howe, Nathanael	*U.S.A.* .	1764–1837
Howell, James	*Welsh* ..	1594 ?–1666
Howitt, Mary (née Botham).	..	1799–1888
Hugo, Victor Marie	.. *French* .	1802–1885
Hume, David ..	*Scot* ..	1711–1776
Hunt, James Henry Leigh..	..	1784–1859

Huntington, William S. S...	..	1745–1813
Hurdis, James.	..	1763–1801
Hutcheson, Francis, the Elder	.. *Scot* ..	1694–1746
Hutchinson, Horatio Gordon	..	*b.* 1859
Huxley, Thomas Henry	..	1825–1895

I

Ibsen, Henrik..	*Norwegian*..	1828–1906
Ingelow, Jean..	..	1820–1897
Ingram, John Kells	.. *Irish* ..	1823–1907
Ireland, William Henry	..	1777–1835
Irving, Washington	.. *U.S.A.*. .	1783–1859
Isidore, St., Hispalensis	.. *Spanish*	560–636
Isidore, St., of Pelusium	.. *Greek* ..	370 ?–450 ?

J

Jacobi, Johann Georg	.. *German* .	1740–1814
James I, of Scotland	.. *Scot* ..	1394–1437
James, George Payne Rainsford	..	1799–1860
Jefferson, Thomas	.. *U.S.A.* ..	1743–1826
Jeffrey, Francis Lord Jeffrey..	*Scot* ..	1773–1850
Jennings, Chas., reputed librettist of Handel's " Saul," 1738.		
Jenyns, Soame .	..	1704–1787
Jerome, Jerome Klapka	..	*b.* 1859
Jerome, St. (Eusebius Hieronymus Sophronius)	.. *Roman*..	331–420
Jerrold, Douglas William	..	1803–1857
John of Salisbury, Bishop of Chartres	..	*d.* 1180
Johnson, Esther, " Stella " ..	..	1681–1728
Johnson, Samuel	..	1709–1784
Jones, Henry Arthur	..	*b.* 1851